# The FBI Encyclopedia

For Heather

# The FBI Encyclopedia

MICHAEL NEWTON

McFarland & Company, Inc., Publishers
*Jefferson, North Carolina, and London*

ISBN 0-7864-1718-8 (illustrated case binding : 50# alkaline paper) ∞

LIBRARY OF CONGRESS CATALOGUING DATA ARE AVAILABLE

British Library cataloguing data are available

*On the front cover: ©2003 EyeWire Images*

Manufactured in the United States of America

*McFarland & Company, Inc., Publishers
Box 611, Jefferson, North Carolina 28640
www.mcfarlandpub.com*

# Contents

*There is always the possibility that a secret police may become a menace to free governments and free institutions because it carries with it the possibility of abuses of power which are not always quickly apprehended or understood. The enormous expansion of federal legislation, both civil and criminal, in recent years, however has made a Bureau of Investigation a necessary instrument of law enforcement.*

*But it is important that its activities be strictly limited to the performance of those functions for which it was created and that its agents themselves be not above the law or beyond its reach. The Bureau of Investigation is not concerned with political or other opinion of individuals. It is concerned only with their conduct and then only with such conduct as is forbidden by the laws of the United States. When a police system passes beyond these limits, it is dangerous to the proper administration of justice and to human liberty.*

—Attorney General Harlan Fiske Stone,
announcing the appointment of
FBI Director J. Edgar Hoover (1924)

# Preface

*The FBI Encyclopedia* is a product of concentrated research spanning four decades, from the early 1970s to the present day, but in a real sense its origins date from 1959 and my first childhood viewing of *The FBI Story*. My eight-year-old imagination was captivated by the exploits of Hollywood G-man James Stewart, and further fueled by subsequent avid perusal of books and magazine articles that were (at least through 1969) chiefly vehicles of laudatory propaganda for Director J. Edgar Hoover and his intrepid special agents. Not until my college years, in the early 1970s, was it revealed that I and the nation at large had been systematically deceived. The FBI was not—indeed, had never been—what it appeared to be in print or on the silver screen.

The work in hand is my third book dedicated solely to the FBI and the first ever published which presents the full scope of Bureau history in an encyclopedic format. The entries contained herein span nearly a century, from the FBI's creation in 1908 to early 2003. Categorized broadly, the entries are these:

*Biographical entries:* Included in the text are profiles for every FBI director, U.S. president and attorney general from 1908 to 2003; various FBI officials and agents whose activities have left a lasting mark on bureau history; civilian champions and critics of the FBI in government and the news media; notorious fugitives and "public enemies" hunted by the FBI; and various persons whose sociopolitical activities made them targets of FBI surveillance, harassment and "neutralization."

*FBI structure, programs and procedures:* These entries examine the FBI's command structure, its major divisions and their evolution over time, together with specific programs ranging from scientific analysis and undercover operations to political harassment during the illicit "COINTELPRO" campaigns. Special attention is paid to some of the Bureau's more controversial methods (e.g. bugging, wiretapping, break-ins and use of criminal informants).

*Organizational histories:* The FBI has never operated in a vacuum. Organizations profiled in the test include allied or competing law enforcement agencies, together with various groups subjected to FBI investigation and surveillance. The latter range from obvious criminal groups to assemblies of social and political activists deemed "subversive" by various FBI leaders and the presidential administrations they served.

*Legislative profiles:* Various entries examine federal statutes under which the FBI has conducted its most famous and far-reaching investigations, from the Mann Act of 1910 to the USA Patriot Act of 2001. Each legislative entry examines the broad terms of specific laws and the ways in which they were enforced by Bureau agents, variously enhancing or detracting from the FBI's reputation.

*Famous cases:* Entries devoted to specific cases span the full range of FBI history, highlighting the ways in which Bureau priorities and tactics have changed over time. Included are a mixed bag of anarchists, outlaws, kidnappers, "subversives" and serial killers, all of whom contributed in various ways to the FBI's popular image. Selections span the period from Jack Johnson's Mann Act prosecution in 1913 to the Bureau's "war on terrorism" 90 years later.

*General entries:* Finally, a selection of general entries survey the FBI's role in a wide range of subject areas including historical eras (e.g. Prohibition, the World Wars), criminal activity (e.g. lynching, organized crime, police brutality, serial murder, terrorism), and various social movements (e.g. anarchism, civil rights, anti-war protests).

Entries in *The FBI Encyclopedia* are alphabetically arranged. Subjects with discrete entries of their own, when mentioned in another entry, are printed in SMALL CAPITALS the first time they appear. Cross-references are also employed for readers' convenience in locating subjects that might otherwise elude them (e.g. Wingate, Lynn *see* Royer, Jeffrey). Multiple appendices provide additional information on FBI field offices; agents killed in the line of duty; fugitives posted to the Bureau's Ten Most Wanted List; and fictional treatments of the FBI by the American entertainment media.

Thanks are due to several individuals whose kind assistance made completion of this volume possible. They include David Frasier, author and research librarian at Indiana University in Bloomington; Lisa Becker, with the FBI's Violent Crimes/Fugitive Unit; and Heather Locken, generous and forbearing beyond measure.

Every effort has been made to ensure the accuracy of this work. Inevitably, unfolding events at Bureau headquarters, in the "war on terrorism" and on other fronts, will render some entries outdated before they are published. Any updates or notice of errors may be sent to the author in care of the publisher.

# Introduction

Nearly everything you know about the FBI is wrong.

America's most famous law enforcement agency, established more than 90 years ago, has been the subject of countless books, articles, essays, congressional investigations, television programs and motion pictures, coupled with a nonstop flow of press releases from FBI HEADQUARTERS spanning the past seven decades, yet it remains an enigma to most U.S. citizens, deliberately shrouded in mystery.

The purpose of this volume is to lift that veil and let the reader glimpse at least some measure of what lies beneath. The view will not be all-encompassing, because the Bureau guards its secrets closely. Thousands of files and millions of documents remain hidden from public scrutiny, concealed on grounds of privacy or "national security" concerns. Limitations of space and economy further dictate that no single book will ever present a "complete" history of the FBI. Because some readers may know less than others about the Bureau's origins and history, a brief overview is offered here in the same format adopted by the FBI's official Internet website—i.e., specific answers to some frequently asked questions. Here, then, is the FBI-FAQ.

*What is the FBI?*

The Federal Bureau of Investigation is the primary investigative and enforcement arm of the U.S. JUSTICE DEPARTMENT, charged with apprehending individuals who violate various federal statutes.

*What is the FBI's mission?*

At press time for this book, the FBI listed its chief priorities as follow:

1. Protect the United States from terrorist attack.

2. Protect the United States against foreign intelligence operations and espionage.

3. Protect the United States against cyber-based attacks and high-technology crimes.

4. Combat public corruption at all levels.

5. Protect civil rights.

6. Combat transnational and national criminal organizations and enterprises.

7. Combat major white-collar crime.

8. Combat significant violent crime.

9. Support federal, state, local and international partners.

10. Upgrade technology to successfully perform the FBI's mission.

*When was the FBI created?*

Attorney General CHARLES BONAPARTE defied congressional opposition to create an unnamed "special agent force" within the Justice Department on 29 June 1908. President THEODORE ROOSEVELT made the unit a permanent subdivision of Justice on 26 July 1908. On 16 March 1909 the agency was named the Bureau of Investigation. It was renamed the U.S. Bureau of Investigation on 1 July 1932. Eleven months later, on 10 June 1933, it merged with the Prohibition Bureau to become the Division of Investigation. Its present name became official on 1 July 1935.

*Who heads the FBI today?*

At press time, the FBI director was ROBERT SWAN MUELLER III, appointed by President GEORGE W. BUSH in July 2001.

*Who was the longest-serving FBI director?*

J. Edgar Hoover ran the Bureau from 10 May 1924 until his death on 2 May 1972—eight days short of 48 years. Exposure of abuses and corruption under Hoover prompted passage of legislation restricting future FBI directors to a maximum 10-year term. Thus far, no Bureau director since 1972 has completed a full term in office.

*Is the FBI a national police force?*

Yes. Bureau spokesmen deny it, claiming the FBI is merely "an investigative component of the Justice Department," only "one of 32 federal agencies with law enforcement responsibilities," but their denials are disingenuous. "Law enforcement" *is* police work. *All* police forces, by definition, are investigative agencies. FBI agents not only investigate crimes, they also arrest offenders and are empowered to use DEADLY FORCE if resisted. The FBI thus meets all criteria of a police force, and its jurisdiction is truly national, spanning all 50 states, plus Puerto Rico and the District of Columbia.

*When did FBI agents receive police powers?*

FBI agents technically lacked authority to make arrests or carry firearms prior to 17 June 1934, when Congress enacted sweeping new anti-crime legislation, but they were far from helpless in the period from 1908 to 1934. In fact, they jailed thousands of suspects during those years: suspected violators of the MANN ACT (1910), the DWYER ACT (1919), the LINDBERGH Law (1932) and other federal statutes; suspected draft-dodgers in the 1918 "SLACKER RAIDS"; alleged anarchists and "subversives" during the PALMER RAIDS (1919-20), and so on. Those agents were also frequently armed, and FBI memos reveal that each field office maintained a gun vault by 1925. In short, lack of legal authority rarely prevented the FBI from doing as it pleased.

*How did FBI agents get the nickname "G-men"?*

Officially, the term was coined by fugitive GEORGE ("MACHINE GUN") KELLY when agents arrested him for KIDNAPPING in September 1933. In fact, Kelly was arrested by Memphis police and never spoke the word. Its actual source was almost certainly a publicist employed by Hoover or the FBI's CRIME RECORDS DIVISION.

*Is it true, as stated on the Bureau's website, that FBI efforts "resulted in the arrest or demise of all the major gangsters [in America] by 1936"?*

No. The FBI's Depression-era list of "major gangsters" included a few dozen independent bank robbers and kidnappers. None were members of ORGANIZED CRIME, and J. Edgar Hoover steadfastly denied the existence of a national crime syndicate until 1961. Serious FBI pursuit of syndicate mobsters (as opposed to sporadic personal harassment) would not proceed until after Hoover's death.

*Is FBI jurisdiction limited to United States territory?*

No. G-men were empowered to operate in Latin America during WORLD WAR II, and while Hoover craved global authority for intelligence operations, that role was filled by the CENTRAL INTELLIGENCE AGENCY. Today, the FBI maintains a network of "legal attachés" in U.S. embassies around the world and collaborates with foreign police on specific cases. In June 1989 Attorney General RICHARD THORNBURGH authorized G-men to arrest suspected terrorists, drug traffickers and other fugitives abroad, without the consent of foreign nations in which they reside. Such activity amounts to kidnapping under foreign statutes and runs the continual risk of provoking international incidents.

*Is it true that Hoover divorced and insulated the FBI from politics after taking charge in May 1924?*

No federal agency is ever immune to political influence, and Hoover's FBI ranked among the most politicized of all. It is true that Hoover fired some corrupt agents during his initial "cleanup" of the Bureau, but he appointed certain agents (including THOMAS DODD and MELVIN PURVIS) as favors for influential congressmen. He also curried friends in Congress and the White House on his own behalf, thereby shielding himself against investigation and removal from office. At the same time, Hoover used the Bureau to investigate and harass his political enemies, frequently drawing derogatory information from FBI files to blackmail opponents or tip the scales in election campaigns. While Hoover finally fell short of his ultimate goal—the presidency or a lifetime appointment to the U.S. SUPREME COURT — he wielded the FBI as a potent political weapon for nearly half a century.

*Is it true, as stated on the FBI's website, that Hoover "embodied the Progressive tradition" and that "his appointment ensured that the Bureau of Investigation would keep that tradition alive"?*

Yes. Unfortunately, the "progressive" era of Presidents Theodore Roosevelt and WOODROW WILSON was known for its gunboat diplomacy, racial segregation, unfettered lynching of blacks, suppression of LABOR UNIONS, revival of the vigilante KU KLUX KLAN, prosecution of social activists, restrictive immigration laws, mass deportation of "enemy aliens," and a moralistic crusade for PROHIBITION of alcoholic beverages that spawned a national crime syndicate. Hoover embodied all those attitudes and molded the FBI in his own image.

*When was the FBI authorized to conduct DOMESTIC SURVEILLANCE operations?*

As recounted on the Bureau's website, "Authority to investigate [Fascist and Communist] organizations came in 1936 with President [FRANKLIN] ROOSEVELT'S authorization through Secretary of State Cordell Hull. A 1939 Presidential Directive further strengthened the FBI's authority to investigate subversives in the United States, and Congress reinforced it by passing the SMITH ACT in 1940, outlawing advocacy of violent overthrow of the government." In fact, the FBI's domestic spying preceded Roosevelt's order by a quarter-century (the earliest surveillance files so far revealed date from 1911), and it was never limited to "subversives"—a label which Hoover and his successors have applied to journalists, clergymen, mainstream politicians, CIVIL RIGHTS advocates, poets, musicians, attorneys, Supreme Court justices, and anyone with the temerity to criticize the FBI. Bureau tactics have also exceeded any semblance of normal investigation, to include malicious harassment, slander, and employment of *agents provocateur* to promote criminal activity.

*Did the FBI save America from Communist subversion during the Depression and Cold War?*

No. While it is incontestable that Soviet spies operated inside the U.S. (just as American spies operated in Russia and other nations), the FBI's record of capturing them was uneven at best. In several notorious cases, like those of RUDOLF ABEL and JULIUS ROSENBERG, mishandling of evidence delayed arrests and prosecution; G-man ROBERT HANSSEN, meanwhile, sold secrets to the Russians from inside the FBI itself, operating with impunity for nearly a quarter-century. At the same time, Hoover's stable of professional INFORMANTS cultivated Red-baiting hysteria nationwide, fueled the witch hunts of Senator JOSEPH McCARTHY, and testified falsely to defame (and sometimes imprison) innocent persons. By the mid-1950s, inside sources estimated that the American COMMUNIST PARTY would have collapsed without financial support from FBI informants in the ranks.

*How well has the FBI fulfilled its stated mission "to uphold the law through the investigation of violations of federal criminal law"?*

Erratically, at best. While Hoover's FBI rigorously enforced certain statutes (notably those involving BANK ROBBERY, kidnapping, and interstate auto theft), others were largely ignored. Hoover scuttled investigations into white-collar crime and political corruption, thereby protecting such influential friends as CLINT MURCHISON and LYNDON JOHNSON. Subsequent directors chose their own priorities, again with mixed results. Historically, the Bureau's greatest failures lie in the long decades of negligence involving organized crime and civil rights investigations.

*How accurate are FBI crime statistics?*

It varies. Under Hoover, statistics were habitually manipulated in the Bureau's favor, demonstrating higher arrest and conviction rates each year to justify larger appropriations. Creative bookkeeping also bolstered Hoover's alarms at new "crime waves" in progress—which, once again, required more money, agents and equipment for the FBI. Conversely, rigged statistics presented an image of zealous activity in fields (like civil rights) where agents did little or nothing. Today, some statistics (including HATE CRIMES) depend on submissions from local police and bear only marginal resemblance to reality. When FBI statistics contradict each other, as in the field of child abductions, it sometimes appears that communication has broken down within the Bureau itself. As a rule, all government statistics should be taken with a healthy grain of salt, treated primarily as products of bureaucratic self-interest.

*How successful is the FBI in combating TERRORISM?*

As in "normal" crime-fighting, the results have been erratic, aggravated by the Bureau's fluid (and wholly arbitrary) definitions of terrorism. Those definitions, in turn, were influenced by the personal bias of presidents and FBI directors. Thus, Hoover's G-men moved against racial terrorists in the South only when ordered to do so by President Lyndon Johnson in 1964. Likewise, the public attitudes of "pro-life" Presidents RONALD REAGAN and GEORGE H.W. BUSH discouraged agents from tackling ANTI-ABORTION VIOLENCE in the 1980s. By contrast, the "terrorist" label has often been applied to law-abiding dissidents as an excuse for aggressive surveillance. In extreme cases, including those of the SECRET ARMY ORGANIZATION and certain Klan factions led by FBI informants, the Bureau has sponsored and financed acts of terroristic violence. On a national and global scale, the FBI's long feud with the CIA proved detrimental to intelligence collection, and may have contributed to the disasters of 11 September 2001.

*Has the FBI ever "framed" an innocent person?*

Sadly, yes. Corrupt FBI collaboration with Boston mobsters led to the wrongful conviction of four innocent defendants in the 1960s: two died in prison, while two others—PETER LIMONE and JOSEPH SALVATI—were exonerated decades later. In California, BLACK PANTHER PARTY activist ELMER ("GERONIMO") PRATT was framed for murder and spent more than 20 years in prison. G-men have knowingly manipulated or suppressed vital evidence in many other trials, ranging from the SACCO-VANZETTI CASE (1920) to the case of Dr. JEFFREY MACDONALD (1979). Suspicion of FBI FRAME-UPS lingers in the case of alleged murderer LEONARD PELTIER and in other cases involving minority activists.

*Have FBI leaders since Hoover eliminated illegal and abusive tactics?*

Unfortunately, no. While Hoover himself allegedly discontinued the FBI's illegal COINTELPRO campaigns in 1971, identical tactics (including warrantless BUGGING, WIRETAPPING and use of criminal *agents provocateur*) continued at least through the late 1980s. Directors L. PATRICK GRAY III (1972–73) and WILLIAM RUCKLESHAUS (1973) were embroiled in the WATERGATE SCANDAL. Director CLARENCE KELLEY (1973–78) ordered illegal acts against the AMERICAN INDIAN MOVEMENT, PUERTO RICAN NATIONALISTS, and "NEW LEFT" groups. Director WILLIAM WEBSTER (1978–87) used identical tactics against Puerto Rican activists and the COMMITTEE IN SOLIDARITY WITH THE PEOPLE OF EL SALVADOR. Director WILLIAM SESSIONS (1987–93) supervised the bloody RANDALL WEAVER and BRANCH DAVIDIAN fiascos, while promoting the invasive LIBRARY AWARENESS PROGRAM; he was dismissed on accusations of misusing government property and funds. Under Director LOUIS FREEH (1993–2001), the Bureau suffered what journalist Ronald Kessler has termed "colossal mismanagement," including scandals in its LABORATORY DIVISION, false charges against RICHARD JEWELL and WEN HO LEE, and the "misplacement" of some 30,000 documents in the case of TIMOTHY MCVEIGH. Director Robert Mueller, during his first year in office, faced charges that FBI officials persecuted agents for exposing acts of gross negligence, including suppression of advance warnings on the terrorist acts of 11 September 2001.

*How accurately is the FBI portrayed in books, media reports, motion pictures, and on television?*

Quality varies, from straightforward reportage to lurid fantasy. Despite its website's claim that "the FBI does not edit or approve" the work of authors and producers, for many years the Bureau did exactly that. From 1933 until his death, J. Edgar Hoover maintained a stable of friendly journalists and ghostwriters who spared no energy in polishing his image and the Bureau's. From REX COLLIER and COURTNEY RYLEY COOPER to DON WHITEHEAD and EFREM ZIMBALIST, JR., countless authors, editors and entertainers have perpetuated the myth of infallible, incorruptible G-men. If the FBI has suffered from adverse portrayals in the realm of fiction, so historians—and all Americans—have been misled for generations by calculated DISINFORMATION campaigns.

Today more than ever, in the wake of "9-11" and the USA PATRIOT ACT (replete with sweeping new surveillance powers for the FBI and CIA), it is imperative for all Americans to understand the Bureau's history, its tactics and philosophies. Events of 2001-02, with their grim echoes of America's first Red Scare (1919-20), provide a classic illustration of Alphonse Karr's statement that "the more things change, the more they remain the same." Those same events should also remind us of the adage that failure to learn from the mistakes of history dooms us to repeat those mistakes—perhaps at tragic cost.

# A

ABEL, Robert William — Between 1982 and 1997, 42 teenage girls and young women were kidnapped from small towns and suburbs along Interstate Highway 45, between Houston and Galveston, Texas. Many of those were later found dead, described by FBI agents and local authorities as victims of SERIAL MURDER. Despite the four-year focus of attention on Robert William Abel as the single suspect, no evidence has been found to support an indictment, and by early 1998 it appeared that G-men had been mistaken in their choice of targets all along.

The most recent "official" victim in the murder series was 17-year-old Jessica Cain, last seen alive while performing with a community theater group, one night in August 1997. Following the show, Cain left for home, driving alone down I-45, but she never reached her destination. Cain's father found her pickup truck abandoned on the highway's shoulder, and her name was added to the ever-growing victims list.

Suspect Abel, a former NASA engineer and operator of a horseback riding ranch near League City, Texas, first came under suspicion in 1993, when the corpses of four missing girls were found in the desert near his property. FBI agents spent a grand total of two hours with League City police, sketching a PSYCHOLOGICAL PROFILE of the unknown killer based on such traits as "intelligence level" and assumed proximity to the crime scene. Abel's ex-wife added tales of alleged domestic abuse ("externalized anger" in FBI parlance) and claims that Abel sometimes beat his horses (a charge that he staunchly denies). The punch line of the federal profile was direct and to the point — "Serial sexual offender: Robert William Abel."

That profile alone was deemed sufficient to support a search warrant, and police moved in, seeking evidence that included a cache of nude photos described by Abel's ex-wife. In fact, they *did* find photographs, some 6,000 in all, of which precisely two depicted naked women (neither of them victims in the murder spree). No evidence was found at Abel's ranch connecting him with any sort of criminal activity, including cruelty to animals.

Frustrated in their search for clues, League City police took the unusual step of naming Abel publicly as a suspect in the I-45 murder case. Soon he began receiving death threats from neighbors and the relatives of sundry victims. One such, Tim Miller, having lost his daughter Laura to the unknown killer, launched a personal crusade of daily "reminders" to Abel, including armed visits to his home and threats of murder recorded on Abel's answering machine. League City police, convinced that Abel was their man, did nothing to halt the harassment and stalled when Abel volunteered to take a polygraph test. It was early 1998 before Abel got his chance with the polygraph, courtesy of the *20/20* television program. In fact, two tests were administered by a retired FBI agent, with Abel denying any knowledge of the four victims found near his ranch in 1993. He hesitated in response to one surprise question, dealing with rumors of a young victim's drug use, and was rated "untruthful" in respect to that answer, but a second test administered without trick questions found him to be truthful on all counts. FBI agents in Houston called the *20/20* tests "extremely significant," admitting that the four-year-old profile of Abel was "poor quality" work on the part of their Quantico colleagues. In fact, they told the world, Robert Abel had been eliminated as a suspect in their eyes, and even Tim Miller relented in his harassment, offering Abel a televised apology.

Not so the League City police. Abel may indeed be innocent, they say, but since there is no solid evidence to clear him by their own exacting standards, Abel "is still swimming in the pool of suspects." Texas courts have barred Abel from filing a lawsuit to clear his name, ruling that League City police are within their rights to publicize him as a suspect, even when the original FBI profile has been retracted. The real I-45 killer, meanwhile, remains unidentified and presumably still at large.

ABEL, Rudolf Ivanovich — Whenever discussions turned to espionage in America, J. EDGAR HOOVER and "friendly" journalists were quick to cite the case of Col. Rudolf Abel as an example of FBI efficiency in curbing Soviet spies. On closer examination, however, it seems to prove the opposite.

A high-ranking Soviet agent, Abel entered the U.S. illegally from Canada in 1948 and spent the better part of two years criss-crossing the country, establishing contacts and tapping them for information which he then sent back to Moscow. In 1950 Abel established himself as a photographer in Brooklyn, New York, under the alias "Emil R. Goldfus." Operating from a studio on Foster Avenue, he served as chief coordinator for all Russian spies in America, while the FBI remained oblivious.

The bureau got its first break in 1953, when a Brooklyn newsboy received a curious nickel from one of his customers. The coin felt unnaturally light and had a hollow ring when dropped on the pavement. After several bounces it popped open and revealed a strip of microfilm inside. The newsboy gave it to a New York police officer, who in turn delivered coin and film to the FBI. For two years, bureau code-breakers labored in vain to decipher the film's ten columns of five-digit typewritten numbers. G-men in New York likewise failed to identify the newsboy's phantom customer.

There matters rested until April 1957, when Soviet agent Reino Hayhanen approached the CIA in Paris, seeking to defect. On arrival in the U.S., Hayhanen promptly deciphered the nickel code and fingered Rudolf Abel as Russia's top spy in America. On 21 June 1957 Abel was arrested in New York by FBI and Immigration agents. The arrest and subsequent search of Abel's apartment were conducted without warrants, Abel spirited to Texas and held incommunicado for seven weeks while the bureau tried to "turn" him. Recalcitrant despite alleged beatings, Abel was finally charged with espionage, convicted at trial on the basis of Hayhanen's testimony (though Abel denied ever meeting Hayhanen), and sentenced to thirty years in prison. He served four years before he was exchanged, in 1962, for American U-2 pilot Francis Gary Powers. On the eve of his release, FBI agents belatedly found a hidden compartment in Abel's wallet — held in bureau custody for five years — and found more microfilm, this strip confirming Abel's contact with Hayhanen. Abel added insult to injury in 1966, describing how he had managed to destroy a decoding device and taped message from Moscow in the presence of the G-men who arrested him.

FBI reports of the Abel case still try to paint it as a bureau triumph. Ex-agent Robert Lamphere, retired in 1955, published his inside account of the "FBI-KGB war" three decades later. Lamphere omitted any mention of CIA involvement in Reino Hayhanen's defection, implying a surrender to the FBI, then noted that G-men found Abel's Brooklyn photo studio "after some difficulty." Lamphere also blamed the Immigration and Naturalization Service for holding Abel incommunicado in Texas, thus excusing the FBI of any legal impropriety.

**ABERNATHY, Ralph David** — A native Alabamian, born 11 March 1926, Ralph Abernathy was ordained as a Baptist minister at age 22. Three years later he became pastor of the First Baptist Church in Montgomery, Alabama, and there assisted Rev. MARTIN LUTHER KING, JR., in the campaign to desegregate Montgomery's city buses (1955-56). Following that victory, Abernathy helped King found the SOUTHERN CHRISTIAN LEADERSHIP CONFERENCE (SCLC) to coordinate nonviolent protests against racial segregation throughout the U.S. Noteworthy campaigns included

those in Birmingham, Alabama (1963); in St. Augustine, Florida (1964); and in Selma, Alabama (1965). Following Dr. King's 1968 assassination, Abernathy assumed leadership of the SCLC and remained as president until 1977. (Abernathy suspected that King was murdered either by the KU KLUX KLAN or by "someone trained or hired by the FBI and acting under orders from J. EDGAR HOOVER himself.")

FBI surveillance of black leaders was widespread during Hoover's years as director, but Hoover's particular hatred of Dr. King prompted more intense observation and harassment of King's closest advisors. Abernathy's 1,500-page dossier indicates that G-men were tracking his movements as early as 1956, noting the motel where he stayed during a Washington, D.C. convention of the NATIONAL ASSOCIATION FOR THE ADVANCEMENT OF COLORED PEOPLE. In March 1964, a memo headed "Communist Influence in Racial Matters" detailed his room service order at another hotel, in Tampa, Florida. Surveillance clearly intensified when Abernathy succeeded King at the helm of the SCLC, and his name was added to the Bureau's RABBLE ROUSER INDEX on 22 April 1968. Five months later, Bureau spies filed 12 memos concerning Abernathy's "elaborate suite" at a Chicago hotel, during the riotous Democratic National Convention.

Abernathy attended President RICHARD NIXON in January 1969 (with G-men reporting his flight schedule, hotel reservation and rental car information to the White House), but Nixon regarded him as yet another "enemy." On 18 May 1970, Hoover penned a memo recounting a conversation with Vice President SPIRO AGNEW: "The Vice President said he thought he was going to have to start destroying Abernathy's credibility, so anything I can give him would be appreciated. I told him that I would be glad to." (The same memo termed Abernathy "one of the worst.") Another recipient of derogatory material was Rep. John Rooney, chairman of the House Appropriations Committee. Rooney once told black journalist Carl Rowan that the FBI had sent him a tape recording of Dr. King inviting Abernathy to engage in HOMOSEXUAL activity. Rowan explained the comment as a joke, but Rooney took it seriously and spread the story throughout Congress.

Abernathy was aware of Hoover's malignant interest from the mid-1960s onward, and once tailored a sermon for the director personally, knowing that his church was illegally bugged. Upon receiving news of Hoover's death in 1972, Abernathy told reporters, "I am reminded that God conducts the ultimate surveillance." Abernathy died in Atlanta on 17 April 1990.

**ABRAHAM Lincoln Brigade** — The Spanish Civil War of 1936-39 pitted fascist insurgents led by Gen. Francisco Franco against a leftist Popular Front government elected by democratic ballot. On a larger scale, it became a dress rehearsal for WORLD WAR II, as ADOLF HITLER and Benito Mussolini supplied material support to Franco's rebels, while Josef Stalin assisted the loyalist regime. American recruits for the loyalist side — allegedly including members of the Young Communist League — served as members of the Abraham Lincoln Brigade. After Franco's victory, they returned to the U.S. and organized a small veterans' group to commemorate their efforts.

All this smacked of communist subversion to U.S. Attorney General FRANK MURPHY, who ordered prosecution of the alleged Reds in July 1939. FBI agents had investigated the Abraham Lincoln Brigade since September 1938, desisting only when the JUSTICE DEPARTMENT's Criminal Investigation Division halted the probe in April 1939. Now, with Murphy's support, the investigation resumed and twelve members of the brigade were indicted on 3 February 1940, under an obscure federal stature banning recruitment for foreign armies on U.S. soil. FBI agents staged a series of predawn raids on February 6, jailing eleven suspects in Detroit and one in Milwaukee.

Their treatment in FBI custody sparked immediate controversy, as tales of beatings and "third-degree tactics" circulated widely. Years after the fact, FBI apologist Don Whitehead insisted that G-men "were told to be courteous and to avoid any arguments" with the prisoners, but no other raids in bureau history to date had been accomplished in such civilized fashion. Ten days after the raids — and eleven days after Frank Murphy assumed his new seat on the U.S. Supreme Court — Attorney General ROBERT JACKSON dismissed all charges in the case, declaring that he saw "no good to come from reviving in America at this late date the animosities of the Spanish conflict so long as the conflict has ended." Even Spain's new dictator was not inclined to jail opposing foot soldiers, and Jackson declined to prosecute American veterans of the Spanish war while "some degree of amnesty at least is being extended in Spain." Jackson further noted that no efforts had been made to prosecute Americans who joined the Spanish fascist team.

Dismissal of the charges failed to quash the controversy, though. Several major newspapers protested the roundup and FBI handling of suspects, as did more than 100 ministers, a dozen labor unions, and columnist Westbrook Pegler. The *Milwaukee Journal* opined that G-men should "be outright condemned" for their conduct, while the *New Republic*'s editors branded the FBI "an American OGPU." As for J. EDGAR HOOVER, the editorial suggested that the "glamour that surrounds him conceals the growth of a power inconsistent with our conception of democratic institutions." In Washington, Nebraska senator George Norris raised his voice against the bureau, warning that "unless this is stopped, there will be a spy behind every stump and a detective in every closet." Hoover and company, predictably, attributed all criticism to the Communist Party, citing an anonymous INFORMANT's report as proof that Reds had organized to make the case "a national issue."

**ABSCAM** — Initiated by the FBI's New York City field office in 1978, Operation ABSCAM was initially designed to capture purveyors of stolen art and securities. To that end, the bureau established Abdul Enterprises, a bogus "fencing" operation, on Long Island, while convicted swindler Mel Weinberg was recruited to solicit business for a mythical client, Arab sheik Kambir Abdul Rahman. Before year's end, the emphasis of ABSCAM shifted to a probe of political corruption in New Jersey, starting with the office of Camden mayor Angelo Errichetti. Posing as agents of Sheik Rahman, FBI agents offered Errichetti a $25,000 bribe to pave the way for a state casino license. Errichetti not only accepted the bribe, but also introduced the G-men to other greedy officials, including U.S. Senator Harrison Williams, Jr.

As the web of corruption expanded, ABSCAM's focus shifted once again, this time from New Jersey to Washington, D.C. Agents rented a house and equipped it with closed-circuit television cameras, entertaining a parade of venal congressmen who demanded an average of $50,000 each for political favors. The operation ended prematurely on 3 February 1980, when a front-page story was leaked to the *New York Times*, presumably by JUSTICE DEPARTMENT insiders.

ABSCAM was one of the first sting operations to use videotapes in surveillance and as evidence in court. It produced twelve convictions on bribery and conspiracy charges, including seven members of Congress and five other public officials. Aside from Senator Williams in New Jersey, the convicted legislators included Representatives John Jenrette (South Carolina), Richard Kelly (Florida), Raymond Lederer (Pennsylvania), John Murphy (New York), and Michael Myers (Pennsylvania). Appeals on grounds of entrapment were rejected by higher courts.

**ABU-JAMAL, Mumia** — A Philadelphia native, born Wesley Cook on 24 April 1954, Mumia Abu-Jamal described his childhood as "absolutely unremarkable." At age 15 he joined the BLACK PANTHER PARTY and soon became "minister of information" for the Philadelphia chapter. His activities were noted in a series of FBI memos filed between June and October 1969, culminating in a report from FBI HEADQUARTERS (dated 24 October 1969) that read:

"In spite of the subject's age (15 years) Philadelphia feels that his continued participation in BPP activities in the Philadelphia Division, his position in the Philadelphia Branch of the BPP, and his past inclination to appear and speak at public gatherings, the subject should be included in the SECURITY INDEX."

Abu-Jamal reduced his Panther activity in 1970, upon his return to high school and later enrollment in college. He launched a career as a radio commentator in 1973, and in 1980 became president of Philadelphia's Association of Black Journalists. The *Philadelphia Inquirer* praised Abu-Jamal in January 1981 for his "eloquent, often passionate, and always insightful interviews." Controversial broadcasts ultimately led to his dismissal from a local radio station, and Abu-Jamal soon attached himself to MOVE — ostensibly an all-black environmentalist group (some say religious cult) whose members took the surname "Africa." Confrontations with police led to tragedy on 12 May 1984, when officers laid siege to MOVE's Philadelphia compound, fired some 10,000 bullets into the rambling structure, then dropped an aerial bomb that killed 11 persons and incinerated 60 homes, but by that time Abu-Jamal was already imprisoned on unrelated charges.

At 3:54 a.m. on 9 December 1981, Patrolman Daniel Faulkner stopped a car driven by Abu-Jamal's brother, Billy Cook. An altercation followed, during which Faulkner struck Cook with his flashlight. Police received a call at 4:00 a.m., informing them that Faulkner had been shot. Arriving on the scene, they found Faulkner dead from bullet wounds to his back and forehead. Nearby, Abu-Jamal sat on the curb, a pistol close beside him; he had been shot once in the chest with Faulkner's gun.

Despite an alleged hospital confession from Abu-Jamal (which he denied), the evidence was ambiguous at best. Four alleged eyewitnesses offered conflicting versions of the shooting: all agreed that a man had run across the street to confront Faulkner during his brawl with Billy Cook, but two failed to identify Abu-Jamal, while a third initially claimed the shooter had "run away," instead of waiting on the curb near Faulkner's corpse. The "star" witness described Abu-Jamal shooting Faulkner in the back, then standing over his prostrate form to fire multiple close-range shots—but she could not explain why only one round from the point-blank fusillade found its target. Meanwhile, the bullets extracted from Faulkner were too mangled for a ballistics match to the suspect's alleged weapon, though their caliber was "consistent."

Abu-Jamal's murder trial was a fiasco. The defendant's initial efforts to represent himself were deemed disruptive and he was excluded from half the proceedings. Refuting claims of a confession, Abu-Jamal's lawyer produced a report from Officer Gary Wakshul that Abu-Jamal "made no comment" in the emergency room, but Judge Albert Sabo refused to admit the statement or "hold up the trial" by calling Wakshul to testify. The witness who first claimed that Faulkner's slayer "ran away" changed his story in court and fingered Abu-Jamal as the gunman. The jury's guilty verdict on 2 July 1982 was no surprise. Abu-Jamal received a death sentence on 10 July 1982, upheld by Pennsylvania's Supreme Court on 6 March 1989.

While the FBI played no part in Abu-Jamal's prosecution, revelations of its prior interest in young Wesley Cook prompted speculation on a possible FRAME-UP, similar to those suffered by Black Panther ELMER PRATT and other victims of the Bureau's illegal COINTELPRO campaigns. That speculation was buttressed in June 1999, when a new player—one Arnold Beverly—confessed to Faulkner's murder. According to his sworn affidavit Beverly "was hired, along with another guy, and paid to shoot and kill Faulkner," because Faulkner had "interfered with the graft and payoffs made to allow illegal activity including prostitution, gambling, drugs without prosecution in the center city area." Beverly added that Faulkner was shot "before Jamal came on the scene. Jamal had nothing to do with the shooting."

No court has yet evaluated Beverly's statement, but Abu-Jamal was spared from death row in December 2001, when federal judge William Yohn invalidated the penalty phase of the 1982 trial. At the same time, however, Yohn upheld Abu-Jamal's murder conviction, effectively commuting his sentence to life imprisonment. His case remains a global cause célèbre for groups and individuals convinced of Abu-Jamal's innocence.

**ADAMS, J. Gary**—A member of the FBI's SWAT team assigned to the troubled Pine Ridge, South Dakota, Indian reservation in the 1970s, Gary Adams is described in sworn testimony as a bitter enemy of the AMERICAN INDIAN MOVEMENT. He was involved in the shootout that left two agents dead at Pine Ridge, on 26 June 1975, and counted the victims among his best friends. Thereafter, Adams was deeply involved in the search for suspects

in those killings, both around Pine Ridge and nationwide. Published reports of his conduct in that manhunt suggest that Adams frequently crossed the line between normal investigation and a personal vendetta.

On 10 September 1975 Adams interrogated 15-year-old shootout witness MICHAEL ANDERSON in jail, denying Anderson's request for an attorney and recruiting Anderson as a prosecution witness with alleged threats of violence. Twelve days later, Adams grilled 17-year-old Norman Brown, warning him, "If you don't talk to us, you might never walk the earth again." (At trial, in 1976, Both Anderson and Brown recanted their statements to Adams, testifying that their affidavits were false and obtained by coercion.) While questioning another suspect, Adams was recorded urging Leonard Crow Dog to see if he could "outrun the bullet from my M16…. Come on, go for it. I'll give you a head start. All you have to do is run." In March 1976 Adams investigated the vigilante murder of AIM associate ANNA MAE AQUASH, later described by the U.S. Commission on Civil Rights as "at the very least [an] extremely indifferent and careless investigation." (The case remains unsolved today.) No record exists of any FBI investigation or disciplinary action resulting from these unorthodox activities.

**ADAMS, Léonie**—The first female writer placed under federal surveillance, Léonie Adams drew attention from the Bureau of Investigation in 1921, after she published several poems in a leftist magazine, *The Liberator*. Nothing more was added to her file until 1932, when agents noted her affiliation with the League of Professional Groups for [William] Foster and [James] Ford, the COMMUNIST PARTY's candidates for president and vice president. In 1948, as the post-war Red Scare gathered steam, Adams was appointed as Consultant in Poetry for the Library of Congress. An FBI loyalty investigation was requested by the Civil Service Commission in 1949—curiously delayed until after Adams had the job—and G-men reported no evidence of communist sympathies. Aside from describing Adams as "a descendant of President Adams," the reports note that "she believes the Communist movement has stifled free thinking and affected the poetic movement in Russia." Adams resigned her position after one year—an established tradition for the library's poetry consultants—whereupon her FBI file noted that she "terminated employment prior to a decision on loyalty." No further investigation was pursued.

**ADMINISTRATIVE Index**—The FBI's Administrative Index (ADEX) was created to preserve information previously filed in the AGITATOR INDEX and SECURITY INDEX. The Agitator Index was abolished by J. EDGAR HOOVER in spring 1971, followed by the Security Index on 16 September 1971, when Congress repealed emergency detention provisions of the 1950 INTERNAL SECURITY ACT. A memo of 17 September from Richard Cotter, head of the FBI's INTELLIGENCE DIVISION, warned Hoover that "the potential dangerousness of subversives is probably even greater now than before the repeal of the Act, since they no doubt feel safer now to conspire in the destruction of this country." Cotter urged Hoover "to determine if there is any manner in which the essence of the Security Index and emergency detention of dangerous individuals could be utilized under Presidential powers."

Hoover sought advice on the matter from Attorney General JOHN MITCHELL, on 30 September 1971. Mitchell replied on 22 October that "the repeal of the aforementioned Act does not alter or limit the FBI's authority and responsibility to record, file and index information secured pursuant to its statutory and Presidential authority. An FBI administrative index compiled and maintained to assist the Bureau in making readily retrievable and available the results of its investigations into subversive activities and related matters is not prohibited by the repeal of the Emergency Detention Act."

Thus encouraged—and despite a February 1972 directive from Assistant Attorney General Robert Mardian, ordering destruction of FILES collected under the defunct statute—Hoover proceeded to create a new, improved "subversives" list. The ADEX was divided into four categories "representing degrees of dangerousness," and given Hoover's racism, many of those listed were black. Category I included names of "national leaders of black extremist separatist organizations" with other suspected radicals. Category II listed the "secondary leadership" and "active participants" in suspect groups—more specifically, anyone who furthered "the aims and purposes of the revolutionary or black extremist separatist organization with which affiliated." Category III included "rank-and-file membership," plus any "individual[s] who, although not a member of or participant in activities of revolutionary organizations or considered an activist in affiliated fronts, has exhibited a revolutionary ideology." Category IV tossed in the proverbial kitchen sink, listing "individuals whose activities do not meet the criteria of Categories I, II, or III." As if ADEX were not already vague enough, a parallel RESERVE INDEX included names of "teachers, writers, lawyers, etc.," who—while not actively subversive "were nonetheless influential in espousing their respective philosophies."

The ADEX survived its creator. Four months after Hoover's death, on 18 September 1972, FBI Acting Director L. PATRICK GRAY informed Attorney General RICHARD KLEINDIENST that the bureau's list included "[I]ndividuals whether affiliated with organized groups or not, who have shown a willingness and capability of engaging in treason, rebellion, or insurrection, seditious conspiracy, sabotage, espionage, terrorism, guerrilla warfare, assassination of Government officials or leaders, or other acts that would result in interference with or a threat to the survival and effective operation of national, state, or local government."

Exposure of the WATERGATE scandal and the subsequent resignation of President RICHARD NIXON curtailed FBI plans for a mass roundup of American "subversives." A memorandum from Director CLARENCE KELLY, dated 7 June 1973, advised all field offices that the ADEX was "strictly an administrative device" and should play no part "in investigative decisions or policies." From there, it was a short step to final abolition of the index, though specific dates are unavailable and critics remain unconvinced that the files have in fact been destroyed.

**ADMINISTRATIVE Services Division**—Prior to 1993, the FBI's Administrative Services Division (ASD) managed the bureau's financial affairs, including budgets and accounting, payrolls and disbursement vouchers, and procurement; the ASD was also in charge building maintenance and space allocation, as well as all FBI personnel matters (including recruitment and hiring, performance evaluations, employee benefit programs, and training courses provided by independent contractors under the Government Employees Training Act. Furthermore, the ASD was responsible for printing and office supplies at FBIHQ and physical security for bureau facilities in Washington, D.C., and Quantico, Virginia. Finally, it coordinated preparation and presentation of the FBI's budget requests to the Justice Department, Congress, and the Office of Management and Budget. In 1993, Director LOUIS FREEH divided the ASD into two new divisions, the FINANCE DIVISION and the PERSONNEL DIVISION.

**AFRICAN Blood Brotherhood**—Organized in early 1919, the African Blood Brotherhood (ABB) was founded by Cyril V. Briggs, a native of Nevis, in the Leeward Islands. Briggs came to the U.S. in 1905, at age eighteen, and began a journalistic career in 1912. The federal government took umbrage to his editorials opposing black participation in World War I. Briggs established a socialist newspaper, the *Crusader*, which appeared regularly from September 1918 through April 1922. Initially promoting the Hamitic League of the World, seeking self-determination for "all people of Color" worldwide, the *Crusader* soon became the organ of the ABB. In 1919 Military Intelligence branded the *Crusader* a "very extreme magazine," noted for "abuse of the white man," and Bureau of Investigation chief WILLIAM FLYNN agreed.

Infiltration of the ABB began in January 1920, when informant WILLIAM BAILEY joined the group; other BI spies over the next two years included HERBERT BOULIN, WILLIAM LUCAS, and JAMES W. JONES. Aside from Briggs, the ABB's most effective spokesman was Barbados native Richard B. Moore, subjected after March 1920 to what his family later termed "lifetime surveillance," spurred by federal antipathy to his lectures on "straight socialism" and "Negro-ology." Some members of the ABB openly embraced the U.S. COMMUNIST PARTY, while reserving some of their most strident criticism for MARCUS GARVEY's back-to-Africa movement.

In May 1921 Briggs took advantage of the bloody Tulsa race riot to claim a mythical 150 ABB chapters and 50,000 members nationwide. More critically, he praised Tulsa blacks for their armed self-defense against white lynch mobs, thereby prompting BI INFORMANTS to allege that the ABB "fomented and directed the Tulsa riots." Seemingly oblivious to the fact that white rioters started the violence and committed most of the murders, J. EDGAR HOOVER convinced himself that socialists directed and bankrolled black militancy—a view he still maintained, against all available evidence, fifty years later. At the same time, BI infiltrators noted and encouraged the ABB's efforts to win members away from Garvey's Universal Negro Improvement Association (a divide-and-conquer tactic also used against black militants in later years). BI director WILLIAM BURNS ordered "close surveillance" of Briggs in the fall of 1921, apparently convinced that the ABB constituted a "colossal conspiracy against the United States."

Still nothing happened, despite false reports of a black uprising planned for 3 July 1921. Federal interest waned after April 1922, when the *Crusader* went bankrupt and ceased publication. Bureau fears were rekindled in August 1923, after a Michigan raid on the Communist Party revealed tenuous links to the ABB, and informant EARL TITUS was dispatched for a last round of surveillance, supervised by black agent JAMES AMOS. Briggs still claimed 8,722 ABB members, but barely 3,000 were "active," two-thirds of those being women. By early 1924, Briggs had failed in his attempts to unite America's black leaders under a "Negro Sanhedrin," and his "Tiger Scouts" youth auxiliary also likewise failed to prosper. The ABB was defunct by year's end, Hoover's agents distracted by new perils.

**AGEE, James**—A noted American novelist, screenwriter and film critic, James Agee became an object of FBI surveillance in 1937, after he published a poem and two book reviews in a leftist magazine, the *New Masses*. In 1942, following publication of his novel *Let Us Now Praise Famous Men*, a note in Agee's FBI file described him as "formerly a Liberal fellow traveler, but now in opposition to the COMMUNIST PARTY." Interviewed by G-men in 1943, Agee expressed "disappointment" with the communist program in America. Six years later, FBI leaders worried over Agee's friendship with CHARLIE CHAPLIN and his script for a new film, *The Quiet One*. Worse yet, Agee had penned a letter to federal prosecutors denouncing a prime witness in the case of ALGER HISS. Still under sporadic surveillance, Agee died in 1954, three years before his novel *A Death in the Family* was published and won the Pulitzer Prize.

**AGENT Misconduct**—Misconduct by FBI agents is broadly divided into two categories: official misconduct committed in performance of assigned duties, and private activities falling outside the scope of an agent's normal duty. Historically, Bureau leaders have often closed their eyes to such criminal behavior as warrantless BREAK-INS, BUGGING and WIRETAPPING, and they often ordered such activities, with the understanding that "deniability" would be preserved if agents were caught breaking state or federal laws. Under the 48-year rule of Director J. EDGAR HOOVER, the FBI's unwritten motto was "Don't embarrass the Bureau," a perpetual warning to G-men that the worst of all possible sins was getting caught.

Spokesmen for the "modern" FBI insist that such illegal practices died with Hoover in 1972, but the record does not support their portrait of a reformed and squeaky-clean Bureau. Hoover's COINTELPRO harassment campaigns were officially canceled in 1970, but identical techniques were employed against the AMERICAN INDIAN MOVEMENT in 1973-76 and against the COMMITTEE IN SOLIDARITY WITH THE PEOPLE OF EL SALVADOR a decade later. President RONALD REAGAN, himself a one-time FBI INFORMANT, gave tacit approval to criminal activity by pardoning agents convicted of illegal bugging and other crimes under a previous administration. In 1991, undercover agent LINDA THOMPSON was accused of using sex to obtain information from a BANK ROBBERY suspect. (She denies the charge.) Shocking revelations of FBI collusion with Boston gangsters, couched in terms

of an ORGANIZED CRIME investigation, sent ex-agent JOHN CONNOLLY to prison on racketeering charges in 2002. On another front, passage of the USA PATRIOT ACT to counteract TERRORISM in the U.S. after 11 September 2001, sparked protests from civil libertarians that the bad old days of widespread domestic surveillance were making a comeback in the guise of "national security."

Reliable statistics on the number of FBI personnel disciplined for misconduct are sparse and closely guarded. Author Robert Kessler has revealed that in 1990, under Director WILLIAM SESSIONS, 1,304 of the Bureau's 23,700 employees (5.5 percent) were investigated on misconduct charges. Of those, 775 received some disciplinary action ranging from censure to dismissal; in the serious cases, 25 were fired, 12 demoted, and 13 suspended for two weeks or longer. Those fired included four agents and 21 clerks. Another 67 (including 11 agents and 56 clerks) resigned while under investigation. (Director Sessions himself was fired in July 1993 for misusing FBI funds.)

On 9 December 1998, Director LOUIS FREEH announced a new policy of reporting annual disciplinary statistics compiled by the OFFICE OF PROFESSIONAL RESPONSIBILITY (OPR) in order "to reduce job-related misconduct by FBI employees while ensuring that the rights of all are fully protected during the investigation of alleged wrongdoing." The program was short lived, with only three announcements issued: in 1998 (for 1997), 1999 (for 1998), and 2000 (for 1999). An article in the November 2001 *Law Enforcement Bulletin* observes that "[s]ome agencies, including the FBI, issue formal yearly reports on their disciplinary process," but at this writing (in July 2002) no such reports have been released since June 1999.

The three reports published under Director Freeh provide a bit more insight into FBI personnel misconduct, although their value is limited. In 1997, we are told that that 212 of the Bureau's 28,000 employees (99 agents and 113 support employees) were disciplined "for offenses classified as serious misconduct." Of those, 19 were fired and 193 received unspecified "lesser punishments." The report for 1998 (issued in August 1999) states simply that 32 FBI employees were fired during the year, while 269 received "lesser punishment" for unstated offenses. No statistics were offered on the number of agents versus support personnel involved in misconduct, but the total figure (301) represents a 42% increase over 1997. The last report thus far, for 1999 (issued on 7 July 2000), reveals that 278 out of 28,200 Bureau employees were disciplined for unspecified offenses, with 14 dismissed and 264 receiving "lesser punishment." Again, no breakdown was provided between agents and support personnel, and the statistics may be incomplete, since a July 2000 FBI report notes that OPR agents conducted only "about one-fourth of the investigations of employees for serious misconduct."

A sampling of the FBI's more notorious misconduct cases includes—

**1980**—Agents ALAN ROTTON AND STEPHEN TRAVIS are fired and indicted on theft charges in Kansas City. Rotton commits suicide, while Travis is sentenced to prison.

**1980**—Agent H. EDWARD TICKEL, JR., is caught burglarizing FBI headquarters. He initially tries to frame a janitor for the crime, then fails a polygraph test and receives an eight-year prison term.

1984—Agent RICHARD MILLER is convicted and sentenced to prison for espionage.

1985—Miami agent DANIEL MITRIONE, JR., pleads guilty to bribery and possessing 92 pounds of cocaine.

1986—FBI polygrapher HARRY PEEL commits suicide in Florida, during an investigation of his alleged HOMOSEXUALITY.

1986—Cleveland agent ROBERT FRIEDRICK is fired for lying during an investigation of his ties to corrupt TEAMSTERS UNION officials.

1987—FRANK and SUZANNE MONSERRATE, a husband-wife team of agents in Florida, are fired for joining a "swingers" sex club.

1988—Philadelphia agent ANTHONY REZZA is fired for compulsive gambling. He sues the Bureau for discrimination, citing his "disability," and wins the case.

1990—Agent FERNANDO MATA is fired for alerting Cuban intelligence agents to surveillance mounted by the CENTRAL INTELLIGENCE AGENCY. Mata sues the Bureau, charging racial discrimination.

1990—Agent MARK PUTNAM pleads guilty to manslaughter in the strangling of his pregnant mistress.

1996—Agent EUGENE BENNETT is imprisoned for attempting to murder his wife (also an FBI agent) over her lesbian affair with best-selling mystery novelist Patricia Cornwell.

1996—GARY HARLOW, an instructor at the FBI ACADEMY, is fired after a wife-beating incident reveals his theft of Bureau equipment, including seven machine guns and 100,000 rounds of ammunition.

2000—Agent DAVID FARRALL is fired for a drunk-driving incident that killed two motorists in Florida. Local police claim FBI officials first tried to whitewash the crime.

2001—Agent ROBERT HANSSEN admits a 20-year history of spying for Russia and receives a life prison term.

**AGITATOR Index** *see* **Rabble Rouser Index**

**AGNEW, Spiro Theodore**—A son of Greek immigrants, born in Baltimore on 9 November 1918, Spiro Agnew received a law degree from the University of Baltimore in 1947. In 1962, campaigning as a reformer, he was elected chief executive of Baltimore County. Four years later, Agnew was elected governor of Maryland. Republican presidential candidate RICHARD NIXON chose Agnew as his running mate in 1968.

That campaign was well advanced when President LYNDON JOHNSON heard rumors of a Republican effort to sabotage peace negotiations on the VIETNAM WAR. Specifically, Anna Chennault—a Chinese-born Republican activist and leader of Concerned Asians for Nixon—was suspected of urging South Vietnamese leaders to stall the peace talks. Johnson ordered an FBI investigation, which included wiretaps and physical surveillance on Chennault. Three days before the election, on 2 November 1968, FBI eavesdroppers heard Chennault advise a South Vietnamese politician that his country would "get a better deal" from Nixon in the new year. Asked if Nixon knew what she was doing,

Chennault replied, "No, but our friend in New Mexico does." Coincidentally or otherwise, Spiro Agnew spent that afternoon in Albuquerque, making campaign speeches.

J. EDGAR HOOVER, himself a staunch Nixon supporter, reported the conversation to President Johnson on 6 November. Furious, LBJ telephoned Nixon—already the president-elect—and chastised him for meddling in U.S. foreign policy. Hoover subsequently reported the FBI investigation of Agnew and Chennault to Nixon, placing full blame on the Johnson White House.

If Agnew took offense at the snooping, he covered it well. Over the next four years, employed primarily as Nixon's mouthpiece for stinging attacks on the press, "radical liberals" and other targets drawn from the White House enemies list, Agnew repeatedly sought Hoover's help in preparing his inflammatory speeches, once requesting "especially graphic incidents" from classified FILES to smear his critics. A phone call 18 May 1970, for instance, solicited FBI assistance in defaming Rev. RALPH ABERNATHY, a civil rights activist and leader of the SOUTHERN CHRISTIAN LEADERSHIP CONFERENCE. Hoover described the call in a memo: "The Vice President said he thought he was going to have to start destroying Abernathy's credibility, so anything I can give him would be appreciated. I told him that I would be glad to."

Exposure of the WATERGATE SCANDAL in 1972 spelled political doom for Spiro Agnew. Journalists investigating the Nixon administration discovered that Agnew had been taking bribes since 1962, from engineers and architects pursuing government contracts in Maryland. The payoffs had continued after he became vice president, Agnew persistently failing to report the income on his tax returns. Meeting with Nixon on 6 August 1973, Agnew proclaimed himself innocent of any wrongdoing, but his days were numbered. On 10 October 1973 he resigned in disgrace, pleading "no contest" the same afternoon on one count of income tax evasion dating from 1967. Agnew was fined $10,000 and placed on three years' probation. Following his resignation, Agnew told friends he had been threatened by unnamed persons at the Nixon White House and stated, "I feared for my life." He never spoke to Nixon again.

**AHRENS, Robin**—Born 6 May 1952 in St. Paul, Minnesota, Robin Ahrens graduated from Utah State University in 1974, with a bachelor of fine arts degree. She taught school in Idaho until 1980, when she moved to Harrisonburg, Virginia, and enrolled at James Madison University, earning a media specialist degree in 1983. She entered the FBI Academy on 14 October 1984, but her graduation was delayed until June 1985 by an injury suffered in training. On 28 June 1985 Ahrens was assigned to her first active-duty post at the Phoenix field office.

On 4 October 1985, Ahrens was among a group of agents detailed to arrest a suspected armored car bandit. The raid was tragically confused: fellow agents mistook Ahrens for an armed accomplice of their suspect and shot her, resulting in her death on October 5. The first WOMAN AGENT killed on duty, Ahrens was memorialized by having the new Phoenix field office named in her honor.

**AIKEN, Conrad**—A prominent American poet, novelist and

critic, Conrad Aiken was one of several writers investigated by G-men in the 1940s, because of his friendship with indicted poet EZRA POUND. Ironically, the FBI fumbled its first brush with Aiken, when a letter he wrote to ERNEST HEMINGWAY in Cuba was intercepted by the Office of Censorship. That agency misread Aiken's signature as "Allen," but preserved the letter in Pound's file, including Aiken's observation that: "I am afraid, as I told Archie [ARCHIBALD MACLEISH] that we will have to stick our necks out for the rope after Ezra has dropped through the trap. If we do it before, we will make the case worse—if they shoot him, I suggest that a few of us get out on a limb and raise hell."

It never came to that, as Pound was declared mentally unfit for trial, but the FBI launched its own investigation of Aiken on 12 December 1945, seeking to learn "discreetly" whether Aiken planned to appear as a character witness for Pound. The last entry in Aiken's 20-page FBI file offers an FBI critique of a poem he published in *Ramparts* magazine: "Life is a wonder imprisoned in the humdrum. Above all it is brief."

## ALGREN, Nelson

ALGREN, Nelson—An American novelist whose acclaimed works included *The Man with the Golden Arm* and *A Walk on the Wild Side*, Nelson Algren was subject to intermittent FBI surveillance for thirty-five years, compiling a 568-page dossier. He first ran afoul of G-men in 1935, when he joined the League of American Writers (considered a "communist front" by J. EDGAR HOOVER) and later served as executive secretary of the league's Chicago chapter. Friend and fellow author Studs Terkel once remarked that Algren "was always chased [by the FBI] because he was such a natural. He was like a character from one of his books. And he was a clown in a big way. The FBI clowns in a lower class way."

The bureau's pursuit of Algren was confused, at best. Once, when a telephone listed his lover Simone de Beauvoir as the sole occupant of Algren's address, agents filed the name "de Beauvoir" as an Algren "alias." Other reports named Algren as a leader of the COMMUNIST PARTY (a charge he denied) and as a "publicity agent for the ROSENBERGS, executed Communist agents." In 1969, four years before Algren's death, a final report claimed he was "working actively" for the party but "is not known by the name Algren," complaining that he wrote "cleverly and with great facility left wing slanted articles."

## ALIEN Enemy Bureau

ALIEN Enemy Bureau—J. EDGAR HOOVER began his career with the JUSTICE DEPARTMENT on 26 July 1917, as a clerk for the Alien Enemy Bureau, assigned to keep records on suspected violators of the new Alien Enemies Act. Under that statute, aliens were forbidden to own firearms, explosives, radio transmitters, or documents "printed in cipher or in which there may be invisible writing." They were likewise barred from entering or leaving the U.S., or traveling within a half-mile of restricted areas (military bases, munitions depots, selected seaports and the nation's capital). Strict rules of censorship were also imposed.

> An alien enemy shall not write, print, or publish any attack or threats against the Government or Congress of the United States, or either branch thereof, or against the measures or policy of the United States, or against the person or property of any person in the military, naval, or civil service of the United States, or the States or Territories, or of the District of Columbia or of the municipal governments therein.

Finally, male German immigrants were required to register with the federal government on 16 November 1917, females no later than 19 April 1918.

On 18 June 1918 Hoover was promoted to the rank of attorney "reviewing aliens who volunteered for military duty and wanted to become citizens." By September he was screening travel plans as well. Infractions could bring stiff penalties, as when Hoover recommended permanent internment for a German who "engaged in conversation with a negro in which he indulged in pro-German utterances and in derogatory remarks regarding the United States." (A superior overruled that harsh judgment.) Of 4,000 "alien enemies" arrested during WORLD WAR I, fewer than 200 were convicted of any crime. After the war, President WOODROW WILSON pardoned three of those and commuted the sentence of 102 others. The Alien Enemy Bureau was dissolved after the armistice and Hoover moved to a new Justice post in June 1919.

## ALLEN, Fred

ALLEN, Fred—A vaudeville comic who found his greatest success in radio with humorous variety programs, Fred Allen first drew the FBI's attention in 1936, with a slapstick skit depicting the bureau's "third-degree" techniques. The routine portrayed a murder suspect beaten with rubber hoses, who later chokes on a martini olive when the G-men try a gentler approach to obtaining his confession. Despite the potentially controversial subject matter, Assistant to the Director CLYDE TOLSON enjoyed the sketch and so advised J. EDGAR HOOVER, who also found it amusing. So pleased was Hoover, in fact, that he requested a transcript "to be included in our FILES" and sought permission to reprint it in the FBI's in-house magazine, *The Investigator*, suggesting that "the employees of this Bureau would find much amusement in reading your version of third degree tactics."

Encouraged by the warm reception, Allen included FBI agents—and sometimes Hoover himself—in numerous radio skits spanning the next decade. Even his portrayal of "Inspector Bungle, the poor man's J. Edgar Hoover" caused no offense, until a punch line from actor Edward G. Robinson offended Hoover's sense of propriety. Playing his standard gangster role, Robinson wisecracked to Allen that "crime does not pay and neither does going straight." Hoover took umbrage at the joke and protested to Allen's sponsor that "clean living not only pays dividends but is the only decent pattern of human behavior." Unmoved by explanations that the line had been "pure farce and hokum," Hoover remained a staunch critic of Allen's work thereafter, until the comic died in 1956.

## ALLEN, William E.

ALLEN, William E.—Following the resignation of A. BRUCE BIELASKI, William Allen was appointed acting chief of the Bureau of Investigation on 10 February 1919, by Attorney General THOMAS GREGORY. He served until 30 June 1919, when WILLIAM FLYNN assumed control as the bureau's full-time director.

## AMERASIA Case

AMERASIA Case—Published during WORLD WAR II, *Amerasia*

was a periodical concerned primarily with Far Eastern affairs. Its contents naturally interested American intelligence agencies, but never so much as in January 1945, when analyst Kenneth Wells recognized one article as a near-verbatim transcript of a classified report he had recently filed with the OFFICE OF STRATEGIC SERVICES. Wells informed his superiors of the apparent security breach, and OSS agents burglarized *Amerasia*'s office on the night of 11 March 1945. Their search disclosed more classified documents ("dozens" or "thousands"; reports vary) from the OSS, STATE DEPARTEMENT, and Office of Naval Intelligence (ONI). Legally barred from investigating domestic cases, OSS leaders turned their information over to the FBI on 14 March.

Leaping at the chance to crack a spy ring, J. EDGAR HOOVER ordered a series of BREAK-INS and WIRETAPS to discover *Amerasia*'s sources. Targets included publisher Philip Jaffe, editor Kate Mitchell, and freelance reporter Mark Gayn. By late spring, the bureau had identified three leaks in Washington: State Department staffers Emmanuel Larsen and John Service, plus ONI employee Andrew Roth. A break-in at Larsen's apartment confirmed his possession of classified papers, and all six were arrested on 6 June 1945. Only three of the six — Jaffe, Larsen and Roth — were indicted, charged with unauthorized possession of classified government papers.

By that time, the case had begun to unravel. Struck by the ease with which G-men found documents hidden around his apartment, Larsen posted bond and grilled the building's janitor, thereby learning of a previous, illegal search. Confronted with proof of FBI burglary, U.S. attorneys offered Larsen and Jaffe a bargain on 28 September 1945, waiving prosecution in return for payment of small fines. Charges against Andrew Ross were dismissed.

**AMERICAN Civil Liberties Union** — Founded in 1920, the American Civil Liberties Union (ACLU) was created by ROGER BALDWIN to replace his National Civil Liberties Bureau in the wake of WORLD WAR I. For the better part of a century it has provided free legal defense to clients of various races, religions and political persuasions in cases where their constitutional rights are abridged by some official action. With clients ranging from the far left to the neo-Nazi right, the ACLU is ever controversial — and it drew attention from the FBI within months of its creation.

FBI FILES released under the FREEDOM OF INFORMATION ACT reveal that the ACLU was under continual bureau surveillance for nearly half a century, from Baldwin's initial 1924 meeting with J. EDGAR HOOVER to the date of Hoover's death in 1972 (and perhaps beyond). While Hoover feigned sympathy in his first conversation with Baldwin, he hated the "liberal" ACLU and all it stood for — particularly when his own tactics were criticized. Ever resourceful, though, Hoover found ways to block that criticism and corrupt the ACLU's leadership, even as he kept the group under nonstop surveillance, indexing names of its members for wartime custodial detention.

FBI records disclose that MORRIS ERNST, general counsel of the ACLU, exchanged more than 300 personal letters with Hoover between 1939 and 1964, keeping Hoover informed of every move the group made. Obsessed with purging COMMU-

NIST PARTY members from the ACLU, Ernst passed along everything from membership lists and trial strategies to office gossip. An internal report cleared Ernst of "over improprieties" in 1977, but ACLU executive director Aryeh Neier called Ernst's dealings with the FBI "inexcusable and destructive of civil liberties."

He was not the worst, even so. Irving Ferman, director of the ACLU's Washington, D.C. chapter, was described in the same 1977 report as having maintained "the most intensive and extensive and secretive" FBI relationship of any ACLU leader — a relationship described as "friendly and somewhat clubby." Between 1952 and 1959 Ferman delivered reams of documents and correspondence to the bureau, conceding from retirement that "perhaps he was violating his trust with the organization" in the process. Assistant FBI Director LOUIS NICHOLS was sufficiently impressed to praise Ferman for being "as much a soldier as those of us serving the Bureau."

The ACLU's 1977 lawsuit unearthed 41,728 pages of FBI reports dating back to 1917, when Baldwin led the American Union Against Militarism. Spying had intensified in 1940, after ACLU spokesmen opposed a $100,000 congressional appropriation for the FBI. Reports filed in the wake of that *faux pas* noted that Ernest Besig, ACLU director for northern California, was "not a Communist [but] enough of a troublemaker not to be left alone"; in southern California, meanwhile, G-men deemed that "every person" in the ACLU's office "is a Communist."

Exposure of illegal FBI wiretaps in the 1949 JUDITH COPLON case prompted criticism from ACLU board member James Fry, but other leaders of the group dissented, praising the bureau's efforts to purge America of communists. The ACLU's annual report for 1953 found "a heartening expression of principle" in one of Hoover's recent ghost-written articles ("Civil Liberties and Law Enforcement"), alleging that FBI violation of civil rights "seems to be happily infrequent." Lou Nichols lied outright to ACLU staff counsel Herbert Levy, telling him that Hoover considered the ACLU a "very worthwhile organization," and ACLU director Louis Joughin suppressed a pamphlet published by the Philadelphia chapter advising citizens of their rights during an FBI interrogation. Joughin, in his wisdom, deemed the warning "unjustified" and "unwise."

The ACLU's one-sided love affair with Hoover's FBI ended in March 1971, after anti-war protestors stole and published thousands of COINTELPRO documents outlining the bureau's illegal harassment of various political groups. On 29-30 October 1971, the ACLU hosted a sharply critical conference on FBI activities, convened at Princeton University. Surveillance and infiltration of the ACLU allegedly ended with Hoover's death in May 1972, but in light of past history some ACLU members remain unconvinced.

The ACLU continued its role as a thorn in the side of FBI HEADQUARTERS in July 2002, opposing new bids by Attorney General JOHN ASHCROFT to permit sweeping FBI DOMESTIC SURVEILLANCE in locations open to the public, whether or not those persons under surveillance had committed or planned to commit any crimes. Interviewed by the *San Francisco Chronicle*, ACLU spokespersons declared that they had "drawn a line with respect to privacy, political and associational rights that government must not cross even with the best of intentions." President GEORGE W.

BUSH responded from Washington that limits on domestic spying might cripple his administrations "war on TERRORISM." The debate continues.

**AMERICAN Indian Movement** — Patterned after the California-based BLACK PANTHER PARTY, the American Indian Movement (AIM) was organized in Minneapolis during the summer of 1968. Founding member Dennis Banks describes its origin and purpose: "Because of the slum housing conditions; the highest unemployment rate in the whole of this country; police brutality against our elders, women, and children; Native Warriors came together from the streets, prisons, jails and urban ghettos of Minneapolis to form the American Indian Movement. They were tired of begging for welfare, tired of being scapegoats in America and decided to start building on the strengths of our own people; decided to build our own schools; our own job training programs; and our own destiny. That was our motivation to begin. That beginning is now being called 'the Era of Indian Power.'"

As chapters spread across the country, AIM began to garner national attention. Members participated in the 1969 occupation of Alcatraz Island, though AIM did not initiate the move. A 1972 "Trail of Broken Treaties" march on Washington, D.C. climaxed with presentation of a 20-point solution paper to President RICHARD NIXON. The following year, a 71-day occupation of WOUNDED KNEE (South Dakota) included violent clashes with the FBI and U.S. Army. An eight-month trial in 1974 exposed FBI harassment tactics at Wounded Knee and ended with dismissal of charges against all AIM defendants, Judge Fred Nichol declaring: "It's hard for me to believe that the FBI, which I have revered for many years, has fallen to this low estate." Violence flared again in 1975, at Pine Ridge, with two G-men slain in a reservation shootout. Suspect LEONARD PELTIER was convicted in that case, but two other AIM members—DINO BUTLER and BOB ROBIDEAU—were acquitted after pleading that they fired on FBI agents in self-defense.

AIM remains active today, though its programs rarely make national headlines. Minneapolis street patrols were revived in 1986, after a spate of SERIAL MURDERS targeting Native American women. In 1988, after 1,200 Indian graves were looted in Kentucky, AIM successfully promoted legislation making grave desecration a felony. Six years later, a six-month coast-to-coast "Walk for Justice" dramatized the prison ordeal of Leonard Peltier (but failed to win presidential clemency). FBI infiltration and harassment of AIM has presumably ceased, though members still recall an off-the-record comment from one G-man after Wounded Knee: "Half the stuff that went on out there isn't even on paper." In 2000, FBI Director LOUIS FREEH lobbied publicly (and successfully) to discourage President BILL CLINTON from pardoning Leonard Peltier.

**AMERICAN LEGION** — Organized by veterans of the First World War in 1919, the American Legion was created to promote "100% Americanism"—defined by its founders as militant opposition to all things "radical" or "Bolshevik." Violence quickly followed, with at least five deaths resulting by year's end, as Legionnaires attacked unfriendly editors, suspected communists or union strikers. The early Legion plainly favored fascism, as witnessed by its 1923 pledge of honorary membership to Italian dictator Benito Mussolini. Two years later, the national commander granted a newspaper interview that included threats to overthrow the U.S. government.

> "If ever needed [said Owsley], the American Legion stands ready to protect our country's institutions and ideals as the Fascisti dealt with the destructionists who menaced Italy!"
> "By taking over the Government?" he was asked.
> "Exactly that," he replied. "The American Legion is fighting every element that threatens our democratic government — Soviets, anarchists, IWW, revolutionary Socialists and any other 'Red' ....Do not forget that the Fascisti are to Italy what the American Legion is to the United States."

Nine years later, in the spring of 1934, high-ranking Legionnaires attempted to carry out Owsley's threat. Legion representative Gerald MacGuire approached retired Marine Corps general Smedley Butler with a plan to seize the White House from President FRANKLIN ROOSEVELT. Their vehicle, a front group called the American Liberty League, was bankrolled by a consortium of industrial giants opposed to the New Deal, including U.S. Steel, Standard Oil and General Motors. Before the league could recruit its army of a half-million veterans to march on Washington, however, Butler told his story to the FBI and the HOUSE COMMITTEE ON UN-AMERICAN ACTIVITIES. None of the plotters were arrested, but exposure doomed their efforts as financial backing was withdrawn.

On the eve of World War II, American Legion commanders announced their plan to organize a civilian spy network, keeping track of perceived "subversives" from coast to coast. Attorney General ROBERT JACKSON sidetracked the vigilante campaign by authorizing the FBI's American Legion Contact Program, whereby some 40,000 Legionnaires were recruited as "confidential national defense INFORMANTS," reporting gossip about their co-workers and neighbors. So successful was the program, filling J. EDGAR HOOVER'S private FILES with much information he might otherwise have missed, that the program was continued until 1966.

From the 1940s onward, Legionnaires provided Hoover's most dependable forum for speeches attacking communists, civil rights activists, anti-war protesters and other enemies of the FBI, but collaboration was not always peaceful. The Legion's super-patriots took themselves too seriously at times, as during the McCarthy era of the early 1950s. In 1953 Hoover ordered Inspector CARTHA DELOACH to join the Legion and "straighten it out." DeLoach enlisted, rising swiftly to become a post commander, department commander, then national vice-commander. Legionnaires wanted to elect him as their national commander in 1958, but Hoover vetoed the move, deeming the top post "too political." Instead, DeLoach became chairman of the Legion's national public relations commission, insuring that any public criticism of Hoover or the FBI was met by immediate protest from Legion posts nationwide, scripted by ghost writers in the FBI's CRIME RECORDS DIVISION.

**AMERICAN Protective League** —Spawned by xenophobic hysteria during WORLD WAR I, the American Protective League (APL) was organized by Chicago advertising executive Albert Briggs in 1916. Conceived as a private intelligence corps to police aliens and "radicals," the APL attracted 100,000 members in its first three months, topping 250,000 by the end of 1917. Its first step toward legitimacy, in February 1917, was an offer posed to Hinton Claybaugh, agent in charge of the Bureau of Investigation's Chicago field office. Claybaugh gladly accepted the APL's plan to spy on wealthy Germans by putting its members to work as chauffeurs and the like. When Briggs returned a month later, offering the bureau a fleet of seventy-five cars, Claybaugh kicked the proposal upstairs. Bureau chief A. BRUCE BIELASKI discussed the prospect with Attorney General THOMAS GREGORY, and both welcomed the APL as a quasi-official JUSTICE DEPARTMENT auxiliary force.

The bargain made sense at first glance, since the BI had only 265 agents to cover the entire United States. More eyes and hands were needed, but the deal caused trouble from day one. First, Treasury complained that APL detectives carried badges identifying them as "Secret Service" agents. Bielaski and Briggs changed the badges in time for their first joint action in Chicago, raiding offices of the INDUSTRIAL WORKERS OF THE WORLD in September 1917. By early 1918 there were reports of APL members burglarizing homes and offices, but Bielaski ignored it, since his agents sometimes did the same. The next public BI-APL collaboration occurred in March 1918, with a city-wide sweep for draft dodgers. That "slacker" roundup was deemed successful enough to prompt others in Cleveland, Detroit, San Francisco, Philadelphia, Dayton, St. Louis and Birmingham (where members of the KU KLUX KLAN joined in the hunt). Beginning on 3 September 1918, thirty-five BI agents, 2,000 APL vigilantes and scores of local police spent three days sweeping the streets of Manhattan, Brooklyn, Newark and Jersey City, jailing an estimated 75,000 suspects. When the dust settled, only one in 200 of those detained were proved to be "slackers."

Denunciation from the press and U.S. Senate scuttled any plans for further raids and stripped the APL of its official status. Two months later, on 11 November 1918, the armistice canceled any need to hunt draft dodgers in America. The APL was formally disbanded on 1 February 1919. The bureau's next experiment with civilian sleuths would wait until 1940, involving members of the AMERICAN LEGION.

**AMERICAN YOUTH Congress** —Organized on 4 July 1936, the American Youth Congress (AYC) was a consortium of representatives from 60 youth-oriented groups, ranging in political complexion from the Young Women's Christian Association to the leftist American League for Peace and Democracy. It's constitution declared that "our generation is rightfully entitled to a useful, creative, and happy life, the guarantees of which are: full educational opportunities, steady employment at adequate wages, security in time of need, civil rights, religious freedom, and peace." That subversive agenda drew immediate attention from the FBI, and AYC leaders were called to explain themselves before the HOUSE COMMITTEE ON UN-AMERICAN ACTIVITIES in November 1939.

That Washington appearance introduced the group to first lady ELEANOR ROOSEVELT, who praised the AYC's goals and told reporters her personal investigation of the group revealed nothing "to indicate any outside control" by communists or other foreign powers. Joseph Lash, an AYC spokesman and national secretary of the American Student Union, became a special protégé of Mrs. Roosevelt, invited with others to stay overnight at the White House, but he broke from the group over Stalin's alliance with Hitler and later denounced it as communist-controlled. In 1942, FBI agents burglarized AYC headquarters and photocopied the group's records, including correspondence from Mrs. Roosevelt. J. EDGAR HOOVER used that correspondence with "Reds" to justify his further investigations of the first lady, including reports on her alleged extramarital affairs.

**AMES, Aldrich Hazen** —The son of a CENTRAL INTELLIGENCE AGENCY officer, born 26 June 1941, Aldrich Ames worked summer jobs for the agency in his teens and joined full-time in February 1962. He quickly mastered Russian and distinguished himself in handling matters related to the Soviet Union. Lust intervened to sidetrack his career in 1981, while Ames was assigned to Mexico City. There, he met and fell in love with Maria del Rosario Casas Dupuy, a cultural attaché with the Colombian embassy who persuaded Ames to divorce his wife and marry her. Ames soon discovered that his salary could not satisfy Maria's expensive tastes, and his quest for additional money led him to become a mercenary Russian "mole" within the CIA.

Between 1985 and his arrest on 21 February 1994, Ames earned more than $2.5 million by selling classified information to Russian spies, his betrayal continuing beyond the 1991 collapse of the Soviet Union. Aside from delivering thousands of CIA documents, Ames also identified 25 Russian nationals employed as spies by the CIA or FBI. All were arrested by the KGB, with at least 10 subsequently executed. Those losses belatedly prompted a joint CIA-FBI investigation, beginning in 1991, but both agencies somehow ignored Ames's extravagant lifestyle until May 1993, when he was betrayed by a KGB defector. G-men then placed Ames under close surveillance, including phone taps, searches of his household trash (revealing notes from a Russian contact) and retrieval of information stored on his computer. Ames and his wife were both indicted on 26 April 1994, Ames quickly striking a bargain on Maria's behalf. The couple pled guilty to various charges on 28 April, Ames receiving a sentence of life without parole for conspiracy and tax fraud, while Maria received a sentence of five years and three months. Both the FBI and CIA were widely criticized for their apparent negligence in plugging the deadly intelligence leak.

**AMOS, James Edward** —A native of Washington, D.C., born 29 January 1879, James Amos held various jobs after graduating from high school, including positions as a steam engineer, a switchboard operator, and a telephone repairman. He entered law enforcement in the early 1900s, serving as a private investigator with the WILLIAM J. BURNS National Detective Agency and as a bodyguard for President Theodore Roosevelt. Burns was appointed to lead the Bureau of Investigation on 30 June 1919, and he hired Amos as a BI agent two years later, on 24 August 1921. Amos thus became the second of five black BI agents hired in the 1920s (before J. EDGAR HOOVER took control in 1924), and the only one of the five to make federal service a career.

Amos was used primarily to supervise the infiltration and disruption of black organizations, including MARCUS GARVEY's Universal Negro Improvement Association and the AFRICAN BLOOD BROTHERHOOD. He was among the agents who secured information resulting in Garvey's fraud conviction and eventual deportation from the United States. FBI press releases state that he later worked on underworld investigations, targeting New York mobsters LOUIS BUCHALTER and Dutch Schultz, but those claims are difficult to evaluate since the bureau never built a case against either subject. Amos retired on 10 October 1953, at age seventy-three, and died a short time later.

**ANARCHISTS** — In its purest form, anarchism is the belief that all forms of government should be abolished. Historically, some anarchists have gone beyond mere advocacy and attempted to secure their goal by physical attacks on prominent officials in Europe and the United States. Before the advent of Bolshevism, with the Russian revolution of 1917, "radicals" and "enemy aliens" in the U.S. were likely to be branded anarchists regardless of their actual philosophy. The same label was also broadly applied to social reformers and labor organizers, as a later generation of activists would be falsely branded "communist."

America's anarchist panic dated from 1880, with the onset of a major immigration wave from Italy. Several prominent anarchist spokesmen were among the new arrivals, including Luigi Galleani, Errico Malatesta and Carlo Tresca. On 4 May 1886 the Chicago Haymarket BOMBING killed eight policemen and an uncertain number of civilians, while injuring more than 260 others at a rally for striking workers. Eight alleged anarchists (none of them Italian) were convicted of conspiracy, though evidence proved that none of them had thrown the bomb. By 1890 a new nativist, anti-radical movement was growing in America, expanding nationwide from its East Coast epicenter.

Fear of anarchism increased with each reported act of violence. In 1900, Italian anarchist Gaetano Bresci left his adopted home in New Jersey to assassinate King Umberto I of Italy. The following year, anarchist Leon Czolgosz shot and killed President William McKinley in Buffalo, New York. McKinley's successor, THEODORE ROOSEVELT, created the Bureau of Investigation and signed legislation to stifle the anarchist press in 1908. Four years later, two immigrant labor organizers were framed on murder charges (but finally acquitted) during a textile strike at Lawrence, Massachusetts. Colorado's Ludlow massacre of 1914 prompted three anarchists to plot the murder of industrialist John D. Rockefeller (and thus sparked creation of the New York City bomb squad). Two more anarchists were arrested (some say framed) in New York the following year, for plotting to blow up St. Patrick's Cathedral.

"Progressive" president WOODROW WILSON reserved some of his harshest words and legislation for "enemy aliens" on the eve of America's entry into WORLD WAR I. The Bolshevik revolution of 1917 gave nativists a new reason to tremble, but communism

and anarchism (or "syndicalism") were confused in many minds, including that a fledgling clerk at the JUSTICE DEPARTMENT named J. EDGAR HOOVER. War's end brought no cessation of violence, as a wave of strikes, riots and bombings rocked American in 1919. G-men retaliated with the PALMER RAIDS, counting prominent anarchists EMMA GOLDMAN and ALEXANDER BERKMAN among those deported to Russia. Still, the bombings remained unsolved, despite unsubstantiated claims of a confession from New York anarchist ANDREA SALSEDO (killed in Bureau custody on 3 May 1920). Two activist friends of Salsedo, NICOLA SACCO and BARTOLOMEO VANZETTI, were also framed for murder by Massachusetts authorities, with collaboration from the Bureau of Investigation. G-men spent six years tracking sympathizers of the Sacco-Vanzetti defense team, but the pair's execution in 1927 sounded a belated death knell for American anarchism, leaving Hoover's agents free to concentrate their full attention on the COMMUNIST PARTY.

**ANDERSON, George F.** — A U.S. district judge in Boston, George Anderson presided in the 1920 case of *Colyer v. Skeffington*, resulting from the PALMER RAIDS conducted in New England. His reaction to illegal tactics employed by the Bureau of Investigation marked Anderson as a BI "enemy" from that date forward. His questioning of witnesses before the court noted that BI agents had no lawful powers of arrest, but that the Labor Department had reached "an understanding" with the bureau to proceed regardless, following a conference with "Mr. [J. EDGAR] HOOVER and another gentleman from the Department of Justice."

Not only were the various arrests illegal, but BI agents had also abused their search warrants by seizing "radical" literature during the raids. As Anderson reminded William West, assistant superintendent of the Boston field office, "You knew … that no search warrant could be obtained under the laws of the United States or of the Commonwealth of Massachusetts which would authorize the seizure of such literature or evidence as you were after, didn't you?… This was not outlaw property within the laws of the United States or the Commonwealth of Massachusetts, was it?" West grudgingly admitted that his "gun warrants" did not permit seizure of documents, but he had "issued no instructions" to his agents in regard to obeying the law.

As for interrogation of the prisoners, Judge Anderson found that BI methods "left these aliens, many of them uneducated and seriously hampered by their inability to understand English … entirely unprotected from the zealous attempts of the Department of Justice agents to get from them some sort of apparent admission of membership [in radical organizations]. … Aliens … were … easily led into some kind of admission."

Anderson found it especially offensive that prisoners seized in the raids had been jailed from four to five months "as though under sentence for crime." "Even if the arrests had been lawful and the proceedings had been regular throughout," he declared, "it cannot be the law that the alien shall be held beyond a reasonable time, for trial and determination of his right either to go free and earn his living in this country, or to be deported. The fact that the Government has overloaded itself by the wholesale arrest of hundreds of aliens, only a small fraction of whom was there evidence to hold, and thus has caused untoward delay in the cases ... was not the fault of the aliens. Their rights were, within reasonable time, either to be deported or to be allowed their freedom. Their detention, under all the unprecedented and extraordinary circumstances ... was illegal."

Reducing bail for the prisoners from $5,000 and $10,000 to a more reasonable $500, Judge Anderson noted for the record that "none of the aliens were in any way involved, by the use of bombs, guns, or other weapons, in plans of injuring persons or property." Accordingly, he ruled, they were entitled to release.

**ANDERSON, Jack**—Born in 1922, newsman Jack Anderson first gained national prominence in the late 1940s, when he joined DREW PEARSON at the *Washington Post*, helping to produce the nationally syndicated "Washington Merry-Go-Round" column. Ironically, Anderson owed his position to J. EDGAR HOOVER, who informed Pearson that his former aide (Andrew Older) was a communist. Pearson promptly fired Older and hired Anderson to replace him. Anderson, in turn, became friendly with Senator JOSEPH McCARTHY, funneling information from Pearson's private files to McCarthy without Pearson's knowledge. Although forewarned that the files contained unverified allegations, McCarthy quoted the information as factual, thereby losing Anderson's support. In 1951, after publicly questioning the use of FBI agents to escort McCarthy's secretary on a visit to Hawaii, Anderson and Pearson were placed on the Bureau's "no contact" list.

Despite that ostracism, the columnists still praised Hoover effusively through the 1960s, until the relationship finally soured in 1968, when Pearson and Anderson began investigating Senator THOMAS DODD, a former G-man and the FBI's unofficial mouthpiece on Capitol Hill. FBI agents tried to foil that inestigation by stealing some of Anderson's mail, the theft later acknowledged by U.S. Postmaster General Lawrence O'Brien. The columnists retaliated with a December 1968 article in *True* magazine, predicting that America was witnessing "the last days of J. Edgar Hoover." The piece ascribed Hoover's "sainthood" to "40 years or planted press notices," without mentioning that Anderson and Pearson had participated in the charade.

FBI surveillance of Anderson continued into the 1970s, joined by agents of the CENTRAL INTELLIGENCE AGENCY, the INTERNAL REVENUE SERVICE, and Military Intelligence. Anderson turned the tables by interviewing Hoover's neighbors and raiding his garbage cans, reversing the standard FBI "trash cover" to report on Hoover's favorite brand of soap and liquor. Anderson won a Pulitzer Prize for his coverage of Washington scandals in 1972, prompting members of RICHARD NIXON'S staff (including former FBI agent G. GORDON LIDDY) to plot his assassination. Several methods were discussed, including an LSD-induced car crash and a simulated mugging, before the White House ruled that murder was "too severe a sanction." Instead, Nixon aides asked Hoover to help them discredit Anderson. Hoover cheerfully agreed, denouncing Anderson as "the lowest form of human being to walk the earth," a "journalistic prostitute," and "the top scavenger of all columnists" who would "go lower than dog shit for a story."

On 1 May 1972 Anderson's column branded Hoover "the old curmudgeon of law enforcement," detailing decades of FBI harassment against MARTIN LUTHER KING, JR., and others. Furious, Hoover ordered an investigation to identify Anderson's sources within the Bureau, but he never learned the results. Next morning, the director was found dead at his home in Washington, D.C.

**ANDERSON, Maxwell**—An American playwright, born in 1888, Maxwell Anderson won the Pulitzer Prize in 1933 for his play *Both Your Houses*. He was marked for FBI investigation five years later, as a member of the leftist Committee to Save Spain and China. A 1942 memo in Anderson's file noted that he was under surveillance "in connection with Alien control work." The same year saw Anderson listed as a potential candidate for "custodial detention," but the case was later placed on "deferred status." J. EDGAR HOOVER apparently found Anderson suspicious as "a person interested in social legislation," adding periodic memos to his file through 1956. Anderson died in 1959.

**ANDERSON, Michael ("Baby Aim")**—A Navajo Indian born on the reservation at Shiprock, New Mexico, Michael Anderson was the younger brother of an AMERICAN INDIAN MOVEMENT (AIM) leader who organized the seizure of a Fairchild Corporation electronics plant at Shiprock in February 1975. Himself a dedicated AIM member, Anderson was fifteen years old when he traveled with LEONARD PELTIER and other activists to the embattled Pine Ridge (South Dakota) reservation in March 1975. Three months later, on 26 June 1975, he was present when a shootout claimed the lives of two FBI agents at Pine Ridge.

Arrested as a murder suspect in that case, Anderson was interrogated on 11 September 1975 by FBI agent J. GARY ADAMS. His requests for legal counsel were ignored, and Anderson later testified under oath that Adams threatened to "beat [him] up in the cell" unless he provided sworn statements against other suspects, including Leonard Peltier. Anderson testified against murder suspects DINO BUTLER and BOB ROBIDEAU in June 1976, but they were acquitted on a plea of self-defense. At Peltier's 1977 murder trial, Anderson recanted his statements under cross-examination and accused the FBI of soliciting perjury. (Peltier was nonetheless convicted.) Two years later, in Arizona, Anderson died in a car crash while fleeing pursuit by police from the Bureau of Indian Affairs. Friends suspect that he was deliberately killed, but no investigation was made and no autopsy was performed.

**ANDERSON, Sherwood**—An Ohio native, born in 1876, Sherwood Anderson abandoned a successful roofing company in 1912 to launch a new career in literature. He drew attention from the FBI in 1932, after publishing an article in the leftist magazine *New Masses*. Anderson's FBI file suggests flirtation with the COMMUNIST PARTY, although one memo notes that he "violently disliked" party spokesman John Reed. There is no evidence he ever joined the party, but G-men still collected 80-plus "subversive" references to Anderson and his published work. Despite his death in 1941, the FBI continued keeping tabs on Anderson's career and adding to his file through 1956.

**ANDERSON, William**—A retired U.S. Navy captain, decorated hero of WORLD WAR II and former commander of the nuclear submarine *Nautilus*, William Anderson served four terms in the House of Representatives for his native Tennessee. Anderson was a long-time admirer of J. EDGAR HOOVER and the FBI, whose faith in both was shaken by Hoover's November 1970 announcement of the alleged BERRIGAN conspiracy to bomb strategic sites in Washington, D.C. and kidnap government officials. Rising on the floor of Congress, Anderson quoted a passage from Hoover's ghost-written book *Masters of Deceit*, noting the FBI director's supposed belief that "Hypocrisy, dishonesty, hatred, all of these must be destroyed and men must rule by love, charity, and mercy." In contrast to those cherished tenets, Anderson noted, Hoover himself had ignored the Constitution's due process clauses by airing criminal charges in public, without benefit of indictments, and thereby resorted to "tactics reminiscent of McCarthyism."

Hoover ordered an immediate investigation of Anderson, G-men fanning out through Washington with photos of the congressman, asking prostitutes if Anderson had ever been a client. While the results were negative, a bordello madam in Nashville told agents she "thought" Anderson had patronized her house years earlier. Upon receipt of that unsupported charge, Hoover scrawled "whoremonger" across the memo and informed President RICHARD NIXON that Anderson frequented prostitutes. FBI agents in Tennessee also leaked the story to journalists, resulting in Anderson's defeat when he ran for a fifth term in 1972. As one of Hoover's aides later told author Curt Gentry, "Anderson's scalp was hung out to dry as a warning to others who might entertain the same notion."

**ANSLINGER, Harry J.**—A Pennsylvania native, born in 1892, Harry Anslinger went to work for the U.S. War Department in 1917, then shifted to Treasury in 1926. Appointed as Commissioner of Prohibition in 1929, he served barely a year in that position before he was named Commissioner of NARCOTICS in 1930. Anslinger thereafter led the FEDERAL BUREAU OF NARCOTICS (FBN) until his retirement in 1962, campaigning for stricter drug laws and harsh enforcement.

A perennial lightning rod for J. EDGAR HOOVER'S wrath, Anslinger invited that reaction in various ways. He courted national publicity, and Hoover blamed Anslinger for using copycat initials to name his agency (although the "FBI" label was not adopted until 1935, five years after the FBN's creation). The greatest bone of contention was Anslinger's public warnings of an international drug-dealing syndicate. Strong evidence supported Anslinger's contention, but Hoover was incapable of any compromise with enemies, a stance that led him to deny the very existence of ORGANIZED CRIME. Deputy Attorney General William Hundly recalled, years later, that Hoover "got in a big pissing match with Harry Anslinger over at Narcotics, who he didn't like, and Anslinger had the Mafia coming up out of the sewers the same way Hoover had the Communists coming up out of the sewers. So Hoover got himself locked into saying there was no Mafia."

That claim proved humiliating over time. Anslinger tapped exiled Mafioso Charles ("Lucky") Luciano's telephone in December 1946, exposing narcotics traffic from Europe to America. Four years later, he cooperated with Senator ESTES KEFAUVER'S investigation of organized crime, while Hoover and the FBI remained aloof. In 1957, following the mass arrest of Mafia bosses at Apalachin, New York, congressional investigator ROBERT KENNEDY demanded FBI FILES on the various gangsters identified, then infuriated Hoover by delivering the information to Anslinger's FBN, where Kennedy thought prosecution was more likely to result. (In fact, Kennedy found that the FBN had files on all 70 of the arrested mobsters, while the FBI had thin dossiers on only 30.) While Hoover belatedly ordered illegal phone taps on various "top hoodlums," Anslinger recruited the Coast Guard, INTERNAL REVENUE SERVICE and Customs officers to interdict narcotics shipments.

Anslinger retired from the FBN in 1962 and published a book, *The Murderers*, that detailed the growth of international drug cartels since the 1920s. He remained outspoken on the subject until his death, in 1975.

**ANTHRAX Conspiracies**—Anthrax is a spore-forming bacillus deadly to humans, transmitted in three different forms: cutaneous (contracted through the skin), gastrointestinal (ingested orally, while eating), and pulmonary (inhaled by its victims). Various countries, including the U.S., have stockpiled anthrax since the early 1930s, constantly experimenting and refining the disease to make it more effective as a biological weapon. In recent years, the FBI has twice investigated plots to use anthrax within the country, as a TERRORIST weapon, with unfortunate results in both cases.

G-men tackled their first anthrax case in February 1998, when they arrested two men in Las Vegas, Nevada for illegal possession of anthrax. Suspects Larry Wayne Harris and William Leavitt were jailed on 19 February after an INFORMANT claimed they were carrying multiple bags of "military grade anthrax" in the trunk of their car. Harris, identified as a microbiologist and member of the neo-Nazi Aryan Nations, supposedly boasted that he had enough anthrax to "wipe out the city"; the same informant claimed Harris had detailed plans to release bubonic plague toxins in a New York City subway station. (He was already serving 18 months probation on a separate charge of fraudulently obtaining bubonic plague samples by mail.) Leavitt, a Mormon bishop and the proprietor of microbiology labs in Nevada and Germany, was named as a conspirator in the plot. Both suspects were charged with possessing anthrax for use as a weapon, but those charges were dropped after U.S. Army technicians reported that the material seized by G-men was a harmless anthrax vaccine designed for use in animals. Leavitt was released on 22 February, after three days in solitary confinement; Harris was detained for violating his probation, but that charge was also later dismissed.

While the Nevada case turned out to be a comedy of errors, America's next brush with anthrax proved tragic. Between 4 October and 21 November 2001, at least 46 residents of the eastern U.S. tested positive for exposure to anthrax, after a series of infected letters were mailed to various media outlets and government offices. Five of those victims died, including two Washington postal workers, an employee of a Florida tabloid, a New York hospital employee, and an elderly Connecticut woman. Despite a massive nationwide investigation by G-men and U.S. Postal inspectors, including a $1 million reward offer for information leading to the arrest of persons responsible for the anthrax mailings, the case remains unsolved today. FBI failure to crack the case, despite unprecedented effort and publicity, opened the Bureau to harsh criticism from Congress, the media, and the American public at large.

The Bureau's lack of progress was clearly revealed in a series of contradictory media announcements. An unnamed FBI spokesman declared on 8 October 2001 that "this kind of situation points to terrorism or criminal intent." Speculation on suspects abounded, including repeated hints that fugitive USAMA BIN LADEN might be responsible for the anthrax mailings. Two days later, G-men announced that "unique characteristics" of the anthrax found in Florida matched "a strain harvested at an Iowa facility in the 1950s," but they also acknowledged that the lead "may mean absolutely nothing." Agents "confirmed" a foreign terrorist link on 15 October, noting that the wife of a Florida tabloid editor had rented rooms to two terrorists killed in SKYJACKING incidents on 11 September 2001, then discarded it on 9 November, voicing a "near certainty" that the anthrax mailer was "probably a man with a grudge" employed at some U.S. laboratory. G-men traced several of the letters to Trenton, New Jersey, but it brought them no closer to their faceless quarry.

In August 2002 *Newsweek* magazine reported "intriguing new clues" in the Bureau's search for the anthrax killer(s). According to that report, tracking dogs employed to screen a dozen possible suspects "went crazy" at the Maryland home of Dr. Steven Hatfill, a 48-year-old scientist once employed at an Army bioweapons-research lab. *Newsweek* dubbed Hatfill "eccentric ... [f]lamboyant and arrogant," proclaiming that FBI agents were "finally on the verge of a breakthrough" in the frustrating case. Hatfill was placed under round-the-clock surveillance, subjected to a polygraph test (which he reportedly passed), and his home was searched twice without revealing evidence of any criminal activity. Mindful of their embarrassment in the 1996 Olympics bombing, where innocent bystander RICHARD JEWELL was falsely accused in anonymous FBI leaks, a Bureau spokesman told reporters, "We've got to be careful [with Hatfill]. Richard Jewell looms large around here." Still, that did not prevent Attorney General JOHN ASHCROFT from publicly branding Hatfill "a person of interest" in the case, refusing to define the term when challenged by Hatfill's attorneys. Hatfill held a press conference to declare his innocence on 11 August 2002; two days later his attorney filed complaints with the Bureau's OFFICE OF PROFESSIONAL RESPONSIBILITY, alleging misconduct in Hatfill's case. On 4 September 2002 Hatfill was fired from his job at Louisiana State University's biomedical laboratory, after JUSTICE DEPARTMENT officials barred him from working on projects funded by federal grants. A lawsuit for harassment is anticipated at this writing, and the anthrax case remains unsolved.

**ANTI-ABORTION Violence** — One of the U.S. SUPREME COURT's all-time most controversial rulings was delivered on 22 January 1973 in the case of *Roe v. Wade*, declaring that all state laws banning abortions violated the due process clause of the U.S. Constitution's Fourteenth Amendment. Henceforth, the court said, the decision on first-trimester abortions must be left to women and their personal physicians. Fundamentalist religious groups (and politicians courting their votes) opposed the ruling from day one, but resistance got off to a sluggish start. The first "pro-life" demonstration at a women's clinic did not occur until mid-1975, and the first act of violence against a clinic was not recorded until February 1977 (in Cleveland, Ohio).

Statistics logged since that date, however, document a grim campaign of TERRORISM against women's clinics throughout North America. Between 1977 and March 2002 a conservative tally includes: 7 murders (with an eighth reported from Australia); 19 attempted murders; 3 KIDNAPPINGS; 41 BOMBINGS; 163 arson incidents; 81 attempting bombings or arsons; 526 bomb threats; 332 death threats; 368 daylight clinic invasions; 60 burglaries; 420 stalking cases; 8,246 harassing telephone calls; and 33,830 arrests during illegal clinic blockades.

Between 1977 and 1994 the FBI attempted to remain aloof from terrorism targeting women's clinics. The owners of a Cleveland clinic, firebombed on 18 February 1978, requested an investigation of the crime, but FBI HEADQUARTERS refused on 6 April 1978, asserting that the fire did not fall within Bureau jurisdiction as outlined by the Federal Bombing Statute. Following a pattern that prevailed for the next 16 years, FBI spokesmen referred victims to the BUREAU OF ALCOHOL, TOBACCO AND FIREARMS (BATF).

On 12 August 1982 a physician and abortion provider, Dr. Hector Zevallos, was kidnapped with his wife from their home in Edwardsville, Illinois. They were held captive for eight days, then released without injury in the first of many crimes committed by a self-styled "Army of God." G-men investigated the kidnapping without result; three suspects were identified by local police when Dr. Zevallos (though blindfolded) recalled details of their escape route. All three were convicted and sentenced to state prison terms.

As bombing and arson attacks escalated through the 1980s, FBI leaders remained intransigent in their refusal to investigate, taking their cue from anti-abortion statements issued by Presidents RONALD REAGAN and GEORGE H.W. BUSH. Both presidents openly fraternized with "pro-life" extremists, and the Bureau often takes its cue on prioritizing cases from the administration in power. After the attempted bombing of a Norfolk, Virginia clinic on 17 February 1984, a one-page FBI investigative report signed off with the handwritten message "Open and close." (BATF agents arrested the bombers in January 1985; they received prison terms ranging from six to 15 years.) Eleven months later, on 4 December 1984, Director WILLIAM WEBSTER decreed that G-men were barred from investigating clinic attacks since those bombings failed to meet the FBI's definition of "true" domestic terrorism. A *Minneapolis Star and Tribune* editorial, published on 12 December, charged that the Bureau "seems to be policing the cabbage patch with a blind eye to clinic bombings.... Webster's words conveyed the wrong message.... If the FBI isn't investigating whether an organized group or conspiracy is involved, it should be."

The FBI made its first half-hearted investigation of "pro-life" violence a month later, in January 1985. Specifically, agents examined the inflammatory statements of anti-abortion activist Joseph Scheidler, but they remained "unconvinced that Scheidler's war cries met the guidelines for the FBI's intervention." Supreme Court justice Harry Blackmun was the target of a murder attempt in February 1985, at his Virginia home, and while G-men linked the shooting to previous threats from the Army of God, they were unable to identify the snipers.

The FBI received new marching orders from liberal President WILLIAM CLINTON and Attorney General JANET RENO after January 1991, but clinic violence remained a low priority until 10 March 1993, when a fundamentalist gunman murdered Dr. David Gunn in Pensacola, Florida. Over the next week, various congressmen, senators and pro-choice activists demanded that the Bureau investigate an obvious nationwide "pattern of harassment" against women's clinics. When FBI headquarters claimed lack of jurisdiction, Congress passed a new Freedom of Access to Clinic Entrances (FACE) Act, signed into law by President Clinton in May 1994. That legislation makes it a federal crime to "engage in violent or obstructive conduct intended to interfere with people seeking or providing reproductive health services," with jurisdiction handed squarely to the FBI.

Still the Bureau remained sluggish in response, refusing to arrest activist Paul Hill when he violated the FACE Act in Pensacola on 10 June 1994. Hill returned to the clinic with a shotgun on 29 July, killing Dr. John Britton and escort James Barrett, critically wounding Barrett's wife. Incredibly, though Hill was identified by multiple eyewitnesses and local police captured him near the murder scene, an official Bureau website today credits "the FBI's investigation" for Hill's subsequent murder conviction and death sentence!

The Pensacola murders finally elicited a federal reaction of sorts. G-men belatedly charged Paul Hill with minor FACE Act violations and circulated a short list of activists who publicly praised Hill's actions as "justifiable homicide." No charges were filed, and a 1995 investigation of 100 anti-abortion organizations across the U.S. reportedly confirmed the FBI's longstanding claim that no conspiracy between such groups existed. Pro-choice activists remained unconvinced, however, filing civil lawsuits against an Internet website — the "Nuremberg Files" — that listed names and home addresses of various abortion providers. Four physicians received a $108.5 million judgment against webmaster Neal Horsley in 1999, on grounds that some of his posted statements amounted to death threats; that judgment was reduced on appeal in March 2001, but a May 2001 judgment from the 9th Circuit Court of Appeals found Horsley legally liable for statements on his website that constituted "true threats."

G-men, meanwhile, were more concerned with "pro-life activists" engaged in clear-cut felonies. Three such terrorists were added to the Bureau's "TEN MOST WANTED LIST" between 1999 and 2001. They include:

• *James Charles Kopp* (AKA "Atomic Dog") — Active in protests for a decade before he was linked to the sniper slaying of New York physician Dr. Bernard Slepian, in October 1998, Kopp went "underground" and was later suspected in the slayings of two Canadian doctors, Garson Romalis (November 1994) and Hugh Short (November 1996). Added to the Top Ten list on 7 June 1999, Kopp was arrested in France on 29 March 2001. One day later, G-men charged two U.S. activists — Loretta Marra and convicted clinic bomber Dennis Malvassi — with harboring Kopp while he was a federal fugitive.

• *ERIC ROBERT RUDOLPH* — Indicted for the 1996 bombing of Atlanta's Centennial Olympic Village (one dead, 120 injured) and the 1998 bombing of a Birmingham abortion clinic (one dead, one wounded), "pro-life" terrorist Rudolph was added to the Top Ten list on 5 May 1998. He was captured in Murphy, N.C., on May 31, 2003, and as of this writing was being held awaiting trial.

• *Clayton Lee Waagner* — Rated "extremely dangerous" by FBI spokesmen, this self-styled "anti-abortion warrior" was added to the Top Ten list on 21 September 2001, after he escaped from jail in Illinois. Already convicted of car theft and federal firearms violations, Waagner soon became a suspect on BANK ROBBERY and carjacking charges. In October 2001, following a spate of ANTHRAX murders in the eastern U.S., Waagner mailed threatening letters containing white powder to 110 abortion clinics across the country. None of the letters contained anthrax, but the hoax added new federal charges to Waagner's rap sheet. Arrested in Cincinnati on 5 December 2001, Waagner received a prison term of 19 years for theft and firearms violations on 15 August 2002 (that time to be served after completion of his 30-year Illinois sentence). A federal grand jury in Philadelphia indicted Waagner for terrorism (in the anthrax hoax) on 19 September 2002.

**APPEL, Charles A.** — A native of Wahington, D.C., born in 1895, Charles Appel trained as a combat aviator in World War I and later attended George Washington Law School, graduating in 1924. He joined the Bureau of Investigation on 24 October 1924, specializing in document examination. Appel recommended establishment of an FBI Laboratory years before J. EDGAR HOOVER finally approved the concept in 1932, with Appel placed in charge. For several months, Appel was the lab's only full-time employee. His testimony in the LINDBERGH KIDNAPPING case helped persuade a jury that suspect Bruno Hauptmann penned various ransom notes. On the side, Appel also served as the FBI's unofficial historian, writing laudatory accounts of the bureau's exploits for both public and in-house consumption. He retired from the FBI on 31 December 1948.

**AQUASH, Anna Mae Pictou** — A Canadian-born member of the AMERICAN INDIAN MOVEMENT (AIM), Anna Aquash traveled to the Pine Ridge (South Dakota) reservation in March 1975, with LEONARD PELTIER and other AIM members. She was arrested by FBI agents on 5 September 1975, reportedly on weapons charges, and was questioned concerning the June 1975 shootout that killed two G-men at Pine Ridge. When she declined to answer, Agent DAVID PRICE allegedly warned Aquash that he would "see her dead within a year."

Released on bond a few days after the interrogation, Aquash fled to Oregon, but she was traced and arrested there on 14 November 1975, returned to South Dakota for trial on the pending weapons charges. On 24 November Judge Robert Merhige freed Aquash on her own recognizance, trial scheduled for the following day, but Aquash never returned to court. Her corpse was found at Pine Ridge on 24 February 1976, near the site where a victimless hit-and-run accident had been reported one week earlier. Agent Price photographed the death scene but failed to identify Aquash, an oversight repeated when Agent J. GARY ADAMS observed her autopsy. Dr. W.O. Brown, coroner for the Bureau of Indian Affairs, blamed the death on alcohol and exposure, sending Aquash's severed hands to the FBI Crime Lab in Washington for fingerprint identification. By the time she was identified, on 3 March 1976, Aquash had already been buried in an unmarked grave.

Upon receiving notice of Aquash's death, her family demanded an independent review of the case. Aquash was exhumed on 11 March 1976, the second autopsy disclosing an obvious close-range bullet wound in the back of her neck. A bullet was extracted from her left temple, variously described in published reports as a .32- or .38-caliber pistol slug. Dr. Brown grudgingly admitted that "The bullet may have initiated or set in progress the mechanism of death, the proximate cause of which was frostbite." A report by the U.S. Commission on Civil Rights described the FBI's handling of Aquash's murder as "at the very least [an] extremely indifferent and careless investigation." Surviving relatives spoke more bluntly, one declaring: "The FBI wanted the investigation to go cold because they thought it would lead them somewhere that they didn't want to go." The case remains unsolved today.

**ARENDT, Hannah**—A Hanover native, born 14 October 1906, Hannah Arendt became politically active when Hitler's Nazi regime assumed control of Germany in 1933. Her Jewish ancestry made such activity perilous, however, and she emigrated with her husband to the United States in May 1941, pursuing dual careers as an author and professor at Manhattan's New School for Social Research.

The FBI apparently noticed her for the first time on 3 May 1953 after the *Washington Post* published an abridgement of Arendt's earlier article in the liberal magazine *Commonweal*. Titled "'Ex-Communists' Remain Totalitarian at Heart," the piece featured a photo of ALGER HISS prosecution witness Whittaker Chambers and sternly criticized INFORMANTS, noting that the stool pigeon's art "is a duty in a police state where people have been organized and split into two ever-changing categories: those who have the privilege to be the informants and those who are dominated by the fear of being informed upon." For that comment and others like it Arendt was indexed under the heading of "Internal Security—R" (for "Russian"). The last entry in her brief file dates from 1956. Arendt died in New York, of a heart attack while entertaining friends at home, on 4 December 1975.

**ARNAZ, Desi**—The son of wealthy Cuban parents, born Desiderio Alberto Arnaz y de Arche III in 1917, Desi Arnaz moved

to the U.S. with his mother to escape political unrest in 1933. He joined Xavier Cugat's band four years later, afterward branching out to lead his own Latin orchestra. Arnaz married actress LUCILLE BALL in 1940, and together they launched the popular "I Love Lucy" television comedy series in 1951. The following year, when a hospital worker tipped the FBI's Los Angeles field office to Lucy's first pregnancy, J. EDGAR HOOVER telephoned to give Arnaz the news before Lucy announced it. Hoover turned against the couple in 1959, when their Desilu production company premiered "The Untouchables," a new TV series dramatizing the exploits of 1930s Prohibition agent ELIOT NESS. Adding insult to injury, the show's second episode (aired on 22 October 1959) credited Ness with wiping out the BARKER-KARPIS GANG. Arnaz divorced Lucy in 1960 and later remarried. He died in 1986.

**ART Car Museum**—A Houston art museum that opened in 1998, the private Art Car Museum was treated to a visit by FBI and Secret Service agents on 7 November 2001, following an anonymous telephone tip that one of the exhibits "threatened" President GEORGE W. BUSH. The piece, entitled "Secret Wars," was duly examined as a potential threat to U.S. security, FBI spokesman Bob Dogium deciding that "the artwork was not dangerous." The bureau took its lead from Attorney General JOHN ASHCROFT, as Dogium explained: "In line with his directive that we would leave no stone unturned, all these calls are taken seriously and followed up."

Museum docent Donna Huanca held a different opinion. "I think it's the new McCarthyism," she told reporters, adding that she found the G-men "intimidating. They were scaring me." Agents showed particular interest, Huanca said, in a charcoal drawing of President Bush titled "EmptyTrellis," depicting the adverse global impact of proposed Republican environmental legislation. Museum founder Jim Harithas condemned the intrusion as revealing "the potential ... for thought control. Apparently now, any criticism of the president is subject to investigation. Are we supposed to cower in fear?"

**ASHCROFT, John David**—A Chicago native, born 9 May 1942 and raised in Missouri, John Ashcroft was the son and grandson of fundamentalist Pentecostal ministers. He carried that conservative upbringing with him through college and law school, then into the political arena, first as a failed congressional candidate in 1972, then as Missouri's state auditor (1973-75). While serving as the state's attorney general (1976-85), Ashcroft fought court-ordered school desegregation (1977) and was equally opposed to a voluntary busing plan for racial parity in St. Louis (1983). He served two terms as Missouri's governor (1985-93), and was elected to a U.S. Senate seat in 1994. During his single term, Ashcroft sponsored the unsuccessful "Human Life Amendment" (banning abortions even in cases of incest and rape), opposed appointment of black federal judges and voted consistently against federal gun-control and firearms safety legislation. His popularity in Missouri is suggested by the fact that Ashcroft lost his 2000 re-election bid to an opponent who died before election day.

A longtime friend and political ally of the Bush family,

Ashcroft was considered for the post of U.S. attorney general by President GEORGE H.W. BUSH in 1991, but his nomination was ultimately deemed too controversial. President GEORGE W. BUSH had no such qualms in 2001, although Ashcroft was admittedly his second choice (after Montana governor Marc Racicot declined the position). Ashcroft's critics challenged his confirmation on grounds that included his civil rights record, his opposition to abortion and gun control, and his acceptance of an honorary degree from far-right Bob Jones University (where interracial dating was banned until the 1990s and students are taught that the Pope is the Antichrist of Revelation). Confirmed despite that opposition, Ashcroft vowed that his religious views would have no impact on his performance in office — and then spent $8,000 for a drape to hide a bare-breasted statue of Justice at his headquarters in Washington. (Ashcroft later told reporters he "knew nothing" of that decision.)

Ashcroft avoided any major controversy until the TERRORIST attacks of 11 September 2001, whereupon he unleashed a national campaign of arrests unequaled since the PALMER RAIDS of 1919-20. He also campaigned for new powers in the realm of DOMESTIC SURVEILLANCE, complaining that current legislation unduly limited federal WIRETAPPING. Many of Ashcroft's goals were achieved with the enactment of the USA PATRIOT ACT, but Congress stopped short of granting the attorney general's fondest wishes: authority to unilaterally detain and deport on suspicion alone any aliens branded "suspected terrorists" or "who may pose a risk to the national security"; elimination of deportation hearings; and waiver of appeals from deportation orders. Addressing an assembly of American mayors on 25 October 2001, Ashcroft issued a warning to "enemy" aliens: "If you overstay your visas even by one day, we will arrest you. If you violate a local law, we will hope that you will, and work to make sure that you are put in jail and be kept [sic] in custody as long as possible."

Despite his commitment to pursuing terrorists, Ashcroft also found time for collateral campaigns. One pitted him against the state if Oregon, where Ashcroft sought federal injunctions in November 2001 to invalidate a state law approving physician-assisted suicide. Governor John Kitzhaber and state attorney general Hardy Myers struck back with litigation of their own; they were victorious in April 2002, when a federal court denied Ashcroft's authority to nullify state laws. Back in Washington, meanwhile, on 7 December 2001, Ashcroft issued a curious order forbidding FBI agents from checking the names of suspected terrorists against federal firearms purchase records. Bewildered Bureau spokesmen told the media, "This is a sticky one for us. The Justice Department sees things differently than we do." Mathew Nosanchuk, a Justice lawyer under ex-Attorney General JANET RENO, spoke more bluntly, accusing Ashcroft and company of "rejecting their own authority and acting as lawyers for the gun lobby."

Ashcroft's concern for the privacy of gun owners did not extend to America's Muslim community. Appearing on ABC's *This Week* in December 2002, he warned that "People who hijack a religion and make out of it an implement of war will not be free from our interest." At the same time, however, the attorney general sought to conduct his vital work behind an airtight screen of secrecy. While in the Senate, during 1998, Ashcroft had accused Janet Reno of "stonewalling" when she withheld federal prosecutors' memos from Congress; in 2002 Ashcroft claimed the same privilege for himself, prompting Rep. Dan Burton, chairman of the House Judiciary Committee, to express "concern that you have one standard for a Democrat attorney general and another standard for yourself." Ashcroft, unfazed by criticism, dismissed public fears that his nationwide crusade might threaten civil rights, responded in terms reminiscent of J. EDGAR HOOVER: "To those who scare peace-loving people with phantoms of lost liberty, my message is: your tactics only aid terrorists, for they erode our national unity and diminish our resolve."

Critics disagreed, including spokesmen for the AMERICAN CIVIL LIBERTIES UNION and 17 other civil rights organizations who joined forces in a lawsuit filed against the Justice Department on 4 December 2001. That action challenged Ashcroft's arrest and detention without criminal charges of an estimated 1,000 unnamed "suspects" and "material witnesses" in the wake of the 11 September attacks. As if determined to further alienate his critics, Ashcroft chose Christmas Day 2001 for his announcement that Justice would withdraw $500,000 in federal grants earmarked for nationwide DNA testing, to determine whether or not inmates in controversial cases had been wrongfully convicted. The money could be better used for other things, Ashcroft decided — including a new plan to fingerprint, photograph and register Middle Eastern visitors to the U.S.

**ASIAN-American Agents** — FBI agents of Asian-American descent comprise the second-smallest minority within the Bureau (after Native Americans). When Director J. EDGAR HOOVER died in May 1972 there were 15 Asian-American agents out of 8,631 employed (or 8,659, reports vary) — or roughly one-tenth of one percent. The hiring picture has improved since then. In February 1992 there were 151 Asian-American agents in a total force of 10,422 (1.4%), and by 1997 they reportedly numbered 237 out of 10,816 (2.2%). The FBI's website presently offers no ethnic breakdown for agents, but it includes a statement that the Bureau actively recruits among minorities, including Asian-Americans and Pacific Islanders. The progress achieved by that recruiting is undisclosed.

**ATKID** — Between July 1979 and May 1981 police in Atlanta, Georgia compiled a list of thirty African Americans alleged to be victims in a case of SERIAL MURDER. Although six of the dead were men in their twenties, the remainder ranged in age from nine to seventeen, earning the case eternal notoriety as the "Atlanta child murders."

In fact, there was no official consensus on the case, no evidence of a serial killer's ritualistic "signature." Fourteen of the victims were strangled or asphyxiated, but four were stabbed, two were bludgeoned, and another was shot. One victim was drowned, and another's death — apparently caused by falling from a railroad trestle — was initially ruled accidental. Cause of death remains unknown in six cases, including one victim whose body has never been found. Two of the official victims were female, though police and prosecutors later claimed the killer was a male homosexual.

By April 1981 it was apparent that the "child murders" case had gotten out of hand. Community critics denounced the official victims list as incomplete and arbitrary, citing cases like the January 1981 murder of Faye Yearby to prove their case. Yearby, like "official" victim Angel Lenair, was found lashed to a tree by her killer, stabbed to death like four acknowledged "series" victims. Still, police rejected Yearby on grounds that (a) she was female — as were two "official" victims — and (b) that she was "too old" at age twenty-two (this despite the fact that five other victims ranged from age twenty to twenty-eight). Author Dave Dettlinger, in his book *The List* (1983), suggests that sixty-three potential victims were capriciously omitted from the official roster, twenty-five of them *after* a suspect's arrest supposedly ended the murder spree.

FBI agents entered the case (dubbed "ATKID") on 22 June 1980, after six-year-old Latonya Wilson was kidnapped from her Atlanta home. Her skeletal remains were found on 18 October 1980, with cause of death undetermined. Six months later, FBI spokesmen outraged local blacks by announcing that several of the local crimes were "substantially solved," suggesting that the unnamed victims were killed by their own parents. Several corpses had by now been pulled from local rivers, and police staked out the waterways by night. In the predawn hours of 22 May 1981, a rookie officer stationed under a bridge on the Chattahoochie River reported hearing "a splash" in the water nearby, and officers manning the bridge were alerted. Moments later, police and FBI agents stopped a car driven by Wayne Bertram Williams, searching his car and grilling him for two hours before he was released. Two days later, the corpse of 27-year-old ex-convict Nathaniel Cater was pulled from the river downstream, and authorities focused their probe on Wayne Williams.

He seemed an unlikely suspect from the start. An only child of two Atlanta schoolteachers, Williams lived with his parents at age twenty-three, chasing dreams of fame and fortune as a music promoter. He had no criminal record, and police by now had several alternate suspects — including a known pedophile named by multiple witnesses as the August 1980 slayer of "list" victim Clifford Jones — but investigators henceforth dismissed any evidence pointing away from Wayne Williams. Arrested on 21 June 1981, Williams was charged with the murder of Nathaniel Cater, despite testimony from four witnesses who saw Cater alive two days after the infamous "splash." On 17 July 1981, while newspapers trumpeted the capture of Atlanta's "child killer," Williams was indicted for killing two adult males — Cater and 21-year-old ex-convict Jimmy Payne, found dead on 27 April.

At trial, beginning in December 1981, prosecutors portrayed Williams as a violent homosexual and racist, so disgusted with his own race that he hoped to wipe out future generations by killing black children before they could breed. No motive was presented for slaying of adult ex-convicts, but one witness claimed to have seen Williams holding hands with Nathaniel Cater on 21 May, a few hours before "the splash." Defense attorneys countered with testimony from a woman who admitted having "normal sex" with Williams, but the prosecution won a crucial victory when the court admitted testimony on ten other deaths from the "child murders" list. One of those included was 12-year-old Clifford Jones, whose identified killer (not Williams) would be convicted in 1981 of attempted rape and sodomy in an unrelated case. Another was 15-year-old Terry Pue, whose corpse reportedly yielded unidentified fingerprints in January 1981, but no link to Wayne Williams was ever established in court.

The most impressive evidence of guilt was offered by a team of FBI experts, describing hairs and fibers found on several of the "pattern" victims. Testimony indicated that fibers matching a brand of carpet found inside the Williams home (and thousands of others) had been retrieved from several corpses. Furthermore, six bodies (including that of Clifford Jones) allegedly bore fibers from the trunk liner of a 1979 Ford automobile owned by the Williams family. Clothing of another victim also yielded carpet fibers from a second car, a 1970 Chevrolet owned by Williams's parents. Curiously, jurors were *not* informed of multiple eyewitness testimony naming a different suspect in the Jones case, nor were they advised of a critical gap in the prosecution's fiber evidence.

Specifically, Wayne Williams had no access to the cars in question when three of the six "fiber" victims were killed. His father took the Ford in for repairs at 9:00 A.M. on 30 July 1980, some five hours before victim Earl Terrell vanished that afternoon, and Terrell was long dead before Williams got the car back on 7 August. It was returned to the shop on 8 August, still refusing to start, and a new repair estimate was so expensive that Wayne's father refused to pay, abandoning the vehicle. Meanwhile, victims Clifford Jones and Charles Stephens were kidnapped on 20 August and 9 October respectively, but the 1970 Chevrolet in question was not purchased until 21 October, twelve days *after* Stephens's death.

Blissfully ignorant of such discrepancies, jurors convicted Wayne Williams of two murders on 27 February 1982. Two days later, after he received a double life sentence, the Atlanta "child murders" task force was officially disbanded, spokesmen declaring that twenty-three of thirty "list" cases were considered solved with his conviction, even though no further charges had been filed. The other seven cases, still open, remain unsolved to this day.

In November 1985 a new team of lawyers uncovered onceclassified documents from an investigation of the KU KLUX KLAN, conducted by the Georgia Bureau of Investigation during 1980 and 1981. A spy inside the Klan reported that KKK members were "killing the children" in Atlanta, in hopes of provoking a race war. One Klansman in particular was caught on tape, boasting that he had strangled "list" victim Lubie Geter in January 1981. The same INFORMANT reported that "after twenty blackchild killings they, the Klan, were going to start killing black women." Perhaps coincidentally, Atlanta police records note the unsolved murders of numerous black women between 1980 and 1982, with most of the victims strangled.

Disclosure of new evidence and suspects has failed to liberate Wayne Williams from prison. Georgia's Supreme Court denied his latest bid for a new trial on 14 December 2001, rejecting assertions of prosecutorial misconduct. Retired FBI agents JOHN DOUGLAS and ROBERT RESSLER, meanwhile, continue to cite the Atlanta case as triumph of FBI PSYCHOLOGICAL PROFILING.

**AUDEN, Wystan Hugh**—A native of York, England, born 21 February 1907, W.H. Auden published his first book of verse in 1928 and emigrated to the United States eleven years later, becoming a naturalized American citizen in 1946. Shortly after his arrival, in 1939, he drew attention from the FBI by contributing an article to the leftist magazine *New Masses*. One memo in his 28-page bureau file notes Auden's membership in a "group of young poets who were all strongly oriented to the Left, some of them being orthodox Communists." Auden himself "was never in complete agreement with the Communist doctrine," another report suggests, but was "simply in rebellion" against "the upper bourgeoise [*sic*] into which he was born." G-men discovered that Auden had also driven an ambulance for Spanish Loyalist troops in 1937, and compounded his alleged subversion by marrying the daughter of another FBI target, THOMAS MANN.

Surveillance of Auden continued throughout his tenure as Chancellor of the American Academy of Poets, from 1954 through 1973. A piece of intercepted mail from 1959 contained birthday greetings to Auden from "a secret admirer," and the FBI was still on his case in 1965, when Jack Valenti, then an aide to President LYNDON JOHNSON, requested a background check on grounds that Auden had been nominated for the Presidential Medal of Freedom. No response to the query is found in Auden's file, but it was presumably derogatory, since he never received the award. By the early 1970s, Auden divided his time between the U.S. and Austria. He died in Vienna on 28 September 1973.

**AUTHORS League of America**— The Authors League of America and its affiliated professional guilds were marked for FBI infiltration in October 1941 and remained under scrutiny for alleged "subversive" activities through the administration of President DWIGHT EISENHOWER. Prior to active infiltration of the league, FBI headquarters maintained a file of bulletins published by the organization dating back to 1936, when the league published an article on censorship and "condemn[ed] several federal bills pending because of their repressive measures." Various writers affiliated with the league or its subsidiaries — the Authors Guild and the Dramatists Guild — were also subjected to individual surveillance on the basis of their alleged "radical" or "communist" sympathies.

After WORLD WAR II the Authors League was targeted by G-men as an "Internal Security — C" (communist) matter. A memo from J. EDGAR HOOVER to the New York field office ordered immediate investigation to determine "Communist infiltration of the Authors League of America." Fearing a publicity backlash if the probe was publicized, Hoover ordered that "In view of the nature of this group, the investigation must be most discreet and at this time should be limited to establishing the history, background, officers and nature of the group and the extent of Communist infiltration, influence or control. A complete review of your field office file should be made and any outside inquiries should be limited to your confidential INFORMANTS and established and reliable sources of information." League members of particular concern to Hoover included LILLIAN HELLMAN, JOHN HERSEY and REX STOUT, though many others were subjected to surveillance as the investigation expanded.

The bureau never failed to find subversion when its agents started looking, supplied in this case by anonymous informants who declared that the Authors League was "at least Communist infiltrated." Based on that finding, and "due to Communist infiltration" now accepted as fact, the FBI circulated reports on the league to various military intelligence agencies. By 1952 the probe had broadened to include leaders and members of the Radio Writers Guild, targeted for its opposition to blacklisting of authors and entertainers. Fueled by FBI memos and spies, the U.S. Senate Judiciary Committee issued a report denouncing the guild for its alleged "constant derision of the capitalistic system, and a constant derision of the average citizen, and there is no such thing in their scripts as a decent banker and a decent lawyer."

Surveillance of the Authors League intensified in 1953, expanding into Canada on Hoover's orders. In August 1953, an FBI-friendly reporter for *American Mercury* magazine penned an article titled "Reds in Your Living Room," claiming that communists "already had control" of the Radio Writers Guild and contending that formation of the fledgling Television Writers of America meant that "the Communist Party has set up a potent weapon to assail you right in your living room!" Perhaps predictably, no "communist" programs were identified by name.

FBI opinion on the league moderated slightly in 1954, the New York field office reporting that "According to informants of known reliability, the Authors League of America is Communist infiltrated but not Communist dominated." A year later, in late 1955, the same office reported to Hoover that its informants had no further knowledge of "current Communist activity to infiltrate" the league, whereupon Hoover ordered the league's file to be placed on "closed status." That order notwithstanding, press clippings and memos about the league and its various members were added to the file through 1962, when Philip Dunning, editor of the Dramatists Guild Bulletin, wrote to thank Hoover for an autographed photo. "I shall prize it highly," Dunning wrote.

# B

**BAILEY, William A.**—A 35-year-old black New Yorker hired by the Bureau of Investigation in January 1920 to report on "radical Negro activities," William Bailey infiltrated the AFRICAN BLOOD BROTHERHOOD and informed on its members. He volunteered to work for leader Cyril Briggs on the *Crusader*, a Brotherhood publication, and concentrated on the group's small procommunist faction. Bailey's reports, invariably signed "WW," also occasionally mentioned the NATIONAL ASSOCIATION FOR THE ADVANCEMENT OF COLORED PEOPLE. He was replaced in March 1920 by informant WILLIAM LUCAS, and subsequently infiltrated MARCUS GARVEY'S Universal Negro Improvement Association in Harlem, unable to support bureau suspicions that UNIA members were "drilling with firearms." Although supported by the bureau, Bailey was never a regular agent.

**BALDWIN, James**—Ranked among America's foremost black authors, James Baldwin was born in Harlem on 2 August 1924. He left New York for Paris at age twenty-four, logging his first notation in FBI files three years later, pursuant to ongoing surveillance of fellow author RICHARD WRIGHT. (G-men noted that Baldwin had criticized Wright for his "Uncle Tom Literature methods.") Baldwin published his first novel, *Go Tell It on the Mountain*, to critical acclaim in 1953. More books and plays followed, but the Bureau ignored him until 1960, when he returned to the U.S. and joined a pro-communist group, the Fair Play for Cuba Committee. A year later, FBI memos noted that Baldwin "supported organizations that supported integration" and had called for abolition of the HOUSE COMMITTEE ON UN-AMERICAN ACTIVITIES. Worst of all, he had publicly "criticized the Director" [J. EDGAR HOOVER].

Soon after that notation, Hoover inquired of his aides, "Is Baldwin in our SECURITY INDEX?" Agents replied that he was listed in the bureau's RESERVE INDEX, but subsequent activism in favor of black civil rights earned Baldwin a promotion to the ADMINISTRATIVE INDEX, where he was rated "dangerous." (That rating came after a 1963 meeting with Attorney General ROBERT KENNEDY, in which Baldwin urged Hoover's dismissal.) In 1964 Baldwin was one of eight persons targeted for special harassment under Hoover's COINTELPRO campaign against the SOCIALIST WORKERS PARTY (SWP). G-men mailed Baldwin at least one anonymous letter, crafted to "bring discredit" on the SWP's work on behalf of black CIVIL RIGHTS. In 1969, another bureau scheme involved recruiting members of the KU KLUX KLAN to read Baldwin's novel *Another Country* and "determine whether it is suitable reading for college students."

Baldwin remained an object of FBI interest to the end of his life, his file accumulating 1,459 pages of derogatory information.

Exposure of his homosexuality prompted Hoover to pen a memo branding Baldwin "a well known pervert," and a 1966 report from the Air Force Office of Special Investigations detailed Baldwin's eviction from an Istanbul apartment for "having homosexual parties." Baldwin's last book, *The Evidence of Things Not Seen* (1985), criticized FBI performance in the ATKID case. He died in France on 1 December 1987.

**BALDWIN, Roger**—A native of Wellesley, Massachusetts, born in 1884, Roger Baldwin was a lifelong pacifist who organized the American Union Against Militarism in 1917. A year later, he created the National Civil Liberties Board to defend conscientious objectors imprisoned for their refusal to fight in WORLD WAR I. By 1920, with America's first "Red Scare" in full swing, his brainchild had adopted its present identity, as the AMERICAN CIVIL LIBERTIES UNION.

An enduring mystery surrounds Baldwin's personal relationship with FBI Director J. EDGAR HOOVER. He met Hoover for the first time in 1924 and blindly accepted Hoover's self-description as an "unwilling" participant in the 1920 PALMER RAIDS. Emerging from that meeting to describe Hoover as a "decent enough fellow," Baldwin was clearly under the director's spell. "For quite a few years," Baldwin later said, "we had no difficulty with Mr. Hoover. As a matter of fact, I saw him half a dozen times. And much of the complaints that we had about FBI men he handled rather diplomatically. But it turned out to be false. Mr. Hoover was a real menace, a sort of political policeman. He established a political secret service, and we didn't know much about it."

Part of that blindness was willful. In January 1925, when Hoover complained to Baldwin that certain liberal magazines planned exposés of illegal FBI surveillance, Baldwin asked Hoover to keep him informed "so that we may correct them." Unmoved by such cooperative spirit, Hoover ordered his G-men to burglarize the ACLU's New York office on 26 February 1929 and examine all records for the previous year. Contrary evidence notwithstanding, Baldwin told ACLU board members in 1933 that Hoover's obsession with communism was "pretty well exhausted." Unknown to Baldwin, Hoover slated him for custodial detention in 1940, ranking Baldwin as both a communist and one of those "individuals believed to be the most dangerous and who in all probability should be interned in event of war."

By age sixty-six, in 1950, Baldwin's behavior was disruptive enough for the ACLU executive board to vote that he "be entirely relieved from executive responsibilities." In 1977, a FREEDOM OF INFORMATION ACT lawsuit revealed more than 41,000 pages of FBI reports on Baldwin and the ACLU spanning five decades. An internal report soft-pedaled Baldwin's relationship with Hoover, terming it "adversarial, otherwise cordial but distant," yet bureau files reveal that Baldwin denounced at least one ACLU member to the FBI as a communist "fellow traveler." Baldwin died in August 1981, at age 97.

**BALL, Lucille**—Born at Jamestown, New York on 6 August 1911, Lucille Ball began acting at age 17 and launched a parallel modeling career three years later. She met Cuban entertainer DESI ARNAZ in 1940 and they married that November. From 1951 through 1957 they starred together in *I Love Lucy*, arguably the most popular American television series of all time. They divorced in 1960, and Ball thereafter starred in several other TV situation comedies.

FBI interest in Lucille Ball initially sprang from Director J. EDGAR HOOVER'S infatuation with celebrities. When Ball became pregnant with the couple's first child in 1952, a hospital source tipped the Bureau's Los Angeles field office and Hoover telephoned to give Desi Arnaz the good news before Lucy could tell him. A year later, the HOUSE COMMITTEE ON UN-AMERICAN ACTIVITIES received information that Ball was aligned with the COMMUNIST PARTY. G-men investigated and confirmed Ball's report that she registered to vote as a communist in 1936, at the insistence of her grandfather. Lucy's patriotism was thus confirmed (and 142 edited pages of her dossier are available for viewing on the FBI's website). Ball died on 26 April 1989, of a ruptured aorta.

**BANDIDOS Motorcycle Club**—An "outlaw" motorcycle gang organized in Texas, the Bandidos filed incorporation papers in February 1978, but various chapters were active at least five years earlier, linked to three murders near El Paso in 1973. A racist group whose constitution specifically denies membership to "fat Mexicans," the Bandidos ranked as America's fastest-growing motorcycle gang in the 1980s, with 30 chapters and 500 members. Though still concentrated in Texas, chapters were found in Alaska, Colorado, Louisiana, Mississippi, New Mexico, South Dakota, Washington—and Australia.

Authorities say the Bandidos earn most of their money from drugs, extortion, prostitution, gun-running, contract murders, welfare fraud and fencing of stolen goods. Like other crime syndicates before them, the Bandidos have begun to infiltrate legitimate business: one Texas member owned 20 small businesses in 1981, valued at $12 million. Violence is habitual, including many homicides. In November 1978, Bandidos ambushed U.S. Attorney Jim Kerr in Austin, nearly killing him. Six months later, several gang members failed FBI polygraph tests in the murder of federal judge John Wood at San Antonio, but the actual assassin proved to be an outside contract killer, Charles Harrelson (father of actor Woody Harrelson). In Sydney, Australia, Bandidos fought a year-long gang war with another motorcycle gang, the Commancheros, during 1983-84. Seven persons died, with 21 wounded, in a shootout between the two gangs on 2 September 1984.

That same year, back in Texas, FBI Agent Dennis Dufour was assigned to crack the gang's Lubbock chapter, accused of ter-

rorizing locals, after a Bandidos lawsuit for police harassment virtually paralyzed local law enforcement. Dufour posed as the new owner of the Sidebuster saloon, purchased by the Bureau after Bandidos threatened and assaulted the female proprietor. An experienced motorcyclist who owned several bars in New Orleans prior to joining the FBI, Dufour stood 6 feet 2 inches and weighed 235 pounds, the very image of a rugged biker with long hair, a beard, and a phony criminal record provided by FBI headquarters. Assisted briefly by undercover agent JOSEPH PISTONE, who delivered $250,000 for a Bureau-approved drug deal, Dufour spent 10 months fraternizing with Bandidos and collecting evidence against them. The operation climaxed on 21 February 1985, when raiders arrested 80 gang members in eight states. Most pled guilty to NARCOTICS, firearms and racketeering charges. (Member Michael Smith sued the feds for $22 million in September 1985, claiming selective prosecution, but his case was dismissed.) The Sidebuster bar closed permanently, but the Bureau turned a $60,000 profit on its operation while the sting was in progress.

**BANISTER, Guy**—A Louisiana native and 20-year FBI agent, Banister spent the early 1950s as special agent in charge of the Chicago field office, where he ran the Bureau's "Red Squad" and forged intimate ties with leaders of ORGANIZED CRIME. The combination of mob ties and fanatical anticommunism followed Banister into retirement, in 1955, following major surgery and a doctor's warning to Banister's wife that "as a result of brain damage he would develop increasingly unpredictable, erratic conduct."

That trait was amply displayed in New Orleans, where Banister set up shop as a private investigator, widely known for his associations with Mafia kingpin Carlos Marcello and various far-right political causes. Banister joined the paramilitary MINUTEMEN in 1960 and subsequently founded his own World Anti-Communist League, collaborating with Cuban exiles and the CENTRAL INTELLIGENCE AGENCY in plots to overthrow Fidel Castro's regime. Other far-right associations included membership in the John Birch Society and the anti-Castro Friends of Democratic Cuba. On a 1961 visit to Europe, Banister reportedly conferred with French army officers plotting the assassination of President Charles DeGaulle. In his spare time, Banister published a racist newsletter, the Louisiana Intelligence Report, that described America's civil rights movement as a communist conspiracy.

Despite retirement, extremist connections and worsening alcoholism, Banister apparently retained close ties with his former FBI colleagues. Aaron Kohn, director of the New Orleans Crime Commission, reports that Banister "was still in touch with J. EDGAR HOOVER after he left" the FBI, and Banister's secretary, Delphine Roberts, confirmed that "Mr. Banister was still working for them. I know he and the FBI traded information." The FBI would be embarrassed by those links in 1963, withholding information on Banister from the Warren Commission's investigation of the JFK ASSASSINATION.

One item kept tightly under wraps was Banister's personal association with accused assassin LEE HARVEY OSWALD. In August 1963, while Oswald was making a name for himself in New Orleans as a pro-Castro activist, he shared office space with Banister's detective agency, Banister once telling Delphine Roberts, "He's with us. He's associated with the office." Another frequent visitor was pilot David Ferrie, an associate of Oswald from his teens, lately employed as a private pilot for mobster Marcello. One of Banister's detectives, Jack Martin, accused Ferrie and Oswald of plotting the JFK murder together, then recanted after a drunken Banister pistol-whipped him in public. FBI agents ignored Martin's report, withholding any mention of Banister and his strange associates from the Warren Commission. Banister died of an apparent heart attack, found in bed with a pistol by his side, before the Commission rendered its "lone assassin" verdict in 1964.

**BANK Robbery**—America's first bank robbery was actually a nocturnal burglary. Englishman Edward Smith used a set of duplicate keys to steal $245,000 from New York's City Bank of Wall Street on 31 March 1831, spending $60,000 of his loot before he was captured and sentenced to five years in prison. The pattern of midnight break-ins continued until February 1866, when the James-Younger gang staged the first daylight holdup at Liberty, Missouri, escaping with $15,000 in gold coins and $45,000 in bonds.

For the next half-century, bank robbery remained a strictly local crime. Federal agents might arrest bandits who robbed U.S. mail shipments, but interstate pursuit of other outlaws was left to such private firms as Wells Fargo and the PINKERTON DETECTIVE AGENCY. The 1930s bestowed celebrity status on a new generation of bank robbers, including JOHN DILLINGER, CLYDE BARROW, GEORGE ("BABY FACE") NELSON, CHARLES ("PRETTY BOY") FLOYD and the BARKER-KARPIS GANG, but G-men who wanted a piece of the action were forced to seek warrants on relatively minor charges such as violation of the DYER ACT (forbidding transportation of a stolen car across state lines). That changed in June 1934, with passage of new legislation making it a federal crime to rob any bank insured by the U.S. government. Over the next three years, Director J. EDGAR HOOVER owed his most flamboyant headlines to the hunt for big-name bandits nationwide.

Eradication of celebrity outlaws in the late 1930s did not eliminate bank robbery, however; quite the reverse, in fact. American bank heists peaked in 1996 with a total of 7,562 (for an average of one per hour), and while that figure had declined to 5,913 by the end of 1999, bandits were stealing more in each holdup (an average of $4,437, versus $4,015 in 1995). Despite the routine nature of such crimes, certain cases still stand out. A few examples include:

1974—Newspaper heiress Patricia Hearst, kidnapped by the SYMBIONESE LIBERATION ARMY, joined her captors in two California bank holdups, one resulting in the death of a female customer. Despite pleas of "brainwashing," Hearst was convicted and sentenced to prison.

1978—The first bank robbery by telephone transferred a record take of $10.5 million from one account to another at Security Pacific National Bank in Los Angeles, on 28 October. The theft went unnoticed until FBI agents contacted the bank eight days later.

1979—Another wire transfer removed $1.1 million from City National Bank in New York, on 25 March. Banking officials professed themselves "unusually concerned" about the potential for future robberies of this kind.

1981—America's youngest bank robber used a toy pistol to steal $118 from the New York Bank for Savings on 25 February. The unnamed nine-year-old, reportedly truant from school since 1979, surrendered to G-men on 27 February. He was arraigned as a juvenile in family court and released to his parents.

1986—Agents in Miami confronted bandits WILLIAM MATIX and MICHAEL PLATT on 11 April, after a series of violent bank and armored car holdups. The resultant firefight killed both gunmen and two agents, while leaving five more G-men wounded.

1993—Los Angeles gang member Robert S. Brown received a 23-year sentence in federal court for training teenage boys to carry out a four-year series of bank heists. FBI spokesmen linked Brown and accomplice Donzell Thompson (sentenced to 25 years) to a stunning total of 175 robberies in California and Nevada, the worst spree of serial bank robberies in U.S. history.

**BAPBOMB**—Birmingham, Alabama's Sixteenth Street Baptist Church has a long history of involvement in the black CIVIL RIGHTS movement. In 1946, after it hosted a meeting of the Southern Negro Youth Congress, police commissioner EUGENE ("BULL") CONNOR visited the pastor and warned him that if such activities continued, God—acting through the KU KLUX KLAN—might "strike the church down." Seventeen years later, when the church served as a rallying point for demonstrators led by Dr. MARTIN LUTHER KING, JR., that threat was realized. On Sunday, 15 September 1963, a powerful bomb rocked the church. Four adolescent girls—Addie Mae Collins, Denise McNair, Carole Robertson and Cynthia Wesley—were killed in the blast; a fifth, Sarah Jean Collins, was permanently blinded in one eye.

Klan members were the prime suspects, with several names provided by GARY ROWE, an FBI INFORMANT in the KKK since 1960. Director J. EDGAR HOOVER called the investigation—code named BAPBOMB—the Bureau's most intensive manhunt since the killing of JOHN DILLINGER, yet it was marked from the beginning by what journalist Diane McWhorter aptly calls a "leisurely pursuit of witnesses." When local police sought information on prime suspect Robert Chambliss, a violent Klansman known to his friends as "Dynamite Bob," G-men falsely reported that they had mounted constant surveillance on Chambliss's home the night before the bombing and observed nothing irregular. Results of FBI polygraph tests on Chambliss and other Klan suspects were likewise withheld from Birmingham authorities, perhaps because Connor's police force was known to be heavily infiltrated with Klansmen. Governor George Wallace "beat the Kennedy crowd to the punch" soon after the bombing, when suspects Chambliss, Charles Cagle and James Hall were charged with misdemeanor counts of possessing unregistered dynamite. All three were convicted and sentenced to six months in jail, their sentences suspended by the court. A few days later, James Hall joined Rowe (and countless other Klansmen) on the FBI's payroll as a full-time informant, vowing to help solve the BAPBOMB case.

In 1964 the Bureau obtained tape recordings of Klansman Thomas Blanton, Jr., discussing details of the church bombing with his wife in their home. Later reports claimed the tapes were "barely audible" without computer enhancement, unavailable in the 1960s, but the issue remains contested today. Before year's end, G-men knew beyond doubt that the bombers were Blanton, Chambliss, Herman Frank Cash and Bobby Lee Cherry. In 1965 Hoover ruled out prosecution on grounds that chances of conviction by an Alabama jury were "remote." A five-year federal statute of limitations officially closed the case in 1968, yet FBI historian Robert Kessler contends that "the investigation continued until 1971."

Be that as it may, the Blanton tapes and other BAPBOMB evidence went into storage after Hoover's death in 1972, and FBI HEADQUARTERS made no initial offer of assistance five years, when Alabama Attorney General Bill Baxley reopened the investigation. Finally, after Baxley threatened to hold a Washington press conference with survivors of the four slain girls, G-men released a portion of their FILE on Robert Chambliss, while withholding all material on Blanton and the other bombers. Chambliss was indicted for murder in September 1977 and convicted two months later, largely on the testimony of a niece who heard him boasting of the crime in 1963. Chambliss received a life prison term with a 10-year minimum before parole; he died in custody, in 1985.

Accounts vary as to what the FBI did next, and when. Robert Kessler maintains that Birmingham agent-in-charge G. Robert Langford reopened the BAPBOMB case in 1993 "without telling headquarters," and that he subsequently "found" the Blanton tapes (allegedly mislaid and forgotten since 1972). An alternate report, published in April 2000, claimed that the FBI reopened its investigation in 1997, after the chance discovery of "new and credible" evidence—i.e., the tapes maintained in Bureau files since 1964. In either case, bomber Herman Cash died in 1994 without facing criminal charges. A grand jury convened to study the case in November 1998, its review culminating in the May 2000 arrest of aging Klansmen Blanton and Cherry on charges of first-degree murder. Even then, controversy endured: Cherry claimed G-men had offered to reduce the charges if he would "lie" under oath about Blanton; Blanton's daughter told reporters, "The FBI told dad, 'We're going to pin it on somebody. We don't care who.'" Agent Craig Dahle of the Birmingham field office denied the charges, telling reporters, "It wouldn't happen that way."

Thomas Blanton was convicted of murder on 1 May 2001 and sentenced to life imprisonment. A year later, on 22 May 2002, Bobby Cherry was convicted and received an identical sentence. In the wake of Blanton's conviction, Bill Baxley voiced outrage at the FBI's long suppression of recordings and other evidence in the case. "What excuse can the FBI have for allowing Mr. Blanton to go free for 24 years with this smoking-gun evidence hidden in its files?" he asked. "If we had had those tapes, we would have unequivocally been able to convict Blanton [in 1977]. The FBI, for all intents and purposes, gave a 'get out of jail free card' to Tommy Blanton." Former assistant attorney general John Yung recalled of the 1977 Chambliss prosecution, "[The

FBI] denied having any more evidence than what they gave us, and it was hard enough getting what we got." Director LOUIS FREEH agreed, calling the BAPBOMB case "a disgrace to the FBI" and telling the media, "That case should have been prosecuted in 1964. It could have been prosecuted in 1964. The evidence was there."

Agent Dahle, in Birmingham, told reporters there was "no easy answer" to Baxley's questions, but insisted, "I think it is wrong to assert that there was any effort to block anything." Newsman Kessler blamed the whole thing on simple ignorance: "Instead of withholding evidence from Alabama Attorney General Baxley in 1977, as Baxley claimed, the FBI did not realize it had the material." And while that assertion strained credulity, Kessler went even further, giving the Bureau credit for Alabama's state prosecution of Tom Blanton. "Because of the tenacity of Langford ... and ... others involved," Kessler wrote, "the FBI had brought to justice a man who had blown up four girls because of the color of their skin."

**BARAKA, Amiri**—A black poet and playwright, born LeRoi Jones in 1934, Amiri Baraka first drew FBI attention when he attended a reception for Fidel Castro in New York City, on 24 September 1960. In 1961 the bureau noted his membership in the Monroe Defense Committee, established to defray legal expenses for black activist ROBERT F. WILLIAMS (falsely accused of KIDNAPPING in North Carolina). On 9 November 1961, G-men noted Baraka's election as president of the Fair Play for Cuba Committee's New York chapter. A report dated 2 May 1968 alleged that Baraka had received bomb recipes from an unnamed Swedish correspondent, complete with a notation of "suggested targets: Government or public buildings, especially police stations, banks, courthouses, post offices, schools, transportation systems, gas stations, radio and telephone buildings, newspapers, all communications facilities." No charges were filed in that case, and Baraka dismissed it as the prelude to a frame-up: "If you ever get busted, then they can say, well he received this mail—they're making a case against you."

By 1970, Baraka was a target of full scale COINTELPRO operations planned in Washington. On 30 October 1970, the FBI had a STATE DEPARTMENT attaché in Sweden send Baraka a bogus letter, allegedly written by a black U.S. Army deserter. The letter, designed to spread dissension within the BLACK PANTHER PARTY, claimed that its (mythical) author was romantically involved with someone "who works in a Swiss bank handling numbered accounts"—including one established by American Panthers who were stealing party funds and hiding them abroad. When Baraka ignored that letter, another was forged on 11 November 1970 and sent to Black Panthers in New Jersey, denouncing Baraka as a "Tom Pig" who "uses people's money for liberation soul power to line his pockets." In 1972, the FBI plastered Newark's ghetto with "WANTED" posters naming Baraka as an agent of the CENTRAL INTELLIGENCE AGENCY, again without result.

Despite a notable lack of success in discrediting Baraka, the bureau compiled 2,000 pages of derogatory information at FBI HEADQUARTERS, sometimes keeping Baraka under 24-hour surveillance. Exposure of the covert campaign, years later, confirmed Baraka's suspicions. "We thought they were there all the time," he told interviewer Natalie Robins. "All the time."

**BARKER-KARPIS Gang** — The Great Depression's largest, most successful gang of bank robbers and kidnappers was a loosely-knit coalition of felons, including thirty-odd bandits who came and went as the spirit moved them, joining up for a heist or two, then drifting off to pull odd jobs on their own. Between October 1931 and September 1933, the gang robbed at least seven banks, stealing an estimated $569,000; ransom KIDNAPPING added another $300,000 to the pot. Along the way, they killed at least ten persons, six of them policemen, yet the FBI had no inkling of the gang's existence until April 1934.

Part of the problem was pure dumb luck. Two local hoodlums were wrongly convicted after Barker-Karpis outlaws murdered an Arkansas lawman, in November 1931. A month later, police mistakenly blamed the Albert Kimes gang for killing a Missouri sheriff slain by the Barkers. Three "innocent" escaped convicts were jailed following a Kansas bank holdup the gang pulled in June 1932. G-man MELVIN PURVIS tried in vain to convict bootlegger ROGER TOUHY for the gang's first kidnapping, in June 1933. Three months later, GEORGE ("MACHINE GUN") KELLY and CHARLES ("PRETTY BOY") FLOYD were blamed for a Barker-Karpis holdup in Chicago. The gang was still unknown to federal agents when it kidnapped banker Edward Bremer in January 1934, collecting a $200,000 ransom.

By that time, leadership of the gang rested in the hands of three men: 34-year-old Arthur ("Dock") Barker, his 31-year-old brother Fred, and 25-year-old Canadian native Alvin ("Old Creepy") Karpis. Two other Barker boys had missed the crime spree: Herman, the eldest, had shot himself to avoid arrest in 1927; Lloyd, the next in line, had been drawn a life sentence in 1922 and would not hit the streets again until 1938. Other frequent members of the gang included fugitive Frank Nash, whose 1933 arrest would spark the KANSAS CITY MASSACRE, and Thomas Holden, later famous as the first man posted to the FBI's "TEN MOST WANTED" LIST.

Agents got their first hint of the Barker-Karpis gang's existence on 3 April 1934, from an unexpected source. Bandit Eddie Green, a DILLINGER gang member, was ambushed that day in St. Paul, Minnesota, fatally wounded while fleeing (unarmed) from G-men. He survived until 11 April, semiconscious, babbling details of his various associates while his wife filled in more details. Among other tidbits, it was revealed that the Barker boys and Karpis often traveled with an older woman who "posed as their mother."

With names in hand at last, the end was near. A fingerprint linked Dock Barker to the Bremer kidnapping, while witnesses named Karpis as an accomplice. The two were indicted for that crime, along with nine others, on 4 May 1934. Melvin Purvis led the team that captured Dock Barker in Chicago, on 8 January 1935. Clues found in his apartment led G-men to Oklawaha, Florida on 16 January, where Fred Barker died in a four-and-a-half-hour battle. Also found dead in the bullet-riddled cottage was Fred's mother, 62-year-old Arizona Donnie Barker — soon to

be known nationwide as "Ma" Barker, the Midwest Bandit Queen.

Almost before the gun smoke cleared in Florida, J. EDGAR HOOVER and a team of "friendly" journalists began to spin the legend of Ma Barker and her "viper's brood." Bereft of evidence, the media reports — some bearing Hoover's by-line — depicted Ma Barker as the "brains" of the gang, plotting crimes with military precision, dividing the loot, and ordering one-way rides for suspected stool-pigeons. Years later, Alvin Karpis told a different story, describing Mrs. Barker as a simple-minded old woman who traveled with her sons because she had no other family, no home.

Karpis was still at large in 1935, however, stealing $106,000 in two Ohio holdups, eluding traps in Arkansas and New Jersey. Hoover, meanwhile, suffered embarrassment in April 1936, when Senator KENNETH MCKELLAR forced the director to admit that he had never made an arrest. Fuming, Hoover spread stories that Karpis had threatened his life, proclaiming an intent to nab "Public Enemy No. 1" on his own. The director got his chance in New Orleans on 1 May 1936, in a scene described by Don Whitehead.

> As Hoover and his men approached the apartment building by automobile, Karpis and a companion unexpectedly walked out the door. …Karpis climbed into his automobile. Hoover ran to the left side of the car and Assistant Director Earl Connelly to the right side. Hoover reached into the car and grabbed Karpis before he could reach for a rifle in the back seat.

In fact, as Karpis told the tale, he and cohort Fred Hunter were sitting unarmed, in a car with no back seat, when a dozen G-men surrounded the vehicle. Only after Karpis and Hunter were frisked for weapons was Hoover summoned from hiding, around a nearby corner, to make his "personal arrest." Even then the embarrassment continued, since no one in the raiding party had brought handcuffs. Karpis and Hunter were finally bound with FBI neckties and hustled into a waiting car.

Dock Barker, convicted of the Bremer kidnapping on 6 May 1935, was sentenced to life and packed off to Alcatraz. Karpis pled guilty to the Hamm kidnapping and joined Barker on The Rock in 1936. Dock died in a bungled escape attempt, on 13 January 1939. Karpis was paroled and deported to Canada in January 1969. He moved to Spain in 1973 and died there, from an overdose of sleeping pills, on 26 August 1979.

**BARI, Judi** — On 24 May 1990 EARTH FIRST! activists Judi Bari and Daryl Cherney left Oakland, California en route to Santa Cruz and a scheduled meeting with fellow environmentalists. Just before noon, a pipe bomb exploded beneath the driver's seat of Bari's car, shattering her pelvis and dislocating her spine, wounding Cherney in the face with shrapnel. Agents from the BUREAU OF ALCOHOL, TOBACCO AND FIREARMS launched an investigation of the bombing, but they were soon displaced by G-men and Oakland police, after FBI spokesmen declared the BOMBING an act of domestic TERRORISM. On 25 May Oakland police announced the arrest of Bari and Cherney, on charges of possessing and transporting a bomb. Sweeping raids throughout the Bay Area failed to reveal Earth First's alleged "bomb factory," and prosecutors dropped all charges in the case on 17 July 1990.

Bari and Cherney, though vindicated, were not content to let the matter rest. Research informed them that RICHARD W. HELD, agent-in-charge of the Bureau's San Francisco field office, had a long history of involvement in illegal COINTELPRO operations, including actions against the BLACK PANTHER PARTY, the AMERICAN INDIAN MOVEMENT, and PUERTO RICAN NATIONALISTS. Those campaigns included widespread use of criminal *agents provocateur* to incite or commit violent acts, thus leading Bari and Cherney to believe that G-men or their hirelings may have planted the bomb as part of a FRAME-UP or attempted murder. On 8 April 1991 Bari and Cherney sued the Bureau and the Oakland Police Department, charging false arrest, libel, and violation of their civil rights.

Bari would not live to see the case resolved. She died of breast cancer on 2 March 1997, with the long-running discovery phase still in progress, but executors of her estate kept up the fight. Attorneys for the plaintiffs collected 7,000 pages of FBI and police files, with another 6,000 pages of sworn testimony from official and civilian witnesses. On 15 October 1997 a federal judge ruled that six G-men and three Oakland policemen should face trial on the charges, while ex-Agent Held and others were dismissed from the lawsuit on a grant of "qualified immunity." More delays followed, including a postponement occasioned by the terrorist SKYJACKINGS of 11 September 2001, when both sides agreed that the catastrophe might influence jurors.

The Bari-Cherney trial began at last on 8 April 2002. On 15 May Judge Claudia Wilken dismissed two more defendants, former G-men John Conway and Walter Hemje, from the case on grounds of insufficient evidence. Finally, after six weeks of testimony and 11 days of deliberation, the 10-member jury returned its verdict on 11 June 2002. The panel found that six remaining defendants had indeed violated Bari and Cherney's constitutional rights to free speech and protection from unlawful searches, awarding damages in the amount of $4.4 million. Those found guilty by the jury included retired G-men Frank Doyle, John Reikes and Phil Sena; Oakland police Sgt. Robert Chenault; retired Oakland police Sgt. Michael Sitterud; and former Oakland Lt. Mike Sims (now with the Tracy Police Department). A seventh defendant, former FBI agent Stockton Buck, was cleared on all counts. The jury's award included $2.9 million for Bari's estate ($1.6 million in compensatory damages, $1.3 million punitive) and $1.5 million to Cherney ($850,000 compensatory and $650,000 punitive). The various defendants filed a notice of appeal on 6 September 2002, claiming that the jury's award was "excessive" and "unsupported by evidence."

**BARNES, Djuna** — A New York native, born 12 June 1892, Djuna Barnes published her first collection of poetry — *The Book of Repulsive Women* — in 1915. She moved to Paris six years later, there emerging as a popular avant-garde writer of the 1930s. Her most famous novel, *Nightwood* (1936), examined the sexual affairs of five protagonists, both homosexual and "straight." She returned to the United States and a reclusive life in 1940, avoiding FBI notice until the mid-1960s, when she published a poem in the leftist magazine *Ramparts*. G-men were seemingly more interested in *Ramparts* than in Barnes, using her file to stash a 25-page review of the magazine. Included was a memo from the CENTRAL INTELLIGENCE AGENCY, noting that two dozen *Ramparts* contributing authors had "most frequently and most vehemently expressed major Communist themes in their published articles." Barnes died in Greenwich Village in 1982, apparently without further attention from the FBI.

**BARR, William Pelham** — A Virginia native, born 23 May 1950, William Barr was the second attorney general to serve President GEORGE H.W. BUSH. He assumed office on 20 November 1991 and soon developed a disdain for FBI Director WILLIAM SESSIONS that rivaled the hostile feelings of predecessor RICHARD THORNBURGH. Communications from retired agents confirmed Barr's suspicion that Sessions was abusing his office, whereupon an investigation was launched by the JUSTICE DEPARTMENT'S self-policing OFFICE OF PROFESSIONAL RESPONSIBILITY (OPR). The OPR's report deemed Sessions's misconduct serious enough that the president should consider removing him from office, but Bush took no action on that recommendation, leaving the problem to President WILLIAM CLINTON and Attorney General JANET RENO. Barr actively opposed investigation of the IRAN-CONTRA SCANDAL, and on 9 December 1992 he rejected congressional demands for an independent prosecutor to investigate possible criminal involvement by government officials in loans to Iraq. Two weeks later, President Bush pardoned six former aides convicted of perjury during investigations of the conspiracy. Barr left office on 15 January 1993.

**BARROW, Clyde Chestnut** — A notorious bandit, Texas born in 1909, Clyde Barrow teamed with girlfriend Bonnie Parker, brother Ivan ("Buck") Barrow and a revolving cast of sidekicks to terrorize bankers and merchants from Texas to Missouri in the early 1930s. The gang was strictly small-time, robbing local stores and gas stations more often than banks, with their largest haul reported as $7,100. Explosive violence marked the gang's progress, claiming at least a dozen lives in holdups and shootouts with police. A federal judge charged Clyde and Bonnie with violating the DYER ACT in May 1933, and while FBI agents were assigned to pursue the gang, they never came close. A posse led by Texas Ranger Frank Hamer ambushed the couple near Gibsland, Louisiana on 23 May 1934 and riddled them with 167 bullets. The gang's exploits were fictionalized by Hollywood in 1967, in the critically acclaimed film *Bonnie and Clyde*.

**BARROW, James W.** — A native of New York City, James Barrow joined the FBI's New York field office as a mimeograph operator on 1 July 1959, while working toward a degree in psychology from St. Francis College in Brooklyn. When Attorney General ROBERT KENNEDY pressured J. EDGAR HOOVER to integrate the Bureau, Barrow became one of the first blacks (with AUBREY LEWIS) to attain the rank of special agent since the early 1920s. Appointed as a special agent on 25 June 1962, Barrow served in the St. Louis field office for a year, then was assigned to the Bureau Language School to learn Spanish. Upon completion of that course, he subsequently served with field offices in Miami (1964-67), Newark (1967-70), Detroit (1970-72), and

Tampa, Florida. By 1989, he was one of three Equal Opportunity Counselors for the Tampa field office.

**BAUGHMAN, Thomas Franklin**—J. EDGAR HOOVER'S closest friend at George Washington University Law School, Thomas Baughman joined the U.S. Army in 1917 and was discharged as a captain after WORLD WAR I. He joined the Bureau of Investigation's GENERAL INTELLIGENCE DIVISION at age twenty-two, on 22 October 1919, and assisted Hoover in managing the notorious PALMER RAIDS that followed soon after. Maintaining his friendship with Hoover through the 1920s (and sacrificing his first marriage to the director's demands for "voluntary overtime"), Baughman was appointed as a supervisor of headquarters staff, making him the third most powerful BI official. In 1928 he replaced HAROLD NATHAN in the number-two spot, as assistant director, but Baughman held that post for less than a year. as Nathan reassumed the job. When CLYDE TOLSON filled a newly created post as assistant to the director in 1936, Baughman was picked as his aide, but he soon left that job as well, transferred to the FBI ACADEMY as a firearms instructor. Baughman held that position until he retired in 1949 and waged a nonstop battle with alcohol for the remainder of his life. Annual Christmas cards from Hoover were Baughman's sole contact with Hoover, his one-time best friend, in those declining years. He died of cancer in Florida on 8 September 1971.

**BAUM, Vicki**—An Austrian native, born to Jewish parents in Vienna during 1888, Vicki Baum published her first novel—*People in a Hotel*—in 1929. The book was adapted for Hollywood three years later and won the Oscar for best picture in 1932. Baum immigrated to the U.S. around that time and became a successful Hollywood scriptwriter. Naturalized in 1938, she refrained from any noteworthy political activity but still rated a brief FBI file. No substantive information was included, beyond notations that the bureau carried out a "review of the files" seeking her name in February 1954 and again in May 1957. In 1988, queried by author Alexander Stephan, the FBI reported that "[n]o investigation has been conducted by this Bureau concerning the above-named individual."

**"BEARDS"**—Nicknamed for their non-regulation hirsute disguises, "The Beards" were FBI agents assigned to an UNDERCOVER OPERATION against the "NEW LEFT" between 1970 and 1973. They were initially detailed to infiltrate the WEATHERMAN UNDERGROUND, although surveillance later extended to other groups including the White Panther Party and the old-line INDUSTRIAL WORKERS OF THE WORLD. G-men were recruited for the unit from field offices where concentrated Weatherman activity had been reported, including New York City, Chicago, Cleveland, Los Angeles, San Francisco and Washington, D.C. Sometimes at odds with FBI HEADQUARTERS, dubbed "Disneyland East" by squad members, the Beards continued their activities for more than a year after the death of Director J. EDGAR HOOVER, under the regimes of Acting Directors L. PATRICK GRAY and WILLIAM RUCKLESHAUS, and under Director CLARENCE KELLY.

Known to their New Left contacts by such nicknames as Ro-

dent, Panda, Walrus and Buddha, the Beards extended their operations from DOMESTIC SURVEILLANCE to FOREIGN OPERATIONS in Canada. Many of their investigative techniques were illegal, including frequent BREAK-INS that led to subsequent criminal indictments of FBI supervisors EDWARD MILLER and W. MARK FELT. Years later, squad member CRIL PAYNE published an account of his service with the Beards, including illegal drug use and prolific sexual activity with New Left suspects and INFORMANTS. The squad's continued operation through 1973 belied FBI claims that illicit COINTELPRO campaigns were discontinued in the spring of 1971.

**BECKWITH, Byron De La, Jr.**—An outspoken white supremacist in Mississippi, Byron De La Beckwith was associated with various extremist groups, including the CITIZENS' COUNCILS and the KU KLUX KLAN. His most notorious criminal action was the 12 June 1963 ambush murder of Medgar Evers, state leader of the NATIONAL ASSOCIATION FOR THE ADVANCEMENT OF COLORED PEOPLE, for which he eluded punishment until 1994.

The case should have been open-and-shut, since Beckwith left his rifle at the crime scene in Jackson, Mississippi. J. EDGAR HOOVER claimed his agents identified Beckwith from a "partial fingerprint" found on the rifle, although it is physically impossible to make a confirmed match with incomplete prints. An alternate story, leaked years later, paints a darker picture of the FBI's technique. In that version, a felon facing long prison time (named in some published reports as alleged mobster Gregory Scarpa) was offered freedom if he could identify Evers's assassin. Scarpa (or whomever) reportedly kidnapped a member of the Jackson Citizens' Council and drove his hostage to a deserted house in the Louisiana swamps, where he bullied and beat his victim into giving up Beckwith's name. FBI agents crouched outside an open window, taking notes, and then matched Beckwith's military records to the partial fingerprint. According to author Gerald Astor, Scarpa received $1,500 from the Bureau for expenses and served no time on his latest federal charge.

FBI spokesmen deny the kidnap story and cling to their fingerprint fable, though a simpler means of tracing Beckwith's rifle would have been to track its serial number from manufacture to sale. However the I.D. was achieved, it produced Beckwith's arrest by FBI agents on 22 June 1963, charged with conspiracy to violate his victim's civil rights. That charge was never tried in federal court, however, even after Beckwith walked away from two mistrials on state murder charges, in February and April 1964. G-men obtained additional evidence in August 1965, after Beckwith confessed the murder at a KKK rally, but reports of that incident from multiple INFORMANTS were suppressed. FBI agents did arrest Beckwith in September 1973, for transporting weapons and explosives across state lines, but a federal jury acquitted him on 15 January 1974. Louisiana prosecutors were luckier with state charges in that case, convicting Beckwith on 16 May 1975. He served most of a five-year sentence and was freed on 13 January 1980.

Another decade passed before Mississippi authorities ordered Beckwith's retrial in the Evers slaying. FBI headquarters still remained aloof, but Beckwith's 1965 admission of guilt was gleaned from a biography of Rev. Delmar Dennis, employed by the Bureau as a KKK informant at the time. Beckwith was finally convicted of murder on 4 February 1994 and sentenced to life imprisonment. He died in prison on 22 January 2001.

**BEHRMAN, Samuel Nathan** — A prolific American playwright, born in Massachusetts on 9 September 1893, S.N. Behrman earned his first FBI memo in 1938, for writing President FRANKLIN ROOSEVELT to suggest a U.S. embargo against Nazi Germany. Nearly two decades later, in 1957, Warner Brothers considered hiring Behrman to write a screenplay for *The FBI Story*, first contacting the bureau to check him out. The studio felt that "from a craftsmanship standpoint Behrman was one of the best writers in the field," but executives were still obliged to ask Washington if his employment "would be embarrassing" to the FBI. An aide to J. EDGAR HOOVER opined that Behrman was "not the type of person we would want to be identified with," a judgment Hoover affirmed by scribbling "Right" in the memo's margin. Warner Brothers took the hint and hired Oscar-winner Richard Breen to write the script, instead. Behrman died in New York City on his eightieth birthday, 9 September 1973.

**BELL, Griffin Boyette** — Georgia attorney Griffin Bell, born at Americus on 31 October 1918, served 14 years as a federal judge (1962–76) before took office as Attorney General under President JAMES CARTER on 26 January 1977. His administration was the first to aggressively pursue FBI undercover campaigns against ORGANIZED CRIME and official corruption, including the ABSCAM and UNIRAC sting operations, though final prosecution was deferred until the 1980s. Bell also secured the first-ever indictments of high-ranking FBI officials, including former director L. PATRICK GRAY and Acting Associate Director MARK FELT, for authorizing illegal BREAK-INS and other outlawed techniques of domestic surveillance. Bell resigned on 16 April 1979, before the defendants in that case were convicted, and returned to private practice in Atlanta.

**BEMELMANS, Ludwig** — A prolific author and illustrator, born 27 April 1898 in Austria, Bemelmans immigrated to New York at age sixteen and served in the U.S. military during WORLD WAR I. The FBI started a file on Bemelmans in April 1944, following publication of his novel *Now I Lay Me Down to Sleep* (1943). The book included a reference to the bureau as "the Gestapo," spoofing its investigation of a character named Bob Sherwood, apparently in reference to real-life FBI target ROBERT SHERWOOD. Despite those jibes, the bureau never launched a full-scale investigation of Bemelmans since, as one G-man critic reported, "on the whole it is a well-written novel and quite entertaining in places."

**BENÉT, Stephen Vincent** — Born in 1898, author and poet Stephen Vincent Benét was first investigated by the FBI for alleged "subversive" attitudes and writings in 1938. (His brother William was indexed at the same time, for supporting the Loyalist side in the Spanish Civil War.) In 1943, agents sought to interview Benét concerning another poet, MURIEL RUKEYSER, only to learn that learn that Benét "had died almost two months ago." In place of an interview, the G-men quoted from an article in which Benét called Rukeyser "a revolutionary" but opined that her poetry "contains no direct appeal to the proletariat, and her symbols of revolt are imaginary." Eleven years after his death, in 1954, the FBI was still upset when one of his scripts was rebroadcast on CBS Radio.

**BENNETT, Eugene and Marguerite** — FBI agent Eugene Bennett was dismissed from the Bureau in 1993, after he pled guilty to fraud and obstruction in a criminal case involving theft of FBI funds. He received a one-year prison sentence on those charges, and his wife Marguerite — also an agent — resigned after admitting she had lied under oath to protect her husband. No criminal charges were filed against Marguerite Bennett, and the case was forgotten until 1996, when the couple made headlines again, in the midst of a bitter divorce.

On 23 June 1996 Eugene Bennett kidnapped a Virginia clergyman, Rev. Edwin Clever, at gunpoint and forced Clever to call Marguerite, telling her she was needed at the Prince of Peace United Methodist Church in Manassas, to deal with an unspecified emergency. Marguerite suspected her estranged husband was behind the call, arming herself with a pistol and pepper spray before she drove to the church. There, she found Eugene armed with a gun and Rev. Clever wrapped with "explosives" which proved to be Play-Doh. A confrontation ensued, Marguerite blinding Eugene with the pepper spray and firing at him with her pistol as he fled. (She missed.) Police responding to the call found real explosives scattered around Prince of Peace, and more stashed in a locker at Northern Virginia Community College in Woodbridge (where Marguerite worked as a police supervisor). Eugene surrendered to police and FBI agents after a brief standoff, explaining the delay by saying that he had to lock his "evil alter-ego Ed" in the garage.

In custody, Eugene Bennett blamed his actions on Marguerite's lesbian affair with best-selling mystery author Patricia Cornwell (whose novels feature agents from the FBI ACADEMY at Quantico, Virginia). At the time of the incident, Cornwell was attending the Academy at the special invitation of Director LOUIS FREEH. Prosecutors countered with a claim that Eugene planned to end the costly divorce fight by killing his wife, collecting $1 million in life insurance, and claiming custody of their two young children. At trial, Eugene pled insanity, but jurors found him competent and convicted him of nine felony counts on 11 February 1997. The panel recommended a 61-year sentence, but Judge Richard Potter imposed a reduced sentence of 23 years. After nearly a year of denials, author Cornwell acknowledged a brief liaison with Marguerite Bennett to Vanity Fair magazine, in April 1997. "If I broke up their marriage," Cornwell said, "it was only because I told Margo if she didn't get away from him he would probably kill her."

**BENTLEY, Elizabeth Terrill** — A native of New England, born in 1908, Elizabeth Bentley graduated from Vassar and moved on to post-graduate work in Italy, where she witnessed the rise of fascism, simultaneously appalled by its brutality and drawn to the communists who opposed Benito Mussolini. Upon returning to the U.S., she joined the COMMUNIST PARTY and was assigned in 1938 to work as a courier for Soviet spy Jacob Golos. (Convicted in 1940 of failure to register as a foreign agent, Golos received a four-month suspended sentence.) Bentley and Golos soon became lovers, their affair terminated by his death from a heart attack in 1943. Thereafter, she was reportedly assigned to other Russian "handlers" and continued to serve them through the end of WORLD WAR II.

In August 1945, soon after V-J Day, Bentley approached G-men at the FBI's New Haven, Connecticut field office. She confessed her role as a Soviet spy and sketched the broad outlines of a vast ESPIONAGE network operating within the U.S. government. Her claims were reported to FBI HEADQUARTERS, but Director J. EDGAR HOOVER delayed follow-up interviews for nearly three months. His motive for stalling was twofold: aside from the embarrassment of learning that the FBI had failed to crack a huge Russian spy ring operating from Washington since 1938, there were also problems with Bentley herself. Author Ellen Schrecker summarizes Bentley's drawbacks in her study of the post-war Red Scare, *Many Are the Crimes* (1998):

> She was not a reliable informant. Even filtered through the bureaucratic prose of the FBI agents who debriefed her, the early statements of this melodramatic, unstable, and alcoholic woman seem slightly hysterical, filled with references — later edited out — to alleged advances from various men. She also fabricated parts of her original account and, like Louis Budenz, had a propensity for coming up with fresh information that would keep her services in demand. By 1953, even the Bureau, which sometimes had to baby-sit her through her drinking binges, had become exasperated with Bentley's tendency to embellish her testimony with new and important details.

There was also a persistent question concerning Bentley's loyalty, since she admitted receiving $2,000 from Soviet agents in October 1945, two months after her first approach to the FBI. Still, when debriefed in detail for the first time on 7 November 1945, she spun a tale involving spies within the U.S. Treasury Department, led by economist Nathan Silvermaster, including future celebrities ALGER HISS and HARRY DEXTER WHITE. Bentley initially named 14 government contacts, but her memory improved with passing time; later interviews named 43 alleged traitors, and the list topped 100 by the time she testified before the HOUSE COMMITTEE ON UN-AMERICAN ACTIVITIES (HUAC) in 1948. Meanwhile, a federal grand jury empanelled in 1947 dismissed Bentley's testimony as incredible and refused to indict the original suspects. Rebounding from that embarrassment, FBI sources leaked her testimony to conservative journalist Frederick Woltman, who published a series of articles promoting Bentley as the "Red Spy Queen."

Media hype notwithstanding, Bentley's subsequent HUAC testimony proved so erratic, contradictory, and totally devoid of supporting evidence that critics assailed the committee for mounting a partisan attack on FRANKLIN ROOSEVELT'S New Deal. Although shielded by immunity in her congressional testimony, Bentley faced potential litigation when she repeated her charges in forums such as NBC's "Meet the Press." The first to sue (and

win a $10,000 settlement from her television sponsors) was alleged spy WILLIAM REMINGTON. Once again, Bentley could produce no evidence of espionage, but a federal grand jury — chaired by an attorney with financial interest in Bentley's forthcoming memoirs — finally indicted Remington on a dubious perjury charge. Convicted at his second trial, Remington was subsequently murdered by federal prison inmates.

Curiously, the event that J. Edgar Hoover feared most — public criticism of his failure to crack Bentley's spy ring before it dissolved at war's end — never occurred. Before her moment in the limelight faded, Bentley even managed to assist Hoover in his long-running feud with the OFFICE OF STRATEGIC SERVICES (OSS) and its postwar successor, the CENTRAL INTELLIGENCE AGENCY (CIA). In a petty act of spite, Hoover had ordered agents of the Bureau's wartime SPECIAL INTELLIGENCE SERVICE to destroy all records of their work in Latin America, thus ensuring that the CIA would have to start from scratch. When CIA leaders protested the move, Hoover sent Bentley back to HUAC with claims that the OSS had been "infiltrated by Communists." Specifically, she named 14 alleged traitors within the intelligence unit — and once again, no evidence beyond her word was offered to support the charges.

**BERKMAN, Alexander**—A native of Russia, born in 1870, Berkman was a committed ANARCHIST by the time he emigrated to America in 1888. Four years later, galvanized by company violence against striking employees of the Carnegie steel empire, Berkman attempted to kill company chairman Henry Clay Frick in Pittsburgh. Frick survived the attack, despite being shot three times at close range and stabbed with a poisoned blade. Berkman was convicted of attempted murder and received a 22-year prison sentence (three times the maximum term allowed for his offense under Pennsylvania law at the time). He served fourteen years, much of it in solitary confinement, and published Prison Memoirs of an Anarchist soon after his release.

With EMMA GOLDMAN and other radicals, Berkman opposed American entry into WORLD WAR I, a stance that put him in conflict with the White House and the Bureau of Investigation. In July 1917, Berkman and Goldman were indicted on charges of conspiring to induce draft evasion among young American men. No evidence existed that either defendant had counseled future soldiers to avoid the draft, but prosecutor Harold Conant used wartime hysteria to win convictions, falsely alleging that the pair were supported by "German money" and hinting that Goldman had been somehow involved in the 1901 assassination of President William McKinley. Both were still in prison, serving two-year terms, when J. EDGAR HOOVER wrote a memo to federal prosecutor John Creighton on 22 August 1919, urging their deportation as "beyond doubt, two of the most dangerous anarchists in this country [who] if permitted to return to the community will result in undue harm [sic]." With Creighton's approval, Hoover personally prepared the deportation cases against Berkman and Goldman as "undesirable aliens." They were among 249 aliens deported aboard the *Buford*— dubbed the "Soviet Ark"— on 21 December 1919.

Berkman spent two years in Russia, but his anarchism

pleased the new Bolshevik regime no better than it had the Bureau of Investigation, and he was finally exiled to Europe, dividing his final years between Germany and France. Gravely ill in 1936, he committed suicide shortly before the outbreak of the Spanish Civil War.

**BERRIGAN, Daniel and Philip**—Brothers Daniel and Philip Berrigan chose the Catholic priesthood as their vocation, ordained in 1952 and 1955 respectively, but they were not content to lead a cloistered existence confined to ritual and theological debates. Philip participated in his first public demonstration, for racial integration of a Mississippi airport terminal, in 1963. By 1966 the brothers were committed to protests against the VIETNAM WAR, assisted by a group of like-minded nuns and laymen collectively known as the "East Coast Conspiracy to Save Lives."

In October 1967 Philip led a raid against a Baltimore draft board, destroying Selective Service records. He received a six-year prison term for that offense but was free on appeal when he joined brother Daniel and seven other protesters for another demonstration on 17 May 1968. Invading the draft board at Catonsville, Maryland, the Berrigan group removed hundreds of files and burned them with homemade napalm. For that offense, Philip received an additional 42 months in jail, while Daniel was sentenced to three years. The brothers exhausted their appeals, then failed to surrender as scheduled on 9 April 1970. FBI agents found Philip Berrigan in Brooklyn six days later; Daniel was arrested in Rhode Island on 11 August 1970.

There the matter rested for three months, until FBI Director J. EDGAR HOOVER appeared before the Senate Subcommittee on Supplemental Appropriations, seeking an additional $14.5 million to hire 1,000 new agents. Hoover justified the request by citing a new national menace, an "incipient plot" by the Berrigans and others to "blow up underground electrical conduits and steam pipes serving the Washington, D.C. area in order to disrupt Federal Government operations." Hoover added that "The plotters are also concocting a scheme to kidnap a highly placed government official. The name of a White House staff member has been mentioned as a possible victim."

Hoover's "proof" of the plot was a bundle of love letters, smuggled in and out of jail between Philip Berrigan and Sister Elizabeth McAlister. Friends told the press that McAlister saw herself as "a modern Joan of Arc," as committed to the anti-war movement as she was to her covert affair with Father Philip. McAlister's letters—carried to Berrigan and photocopied for the FBI by INFORMANT/*provocateur* Boyd Douglas, Jr.—suggested placing White House aide HENRY KISSINGER under "citizen's arrest" to stop the war in Vietnam. Hoover had informed Kissinger and President RICHARD NIXON of the "plot" in September 1970. Nixon seemed to take it seriously, but Kissinger had shrugged it off with a joke about "sex-starved nuns."

Although Hoover's report to the Senate was offered behind closed doors, FBI staffers leaked his statement to the media, thereby igniting a firestorm of controversy. Tennessee congressman WILLIAM ANDERSON attacked Hoover's resort to "tactics reminiscent of McCarthyism" on the floor of the House (thus bring-

ing down the full wrath of the FBI upon his head), while President Nixon told reporters, "The JUSTICE DEPARTMENT is looking into the testimony that Mr. Hoover has given and will take appropriate action if the facts justify it." In fact, Attorney General JOHN MITCHELL had already found the evidence insufficient to support criminal charges, and he was furious at Hoover's breach of Justice Department guidelines on pretrial statements to the press. Still, after a meeting at the White House, Mitchell felt compelled to prosecute the "plotters" in an effort "to get Hoover off the hook."

On 12 January 1971 a federal grand jury indicted six defendants on charges of conspiring to kidnap Henry Kissinger and to bomb the heating systems of various government buildings in Washington. Those charged included Philip Berrigan, Sister McAlister, Father Neil McLaughlin, Father Joseph Wenderoth, Anthony Scoblick (a married priest), and Dr. Eqbal Ahmad. Daniel Berrigan and six others were named as co-conspirators but were not charged, although Hoover had described Father Daniel as one of the conspiracy's "principal leaders." A second indictment was handed down on 30 April 1971, adding a seventh defendant (John Glick) and expanding the charges to include counts of destroying government property (draft files) and conspiracy to possess illegal explosives. On 5 April 1972, following an 11-week trial with former Attorney General RAMSEY CLARK chairing the defense team, Berrigan and McAlister were convicted on seven counts of smuggling letters in and out of Lewisburg prison. Jurors deadlocked at 10-to-2 in favor of acquitting the other defendants, and all remaining charges were dismissed in July 1972—two months after Hoover's death. Hoover lived long enough to claim victory in the case, and to attack one last enemy. Reporter Jack Nelson had written several articles about the Berrigan trial for the *Los Angeles Times*, commenting on the prosecution's ephemeral evidence and enraging Hoover to the point that Hoover sought a personal audience with the paper's publishers. In that meeting, Hoover denounced Nelson as a drunken liar who had spread false rumors of the director's alleged HOMOSEXUALITY. Nelson's employers took the charges with a grain of salt and left him to his work.

Philip Berrigan emerged from prison unrepentant, left the priesthood to marry Elizabeth McAlister, and pursued anti-war activism for the rest of his life. His "Plowshares" campaigns took their title from scripture (Isaiah 2:4) and typically involved demonstrators pounding on military weapons or vehicles with their fists, sometimes splashing instruments of war with blood. Twice nominated for the Nobel Peace Prize, the Berrigan brothers led more than 50 demonstrations around the U.S. between 1980 and 1997. Philip and seven others were jailed in 1980 for pounding on the nose cones of nuclear missiles in Pennsylvania. Eight years later, Berrigan went back to prison for punching cruise missile launchers aboard a Navy destroyer in Virginia. In 1993 he was sentenced for assaulting an jet fighter plane in North Carolina. In February 1997 Philip and five others invaded a foundry in Maine, boarded an unfinished Navy destroyer, then bashed the ship's controls with hammers and splashed the decks with bottles of their own blood. For that stunt, the "Plowshares 6" received terms of six to 27 months in federal prison. Berrigan was released in time to attack a pair of U.S. warplanes in Maryland, in December 1999, and was sentenced with three companions to 30-month prison terms. (Poor health prevented Daniel Berrigan from joining in the latest foray.)

Following the terrorist attacks of 11 September 2001, Berrigan's jailers placed him in solitary confinement "for his own protection." (An identical lockdown was ordered for LEONARD PELTIER, at a different federal prison.) Released three months later, Philip Berrigan died of cancer on 8 December 2002. His parting words: "I die with the conviction, held since 1968 and Catonsville, that nuclear weapons are the scourge of the earth; to mine for them, manufacture them, deploy them, use them, is a curse against God, the human family, and the earth itself."

**BIDDLE, Francis Beverley**—Born in Paris of American parents on 9 May 1886, Francis Biddle was the fourth and last attorney general to serve President FRANKLIN ROOSEVELT. He assumed office on 5 September 1941. His sporadic attempts to restrict illegal FBI surveillance techniques, authorized by his predecessors in office, were rarely successful. Despite a November 1941 agreement that J. EDGAR HOOVER would report ongoing FBI operations to Biddle, the FBI director still dealt privately with President Roosevelt whenever possible. When Biddle did attempt to limit FBI excesses he was overruled by FDR, who condoned (or secretly ordered) various illicit activities.

America's entry into WORLD WAR II was the first real test of Biddle's authority. He approved detention of "dangerous" German and Italian immigrants, but refused Hoover's request for mass arrests of Communists since the Soviet Union was a U.S. ally. Biddle also ordered the abolition of Hoover's CUSTODIAL DETENTION INDEX in July 1943, on grounds that the "classification system is inherently unreliable"; he added that the Bureau's "proper function" was to investigate those "who may have broken the law," with that purpose "not aided by classifying persons as to dangerousness." Biddle ordered that all Custodial Detention dossiers should be clearly stamped as cancelled and unreliable, with a warning that "There is no statutory authorization or other present justification" for maintaining such files. Hoover responded in August 1943 by renaming his list the SECURITY INDEX, instructing all FBI field offices that such files must be "strictly confidential and should at no time be mentioned or alluded to in investigative reports or discussed with agencies or individuals outside the Bureau."

Biddle disapproved of Hoover's wide-ranging investigations into legitimate political dissent, but he rarely took steps to curtail FBI snooping. In 1941, when Biddle ordered an end to surveillance of liberal groups and labor unions, Hoover complained to FDR that Biddle's restrictions would hamper "investigations into situations involving potential danger to the Government of the United States" and "will make utterly impotent the work of the FBI in subversive fields." (Roosevelt sided with Hoover.) Later, when Biddle refused to prosecute certain right-wing critics of the New Deal whom Hoover branded "subversive," Hoover told Roosevelt that FBI investigations had been "blocked by the Attorney General again and again." Furthermore, he said, "until some of the Attorney General's instruc-

tions have been changed … agents could not operate." (Again, Biddle was overruled.)

Six weeks after Roosevelt's death, on 30 June 1945, President HARRY TRUMAN demanded and received Biddle's resignation. Successor THOMAS CLARK would prove to be more pliable, ranked by Hoover as one of his favorite attorneys general. Biddle died of a heart attack at Wellfleet, Massachusetts on 4 October 1968.

**BIELASKI, Alexander Bruce**—A. Bruce Bielaski and his brother Frank got their start in law enforcement as operatives of the PINKERTON DETECTIVE AGENCY. Bruce initially joined the Bureau of Investigation under chief STANLEY FINCH, overseeing many of the day-to-day activities as Finch's second in command. Attorney General GEORGE WICKERSHAM appointed Bielaski to succeed Finch on 30 April 1912. The next five years were fairly uneventful, aside from Bielaski's establishment of the first training school for Bureau agents, but America's entry into WORLD WAR I changed everything. Pursuit of draft dodgers thereafter consumed Bielaski's attention, and a manpower shortage prompted his unwise approval of collaboration with the vigilante AMERICAN PROTECTIVE LEAGUE. APL "detectives" were much in evidence during the "SLACKER" RAIDS of 1918, marked by widespread brutality and illegal arrests. Controversy surrounding those raids prompted Bielaski's resignation on 10 February 1919, with WILLIAM ALLEN named as his successor. (Two decades later, brother Frank Bielaski would serve as director of investigations for the OFFICE OF STRATEGIC SERVICES, playing a key role in the *AMERASIA* CASE.)

**BIN LADEN, Usama**—The son of an oil-rich Arab family, born in Saudi Arabia in 1957, Usama Bin Laden is regarded by some investigators as the foremost exponent of Muslim TERRORISM in the world today. Other experts believe he was killed by U.S. troops in Afghanistan, sometime in late 2001 or early 2002, but evidence remains elusive and Bin Laden still occupies a position on the FBI's "TEN MOST WANTED" LIST, with a reward of $27 million offered for information leading to his arrest and conviction on various charges.

Bin Laden is (or was) the leader of a Middle Eastern terrorist organization known as Al-Qaeda ("The Base"), blamed by various investigators for some or all of the following incidents:

*5 November 1990*—The assassination of Rabbi Meir Kahane, shot in New York City by Egyptian national El Sayed a Nosair, whose writings were later found to contain plans for BOMBINGS of the WORLD TRADE CENTER and other local targets.

*19 December 1992*—An attack on a hotel in Aden, Yemen, where 100 U.S. servicemen were lodging en route to Somalia. Two Austrian tourists were killed, but the American troops escaped injury. Bin Laden claimed responsibility.

*26 February 1993*—A truck bombing at the World Trade Center in New York, killing six persons and wounding more than 1,000.

*24 June 1993*—A bomb plot by followers of Sheik Omar Abdel-Rahman (allegedly linked to Bin Laden) targeting the Holland Tunnel, the United Nations, the George Washington Bridge and other famous landmarks.

*3 October 1993*—The downing of a U.S. attack helicopter

with loss of 18 lives in Mogadishu, Somalia, reportedly executed by Al-Qaeda-trained guerrillas.

*11 December 1994*— The bombing of a Philippine Airlines 747 jet bound from Manila to Tokyo, killing one passenger. The incident was allegedly a test-run by World Trade Center bomber Ramzi Ahmed Yousef, financed by Bin Laden, in a conspiracy to destroy 12 U.S. airliners.

*13 November 1995*— The bombing of U.S. Army headquarters in Riyadh, Saudi Arabia, killing seven persons and wounding 31.

*25 June 1996*— The bombing of the Khobar Towers apartments at a U.S. military base in Dhahran, Saudi Arabia, with 19 Americans killed and 372 wounded.

*7 August 1998*— The synchronized bombings of U.S. embassies in Nairobi, Kenya and in Dar es Salaam, Tanzania. A total of 224 victims died (including 12 Americans), while some 4,585 were injured. Four members of Al-Qaeda were later convicted and sentenced to life imprisonment.

*14 December 1999*— The arrest of Ahmed Ressam, a bomber trained by Al-Qaeda, as he crossed the border from Vancouver, Canada with explosives intended for bombings of three U.S. airports during millennium celebrations.

*3 January 2000*— A failed attempt to damage a U.S. Navy destroyer, *The Sullivans*, with an explosive-laden skiff. (The skiff sank harmlessly on its approach.)

*6 January 2000*— The arrest of two Al-Qaeda operatives in Vermont, shortly after their arrival from Canada. Both are suspected of involvement in the foiled millennium bombing plots.

*12 October 2000*— The bombing of the *USS Cole*, anchored in Aden, with a loss of 17 sailors killed and 39 wounded.

President WILLIAM CLINTON reportedly ordered agents of the CENTRAL INTELLIGENCE AGENCY to kill Bin Laden following the August 1998 embassy bombings in Africa, but the CIA failed to carry out that assignment. On 7 June 1999 Bin Laden was added to the FBI's "Top Ten" list, but G-men were unable to reach their quarry in Afghanistan, where he was sheltered by the Muslim fundamentalist Taliban regime. President GEORGE W. BUSH ordered federal agents to "back off" their investigation of Bin Laden's family in early 2001, including relatives in the United States, but that command was rescinded in the wake of catastrophic SKYJACKINGS carried out by Al-Qaeda guerrillas on 11 September 2001. In the wake of that disaster, reporters for the British Broadcasting Company revealed that President Bush earned his first million dollars in the early 1980s, from an oil company funded in part by the Bin Laden family.

The "9-11" disasters prompted Bush to declare a global (if selective) "war on terrorism" that included military strikes against Afghanistan. The Taliban regime was toppled, but Bin Laden once again eluded capture. In May 2002 media reports exposed an FBI memo, dated three months earlier, revealing that evidence on Bin Laden's activities had been inadvertently destroyed during a routine purge of e-mails captured by DOMESTIC SURVEILLANCE programs on the Internet, but it made little difference with no defendant in custody. On 17 July 2002 FBI counterterrorism chief Dale Watson declared his belief that Bin Laden was dead, presumably killed at some point in the U.S. assault on Afghanistan, but his view was not the official Bureau line. Four months later, on 13 November, USA Today reported that G-men and CIA agents were still "scouring the world" in search of Bin Laden, without success. Expert opinions are divided on the authenticity of an audio tape, aired two weeks later, which reportedly contained new threats from Bin Laden against the U.S. and its allies.

**BLACK Agents**—The Bureau of Investigation had no black agents until 1919, when JAMES WORMLEY JONES was hired specifically to infiltrate black "radical" groups and report on their activities. Four more black agents were hired in 1921–22, but of the original five only JAMES AMOS remained as a long-term Bureau employee. In addition to surveillance on black activists, various sources claim Amos was assigned to investigate New York mobster Dutch Schultz, but the Bureau never arrested Schultz and he was killed by rival racketeers in 1935. No details are available for Amos's career between that time and his retirement in 1953.

No other black agents were hired between 1922 and 1962. With the onset of WORLD WAR II, Director J. EDGAR HOOVER reclassified his various servants and chauffeurs as "agents" to make them exempt from conscription, sending JAMES CRAWFORD and SAMUEL NOISETTE through abbreviated (and segregated) courses at the FBI ACADEMY to lend the sham an air of authenticity, but none of those faux G-men performed any investigative functions. Attorney General ROBERT KENNEDY ordered Hoover to integrate the Bureau in 1962, whereupon JAMES BARROW and AUBREY LEWIS became the first black recruits to share classes with white trainees at the academy. Reports conflict on the total number of black agents employed at Hoover's death in May 1972, with different accounts claiming 63 or 70 amidst a total of 8,631 (or 8,659) agents—still less than one percent in any case.

As with other ethnic minorities, hiring and promotion of black agents has improved since Hoover's death. In February 1992 there were 510 black agents among 10,422 (4.9 percent); five years later there were 606 among 10.816 (5.6 percent). John Glover became the first black special agent in charge (of the Milwaukee field office) in February 1979, and he was promoted to serve as the first black executive assistant director in April 1986. Sylvia Mathis became the first black WOMAN AGENT in February 1976, while Carolyn Morris was appointed to serve as the first black female assistant director in October 1995. In September 1990, Jimmy Carter was chosen to supervise FBI recruitment in the black community. (EDWIN WOODRIFFE took dubious honors as the first black G-man killed on duty in January 1969.)

Still, racial tension and problems remained. In August 1990 Director WILLIAM SESSIONS settled a lawsuit filed by ex-agent Donald Rochon, alleging racial harassment by his white superiors and fellow agents in the Chicago, Omaha and Philadelphia field offices. Sessions agreed to a financial settlement and disciplined 11 subordinates for either harassing Rochon or ignoring his complaints. (That decision and a similar settlement with HISPANIC AGENTS led white G-men to dub the director "ConSessions.") A December 1990 internal survey found 40 percent of black agents reporting that management was "sometimes" insensitive to racial harassment or discrimination. In April 1991, when 230 members of BADGE (Black Agents Don't Get Equality) met in Washington to discuss a class action lawsuit, Director Sessions asked them to meet with him instead. A year of intense negotiations followed, climaxed by the director's agreement to place 19 blacks in supervisory or relief supervisory posts, while taking other steps to improve training and promotion of black agents.

The FBI's website presently offers no ethnic breakdown on agents, but public statements affirm a commitment to equal opportunity hiring and promotion. It remains to be seen if good intentions can finally overcome tradition.

**BLACK, Fred B., Jr.**—A lobbyist for the aerospace industry in Washington, D.C., Fred Black was convicted of income tax evasion in 1964. At the time of his conviction, federal prosecutors were unaware of illegal FBI bugs installed in Black's hotel room during early 1963, but they learned of the BUGGING in 1965, when G-men inadvertently tipped their hand during briefings on another case. Black's lawyers appealed his conviction to the U.S. SUPREME COURT in 1966, whereupon Attorney General NICHOLAS KATZENBACH informed the court of the covert eavesdropping. On 13 June 1966 the court ordered the JUSTICE DEPARTMENT to submit a brief on its bugging policy, thereby sparking a bitter feud between Katzenbach and J. EDGAR HOOVER.

In essence, Katzenbach refused to tell the court that FBI bugging in the Black case had been specifically authorized, or that bugging in general was reviewed and approved by the Justice Department. Hoover called on various contacts, including the White House, U.S. senators and Supreme Court Justice ABE FORTAS (himself an FBI INFORMANT) to make Katzenbach revise the language of his brief, but Katzenbach refused. The brief as finally submitted made it clear that no specific federal statute or executive order authorize FBI bugging, although eavesdropping in the Black case had been approved by Attorney General ROBERT KENNEDY. Largely as a result of the Black case, and before it was heard by the Supreme Court, FBI bugging was restricted under new guidelines from Katzenbach, issued on 30 March 1965.

**BLACK Nationalist Photograph Album**—This FBI record of black militants in the U.S. began in March 1968, coordinated with the bureau's AGITATOR INDEX. Field offices were ordered to obtain and submit "visual material relating to violence by black extremists," more specifically "clear, glossy 8" by 10" photographs" of said persons in action. Copies of the mug book were then circulated back to the field offices with a Racial Calendar highlighting "the dates of ... racial events." Copies were also furnished to the CENTRAL INTELLIGENCE AGENCY and the Royal Canadian Mounted Police, to facilitate surveillance outside the United States. The album ultimately included 484 activists of various political persuasions. Only death qualified to remove a subject from the collection, as when Hakim Jamal was murdered by members of a rival militant organization in Massachusetts. (Even then, the Boston field office needed Washington's permission to extract Jamal's photo from the album.) Shortly before his death in 1972, J. EDGAR HOOVER renamed the collection, calling it the Extremist Photograph Album, with photos of some two dozen KU KLUX KLAN members included.

**BLACK Panther Party for Self-Defense**—The Black Panther Party was organized in October 1966 by Huey Newton and Bobby Seale, two students at Merritt College in Oakland, California. Combining Maoist politics with the teachings of MALCOLM X, they devised a party program that included freedom, full employment, decent housing, improved educational facilities, liberation of all black men held in American prisons, exemption from military service for all blacks, and "an immediate end to police brutality and murder of black people." To the latter end, Panthers armed themselves and "patrolled" police in the ghetto, advising black prisoners of their constitutional rights. Less confrontational (but more successful) party programs included free breakfast service for children, provision of free health care, and campaigns against NARCOTICS traffickers. Soon, spokesmen of STUDENTS FOR A DEMOCRATIC SOCIETY hailed the Panther Party as "the vanguard of an anticapitalist revolution involving the whole of American society."

FBI Director J. EDGAR HOOVER seems to have taken that overblown rhetoric seriously, describing Black Panthers as the single greatest threat to America's internal security. Reports suggest that there were never more than 1,200 Panthers nationwide, but many white police and politicians shared Hoover's view, exacerbated by a series of violent clashes in late 1967 and early 1968. (Hoover's reaction may have been conditioned by an article in *The Black Panther*, declaring that "We need Black FBI agents to assassinate J. Edgar Hoover, [Attorney General] JOHN MITCHELL and [President] RICHARD NIXON.") FBI HEADQUARTERS was ready to act in February 1968, when a merger was proposed between the Panther Party and the STUDENT NONVIOLENT COORDINATING COMMITTEE (SNCC). In return for collaboration with the party, SNCC leader STOKELY CARMICHAEL was named honorary prime minister, while H. RAP BROWN became the party's minister of justice and JAMES FORMAN was appointed minister of foreign relations. G-men quickly disrupted the alliance by planting evidence that Carmichael was an undercover agent of the CENTRAL INTELLIGENCE AGENCY, then warning Carmichael's family of an impending "hit" by Panther gunmen.

That Bureau "victory" set the tone for future COINTELPRO operations directed against the Panthers. In November 1968 Hoover ordered FBI field offices "to exploit all avenues of creating ... dissension within the ranks of the BPP"; he also demanded "imaginative and hard-hitting counterintelligence measures aimed at crippling the BPP." To that end, California G-men engineered a shooting war between Panthers and members of the rival US organization, using INFORMANTS and *agents provocateur* on both sides to keep the action going. At least four Panthers were killed by US gunmen before the feud ended, mute testimony to the claim of ex-Agent M. WESLEY SWEARINGEN that "Hoover wanted the Panthers in jail or dead." A similar effort in Chicago sparked violence between the Panthers and members of a volatile street gang, the BLACKSTONE RANGERS. Between December 1967 and December 1969, at least 28 Panthers were killed by police or rival militants — many of whom, on closer inspection, proved to be FBI hirelings.

Prosecution was another angle of attack, although with less certain results. In 1969 alone, 348 Panthers were jailed across America on various felony charges, costing the party more than $200,000 in bail premiums. In April of that year, G-men and New York police charged 21 Panthers with conspiracy to commit murder and arson, but all were finally acquitted at trial. A month after those arrests, on 15 May 1969, Hoover issued a memo commanding all agents to "destroy what the BPP stands for." When the San Francisco field office objected to persecuting innocent persons, Hoover scolded the agent in charge with a memo, dated 27 May, that read:

> A review has been made of ... your thoughts on the Counterintelligence Program (CIP). Your reasoning is not in line with Bureau objectives as to our responsibilities under the CIP.
>
> ... You have previously been instructed to review your files concerning [the Panther] newspaper to determine whether we could disrupt the mailings of the publication. Your answer stated that you were not in a position to do this. You must immediately take positive steps to insure that we will be in a position to accomplish CIP objectives including the disruption of the mailing of their publication....
>
> ... You state that the Bureau under the CIP should not attack programs of community interest such as the BPP "Breakfast for Children." ... You have obviously missed the point. The BPP is not engaged in the "Breakfast for Children" program for humanitarian reasons. This program was formed by the BPP for obvious reasons, including their efforts to create an image of civility, assume community control of Negroes, and to fill children with their insidious poison....
>
> The CIP in the San Francisco Office must be reevaluated. During the reevaluation, give thorough consideration to the adequacy of the personnel assigned. Insure that you are utilizing the best personnel available in this program. Advise the Bureau of the results of your reevaluation by June 9, 1969.

Stung by Hoover's rebuke, San Francisco agents mounted an aggressive campaign against the Panther Party. "There was a tremendous fear of Hoover out there," Agent Charles Gain later recalled. "It was almost all they could talk about. They were afraid of being sent to some awful post in Montana."

Other FBI field offices "got the point" without warnings from Hoover. In Detroit, agents drafted spurious extortion letters in the party's name, addressed to local businessmen. In Los Angeles, FBI informant MELVIN SMITH provided information on a nonexistent cache of weapons, prompting police to raid the local Panther office in December 1969. Four days later, members of the CHICAGO POLICE DEPARTMENT used a floor plan drawn by G-men and informant WILLIAM O'NEAL to raid the home of party leader FRED HAMPTON, riddling him with bullets as he lay asleep in bed.

By April 1970 Hoover was determined to split the Panther Party along east-west lines, concocting a feud between Bobby Seale in California and rival Eldridge Cleaver. G-men mailed a letter to Cleaver in Algiers, claiming that Seale and others planned to kill him, and Hoover graced the team with "incentive rewards" after Cleaver issued a communiqué expelling his enemies from the party. A second letter warned Melvin Newton (Huey's brother) of an alleged murder plot by Cleaver loyalists. The technique of "SNITCH-JACKETING" also produced several shooting, prompting

the San Francisco field office to ask Washington if "we are ready to assume responsibility for the death of BPP members we 'set up' as FBI informants." The answer was affirmative, as Assistant Director WILLIAM SULLIVAN wrote on 15 May 1970, reminding all concerned that the "[p]urpose of counterintelligence action is to disrupt BPP and it is immaterial whether facts exist to substantiate the charge. If facts are present, it aids in the success of the proposal but the Bureau feels that ... disruption can be accomplished without facts to back it up." Such was the case in 1972, when G-men and informants joined forces with the Los Angeles Police Department to frame Panther ELMER ("GERONIMO") PRATT on a false murder charge.

The FBI's Panther hunt did not end with Hoover's death in May 1972 or with the party's subsequent dissolution. Imprisoned Panthers were still subject to surveillance and harassment under the Bureau's PRISACTS (Prison Activists) program targeting "extremist, revolutionary, terrorist, and subversive activities in penal institutions." PRISACTS was launched in 1974 "with the primary goals of promoting liaison and cooperation between the FBI and prison administrators nationwide relative to above elements, and to generally provide for two-way exchange of information."

G-men also pursued the scattered party veterans still at large, including ex-Panther Joanne Chesimard. Linked to a robbery and shootout in New Jersey during May 1973, Chesimard was indicted for a wide range of East Coast crimes, but courts dismissed three cases and juries acquitted her in two others. Finally convicted on the original counts in March 1977, she escaped from prison in November 1979 and surfaced in Cuba eight years later, to promote her autobiography. Huey Newton also fled to Cuba, dodging charges for the murder of an Oakland prostitute in 1974, then returned in 1977 to face trial. Two juries failed to reach a verdict in the case. Newton was killed in Oakland on 22 August 1989, in what police described as a drug dispute. A member of the rival Black Guerrilla Family was convicted of Newton's murder in 1991.

**BLACKSTONE Rangers**—An all-black Chicago street gang, alternately known as the Black P. Stone Nation, the Blackstone Rangers attracted FBI attention for the first time on 18 December 1968, when leader Jeff Fort convened a meeting with FRED HAMPTON and other officers of the BLACK PANTHER PARTY'S Chicago chapter. A few hours earlier, gunfire had been exchanged between the groups, leaving one Panther wounded, while 12 Panthers and five Rangers were arrested. WILLIAM O'NEAL, an FBI INFORMANT in the Panther Party, described the meeting for his handlers.

> Everyone went upstairs into a room which appeared to be a gymnasium, where Fort told Hampton and [STUDENT NONVIOLENT COORDINATING COMMITTEE activist Bobby] Rush that he had heard about the Panthers being in Ranger territory during the day, attempting to show their "power" and he wanted the Panthers to recognize the Rangers['] "power." ... Fort then gave orders, via walkie-talkie, whereupon two men marched through the door carrying pump shotguns. Another order and two men appeared carrying sawed off carbines then eight more, each carrying a .45 caliber machine gun, clip type, operated from the shoulder or hip, then oth-

ers came with over and under type weapons…. After this procession Fort had all the Rangers present, approximately 100, display their side arms and about one half had .45 caliber revolvers. Source advised that all the above weapons appeared to be new….

Source advised nothing was decided about the two groups joining forces, however, a decision was made to meet again on Christmas day. Source stated that Fort did relate that the Rangers were behind the Panthers but that they were not to be considered members. Fort wanted the Panthers to join the Rangers and Hampton wanted the opposite, stating that if the Rangers joined the Panthers, then together they would be able to absorb all the other Chicago gangs…. Source advised that based on conversations during this meeting, Fort did not appear over anxious to join forces with the Panthers, however, neither did it appear that he wanted to terminate meeting for this purpose.

The Christmas meeting dissolved into arguments and brought the coalition no closer. On 27 December Fort allegedly telephoned Hampton and warned that Chicago Panthers had 24 hours to join the Rangers "or else." Later that week, when Panthers criticized Fort's "lack of commitment to black people generally," Fort vowed to "'take care' of individuals responsible for the verbal attacks."

The FBI stepped in at that point, to make matters worse. MARLIN JOHNSON, agent in charge of the Chicago field office, wrote to FBI HEADQUARTERS on 10 January 1969, proposing a COINTELPRO operation against the Rangers and Panthers. Specifically, Johnson wanted to prepare and mail a letter to Jeff Fort, reading:

Brother Jeff,

I've spent some time with some Panther friends on the west side lately and I know what's been going on. The brothers that run the Panthers blame you for blocking their thing and there's supposed to be a hit out for you. I'm not a Panther, or a Ranger, just black. From what I see these Panthers are out for themselves not black people. I think you ought to know what their [sic] up to, I know what I'd do if I was you. You might hear from me again.

A black brother you don't know

As Agent Johnson explained to Director J. EDGAR HOOVER: "It is believed that the [letter] may intensify the degree of animosity between the two groups and occasion Forte [sic] to take retaliatory action which could disrupt the BPP or lead to reprisals against its leadership…. Consideration has been given to a similar letter to the BPP alleging a Ranger plot against the BPP's leadership; however, it is not felt that this would be productive principally because the BPP … is not believed to be as violence prone as the Rangers, to whom violent type activity — shooting and the like — is second nature."

Hoover's response to Johnson, dated 30 January 1969, made it clear that headquarters had no objection to provoking murder. The plan was authorized with orders to "[u]tilize a commercially purchased envelope for this letter and insure that the mailing is not traced to the source." Johnson was also instructed to "Advise the Bureau of any results obtained by the above mailing."

The first result was a threat against Hampton, with Fort vowing to "blow his head off." G-men kept the pot boiling with another letter in March 1969, this one addressed to Hampton.

Brother Hampton:

Just a word of warning. A Stone friend tells me [name deleted] wants the Panthers and is looking for somebody to get you out of the way. Brother Jeff [Fort] is supposed to be interested. I'm just a black man looking for blacks working together, not more of this gang banging.

Informant O'Neal engineered the next armed clash between Panthers and Rangers on 2 April 1969, but no injuries resulted and Hampton managed to keep the simmering violence in check until his death at police hands eight months later. The Rangers/Nation subsequently changed its name to El Rukn tribe of the Moorish Science Temple of America, and later still to El Rukn, Sunni Muslims. Jeff Fort (aka "Prince Iman Malik") remained in charge despite ongoing problems with the law. In 1972 Fort and others were convicted of swindling the U.S. government out of nearly $1 million in a job-training scam. Parole from Leavenworth federal prison in 1976, Fort remained at liberty for six years, until he was charged with drug smuggling in Texas. Conviction on that charge earned him a 13-year sentence, but the worst was yet to come. In 1987 members of El Rukn bought a rocket launcher from an undercover federal agent and were promptly charged with participation in a TERRORISM-for-hire agreement with the Libyan government. Jeff Fort, named as the "mastermind" of the alleged conspiracy, received a 175-year prison term, plus 75 additional years for the murder of a rival gang leader.

In the early 1990s, 56 El Rukn members were tried and convicted in federal court on racketeering charges. Evidence produced in subsequent appeals disclosed that "shamefully lax" security measures by federal prosecutors and agents of the BUREAU OF ALCOHOL, TOBACCO AND FIREARMS had allowed key inmate-witnesses free access to drugs, liquor, sex, pornography and other luxuries generally barred in prison. Those witnesses were also furnished copies of secret grand jury minutes to "assist" them in perfecting their testimony prior to trial. Chief prosecutor William Hogan, himself investigated for misconduct by the JUSTICE DEPARTMENT after several El Rukn verdicts were overturned on appeal, later complained that agents from the OFFICE OF PROFESSIONAL RESPONSIBILITY were "rank amateurs" who "had no experience in dealing with the witnesses and no appreciation of the realities and practicalities" of trying a criminal case. A federal judge later found that while most of the charges concerning misconduct were true, the violations occurred "without Hogan's prior knowledge."

BLOCH, Ernst — A German philosopher, born 8 July 1885, Ernst Bloch emigrated to Paris in 1935 and settled in New York City two years later. The FBI first took note of him on 13 November 1940, after an anonymous accusation suggested Bloch's involvement in espionage and "possible UnAmerican activities." The search went nowhere, but interest was renewed on 11 May 1942, after exiled writer BUDO UHSE sent Block a telegram from Mexico City. The cable was intercepted in New York and seemed to confuse G-men, who noted: "Meaning of telegram not clear but believed possibly to be of subversive nature." Subsequent memos from 1942 note Bloch's "glorification of the Soviet Union" and "sarcastic references to the Second Front" in WORLD WAR II.

Bloch became a naturalized American citizen on 17 March 1947, then abruptly returned to East Germany in 1948 and held a teaching post at the University of Leipzig. In September 1953, the FBI's Boston field office tried to prevent Bloch from reentering the U.S., establishing a "National Stop with the U.S. Customs Service." G-men noted Bloch's move to West Germany, following erection of the Berlin Wall, and followed his visit to England in May 1962. While apparently regarding Bloch as an East German intelligence agent, the bureau never built a case and filed no charges. Bloch died at Tübingen on 4 August 1977.

**BODENHEIM, Maxwell** — A Mississippi native, born in 1893, Bodenheim published regularly between 1918 and the early 1930s, while living in Chicago and New York. His FBI file was opened in 1936, with reports that he had published articles in the leftist magazine *New Masses* and that on 1 May 1936 "he was photographed at the May Day Parade carrying a Communist flag and selling the Daily Worker." Several INFORMANTS reported that Bodenheim was a member of the COMMUNIST PARTY from 1932 to 1940, though another expressed "doubts whether he was ever sober enough to attend the meetings." Bodenheim joined the Federal Writers Project in 1938 but was fired two years later, for failure to divulge his communist associations.

Interviewed by G-men in 1940, Bodenheim said he had resigned from the Communist Party in protest against Russia's invasion of Finland. As Bodenheim later described the interview to colleague BEN HECHT, "The galoriously [sic] democratic FBI has threatened me with arrest and a trial for perjury unless I turn stool pigeon and informer and give reams of information regarding names of Party members, places where members recruited others, etc., in return for which the government would restore my $21.90 WPA job (just a little deal between friends). If I do not sign certain papers the FBI declares that I will be arrested."

No arrest was forthcoming, and the bureau seemingly lost interest. In 1954, Bodenheim and his wife were murdered in New York City by a gunman who told arresting officers, "I killed two communists. I ought to get a medal." On learning of the murders, J. EDGAR HOOVER telegrammed the New York field office, ordering his agents to withhold "information concerning subversive behavior" of the Bodenheims from New York police unless Hoover personally ordered its release. The motive for that order is unknown.

**BOGAN, Louise** — A native of Maine, born in 1897, Louise Bogan published her first work in the early 1920s but avoided FBI attention until September 1937, when she was indexed for contributing a poem to *The Nation*, a liberal weekly magazine. Eleven subsequent "name-checks" were included in her file, without adding further "subversive" connections. The bureau apparently missed Bogan's 1945 appointment to serve as Consultant in Poetry to the Library of Congress. She served as poetry editor of *The New Yorker* for thirty-eight years, and died in New York City during 1970.

**BOGGS, Thomas Hale Sr.** — Louisiana representative Hale Boggs Sr. was selected by President LYNDON JOHNSON in 1963 to serve on the Warren Commission investigating the JFK ASSASSINATION. At a closed commission hearing on 9 December 1963, Boggs declared that the FBI's five-page report indicting LEE HARVEY OSWALD as the lone assassin "leaves a million questions" unanswered. Boggs was also disturbed by evidence linking Oswald to the FBI, telling colleagues, "I don't even like to see this being taken down. I would hope that none of these records are circulated to anybody." Boggs got his wish in that case, but later publicly questioned the commission's final report, citing "strong doubts" about the controversial "single bullet theory."

By January 1971, Boggs had risen to serve as majority leader of the 92nd Congress. Four months later, on 5 April 1971, he called for J. EDGAR HOOVER'S resignation, declaring that the FBI had tapped his phone, along with those of other congressmen and senators. Boggs accused the FBI of adopting "the tactics of the Soviet Union and Hitler's Gestapo," repeating the charges in a second speech on 22 April. Hoover retaliated by leaking a list of Boggs's drinking binges to Bureau-friendly journalists, but the feud was inconclusive. Hoover retained his office and Boggs was among those who offered laudatory eulogies for the late director in May 1972. Five months later, while campaigning for Rep. Nicholas Begich in Alaska, Boggs disappeared on a flight from Anchorage to Juneau. No trace of his aircraft has ever been found.

**BOMB Data Center** — Inaugurated in the early 1970s as part of the FBI's TRAINING DIVISION, the Bomb Data Center was reassigned to the LABORATORY DIVISION in 1987, later transferred to Quantico, Virginia as part of the Forensic Science Research and Training Center. Today it is an international clearinghouse for bombing investigations, as well as a state-of-the-art training facility for bomb disposal experts. The center's staff collaborates with other law enforcement agencies on matters related to explosives and offers support during special events that require unusual security precautions.

**BOMBING** — Despite the absence of specific legal mandates, the FBI has been involved in bombing investigations since 1919, when a series of bungled bombing attempts were blamed on ANARCHIST immigrants. Those crimes remain unsolved, despite the dubious confession (and highly suspicious "suicide") of suspect ANDREA SALSEDO, but they provided a pretext for the sweeping PALMER RAIDS of 1919-20. In retrospect, some historians suspect that the wave of attacks were in fact carried out by right-wing provocateurs, to fuel animosity against so-called "enemy aliens."

The 1919 bombings claimed only two lives — a pair of clumsy bombers killed by their own "infernal machine" — but the next blast blamed on anarchists was catastrophic. On 16 September 1920 a wagon loaded with explosives detonated on New York's Wall Street, outside the offices of financier J.P. Morgan. The blast killed 30 persons and wounded 300, while causing extensive property damage. Future FBI director J. EDGAR HOOVER declared that he was taking personal responsibility for the investigation — but that case, too, remained unsolved.

Bombings by urban racketeers were routine during PROHI-

BITION and the Great Depression, but Hoover's FBI denied the existence of ORGANIZED CRIME until 1961 and dismissed all such crimes as matters for local police. G-men took a similar view of racist bombings in the South, when African Americans began "invading" formerly white neighborhoods in the late 1940s. The U.S. SUPREME COURT'S school desegregation rulings of 1954-55 prompted a revival of the KU KLUX KLAN and redirected southern bombers toward public buildings including schools, churches and synagogues, but the FBI remained aloof. When a SOUTHERN CONFERENCE ON BOMBING was organized in 1958 to investigate the escalating demolition campaign, Hoover refused to let his agents participate. The CIVIL RIGHTS Act of 1960 empowered G-men to investigate racist bombings, on a "presumption" that explosives had been transported across state lines, but the Bureau's conviction count held steady at zero until 1963. That May, in Birmingham, witness ROOSEVELT TATUM reported that a city police car had delivered a bomb that wrecked the home of A.D. King (brother of Dr. MARTIN LUTHER KING, JR.) G-men took Tatum's statement, then charged him with lying to federal agents. Upon conviction, he was sentenced to one year and a day in prison.

The Tatum case was followed, four months later, by the death of four young girls in a Birmingham church bombing. FBI agents called their BAPBOMB manhunt the Bureau's greatest effort in 30 years, but no charges were filed against four identified bombers. The first suspect would not face trial until 1977, with state prosecution obstructed by FBI foot-dragging. Another quarter-century elapsed before FBI HEADQUARTERS released a taped confession from one of the bombers, recorded in 1964, and thus permitted two more overdue convictions. Frustrated by the wrist-slap sentences doled out to Klan bombers in Mississippi, meanwhile, agents of the FBI's illegal COINTELPRO campaign used an INFORMANT (himself a known murderer) to arrange the ambush of two nightriders at Meridian in 1968.

By that time, right-wing bombings had largely given way to attacks by PUERTO RICAN NATIONALISTS and groups of the "NEW LEFT," including the WEATHERMAN UNDERGROUND. FBI agents were more highly motivated (and thus more successful) in their pursuit of leftist suspects, but disturbing echoes from a bygone era suggested that some of the defendants were entrapped by federal agents — or were altogether innocent. Various trials and congressional hearings revealed that a small army of FBI *agents provocateur* had been employed to make various New Left groups seem "violence prone." In that pursuit informants such as HORACE PACKER, LARRY GRATHWOHL, THOMAS TONGYAI, Joe Burton and others not only encouraged acts of violence, but provided radical groups with weapons and explosives at government expense. An informant in Seattle was ordered to arrange the bombing of a bridge, with charges set to kill the would-be saboteurs. Disgusted by the order to commit premeditated murder, he resigned and told his story to defense attorneys in the trial of the "Seattle Seven."

In San Diego, meanwhile, the FBI itself created a TERRORIST group called the SECRET ARMY ORGANIZATION, recruiting former members of the MINUTEMEN and furnishing an arsenal of guns and explosives used in several bombings and the attempted

murder of a college professor. A similar case, though apparently unauthorized by FBI headquarters, involved Agent DAVID HALE, assigned to the underworld beat in Tucson, Arizona. Between July 1968 and August 1969 Hale hired two thugs to plant more than a dozen bombs on property owned by known mobsters, hoping to touch off a war between competing Mafia families.

In 1972 a new Federal Bombing Statute defined responsibility for cases involving explosives. Henceforth, U.S. Postal inspectors would investigate mail-bombings and bombing attacks against post offices, while the FBI handled bombings of federal property excluding Postal and Treasury facilities. The Treasury Department's BUREAU OF ALCOHOL, TOBACCO AND FIREARMS (BATF) is responsible for all other bombings within the U.S. unless those bombings are designated acts of TERRORISM — in which case they revert to FBI jurisdiction.

Unfortunately, the new legislation created more problems than it solved. Long accustomed to manipulating facts and language, often applying the "terrorist" label to justify sweeping campaigns of DOMESTIC SURVEILLANCE against groups with no criminal history, the Bureau used the tag as an exclusionary tool, unloading cases it had no desire to handle. A prime example lay in the realm of ANTI-ABORTION VIOLENCE, where FBI Director WILLIAM WEBSTER declared in 1984 that coordinated bombings of women's clinics across the country did not fit the Bureau's narrow definition of terrorism. Various cases involving the KKK and neo-Nazi criminals were likewise rejected — until BATF agents completed their investigation and suspects were indicted. BATF historian James Moore describes what happened once the cases were perfected:

> The FBI liked these cases, liked them so much that, notwithstanding their minor assistance in no more than three [of 10] investigations, they issued an official report taking full and exclusive credit for almost all of them. The sad news is that 85 percent of all the cases the G-men claimed in that report were actually ATF's. The nice news is that the FBI might really deserve credit for 15 percent of the cases they claimed.

BATF agents also shared involvement (while G-men claimed primary credit) for solution of the VANPAC mail-bombing case (1989-90) and the lethal Oklahoma City bombing of April 1995 that ultimately led to conviction and execution of TIMOTHY MCVEIGH. When left to their own devices on bombing cases, modern FBI agents often do no better then their predecessors from the years immediately after WORLD WAR I. Elusive "Unabomber" THEODORE KACZYNSKI outwitted Bureau lab technicians and PSYCHOLOGICAL PROFILERS for 18 years, until a relative betrayed him for the FBI's $1 million reward in 1996. That same year, G-men falsely accused security guard RICHARD JEWELL of planting a deadly bomb in Atlanta's Olympic Park; attention later focused on ERIC RUDOLPH, accused in 1998 of bombing as Alabama abortion clinic, but following the Alabama bombing Rudolph vanished into the wilderness of the North Carolina mountains and remained in hiding until 2003, when he was captured in a chance encounter with local police. Worse yet, the case of JUDI BARI — an environmental activist accused of transporting illegal explosives — evoked grim echoes of the Hoover years. Bari and codefendant Daryl Cherney were acquitted of building the car bomb that nearly claimed their lives in May 1990, and FBI agents led by former COINTELPRO operative RICHARD W. HELD are suspected of planting the bomb themselves.

FBI agents once again joined forces with the BATF in February 1993, when a bombing at New York's WORLD TRADE CENTERS killed six persons and injured 1,042, inflicting property damage in excess of $500 million. Four suspects were convicted in that case the following year and received 240-year prison terms; a fifth was posted to the FBI's "TEN MOST WANTED" LIST and was captured in Pakistan on 7 February 1995. August 1998 witnessed terrorist bombings of U.S. embassies in Kenya and Tanzania, with 224 persons killed and over 5,000 injured. FBI agents joined the international manhunt, climaxed by the 2001 conviction and imprisonment for life of four Muslim extremists. Alleged mastermind USAMA BIN LADEN was added to the Bureau's "Top Ten" list, but he remains at large after plotting the catastrophic SKYJACKINGS of 11 September 2001.

**BOMPENSIERO, Frank**—Born in 1905, Frank Bompensiero was for many years considered one of the American Mafia's most efficient contract killers. Operating from southern California, with his home in San Diego, "Bomp" carried out lethal assignments for underworld leaders as far east as Detroit, and reportedly specialized in strangling his victims with a technique nicknamed the "Italian rope trick." In 1967, after being charged with fraud, Bompensiero became a paid INFORMANT for the FBI and charges were dismissed. Over the next decade, while feeding information on his cohorts to the Bureau, Bompensiero continued his own criminal activities (including the high-profile 1975 murder of San Diego real estate broker Tamara Rand). He went too far in 1976, when he introduced several Los Angeles mobsters to a pornography business operated by G-men. The sting operation resulted in several arrests and left Bompensiero marked for death as a stool pigeon. Vengeance overtook him in February 1977, when he was ambushed outside his Pacific Beach apartment and shot four times in the head by an unidentified assassin. The scam resulting in his death was apparently designed by the FBI to net an even bigger fish, informant ALADENA ("JIMMY THE WEASEL") FRATIANNO.

**BONAPARTE, Charles Joseph**—A grandnephew of French emperor Napoleon Bonaparte I, born in 1851, Charles Bonaparte was appointed by President THEODORE ROOSEVELT to serve on the Board of Indian Commissioners in 1902. He later served as Secretary of the Navy (1905) and as an assistant to Attorney General Philander Knox, dedicated to pursuing "bad men in public office." Bonaparte succeeded Knox as Attorney General on 17 December 1906 and continued his policy of prosecuting corrupt officials, a circumstance that won him few friends in Congress. Denied the use of SECRET SERVICE agents and legally barred from recruiting his own detectives, Bonaparte defied Congress by creating a team of agents on 30 June 1908. Congressional critics were outraged, but there was little they could do to block the move after Roosevelt issued a presidential order supporting Bonaparte on 26 July 1908.

The original force had no formal name or function, described by historian Francis Russell as "an odd-job detective agency with fuzzy lines of authority and responsibility." Bonaparte vowed that his "special agents" would abstain from any investigation of private morality, confining their attention to antitrust cases and similar federal crimes. That promise would be forgotten after passage of the MANN ACT in 1910, but Bonaparte was already gone, leaving office on 4 March 1909. He returned to private legal practice in his native Baltimore, working until his death in 1921.

**BOULIN, Herbert S.**—Little is known of Herbert Boulin's early life, beyond the fact that he came from Jamaica, finding his way to New York City sometime in the late 19th or early 20th century. By the end of WORLD WAR I he was established as a Harlem businessman, proprietor of a company that manufactured black dolls for African American children. The Bureau of Investigation recruited Boulin in 1920, to infiltrate various black "radical" groups including the NATIONAL ASSOCIATION FOR THE ADVANCEMENT OF COLORED PEOPLE, the AFRICAN BLOOD BROTHERHOOD, and MARCUS GARVEY'S Universal Negro Improvement Association.

Signing his reports with the code name "P-138," Boulin supplied reams of information on his assigned targets between July 1920 and August 1921. He shadowed NAACP leader W.E.B. DuBois, ingratiated himself with Garvey, and spent most of each day at "radical" hangouts or rallies, collecting anecdotes and literature for delivery to his white supervisors. G-men were disappointed to hear that one of their primary targets, the *CHICAGO DEFENDER*, often criticized socialists and communists, but Boulin's reports on the African Blood Brotherhood were more encouraging. He judged that "this organization is becoming and will become a serious menace to society," because it "has the object of killing white people and to foment and start a massacre of white people whenever there is the slightest sign of race friction."

Rhetoric was one thing, but the Bureau wanted results. Boulin was ordered to get evidence supporting an indictment of Marcus Garvey on federal MANN ACT charges, for crossing state lines with his mistress, but Boulin failed to produce. He was dismissed from service after 13 months, but Boulin missed the covert life so much that he soon abandoned doll-making and opened a private detective agency, advertising himself as a former JUSTICE DEPARTMENT employee. Only then did Marcus Garvey and others learn that they had been betrayed.

**BOWLES, Jane Auer**—Born in New York City on 22 February 1917, Jane Auer was raised on Long Island and married writer-composer Paul Bowles in 1938. She published her first novel, *Two Serious Ladies*, in 1943. FBI agents began collecting information on Bowles in 1945, after her name surfaced in their investigation of another target. She admitted membership in the U.S. COMMUNIST PARTY from December 1938 to March 1939, when she was "willingly dropped" on grounds that she was not "serious enough." Bowles and her husband lived abroad from 1947 onward, mostly in Tangier. Her FBI FILE remained inactive until 1958, when a new probe was started under the heading "Security matter — Communist." No incriminating evidence had been uncovered by the time of her death in 1973.

**BOYLE, Kay** — An American author of more than thirty books, Kay Boyle was born in St. Paul, Minnesota and raised in Cincinnati. She moved to France with her first husband at age twenty-one, in 1923, and there remained until 1941. The FBI started a file on her, meanwhile, after an INFORMANT (later judged "unreliable") described her to G-men in 1940 as "an organized Communist." Agents interviewed Boyle in 1943 concerning her relationship with EZRA POUND, whom she described as "a dreadful man" feigning insanity to escape trial on sedition charges. (The bureau file falsely alleged that Boyle "had a clandestine affair" with Pound "before WORLD WAR I," when she was barely ten years old. In 1943 the file recorded Boyle's marriage "to a private in the United States army whose name was Franckenstein and who was supposedly a citizen of Austria" — in fact Baron Joseph von Franckenstein soon deployed as an agent behind Nazi lines in Europe.

In 1947, now a U.S. citizen and diplomat, Franckenstein was posted to Germany, where Boyle also resided. Ex-communist and paid informant Louis Budenz named Boyle as a member of the COMMUNIST PARTY, and the label stuck despite her firm denials. Franckenstein's career was interrupted in 1952, after associates of Senator JOSEPH MCCARTHY called him before a loyalty board, and while he was later reinstated, Boyle found herself blacklisted as a writer for American magazines, listed as a candidate for possible detention in the FBI's SECURITY INDEX. Following Franckenstein's death in 1963, Boyle returned to the U.S. and settled in San Francisco, involving herself in the student protest movement. Although removed from the Security Index in 1963, Boyle remained an object of FBI interest. When she visited Cambodia in July 1966, Deputy Associate Director CARTHA DELOACH speculated that funding for her "jaunt may have come from subversive sources." DeLoach suggested that "current information" about Boyle should be leaked to an unnamed newspaper columnist, to which J. EDGAR HOOVER replied, "I concur." Boyle's trip to Cambodia and the FBI's response led the Peace Corps to reject her services in 1966.

Boyle remained active on the left, despite bureau harassment. In 1967 she joined the anti-VIETNAM WAR PROTEST movement and was jailed for "disrupting activities and functions" at the Oakland draft board. Four years later, G-men noted that she still had "many contacts in the subversive and racial fields." Incredibly, in 1976, the FBI considered recruiting Boyle as an informant, but dropped the plan because of "her background, her advanced age, and lack of asset potential." Her 355-page file was thereafter closed. Boyle died in California on 27 December 1992.

**BRADY Gang** — Led by Alfred James Brady, an Indiana native born 25 October 1910, this four-man gang terrorized the Midwest between October 1935 and October 1937, pursuing Brady's stated goal to "make JOHN DILLINGER look like a piker." Other members of the gang included Rhuel James Dalhover, Clarence Lee Shaffer, Jr., and Charles Geiseking.

The outfit started small, stealing $18 from an Indiana theater on 12 October 1935. Over the next two months they robbed an estimated 150 stores and gas stations in Indiana and Ohio, wounding two Crawfordsville, Indiana policemen during a holdup on 30 November 1935. During March and April 1936 the Brady gang concentrated on Ohio jewelry stores, bagging some $45,000 in four robberies, breaking the pattern to rob a grocery store and kill the clerk on 22 April.

Arrests soon followed. Brady was jailed in Chicago on 22 April 1936; Shaffer was captured in Indianapolis on 11 May; Dalhover was seized by Chicago police on 15 May; and Geiseking was nabbed in Kentucky on 12 September 1936. Confined together in Greenfield, Indiana, Brady, Dalhover and Shaffer escaped on 11 October 1936. Two days later, a federal complaint was filed against them, charging interstate transportation of stolen property, and FBI agents joined the chase.

The gang next turned to BANK ROBBERY, bagging $7,800 from four Indiana holdups between 23 November 1936 and 25 May 1937. They shot their way out of a police trap in Baltimore, on 7 August 1937, leaving a small arsenal of weapons behind. A Wisconsin bank heist followed, netting $7,000 on 23 August, and the gang was suspected of killing an Ohio highway patrolman on 28 September 1937.

Their luck ran out two weeks later, in Bangor, Maine. Brady had ordered a submachine gun from a local gun store, and FBI agents were alerted, ready to strike when the gang returned to collect the weapon on 12 October. Brady and Shaffer died in an exchange of gunfire with G-men, while Dalhover was captured alive, convicted of murder in Indiana and executed on 18 November 1938. Author Stephen King later fictionalized the gang's final bloody moments as a vignette in his horror novel *It*.

**BRANCH Davidian Sect** — The Branch Davidian sect is a fundamentalist Christian denomination organized in the 1930s, after Bulgarian immigrant Victor Houteff led a small group of defectors from the parent Seventh-Day Adventist (SDA) church. Houteff established his own Davidian SDA church outside Waco, Texas, and leadership passed to his widow with Houteff's death in 1955. Mrs. Houteff predicted the return of Christ at Easter 1959, but the failure of that prophecy produced another rift, various members departing while a hard core of 50 believers — renamed Branch Davidians — remained at the Waco compound ("Mt. Carmel") under "prophet" Ben Roden. Roden died in 1978, ceding leadership to his widow Lois, but her subsequent death left son George Roden vying for control of the sect with 25-year-old Vernon Howell, alias "David Koresh." A period of bitter conflict, including a nocturnal shootout at Mt. Carmel in November 1987, left Koresh in charge of the sect. His behavior grew increasingly bizarre, including collection of high-powered weapons, recruitment of a private security team (the "Mighty Men"), and a 1989 decree that only he (Koresh) was entitled to marry or have sex.

By November 1992 agents from the BUREAU OF ALCOHOL, TOBACCO AND FIREARMS (BATF) had multiple reports on file that Koresh was stockpiling illegal weapons and explosives. For three months, they planned a "surprise" raid on the Mt. Carmel compound, but Koresh was apparently forewarned. When BATF agents stormed the sect's camp on 28 February 1993, a deadly firefight erupted, killing four agents and six Branch Davidians, leaving another 26 persons wounded (including Koresh). BATF leaders requested FBI assistance, and the Bureau's HOSTAGE RESCUE TEAM was dispatched to Waco. Deeming a fresh assault potentially disastrous, the two agencies laid siege to Mt. Carmel with 700 officers and a fleet of armored vehicles. By early April 1993, FBI leaders feared that the standoff—complete with sensory assaults from floodlights and loudspeakers blaring at night—might drag on forever, their embarrassment compounded day by day. The Branch Davidians, meanwhile, apparently viewed the siege as fulfillment of Koresh's prediction that an "apocalyptic" showdown with the U.S. government would presage Christ's return.

FBI strategists approached Attorney General JANET RENO on 16 April 1993, with a plan to break the siege by unleashing tear gas within the Davidian complex. Reno rejected the plan, then changed her mind on 17 April, after G-men promised that no potentially inflammatory gas canisters would be employed. The tanks moved in at 6:02 a.m. on 19 April, receiving gunfire as they sprayed gas into the cluster of occupied buildings. Gassing proceeded for six hours, until flames were sighted at 12:07 p.m. Gunfire echoed from within the compound at 12:25, and flames soon devoured the rambling structure. Nine Davidians escaped the blaze; Koresh and 75 others lay dead in the rubble, including 25 children below the age of 15 years.

Investigators claimed that the fire was deliberately set by cult members, apparently to initiate mass-suicide. Autopsy results showed that Koresh died from a gunshot to the forehead, while second-in-command Steve Schneider was shot in the mouth. Seventeen others, including five children, were also shot before the flames reached them, and a two-year-old boy was apparently stabbed to death. Eleven surviving Davidians were charged with murder and conspiracy to murder federal agents. All were acquitted on those counts at trial, but five were convicted of manslaughter and received 40-year prison terms; four others were sentenced to terms between three and 20 years for lesser crimes.

A series of investigations followed the Waco disaster. At the first hearing, before the House Judiciary Committee on 28 April 1993, Reno and other key officials defended their assault as the only means of protecting Davidian children from physical and sexual abuse inside the compound. A separate report, issued by former Assistant Attorney General Edward Dennis, Jr., on 8 October 1993, acknowledged various FBI tactical errors, but concluded that "[u]nder the circumstances, the FBI exhibited extraordinary restraint and handled this crisis with great professionalism." Four days later, a *New York Times* editorial dismissed the Dennis report as a "whitewash." Outside Washington, members of the rapidly-growing MILITIA MOVEMENT armed and trained in anticipation of similar showdowns, and terrorist TIMOTHY MCVEIGH chose the second anniversary of the Mt. Carmel blaze as his target date for bombing Oklahoma City's Alfred P. Murrah Federal Building, with a loss of 168 lives.

A new Congress, dominated by Republicans, reviewed the Waco tragedy in July 1995, and its report—issued 12 months

later—was predictably more critical of Reno's choices, calling her acceptance of the tear-gas plan "premature, wrong, and highly irresponsible." Criticism aside, there were no consequences for agents involved in the Branch Davidian fiasco. Two BATF agents in charge of the initial raid were fired, then reinstated on appeal. No FBI agents were disciplined, and Attorney General Reno defended their conduct of the final assault until August 1999, when Bureau spokesmen finally admitted lying for the past six years about their use of military-style inflammatory tear-gas canisters. Despite their promises to Reno beforehand, volatile grenades had been used at Mt. Carmel—but agents now insisted they had "bounced off" the buildings without setting fire to the compound. Reno declared herself "very, very upset" by the admission of deceit, but the renewed debate produced no disciplinary actions, either for the Waco siege or for misleading the attorney general. A federal lawsuit filed by Davidian survivors, seeking $675 million in damages for wrongful death of those killed on 19 April 1993, was dismissed by a federal court in September 2000, with a ruling that FBI and BATF agents were not responsible for the fire or resultant loss of life.

**"BRASCO, Donnie"** *see* **PISTONE, Joseph**

**BREAK-INS**—"Black bag jobs," in FBI parlance, are break-ins conducted on private property for purposes of BUGGING, WIRETAPPING, or obtaining information by some other means (including theft or photocopying of documents and mail). It is unknown precisely when Bureau agents began to indulge in burglary, since records of criminal activity are often missing or misleading. In the 1970s, FBI spokesmen called to account for the agency's crimes admitted a total of 239 illegal break-ins between 1942 and 1966, but the record was clearly incomplete. During investigations of the TEAPOT DOME SCANDAL (1923-24) G-men burglarized the offices of Montana senators THOMAS WALSH and BURTON WHEELER, to subvert prosecution of corrupt government officials, and there is no reason to suppose those break-ins were the Bureau's first.

Burglary was a regular feature of FBI investigations under Director J. EDGAR HOOVER, whose only concern for violations of the law was that the Bureau should avoid exposure and embarrassment. In 1942 G-men invaded officers of the American Youth Congress and photographed correspondence from First Lady ELEANOR ROOSEVELT. Three years later, the *AMERASIA* CASE collapsed in court upon revelation of illegal entries by the FBI and OFFICE OF STRATEGIC SERVICES. Attorney General HERBERT BROWNELL approved warrantless break-ins and bugging on 20 May 1954; one day later, Hoover privately extended the authorization to any "important" criminal case. By 1957 leaders of ORGANIZED CRIME were targeted for burglary under the FBI's TOP HOODLUM PROGRAM. Assistant Director WILLIAM SULLIVAN described the ethos of illegal break-ins in a memo to colleague CARTHA DELOACH, dated 19 July 1966. That memo read:

> The following is set forth in regard to your request concerning what authority we have for "black bag" jobs and for the background of our policy and procedures in such matters.

We do not obtain authorization for "black bag" jobs from outside the Bureau. Such a technique involves trespass and is clearly illegal; therefore it would be impossible to obtain any legal sanction for it. Despite this, "black bag" jobs have been used because they represent an invaluable technique in combating subversive activities of a clandestine nature aimed directly at undermining and destroying our nation.

The present procedure in the use of this technique calls for the Special Agent in Charge of a field office to make his request for the use of the technique to the appropriate Assistant Director. The Special Agent in Charge must completely justify the need for the use of the technique and at the same time assure that it can be safely used without any danger of embarrassment to the Bureau. The facts are incorporated in a memorandum which, in accordance with the Director's instructions, is sent to Mr. [CLYDE] TOLSON or to the Director for approval. Subsequently this memorandum is filed in the Assistant Director's office under a "Do Not File" procedure.

In the field the Special Agent in Charge prepares an informal memorandum showing that he obtained Bureau authority and this memorandum is filed in his safe until the next inspection by Bureau Inspectors, at which time it is destroyed....

We have used this technique on a highly selective basis, but with wide-ranging effectiveness, in our operations. We have several cases in the ESPIONAGE field, for example, where through "black bag" jobs we determined that suspected illegal agents actually had concealed on their premises the equipment through which they carried out their clandestine operations.

Also through the use of this technique we have on numerous occasions been able to obtain material held highly secret and closely guarded by subversive groups and organizations which consisted of membership lists and mailing lists of these organizations....

Through the same technique we have recently been receiving extremely valuable information concerning political developments in the Latin American field, and we also have been able to use it most effectively in a number of instances recently, through which we have obtained information concerning growing [deleted] intelligence activities directed at this country.

In short, it is a very valuable weapon which we have used to combat the highly clandestine efforts of subversive elements seeking to undermine our Nation.

Hoover penned an order across the bottom of Sullivan's memo, declaring that "No more such techniques must be used" —but still they continued. In July 1970 the White House-approved HUSTON PLAN echoed Sullivan's memo, outlining a series of "clearly illegal" techniques to be used against political "enemies" of President RICHARD NIXON. Hoover initially balked at participating in the program, then agreed with the proviso that Attorney General JOHN MITCHELL should personally approve each instance of G-men breaking the law. Eight months later the tables were turned, when burglars invaded the FBI RESIDENT AGENCY at MEDIA, PENNSYLVANIA and escaped with thousands of classified documents detailing the Bureau's illicit COINTELPRO operations. Hoover canceled those programs a month later. Publication of those papers touched off a flurry of lawsuits, including a $27 million action filed by leaders of the SOCIALIST WORKERS PARTY (targets of 92 documented break-ins between 1960 and 1966).

It was finally another break-in, planned in part by ex-FBI agent G. GORDON LIDDY, which doomed the Nixon administration. In August 1973, as the WATERGATE SCANDAL unfolded,

Nixon told reporters that similar burglaries had been carried out "on a very large scale" under predecessors JOHN KENNEDY and LYNDON JOHNSON. The next day, FBI spokesmen acknowledged using the same "old, established investigative technique" for 30-odd years in "national security" cases, but they clung to the fiction that illegal break-ins ceased in July 1966. The CHURCH COMMITTEE'S 1976 report on FBI abuses tabulated 697 bugging incidents and 26,287 illegal mail-openings between 1958 and 1974, but the senators strangely accepted Director CLARENCE KELLEY'S assertion that G-men committed only 239 burglaries between 1942 and 1966. Retired agent M. WESLEY SWEARINGEN challenged Kelley's statement, claiming personal knowledge of more than 500 break-ins committed in Chicago alone, between 1952 and 1957.

Critics found a certain irony in Kelley's May 1976 statement that the FBI should never again occupy the "unique position that permitted improper activity without accountability," when his own agents were accused of using COINTELPRO-style techniques against the AMERICAN INDIAN MOVEMENT and PUERTO RICAN NATIONALISTS. In November 1980 former acting associate director W. MARK FELT and former assistant director EDWARD MILLER were convicted of authorizing illegal break-ins around New York City in the 1970s, but President RONALD REAGAN pardoned both defendants four months later. Soon, Reagan's own administration was using identical techniques against political dissenters, notably the COMMITTEE IN SOLIDARITY WITH THE PEOPLE OF EL SALVADOR.

It would be comforting to think that FBI leaders have finally abandoned use of illegal techniques, after skirting or breaking the law for almost a century, but recent events provide no such assurance. After the events of September 2001, in the fervor of a global "war on TERRORISM" that includes sweeping new surveillance powers embodied in the USA PATRIOT ACT, vigilance remains essential in respect to every U.S. law enforcement agency.

**BRECHT, Bertolt Eugen Friederich**—Born at Augsburg, Bavaria on 10 February 1898, Bertolt Brecht became an ardent Marxist after WORLD WAR I. ADOLF HITLER'S rise to power prompted Brecht to leave Germany in 1933, settling first in Switzerland, then Denmark. In 1941 he emigrated to Los Angeles, by way of the Soviet Union. Automatically suspect to U.S. intelligence agencies as both a German immigrant and communist, Brecht was investigated by the FBI and OFFICE OF STRATEGIC SERVICES for his involvement with the Free Germany Movement, based in Mexico. Brecht's 1,100-page FBI FILE includes the observation that "Subject's writings ... advocate overthrow of Capitalism, establishment of Communist State and use of sabotage by labor to attain its ends." Though not himself a scriptwriter, Brecht was summoned to testify before the HOUSE COMMITTEE ON UN-AMERICAN ACTIVITIES in October 1947, during that body's investigation of "subversion" in the motion picture industry. Brecht denied membership in the COMMUNIST PARTY, then left the U.S. for Switzerland the day after he testified. Settled in East Berlin by 1948, he received the Lenin Peace Prize for his work in 1954. Two years later, on 20 March 1956, an "urgent" telegram from the bureau's New York field office warned

J. EDGAR HOOVER that Brecht was expected to visit a Manhattan theater, where one of his plays was being performed. Hoover responded that Brecht "is of sufficient importance to international Communism that the Bureau should be aware of all his activities and contacts," but the playwright failed to appear, a local master of ceremonies joking with the audience that "We certainly fooled the FBI this time." Five months later, Brecht was dead, the victim of a heart attack in East Berlin, on 14 August. Years of FBI BUGGING, physical surveillance, intercepted mail and "trash covers" failed to develop a criminal case against Brecht or to link him with any subversive activities.

**BRILAB** — Named with an anagram of *bri*bery and *lab*or, Operation BRILAB was launched in 1979 to snare allegedly corrupt politicians and LABOR UNION officers in the southern U.S. G-men recruited Joseph Houser, convicted of insurance fraud in federal court, to spearhead their campaign in conjunction with an undercover FBI agent. The results were a mixed bag and remain intensely controversial to the present day.

In Texas, Houser and his FBI partner approached Billy Clayton, speaker of the state House of Representatives, offering an insurance plan designed to save the state more than $1 million in premiums. During those negotiations, Clayton was offered and accepted a campaign contribution from Houser, but he rejected Houser's offer to split future proceeds from the insurance deal. Federal prosecutors charged Clayton with accepting bribes to approve the insurance transaction, but he was acquitted at trial, with jurors finding that no explicit bribe had ever been proposed or accepted.

The FBI had better luck in Louisiana, where bribery indictments were filed against Mafia boss Carlos Marcello and Charles Roemer II, commissioner of administration for Louisiana's governor. Both defendants were convicted at trial in April 1981, Marcello for bribing state officials to receive insurance kickbacks, Roemer for allegedly accepting bribes. Both received seven-year prison terms, but their convictions were reversed on appeal. A second federal conviction, for conspiracy to bribe a federal judge, finally sent Marcello to prison in June 1983.

The only defendant finally imprisoned in the BRILAB case was California mobster Jimmy Regace, aka "Dominick Brooklier." Sentenced to a five-year prison term for bribery in 1983, the aged Regace served 11 months before dying of natural causes at the federal lockup in Tucson, on 18 July 1984. Critics of BRILAB and sting operations in general maintain that such techniques constitute unlawful entrapment and lend themselves to persecution of innocent persons, while wasting limited government resources.

**BROOKINGS Institution** — The Brookings Institution is a private non-profit organization that seeks to improve the performance of American institutions, the effectiveness of government programs, and the quality of U.S. public policy. Since 1916, when it began life as the Institute for Government Research (renamed for St. Louis philanthropist Robert Somers Brookings in 1927), the group has functioned as "a bridge between scholarship and public policy," researching various critical subjects and critiquing

government efforts to cope with various problems. Its stated goals include "bringing new knowledge to the attention of decision-makers and affording scholars a better insight into public policy issues." In 1940 the BYRD COMMITTEE retained Brookings scholars to compare FBI efficiency with the performance of six other federal law enforcement agencies.

Such efforts are predictably unwelcome to dogmatic regimes that operate covertly in defiance of the law. President RICHARD NIXON, obsessed with pursuit of those who had leaked the so-called "PENTAGON PAPERS" to various newspapers in 1970, decided that "liberal Democrats" at the Brookings Institution had played some role in the affair. The evidence: a paper reviewing U.S. involvement in the VIETNAM WAR, written for Brookings by ex-Pentagon employee Leslie Gelb. White House conspirator Charles Colson wrote a memo to Nixon aide John Ehrlichman on 6 July 1971, saying in part: "It looks to me like we may soon expect another installment in the Pentagon Papers written by the same authors but doubtless more up to date.... In my opinion this should be promptly investigated."

White House "plumber" John Caulfield later claimed that he was summoned to Colson's office in the second week of July 1971, there informed that President Nixon recognized "a high priority need to obtain papers from the office of a gentleman named Leslie Gelb" at the Brookings Institution. Colson also had a plan, according to Caulfield: "The suggestion was that the fire regulations in the District of Columbia could be changed to have the FBI respond to the scene of any fire in the district and that if there were to be a fire at the Brookings Institute [sic] that the FBI could respond and obtain the file in question from Mr. Leslie Gelb's office." While no specifics were discussed, Caulfield inferred that he was being told to set the fire himself.

Caulfield, himself no stranger to criminal activity, reportedly deemed the plan "asinine" and reported it to presidential counsel John Dean. Dean, in turn, warned Ehrlichman against pursuing the "insane" conspiracy, and Ehrlichman allegedly ordered Colson to forget the plan. Colson, for his part, denies any knowledge of the plot (though a friend later told author J. Anthony Lukas that Colson may have suggested the plan as "a joke").

**BROOKS, Van Wyck** — A native of Plainfield, New Jersey, born in 1886, Van Wyck Brooks graduated from Harvard in 1908 and published his first book on American history, *The Wine of the Puritans*, the following year. The FBI opened a file on Brooks in 1935, after finding his name on the membership roll of the Authors League of America, and maintained a close watch on him for the remainder of his life. Every petition Brooks signed and every group he joined was duly noted, among them the Golden Book of Friendship with the Soviet Union (1937), the War Writers Board (1941), a petition to abolish the HOUSE COMMITTEE ON UN-AMERICAN ACTIVITIES (1943), and the NATIONAL ASSOCIATION FOR THE ADVANCEMENT OF COLORED PEOPLE'S Legal Defense and Educational Fund Committee of One Hundred (1958). One memo skeptically observes that Brooks "reputedly received" a Pulitzer Prize, in fact awarded for *The Flowering of New England* (1936). Brooks died in 1963, and a censored version of his 72-

page dossier was later released under the FREEDOM OF INFORMATION ACT.

## BROUN, Heywood Campbell

BROUN, Heywood Campbell—A Brooklyn native, born 7 December 1888, Heywood Broun was the son of an English immigrant who had established a successful print shop in the city. He entered Harvard University in 1906, and there befriended left-wing activist JOHN REED. Upon graduating in 1910, Broun worked as a sports reporter for the *New York Morning Telegraph*, then transferred to the *New York Tribune* in 1912 and served as a correspondent in France during WORLD WAR I. From 1921, as a columnist with the *New York World*, Broun was known for his campaigns against censorship and racial discrimination, and for supporting the defense in the SACCO-VANZETTI CASE. In 1930 he ran for Congress as a Socialist and was defeated. The Socialist Party expelled him three years later, after Broun appeared with members of the COMMUNIST PARTY at a rally demanding release of political prisoners. The same year (1933), Broun helped establish the American Newspaper Guild and served as its first president. He died at Stamford, Connecticut on 18 December 1939.

It is unknown when the Bureau decided to index Heywood Broun. The single memo in his Bureau dossier includes notations ranging from 1935 (when G-men called him a member of the Communist Party) to 1952, when a notation claimed he might have been "a Communist in 1935 or 1936." A copy of that memo was curiously furnished to the HOUSE COMMITTEE ON UN-AMERICAN ACTIVITIES in 1951, when Broun had been dead for 12 years.

## BROWN, Hubert Geroid

BROWN, Hubert Geroid—The man known to a generation of activists and police as H. Rap Brown was born in Baton Rouge on 4 October 1943. While attending Southern University in New Orleans (1960–64) he joined the STUDENT NONVIOLENT COORDINATING COMMITTEE (SNCC) and participated in various CIVIL RIGHTS demonstrations. Brown became SNCC's Alabama project director in 1966, then national director after STOKELY CARMICHAEL left that post in May 1967.

The FBI was well aware of SNCC and Brown by then, but G-men apparently made no move against Brown for another two months. On 24 July 1967 Brown delivered a speech in strife-torn Cambridge, Maryland, advising his black audience to "get yourselves some guns" and "burn this town down" if their demands for reform were not met. He singled out a local all-black elementary school, calling it a "firetrap" and declaring, "You should have burned it down long ago." Arsonists torched the school hours later, whereupon Maryland authorities charged Brown with arson and inciting a riot. Federal charges of unlawful flight were filed the same day, and Brown was arrested at Washington National Airport on 26 July. (FBI Director J. EDGAR HOOVER told White House aide Marvin Watson, "I took the occasion to have a Negro Agent participate in the arrest.") Brown posted $10,000 bond the following day and was freed with a hearing scheduled for 22 August. Meanwhile, more charges were filed on 19 August 1967, when G-men arrested Brown for carrying firearms across state lines while under indictment. On 18 September a federal judge ordered Brown not to leave New York except for court appearances related to his case.

By that time, Hoover had added Brown's name to a short list of black "extremists" singled out for "particular attention" under the FBI's illegal COINTELPRO campaign against "Black Nationalist-Hate Groups." When Brown and SNCC ally JAMES FORMAN denounced Zionist expansionism at a National Convention for New Politics in 1967, G-men launched a smear campaign branding them anti-Semites. Upon learning that Brown had borrowed a car from the federally-funded Harlem Youth Opportunities Unlimited office, FBI spokesmen branded HARYOU a "hate school." In testimony before the KERNER COMMISSION, Hoover blamed most of 1967's ghetto rioting on "the exhortations of 'Black Power' advocates Stokely Carmichael and H. Rap Brown."

The FBI's campaign accelerated in early 1968. Brown flew to California on 17 February, to announce SNCC's merger with the militant BLACK PANTHER PARTY, including his own appointment to serve as the party's "minister of justice." The trip violated Brown's travel restrictions and G-men jailed him again on 20 February, filing additional charges for Brown's alleged threats against the life and family of black agent William Smith, Jr., (Brown maintained that he simply called Smith an "Uncle Tom.") Elsewhere, the Bureau forged ahead with plans to "foster a split" between SNCC and the Panthers, a campaign that included "SNITCH-JACKETING" and anonymous death threats telephoned by FBI agents to Stokely Carmichael and others. A Hoover memo dated 4 March 1968 ranked Brown among the Bureau's top five "targets," commanding all FBI field offices to "prevent the rise of a 'messiah'" in the black community.

Brown missed the opening day of his Maryland arson trial on 4 May 1970, and Hoover added his name to the FBI's "TEN MOST WANTED" LIST two days later. On 16 October 1971 Brown and three accomplices robbed the Red Carpet Lounge in Manhattan, trading shots with police as they fled. Brown was wounded twice before police arrested him on the roof of a nearby apartment building. Authorities seized two shotguns, a carbine, three pistols and 300 rounds of ammunition from the bandits. Upon conviction, Brown received a sentence of five to 15 years in prison. He converted to Islam while incarcerated and emerged from Attica Prison in 1976 as Jamil Abdullah Al-Amin.

Resettled in Atlanta, Al-Amin opened a grocery store and assumed leadership of the Atlanta Community Mosque. Neighbors praised his efforts to rid the West End neighborhood of prostitution and NARCOTICS. By 1978, installed as leader of the National Ummah—one of America's largest Black Muslim sects—Al-Amin told a reporter from the *Washington Post*, "I don't miss the Sixties."

Still, trouble dogged him. In 1994 several members of Al-Amin's mosque were convicted of smuggling weapons to Muslims in New York. A year later Al-Amin was accused of assault in a nonfatal shooting; victim William Miles later recanted and claimed police had pressured him to name Al-Amin as the shooter. In May 1999 Cobb County authorities charged Al-Amin with receiving stolen property and impersonating a police officer. (Investigation showed that Al-Amin possessed a legitimate auxiliary policeman's badge.) That case dragged into March 2000, when two Fulton County deputies tried to serve a Cobb County arrest warrant at Al-Amin's store. Both officers were shot with an assault rifle, one fatally. The survivor named Al-Amin as the gunman and murder charges were filed. FBI agents arrested Al-Amin on 20 March 2000, at White Hall, Alabama. G-man Ron Campbell later confessed under oath that he kicked and spat on Al-Amin as the suspect lay handcuffed and helpless, telling him, "This is what we do to cop killers."

Legal maneuvers and the terrorist SKYJACKINGS of 11 September 2001 delayed Al-Amin's trial until February 2002. On 9 March jurors convicted Al-Amin on 13 felony counts, including murder, aggravated assault on a police officer, obstruction and possession of a firearm by a convicted felon. The court imposed a term of life imprisonment.

**BROWNELL, Herbert, Jr.**—A native of Peru, Nebraska, born 20 February 1904, Herbert Brownell, Jr,. spent most of his life in New York, where he practiced law and immersed himself in Republican Party politics. He served in the New York state assembly (1933-37) and as chairman of the Republican National Committee (1944-46). In 1948 he managed the presidential campaign of GOP contender THOMAS DEWEY, encouraging covert support from FBI Director J. EDGAR HOOVER. Brownell assumed office as attorney general on 21 January 1953, under President DWIGHT EISENHOWER.

Brownell's term of office spanned the worst of the Red Scare propelled by Senator JOSEPH MCCARTHY, and the attorney general had no qualms about fanning the flames of hysteria. On 6 November 1953 he addressed a group of Chicago businessmen, accusing ex-President HARRY TRUMAN of coddling traitors in government and citing FBI reports on the "spying activities" of economist HARRY DEXTER WHITE as proof of those claims. (In fact, Bureau FILES contained no evidence against White, merely unsupported allegations.) On 17 November Brownell expanded his charges before the SENATE INTERNAL SECURITY SUBCOMMITTEE, accompanied by Hoover. Once again, the witnesses declined to support their sweeping accusations with anything resembling evidence.

On 20 May 1954, in response to urgings from Hoover, Brownell issued a secret memo that approved illegal BREAK-INS and BUGGING in cases of "national security." According to Brownell, "For the FBI to fulfill its important intelligence function, consideration of internal security and the national safety are paramount and, therefore, may compel the unrestricted use of this technique in the national interest." Recognizing that his order violated many state and federal laws, Brownell warned Hoover that he "would be in a much better position to defend the Bureau in the event there should be a technical trespass if he had not heretofore approved it." One day later, Hoover unilaterally expanded Brownell's order to include "important" criminal cases, thus giving the Bureau a license to burglarize any target he selected.

Two years later, in March 1956, Brownell invited Hoover to address Eisenhower's Cabinet on the subject of racial turmoil in the South. Hoover used the occasion to praise the segregationist CITIZENS' COUNCILS and to dismiss the growing, increasingly violent KU KLUX KLAN as "pretty much defunct." He blamed recent unrest on the U.S. SUPREME COURT'S school desegregation rulings of 1954-55, noting that behind fears of "mixed education … stalks the specter of racial intermarriage." Hoover denounced the NATIONAL ASSOCIATION FOR THE ADVANCEMENT OF COLORED PEOPLE and other CIVIL RIGHTS groups for preaching "racial hatred," then produced a chart on the decline of LYNCHING to support his claim that Bureau intervention in the South was not required.

Herbert Brownell left office on 8 November 1957, replaced as attorney general by WILLIAM ROGERS. He returned to the practice of law in New York and died there, of cancer, on 1 May 1996.

**BRUCKNER, Ferdinand**—Born Theodor Tagger at Vienna, Austria on 26 August 1891, Ferdinand Bruckner (his pen name) became a famous playwright and stage director under the Weimar Republic. His opposition to Nazism forced Bruckner to flee his homeland for sanctuary in the U.S., but FBI agents found his motives suspect, noting Bruckner's affiliation with other leftist exiles in New York City. In 1944 Bruckner collaborated in founding Aurora Verlag, a publishing house for exiled authors which an erroneous FBI report (dated 26 February 1947) described as being "designed principally for German Prisoners of War in the United States."

Bruckner became a naturalized U.S. citizen in August 1946, despite the Bureau's continuing surveillance and collection of material for a FILE labeled "Security Matter—C" (for "communist"), but his career languished in America. Of the 11 plays Bruckner wrote while living in New York, only one was produced (*Nathan the Wise*, 1942), and five have never been published. Bruckner left New York for Berlin in 1949 and was stripped of his U.S. citizenship after five years abroad, in June 1954. He died in Berlin on 5 December 1958.

**BRUNETTE, Harry**—A small-time bank robber of no great reputation in the 1930s, Harry Brunette is remembered today primarily because he was selected by the FBI for propaganda purposes. Without that special (and unwelcome) attention, he would almost certainly have been arrested by local police, routinely convicted, and long since forgotten. As luck would have it, though, Director J. EDGAR HOOVER came under fire in early 1936, forced by U.S. Senate critic KENNETH MCKELLAR to admit that he (Hoover) had never made an arrest. Embarrassed, Hoover solved that problem in May 1936 with the staged capture of ALVIN KARPIS, but he still hoped to perform the same service for Associate Director CLYDE TOLSON. Harry Brunette became the next target, traced to a New York City hideout on 14 December 1936.

Where the Karpis capture had been carefully managed, pulled off without firing a shot, the Brunette raid was a study in chaos. New York police initially located Brunette, sought with accomplice Merle Vandenbush for several holdups and the kidnapping of a New Jersey state trooper, and they notified FBI HEADQUARTERS as a professional courtesy. Hoover rushed to the scene with a small army of agents, and after conferring with police, agreed to raid the hideout at 2:00 p.m., when Brunette was normally asleep. He then reversed himself and ordered a full-scale assault at midnight, 14 hours ahead of schedule, while detectives on stakeout duty watched in shock. The *New York Times* reported that when officers on site asked Hoover what he was doing, the director "merely shrugged his shoulders."

Things quickly went from bad to worse. An FBI agent tried unsuccessfully to shoot the lock off Brunette's door, whereupon Brunette returned fire. Gas grenades were lobbed into the small apartment, setting it ablaze. When firefighters arrived, the situation degenerated even further. As a *Newsweek* reporter observed: "Amid the hubub, a flustered G-man poked a submachine gun at a husky fireman. 'Dammit, can't you read?' growled the fireman, pointing at his helmet. 'If you don't take that gun out of my stomach I'll bash your head in.'" Brunette finally surrendered and Tolson was duly photographed leading the bandit away from his bullet-riddled hideout, but the raiders missed Merle Vandenbush entirely.

The next morning, New York Police Commissioner Lewis Valentine and his New Jersey counterpart voiced outrage at what they perceived as an FBI double-cross that had risked lives needlessly while permitting Vandenbush to escape. Hoover, back in Washington, dismissed the "unjustified and petty criticism" of his presumed inferiors. Two months later, local authorities captured Merle Vandenbush without firing a shot. The fugitive reported that he had been on his way to meet Brunette when the battle erupted. At one point, Vandenbush said, he had been close enough to tap Hoover on the shoulder, but he had opted for escape instead.

**BUCHALTER, Louis ("Lepke")**—America's foremost labor racketeer of the Great Depression, Louis Buchalter ranked among the leading figures of ORGANIZED CRIME in New York. Between 1927 and 1939 he extorted millions of dollars from various industries and LABOR UNIONS, enforcing his demands with a crew of pitiless killers whom the press nicknamed "Murder Incorporated." In 1937 a federal NARCOTICS indictment drove Lepke into hiding. New York prosecutor THOMAS DEWEY also wanted him, on murder charges, but a $50,000 reward failed to disclose that Buchalter lived in an apartment next door to Brooklyn police headquarters. At last, when unrelenting pressure on the New York syndicate made Buchalter a liability to business, friends of the mobster approached columnist WALTER WINCHELL to negotiate a deal. Buchalter naïvely accepted a promise that state charges would be dropped if he surrendered to FBI Director J. EDGAR HOOVER. Author DON WHITEHEAD offered the Bureau's official version of that event in *The FBI Story* (1956).

> On the night of August 24, 1939, Director Hoover walked alone through New York City's streets to the corner of 28th Street and Fifth Avenue. And there the hunted man, Buchalter, surrendered to him. The FBI got Buchalter, and Winchell got an exclusive story. Buchalter was turned over to state authorities and later was executed for murder.

Except for the final sentence, Whitehead's account is false in all particulars. Hoover had a dozen armed G-men staked out at the rendezvous point before he "walked alone" (in fact driving) to meet Buchalter. Lepke arrived in a limousine with Winchell,

then climbed into Hoover's waiting car. And Winchell—who later claimed Hoover was "disguised in dark glasses to keep him from being recognized by passersby"—missed the exclusive when Hoover called a press conference to announce the capture at 11:15 p.m., stressing that Dewey and the NEW YORK POLICE DEPARTMENT played no part in Lepke's apprehension.

Nor was Buchalter's transfer to state custody as simple as Whitehead makes it sound. Tom Dewey immediately demanded custody of Buchalter for trial on murder charges, but Hoover refused even to let Dewey question the prisoner. Attorney General FRANK MURPHY tried to intercede on Dewey's behalf, but Hoover told his nominal superior, "The man doesn't live who can break my word to the underworld." Lepke was convicted on federal drug charges in 1939 and received a 14-year prison term. Still Hoover blocked Dewey's access, until rumors surfaced in the press that Democratic Party leaders were protecting Lepke in an effort to conceal his White House connections. Furious, President FRANKLIN ROOSEVELT ordered Lepke delivered to state authorities. He was convicted of murder in September 1941 and executed in March 1944—the only high-ranking member of organized crime put to death in American history. Despite the FBI's minor role in his story, Lepke's case is still cited by Bureau publicists as an example of how the FBI "eradicated gangsters" in the 1930s.

**BUCK, Pearl S.**—A daughter of Presbyterian missionaries, Pearl Sydenstricker was born at Hillsboro, West Virginia on 26 June 1892. Her parents soon returned to their religious work in China and raised Pearl there until 1910, when she returned to the U.S. and entered Randolph-Macon Woman's College. Upon graduating in 1914 she returned to China as a teacher, and there married agriculturalist John Buck three years later. Her novel *The Good Earth* (1931) sold 1.8 million copies in its first year of publication. Three years later Buck returned permanently to the U.S., divorced her first husband (1935) and married her publisher. In 1936 she was made a member of the National Institute of Arts and Letters. In 1938 she became the third American to win a Nobel Prize for literature (following SINCLAIR LEWIS and EUGENE O'NEILL).

FBI Director J. EDGAR HOOVER made a habit of investigating Nobel laureates, and Buck was no exception, though her initial contact with the FBI was cordial. Her dossier apparently opened with a letter from Hoover himself, in September 1938, complimenting Buck on a recent KIDNAPPING story in *Cosmopolitan* magazine and praising *The Good Earth* for its "keen understanding of human nature." Hoover invited Buck to tour FBI HEADQUARTERS as his guest, but 12 years elapsed before she accepted the offer. By then Hoover's admiration had soured, demonstrated by a memo reading: "Have someone else talk to her. My impression is that she is way to the left to say the least." In 1956, when officers of Kraft TV Theater asked Hoover to participate in their production of "Ransom"—the same story Hoover had praised in 1938—the director curtly replied: "Certainly not in anything Pearl Buck has anything to do with."

What caused the change in Hoover's attitude? The censored pages of Buck's FILE, released under the FREEDOM OF INFORMATION

ACT, reveal that G-men were suspicious of her membership in the Women's International League for Peace and Freedom; Hoover was also put off by Buck's attendance at a banquet supporting veterans of the ABRAHAM LINCOLN BRIGADE. Hoover deemed Buck "a little too liberal," and he was especially put off by her role as "a champion of the colored races." In 1941-42 Buck angered the Bureau by writing a series of articles for the Post War World Council that criticized racial segregation in the U.S. armed forces. (An unknown FBI critic scrawled "Sabotage" and "Lies" across the clippings filed in Buck's dossier.) Under the heading of "Communist affiliation," G-men noted: "Although it is not believed from the information available that Miss Buck is a Communist, her active support of all programs advocating racial equality has led her to associate with many known Communists and other individuals of varying shades of political opinions."

Hoover declined to list Buck's name in the FBI's SECURITY INDEX, noting a paucity of evidence that "subject has advocated overthrow of the government of the United States," but the dossier still branded Buck as "an outspoken person whose political sympathies at times paralleled those of the COMMUNIST PARTY." Her novels were removed from U.S. libraries abroad by Red-hunter ROY COHN, and a background check requested by the EISENHOWER White House prompted Hoover to report: "This bureau's files contain many allegations [sic] in her writings and speeches that have been against universal military training, militarism, racial segregation, and has been [sic] critical of the government of Chiang Kai-shek." G-men continued filing memos on Buck until her death at Danby, Vermont on 6 March 1973. More than three decades later, 77 pages of her 280-page dossier still remain classified "in the interest of national security."

**BUCKLEY, William Frank, Jr.**—A New York City native, born in 1925, William F. Buckley Jr. graduated with honors from Yale University, then lampooned the values of his alma mater in his first book, *God and Man at Yale* (1951). Three years later he rose to the defense of Red-baiting Senator JOSEPH MCCARTHY with *McCarthy and His Enemies*, a volume hailed by columnist WALTER WINCHELL before its release as "a sure best-seller." The FBI knew Buckley well by that time, having first indexed his name on 22 November 1941, in a report erroneously claiming that his father (president of a Venezuelan oil company) had given Buckley a Connecticut farm at age 13.

Thus began a 690-page FBI FILE that charts Buckley's rise and fall in the esteem of Director J. EDGAR HOOVER. On 7 February 1948 Buckley was listed in Bureau notes with the other college representatives attending a convention in Boston. A year later, as editor of the *Yale Daily News*, he was so angered by anti-FBI articles published in the rival *Harvard Crimson* that he invited Bureau spokesmen to state their case at a campus debate. Hoover dispatched Assistant to the Director LOUIS NICHOLS, despite a personal statement that read: "I don't like this at all. As I understood originally they wanted us to meet informally and to outline our policies and problems and answer questions for honest enlightenment. Now it has degenerated into a public assembly as a debate. We can't arbitrarily set up conditions other than not discussing pending matters and we can't very well say who is

to be invited and who can ask questions. I will approve Nick going but I will do so reluctantly." All fears aside, Buckley later told author Natalie Robins that Hoover was "just oleaginous" over the debate's success. In 1951, Buckley claimed, he was offered a job with the Bureau, Nichols promising to waive the mythical law-school requirement, but he declined the post to complete his next book.

Buckley's friendly relationship with FBI HEADQUARTERS endured for another 16 years. When he launched the conservative *National Review* in 1955 a memo to Hoover from one of his aides declared: "I think the Director would be interested in looking at it. ... It is believed that this journal and the writers connected with it may be of some value to the Bureau." Hoover promptly opened a new file on the magazine, including an article from the 12 August 1955 issue of *COUNTERATTACK* that called Buckley "an effective foe of Communism." Various letters and clippings sent by Buckley to Nichols bear parenthetical notes identifying Buckley as "the outspoken anti-communist." Still, it was not all puffery. In 1959 the Bureau's Publications Section noted that a "quick review" of Buckley's *Up from Liberalism* "indicates that it is neither a balanced nor an effective presentation." Three years later, Buckley — now "a controversial figure"—visited FBI headquarters with his son, a memo noting that they "visited briefly" with Hoover. In 1964 a tardy G-man noted the premiere of Buckley's column "On the Right," apparently unaware that it had debuted two years earlier.

The Buckley-Hoover relationship suffered a fatal rift in May 1967, when the *National Review* published a parody of the "liberal" *New York Times*. The send-up included an article reporting that Hoover had resigned after being arrested on a morals charge. Furious at this "new low in journalism," Hoover struck Buckley from the FBI's list of Special Correspondents and Assistant Director CARTHA DELOACH called Buckley at home, declaring that "the entire FBI was outraged," haunted by fears that "there would be many people who would accept the article at face value." (Ironically, in 1967 Buckley received an award naming him Best Columnist of the Year.)

Hoover never forgave Buckley the perceived insult, though Buckley later claimed (despite DeLoach's call) that he knew nothing of the director's wrath for years afterward, until his dossier was released under the FREEDOM OF INFORMATION ACT. In 1969 Buckley invited Hoover and others to join him in a libel suit against Olympia Press, for listing their names in *The Homosexual Handbook*, but Hoover ignored the overture, privately citing concerns over bad publicity and the fact that "Buckley indicates no financial target that would make the lawsuit profitable in the money sense." That fall, as part of an ongoing COINTELPRO campaign, G-men sent Buckley an anonymous letter "setting forth Yale University sanctions of BLACK PANTHER PARTY activities on the Yale campus during May 1969." The goal was to produce a Buckley column attacking the Panthers, and while Buckley later denied receiving the letter he *did* write such a column on 13 November 1969.

Hoover's enmity toward Buckley fluctuated toward the end of the director's life. In 1970, invited to appear on Buckley's television talk show *Firing Line*, Hoover penned a terse memo: "No.

Buckley recently [*sic*] wrote a vicious column on the FBI." A second parody confused the Bureau's staff in 1971, as Buckley spoofed the PENTAGON PAPERS in a column titled "The Secret Papers They Didn't Publish." G-men produced a seven-page analysis calling the article "disjointed and lacking in continuity," but they apparently missed the joke — until Buckley announced it to the media five days later. Even so, Hoover swallowed his spite long enough to thank Buckley for another 1971 column, in which he praised the FBI and denounced LILLIAN HELLMAN'S Committee for Public Justice seminar at Princeton University. Two years after Hoover's death, when new director CLARENCE KELLEY was invited to appear on *Firing Line*, he echoed Hoover's refusal — and the 1967 satire was again cited as one reason for declining.

On balance, Hoover's malice failed to trouble Buckley, who won an Emmy award for TV program achievement (1969), an American Book Award for best mystery (*Stained Glass*, 1980), and a Presidential Medal of Freedom from GEORGE H.W. BUSH (1991). Buckley remained as editor-in-chief of *National Review* until 1990, while publishing numerous books and maintaining a column that runs in some 300 daily newspapers. On balance, while still pleading ignorance of the one-sided FBI feud, Buckley told author Natalie Robins, "It was plain stupid for Hoover to get sore at me, plain dumb. Suppose I had gotten sore at him? I could have done much more damage than he could have done to me."

**BUGGING**— "Bugging"— the covert installation of electronic listening devices — is a form of surveillance which the FBI has utilized for decades to collect information on criminal suspects and spies, as well as countless individuals with no involvement in any illegal activity. In conjunction with WIRETAPPING, bugs supply much of the material credited to unnamed "confidential sources" or "reliable sources" in FBI FILES. Because installation of eavesdropping equipment frequently involves BREAK-INS on private property, many Bureau bugging operations have been carried out in violation of the U.S. Constitution's Fourth Amendment

Director J. EDGAR HOOVER recognized the illegality of most FBI bugging raids, and while he rarely shied away from breaking state or federal laws, Hoover required that each illegal operation be cleared in advance by his office. Whether agents in the field obeyed that dictum is impossible to say, since Hoover also created elaborate procedures for hiding illicit orders and contraband intelligence in the Bureau's FILES. Exposure of a bug could jeopardize prosecution in some cases, but Attorney General ROBERT JACKSON promised Hoover in June 1940 that "confidential sources" would not be compromised "without the prior approval of the Bureau." Another 11 years passed before Hoover sought guidance on bugging procedures from Attorney General J. HOWARD MCGRATH, in October 1951. McGrath replied on 26 February 1952 that "I cannot authorize installation of a microphone involving a trespass under existing law," but FBI bugging continued, albeit on a smaller scale. On 20 May 1954 Attorney General HERBERT BROWNELL authorized break-ins and bugging in "national security" cases, a grant of power which Hoover unilaterally extended to "important" criminal cases the following day. By late 1957 the Bureau's TOP HOODLUM PROGRAM had extended illegal bugging to selected leaders of ORGANIZED CRIME.

Various presidents from FRANKLIN ROOSEVELT to RICHARD NIXON authorized illegal surveillance of political adversaries, allies, journalists, public figures and others who had committed no crimes and were suspected of none. Bugging of Dr. MARTIN LUTHER KING, JR., was authorized by Attorney General ROBERT KENNEDY, and President LYNDON JOHNSON enjoyed listening to FBI tapes of King's sexual encounters with various women. In 1964 Johnson also ordered bugging of various hostile delegates to the Democratic National Convention. A July 1970 memo from Nixon aide Charles Huston outlined a series of "clearly illegal" DOMESTIC SURVEILLANCE campaigns, and while Hoover voiced doubts about the HUSTON PLAN, he told Attorney JOHN MITCHELL that the FBI would "implement the instructions of the White House at your direction." To protect himself from criticism, Hoover added that he would "continue to seek your specific authorization" each time G-men were asked to break the law.

New federal legislation, meanwhile, had expanded FBI authority to use bugs and wiretaps. The Omnibus Crime Control and Safe Streets Act of June 1968 approved bugs and wiretaps under court order, while preserving the president's power to order surveillance in cases of "national security." Two years later, in October 1970, the Racketeer Influence and Corrupt Organization (RICO) Act broadened the scope of eavesdropping against organized crime. Legal requirements notwithstanding, though, the FBI continued illicit bugging on a daily basis. Subsequent disclosures by the CHURCH COMMITTEE revealed 697 incidents of bugging in the Bureau's COINTELPRO campaigns, between 1960 and 1974. (Claims that statistics on COINTELPRO bugging between 1956 and 1959 were "not available" are scarcely credible, but the figures remain undisclosed.)

Today, most Bureau bugging is carried out by units variously known as Technical Support Squads (TSS) or Special Operations Groups (SOG). The New York City field office maintained 15 such teams in the 1980s, and their schedule was so crowded that some agents claimed the initials TSS stood for "Tough Shit Squad," after the number of requests for bugs and wiretaps commonly denied by heavy workloads. A decade later, new technology had projected bugging into cyberspace and sparked new controversy, after G-men used surveillance software to monitor keystrokes on a New Jersey mobster's personal computer. Prosecutors used the evidence thus collected to charge Nicodemo Scarfo, Jr., with running a $5 million bookmaking and loansharking operation in the Garden State.

**BULGER, James Joseph, Jr.**—A Boston native, born 3 September 1929, James ("Whitey") Bulger served time in Alcatraz for BANK ROBBERY and emerged from prison in the early 1960s to seize control of Boston's mostly-Irish Winter Hill Gang. He was assisted in that conquest by a ruthless temperament, a brother who served as president of the Massachusetts state senate, and by the FBI's Boston field office. Boston G-man JOHN CONNOLLY, JR., had grown up with the Bulger brothers, and he welcomed the chance to recruit Winter Hill gang leaders for the Bureau's Top Echelon INFORMANT Program, ignoring criminal activities of selected mobsters in return for tips about their Italian-American rivals. Over the next three decades, as described by Bureau historian

Robert Kessler, "the FBI ran a protection racket for the Winter Hill Gang in return for their information on the New England Mafia and the ego gratification of recruiting informants." Connolly and others also accepted cash from Bulger in exchange for services rendered, while joining in the FRAME-UPS of PETER LIMONE, JOSEPH SALVATI and other innocent persons for murders they did not commit.

The symbiotic relationship broke down in 1995, when a joint task force composed of agents from the DRUG ENFORCEMENT ADMINISTRATION and the INTERNAL REVENUE SERVICE secured evidence leading to Bulger's indictment on racketeering charges. Boston agents warned Bulger of the impending charges and he fled into hiding, accompanied by Catherine Elizabeth Greig, a dental hygienist 22 years his junior. On 19 August 1999 Bulger's name was added to the Bureau's "TEN MOST WANTED" LIST, with a $250,000 reward offered for information leading to his capture. A new indictment, in September 2000, charged Bulger and side-kick Stephen FLEMMI with additional crimes, including 21 gangland murders. Those charges, coupled with disclosure of the FBI's complicity in his escape, boosted the reward for Flemmi's capture to $1 million on 29 November 2000, but so far there have been no takers. Oklahoma prosecutors charged Bulger and Flemmi with a 1981 Tulsa murder on 13 March 2001, in yet another case where Boston G-men had suppressed incriminating evidence. Ex-agent Connolly was convicted of racketeering and obstructing justice in May 2002, while his childhood friend remained at large.

**BUREAU of Alcohol, Tobacco and Firearms** — The U.S. government has collected tax on alcoholic beverages since 1791, but the Treasury Department's modern Bureau of Alcohol, Tobacco and Firearms (BATF) properly traces its lineage to the PROHIBITION Bureau active between 1920 and 1933. That unit was briefly transferred to the JUSTICE DEPARTMENT in June 1933, merging with the FBI to create a new Division of Investigation, but its life ran out with Repeal six months later. After the demise of Prohibition's "noble experiment," Treasury created a new Alcohol Tax Unit to pursue recalcitrant bootleggers. (As late as 1963, 5,500 suspects were charged with distilling or selling untaxed alcohol; the number dropped to 75 in 1979.) Guns were added to the mix in 1934, with passage of the National Firearms Act (which taxed, but did not ban, such "gangster weapons" as machine guns, silencers and sawed-off shotguns). The federal Gun Control Act of 1968 extended those taxes to "destructive devices," but BATF remained a division of the INTERNAL REVENUE SERVICE until July 1972, when it became a separate agency at Treasury. That same year witnessed passage of the Federal BOMBING Statute, which divided jurisdiction in explosives cases as follows:

• U.S. Postal inspectors are responsible for mail-bombs and bombings of post offices;

• The FBI investigates all bombings of federal property other than post offices or Treasury facilities;

• BATF takes primary responsibility for all other bombings *unless* the incidents are officially designated as acts of TERRORISM, in which case G-men assume control of the investigation.

In a nation where the phrase "gun control" sparks acrimonious debate from coast to coast, BATF was bound to be a controversial agency. It did not help that John Caulfield, appointed by President RICHARD NIXON to lead BATF, was soon exposed as a hush-money bagman in the WATERGATE SCANDAL. In 1979 BATF's critics told the U.S. Senate that "75 to 80 percent of BATF cases brought [to trial in Maryland and Virginia] involved defendants who had no criminal intent, but were enticed by bureau agents into violating technical requirements, which the defendants did not know existed." President JAMES CARTER, near the end of his term in office, considered transferring most of BATF's criminal work to Justice, but the shift was never made. President RONALD REAGAN hoped to dismantle the unit entirely, thus repaying political debts to the National Rifle Association, but he succeeded only in cutting BATF's budget and manpower.

Still BATF endured, often struggling in an adversarial relationship with the FBI. As BATF historian James Moore reports, "The FBI has had a deep and lasting impact on the ATF, and the effects were clearest and most destructive in terrorist cases." According to the BATF, conflict arose primarily when G-men manipulated their definition of "terrorism" to avoid unwanted cases (notably those involving ANTI-ABORTION VIOLENCE and the KU KLUX KLAN) or when they claimed credit for cases solved by BATF agents. Moore describes 10 such cases with 50 defendants, in which Bureau spokesmen claimed credit after the fact.

Two of the FBI's most embarrassing cases from the 1990s began as BATF operations. The first, from Idaho, involved a four-year BATF campaign to entrap neo-Nazi RANDY WEAVER in illegal arms transactions. When he was finally charged and refused to surrender, agents of the U.S. MARSHALS SERVICE were sent to arrest him, sparking a shootout that killed Weaver's son and a federal officer. The FBI's HOSTAGE RESCUE TEAM took over at that point and matters quickly went from bad to worse, resulting in the death of Weaver's wife and a $3.1 million settlement to her survivors. Eight months later, another BATF squad attacked the BRANCH DAVIDIAN religious sect near Waco, Texas. Six persons died in the clash, and G-men moved in for a siege that ended with the fiery deaths of nearly 80 more on 19 April 1993.

There were success stories, as well. In 1989-90, BATF agents shared responsibility for solution of the deadly VANPAC mail-bombing case. Two days before the Waco raid, on 26 February 1993, FBI and BATF agents launched a successful joint investigation of a terrorist bombing at New York's WORLD TRADE CENTER. And when right-wing fanatic TIMOTHY MCVEIGH bombed Oklahoma City's federal building, killing 168 persons on the second anniversary of the Waco holocaust, BATF agents took the lead in processing evidence from the crime scene. After the catastrophic SKYJACKINGS of 11 September 2001, as President GEORGE W. BUSH sought to reorganize America's "homeland security" apparatus, there were renewed calls for BATF's relocation from Treasury to Justice. FBI spokesmen hailed the proposed move on 12 November 2002, with a press release that read:

> The FBI supports the proposed transfer of the criminal enforcement authorities of the Bureau of Alcohol, Tobacco, and Firearms (ATF) to the Department of Justice (DOJ). We have been working closely with the DOJ and with the Treasury Department to

ensure that any legislation effectuating such a transfer would preserve the ATF's existing criminal and regulatory enforcement authorities.

**BURNETT, Alfred**—A twice-convicted felon in Seattle, Alfred Burnett was awaiting trial on robbery charges in January 1970, when he was suddenly released from the Kings County jail over objections from his parole officer. Burnett subsequently pled guilty in that case but remained at large, again despite the parole officer's demand that he be jailed for failure to appear for sentencing on another charge. The FBI's Seattle field office overruled Burnett's parole officer in each case, naming Burnett as an INFORMANT who supplied the Bureau with "valuable information" on ghetto violence and the BLACK PANTHER PARTY. More specifically, he was assigned to locate Jimmy Davis, a Panther suspected of involvement in one or more recent BOMBINGS.

Burnett never located Davis, but he compromised by targeting a friend of Davis's, 22-year-old VIETNAM WAR veteran Larry Ward. After some haggling, Ward apparently accepted Burnett's offer of $75 to plant a bomb at Seattle's Hardcastle Realty Company on the night of 14 May 1970. Burnett supplied the bomb, then alerted G-men and police to the impending crime. According to his later statements, "The police wanted a bomber and I gave them one." Burnett insists that he "distinctly told them it was Ward instead of [Davis]" and "that he was unarmed." Be that as it may, when Ward arrived on foot at Hardcastle Realty, carrying Burnett's bomb, he was surrounded by Seattle squad cars and killed in a barrage of gunfire. Adopting a remorseful pose after the fact, Burnett maintained, "I didn't know Larry Ward would be killed."

Seattle police were equally surprised, if we believe their later statements (although the city's mayor had publicly advocated killing bombers as a "deterrent" to future attacks). John Williams, chief of the Seattle Police Department's intelligence unit, blamed FBI agents for Ward's death. "As far as I can tell," Williams told Senate investigators, "Ward was a relatively decent kid. Somebody set this whole thing up. It wasn't the police department." FBI agents protected Burnett, now marked as an informer, by securing his transfer from state prison to federal custody.

**BURNS, William J.**—A Baltimore native, born "around 1860" and raised in Ohio, William Burns worked briefly as a SECRET SERVICE agent (and later chief) before retiring in 1909 and founding his own Chicago-based William J. Burns International Detective Agency. In 1910 Burns was credited with solving the BOMBING of the *Los Angeles Times*, though some critics called the case a FRAME-UP. A year later, according to reports filed by Attorney General GEORGE WICKERSHAM, Burns stacked the trial juries of Oregon Senator John Mitchell and Representative John Williams with political enemies, thus securing dubious convictions on land-fraud charges. Before the U.S. entered WORLD WAR I, Burns was also employed as an agent of British Intelligence.

Despite that checkered background—or perhaps because of it—Burns was tapped by Attorney General HARRY DAUGHERTY (a personal friend) on 18 August 1922 to head the Bureau of Investigation. Burns took office four days later, while young J.

EDGAR HOOVER was promoted to serve as the Bureau's first assistant director. That same afternoon, G-men in Michigan illegally raided a meeting of the COMMUNIST PARTY, seizing membership records and other documents. That action set the tone for Burns's tenure as director, during which the Bureau was used as a partisan political weapon, pursuing "radicals" and LABOR UNIONS, breaking strikes, maintaining FILES on Democratic congressmen, and generally protecting the corrupt regime of President WARREN HARDING.

Burns also kept files on the party affiliations and political connections of his agents, whose number increased from 346 to 441 at the end of his tenure. (Clerical staff decreased by 78 during the same period, for an overall net increase of 17 Bureau employees.) Some of the new G-men were hired as favors to influential politicians; others were drawn from the ranks of private detective agencies, notorious as corrupt strikebreakers. (The worst of the lot was probably GASTON MEANS, hired in October 1921 to handle "special assignments of a confidential nature.") When Congressman OSCAR KELLAR objected to Bureau involvement in a national railroad strike, G-men raided his office in September of 1922. A year later, in the midst of the TEAPOT DOME SCANDAL, Burns and Hoover sent agents to investigate the administration's leading critics, Montana senators THOMAS WALSH and BURTON WHEELER.

While Hoover later took pains to distance himself from Burns, he also learned a great deal from the aging director—including the use of scare tactics and dubious statistics to milk appropriations from Congress. Hoover accompanied Burns on his various trips to Capitol Hill, where Burns warned credulous lawmakers of the latest "menace" and impressed them with news of the Bureau's achievements. In 1922, for instance, Burns told the House Appropriations Committee that Bolshevik strategy in America—

> principally consists of urging the working man to strike, with the ultimate purpose of bringing about a revolution in this country…. Radicalism is becoming stronger every day in this country. They are going about it in a very subtle manner. For instance, they have schools all over the country where they are teaching children 4 and 5 years old, and they are organizing athletic clubs through the country. I dare say that unless the country becomes aroused concerning the danger of this radical element in this country, we will have a very serious situation.

Where finances were concerned, Burns fell back on the DYER ACT to claim that G-men had "recovered" thousands of stolen cars across the U.S. (most of them retrieved in fact by local police). Playing a tune that Hoover would echo for the next 50 years, Burns told the House in 1922, "The value of automobiles recovered by our service amounts to more than our appropriation."

The Teapot Dome investigation snowballed after President Harding's sudden death in August 1923, and Burns was one of those called before Congress to explain his behavior. Burns admitted using G-men to investigate Senators Walsh and Wheeler, but the interrogation skirted his apparent role in the May 1923 shooting death of JUSTICE DEPARTMENT employee Jess Smith. Attorney General HARLAN STONE demanded Burns's resignation on 9 May 1924, and after a brief spell of defiance, Burns complied the next day, replaced as director by J. Edgar Hoover. (The modern FBI's Internet website erroneously claims that Burns remained in office until 14 June 1924.)

Resignation did not end his involvement with the Teapot Dome conspirators, however. When the trial of ex-Secretary of the Interior Bernard Fall finally opened in October 1927, Burns (now back at the helm of his detective agency) was hired to shadow the jurors. A mistrial was declared, and Burns narrowly escaped conviction on a charge of criminal contempt. The near-miss drove him into retirement at Sarasota, Florida, where he passed his final years penning "true" accounts of his more famous cases. At his death, on 14 April 1932, the *Washington Post* hailed Burns as "probably the most famous individual in the detective business during his active years."

**BUSH, George Herbert Walker**—A Milton, Massachusetts native, born 12 June 1924, George H.W. Bush was decorated for bravery as a U.S. Navy pilot during WORLD WAR II. He graduated from Yale in 1948 and then moved to Texas, where he made a fortune from various oil companies over the next 18 years. Twice defeated in campaigns for the U.S. Senate (1966 and 1970), Bush served as a Texas congressman (1967-71), as chairman of the Republican National Committee (1973-74), in the U.S. Liaison Office at Beijing (1974-75), and as director of the CENTRAL INTELLIGENCE AGENCY (1976-77). In 1980 he was RONALD REAGAN'S chief opposition for the Republican presidential nomination, finally elected to serve as Reagan's vice president (1981-89).

Two weeks after their first election, on 18 November 1980, Reagan and Bush visited Washington, D.C. for a closed-door meeting with leaders of the TEAMSTERS UNION, including JACKIE PRESSER, an Ohio mobster and FBI INFORMANT. Soon after that meeting, Presser—an eighth-grade dropout facing nonstop federal investigations for corruption—was appointed to serve the Reagan-Bush transition team as a "senior economic adviser." In January 1982 Bush was named to lead Reagan's "war on drugs," announcing that his national strike force would include 43 FBI agents and 130 Customs officers. The futile "war" was conducted in such secrecy that spokesmen for the General Accounting Office complained to Congress and the JUSTICE DEPARTMENT, while a Coast Guard commander in Miami dismissed the campaign as "an intellectual fraud." In 1984 Reagan sent Bush to Ohio, where he received another Teamster endorsement. Appearing arm-in-arm with Presser, Bush told the audience, "We couldn't be more pleased. We're very, very grateful, I'll tell you, and we will work, work hard to earn the confidence of your members." When reporters asked about Presser's legal problems, Bush replied, "We have a system of justice in this country that people are innocent until proven guilty. There have been a lot of allegations; the endorsement has nothing to do with that."

Bush was elected president in November 1980, again with outspoken Teamsters support. (Union president William McCarthy, a confessed participant in illegal kickbacks, was soon named to the President's Drug Advisory Council.) One week after his inauguration, Bush promised federal bail-outs for a series of savings and loan corporations looted by their proprietors—

including Denver's Silverado S&L, run by son Neil Bush. Exposure of Bush's involvement in the Reagan-era Iran-Contra scandal embarrassed the White House and sent various aides to prison for perjury. Attorney General WILLIAM BARR obstructed the ongoing investigation, refusing congressional demands for an independent prosecutor in that case, and Bush ultimately pardoned six of his associates who were convicted for lying to Congress.

Bush was informed of misconduct by FBI Director WILLIAM SESSIONS in early 1992, and while a report from the Justice Department's OFFICE OF PROFESSIONAL RESPONSIBILITY recommended presidential action against Sessions, Bush left him in place and uncensured. In August 1992 the FBI's lethal Ruby Ridge, Idaho standoff with RANDY WEAVER sparked new controversy about Bureau tactics. Coupled with Bush's comments on the advent of a "New World Order," the Weaver case served as a catalyst for the violent MILITIA MOVEMENT in America. Economic recession doomed Bush's reelection hopes, and he was defeated by WILLIAM CLINTON in November 1992.

**BUSH, George Walker**—The eldest son of President GEORGE H.W. BUSH, George W. Bush—or "Dubya"—was born at New Haven, Connecticut on 6 July 1946. He followed a family tradition by attending Yale University (1964-68), and thereafter avoided combat service in the VIETNAM WAR by joining the National Guard. (Commanders at his final post say Bush was inexplicably absent during the final 12 months of his term.) Following his discharge, Bush somehow prospered from a series of failed business ventures—his $848,00 windfall from Harken Energy before its collapse prompted a 1991 Securities and Exchange Commission investigation for insider trading—and made his first $1 million from a petroleum company funded by relatives of future terrorist USAMA BIN LADEN.

Bush lost his first political race (for Congress, 1978), but subsequently served as governor of Texas (1995-2000) while building support for himself as a Republican presidential candidate. In November 2000 Bush trailed his Democratic opponent by 539,000 votes, but he carried the electoral college after charges of vote fraud in Florida (where brother John Bush served as governor) produced an appeal to the U.S. SUPREME COURT. There, in December, five justices appointed by Bush's father or by predecessor RONALD REAGAN found that Bush might suffer "irreparable harm"—i.e., loss of the election—if contested votes were recounted in Florida.

Bush's first year in office was beset by controversy, including his links to the expanding ENRON SCANDAL, the hotly-contested appointment of Attorney General JOHN ASHCROFT, and reports from the JUSTICE DEPARTMENT that Bush had ordered federal agents to "back off" investigation of the Bin Laden family's ties to global TERRORISM. The latter move was especially troubling, in light of Usama Bin Laden's role in the catastrophic SKYJACKINGS of 11 September 2001. Bush's announcement of a worldwide "war on terrorism" and Ashcroft's dragnet arrests of Muslim immigrants in the U.S., were followed by passage of the USA PATRIOT ACT (including vast expansion of surveillance powers for the FBI and the CENTRAL INTELLIGENCE AGENCY). At this writing (in December 2002) Bush's campaign has failed to apprehend any major terrorist subjects, and the person(s) responsible for a series of ANTHRAX murders in 2001 remain unidentified.

**BYARS, William, Jr.** — The son of Texas oilman WILLIAM BYARS, SR., a wealthy friend and patron of FBI Director J. EDGAR HOOVER, William Byars, Jr., was born in 1937 and met Hoover frequently during summers spent at CLINT MURCHISON'S Del Charro Hotel at La Jolla, California. A college student in the early 1960s, later described by author Anthony Summers as "a part-time filmmaker, a fitness enthusiast and dilettante," Byars shared his memories of Hoover with Summers in a 1988 interview. On several occasions Byars recalled Hoover "raving about [Attorney General] ROBERT KENNEDY, saying god-awful things about him. He despised him and didn't hide the fact." In the summer of 1964 Byars questioned Hoover about the JFK ASSASSINATION: "I asked him, 'Do you think Lee Harvey Oswald did it?' and he looked at me for quite a long time. Then he said, 'If I told you what I really know, it would be very dangerous to this country. Our whole political system could be disrupted.' That's all he said, and I could see he wasn't about to say any more."

Byars and one of his California friends, Charles Krebs, also corroborated longstanding rumors of Hoover's HOMOSEXUALITY. Byars's home in Laurel Canyon was known as a site of frequent gay parties, allegedly attended on occasion by Hoover and constant companion CLYDE TOLSON. "It was accepted in our circle that Hoover and Tolson were homosexual," Krebs told Summers. "The impression I had from Byars was that Hoover and Tolson had had a sexual relationship with each other when they were younger, but not anymore. They were just two old aunties together in old age, but they were queens. On three occasions that I knew about, perhaps four, boys were driven down to La Jolla at Hoover's request." Krebs also described multiple occasions when Hoover and Tolson were chauffeured to a La Jolla gay bar, seeking teenage boys. Byars, who fled the U.S. in 1973 after his indictment for producing pornographic films, confirmed the stories in his 1988 interview with Summers.

**BYARS, William Sr.** — One of several Texas oilmen who befriended FBI Director J. EDGAR HOOVER, William Byars Sr. was a close associate of CLINT MURCHISON who frequently vacationed with Hoover and constant companion CLYDE TOLSON at Murchison's Del Charro Hotel in La Jolla, California. With Murchison, Byars introduced Hoover to various risk-free investment opportunities, guaranteeing in advance that Hoover would suffer no loss if the projects should fail. Byars was also a heavy financial supporter of Presidents DWIGHT EISENHOWER and LYNDON JOHNSON, the latter a fellow Texan. Hoover's telephone logs for 22 November 1963 reveal that he made only three calls after receiving word of the JFK ASSASSINATION — to Attorney General ROBERT KENNEDY, the SECRET SERVICE, and to William Byars. Subsequent research by author Anthony Summers revealed that Byars met with Dallas mobster JACK RUBY on at least one occasion before Ruby killed alleged presidential assassin LEE HARVEY OSWALD. Byars died in 1965, but his son, WILLIAM BYARS, JR., subsequently corroborated rumors of Hoover's HOMOSEXUALITY.

**BYNNER, Harold Witter** — Born on 10 August 1881, future poet Witter Bynner developed a lifelong enthusiasm for Far Eastern culture and philosophy while a student at Harvard. He toured Japan in 1917 and returned to the U.S. with a passion for translating Asian poetry, explaining that his work with Chinese verse gave him "a newer, finer, and deeper education than ever came to me from the Hebrew or the Greek."

It was politics, rather than geography, which prompted the FBI to open a FILE on Bynner in 1937, after noting his membership in the Medical Bureau to Aid Spanish Democracy and finding his name on a letterhead of the American Committee for the Defense of [Leon] Trotsky. Bynner compounded his offense in 1943, by signing a petition to abolish the HOUSE COMMITTEE ON UN-AMERICAN ACTIVITIES, and a year later G-men noted his attendance at a party thrown for Robert Oppenheimer, a nuclear physicist at the Los Alamos testing facility who was later branded a security risk on the basis of his leftist associations. Around the same time, the El Paso (Texas) Office of Censorship opened a letter that mentioned Bynner in passing, and FBI assistance was solicited. The Bureau's answer described Bynner as an "American poet, very much interested in all things Chinese." Agents abandoned their surveillance of Bynner in 1954, and he died in 1968. When his censored dossier was released under the FREEDOM OF INFORMATION ACT, the most curious item therein was an unexplained list of names, including Bynner's with such nondescript targets as the "Cozy Inn Bar," the "Courtesy Hotel," and the "Cat Gang."

**BYRD Committee** — In 1937 Virginia senator Harry Byrd chaired a committee appointed to investigate the relative efficiency of various federal executive agencies. Included in its study were the FBI, the U.S. Postal inspector's service, the Treasury Department's SECRET SERVICE, the INTERNAL REVENUE SERVICE and U.S. Customs. Scholars from the BROOKINGS INSTITUTION were employed to review statistics submitted by various agencies (convictions, cash recoveries, etc.), and they reported that both the Secret Service and U.S. Postal inspectors produced conviction rates superior to the FBI's by a factor of five or six to one. FBI statistics initially looked better on paper, but the Brookings scholars found them falsely inflated by an average of 33 percent. The committee's final report had more to say about Director J. EDGAR HOOVER'S abuse of statistics.

> The Director of the Federal Bureau of Investigation referred in March 1936 to the "armed forces of crime which number more than 3 million active participants." Three months later he stated that "the criminal standing army of America" numbered 500,000, "a whole half-million of armed thugs, murderers, thieves, firebugs, assassins, robbers, and hold-up men." About six months afterward he gave the total criminal population as 3,500,000 and the number of crimes as 1,500,000. Five months later he stated that 4,300,000 persons were engaged by day and by night in the commission of felonies and estimated that 1,333,526 major felonies were committed in the United States during the year 1936....
>
> In an address about a year ago [23 April 1936], he stated that "the files of the Bureau of Investigation show that there are actually 3 million convicted criminals. Beyond this there are enough more with police records to demonstrate that an average of one

out of every twenty-five persons in the United States of America has at least had his brush with law-enforcement agencies and is inclined toward criminality."

In the same address he declared that "there are today in America 150,000 murderers roaming at large"; but it appears from [the FBI's] UNIFORM CRIME REPORTS that in 987 cities with a population of 35,450,666 the police were cognizant of only 3,582 cases of criminal homicide, and of these 2,936 or 81.9 per cent had, according to the police, been cleared by arrest.

The committee attributed Hoover's errant statistics to "guesswork," although their frequent spurious precision might suggest deliberate fabrication. The Byrd Committee concluded its review by noting a persistent American "fear that a strong Federal police force might be used as an instrument of oppression," further warning that concentration of police powers in federal hands "may weaken the incentives for better State and local enforcement."

# C

**CALDER, Alexander**—Born in 1898 at Lawton, Pennsylvania, third-generation sculptor Alexander ("Sandy") Calder ranks among America's best-known artists. He was also a subject of interest to the FBI, with portions of his 31-page file still classified as secret, three decades after his death, "in the interest of national defense or foreign policy."

The first memo in Calder's file dates from 1954 but reports his 1941 membership in the American Artist Congress, branded "typical of Communist created and controlled organizations" by the California Committee on Un-American Activities. Worse yet, Calder's name had appeared in support of the American-Russian Institute, soliciting funds to bankroll a Russian art exhibit in the United States. That information was regurgitated when the U.S. STATE DEPARTMENT sought a background check on Calder, in 1957. In 1964, when LYNDON JOHNSON'S White House made a similar request, the FBI reported Calder's sponsorship of an April 1961 rally in New York City, seeking abolition of the HOUSE COMMITTEE ON UN-AMERICAN ACTIVITIES. Living in France by 1966, Calder earned another black mark in his bureau file when he returned for a peaceful demonstration against the Vietnam War. Memos from 1967 and 1968 note Calder's continuing involvement in the anti-war movement, while a note from 1970 lists him among supporters of seven defendants charged with conspiracy in Chicago, for disrupting the 1968 Democratic Convention. Aides to President RICHARD NIXON requested another name-check on Calder and his wife in 1974, pursuant to ongoing anti-war activities. Calder died in 1976, having outlived J. EDGAR HOOVER by four years.

**CALDWELL, Erskine**—A native of Coweta, Georgia, born 17 December 1903, Erskine Caldwell moved to Maine in 1926 and began to write for various magazines, including the leftist *New Masses*. The FBI overlooked him until 1932, when the first entry in his file described Caldwell as a leader of the League of Professional Groups for Foster and Ford [COMMUNIST PARTY candidates for president and vice president]. In 1935 Caldwell was indexed for participation in the League of American Writers, while a 1938 memo branded him a "fellow traveler of Communists."

That same year, Caldwell complained to the FBI of threatening letters received in New York, but G-men were unable to identify the author who signed himself "C.Y.A." In 1940 an "unknown outside source" tipped the bureau that Caldwell and his wife "have been members of the CP [Communist Party] for a long time." Labeled "an outstanding propagandist for Communism" in later FBI memos, Caldwell reported another threatening letter in 1952, dismissed by the bureau as having been written by "a typical crack-pot." Nine years later, Caldwell telephoned the San Francisco field office to discuss his 1959 endorsement of a Russian translator hired by the State Department. He belatedly suspected that the person might be an "imposter," and while bureau files suggest a possibility of espionage afoot, with two persons using the same name interchangeably, no disposition of the matter was recorded. No further contact with the bureau was recorded prior to Caldwell's death at Paradise Valley, Arizona, on 11 April 1987.

**CALLAHAN, Nicholas P.**—Nicholas Callahan began his FBI career in 1936, as a clerk in the IDENTIFICATION DIVISION, and held that post until he was appointed as a full-fledged agent in 1939. Over the next seven years he served in the Dallas, Newark, Baltimore and Philadelphia field offices. Recalled to FBI HEADQUARTERS in 1946, he was promoted to the rank of deputy assistant director (otherwise known as the "number one man") in the Administrative Division, where he controlled the Bureau's Confidential Fund from 1946 through 1973. More promotions followed: to inspector (1948), assistant director of the Administrative Division (1959), and finally associate director of the FBI (1973).

In theory, the Confidential Fund was reserved for payment of INFORMANTS and similar expenses, but subsequent investigation by JUSTICE DEPARTMENT auditors in 1976 revealed widespread mismanagement and misappropriation of funds under Callahan and his immediate superior, JOHN MOHR. Together, they required that all FBI surveillance equipment be purchased from a firm owned by a close friend of Mohr's, at prices marked up from 40 to 70 percent above normal retail. That sweetheart system wasted at least $75,000, while another $23,000 was spent on entertainment of politicians and foreign law enforcement officers, falsely billed to the government as "travel vouchers" that were never repaid (as required under federal law at the time). Callahan also withdrew another $39,590.98 from the FBI RECREATIONAL ASSOCIATION coffers between 1951 and 1972, earmarked for an untraceable "Library Fund." In 1972, following J. EDGAR HOOVER'S death, Callahan and Mohr destroyed most records of the Confidential Fund, Library Fund and the FBI Recreational Association, but enough remained in 1976 to condemn Callahan. Before year's end, Director CLARENCE KELLEY demanded Callahan's resignation, citing evidence of corruption and unspecified "abuses of power."

In Callahan's case, profiteering from the FBI exceeded claims of disappearing cash. He also received numerous "gifts" from the Bureau, including a customized coat of arms, a dresser-top valet, and a portable wine-cask liquor cabinet. Technicians in the FBI's Exhibits Section kept busy on Callahan's behalf, silk-screening a felt table top for board games, trimming his doors at home to fit new carpeting, constructing walnut shelves and fishing pole racks, assembling lath fences to halt sand erosion at his beach house, printing maps with directions to said beach house, fashioning Styrofoam nautical decorations for the beach house, waterproofing the roof of a shed, crafting a house sign for Callahan's daughter, framing personal photos, fabricating plastic stack tables and a desk memento for friends, servicing Callahan's personal vehicles, and "loaning" the associate director film and cameras for personal photographs.

Callahan's loyalty to top men in the Bureau was further rewarded upon the death of Associate Director CLYDE TOLSON. Callahan received a $28,000 bequest in Tolson's will, but legal challenges eventually required that he and other beneficiaries pay 10 percent of their inheritance to Tolson's favorite charities. Callahan died on 12 November 1997.

**CAPGA** —After 20 years of public denials that ORGANIZED CRIME existed in America, FBI Director J. EDGAR HOOVER launched his first campaign against the mob in 1946. The operation began when Chicago gangster James Ragen approached the local Bureau field office, complaining of syndicate attempts to muscle in on his wire service, Continental Press, which supplied daily race results to illegal bookmakers from coast to coast. Without reversing his public stance on syndicated crime, Hoover ordered a local investigation code-named CAPGA — an acronym for "*Cap*one *Ga*ng," referring to the underworld successors of ALPHONSE CAPONE who dominated Chicago's rackets.

There followed a campaign of covert surveillance, accompanied by illegal BREAK-INS and WIRE-TAPPING normally reserved for targets thought to hold left-of-center political beliefs. The CAPGA operation failed to help James Ragen: he was gravely wounded in a drive-by shooting on 24 June 1946, and subsequently poisoned with mercury by persons unknown at Michael Reese Hospital, when it appeared he might recover from his injuries. The CAPGA unit was dissolved soon after Ragen's death, in August 1946. Deputy Associate Director CARTHA DELOACH, ever loyal to Hoover's memory, reported years later that "quite suddenly, the attorney general, TOM CLARK, told us to discontinue our operations." Eleven more years would pass before the FBI took another crack at organized crime, with Hoover's "TOP HOODLUM PROGRAM" of 1957.

**CAPONE, Alphonse** —Arguably America's most flamboyant mobster from the Roaring Twenties, "Scarface Al" Capone was born in Brooklyn on 17 January 1899. Around age twenty, sought for questioning on murder charges, he moved to Chicago and found "muscle" work with mob boss Johnny Torrio. Rising swiftly through the ranks during Chicago's bootleg wars, Capone replaced Torrio in January 1925 and waged ruthless campaigns to suppress his competitors, climaxing with the machine-gun massacre of seven rivals on 14 February 1929. As described by Don Whitehead in *The FBI Story*, "Capone was virtually untouchable for years. But finally he made a slip and the FBI went after him."

Thus began the legend that the bureau and J. EDGAR HOOVER "got" Capone. In fact, the mobster's "slip" involved evasion of a federal subpoena calling him to testify in a Chicago liquor trial. Capone claimed illness, but G-men trailed him to the race track and watched him fly off for a Caribbean vacation. Arrested for contempt of court on 27 March 1929, Capone posted $5,000 bond and was instantly released. Six weeks later, unknown to the bureau, he led Chicago's delegation to a gangland conference in Atlantic City, where details of a national crime syndicate were arranged. On 16 May, by prearrangement with police, Capone was jailed in Philadelphia for carrying a pistol and received a one-year prison sentence, thereby hoping to appease some of the outrage generated by the St. Valentine's Day massacre. He served ten months, paroled on 16 March 1930.

The Chicago contempt charge caught up with Capone on 25 February 1931, when he received a six-month jail term. He was still confined on that charge when the INTERNAL REVENUE SERVICE indicted him for income tax evasion. On the eve of that trial, Hoover's G-men slapped Capone with some 5,000 bootlegging charges, but all were swiftly dismissed. Convicted of tax evasion on 17 October 1931, Capone was sentenced to eleven years in prison, paroled 16 November 1939. He died on 25 January 1947, a victim of untreated syphilis.

**CAPOTE, Truman** —A native of New Orleans, born Truman Streckfus Persons on 30 September 1924, Capote became one of modern America's most famous (and flamboyant) authors. The FBI first took notice of him on 13 December 1956, after learning that an unidentified surveillance target owned a copy of *The Muses Are Heard*, Capote's nonfiction account of an American drama troupe touring the Soviet Union. Thus began his 185-page file, fattened in 1959, when a Random House staffer called the FBI on Capote's behalf, seeking assistance on research for Capote's "nonfiction novel" *In Cold Blood.* Deputy Associate Director CARTHA DELOACH denied the request, asserting that the bureau "could not insert itself in a local murder case," but he later noted that "Mr. HOOVER liked *In Cold Blood* very much."

Hoover did not like much else about Capote, though. Aside from being HOMOSEXUAL, Capote was also deemed a dangerous radical. An FBI report of 18 April 1960 noted that he "supports the Revolution" in Cuba, and eight days later he was listed as a member of the leftist Fair Play for Cuba Committee. Most of Capote's file concerns Cuba, in fact, though he left the FPCC in 1963. Capote died in Los Angeles on 25 August 1994.

**CARMICHAEL, Stokely**—Born at Port of Spain, Trinidad on 29 June 1941, Stokely Carmichael immigrated to New York City with his family at age 11, graduated from the prestigious Bronx High School of Science in 1960, and thereafter studied philosophy at Howard University (1960-64). At Howard, Carmichael joined the STUDENT NONVIOLENT COORDINATING COMMITTEE (SNCC) and participated in the 1961 FREEDOM RIDES, spending seven weeks in jail at Jackson, Mississippi. Following his graduation with honors from Howard University, Carmichael joined SNCC's 1964 campaign to register black voters in "Bloody Lowndes" County, Alabama. There, he helped organize the Lowndes County Freedom Organization, which chose a snarling black panther as its emblem. Elected to serve as chairman of SNCC in 1966, he charted a militant course toward "Black Power" and joined colleague H. RAP BROWN in deleting "Nonviolent" from the organization's title.

By that time, Carmichael was already a subject of interest to J. EDGAR HOOVER and the FBI. Attorney General ROBERT KENNEDY had demanded a Bureau background check on Carmichael and five others after they staged an impromptu sit-in at Kennedy's office. A short time later, as a Mississippi Freedom Democratic Party delegate to the 1964 Democratic National Convention, Carmichael had been subjected to illegal FBI WIRETAPPING on orders from President LYNDON JOHNSON. In the wake of 1967's ghetto rioting, Hoover advised the KERNER COMMISSION that the violence derived from the "catalytic effect of extremists" and from the "vicious rhetoric" of black spokesmen like Carmichael, Brown, and Dr. MARTIN LUTHER KING, JR., Hoover specifically named Carmichael, Brown and King as "rabble rousers who initiate action and then disappear," while cities went up in flames.

Aside from ghetto activism, the year 1967 also witnessed Carmichael's expansion into VIETNAM WAR PROTESTS. One of his speeches particularly outraged the White House, when Carmichael declared that America's war in Asia "is for the birds—Lynda Bird, Lucy Bird, and Lady Bird." Roger Wilkins, then the highest-ranking African American in the JUSTICE DEPARTMENT, recalled that President Johnson "despised us ... because we wouldn't put Stokely Carmichael in jail." Johnson pressed Assistant Director CARTHA DELOACH to learn "if the FBI knew anything regarding the activities of King [or] Carmichael" and suggested an investigation by the HOUSE COMMITTEE ON UN-AMERICAN ACTIVITIES, but DeLoach discouraged that plan,

noting that public hearings "might react to their advantage rather than hurting them." At the same time, Assistant Attorney General Fred Vinson reported receiving "50 letters a week from Congress," demanding that "people like Carmichael be jailed."

Hoover and his G-men shared that sentiment, but they had difficulty finding evidence that would support a trial. On 25 August 1967 Hoover demanded "intensified action" against SNCC and five other activist groups. Assistant Director WILLIAM SULLIVAN's Domestic Intelligence Division planted an INFORMANT close to Carmichael, in the person of bodyguard Peter Cardoza, but later admitted that Cardoza was "a real discipline problem for the Bureau." The Bureau's sense of urgency intensified on 17 February 1968, when SNCC announced a merger with the militant BLACK PANTHER PARTY and Carmichael was named as the party's honorary prime minister. Two weeks later, a new Hoover memo ranked Carmichael among five "primary targets" for harassment in a drive to "prevent the rise of a 'messiah' who could unify, and electrify, the militant black nationalist movement."

William Sullivan—who personally donned a disguise to shadow Carmichael during the Poor People's March on Washington in spring 1968—considered Carmichael the only true "messiah" prospect on the list, dismissing the others as either too old or lacking "the necessary charisma." Accordingly, the FBI devised a plan to undermine Carmichael (and place his life at risk) by means of "SNITCH JACKETING." A memo to Hoover from the New York City field office, dated 10 July 1968, recommended that:

> ...consideration be given to convey the impression that Carmichael is a CIA informer. One method of accomplishing [this] would be to have a carbon copy of an informant report supposedly written by Carmichael to the CIA carefully deposited in the automobile of a close Black Nationalist friend.... It is hoped that when the informant report is read it will help promote distrust between Carmichael and the Black Community.... It is also suggested that we inform a certain percentage of reliable criminal and racial informants that "we have it from reliable sources that Carmichael is a CIA agent. It is hoped that the informants would spread the rumor in various large Negro communities across the land.

Two months later, with that plan still in the works, New York G-men reported to Hoover that "On 9/4/68, a pretext phone call was placed to the residence of Stokely Carmichael and in the absence of Carmichael his mother was told that a friend was calling who was fearful of the future safety of her son. It was explained to Mrs. Carmichael the absolute necessity for Carmichael to "hide out" inasmuch as several BPP members were out to kill him. Mrs. Carmichael appeared shocked upon hearing the news and stated she would tell Stokely when he came home."

The murder plot was an FBI fabrication, but Carmichael left on an extended tour of Africa the next day, seizing the opportunity to speak out against U.S. foreign policy in his travels. (The STATE DEPARTMENT suspended his passport for 10 months, upon his return.) In Carmichael's absence, the Bureau's San Francisco field office wrote Hoover of its plans to "assist" the Panther Party in expelling Carmichael. On 5 September 1970 Panther chief

Huey Newton declared, "We ... charge that Stokely Carmichael is operating as an agent of the CIA."

By that time, Carmichael had resigned from leadership of SNCC and U.S. with his new bride, South African singer Miriam Makeba. They settled in Guinea, West Africa, where Carmichael changed his name to Kwame Ture (in honor of early Pan-Africa spokesmen Kwame Nkrumah and Sékou Touré). In Guinea, Ture founded the All-African People's Revolutionary Party and became an aide to Guinea's Prime Minister, Ahmed Sekou Ture. A proponent of "scientific socialism" for the last three decades of his life, Ture/Carmichael died at Conakry, Guinea on 15 November 1998. To the end of his life, he habitually answered his telephone: "Ready for the revolution."

**CARNEGIE, Dale**—A child of poor Missouri farmers, born Dale Carnagey in 1888, America's future prophet of salesmanship moved to New York City in 1912, teaching his first public speaking class at the YMCA. Three years later he published his first book, *Talking to Win*, later changing the last two letters of his surname to match that of the fabulously wealthy Carnegie industrial clan. On 5 August 1936, J. EDGAR HOOVER ordered the FBI Communications Section to buy a copy of Carnegie's *Public Speaking and Influencing Men in Business*. The following year, Hoover "suggested" that Carnegie's most famous tome—*How to Win Friends and Influence People*—should be "adopted for parallel reading by all new Special Agents during the original training school."

The admiration was mutual. In 1938 Carnegie volunteered space in his newspaper column to Hoover "in your fight against crime." Hoover reciprocated with an invitation to FBI headquarters for a personal confab and "tour of inspection." The relationship apparently cooled during WORLD WAR II, secretary HELEN GANDY responding to Carnegie's request for an interview with the terse observation that Hoover's "duties with the war program have made it impossible for him to tell when he would be in New York again." Whatever the relationship, it was clear from Hoover's style that he ignored Carnegie's principles of leadership, especially No. 4: "Talk about your own mistakes before criticizing the other person." Collection of memos in Carnegie's file continued until his death, in 1955.

**"CARNIVORE"**—Created in February 1997 and nicknamed "Omnivore," this Internet "sniffer" device was renamed "Carnivore" in June 2000 to support the FBI's assertion that it captures only "meaty" data authorized for interception by federal court orders in criminal cases. Bureau publicists maintain that "[t]he Carnivore device provides the FBI with a 'surgical' ability to intercept and collect the communications which are the subject of the lawful order while ignoring those communications which they are not authorized to intercept. This type of tool is necessary to meet the stringent requirements of the federal wiretapping statutes."

Given the FBI's long history of illegal surveillance and flagrant evasion of federal statutory limitations, civil libertarians were naturally concerned by the implications of Carnivore's Internet scanning. On 18 July 2000, one week after the system's existence was broadcast, leaders of the Electronic Information Privacy Center (EPIC) filed a FREEDOM OF INFORMATION ACT request seeking all available data on the system's operation and capabilities. EPIC subsequently filed a federal lawsuit when the JUSTICE DEPARTMENT failed to meet its statutory deadline for disclosure. On 2 August 2000, U.S. District Judge James Robertson ordered the FBI to report back by 16 August, identifying the amount of material at issue and providing a timeline for its release. The bureau subsequently reported that 3,000 pages of "responsive" material had been located, but no deadline for release was forthcoming. In late January 2001 the FBI revised its previous estimate, asserting that only 1,756 pages of Carnivore data existed; 1,502 heavily edited pages were ultimately released, while another 254 were withheld in their entirety.

Based on the partial documents released, computer experts have challenged the FBI's description of Carnivore as a "surgical" sniffer. In fact, as EPIC's David Sobel notes, "The little information that has become public raises serious questions about the privacy implications of this technology. The American public cannot be expected to accept an Internet snooping system that is veiled in secrecy." Analysts note that Carnivore can theoretically scan millions of e-mails per second, processing up to six gigabytes of data per hour. Critics remain skeptical of FBI claims that "the system is not susceptible to abuse because it requires expertise to install and operate."

**CARROLL, Joseph F.**—Born in 1910, Joseph Carroll joined the FBI at age 30 and served as an agent for seven years, thereafter resigning to lead the newly created U.S. Air Force Office of Special Investigations (OSI). That post made responsible for espionage and counterintelligence activities, as well as internal reviews of the Air Force itself. In 1959 Carroll was appointed to serve as Air Force chief of staff in Europe. Two years later, following the Bay of Pigs fiasco, President JOHN KENNEDY chose Carroll to head a new Defense Intelligence Agency (DIA), coordinating activities of the U.S. intelligence community to avoid redundancy and minimize future embarrassment. Carroll retired in 1969 and died in 1991.

**CARTER, James Earl, Jr.**—Born at Plains, Georgia on 1 October 1924, James Carter served in the U.S. Navy (1946-53) before resigning to join the family farm and warehouse business. He subsequently entered Democratic Party politics, serving as chairman of the Sumter County school board (1955-62), in the state senate (1963-66) and as governor of Georgia (1971-75). Assisted by the WATERGATE SCANDAL and disclosures of the CHURCH COMMITTEE, Carter campaigned for president in 1976 with the motto "I'll never lie to you," and thus defeated incumbent GERALD FORD.

Despite Carter's commitment to integrity, his administration was not immune to scandal. Campaign manager Bert Lance was forced to resign as director of the Office of Management and Budget in September 1977, following indictment on 33 counts related to his shady banking practices in Georgia. (A court dismissed 14 counts, jurors acquitted Lance on six, and the rest were dropped in exchange for a consent decree vowing that Lance would henceforth obey the law.) A greater embarrassment was brother Billy Carter, who accepted $220,000 from alleged Libyan TERRORIST ringleader Muammar Qaddafi while failing to register as a foreign agent.

In regard to the FBI, Carter responded to the revelations of abuse under Director CLARENCE KELLEY by deciding that a judge should be the Bureau's next director. Attorney General GRIFFIN BELL suggested three candidates, and Carter chose WILLIAM WEBSTER, confirmed as director in February 1978. Spurred by the conviction of FBI officials EDWARD MILLER and MARK FELT for ordering illegal BREAK-INS, Carter's EXECUTIVE ORDER 12036 restricted Bureau activities in the fields of foreign intelligence and DOMESTIC SURVEILLANCE. On 25 October 1978 Carter signed the Foreign Intelligence Surveillance Act, creating a special secret court to review government appeals for permission to indulge in WIRETAPPING or BUGGING of foreign agents.

On the domestic front, UNDERCOVER OPERATIONS against corrupt officials and members of ORGANIZED CRIME became more frequent and successful under Carter, producing indictments against Mafia leaders in Buffalo, Chicago, Cleveland Detroit, Kansas City, Los Angeles, Milwaukee, New Orleans, Philadelphia, Rhode Island and Tucson. Ironically, while most of those cases would end with convictions, their protracted litigation dragged on into the 1980s and President RONALD REAGAN reaped the credit (though he personally showed no enthusiasm for prosecuting mobsters). Where venal politicians were concerned, sting operations such as BRILAB produced sufficient controversy that Attorney General BENJAMIN CIVILETTI established new guidelines for FBI undercover operations in the final days of the Carter administration.

Those final days were hastened by the Iranian revolution and a militant seizure of the U.S. embassy in Teheran on 4 November 1979, one year to the day before the 1980 presidential election. Carter was defeated in that race and retired to private life — which, in his case, meant a more hectic schedule of foreign travel and diplomatic negotiations than ever before. In 2002 he received a Nobel Peace Prize for his efforts to resolve the long-running Arab-Israeli conflict in the Middle East.

**CATHER, Willa** — Born Willella Sibert Cather in Virginia, on 7 December 1873, this famous American novelist rated a brief (six-page) FBI file which remains closed to public scrutiny despite her death, in New Hampshire, on 24 April 1947. The Bureau excuses its continuing secrecy on grounds that most of the material in Cather's file pertains to a different, unidentified person.

**CENTRAL Intelligence Agency** — Before WORLD WAR II the U.S. maintained no permanent agency to conduct foreign ESPIONAGE. In July 1941 President FRANKLIN ROOSEVELT created the Office of the Coordinator of Information under chief WILLIAM DONOVAN, renamed the OFFICE OF STRATEGIC SERVICES (OSS) in 1942. FBI Director J. EDGAR HOOVER hated Donovan and refused to withdraw his SPECIAL INTELLIGENCE SERVICE (SIS) agents from Latin America, a feud resolved in Hoover's favor when Roosevelt gave the FBI primary jurisdiction over espionage cases in the western hemisphere. The OSS was dissolved in 1945, but President HARRY TRUMAN created a new Central Intelligence Group on 22 January 1946 (renamed with its present title in 1947). Hoover demanded control of the new organization, but Truman refused. When Hoover persisted, Truman committed the unpardonable sin of telling Hoover, "You're getting out of bounds." Thus began Hoover's seven-year feud with Truman and an FBI-CIA rivalry that endures to the present day.

Hoover struck his first blow when he was commanded to deliver all FBI operations in Latin America to the new agency. Instead, he ordered all SIS agents south of the border to burn their FILES and dismiss their INFORMANTS. A CIA agent later described the result: "The only thing I found when the Bureau left was a row of empty safes and a pair of rubber gloves in what had been an FBI darkroom." When called to account for his childish insubordination, Hoover produced testimony from professional informant ELIZABETH BENTLEY to suggest that the OSS — and by extension, its successor organization — had been heavily infiltrated by communists. At the same time, to Hoover's chagrin, some of his key SIS agents defected to the CIA, thus enabling the agency to reestablish links throughout Latin America.

Hoover managed to block William Donovan's appointment as director of the CIA, but he was equally unhappy with the President DWIGHT EISENHOWER's selection of ALLEN DULLES in 1953. Hoover regarded the whole Dulles family as suspect, dubbing them "internationalists" with "communist leanings." Hoover maintained a thick file on Dulles prior to 1953, including rumors of his numerous love affairs, and the dossier grew rapidly after Dulles was installed as CIA director. Hoover's enmity only increased as Dulles took steps to weed out or neutralize FBI "moles" within the agency. A rare moment of cooperation arrived in 1954, when the FBI and CIA drafted an agreement that effectively put both above the law: in the event that an agent of either group was caught breaking the law in pursuit of a "national security" case, Hoover and Dulles agreed, the offender would be reported to his own superiors without involving any other law enforcement agency. Since BREAK-INS and other criminal acts were routinely approved in advance by FBI HEADQUARTERS, the agreement added one more layer of insulation between Hoover and a potentially disastrous scandal.

In the early 1960s Hoover kept abreast of CIA collaboration with leaders of ORGANIZED CRIME in their efforts to kill Cuban leader Fidel Castro, and he was constantly aware of CIA trespasses in the field of DOMESTIC SURVEILLANCE (legally barred to the CIA by terms of its charter). On occasion the FBI performed BUGGING and WIRETAPPING missions at the CIA's request, but Hoover was as likely to betray the rival agency as to provide assistance.

Rivalry between the FBI and CIA took a drastic turn for the worse in 1970, as a result of a missing-person case in Denver. Professor Thomas Riha, an instructor in Russian history at the University of Colorado who also worked part time for the CIA, had vanished from home without explanation in 1969. The FBI knew his whereabouts but refused to share the information until early 1970, when an agent in Denver leaked details to the CIA's station chief. Hoover learned of the betrayal and demanded the G-man's name, but CIA spokesmen refused to divulge it as "a point of honor and personal integrity." Hoover's response was a furious memo: "This is not satisfactory. I want our Denver office to have absolutely no contacts with CIA. I want direct liaison here with CIA terminated & any contact with CIA in the future to be only by letter."

Hoover's rift with the CIA inspired President RICHARD NIXON to seek ways of consolidating America's intelligence agencies. One result was the HUSTON PLAN, staunchly opposed by Hoover and exposed after his death in the midst of the WATERGATE SCANDAL. Hoover's passing generally improved the FBI-CIA working relationship, but natural rivalry tempered with 25 years of outright hostility ensured that the two agencies would always deal with one another at arm's length. The nearest thing to a bridge was achieved in May 1987, when FBI Director WILLIAM WEBSTER resigned after nine years with the Bureau to become director of the CIA. Still, 14 years later, critics charged that stinginess with information had prevented G-men and CIA agents from cooperating to prevent the catastrophic SKYJACKINGS of 11 September 2001.

**CHANDLER, Albert Benjamin**—A native of Corydon, Kentucky, born 14 July 1898, A.B. ("Happy") Chandler served as governor from 1936 to 1939, then occupied a U.S. Senate seat from 1939 until 1945. He resigned that year to serve as national baseball commissioner, a post he held until 1951. Reelected as Kentucky's governor in 1955, he supported court-ordered school desegregation between 1956 and 1959. Subsequent gubernatorial races in 1963, 1967 and 1971 were unsuccessful.

In May 1970, Chandler physically assaulted a student peace demonstrator on the University of Kentucky campus in Lexington. J. EDGAR HOOVER learned of the incident and sent a personal letter of commendation to Chandler for the criminal assault, stating that if such "prompt action" were taken across the country, student protests would be eliminated. Chandler's reaction to the note is unrecorded. He died at Versailles, Kentucky on 15 June 1991.

**CHAPLIN, Charles Spencer**—A British subject, born 16 April 1889, Charlie Chaplin was raised in London's slums. His father was a vaudeville performer and Chaplin followed the family tradition, joining a traveling music-hall troupe at age 21. He immigrated to the U.S. and joined Mack Sennett's Keystone Studios in 1913, directing and starring in silent comedies that featured his alter-ego, the Tramp. By 1919 Chaplin had built his own movie studio and co-founded United Artists with Douglas Fairbanks, Mary Pickford and director David Wark Griffith. That move—and his huge fan base—granted Chaplin unique independence in an era when Hollywood studio heads controlled most of the U.S. motion picture industry.

The Bureau of Investigation noted Chaplin's liberal politics in 1922, but most of his 2,063-page dossier revolved around investigations started in the 1940s. The first was opened in 1943, after actress Joan Berry filed a paternity suit against Chaplin, naming him as the father of a child she expected to deliver that October. Blood tests exonerated Chaplin, but since the results were then deemed inadmissible in California courts, he was

nonetheless ordered to make modest support payments until the child's eighteenth birthday. In the meantime, federal prosecutors charged Chaplin with a MANN ACT violation and with violating Barry's CIVIL RIGHTS, but both counts were dismissed in 1945. Despite that fact, Barry's case provides the bulk of Chaplin's FBI FILE, with two massive reports (dated 25 February 1944 and 4 May 1944) providing 450 pages, while additional memos and newspaper clippings account for another 800 pages. The clippings reveal Chaplin's emergence as an ideological pawn of right- and left-wing journalists, the former painting him as a villainous satyr while the latter portray him as a hapless victim.

FBI Director J. EDGAR HOOVER was more interested in Chaplin's politics than in his sex life. That interest intensified after WORLD WAR II, with the advent of a new Red scare focused on Hollywood. FBI HEADQUARTERS dusted off a 1923 article praising Chaplin in the Soviet newspaper *Pravda*, and Hoover requested an update on Chaplin's political activities from the Los Angeles field office. He received a 23-page report on 6 August 1947, and the mass of paperwork would ultimately grow to 726 pages detailing Chaplin's alleged "subversive" tendencies. Chaplin and his family returned to London in September 1952, for a film premiere, and Attorney General JAMES MCGRANERY revoked the star's reentry permit two days later, demanding that Chaplin prove himself morally and politically fit before he returned to the U.S. G-men spent most of that fall and winter seeking evidence to bar Chaplin's return, and while they found no evidence of any criminal activity, Chaplin elected to spend the rest of his life at a villa near Vevey, Switzerland.

The Los Angeles field office officially closed Chaplin's case on 10 July 1953, at Hoover's instruction, but the FBI kept tabs on Chaplin for the rest of his life. Notations were added to his file in 1962, when Chaplin received two honorary degrees from the British University. G-men were watching in 1972, when Chaplin briefly returned to accept an Academy Award in Hollywood, and they filed a memo when he was knighted in 1975. Two years later, on 25 December 1977, Chaplin died at home in Switzerland. His dossier should logically have ended there, but the FBI filed updates when his corpse was stolen for ransom on 2 March 1978. A psychic telephoned the Bureau's field office in Portland, Maine with hints on where the body might be found, but agents ignored the tip. The culprits were arrested on 17 May 1978, and Chaplin's corpse was found in a cornfield and restored to its proper resting place.

**CHEEVER, John**—Born in 1912, acclaimed novelist and short story author John Cheever apparently drew FBI attention for the first time on 18 June 1965. Contents of his four-page file reveal at least one bureau tap on Cheever's telephone, but the motive for surveillance remains obscure, since most of the remaining documents were blacked out by FBI censors prior to their release under the FREEDOM OF INFORMATION ACT. It is known that copies of one report on Cheever were sent to bureau field offices in Louisville, New Orleans, New York and Washington, as well as FBI legal attachés in Bonn and London, but again the reasons are unknown. Another cryptic report from Cleveland, filed in 1969, quotes a nameless informant as stating that "he did not know the

Cheever family personally." Cheever died in 1982, unaware of the FBI's apparently pointless surveillance.

**CHICAGO Defender**— Publisher Robert Abbott produced the first issue of the *Chicago Defender* on 5 May 1905, after spending 25 cents to print 300 copies. The newspaper was an immediate success, claiming 67,000 nationwide subscribers by 1917. Its articles angered white racists by condemning LYNCHING and race riots (primarily a white activity until the 1960s), and by urging blacks to leave the rural South in favor of northern cities where jobs were abundant. During WORLD WAR I, bigots complained that the *Defender* was in league with Germany, working to incite a black revolt against the status quo.

Those complaints reached the Bureau of Investigation, where chief A. BRUCE BIELASKI ordered three investigations of the *Defender*'s alleged subversive activity between 1917 and 1919. G-men worked with agents from the post office and military intelligence to suppress the newspaper by any means available, blaming the *Defender* for several riots that were, in fact, white massacres of African Americans. When Chicago blacks defended themselves against white mobs in July 1919, killing 15 would-be lynchers (versus 23 blacks killed, with more than 1,000 homes burned), it was viewed as further evidence of the *Defender*'s "subversive" impact.

Postal authorities never found an excuse to ban mailing of the *Defender*, but G-men kept watch on the paper, shadowing its publisher and reporters. By mid-1921 J. EDGAR HOOVER required each Bureau field office to file a "Monthly Report on Radical Publications," and the *Defender* was promoted to "ultraradical" status for articles including its "vicious" denunciation of the violent KU KLUX KLAN. (Klan threats to the *Defender*'s staff were ignored by the Bureau.) Federal interest in the *Defender* waned over time, as Hoover and his agents were distracted by "enemy aliens" and the COMMUNIST PARTY, then by a rash of BANK ROBBERY and KIDNAPPING in the 1930s. In 1940, publisher Abbott's nephew and heir, John Sengstacke, assumed control of the *Defender* and founded the National Negro Publishers Association (now the National Newspaper Publishers Association). Sengstacke changed the paper's title to the *Chicago Daily Defender* in 1956, adding it to a chain of newspapers that eventually included the *Pittsburgh Courier*, Detroit's *Michigan Chronicle* and the *Tri-State Defender* in Memphis. Sengstacke remained as publisher until his death in May 1997.

**CHICAGO Police Department**—Best known until 1968 for its corrupt alliance with ORGANIZED CRIME, the Chicago Police Department has also been extremely active in political surveillance—so active, in fact, that author Frank Donner once dubbed Chicago "the national capital of police repression." Official conflict with ANARCHISTS and LABOR UNIONS dates from the 19th century, while later targets of surveillance and harassment included the COMMUNIST PARTY and the INDUSTRIAL WORKERS OF THE WORLD. FBI agents kept abreast of those campaigns and cooperated when they could, while ignoring (and publicly denying) the existence of syndicated crime in the Windy City. Occasional insults, such as G-man MELVIN PURVIS's decision to capture JOHN DILLINGER

without informing local police, never truly jeopardize the joint pursuit of persons and organizations branded "subversive."

By 1960 Chicago's intelligence unit had collected files on 117,000 "local individuals," plus 141,000 out-of-towners and some 14,000 suspect organizations. Subjects included the STUDENTS FOR A DEMOCRATIC SOCIETY and its offshoot WEATHERMAN UNDERGROUND, the SOUTHERN CHRISTIAN LEADERSHIP CONFERENCE, and various organizations opposed to the VIETNAM WAR. Agents of the FBI's Chicago field office frequently shared information with police, as in Chicago's 1966 campaign against JOIN (Jobs or Income Now), which climaxed with a raid on the group's office. Two years later, televised incidents of POLICE BRUTALITY during the Democratic National Convention shocked America. (Congressional investigators dubbed the incident a "police riot.") At the same time, in 1968-69, police collaborated with the FBI's illegal COINTELPRO operations against the BLACKSTONE RANGERS and the BLACK PANTHER PARTY. Armed with floor plans drawn by an FBI INFORMANT, Chicago police invaded the home of Chicago Panther chief FRED HAMPTON in December 1969 and killed him while he slept. (It now appears that Hampton was drugged before the raid, by the same Bureau informant who sketched his apartment for police.)

In 1970 the Chicago police department had 382 officers assigned to its intelligence unit, 49 committed full-time to investigation of "subversive" activities (as opposed to actual crimes). Citywide, more than 1,000 federal, state and city agents were engaged in UNDERCOVER OPERATIONS, spending an estimated $2 million that year in pursuit of alleged traitors. Chicago's Subversive Activities Unit received a broader mandate in 1971, ordered "through covert and over activity" to gather intelligence on all "organizations and individuals which present a threat to the security of the country, state or city." That mandate was renewed in 1973, with a special "dirty tricks" campaign inaugurated in 1974, to "neutralize" various targets by causing them "to cease or change direction." Exposure of illicit activities embarrassed the department in 1974, and by year's end police spokesmen admitted destroying files on 1,300 organizations and 105,000 individuals (thus concealing the names of 220 informants). No surveys of police surveillance have been made since the 1970s, but minority groups and civil libertarians suggest that the problem is ongoing.

**CHILD Abduction**—It is a cause for some alarm that no American governmental agency keeps accurate statistics on children kidnapped each year. In 1984 the U.S. Department of Health and Human Resources estimated that 1.8 million children vanish from home annually: 95 percent were listed as runaways, and 90 percent of those returned home within two weeks, leaving 171,000 children at large on the streets, their whereabouts unknown. Five percent of the missing—some 90,000—were identified as abductees, with 72,000 kidnapped by parents in custody disputes. The other 18,000 were simply gone.

The FBI cast doubt on those statistics in 1987, reporting that its agents investigated only 150 "stranger abductions" of children between 1984 and 1986, but what does that disclaimer prove? G-men normally remain aloof from kidnap cases in the absence of ransom demands or interstate abduction, and they take no notice of alleged runaways. Indeed, the FBI statistics are suspect, since bureau spokesmen radically changed their tune in 1995, admitting reports of 300 stranger abductions *per year* in the United States.

One response to that crisis is the Child Abduction and Serial Killer Unit (CASKU), created by Congress in 1994. As described in FBI literature, the unit consists of a chief and twelve agents, nine of whom hold unspecified "advanced degrees." While dominated by the FBI, CASKU also includes representatives of the U.S. SECRET SERVICE, the U.S. Customs Service, the U.S. Postal Service, the DRUG ENFORCEMENT ADMINISTRATION, and the BUREAU OF ALCOHOL, TOBACCO AND FIREARMS. According to its mission statement, "CASKU's primary objective is the safe return of the victim." Any successes in that area to date have been kept carefully under wraps.

**CHRISTIAN Front**—The brainchild of Detroit's Rev. Charles Coughlin, a Catholic priest known for his radio diatribes attacking Jews and President FRANKLIN ROOSEVELT, the Christian Front was organized in early 1938. Instructions printed in Coughlin's newsletter *Social Justice*, on 22 May 1938, urged would-be leaders of the movement to

> Let your organization be composed of no more than 25 members. After a few contacts with these 25 persons you will observe that two of them may be capable of organizing 25 more. Invite these capable people to do that very thing.

The Christian Front's first and largest chapter was organized in New York City, where it met weekly in the basement of the Church of St. Paul the Apostle. Some members affected Nazi-style uniforms, banding together in "goon squads" notorious for their verbal and physical assaults on Jewish merchants. On 31 July 1939 *Social Justice* hailed the Front as "the inevitable counteraction to Communism" and "a protector of Christianity and Americanism." A nationwide membership of five million was predicted for the following year.

On 14 January 1940, journalists were summoned to the FBI's New York field office, where J. EDGAR HOOVER personally announced the arrest of seventeen Christian Fronters, charged with stealing weapons from a National Guard armory as part of a "vast plot" to overthrow the U.S. government and establish a fascist dictatorship. When one of the reporters asked how such a small group could execute a "vast" conspiracy, Hoover replied (inaccurately), "It only took twenty-three men to overthrow Russia."

At trial, in April 1940, the Christian Front defendants were accused of plotting to foment race warfare in America. As outlined by the prosecution, "the ultimate idea was to incite Jews to riot and then have a revolution and a counter revolution." Despite testimony from FBI INFORMANT Denis Healy that the Front was "growing by leaps and bounds," training special teams "to eradicate the Jews," hard evidence of criminal conspiracy was slim to nonexistent. Defense attorneys questioned Healy's role and cast doubt on his actions as an *agent provocateur*. None of the defendants were convicted, but public embarrassment did not

prevent Hoover from trying a similar ploy thirty years later, against the BERRIGAN brothers.

**CHURCH Committee**—Idaho senator Frank Church served as chairman of the U.S. Senate's Select Committee on Government Intelligence Activities, better known as the Church Committee. Active during the term of the 94th Congress (1975-77), it took public and private testimony from hundreds of witnesses and collected thousands of classified FILES from the FBI, the CENTRAL INTELLIGENCE AGENCY, the INTERNAL REVENUE SERVICE, the NATIONAL SECURITY AGENCY and other federal investigative bodies. The committee issued 14 reports before it was dissolved, but much of the original reference material remained secret until 1992, when passage of the JFK ASSASSINATION Records Collection Act declassified more than 50,000 documents.

After interrogating FBI officials, INFORMANTS and victims of harassment, the Church Committee had this to say about J. EDGAR HOOVER'S motives for initiating illegal "COINTELPRO" campaigns:

> Protecting national security and preventing violence are the purposes advanced by the Bureau for COINTELPRO. There is another purpose for COINTELPRO which is not explicit but which offers the only explanation for those actions which had no conceivable rational relationship to either national security or violent activity. The unexpressed major premise of much of COINTELPRO is that the Bureau has a role in maintaining the existing social order, and that its efforts should be aimed toward combating those who threaten that order.

With respect to FBI claims that COINTELPRO activities were discontinued after May 1971, Senator Church and his colleagues reported:

> The Committee has not been able to determine with any greater precision the extent to which COINTELPRO may be continuing. Any proposals to initiate COINTELPRO-type action would be filed under the individual case caption. The Bureau has over 500,000 case files, and each one would have to be searched. In this context, it should be noted that a Bureau search of all field office COINTELPRO files revealed the existence of five operations [conducted after May 1971]. A search of all investigative files might be similarly productive.

More disturbing than concealment of records, however, was the committee's discovery that "[a]ttitudes within and without the Bureau demonstrate a continued belief by some that covert action against American citizens is permissible if the need for it is strong enough." Based on that conclusion, the committee declared in its final report that:

> The American people need to be assured that never again will an agency of the government be permitted to conduct a secret war against those citizens it considers threats to the established order. Only a combination of legislative prohibition and Departmental control can guarantee that COINTELPRO will not happen again.

Ending on a pessimistic note, the Church Committee noted that "Whether the Attorney General can control the Bureau is still an open question." In fact, as events since 1976 have revealed, neither the JUSTICE DEPARTMENT nor the White House has been able to restrain FBI DOMESTIC SURVEILLANCE—if, in fact, they had any serious inclination to do so.

**CITIZENS' Councils**—The first Citizens' Council was organized in Sunflower County, Mississippi, in July 1954, in response to the U.S. Supreme Court's order for desegregation of public schools. Its slogan — "Never!" — fairly summarized the organization's attitude on compliance with civil rights laws, although the Councils adopted a "respectable" façade in contrast to the violence of the KU KLUX KLAN. According to their spokesmen, the Councils preferred "education" (generally consisting of accusations that civil rights leaders were communists or sexual deviants) and "peaceful" economic measures (such as boycotts and dismissal of black activists from their jobs). Active in eleven southern states by 1960, the Councils also planted scattered outposts in the North and West, where racial crises were reported.

J. EDGAR HOOVER rendered his verdict on the Citizens' Councils on 1 March 1956, in a report on southern race relations offered to the cabinet of President DWIGHT EISENHOWER. In that statement, Hoover blamed "the specter of racial intermarriages" and "mixed education" for mounting violence in Dixie, noting that "Delicate situations are aggravated by some overzealous but ill-advised leaders of the NAACP and by the COMMUNIST PARTY, which seeks to use incidents to further the so-called class struggle." Hoover deemed the 50,000-member KKK "pretty much defunct," while the Citizens' Councils enlisted "the leading citizens of the South," including "bankers, lawyers, doctors, state legislators and industrialists."

In fact, Hoover knew — or should have known — that members of the "respectable" Councils openly collaborated with the Klan in several states and were responsible for many acts of violence on their own. Council members in Birmingham, Alabama assaulted black singer Nat ("King") Cole during a 1956 concert and castrated a second victim in 1957. BYRON DE LA BECKWITH, the assassin of civil rights activist Medgar Evers, was a prominent member of the Mississippi Citizens' Council. Threats from known members of the Mississippi Council also preceded the shooting of NAACP activists GEORGE LEE and GUS COURTS. Emmett Miller, founder of the Council in Little Rock, Arkansas, was jailed for planting dynamite at an all-black college in 1960, but charges were dropped after FBI leaders refused to identify their informants in that case. (A second Arkansas Council leader, E.A. Lauderdale, was imprisoned for bombings in a separate case.) Elsewhere — in Texas, Tennessee and Louisiana — Council meetings erupted into full-scale riots against blacks.

Despite such incidents, the FBI refrained from launching an investigation of the Councils, even when requested by members of the U.S. Civil Rights Commission. BURKE MARSHALL, assigned to the Commission by Attorney General ROBERT KENNEDY, complained, "We have never had any formal [FBI] investigation of the Mississippi Council. We have also had no results from suggestions that the bureau should keep itself informed in the same way it does with the Klan." No such investigation was forthcoming, but the Councils faded away in the latter 1960s, abandoned by die-hard racists when their "peaceful" methods failed

to preserve segregation. Hoover's admiration for the movement was never publicly renounced.

**CIVIL Rights**—In 1953, after Florida governor Allan Shivers criticized the FBI for "snooping" in a civil rights case already investigated by state authorities, Director J. EDGAR HOOVER indignantly replied:

> We of the FBI certainly have no apologies to make to anyone for doing our duty in carrying out the instructions of the Attorney General in enforcing the law of the land. Should the day ever come when the Director of the Federal Bureau of Investigation has the discretion of choosing those laws which his service will enforce, then indeed we will have a Gestapo, and I can assure you I would have no part of it.

The irony of that statement, revealed at his death nearly two decades later, was that Hoover had routinely stalled, sidetracked and buried civil rights investigations throughout his tenure as director. Ultraconservative political philosophy tainted Hoover's every move where race relations were concerned, and his personal racism verged on the pathological, affecting even cases where no racial issues were involved. (In 1949, when Attorney General TOM CLARK asked Hoover to investigate the attempted murder of union leader Victor Reuther, the strange answer came back: "Edgar says no. He says he's not going to get involved every time some nigger woman gets raped.")

Congress passed its first federal statutes to protect the rights of black Americans in 1866 and 1870, the latter specifically designed to punish crimes committed by the KU KLUX KLAN. Over the next 10 years, however, various decisions by the U.S. SUPREME COURT combined to restrict U.S. authority in civil rights cases. By the time the FBI was created in 1908, those rulings generally restricted federal prosecution to state officials who conspired specifically to violate a victim's civil rights (as in preventing blacks from voting). HATE CRIMES committed by private individuals or groups without official collusion were thereby excluded, and no prosecution was undertaken without evidence of a conspiracy to deprive the victim(s) of specific federally protected rights.

That situation suited Hoover perfectly, and he used judicial precedent to justify inaction in cases where the FBI had clear jurisdiction. From 1939 to 1947 the Bureau accepted complaints alleging federal civil rights violations but investigated those complaints only at the specific request of the JUSTICE DEPARTMENT'S Criminal Investigation Division. Attorney General Clark revised the policy in April 1947, authorizing G-men "to conduct preliminary investigations of any civil rights complaints or incidents upon its own motion," but Hoover told his aides that Clark's directive was "not to be construed as changing the existing instructions." Attorney General J. HOWARD McGRATH raised the ante in December 1951 telling Hoover: "I wish to make it clear that the Bureau can in the first instance originate, initiate, and carry through to a conclusion any investigation within its jurisdiction." More specifically, McGrath granted "blanket authority to conduct full and complete investigations in [civil rights] cases." Hoover, with no interest in such matters, ordered all field offices to proceed on "undesirable" or "potentially embarrassing" cases only with direct orders from FBI HEADQUARTERS. By October 1952 he had persuaded Attorney General JAMES MCGRANERY to rescind McGrath's directive altogether.

Under President DWIGHT EISENHOWER, while a more liberal Supreme Court increased pressure on the civil rights front, Hoover staged a one-man battle to eliminate such cases from the FBI's workload. By 1958 he had secured revisions in Justice Department policy on matters ranging from PEONAGE to POLICE BRUTALITY, declaring all previous guidelines "permissive rather than mandatory." Henceforth, the Bureau refused even preliminary civil rights investigations without specific orders from the Attorney General on a case-be-case basis — and even when such orders were received, as in the Mississippi cases of victims GUS COURTS and GEORGE LEE, G-men habitually reported "insufficient evidence" for prosecution. When Klansmen turned to widespread BOMBING in the 1950s, striking integrated schools and other public buildings, the FBI largely ignored it. Hoover forbade his agents from cooperating with the SOUTHERN CONFERENCE ON BOMBING, and a special bombing clause in the Civil Rights Act of 1960 — permitting FBI investigation of such cases on a "rebuttable presumption" that explosives were transported interstate — did nothing to improve the Bureau's record of arrests.

In lieu of performance, Hoover relied on statistics to paint the FBI as a veritable beehive of civil rights activity. Before 1959 the Bureau's annual reports tabulated the number of civil rights investigations conducted each year — e.g., 1,269 in 1958 — without disclosing the number of indictments or convictions. Starting in 1959, FBI reports listed the number of civil rights complaints *received*, without even tabulating the investigations authorized. The result was a paper façade of devoted attention, with little of nothing behind it. In the five years between 1960 and 1964, for example, the FBI "handled" 11,328 civil rights cases and obtained only 14 convictions (barely one-tenth of one percent).

Despite such minimal results, friendly journalists played Hoover's numbers game to cast the FBI as a bastion of civil rights protection. Authors Harry and Bonaro Overstreet provide a typical example, from *The FBI in Our Open Society* (1969). They write:

> In 1961, at the [Justice] department's request, the FBI conducted a survey of 294 cities in 17 states to determine whether or not interstate bus passengers were being subjected to segregationist practices. Evidence of segregation was found in 97 cities. Armed with this evidence, the department secured from the Interstate Commerce Commission a ruling to end such practices.

A casual reader might infer that the FBI ended segregation in interstate travel by bus, but such is not the case. The Overstreets omit all mention of the 1961 FREEDOM RIDES, organized by the CONGRESS OF RACIAL EQUALITY to test southern compliance with previous Supreme Court orders requiring integration of all interstate transportation facilities. When the mixed group of riders rolled southward in May 1961, FBI agents provided their itinerary to Alabama policemen known as members or associates of the KKK. FBI INFORMANTS in the Klan warned G-men of a conspiracy between Klansmen and Birmingham police to assault

the freedom riders (the plot itself a federal crime), but agents allowed the riots to proceed on schedule, filming the attacks from a safe distance. Years later, the FBI was sued by two injured riders and lost its case in federal court.

Hoover's stubborn inaction on civil rights cases stood in sharp contrast to his frantic pursuit of any and all minority groups that pressed their case for equal treatment under law. Without exception, Hoover regarded such organizations as "radical," "subversive," and/or "Communist-infiltrated." From 1919 to the moment of his death in 1972, Hoover authorized sweeping (frequently illegal) surveillance and harassment of such groups as MARCUS GARVEY'S Universal Negro Improvement Association, the AFRICAN BLOOD BROTHERHOOD, the NATIONAL ASSOCIATION FOR THE ADVANCEMENT OF COLORED PEOPLE, the NATION OF ISLAM, the STUDENT NONVIOLENT COORDINATING COMMITTEE, the SOUTHERN CHRISTIAN LEADERSHIP CONFERENCE and the BLACK PANTHER PARTY. Subsequent FBI directors extended those investigations to the AMERICAN INDIAN MOVEMENT and similar groups, employing the same illicit tactics. In 2002, following the terrorist attacks of "9-11," Muslim Americans complained of identical surveillance and harassment by the Bureau under Director ROBERT MUELLER III and Attorney General JOHN ASHCROFT.

The modern FBI's Internet website lists 10 Bureau priorities. Protecting civil rights ranks fifth, in the middle of the pack, but long-term observers of FBI performance recall the traditional gap between lip service and real-world performance. They also recall that if Truth is the first casualty in a self-declared war (against terrorism, crime, or any other "enemy"), civil liberties are typically the next to fall.

**CIVILETTI, Benjamin Richard** — Born at Peekskill, New York on 17 July 1935, Benjamin Civiletti served as President JAMES CARTER'S second attorney general. He assumed office on 16 August 1979 and remained until the inauguration of President RONALD REAGAN on 19 January 1981. Civiletti's primary contribution came a mere two weeks before he left office, with the issuance of new guidelines governing FBI UNDERCOVER OPERATIONS on 5 January 1981. Those rules, created in the wake of controversy over the BRILAB and CORKSCREW operations in 1980, remain in force today with only minor alterations.

Civiletti's guidelines divided Bureau undercover operations into two broad categories. The first, requiring approval from the FBI director and the Bureau's Undercover Operations Review Committee, include all investigations lasting longer than six months and/or involving any of various "sensitive" areas: foreign governments; religious or political organizations; public officials; the news media; domestic security; any case where an agent might break the law (except for buying or selling stolen property and/or concealing his/her identity); any case where an agent will pose as a lawyer, doctor, journalist or member of the clergy; any case where an agent may attend meetings between the target and his/her attorney; or any case involving significant risk of physical injury or financial loss.

**CLARK, Thomas Campbell** — A native Texan, born 23 September 1899, Tom Clark served with distinction in WORLD WAR I before entering private law practice. President HARRY TRUMAN chose him to replace Attorney General FRANCIS BIDDLE, with Clark assuming office on 1 July 1945. A great friend of J. EDGAR HOOVER, Clark was also close to CLINT MURCHISON and WILLIAM BYARS, SR., the oilmen who financed many of Hoover's vacations. Under Clark, G-men had a virtual free hand for illegal surveillance techniques, an aide explaining that Clark "didn't want to know who was tapped or who wasn't tapped" by Hoover's eavesdroppers.

As a staunch anticommunist in the Red-baiting 1940s, Clark initiated the SMITH ACT prosecution of COMMUNIST PARTY leaders in 1948; he also worked hard to deport alleged "subversives," Clark's administration witnessing the JUSTICE DEPARTMENT'S closest cooperation with Immigration since the days of Attorney General A. MITCHELL PALMER (a crusading partnership renewed 50 years later by Attorney General JOHN ASHCROFT). Unfortunately, Clark was not so zealous when it came to prosecuting members of ORGANIZED CRIME. In May 1947 he personally dismissed fraud charges against leaders of the Chicago Mafia, and three months later arranged early parole for the same gangsters, serving federal time for extortion. When Congress sought to investigate the latter case, Clark withheld parole records. Nearly two decades later, an FBI bug in Chicago caught one of those paroled, notorious mobster Murray ("The Camel") Humphreys, explaining how the early parole was arranged. "The trick was to get to Tom Clark," Humphreys boasted. "Finally, a deal was made: If he had the thick skin to do it, he'd get the next appointment to the Supreme Court."

That promise was kept in October 1949, when President Truman appointed Clark to the nation's highest court. The *Chicago Tribune* greeted the announcement with a call for Clark's impeachment, noting the ex-attorney general's "utter unfitness for any position of public responsibility, and especially for a position on the Supreme Court." Clark displayed his "thick skin" by remaining on the court until 1967, resigning then to avoid potential conflicts of interest when his son became attorney general under President LYNDON JOHNSON. J. Edgar Hoover, meanwhile, had buried the Chicago recordings that incriminated his favorite attorney general of all time. Clark died on 13 June 1977.

**CLARK, William Ramsey**—A Dallas native, born 18 December 1927, Ramsey Clark was the son of Attorney General and Supreme Court justice THOMAS CLARK. He joined the JUSTICE DEPARTMENT under President JOHN KENNEDY and served primarily in the civil rights field. Clark led the U.S. marshals assigned to protect black student James Meredith at the University of Mississippi in 1962, coordinated federal operations in Birmingham the following year, and played a key role in writing the Civil Rights Act of 1964. Promoted to Assistant Attorney General in 1965, he was present in Selma, Alabama, during Dr. MARTIN LUTHER KING'S campaign to register black voters.

President LYNDON JOHNSON appointed Clark as Acting Attorney General on 3 October 1966, and Clark assumed the permanent office on 2 March 1967. He clashed instantly with J. EDGAR HOOVER, whom Clark dismissively labeled "the old man

down the hall." Staunchly opposed to FBI BUGGING and other illegal surveillance techniques, Clark issued sweeping directives against such behavior, except in special cases dealing with national security. (In that vein, Clark rejected Hoover's plea to bug the rooms of hopeful presidential candidates at the 1968 Democratic Convention.) Hoover retaliated with a torrent of peevish memoranda, prompting Clark to observe that "Hoover would memo you to death. An attorney general could have spent literally all his time preparing memos back to the director."

The feud between Hoover and Clark went beyond mere procedural details, plumbing the depths of bitter enmity. Clark denounced Hoover's endless pursuit of the COMMUNIST PARTY as a "terribly wasteful use of very valuable resources," while lampooning the director's "self-centered concern for his own reputation." Hoover fired back in kind, branding Clark "a jellyfish" and the worst attorney general of the century. In fact, Hoover confided to friendly journalists, Clark was "nothing but a hippie. I went over there once and his wife was barefoot. What kind of person is that?"

Despite their quarrels, Clark stopped short of reforming the FBI. He once declared the prosecution of renegade G-men his "highest priority," but none were indicted while Clark held office. He likewise failed to investigate complaints from within the FBI itself of Hoover's profiteering and autocratic rule. Clark *did* propose appointment of a "single oversight officer" to supervise all federal investigative agencies, noting that "from many standpoints it was desirable for Mr. Hoover to be removed from running of the FBI," but President Johnson dismissed the plan as "too ambitious and too heavy to take on." In the end, Johnson regretted his choice for attorney general, telling friends, "I thought I had appointed Tom Clark's son. I was wrong."

Notwithstanding that lack of support, Clark remained through the end of Johnson's administration, stepping down with the rest of the LBJ team in January 1969. A controversial visit to North Vietnam in 1972 failed to help Clark with abortive U.S. Senate campaigns in 1974 and 1976. He remains an outspoken critic of U.S. policies abroad, and has published a book analyzing American "war crimes" in the 1991 Gulf War.

**CLARKE, Floyd I.**—An Arizona native, Floyd Clarke joined the FBI in 1964, specializing in matters related to ORGANIZED CRIME. In 1977 he became assistant special agent in charge of the Philadelphia field office, afterward promoted to inspector (1979) and special agent in charge of the Kansas City field office (1980). In 1982 he was assigned to FBI Headquarters as assistant director of the CRIMINAL INVESTIGATION DIVISION, promoted to executive assistant director of Administration in 1989. On 18 July 1989 Director WILLIAM SESSIONS appointed Clarke to serve as first deputy director. When Sessions was fired four years later, on 19 July 1993, President WILLIAM CLINTON named Clarke acting director of the FBI, a post he held until Director LOUIS FREEH took office on 1 September 1993. Clarke then returned to his post as deputy director, retiring from the bureau in February 1994.

**CLEGG, Hugh H.**—Born 17 July 1898 in Mathiston, Mississippi, Hugh Clegg joined the FBI on 12 August 1926. He rose rapidly through the ranks, serving as special agent in charge of the Atlanta, Chicago and Washington, D.C. field offices. In 1932 he was appointed to serve as assistant director to J. EDGAR HOOVER. In 1935 Clegg became the first head of the FBI National Academy, serving simultaneously as assistant director of the TRAINING and INSPECTION DIVISIONS. In 1940-41 he studied wartime intelligence and security techniques in England, with the British intelligence service. Following retirement from the FBI in 1954, Clegg served as assistant to the president of the University of Mississippi from 1956 to 1971. He died at Anguilla, Mississippi on 12 December 1979.

**CLINTON, William Jefferson** — Born William Jefferson Blythe IV at Hope, Arkansas on 19 August 1946, Bill Clinton graduated from Georgetown University (1969) and Harvard Law School (1973) before pursuing a political career in his home state. He lost his first campaign (for Congress, 1974), but subsequently served three terms as governor (1979-81, 1983-92) and two terms as President of the United States (1993-2001). Clinton's administration was haunted by controversy, with critics raising charges of immorality and corruption while Clinton blamed a "vast right-wing conspiracy" intent on crippling his socio-economic agenda. Clinton was impeached by the House of Representatives in December 1998, charged with perjury and obstruction of justice relative to his sexual liaison with a White House intern, but the Senate acquitted him on all counts.

The FBI and JUSTICE DEPARTMENT aroused nearly as much controversy under Clinton as did the president's private life and financial affairs. Attorney General JANET RENO was repeatedly accused of "stonewalling" investigations into alleged Democratic Party misconduct, while the FBI seemed constantly mired in scandal. The BRANCH DAVIDIAN siege of 1993 provided impetus for a violent MILITIA MOVEMENT in the U.S. and apparently motivated TIMOTHY MCVEIGH to bomb an Oklahoma City federal building, killing 168 persons in April 1995. President Clinton fired FBI Director WILLIAM SESSIONS in July 1993 and replaced him with LOUIS FREEH, but the Bureau's problems continued, including the RICHARD JEWELL and WEN HO LEE cases and persistent scandals involving the FBI's LABORATORY DIVISION. Press reports revealed that a White House aide Anthony Marcecha had requested FBI FILES on some 900 persons during 1993-94, including 400 REAGAN-BUSH employees, but Clinton spokesmen termed the requests "inadvertent." In the realm of TERRORISM, Clinton authorized the CENTRAL INTELLIGENCE AGENCY to kill fugitive terrorist USAMA BIN LADEN, but the contract was never executed. At home, Clinton pushed Congress to expand FBI investigative powers and expedite deportation of suspected terrorists, but the Anti-Terrorism Act of 1996 failed to expand the Bureau's authority.

**COHN, Roy Marcus** — A New York City native, born 20 February 1927, Roy Cohn was the son of a judge prominent in the Democratic Party. He graduated from Columbia Law School and was admitted to the bar at 21, using his family connections and friendship with columnist GEORGE SOKOLSKY to land work as an assistant U.S. attorney in Manhattan. Cohn was among the federal prosecutors of 11 COMMUNIST PARTY leaders tried for SMITH ACT violations in 1948, and three years later he helped prosecute JULIUS AND ETHEL ROSENBERG. That victory set the stage, in 1952, for his appointment as chief counsel to Senator JOSEPH MCCARTHY's Red-hunting Committee on Government Operations. With young protégé (and alleged lover) G. David Schine, Cohn toured Europe and purged U.S.-supported libraries of "subversive" literature. He also served as a frequent conduit of classified information passed to McCarthy by top-level aides of FBI Director J. EDGAR HOOVER.

In 1953, when McCarthy launched his crusade against alleged communists in the U.S. Army, military sources leaked the story that Cohn had abused his congressional privilege in a vain attempt to spare Schine from the draft. When that failed, it was claimed, he brought new pressure on the Army to win Schine special privileges. A year after that story broke, in December 1954, McCarthy was censured by the Senate and soon left office to die in obscurity. (Cohn, Hoover and Vice President RICHARD NIXON attended McCarthy's funeral in 1957.) Cohn was more fortunate, retreating to private practice in New York, earning a reputation for his links to high-ranking figures in ORGANIZED CRIME. He also maintained close ties to FBI HEADQUARTERS and played a pivotal role in soliciting LEWIS ROSENSTIEL's donation to create the J. EDGAR HOOVER FOUNDATION.

In 1964, while federal prosecutors tried in vain to jail Cohn for his various shady activities, Cohn encouraged Missouri senator Edward Long to convene public hearings on illegal government DOMESTIC SURVEILLANCE techniques. Author Anthony Summers contends that Cohn made that move with Hoover's blessing, as part of a campaign to embarrass Attorney General ROBERT KENNEDY. Around the same time, Cohn was instrumental in an FBI plot to derail the vice presidential hopes of New Jersey congressman Cornelius Gallagher. (Two decades later, Cohn signed an affidavit attesting that G-men slandered Gallagher's wife to prevent President LYNDON JOHNSON from choosing Gallagher as his 1964 running mate.)

Cohn ran out of luck in the 1980s, disbarred from practicing law on grounds of unethical and unprofessional conduct. (Among other offenses, he had forged Lewis Rosenstiel's signature to a false codicil while his client lay comatose and dying.) At the same time, decades of thinly-veiled and reckless HOMOSEXUAL activity caught up with Cohn in the form of AIDS. Cohn died in New York, from complications of the disease, on 2 August 1986.

**"COINTELPRO"** — The FBI's official history, reported on the Bureau's Internet website, provides the following information on so-called COINTELPRO (counter*intel*ligence *pro*gram) operations in the midst of a section devoted to "The Vietnam War Era." The description reads as follows:

> No specific guidelines for FBI Agents covering national security investigations had been developed by the [RICHARD NIXON] Administration or Congress; these, in fact, were not issued until 1976. Therefore, the FBI addressed the threats from the militant "New Left" as it had those from Communists in the 1950s and the KKK in the 1960s. It used both traditional investigative tech-

niques and counterintelligence programs ("Cointelpro") to counteract domestic terrorism and conduct investigations of individuals and organizations who threatened terroristic violence. Wiretapping and other intrusive techniques were discouraged by Hoover in the mid-1960s and eventually were forbidden completely unless they conformed to the Omnibus Crime Control Act. Hoover formally terminated all "Cointelpro" operations on April 28, 1971.

That passage, pretending to describe a campaign of criminal activity perpetrated under the COINTELPRO label, is a classic piece of FBI DISINFORMATION. Within a span of 113 words it rewrites history concerning illegal WIRETAPPING (banned by Congress in 1934, and by U.S. SUPREME COURT rulings in 1937 and 1939); falsely identifies the targets of COINTELPRO harassment as "terrorists"; implies that COINTELPRO campaigns occurred only during the first 28 months of the Nixon administration (i.e., January 1969 through April 1971); falsely claims that J. EDGAR HOOVER "discouraged" illegal surveillance techniques; and claims (again, falsely) that such techniques have not been used by G-men since 1971.

The FBI has used illegal techniques, including wiretaps, BREAK-INS and BUGGING since its creation in 1908. Other classic techniques employed from the start, including FRAME-UPS and use of corrupt INFORMANTS as *agents provocateur* to promote criminal activity among surveillance targets, were also staples of various COINTELPRO operations during the 25 years when that label was applied to FBI harassment and disruption campaigns. And while the embarrassing practice was officially discarded in 1971, evidence from the FBI's own FILES clearly proves that identical abuses have continued without interruption to the present day.

The first official COINTELPRO campaign was launched by FBI HEADQUARTERS on 28 August 1956. It targeted the COMMUNIST PARTY, and its goals were described in a memo from Alan Belmont, head of the Bureau's Internal Security Section.

> During its investigation of the Communist Party, USA, the Bureau has sought to capitalize on incidents involving the Party and its leaders in order to foster factionalism, bring the Communist Party (CP) and its leaders into disrepute before the American public and cause confusion and dissatisfaction among rank-and-file members of the CP.
>
> Generally, the above action has constituted harassment rather than disruption, since, for the most part, the Bureau has set up particular incidents, and the attack has been from the outside. At the present time, however, there is existing within the CP a situation resulting from the developments at the 20th Congress of the CP of the Soviet Union and the Government's attack on the Party principally through prosecutions under the SMITH ACT of 1940 and the Internal Security Act of 1950 which is made to order for an all-out disruptive attack against the CP from within. In other words, the Bureau is in a position to initiate, on a broader scale than heretofore attempted, a counterintelligence program against the CP, not by harassment from the outside, which might only serve to bring the various factions together, but by feeding and fostering from within the fight currently raging.

On 8 May 1958 Hoover sent Attorney General WILLIAM ROGERS a progress report on the FBI's effort "to promote disruption within the ranks of the Communist Party, including use of paid infiltrators to spark "acrimonious debates" and "increase factionalism." A flurry of anonymous letters was also employed to generate "disillusionment [with] and defection" from the party. Six months later, on 8 November 1958, Hoover briefed President DWIGHT EISENHOWER'S full cabinet on the continuing effort, distributing a 36-page "Top Secret" summary. That booklet read, in part:

> To counteract a resurgence of Communist Party influence in the United States, we have a … program designed to intensify confusion and dissatisfaction among its members. During the past few years, the program has been most effective. Selective informants were briefed and trained to raise controversial issues within the Party. In the process, they may be able to advance themselves to high positions. The INTERNAL REVENUE SERVICE was furnished the names and addresses of Party functionaries…. Based on this information, investigations have resulted in 262 possible income tax evasion cases. Anticommunist literature and simulated Party documents were mailed anonymously to carefully chosen members.

FBI files later revealed that during the years 1957-60, 266 individual COINTELPRO campaigns were mounted against the Communist Party in America. In the year 1960 alone, those campaigns involved 114 illegal wiretaps, 74 warrantless bugs, and 2,342 pieces of private mail read by G-men in violation of federal law. Hoover "discouraged" none of it; in fact, he required that headquarters approve each specific criminal act in advance.

On 10 January 1961, Hoover briefed President JOHN KENNEDY and Attorney General ROBERT KENNEDY on the campaign's progress, including:

> … penetration of the Party at all levels with security informants; use of various techniques to keep the Party off-balance and disillusion individual communists concerning communist ideology; investigation of every known member of the CPUSA in order to determine whether he should be detained in the event of a national emergency…. As an adjunct to our regular investigative operations, we carry on a carefully planned program of counterattack against the CPUSA….

One of those "carefully planned programs," launched on 4 October 1966, was dubbed Operation Hoodwink. As described in the kick-off memo, Hoodwink was "designed to provoke a dispute between the Communist Party, USA, and La Cosa Nostra" (otherwise known as the Mafia). Ideally, G-men hoped that American communists and members of ORGANIZED CRIME would "expend their energies, time, and money attacking each other. This would help neutralize the activities of both groups which are detrimental to this country." The Bureau's New York City field office recommended a method of sparking the feud.

> This technique consists of anonymously forwarding one leaflet to a local La Cosa Nostra leader attacking the labor practices of one of his enterprises. The leaflet would ostensibly be published by a local Party unit. A note with the leaflet would give the impression that it has received wide circulation.

Instead of vetoing the suggestion, with its clear potential for provoking lethal violence, Hoover suggested an even more aggressive campaign in a memo dated 5 October 1966. It read:

New York is authorized to mail the anonymous letters and leaflet set out ... as the beginning of a long-range program to cause a dispute between La Cosa Nostra (LCN) and the Communist Party, USA.... To strengthen this alleged attack, add a last sentence to the leaflet: "Let's show the hoodlums and the bosses that the workers are united against sweatshops."

Take the usual precautions to insure this mailing cannot be associated with the Bureau and advise of tangible results. New York should also submit follow-up recommendations to continue this program.

The Party has been the subject of recent BOMBINGS, a typical hoodlum technique. Consider a spurious Party statement blaming the LCN for the bombings because of "Party efforts on behalf of the workers." This statement could be aimed at specific LCN members if appropriate.

In developing this program, thought should also be given to initiating spurious LCN attacks on the CPUSA, so that each group would think the other was mounting a campaign against it. The Bureau very much appreciates New York's careful analysis of this program and the initial "low-key" technique suggested.

It is difficult to guess what actions Hoover may have deemed excessive, when bombing and other acts of deadly violence were deemed "low-key." The campaign failed to produce a gang war as desired, but the FBI was still trying in early 1968, when similar spurious letters were sent from alleged party members to the mob-affiliated TEAMSTERS UNION in Philadelphia.

Hoover's campaign to disrupt the Communist Party proved so successful that a second COINTELPRO operation was launched in 1960, this one targeting a wide spectrum of PUERTO RICAN NATIONALISTS. Hoover's initial memo on the subject, dated 4 August 1960, advised his subordinates that:

The Bureau is considering the feasibility of instituting a program of disruption to be directed against organizations which seek independence for Puerto Rico through other than lawful, peaceful means.

Because of the increasing boldness apparent in the activities of such organizations, their utter disregard for the will of the majority, the inevitable communist and/or Soviet effort to embarrass the United States, and the courage given to their cause by Castro's Cuba, we must make a more positive effort, not only to curtail, but to disrupt their activities.

San Juan and New York should give this matter studied consideration and thereafter furnish the Bureau observations, suggestions and recommendations relative to the institution of such a program to reach the Bureau no later than 3-25-60 [sic].

In considering this matter, you should bear in mind the Bureau desires to disrupt the activities of these organizations and is not interested in mere harassment. No action should be taken in this program without Bureau authority at any time.

There followed a familiar war of nerves, including use of infiltrators to "raise controversial issues at meetings, raise justifiable criticisms against leaders and take other steps which would weaken" various nationalist groups; circulation of anonymous letters and planted news stories to sow dissent among *independistas*; and pursuit of other means by which "the nationalist elements could be pitted against the communist elements to effectively disrupt some of the organizations." When nationalist leader Juan Mari Bras suffered a near-fatal heart attack on 21 April 1964, FBI memos gloated that one of the Bureau's anony-

mous letters "certainly did nothing to ease his tensions for he felt the effects of the letter deeply.... This particular technique has been outstandingly successful and we shall be on the lookout to further exploit our achievements in this field." Another memo, dated 15 December 1967, boasted that COINTELPRO operations in Puerto Rico had served to "confuse the independentist leaders, exploit group rivalries and jealousies, inflame personality conflicts, emasculate the ... strength of these organizations and thwart any possibility of pro independence unity."

Far from ending in April 1971, illegal disruption campaigns against Puerto Rican nationalist groups and leaders escalated over the next two decades, becoming markedly more violent after COINTELPRO veteran RICHARD W. HELD took charge of the San Juan field office in 1978. The new phase of psychological warfare included vigilante bombings, beatings and murders of nationalist leaders, investigated but never solved by the FBI. Sworn depositions taken from G-men in 1985 acknowledged use of illegal bugs and wiretaps, while a former secretary with the San Juan field office blamed agents for a 1978 firebombing at the home of Juan Mari Bras. Agent Helm was rewarded for the campaign in 1988, with promotion to serve as special agent in charge of the San Francisco field office.

The Bureau's third formal COINTELPRO target, beginning in October 1961, was the SOCIALIST WORKERS PARTY (SWP). Any claim that COINTELPRO actions were reserved for "terrorists" is laid to rest by Hoover's memo of 12 October 1961, inaugurating his new campaign with a complaint that the SWP

... has, over the past several years, been openly espousing its line on a local and national basis through the running of candidate for public office and strongly directing and/or supporting such causes as Castro's Cuba and integration problems in the South. The SWP has been in frequent contact with international Trotskyite groups stopping short of open and direct contact with these groups.... It is felt that a disruption program along similar lines [to COINTELPRO-CPUSA] could be initiated against the SWP on a very selective basis. One of the purposes of this program would be to alert the public to the fact that the SWP is not just another socialist group but follows the revolutionary principles of Marx, Lenin and Engels as interpreted by Leon Trotsky.... It may be desirable to expand the program after the effects have been evaluated.

In fact, the "new" COINTELPRO-SWP was not new at all. FBI records, later released under the FREEDOM OF INFORMATION ACT, reveal that between 1943 and 1963, G-men logged 20,000 days monitoring wiretaps on SWP telephones and 12,000 days monitoring bugs illegally planted in SWP homes and offices. The same 20-year period witnessed 208 FBI break-ins against the SWP, with 9,864 party documents stolen or photographed during burglaries. Separate COINTELPRO records, perhaps including some overlap with the previous statistics, confirm 46 disruptive campaigns against the SWP through 1971, with 80-plus break-ins staged to photograph more than 8,000 documents during the same period.

Some of the Bureau's specific anti-SWP campaigns included disruption of the party's support for frame-up victim ROBERT F. WILLIAMS, a black CIVIL RIGHTS leader falsely charged with KID-

NAPPING in North Carolina, and a successful effort to drive SWP member Morris Starsky from his teaching post at Arizona State University. According to a memo from the Phoenix field office, dated, 1 October 1968, Professor Starsky was chosen for character assassination because:

> MORRIS J. STARSKY, by his actions, has continued to spotlight himself as a target for counterintelligence action. He and his wife were both named as presidential electors by and for the Socialist Workers Party when the SWP in August, 1968, gained a place on the ballot in Arizona. In addition they have signed themselves as treasurer and secretary, respectively of the Arizona SWP. Professor STARSKY's status at Arizona State University may be affected by the outcome of his pending trial on charges of disturbing the peace. He is alleged to have used violent, abusive and obscene language against the Assistant Managing Director of Gammage Auditorium at ASU during the memorial services for MARTIN LUTHER KING last April. Trial is now scheduled for 10/8/68 in Justice Court, Tempe, Arizona.

Rather than await the outcome of that trial, G-men mailed a series of scurrilous letters to the university's faculty committee, signed by "concerned ASU alumni" and accusing Starsky of various unethical (or criminal) activities. Starsky's dismissal from the faculty was rated a success for the Bureau's COINTELPRO-SWP. Parallel COINTELPRO operations were also undertaken against an SWP affiliate, the Young Socialist Alliance (YSA), and records from those campaigns prove that the operation did not end in April 1971, as the FBI claims. In fact, a memo sent to headquarters on 20 June 1973 referred to the Bureau's recent receipt of "items stolen from the YSA local office" in New York City.

Next on tap for the COINTELPRO treatment, however reluctantly on Hoover's part, were various factions of the KU KLUX KLAN. Spurred by President LYNDON JOHNSON, the FBI inaugurated its COINTELPRO — WHITE HATE GROUPS on 2 September 1964. By the time action was suspended in April 1971, G-men had undertaken 287 separate operations against Klansmen in various states. "SNITCH-JACKETING" was a favorite technique, apparently prompting Mississippi Klansmen to murder one of their colleagues in 1965, but the KKK was seemingly spared the more aggressive techniques employed against targets on the political left. Informants such as GARY ROWE were encouraged to spread dissension in Klan ranks by any means available, including serial adultery with the wives of brother Klansmen, but G-men often sheltered Klan spies who committed acts of violence against southern blacks or civil rights workers.

Aside from the 1968 incident wherein a Mississippi Klan informant was paid to arrange the police ambush of two racist bombers, leaving one dead and the other gravely wounded, FBI anti-Klan operations consisted primarily of bush-league harassment. Familiar anonymous letters accused Klan leaders of financial and/or sexual impropriety. The FBI prepared a joke book titled *United Klowns of America*, described in headquarters memos as "light in presentation" but still "a serious effort at counterintelligence." G-men also created a front group, the National Committee for Domestic Tranquility, that was described in FBI reports as "a Bureau-approved vehicle for attacking Klan policies and disputes from a low-key, common sense, and patriotic position."

Claiming active chapters in 11 states, the paper group published a regular newsletter urging Klansmen to quit the KKK and support "our boys" fighting in the VIETNAM WAR. The Bureau had 2,000 Klan informants on its payroll by September 1965, when G-men assisted the HOUSE COMMITTEE ON UN-AMERICAN ACTIVITIES with a public investigation of the Klan. Friendly authors like DON WHITEHEAD described a series of physical confrontations between FBI agents and Klansmen, prompting Hoover to boast that Klan members were "afraid to 'mix' with our Agents," but no such showdowns have been reliably documented.

The Bureau's last official COINTELPRO operation, targeting "Black Nationalist-Hate Groups," was launched on 25 August 1967, with a memo from Hoover that read:

> The purpose of this new counterintelligence endeavor is to expose, disrupt, misdirect, discredit, or otherwise neutralize the activities of black nationalist, hate-type organizations and groupings, their leadership, spokesmen, membership, and supporters, and to counter their propensity for violence and civil disorder. The activities of all such groups of intelligence interest to this Bureau must be followed on a continuous basis so we will be in a position to promptly take advantage of all opportunities for counterintelligence and to inspire action in instances where circumstances warrant. The pernicious background of such groups, their duplicity, and devious maneuvers must be exposed to public scrutiny where such publicity will have a neutralizing effect. Efforts of the various groups to consolidate their forces or to recruit new or youthful adherents must be frustrated. No opportunity should be missed to exploit through counterintelligence techniques the organizational and personal conflicts of the leaderships of the groups and where possible an effort should be made to capitalize upon existing conflicts between competing black nationalist organizations.

The scope of Hoover's plan was demonstrated by a list of target organizations, ranging from the wholly nonviolent CONGRESS OF RACIAL EQUALITY and SOUTHERN CHRISTIAN LEADERSHIP CONFERENCE (SCLC) to the more militant STUDENT NONVIOLENT COORDINATING COMMITTEE (SNCC), and the separatist NATION OF ISLAM. Of the lot, only the Nation of Islam truly qualified as a "black nationalist" group, and none of the other organizations came close to preaching "race hatred" except in Hoover's private definition of the term.

The campaign undertaken in 1967 was merely an extension of FBI harassment directed at sundry black activists since 1919. MARCUS GARVEY was an early victim of such methods, and his case was far from unique. As in previous COINTELPRO campaigns, G-men worked overtime concocting anonymous letters and leaflets, cartoons and press leaks to embarrass black leaders. Adultery was a favorite charge, highlighting the white racist's frequent preoccupation with black sexuality. False arrests and frame-ups were routine, as the Bureau coordinated its efforts with local police departments throughout the U.S. *Agents provocateur* encouraged various targets to break the law, often supplying guns or other contraband at FBI expense in order to facilitate arrests. It mattered not to FBI headquarters that G-men were the true felons in such cases; any excess was permissible in the name of forestalling "black revolution."

On 29 February 1968, a new memo warned Bureau field

offices of a "tremendous increase in black nationalist activity," demanding that the COINTELPRO campaign launched six months earlier "should be expanded and [its] goals should be re-iterated to the field." Four days later, another headquarters memo reminded all G-men of their duty to "prevent the coali-tion of militant black nationalist groups"; "prevent the rise of a 'messiah' who could unify, and electrify, the militant black na-tionalist movement"; "prevent violence on the part of black na-tionalist groups"; "prevent militant black nationalist groups and leaders from gaining respectability"; and "prevent the long-range growth of militant black nationalist organizations, especially among youth."

The four groups named specifically as "primary targets" in Hoover's memo of 4 March 1968 were the SCLC, SNCC, the Na-tion of Islam and the REVOLUTIONARY ACTION MOVEMENT, (RAM) but the director's focus was already shifting toward the California-based BLACK PANTHER PARTY, soon named by Hoover as "the greatest threat to the internal security of the country." FBI files from the late 1960s reveal that Hoover's commitment to "prevent violence" by black militants was a cynical sham. In fact, from southern California to Chicago and New York, G-men did everything within their power to *cause* violence between rival groups, pitting Black Panthers against, promoting street warfare between Black Panthers and Ron Karenga's US (United Slaves) and the BLACKSTONE RANGERS, encouraging members of the militant Jewish Defense League to attack black spokesmen whom the FBI accused of anti-Semitism. Multiple deaths resulted from the Bu-reau's effort to "exploit conflicts" between militant groups in southern California and elsewhere.

When not promoting murder, FBI agents indulged in more conventional forms of harassment, including collaboration with local police in a systematic campaign of raids and false arrests. FBI memos from 1967 boast that RAM members were "arrested on every possible charge until they could no longer make bail" and thus "spent most of the summer in jail." The following year, police cooperating with an FBI *agent provocateur* invaded the Chicago Black Panther office and killed chairman FRED HAMPTON while he slept. In California, Panther member ELMER PRATT was framed for murder and spent most of three decades in prison. Other police actions and prosecutions are equally suspect, in-cluding the death sentence handed to Philadelphia Panther MUMIA ABU-JAMAL for allegedly killing a white patrolman.

The FBI's last official COINTELPRO campaign began with a memo dated 9 May 1968, which read in part:

Our Nation is undergoing an era of disruption and violence caused to a large extent by various individuals generally connected with the NEW LEFT. Some of these activists urge revolution in America and call for the defeat of the United States in Vietnam. They continually and falsely allege police brutality and do not hesitate to use unlawful acts to further their so-called causes. The New Left has on many occasions viciously and scurrilously at-tacked the Director and the Bureau in an attempt to hamper our investigation of it and to drive us off the college campuses. With this in mind, it is our recommendation that a new Counterintel-ligence Program be designed to neutralize the New Left and the Key Activists. The Key Activists are those individuals who are the moving forces behind the New Left and on whom we have in-tensified our investigations.

The purpose of this program is to expose, disrupt and other-wise neutralize the activities of this group and persons connected with it. It is hoped that with this new program their violent and illegal activities may be reduced if not curtailed.

FBI headquarters apparently missed the irony of commit-ting criminal acts in order to "reduce illegal activities," but there can be no doubt that Bureau informants and *agents provocateur* significantly increased violence on the part of various New Left organizations. A partial list of those felons who received their salaries and orders from the Bureau would include: HORACE PACKER, who admitted supplying student radicals in Seattle with drugs, weapons, and components for Molotov cocktails; ALFRED BURNETT, who built and supplied the bomb carried by Vietnam veteran Larry Ward on the day he was ambushed and killed by Seattle police, in May 1970; ROBERT HARDY, who supplied "90 percent" of the burglary tools used by radicals to invade a New Jersey draft board; CHARLES GRIMM, a participant in arson and student riots at the University of Alabama; LARRY GRATHWOHL, who participated in the 1969 bombing of a Cincinnati school; WILLIAM LEMMER, arrested with illegal weapons and held for psy-chiatric evaluation after infiltrating Vietnam Veterans Against the War (VVAW); REINHOLD MOHR, jailed while trying to sell Ohio VVAW members a rocket launcher and machine gun; and Howard Godfrey, employed by G-men to lead the violent SECRET ARMY ORGANIZATION in California, whose violent acts including bombings and attempted murder of a university professor.

With such individuals on the payroll, it is perhaps no sur-prise that former radicals from the New Left era blame the FBI itself for a majority of bombings and similar acts attributed to the movement. A memo from the Philadelphia field office, dated 29 May 1968, explained why the time-honored methods of slan-der through press leaks and unsigned letters proved ineffective against New Left targets.

The disruption of the "New Left" through counterintelligence activities poses problems which have not been previously present in this phase of our work. Whereas the Communist Party and similar subversive groups have hidden their indiscretions and gen-erally shunned publicity, the New Left groups have flaunted their arrogance, immorality, lack of respect for law and order, and thrived on publicity. Communal living quarters for unmarried male and female members of the New Left have been advertised as a badge of "free-thinking" individualism. Adherence to prin-ciples of Marxism has been freely acknowledged. Members of the STUDENTS FOR A DEMOCRATIC SOCIETY (SDS) have openly ad-mitted their affiliations and their adherence to anarchistic ideas.

Still, the Bureau was unwilling or unable to abandon its tra-ditional techniques. An order from Hoover, dated 5 July 1968, laid out a 12-point strategy for disrupting the New Left nation-wide. Hoover's "suggestions" included:

1. Preparation of a leaflet designed to counteract the im-pression that Students for a Democratic Society (SDS) and other minority groups speak for a majority of students at universi-ties....

2. The instigating of or the taking advantage of personal conflicts or animosities between New Left leaders.

3. The creating of impressions that certain New Left leaders are informants for the Bureau or other law enforcement agencies.

4. The use of articles from student newspapers and/or the "underground press" to show the depravity of New Left leaders and members....

5. Since the use of marijuana and other narcotics is widespread among members of the New Left, you should be alert to opportunities to have them arrested by local authorities on drug charges....

6. The drawing up of anonymous letters regarding individuals active in the New Left. These letters should set out their activities and should be sent to their parents, neighbors and the parents' employers....

7. Anonymous letters or leaflets describing faculty members and graduate assistants in the various institutions of higher learning who are active in New Left matters.... Such letters could be signed "A Concerned Alumni" or "A Concerned Taxpayer."

8. Whenever New Left groups engage in disruptive activities on college campuses, cooperative press contacts should be encouraged to emphasize that the disruptive elements constitute a minority of the students and do not represent the conviction of the majority....

9. There is a definite hostility among SDS and other New Left groups toward the Socialist Workers Party (SWP), the Young Socialist Alliance (YSA), and the Progressive Labor Party (PLP). This hostility should be exploited wherever possible.

10. ... New Left groups are attempting to open coffeehouses near military bases in order to influence members of the Armed Forces.... [F]riendly news media should be alerted to them and their purpose....

11. Consider the use of cartoons, photographs, and anonymous letters which will have the effect of ridiculing the New Left....

12. Be alert for opportunities to confuse and disrupt New Left activities by disinformation....

The Nixon administration assisted FBI efforts against the New Left with multiple conspiracy charges against movement leaders, resulting in trials described by historian William Manchester as "an unparalleled series of judicial disasters for the government." In terms of curbing leftist violence, the Bureau's campaign was a resounding failure. A majority of the 862 alleged bombings or bombing attempts recorded by G-men between January 1969 and April 1970 remain unsolved (perhaps because investigation would expose the crimes committed by *agents provocateur* on the FBI payroll). Of 13,400 persons arrested in New Left demonstrations during May 1971, 12,653 were discharged without trial; 122 were convicted, while another 625 pled guilty or no contest, but all such pleas were voided and expunged by a federal court in 1974, on grounds of police coercion. In January 1975 the victims of mass arrest from May 1971 were awarded $12 million in punitive damages. The New Left, meanwhile, collapsed in 1972 after its *raison d'être* was removed by American withdrawal from South Vietnam.

The FBI's harassment network suffered terminal embarrassment in March 1971, after burglars invaded the RESIDENT AGENCY located in MEDIA, PENNSYLVANIA and stole several thousand COINTELPRO documents, which soon found their way to the press. Hoover officially canceled all COINTELPRO activities a month later, although their full scope would not be revealed until several years after his death. According to records exposed by the CHURCH COMMITTEE in 1975, the FBI mounted at least 2,218 separate COINTELPRO actions against various groups and individuals between 1957 and 1971; those illegal campaigns included at least 1,884 illegal wiretaps and 583 warrantless bugs, plus 55,804 pieces of mail illegally opened and read by G-men.

It would be comforting to believe the FBI's claim that such methods have not been used since April 1971, but evidence to the contrary is plentiful. The Church Committee found that during 1972-74, despite the alleged ban on all COINTELPRO techniques, FBI agents installed another 421 illegal wiretaps and 114 warrantless bugs, while stealing another 2,042 pieces of personal mail. As embarrassing as those disclosures were (or should have been), they still had no apparent impact on the Bureau's dedication to business as usual. Organizations including the AMERICAN INDIAN MOVEMENT (AIM), EARTH FIRST!, the COMMITTEE IN SOLIDARITY WITH THE PEOPLE OF EL SALVADOR, and various Puerto Rican nationalist groups suffered attacks indistinguishable from "banned" COINTELPRO techniques throughout the 1970s, 1980s and early 1990s. (On 26 November 1973, some 31 months after all such programs supposedly ended, the aforementioned Agent Richard W. Held penned a memo to headquarters, suggesting that "Los Angeles and Minneapolis consider possible COINTELPRO measures to further disrupt AIM leadership.") "TERRORISM" remains a frequent excuse for extralegal measures on the part of federal agents, and sweeping provisions of the new USA PATRIOT ACT suggest that use of such methods may be increasing, rather than declining in the future.

**COLBURN, Wayne B.**—Born in 1907, Wayne Colburn joined the U.S. MARSHALS SERVICE late in life, at age 55. He served in an administrative capacity until 1970, when Attorney General JOHN MITCHELL appointed Colburn to replace Director Carl Turner (forced to resign over charges of graft and corruption). Colburn sought to reform the service, but found it no easy task in the shadow of President RICHARD NIXON's scandal-ridden regime. After Attorney General Mitchell resigned in disgrace, replacement RICHARD KLEINDIENST granted the Marshal's service full bureau status on 10 May 1973; Attorney General ELLIOT RICHARDSON revoked that status on 17 October 1973, but his successor WILLIAM SAXBE restored it in May 1974. Through all the waffling, appointment of marshals remained political, with candidates nominated by members of the U.S. Senate.

Colburn's primary contribution to the service was the creation of the Special Operations Group (SOG), an elite SWAT team designed to cope with crises. One persistent target of SOG marshals in the early 1970s was the AMERICAN INDIAN MOVEMENT, confronted at Alcatraz Island and the Twin Cities Naval Air Station in 1971, then at WOUNDED KNEE, South Dakota in

1973. FBI agents joined the SOG at Wounded Knee, sporadic gunplay leaving two Native Americans dead and one marshal paralyzed for life. (Attorney General KLEINDIENST vetoed Colburn's plan to break the siege with a frontal assault by armored vehicles.) Colburn retired in May 1976 and died at home in California, on 21 June 1983.

**COLE, John M.**—A 41-year-old program manager for FBI foreign intelligence investigations covering Afghanistan, India and Pakistan, John Cole addressed a letter to Director ROBERT MUELLER III in early 2002, reporting that the Bureau's counterintelligence and counterterrorism training "has declined drastically in recent years as part of a continuing pattern of poor management." Cole also reported a perceived security lapse in the screening and hiring of FBI translators. "I thought we had all these new security procedures in place, in light of [traitorous G-man ROBERT] HANSSEN," Cole told the *Washington Post*, "but no one is going by the rules and regulations and whatever policy may be implemented."

Cole's letter was referred from FBI HEADQUARTERS to the JUSTICE DEPARTMENT's Office of the Inspector General, which confirmed an ongoing investigation in June 2002. No result of that investigation has yet been announced, though Cole's public statements — coupled with those of other FBI whistle-blowers — prompted leaders of the U.S. Senate Judiciary Committee to question FBI procedures in the midst of President GEORGE W. BUSH's "war on TERRORISM."

**COLLIER, Rex**—Rex Collier, a reporter for the *Washington Star*, was the first of many journalists listed as "friendly" by FBI HEADQUARTERS under the administration of J. EDGAR HOOVER, a designation meaning they could be trusted to publish favorable items on the Bureau and attack Hoover's critics on command. Collier penned his first laudatory article on Hoover in 1929, and six years later helped negotiate a contract that gave Hoover complete control over the "G-Men" radio series based on famous Bureau cases. A year later, Collier himself launched the "War on Crime" comic strip that ran from 1936 to 1939, its stories "based on official files" and produced "with the consent and cooperation of the Federal Bureau of Investigation." He also joined forces with COURTNEY RYLEY COOPER as a ghost writer of many Hoover speeches. In 1950, Collier was one of the first reporters to attack author MAX LOWENTHAL's critical study of the FBI. On the night JULIUS and ETHEL ROSENBERG were executed in New York for ESPIONAGE, 19 June 1953, Collier spent the evening with Assistant Director LOUIS NICHOLS, at the latter's home in Virginia. J. Edgar Nichols later told author Anthony Summers that Collier and his father "went around the house turning off the lights, so they would have more electricity at Sing Sing to electrocute the Rosenbergs. It was symbolic." Half a century later, Collier's praise for the FBI LABORATORY may still be found on the Bureau's website.

**COMMITTEE in Solidarity with the People of El Salvador**—The FBI's four-year pursuit of the Committee in Solidarity with the People of El Salvador (CISPES) began in June 1981, when Salvadoran native Frank Varelli approached the Dallas field office with a tale of right-wing Central American murder squads roaming around the U.S. Agent Gary Penrith, second in command of the Dallas FBI, sent an inquiry to the CENTRAL INTELLIGENCE AGENCY and secured a reply that Varelli's information might be accurate. (In fact, it was false.) By that time, Varelli had expanded his story to include CISPES, a group created to solicit funds for humanitarian aid to war-torn El Salvador. Varelli insisted that CISPES was the leftist counterpart of his mythical right-wing assassins, and the Bureau took him at his word. In September 1981 a criminal investigation was opened, seeking evidence that CISPES members had violated the federal Foreign Agents Registration Act. G-men found no evidence of any illegal acts, and the case was officially closed in February 1982.

FBI historian Robert Kessler reports (in *The Bureau*, 2002) that "[b]ecause of poor supervision by headquarters, the Dallas office reopened the CISPES case two years later," but records declassified in January 1988 indicate that the CISPES investigation resumed in March 1983 on direct orders from FBI HEADQUARTERS, employing Attorney General WILLIAM SMITH's expanded guidelines for "foreign counterintelligence — international TERRORISM" cases. Kessler further states that the investigation "had no political motives," and while headquarters instructed G-men that "the purpose of the investigation was not to investigate the exercise of First Amendment rights of CISPES members," agents proceeded as they might have done for any COINTELPRO operation ordered by late Director J. EDGAR HOOVER. A headquarters memo issued to all field offices on 28 October 1983 commanded agents to develop "information on the locations, leadership, and activities of CISPES chapters within each field offices' jurisdiction."

Before the CISPES surveillance finally ended on 18 June 1985 (without producing any criminal charges), the FBI had opened new FILES on 2,375 individuals and 1,330 organizations found to have some marginal link with CISPES or its members. The other groups included more than 100 organizations opposed to President RONALD REAGAN's Central American policies, plus local chapters of the United Auto Workers and the National Education Association. The writings of one CISPES clergyman were cited in an FBI report as evidence of a "mind totally sold on the Marxist Leninist philosophy." When one G-man reported that a group he had investigated was nonviolent and legitimate, FBI headquarters refused his suggestion to drop surveillance; instead he was ordered to "consider the possibility" that the orginization "may be a front org for CISPES." A memo from the New Orleans field office, dated 10 November 1983, advised Director WILLIAM WEBSTER that:

> It is imperative at this time to formulate some plan of attack against CISPES and specifically, against individuals ... who defiantly display their contempt for the U.S. Government by making speeches and propagandizing their cause while asking for political asylum.
>
> New Orleans is of the opinion that Departments of Justice and State should be consulted to explore the possibility of deporting these individuals or at best denying their re-entry once they leave.

A subsequent review of the CISPES investigation by the House Committee on Civil and Constitutional Rights found that all 59 FBI field offices were involved in the futile search for "subversive" activity. The committee also documented 50 unsolved BREAK-INS committed during the same period, targeting churches, homes and offices of persons opposed to Reagan's Central American policies. FBI spokesmen denied any Bureau involvement in those burglaries, and while Director WILLIAM SESSIONS confessed that "the scope of the investigation was unnecessarily broadened" in October 1983, he called the case "an aberration" in FBI behavior. One agent was disciplined for his role in the CISPES case: G-man Daniel Flanagan, assigned as Frank Varelli's case officer in Dallas, confessed to stealing money earmarked for Varelli and resigned after reimbursing the FBI $1,000.

**"COMMUNAZIS"** — Between 1933 and 1941, numerous writers, artists and other intellectuals fled Europe to escape the rising tide of fascist repression. The exodus began in Nazi Germany and spread thereafter as ADOLF HITLER and his allies devoured the continent, driving Jews, pacifists, communists and all manner of "liberals" from Austria, Czechoslovakia, France and "neutral" Spain (controlled by fascist dictator Francisco Franco). Many of those exiles fled to the United States, while another large colony gathered in Mexico. Collectively, they were viewed with suspicion by many Americans, including FBI Director J. EDGAR HOOVER. Various government reports from the era lumped the refugees together, as if they were all of one mind, and dubbed them "Communazis."

The label reveals a confused approach to the exile problem, doubtless exacerbated by the Nazi-Soviet non-aggression pact of 1939-41. That brief truce between Hitler and Josef Stalin encouraged some shallow thinkers to believe that Nazism and communism were "the same," lumped together under the broad umbrella of "un-American" activities, with Nazism sometimes incorrectly dubbed "brown bolshevism." Hoover's G-men were fond of the "Communazi" tag, but they probably did not create it. The term is also found in STATE DEPARTMENT documents and in the title of a newspaper column written by Red-hunter Jack Tenney, chairman of the California Senate Fact-finding Committee on Un-American Activities. Strangely, while J. Edgar Hoover was happy to lump all exiles together, calling them servants of amorphous "totalitarianism," he seized on any public criticism of fascist dictatorships to brand its author a communist. That personal quirk was especially ironic after America's entry into WORLD WAR II, when the U.S. allied itself with Soviet Russia to crush Hitler's Axis.

**COMMUNIST Labor Party** — On 30 August 1919 the Socialist Party of America split in a rift between right- and left-wing members. Some 10 percent of the latter — an estimated 10,000 persons, mostly English-speaking immigrants — organized the Communist Labor Party (CLP) that same afternoon. The remainder, chiefly immigrants who spoke little or no English, created the COMMUNIST PARTY (CP) two days later. Attorney General A. MITCHELL PALMER considered both groups equally dangerous and members of both were marked for deportation under the Immigration Act of 1918 (banning any immigrants or advocated violent overthrow of the U.S. government).

The extent of government infiltration already achieved with both groups was demonstrated on 27 December 1919, when future FBI director J. EDGAR HOOVER penned a memo instructing all INFORMANTS in the CLP and the CP to arrange simultaneous meetings on the night of 2 January 1920 and thereby "facilitate arrests." The sweeping PALMER RAIDS conducted that night jailed thousands of CP members, but only 300 from the CLP. Over Hoover's objections, Secretary of Labor LOUIS POST released all 300 on their own recognizance, pending a hearing to decide their fate. That hearing convened in April 1920 and received Hoover's testimony that the CLP was "a gang of cutthroat aliens who have come to this country to overthrow the government by force." Nonetheless, Assistant Secretary of Labor WILLIAM WILSON decreed that membership in the CLP was not a deportable offense, since members were not required to accept (or even know) the party's goals as a condition of membership. Charges against all 300 detainees were therefore dismissed.

The Palmer raids had the desired effect, however, despite the small number of subjects finally deported. By the time the CLP and CP merged in early 1921, combined membership had shriveled to an estimated 5,700 nationwide. Former CLP organizer Benjamin Gitlow put a brave face on his party's collapse, declaring that "the raids helped the communist party separate the wheat from the chaff."

**COMMUNIST Party** — The U.S. Communist Party (CP) was organized on 1 September 1919, following a split in the Socialist Party of America. Estimates of its initial membership range from 25,000 to 60,000 members, but none are truly reliable, since various left-wing groups joined the party *en masse* without consulting their individual members. Whatever the party's actual size, however, it was viewed as a national menace by Attorney General A. MITCHELL PALMER and his aide at the helm of the GENERAL INTELLIGENCE DIVISION, young J. EDGAR HOOVER. Within a month of the CP's creation, Hoover had drafted a blanket indictment of its philosophy under the Immigration Act of 1918. In a brief to Palmer he declared:

> From the examination of ... the manifesto of the Communist International and the manifesto of the Communist Party of America, we find advocation of doctrines to the overthrow of the Government of the United States, not by parliamentary action but by direct action or mass action, which ... means force and violence. Thus the Communist Party of America stands indicted under the act of October 16, 1918. However, in order that there may be no doubt as to the responsibility of individual members of the Communist Party of America, we have but to examine the application for membership which each member must sign upon entering the organization. The following is a statement taken from the application: "The undersigned, after having read the constitution and program of the Communist Party, declares his adherence to the principles and tactics of that party and the Communist International; agrees to submit to the discipline of the party as stated in its constitution; and pledges himself to actively engage in its work."

It was enough for Palmer, and plans were laid for a mass roundup of CP members on 2 January 1920. Hoover drafted a letter, afterward signed by Frank Burke, assistant director of the

Bureau of Investigation, and sent to G-men in 33 major cities on 27 December 1919, which read: "You should arrange with your undercover INFORMANTS to have meetings of the Communist party and COMMUNIST LABOR PARTY on the night set. ... This, of course, would facilitate the making of arrests." Officials of the LABOR DEPARTMENT issued 3,000 blank arrest warrants for the PALMER RAIDS, but an estimated 10,000 suspects were jailed nationwide by the dragnet. Of those, some 6,500 were released upon discovery that they were U.S. citizens or because they were simply friends and relatives of alleged communists, arrested to maintain secrecy during the sweeps. Of the remaining 3,500, a mere 556 were finally deported. Federal judge GEORGE ANDERSON, reviewing Hoover's conduct in the raids and the use of informants to arrange party meetings, declared on 24 April 1920 that the federal government apparently "operates some part of the Communist party in this country."

The raids, as desired, had a chilling effect on communist activity in the U.S. Party membership dwindled to an estimated 10,000 by the end of 1920, and half that number the following year. Still, surveillance and harassment of Reds remained one of the Bureau's top priorities. On the very day Director WILLIAM BURNS was sworn into office, 22 August 1922, G-men illegally raided a CP meeting in Michigan and seized party documents. State and local authorities collaborated in the nationwide campaign, as did the FISH COMMITTEE and other investigative bodies. Party membership received a boost with the arrival of the Great Depression, and G-men heightened their vigilance accordingly. In September 1939 President FRANKLIN ROOSEVELT gave the FBI virtual carte blanche to investigate "matters relating to ESPIONAGE, sabotage, and violations of the neutrality agreements." Hoover unilaterally added the phrase "subversive activities" to that mandate and used Roosevelt's order as a Red-hunting license.

Passage of the 1940 SMITH ACT also encouraged Hoover, with its ban on membership in groups that advocated toppling the government by force, but prosecutions were delayed until after WORLD WAR II, since Soviet Russia was then an American ally. Twelve CP leaders were indicted in June 1948 for advocating revolution, although they had made no attempt to achieve it. Convicted four months later, they lost an appeal to the U.S. SUPREME COURT in 1951 and were consigned to prison for their thoughts and words alone. Thus far, no CP member had been charged with spying for the Soviets or any other criminal activity beyond the realm of theory.

Observers estimate that the CP's membership declined from 46,000 in 1946 to 22,000 in 1955. Many of those who remained were FBI informants — including the party's second in command, Morris Child, recruited by the Bureau as "Agent 58" in 1954. Two years later, in 1956, brutal Soviet reactions to uprisings in Poland and Hungary finished the CP for all practical purposes, leaving it with fewer than 10,000 members nationwide. Hoover chose that moment to launch an aggressive new campaign against the party, designated as the FBI's first "COINTELPRO" operation. The program's introductory memo, dated 28 August 1956, declared:

> During its investigation of the Communist Party USA, the Bureau has sought to capitalize on incidents involving the Party and its leaders in order to foster factionalism, bring the Communist Party (CP) and its leaders into disrepute before the American public and cause confusion and dissatisfaction among rank-and-file members of the CP.
>
> Generally, the above action has constituted harassment rather than disruption, since, for the most part, the Bureau has set up particular incidents, and the attack has been from the outside. At the present time, however, there is existing within the CP a situation resulting from the developments at the 20th Congress of the CP of the Soviet Union and the Government's attack on the Party principally through prosecution under the Smith Act of 1940 and the Internal Security Act of 1950 which is made to order for an all-out disruptive attack against the CP from within. In other words, the Bureau is in a position to initiate, on a broader scale than heretofore attempted, a counterintelligence program against the CP, not by harassment from the outside, which might only serve to bring the various factions together, but by feeding and fostering from within the internal fight currently raging.

To that end, G-men planted false newspaper stories about the CP; mailed anonymous letters to CP members, their spouses, relatives and other friends; made hundreds of nuisance phone calls, and so forth. Personal accusations raised against individual targets included claims of adultery, HOMOSEXUALITY, venereal disease and various financial irregularities. Some of the allegations were true, but many more were fabricated. Employers and coworkers were sometimes informed of a target's CP affiliation, provoking ostracism or dismissal. "Selective law enforcement" was employed, including harassment by local police and tax audits by the INTERNAL REVENUE SERVICE. Over the next 15 years, attacks on the Communist Party accounted for more than half of the FBI's acknowledged COINTELPRO operations — 1,388 out of 2,370.

The covert war was not entirely secret. Hoover briefed Attorney General WILLIAM ROGERS in a memo dated 8 May 1958, and addressed President DWIGHT EISENHOWER'S full cabinet on the subject six months later, complete with a 36-page "Top Secret" booklet outlining the campaign to date. As Hoover explained in those pages:

> To counteract a resurgence of the Communist Party influence in the United States, we have a ... program designed to intensify confusion and dissatisfaction among its members. During the past few years, the program has been most effective. Selective informants were briefed and trained to raise controversial issues within the Party. In the process, they may be able to advance themselves to high positions. The Internal Revenue Service was furnished the names and addresses of Party functionaries.... Based on this information, investigations have been instituted in 262 possible income tax evasion cases. Anticommunist literature and simulated Party documents were mailed anonymously to carefully chosen members.

There had been no "resurgence" of CP strength, in fact, and Hoover's briefing barely scratched the surface of FBI harassment techniques. Three years later he provided a similar incomplete briefing for Attorney General ROBERT KENNEDY, who apparently raised no objections. Writing for *The Nation* in September 1962, ex-agent JACK LEVINE revealed that 1,500 of the CP's estimated 8,500 remaining members were informants on the Bureau's payroll. He also suggested that Hoover had been disingenuous in his promotion of the CP as a national menace. Levine wrote:

> By 1960 the end of the Communist Party U.S.A. as a viable organization was already in sight. In a highly confidential memorandum to all Bureau Offices, Hoover announced that the development of additional Communist Party informants, except at the highest policy making levels, would serve no useful purpose.
> … The Supervisor in charge of the Communist Party desk at FBI headquarters in Washington, during a briefing of Agent personnel on recent developments in the Party, summed up the situation as well as anyone when he said: "The Communist Party U.S.A. has long ago become a paper tiger. The hard core members have been reduced in size to a manageable bunch of harmless crackpots. We here at the Bureau are starting to feel sorry for them."

Not sorry enough, however, to leave them in peace. As a matter of fact, in 1966 the FBI devised a plan to instigate deadly conflict between the CP and members of ORGANIZED CRIME. Dubbed "Operation Hoodwink," the plot was hatched in a memo dated 4 October 1966.

> The purpose of this memorandum is to recommend a long-range counterintelligence program designed to provoke a dispute between the Communist Party, USA, and La Cosa Nostra under the code name of Hoodwink.
> A dispute between the Communist Party, USA, and La Cosa Nostra would cause disruption of both groups by having each expend their energies, time, and money attacking the other. This would help neutralize the activities of both groups which are detrimental to this country.
> La Cosa Nostra has no sympathy for the communists. The Communist Party, USA, and La Cosa Nostra come in contact with each other in the labor field where hoodlums operate businesses under "sweatshop" conditions. By making it appear that the Party is attacking hoodlum labor practices, over a period of time we could provoke a bitter dispute between the two organizations.
> The New York Office has recommended a specific technique to initiate this program. This technique consists of anonymously forwarding one leaflet to a local La Cosa Nostra leader attacking the labor practices of one of his enterprises. The leaflet would ostensibly be published by a local Party unit. A note with the leaflet would give the impression that it had received wide circulation.

Hoover authorized the mailing on 5 October, with a twist. His answering letter read, in part:

> Take the usual precautions to insure this mailing cannot be associated with the Bureau and advise of tangible results. New York should also submit follow-up recommendations to continue this program.
> The Party has been the subject of recent BOMBINGS, a typical hoodlum technique. Consider a spurious Party statement blaming the LCN for the bombings because of "Party efforts on behalf of the workers." This statement could be aimed at specific LCN members if appropriate.
> In developing this program, thought should also be given to initiating spurious LCN attacks on the CPUSA, so that each group would think the other was mounting a campaign against it.
> The Bureau much appreciates New York's careful analysis of this program and the initial "low-key" technique suggested.

Operation Hoodwink continued into 1968, but its "tangible results" in terms of urban mayhem are unknown. A year later, with the CP on its last legs, G-men found themselves reduced to attacking dumb animals. Assistant Director WILLIAM SULLIVAN recalled:

> Even though the CPUSA was finished we kept after them. Early in 1969 we learned that the Soviet Union planned on sending [CP chief Gus] Hall a gift of some expensive stallions and mares which Hall planned to ship to his brother's farm in Minnesota. They expected to breed thoroughbreds and sell the colts to help fill the coffers of the party. On learning about the impending gift to Hall, one of the imaginative men in my division came up with an idea [which Hoover approved]. He contacted a veterinarian, and without telling him what it was about, got the doctor to agree to inject the horses with a substance that would sterilize them before they were taken off the ship in New York.

Sullivan finally tired of the charade, and while addressing an audience of Virginia newspaper editors on 12 October 1970 he revealed that the CP posed "no significant threat to national security" in the U.S. The party was so shrunken, he revealed, that only four members resided in the U.S. capital — but an entire squad of agents from the Washington field office was assigned to watch them constantly. Hoover soon compelled Sullivan to resign with charges of "insubordination," but the damage was done. A "national menace" had been laid to rest after 50 years, forcing the FBI to search for other enemies.

**COMPUTER Crimes** — Law enforcement agencies traditionally lag behind criminal elements in the adoption of new technology. Unhampered by monetary constraints or conservative attitudes, criminals have led the way from horseback travel to cars and aircraft, from muskets and six-guns to high-powered automatic weapons. So it is in the ethereal domain of "cyberspace," where computer technology permits a bandit to rob banks in New York or Seattle without leaving his home in Moscow, Manila or Tokyo; where child pornography can reach a global audience without a penny spent on postage; and where spies can glean no end of secrets from the Internet, without the risk of breaking into vaults or military camps.

The FBI has long made use of computers — for communication, in its VICAP program, analyzing FINGERPRINTS and so on — but it was August 1991 before the Bureau's LABORATORY DIVISION announced creation of a Computer Analysis and Response Team to support ongoing investigations. By February 1997 computer-crimes units were active in the Washington, New York, Los Angeles and San Francisco field offices, connected to the National Infrastructure Protection Center in Washington, D.C. and the JUSTICE DEPARTMENT'S Internet Fraud Complaint Center. Together, those units and the agents trained within them were confronted with a range of criminal activity that would have been literally unimaginable 10 years earlier.

Computer crimes are broadly divided into two categories: crimes committed with or facilitated by computers, and crimes in which computers are the targets. The former class includes a wide variety of offenses, including all manner of fraud, identity theft, transmission of child pornography, extortion or ransom demands, intellectual property theft (copyright violations), stalking, money laundering, and so forth. The latter (often dubbed "hacking" or "cracking") includes ESPIONAGE, theft of trade secrets or other commercial information, looting of bank accounts, alteration or destruction of official records, sabotage of computer systems, disruption of transportation and communications, writing of "malicious codes" (computer "worms" and "viruses"), or acts of long-distance TERRORISM. In the wake of the catastrophic SKYJACKINGS on 11 September 2001, the Bureau opened a computer tip line for reports of alleged terrorist activity across America. A month later President GEORGE W. BUSH created a new Critical Infrastructure Board, ordered to safeguard "the people, economy, essential human and government services and national security of the United States" by protecting vital computer networks. Civil libertarians, meanwhile, expressed concern that the Bureau's "CARNIVORE" software might inaugurate a new age of illegal DOMESTIC SURVEILLANCE on the Internet.

The FBI's war on "cybercrime" has produced some unfortunate embarrassments. In December 2001 the Bureau's monthly *Law Enforcement Bulletin* described five "new insidious viruses" that did not exist. Apparently, the editors had been deceived by jocular small talk on some Internet newsgroup, described by one observer as "the equivalent of geek knock-knock jokes." A more serious problem, revealed in August 2002, was the unexplained disappearance of several hundred laptop computers. More than half of the FBI's laptops — 8,000 out of 15,077 — were authorized to store "secret" or "top secret" data, but Justice Department auditors found Bureau records so confused and incomplete that they were unable to say whether critical information had been compromised. The same audit revealed bizarre lapses in the FBI's accounting procedures. Whereas Bureau rules demand an inventory of physical property every two years, the last inventory prior to 2001 was conducted in 1993. Some reports of missing property (including firearms) were not filed for 23 years after the initial loss, and the *average* reporting time for a loss was four years. Employees responsible for losing the expensive laptops were disciplined in only four percent of all cases.

Even that report paled, however, beside the Bureau's embarrassment in a case of computerized child pornography. While agents worked overtime on Internet sting operations like "Candyman," arresting purveyors of child pornography around the country and jailing them for terms of 30 years or more, it was revealed that one of their own — FBI bomb technician CHARLIE ENGLISH, JR. — had been trading contraband photos himself. Dismissed from the Bureau, he faced trial on charges bearing a maximum sentence of 15 years in prison.

**CONGRESS of Racial Equality** — Originally called the Committee of Racial Equality, CORE was founded in 1942 by an interracial group of college students in Chicago, dedicated to Mahatma Gandhi's principle of nonviolent resistance to injustice. More conservative CIVIL RIGHTS groups such as the NATIONAL ASSOCIATION FOR THE ADVANCEMENT OF COLORED PEOPLE opposed such "direct action" tactics, and the FBI wasted no time in marking CORE as a "radical" organization. By the summer of 1942 a full Bureau investigation was under way, including an il-

legal "mail cover" on Rev. Archibald Carey's African Methodist Episcopal Church, where CORE had its office.

CORE members staged sit-in demonstrations to protest segregation in 1942, 18 years before the concept was "discovered" by another generation of students in North Carolina, and founding member (later National Director, 1953-66) James Farmer toured the country with colleague BAYARD RUSTIN, recruiting activists for future campaigns. G-men shadowed their every move, reporting to FBI HEADQUARTERS on various localized demonstrations. In April 1947, a full 14 years before the more famous FREEDOM RIDES, CORE sent an integrated group of 16 men on a "Journey of Reconciliation" to the South, testing a U.S. SUPREME COURT order for desegregation of interstate buses and depots. (They were repeatedly arrested.)

Between 1954 and 1965, CORE focused its attention on desegregation protests and black voter registration efforts in the South. Its members were involved in every major civil rights campaign of that turbulent era, and Farmer ranked among the "Big Six" U.S. civil rights leaders. In 1961, seeking federal protection for its Freedom Riders, CORE furnished FBI agents with their bus itineraries. Instead of guarding the protesters, though, G-men delivered the information to racist police and members of the KU KLUX KLAN, while providing columnist FULTON LEWIS, JR., with material on "Red" links to the protest and feeding segregationist Sen. Strom Thurmond WIRETAP information suggesting that two alleged communists hoped to start a CORE chapter in San Francisco.

Bureau relations with CORE were ambiguous throughout the 1960s. FBI headquarters freely leaked information to "reliable, intelligent" leaders of the group who "expressed concern over possible 'radical' influences," and Assistant Director CARTHA DELOACH met with Farmer in 1963 to discuss "the possibilities of the FBI advising him on a confidential basis whenever members of the COMMUNIST PARTY sought to infiltrate and take advantage of CORE." Julius Hobson, director of CORE's Washington, D.C. chapter was fired in 1964 for being "too militant," and while the FBI may have influenced that decision, Assistant Director Alex Rosen later identified Hobson as "one of the Bureau's most effective contacts."

FBI surveillance of CORE escalated in 1964, when CORE helped organize Mississippi's "Freedom Summer" project, resulting in a series of murders that finally forced J. EDGAR HOOVER to take action against the KKK. At the same time, Assistant Director WILLIAM SULLIVAN'S Domestic Intelligence Division established a Communist Infiltrated Racial Matters (CIRM) unit to report on alleged Red penetration of CORE and other civil rights groups. In March 1965 Alabama congressman George Andrews transmitted an "urgent request" from Klan-allied Gov. George Wallace for any available "information indicating communist connections on the part of civil rights leaders," including James Farmer, and Hoover's office rapidly complied.

James Farmer retired from leadership of CORE in 1966, replaced by the more militant Floyd McKissick, who endorsed STOKELY CARMICHAEL'S call for "Black Power" in America. A Hoover memo on "Black Nationalist Hate Groups," dated 25 August 1967, called for "intensified attention ... to expose, disrupt, misdirect, discredit, or otherwise neutralize" a short list of civil rights groups with "backgrounds of immorality, subversive activity, and criminal records." The list included CORE and several others with no history of violence. G-men in the field found communist influence on CORE to be "negligible," but they still insisted that McKissick and successor Roy Innis condoned "violence as a means to obtaining Negro rights." Accordingly, in March 1968, CORE's file was moved from the FBI's "COMIN-FIL" category to a special "Racial Matters" section, later filling its own subsection in Hoover's RABBLE ROUSER INDEX. Surveillance of CORE presumably ended with Hoover's death, although corroboration of that fact remains impossible. CORE survives today, headquartered in New York, with Roy Innis as national director.

**CONNOLLY, John J., Jr.**—A native of South Boston, born in 1940, John Connolly was a childhood neighbor and admirer of future mob boss JAMES ("WHITEY") BULGER. By 1975, as an agent of the FBI's Boston field office, Connolly was assigned to recruit "Top Echelon INFORMANTS" in the Bureau's campaign against ORGANIZED CRIME. In the process, he forged an alliance with Bulger's ruthless Winter Hill Gang against the New England Mafia, forging an illicit combination that had tragic consequences for all concerned.

Recruitment of Bulger as an informant made Connolly a "star" within the FBI, a status he enjoyed until his retirement from active service in 1990. Bulger's tips enabled the Boston field office to score impressive victories against the Irish mob's Italian competitors, but those victories came at a price. Connolly (and others in the Boston field office) had become as corrupt as the mobsters with whom he fraternized. On a government salary of $60,000 per year, he purchased a $400,000 home in Boston and a $300,000 summer retreat at Cape Cod. In exchange for that largess, Connolly and other G-men tipped Bulger and his gang to impending sting operations and shielded them from prosecution on various charges (including multiple murder). At least four innocent defendants suffered FRAME-UPS and were jailed for life on false murder charges, while Bulger and his trigger men went free. (Two of those scapegoats, PETER LIMONE and JOSEPH SALVATI, would survive to win exoneration after 30 years in prison.)

Bulger's free ride ended after Connolly retired in 1990, to accept a lucrative post with Boston Edison. A new task force, including agents from the DRUG ENFORCEMENT ADMINISTRATION, built a NARCOTICS case against Bulger in 1995, but friendly G-men warned him once again and he escaped. (At this writing, in December 2002, Bulger is a fugitive from justice on the Bureau's "TEN MOST WANTED" LIST, with a $1 million reward outstanding for information leading to his capture.) Details of the FBI's protection racket were exposed in 1998, during pretrial hearings for Bulger associate Stephen FLEMMI. In 1999 Connolly was indicted for accepting bribes and sharing the money with his former supervisor, Agent John Morris. A second indictment, handed down in 2002, charged Connolly with leaking information to Bulger and Flemmi that led to three murders.

Connolly's trial opened in Boston on 6 May 2002, with the defendant facing eight counts of racketeering, racketeering conspiracy, conspiracy to obstruct justice and making false statements. Co-defendant Stephen Flemmi was charged with one count each of obstructing justice and conspiracy to obstruct justice. Prosecution witnesses included a motley collection of convicted mobsters, confessed killers, and disgraced former G-men. John Morris, testifying under a grant of immunity, wept on the witness stand as he admitted taking $7,000 in bribes from Bulger and soliciting $5,000 more from an unnamed Mafia bookie (also an FBI informant). Connolly's defense attorney blasted the government's witnesses, declaring that "you've never seen a bigger group of thieves and liars in your life," while U.S. Attorney Michael Sullivan told the jury, "John Connolly became a Winter Hill gang operative masquerading as an FBI agent." Jurors dismissed Connolly's pleas of innocence and convicted him on 28 May 2002.

With sentencing scheduled for August, federal judge Edward Harrington took the unusual step of writing a letter to colleague Joseph Tauro, presiding over Connolly's trial and sentencing. The unsolicited correspondence recalled Harrington's days as a U.S. attorney, working with Connolly in Boston, and advised Tauro, "I always held Mr. Connolly in the highest regard and considered him to be a man of the highest character and ability. I respectfully ask that, in deciding Mr. Connolly's appropriate punishment, you consider the contribution he made to the government's campaign against organized crime, as well as the risks and complexities inherent in the duties he was asked to undertake in carrying out the policy of the United States government." On 16 September 2002 Judge Tauro sentenced Connolly to a 10-year prison term (instead of the maximum 20 years) and rejected a defense motion that Connolly be freed on bond to settle affairs before incarceration. At last report, Connolly still faced wrongful-death litigation from survivors of three men—John Callahan, Richard Castucci (another FBI informant) and Brian Halloran—allegedly murdered as a result of Connolly's leaks to the Winter Hill gang. Relatives of those seek $35 million in damages from Connolly and the FBI.

**CONNOR, Eugene ("Bull")**—Born at Selma, Alabama on 11 July 1897, Theophilus Eugene Connor dropped out of high school to work as a railroad telegrapher and radio sportscaster (where he earned his famous nickname for fabricating plays and statistics—i.e., "shooting the bull"—during broadcasts). In 1934 he was elected to the Alabama state legislature; three years later he won election as Birmingham's commissioner of public safety, commanding the city's police and fire departments. Connor held that post until 1953, declining to seek reelection that year in the wake of a 1951 sex scandal. He was returned to office in 1957, on a pledge maintain strict racial segregation in the face of mounting CIVIL RIGHTS protests, and maintained his post until Birmingham changed its form of municipal government in 1963.

Connor's die-hard commitment to segregation placed him in collaboration with the violent KU KLUX KLAN, protecting nightriders responsible for 40-plus racial BOMBINGS between 1948 and 1963. Under Connor, the city was nicknamed "Bombingham," while its largest black neighborhood was dubbed "Dynamite Hill." On the rare occasions when he addressed the problem at all, Connor habitually blamed blacks for the crimes. "We know Negroes did it," he told reporters after three black churches were bombed in January 1962. "Everybody we talk to who knows anything about it says they saw Negroes running away from the churches." An FBI memo filed on 7 December 1957, following the demolition of a black-owned home, reported that "Connor did not intend to attempt to solve this bombing." Seven months later, on 24 July 1958, FBI HEADQUARTERS ordered the Birmingham field office "to hold contacts with Connor to a minimum in view of his unsavory background." Connor reciprocated in October 1958, instructing his police to share no information with G-men on pending civil rights cases. (During the last decade of Connor's reign, Birmingham officers were unofficially barred from attending the FBI NATIONAL ACADEMY.)

The breakdown in communications hardly mattered by that time, since FBI INFORMANTS in the Klan kept G-men fully advised of Connor's negligence where acts of TERRORISM were concerned. One such informant, GARY ROWE, advised agents of Connor's April 1961 agreement to let Klansmen assault participants in the integrated "FREEDOM RIDES" without police interference. Rather than warn the demonstrators, however, FBI agents provided Birmingham police (including an officer known for his ties to the Klan) with an itinerary of the buses, thereby facilitating violent attacks at Anniston and at Birmingham's Trailways bus depot. Following the latter riot, on 14 May 1961, Connor explained the absence of police by claiming that most officers had gone home to celebrate Mother's Day.

Stripped of his office via popular vote and court orders in 1963, Connor was elected the following year to serve as president of Alabama's Public Service Commission. He held that post until 1972, when a series of strokes left him disabled and forced his resignation. A final stroke claimed Connor's life on 26 February 1973.

**COOLIDGE, John Calvin**—A Vermont native, born 4 July 1872, Calvin Coolidge served as governor of Massachusetts in 1919 and 1920, earning national recognition when he broke the 1919 Boston police strike. The publicity surrounding that performance won Coolidge nomination as WARREN HARDING'S vice president in 1920, and he inherited the White House upon Harding's death in August 1923. Coolidge emerged personally unscathed from the TEAPOT DOME SCANDAL, exposed after Harding's demise, and he won election by a landslide in 1924, inspiring public confidence with admonitions that "the business of America is business."

Harding's administration did nothing to stem the corruption spawned by Prohibition and the rise of ORGANIZED CRIME in America, but his April 1924 appointment of Attorney General HARLAN FISKE STONE led to a cleanup at the Bureau of Investigation and installed J. EDGAR HOOVER as director. Perhaps anticipating the imminent stock market crash, Coolidge declined to run for reelection in 1928, leaving successor HERBERT HOOVER to confront the ensuing Great Depression. Coolidge retired to Massachusetts, where he died on 5 January 1933.

**COOPER, Courtney Ryley**—A Kansas City native, born in 1886, Courtney Ryley Cooper ran away from home to become a circus clown at age 16, later serving as a publicist for William "Buffalo Bill" Cody and as a reporter for various newspapers. In 1912 he launched a new career as a freelance writer, ultimately publishing some 750 magazine articles and short stories, plus more than 30 books. One critic complained that Cooper's work was "not always written with entire regard for actualities," but his melodramatic style appealed to FBI Director J. EDGAR HOOVER, and Hoover biographer Athan Theoharis has called Cooper "probably the most important of all Hoover's publicists during the critical 1930s."

Cooper's first contact with the FBI came in 1933, when he was assigned to research a crime article for *American Magazine*. The finished product pleased Hoover so much that Cooper found himself promoted to the head of the Bureau's favored-journalist roster, later serving as Hoover's speech writer and literary "ghost" for the director's first book, *Persons in Hiding* (1938). In addition to his yeoman service behind the scenes, Cooper ranked among Hoover's most ardent defenders in case of attack by unsympathetic reporters. (When one journalist described Hoover as short and fat, Cooper fired back with a description of the FBI chief as "a well-built man, tall, but sufficiently well-proportioned to make his height less apparent.") In return for services rendered, Cooper was granted entrée to Hoover's inner circle, frequently joining the director on fishing trips with confidants CLYDE TOLSON and GUY HOTTEL.

The Cooper-Hoover relationship apparently soured in early 1940, for reasons still unknown. The break-up may have been occasioned by Cooper's return to circus life, manifested in April 1940 by his acceptance of a publicist's job with the Ringling Brothers and Barnum & Bailey Circus at a salary of one cent per year. On 27 September 1940 Cooper checked into a two-room suite at New York's Park Central Hotel, where employees found him hanging from a steam pipe in the closet two days later. Hoover was among 150 mourners at Cooper's funeral, on 1 October 1940, but Cooper's widow subsequently blamed Hoover for her husband's suicide, citing some unspecified "wrong" on the director's part.

**COPLON, Judith**—A Brooklyn native, born in 1921, Judith Coplon joined the Young Communist League while a student at Barnard College. That fact was discovered by FBI agents when she later applied for a job with the JUSTICE DEPARTMENT, but Coplon was hired anyway and later received a letter of commendation from Attorney General TOM CLARK. Her past apparently forgotten, G-men suspected nothing until a cryptanalyst with the Army Security Agency cracked a KGB code in 1948, translating messages that referred to an unnamed Russian spy at Justice. The agent was identified as a woman, once employed in New York, transferred to Washington, D.C. in January 1945. The description fit Coplon, still employed at Justice as a political analyst in the Foreign Agents Registration Section.

G-men began their full-press investigation of Coplon on 4 January 1949. They tapped her home and office telephones, as well as phones belonging to her parents and her lover (a Justice

Department attorney); they also rented a flat across the street from Coplon's apartment and followed everywhere she went. The surveillance paid off on 16 January, when Coplon visited New York and met with Valentin Gubitchev, a member of Russia's delegation to the United Nations. A second meeting was observed on 18 February, and a third on 4 March 1949, protracted over 99 minutes as Coplon and Gubitchev tried to outwit their FBI shadows. Agents arrested both suspects and found 28 FBI documents in Coplon's purse. Most were "data slips," summarizing the contents of various FILES, but Coplon also carried a false memo planted on orders from FBI Director J. EDGAR HOOVER.

Both defendants were indicted for ESPIONAGE in New York; Coplon was also indicted in Washington, on a separate charge of stealing government documents. That case went to trial on 26 April 1949, with prosecutors anticipating an easy victory. Their case hit a snag when defense attorney Archibald Palmer requested access to the "raw files" summarized by various FBI data slips found in Coplon's possession at her arrest. Hoover, alerted to the threat of exposure, urged Attorney General Clark to seek a mistrial, but Clark refused to intervene. Judge Albert Reeves ordered release of the files, ruling that the prosecution "could not insist on the importance of the documents to national security and at the same time use national security as a reason for refusing to reveal their contents."

The press had a field day with Hoover's secret files, including accusations of communist activity by various Hollywood celebrities and a strange report from Brooklyn, recording an IN-FORMANT's complaint that one of his neighbors liked to walk around nude. Don Whitehead, in *The FBI Story* (1956), claims that "Only a small portion of the information in the file was relevant to the government's case against Coplon. Much of it, in the course of normal procedure, would have been tossed out as a matter of course. The FBI files were ridiculed as a storehouse of gossip and the trivia were given prominence above all else." In fact, we know today that Hoover discarded *nothing*, however bizarre, unless destruction of a file somehow protected him. And every item was completely relevant to Coplon's case, since the government accused her of providing vital secrets to the Soviets.

The media furor was one thing, but Coplon still had to explain why she stole *any* documents at all. Her lawyer used a romantic defense, claiming that Coplon had been "crazy" in love with Gubitchev, a slave to his every demand. Coplon's lawyer also requested a hearing to discover whether the investigation of his client had involved illegal WIRETAPPING, but Judge Reeves accepted false denials from Justice on that point and denied the motion. Jurors dismissed the "love" defense and convicted Coplon 30 June 1949, whereupon she received a 10-year prison term. The NATIONAL LAWYERS GUILD, meanwhile, called in vain for a full-scale investigation of FBI DOMESTIC SURVEILLANCE (which would have revealed illegal BREAK-INS at the guild's own offices dating back to 1924).

Judge Sylvester Ryan, in New York, proved more receptive to the notion of exploring FBI wiretap procedures. A pretrial hearing on the subject convened in December 1949, revealing that G-men had lied under oath about tapping Coplon's phones and that Hoover himself had ordered the wiretap logs destroyed

"in view of the imminence of her trial." Frightened by a defense subpoena for telephone records from New York and Washington, Hoover warned phone company officers to cover their tracks, meanwhile complaining to his aides that if Coplon's maneuver succeeded "all wiretapping is through." The New York trial finally proceeded, with Coplon and Gubitchev convicted on 7 March 1950, both sentenced to 15 years in prison.

As it happened, neither defendant would ever serve time. Gubitchev's sentence was suspended in favor of deportation, while Coplon remained free on $40,000 bond pending appeal. On 5 December 1950 the U.S. Circuit Court of Appeals overturned both convictions. The Washington case was thrown out on grounds that G-men had continued tapping Coplon's phones after she was arrested, illegally eavesdropping on conversations with her attorney. Dual grounds were cited for the New York reversal: Coplon's arrest without a warrant was illegal, and Judge Reeves had erred in refusing to explore the issue of illicit wiretaps. Congress solved the warrant problem on 28 December 1950, passing at Hoover's request a new law permitting warrantless arrests in cases of espionage, sabotage and other major crimes. Still, the new law was not retroactive, and the illegal arrest in New York barred introduction at any future trial of the papers taken from her purse on 4 March 1949.

Prosecutors could not try Coplon without evidence, but Hoover argued bitterly against dismissal of the charges. Over the next 17 years he persuaded five attorneys general to leave the case open, held in abeyance while he played a pointless game of nerves with Coplon. Attorney General RAMSEY CLARK, whose father filed the original case against Coplon, finally dropped the charges over Hoover's angry protests in 1967. At the time, it was simply one more incident that led Hoover to brand the younger Clark "a jellyfish."

**COUNTERATTACK**— Variously subtitled *The Newsletter of Facts on Communism* or *Facts to Combat Communism, Counterattack* was a weekly newsletter launched in 1946 by three retired FBI agents. Published in New York by a firm called American Business Consultants, which also produced the magazine *Red Channels, Counterattack* was initially funded by right-wing industrialist Alfred Kohlberg and Father John Cronin, a Catholic priest who placed Red-baiting ahead of his pastoral duties in the 1940s and '50s. Armed with their FBI training and a handful of COMMUNIST PARTY defectors employed as "fact checkers," the editors of *Counterattack* lined their pockets by accusing public figures of disloyalty — or by "clearing" them for a price. If not precisely blackmail or extortion, it was close enough. Hollywood studios, radio/television networks, labor unions and other commercial entities paid *Counterattack* to vet their employees, or to smear the competition with a taint of crimson.

One early target of the newsletter, in 1947, was playwright ARTHUR MILLER, condemned as a subversive on general principles and more specifically for allowing *All My Sons* to be produced in postwar Germany, where *Counterattack* feared "it would help Stalin in his efforts to convince the Germans that the U.S. is controlled by heartless plutocrats." If that was not bad enough, the newsletter accused Miller of "twisting the facts in a central situation in his play!" Another object of FBI interest, author AL-DOUS HUXLEY, was denounced by *Counterattack* in 1952 for supporting the notion of peace between the U.S. and Russia. Outspoken conservative WILLIAM BUCKLEY, JR., by contrast, was praised in August 1955 as "an effective foe of Communism." Accusations from *Counterattack* also surface in many FBI dossiers from the Red-hunting era, providing a clear illustration of the rumor-mongering that underlay many Bureau "loyalty" investigations. The newsletter ceased publication in the late 1950s, replaced by more blatant appeals to racism as CIVIL RIGHTS issues preoccupied far-right conspiracy theorists.

**COURTS, Gus**—A son of former slaves, born in 1889, Gus Courts joined Rev. GEORGE LEE in 1954 to organize Belzoni, Mississippi's first chapter of the NATIONAL ASSOCIATION FOR THE ADVANCEMENT OF COLORED PEOPLE. Despite threats and harassment from members of the segregationist CITIZENS' COUNCIL, Courts and Lee managed to register 92 black voters around Belzoni over the next 12 months. Courts carried on alone after Lee was murdered by nightriders in May 1955, while threats on his life multiplied. FBI agents briefly investigated Lee's murder, without result, but Director J. EDGAR HOOVER declared (falsely) that his agents were legally barred from protecting CIVIL RIGHTS activists in the South.

On 25 November 1955, Courts was wounded by gunshots fired from a passing car in Belzoni. The town's police chief declined to take action, telling reporters, "Let the Naps [white slang for NAACP members] investigate. They won't believe anything I say anyway." Sheriff Isaac Shelton, meanwhile, repeated his verdict from the Lee murder. When asked if the latest shooting was related to civil rights issues, Shelton told reporters, "Hell, no. Some nigger had it in for him, that's all."

Attorney General HERBERT BROWNELL, JR., told the press that FBI agents "automatically" launched an investigation of the crime, but their tactics were self-defeating. G-men interviewed Courts briefly in the hospital, then never spoke to him again. When his physician produced the shotgun pellets taken from Courts's body, two agents from the Memphis field office told him to "keep them." The projectiles were never collected, though Brownell later insisted that "all evidence" in the case was delivered by G-men to local authorities. The case was never solved, and Hoover's statements to President DWIGHT EISENHOWER'S cabinet cast doubt on the director's willingness to solve HATE CRIMES. In that presentation, Hoover called Citizens' Council members "the leading citizens of the South," while he blasted the NAACP and the U.S. SUPREME COURT for promoting "racial hatred."

**COWLEY, Malcolm**—A native of Belsano, Pennsylvania, born in 1898, Malcolm Cowley ranked as one of America's foremost literary critics and social historians, serving as chancellor of the American Academy of Arts & Letters from 1966 through 1976. Long before that, however, the FBI had opened a file on Cowley, beginning with his support for Spanish Loyalist forces in 1936 and writings for the liberal *New Republic*. The dossier included thirty single-spaced typewritten pages by 1942, when

Cowley went to work for the U.S. Office of Facts and Figures in Washington, D.C. Cowley was shown a copy of the file by ARCHIBALD MACLEISH and became "obsessed with the desire to set the record straight."

> I began to feel like K— in Kafka's "The Trial." I went to see high officials in the Department of Justice to press for a hearing. To one of them I made the obvious remark that most of the FBI investigators seemed pretty stupid. "Of course," he said. "You don't expect us to get *bright* law-school graduates, do you, for $65 a week?"

In March 1947, following an FBI-inspired attack by right-wing columnist WESTBROOK PEGLER, Cowley "left Washington with my FBI dossier still full of more falsehoods and unsupported assertions than you could find in any three of Hitler's speeches." Two years later, Cowley appeared as a defense witness for ALGER HISS, recounting conversations with prosecution Whittaker Chambers which contradicted the government's claims against Hiss. "And after that," Cowley recalled, "I really got out of politics, completely." He died at Sherman, Connecticut in 1989.

**COWLEY, Samuel P.**—A native of Franklin, Idaho, born 23 July 1899, Samuel Cowley was a devout Mormon who conducted missionary work in Hawaii between 1916 and 1920. He graduated from George Washington University's law school in 1928, licensed to practice law in Utah and the District of Columbia. Cowley joined the FBI in March 1929 and was assigned to headquarters in October 1932. He was promoted to inspector on 1 July 1934, placed in charge of the bureau's Midwest "flying squad" that pursued JOHN DILLINGER and suspects deemed responsible for the KANSAS CITY MASSACRE.

Cowley's role in the Dillinger manhunt assumed greater importance as a personal rift developed between J. EDGAR HOOVER and Chicago G-man MELVIN PURVIS. After Purvis resigned from the FBI in August 1935, Hoover launched a campaign to erase his name from bureau history, publicly crediting Sam Cowley with the apprehension of Dillinger and CHARLES ("PRETTY BOY") FLOYD. Briefly credited with killing Dillinger himself, Cowley was afterward enshrined as the mastermind behind the FBI's pursuit, Hoover insisting that Cowley "mapped the campaign, working from a secret office with unlisted telephones, and it was this campaign which led to Dillinger's death." That revision of history was facilitated by Cowley's own death, on 28 November 1934, from wounds he suffered in an Illinois shootout with bank robber GEORGE ("BABY FACE") NELSON. Cowley's widow afterward became an FBI clerk, serving the bureau from September 1936 through July 1948.

**COZZENS, James Gould**—A Chicago native born in 1903, conservative novelist James Cozzens ran afoul of J. EDGAR HOOVER in 1942, over the content of his novel *The Just and the Unjust*. Hoover, who had applauded comic FRED ALLEN'S radio portrayal of FBI third-degree methods six years earlier, now took offense at Cozzens's "unfounded insinuations and accusations that the FBI uses third degree methods" and that G-men "would perjure themselves and withhold evidence on the witness stand during a trial." Hoover ordered that "a letter be prepared to the publishers ... as well as the author straightening them out," and files were scoured for any prior references to Cozzens or his publisher. Still unsatisfied, Hoover urged his agents to conceal their FBI affiliation and write angry letters to the Book-of-the-Month Club, denouncing its selection of this "most libelous" novel as a featured selection. (The club kowtowed, noting Hoover's complaint in a special mailing to its 500,000 members, pleading that "any unfair reflection upon the FBI ... is ... regretted.") Hoover climaxed his campaign by sending terse notes to various reviewers of the novel, prompting the New York *Herald Tribune*'s literary editor to write back, reminding the director his "argument is with Mr. Cozzens" and not with literary critics. Cozzens died in 1978, leaving a 141-page file in the bureau archives.

**CRAIG, Arthur Ulysses**—A Missouri native, born in 1871, Arthur Craig earned a degree in electrical engineering from the University of Kansas in 1895, becoming the first black graduate in that field. He taught electrical engineering at the Tuskegee Institute from 1896 to 1901, then spent the next 17 years as a teacher and high school principal in Washington, D.C. (where he also ran a small poultry farm and dairy in his spare time). Craig served with the Food Administration's Negro Press Section during WORLD WAR I, and was recruited by the Bureau of Investigation for UNDERCOVER OPERATIONS near the end of 1918.

Craig's first assignment as an INFORMANT was to infiltrate the Liberty League, a "radical" group that urged blacks to defend themselves against white rioters and lynch mobs. Recalled to covert duty during the "Red Summer" of 1919, Craig joined a variety of black organizations, including the NATIONAL ASSOCIATION FOR THE ADVANCEMENT OF COLORED PEOPLE (NAACP) and MARCUS GARVEY'S Universal Negro Improvement Association (UNIA), signing his reports "C-C." J. EDGAR HOOVER, still five years away from total control of the Bureau, ordered Craig to focus his attention on Garvey and a "radical" black newspaper, the *Messenger*, published by A. PHILLIP RANDOLPH, whereupon Craig found a job writing for the suspect publication. He also mailed copies of Garvey's *Negro World*, while reporting from the UNIA that "the spirit of these meetings is decidedly unAmerican."

Newark G-men distracted Craig from his primary mission in 1919, with claims that gun parts stolen from Remington Arms in Connecticut were stockpiled at the NAACP's national headquarters on Fifth Avenue, in Manhattan. Craig prowled the office in vain, but found nothing. Another red herring took him to Baltimore, on a mission to expose links between black radicals and the INDUSTRIAL WORKERS OF THE WORLD. On arrival, Craig found that his primary suspect, longshoreman Ollis Brown, was in fact a bitter enemy of the IWW.

Hoover dismissed Craig in late September 1919, after Craig failed to produce hard evidence of federal MANN ACT violations against Marcus Garvey. Craig went on from Bureau service to pursue disparate careers as a mechanic, draftsman, teacher, heating engineer and editor of a Harlem newspaper. He died in 1959.

**CRAWFORD, James E.**—One of the FBI's few African American employees prior to 1962, James Crawford was initially hired in 1935 to work as Associate Director CLYDE TOLSON'S office "boy" and chauffeur, but J. EDGAR HOOVER commandeered Crawford's services the following year, when his own chauffeur died. Thereafter, Crawford served Hoover as a combination driver, gardener, dog-walker and general handyman, his after-hours household chores performed at taxpayers' expense. In the occasional absence of Hoover's black maid, Crawford filled in as cook and housekeeper, donning a white dinner jacket to wait on special dinner guests at Hoover's home. Crawford's wife would later complain that he "worked 15 hours a day, seven days a week" for Hoover, including holidays.

In 1941, fearing that Crawford would be drafted into military service during WORLD WAR II, Hoover appointed Crawford as a "special agent," sending him through a brief (and segregated) training course at the FBI ACADEMY. Crawford was issued a pistol but never took possession of it, and despite occasional press reports to the contrary, he never worked a Bureau case or served as Hoover's bodyguard. Hoover occasionally referred to Crawford, office majordomo SAMUEL NOISETTE and his other chauffeurs around the country when asked if the Bureau had any black agents, but none were assigned to anything resembling investigative duties.

Crawford officially resigned in January 1972, but he continued daily work at Hoover's home and it was he who found Hoover dead in his bedroom on 2 May 1972. Bureau reports attributed the discovery to maid Annie Fields, perhaps (as author Curt Gentry suggests) to avoid troubling questions about why a retired "agent" was performing menial chores at Hoover's home. In the days after Hoover's death, Crawford was one of several persons seen by neighbors, removing cartons from the house that were presumed to contain Hoover's private FILES.

Crawford was a beneficiary to Hoover's will, receiving half of the late director's used clothing and a $2,000 bequest paid out over 36 months. Still serving the Bureau despite Hoover's passing, Crawford frequently drove Tolson to the cemetery, Tolson waiting in Crawford's car while Crawford placed flowers on the grave. He was at Tolson's hospital bedside when Tolson died in April 1975, this time inheriting all Tolson's clothing plus $27,000 in cash. A legal challenge to the will forced Crawford and the other beneficiaries to pay 10 percent of their windfall to Tolson's favorite charities.

**CRIME Records Division**—Encouraged by journalist COURTNEY RYLEY COOPER, FBI Director J. EDGAR HOOVER created the bureau's Publications Section in 1935, to generate favorable publicity. The Publications Section was supplanted by a new Research Division on 13 July 1936, officially renamed the Crime Records Division (CRD) on 16 September 1938. Whatever its name and officially designated task, the CRD's primary function from 1935 to 1972 consisted of preserving and inflating the FBI's reputation at home and abroad.

To that end, CRD agents and clerical staff served as Hoover's uncredited ghost writers, churning out four books, scores of magazine articles and hundreds of speeches for which the director claimed sole credit. Hoover received thousands of dollars in royalties from four ghost-written books—*Persons in Hiding* (1938), *Masters of Deceit* (1958), *A Study of Communism* (1962) and *J. Edgar Hoover on Communism* (1969)—while laundering his income through the FBI RECREATIONAL ASSOCIATION to avoid paying taxes. As biographer Curt Gentry reports, "it was a standing joke among the agents that the director not only didn't write his own books; he hadn't even read them."

Aside from launching Hoover's literary career, Crime Records worked tirelessly to assist friendly journalists, script writers and authors (notably including DON WHITEHEAD, author of *The FBI Story*). An equally important CRD assignment was promotion of the bureau during Hoover's annual congressional appearances, pleading for ever-larger appropriations. While Hoover consistently boasted to Congress of the FBI's impressive "conviction rate," the statistics cited invariably included defendants who pled guilty without facing trial. In 1968, for example, Hoover claimed an FBI conviction rate of 96.7 percent; in fact, of some 483,000 criminal cases investigated by G-men that year, barely 13,000 resulted in guilty verdicts at trial, for an actual conviction rate of 2.6 percent. The bureau's record in CIVIL RIGHTS was even worse: fourteen convictions out of 11,328 cases investigated between 1960 and 1964, barely one-tenth of one percent. Overall, FBI-obtained convictions during any given year amount to roughly one percent of all criminal convictions obtained in the United States.

The Crime Records Division survived its creator by less than a year. Acting Director L. PATRICK GRAY renamed CRD the Crime Research Division in October 1972, but soon abolished it completely, dispersing the unit's 200 employees to other administrative tasks. Still, despite CRD's passing, FBI manipulation of crime statistics continues. On 28 December 2001, bureau spokespersons announced their plan to create "a new crime classification" for the estimated 3,000 victims killed in tri-state terrorist attacks on 11 September. As explained to the press, the bureau's goal was "prevent the dozens of kidnappings, thousands of deaths and billions of dollars in property damage stemming from the attacks from giving New York, Virginia and Pennsylvania aberrant crime rates." So far, the FBI's "new classification" of murder remains nameless.

**CRIMINAL Investigative Division**—The FBI's Criminal Investigative Division (CID) was created in 1977 by combining the former GENERAL INVESTIGATIVE DIVISION, the SPECIAL INVESTIGATIVE DIVISION, and elements of the INTELLIGENCE DIVISION. The new division handles investigation of ORGANIZED CRIME, NARCOTICS offenses, white-collar crimes, crimes on government reservations, CIVIL RIGHTS cases, federal fugitives, interstate theft, and government job applicants. The CID's Organized Crime and Drug Sections were merged in June 1992, creating a new Organized Crime/Drug Branch to consolidate domestic and international investigations. A Violent Crimes and Major Offenders Program was created within the CID on 21 June 1989, with "violent crimes" including KIDNAPPING, SKYJACKING and assaults on federal agents. Domestic TERRORISM was added to the list on 3 March 1993, then shifted to the NATIONAL SECURITY DIVISION in 1994. Since 1994 the CID's International Relations Branch has

overseen the FBI's LEGAT PROGRAM, thus assuming duties once performed by the OFFICE OF LIAISON AND INTERNATIONAL AFFAIRS.

**CRIMINAL Justice Information System**—Created on 24 February 1992 and based at Clarksburg, West Virginia, the FBI's Criminal Justice Information System (CJIS) combines the functions of the NATIONAL CRIME INFORMATION CENTER, the UNIFORM CRIME REPORTS program, and the former IDENTIFICATION DIVISION. The CJIS provides state-of-the-art identification and information services to local, state, federal and international law enforcement agencies. Originally led by Assistant Director G. Norman Christensen, CJIS today has three deputy directors in charge of administrative support services, engineering, and policy and liaison.

**CRITICAL Incident Response Group**—Following adverse publicity attending the RANDY WEAVER incident in 1992 and the Waco, Texas BRANCH DAVIDIAN siege of 1993, FBI leaders determined that a new unit was required to deal with violent crimes and crises. The result, founded in 1994 and based at Quantico, Virginia, was the Critical Incident Response Group (CIRG). Its major divisions include an Operations Support Branch (including Crisis Management, Special Operations and an Underground Safeguard Unit), a Tactical Support Branch (including the FBI HOSTAGE RESCUE TEAM and a SWAT Training Unit), and the NATIONAL CENTER FOR ANALYSIS OF VIOLENT CRIME (including specialists in PSYCHOLOGICAL PROFILING). CIRG's special agent in charge also supervises the FBI units tasked with investigating CHILD ABDUCTION and SERIAL MURDER.

**CROW DOG, Leonard**—A resident of South Dakota's ROSEBUD RESERVATION and a recognized Brulé Lakota holy man, Leonard Crow Dog was widely considered the spiritual leader of the AMERICAN INDIAN MOVEMENT (AIM) in the early 1970s. He helped organize AIM's "Trail of Broken Treaties" protest in 1972 and he participated in the WOUNDED KNEE SIEGE a year later, transporting supplies to demonstrators from the Independent Oglala Nation and subsequently helping to negotiate their surrender. In the wake of that siege, Crow Dog was one of five AIM members arrested by FBI agents, held in lieu of $35,000 bond pending resolution of the "Wounded Knee Leadership" trials. All charges against defendants Russell Means and Dennis Banks were dismissed in September 1974, with the court citing FBI misconduct; federal counts against Crow Dog and two other defendants were reduced from 11 counts to three.

Crow Dog was finally tried for his role in an incident occurring on 11 March 1973, wherein six members of the vigilante GUARDIANS OF THE OGLALA NATION (GOON) illegally posed as U.S. postal inspectors to infiltrate AIM's headquarters. The criminals were detained and disarmed, but no charges were filed against them for impersonating federal officers. Instead, the FBI charged Crow Dog and company with assault, robbery, and "interfering with federal officers." Convicted on those charges in 1974, Crow Dog received an eight-year prison sentence but was released on probation.

A nephew of Crow Dog's, AIM member Andrew Stewart, was shot and killed on 25 July 1975, on the PINE RIDGE RESERVATION. Two GOON members present at his death subsequently visited Crow Dog's home and assaulted another relative on 2 September 1975. When the two men returned and lost a second fight with Crow Dog's friends, they filed a complaint alleging unprovoked assault. G-men responded on 5 September with an airborne raid on Crow Dog's home, ransacking the house and arresting Crow Dog. An audio tape of the raid reveals Agent J. GARY ADAMS ridiculing Crow Dog's religious artifacts and urging Crow Dog to see if "you can outrun my M-16 [assault rifle]." On 28 November 1975 an all-white jury convicted Crow Dog of "aiding and abetting" an assault on the GOONs, and he received a five-year prison term. (During the trial, GOONs attacked and burned the home of Crow Dog's parents, at Grass Mountain, South Dakota.)

A third federal case was filed against Crow Dog in January 1976, stemming from an incident occurring on 25 March 1975. In that case, three white strangers reeking of liquor had invaded Crow Dog's home, making crude propositions to Crow Dog's wife and punching him when he told them to leave. The three were finally ejected, only to file yet another complaint. Prosecutors claimed that "victim" Royer Pfersick was an FBI INFORMANT, thereby justifying charges of assault on a federal officer. Convicted by another all-white jury, Crow Dog received his second five-year sentence, running consecutively with the previous jail term. Shuffled through nine different prisons in the next six months, Crow Dog lost 45 pounds and was diagnosed by prison doctors as suffering from a brain tumor. The doctors wanted to operate without Crow Dog's permission, but they were finally dissuaded by pleas from Amnesty International and the National Council of Churches. The tumor diagnosis proved false, and Crow Dog was finally released from Leavenworth on 21 March 1977.

**CUMMINGS, Edward Estlin**—Born at Cambridge, Massachusetts on 14 October 1894, E.E. Cummings published his first poems at age eighteen, in the *Harvard Monthly*. He drove an ambulance in France during WORLD WAR I, until French authorities jailed him in 1917, on suspicion of disloyalty. Released on 1 January 1918, he was drafted into the U.S. Army and served until the armistice. A prolific author who published hundreds of poems, Cummings won the Guggenheim Fellowship twice, in 1931 and 1951. FBI agents opened a file on him in 1955, after learning that he had translated "a small paperback publication called *The Red Front*," written by French communist Louis Aragon. According to bureau reviewers, Aragon's work "inferred [*sic*] the revolution would be bloody." The pamphlet's publisher advertised other works said to "support Communism by inference," but no other derogatory material was found on Cummings, and his file never grew beyond six pages. He died at North Conway, New Hampshire on 3 September 1962.

**CUMMINGS, Homer Stillé**—Born in Chicago on 30 April 1870, Homer Cummings spent most of his life in Connecticut, where he rose rapidly through Democratic party ranks. He served briefly in Congress (1902), later making unsuccessful bids for a U.S. Senate seat (1916) and the White House (1920). President FRANKLIN ROOSEVELT chose Cummings as his first attorney general, installed on 4 March 1933. He served until January 1939, his term in office coinciding with the FBI's expansion into headline "gangbusting" and covert investigation of "subversive" activities.

Driven by such incidents as the LINDBERGH and URSCHEL kidnappings, coupled with the KANSAS CITY MASSACRE, Cummings declared a federal war on crime that perfectly suited J. EDGAR HOOVER'S desire to broaden bureau authority. While reorganizing the JUSTICE DEPARTMENT, Cummings merged the Bureau of Investigation with the Prohibition Bureau and the Bureau of Identification to create a new Division of Investigation on 10 June 1933. Two years later, on 1 July 1935, he christened the new agency the Federal Bureau of Investigation. Between those two events, on 19 April 1934, Cummings announced a Twelve Point Crime Program complete with legislation to expand bureau authority and make a long list of offenses federal crimes. His national conference on crime, convened in December 1934, helped publicize the new campaign—so much so, in fact, that a 1935 article by journalist Milton Mayer referred to "Mr. Cummings's crime wave."

Congress rejected some of the Cummings-FDR proposals, but FBI agents were finally granted authority to carry firearms, serve warrants and make arrests (activities some agents had pursued illegally since 1908). The Seventy-third Congress also added more laws to the U.S. criminal code than all previous Congresses combined. Among the new federal offenses were BANK ROBBERY; murder of a federal agent or employee of a federally insured bank; possession of unregistered "gangster" weapons (including machine guns, sawed-off shotguns and silencers); and a mixed bag of interstate crimes including KIDNAPPING, extortion, racketeering, and transportation of stolen property.

As the "crime war" wound down and a new war loomed in Europe, President Roosevelt ordered sweeping FBI investigation of "subversive" activity including "general activities—Communist and Affiliated Organizations, Fascist, Anti-Fascist movements, and activities in Organized Labor organizations." Hoover received his orders from FDR on 1 September 1936 and launched his campaign four days later, belatedly informing Cummings on 10 September. Cummings endorsed the plan and broadened its scope, instructing Hoover to collaborate with the State Department, military and naval intelligence.

Broken by his failure to help FDR "pack" the Supreme Court with liberal justices, Cummings resigned as attorney general on 2 January 1939, replaced by FRANK MURPHY. Following retirement, Cummings practiced law in Washington, D.C. and remained active in Democratic politics, serving as a presidential elector from Connecticut in 1940 and 1944. He died in Washington on 10 September 1956.

**CUSTODIAL Detention Index**—Following the European outbreak of WORLD WAR II in September 1939, J. EDGAR HOOVER devised a new program targeting "individuals, groups and organizations engaged in ... subversive activities, or espionage activities, or any activity that was possibly detrimental to the internal security of the United States." Immediate subjects of interest were all "persons of German, Italian, and Communist sympathies," together with any others whose "interest may be directed primarily to the interest of some other nation than the United States." Those "whose presence at liberty" was deemed "dangerous to the to the public peace and safety of the United States Government" were to be "discreetly" listed in a new Custodial Detention Index, slated for mass arrest if America entered the war.

Lacking any vestige of legal authority for his new campaign, Hoover sought and received secret approval from Attorney General ROBERT JACKSON in June 1940. Jackson's successor, Attorney General FRANCIS BIDDLE, authorized arrest of German and Italian enemy aliens in 1942, but U.S. citizens were not affected and communists were likewise omitted since the Soviet Union was an American ally. In July 1943 Biddle ordered Hoover to discontinue the program, noting that the FBI "classification system is inherently unreliable" and that the bureau's proper law enforcement function "is not aided by classifying persons as to dangerousness." In typical fashion, Hoover avoided Biddle's order with an August 1943 memorandum informing subordinates that "Henceforth, the cards known as Custodial Detention cards will be known as SECURITY INDEX." Fearing discipline for insubordination, Hoover insisted that the new list be "strictly confidential and should at no time be mentioned or alluded to in investigative reports or discussed with agencies or individuals outside the Bureau." Under its new name, the index endured for another 28 years, finally abolished in fall 1971.

# D

**DAUGHERTY, Harry Micajah**—An Ohio native, born at Washington Court House on 26 January 1860, Harry Daugherty was a lifelong Republican activist known for his talents as a political manipulator. He was also a close friend of WARREN HARDING and served as manager of Harding's presidential primary campaign in 1920. As his reward for that victory, Daugherty was appointed to serve as attorney general on 4 March 1921.

Harding's regime is remembered today as one of the most corrupt in U.S. history, and Daugherty's performance was no exception. He quickly transformed the JUSTICE DEPARTMENT into a "Department of Easy Virtue" that became a national laughingstock. Daugherty's top priority appeared to be concealing crimes committed by Harding's "Ohio Gang," including the notorious TEAPOT DOME SCANDAL. To that end, acting in concert with Bureau chief WILLIAM BURNS and assistant chief J. EDGAR HOOVER, he launched a campaign of surveillance and character assassination against congressional critics, including Senators THOMAS WALSH and BURTON WHEELER.

Harding's death in August 1923 brought CALVIN COOLIDGE to the White House, and increasing heat from Congress and the courts placed Daugherty in an untenable position. Coolidge demanded his resignation on 28 March 1924 and replaced Daugherty with HARLAN STONE 10 days later. Daugherty was subsequently indicted on charges of conspiracy to defraud the U.S. government, but two hung juries spared him from prison and the charges were dismissed in 1927. He died at Columbus, Ohio on 12 October 1941.

**DAVIDSON, Alaska P.**—Born in 1868, Alaska Davidson completed only three years of public school education but was still described by friends as "very refined." On 11 October 1922, at age fifty-four, she was appointed by Chief WILLIAM BURNS to serve as the Bureau of Investigation's first female "special investigator." Davidson was trained in New York before assignment to the Washington, D.C. field office, but no record of her work survives today. J. EDGAR HOOVER assumed control of the BI on 10 May 1924 and ordered each field office to evaluate its personnel, with an eye toward dismissal of "unqualified" agents. Washington's special agent in charge reported that his office had "no particular work for a woman agent," whereupon Hoover requested and received Davidson's resignation on 10 June 1924.

**DAVIS, Angela Yvonne**—A native of Birmingham, Alabama, born 26 January 1944, Angela Davis was the daughter of African American schoolteachers who maintained friendships with members of the COMMUNIST PARTY. As a teenager she spent two years in Germany (1960-62), at the Frankfurt School, and later studied at the University of Paris (1963-64). Upon her return to the U.S., Davis graduated with honors from Brandeis University (1965), then returned to Germany for graduate research. She earned her master's degree from the University of California in 1968. That same year, she joined both the Communist Party and the BLACK PANTHER PARTY, political choices that prompted Governor RONALD REAGAN to dismiss her after one year as an assistant professor of philosophy at the University of California in Los Angeles.

Thus unencumbered by daily employment, Davis threw herself full-time into radical politics, specifically the struggle to liberate a group of black convicts at Soledad Prison whom she regarded as political prisoners. Romance blossomed between Davis and one of the convicts, "Soledad Brother" George Jackson, and Davis hired Jackson's younger brother (Jonathan) as her personal bodyguard. Jonathan Jackson was killed, with several others, during an ill-conceived bid to liberate several convicts from the Marin County courthouse at San Rafael, California, on 7 August 1970. A routine trace of Jackson's weapons revealed that three had been purchased by Davis at various times between January 1968 and July 1970. On 14 August 1970 a California grand jury charged Davis with murder, kidnapping and conspiracy; federal charges of unlawful flight were added two days later, and on 18 August she became the third woman added to the FBI's "TEN MOST WANTED" LIST.

Two months later, on 13 October 1970, Bureau surveillance on a male acquaintance led to Davis's arrest in New York City. Her friend, David Poindexter, was charged with harboring a federal fugitive, but a jury acquitted him on 12 April 1971. Legal maneuvers delayed Davis's trial until March 1972. Davis declared that Jonathan Jackson had taken her guns for the Marin County jailbreak without her permission and jurors believed her, acquitting Davis of all counts on 4 June 1972.

Taking advantage of her notoriety, Davis founded the National Alliance Against Racist and Political Repression, which remains active today. She resumed teaching and campaigned unsuccessfully as the Communist Party's vice presidential candidate in 1980. A prolific author and lecturer, she also serves on the Advisory Board of the Prison Activist Resource Center, working tirelessly to expose the inequities of what she calls the U.S. "punishment industry." In April 1999, a lecture at the University of Wisconsin in Milwaukee left students so inspired that they organized the Angela Davis Copwatch and Campaign Against Racial Profiling.

**DAWSON, Edward**—A native of New Jersey, born in 1921, Edward Dawson dropped out of school in the seventh grade. In 1942, following two charges of insubordination in the U.S. Army, he was convicted of going AWOL; Dawson escaped from the brig in 1943 but was recaptured, convicted in his second court-martial of desertion and another AWOL charge. He was working as a self-employed contractor in Greensboro, North Carolina when he joined the United Klans of America (UKA) in 1964. Once a member of the UKA's state board and an officer in the Klan's security guard, Dawson was convicted of a TERRORIST shooting incident in 1967 and served nine months in prison. Sometime during his incarceration or immediately after his release, he was recruited as a paid INFORMANT for the FBI.

Bureau records suggest that Dawson received his first federal payoff on 7 November 1969, but questions surround his role in a violent incident from 4 July 1969, wherein a black girl was wounded and a police car riddled with bullets after a Klan rally at Swan Quarter, North Carolina. Dawson subsequently left the UKA—"coincidentally" in November 1969—and joined in founding the rival North Carolina Knights of the KU KLUX KLAN.

He remained with that faction (and served as an officer of another group, the Confederation of Independent Orders) while reporting to the Bureau and presumably disrupting Klan affairs on behalf of the FBI's COINTELPRO campaign against white hate groups. Dawson supposedly received his last FBI check on 31 August 1976, around the same time he was elected "grand dragon" of the North Carolina Knights, but he may have continued work as a federal informant—and in any case, he was doubling as an informant for the Greensboro Police Department while remaining active in Klan affairs.

Although uncertain of Dawson's loyalty, Greensboro detectives showed him a copy of the parade permit for a "Death to the Klan" demonstration planned by the local Communist Workers Party for 3 November 1979. That document revealed the starting point of the parade, and the fact that demonstrators would be unarmed. Dawson immediately began agitating for Klansmen and neo-Nazis to meet the parade, making personal contacts with various groups and distributing posters. As one Klansman later told the press, "We'd never have come to Greensboro if it wasn't for Ed Dawson berating us." Meanwhile, Dawson warned authorities on 31 October and again on 3 November that Klansmen were coming to the protest heavily armed, but police declined to intervene. On 3 November 1979 a Klan firing squad ambushed the marchers, killing five persons and wounding nine others. Six defendants were acquitted of murder charges by an all-white jury on 17 November 1980; similar charges filed against 13 others were dismissed on 26 November 1980. The original six defendants faced trial again in 1985, this time on federal CIVIL RIGHTS charges: five were acquitted, while one received a six-month sentence in a prison work-release program. Dawson's role in the bloody incident was never satisfactorily examined.

**DEADLY Force**—The FBI maintains a Hall of Honor for its agents killed on duty, whether by accident or "adversarial action." [See the Appendix.] Likewise, the INTERNATIONAL ASSOCIATION OF CHIEFS OF POLICE keeps detailed records of every U.S. law enforcement officer slain in the line of duty. By contrast, no agency (public or private) has ever attempted to count (much less identify by name) the thousands of "civilians" killed by police in America. The discrepancy is natural, since law enforcers killed on duty are invariably portrayed as heroes and martyrs, while those killed by police are typically dismissed as criminals who "asked for it" and "had it coming." Still, in a society that claims to value freedom and equality above all else, it is incumbent on all citizens to study the uses which their authorized defenders make of deadly force.

Official histories of the FBI, from DON WHITEHEAD's *The FBI Story* (1956) to the Bureau's modern Internet website, uniformly stress that G-men had no legal authority to carry firearms or make arrests before 18 June 1934, when Congress passed a clutch of new laws to facilitate the federal "war on crime." The point is made repeatedly, in an attempt to show how courageous agents performed their duties from 1908 to 1934 with one hand tied behind their backs, striving against near-impossible odds. Unarmed in their contest with criminal hordes, still they managed to carry the day.

A closer look at Bureau history, however, proves the legend false. G-men may have been barred by law from packing "heat" before June 1934, but a memo from J. EDGAR HOOVER to all FBI field offices, dated 24 March 1925, ordered special agents in charge to store certain sensitive FILES "in either the gun vault or the SAC's safe." Hoover biographer Athan Theoharis further reports that Hoover subordinates CLYDE TOLSON and GUY HOTTEL were "regularly armed" throughout the late 1920s and early 1930s, whenever they appeared with Hoover in public. By 1933, Hoover had started recruiting "HIRED GUNS" from other law enforcement agencies and G-men sported guns on some of their assignments, notably the arrest of fugitive Frank Nash which led to the KANSAS CITY MASSACRE of 17 June 1933. FBI records, revealed 60 years after the fact, prove that Nash and two of the four lawmen killed that afternoon were shot accidentally by an agent armed with an unfamiliar weapon.

Unfazed by the massacre and subsequent cover-up, Attorney General HOMER CUMMINGS issued a public command for G-men to use deadly force in January 1934, a full six months before they were legally empowered to do so. "Shoot to kill," Cummings ordered, "and then count to ten." Agents scored their first kill on 3 April 1934, when they shot Eddie Green, a member of the JOHN DILLINGER gang, in St. Paul, Minnesota. (Green was unarmed at the time.) Nine days later, Bureau gunmen killed William Phillips, a member of the TRI-STATE GANG, in Washington, D.C. On 22 April 1934, Chicago G-man MELVIN PURVIS tried to corner the Dillinger gang at Wisconsin's Little Bohemia Lodge, but the effort went tragically wrong: agents shot three innocent bystanders, killing one, and lost one of their own to gangland guns before the bandits fled unscathed.

Another two years elapsed before Hoover was called to account for his bureau's use of deadly force. The May 1936 exchange between Hoover and Senator KENNETH MCKELLAR was recorded for posterity in the *Congressional Record*:

> McKellar: How many people have been killed by your Department since you have been allowed to use guns?
>
> Hoover: I think there have been eight desperadoes killed by our agents and we have had four agents in our service killed by them.

Inexplicably, Hoover was wrong on both counts. Only six fugitives had been killed by G-men since June 1934, including Dillinger (July 1934), CHARLES ("PRETTY BOY") FLOYD (October 1934), GEORGE ("BABY FACE") NELSON (November 1934), and three members of the BARKER-KARPIS GANG (all in January 1935). During the same period, only three agents were killed: Agents SAMUEL COWLEY and Herman Hollis were shot by Baby Face Nelson on 17 November 1934, while Agent Nelson Klein was killed by an Indiana car thief on 16 August 1935. Hoover's statistics are only accurate if he began counting fatalities in April 1934, two months *before* his men were authorized to carry guns.

FBI gunplay declined markedly after the bloody demise of the BRADY GANG in 1937, as G-men spent more time in pursuit of "Reds" and less on the trail of roving bank robbers. Still, sporadic incidents have called attention to the Bureau's use of deadly force, raising questions about its application in specific circumstances.

An epidemic of SKYJACKING in the early 1970s challenged FBI agents, as the Bureau was charged with enforcement of federal laws banning aircraft piracy. The initial response was somewhat chaotic: between July 1971 and August 1972, G-men engaged in four shootouts with airline hijackers, killing three suspects and wounding two others; sadly, three passengers were also shot (one fatally) in the same encounters. A fifth incident, in October 1971, ended tragically after FBI snipers flattened the tires of a hijacked airliner in Jacksonville, Florida. Alarmed by the gunfire, the hijacker murdered his wife and the pilot before committing suicide.

The 1970s also exposed a chaotic, sometimes ruthless FBI response to "radicals" and militant racial minorities. During the WOUNDED KNEE SIEGE of 1973, COINTELPRO agent RICHARD W. HELD complained to headquarters that G-men had been ordered "to aim to wound rather than kill" members of the AMERICAN INDIAN MOVEMENT (AIM). Henceforth, Held declared, "the FBI will insist upon taking charge from the outset and will not countenance any interference on an operational basis with respect to our actions." Six months later, in May 1974, reporters for *The Nation* described G-men lobbing military antipersonnel grenades into a Los Angeles bungalow where members of the fugitive SYMBIONESE LIBERATION ARMY subsequently burned to death. Back on South Dakota's PINE RIDGE RESERVATION, two agents died in a firefight with AIM members on 26 June 1975. Bureau leaders expected a speedy murder conviction for confessed shooters DARRYL BUTLER and ROBERT ROBIDEAU, but jurors acquitted both defendants on a plea of self-defense, suggesting that the agents were engaged in an illicit use of deadly force when they were killed.

G-men continued to draw criticism for their use of force in the 1980s and 1990s. ROBIN AHRENS, the first WOMAN AGENT killed on duty, was accidentally shot by fellow agents while trying to arrest a fugitive October 1985. Six months later, the bloodiest shootout in Bureau history left two agents dead and four wounded in Miami; bandits WILLIAM MATIX and Michael Platt also died in the battle, which led to revisions in FBI training and choice of firearms. August 1992 witnessed the RANDALL WEAVER siege at Ruby Ridge, Iowa, where Bureau rules of engagement were altered to include a "shoot on sight" order, resulting in the death of Weaver's wife. FBI sniper LON HORIUCHI escaped prosecution in that case, but five Bureau officials were suspended on suspicion of destroying crucial documents and Weaver's wrongful death lawsuit was settled out of court for $3.1 million. FBI marksmen claimed no lives in the BRANCH DAVIDIAN siege at Waco, Texas, but Bureau efforts to crack the 51-day stalemate with armored vehicles produced a fire of disputed origin that killed 79 persons on 19 April 1993.

Thus far, we have considered only cases wherein use of deadly force might be presumed legitimate in light of serious resistance from suspected felons. If such cases were the only ones on file, some excuse might be offered even for the death of unarmed suspects and innocent bystanders. Unfortunately, there are *other* cases where the Bureau's use of lethal force seems clearly both malicious and illegal. Two suspects detained for simple questioning, ANDREA SALSEDO (1920, New York) and JOHN

PROBASCO (1934, Chicago), plunged to their deaths from skyscraper windows while in FBI custody; both cases were logged as "suicides," but a witness reported agents beating Salsedo moments before his fall, while Chicago G-men were said to routinely dangle recalcitrant witnesses from their 19th-story window as a means of loosening tongues. FBI *agents provocateur*, including ALFRED BURNETT and WILLIAM O'NEAL, were responsible for fatal shootings executed by local police under suspect circumstances. (Burnett constructed a bomb and hired victim Larry Ward to plant it at a Seattle site where police lay waiting in ambush; O'Neal apparently drugged subject FRED HAMPTON several hours before police invaded Hampton's Chicago apartment and shot him while he slept.) Worse yet, in 1970 the San Diego field office helped right-wing extremists create the SECRET ARMY ORGANIZATION (SAO), providing (and later concealing) weapons that SAO members used in attempts to murder a "radical" college professor.

In light of those incidents and others detailed in this volume, it is clear that use of deadly force (like DOMESTIC SURVEILLANCE) remains an area where oversight by some reviewer(s) independent of the FBI is critical. To date, the JUSTICE DEPARTMENT has displayed no willingness to fill that vital role.

**DeLOACH, Cartha Dekle** —A Georgia native, born 20 July 1920, Cartha ("Deke") DeLoach graduated from Florida's Stetson University and remained there for law school, though he failed to complete his graduate study. On 31 August 1942 he was hired as a clerk with the FBI's IDENTIFICATION DIVISION, elevated to the rank of special agent on 14 December 1942, with subsequent assignments to the Norfolk, Virginia and Cleveland, Ohio field offices. G-men lost their automatic draft deferments the following year, and DeLoach joined the U.S. Navy in November 1944, spending the last nine months of WORLD WAR II in the athletic department of a naval air station in landlocked Oklahoma.

Rejoining the Bureau after his discharge, DeLoach briefly occupied Akron, Ohio's RESIDENT AGENCY, before he was recalled to FBI HEADQUARTERS as a supervisor in the Security Division (later the Domestic Intelligence Division). From December 1951 to October 1953, DeLoach served as an inspector for the Training and Inspection Division. It was during 1953 that Director J. EDGAR HOOVER selected DeLoach to solve the FBI's "AMERICAN LEGION problem." Specifically, the Legion's amateur Red-hunters had made a series of demands for the Bureau to investigate specific individuals as possible "subversives." Their meddling annoyed Hoover, and he ordered DeLoach to "straighten it out" from the inside. DeLoach joined the Legion and rose swiftly through its ranks, until by 1958 he was poised for election as national commander. Hoover vetoed the move as "too political," and DeLoach settled for appointment as chairman of the Legion's national public relations commission, a post that enabled him to control the group's various publications and statements to the media.

Meanwhile, in October 1953, DeLoach had left Training and Inspection to serve as an aide to Associate Director CLYDE TOLSON. At the same time, he doubled as FBI liaison to the CEN-TRAL INTELLIGENCE AGENCY, former G-man Robert Lamphere recalled that DeLoach "reflected the director's negative attitude toward the CIA by working to exacerbate the problems between the 2 agencies, rather than damp then down." That conflict was resolved in March 1954, when DeLoach transferred to the critical CRIME RECORDS DIVISION, heart of the Bureau's various "DISINFORMATION" campaigns. January 1959 found him in command of Crime Records, promoted to assistant director four months later. He remained at that post until his promotion to serve as Assistant to the Director for Investigations in 1965.

By that time, in the wake of the JFK ASSASSINATION, DeLoach had assumed a critical role in the Bureau, serving as FBI liaison to President LYNDON JOHNSON. Johnson called on DeLoach for information and advice at all hours, ordering a special White House hot-line installed beside DeLoach's bed for late-night emergencies. As Hoover neared mandatory retirement age, DeLoach was sent to get a presidential waiver and LBJ cheerfully complied on 8 May 1964. Part of the payback, three months later, was DeLoach's assignment to lead a 30-man surveillance team at the Democratic National Convention in Atlantic City, New Jersey. Johnson worried that civil rights activists might disrupt the convention, or that hostile delegates might draft ROBERT KENNEDY as their presidential candidate, but DeLoach's G-men used their skill at WIRETAPPING and BUGGING to keep LBJ ahead of the game.

Around the same time, DeLoach went in search of larger appropriations to complete the new FBI building, authorized by Congress in 1962. (Cost overruns would top $102 million by the time it was completed in 1972.) He approached Roy Elson, administrative aide to sympathetic Senator Carl Hayden, but Elson had reservations about the increased price tag. As Elson later described the event to author Robert Kessler, DeLoach "was persistent"; he "hinted" at possible disclosure of "information that was unflattering to my marital situation and that the senator might be disturbed." More specifically, Elson claims that DeLoach mentioned "information about my sex life" involving "more than one girl." Elson called his bluff, requesting proof, whereupon DeLoach "started backing off" and claimed he was "only joking." Thirty years after the fact, Elson still regarded the conversation as "attempted blackmail."

Such episodes only enhanced DeLoach in Hoover's eyes, since the director had been playing blackmail games for over 40 years. On 31 December 1965 he promoted DeLoach to the FBI's number-three spot, as deputy associate director. Widely regarded as Hoover's heir apparent, DeLoach surprised FBI-watchers by retiring from the Bureau on 31 July 1970 and moving to New York as Pepsico's vice president of corporate affairs. He held that job until 1985, then "retired" a second time and moved to Hilton Head Island, South Carolina, as chairman of the board for the Lighthouse Mortgage Corporation. Ten years later DeLoach published his memoirs, entitled *Hoover's FBI*, in which he hailed the late director as "a rare individual" possessed by "a nobility of purpose" that outshone his minor faults.

**DENNIS, Delmar** —A Mississippi minister who supported racial segregation, Delmar Dennis joined the KU KLUX KLAN in March

1964, but he grew disillusioned several months later, after witnessing a series of violent incidents. Dennis decided to quit the Klan, but FBI agents pursuing the MIBURN case visited him in September 1964, persuading Dennis to remain in the group and report its clandestine activities. In that role, Dennis rose through Klan ranks to become a "Titan," commanding Klan members in a 10-county region of eastern Mississippi. In August 1965 he reported Klansman BYRON DE LA BECKWITH'S confession to the June 1963 murder of NAACP leader Medgar Evers, but the FBI chose not to act. He finally broke cover in October 1967, as a prosecution witness at the federal trial of Klansmen charged with killing three civil rights workers in June 1964. After going public, Dennis toured briefly as a traveling speaker for the far-right John Birch Society, denouncing both the KKK and the civil rights movement as tools of Moscow. He mounted a hopeless presidential race in 1988, winning 3,476 votes as a candidate of the American Party. Six years later, back in Mississippi, Dennis was a key witness at the third trial of Byron De La Beckwith for the Evers slaying. Beckwith was convicted of murder on 4 February 1994 and subsequently died in prison.

**DE VOTO, Bernard Augustine** — Born at Ogden, Utah on 11 January 1897, Bernard De Voto was the son of a Catholic father and a Mormon mother. He taught English at Northwestern University from 1922 through 1927 and at Harvard from 1929 to 1936, simultaneously pursuing a prolific writing career. De Voto moved to New York City in 1936 and served for two years as editor of the *Saturday Review of Literature*. His trilogy of books on western U.S. history won him a Pulitzer Prize in 1947 and a National Book Award in 1952.

De Voto first drew FBI attention in 1944, when he served on a committee opposed to literary censorship. G-men noted that De Voto tried to force a test case by purchasing a copy of Lillian Smith's novel *Strange Fruit*, which "championed Negro rights." A year later, his attendance at a New York "Win the Peace" rally was noted, but most of De Voto's 207-page file concerns a column he wrote for *Harper's* magazine in October 1949. That column charged that Hoover's FBI "shatters the reputations of innocent and harmless people" by collecting a "hash of gossip, rumor, slander, backbiting, malice, and drunken invention" which "is permanently indexed in FBI files." De Voto worried that "honest men are spying on their neighbors for patriotism's sake" and opined that "it has gone too far." Worse yet, he urged that "people interviewed in the loyalty program should refuse to give any information to FBI agents" outside of open courtroom proceedings.

J. EDGAR HOOVER was outraged, instantly placing both De Voto and *Harper's* on the FBI's "Do Not Contact" list. As part of his counterattack, Hoover noted that De Voto "had among his collection of books a copy of *Das Kapital* which he prized very highly," noting further that De Voto "was the son of a fallen away Catholic priest ... and that he himself was a fallen away Catholic." Equally telling, he reported that on one occasion De Voto "was unshaven, wearing a loose and somewhat soiled sport shirt and a pair of baggy summer slacks of dark hue." Hoover's malice pursued De Voto beyond the grave, including preparation

of a pro-FBI magazine article by John Shuttlesworth in 1959, four years after De Voto's death. The piece branded De Voto "a professional apologist for Communism or misguided innocent," warning Americans that other "De Votos are at work today" in the United States.

**DEWEY, Thomas Edmund** — A native of Owosso, Michigan, born 24 March 1902, Thomas Dewey spent most of his life in New York. There, in the 1930s, he built a reputation as a high-profile "gangbuster" while variously serving as a district attorney, U.S. attorney, and special prosecutor. Among the leaders of ORGANIZED CRIME he pursued, two stand out: Charles ("Lucky") Luciano, convicted (some say framed) for prostitution in 1936; and LOUIS ("LEPKE") BUCHALTER, executed for murder in 1944. At the same time, unverified rumors persist that Dewey (or his Republican cronies) accepted large bribes from various mobsters to finance his political campaigns. Luciano himself claimed to have procured release from prison with a $75,000 "donation" to Dewey's war chest.

FBI Director J. EDGAR HOOVER hated and feared Thomas Dewey. The hatred arose from Dewey's publicity campaigns, which sometimes eclipsed Hoover's own self-promotion while casting doubt on the FBI's reputation as a crime-smashing organization. (Hoover denied the existence of organized crime while Dewey sent its leaders to prison, and the Bureau suffered by comparison.) The fear derived from Hoover's knowledge that Dewey despised him in turn and would likely dismiss him if Dewey ever fulfilled his presidential ambitions. Thus was born one of the more peculiar feuds in U.S. political history.

In October 1942, during Dewey's first successful campaign to become New York's governor, Hoover ordered a review of FBI files to prepare a summary memo on Dewey, to "be filed for future reference." Disappointed by the dearth of derogatory information uncovered, Hoover watched nervously as Dewey occupied the governor's mansion, then challenged FRANKLIN ROOSEVELT'S third-term bid for the White House in 1944. Dewey tried again in 1948, and this time pollsters almost universally predicted he would win.

Convinced that Dewey meant to fire him on inauguration day, Hoover chose a risky course of action, secretly throwing the FBI's weight behind Dewey and against incumbent HARRY TRUMAN. In the Republican primary race, Hoover ordered LOUIS NICHOLS, head of the Bureau's CRIME RECORDS DIVISION, to supply Dewey with "dirt" on lead contender Harold Stassen, thus enabling Dewey to triumph in a May 1948 radio debate and secure the GOP nomination a month later. After the Republican convention in Chicago, Hoover deluged Dewey's camp with derogatory material on Truman, including Truman's ties to the corrupt Pendergast machine in Missouri, the foibles of Attorney General TOM CLARK, and the threat of "communists in government," ranging from ALGER HISS to HARRY DEXTER WHITE. In return for his help, Hoover was promised promotion to serve as attorney general, with inseparable companion CLYDE TOLSON at his side and Nichols in charge of the FBI. After a "suitable interval," Hoover would be named to a lifetime position on the U.S. SUPREME COURT, where no hostile president could touch him.

Those plans collapsed on 2 November 1948, when Truman beat Dewey by a margin of some 2.1 million votes. Assistant Director WILLIAM SULLIVAN recalled that "heavy gloom" settled over FBI HEADQUARTERS on 3 November, with Hoover irrationally blaming Lou Nichols for Dewey's defeat. Only after the election, in December 1948, did Hoover confirm Dewey's plans to remove him as FBI director. One report to that effect came from E.E. Conroy, special agent in charge of the New York field office; another, including Dewey's alleged threat to put Hoover in prison, came from California INFORMANT "T-10" (known publicly as actor RONALD REAGAN), who overheard the comment during one of Dewey's campaign trips to Los Angeles.

Dewey, meanwhile, retained his post as New York's governor until 1955, then retired from politics. Throughout the latter 1950s and early 1960s he was employed by ex-bootlegger LEWIS ROSENSTIEL, as general counsel for Schenley Industries. Dewey died in New York on 16 March 1971.

**DICKSON, Bennie and Stella** — A young husband-wife holdup team, the Dicksons committed their first BANK ROBBERY on Stella's sixteenth birthday, 25 August 1938. The take from that South Dakota heist was disappointing, a mere $2,174, but they did better on their second try, stealing $47,233 on 31 October 1938. Police trailed the couple to Topeka, Kansas, where they shot their way out of a trap on 24 November. A second battle with lawmen, this one in Michigan, earned Stella the nickname "Sure Shot." FBI agents finally cornered Bennie Dickson at a St. Louis hamburger stand on 6 April 1939, killing him when he reached for a pistol. Stella was captured in Kansas City the following day, returned to South Dakota for trial. Upon conviction of bank robbery she received a 10-year prison sentence.

**DIES, Martin, Jr.** — A second-generation congressman, Martin Dies, Jr., was born at Colorado City, Texas on 5 November 1900. He attended Wesley College in Texas and Virginia's Cluster Springs Academy before graduating from the University of Texas in 1919. A year of legal study at National University in Washington, D.C. (now George Washington University) won him admission to the Texas bar in 1920. After nine years of private practice and service as a district judge, Dies was elected to Congress in 1930 and served seven terms in the House (1931-45). His zeal for pursuing "subversives" paid off in 1938, when Dies was named chairman of the newly-created HOUSE COMMITTEE ON UN-AMERICAN ACTIVITIES (HUAC).

Dies fell into conflict with the FBI that same year, when he sought to borrow G-men as investigators for his Red-hunting committee. Director J. EDGAR HOOVER shared HUAC's aversion to all things left-of-center, but he would never relinquish control of his agents. That judgment was validated on 6 July 1938 when a HUAC aide, E.K. Gubin, informed FBI HEADQUARTERS that Dies had ordered "certain of the Investigators to confiscate anything that they wanted in any business office to which they were sent ... and not worry particularly about legal procedure." (Two HUAC sleuths and a Philadelphia police officer were later indicted for stealing two tons of documents from the COMMUNIST PARTY.) Despite his misgivings, Hoover arranged a secret

1939 meeting between Dies and attorney MORRIS ERNST of the AMERICAN CIVIL LIBERTIES UNION, where Ernst agreed to purge his staff of communists in return for HUAC's agreement that the ACLU was not a "Communist front."

The FBI-HUAC relationship worsened after Dies described Hoover's men as "a bunch of boy scouts" afraid to soil their hands with aggressive Red-hunting. In fact, Dies maintained, the Bureau had overlooked hordes of potential saboteurs throughout the nation, more than 5,000 in Detroit alone. In January 1940, after Philadelphia's top G-man attended Dies's speech to the Penn Athletic Club, Hoover issued a directive reading: "I think it is undesirable for our agents to attend such affairs. There can be placed misinterpretation upon such attendance to our embarrassment." Assistant Director EDWARD TAMM followed up with a reprimand "pointing out that Mr. Dies has been accusing the [JUSTICE] DEPARTMENT of investigating him and ... even alleging that the Bureau is being used by the White House to whitewash the purportedly astounding conditions that he has uncovered." When Attorney General ROBERT JACKSON publicly attacked Dies on 23 November 1940, Hoover ordered all field offices to forward his remarks "to all friendly newspaper contacts in your district to insure ... the widest possible coverage." Five days later, after Dies carried his complaints to President FRANKLIN ROOSEVELT, Hoover rebuked Dies for holding "the FBI up to ridicule." (Dies emerged from the White House meeting to claim that FDR had told him, "Some of my best friends are Communists." A secret tape of their conversation disproved the allegation.)

By 1941, when HUAC descended on Hollywood, G-men found themselves in the curious position of aiding the committee while collecting "dirt" on its chairman. A memo from headquarters to the Los Angeles field office ordered agents to collect and report "any information ... with respect to testimony furnished before the Dies Committee which caused undue hardships on private citizens." (This marked the only occasion in his life when Hoover displayed any sympathy for victims of a congressional witch hunt.) The feud climaxed on 3 December 1941, when Ed Tamm visited Dies and revealed Bureau knowledge of a $2,000 bribe Dies had accepted, in return for legislation permitting a Jewish refugee to enter the U.S. from Cuba. Dies immediately ceased all criticism of the FBI, and the report was buried in Hoover's top-secret "Official/Confidential" FILE.

Although victorious, Hoover could not resist indulging in clandestine overkill. FBI surveillance of Dies continued, and in 1943 Hoover furnished President Roosevelt with evidence of Dies's links to rabid anti-Semite Gerald L.K. Smith. Dies declined to seek reelection in 1944 and returned to private legal practice for nearly a decade. He was elected to Congress again in 1952 and served three more terms, then retired for good in January 1959. He died at Lufkin, Texas on 14 November 1972.

**DILLING, Elizabeth** — Chicago born to an affluent family on 19 April 1894, Elizabeth Dilling traveled widely before a 1931 visit to the Soviet Union left her "transformed" and committed to battling global communism. Her first book on the subject, *The Red Network* (1934), was a compilation of rumor and slander listing some 500 organizations and 1,300 individuals as members of a worldwide communist conspiracy. Groups branded as "Red" included the YMCA, the Federal Council of Churches of Christ, and the AMERICAN CIVIL LIBERTIES UNION. Individuals listed included ELEANOR ROOSEVELT, Mahatma Gandhi, Albert Einstein, U.S. SUPREME COURT Justice Felix Frankfurter, and Sigmund Freud (indexed because of his alleged contention that "religious ideas are illusions"). Her second book in a similar vein, *The Roosevelt Red Record and Its Background*, was published in 1936. Later denials notwithstanding, evidence from FBI files suggests that J. EDGAR HOOVER made extensive use of *The Red Network* while building his own files on "subversive" groups and persons in America.

With the approach of WORLD WAR II, Dilling devoted herself to praising Adolf Hitler's Third Reich and opposing U.S. intervention in support of Allied nations. She led a "Mother's Movement" to picket the U.S. Senate in February 1941, opposing passage of the Lend-Lease Act, but her published broadsides increasingly focused on Jews and communists—whom she regarded as one and the same. Invited to speak at the University of Chicago, she informed a student audience that "You are all guinea pigs of Stalin. The University of Chicago is a Red school." Indicted with other Nazi propagandists for sedition in 1942, Dilling won dismissal of all charges four years later, on grounds that she had been denied a speedy trial.

In the postwar era, Dilling continued her activities with a sideline in race-baiting, finding a new audience in groups like the John Birch Society and the segregationist CITIZENS' COUNCILS. She survived into the 1960s, opposing racial integration and attacking President LYNDON JOHNSON for his "lack of commitment to victory" in Vietnam. Her later published works, including *Jewish Religion* and *The Plot Against Christianity* are still offered for sale by neo-Nazi groups around the country, while a web site maintained by the KU KLUX KLAN recently praised Dilling as "a beaughtiful [*sic*] and gifted woman."

**DILLINGER, John Herbert**—Arguably the most famous fugitive ever pursued by the FBI, John Dillinger was born in Indianapolis on 22 June 1903. He grew up wild, a classic juvenile delinquent, and deserted from the navy at age 21. A year later, in September 1924, he was arrested for mugging an elderly grocer. Dillinger pled guilty on advice of counsel, expecting leniency, but the judge decided to make an example of him, slapping Dillinger with a sentence of two to 20 years. He served eight years and eight months, befriended by a list of hard-core thieves including Harry Pierpont, Charles Makley, Homer Van Meter, Russell Clark and John Hamilton. Prior to his release, on 22 May 1933, Dillinger had sworn to help his friends escape and join him in a new career of BANK ROBBERY.

To that end, Dillinger joined the "White Cap" gang and launched a series of holdups, ranging over Indiana and Ohio. Between June and September 1933 they stole an estimated $51,200 from five banks, plus lesser amounts from various shops. Dillinger arranged for a box of pistols to be smuggled past guards at Indiana's state prison, but he missed the main event. Arrested for an Ohio bank job on 22 September 1933, he was in jail when 10 inmates escaped from the pen four days later.

The fugitives stole $14,993 from an Ohio bank on 3 October 1933 and rescued Dillinger from the jail at Lima nine days later, killing Sheriff Jesse Sarber in the process. Armed with weapons stolen from small-town police stations, the gang lifted $75,000 from an Indiana bank on 23 October and $28,000 more from a Wisconsin holdup on 20 November 1933. Three days after Christmas, Illinois authorities named Dillinger "Public Enemy No. 1." On 15 January 1934 he was accused of killing a policeman, during the $20,000 holdup of a bank in East Chicago, Indiana.

The gang sought to cool off in Tucson, but local authorities recognized their faces from mug shots published in a magazine. Arrested en masse, they were shipped north to face trial for murder—Dillinger for the Indiana patrolman; Pierpont, Makley and Russell Clark for Sheriff Sarber in Ohio. Dillinger would never see his friends again, but he escaped from jail at Crown Point on 3 March 1934, using either a hand-carved wooden gun or a pistol smuggled by his lawyer (reports vary). In flight, he drove a stolen car across state lines and thus became a federal fugitive, sought by FBI agents for violation of the DYER ACT.

Of the original gang, only Dillinger and John Hamilton remained at large. They were soon reunited, teaming with Homer Van Meter, GEORGE ("BABY FACE") NELSON and a rotating cast of accomplices on a new crime spree. Three days after Dillinger's escape from Crown Point, they stole $49,500 from a bank in Sioux Falls, South Dakota. A week later, the gang tapped a bank in Mason City, Iowa for $52,000. Relaxing in St. Paul, Minnesota, Dillinger and Van Meter shot their way out of an FBI trap on 31 March 1934. Gang member Eddie Green was less fortunate, mortally wounded by G-men who found him unarmed three days later.

After looting another police station for weapons, the gang retreated to Emil Wanatka's Little Bohemia Lodge, near Rhinelander, Wisconsin. An INFORMANT tipped Chicago agent MELVIN PURVIS to Dillinger's whereabouts, and Purvis led a raiding party north to surprise the gang. The nocturnal raid, on 22 April 1934, was a fiasco. Agents shot three innocent bystanders, killing one of them, while Dillinger and four cohorts escaped through the woods. Fleeing on foot to a nearby hamlet, Baby Face Nelson killed Bureau agent W. Carter Baum and wounded two other lawmen, then stole a car and vanished. John Hamilton was fatally wounded the following day, while crashing a Minnesota roadblock with Dillinger and Van Meter, but months would pass before authorities confirmed his death.

Meanwhile, the search for Dillinger was stalled. Embarrassed by Little Bohemia, J. EDGAR HOOVER appointed Agent SAMUEL COWLEY to supervise the Dillinger manhunt, a first sign of the director's mounting displeasure with Purvis. On 28 May 1934, Dillinger underwent plastic surgery at the Chicago home of elderly burglar JAMES PROBASCO. One day later, Melvin Purvis told reporters he believed that Dillinger was dead. Unimpressed by that announcement, Attorney General HOMER CUMMINGS named Dillinger the nation's first "Public Enemy No. 1" on 22 June 1934. Eight days later, Dillinger's gang stole $29,890 from a bank in South Bend, Indiana, killing a policeman as they fled.

Dillinger was finally betrayed by brothel madam Anna

Cumpanas and her boyfriend MARTIN ZARKOVICH, a corrupt detective from East Chicago. Together, they arranged for G-men to confront Dillinger at Chicago's Biograph Theater, on the night of 22 July 1934. Surrounded as he left the theater, Dillinger allegedly reached for a pistol and was cut down in a barrage of shots that also wounded several bystanders. Rumors persist that Dillinger's corpse was plundered en route to the morgue, Zarkovich stealing several thousand dollars from the outlaw's pockets, while Purvis helped himself to Dillinger's rub ring and diamond stickpin.

Long after the fact, author Jay Robert Nash cited various discrepancies in Dillinger's autopsy report, promoting a theory that Dillinger escaped justice and left small-time hoodlum "Jimmy Lawrence" to die in his place. Most crime historians dismiss that claim, but Nash did uncover evidence that Dillinger may have been unarmed at the Biograph. Tracing the serial number of a Colt pistol displayed for years at FBI HEADQUARTERS, Nash proved conclusively that the gun was manufactured months after Dillinger died. Author William Helmer proposes an alternate theory, that Dillinger *was* armed on 22 July 1934, but that J. Edgar Hoover claimed his pistol as a personal keepsake, replacing it with a "ringer" in the FBI trophy case.

Whatever his ultimate fate, Dillinger remains as famous in death as in life, a virtual icon of FBI history. The mock theater on HOGAN'S ALLEY, at the FBI ACADEMY, is called the Biograph. Its marquee advertises *Manhattan Melodrama*, the last film viewed by Dillinger before he stepped outside and into history.

**"DIRTY Dozen"**—In early 1976 FBI HEADQUARTERS learned that the Bureau would soon be investigated for its use of illegal DOMESTIC SURVEILLANCE techniques against the WEATHERMAN UNDERGROUND organization. Assistant Attorney General J. Stanley Pottinger was placed in charge of the probe, recruiting as his researchers 12 G-men he identified "as being more loyal to the United States than to the FBI." That lapse in loyalty outraged many other agents, who promptly dubbed Pottinger's team "the Dirty Dozen," after a novel and Hollywood film depicting military convicts drafted for a suicide mission in WORLD WAR II. The colorful nickname survived even after Pottinger doubled the size of his investigative team.

The Dirty Dozen's exploits are known today only from the vague and rumor-ridden memoirs of retired G-man CRIL PAYNE, published in 1979. According to Payne, the squad "conducted an armed assault" on FBI headquarters, seizing control of several offices and rifling through the files in search of evidence. "According to rumor," Payne writes, they found "practically nothing" of value to Pottinger. Payne speculated that a "loyal" member of the Dirty Dozen may have tipped his FBI colleagues in advance of the raid, but speculation is fruitless, since no other record of the alleged "armed assault" has surfaced to date.

**DISASTER Squad**—The FBI Disaster Squad was created in 1940, following the death of two bureau employees in an airplane crash. G-men quickly discovered that no one at the scene knew how to identify the burned and mangled bodies, whereupon a new unit was organized to deal with future crises. Noteworthy incidents investigated by the Disaster Squad include the Jonestown, Guyana cult suicides of 17 November 1978; the Mount St. Helens eruption of 18 May 1980; the space shuttle *Challenger* explosion of 28 January 1986; the Pan Am Flight 103 bombing of 21 December 1988; and TWA FLIGHT 800 crash of 17 July 1996. The Disaster Squad consists of non-agent latent fingerprint specialists and others who use any means available, including medical X-rays and dental records, to identify victims of various catastrophes.

**"DISINFORMATION"**—The term "disinformation," coined in the 1950s by some forgotten intelligence agent, refers to fabrication or manipulation of information to deceive an enemy. Such activities are routine in the realm of ESPIONAGE, where agents are frequently planted or "turned" to furnish an opponent with misleading data, but the tactic's use has not been limited to wartime or to adversarial relationships with foreign powers. As practiced by the FBI, it has been used to deceive the American public, milk greater appropriations from Congress, disrupt legitimate political activities, spark deadly violence between militant groups, and to imprison innocent defendants.

Long before disinformation had a formal name, G-men were well acquainted with its uses. By the time America entered WORLD WAR I, Bureau INFORMANTS and *agents provocateur* were active within such groups as the Socialist Party of America and the INDUSTRIAL WORKERS OF THE WORLD, working overtime to create dissension and discord. False accusations of theft were a favorite technique, along with "SNITCH-JACKETING" (the malicious branding of loyal party members as police informers). The postwar Red Scare offered a wide range of new targets for slander and harassment, ranging from the COMMUNIST PARTY to the AFRICAN BLOOD BROTHERHOOD, the NATIONAL ASSOCIATION FOR THE ADVANCEMENT OF COLORED PEOPLE, and MARCUS GARVEY'S Universal Negro Improvement Association. Throughout the Great Depression, WORLD WAR II and the ensuing Cold War, FBI HEADQUARTERS fueled paranoia of a vast Red conspiracy by leaking false or unsubstantiated information to congressional witch hunters such as the HOUSE COMMITTEE ON UN-AMERICAN ACTIVITIES, the SENATE INTERNAL SECURITY SUBCOMMITTEE, and Wisconsin Senator JOSEPH MCCARTHY. Those campaigns not only filled Bureau coffers with millions of dollars to fight the "Red Menace," but also cemented FBI Director J. EDGAR HOOVER'S alliance with right-wing political leaders and allowed him to punish various "subversives" and (an ever-growing list of targets that included blacks, liberals and anyone who dared to criticize the FBI).

Hoover was adept at fabricating "crime waves" and "threats to national security," ranging from practitioners of BANK ROBBERY and KIDNAPPING in the 1930s, Communists and NAZI SABOTEURS in the 1940s, JUVENILE DELINQUENCY in the 1950s, CIVIL RIGHTS "extremists" in the 1960s, and "NEW LEFT" radicals in the 1970s. The FBI's CRIME RECORDS DIVISION served for many years as Hoover's personal disinformation machine, ghost-writing books and articles under Hoover's by-line (which he sold for personal profit) and manipulating crime statistics to "document" Hoover's current menace-of-the-moment. In its most extreme form, under the illegal "COINTELPRO" operations that began in 1956, those tactics escalated to include deliberate FRAME-UPS of innocent persons whom Hoover and his aides sought to remove from American society. G-men also perjured themselves in court to protect racist police and members of ORGANIZED CRIME, as revealed in the ORANGEBURG MASSACRE case and the scandal surrounding Boston mobster JAMES BULGER.

FBI mythology insists that such illicit actions were a fleeting aberration, stamped out a year before Hoover's death in May 1972, but identical tactics were employed against the AMERICAN INDIAN MOVEMENT (1973-76), the COMMITTEE IN SOLIDARITY WITH THE PEOPLE OF EL SALVADOR (1981-85), PUERTO RICAN NATIONALISTS (through 1988, at least), EARTH FIRST! (1989-90) and others. In an era when Attorney General JOHN ASHCROFT champions secrecy and expanded use of DOMESTIC SURVEILLANCE to combat TERRORISM, civil libertarians maintain that constant vigilance is needed to prevent the FBI from lapsing into its bad habits of the past.

**DÖBLIN, Bruno Alfred**— A Jewish novelist who fled his native Germany when Adolf Hitler rose to power, Döblin settled first in France and then in California. He was shadowed and questioned at various times by the FBI, the Immigration and Naturalization Service, and the OFFICE OF STRATEGIC SERVICES (OSS). Aside from his status as a potential "enemy alien," authorities questioned Döblin's relationship with writer THOMAS MANN and his several excursions into Mexico between May 1939 and March 1941. No evidence of criminal or "subversive" activity was discovered, however, and Döblin was recruited by the OSS to help "re-educate" Germans after WORLD WAR II. Although himself a convert to Catholicism, Döblin advised Jewish exiles against returning to Germany, noting that "the roots of Hitlerism run deep." Döblin died on 26 June 1957, at age 78.

**DOCTOROW, Edgar Laurence**—A New York native, born 6 January 1931, novelist E.L. Doctorow served as editor for the New American Library from 1965 to 1964 and as editor-in-chief of Dial Press from 1964 through 1969. The latter job brought him to J. EDGAR HOOVER's attention on 13 February 1968, when Doctorow wrote a letter asking Hoover to provide a foreword for a forthcoming book by Alwin Mosow, revealing details of an international narcotics conspiracy. Hoover declined to cooperate, perhaps because the volume was prepared with help from the rival BUREAU OF NARCOTICS, but Doctorow's letter became the first entry in a file that ultimately included twenty-four pages.

In 1971 Doctorow published his third novel, *The Book of Daniel*, which examined the federal prosecution of JULIUS and ETHEL ROSENBERG, but FBI agents were more interested in his 1980 participation in the Fourth Soviet-American Writers Conference, held in Los Angeles. Nine pages of Doctorow's file concern that event, primarily documents collected from the U.S. State Department, and three more pages remain classified today "in the interest of national defense."

**DODD, Thomas Joseph**—A Connecticut native, born on 15 May 1907, Thomas Dodd prevailed on Attorney General HOMER CUMMINGS to arrange an FBI appointment in 1933, as a springboard to future political office. Director J. EDGAR HOOVER accepted Dodd as an agent, but his tenure was brief. Dodd resigned from the Bureau after one year and resumed private legal practice until he was elected to the House of Representatives in 1953, and to the U.S. Senate six years later. Although Hoover once described Dodd in a personal memo as "absolutely no good ... a scoundrel," Dodd remained on good public terms with the FBI and made dozens of dozens of speeches praising Hoover. His friendship grew more valuable with time, as Dodd became chairman of the SENATE INTERNAL SECURITY SUBCOMMITTEE, while also serving on the Senate's Judiciary and Foreign Relations Committees.

Aside from praising Hoover on the Senate floor and denouncing his critics, Dodd also provided more practical aid to the Bureau. In 1966, for instance, Dodd interceded on Hoover's behalf with the STATE DEPARTMENT, after Abba Schwartz in the Bureau of Security and Consular Affairs sought to dismiss passport director Frances Knight (successor to Hoover ally RUTH SHIPLEY) for authorizing surveillance of prominent Americans traveling abroad. Knight complained to Hoover, who in turn contacted Dodd. Dodd spoke to Secretary of State Dean Rusk, and Schwartz was summarily fired, while Knight kept her post and continued to spy on subjects of interest to the FBI. Dodd also helped secure Hoover's job in 1963 and 1965, by scuttling proposed legislation that would have required Senate confirmation of the FBI's director. The Bureau reciprocated by tipping Dodd off to pending investigations of his finances, providing a car and driver when he visited New York on personal business, and tailing staff members who displeased the senator.

Dodd's ultimate failings were greed and ambition. He practiced nepotism, charged exorbitant speaking fees while parroting scripts prepared by right-wing special interest groups, and billed his constituents for routine services normally performed free of charge. In 1963 Dodd angered Hoover by suggesting that Congress, rather than the FBI, should investigate the JFK ASSASSINATION, but appointment of the Warren Commission resolved that dilemma. When columnists DREW PEARSON and JACK ANDERSON broke the story of Dodd's personal corruption in 1966, G-men grilled Dodd's staffers in search of a leak and stole Anderson's mail in an effort to scuttle his research. As former aide James Boyd told author Anthony Summers, "Nothing could have been more effective for intimidating potential witnesses into silence.... FBI agents had been instructed not to take any information concerning Dodd." On the side, Dodd hired a former G-man to burglarize Anderson's office and rifle his trash can for clues.

Dodd's luck ran out when Hoover was informed of a comment made to reporters, wherein Dodd expressed a desire to lead the FBI or CIA, remarking that "I may end up in one or the other." FBI support was instantly withdrawn, leaving Dodd to fend for himself. The Senate censured him on 3 June 1967, by a vote of 92 to 5, and Connecticut Democrats denied him renomination in 1970. Dodd died of a heart attack in 1971.

**DOMESTIC Surveillance**—In 1908 the congressmen who opposed creation of a detective force within the JUSTICE DEPARTMENT voiced their determination that "No general system of spying upon and espionage of the people, such as has prevailed in Russia, in France under the Empire, and at one time in Ireland, should be allowed to grow up." Attorney General CHARLES BONAPARTE dismissed those fears as groundless, insisting that innocent persons should have no qualms about policemen studying their every move. In fact, the fledgling Bureau of Investigation's jurisdiction was narrowly restricted to investigation of specific federal crimes, but the concerns of those early opponents in Congress soon proved prophetic.

The earliest known FBI file on private political expressions dates from 1911, but it would not be an isolated case. Presidents and attorneys general soon realized that the Bureau was a handy tool for investigating or blackmailing political enemies, and pursuit of "radicals" or ANARCHISTS soon became routine. If those radicals were blacks or immigrants, so much the better. During WORLD WAR I the Bureau's jurisdiction legally extended for the first time into "national security," including investigations of sabotage and ESPIONAGE, protection of war-related industries, and prosecution of neutrality violations. A new Radical Division was created in 1918 to hunt "enemy aliens," soon renamed the GENERAL INTELLIGENCE DIVISION (GID) with young J. EDGAR HOOVER at the helm. By 1922, in the wake of the first great Red Scare and the PALMER RAIDS, Hoover had compiled 450,000 index cards on various "subversive" groups and individuals, ranging from the COMMUNIST PARTY and INDUSTRIAL WORKERS OF THE WORLD to MARCUS GARVEY'S Universal Negro Improvement Association and the NATIONAL ASSOCIATION FOR THE ADVANCEMENT OF COLORED PEOPLE.

Attorney General HARLAN STONE, while appointing Hoover to lead the Bureau in 1924, disbanded the GID and accepted Hoover's promise that future investigations would be strictly limited to crimes against the U.S. government. Unfortunately, Stone's blind faith in Hoover made it inconceivable to Stone that his trusted aide would lie. In fact, while Hoover acquiesced in dissolution of the GID, he kept his FILES intact and escalated his surveillance of "subversive" groups across the nation, collecting dossiers on thousands of Americans who ran the full gamut from laborers and housewives to presidents and justices of the U.S. SUPREME COURT. Most had committed no crime, but their inclusion in the Bureau's files was justified on grounds of "national security."

President FRANKLIN ROOSEVELT legitimized a portion of that spying on 25 August 1936, when he requested an FBI report on communist and fascist activities in the U.S. Citing a World War I statute that permitted investigations upon request from the STATE DEPARTMENT, Roosevelt enlisted Secretary of State Cordell Hull to give his order the force of law. On 5 September 1936 Hoover issued a directive commanding all FBI field offices to report "any information relating to subversive activities on the part of any individual or organization, regardless of the source from which this information is received." On 2 November 1938, FDR approved Hoover's request to expand domestic surveillance activities in "strictest confidence" and without passage of "additional legislation." The Bureau's new authority went public on 6

September 1939, when Roosevelt authorized the Bureau to "take charge of investigative work relating to espionage, sabotage, and violations of the neutrality regulations." Police across the U.S. were pertinent information with FBI HEADQUARTERS. Eight months later, on 21 May 1940, Roosevelt issued a secret directive that approved FBI WIRETAPPING (with prior approval from the attorney general) in "national defense" investigations. Congress officially broadened the scope of "subversive" activities in June 1940, with passage of the SMITH ACT (providing criminal penalties for any group or person advocating violent overthrow of the U.S. government, whether or not the deed was actually attempted).

Domestic surveillance was big business for the FBI. In 1945 the Bureau's budget was $44 million—up from $8.7 million in 1940—with 81 percent earmarked for "national defense." Hoover resurrected the GID in 1941, calling it the National Defense Division, then renamed it the Security Division two years later. By the end of 1945 it was apparent that FBI "internal security" work was neither temporary nor war-related. In fact, over the next decade Hoover collaborated freely in creation of a new Red Scare, feeding a mixture of fact, innuendo and DISINFORMATION to a cast of witch-hunters including RICHARD NIXON, JOSEPH MCCARTHY, the HOUSE COMMITTEE ON UN-AMERICAN ACTIVITIES and the SENATE INTERNAL SECURITY SUBCOMMITTEE. Two-thirds of all FBI reports issued in the late 1950s concerned themselves with the "Red menace"; by 1960 G-men had complied 432,000 new dossiers on alleged subversive individuals and groups. Ironically, a number of significant Soviet spies were overlooked in the process, until brought to the Bureau's attention by outside agencies including the CENTRAL INTELLIGENCE AGENCY, the Royal Canadian Mounted Police and Britain's MI-6.

The Red scare was winding down in 1956, when Hoover declared a new secret war of his own under the code name "COINTELPRO"—short for *counterintelligence programs*. Over the next 15 years, before the illegal campaigns were officially terminated, G-men mounted 2,340 acknowledged attempts to "disrupt" and "neutralize" various political organizations, including the Communist Party, the SOCIALIST WORKERS PARTY, various black militant groups, the KU KLUX KLAN and sundry factions of the "NEW LEFT." As before, most of the targets had committed no crime; those with criminal histories, meanwhile, were not investigated with an eye toward prosecution, but rather for means of harassment including FRAME-UPS of innocent persons and entrapment by criminal *agents provocateur*.

The COINTELPRO campaigns allegedly ended a year before Hoover's death, but documents later released under the FREEDOM OF INFORMATION ACT prove that the "COINTELPRO" label was applied to ongoing operations through 1973 and identical tactics were employed against "suspected terrorists" as recently as 1990. Director CLARENCE KELLEY (1973-78) came close to resurrecting Hoover's GID when he assigned domestic surveillance chores to a "new" General Investigative Division. A 1976 report from the government's General Accounting Office reveals that combined domestic and foreign intelligence cases accounted for 20 percent of the Bureau's workload between 1965 and 1975, but the actual breakdown remains classified. Deception was still the order of the day, as revealed in a 1978 lawsuit seeking to enjoin FBI political surveillance in Chicago: under oath, Bureau spokesmen were compelled to admit that 258 Windy City informants had lately been reclassified from "domestic security" work to "foreign counterintelligence," although their targets had not changed.

Presidential candidate RONALD REAGAN—an FBI informant in the 1940s who later collaborated with Bureau surveillance as governor of California (1967-75)—assailed incumbent JAMES CARTER in 1980 for failing to curb domestic security threats from the Soviet Union and Islamic extremists. Reagan called for an "unleashing" of U.S. intelligence agencies, implying that investigative guidelines restricting criminal behavior by the FBI and CIA placed American in danger. Soon after his inauguration, President Reagan removed those restrictions and empowered the FBI to "anticipate or prevent crime" by investigating groups or individuals who "advocate criminal activity or indicate an apparent intent to engage in crime." (Reagan also pardoned former FBI officials recently convicted of ordering illegal BREAK-INS in the 1970s, thus sending a clear message to G-men who favored "black bag jobs.")

Domestic security investigations reportedly declined under President GEORGE H.W. BUSH, with the collapse of the Soviet Bloc during 1989-91, but threats of TERRORISM soon replaced the brooding menace of Reagan's "Evil Empire." That threat continued through the 1990s, with attacks from foreign enemies and the rise of a home-grown, heavily armed MILITIA MOVEMENT. The disastrous SKYJACKINGS of 11 September 2001 obliterated memories of reckless and illegal conduct by U.S. intelligence agencies and renewed calls for sweeping surveillance to prevent future attacks. That outcry eased passage of the USA PATRIOT ACT, including broad surveillance powers, but G-men were active even before the new law was enacted. By mid-October 2001, 159 American colleges had delivered information on their foreign students to FBI headquarters, while surveillance (some say harassment) of Muslim Americans and immigrants became routine. On 30 May 2002 Attorney General JOHN ASHCROFT announced that G-men would henceforth be permitted to spy on domestic organizations without demonstrating any evidence of criminal behavior. The rationale: limits on domestic surveillance provide "a competitive advantage for terrorists who skillfully utilize sophisticated techniques and modern computer systems to compile information for targeting and attacking innocent Americans," according to Ashcroft. "Our philosophy today is not to wait and sift through the rubble following a terrorist attack." Critics like Laura Murphy of the AMERICAN CIVIL LIBERTIES UNION reply that "The government is rewarding failure. When the government fails, as it increasingly appears to have done before September 11, the [GEORGE W.] BUSH administration's response is to give itself new powers rather than seriously investigate why the failures occurred."

Ironically, the FBI itself may yet turn out to be the final loser in the frenzy to investigate terrorists and "enemy aliens." On 16 November 2002 White House security advisors announced their consideration of plans to create "a new domestic spy agency" that "would take over responsibility for counterterrorism spying and analysis from the FBI." Director ROBERT MUELLER grudgingly admitted that the Bureau "has not yet made the huge changes needed" since the 9-11 terrorist attacks, but he "believe[d] it can eventually do so." In fact, Mueller declared on 22 December 2002, "creating a new agency from whole cloth" would be "a step backward in the war on terrorism." What the FBI (and the nation) really needed, according to Mueller, was a larger force of G-men better trained, better equipped, and better funded to protect Americans from terrorists — and from themselves.

**DONOVAN, William Joseph**—A native of New York City, born 1 January 1883, attorney "Wild Bill" Donovan emerged from WORLD WAR I with a Congressional Medal of Honor for his combat service in France. Despite publicity surrounding his wartime exploits, Donovan lost his bid to become New York's lieutenant governor in 1922. He rebounded by joining the JUSTICE DEPARTMENT, first as U.S. attorney for the Western District of New York (1922-24), then as an assistant to Attorney Generals HARLAN STONE and JOHN SARGENT (1924-29).

Donovan suffered his first clash with FBI Director J. EDGAR HOOVER in October 1924, while serving as chief of the department's Criminal Division. Hoover had promised to cease DOMESTIC SURVEILLANCE on various nonviolent "radical" groups in May 1924, but he reneged five months later, arguing to Donovan that while the Bureau "theoretically ... [had] no right to investigate such activities," spying should continue regardless. Donovan disagreed, and while his veto failed to terminate illegal FBI surveillance, Hoover never forgave the rebuff. In January 1925, two months from retirement, Attorney General Stone accepted Hoover's recommendation that "politicians" like Donovan should have no control over Bureau affairs. Donovan was transferred to the Anti-Trust Division, where he remained until leaving Justice for greener pastures in 1929.

In 1928, while still employed at Justice, Donovan served as the chief strategist for HERBERT HOOVER'S winning presidential campaign. In return, he was promised appointment as the next attorney general, but President Hoover backed out of the deal under "considerable pressure" from opponents whose number included J. Edgar Hoover, the Anti-Saloon League and the KU KLUX KLAN (opposed to Donovan because he was a Catholic). Donovan refused an alternate appointment as governor of the Philippines and retired to private practice, including service as a personal investigator for such millionaire clients as J.P. Morgan and the Rockefellers.

Donovan made no secret of his wish to be America's first Catholic president, but his next political foray, running for governor of New York in 1932, produced another defeat. FBI agents kept Donovan under sporadic surveillance, and while his activities were "duly reported to the President," no significant derogatory information was discovered. Donovan was a former law school classmate of President FRANKLIN ROOSEVELT, and while the two men were political rivals, FDR recognized Donovan's courage and ingenuity, selecting him in early 1941 to lead the Office of the Coordinator of Information, renamed the OFFICE OF STRATEGIC SERVICES (OSS) in June 1942. J. Edgar Hoover opposed the new group by any name, coveting foreign intelligence work for the FBI exclusively, and he obstructed Donovan at every turn. Hoover withheld advance warning of the PEARL HARBOR AT-TACK from OCI and the White House in 1941, then persuaded Roosevelt to bar Donovan's agents from Latin America during WORLD WAR II. Meddling in foreign ESPIONAGE, Hoover success-fully opposed Donovan's 1943 plan to infiltrate Soviet secret po-lice headquarters in Moscow, then complained that OSS coop-eration with America's Russian allies had flooded the U.S. with enemy spies (none of whom were identified or apprehended by G-men). On balance, Donovan complained to Attorney General FRANCIS BIDDLE that "the Abwehr [Nazi Intelligence] gets better treatment from the FBI than we do."

Donovan was also well aware of Bureau snooping into his personal life. He branded Hoover a "moralistic bastard," and re-taliated with some spying of his own. Author Anthony Summers reports allegations that Donovan's agents obtained photographs of Hoover engaged in HOMOSEXUAL activity with Associate Di-rector CLYDE TOLSON, but the photos never surfaced and those rumors remain unverified.

In November 1944 Donovan proposed a structure for Amer-ica's postwar intelligence service, which Hoover predictably op-posed. President HARRY TRUMAN dissolved the OSS in 1945 and waited another two years before replacing it with a new CENTRAL INTELLIGENCE AGENCY (CIA). Donovan, having failed to capture New York's nomination for the U.S. Senate in 1946, hoped to lead the CIA, but Hoover and others successfully blocked his nomi-nation. Appointed by President DWIGHT EISENHOWER as ambas-sador to Thailand, Donovan served from 1953 to 1955, then re-turned to private legal practice. He suffered his first major stroke in February 1957 and died two years later, on 8 February 1959. A letter of condolence, prepared by the FBI's CRIME RECORDS DI-VISION for Hoover's signature, elicited no response from Dono-van's widow.

**DOS PASSOS, John** — A Chicago native, born 14 January 1896, John Dos Passos served as an ambulance driver in France during WORLD WAR I, afterward using the experience to write his first novel, *One Man's Initiation: 1917* (1920). Educated at Harvard and widely identified with radical causes, he published a short story ("Facing the Chair") which dealt with the SACCO-VANZETTI case and his "USA" trilogy of novels — *The 42nd Parallel* (1930), *1919* (1932), and *The Big Money* (1936) — charted the growth of Amer-ican materialism, climaxed by the onset of the Great Depression. In 1930 Dos Passos joined THEODORE DREISER and four other writers to investigate company terrorism directed at striking coal miners in Harlan County, Kentucky, but two decades later he told FBI agents "he got the impression that the National Miners Union was controlled by the COMMUNIST PARTY" and was "try-ing to make a monkey out of him."

The bureau began charting Dos Passos's radical career in 1923, after his name appeared on a letterhead of the Ameri-can Committee for Relief of Russian Children. A 1937 memo "reliably reported" that Dos Passos was "close to Communist Party Headquarters in New York City," but his membership remains disputed by historians and biographers. By 3 June 1952, when he sat for an interview with G-men, Dos Passos

had drifted to the far right. As recorded by the agents on that occasion:

> At the outset of the interview, Dos Passos informed that he was never a member of the Communist Party, although he related that he had close associations with the Communist Party at var-ious times. He pointed out that inasmuch as he was never a mem-ber ... he was not in a position to definitely state that a person was a Communist....
>
> He remarked that he had been to Russia ... in the fall of 1921 at about the time the Soviets took over. He claimed that he was traveling at this time as a tourist and was attracted to the coun-try.... Concerning various front organizations organized during this period such as the American Committee for Relief of Rus-sian Children, Dos Passos claimed that he could not recall specifically this organization but he did lend his name ... because he was interested in cementing relations with the Soviet Union and seeing that the Soviet Union was recognized.... He pointed out, however, that there were occasions when his name was used without his authorization.... During the interview Dos Passos appeared to be cooperative but was hazy concerning details....

In 1970 aides to President RICHARD NIXON requested an FBI background check on Dos Passos, prior to inviting him for din-ner at the White House. Hoover's responding memo noted: "The files indicate that Dos Passos first had sympathy for the Soviet Union in 1923. He next showed an interest in the civil war in Spain.... In 1937, Dos Passos was reported to be sympathetic to the Trotskyites." Things had improved by 1947, when "Dos Pas-sos indicated to a bureau agent in Boston that his political sym-pathies were now 'to the right'," and he had supplied a foreword for rightist author WILLIAM F. BUCKLEY, JR.'s book *Up From Lib-eralism* in 1959. Still, it was not enough to please Hoover. Dos Passos died in Baltimore on 28 September 1970, but the FBI con-tinued adding memos to his file through 1974.

**DOUGLAS, John Edward** — A Brooklyn native, born in 1945, John Douglas was rejected by Cornell University and carried a "D" average at Montana State College before he joined the U.S. Air Force, in 1966, to avoid infantry service in the VIETNAM WAR. While stationed in New Mexico, Douglas finished his bachelor's degree and became close friends with an FBI agent assigned to the nearby RESIDENT AGENCY. On leaving the service in 1970, Douglas joined the Bureau, serving with the Detroit and Mil-waukee field offices before he returned to the FBI ACADEMY for training as a hostage negotiator. There, he met instructor ROBERT RESSLER, assigned to the Behavioral Science Unit devoted to PSY-CHOLOGICAL PROFILING of unknown offenders. Douglas trans-ferred to Behavioral Science in 1977 and joined Ressler in push-ing for creation of the VIOLENT CRIMINAL APPREHENSION PROGRAM. Ressler retired in 1990 and Douglas replaced him as head of Behavioral Science (later renamed Investigative Support Services), holding that post until his own retirement in 1995.

While involved on the periphery of many infamous SERIAL MURDER cases, often described as the real-life model for fictional G-man Jack Crawford in the novels *Red Dragon* and *The Silence of the Lambs*, Douglas never pursued or arrested a serial killer himself. Still, the job had its dangers, including a schedule so hec-tic and stressful that it drove Douglas to a near-fatal brain hemorrhage in December 1983, while visiting Seattle to consult on the case of the "Green River Killer."

In retirement, Douglas has pursued a lucrative new career in true-crime writing, TV talk-show appearances, and private consultation on cases including the JonBenét Ramsey murder of 1996. Ironically, Douglas's celebrity has evoked public hostility from his one-time mentor, Robert Ressler (himself an author and frequent guest on sundry television programs). Ressler has denounced Douglas for his "flamboyance" and dubbed him "a Hollywood type of guy," while questioning Douglas's "gut instinct" that JonBenét Ramsey's parents are innocent of her murder. Ressler has also taken shots at Douglas's work for the FBI, telling this author in February 1998 that Douglas's profile of "Unabomber" THEODORE KACZYNSKI was "all wrong." Douglas, for his part, has thus far declined to engage in public squabbling with his former boss.

**DOUGLAS, William Orville**—A native of Maine, Minnesota, born 16 October 1898, William O. Douglas was raised in Yakima County, Washington and served in the U.S. Army during WORLD WAR I. He attended Columbia University Law School and later became a professor of law (1927-36). Douglas joined the Securities and Exchange Commission in 1936 and served as its chairman from 1937 to April 1939, when he was appointed to the U.S. SUPREME COURT by President FRANKLIN ROOSEVELT. Over the next 36 years, until his retirement in November 1975, Douglas was one of the court's most liberal voices, rejecting any infringement on freedom of speech or the press.

That attitude made Douglas an instant enemy in the person of FBI Director J. EDGAR HOOVER. It is unclear precisely when Hoover began subjecting Justice Douglas to illegal WIRETAPPING and BUGGING, but the director was greatly relieved when President Roosevelt canceled plans to draft Douglas as his running mate in 1944. (If chosen, Douglas would have become president with Roosevelt's death in 1945 and may well have removed Hoover from office.) Records declassified under the FREEDOM OF INFORMATION ACT later revealed that Douglas was subjected to electronic eavesdropping under every presidential administration from HARRY TRUMAN'S to that of RICHARD NIXON. He was also placed on the FBI's "watch list," marked for physical surveillance during his travels abroad. In June 1953, after Douglas issued a last-minute stay of execution for JULIUS and ETHEL ROSENBERG, Hoover made a point of passing on derogatory information from his dossier to President DWIGHT EISENHOWER.

Douglas learned of the FBI's snooping in 1966, when his swing vote in the FRED BLACK case was leaked in advance of the court's announced decision. Douglas asked Chief Justice EARL WARREN how often the court's conference room was checked for bugs, and Warren replied that it never had been. Investigating the matter, Warren learned that a professional "sweep" would cost $5,000—but G-men offered to do it for free. Warren gladly accepted and appeared to trust the all-clear report he received from FBI HEADQUARTERS, but Douglas was less easily convinced. Over time he would declare a "moral certainty" that "all Supreme Court wires were tapped" at various times, by culprits including the Bureau, the CENTRAL INTELLIGENCE AGENCY and the National Security Council.

Douglas was also the target of at least one BREAK-IN, for which he blamed G-men acting on orders from Hoover and President LYNDON JOHNSON. Near completion of his memoirs in autumn 1968, Douglas suffered a setback when burglars invaded his chambers and stole part of the manuscript relating details of Johnson's financial and political chicanery. Douglas recreated the chapter from memory, but he was never truly satisfied with the result—and he never forgave either Johnson or Hoover.

In 1969, as President Nixon prepared to stack the Supreme Court with conservative judges, Hoover prepared a short list of incumbents he deemed vulnerable to impeachment. Douglas was first on the list, selected for his liberal voting record, his "immoral" private life (four marriages, the latest at age 67), and his role as a director of the Albert Parvin Foundation at a salary of $12,000 per year. Hoover had learned that Parvin's stock portfolio included part-ownership of a Las Vegas casino, and he used the fact to falsely imply that Douglas had ties to ORGANIZED CRIME. After Douglas survived a Nixon-ordered tax audit by the INTERNAL REVENUE SERVICE, Hoover supplied derogatory material to Rep. GERALD FORD, spearheading the impeachment drive in Congress. The newest item was Hoover's claim that a "pornographic" magazine—the *Evergreen Review*—had published an excerpt from Douglas's latest book, *Points of Rebellion*. (Hoover also supplied White House aide H.R. HALDEMAN with transcripts of a wiretapped conversation detailing Douglas's strategy for opposing impeachment, taped on 25 June 1970.) The House of Representatives was unimpressed by Ford's presentation, exonerating Douglas of all charges in a 924-page report. Ironically, Douglas later revealed that he had penned his resignation in 1969, but the Nixon-Hoover assault had persuaded him "to stay on indefinitely until the last hound dog had stopped yapping at my heels."

In fact, Douglas outlasted his enemies, witnessing Hoover's death and Nixon's resignation in disgrace before he finally retired on 12 November 1975. His term on the Supreme Court—36 years and 7 months—is the prevailing record and seems likely to remain so. Douglas died on 19 January 1980.

**DREISER, Theodore**—An Indiana native, born in 1871, Dreiser began his writing career as a reporter for the *Chicago Globe* in 1892 and published his first novel (*Sister Carrie*) eight years later. The first entry in his 240-page FBI file concerned Dreiser's 1927 visit to Russia and his public endorsement that same year of Workers International Relief, a group sponsored by the COMMUNIST PARTY. Dreiser also protested the 1927 execution of SACCO and VANZETTI. In 1930 he told the Soviet newspaper *Izvestia* that he foresaw "a possibility Russia in the near future would overshadow Western capitalism in importance." The following year, Dreiser joined JOHN DOS PASSOS and other writers to visit striking coal miners in Harlan County, Kentucky. Mine owners noted that Dreiser was accompanied by his mistress—described in FBI reports as having "positively no literary acumen"—and he was indicted for adultery. Dreiser left Kentucky before police could jail him, and the charge was dismissed two years later. G-men gleefully noted that in his own defense, "Dreiser claimed impotency."

Overall, the Bureau regarded Dreiser as "a great American novelist, but not a great American." Surveillance continued through the 1930s, noting his support for leftist groups and causes, one INFFORMANT telling agents that in 1939 Dreiser informed a group of fellow authors, "We are intellectual shock troops that should speed the gospel of Moscow." Dreiser denied membership in the Communist Party when agents questioned him at his California home, in June 1939, and subsequent reports confirm the FBI's opinion that Dreiser "is not believed to have ever been an actual Party member." Nonetheless, he was listed as a potential candidate for CUSTODIAL DETENTION in 1941 and remained in the FBI's SECURITY INDEX after J. EDGAR HOOVER changed the program's name in 1943. While Hoover maintained an interest in Dreiser's sex life, a 1943 memo from Attorney General FRANCIS BIDDLE advised that prosecution under the MANN ACT had been vetoed "in the absence of commercialism."

By May 1945, seven months before his death, the FBI was pleased to rate Dreiser as "a 'has-been' in the literary field," noting that Dreiser produced "very little writing and what little work he does put out is not in great demand by publishers." Still, it rankled Hoover two months later, when the *Daily Worker* headlined "Theodore Dreiser Joins Communist Party." The Bureau pursued Dreiser's memory for 13 years after his death, adding the last item to his file on 31 July 1958. A full 42 pages of his dossier remain "classified" today, while much of the rest is heavily censored.

**DRUG Demand Reduction Program** —Inaugurated on 27 June 1984, under Attorney General WILLIAM FRENCH SMITH, this program involves collaboration between the FBI and the DRUG ENFORCEMENT ADMINISTRATION to publicize the dangers of drug abuse and the FBI's role in America's "war on drugs." As part of the campaign, athletic coaches, sports figures, media celebrities (and even cartoon characters) have been recruited in an effort to reduce youthful drug abuse. Each field office has a Drug Demand Reduction coordinator, who arranges for the FBI to "adopt" local schools and steer young people away from drugs, toward more constructive forms of recreation. Director WILLIAM SESSIONS shifted the program to the FBI's Research Unit, Office of Congressional and Public Affairs, in April 1988. Five years later, Director LOUIS FREEH moved it once again, this time into the CRIMINAL INVESTIGATIVE DIVISION.

**DRUG Enforcement Administration (DEA)** —Created on 1 July 1973, the DEA is a direct descendant of the earlier FEDERAL BUREAU OF NARCOTICS and thus inherited its predecessor's long-running feud with the FBI, manifested in the 1970s as competition for publicity and funding. The first known collaborative effort between the two agencies occurred in 1980, when G-men joined the staff of the Southwest Border Intelligence Center at El Paso, Texas (founded six years earlier by members of the DEA, Customs, Immigration, and the BUREAU OF ALCOHOL, TOBACCO AND FIREARMS (BATF). FBI agents were still not officially involved in NARCOTICS cases at that point, but rather shared in-

formation on a variety of interstate and international investigations.

The picture changed with RONALD REAGAN'S inauguration as president in 1981. While pledged to a campaign of "law and order," Reagan and his aides had a history of underworld connections dating from the 1930s. Soon after taking office, Reagan fired DEA administrator Peter Bensinger and replaced him with an assistant FBI director, Francis Mullen, in a surprise move that sparked criticism in Congress. (Investigators charged that Mullen's appointment might be a reward for his role in concealing Labor Secretary Raymond Donovan's ORGANIZED CRIME connections during Senate confirmation hearings.) On 28 January 1982 Attorney General WILLIAM SMITH announced a new "war on drugs," personally commanded by Vice President GEORGE H.W. BUSH. As part of that effort, the FBI and DEA were henceforth given concurrent jurisdiction in narcotics cases, with Mullen reporting to FBI HEADQUARTERS. (Director WILLIAM WEBSTER opposed the move, on grounds that it would make G-men more susceptible to corruption, but his protests fell on deaf ears at the White House.) Curiously, at the same time the "war" was declared, Reagan proposed a 12% cut in the DEA's budget, requiring the dismissal of 211 agents and 223 support personnel. By March 1982 the AMERICAN CIVIL LIBERTIES UNION, Coast Guard officers and others had publicly condemned the Reagan drug war as a "fraud in terms of being serious proposals to reduce crime."

The new system produced an uneasy division of labor between the FBI and DEA, with G-men devoting most of their efforts to pursuit of top-echelon drug smugglers, leaving DEA agents to handle the dangerous street action. In practical terms, the DEA revised its personnel requirements to demand college diplomas, but its employees retained protection from the civil service system (unlike FBI personnel). A DEA training facility was established at the FBI ACADEMY in 1985, with agents practicing their pursuit and arrest techniques on HOGAN'S ALLEY.

The FBI-DEA collaboration has produced a spotty record of success, failure, and occasional embarrassment. The jointly-sponsored Drug Demand Reduction Program, launched in June 1984, had no appreciable impact on the U.S. narcotics marketplace, but certain criminal investigations have proved more impressive. In 1985 G-men helped pursue the killers of DEA agent Enrique Camarena, their efforts producing 22 indictments in California and 24 convictions in Mexico (including several Mexican police officers). In November 1986 another joint investigation indicted leaders of the Medellin, Colombia cocaine syndicate; reputed leader Carlos Lehder Rivas was captured and extradited to the U.S. in February 1987. A year later, in February 1988, Panamanian dictator Manuel Noriega and 16 associates were indicted on drug smuggling and money laundering charges, after an FBI-DEA investigation. (Noriega remained at large until President Bush sent troops to abduct him from Panama City in May 1989.) In 1992 the FBI and DEA collaborated with the Coast Guard and BATF to create a National Drug Intelligence Center based at Johnstown, Pennsylvania. Efforts to control the flow of drugs continue today, producing sensational headlines but no realistic prospect of ending the illicit traffic.

**DUCKSTEIN, Jessie B.**—Only three WOMAN AGENTS are known to have served the FBI between 1908 and 1972. The second, Jessie Duckstein, was already in her forties when Attorney General HARRY DAUGHERTY appointed her as a temporary stenographer/typist at the Bureau's Washington, D.C. headquarters on 11 August 1921. By July 1923 she had been promoted to serve as confidential secretary to Director WILLIAM BURNS. Four months later, Duckstein asked to serve as a special agent and Burns officially changed her title on 20 November 1923. She was assigned to the Washington, D.C. field office and served there for the next six months, although Special Agent in Charge E.R. Bohner denied any need for female agents in the nation's capital. Following Director Burns's resignation on 9 May 1924, Bohner communicated his opinion to Acting Director J. EDGAR HOOVER. Hoover demanded Duckstein's resignation on 16 May 1924 and she left Bureau service the same day.

**DULLES, Allen Welsh**—The second son of a Presbyterian minister, born at Watertown, New York on 7 April 1893, Allen Dulles was reared in a family that valued public service and where world affairs were frequently discussed. He received a bachelor's degree from Princeton University in 1914 and a master's two years later, moving from the classroom into diplomatic service with the STATE DEPARTMENT. He spent WORLD WAR I in Switzerland, engaged in thinly-veiled ESPIONAGE, and later joined older brother John Foster Dulles on President WOODROW WILSON'S staff at the Versailles Peace Conference.

Growing dissatisfied with his salary and prospects at State, Dulles earned a law degree from George Washington University in 1926 and the following year joined the New York firm where his brother was a partner. Still unable to reject the call of statesmanship, however, he doubled in 1927 as legal advisor to the American delegation attending the Geneva Disarmament Conference. In 1940 Dulles met WILLIAM DONOVAN at the Republican National Convention, and Donovan invited him to join a new intelligence agency in the making. Formally inaugurated as the Office of Coordinator of Information in October 1941, the group would later be known as the OFFICE OF STRATEGIC SERVICES (OSS). Dulles served ably under Donovan during WORLD WAR II and afterward, until President HARRY TRUMAN disbanded the OSS in 1945. After two years away from the cloak-and-dagger trade, he joined the fledgling CENTRAL INTELLIGENCE AGENCY (CIA) in 1947 and became its deputy director four years later.

By that time, FBI Director J. EDGAR HOOVER had been tracking Dulles for at least a decade. He regarded the whole Dulles clan with suspicion, dubbing them "internationalists" as if it were a mortal insult. In 1942 G-men reported that Allen's sister, Eleanor Dulles, was engaged in a cover love affair with a Polish college professor who had lately applied to the Bureau for work as a translator. Hoover rejected the man on those grounds alone, but he soon found employment with Donovan and the OSS. (The affair, meanwhile, reportedly continued with thrice-weekly trysts for the next 14 years.)

Hoover opposed President DWIGHT EISENHOWER'S selection of Allen Dulles to lead the CIA in February 1953 (soon after brother John was named secretary of state). It marked one of the rare occasions when Hoover and William Donovan agreed on anything, although for different reasons. While Hoover feared Dulles's mythical "leftist tendencies," Donovan questioned his former subordinate's leadership skills. He regarded Dulles as a first-rate spy but a hopeless administrator—and he told Dulles as much in private conversation. Later, Donovan told a third party, "God help America if he heads up the CIA. It's like making a marvelous telegraph operator the head of Western Union." Still, Eisenhower forged ahead with the appointment and FBI-CIA relations remained chilly for the next eight years. The one brief thaw, in February 1954, involved a mutual agreement that neither agency would report the other's operatives to police if they were caught breaking the law. A simple phone call to the errant agent's supervisor would suffice—and thus effectively place both organizations above the law.

Dulles withstood FBI infiltration and attacks from Red-hunting Senator JOSEPH MCCARTHY in the 1950s, but his luck ran out in the first year of President JOHN KENNEDY'S administration. Dulles had begun planning an invasion of Cuba under President Eisenhower, and he persuaded Kennedy to follow through on the doomed effort in April 1961, resulting in the Bay of Pigs fiasco that pushed America toward the Cuban Missile Crisis and a threat of nuclear war with the Soviet Union. Although convinced that the invasion might have succeeded with stronger U.S. backing, Dulles ultimately took responsibility for its failure and resigned from the CIA in September 1961. Twenty-six months later, Kennedy was dead and Dulles was one of those appointed by President LYNDON JOHNSON to investigate the JFK ASSASSINATION. At one point during the investigation, after a discussion of alleged assassin LEE HARVEY OSWALD'S employment as a paid FBI INFORMANT, Dulles opined, "I think this record ought to be destroyed." His final endorsement of the commission's lone-gunman theory was half-hearted at best: "I don't think it can [be proved] unless you believe Mr. Hoover, and so forth and so on, which probably most people will."

In retirement, Dulles wrote extensively about intelligence, forever defending the OSS and the early CIA, steadfastly denying (in spite of voluminous evidence to the contrary) that either agency had ever violated presidential orders or the terms of their respective charters. (Both were barred by law from conducting DOMESTIC SURVEILLANCE inside the United States, but documents released under the FREEDOM OF INFORMATION ACT demonstrate habitual violation of the law by both agencies.) Dulles died in Washington, of influenza complicated by pneumonia, on 29 January 1969.

**DUPEE, Frederick W.**—American literary critic and biographer F.W. Dupee became editor of the leftist *Partisan Review* in 1937, but the FBI overlooked him until May 1939, when a keen-eyed G-man noted his name on the journal's letterhead. By that time, Bureau observers decided, the *Review* had "no commitments to any political party," although it was "formerly associated with the COMMUNIST PARTY." Still, it was determined, the editors were "a group of self-styled revolutionists" who "still adhered to their Marxian revolutionary theories." The last entry was added to Dupee's file in 1968, noting his presumed link to the

BLACK PANTHER PARTY via sponsorship of the International Committee to Defend Eldridge Cleaver.

**DYER Act**—After the MANN ACT of 1910, the Bureau of Investigation received its next great boost in manpower and authority from the National Motor Vehicle Theft Act, more commonly known as the Dyer Act (after its primary sponsor, Missouri congressman Leonidas Dyer). Passed on 28 October 1919, in response to fears of a new "crime wave," the law imposed harsh sentences — up to 10 years in prison, plus fines — on anyone who drove a stolen car across state lines. Charged with enforcement of the Dyer Act, the Bureau rapidly expanded from 301 agents and 329 support personnel in 1919, to 579 agents and 548 support personnel in 1920.

The Dyer Act was a financial godsend for the Bureau, as G-men claimed credit for stolen cars recovered by local police, and their leaders used the rigged statistics to obtain increased congressional appropriations. Chief WILLIAM BURNS set the tone in 1922, telling Congress that the value of stolen cars recovered "amounts to more than our appropriations" for the year. Watching from the sidelines, future J. EDGAR HOOVER studied his boss's technique and refined it during his 48 years as FBI director. By 1970, pleading for a budget in excess of $256 million, Hoover would tell Congress that his agents had recovered 30,599 stolen cars and convicted 3,694 auto thieves in 1969.

The Dyer Acts second benefit to G-men was its service as a "handle" on high-profile cases that otherwise fell outside FBI jurisdiction. Many notorious outlaws, including CLYDE BARROW and JOHN DILLINGER, were pursued for Dyer Act violations at a time when federal agents had no authority to arrest them for the more serious crimes of BANK ROBBERY and murder. Another felon, young Charles Manson, was jailed on a Dyer Act violation in 1951, two decades before he gained global notoriety with the Tate-LaBianca murders in Los Angeles.

No further federal intervention on auto theft occurred until 1969, when Congress required that all road-going motor vehicles must have a registered vehicle identification number (VIN).

After 1 January 1980, VINs were required to use a uniform 17-character format. The Motor Vehicle Theft Law Enforcement Act of 1984, aimed at professional "chop shops," required manufacturers of designated "high-theft" passenger car lines to put the VIN on the engine, the transmission, and 12 major body parts (with criminal penalties imposed for altering or removing those numbers). The same law brought interstate traffic in stolen cars or auto parts under federal racketeering statutes and imposed stiff penalties for export violations. Another 1984 statute, the Comprehensive Crime Control Act, made it a federal offense to counterfeit or forge motor vehicle title certificates. Responding to a national wave of "carjacking," the Anti-Car Theft Act of 1992 made armed auto theft a federal crime, and created a new offense making it a federal crime to own, operate, maintain, or control a chop shop. Two years later, the Motor Vehicle Theft Prevention Act (part of the Violent Crime Control and Law Enforcement Act of 1994), required the Attorney General to develop, in cooperation with the States, a national voluntary motor vehicle theft prevention program, in which a car's owner may sign a consent form authorizing law enforcement officers to stop the car if it is being operated under specified conditions — e.g., at unusual hours or in certain high-crime neighborhoods. Participating motorists must display a program decal on their cars. The Violent Crime Control and Law Enforcement Act also made carjacking where death results a federal crime punishable by death.

FBI recovery of stolen cars has not always been a painless operation. In 1981, during an investigation of interstate auto theft dubbed Operation RECOUP, G-men established a bogus used-car dealership to ensnare racketeers dealing in stolen vehicles. In the process, agents not only purchased "hot" cars, but also sold them to innocent third parties, in full knowledge that the buyers would lose title to their cars (and lose their money) when the operation was concluded. By October 1982 agents had confiscated more than 250 vehicles from innocent buyers, and the "sting" resulted in multiple lawsuits charging the Bureau with fraud.

# E

**EARTH First!**—Inspired by Edward Abbey's novel *The Monkeywrench Gang* (1975), Earth First! was organized in 1980 with a motto of "No Compromise in Defense of Mother Earth!" The group's "monkeywrenching" tactics included removal of surveyor stakes from Forest Service logging roads, vandalism of logging and mining equipment, and "spiking" of trees slated for harvest by loggers. FBI agents placed Earth First! under sporadic surveillance almost from its beginning, but interest intensified in May 1987, when a California sawmill employee was maimed after his saw blade shattered on a hidden nail. Henceforth, the Bureau regarded Earth First! as a "terrorist" organization and treated its members accordingly. (Critics note the FBI's foot-dragging on ANTI-ABORTION VIOLENCE, including murders and BOMBINGS of medical clinics, during the same time period.)

Between 1988 and 1990 G-men mounted a full-scale effort to infiltrate Earth First! with undercover agents and paid INFORMANTS. Documents later revealed in response to a lawsuit disclose that the group's Arizona chapter was subjected to a "COINTELPRO"-style campaign from 1988 to 1990, including use of an *agent provocateur* who persuaded Earth First! members to cut down a rural power line. G-man Michael Fain provided the necessary tools, instructed Earth First! members in their use and drove them to the target, then arrested them as they were acting out his plan. More sinister intensions were suggested by the operation's code name: "Thermcon," which stood for "Thermite Conspiracy" in FBI jargon. Since Earth First! had never used thermite (a military-style incendiary), its members now believe agents planned a FRAME-UP involving illegal explosives, but the plan never came to fruition. It may be no coincidence that California Earth First! activists JUDI BARI and Darryl Cherney were nearly killed on 24 May 1990, when a bomb exploded in Bari's car. FBI agents and members of the Oakland Police Department rushed to charge Bari and Cherney with transporting illegal explosives, but the case was dropped for lack of evidence. Bari and Cherney responded with a federal lawsuit for violation of their civil rights and were victorious in June 2002, winning a $4.4 million judgment against several G-men and Oakland detectives.

The 12-year pursuit of justice in that case revealed a mass of classified FBI documents, including 7,000 pages from law enforcement FILES and 6,000 more of sworn testimony. While San Francisco agent-in-charge RICHARD W. HELD pleaded faulty memory to avoid revealing Bureau activities, he could not conceal all of the FBI's moves against Earth First! In one instance, agents had targeted a subject named Mark Berry, whose only link to Earth First! was his friendship with a subject of the Arizona "Thermcon" sting operation. In pursuit of nonexistent crimes, the agents subjected Berry to WIRETAPPING and physical surveillance, read his mail, and circled his home with aircraft. Once, a pregnant WOMAN AGENT and her male partner visited Berry's cabinet shop, in the guise of a married couple seeking baby furniture. It came to nothing and the Thermcon file was officially closed in January 1990, but Agent Held's San Francisco office kept adding new reports until March — two months before the Bari/Cherney bombing. Earth First! abandoned "monkey-wrenching" after 1990, supplanted in that regard by the EARTH LIBERATION FRONT.

**EARTH Liberation Front** — Unhappy with the moderate course of action charted by the environmentalist group EARTH FIRST! after 1990, more radical activists met to organize the Earth Liberation Front at Brighton, England in 1992. According to its video, *Igniting the Revolution*, ELF sprang from a realization "that to be successful in the struggle to protect the Earth, more extreme tactics must be utilized." The first such actions on record, from October 1996, include the burning of a U.S. Forest Service truck in Detroit and the destruction of an Oregon ranger station (caus-

ing $5.3 million in damage). Since then, a six-year series of arson incidents claimed by ELF include attacks on a fur breeders co-op ($1 million damage); a fast-food restaurant ($400,000); a ski resort ($12 million); a U.S. Forest Industries facility ($500,000); a Michigan State University research facility ($400,000); Boulder, Colorado's Legend Ridge mansion ($2.5 million); a Minnesota genetics research lab ($250,000); plus various homes, commercial offices and vehicles. Small-scale activities include roving acts of vandalism and tree-spiking.

The FBI investigates ELF as a terrorist organization, but its efforts have produced no noteworthy results thus far. On 5 April 2001 G-men raided the Portland, Oregon home occupied by ELF spokesmen Craig Rosebraugh and Leslie James Pickering, seeking evidence in recent arson attacks, but they came away empty-handed. Frank Ambrose, a 27-year-old "suspected" ELF activist, was charged with tree-spiking in Bloomington, Indiana around the same time, but prosecutors dismissed the charges "in the interests of justice" on 13 September 2001, after declaring their suspicion of "a widespread conspiracy" behind the tree-spiking incidents. Defense attorney Richard Kammen took a different view of the dismissal. "It was very clear," he told reporters, "that the state's case was based on wild speculation without any support of the facts. There just wasn't any evidence."

ELF, meanwhile, seemed intent on carrying its battle to the enemy. Protesters picketed the Bloomington FBI office during a "Week of Resistance" in April 2001, and ELF's website went further, declaring that the group would henceforth target "FBI offices and U.S. federal buildings," "liberal democracy," and even "industrial civilization" at large. Thus far, no such sweeping attacks have occurred.

**EASTMAN, Max** — A lifelong socialist, Max Eastman was a native of New York state, born in 1883. One of his early forays into politics involved membership in the Men's League for Women's Suffrage. In 1912, with outspoken communist JOHN REED, Eastman founded *The Masses*, which he described as "a magazine with a sense of humor and no respect for the respectable."

The magazine also opposed American entry into WORLD WAR I with such vehemence that it was driven out of business by government pressure in 1918 (reemerging soon thereafter as *The Liberator*). Eastman, for his part, was charged with violating the 1917 espionage act, but charges were dismissed after juries deadlocked at two trials, in April 1918 and January 1919. Still, Eastman remained a subject of surveillance by the Bureau of Investigation and other agencies. A bureau report of 23 June 1919 indicates that agents were reading his mail, marking Eastman as one of the first American writers (with LINCOLN STEFFENS) to be targeted for illicit "mail covers." That same year, future president FRANKLIN ROOSEVELT, while serving as assistant secretary of the navy, reported to Attorney General A. MITCHELL PALMER on a speech Eastman delivered in Seattle.

Eastman subsequently spent two years in Soviet Russia, from 1922 to 1924, while the BI under WILLIAM BURNS pursued his every move. Eastman's file would ultimately total some 369 pages, including a memo that labeled him "one of the most dangerous radical socialists [*sic*] in America, a true believer in free love." Even Eastman's dining habits were of interest to G-men, another memo noting that "he eats frequently at 'Dutch Oven' in the basement of the [Liberal] Club, at Polly's, etc." As for sex, the BI noted that Eastman "is married, but the general consensus of opinion around Washington Square is that he is a dangerous man where women are concerned. Even experienced literary and stage women 'shy clear' of handsome Max Eastman."

For all his early radicalism, Eastman underwent a drastic change in the early 1940s, veering sharply to the right. In the wake of WORLD WAR II he emerged as an ardent supporter of witch-hunting Senator JOSEPH MCCARTHY and the HOUSE COMMITTEE ON UN-AMERICAN ACTIVITIES. For the last quarter-century of Eastman's life, until his death in 1969, he served as a roving reporter for the arch-conservative *Reader's Digest*.

**EDMONDS, Sibel** — Sibel Edmonds was hired by the FBI in September 2001, as a WIRETAP translator in the Washington field office. She was among 400 translators hired by the FBI over a two-year period, to reduce what Director ROBERT MUELLER described as an "accumulation of thousands of hours of audio tapes and pages" left untranslated from various surveillance operations. Pressure to translate those conversations mounted in the wake of catastrophic terrorist attacks on 11 September 2001, with corresponding emphasis on watching groups of Middle Eastern origin.

Edmonds was fired in March 2002, after she wrote a letter to FBI Counterterrorism chief Dale Watson, expressing concern for lax security in the Washington field office. Specifically, Cole revealed that one of her coworkers belonged to a group under FBI surveillance, that the same coworker had "unreported contacts" with a foreign government official being wiretapped by the Bureau, and that the employee in question failed to translate two communications from that suspect official. Rather than investigate the matter, FBI officials dismissed Edmonds for "disruptiveness," but she took her case to Congress after COLLEEN ROWLEY'S case made national headlines that spring. Under pressure from the U.S. Senate, G-men finally examined Edmonds's story and admitted that her allegations were true.

In addition to alleged malfeasance on the job, Edmonds reported that her coworker — identified in *Washington Post* reports as a 33-year-old U.S. citizen of Arab ancestry — and the coworker's husband (a U.S. military officer) had tried to recruit Edmonds for the same unidentified group. According to Edmonds, the coworker's husband told her, "It's a very good place to be a member. There are a lot of advantages of being with this organization, and one of the greatest things about it is you can have an early, an unexpected early retirement. And you will be totally set if you go to that specific country." Edmonds interpreted the conversation as an effort to recruit her for espionage within the FBI, but G-men showed no interest in her report. After she was fired Edmonds wrote to the JUSTICE DEPARTMENT'S inspector general that "Investigations are being compromised. Incorrect or misleading translations are being sent to agents in the field. Translations are being blocked and circumvented." Even then, with Senate investigators calling for an explanation, Bureau spokesmen reported that they "could not corroborate" alleged efforts to recruit Edmonds for the suspect organization.

**EHRLICHMAN, John D.** — A native of Tacoma, Washington, born 20 March 1925, John Ehrlichman graduated from Stanford University School of Law in 1951 and was a partner in a Seattle law firm until 1968, when he became tour director for RICHARD NIXONS's second presidential campaign. Following Nixon's victory in November 1968 Ehrlichman was designated presidential counsel (1968), then appointed presidential assistant for domestic affairs (1969-73). In that post he played a critical role in the WATERGATE SCANDAL that finally drove Nixon from office in disgrace.

Nixon made Ehrlichman his chief liaison with FBI Director J. EDGAR HOOVER, a buffer of sorts to forestall personal meetings at the White House. Of his hour-long introduction to Hoover, Ehrlichman recalled that Hoover "did all the talking" from behind his desk, mounted on a six-inch dais that permitted him to look down on visitors. Hoover, apparently unimpressed, informed Assistant Director WILLIAM SULLIVAN in May 1969 that Ehrlichman and Nixon aide H.R. HALDEMAN belonged to "a ring of homosexuals at the highest levels of the White House." The rumor reached Attorney General JOHN MITCHELL in June, and President Nixon reluctantly ordered an FBI investigation, which Hoover assigned to Deputy Associate Director MARK FELT. Questioned about specific suspect dates, Ehrlichman later wrote, "I had a good alibi for the dates alleged. I was elsewhere with other people, including a satisfactory number of women." Hoover duly closed the case but Ehrlichman never forgot it, agitating thereafter for the director's removal.

Still there were appearances to be observed, and Ehrlichman joined Nixon for dinner at Hoover's home on 1 October 1969. (Steaks were flown in from CLINT MURCHISON's Texas ranch for the occasion.) Hoover regaled his guests with tales of FBI BREAK-INS, noting that Nixon raised no objection and seemed to admire the illegal technique. "At the end of the evening," Ehrlichman wrote in his memoirs, "Hoover would have had every reason to think he was authorized to do 'black bag' jobs." He nonetheless resisted some White House requests for burglaries and WIRE-TAPPING, prompting Nixon's team to propose the alternate HUSTON PLAN as a means of circumventing FBI resistance.

Ehrlichman, meanwhile, was deeply immersed in Nixon's illegal activities. He vetoed certain zany plans, including a scheme to firebomb the BROOKINGS INSTITUTION as a means of letting G-men loot its files, but he routinely approved other criminal acts, including a burglary at Dr. Lewis Fielding's office (seeking information on unauthorized release of the PENTAGON PAPERS by Fielding's patient, Daniel Ellsberg). In early 1973, when the Watergate scandal tainted acting FBI director L. PATRICK GRAY, Ehrlichman had no sympathy, telling White House counsel John Dean, "I think we ought to let him hang there. Let him twist slowly, slowly in the wind." A month later it was Ehrlichman's turn on the gallows, forced to resign with H.R. Haldeman.

Criminal charges followed, including allegations of obstructing justice, conspiracy to violate Dr. Fielding's civil rights and perjury before a federal grand jury. Ehrlichman was convicted on all counts in 1975, and given a five-year prison term. Nixon refused his plea for a pardon and Ehrlichman served 18 months, paroled in 1978. He published his memoirs, *Witness to*

*Power*, in 1982 and subsequently turned to fiction while working simultaneously as a conservative radio commentator. Ehrlichman died in Atlanta on 14 February 1999.

**EINSTEIN, Albert** — Arguably the world's greatest scientist of the 20th century, Albert Einstein was born at Ulm, Germany in 1879. He left his homeland and renounced German citizenship at age 16, becoming a citizen of neutral Switzerland in 1901. Four years later Einstein published his special theory of relativity, including the famous formula "$E = mc^2$." He moved to Berlin in April 1914 and signed his first antiwar petition four months later, at the outbreak of WORLD WAR I. In 1915 Einstein joined an antiwar organization, the Organization for a New Fatherland, that was later banned by law. November of that year saw publication of his general theory of relativity, portraying gravity as warped space-time.

Einstein's attraction to controversial causes lasted beyond war's end. In 1921 he made his first visit to the U.S. with Zionist leader Chaim Weizmann, soliciting funds for a new Hebrew University in Jerusalem. A year later, while a member of the League of Nations Committee on Intellectual Cooperation, he received the Nobel Peace Prize. (Russia's COMMUNIST PARTY seized upon the occasion to denounce his theory of relativity as "reactionary.") In 1925 Einstein joined Gandhi in signing a manifesto against compulsory military service.

The rise of Nazism in Germany encouraged Einstein to leave once again, but he faced opposition in 1932, when he sought a visa to teach at the University of California. Specifically, a far-right organization called the Woman Patriot Corporation sent the STATE DEPARTMENT a 16-page letter arguing that Einstein should be barred from U.S. soil because his pacifism and internationalist views constituted "direct affiliation with Communist and anarcho-communist organizations and groups." Officials at State took the claim seriously enough to grill Einstein on his politics, with the result described in a dispatch from the Associated Press:

> Professor Einstein's patience broke. His usual genial face stern and his normally melodious voice strident, he cried: "What's this, an inquisition? Is this an attempt at chicanery? I don't propose to answer such silly questions. I didn't ask to go to America. Your countrymen invited me; yes, begged me. If I am to enter your country as a suspect, I don't want to go at all. If you don't want to give me a visa, please say so. Then I'll know where I stand."

Within hours of that story's publication, State Department spokesmen announced that Einstein and his wife would receive their visas the following day. The couple set sail for the U.S. on 10 December 1932 and arrived on 12 January 1933. When ADOLF HITLER assumed political control of Germany later that month, Einstein found himself cast into permanent exile. He soon moved to Princeton with an appointment to the Institute for Advanced Study. Questions concerning his politics lingered, and despite a September 1933 statement to the *London Times* that he had "never favored Communism and do not favor it now," the FBI continued filing reports on such subjects as Einstein's support for Loyalist Spain (he later declared himself "ashamed" for not backing the cause more strongly) and his efforts to obtain U.S. entry visas for other fugitives from Nazi persecution.

In August 1939 Einstein addressed his first letter to President FRANKLIN ROOSEVELT, warning that Germany was attempting to build an atomic bomb. On 22 June 1940, Einstein praised America in a public address, declaring, "In this country, it has been generations since men were subject to the humiliating necessity of unquestioning obedience. Ironically, one month later, Einstein was denied a security clearance to work on the Manhattan Project because of his failure to conform. Army Intelligence had asked the FBI's opinion of his loyalty, and while no evidence of any treasonous activity existed in his file, Director J. EDGAR HOOVER added a "Biographical Sketch" replete with lies and half-truths, including claims that Einstein "has been sponsoring the principal Communist causes in the United States" and that "in Berlin, even in the political free and easy period of 1923 to 1929, the Einstein home was known as a Communist center and clearing house." Concluding, Hoover wrote: "In view of his radical background, this office would not recommend the employment of Dr. Einstein on matters of a secret nature, without a very careful investigation, as it seems unlikely that a man of his background could, in such a short time, become a loyal American citizen."

Hoover's condemnation might bar Einstein from building a nuclear bomb, but it did not stop him from becoming a U.S. citizen on 1 October 1940. Three years later, the U.S. Navy's Bureau of Ordnance saw fit to hire Einstein as a consultant on development of high-speed torpedoes. Einstein wrote to Roosevelt again in March 1945, introducing a friend (Leo Szilard) who opposed wartime use of America's new atom bomb, but FDR died before reading the message. Three months later, President HARRY TRUMAN unleashed two of the dreaded weapons on Japan and thereby inaugurated the Nuclear Age.

Undeterred by the onset of the Cold War and a new Red Scare, Einstein agreed in May 1946 to lead the Emergency Committee of Atomic Scientists, raising money for anti-bomb organizations. Four months later, a fresh outbreak of racist brutality in the South prompted him to sign on as co-chairman of the American Crusade to End LYNCHING. Both were "subversive" causes, according to J. Edgar Hoover, and FBI surveillance of Einstein escalated accordingly. A notation in his file from the period claimed that Einstein "in the past has been used by various Communist Front organizations as a 'big name' 'innocent' sponsor." FBI HEADQUARTERS took note when Einstein appealed on behalf of the SMITH ACT defendants in 1948, and again when he sought clemency on behalf of JULIUS and ETHEL ROSENBERG. (Einstein argued in a letter to Judge Irving Kaufman that there were in fact no real "atomic secrets" to be stolen by a ring of spies.) By that time, years of surveillance had taken their toll on Einstein. At a 1948 dinner party he told Poland's ambassador to the U.S., "I suppose you must realize by now that the U.S. is no longer a free country, that undoubtedly our conversation is being recorded. The room is wired, and my house is closely watched." Hoover proved him correct in that instance by adding the private remark to Einstein's dossier.

On 30 January 1950, following Russia's detonation of a new

hydrogen bomb, President Truman announced a crash program to build similar weapons for America. Einstein appeared on ELEANOR ROOSEVELT'S television show two weeks later, warning that such weapons could spell the end of life on Earth. The same day those remarks were reported in the *Washington Post*, Hoover ordered his chief of domestic intelligence to draft a new report on Einstein. Hastily completed in two days, the document still found no grounds for prosecution. It left G-men grasping at straws, as when they pursued a report that Einstein had invented a robot capable of dominating human minds. Another wild story—also proved false—had Einstein's son held hostage in Russia, compelling his support for "Communist causes."

At the same time, in March 1950, the Immigration and Naturalization Service asked Hoover to furnish "any derogatory information contained in any file" on Einstein. A second letter from the INS assured Hoover that "this naturalized person, notwithstanding his world-wide reputation as a scientist, may properly be investigated for possible revocation of naturalization." Agents thought they had found the key in 1951, briefly branding Einstein's secretary and housekeeper as a Soviet agent, but the hot tip led to another dead-end. A year later Einstein was offered the presidency of Israel, but he declined.

A fresh storm broke around Einstein in May 1953, when Brooklyn schoolteacher William Frauenglass—subpoenaed to testify before the SENATE INTERNAL SECURITY SUBCOMMITTEE—wrote to Einstein with a plea for advice. Einstein's reply, published by the *New York Times* in June, urged Frauenglass: "Refuse to testify." Editors of the "liberal" *Times* ran a front-page editorial on 12 June 1953, denouncing Einstein's advice as "illegal," "unnatural" and "unwise." Again Hoover took note. By the close of 1954 his agents calculated that Einstein had served as honorary chairman for three Communist organizations over the past 17 years; during the same period he had furthermore joined, sponsored or otherwise become affiliated with 50 Communist front groups.

All that, and the long war was about to end. On 11 April 1955 Einstein joined Bertrand Russell in issuing a manifesto to all nations of the world, urging them to renounce nuclear weapons. Seven days later, Einstein died at age 76. Hoover officially closed his dossier a few days later, noting, "It is not believed that additional investigation in the matter is warranted."

The Bureau's dossier on Einstein was exposed in 1983, when Florida professor Robert Schwartz wrote an article about it for *The Nation*. Even then, at least a quarter of the file was classified, blacked out by FBI censors, until author Fred Jerome sued to retrieve the rest under the FREEDOM OF INFORMATION ACT. Even now, with Jerome's detailed study in print, it is unclear how much material was actually filed on Einstein. Different published reports on the subject cite his dossier as including 1427, 1535 or 1800 pages.

**EISENHOWER, Dwight David**—A native of Denison, Texas, born 14 October 1890, Dwight Eisenhower was a career soldier who commanded Allied operations in Europe during WORLD WAR II. Upon retirement from the Army, Eisenhower served as president of Columbia University from 1948 through 1952, when he mounted a successful campaign for the White House. Incumbent HARRY TRUMAN declined to seek a second term, leaving war hero "Ike" to face Democratic hopeful ADLAI STEVENSON that November. Eisenhower ran on a promise to drive "crooks and cronies" from Washington, and he won by a landslide despite the pervasive taint of scandal borne by running mate RICHARD NIXON.

Soon after his inauguration, concerned by rumors that FBI Director J. EDGAR HOOVER "had been out of favor in Washington," Ike summoned Hoover to the White House "to assure him that I wanted him in government as long as I might be there and that in the performance of his duties he would have the complete support of my office." A grateful Hoover paid the first installment on that debt soon after, when he tipped Eisenhower that a White House aide (the son of a prominent GOP senator) was HOMOSEXUAL, thereby permitting Eisenhower to avoid potential scandal and dismiss the young man quietly. By the end of his first year office, according to Assistant Director WILLIAM SULLIVAN'S memoirs, Eisenhower "blindly believed everything the director told him, never questioned a word.... He may have been a great general but he was a very gullible man, and Hoover soon had him wrapped right around his finger."

Ike's concern for "internal security" during the 1950s essentially mirrored Hoover's. In April 1953 Eisenhower issued EXECUTIVE ORDER 10450, establishing a LOYALTY PROGRAM that reserved federal jobs for persons of "unswerving loyalty" to the U.S. At the same time, Attorney General HERBERT BROWNELL gave the FBI virtual carte blanche for unfettered DOMESTIC SURVEILLANCE on cases of national security. It seems that Eisenhower never learned of Hoover's covert support for Red-hunting Senator JOSEPH MCCARTHY, who considered the new Republican White House team as "soft on Communism" as Truman's departed Democrats.

On 13 May 1955 McCarthy aide Don Surine contacted Assistant Director LOUIS NICHOLS "in confidence" to report "scuttlebut" [*sic*] that had considered getting a divorce in 1944, "at a time when General Eisenhower was allegedly having an affair with Kay Summersby, the British WAC. General [George] Marshal[l] is reported to have squelched the idea of the divorce and to have engaged in maneuvering which broke up the affair with Kay Summersby." Four months later, Surine contacted Nichols again "to confidentially advise that Kay Summersby ... has been staying at the Shoreham Hotel [in Washington] for the last 30 to 45 days under an assumed name."

Hoover already had a FILE on Summersby. Her first husband had divorced her for adultery in 1943, and during World War II she served as Eisenhower's confidential secretary, aide and driver. At the time Surine contacted Nichols, she was married to Wall Street stockbroker Reginald Morgan. Hoover ordered Nichols to "See if we can discreetly get the name" she was using at the Shoreham Hotel, but Summersby was gone by the time G-men arrived and they never discovered her secret. A second, similar report on Eisenhower's love life was derived from a Detroit wiretap, in which two mobsters referred to a well-known Washington attorney. The lawyer, one said, had "a good-looking wife. He says Ike has been trying to get into her pants."

Despite such foibles (or malicious rumors, as the case may be), Eisenhower managed to avoid the kind of scandals that dogged some of his successors. Upon retirement from politics in 1961, his general's rank was restored by the Army, but it signaled no return to active duty. Settled on a spacious ranch at Gettysburg, Pennsylvania — bankrolled by CLINT MURCHISON and other wealthy friends he shared with Hoover — Ike published his memoirs in three volumes, between 1963 and 1967. He died at Walter Reed Army Hospital in Washington, following a series of heart attacks, on 28 March 1969.

**EISEMANN-SCHIER, Ruth**—A native of Honduras, born in 1942, Ruth Eisemann-Schier was living in the U.S. and working as a biological researcher when she met ex-convict Gary Steven Krist, three years her junior, in 1968. Despite his criminal record dating from age 14, Eisemann-Schier found herself strongly attracted to Krist and soon fell in line with his plans for a high-stakes ransom KIDNAPPING. The target was 20-year-old Barbara Jane Mackle, a freshman at Emory College in Atlanta, Georgia. Mackle's father was a millionaire Florida land developer and personal friend of president-elect RICHARD NIXON, well able to meet Krist's ransom demands.

In the week before Christmas 1968, Mackle and her mother were registered at an Atlanta motel. Barbara was suffering from a bout of influenza and had left her dormitory to avoid infecting her roommates. Krist and Eisemann-Schier invaded the motel room in the predawn hours of 17 December, brandishing pistols and subduing Mackle's mother with chloroform, leaving her bound on the bed. They next drove Mackle 20 miles northeast of town and buried her alive in a box equipped with an air pump, food and water, and a battery-powered lamp. A ransom note buried in the Mackles' front yard at Coral Gables, Florida demanded $500,000 in old $20 bills for Barbara's safe return.

The family followed orders, running a specified ad in a Miami newspaper on 18 December, nervously awaiting instructions for the ransom's delivery. The drop was arranged for 19 December on a causeway leading to uninhabited Fair Isle, in Biscayne Bay. Robert Mackle lost his way in darkness and arrived an hour late at the drop point, but Krist confirmed the payoff via telephone. He barely had the bag in hand when a policeman on routine patrol mistook Krist for a burglar and gave chase. The kidnapper escaped on foot, but clues from his abandoned car identified both suspects for the FBI. Meanwhile, at 12:30 a.m. on 20 December, a telephone call to the Bureau's Atlanta field office directed G-men to the site where Barbara Mackle was buried. Exhumed after 83 hours below ground, she was found alive and well. Arrest warrants were issued for Krist and Eisemann-Schier the same day; Krist was added to the FBI's "TEN MOST WANTED" LIST on 20 December, while Eisemann-Schier joined the roster eight days later.

In headlong flight, Krist used some of the ransom money to purchase a boat in South Carolina, but a Coast Guard helicopter spoiled his escape plan, trailing him until he abandoned his craft on Hog Island, in Charleston Harbor. Captured by Sheriff Richard McLeod on 22 December 1968, Krist was held in lieu of $500,000 bond. A Georgia grand jury indicted Krist and Eise-mann-Schier for kidnapping on 3 January 1969. Eisemann-Schier remained at large until 5 March 1969, when she applied for a nursing job as "Donna Sue Wills," in Norman, Oklahoma. A fingerprint check, required of all Oklahoma nursing applicants, revealed her true identity and she was taken into custody by FBI agents.

A Georgia court convicted Gary Krist of kidnapping on 26 May 1969, whereupon he was sentenced to life imprisonment. (Krist also confessed to a series of murders allegedly committed between 1959 and 1967, but no additional charges were filed.) Ruth Eisemann-Schier pled guilty to kidnapping charges on 29 May 1969 and received a seven-year sentence. She served three years in prison and was deported to her native Honduras upon her release.

**EL PASO Intelligence Center**—Established in 1974 as the Southwest Border Intelligence Center and later renamed for its location at El Paso, Texas, this facility was initiated as a joint operation of the DRUG ENFORCEMENT AGENCY; the Immigration and Naturalization Service; the BUREAU OF ALCOHOL, TOBACCO AND FIREARMS; the U.S. Customs Service; and the U.S. Coast Guard. The FBI became a participating agency in 1980, followed in 1983 by the INTERNAL REVENUE SERVICE, the U.S. Marshals Service, and the Federal Aviation Administration. Agencies collaborating at the center — known as EPIC for short — are variously concerned with smuggling of aliens, NARCOTICS and weapons. A more recent concern, since 11 September 2001, is the joint investigation of alleged TERRORIST activity in the Southwest and Mexico.

**ELIOT, Thomas Stearns**—A native of St. Louis, born in 1888, T.S. Eliot became a British citizen in 1927 and won the Nobel Prize for literature in 1948. His curious two-page FBI file, opened in March 1949, consists of two clippings from *The Daily Worker*, attacking Eliot as an "anti-Semite" friend of EZRA POUND. In fact, Eliot had been denounced by the American COMMUNIST PARTY more than a decade earlier, branded "anti-people and fascist-minded," and while such condemnation might have marked him as a patriot in other circumstances, friendship with Pound placed an indelible black mark beside his name. No further additions were made to his file before Eliot died in 1965.

**ENGINEERING Research Facility**—Housed on the FBI ACADEMY grounds at Quantico, Virginia, the bureau's Engineering Research Facility is part of the larger INFORMATION RESOURCES DIVISION. Its staff reportedly includes engineers, mathematicians, technicians, analysts, "technically trained agents," and support personnel who provide technical assistance for field investigations, supply electronic surveillance equipment and monitor security in all FBI facilities. The unit also runs a training program for special agents and electronics technicians employed by the bureau.

**ENGLISH, Charles, Jr.**—A Bureau bomb technician based in Mobile, Alabama, Charles English, Jr., was indicted in September 2001 for possessing child pornography and sending a computer disk of pornographic photos through the U.S. mail (in November 1998). The indictment was sealed until a team of G-men from FBI HEADQUARTERS arrived to arrest English on 17 October 2001. Assistant U.S. attorney Michael Nicrosi told a federal magistrate that English asked an unnamed person to download the illicit images onto a computer disk, explaining the request with a false claim that he (English) was involved in a child pornography investigation. Agent Chuck Middleton, in charge of the FBI's Mobile field office, told reporters that English had been fired as a result of an internal investigation. No resolution of the case had been announced at press time for this volume, but prosecutors stress that an indictment is merely an accusation of criminal conduct and not proof of crime. Possession of child pornography carries a maximum penalty of five years in prison; mailing pornography is a separate offense, with a maximum penalty of 15 years.

**ENRON**—Founded in 1985, the Enron corporation began trading natural gas commodities four years later and launched the first global commodity trading website in November 1999. Nine months later, Enron chairman Kenneth Lay contributed more than $290,000 to the campaign fund of GOP presidential candidate GEORGE W. BUSH. It came as no surprise, therefore, when Lay was appointed as an advisor to President-elect Bush's transition team in January 2001, while Enron backer Patrick Wood III became Bush's chairman of the Federal Energy Regulatory Commission. Top Bush advisor Karl Rove waited another six months to divest himself of Enron stock worth $100,000, all the while meeting with Enron officials to plan the new administration's energy policy (including tax cuts and expanded drilling in protected areas). On 16 October 2001, following conversations between Lay and Commerce Secretary Donald Evans, Enron stunned investors with a report of $618 million in losses and a $1.2 billion reduction in shareholder equity. The SEC launched an investigation into rumored conflicts of interest, while the INTERNAL REVENUE SERVICE revealed Enron's $50,000 campaign contribution to House Majority Whip Tom DeLay.

The scandal spread from there. In November 2001 Enron filed documents with the SEC "revising" its financial statements for the past five years to account for $586 million in losses. A month later the company filed for Chapter 11 bankruptcy protection, dismissed 4,000 employees and borrowed $1.5 billion to keep operating while in bankruptcy. The JUSTICE DEPARTMENT announced a criminal investigation of Enron on 10 January 2002, but Attorney General JOHN ASHCROFT recused himself on grounds that Enron had donated $57,499 to his Missouri political campaigns in 1999-2000. Twelve days later, an ex-Enron employee revealed mass shredding of documents after the SEC investigation was announced in October 2001. FBI agents began pursuing that claim on 23 January 2002, and Ken Lay resigned as Enron's CEO the same day. On 25 January former Enron vice chairman J. Clifford Baxter was found dead in his car, an apparent suicide.

With Attorney General Ashcroft sidelined, the Justice Department instructed President Bush to preserve all documents related to his dealings with Enron, and White House aides agreed. Skeptics questioned whether the warning came too late, but Senate investigators were preoccupied with Kenneth Lay and his associates, as past and present Enron executives claimed their Fifth Amendment privilege to avoid giving testimony. The White House also favored stony silence, prompting the General Accounting Office to file an unprecedented lawsuit against Vice President Dick Cheney on 23 February 2002, demanding release of documents detailing his involvement with Enron and President Bush's energy task force. (At this writing, in January 2003, Cheney was appealing court orders to release those documents.) In March 2002 Army Secretary Thomas White—another ex-Enron executive, holder of 200,000 company shares—publicly denied any improper contact with Enron colleagues; at the same time, he released a list of 44 previously undisclosed phone calls to Enron officials preceding sale of his stock.

In April 2002, while President Bush belatedly called for imprisonment of dishonest corporate executives, the House passed accounting reform legislation including stricter oversight and disclosure provisions. August 2002 saw the first Enron conviction, as former executive Michael Kopper pled guilty to money laundering and wire fraud. Three weeks later, on 13 September 2002, three British bankers were indicted on wire-fraud charges related to the Enron case. Andrew Fastow, Enron's onetime chief financial officer, was indicted by a federal grand jury on 31 October 2002. His charges included 78 counts of wire and mail fraud, money laundering and conspiracy to inflate Enron's profits. More indictments are likely, but it remains to be seen if the scandal will further taint the White House and Justice Department.

**ERNST, Morris L.**—A New York lawyer, born in 1888, Morris Ernst spend nearly a quarter-century as general counsel for the AMERICAN CIVIL LIBERTIES UNION (ACLU). At the same time, he also represented private clients who included WALTER WINCHELL and FBI Director J. EDGAR HOOVER. Unknown to his ACLU colleagues at the time, Ernst also served as an FBI "mole" within the group, neutralizing ACLU criticism of the Bureau, reporting private conversations and furnishing FBI HEADQUARTERS copies of personal (even privileged) correspondence. These activities seemingly sprang from a combination of Ernst's own anticommunist beliefs and his admiration for Hoover. Journalist Curt Gentry, in his definitive biography of Hoover, branded Ernst a "fanatic champion" of the FBI and its director.

Throughout his tenure with the ACLU Ernst ardently defended the FBI in a series of speeches and articles prepared with assistance from ghost writers in the Bureau's CRIME RECORDS DIVISION. More troubling was his 1949 offer to become a defense attorney for accused atom bomb spies JULIUS and ETHEL ROSENBERG on behalf of the FBI. Memos from Assistant Director LOUIS NICHOLS reveal that Ernst suggested the plan "on only one ground, that he could make a contribution" to the FBI. Ignoring the obvious (and illegal) conflict of interest, Ernst opined that "this would be a terrific story and probably would be most helpful to the Bureau." The Rosenbergs declined his aid, but Ernst still used his influence to persuade ACLU leaders that there were "no civil liberties issues involved" in the case.

Throughout the Red Scare that followed WORLD WAR II,

Ernst never challenged any FBI activity, including Bureau leaks of classified information to Senator JOSEPH MCCARTHY and the HOUSE COMMITTE ON UN-AMERICAN ACTIVITIES (HUAC). His adulation for the Bureau and for Hoover personally is revealed in a series of fawning letters Ernst penned to Hoover, Nichols and Associate Director CLYDE TOLSON. On 12 July 1949, for example, he wrote to Hoover, "I am flattered to be associated with you." Four months later, on 25 November, he wrote to the director, "I am fast becoming known as the person to pick a fight [with] in relation to the FBI." Still, he received little in return for his tireless service. The FBI ran background checks on a few individuals for Ernst, and in 1939 Hoover arranged a private meeting with Congressman MARTIN DIES, where Ernst vowed to expel known Reds from the ACLU in return for HUAC's lifting its brand as a "Communist front" organization. Otherwise, Ernst's "friendship" with the Bureau was a decidedly one-way street.

And a tenuous one, at that. On 13 February 1948 Ernst angered Hoover by suggesting that Hoover was "getting a little thin-skinned" on the subject of LOYALTY PROGRAMS, and that he was "probably writing too many letters making corrections of attacks on the FBI." Ernst tried to smooth Hoover's ruffled feathers in December 1948, by negotiating an FBI movie deal in Hollywood, but his help was rejected. A year later, on 3 December 1949, he made matters worse by asking Nichols to "Tell Edgar that I am worried about him for the first time," concerning a recent outburst that "bespeaks some degree of insecurity."

Though angry, Hoover still had use for Ernst in 1950, as author MAX LOWENTHAL prepared to publish his scathing critique, *The Federal Bureau of Investigation*. Hoover asked Ernst to contact Lowenthal's publisher with word that "the book was filled with distortions, half-truths and incomplete details as well as false statements," but Ernst declined for the sake of appearances. Instead of a frontal assault, he suggested that G-men recruit allies at the Library of Congress to suggest a new and "less confusing" title for Lowenthal's book. When that scheme failed to do the trick, Ernst prepared an article with help from Nichols and the Crime Records Division, published in *Reader's Digest* as "Why I no longer fear the FBI" (December 1950).

Ernst had no further value to the FBI after he left the ACLU in 1954, but he still sought to keep up his "friendship" with Hoover and company. Any hope of an amicable relationship was doomed on 22 December 1955, when Ernst penned a letter to Hoover reporting that "some silly Republicans" hoped to nominate Hoover for president in 1956. Ernst assured Hoover that he had done his best to dissuade them from such "nonsense," going on to write: "I hope you will not deem it unkind for me to say that I like you as head of the FBI, but not as President or even a candidate for that office." Henceforth, Hoover refused Ernst's calls and their erratic correspondence was conducted at arm's length, through Lou Nichols. Nearly a decade later, in 1964, Ernst still defended Hoover as "a treasured friend" in testimony before the U.S. Senate, but Clyde Tolson laid that illusion to rest the same year, when he placed Ernst's name on the director's "in absence of" list (meaning that any time he called or wrote Hoover would be reported "out of town"). Curt Gen-

try writes that Tolson took that action "in a bizarre fit of jealous rage," and that Ernst was "shattered" by the end of his long relationship with Hoover. He outlived Hoover by four years, dying in 1976.

Controversy still surrounds Ernst's ties to the FBI. Hoover periodically denied any personal link to Ernst, but in October 1971 he confirmed to a *Los Angeles Times* reporter that Ernst had been his "personal attorney for many years." Ernst likewise confirmed that relationship to Curt Gentry in 1975, though senility prevented him from recalling any specific details. Still, he remembered "grand and glorious nights at the Stork Club" with Hoover and Walter Winchell, reporting that he still admired Hoover "as much as any other." Eight years after Ernst's death, Harrison Salisbury analyzed his correspondence with Hoover for *The Nation* (1 December 1984) and concluded: "On balance, it seems clear that Ernst's greatest value to the Bureau was as publicist, a sort of *Good Housekeeping* seal of approval."

**ESPIONAGE** — Although FBI agents were assigned to enforce the Espionage Act of 1917 during WORLD WAR I, their service under that statute had less to do with bagging foreign spies than with investigating critics of military conscription. Secret operatives were captured on occasion, but the Bureau's first major espionage case began in 1935, when agents from the New York City field office uncovered a German spy ring led by Guenther Rumrich. The breakthrough was tempered by embarrassment, since the ring had been active since 1927, and another three years passed before 18 suspects were indicted on 20 June 1938. Even then, 14 escaped, leaving Rumrich and three others to face trial and receive 10-year prison terms in December 1938.

A month before that trial, President FRANKLIN ROOSEVELT approved Hoover's proposal to expand the FBI's espionage investigations in collaboration with the Army's Military Intelligence Division and the Office of Naval Intelligence. FBI statistics reveal a dramatic surge in espionage cases around that time, from an average of 35 cases per year through 1937, to 634 in 1938 and a "projected total" of 772 in 1939. No total figures are available for the duration of WORLD WAR II, but figures provided by the FBI to author William Breuer and published in his volume *Hitler's Undercover War* (1989) betray a less impressive conviction rate. According to the Bureau's own figures, it convicted only 100 spies between 1937 and 1945, including 68 American citizens, 25 Germans, and one agent each from Austria, Canada, Colombia, Portugal, Russia, South Africa and Spain. The war's most dramatic spy investigation, the AMERASIA CASE of 1945, was thrown out of court because G-men and agents from the OFFICE OF STRATEGIC SERVICES committed illegal BREAK-INS when they should have known better.

Counterespionage work was no easier in the Cold War. ELIZABETH BENTLEY volunteered her services to the Bureau as an INFORMANT in 1945, describing her wartime work with the Jacob Golos spy ring, but again the Bureau was embarrassed at having missed the operation entirely while it was active in New York City, beginning in 1938. This time, Bentley's information was insufficient to win a single indictment — a problem she suffered again with her subsequent charges against WILLIAM REMINGTON and HARRY DEXTER WHITE. G-men caught JUDITH COPLON red-handed, passing classified documents to a foreign agent in 1949, but she escaped punishment in the end because of the Bureau's addiction to illegal WIRETAPPING. Accused traitor ALGER HISS, likewise, could not be convicted on the ever-changing testimony of professional witness Whittaker Chambers, though he was finally imprisoned on a dubious perjury charge. Even the FBI's "victory" in the case of JULIUS and ETHEL ROSENBERG stands tainted today, in light of revelations that Ethel was framed and wrongly executed in a vain effort to make Julius confess.

The FBI has fared better with espionage cases since Hoover's passing. In May 1978 G-men arrested three Soviet citizens employed by the United Nations for trying to buy official secrets from a U.S. Navy officer. One slipped through the net on diplomatic immunity, but his accomplices were convicted and sentenced to 10 years in prison. JOHN WALKER'S spy case played out in 1985, and six years later Bureau agents joined forces with their rivals at the CENTRAL INTELLIGENCE AGENCY to pursue ALDRICH AMES, finally indicted with his wife in 1994. September 1996 witnessed the arrest of Robert Kim, an analyst with the Office of Naval Intelligence, for passing secrets to agents of South Korea. Two months later, former CIA station chief Harold Nicholson was charged with selling the names of his overseas colleagues and foreign contacts to Russia in the 1990s. In August 2001, retired Air Force sergeant Brian Regan was charged with conspiring to commit espionage while employed as a contractor at the National Reconnaissance Office, a Pentagon agency that designs and builds spy satellites. The Bureau took its own hits in those busy years, beginning with the arrest of G-man RICHARD MILLER in October 1984. He was the first FBI agent ever arrested for espionage, but he would not be the last. Supervisor EARL PITTS faced charges in December 1996, for selling Bureau secrets to Russia over the past decade. Even that disclosure was eclipsed, however, by the 2001 revelation that high-ranking G-man ROBERT HANSSEN had been spying for the Russians more or less continuously since 1979.

Even when its agents are on the right side, problems remain with the FBI's handling of some espionage cases. A report from the General Accounting Office, released on 15 August 2001, charged that when the Bureau uncovers spies, it does not always tell federal prosecutors that U.S. laws have been broken. Furthermore, the same report alleged, when revelations *were* made to the JUSTICE DEPARTMENT, they sometimes came too late to be of any value. Senator Fred Thompson, speaking for the U.S. Senate's Governmental Affairs Committee, noted that delays facilitating coordination of various intelligence agencies proved fatal to prosecution in some cases. "Opportunities may be lost to preserve and enhance the government's option of bringing criminal prosecutions against spies, terrorists or other criminals," Thompson told reporters.

**EVANS, Courtney**—FBI agent Courtney Evans initially met JOHN KENNEDY in 1957, when Evans was assigned as Bureau liaison to the U.S. Senate Labor Rackets Committee. Senator Kennedy was a member of that committee, and younger brother ROBERT KENNEDY was the committee's chief counsel, zealously pursuing members of the TEAMSTER'S UNION on cor-

ruption charges. In 1961, when John Kennedy became president and named Robert as attorney general, Director J. EDGAR HOOVER appointed Evan to serve as FBI liaison to the JUSTICE DEPARTMENT. He also headed the Bureau's Special Investigative Division in the early 1960s, after Attorney General Kennedy ordered the FBI to begin WIRETAPPING and BUGGING leaders of ORGANIZED CRIME. It was primarily through Evans that Hoover and Kennedy communicated on such matters as the FBI's "COINTELPRO" operations and surveillance on Dr. MARTIN LUTHER KING, JR., Evans quit the FBI in 1964 to practice law.

**EXECUTIVE Orders**—Executive orders are presidential decrees concerning the administration of the U.S. government. Orders which have affected the FBI's operations include the following, presented chronologically:

*3 June 1941:* Executive Order 8766, issued by President FRANKLIN ROOSEVELT, exempted all FBI personnel from Civil Service and placed them within the "Excepted Service" category, permitting J. EDGAR HOOVER to promote, demote or dismiss personnel without restriction. (Subsequent legislation offered certain protection to whistle-blowers, though retaliation for "embarrassing the Bureau" is routine and sparked a successful lawsuit as recently as 1998.)

*22 March 1947:* Executive Order 9835, from President HARRY TRUMAN, established the Federal Employees Loyalty Program, wherein FBI agents investigated all job applicants (or current employees, at an agency's request, if derogatory information was received). In practice, the reports often included malicious gossip and unfounded charges from sources whose names were withheld.

*28 April 1951:* In Executive Order 10241, President Truman eliminated requirements for proof of disloyalty, thereafter permitting government employees to be dismissed on the basis of mere accusations alone when a review board found "reasonable doubt as to their loyalty to the Government of the United States."

*27 April 1953:* Executive Order 10450, from President DWIGHT EISENHOWER, replaced the Truman loyalty review program and authorized the heads of various government departments to summarily fire "disloyal" employees. Henceforth, employees were required to demonstrate "complete and unswerving loyalty to the United States."

*14 October 1953:* With Executive Order 10491, President Eisenhower authorized suspension of any government employee who claimed Fifth Amendment rights during interrogation by any congressional committees investigating "alleged disloyalty or other misconduct." FBI files, often filled with unsubstantiated gossip, remained a primary source of such accusations lodged by the HOUSE COMMITTEE ON UN-AMERICAN ACTIVITIES and similar bodies.

*2 August 1954:* Eisenhower's Executive Order 10548 permits suspension of any government worker whose alleged illness or mental condition might "cause significant defect in the [employee's] judgment or reliability." Again, material from FBI files could result in suspension, whether or not it was substantiated.

*20 February 1960:* Eisenhower's Executive Order 10865

stripped government employees of their Sixth Amendment right to confront accusers whenever an anonymous informer "has been engaged in obtaining intelligence information for the Government and ... disclosure of his identity would be substantially harmful to the national interest."

*2 July 1971*: Executive Order 11605, from President RICHARD NIXON, expanded the scope of organizations deemed "subversive" to include groups allegedly threatening state or local governments, plus any group involved in "civil disorders" or which obstructed "the recruiting and enlistment service of the United States, impeding officers of the United States, or related crimes and offenses." The order thus legitimized FBI surveillance of various CIVIL RIGHTS groups, NEW LEFT organizations, and groups involved in VIETNAM WAR PROTESTS.

*4 June 1974*: Nixon's Executive Order 11785 abolished the attorney general's list of proscribed "subversive" organizations and broadened the definition to include participation in any group "which unlawfully advocates or practices the commission of acts of violence to prevent others from exercising their rights under the Constitution or laws of the United States or of any state, or which seeks to overthrow the Government of the United States or subdivision thereof by unlawful means." A JUSTICE DEPARTMENT pronouncement of 11 November 1974 explained that "It is not necessary that a crime occur before the investigation is initiated, but only that a reasonable evaluation of the available information suggests that the activities of the organization may fall within the prescription of the Order." Thus, surveillance of any and all dissident groups was approved.

*18 February 1976*: Executive Order 11905, by President GERALD FORD, attempted to "clarify the authority and responsibilities" of U.S. intelligence agencies, allegedly striving to insure that their activities "are conducted in a Constitutional and lawful manner and are never aimed at our own citizens." Having said that, Ford permitted any form of DOMESTIC SURVEILLANCE approved by the heads of various agencies, subject to theoretical White House review. Secrecy was further guaranteed by minimizing congressional oversight and requiring all executive branch officials and government contractors to sign an oath of confidentiality concerning "intelligence sources and methods."

*24 January 1978*: Executive Order 12036, from President JAMES CARTER, tightened administrative controls over the activities of U.S. intelligence agencies, while domestic surveillance was still permitted without proof of criminal activity. The president reserved authority to order investigations of suspected foreign agents "without a judicial warrant," and the CENTRAL INTELLIGENCE AGENCY was granted authority to conduct domestic operations "in coordination with the FBI and subject to the approval of the Attorney General."

*4 December 1981*: Executive Order 12333, from President RONALD REAGAN (himself a onetime FBI informer), permits the FBI, upon request from other intelligence agencies, to "collect foreign intelligence or to support foreign intelligence collection requirements" within the U.S. In effect, this order eliminated even the minimal restrictions on CIA domestic spying imposed by President Carter's Executive Order 12036.

*15 July 1996*: Executive Order 13010, from President WILLIAM CLINTON, created the President's Commission on Critical Infrastructure Protection to study potential terrorist threats. It also created a new Infrastructure Protection Task Force within the justice department, "to facilitate the coordination of existing infrastructure protection efforts in the interim period, while the PCCIP conducted its analysis and developed long-term recommendations." The end result, in 1998, was creation of a new FBI National Infrastructure Protection Center.

*14 July 1999*: President Clinton's Executive Order 13130 established a 20-member National Infrastructure Assurance Council designed to "enhance the partnership of the public and private sectors in protecting our critical infrastructure and provide reports on this issue to the President as appropriate." The FBI, while not directly involved, would share responsibility for security measures.

*8 October 2001*: Executive Order 13228, from President GEORGE W. BUSH, established a new Office on Homeland Security "to develop and coordinate the implementation of a comprehensive national strategy to secure the United States from terrorist threats or attacks." A Homeland Security Council was also created, including the FBI's director and director of the CIA as members.

*16 October 2001*: Executive Order 13321, from President Bush, revoked Order 13130 [see above] and created the President's Infrastructure Protection Board to "recommend policies and coordinate programs for protecting information systems for critical infrastructure, including emergency preparedness communications, and the physical assets that support such systems." One of the board's 27 members if the director of the FBI's National Infrastructure Protection Center.

**EXECUTIVE Training Programs** —In its quest for professionalism, the FBI has established various executive training programs for its own personnel and members of other law enforcement agencies. In 1976, Director CLARENCE KELLEY inaugurated the National Executive Institute, a 15-day course designed to hone the skills of high-ranking officers in large American police departments. A program geared toward leaders of smaller police agencies, the Law Enforcement Executive Development Seminar, was launched in 1981. A third training course, the seven-day National Law Institute, opened in 1984 to train local prosecutors and police legal advisors. Unlike the FBI NATIONAL ACADEMY, these courses stress administrative duties rather than the day-to-day investigative tasks of modern law enforcement.

**EXTERNAL Affairs Division** — A short-lived subdivision of the FBI, External Affairs was created by Director CLARENCE KELLEY in 1973, to replace the CRIME RECORDS DIVISION which handled most FBI publicity prior to its abolition by Acting Director L. PATRICK GRAY. The new division included offices of Congressional Services, Press Services, Correspondence and Tours, plus a Research Section. It also initially supervised the FBI's FREEDOM OF INFORMATION ACT Section, but that unit was transferred to the Office of Legal Counsel in 1974. A new Crime Resistance Program joined the External Affairs menu from 1975 to 1977, and Kelley created an additional Speech Unit to prepare his public addresses in 1977. Director Kelley was apparently dissatisfied with the division's performance however, and he abolished External Affairs before the end of 1977, absorbing its ninety-five employees into he personal staff. To maintain the traditional flow of pro-FBI publicity, a new Public Affairs Office was established, subdivided into Media Services and a Research Unit. Housed today at the FBI ACADEMY, Public Affairs "is responsible for all media and public relations for the TRAINING DIVISION of the FBI." By any name, its personnel remain in charge of "spin" control, promoting the bureau's side of any controversy that arises.

# F

**FARLEY, James Aloysius** — Born at Grassy Point, New York on 30 May 1888, James Farley was a lifelong Democratic Party stalwart. He served as the party's New York secretary from 1928-30, as its New York state chairman from 1930-44, and as chairman of the Democratic National Committee from 1932-40. His most important political connection was a longtime friendship with FRANKLIN ROOSEVELT, whose presidential campaigns Farley managed in 1932 and 1936. His reward for success in those races was appointment to serve as U.S. Postmaster General (1933-40) and, unofficially, as Roosevelt's chief of political patronage.

The latter position led Farley into a clash with FBI Director J. EDGAR HOOVER soon after Roosevelt's 1932 election to the White House. Farley hoped to replace Hoover with Val O'Farrell, a former member of the NEW YORK POLICE DEPARTMENT turned private detective. On learning of Farley's choice, Hoover launched an FBI investigation of O'Farrell's background and procured sufficient "dirt" to spoil O'Farrell's chances with Attorney General HOMER CUMMINGS. Among the items uncovered were reports of O'Farrell's bankruptcy filing in 1919; his role in a celebrity divorce from 1920; charges of bribery and filing a false affidavit while he was still a policeman; and reports that he served as a personal bodyguard for mobster Dutch Schultz in 1932. (Ironically, it was O'Farrell, not the FBI, who broke the news of a right-wing plot to oust Roosevelt from the White House by force in 1934.)

Farley made another unsuccessful attempt to replace Hoover in 1935, but by that time the president had come to depend on Hoover's clandestine services and the director's post was secure. The same could not be said for Farley, though, when he opposed FDR's third-term campaign in 1940. Roosevelt suspected Farley of leaking derogatory material to anti-New Deal journalist Ray Tucker, and the president asked Hoover to install WIRETAPS on Farley's telephones. FBI Inspector QUINN TAMM later claimed that Hoover refused the assignment on "ethical" grounds, but volunteered to tap Tucker's phones instead (thus resolving a grudge from 1933, when one of Tucker's articles in *Colliers* magazine described Hoover walking with "mincing steps"). Following his 1940 ouster as postmaster general, Farley never held another public office, but he remained active in politics, serving as a New York delegate to Democratic National Conventions in 1940, 1944, 1948, 1952, 1960 and 1968. He died in New York City on 9 June 1976.

**FARNSWORTH, John S.** — A Cincinnati native, born in 1893, John Farnsworth graduated from the Annapolis Naval Academy in 1915 near the top of his class. After service at sea in WORLD WAR I, Farnsworth returned to Annapolis and studied aeronautical engineering, pursuing that subject further at the Massachusetts Institute of Technology in 1923. Back in uniform as a flight instructor, then commander of a Navy fighter squadron, Farnsworth married the daughter of a wealthy Virginia family and began to live beyond his means. Debt-ridden, Farnsworth borrowed money from a sailor and refused to pay it back, prompting his dishonorable discharge from the Navy in 1927. Thereafter shunned by commercial shipping lines and foreign navies alike, Farnsworth was saved from destitution when he offered himself to Japan as a spy.

Beginning in 1933, Farnsworth received an average $300 per month from Japanese agents while milking old friends in the Navy for all they were worth, transmitting reams of information back to Tokyo. The items he delivered over time included code books; maps and sketches of strategic targets; photographs and models of new Navy equipment; specifications for most Navy guns then in service; detailed information on the aircraft carriers *Ranger* and *Saratoga*; and a top-secret Navy manual, *The Service of Information and Security*. Agents with the Office of Naval Intelligence discovered Farnsworth's betrayal in 1934, after he stole classified documents from a friend's office in Washington, and reported him immediately to the FBI. G-men placed him under 24-hour surveillance, including WIRETAPS, but still Farnsworth remained at large as an active spy for nearly two years, while agents tried in vain to identify his Japanese contacts. Farnsworth's tenure as a spy ended in July 1936, when he approached journalist FULTON LEWIS, JR., with an offer to sell his story for $20,000. Lewis stalled for time, recording Farnsworth's statement, and then called Washington police, who in turn alerted the FBI. Only then was Farnsworth arrested, held for trial on espionage charges that earned him a prison term of four to 20 years in February 1937. His Japanese contacts, identified by Farnsworth as Commander Yoshiashi Ichimiya, Commander Akira Yamaki and a journalist named Sato, were not indicted with Farnsworth. They were still at large when Japanese bombers raided the U.S. naval base at PEARL HARBOR, in December 1941.

**FARRALL, David**—A probationary agent with the FBI's Miami field office, 36-year-old David Farrall was driving the wrong way on Interstate 95, when he struck another vehicle in the early morning hours of 23 November 1999. Two passengers in the other car, brothers Craig Chambers and Maurice Williams, were killed instantly. Investigators from the Florida Highway Patrol initially blamed the deceased, naming Farrall as the "victim" of a wrong-way driver, then revised that story to admit "mistakes" in their original report. FHP spokesmen cited "a misinterpretation of physical evidence," insisting that "there was no cover-up," but Trooper Rene Guillen insisted that his supervisors dictated the final content of his accident report, exonerating Agent Farrall despite a blood alcohol content of .17 (more than twice Florida's legal limit for drivers). On 23 December 1999 the highway patrol apologized to relatives of the two victims, Maj. Richard Carpenter announcing: "It's been determined from the physical evidence that the Farrall vehicle was in fact going the wrong way on the interstate at the time of the collision."

Media investigation revealed that following the crash, Agent Farrall had been admitted to North Broward Medical Center under an assumed name, under guard by FBI agents who blocked reporters from questioning Farrall. Later, when forced to testify under subpoena, two FBI agents—including Miami's assistant special agent in charge—admitted knowing that Farrall was drunk on the night of the accident and withholding that information from state investigators. Farrall, meanwhile, remained on leave with pay until 7 April 2000, when he was dismissed following "a comprehensive internal inquiry by the FBI's OFFICE OF PROFESSIONAL RESPONSIBILITY." Bureau spokesmen now termed the accident "tragic"—but no other personnel were disciplined for their apparent efforts to conceal the truth.

Charged with six criminal counts, Farrall continued to insist that he was innocent, attorneys dismissing his initial blood-alcohol reading as "faulty." In February 2001 a court granted Farrall permission to recreate his last meal of 23 November 1999 (including two pitchers and one pint of beer) under medical supervision, with blood drawn at 20-minute intervals to determine how fast his body metabolized alcohol. The results of that test were still under wraps when jury selection began for Farrall's trial on 21 June 2001. Motions for a change of venue were denied, but jury selection was stalled by 9 July, when Judge Marc Gold dismissed two counts of driving with an unlawful blood-alcohol level, ruling that prosecutors were required to prove "impairment" as a cause of the crash. Farrall still faced two counts each of DUI manslaughter and vehicular homicide, with a potential maximum 30-year sentence. Prosecutors appealed the decision

and the criminal trial was rescheduled for November 2001. Meanwhile, Farrall was given a 3 August 2001 deadline for his response to a $50 million civil lawsuit filed against him by relatives of the two slain youths. A second lawsuit—this one for $100 million, filed against the FBI and Farrall's Miami supervisors on 9 November 2001—further delayed the criminal proceedings.

**FARRELL, James T.**—A Chicago native, born 7 February 1904, novelist James Farrell supported the COMMUNIST PARTY between 1932 and 1935, that link discovered by the FBI in 1934, after an INFORMANT reported Farrell's signing of a petition sponsored by the National Committee for the Defense of Political Prisoners. A year later, G-men noted his membership in the American Writers Congress. By 1937 Farrell had become an outspoken defender of Leon Trotsky, thereby alienating himself from the party at large, but FBI agents failed to draw a distinction between leftist ideologies, noting that Farrell "was aiding the Trotskyists even more than if he were an enrolled Party member."

In the 1940s Farrell attached himself to the SOCIALIST WORKERS PARTY, serving as chairman of that group's Civil Rights Defense Committee from 1941 to 1945. In 1948 FBI reports noted that Farrell had contributed to a fund for "drugs and medicine" on behalf of the "Vietnamese in their war against the French." Agents were still collecting Farrell's novels and articles in 1955, when he surprised them by opposing repeal of the 1950 internal security act. Citing a communist conspiracy among those who opposed the statute, Farrell noted that critics "overlook or ignore the fact that the association of American Communists with Communists of other countries is for the avowed purpose of overthrowing democratic government by any means, including force and violence." Apparently satisfied to hear his own opinions flow from Farrell's lips, J. EDGAR HOOVER discontinued any further investigation of the writer. Farrell died in 1979, at age seventy-four.

**FAST, Howard**—The son of a New York City factory worker, born in 1914, Howard Fast published his first novel at age twenty. FBI Director J. EDGAR HOOVER, in his ghost-written volume *Masters of Deceit*, described Fast as "one of the [Communist] Party's best-known writers, later to become bitterly disillusioned," but that process spanned several decades. Fast himself, in October 1957, told an interviewer, "I have known Communists, been affected by Communists, read Communist literature and believed it, ever since 1933." Fast apparently attended meetings of the JOHN REED Club that year, although FBI agents later described it erroneously as "the Tom Paine Club of the COMMUNIST PARTY" (apparently confused by the title of Fast's 1943 novel, *Citizen Tom Paine*). It was 1943 before Fast actually joined the party himself, remaining active until 1956 or 1958 (accounts vary). His political attitude is perhaps best summarized by a 1951 essay on May Day demonstrations, wherein he declared that "anything which does you some good and takes a nickel out of the boss's pocket is subversive."

Summoned before the HOUSE COMMITTEE ON UN-AMERICAN ACTIVITIES in 1950, Fast claimed his Fifth Amendment privilege to avoid giving testimony and was sentenced to three months in prison for contempt of Congress, after refusing to name fellow party members. Blacklisted for his political associations, Fast founded Blue Herron Press on his own and continued to publish throughout the post-war Red Scare. His novel *Spartacus*, published in 1951, helped defeat the Hollywood blacklist nine years later, when alleged "subversive" Dalton Trumbo was employed to write the screenplay. Fast's FBI file, weighing in at 1,603 pages, was one of the longest ever compiled on an American author. He published his autobiography, *Being Red*, in 1991.

**FAULKNER, William** — Born 25 September 1897 at New Albany, Mississippi, William Faulkner became the Magnolia State's most famous author, winning the Nobel Prize for literature in 1949. A decade prior to that achievement, on 7 February 1939, the FBI opened a file on Faulkner after learning that he had signed a petition requesting that the U.S. embargo on the Spanish Republic be lifted. Federal suspicion of Faulkner deepened in 1951, after he joined in efforts to save the life of Willie McGhee, a black man condemned for allegedly raping a white woman at Laurel, Mississippi six years earlier. (Investigation of that case revealed that the alleged victim had initiated a romantic liaison with McGhee, alleging rape only after her husband discovered the affair. Those revelations notwithstanding, McGhee was executed on 8 May 1951.) The bureau's file on Faulkner also includes memos on his own extramarital affairs, dating from 1957. Faulkner was hospitalized at Oxford, Mississippi after falling from a horse on 17 June 1962; he died on 7 July, from a heart attack.

**FBI Academy** — One of J. EDGAR HOOVER'S primary goals, upon assuming command of the Bureau in 1924, was to establish a more professional agency. That meant formalized training for agents, but the none was provided by the JUSTICE DEPARTMENT. Director WILLIAM BURNS established brief training courses for new agents — a few days in length, followed by practical work with Bureau veterans, but the short-lived program was confined to the New York field office. Hoover expanded the program in 1928, shifting its locus to Washington, D.C. and the nearby Marine Corps training base at Quantico, Virginia. By 1941, new agents spent 16 weeks in training, including some 600 hours of classroom instruction and practical work with agents from the Washington field office. The length of training was slashed to eight weeks during WORLD WAR II and the post-war Red panic, then returned to 16 weeks in 1953. The "new" FBI Academy, still located adjacent to the Quantico Marine Corps base, opened six days after Hoover's death, on 8 May 1972.

During Hoover's reign as director, the FBI Academy served as much to indoctrinate trainees in Bureau political philosophy as it did to prepare them for field work. Prior to integration of the FBI, agents including JACK LEVINE and NORMAN OLLESTAD report that academy instructors routinely referred to African Americans as "niggers," while maintaining that the CIVIL RIGHTS movement was part of a larger Communist conspiracy to destroy the U.S. Far-right literature from groups like the John Birch Society was also incorporated into lessons on communism and related subjects. A more important function than political indoctrina-

tion, though, was the inculcation of loyalty to Hoover himself. Trainees were "encouraged" to purchase copies of Hoover's various ghost-written books, as well as author DON WHITEHEAD'S laudatory history of the Bureau, *The FBI Story*.

Today, in addition to training FBI agents, the academy also trains agents of the DRUG ENFORCEMENT ADMINISTRATION. A collateral program, the FBI NATIONAL ACADEMY, trains police officers from around the U.S. and from foreign countries. The FBI Academy also houses the Bureau's Investigative Support Services unit (formerly Behavioral Science) which attempts to solve SERIAL MURDERS and other crimes by means of PSYCHOLOGICAL PROFILING.

**FBI Alumni Association** — Organized as the Society of Former FBI Women in May 1973, this group was created for retired female employees of the Bureau. Since no WOMEN FBI AGENTS were hired during J. EDGAR HOOVER'S 48 years as director, membership was initially limited to retired clerical personnel (including 1,200 members in 26 chapters by 1987). In 1992 the group voted to admit men, including former special agents, and its name was formally changed two years later.

**FBI Background Investigation Contract Service** — Staffed by former FBI agents, this unit carries out background investigations of Bureau job applicants and presidential appointees (cabinet members, federal judges, White House staff, etc.). The use of retired personnel frees active-duty FBI agents to perform more important tasks.

**FBI Headquarters** — FBI headquarters (FBIHQ) is located in Washington, D.C., known during Director J. EDGAR HOOVER'S tenure as the "Seat of Government" (or "SOG"). All commands theoretically flow from this pinnacle of the Bureau pyramid, while information collected in "the field" presumably finds its way back to headquarters. Because FBI employees have long been exempt from protections of the Civil Service Act, at the insistence of various directors beginning with Hoover, the authority of FBIHQ over agents and clerical personnel is virtually absolute.

Frequent changes in nomenclature and responsibility at FBIHQ make it impossible to predict the exact chain of command on any given day, but the structure here described prevailed as of November 2002. Supreme command of the Bureau is vested in the *Office of the Director*, operating with assistance from the following aides:

*Chief Technology Officer* — Responsible for supervising implementation of the FBI's "Trilogy Project" (a three-year information technology infrastructure upgrade initiative) and related technological projects.

*Executive Secretariat* — Managing "high-level" mail to and from the JUSTICE DEPARTMENT or other government agencies, members of Congress, and influential members of the public.

*OFFICE OF THE GENERAL COUNSEL* — Providing legal advice to the director and other FBI leaders, researching legal questions in respect to law enforcement or national security, and coordinating the defense of civil lawsuits filed against the Bureau.

*Office of Inspections* — Responsible for reviewing FBI investigative and administrative programs "to ensure their economic value and effective compliance with objectives, governing laws, rules, regulations and policy."

*OFFICE OF PUBLIC AND CONGRESSIONAL AFFAIRS*—The Bureau's public relations department, including maintenance of the FBI website and tours of FBIHQ.

*Community Outreach Program*— Putting a "human face" on FBI operations and encouraging minority recruitment as may be deemed appropriate.

*Office of Strategic Planning*— Tasked "to enable the successful implementation and achievement of the Director's vision and national priorities" by means of advice, assessment and strategic planning.

The FBI's director delegates authority to a number of executive assistant directors, whose authority within the Bureau is theoretically equal. The first of those listed on the FBI's Internet website is the *Executive Assistant Director for Criminal Investigations*. The departments under his (or her) control presently include:

*Criminal Investigative Division*— Charged with investigation of all federal crimes falling within FBI jurisdiction except COMPUTER CRIMES (see below). The wide-ranging mandate includes crimes committed on government property, various interstate crimes, assorted frauds, corruption of public officials and pursuit of federal fugitives. Subdivisions of this section include the Art Theft Program; the Asset Forfeiture Program (dealing primarily with NARCOTICS cases); the CIVIL RIGHTS Section; the Crimes Against Children Program (including prosecution of child pornography distributors); the Financial Crimes Section; an Internet Fraud Complaint Center; the Jewelry and Gem Program (retrieving stolen jewels); and the ORGANIZED CRIME Section.

*Cyber Crime Division*— Created in the mid-1990s, responsible for investigation of all computer crimes and intellectual property theft.

Next in line on the Bureau's website (but ranked first among the FBI's public priorities for 2002) is the *Executive Assistant Director for Counterterrorism/Counterintelligence*. Subdivisions of his domain in the campaign to curb TERRORISM and ESPIONAGE include:

*Office of Intelligence*— Vested with general responsibility for oversight of the Bureau's intelligence program.

*Counterintelligence Division*— Charged with investigation of cases including espionage, overseas homicide, protection of foreign guests and officials, domestic security and nuclear extortion. Also included is the FBI's Security Countermeasures Program, responsible for background investigations and various issues of physical security.

*Awareness of National Security Issues and Response* (ANSIR)— Another of the Bureau's several public relations departments, assigned to "educate" the public on the need for expanded FBI authority, funding and increased personnel.

*Counterterrorism Division*— Consolidating and coordinating various FBI campaigns against terrorism. This unit includes the National Infrastructure Protection Center (geared to threat assessment and response to physical attacks on the U.S.) and the

National Domestic Preparedness Office (assisting and coordinating state and local responses to incidents involving weapons of mass destruction).

The *Executive Assistant Director for Law Enforcement Services* supervises one of the FBI's most diverse sections. Its various subdivisions include:

*CRITICAL INCIDENT RESPONSE GROUP*—Facilitating FBI response to high-risk crises, including hostage situations, terrorist incidents, child abductions and the like.

*International Operations*— Promoting FBI relations with foreign law enforcement and security agencies, primarily through the Bureau's LEGAL ATTACHÉ PROGRAM.

*Language Services Section*— Providing critical translation and foreign language training via the FBI's Foreign Language Program and the Contract Linguist Program.

*Office for Law Enforcement Coordination*— Charged with improving FBI communication and sharing of information with state and local police or other public safety agencies. The Bureau has historically failed in this area, and complaints from various U.S. police departments suggest there has been little improvement since the terrorist attacks of 11 September 2001.

*Strategic Information Operations Center*— Often said to act at cross purposes with the Office of Law Enforcement Coordination, the SIOC "serves as a focal point for information management, coordination, and operational support Bureau wide"— in short, releasing only that information deemed advantageous by FBI leaders.

*CRIMINAL JUSTICE INFORMATION Services Division*— Including the Bureau's Fingerprint Identification Program, the Integrated Automated Fingerprint Identification System, the NATIONAL CRIME INFORMATION CENTER, and the Uniform Crime Reporting Program, this division serves as the FBI's central repository for criminal justice information.

*LABORATORY DIVISION*—Responsible for various forensic testing and analysis, including crime scene searches, DNA testing, and any other scientific services required by the Bureau.

*TRAINING DIVISION*—Including both the FBI ACADEMY (for Bureau special agents) and the FBI NATIONAL ACADEMY (for law enforcement personnel outside the FBI).

The FBI's *Executive Assistant Director for Administration* ranks last in website listings but effectively controls the daily workings of the FBI. Departments under his or her immediate control include:

*Office of Equal Employment Opportunity Affairs*— Created to eliminate discrimination in hiring of FBI personnel. "Special emphasis programs" are identified as follows: American Indian/Alaskan Native; Asian American/Pacific Islander, Black Affairs; Federal Women, Hispanic Employment; Selective Placement (of handicapped employees, including disabled veterans); and Upward Mobility.

*Office of the Ombudsman*— The FBI grievance machine, described in Bureau press releases as existing "to help all FBI employees seeking fair and equitable solutions to situations that cause stress and interfere with their ability to perform assigned duties."

*OFFICE OF PROFESSIONAL RESPONSIBILITY*—Created to investigate and punish serious misconduct (including criminal activity) on the part of FBI employees. Despite the units best efforts, Bureau field offices still face accusations of whitewashing AGENT MISCONDUCT.

*Administrative Services Division*— Handling all aspects of FBI personnel management and recruitment, this division also has responsibility for physical security of all FBI facilities.

*Finance Division*— Responsible for all FBI budgetary and fiscal matters, financial planning and so forth. The division's assistant director is the Bureau's chief financial officer and serves as chairman of the FBI Contract Review Board.

*Information Resources Division*— Provides centralized management and planning for information resources within the FBI. As part of that program, "architectures are developed and maintained that specify how information is to be collected, managed, and used."

*Records Management Division*— Revived under Director ROBERT MUELLER in his reorganization of FBIHQ, Records Management is assigned "to ensure executive direction and full-time oversight over all records policy and functions, consolidating all records operations to ensure consistency, thoroughness and accountability." Presumably it should eliminate embarrassing incidents such as the "loss" of several thousand documents related to domestic terrorist TIMOTHY MCVEIGH.

*Freedom of Information/Privacy Acts Section*— Handling all requests for disclosure of FBI FILES under the FREEDOM OF INFORMATION ACT, this section reviews and censors documents prior to release, sometimes prompting lawsuits from dissatisfied media outlets or individuals.

*Security Division*— Described in Bureau publications as "responsible for ensuring the integrity of FBI employees, contractors, visitors, information systems, and facilities"— an endless task beset by controversy on all sides.

**FBI National Academy**—Like most other divisions of the Bureau, the FBI National Academy has passed through several incarnations since its debut in 1935. It was originally called the FBI Police Training School, renamed the FBI National Police Academy in 1936, and finally received its present name in 1945. Its facilities lie adjacent to the FBI ACADEMY and the U.S. Marine Corps base at Quantico, Virginia. Since 1972 the University of Virginia has collaborated with both FBI academies as "partners in the quest for police professionalization," offering additional courses in criminal law, forensic science, and so forth. Some 1,200 students per year pass through the FBI National Academy, drawn from state and local law enforcement agencies throughout the U.S. and around the world

As of 2001, an estimated 29,000 police officers had graduated from the FBI National Academy. Of those, 15,000 elected to join an alumni organization, the FBI National Academy Associates, gathered in 44 U.S. and four international chapters. The group holds an annual meeting, in conjunction with yearly conventions of the INTERNATIONAL ASSOCIATION OF CHIEFS OF POLICE, and there is reason to suspect that its purposes are more than social. Ex-agent WILLIAM TURNER reports that under J. EDGAR HOOVER'S FBI regime, National Academy graduates were con-

tacted every 30 days by agents from the field office nearest to their homes, often seeking information on the inner workings of the graduate's agency. As one California police chief told Turner, "The FBI doesn't realize that National Academy graduates aren't FBI agents, but that their first loyalty is to the department." Admission to the National Academy was also sometimes used as a reward for "friendly" police departments — or withheld as punishment, as in the case of Hoover's long-running feud with Los Angeles police chief WILLIAM PARKER.

Instructors at the National Academy are not responsible for how their students utilize their newfound skills, once they return home with diplomas in hand. Critics suggest that agents from certain oppressive regimes should be excluded until their governments desist from flagrant human rights violations, but the Bureau does not discriminate against right-wing military juntas. One of the National Academy's most notorious graduates was Daniel Mitrione Sr., assigned by the CENTRAL INTELLIGENCE AGENCY in 1969 to lead Uruguay's Office of Public Safety. Prior to his July 1970 abduction and execution by Tupamaros guerrillas, Mitrione schooled Uruguayan police and soldiers in the fine points of torture, once advising a colleague: "When you get what you want — and I always get it — it may be good to prolong the [torture] session a little to apply another softening-up. Not to extract information now, but only as a political measure, to create a healthy fear of meddling in subversive activities." An associate of Mitrione, Manuel Hevia Cosculluela, reported that Mitrione once "personally tortured four beggars to death with electric shocks." In death, Mitrione's name graced the FBI's "Wall of Honor," as an academy graduate killed in the line of duty. (Mitrione's son later became an FBI agent but failed to demonstrate the "right stuff": in 1985 he received a 10-year prison term for bribery and drug trafficking.)

**FBI Recreational Association**—Created on 5 December 1931 as the U.S. Bureau of Investigation Athletic Association, later renamed the FBI Recreational Association (FBIRA), this organization was ostensibly created "to promote and encourage athletics as a means to better health, to stimulate fair play, and to create a better understanding of each other." Dues were mandatory from all FBI employees, whether or not they participated in the FBIRA, and no accounting was made as to how those funds were spent. Aside from publishing a monthly magazine, *The Investigator*, little was known about FBIRA expenditures, a situation that finally led to complaints from the rank and file. At one point, a field agent was added to the FBIRA's five-man board of directors, but his first question — asking how much money the group's fund contained — was met with what Assistant Director WILLIAM SULLIVAN called "a very heavy silence." The agent was soon removed from the board, while control of the FBIRA returned exclusively to FBI HEADQUARTERS personnel.

Author Curt Gentry, in his masterful biography of J. EDGAR HOOVER, bluntly describes the FBIRA as "Hoover's personal money-laundering operation." The group received a portion of Hoover's royalties from ghost-written books and film sales, including $71,000 in royalties from his book *Masters of Deceit*. In 1965, when ABC television contracted to produce *The FBI*,

Hoover insisted that the network also purchase rights to *Masters of Deceit* for an additional $75,000. That money, plus $500 per episode during the show's nine-year run, were paid directly to the FBIRA. Altogether, Gentry estimates that royalty payments to the FBIRA exceeded $200,000 during Hoover's lifetime.

What happened to that money? Many of the FBIRA's records were destroyed after Hoover's death, but some of the expenditures are traceable. Ex-agent WILLIAM TURNER reports that local field offices tapped FBIRA coffers to purchase expensive whiskey and two dozen roses for Hoover's hotel room, every time the director took one of his "working vacations" to race tracks around the U.S. Between 1958 and 1972, some $55,000 was spent on receptions for students and guests at the FBI NATIONAL ACADEMY. Another $2,000 went for other public relations activities. Deputy Assistant Director NICHOLAS CALLAHAN personally withdrew $39,590.98 between 1951 and 1972, for a "Library Fund" that proved otherwise untraceable. Soon after Hoover's death, Callahan and Assistant to the Director JOHN MOHR discontinued the Library Fund and destroyed all its records. Auditors for the JUSTICE DEPARTMENT waited for Hoover confidant CLYDE TOLSON to die, in April 1975, before they examined FBIRA financial records. Their report declares: "There is no evidence that these Bureau officials converted the money to their own use and, therefore, no evidence of criminal intent." Curt Gentry, meanwhile, reports that "One of the deepest and darkest of all the FBI's secrets was that America's number one law enforcement officer was himself a crook."

The FBIRA survives, operating a store at Quantico, Virginia to generate funds. It is officially a nonprofit organization, with membership limited to active-duty FBI personnel, governed by a board of directors. Covert abuses from the Hoover era have presumably ceased to occur.

**FEDERAL Bureau of Narcotics**—America's first federal law restricting use of opium and other NARCOTICS was the 1906 Pure Food and Drug Act. Three years later Congress passed the Opium Exclusion Act. The Harrison Narcotics Act was passed in 1914, taxing and regulating the sale and distribution of narcotics. None of these laws were enforced by the Bureau of Investigation, and a Federal Narcotic Control Board was finally established in 1922 to oversee federal drug programs. That in turn became the Federal Bureau of Narcotics in July 1930, when President HERBERT HOOVER appointed HARRY ANSLINGER as the first U.S. Commissioner of Narcotics, operating from the Treasury Department.

Anslinger pursued drugs, their sellers and users with a crusading zeal that sometimes drove him to exaggerate (or fabricate) the alleged harmful effects of certain substances. (Marijuana is a case in point, with the era of "reefer madness" hysteria fostered in large part by FBN propaganda.) At the same time, Anslinger alienated FBI Director J. EDGAR HOOVER by naming and indicting members of ORGANIZED CRIME, while Hoover steadfastly denied that such groups as the Mafia even existed. In pursuit of ever more restrictive legislation, Anslinger's FBN successfully lobbied for passage of the 1937 Marijuana Tax Act, the 1942 Opium Poppy Control Act, the 1951 Boggs Act (imposing harsher penalties for drug offenses), and the 1956 Narcotics Control Act (stiffening penalties once again, while it ensured federal primacy in suppressing illegal drug traffic).

In 1962 the White House Conference on Narcotics and Drug Abuse recommended dismantling the FBN in favor of programs including drug treatment and preventing diversion of dangerous drugs from legitimate channels, but the FBN hung on until 1968, when President LYNDON JOHNSON transformed it into the Bureau of Narcotics and Dangerous Drugs. The name switch also brought a bureaucratic change of scene as the BNDD was moved from Treasury to the JUSTICE DEPARTMENT. On 1 July 1973 the agency's name was renamed once again, becoming the DRUG ENFORCEMENT ADMINISTRATION.

**FELT, W. Mark**—A native of Twin Falls, Idaho, Mark Felt graduated from the University of Idaho in 1935 and moved to Washington, D.C. the following year, where he studied law at night while working in the office of Idaho senators James Pope and D. Worth Clark. Admitted to the District of Columbia bar in 1941, he soon obtained a post on the Federal Trade Commission, then joined the FBI on 19 January 1942. From the beginning of his Bureau service, Felt was fast-tracked for FBI stardom, spending barely three months each in the Houston and San Antonio field offices before he was transferred to FBI HEADQUARTERS as a supervisor in the ESPIONAGE Section. There he spent the remainder of WORLD WAR II, then transferred to Seattle for two years and subsequently served as a firearms instructor at the FBI ACADEMY.

In 1954, after a stint investigating employees of the Atomic Energy Commission, Felt was back at headquarters as an inspector's aide, followed by tours of duty in New Orleans and Los Angeles. He served as agent in charge of the Salt Lake City field office before moving on to Kansas City, active in both posts as a prime mover of the Bureau's TOP HOODLUM PROGRAM. In September 1962 he returned to headquarters once more as deputy assistant director in charge of the Training and Inspection Division. November 1964 saw him promoted to chief inspector, as head of the Inspection Division, where he spent the next six years. While there, Felt was assigned by Director J. EDGAR HOOVER to personally interrogate a group of alleged HOMOSEXUALS on President RICHARD NIXON'S White House staff. (No evidence of impropriety was found.) Hoover also ordered Felt to "control" Assistant Director WILLIAM SULLIVAN, a job which Felt interpreted as requiring WIRETAPS on Sullivan's phones and recruitment of his secretaries as INFORMANTS.

In 1971 Felt was promoted to deputy associate director, ranking third in command of the FBI behind Associate Director CLYDE TOLSON. When Hoover died in May 1972 and Tolson subsequently retired, Felt was elevated to acting associate director under Acting Director L. PATRICK GRAY III. He served briefly as acting director following Gray's resignation on 27 April 1973, then retired from the Bureau on 22 June 1973. (In the midst of the WATERGATE SCANDAL, Felt was named as a possible "Deep Throat" informer for the *Washington Post*, but he denies playing any such role.)

Trouble caught up with Felt five years after he retired. It began in August 1976, when JUSTICE DEPARTMENT investigators at the New York City field office found documentary evidence of illegal BREAK-INS committed by G-men between 1956 and 1973. (The records, part of Hoover's elaborate "Do Not File" system instituted in 1942, should have been destroyed at six-month intervals but somehow were ignored.) That discovery in turn led probers to the records of Squad 47, a special FBI unit assigned to track fugitive members of the WEATHER UNDERGROUND during the Nixon years. Agents had repeatedly burglarized homes of the fugitives' friends, with surviving memos indicating that the break-ins were approved by Acting Director Gray, by Felt, and by Assistant Director EDWARD MILLER. Attorney General GRIFFIN BELL filed charges against all three and they were indicted by a federal grand jury on 10 April 1978.

Gray denied all knowledge of the break-ins and his case was severed from the others. Felt and Smith faced trial in 1980 on charges of conspiring to violate the CIVIL RIGHTS of five persons whose homes were burglarized by G-men. Felt claimed that the FBI was entitled to make warrantless searches "in cases of national security involving foreign-directed terrorism" (thus persisting in the fiction that Russian agents controlled the American "NEW LEFT"), and furthermore asserted that Director Gray had blanket approval to authorize "black-bag jobs." Gray predictably denied it, while ex-President Nixon and five former attorneys general likewise testified that they had never authorized illegal break-ins by the FBI. Prosecutors noted that the actions of Squad 47 were merely the tip of the iceberg, citing "tons of examples of [illegal] entries that continued from 1966 to 1972." Jurors convicted Felt and Miller on 6 November 1980; one month later they were fined $8,500 each. President RONALD REAGAN, himself a former FBI informant, granted the defendants a full pardon on 26 March 1981, claiming that Felt and Miller had served "with great distinction" and acted "in good faith" while pursuing radical leftists. The next day, Richard Nixon sent each defendant a bottle of champagne.

**FERBER, Edna** — Born at Kalamazoo, Michigan on 15 August 1885, Ferber moved to Wisconsin with her family at age twelve. Active in journalism following her high school graduation, she later became a prolific novelist and won the Pulitzer Prize in 1924 for *So Big*. She inadvertently came to FBI attention as a result of the LINDBERGH kidnapping case, while attending the New Jersey trial of suspect Bruno Hauptmann. J. EDGAR HOOVER, apparently incensed by Ferber's remark that "the revolting faces of those who are watching this trial [are] an affront to civilization," ordered an investigation that resulted in an 89-page file on Ferber's activities. In 1937 Hoover noted that she was a member of the Women's International League for Peace and Freedom, along with novelist PEARL BUCK and others. Hoover apparently lost interest in Ferber thereafter. She died of cancer, in New York City, on 16 April 1968.

**FEUCHTWANGER, Lion Jacob** — A German novelist, born in Munich on 7 July 1884, Lion Feuchtwanger made his first tour of the United States in November 1932. A few months later, Nazi propaganda minister Josef Goebbels declared Feuchtwanger "the worst enemy of the German people," stripping the author of his

citizenship, university degrees, and all personal property. Living in exile, Feuchtwanger visited Moscow in 1937 and was twice interned in France, in 1939 and 1940. He escaped through Portugal and Spain to the United States, reaching New York in October 1940, and later settled in Los Angeles, near his friends BERTHOLT BRECHT and THOMAS MANN.

Feuchtwanger's politics and personal associations made him a natural target for the FBI, along with Immigration, the STATE DEPARTMENT, and the OFFICE OF STRATEGIC SERVICES. All maintained dossiers on Feuchtwanger, with Immigration's and the Bureau's running close to 1,000 pages. INFORMANTS kept track of his movements, reporting his meetings with Brecht, Mann and other "subversives," tipping G-men that Feuchtwanger had joined his friends in August 1943 to "endorse the Moscow manifesto" of the National Committee for Free Germany. The 43 major reports in Feuchtwanger's FBI file include documents from field offices in Albany, El Paso, Los Angeles, Milwaukee, New York City, Phoenix and San Francisco. A typical observation reports that Feuchtwanger "appears to take Russian pretense for reality still and to see a fundamental difference between the HITLER and Stalin regime.... [T]he Germany and the Russia of today ... are run by a gang of robbers and cutthroats with a hoodlum at the head.... Neither Hitler nor Stalin has any different ideals from AL CAPONE. Feuchtwanger is not sufficiently familiar with the Capone type to be able to recognize it." The remainder of the dossier contains selected quotes from Feuchtwanger's work and clippings from various publications referring to his alleged "Communist" activities.

It is clear from the FBI's file, obtained by author Alexander Stephan under the FREEDOM OF INFORMATION ACT, that G-men read Feuchtwanger's mail on at least 40 separate occasions, while providing copies to Immigration, Army Intelligence, the State Department and the INTERNAL REVENUE SERVICE. As early as 4 June 1941, Director J. EDGAR HOOVER sent Immigration officials a "Personal and Confidential" memo urging that "all legal and proper methods be used to effect [Feuchtwanger's] deportation." That effort failed, but Hoover kept up the pursuit; he personally vetoed two requests from the Los Angeles field office to close Feuchtwanger's file, in 1946 and 1949, "due to inactivity." Feuchtwanger's application for U.S. citizenship, filed in 1948, was never approved, and from 1954 onward his name appeared consistently on weekly lists of "racketeers and subversives" who were "being considered under the Denaturalization and Deportation Program." Feuchtwanger died in Los Angeles, of stomach cancer, on 21 December 1958. The Bureau recorded terms of his will and continued filing memos on his case into September 1960 (their contents entirely censored prior to public release).

**FIELD Offices** *see* the Appendix

**FIELDS, W.C.** — A Philadelphia native, born William Claude Dunkenfield on 9 April 1879 or 29 January 1880 (accounts vary). The other facts of his childhood are equally vague and contradictory, but he apparently quit school at an early age, devoting himself to billiards, cards and juggling. Around age 15 he became a professional juggler, soon adding comedy to his vaudeville stand-up routine and billing himself as W.C. Fields. By the early 1900s some critics called him the world's greatest juggler, praising his performances in Europe. Fields joined the Ziegfeld Follies in 1915, played his first starring role on Broadway in 1923, and made his first silent film two years later. A move to Hollywood followed the demise of silent movies, and Fields soon perfected the persona of a misanthropic drunkard (said by some acquaintances to mirror his off-screen personality). His classic films included *It's a Gift* (1934), *David Copperfield* (1935), *The Man on the Flying Trapeze* (1935), *You Can't Cheat an Honest Man* (1939), *The Bank Dick* (1940), *My Little Chickadee* (1940), and *Never Give a Sucker an Even Break* (1941).

FBI Director J. EDGAR HOOVER followed the actor's career from afar and surprised Fields one day in the late 1930s with a visit at his California home. Fields, so flustered by the top G-man's arrival that he repeatedly called Hoover "Herbert," was even more surprised when Hoover raised the subject of three miniature portraits of "a certain lady in Washington." The cameos, prepared for Fields by artist John Decker, depicted First Lady ELEANOR ROOSEVELT; when turned upside-down they presented an exaggerated likeness of female genitalia. Fearing arrest for possession of obscene material, Fields initially denied that the paintings existed, but Hoover persevered until Fields agreed to produce them. Gratified by Hoover's jovial response, Fields presented all three as a gift to the director, pleading only that they should not be displayed until "there's a change in the administration." Hoover agreed to the stipulation, but he made a habit of showing the cameos to favored male visitors, when they were shown into his recreation room. Biographer Curt Gentry notes that the paintings were not listed in the final inventory of Hoover's estate, suggesting that "a certain former assistant director" absconded with the cameos after Hoover's death in 1972.

Fields, for his part, had no time to worry about the fate of his paintings. Illness related to alcoholism soon destroyed both his health and his career, relegating him to minor roles after 1941. He died at Pasadena, California on 25 December 1946.

**FILES**—As an "intelligence" agency, the FBI stands or falls on its ability to collect information—names, dates, addresses, details of events, correspondence and conversations. Without that constant flow of data, the Bureau has no reason to exist. Each piece of information is examined, analyzed, digested—and inevitably filed.

We live in a computer age, but the FBI Building in Washington stands on a literal mountain of paper. Author Robert Kessler, in his book *The FBI* (1993), reports that files maintained at FBI HEADQUARTERS alone—excluding 56 FIELD OFFICES, roughly double that number of RESIDENT AGENCIES and an ever-growing number of "LEGAL ATTACHÉ" offices abroad—contain enough documents to equal the height of 275 Washington Monuments. The central index for those files contained 75 million names in 1992 and added new ones at a rate of some 830,000 per year. It may not be the largest set of files on earth, but it certainly ranks high among those with potential for grievous abuse.

The Bureau began collecting files from the moment it was organized in 1908. In 1919, during its first three months of life,

the GENERAL INTELLIGENCE DIVISION (with young J. EDGAR HOOVER in charge), compiled dossiers on 60,000 suspected radicals or leftist organizations; a year later, the total had topped 200,000; in 1921 Hoover had an estimated 450,000 names on file. The GID was soon abolished—at least in name—but its files lived on, with investigation of some targets continuing for years beyond their deaths.

Upon his promotion to serve as the Bureau's director in April 1924, Hoover promised Attorney General HARLAN STONE that he would restrict future investigations to persons suspected of federal crimes. It was a calculated lie, which Stone only discovered years later, after his elevation to the U.S. SUPREME COURT. In the meantime, Hoover continued collecting information on anyone and anything that caught his eye. On 25 March 1925 he opened a new "Obscene File," instructing all field offices to collect "any obscene matter of any nature whatsoever" and mail it to Washington. Envelopes were to clearly bear "in large type or letters the word 'OBSCENE,' in order that the nature of the contents may be noted at a glance." Material should be collected, Hoover said, "even though no Federal violation exists ... in order to increase the effectiveness of the Obscene Files." The files were not restricted to routine pornography, by any means: one item from 1954 was the transcript of a Detroit wiretap, including references to the alleged sexual affairs of President DWIGHT EISENHOWER. The Obscene File's political blackmail potential was clearly indicated by a Hoover memo dated 10 July 1946:

> Each obscene literature investigation possesses potential publicity value because of the very nature of the investigation. Every Special Agent in Charge should closely follow obscene matter investigations in order that consideration may be given to obtaining proper publicity in appropriate cases. Where it is contemplated that publicity will result from the Bureau's investigation of an obscene matter case, it is the responsibility of the Special Agent in Charge to make certain that the Bureau is notified in advance of any contemplated arrest, arraignment, or other development prior to the time that any publicity is released.

Throughout Hoover's reign as director (1924-72), material was routinely leaked to "friendly" journalists, politicians, and various investigative bodies (including the HOUSE COMMITTEE ON UN-AMERICAN ACTIVITIES and the SENATE INTERNAL SECURITY SUBCOMMITTEE). Hoover habitually denied those leaks, but his covert contributions were apparent from coast to coast—in campaign speeches and gossip columns, in the literature of right-wing vigilante groups, in the dismissal of alleged "subversives" from their jobs, and in opposition to a federal holiday honoring Dr. MARTIN LUTHER KING, JR., The crime of releasing that classified data was compounded by the fact that so much of it was false—a compilation of unfounded speculation, gossip and malicious innuendo. The FBI filed *everything*, and headquarters was always eager to pleas for derogatory information were made in the name of "national security."

Even then, some material was too "sensitive" to share, particularly data collected by means of illegal BREAK-INS, WIRETAPPING and BUGGING. In 1942 Hoover instituted a new "Do Not File" system for especially incriminating documents. Any reports or memos so labeled were excluded from the Bureau's central records index and routed directly to headquarters, where they were consigned to special files in the offices of Hoover, Associate Director CLYDE TOLSON, or Assistant Director LOUIS NICHOLS. At the field office level, Do Not File material was preserved in the guise of "informal" memos, one for each authorization of an illegal "black bag" job, which were locked in the office safe "until the next inspection by Bureau Inspectors, at which time it is destroyed."

Hoover devised yet another evasive technique, the so-called "JUNE Mail" filing system, on 29 June 1949. Those files were initially created to hide FBI correspondence with "the most sensitive sources, such as Governors, secretaries to high officials who may be discussing such officials and their attitudes," along with references to "highly confidential or unusual investigative techniques" (i.e., illegal bugs and wiretaps). Like the Do Not File material, JUNE Mail reports were kept separate from the central files, in a Special File Room at FBI headquarters. This system survived its creator and remained in use until Director WILLIAM WEBSTER formally abolished it in November 1978.

On 19 March 1953 Hoover ordered all senior FBI officials to destroy the contents of their "office files" at regular intervals — specifically, every six months for assistant directors and every 90 days for supervisors. The following year, a new "summary memorandum" program was launched to collect background information on members of Congress (expanded in 1960 to include gubernatorial candidates and candidates for Congress). These reports had no place in the main body of FBI records. Rather, they were stored first in the Research unit and later in the Administrative unit at headquarters. The "summary memorandum" program was an extension of Hoover's longstanding file on various senators and representatives, kept in his office. By the early 1970s, the FBI had personal files — as opposed to criminal records or legitimate investigative files — on an estimated 25 million Americans.

Security was paramount for FBI files — except when Hoover himself chose to leak them — but no protective system is perfect. On 8 March 1971 burglars struck the Bureau's resident agency at MEDIA, PENNSYLVANIA and stole several thousand documents which were later sent to the press and to selected members of Congress. As a result of that exposure, Hoover was forced to terminate the Bureau's illegal "COINTEPLRO" operations — at least under that code name. He also closed one-fifth of the FBI's resident agencies in a move to forestall further losses, but the damage was done and his reputation never recovered from those initial revelations of lawless DOMESTIC SURVEILLANCE.

Lifelong Hoover secretary HELEN GANDY later revealed that Hoover kept three sets of confidential files in his office. They included an Official and Confidential File, a Personal and Confidential File, and an untitled block of documents described as "about a drawer and one half of Bureau files which were kept in his office under lock and key." The latter items, Gandy claimed, were stored in Hoover's office "for safekeeping" because they contained "highly confidential Bureau information." In May 1972, following Hoover's death, a large number of those files disappeared and were never seen again. Controversy still surrounds their disposal, with conflicting stories told by Gandy and others involved in their hasty move from Hoover's office to his private residence.

In July 1975 the JUSTICE DEPARTMENT belatedly ordered G-men to investigate whether "any official files were removed from Mr. Hoover's office to his residence following his death and may have been subsequently removed from that address following the death of Clyde A. Tolson." The final report concluded that Helen Gandy removed 35 drawers of Hoover's "personal" files but took no official documents. Gandy herself admitted removing only four filing cabinets — a total of 10 drawers — but agreed that they all concerned Hoover's "personal business affairs." Furthermore, Gandy said those papers were preserved intact until their transfer to the Valley Forge archives of the J. EDGAR HOOVER FOUNDATION. A truck driver who hauled the files contradicted Gandy, reporting that he moved "20 to 25 file cabinets" from FBI headquarters to Hoover's home. One cabinet opened in transit, allowing the driver to glimpse "light colored folders inside with the contents of each folder roughly one inch thick." (Spokesmen for Justice concluded that the trucker suffered from "jumbled recollection of the facts due to the passage of over three years since Mr. Hoover's death.")

FBI files and their "sensitive" contents remain a matter of concern to the present day. While bureaucratic foot-dragging stalls release of ancient documents under the FREEDOM OF INFORMATION ACT and censorship renders many of the declassified files illegible, outside individuals and agencies work overtime to crack the Bureau's files by less orthodox means. On 25 October 2001 two Nevada law enforcement officers pled guilty to federal conspiracy charges involving a secrets-for-sale scandal that rocked the FBI's Las Vegas field office. Maria Emeterio (a former investigator for the Nevada attorney general's office) and Mary Weeks (a Las Vegas Municipal Court intake services officer) faced a maximum of five years each in federal prison after admitting they sold stolen FBI files to a private investigator. James J. Hill, a former security analyst at the Las Vegas field office, pled guilty in the same case, admitting that he earned thousands of dollars selling FBI files between 1999 and June 2001. The investigation continues, in pursuit of attorneys and others who purchased the stolen material.

**FINCH, Stanley Wellington**—A native of Monticello, New York, born 20 July 1872, Stanley Finch attended five different colleges before accepting a clerical post with the JUSTICE DEPARTMENT in at age 21. In short order, he was promoted to chief bookkeeper, examiner, special examiner, and finally chief examiner at Justice. Finch graduated from the National University Law School in Washington, D.C. in 1908, around the same time that Attorney General CHARLES BONAPARTE defied Congress by creating the Bureau of Investigation. Bonaparte appointed Finch to lead the new detective unit on 26 July 1908, maintaining his title as Chief Examiner. Finch remained through the BI's period of frenetic MANN ACT prosecutions, replaced at the helm by A. BRUCE BIELASKI on 30 April 1912.

After leaving the Bureau, Finch was appointed as the Justice Department's special commissioner for the suppression of "white slavery," operating from Baltimore until he resigned in

1913. Returning to Justice nine years later, Finch was named special assistant to the attorney general in the Anti-Trust Division, where he served until 1925. Engaged in private enterprise and legal practice over the next six years, Finch was drawn back to Justice once again in 1931, serving as an inspector for the Bureau of Prisons through 1934. In January 1935 Attorney General HOMER CUMMINGS reinstated Finch as an auditor, but he regained his old chief examiner's rank in January 1940, thus bringing his career full-circle before he retired, later in 1940. Finch died in 1951.

**FIREARMS and Toolmarks Unit** — The FBI LABORATORY DIVISION'S oldest and best-known unit handles an average 1,100 cases per year, matching bullets to suspect weapons by their markings and examining other evidence were impressions have been left on sundry surfaces including metal, wood, plastic and glass. At last report the Bureau's gun collection included hundreds of confiscated weapons, some dating from cases in the 1930s, and its ammunition file included samples from some 13,792 different brands and calibers manufactured in the U.S. and abroad.

Although the FBI has built its reputation to a fair extent on ballistics evidence, some of its most famous cases remain controversial, the verdicts still open to question. G-men were not directly involved in the 1920 SACCO-VANZETTI CASE, but they were clearly aware that ballistics reports had been falsified and misrepresented by state experts in a deliberate FRAME-UP. Thirteen years later, in the case of the KANSAS CITY MASSACRE, FBI technicians stalled for a year before linking one of the murder slugs to a weapon owned by notorious bandit CHARLES ("PRETTY BOY") FLOYD. When Floyd and cohort Adam Richetti were charged with that crime, FBI HEADQUARTERS concealed the fact that several of the victims killed in Kansas City were actually shot by an FBI agent, illegally armed with an unfamiliar weapon.

Similar problems have been seen in more recent cases. Following the JFK ASSASSINATION, FBI marksmen found the alleged assassin's rifle defective to the point that they could not aim it without repairing the telescopic sight — but Director J. EDGAR HOOVER still maintained that the rifle had inflicted all wounds suffered by the president and Texas governor John Connally. Five years later, a similar hasty verdict was rendered in the death of Dr. MARTIN LUTHER KING, despite a failure of ballistics testing and conflicting eyewitness testimony. (In November 1999 the judge who sentenced alleged killer James Earl Ray to prison for King's slaying publicly declared that he did not believe the rifle tested by FBI agents was the murder weapon.) Two months after King's death, the RFK ASSASSINATION found G-men delivering another "lone assassin" verdict, despite the fact that their suspect's revolver had seemingly fired nearly twice its eight-shot capacity without reloading.

Similar problems continued at Firearms and Toolmarks long after Hoover's death. One notorious case, the RANDY WEAVER siege of 1992, found the unit performing 350 examinations on 199 different pieces of evidence, generating 12 separate reports. At Weaver's trial, FBI reconstructions of the shootout were dismantled by defense expert Lucien Haag and Weaver was acquit-

ted of murder charges. Afterward, federal prosecutors sent a scathing report to the JUSTICE DEPARTMENT, declaring: "With all due respect to the [unit's] supervisor [trial witness James Cadigan], it was quite obvious that Mr. Haag was quite out of the supervisor's league when it came to not only shooting reconstruction but ballistic and firearms identification." In fact, the 13-page memo concluded, the FBI's laboratory seemed to be "out of touch with forensic reality."

**FIREARMS Training Facility** — Originally located at Fort Dix, New Jersey, the Firearms Training Facility currently operates in Montgomery County, Texas, under the aegis of the Bureau's Houston field office. It is a cooperative joint facility built by the FBI, the Department of Defense and the Conroe (Texas) Police Department, used to train state, federal and local law enforcement officers in state-or-the art combats techniques. Its guiding proposition is that "no more names be added to the wall," referring simultaneously to the Wall of Honor for fallen agents at the FBI ACADEMY and to the Law Enforcement Memorial in Washington, D.C.

**FISH Committee** — In June 1930, eight years before the HOUSE COMMITTEE ON UN-AMERICAN ACTIVITIES was created, New York congressman Hamilton Fish led a Special House Committee to investigate Communist activities in the U.S. FBI Director J. EDGAR HOOVER was called to testify as an "expert" witness, though biographer Richard Powers reports that his testimony consisted primarily of "stories about Communist atrocities drawn from his pre-1924 briefs and investigations" conducted for Attorney General A. MITCHELL PALMER. Though dated, his presentation still impressed the committee and visiting reporters. The *Washington Star* opined on 13 June 1930 that Hoover "made a strong impression. ... Uncle Sam's boyish looking Sherlock Holmes reeled off facts and figures that carried deep conviction with the committee, who soon discovered it had before it a man who knows his onions." In fact, the committee suggested to Attorney General WILLIAM MITCHELL that the Bureau of Investigation should launch a new investigation of Red "sabotage," but Mitchell declined, suggesting that the LABOR DEPARTMENT was better equipped for that task.

**FITZGERALD, F. Scott** — It is a measure of the MCCARTHY era's paranoia that FBI agents were assigned to collect information on novelist Francis Scott Key Fitzgerald, 11 years after his death. The novelist's file was opened on 21 August 1951, with a report that one of his short stories — "A Diamond as Big as the Ritz" — had been selected for production as a Broadway musical. Born 24 September 1896, Fitzgerald was best known for his novels, including *This Side of Paradise, Tender is the Night,* and *The Great Gatsby.* Despite his death from a heart attack on 21 December 1940, G-men were still concerned about his work, although the FBI file notes that Fitzgerald "was merely heard to be a Red." Another target of FBI surveillance, HOWARD FAST, confirmed that Fitzgerald was in fact a member of the COMMUNIST PARTY, but federal agents failed to note the affiliation while he was alive.

**FLEMMI, Vincent J.**—As associates of Boston mobster JAMES ("WHITEY") BULGER, Vincent Flemmi (AKA "Jimmy the Bear") and his brother Stephen ("The Rifleman") Flemmi benefited from Bulger's corrupt alliance with the FBI's Boston field office. G-men including JOHN CONNOLLY and H. Paul Rico, both assigned to the local ORGANIZED CRIME squad, accepted bribes from Bulger's Winter Hill gang and protected its operations in return for tips on the activities of rival mobsters. On 10 March 1965 an IN-FORMANT warned Agent Rico that Vincent Flemmi planned to murder Chelsea gangster Edward Deegan. Rico failed to intervene, and Deegan was killed two days later. On 13 March the same informant told Rico that Flemmi and contract killer Joseph Barboza had watched three other thugs perform the execution, but G-men suppressed that information because Barboza was also a prized FBI informant. Reports of the incident were forwarded to Director J. EDGAR HOOVER, who took no steps to correct the situation. In fact, Flemmi himself was recruited for the FBI's Top Echelon Informant program three months later. His file contained a memo from the agent in charge of the Boston field office (dated 4 June 1965), noting that Flemmi's handler "believes that Flemmi murdered Deegan" and that "from all indications, he is going to continue to commit murder."

Suppressing evidence of homicide was bad enough, but Boston G-men also joined Flemmi and Barboza in a FRAME-UP of four innocent men who received life sentences for Deegan's murder despite the fact that they played no part in the crime. Two of those framed died in prison; the others — defendants PETER LIMONE and JOSEPH SALVATI — were exonerated after more than 30 years in custody and filed huge lawsuits against the FBI. Barboza was murdered by rival mobsters in 1976. Vincent Flemmi was convicted of attempted murder in an unrelated case; he died in prison in 1979. Brother Stephen was convicted on racketeering charges and money laundering charges in 2001. James Bulger escaped, with help from the FBI, and remains a fugitive at large. Agent Connolly was later convicted of racketeering and received a 10-year prison term. Federal prosecutors reported that other G-men involved in the case were saved from prison by the statute of limitations on their various crimes.

**FLOYD, Charles Arthur ("Pretty Boy")**—A Georgia native, born 2 February 1904, Charles Floyd moved to Oklahoma with his family as a child and is chiefly identified with that state today. Accused of 40 bank robberies and ten murders, he attained mythic status on a par with that of JOHN DILLINGER in the Great Depression, despite the fact that his largest known take from a bank job was less than $4,000.

Floyd's first known brush with the law was a May 1929 vagrancy arrest in Colorado. By year's end he was jailed twice more in Kansas City, briefly held "for investigation" in September and November 1929. His first confirmed BANK ROBBERY occurred at Sylvania, Ohio on 5 February 1930. A month later, on 8 March, he was arrested with two cohorts on suspicion of killing an Akron, Ohio policeman. When those charges failed to stick, he was delivered to Toledo authorities on 20 May, convicted of bank robbery on 24 November 1930 and sentenced to a prison term of 12 to 15 years. Floyd escaped from the train bearing him to prison, on 10 December 1930, and was never recaptured.

If any doubt remained, the near-miss with prison made Floyd a confirmed outlaw. On 25 March 1931, in Kansas City, he joined comrade Bill ("The Killer") Miller to murder brothers Wallace and William Ash, either for suspicion of informing or in a dispute over women (reports vary). Sadie Ash, mother of the victims and herself a local underworld character, is generally credited with giving Floyd his "Pretty Boy" nickname in conversations with police. Floyd and Miller stole $1,600 from an Ohio bank on 14 April 1931, but police spotted the pair with their girlfriends two days later, in Bowling Green. A wild shootout left Miller and a patrolman dead, the women arrested, while Floyd alone escaped. Three months later, on 21 July, he killed a federal Prohibition agent during a raid on his Kansas City hideout.

Floyd soon returned to Oklahoma, hiding out in the lawless Cookson Hills and launching a series of small-time bank jobs that netted him an estimated $18,021 (from 14 holdups) between August 1931 and November 1932. Stories spread of Floyd burning mortgage papers in banks he robbed, and while no such events are documented, the tales earned him a "Robin Hood" reputation among the poor farmers who frequently offered him shelter. Floyd's holdups were minor, by standards of the era, but bankers used their influence to generate frantic police activity. February 1932 saw Floyd and sidekick Adam Richetti cornered three times in Tulsa, but they shot their way clear of each trap. On 6 April 1932 Floyd slipped through another ambush at Bixby, killing a state investigator in the process.

Anxious for a change of scene, Floyd and Richetti shifted their activities to Missouri, stealing $3,000 from an Ash Grove bank on 11 January 1933. They surfaced next on 16 June, kidnapping Sheriff William Killingsworth from Bolivar, Missouri, dropping him (and a civilian hostage) that night near Kansas City. The next day, 17 June 1933, witnessed the bloody KANSAS CITY MASSACRE, with four lawmen (including BI agent Raymond Caffrey) killed while transporting fugitive Frank Nash to prison at Leavenworth. Survivors of the shooting initially blamed nearly every notorious Midwestern gangster *except* Floyd and Richetti for the murders. Another 13 months would pass before bureau ballistics experts claimed to link a single cartridge from the crime scene with one of Floyd's pistols. By that time, Floyd had spent a year in hiding with Richetti and was ready to resume his bank-robbing career.

Their first confirmed score since the Kansas City slayings — at Tiltonsville, Ohio on 19 October 1934 — brought the bandits a pitiful $500. Their car broke down near Wellsville on 21 October, and Richetti was caught the same day, held over for trial (and eventual execution) on Missouri murder charges. Floyd remained at large until 22 October, when a squad of BI agents and local police led by MELVIN PURVIS trapped him at a farm near East Liverpool, Ohio. According to FBI spokesmen, Floyd was mortally wounded by gunfire while fleeing on foot from authorities and he died moments later, after confirming his identity to Purvis. Forty years later, retired East Liverpool policeman Chester Smith told a different story, claiming that Floyd was wounded only in the arm (by Smith) before Purvis tried to question him.

Instead of confessing to the Kansas City murders, Floyd allegedly cursed Purvis, whereupon Purvis ordered a nearby G-man to "shoot into him."

FBI supporters dismissed Smith's story and questioned his long delay in reporting the alleged execution. Smith replied that he had feared FBI retribution, but passing time and the death of colleagues who participated in the raiding party had encouraged him to tell the truth. As proof, Smith produced a .45-caliber submachine gun bullet, allegedly extracted from Floyd's body, which later tested positive for traces of human blood. Further credence was added to Smith's tale in 1997, when newly-declassified FBI files revealed that most of those killed in the 1933 massacre were shot accidentally by a federal agent illegally armed with an unfamiliar weapon.

**FLYNN, William James**—A native of New York City, born 18 November 1867, William Flynn joined the U.S. SECRET SERVICE in 1897 and remained until 1917, spending his last five years as chief of that agency. Attorney General A. MITCHELL PALMER appointed Flynn to lead the Bureau of Investigation on 30 June 1919, and he assumed control the following day.

In announcing Flynn's selection, Palmer dubbed him America's top "ANARCHIST chaser," reporting that "He knows all men of that class. He can pretty nearly call them by name." That qualification seemed critical in July 1919, with a series of apparent anarchist bombings still unsolved from three months earlier. Flynn launched his ultimately fruitless search for the bombers with an announcement that they were "connected with Russian Bolshevism, aided by Hun money"—but in fact he had no idea who they were. Flynn was present in New York for the brutal interrogation of suspect ANDREA SALSEDO, but the bombings were never solved.

Chief Flynn had better luck as a strikebreaker, although the Bureau had no legal authority to investigate LABOR UNIONS. Nonetheless, he would later boast of his tenure in office, "During the steel strike, coal strike and threatened railway strikes, secret agents moved constantly among the more radical of the agitators and collected a mass of evidence." He went even further beyond his legitimate jurisdiction on 12 August 1919, with an order for "all special agents and employees" to launch "a vigorous and comprehensive investigation" of anarchists, communists and "kindred agitations." Alien radicals were the initial targets, but Flynn further instructed his men: "You will also make full investigation of similar activities of citizens of the United States with a view to securing evidence which may be of use in prosecutions under the present existing state or federal laws or under legislation of that nature which may hereinafter be enacted." One subordinate who hastened to obey was young J. EDGAR HOOVER, then in charge of the Red-hunting GENERAL INTELLIGENCE DIVISION. Five months later, in the wake of the notorious PALMER RAIDS, Flynn claimed that his efforts had averted a revolution in the U.S.

Public outcry over those raids and the Bureau's sweeping infringement of civil liberties ultimately drove both Flynn and Palmer from office. Attorney General HARRY DAUGHERTY replaced Flynn with Director WILLIAM BURNS on 22 August 1921, as part of President WARREN HARDING's attempt to restore "normalcy." Flynn died in 1933.

**FORD, Gerald Rudolph**—An Omaha native, born Leslie Lynch King, Jr., on 14 July 1913, Gerald Ford was raised and studied law in Michigan. After serving with the Navy in WORLD WAR II he was drawn to politics, running for Congress from Grand Rapids in 1948. FBI Director J. EDGAR HOOVER arranged Bureau support for Ford's campaign, and Ford repaid the favor in 1949, using his maiden speech in the House to request a pay raise for Hoover. They were close friends thereafter, and Ford served as Hoover's "eyes" inside the Warren Commission, appointed to investigate the JFK ASSASSINATION. Before the committee's final report was issued in 1964, Ford opposed public criticism of the FBI's failure to inform SECRET SERVICE agents that LEE HARVEY OSWALD lived in Dallas and worked in a building along President Kennedy's final motorcade route. Chairman EARL WARREN overruled Ford's objection and insisted that the comment be included.

In 1970 Ford spearheaded President RICHARD NIXON's campaign to impeach U.S. SUPREME COURT Justice WILLIAM O. DOUGLAS. As House minority leader, Ford introduced a resolution to investigate Douglas's fitness for continued service on the court, but the Democratic chairman of the House Judiciary Committee blocked that effort on 21 April with counter resolution to investigate Ford's charges. Nixon, undeterred, called on Hoover for help. The director sketched their conversation in a memo dated 5 June 1970.

> Douglas had an article in one of those magazines. I said he did—a magazine that is pornographic. I said the attitude of Douglas and Black is they won't look at a pornographic motion picture like "I Am Curious—Yellow." The President asked if he had Jerry Ford call me, would I fill him in on this; that he is a good man. I told him I would.

The introduction was unnecessary, given Hoover's history with Ford, but Hoover's assistance in the impeachment drive achieved nothing. Three years later, on 6 December 1973, Ford became Nixon's third vice president and succeeded him when Nixon resigned in August 1974. A month later Ford granted Nixon a "full, free and absolute pardon" for any crimes he had "committed or may have committed." Charges of a "corrupt bargain" were inevitable, but no hard evidence ever surfaced that Ford was handed the White House in exchange for keeping Nixon out of prison.

True to his roots in the Red-hunting 1940s, President Ford did his best to protect the FBI and the CENTRAL INTELLIGENCE AGENCY from harm as their crimes were exposed in 1975-76, by the CHURCH and PIKE COMMITTEES. Ford recommended suppression of the Pike Committee's final report until it was reviewed by censors from the executive branch and Congress agreed: the report has not been released to this day. On 24 November 1974 Congress overrode Ford's veto of amendments broadening the FREEDOM OF INFORMATION ACT'S disclosure requirements and subjecting FBI records to mandatory disclosure (with specified exceptions). On 18 February 1976 Ford issued EX-

ECUTIVE ORDER 11905, broadly outlining the authority and responsibility of U.S. intelligence agencies. While ostensibly aimed at curbing abuses, the order still permitted CIA surveillance "against United States persons in the United States" if its targets were "reasonably believed to be acting on behalf of a foreign power or engaging in ... activities threatening the national security."

Ford suffered two near-misses with death in September 1975, ironically both on visits to San Francisco. In the first instance, on 5 September, he was threatened with a pistol by a member of the Charles Manson "family" but the would-be killer's gun misfired. Less than three weeks later, on 22 September, SARAH JANE MOORE fired a shot at Ford but a bystander deflected her aim. At trial in 1976, where she received a life sentence, evidence revealed that Moore had once been a paid FBI INFORMANT.

Ford was defeated in his 1976 reelection bid, largely because of the Nixon pardon and lingering public anger over the WATERGATE SCANDAL. In 1999 he was awarded the Presidential Medal of Freedom.

**FOREIGN Operations**—Many Americans believe that a strict division of labor exists between the FBI and the CENTRAL INTELLIGENCE AGENCY, with the Bureau confined to domestic operations and the CIA barred by law from collecting intelligence on U.S. soil. In fact, neither presumption is true, and FBI agents have operated in foreign countries for over six decades.

The official beginning of FBI foreign intelligence work dates from 24 June 1940, when President FRANKLIN ROOSEVELT authorized Bureau investigations in Latin America. The FBI's Special Intelligence Service (SIS) was created to pursue foreign investigations, staffed at its peak by 360 G-men and 500 support personnel. Later, when the OFFICE OF STRATEGIC SERVICES (forerunner of the CIA) was created, FBI Director J. EDGAR HOOVER demanded and received a presidential order barring OSS agents from pursuing leads in the western hemisphere. SIS agents remained in place until 1946 and burned their files (on Hoover's orders) rather than deliver them to CIA replacements.

FBI collaboration with INTERPOL had been interrupted during WORLD WAR II, but it resumed—at least sporadically— in 1946. Frequently disrupted over the next 30 years by Cold War disputes, that link still maintained a continuing FBI role in foreign investigations. At the same time, G-men were assigned to various U.S. embassies abroad as "LEGAL ATTACHÉS," thus maintaining contact with outside intelligence agencies and dabbling in criminal cases beyond their lawful jurisdiction. FBI FILES released long after the fact reveal that agents began spying on Canada's PIERRE TRUDEAU in 1952 and continued for the next three decades, through his tenure as prime minister. In 1965, when President LYNDON JOHNSON planned his military invasion of the Dominican Republic, he bypassed the CIA and sought information on native political leaders from FBI HEADQUARTERS.

Recent FBI leaders have differed on the importance and desirability of Bureau overseas activity, but their mandate was established on 21 June 1989, when Attorney General RICHARD THORNBURGH authorized G-men to arrest suspected terrorists, drug traffickers and other fugitives abroad, without consent from the nations in which they reside. According to reports, that power has been exercised—but sparingly, since Thornburgh's order lacked any legal authority and such arrests amount to criminal KIDNAPPING. FBI Director WILLIAM SESSIONS opposed expansion outside the U.S., while successor LOUIS FREEH held a contrary view. In June 1994 Freeh sent Bureau spokesmen to meet with senior officials from 11 European nations—Austria, the Czech Republic, Estonia, Germany, Hungary, Latvia, Lithuania, Poland, Russia, the Slovak Republic and Ukraine—to promote coordination of major criminal investigations. Three months later a joint NARCOTICS operation with Italian authorities jailed 29 suspects in the U.S. and 74 in Italy.

Foreign operations have become even more diverse and urgent for the FBI in its campaign against TERRORISM. Agents were dispatched to Kenya and Tanzania in 1998, following the bombings of U.S. embassies in those nations (allegedly planned by fugitive USAMA BIN LADEN). In 1999 FBI forensic teams were sent to Bosnia, Rwanda and Yugoslavia to examine evidence of war crimes and genocidal "ethnic cleansing." A year later the experts were in Yemen, after suicide-bombers killed 17 sailors and injured more than 30 aboard the USS *Cole*.

FBI history teaches that no authority, once granted, is ever willingly surrendered. In November 2001 an FBI press release announced that Bureau spokesmen had "asked Congress for more money to increase its permanent presence in Canada to prevent terrorist attacks and deter cross-border crime." (Canadians were not consulted for their view of the plan.) Nine months later, a *Los Angeles Times* report from Pakistan revealed that G-men were "working undercover with local security forces who have a long history of human rights abuses." (On 8 January 2003 G-men and Pakistani authorities engaged in a battle with alleged terrorists, capturing two suspects supposedly linked to fugitive terrorist Usama Bin Laden.) Bureau leaders have also publicly debated the hypothetical surrender of prisoners to foreign police agencies for torture in terrorist cases, where niceties of American law forbid use of third-degree tactics. Civil libertarians at home are not encouraged by the FBI's apparent drift toward collaboration with (and imitation of) Third World totalitarian regimes.

**FORENSIC Science Research and Training Center**—As its name suggests, this section of the FBI ACADEMY at Quantico, Virginia provides research, training and operational support in the various forensic sciences, both for FBI personnel and for various outside agencies. Staff members participate in forensic science conferences around the world and publish the quarterly *Crime Laboratory Digest* in conjunction with the American Society of Crime Laboratory Directors.

**FORMAN, James**—A Chicago native, born 5 October 1928, James Forman graduated from Roosevelt University and afterward worked as a journalist, covering the Little Rock, Arkansas desegregation crisis of 1956-57 for the *CHICAGO DEFENDER*. In 1961, as a member of the STUDENT NONVIOLENT COORDINATING COMMITTEE (SNCC), he participated in the FREEDOM RIDES and was present in North Carolina during events that led to the wrongful prosecution of black activist ROBERT F. WILLIAMS on KIDNAPPING charges. Later that year, Forman became SNCC's executive secretary and held the post until 1966.

As one of the country's "Big Six" CIVIL RIGHTS leaders in the 1960s, Forman became a natural target of FBI surveillance and harassment. The situation was not improved by Forman's frank descriptions of the Bureau was "the enemy of black people." In 1964, while attending the Democratic National Convention, Forman was one several activists targeted for illegal FBI WIRETAPPING on orders from President LYNDON JOHNSON. That summer, Forman reported increasing "pressure on SNCC" to sever its connection to the NATIONAL LAWYER'S GUILD, opining that said pressure emanated "from the heartland of the administration itself." BURKE MARSHALL, assistant attorney general for civil rights, personally "pleaded with [SNCC] to go slow" in pursuit of black voter registration, and at least one Big Six rival apparently served as an FBI INFORMANT against Forman. An August 1964 report, summarizing a meeting between Assistant Director Cartha DeLoach and ROY WILKINS, head of the NATIONAL ASSOCIATION FOR THE ADVANCEMENT OF COLORED PEOPLE, says "Wilkins advised … that James Forman, whom other Negroes refer to as 'the Commissar,' was actually the man in charge of SNCC and that John Lewis was merely a front man…. Wilkins also felt that Forman had brought Lewis instructions from the CP [COMMUNIST PARTY]."

By March 1965 Attorney General NICHOLAS KATZENBACH had grown concerned over SNCC's role in the Selma, Alabama voting rights campaign — and more specifically Forman's alleged threat "to send some of the toughest SNCC members to Washington, with a view of demonstrating here." Katzenbach requested FBI "intelligence" on Forman, and surveillance intensified. In 1967, after Forman and colleague H. RAP BROWN led a floor fight at the National Convention on New Politics to condemn Zionist expansionism, G-men launched a whispering campaign to accuse the pair of "anti-Semitism." Harassment increased after 17 February 1968, when SNCC announced a short-lived merger with the BLACK PANTHER PARTY and Forman was named as the party's Minister of Foreign Affairs (corresponding with his post as SNCC's director of international affairs). FBI agents managed to disrupt the SNCC-Panther alliance with a variety of illegal techniques that included anonymous telephone calls to Forman's home, declaring that a nonexistent Panther hit team planned to "get him." (The same tactic was used against STOKELY CARMICHAEL.)

Internal dissension led to Forman's expulsion from SNCC in 1968, whereupon he joined the League of Revolutionary Black Workers. In April 1969, with other League members, Forman took charge of the Detroit-based National Black Economic Development Conference (NBEDC). A month later Forman interrupted services at the Riverside Church in New York City to read his "Black Manifesto," including a demand that white churches pay $500 million to American blacks as reparations for 250 years of slavery. FBI Director J. EDGAR HOOVER immediately launched a "racketeering" investigation, seeking evidence to prosecute Forman for "extortion," but no charges were filed. In March 1971, after a break-in at the MEDIA, PENNSYLVANIA FBI office revealed

illegal COINTEPLPRO campaigns against numerous organizations, Hoover warned Attorney General JOHN MITCHELL that covert INFORMANTS within Forman's NBEDC were "in serious personal jeopardy. Even death is a possibility." (In fact, none were harmed in any way.) Forman published his memoirs in 1972, the year of Hoover's death, and he remains active in issues pertinent to African Americans.

**FOXWORTH, Percy E. ("Sam")** — Born at Purvis, Mississippi on 29 November 1906, Percy Foxworth attended public school in the Magnolia State, then studied accounting at Chicago's Walton School of Commerce. He became an FBI agent on 21 March 1932, thereafter logging service with field offices in Jacksonville, Florida; Oklahoma City; New York City; and Washington, D.C. It was a short step from the final posting to FBI HEADQUARTERS, as assistant chief of the Bureau's Investigative Division. From there, Foxworth served briefly as special agent in charge of the Newark field office, then returned to headquarters as assistant director of the Administrative Division, and later the Domestic Intelligence Division. With the outbreak of WORLD WAR II in Europe, J. EDGAR HOOVER named Foxworth assistant director in charge of the New York field office.

It was in that capacity that Foxworth encountered British double-agent Dusan Popov, dispatched from London to the U.S. in August 1941 with warnings of an impending Japanese attack on PEARL HARBOR, Hawaii. Foxworth examined the Axis plans, concluding that they seemed "too precise." In fact, as Foxworth acknowledged, the information "spell[ed] out in detail exactly where, when, how and by whom we are to be attacked." His final judgment: "If anything, it sounds like a trap." Still, Foxworth arranged a meeting between Popov and Hoover, warning Popov in advance that he must "walk in step." Foxworth further advised that "Searching for the truth beyond your reach may be dangerous. It may stir up an idea in Mr. Hoover's head…. Mr. Hoover is a very virtuous man." The actual meeting amounted to a one-sided shouting match, with Hoover denouncing Popov's "playboy" lifestyle and rejecting his information out of hand.

In the wake of Pearl Harbor and America's entry to the war, Foxworth received additional responsibility as head of the Bureau's National Defense Office in New York, a post which placed him in charge of the SPECIAL INTELLIGENCE SERVICE, supervising G-men throughout South America. It would be his last assignment. On 15 January 1943, Foxworth and Agent Harold Haberfield died (with 33 others) in a plane crash near Paramaribo, Dutch Guiana (now Suriname). At the time of the crash, Foxworth and Haberfield were en route to North Africa, embarked on "a secret mission of critical importance" for General DWIGHT EISENHOWER. The cause of the plane crash was never determined. Foxworth's presumed remains, combined with those of 34 other victims in a single casket, were returned to the U.S. for burial in 1948. Meanwhile, a liberty ship bearing his name was launched in February 1944.

**FRAME-UPS** — In *The FBI Story* (1956), author DON WHITEHEAD wrote of the Bureau's commitment to justice:

The FBI is not a robot of efficiency. It is a human organization like all others, subject to mistakes in judgment and procedures in making investigations.

In every case of error — and they are a minute fraction of a percentage in the total of FBI investigations — the failure has been one of mechanics and not the result of intent. Over and over, [Director J. EDGAR] HOOVER had drilled into agents the absolute necessity for making such complete inquiries that there "can be no margin for error" and that even though there was no intent to do injury, it was wrong when an injury was done. This attitude represents the wide difference between the FBI and the police of a totalitarian state.

Today, in light of discoveries made during various criminal cases and in thousands of FBI documents released under the FREEDOM OF INFORMATION ACT, we know that Whitehead's portrait of the FBI was false throughout, and that the passage quoted here is rife with bitter irony. In place of rare and instantly-corrected "errors," we know that G-men deliberately and repeatedly framed innocent defendants in multiple cases spanning more than half a century, suppressing or fabricating evidence to suit their needs, offering perjured testimony from agents and hired INFORMANTS alike. Far from chastising or dismissing the guilty in those cases, Hoover frequently rewarded them with promotion, commendations and "merit bonuses" of cash.

The earliest known frame-up with FBI involvement was the SACCO-VANZETTI CASE of 1920. G-men did not participate in the state prosecution, but they were clearly aware of false evidence introduced at trial and they subverted the defense by urging paid informants to steal money from funds collected for legal expenses. Similar activities were recorded in the prosecution of black nationalist MARCUS GARVEY. In the 1930s Chicago FBI agents framed bootlegger ROGER TOUHY on two separate KIDNAPPING charges before finally sending him to prison for a crime that never occurred. False evidence was likewise introduced in the 1933 CHARLES URSCHEL kidnapping case, to convict defendant Kathryn Kelly. That same year, FBI HEADQUARTERS suppressed evidence that several victims of the KANSAS CITY MASSACRE were accidentally shot by a federal agent illegally armed with an unfamiliar weapon. In place of that embarrassing truth, the Bureau blamed fugitives Adam Richetti and CHARLES ("PRETTY BOY") FLOYD for the killings, using perjured testimony and dubious ballistics evidence. Richetti was executed for the crime, while Floyd died "resisting arrest." (Persuasive evidence suggests he was executed on orders from Chicago agent MELVIN PURVIS.)

In the Red Scare that followed WORLD WAR II, agents increasingly turned their attention to jailing alleged members of the COMMUNIST PARTY, often using suspiciously flexible testimony from professional witnesses such as ELIZABETH BENTLEY and Whittaker Chambers. While their sworn statements never secured a conviction for ESPIONAGE, Bentley and Chambers did help the government imprison defendants WILLIAM REMINGTON and ALGER HISS on perjury charges. (In the Hiss case, RICHARD NIXON later boasted that the prosecution "built a typewriter" to link the defendant with purloined documents.) The era's most famous case was that of "atom bomb spies" JULIUS and ETHEL ROSENBERG. Today, while controversy endures over Julius's guilt, most students of the case acknowledge that Ethel was framed

(and later executed) in a failed attempt to make her husband name his presumed accomplices.

Hoover's agents had no scruples when it came to framing CIVIL RIGHTS activists or members of various organizations, including the BLACK PANTHER PARTY and the REVOLUTIONARY ACTION MOVEMENT. One California Panther, ELMER ("GERONIMO") PRATT, was framed for murder by G-men and local police, serving nearly three decades in prison before he was finally exonerated. In Boston, similar tactics were used to protect FBI informants in ORGANIZED CRIME. Agent JOHN CONNOLLY received a 10-year prison sentence for his corrupt alliance with mobster JAMES BULGER, including the deliberate frame-up of four innocent defendants who were convicted on murder charges in the 1960s. Two of those men died in prison; survivors PETER LIMONE and JOSEPH SALVATI were vindicated after serving more than three decades, while FBI agents suppressed proof of their innocence.

In 1970 Hoover regaled Congress with details of an alleged plot to kidnap Secretary of State HENRY KISSINGER and to blow up various targets around Washington, D.C. Attorney General JOHN MITCHELL had already rejected the case as a mixture of half-truth and fantasy, but Hoover's public statements prompted Mitchell to charge several defendants, including anti-war protesters DANIEL and PHILIP BERRIGAN. Most of the charges were later dismissed, but Philip Berrigan and his girlfriend were convicted on a misdemeanor of smuggling love letters in and out of prison. Mitchell later privately admitted that he filed the charges only "to get Hoover off the hook" with critics of his fantastic claims.

Hoover's death in 1972 did little or nothing to change the FBI's *modus operandi*. Identical tactics, including entrapment and perjured testimony, were used against the AMERICAN INDIAN MOVEMENT (AIM) under Director CLARENCE KELLEY, with embarrassing results. Charges filed against AIM leaders for the 1973 WOUNDED KNEE SIEGE were thrown out of court by a federal judge based on FBI misconduct, and two AIM members charged with killing G-men on the PINE RIDGE RESERVATION in 1975 were acquitted on a plea of self-defense. The record of proceedings that convicted AIM member LEONARD PELTIER in the same case strongly suggests that illegal tactics were employed, including perjury, suppression of evidence and intimidation of witnesses. Another who suffered false imprisonment was JOHN LARRY RAY, brother of Dr. MARTIN LUTHER KING'S alleged assassin. Judge WILLIAM WEBSTER, who sentenced Ray to prison for driving the getaway car in a BANK ROBBERY where both alleged robbers were cleared of all charges, later succeeded Clarence Kelley as director of the FBI.

Based on FBI performance in those cases, serious doubts have been raised about others, including the North Carolina murder case of Dr. JEFFREY MCDONALD, the Pennsylvania death sentence of alleged cop-killer MUMIA ABU-JAMAL, and the terrorism charges filed in 1990 against EARTH FIRST! activists JUDI BARI and Darryl Cherney. (That case was later dismissed, and the defendants won a $4.4 million judgment against G-men and Oakland, California police officers for violating their civil rights.) After more than eight decades of illegal and unethical behavior, prudence dictates that every charge filed on the basis of FBI investigations should be closely scrutinized. To date, no agent in the Bureau's history has been prosecuted or fired for framing an innocent person.

**FRANK, Bruno**—A German novelist and playwright, born in 1887, Bruno Frank emigrated to the United States in 1938. Soon after his arrival, in August of that year, he drew attention to himself by denouncing the HOUSE COMMITTEE ON UN-AMERICAN ACTIVITIES before a Hollywood meeting of the Anti-Nazi League. He subsequently wrote the screenplay for *The Hunchback of Notre Dame* (1939), but FBI agents were more interested in his political and personal connections. In July 1943 they interviewed him concerning his friendship with exiled writer THOMAS MANN, and while historian Alexander Stephan says Frank was "never accused of being Marxist," G-men did note his attendance at an August 1943 gathering, chaired by BERTHOLT BRECHT, to draft a statement supporting the National Free Germany Committee's "Moscow manifesto." Agents also intercepted Frank's correspondence with the Free Germany unit in Mexico, whose *El Libro Libre* reprinted Frank's novels. Frank was granted U.S. citizenship in January 1945, despite a confused FBI report claiming that "He has been reported as pro-Nazi, a close associate of known COMMUNIST PARTY members and is possibly communistic himself." The Bureau closed Frank's file six months later, on 22 June 1945, with a *New York Times* clipping announcing his death from a heart attack.

**FRANK, Leonhard**—A German native, born at Würzburg on 4 September 1882, Leonhard Frank worked first as a commercial artist in Munich, then turned to writing after he moved to Berlin. His outspoken pacifism required Frank to live in Switzerland during WORLD WAR I. Home again in 1919, he enjoyed critical success under the Weimar Republic, but returned to Switzerland in 1933, after ADOLF HITLER's Nazis banned his work. Frank made his way to France in 1938, and from there to the U.S. in 1940. On arrival in Los Angeles, Warner Brothers gave Frank a one-year "lifesaver" contract, but he never found a lasting place in Hollywood and endured a life of near-poverty throughout WORLD WAR II.

The FBI, meanwhile, was concerned with Frank's pacifism, which L.A. special agent in charge R.B. Hood equated with a "leftist" persuasion. Hood's agents staged BREAK-INS at Frank's apartment, copied his address book ("approximately twenty-one names and addresses"), noted the address of his favorite gas station, and filed anonymous letter denouncing Frank as subversive. Frank returned to Germany in 1950, and the FBI closed his file four years later, with a memo from New York lamenting the "paucity of derogatory information" available. Other agencies continued to pursue him overseas, including the CENTRAL INTELLIGENCE AGENCY, U.S. Army and Air Force Intelligence. Frank's German citizenship (revoked by the Gestapo in 1934) was restored in March 1952, and he died in Munich on 18 August 1961. The Bureau filed its last report on Frank, received from Army Intelligence, seven months after his death.

**FRANK, Waldo**—A native of New Jersey, born in 1889, Waldo Frank was a prominent Jewish novelist, social historian and political activist. He was also an outspoken socialist, writing for the magazine *New Masses* in September 1932 that his "movement toward the left" was "a steady, logical evolution." FBI agents first took note of him the same year, as a member of the National Committee for the Defense of Political Prisoners, and they pursued him ardently thereafter, bulking up his file to some 565 pages by the time he died in 1967.

In 1962 Frank became chairman of the Fair Play for Cuba Committee (FPCC), generally regarded as a communist front group sympathetic to Fidel Castro. His assumption of that post capped two decades of interest in Latin American affairs, including lecture tours of South America in the 1940s and a 1948 visit to Puerto Rico, where he urged young people to "retain their Spanish language and resist cultural absorption by the United States," which Frank termed "an imperialist nation." At the same time, G-men reported, Frank was criticized by doctrinaire communists for telling Latin American youth that they could "learn more from Gandhi than from Stalin."

Two years before Frank's alignment with the FPCC, G-men had already launched a new investigation of his activities under the heading "Waldo Frank/Internal Security—Cuba." After Frank published *The Prophetic Island: A Portrait of Cuba*, agents schemed to prosecute him as "an unregistered agent of a foreign government," but the effort never bore fruit. Not only was Frank suspect as an ally of Cuba, but his latest publisher—Beacon Press, in Boston—was equally subversive in FBI eyes, agents noting that is was "affiliated with [the] American Unitarian Association which in [the] late 1940s and early 1950s was critical of [the American government's] loyalty program." Worse yet, in November 1958 the Unitarian Association's "official publication ... carried an article which was critical of ... *Masters of Deceit*," a book ghost-written for J. EDGAR HOOVER's personal profit by the FBI CRIME RECORDS DIVISION.

In 1963 the FBI retained an unidentified critic to review *The Prophetic Island*, his report noting with high irony that "the book is typical of the non-objective style of writing for which Waldo Frank is noted." This nameless "expert in the field of Latin American History and politics" assured his bureau sponsors that "he did not consider the book to be an example of scholarship, nonetheless he could not testify that the book was in fact propaganda rather than an expression of the author's personal view of the events." On 27 March 1963 Frank appeared before the SENATE INTERNAL SECURITY SUBCOMMITTEE, testifying (as interpreted by the FBI) that "he has never been a communist and that his activities on behalf of subversives are matters of principle." Two months later, citing Frank's advanced age, Hoover placed the writer's file on "inactive status," but 1964 still saw his name included in the FBI's RESERVE INDEX for possible future detention. Frank's name remained on the list until his death in 1967, at age seventy-eight.

**FRATIANNO, Aladena ("Jimmy the Weasel")**—A Cleveland native, born in 1913, Aladena Fratianno turned to crime at an early age and reportedly earned his famous nickname for his skill at eluding police after snatch-and-run thefts from street vendors.

He grew into a ruthless killer and a "made man" of the U.S. Mafia. Facing conviction on various federal charges, Fratianno turned INFORMANT for the FBI — a role that did not prevent him from rising to the post of acting Mafia boss in Los Angeles while still on the Bureau's payroll. After his role as a spy was revealed, Fratianno testified at a series of trials that sent some of his former friends to prison. G-men describe him as the highest-ranking Mafioso turncoat prior to their recruitment of SALVATORE GRAVANO in New York, more than a decade later. Still, there are questions surrounding Fratianno's credibility in some cases — e.g., he once named the alleged gunman who had "clipped" Reno gambler Mert Wertheimer in the 1950s, when in fact Wertheimer died of leukemia. Fratianno likewise died peacefully, of natural causes, in 1993.

**FREEDOM of Information Act** — Signed by President LYNDON JOHNSON on 4 July 1966, the Freedom of Information Act required (subject to broad exemptions) the public release of specified federal agency and department records. Thousands of FBI FILES have been declassified under this act, though most documents released are heavily censored to remove names of Bureau personnel, INFORMANTS, and various other details. Some items thus cleared for "release" are entirely blacked out or else rendered meaningless by deletions.

In 1974 Congress amended the law to broaden its disclosure requirements and to impose mandatory disclosure on FBI records (again, with specified exceptions). President GERALD FORD vetoed the amendments, but Congress overrode his veto on 21 November 1974. The act was further amended under President RONALD REAGAN, on 17 October 1986, to exempt specified law enforcement investigative material from release and to present FBI officials with a new evasive option: henceforth, they were no longer required even to confirm or deny that files exist for ongoing criminal investigations or active informants.

Specific exceptions to disclosure under the act presently include: properly classified national security information; federal agency rules governing personnel practices; information exempted under law by Congress, (e.g., classified nuclear weapons data or intelligence sources and methods); trade secrets or commercial and financial information; internal agency deliberative documents; information related to personal privacy; law enforcement investigation records; financial institution records; and oil well data, including geological maps of wells.

**FREEDOM Rides** — The "freedom ride" movement was designed to test court orders requiring racial desegregation in interstate transportation. The first rides were organized by the CONGRESS OF RACIAL EQUALITY (CORE) in 1947, after the U.S. SUPREME COURT'S ruling in *Morgan v. Virginia*, which ordered integrated seating on interstate buses. Several CORE members were arrested in southern states despite the court's ruling, but the demonstrations passed without much fanfare.

Such was not the case in 1961, when the Supreme Court's ruling in *Boynton v. Virginia* expanded the *Morgan* decision, ordering desegregation of all terminal accommodations related to interstate commerce. Black activist JAMES FARMER planned a new round of freedom rides that spring, forging an alliance between CORE and the STUDENT NONVIOLENT COORDINATING COMMITTEE. Opposition was swiftly mounted by the KU KLUX KLAN, acting in collaboration with racist law enforcement officers. J. EDGAR HOOVER, meanwhile, insisted that the FBI could not protect the freedom riders because it was "not a police agency." Instead, Hoover decreed, the Bureau would "fulfill its law enforcement function" by keeping state and local police informed of the riders' itinerary — even when those officers were known as members or friends of the KKK.

An integrated team of freedom riders, seven blacks and six whites, left Washington, D.C. on 4 May 1961. They traveled on two buses, one Greyhound and one Trailways, with plans to test accommodations at various depots along their route through Dixie. Police in Charlotte, North Carolina and Winnsboro, South Carolina defied the Supreme Court's order by arresting several riders, but the first violence occurred on 9 May, at Rock Hill, South Carolina, where three demonstrators were assaulted by white thugs. Rock Hill police were slow in arriving at the depot, suggesting possible collusion with the racists.

By that time, FBI HEADQUARTERS knew that police and Klansmen in Alabama were planning a violent reception for the freedom riders. Birmingham police commissioner EUGENE ("BULL") CONNOR had communicated with the KKK through Sgt. Thomas Cook (a known ally of the Klan, described by journalist Diane McWhorter as "Bull Connor's personal detective") that police would grant the Klan 15 minutes of uninterrupted mayhem at the local bus station when freedom riders arrived on 14 May. Connor wanted the riders beaten until they "looked like a bulldog got ahold of them"; he also specifically ordered that black demonstrators be stripped of their clothing, so that police could arrest them on charges of indecent exposure when they fled the terminal naked. GARY ROWE, an FBI INFORMANT in the local Klan, warned G-men of the plot, but Hoover failed to inform Attorney General ROBERT KENNEDY of the impending riots.

Agents *did* warn police in Anniston, Alabama, where the riders were scheduled to stop before proceeding to Birmingham, but their effort was wasted. Officers were nowhere to be seen on 14 May, when Klansmen attacked the Greyhound bus, beat its passengers, then set the bus on fire. (The wounded riders were transported to a local hospital, where the white staff refused to treat them.) When the Trailways bus reached Anniston, Klansmen rushed aboard and beat several of the riders, inflicting permanent brain damage on Dr. Walter Bergman. FBI agents watched and took notes as the bus, with Klansmen still aboard, proceeded on its way to Birmingham.

Another racist mob, at least 1,000 strong, was waiting at the Trailways terminal in Birmingham. Police kept their promise, giving the TERRORISTS 15 minutes to beat the demonstrators, black bystanders and various journalists before the first squad car arrived. Informant Gary Rowe was photographed while beating one of the riders, his picture displayed on the front page of a Birmingham newspaper, but G-men kept the news of their informant's criminal activity a secret from FBI headquarters. Bull Connor explained his department's failure by noting that 14 May was Mother's Day, claiming most of his officers were at home with their families. He also told the press, "Our people of Birmingham are a peaceful people, and we never have any trouble unless some people come into our city looking for trouble."

Those riders still able to travel, reinforced by others, continued to the state capital at Montgomery on 20 May 1961. Despite FBI warnings of Klan riot plans, Police Commissioner Lester Sullivan stationed no men at the bus depot. Another melee erupted, again with G-men on the sidelines, snapping photographs and taking notes. They made no move to intervene when JOHN SEIGENTHALER, a personal aide to Attorney General Kennedy, was clubbed unconscious and left bleeding on the ground for 25 minutes. Medical aid was slow in arriving, Commissioner Sullivan later explained, because every "white" ambulance in Montgomery had "broken down" at the same moment. Attorney General Kennedy finally dispatched 500 U.S. MARSHALS to Montgomery, where they held a mob of 3,000 racists at bay outside Rev. RALPH ABERNATHY'S church on the night of 21 May.

Having failed to prevent the violence in Alabama, G-men next opened a case file (code-named FREEBUS) to press charges in the Anniston attack. Four Klansmen were arrested on 22 May, while federal judge Frank Johnson issued a sweeping injunction against further violence by various Klan factions. On 1 September 1961 a federal grand jury indicted nine suspects for their role in the Anniston Greyhound attack. Five defendants were convicted in January 1962 and received one year's probation in return for their promise to sever all ties to the Klan. No one was ever charged or punished for the riots in Birmingham and Montgomery.

The freedom rides were a fading memory by August 1961, when black activist ROBERT WILLIAMS invited some of the riders to join in protests against segregation at Monroe, North Carolina. The riders arrived on 21 August and were soon under attack by local Klansmen. One demonstrator was shot and two others beaten on 25 August; the following day, residents of Monroe's black district erected street barricades to keep Klan raiding parties from their homes. A white couple drove into the battleground by mistake and were briefly escorted to a nearby home for their own safety, whereupon Monroe authorities and FBI agents joined forces to charge Robert Williams with KIDNAPPING.

More than two decades after the Birmingham riots, in 1983, injured freedom riders Walter Bergman and James Peck filed lawsuits against the FBI. Noting that G-men knew of the Klan's riot plans in advance and did nothing to stop them, while concealing their own informant's role in the violence, a federal court found the FBI liable for injuries suffered by Bergman and Peck. On 17 February 1984 Bergman was awarded $45,000 in damages, while Peck received $25,000.

**FREEH, Louis Joseph**—A Jersey City native, born 6 January 1950, Louis Freeh was an altar boy and Eagle Scout who attended Rutgers University on a scholarship and graduated Phi Beta Kappa in 1971. He received his J.D. degree from Rutgers University Law School three years later, serving on the staff of a New Jersey senator in 1974-75. He entered the FBI in 1975 and was initially assigned to the New York City field office, then promoted to a supervisory role on ORGANIZED CRIME investigations

at FBI HEADQUARTERS (1980). Freeh left the Bureau to become a U.S. attorney in New York City (1981-91), earned an LL.M. in criminal law from New York University Law School (1984) and served as a special prosecutor on the VANPAC case (1990). From the JUSTICE DEPARTMENT, he moved on to become a federal judge in New York (1991-93).

When FBI Director WILLIAM SESSIONS was fired in disgrace, President WILLIAM CLINTON chose Freeh to replace him. Both parties initially regarded Freeh as the ideal candidate, and he was confirmed without opposition. At his swearing-in ceremony, on 1 September 1993, Clinton called Freeh "the best possible person to head the FBI as it faces new challenges and a new century." In his new post, Freeh moved to expand the FBI's FOREIGN OPERATIONS and cut headquarters staff by 37 percent in 12 months, transferring 450 agents from Washington to various field offices around the country. In his first staff meeting, Freeh urged assistant directors to "talk straight" and "tell me if I'm full of shit," but subordinates soon realized that Freeh resented conflicting opinions. "Freeh killed the messenger," one Bureau official told journalist Robert Kessler. "After a while, there were no more messengers." Kessler himself would criticize Freeh for "colossal mismanagement" over the next eight years, claiming that he ultimately "left the FBI in a shambles."

One major problem was the adversarial relationship Freeh developed with President Clinton and Attorney General JANET RENO during Clinton's second term. Freeh urged appointment of a special prosecutor to investigate charges of Democratic campaign financial scandals during the 1996 election, and he carried the debate to Congress when Reno refused. The clash went public in December 1997, and while Reno described herself to reporters as "a great admirer" of Freeh, they were constantly at odds. President Clinton publicly declined to give his FBI director a vote of confidence, and in private (according to columnist Robert Novak) described Freeh "in three unspeakably vulgar words." Freeh dismissed suggestions that he resign, whereupon Justice leaders moved to censure him for the FBI's performance in the RANDY WEAVER and BRANCH DAVIDIAN sieges. (Freeh had been a federal judge when those events occurred, but critics charged him with participating in subsequent cover-ups.) Assistant Attorney General Stephen Colgate, tasked with making the final decision, refused to censure Freeh on grounds that "I just didn't think it was necessary. Freeh was a small part of it."

Freeh's tenure was burdened with scandal, including exposure of malfeasance in the Bureau's LABORATORY DIVISION; the cases of RICHARD JEWELL and WEN HO LEE; the unexplained loss of numerous weapons and laptop computers; and the "accidental" misplacement of more than 30,000 documents relevant to the case of Oklahoma City bomber TIMOTHY MCVEIGH. Overall, the public impression was one of mismanagement from top to bottom, with strong suggestions of malicious intent in some cases. Freeh announced his retirement from the Bureau on 1 May 2001, effective on 22 June. By July 2001 he was installed ("ironically," Robert Kessler wrote) as senior vice chairman for administration of MBNA, a major credit card company based in Wilmington, Delaware.

**FROST, Robert** — Born in San Francisco on 26 March 1874, "America's favorite poet" won the Pulitzer Prize in 1924, received nearly a score of honorary degrees from universities around the country, and was honored by a special resolution of the U.S. Senate in 1950, on his seventy-sixth birthday. Frost's FBI file began in 1942, when agents clipped his entry from *Current Biography* and preserved it for no apparent reason. Sixteen years elapsed before the next notation, in 1958, marking Frost's appointment to serve as a Consultant in poetry at the Library of Congress. His name was also mentioned in a 1958 internal security reference to some unidentified third party, with a marginal note and arrow branding Frost a "Communist." Summoned to read one of his poems at President JOHN KENNEDY'S 1961 inauguration (an event unmentioned in his bureau file), Frost was honored the following year with a Congressional Gold Medal. The same year, FBI agents duly noted Frost's visit to the Soviet Union, where he met with Premier Nikita Khrushchev. Translation of a Russian newspaper article told G-men that "Frost advised he is not a Communist or a Socialist but he believes that socialism is the only system that can deal with the economic problems of the millions of people in the world." He died of an embolism on 29 January 1963, never knowing that the FBI had placed him under scrutiny.

# G

**GALLAGHER, Cornelius Edward** — A native of Bayonne, New Jersey, born 2 March 1921, Cornelius Gallagher served with the U.S. Army in Europe during WORLD WAR II. He graduated from John Marshall College in 1946 and from John Marshall Law School two years later, admitted to the bar in 1949. He returned to military service during the Korean War, then entered Democratic Party politics in 1953. He was elected to Congress from Bayonne in 1958 and served seven terms. By 1964 he was a member of the House Committee on Government Operations, collecting information for a Subcommittee on Invasion of Privacy which he hoped would expose illegal government BUGGING and WIRETAPPING.

FBI Director J. EDGAR HOOVER approved of the plan — with a twist. The Bureau would admit certain illicit DOMESTIC SURVEILLANCE while blaming it all on Hoover's worst enemy, former Attorney General (then Senator) ROBERT KENNEDY. To that end, Assistant Director CARTHA DELOACH drafted a letter asking Attorney General NICHOLAS KATZENBACH to provide Gallagher's subcommittee with JUSTICE DEPARTMENT authorizations for illegal surveillance on Dr. MARTIN LUTHER KING, JR., and various Las Vegas casinos. Attorney ROY COHN dictated the letter to Gallagher's secretary, and she prepared it for his signature. On seeing it for the first time, Gallagher was "very unhappy" and telephoned Cohn, who explained that Hoover was "sick and tired" of criticism for domestic spying and "furious with Senator Kennedy, who was blaming it on Hoover." The director saw Gallagher's committee as a means to "relieve himself of the public criticism," but Gallagher refused to cooperate. Cohn tried to persuade him, then warned, "You'll be sorry. I know how they work."

Gallagher's hearings proceeded without Hoover's seal of approval, exposing FBI malfeasance years before the CHURCH and PIKE COMMITTEES undertook a similar task in 1975-76. At once, FBI sources began to furnish friendly gossip columnists with derogatory information on Gallagher and his family. In 1967 a *Life* magazine article branded him a "tool and collaborator" of New Jersey mobster Joseph Zicarelli. A year later, on 9 August 1968, a longer *Life* story professed to expose details of Gallagher's Mafia ties, ironically based on transcripts from FBI wiretaps in New Jersey. In one chilling conversation, a mob hit man (and FBI INFORMANT) claimed Gallagher had summoned him to remove a corpse from the basement of Gallagher's home.

The media assault left Gallagher reeling, but FBI HEADQUARTERS was not yet satisfied. DeLoach called Cohn and told him, "If you still know that guy you had better get word to him to resign from Congress." If Gallagher refused, DeLoach threatened, the Bureau would leak stories that a Jersey mobster had died from a seizure while having sex with Gallagher's wife. Informed of that threat, Gallagher braced himself to retaliate in kind. He previewed a speech for Cohn in which he planned to say: "It has been called to my attention that the Director of the FBI and the Deputy Director of the FBI have been living as man and wife for some 28 years at the public's expense. As a member of Congress we have an oversight duty and that oversight is to make sure that the funds which go to the FBI are properly spent." In short, Gallagher warned Cohn, "I may go down, but I'm taking that old fag with me."

Cohn, who recalled the conversation in his memoirs, promptly called DeLoach and made a deal. In return for Gallagher's silence on the matter of Hoover's alleged HOMOSEXUAL-

ITY, FBI spokesmen would admit that the New Jersey wiretap logs were fraudulent. G-men kept their bargain but the whispering campaign against the Gallaghers continued. In 1972 Gallagher was charged with income tax evasion, conspiracy and perjury. He pled guilty on the tax charge and received a two-year prison sentence, with a $10,000 fine. In his final speech to Congress, on 19 April 1972, Gallagher declared:

> Mr. Speaker, this is corruption at its worst and the central figure is J. Edgar Hoover. It is he whose unchecked reign of absolute power has intimidated Congress to the extent that a serious question has not been asked about his management of the FBI for 10 years — maybe longer. He has become the American Beria, destroying those who threaten his empire, frightening those who should question his authority, and terrorizing those who dissent from his ancient and anachronistic view of the world.

On a personal note, Gallagher said, "I doubt if even [Nazi propaganda minister Josef] Goebbels had the terrible capacity of a DeLoach to spread the big lie, nor could Goebbels exceed the filthy mind of a DeLoach."

Rumors about Gallagher and his wife circulated around Washington and New Jersey for years afterward, until Roy Cohn signed an affidavit in 1986, admitting that the couple had been persecuted by an FBI smear campaign designed to drive them both from public life. Cohn died three months later from complications related to AIDS.

**GANDY, Helen W.** — A New Jersey native, born in 1896, Helen Gandy graduated from high school in Bridgeton, then moved to Washington, D.C. and took courses at various colleges without earning a degree. She joined the DEPARTMENT OF JUSTICE as a file clerk and messenger in early 1918, but by 25 March she had settled into the position that would consume the rest of her life, serving as personal secretary to J. EDGAR HOOVER. Hoover promoted Gandy to "office assistant" in August 1937 and named her "executive assistant to the director" on 1 October 1939, but her duties never varied: she handled Hoover's correspondence, screened his visitors, and presided beyond his death over the FBI director's secret FILES. On Gandy's 25th anniversary, Hoover wrote: "You have been my right arm in the Bureau and when its history is finally written…you will occupy an important part of the introduction, in the body, and in the epilogue of this presentation." (In fact, when author DON WHITEHEAD published that official history in 1956, Gandy was mentioned exactly once — in a single-sentence footnote.)

Gandy's influence within the FBI should not be judged by her desk-bound status, however. G-men frequently complained that she exceeded her authority by screening Hoover's mail, or by diverting files and visitors before they reached his inner sanctum. Hoover's closest aides at FBI HEADQUARTERS were dubbed "Gandy dancers" by agents in the field, and Hoover biographer Curt Gentry notes that "[m]any a career in the Bureau had been quietly manipulated by her," for good or ill. Her impact was even more profound after Hoover's death on 2 May 1972, when Gandy undertook destruction of the late director's "Personal and Confidential Files."

Controversy endures to this day over precisely which files were purged by Gandy in the aftermath of Hoover's death. (She officially retired from the Bureau the day Hoover died, but worked at shredding his files through mid-July 1972.) In testimony before Congress, Gandy claimed that she removed four file cabinets (a total of 10 drawers) from Hoover's office to his home, where the contents were examined and shredded. (The truck driver who moved the files described "20 to 25" cabinets.) She also admitted shredding items of personal correspondence at FBI headquarters between 2 May and 12 May, allegedly with the permission of Acting Director L. PATRICK GRAY III. (Gray denied approving Gandy's actions.) Gandy swore under oath that she "systematically" and "very carefully" examined "every single page" of "every personal file" before they were shredded and discovered nothing of an official nature in the stash, "not even his badge." She wavered on whether the shredding was ordered by Hoover prior to his death, or afterward by Associate Director CLYDE TOLSON, but when asked for proof that no official documents were shredded Gandy replied, "As I say, you just have my word."

Gandy received a $5,000 bequest in Hoover's will. She remained in Washington until the 1980s, then moved to DeLand, Florida and died there on 7 July 1988.

**GARDNER, Erle Stanley** — Born at Malden, Massachusetts on 17 July 1889, Erle Stanley Gardner dropped out of college but was later admitted to the California bar, in 1917, after three years as a law-firm typist. He practiced law full-time until 1933, when the commercial success of his first three Perry Mason mystery novels allowed him to retire from the courtroom. Gardner eventually published over 140 novels and found one of his greatest fans in the person of J. EDGAR HOOVER. Despite Hoover's fondness for Gardner's fiction, an FBI file was opened on Gardner in November 1943, when he was commissioned to cover a murder trial in the Bahamas.

Seven years later, Hoover soured on Gardner following publication of a magazine article, prepared with FBI assistance, in which Gardner described a suspect being "hounded" by the bureau. In 1959 Gardner wrote a letter to Hoover, asserting that his private "Court of Last Resort" deemed innocent a suspect recently jailed by G-men on kidnapping. Hoover urged his subordinates to "analyze point by point the issues raised by Gardner," but a subsequent meeting saw Gardner labeled "most difficult to interview" and "possessed of a disjointed personality"; worse yet, agents deemed him "capricious, wasting time talking about himself and his opinions while he refuses to get down to facts." Gardner later apologized for his "erroneous impression" of the FBI's case, but CLYDE TOLSON deemed that letter undeserving of an answer, to which Hoover added: "I concur." Two years later, when Gardner wrote Hoover that he was "still working" on the same case, Hoover filed a memo noting that "We have experienced considerable difficulty" with Gardner. Gardner died at home on 11 March 1970.

**GARVEY, Marcus Mosiah** — A native of Jamaica, born 17 August 1887, Marcus Garvey was the first internationally recognized spokesman of the black nationalist movement. He founded the

Universal Negro Improvement Association (UNIA) in 1914, with the ambitious goal of solving all problems suffered by his race worldwide, and Garvey carried his message to New York City in 1916. There, two years later, he established the *Negro World* as his movement's national newspaper, preaching his back-to-Africa message from Harlem's Liberty Hall and on various nationwide tours. The new "Black Moses" had an estimated 2 million followers by 1919, a year after G-men opened their first dossier on his movement.

J. EDGAR HOOVER, then at the helm of the Bureau's Red-hunting GENERAL INTELLIGENCE DIVISION, made his first move against Garvey on 15 September 1919, with a memo asking Immigration officials whether they had any concrete plans to deport him. The negative response galvanized Hoover, and he set about pursuing Garvey with the few black troops at his disposal, notably Agent JAMES JONES and a team of INFORMANTS that included WILLIAM BAILEY, HERBERT BOULIN, ARTHUR CRAIG and WILLIAM LUCAS. Despite their best efforts, though, Hoover was forced to admit that "Unfortunately ... he has not as yet violated any federal law whereby he could be proceeded against on grounds of being an undesirable alien, from the point of view of deportation."

That was not from lack of trying on the Bureau's part. Agents and informants shadowed Garvey everywhere, hoping to catch him in a MANN ACT violation when he crossed state lines with mistress Amy Jacques, but they never caught Garvey and Jacques *in flagrante delicto*. When Garvey was elected "Provisional President of Africa" at a salary of $12,000 per year, INFORMANT Boulin interviewed disgruntled UNIA members, but he found no basis for a legal complaint. Agent Jones encouraged UNIA defectors to sue Garvey for unpaid salaries, but the lawsuits were merely a nuisance. Jones also reported that Garvey had siphoned some $46,000 from the UNIA's death benefits fund, but he could not make the accusation stick.

Hoover finally found his weapon in the form of Garvey's Black Star shipping line. Thousands of UNIA supporters had purchased stock in the line at $5 per share, convincing Hoover that it must be "a racket." Garvey was arrested for mail fraud on 12 January 1922 and formally indicted two weeks later by a federal grand jury. Black support for Garvey faltered in July, after G-men leaked reports of his secret meeting with KU KLUX KLAN leaders. Agent Jones "encouraged" prosecution witnesses throughout Garvey's trial, beginning on 18 May 1923, and Garvey was convicted the following month, sentenced to five years in prison. The conviction was upheld on appeal, in February 1925, and Garvey ultimately served 33 months in Atlanta's federal prison. President CALVIN COOLIDGE commuted Garvey's sentence in 1927 and ordered him deported as an undesirable alien. Garvey's later attempts to revive the UNIA were fruitless, though the *Negro World* continued publishing through 1933. Garvey died in England, in 1940.

**GENERAL Intelligence Division**—The FBI's General Intelligence Division was created by Assistant Chief Frank Burke on 1 August 1919, soon after the BOMBINGS allegedly perpetrated by ANARCHISTS in Washington, D.C. and elsewhere around the U.S.

Its mission was to collect and collate information on "radical" groups and individuals throughout the country. Young J. EDGAR HOOVER was placed in charge of the unit and soon amassed 200,000 FILES on various targets, increasing to 450,000 by 1921. Aside from suspected revolutionaries and "enemy aliens," the GID also conducted DOMESTIC SURVEILLANCE against various LABOR UNIONS and employed INFORMANTS to infiltrate black organizations which Hoover deemed "subversive"—i.e., all of them. A special "IWW division" of the GID worked solely on cases involving the INDUSTRIAL WORKERS OF THE WORLD, ordered by Hoover to find evidence supporting deportation of 500 "leading alien agitators." At the same time G-men mounted an investigation of social reformer Jane Addams, spurred by her membership in the "radical" NATIONAL ASSOCIATION FOR THE ADVANCEMENT OF COLORED PEOPLE. By January 1920 Hoover was able to report that "conditions among the negroes [*sic*] throughout the country are said to be rather quiet."

He could say the same for the Bureau's political front, where GID agents and informants under Hoover's command organized the chaotic PALMER RAIDS of 1919-20, arresting thousands of persons linked to the Union of Russian Workers, the COMMUNIST PARTY and the COMMUNIST LABOR PARTY. Some were later deported, including anarchists ALEXANDER BERKMAN and EMMA GOLDMAN, but most were finally released without criminal charges. The resultant outcry and congressional hearings revealed illegal Bureau activities including mass arrests without warrants, confinement of suspects without legal counsel, and frequent beatings of those in custody. Attorney General A. MITCHELL PALMER was driven from office by the scandal, but Hoover's dominant role in the raids was largely ignored.

The GID also survived the Palmer scandal, continuing its pursuit of Reds and blacks under Presidents WARREN HARDING and CALVIN COOLIDGE. The unit's "victories" included the fraud conviction of black nationalist leader MARCUS GARVEY in 1923 and general disruption of various left-wing organizations. Hoover had another near-miss with exposure of his role in the TEAPOT DOME SCANDAL, assigned by Attorney General HARRY DAUGHERTY to investigate and harass administration critics whose number included Senators THOMAS WALSH and BURTON WHEELER. Daugherty was fired in 1924 but successor HARLAND STONE somehow overlooked Hoover's role in the Harding scandals, appointing him as the Bureau's new director. Stone dissolved the GID and ordered Hoover to cease political investigations immediately. Hoover agreed, but the wide-ranging domestic surveillance only increased. The GID's files were vastly expanded over the next 48 years, until Hoover's death in May 1972.

**GEORGE, Paul**—Assigned as a supervisory special agent to the FBI's Detroit field office in 2000, Paul George made the critical mistake of discussing with reporters his views on DOMESTIC SURVEILLANCE. More specifically, he announced, "If there is going to be a Big Brother in the United States, it is going to be us—the FBI." When questioned about the Orwellian analogy, George replied, "There are worse things than having your privacy violated, like murder." Some civil libertarians regard George's view as symptomatic of the FBI's overall attitude and goal.

**GHETTO Informant Program** — J. EDGAR HOOVER blamed the ghetto riots of 1965-67 on a widespread "black nationalist" conspiracy, presumably financed from Moscow. His response, in striking contrast to recommendations for reducing poverty or curbing racism and POLICE BRUTALITY, was an escalation of FBI surveillance on African Americans. Hoover's Ghetto Informant Program, inaugurated in October 1967, was designed to establish thousands of "ghetto listening posts," defined in Bureau documents as "any individual who resides in a ghetto-type area" or "who frequent[s] ghetto areas on a regular basis." Likely candidates included the owners or employees of bars, liquor stores and other ghetto businesses; tenement janitors; cab drivers; bill collectors; and distributors of food, beverages or newspapers. Honorably discharged military veterans and members of veterans' organizations like the AMERICAN LEGION were special favorites, presumed to be conservative patriots.

Ghetto INFORMANTS, once recruited and paid a small stipend, were directed to visit "Afro-American type book stores" in their districts and identify "owners, operators and clientele." They were also asked to monitor street gang members and their activities, watch ex-convicts, and advise the FBI of any "changes in the attitude of the Negro community towards the white community." In theory, the Bureau would thus be forewarned of impending riots at the planning stage, but since the "black conspiracy" existed solely in Hoover's imagination, outbreaks like the riots following the murder of MARTIN LUTHER KING, JR., continued to surprise the FBI.

Once launched, the Ghetto Informant Program became an obsession at FBI HEADQUARTERS. Field agents soon found themselves operating on "a kind of quota system" that required each G-man to recruit a minimum number of black spies. If an agent's normal territory included no ghetto districts, he was ordered to "so specify by memorandum ... so that he will not be charged with failure to perform." Some field offices met the ever-rising quota be reclassifying criminal sources as "ghetto" informants, while others created spies out of thin air, drafting reports from informants who existed only on paper. The zealous New York City field office identified 42 "ghetto areas" within the city's five boroughs, assigning 25 agents full-time to a "racial squad" created solely for recruitment of black informants.

Through such concerted effort, the FBI enlisted 3,248 ghetto informants by the summer of 1968, increasing to some 3,300 at the time President LYNDON JOHNSON left office. Hoover's program was compromised, along with other COINTELPRO operations, by the MEDIA, PENNSYLVANIA BURGLARY in March 1971, but recruitment of "racial ghetto-type informants" accelerated under President RICHARD NIXON, with his fondness for "enemies" lists. By the end of Nixon's first term in office, the Bureau counted 7,500 ghetto informants on its payroll. The program was reportedly discontinued after the WATERGATE SCANDAL and subsequent CHURCH COMMITTEE'S exposure of DOMESTIC SURVEILLANCE abuses, but real-world events since 1975 offer no sound reason to believe such tactics have been wholly abandoned.

**GIANCANA, Sam** — A native of Chicago, born in 1908, Sam ("Momo") Giancana was described in one police report as "a snarling, sarcastic, ill-tempered, sadistic psychopath." Those traits served him well as a member of the notorious 42 Gang and later as a contract killer for the PROHIBITION crime syndicate led by ALPHONSE CAPONE. A prime suspect in three murders by age 20, Giancana used his ruthless talents to rise swiftly through Mafia ranks and dominate Chicago's (some say the nation's) underworld by the late 1950s. At the same time, he was acutely conscious of the mob's public image and once allegedly issued a murder contract on DESI ARNAZ for producing *The Untouchables*, a TV program that glorified ELIOT NESS while portraying members of the Capone gang as vicious thugs. (The contract was not carried out.)

In 1960 Giancana's influence was critical to the presidential election of JOHN F. KENNEDY. "Momo" guaranteed a Democratic majority in Illinois by means of massive vote fraud and later claimed credit for putting Kennedy in the White House. Over the next two years he also collaborated with members of the CENTRAL INTELLIGENCE AGENCY on plots to assassinate Cuban leader Fidel Castro. Instead of the rewards he expected, however, Giancana found himself on a mob "hit list" prepared by Attorney General ROBERT KENNEDY, followed day and night by FBI agents who also targeted Giancana for illegal BUGGING and WIRETAPPING. In June 1963 Giancana took the unprecedented step of suing the Bureau for harassment. Private investigators filmed G-men in their "lockstep" surveillance of Momo — at church, on the golf course, during cemetery visits — and Judge Richard Austin ruled in the plaintiff's favor, fining Chicago agent-in-charge MARLIN JOHNSON $500 and ordering G-men to track Giancana from a "reasonable distance" in the future.

Giancana's recorded threats against the Kennedy brothers made him a prime suspect in the 1963 JFK ASSASSINATION, but FBI Director J. EDGAR HOOVER'S instant "lone-gunman" announcement precluded any serious investigation of mob ties to the killing. Giancana's name was mentioned again in 1968, following the RFK ASSASSINATION, but again the FBI failed to pursue suggestions of conspiracy. Giancana was scheduled as a critical witness when the CHURCH COMMITTEE launched its investigation of FBI and CIA irregularities, but he never had a chance to testify. On 18 June 1975 Momo was murdered in the basement of his Oak Park, Illinois home by a gunman who shot him seven times in the head.

**GIBBONS, Nelson H.** — Nelson ("Skip") Gibbons was once a legendary figure in the FBI. A college football star and ex-Marine, he served as a New York state trooper for seven years prior to joining the bureau. Assigned to the Detroit field office, Gibbons single-handedly exposed a Soviet spy, Kaarlo Tuomi, whose confessions later revealed three more spies in New York and earned the FBI national accolades in July 1963. By that time, however, Gibbons had been hounded from the bureau by J. EDGAR HOOVER, in a classic display of the director's personal malice.

The trouble began in 1958, when Hoover's physician ordered him to lose weight. Determined not to suffer alone, Hoover issued an insurance firm's weight charts to all field offices, insisting that every agent register a "desirable" weight for his height.

Physicians ridiculed the plan, one U.S. Navy doctor branding it "irresponsible," but Hoover was intractable. Even after one agent died in the midst of a crash diet, his widow filing suit against the FBI for wrongful death, Hoover clung to his chart as if it were infallible. Agent Gibbons was five pounds over the limit at his 1960 evaluation, and a physician's opinion that his weight was "medically proper" carried no weight with Hoover. The order came back from Washington: "Lose 5 lbs."

Gibbons next sought a meeting with Hoover. "Although I did not specify a date," he recalled, "I received the stock answer that he would not be available." Two weeks later, in September 1960, Gibbons received an "unsatisfactory" personnel rating and a punitive transfer from Detroit to Mobile, Alabama. The travel papers carried an order for Gibbons to be shipped out again in November 1960, this time to Oklahoma City—a tactic of harassment known in FBI circles as the "Bureau bicycle." On arrival in Oklahoma, SAC WESLEY GRAPP warned Gibbons, "I'm going to give you ulcers." In January 1961 Gibbons received a three-week suspension without pay for allegedly displaying an "unsatisfactory attitude toward the physical requirements of your position." Further requests for a meeting with Hoover were denied, but Assistant Director JOHN MOHR told Gibbons to expect a 30-day suspension if he had not lost five pounds by 2 February 1961.

When Gibbons and friend WILLIAM TURNER filed harassment complaints against SAC Grapp, Hoover deemed their complaints "baseless" and transferred both agents—Gibbons to Butte, Montana, and Turner to Knoxville, Tennessee. An FBI hearing in October 1961 failed to resolve the matter, and Gibbons was next transferred to Alaska. Still he refused to resign, and bureau leaders solved the problem in the fall of 1962, issuing Gibbons a medical discharge for "nervousness" with a monthly pension of $250 for life.

**GINSBERG, Allen**—Hailed as "the voice of the Beat Generation," Allen Ginsberg was a native of Newark, New Jersey, born 3 June 1936. He published his first collection of poetry at age 30, soon attracting interest from the FBI and various other government agencies. Travels to Cuba and Czechoslovakia, outspoken protests against the Vietnam War, and advocacy of legalized marijuana agitated federal investigators to collect a dossier that Ginsberg himself described, in 1987, as "a stack of documents three feet high." (In fact, it contained 919 pages.) Agents detailed Ginsberg's 1949 treatment at a New York psychiatric hospital and his 1954 vagrancy arrest in California (where he was acquitted). In 1959 they branded his mother "a psychotic and a Communist." By 1960, G-men were stealing and reading his mail.

Collateral investigations were pursued by the Treasury Department, Customs and the FEDERAL BUREAU OF NARCOTICS, where even his photograph was apparently regarded as dangerous. FBN agents sent a snapshot of Ginsberg to J. EDGAR HOOVER in 1967, noting that "For possible future use, the photograph has been placed in a locked sealed envelope marked 'Photograph of Allen Ginsberg—Gen. File: ALLEN GINSBERG. The locked sealed envelope has been placed in the vault of this office for safekeeping." A year later, during the chaotic Democratic Conven-

tion in Chicago, G-men investigated Ginsberg for alleged violation of "antirioting laws," noting his public recitation of "unintelligible poems" (in fact, William Blake's "The Grey Monk"). In 1969, FBI memos dubbed Ginsberg "the bearded apostle of opposition and resistance," student INFORMANTS reporting his words from college campus across the U.S. In 1970, when Ginsberg visited Quincy College for a poetry reading, Illinois agents kept watch as part of an ongoing "IS" (Internal Security) case that never bore fruit. Even a passing mention of his name demanded that articles be clipped and filed, as with a piece from the 3 May 1976 issue of *New Times* magazine. Surveillance of Ginsberg apparently ceased thereafter, two decades before his death in New York City, from liver cancer, on 5 April 1997.

**GOLDMAN, Emma**—A Lithuanian Jew, born in 1869, Emma Goldman was 13 when her family moved to St. Petersburg. A wave of anti-Semitic repression in Russia made life nearly unbearable for the Goldmans, prompting Emma to leave school and take a factory job six months after the move. There she was introduced to ANARCHIST philosophy and rebelled when her parents tried to arrange her marriage at age 15. She was packed off to the U.S. in 1885, living with a sister in Rochester, New York. Married briefly to a Russian immigrant in 1889, Goldman soon divorced him and moved to New York City, where she joined the ranks of anarchists led by ALEXANDER BERKMAN and Johann Most.

Berkman was imprisoned for a failed murder attempt in 1892, but Goldman carried on without him, receiving her first prison sentence (one year) in 1893 for urging the poor to take bread "by force." A second jail term followed for distributing information about contraceptives. Berkman was paroled in 1906 and Goldman rejoined him, collaborating on various programs until they were arrested in 1917 for opposing military conscription. Upon release in 1919 they were scheduled for deportation with other anarchists and alleged Bolsheviks captured during the first PALMER RAIDS. Future FBI Director J. EDGAR HOOVER was on hand when the deportees sailed from New York for the Soviet Union aboard the S.S. *Buford*, on 21 December 1919.

Goldman was disillusioned by what she found in Russia, and she left for England in December 1921, after striking workers at Kronstadt were crushed by the Red Army. Alexander Berkman killed himself in 1936 and Goldman—by then 67 years old—traveled to Spain a year later, joining in the armed struggle against Francisco Franco's fascists. She died in 1940, and while J. Edgar Hoover staunchly opposed a plan to bury her in Chicago, Immigration officials permitted her posthumous return.

**GRAF, Oskar Maria**—A Bavarian author, born in July 1894 and best known for his novels depicting peasant life, Oskar Graf fled his homeland to escape Nazi persecution and settled in New York City. FBI agents noted his membership in the German-American Writers' Association, "which organization is alleged to have Communistic tendencies," and while the first entry in his Bureau file is dated 5 May 1943, it reveals that G-men and members of the NEW YORK POLICE DEPARTMENT's notorious Alien Squad had actually searched Graf's home three months earlier, on 13 February. "No contraband was found" in that raid, nor was Graf intimidated by interrogation over his "sympathies and tendencies." Finally, the frustrated agents subjected Graf to a secret "mail cover" operation, illegally stealing and reading letters received at his home.

A report by E.E. Conroy, in charge of the New York field office, explains that Graf was denounced to the FBI by an unnamed INFORMANT who described Graf as "an individualist, though with strong Communist leanings." Remarkably confused, agents reported that while Graf allegedly wrote for Red publications in Russia and was "lavishly wined and dined in Moscow," his work was also praised in Nazi Germany, "where Dr. Groebbls [sic] found no fault with his printed outpourings." The FBI pursued Graf long after he became a U.S. citizen, employing German sources to record his movements during post-war visits to his former homeland. The last entry to Graf's dossier was filed in June 1964. Graf died in New York three years later, on 28 June 1967.

**GRAPP, Wesley G.**—G-man Wesley Grapp got his first taste of controversy in 1959, while serving as special agent in charge (SAC) of the Oklahoma City field office. In June of that year, federal prison inmates Kathryn Kelly (widow of GEORGE "MACHINE GUN" KELLY) and her mother, Ora Shannon, were released on bond pending appeal of their 1933 convictions in the CHARLES URSCHEL kidnapping. After years of appeals, Kelly had finally uncovered FBI documents disputing ancient testimony that her handwriting matched that of the Urschel ransom note, and a federal judge ordered the Bureau to produce its records on the case. After reviewing his files, SAC Grapp informed FBI headquarters on 15 October 1959 that surviving records contained no evidence of a handwriting match to Kelly. If that fact was revealed, Grapp advised, it might result in "some embarrassment to the Bureau." Accordingly, the records were withheld and the defendants remained at liberty, after losing 23 years of their lives to an apparent frame-up.

By the mid-1960s, SAC Grapp "was a household name inside the Bureau," described by one observer as "an iron disciplinarian of the most zealous sort." That quality was demonstrated in the case of Agent WILLIAM TURNER, hounded from the FBI by punitive actions of Grapp and J. EDGAR HOOVER in 1961, after Grapp took offense over Turner's routine request for a transfer from Oklahoma City to Los Angeles. Other agents were also driven from the Bureau by Grapp, who threatened to "get something on them" and push for their dismissal if they refused to resign. Ex-agent Turner goes further, in *Hoover's FBI: The Men and the Myth* (1970), suggesting that Grapp's harassment may have driven one G-man to suicide.

Through it all, Grapp remained well-connected and well-regarded in the FBI, strong enough to defy Hoover's order for a transfer to Los Angeles in 1967 and escape punishment. Grapp subsequently took the L.A. posting and handled COINTELPRO operations for that office, but it marked the end of his career. Following Hoover's death in May 1972, successor L. PATRICK GRAY was deluged with complaints from the field, detailing cases of unfair and autocratic discipline in various field offices. Grapp ranked among the worst offenders, accused of BUGGING his own agents

and dispatching one G-man whose sideburns offended him to a Mojave Desert detail in a car without air-conditioning. Demoted and slapped with a punitive transfer to Minneapolis, slated for "a long road trip to North Dakota" in the dead of winter, Grapp retained a lawyer and negotiated early retirement from the FBI.

**GRASSLEY, Charles Ernest**—A native of New Hartford, Iowa, born 17 September 1933, Charles Grassley served as a member of the Iowa state legislature (1959-74) and in the House of Representatives (1975-81) before his election to the U.S. Senate. In 2001 he emerged as one of the scandal-ridden FBI's most outspoken congressional critics. "Because of one embarrassment after another," he told reporters, "the public has been losing confidence in the FBI. [Director LOUIS] FREEH tried to some extent, but he was not able to change the cowboy culture inside the FBI." Grassley was especially critical of Bureau attempts to silence and punish whistle-blowers within its own ranks after the catastrophic SKYJACKINGS of 11 September 2001. Past and present G-men, meanwhile, resented Grassley's observations, one of them suggesting (presumably with tongue in cheek) that "Senator Grassley is an old Soviet mole still trying to impede the efficiency of the FBI."

**GRATHWOHL, Larry C.**—Ranked among "the most militant members" of the WEATHERMAN UNDERGROUND in the late 1960s, Larry Grathwohl was in fact an FBI INFORMANT whose activities, by his own admission, went far beyond simply observing and exposing the criminal acts of others. Habitually armed with a .357 Magnum revolver and a straight razor, Grathwohl advertised himself to fellow Weathermen as a demolitions expert and offered bomb-making classes for radicals of the "NEW LEFT." He went further still, in fact, and later confessed to the *New York Times* that he participated in the 1969 bombing of a Cincinnati public school.

On 6 March 1970 a federal grand jury in Detroit indicted Grathwohl and 12 other Weathermen for conspiracy to bomb various military and police facilities. A subsequent indictment, issued on 7 December 1972, dismissed charges against Grathwohl and another defendant, while adding radicals to the list. Despite the serious nature of the charges, including the March 1970 firebombing of a Cleveland policeman's home and conspiracy to plant bombs in four states, none of the defendants were ever tried. Grathwohl, meanwhile, vanished into the federal witness protection program and later published a sensational account of his exploits titled *Bringing Down America: An FBI Informer with the Weathermen* (1976).

**GRAVANO, Salvatore ("Sammy the Bull")**—A New York City mobster, born in 1945, Salvatore Gravano—dubbed "The Bull" for his squat, muscular physique—committed at least 19 Mafia contract killings (some accounts claim 36) over two decades beginning in 1970. Through ruthless cunning, he rose to the rank of underboss in the crime family run by "Teflon Don" John Gotti, but personal disputes with Gotti and a threat of life imprisonment on racketeering charges prompted Gravano to turn INFORMANT in 1990. Named as the highest-ranking Mafiosi who ever "rolled over" for the FBI, Gravano subsequently testified at trials which sent 36 mobsters (including Gotti) to federal prison. The reward for his testimony was a five-year prison term and official absolution for his many homicides. In 1997 he published a book (*Underboss*) with author Peter Maas that gave Gravano's side of the defection and painted him as a hero of sorts.

Resettled in Scottsdale, Arizona as "Jimmy Moran," a member of the federal Witness Protection Program, Gravano soon grew tired of the "straight" life and returned to his old criminal habits. On 24 February 2000 Gravano was jailed with 45 others, including his son and daughter, on charges of selling the designer drug Ecstasy to members of a white supremacist group, the Devil Dogs. At its peak, prosecutors said, the drug network was selling pills valued at $300,000 per week. In 2001 Gravano pled guilty on 10 felony counts including conspiracy to sell dangerous drugs, offering to sell or transport dangerous drugs, conducting an illegal enterprise, participating in a criminal syndicate, money laundering and weapons charges. That plea earned him a 20-year term in federal prison. A year later, on 30 October 2002, Gravano received a concurrent 19-year term for his role as founder and mastermind of the Ecstasy ring. Son Gerard Gravano received a nine-year sentence, while daughter Karen Gravano escaped with probation.

**GRAY, Louis Patrick III**—A St. Louis native, born 18 June 1916, L. Patrick Gray III grew up in Houston, Texas and studied at Rice University before proceeding to the U.S. Naval Academy at Annapolis, Maryland. He graduated as a commissioned officer, later serving as a submarine commander in WORLD WAR II and as commander of a submarine flotilla in the Korean War. While still in military service, during 1949, Gray graduated from George Washington University School of Law. After service as assistant to the Joint Chiefs of Staff, he retired from the Navy in 1960 to join RICHARD NIXON'S presidential campaign staff. Following Nixon's defeat, Gray practiced law in New Haven, Connecticut, then rejoined Nixon for the 1968 presidential campaign. By December 1970 he was an assistant attorney general in charge of the JUSTICE DEPARTMENT'S Civil Division, where he prosecuted VIETNAM WAR protesters and defended the FBI against lawsuits filed by would-be WOMEN AGENTS whom Director J. EDGAR HOOVER rejected.

On 3 May 1972, one day after Hoover's death, President Nixon appointed Gray to serve as acting FBI director. His first task was a fruitless effort to discover and retrieve Hoover's secret FILES. Having failed in that mission, Gray quickly established an unsavory reputation in office. Assistant Director Leonard Walters later told journalist Robert Kessler that "Gray would lie regularly" to the press and his subordinates. He also avoided FBI HEADQUARTERS whenever possible. G-men quickly dubbed him "three-day Gray," after the fact that he never appeared at his office on Monday or Friday, habitually taking long weekends at home or visiting different field offices aboard an Air Force jet (billed to the Bureau at more than $100,000 for Gray's 11 months in office).

The positive aspects of Gray's tenure included new initiatives to recruit minority and female agents, but Gray was doomed by the festering WATERGATE SCANDAL. Secret White House tapes reveal that Nixon first discussed firing Gray on 7 March 1973, after Gray (at his Senate confirmation hearing) admitted destroying documents relevant to the Watergate cover-up. Aide JOHN EHRLICHMAN remarked on that occasion, "I think we ought to let him hang there. Let him twist slowly, slowly in the wind." Six days later Nixon said, "Gray should not be the head of the FBI." On 22 March he added, "The problem with [Gray] is he is a little bit stupid." Gray withdrew his name from nomination as FBI director on 5 April 1973 and formally resigned his post on 27 April, returning to private practice in Connecticut.

His difficulties were not past, however. Five years later, in April 1978, Gray was indicted with two other retired FBI officials—W. MARK FELT and EDWARD MILLER—on charges of ordering illegal BREAK-INS around New York City in the early 1970s. Gray requested a separate trial, denying any knowledge of the crimes, and his motion was granted. Felt and Miller were convicted and fined in November 1980, then were pardoned by President RONALD REAGAN in March 1981. Federal prosecutors dismissed their charges against Gray on 11 December 1980, citing lack of evidence.

**GREGORY, Horace**—A Milwaukee native, born in 1898, Horace Gregory was indexed by the FBI in May 1939, after a *New York Times* article identified him as a member of the JOHN REED Club who had signed a protest against "alleged anti-communist propaganda." Gregory's work often criticized middle-class life in America, and while he once wrote that his poetry "has contained social implications that can be resolved only by the success of the COMMUNIST PARTY," G-men found no evidence that he was ever a dues-paying member. A 1932 report linked Gregory to the League of Professional Groups for Foster and Ward—the Communist presidential slate in that election year—and agents thereafter referred to Gregory habitually as a "Revolutionary writer," taking care to note when and where his work was published. Loyalty-security hearings were convened with respect to Gregory in 1948 and 1949, and for his son-in-law in 1953. Ideas aside, no "subversive" activities were uncovered, and his FBI file consists of a paltry 56 pages. Gregory died in 1982.

**GREGORY, Thomas Watt**—Born 6 November 1861, a native of Crawfordsville, Mississippi who lost his father in the Civil War, Thomas Gregory took office as President WOODROW WILSON'S second attorney general on 20 August 1914. Unlike predecessor JAMES MCREYNOLDS, Gregory's administration was both active and controversial. The shrunken Bureau of Investigation regained most of its former strength under Gregory, growing from 122 special agents to 225 and from 39 support personnel to 268. Bureau strength was further enhanced by Gregory's ill-advised approval of a working alliance with the vigilante AMERICAN PROTECTIVE LEAGUE (APL) in February 1917. That collaborative effort got its first controversial workout with the sweeping "SLACKER RAIDS" of 1918, resulting in public outcry against the Bureau's abuses of power. Gregory subsequently helped to draft the equally controversial espionage and sedition acts, continuing JUSTICE DEPARTMENT involvement with the APL's amateur spies throughout WORLD WAR I. Gregory's final contribution was the appointment of Acting Director WILLIAM ALLEN in February 1919, after Director A. BRUCE BIELASKI resigned under fire. Gregory resigned on 4 March 1919 and returned to the practice of law in Texas. He died at Austin on 26 February 1933.

**GRIMM, Charles**—At the height of protests against the VIETNAM WAR and exposure of President RICHARD NIXON'S covert military activities in Cambodia, the FBI employed countless INFORMANTS to infiltrate and disrupt anti-war groups and the "NEW LEFT." One of those, active on the University of Alabama campus in Tuscaloosa, was Charles Grimm, an agitator who received paychecks both from the Bureau and from local police. On 7 May 1970, three days after the KENT STATE SHOOTINGS in Ohio, Grimm burned Dressler Hall on the university campus. One week later, on 14 May, he lobbed incendiary Molotov cocktails into a Tuscaloosa street, and on 18 May he engaged in stoning police officers on the university campus. When questioned about these crimes later, Grimm claimed that his FBI handlers knew everything about his activities and that G-men ordered him to torch Dressler Hall. FBI spokesmen denied the charge, but no investigation of Grimm's allegations was pursued. In light of revelations from other FBI *agents provocateur* during the same period, it seems likely that Grimm's "control" agents were (at the very least) fully aware of his illegal behavior and that they did nothing to restrain him.

**GUARDIANS of the Oglala Nation**—Based on South Dakota's PINE RIDGE RESERVATION, the group aptly known as GOON was created in November 1972 by Oglala tribal president Richard Wilson, an outspoken enemy of the AMERICAN INDIAN MOVEMENT (AIM) who was elected to office with covert support from the Bureau of Indian Affairs (BIA). The group was initially bankrolled by a $62,000 donation from the BIA, provided (in Wilson's words) to create "an auxiliary police force ... to handle people like [AIM leader] Russell Means and other radicals." Wilson first used his GOONs to suppress opposition during a February 1973 impeachment campaign, then rallied them a month later to harass AIM activists during the WOUNDED KNEE SIEGE.

The GOON squad came into its own at Wounded Knee, manning roadblocks, seizing food and medicine intended for AIM members, and joining federal officers to fire some 20,000 rounds of ammunition at AIM activists during a one-sided "battle" on 26 March 1973. A month later, on 20 April, GOON members John Hussman and Emile Richards told reporters they were "fed up" with the siege and "if the government does not move the militants out of Wounded Knee by May 4 we will begin to lead commando-style raids." The FBI raised no protest to that suggestion and Richard Wilson announced that he would support the raiders "100 percent, with whatever is necessary." On 23 April 1973 GOON road blockers detained several JUSTICE DEPARTMENT employees and threatened members of the U.S. MARSHALS SERVICE with firearms. The next day, when marshals tried to disperse the blockade, FBI COINTELPRO agent RICHARD G. HELD arrived to countermand the order. G-men subsequently furnished the GOONs with military-style automatic weapons and ammunition, producing the following results on 26 April 1973:

> The [GOONs] were in the hills with government-issue weapons, M16s, firing on both government and Indian positions. The government troops poured fire into Wounded Knee that night. Wounded Knee security estimated that they took 20,000 rounds from vigilantes and marshals in twelve hours.

Despite their errant gunplay, GOON members were unmolested by FBI agents and BIA police. After the siege was broken they launched a three-year series of reprisals at Pine Ridge, killing at least 69 AIM members or supporters and wounding or assaulting more than 300 by mid-1976. FBI spokesmen claimed a "lack of manpower" prevented them from curbing GOON crimes on federal land—but they still found time and personnel enough to file 40 separate criminal cases against Russell Means during the same period.

Means challenged Wilson for the Oglala tribal presidency in 1974 and won the primary contest with 677 votes to Wilson's 511, but Means somehow lost the GOON-supervised general election by more than 200 votes. A subsequent investigation revealed at least 154 cases of vote fraud plus an "undetermined number" of illegitimate votes by outsiders, but Attorney General WILLIAM SAXBE ignored official recommendations for a new election under federal supervision. Wilson celebrated his "victory" by raising his own salary 300 percent and doling out patronage jobs to a long list of relatives. (Brother George Wilson walked away with a $25,000 yearly salary.) The GOONs received $220,000 for a new headquarters plus a $400,000 "tribal loan" from Washington to augment the group's payroll.

Violence continued unabated on the reservation, meanwhile. A series of GOON provocations, followed by FBI arrests of AIM members, climaxed on 26 June 1975 with a shooting that claimed the lives of Agents Jack Coler and Ronald Williams. Two AIM members who admitted firing on the agents were acquitted at trial on a self-defense plea, but G-men finally convicted suspect LEONARD PELTIER with testimony from "witness" Gregory Clifford, who was facing trial for rape until the FBI dismissed those charges in return for his assistance in the Peltier prosecution. (Clifford disappeared into the federal Witness Protection Program after Peltier's trial, but he resurfaced in March 1987, receiving a 45-year prison term for the brutal sex-murder of a Colorado woman.)

Peltier's incarceration did not end the GOON campaign. In January 1976 GOON members murdered Oglala tribal attorney Byron DeSersa at Pine Ridge. Two suspects in that case, Charles Winters and Dale Janis, plea-bargained for reduced manslaughter charges and received two-year prison terms; their codefendants, Richard Wilson's son and son-in-law, were acquitted on grounds of "self-defense" (though DeSersa was admittedly unarmed when they shot him). Wilson's son-in-law, Charles Richards, hailed from a clan of GOON members so feared at Pine Ridge that neighbors dubbed them "the Manson Family." In May 1979 he was sent to the federal prison at Lompoc, California where Leonard Peltier had been recently transferred. Identified with federal collusion as "Chuck Richardson,"

Richards tried to befriend Peltier in what AIM members later described as an abortive murder plot, but Peltier shunned him and escaped from prison two months later (thereby earning a longer sentence upon his recapture).

Another GOON member from the same family, Benny Richards, was listed as a suspect in the February 1979 arson-slaying of four persons on the Shoshone-Paiute Reservation at Duck River, straddling the Idaho-Nevada border. The victims in that case were the wife and children of AIM leader John Trudell, described in FBI memos as "an extremely effective agitator." That case remains officially unsolved today, along with the majority of crimes committed by GOON vigilantes at Pine Ridge. With the exception of the DeSersa slaying, G-men tasked with enforcing the law on federal property have been unable to solve even one of nearly 400 violent crimes committed by the GOON squad they helped arm and finance in the 1970s.

**GUEVARA de la Serna, Ernesto ("Che")**—A native of Rosario, Argentina, born 14 June 1928, Ernesto graduated from medical school in Buenos Aires in March 1953. Nine months later, shortly after his first meeting with veterans of Fidel Castro's Cuban revolutionary movement, Guevara settled in Guatemala. He was present in June 1954, when right-wing mercenaries supported by the U.S. CENTRAL INTELLIGENCE AGENCY invaded Guatemala and forced the resignation of elected president Jacobo Arbenz. That experience radicalized Guevara, and he fled Guatemala for Mexico City in September 1954. A July 1955 meeting with Castro persuaded Guevara to join the Cuban revolution as a field medic, in which capacity he witnessed Castro's victory over the corrupt regime of dictator Fulgencio Batista. Castro's troops captured Havana on 8 January 1959, and Guevara was declared a Cuban citizen one month later, in honor of his military service.

The FBI's interest in Guevara predated his political awakening by three full years, beginning when agents recorded his passport information during a 1952 visit to Miami. A year after his enlistment with Castro's forces, on 25 July 1956, an FBI report inaccurately reported that Guevara was "a doctor at General Hospital [in Mexico City], although he has never studied medicine." A series of memos filed between August 1959 and June 1965 reported Guevara's public remarks from Havana, Brazil, Algeria, Sudan and Yugoslavia. News clippings were also preserved, including a fanciful item from 28 June 1965, headlined: "Guevara rumored to prepare coup in Guatemala."

The FBI had no legal jurisdiction in any of those countries, but its paper pursuit of Guevara was relentless. In February 1961, G-men noted rumors of an attempt on Che's life. Three months later, a bomb was reportedly thrown at a Rio de Janeiro auditorium where he delivered a speech. In September 1965 Bureau INFORMANTS told Washington that Che suffered from "acute bronchial disease." The following month, he was allegedly captured in Peru. February 1966 brought reports of his death at sea, drowned when his boat was sunk by a Dominican warship, but Che was resurrected the following month for a political rally at Concepcion, Chile. On 4 May 1966 G-men reported that Che "might have been in Peru"; 10 days later they reported him dead since April 1964 (again, while trying to land on Santo Domingo).

Contradictory reports from July 1966 placed Che alive in "southern South America," then killed him off again after a "violent political argument" with Castro supporters in Cuba.

In fact, Che was alive and well. He surfaced in Bolivia on 4 November 1966, as a commander of revolutionary forces opposing that nation's military junta. FBI agents missed the move, reporting his presence in Bolivia for the first time on 13 September 1967. By then, Guevara had less than a month to live. Wounded and captured with 17 other guerrillas on 8 October 1967, he was murdered with two other captives the same day, while in army custody. The Bureau's final reports of Che's death were typically inaccurate, describing a fatal shot to the heart (when in fact he was shot in the neck). Documents describing the FBI's pointless 15-year pursuit of Che Guevara remained classified until 1985, when they were released under the FREEDOM OF INFORMATION ACT.

**GUNDERSON, Ted L.**—Typically described in media reports as "colorful" or "eccentric," Ted Gunderson joined the FBI in December 1951 and spent his first decade with the Bureau pursuing various federal investigations. Thereafter he advanced through the ranks to serve as agent in charge of the Memphis and Dallas field offices. At retirement, in March 1979, he was senior agent in charge of the huge Los Angeles field office, commanding more than 700 subordinates and coordinating FBI operations for most of southern California. Soon after Gunderson retired, Attorney General GRIFFIN BELL recruited him to coordinate security for the summer 1979 Pan American games in San Juan, Puerto Rico. At the same time he established Ted L. Gunderson and Associates, a private investigation firm based at Santa Monica, California. In 1981-82 Gunderson served on the California NARCOTIC Authority, as a consultant to Governor Jerry Brown. In 1984 he was retained as a security consultant for the Los Angeles Olympic Committee.

While Gunderson's FBI service was exemplary and most of his cases since retirement have proved to be routine, some of his activities and statements have made the ex-agent a lightning rod for controversy. One case in point is that of alleged murderer JEFFREY MACDONALD, imprisoned for killing his wife and two daughters in 1970. Gunderson's investigation of the case more than a decade later revealed many discrepancies in the prosecution's evidence and in findings reported by the FBI's LABORATORY DIVISION. Even more controversial is Gunderson's involvement in various high-profile cases where day-care personnel and others stand accused of abusing young children during satanic rituals. Gunderson investigated California's notorious McMartin Preschool case and he was also involved in a Nebraska case that featured accusations of child abuse against President GEORGE H.W. BUSH.

In the course of pursuing those cases, Gunderson had issued various public statements and videotapes that prompt critics to question his motives or his competency. One such tape, advertised for sale in 1999, bore the title *Satanism & the CIA: International Trafficking in Children*. A promotional ad for the video declared that Gunderson "shows the link between Satanic ritual-abuse, drug trafficking and the international trafficking in children by the CIA." Another tape, titled *The New World Order*, was billed as "the most insightful, important information you will find available ... [to] 'connect the dots' of the New World Order." Such topics brought Gunderson into contact with spokesmen for the far-right MILITIA MOVEMENT and prompted critics to accuse him of political extremism. (In 1995 Gunderson told a California militia gathering that the Oklahoma City bombing blamed on TIMOTHY MCVEIGH was actually perpetrated by a "demonic element from within the government.") Gunderson supporters countered with charges of a conspiratorial smear campaign. In 2001, while serving as a defense investigator for an accused murderer in Nevada, Gunderson was slapped with a state citation for operating without a license. State authorities were unimpressed by Gunderson's claim that he tackled the case as an "investigative journalist" and thus required no special permits.

**GUNTHER, John**—Born in Chicago on 30 August 1901, John Gunther was a popular American journalist whose first book in a series of respected sociopolitical surveys, *Inside Europe*, was published in 1936. The FBI opened a file on Gunther that same year, after the *Daily Worker* reported that he had attended a dinner sponsored by the American League Against War and Fascism. In 1937 Gunther sponsored the Friends of the ABRAHAM LINCOLN BRIGADE, but G-men somehow overlooked that "subversive" connection until it was reported by the HOUSE COMMITTEE ON UN-AMERICAN ACTIVITIES (HUAC) in June 1958. Meanwhile, Gunther attracted further scrutiny by joining the AUTHORS LEAGUE OF AMERICA, regarded by J. EDGAR HOOVER as a thinly-veiled communist front.

Despite those left-of-center connections, and a memo declaring that Gunther "certainly slips in some subtle pleading for the U.S.S.R." in his published work, Hoover held an ambiguous attitude toward the author whose later work included *Inside Asia* (1939), *Inside Latin America* (1941) and *Inside Africa* (1955). Hoover granted Gunther a tour of FBI headquarters in 1939, permitting Gunther to fire tommy guns on the bureau target range, and met with him privately in 1957 to discuss a case involving "the Sterns" (otherwise unidentified). Although HUAC found Gunther's books on sale at communist bookstores in June 1958, Hoover made no further additions to the author's 104-page file before Gunther died, on 29 May 1970.

# H

**HABE, Hans**—Born János Békessy in Hungary, on 12 February 1911, Habe worked as a journalist there before moving to Austria and changing his name. He was known in both countries as a popular novelist and "a journalist of dubious professional ethics," who married six wealthy brides in succession and fled to the U.S. when Nazi Germany annexed his adopted homeland. Once established in New York City, he joined a group of exiled writers calling themselves the Emergency Rescue Committee, created to help other writers escape the Gestapo's clutches at home.

Habe approached the FBI to request an interview in May 1942, apparently hoping to make a good impression before some malicious INFORMANT could beat him to the punch with derogatory reports. He claimed to have received threatening letters, but the New York field office determined that "there is definitely no extortion violation in this case," suggesting that Habe's "principle object in calling at the Bureau appeared to be his desire to counteract any reports which might be received at any time relative to his activities having a tinge of international intrigue." Habe presented the agents with a collection exceeding 3,000 press clippings and several hundred flattering reviews of his work. The preemptive strike notwithstanding, G-men later filed an informant's report that "young Hans Habe was in the service of the fascist Heimwehr Movement in Austria." In later life, Habe emigrated to Switzerland and died at Locorno on 29 September 1977.

**HALDEMAN, Harry Robbins**—A Los Angeles native, born 27 October 1926, H.R. Haldeman was an Eagle Scout who served in the Naval Reserve during WORLD WAR II and graduated from the University of California at Los Angeles in 1948. Over the next decade he worked as an advertising executive in New York and California, working in his spare time as an advance man for RICHARD NIXON in various political campaigns (1952, 1956 and 1960). In 1962 he managed Nixon's unsuccessful California gubernatorial campaign. Six years later Haldeman was chief of staff for Nixon's winning presidential campaign, and he maintained the chief of staff's position at the Nixon White House. Nixon later described Haldeman as "a man of rare intelligence, strength, integrity and courage" who "played an indispensable role in turbulent times." Haldeman once described himself more succinctly as "the president's son of a bitch."

In that role, working closely with former UCLA classmate JOHN EHRLICHMAN, Haldeman became a central figure in the morass of conspiracy known today as the WATERGATE SCANDAL. Before his criminal behavior was exposed, however, he dealt frequently with FBI Director J. EDGAR HOOVER to implement Nixon's plans for suppressing political dissent and muzzling critics in the news media. That relationship got off to a rocky start in May 1969, when Hoover named Haldeman and Ehrlichman as suspects in "a ring of homosexuals at the highest levels of the White House." The false charge was disproved by Assistant Director W. MARK FELT, but Haldeman remembered the incident and in November 1970 asked Hoover for a list of "HOMOSEXUALS known and suspected in the Washington press corps." Hoover acknowledged that "we have some of that material" and promised to "get after that right away." He also furnished Haldeman with derogatory information on U.S. SUPREME COURT Justice WILLIAM O. DOUGLAS, collected by means of illegal WIRETAPPING, to assist the White House in an abortive impeachment campaign.

Hoover did not survive to witness the Watergate burglary of June 1972 or the ensuing scandals that doomed Nixon's administration. Haldeman and Ehrlichman resigned in disgrace on 30 April 1973, both subsequently prosecuted and convicted of conspiracy and obstructing justice. Haldeman served 18 months in prison but emerged relatively unscathed. In 1978 he published a memoir, *The Ends of Power*, which accepted personal blame for much of the illegal activity committed and concealed by Nixon's aides. "I put on too much pressure," he wrote, "and in the process laid the groundwork for the mental attitude that 'the job must be done.'" That in turn "badly served the cause when Watergate struck. By then, our whole crew was so strongly indoctrinated in the principle that there were to be results, not alibis, that they simply once again swung into action — doing what they felt was expected of them."

After his release from prison, Haldeman served as vice president of a real estate development firm, while maintaining a financial interest in various hotels and restaurants. He died of cancer at age 67, on 13 November 1993.

**HALE, David Olin** — On 21 July 1968 a bomb exploded at the Tucson, Arizona ranch owned by Detroit mobster Peter ("Horseface") Licavoli. One day later, two explosions damaged the nearby home of transplanted New York gangster Joseph ("Joe Bananas") Bonnano. Over the next year, Tucson was rocked by 15 more BOMBINGS while newspapers carried reports of a "gang war" raging between rival leaders of ORGANIZED CRIME. In fact, as local authorities learned in 1970, the bombing campaign was an FBI "COINTELPRO" operation planned and carried out by Tucson agent David Hale, in a bizarre attempt to set high-ranking mobsters at each other's throats.

As later revealed in sworn courtroom testimony, Agent Hale recruited two local felons to plant the explosive charges on command. On one occasion, fleeing from the scene of an attempted bombing, one of Hale's accomplices was shot and wounded. Hale visited him in the hospital and asked the wounded man to "crimp a cap onto a fuse" for the next scheduled blast, but Hale's accomplice was unable to complete the task with one hand disabled.

A female college student was found shot to death in Tucson after boasting to friends that she and Hale had tried to bomb Joe Bonnano's car, but police ruled her death a suicide.

Agent Hale was suspended from duty when his criminal accomplices went on trial for the bombings in June 1971, and he resigned when a witness named him in court as the plan's mastermind. (After he resigned, FBI spokesmen claimed that Hale was on the verge of being fired because he had accepted cash and gifts from unnamed private citizens.) The bombers were convicted but their judge let them off with a $260 fine, announcing that they had been "taken in, misled, led down that primrose path pointed out" by Agent Hale. According to the judge, the plot was solely Hale's idea, "a frolic of his own that has brought embarrassment to all concerned." No state or federal charges were filed against Hale, and he moved on from the FBI to an executive position in private industry, suggesting that he received a favorable recommendation from FBI HEADQUARTERS.

**HAMMETT, Samuel Dashiell** — Few cases demonstrate the malicious and futile nature of J. EDGAR HOOVER'S domestic surveillance campaigns more clearly than the FBI's long pursuit of renowned mystery author Dashiell Hammett. Incensed by Hammett's politics and lifestyle, Hoover hounded him relentlessly for 27 years, at last trying to carry the one-sided feud beyond the grave.

A Maryland native, born 27 May 1894, Hammett first drew the FBI's attention at age 40. Bureau agents opened a file on him in 1934, suspicious that "subversive" messages might be hidden within the "Secret Agent X-9" comic strip Hammett created for the San Francisco *Call Bulletin*. Four years later, Hammett was notorious enough that members of the NEW YORK POLICE DEPARTMENT's "Red Squad" took special note of him renting a suite at the Plaza Hotel. Bureau critics described Hammett's mystery novels as "extremely lean," while noting that the "pro-Communist padding gets in there, just the same." Doubly critical of Hammett's long affair with suspect playwright LILLIAN HELLMAN, G-men noted that she was one of several "Communists" Hammett employed to write for *PM* magazine in 1940. From his salary, Hammett allegedly contributed $1,000 monthly to the COMMUNIST PARTY, prompting Bureau observers to dub the period his "Stalinist honeymoon."

Hammett joined the U.S. Army in 1942, at age 48, and served until 1945 in the Aleutian Islands, where he edited an army newspaper. Upon his enlistment, Hoover informed military intelligence that Hammett was president of "a Communist-front organization," the League of American Writers, but when that failed to bring about his discharge, Hoover adopted the strange pose of claiming that Hammett had disappeared, with the FBI unable to locate him. If he was found out of uniform, a 1944 memo suggested, the Bureau should "present a case against the subject for impersonation." When G-men finally "found" him again, they established "a casual surveillance" via army INFORMANTS, but the myth of Hammett's wartime vanishing act lived on, post-war FBI documents still insisting that Hammett "claimed to be a Corporal in the United States army, but to date this information has not been verified."

After WORLD WAR II, Hammett continued to irritate G-men by adopting "radical" causes such as the Civil Rights Congress, which opposed police brutality against blacks, and went to jail for contempt in 1951, rather than provide Senator JOSEPH MCCARTHY a list of the group's contributors. (Hammett served as president and as a trustee of the group's bail fund.) He also addressed a reunion of the ABRAHAM LINCOLN BRIGADE, and joined DOROTHY PARKER in efforts to recruit more liberal commentators for national radio networks. With such activities in mind, Hoover ranked Hammett as a "key figure" for surveillance in the 1950s.

One incident memorializing Hoover's personal spite occurred in 1951, when a veterans' group wrote to columnist WALTER WINCHELL, asking why a "pro-Commy" like Hammett would join the army at age 48. Hoover scripted Winchell's reply in a memo reading:

> You ask: "Why would a pro-Commy enlist in our army?" That's easy. Because our army was fighting for Russia. In other words: Only the Commies knew what the last war was all about — a war to make the world safe for Communism. (Don't mention me.) (Just call me professor.)

Winchell returned the favor a short time later, tipping "Professor" Hoover that four fugitive Communist Party leaders were hiding at Hammett's home. G-men visited the house without a warrant on 8 July 1951, whereupon Hammett invited them to search the premises, "which was done with negative results." Winchell, meanwhile, felt obliged to imply that Hammett was involved in a conspiracy to hide the fugitives, reporting to his audience: "The FBI searched the home of Dashiell Hammett … looking for his comrades, the four escaped Red leaders. They went thataway."

In 1958, Hoover targeted Hammett for one of the FBI's early COINTELPRO harassment campaigns, designed to cause dissension within the Communist Party. First, agents included Hammett on a list of persons slated to receive phony articles on FBI target HOWARD FAST, later mailing Hammett Bureau-printed "Communist" leaflets praising the Russian execution of Hungarian protesters. Yet another COINTEPLPRO mailing bombarded Hammett with clippings from *Labor Action*, published by the Independent Socialist League.

Upon Hammett's death, in January 1961, Hoover aide CARTHA DELOACH circulated a memo to dozens of FBI-friendly journalists, urging them to protest the burial of a "Communist" at Arlington National Cemetery. As a parting shot, G-men fattened Hammett's 356-page dossier by inserting a copy of ELIZABETH DILLING'S book *The Red Network*, although Hammett is not mentioned in the text.

**HAMPTON, Fred** — An Illinois native, born in 1948, Fred Hampton was by all accounts a remarkable young man. At age 18 he organized and led a successful campaign to desegregate Chicago swimming pools under the auspices of the NATIONAL ASSOCIATION FOR THE ADVANCEMENT OF COLORED PEOPLE. A year later he was affiliated with the more militant BLACK PANTHER PARTY, marked by G-men as a dangerous radical. Chicago agent-in-charge MARLIN JOHNSON opened a FILE on Hampton in late

1967, which expanded to 12 volumes and some 4,000 pages over the next two years. In February 1968 Johnson requested WIRETAPS on Hampton's mother; three months later Hampton was listed in the Bureau's AGITATOR INDEX as a "key militant leader." By that time Hampton faced local charges of stealing ice cream bars valued at $71. He was convicted in that case, drawing a prison term of two-to-five years, but he was released in August 1969 on an appeal bond.

The FBI was not idle while Hampton fought the theft case in court. Between December 1968 and April 1969, members of the Bureau's illegal COINTELPRO team used anonymous letters to provoke a gang war between Hampton's Panthers and members of the BLACKSTONE RANGERS. WILLIAM O'NEAL, a Bureau INFORMANT and *agent provocateur*, was installed as security chief of the Illinois Panthers in February 1969, later serving as Hampton's personal bodyguard. G-men raided the Chicago Panther office on 4 June 1969, ransacking the building and arresting eight persons in an alleged search for federal fugitives (none of whom were found on the premises).

Soon after that raid, FBI leaders approached members of the CHICAGO POLICE DEPARTMENT, asking them to conduct additional Panther raids. A series of violent clashes ensued, leaving two policemen and two Panthers dead by the end of July, with nine persons jailed on various felony charges. Following the second police raid, on 30 July, "mysterious" fires broke out in the Panther office and caused extensive damage. A third raid, on 21 October 1969, left the remodeled office in a shambles once again. Throughout that series of attacks, authorities found nothing to support FBI claims that the Chicago Panthers had stockpiled illegal weapons.

On 9 November 1969 Chicago agents learned that Hampton was scheduled for promotion to serve as the Panther Party's national chief of staff if incumbent David Hilliard was imprisoned for threatening President RICHARD NIXON. Accordingly, G-men turned up the pressure on local police to destroy Hampton, a campaign that gathered steam after 13 November, when another shootout in Chicago killed two Panthers and two police officers. Eight days later, agents met with representatives of Illinois State's Attorney Edward Hanrahan, providing them with information collected by William O'Neal. The package included a detailed floor plan of Hampton's apartment, with various objects helpfully labeled — including "Fred's bed." That same day, 21 November 1969, the Chicago field office reported to FBI HEADQUARTERS that "[o]fficials of the Chicago police have advised that the department is currently planning a positive course of action relative to this information."

On the night of 3 December 1969 some unknown person sedated Fred Hampton with a dose of secobarbitol before he went to bed. Hampton was unconscious at 4:45 the next morning, when state and local police stormed the apartment. Panther Mark Clark was killed by the first police gunshot as officers burst through the door. Dying, he triggered the only shot fired from a Panther weapon that morning, a shotgun blast into the floor. Police swept through the apartment, firing an estimated 90 shots at unarmed targets. Fred Hampton died in his bed, shot twice in the head at close range with a pistol, execution-style. Five other

Panthers were wounded in the fusillade, and various tenants of the apartment were charged with "attempted murder."

In the wake of Hampton's death, one member of the raiding party (Sgt. Daniel Groth) told reporters, "Our men had no choice but to return fire" during the raid. Ballistic evidence soon gave the lie to that claim, while critics dubbed Hampton's killing an assassination. Agent M. WESLEY SWEARINGEN supported that claim, later testifying under oath that a member of the Bureau's Racial Squad told him, "We gave [police] a copy of the detailed floor plan ... so that they could raid the place and kill the whole lot."

Agent-in-charge Johnson was blasé in his public statements—"What they did with the information was none of our concern"—but he cabled Hoover on 11 December to boast that "The raid was based on information furnished by the informant. ... This information was not available from any other source and subsequently proved to be of tremendous value." He requested a $300 bonus payment for William O'Neal, which Hoover personally approved on 17 December 1969 "for uniquely valuable services which he has rendered over the past several months." (In all, O'Neal earned $30,000 from the FBI between 1969 and 1972.)

In order to preserve appearances, Agent Johnson requested a federal grand jury investigation on 13 December 1969, to determine whether police had violated anyone's civil rights during the Hampton raid. Attorney General JOHN MITCHELL assigned Assistant Attorney General Jerris Leonard to chair the hearings, which began on 21 December. Four months later, an FBI memo of 8 April 1970 disclosed that "AAG Jerris Leonard ... advised SAC Marlin Johnson in strictest confidence that no indictments of police officers are planned.... The above is based on an agreement whereby Hanrahan will dismiss the local indictments against the BPP members." The police, in return for absolution, agreed to keep silent regarding FBI involvement in the raid.

Members of the Clark and Hampton families were not satisfied with the grand jury's findings. In 1970 they filed a $47.7 million lawsuit against Hanrahan and others, charging conspiracy to violate the civil rights of Fred Hampton and Mark Clark. (A new grand jury indicted Hanrahan and 13 police officers for conspiracy in August 1971, but the charges were later dismissed.) Nearly a decade passed before evidence uncovered in that case revealed the Bureau's central role in Hampton's death. Attorneys for the plaintiffs persuaded ex-Agent Swearingen to testify, and the defendants finally settled with a payment of $1.85 million in November 1982. One attorney in the case described that settlement as "an admission of the conspiracy that existed between the FBI and Hanrahan's men to murder Fred Hampton."

**HANSSEN, Robert**—A Chicago native, born in 1945, Robert Hanssen was the only son of a brutal policeman who constantly humiliated him while hounding him to become a doctor. After graduating from Knox College, Hanssen enrolled at Northwestern University's dental school in 1966 and studied there for two years, then dropped out shortly after his marriage in August 1968. He ultimately earned a master's degree in business administration from Northwestern (1973) and became a certified public ac-

countant, then spent two years with the CHICAGO POLICE DEPARTMENT'S Internal Affairs division. Hanssen joined the FBI in January 1976, spending two years on white-collar crime investigations in Indiana, where his supervisors "thought Bob Hanssen walked on water."

Still he was dissatisfied, anxious for a foreign intelligence assignment to make use of the Russian he studied in college. Transferred to New York City in 1978, Hanssen organized a major sting operation to capture Soviet spies, but he was disappointed once again. As a colleague recalled, "He set up this squad ... and well over half the FBI guys called in from home. They didn't want to work on Sunday, so the Russians got away." Thereafter, Hanssen apparently resented the Bureau and decided to betray it for profit. In 1979 he accepted $20,000 from Russian military intelligence (GRU) to reveal various FBI secrets including the identity of Russian double-agent Dmitri Polyakov (executed in 1988 after he was betrayed a second time, by CIA traitor ALDRICH AMES). Hanssen's career as a spy was nearly ruined in 1980, when his wife caught him writing a letter to his Russian paymasters and he confessed his illicit activity. In lieu of surrendering to the Bureau, however, Hanssen consulted a Catholic priest who advised him to stop spying, seek counseling and give the Soviet money to charity.

Religious vows notwithstanding, Hanssen kept spying until 1981, when he was transferred to FBI HEADQUARTERS as a supervisory agent. Two years later he was transferred to the FBI's Soviet Analytical Unit in Washington, then back to New York City as a supervisor in 1985. Aware that G-men did not monitor mail sent to the homes of KGB officers stationed in the U.S., Hanssen wrote to agent Viktor Charkashin in October 1985 and offered to sell classified data for $100,000. His letter—signed "B"—proved his worth by naming three KGB agents secretly serving America. Two were subsequently executed; the third was sentenced to 15 years in a Russian labor camp.

Over the next 15 years Hanssen emerged as one of Russia's most valuable spies in the U.S. He betrayed entire ESPIONAGE networks, while evading detection by his fellow G-men. Returned to headquarters as an intelligence analyst in 1987, he burrowed deeper, using his spare time and advanced computer skills to expose high-level secrets of the FBI, the CENTRAL INTELLIGENCE AGENCY and the NATIONAL SECURITY AGENCY. Moscow was delighted and his coworkers were none the wiser. G-men had their first clear chance to capture Hanssen in 1990, when brother-in-law Mark Wauck, a Chicago FBI agent, grew suspicious of Hanssen's suspicious cash reserves. Wauck told his superiors that Hanssen kept unusual amounts of money at home and that he suspected Hanssen was spying for Russia. The Bureau did nothing and Hanssen continued his illegal operations for another decade. He earned a small fortune from the Soviets but wisely resisted the urge to indulge in extravagant spending. (One deviation from that cautious pattern was his expensive romance with a stripper, whom he once flew to Hong Kong for an inspection tour of the FBI LEGAL ATTACHÉ'S office.)

In the end, it was a Russian double-agent who betrayed Robert Hanssen. In the latter part of 2000 a KGB source supplied G-men with some of the material furnished by Hanssen since 1985. The source did not know Hanssen's name, but finger-prints were lifted from one of the plastic bags that contained certain documents. Thus identified, Hanssen was placed under surveillance (with his office bugged) from 12 December 2000 through 5 February 2001, agents noting the location of a "dead drop" where he left information for his Russian contacts. When Hanssen was arrested en route to make another delivery, on 18 February 2001, he asked the agents who surrounded him, "What took you so long?"

Hanssen confessed his crimes in custody and bargained with federal prosecutors to escape the death penalty. On 6 July 2001 he pled guilty to 13 counts of espionage; 10 months later, on 9 May 2002, he received a prison term of life without parole. Former FBI/CIA Director WILLIAM WEBSTER was appointed to investigate Hanssen's long career as a spy, producing a report highly critical of the Bureau's failures (including a lapse in reviewing its agents' financial records). A month before his final sentencing, it was reported that Hanssen had provided "valuable aid" in closing some of the Bureau's security loopholes against future spies.

**HARDING, Warren Gamaliel** — A political product of the corrupt "Ohio Gang," Warren Harding served as a state legislator (1899-1903), lieutenant governor (1904-05) and U.S. senator (1915-21) before his inauguration as president. Harding was elected on a promise to restore "normalcy" in America after the turmoil of WORLD WAR I and the PALMER RAIDS, but instead he brought new levels of corruption to the capital, revealed after his premature death in the TEAPOT DOME SCANDAL. (Harding's secretary of the interior, Bernard Fall, would be the first cabinet member convicted of crimes committed while in office.)

The Bureau of Investigation's growth stalled under Harding and new chief WILLIAM BURNS, with the agent force expanding from 346 to 401 while support staff was cut from 294 to 189. (The budget also decreased, from $2,342,751 in 1921 to $2,166,997 in 1923.) Many of the new agents were "dollar-a-year men," appointed to the BI by political cronies, anxious to fill their pockets with graft. Attorney General HARRY DAUGHERTY used the Bureau as a blunt instrument to punish striking railroad workers in 1922, and sent agents to raid the offices of his critics in Congress. PROHIBITION enforcement languished, while bootleg gangs took their first steps toward establishment of a national crime syndicate.

President Harding, meanwhile, amused himself with mistress Nan Britton (who bore his child out of wedlock in 1919) and his personal bootlegger. Several historians claim (and one reports as fact) that Harding joined the KU KLUX KLAN soon after his inauguration. The Klan's "Imperial Wizard" confirmed those reports, and while his word is naturally suspect, Klan members nationwide held mourning ceremonies in August 1923, after Harding died of a stroke while traveling. For years afterward, Ohio Klan leaders posted an honor guard at his gravesite.

**HARDY, Robert W.** — On 22 August 1971 FBI Director J. EDGAR HOOVER joined Attorney General JOHN MITCHELL to announce the arrest of 20 anti-VIETNAM WAR activists in or near the Camden, New Jersey federal building. Five days later Mitchell announced the indictment of 28 defendants on charges of destroying government property, interfering with the Selective Service system, and conspiracy to destroy records from the Camden draft board, the FBI's RESIDENT AGENCY and the Army Intelligence office. The defendants (including four Catholic priests and a Lutheran minister) called themselves "America's conscience"; critics and defenders alike dubbed them the "Camden 28."

At trial, the government's key witness was Robert Hardy, an FBI INFORMANT who approached the Bureau in June 1971 with word that a group of "friends" planned to burglarize the Camden draft board. G-men later claimed that they employed Hardy in hopes of capturing the persons who had raided an FBI office at MEDIA, PENNSYLVANIA three months earlier, removing and publicizing documents that exposed the Bureau's illegal COINTELPRO operations, but in fact Hardy's activities went far beyond providing inside information on a criminal conspiracy. At trial, the Camden defendants testified that they had abandoned their burglary plan as hopeless before Hardy joined the group and resurrected the idea. Hardy himself, under oath, admitted proposing a break-in, offering his "expertise at breaking and entering," and providing "90 percent" of the tools used to invade the federal building. Defense attorneys urged the jury to acquit all 28 defendants if the FBI had gone to "intolerable lengths" that were "offensive to the basic standards of decency and shocking to the universal sense of justice." After three days of deliberation, the panel acquitted all 28 defendants on all charges.

**HARLOW, Gary** — Once employed as an instructor at the FBI ACADEMY, Agent Gary Harlow left that post in early 1996 to process top-secret White House clearances for President WILLIAM CLINTON. One night that summer, Harlow assaulted his wife and broke her nose during a domestic quarrel. While under treatment at the hospital, Mrs. Harlow described her husband's private arsenal to physicians and police were notified in turn. Detectives visited the Harlow home and found a cache of hardware that included machine guns, hand grenades, plastic explosives, night-vision gear and over 100,000 rounds of ammunition — all clearly marked "Property of the FBI." Agent Harlow was absent at the time, but officers soon located and arrested him. In his car, they found seven more machine guns. At trial Harlow pled guilty to theft of government property and received a one-year prison sentence. He was dismissed from the Bureau upon conviction, after he confessed to the additional offense of faking White House clearances.

**HART, Moss** — A native of New York City, born 24 October 1904, Hart won the Pulitzer Prize for his drama *You Can't Take It with You* in 1937. He first attracted FBI attention the following year, when his name appeared on a letterhead of the American Committee for Anti-Nazi Literature. Other entries in his file note Hart's support for the National Council of American-Soviet Friendship during WORLD WAR II, his sponsorship of the American Committee for Spanish Freedom (opposing fascist dictator Francisco Franco), and his attendance at a luncheon of the Joint Anti-Fascist Refugee Committee. In 1951 Hart angered Bureau leaders by signing an open letter calling for abolition of the

HOUSE COMMITTEE ON UN-AMERICAN ACTIVITIES. Seven years later, the U.S. Information Agency asked J. EDGAR HOOVER whether Hart's work was suitable for overseas distribution, but the response was not preserved. Hart died in Palm Springs, California on 20 December 1961, but the FBI kept his file open for another seven years, concerned in 1968 that a White House performance of excerpts from *Camelot* and *My Fair Lady* (both directed by Hart) might somehow "embarrass" President LYNDON JOHNSON.

**HATCH Act**—Enacted by Congress in 1939, the Hatch Act barred from federal employment any member of an organization or political party advocating violent overthrow of the U.S. government, thereby justifying various FBI and congressional "loyalty" investigations. The law also restricted political activities by employees of the federal government or the District of Columbia, but those restrictions were somewhat relaxed by amendments enacted in 1993. Details of the law's provisions may be found on the Internet at http://www.fmcs.gov/agency/ogc/federal_hatch_act.htm

**HATE Crimes**—The federal Hate Crimes Statistics Act of 1990 defines these offenses (also termed "bias crimes") as "crimes that manifest evidence of prejudice based on race, religion, sexual orientation, or ethnicity, including where appropriate the crimes of murder, non-negligent manslaughter, forcible rape, aggravated assault, simple assault, intimidation, arson, and destruction, damage or vandalism of property." While various federal statutes impose criminal penalties for interference with free exercise of certain CIVIL RIGHTS, there is presently (as of April 2003) no federal "hate crimes" legislation. Nationwide, 24 states and the District of Columbia have comprehensive hate crimes statutes; 20 more have laws excluding sexual orientation as a factor; while 7 states (Arkansas, Hawaii, Indiana, Kansas, New Mexico, South Carolina and Wyoming) have no legislation in place.

The FBI has been empowered from its creation in 1908 to enforce U.S. civil rights laws, but its zeal in pursuing such cases traditionally depended on attitudes held by the president, the attorney general, and the FBI's director of the moment. J. EDGAR HOOVER made no secret of his disdain for civil rights cases, and during his long tenure as director (1948-72) they were typically ignored unless pressure from superiors forced Hoover's hand.

The Hate Crimes Statistics Act carries no enforcement provisions, but merely requires the FBI to collect and tabulate statistics voluntarily submitted by other law enforcement agencies around the U.S. Upon signing the act in April 1990, President GEORGE H.W. BUSH called it a "significant step to help guarantee civil rights for every American. The faster we find out about these hideous crimes, the faster we can track down the bigots who commit them." Seven years later, addressing a White House Conference on Hate Crimes, President WILLIAM CLINTON echoed that theme: "If a crime is unreported, that gives people an excuse to ignore it."

How well has the statute worked? A detailed study by the Southern Poverty Law Center (SPLC) reveals that while voluntary reports of hate crimes increased from 2,215 to 12,122 between 1991 and 1999, the system remains "seriously flawed." Donald Green, a hate crimes expert at Yale University, went further, telling the SPLC that "the overall numbers are worthless." Among the many problems found with published FBI hate crime statistics, the following stand out:

• Hawaii, with no hate crimes legislation of its own, refuses to participate in the FBI program on grounds that the federal definition of hate crimes is "very broad and subjective."

• Alabama, long a hotbed of the KU KLUX KLAN and similar hate groups, reported "zero" hate crimes statewide for years on end, and has submitted no reports at all for "five or six years."

• In Kansas, only the Wichita Police Department reports hate crimes, and its clerks lag several years behind schedule. As of September 2001, they had not tabulated hate crimes for the years 1999 or 2000.

• In 1999, 83 percent of all reporting jurisdictions claimed "zero" hate crimes for the year. SPLC investigators found that officials in seven states arbitrarily reported "zero" hate crimes to the FBI on behalf of agencies that filed no report for themselves.

• A report from the JUSTICE DEPARTMENT, released in September 2000, found that nearly 6,000 U.S. law enforcement agencies had falsely reported "zero" hate crimes, when one or more offenses within their jurisdiction met the federal definition.

The FBI, meanwhile, makes its share of mistakes even when hate crimes are reported from the hinterlands. Officials in Washington state provided the SPLC with copies of their hate crimes reports for 1999, and comparison with the FBI's published statistics revealed some startling discrepancies: 16 jurisdictions reporting hate crimes were entirely omitted from the FBI's report, while three others showed figures at variance with the original reports.

Based on such negligent errors or willful omissions, the SPLC's auditors concluded that American hate crimes are presently underreported by a factor of some 625 percent—i.e., an estimated 50,000 hate crimes occurring for each 8,000 recorded by the FBI. A case in point was the November 1999 murder of a black teenager in Elkhart, Indiana, gunned down by a prospective member of the Aryan Brotherhood as part of an initiation rite. Police reported the murder as a hate crime, but they missed the FBI's filing deadline for 1999, and Bureau bookkeepers refused to include the incident in their tabulations for 2000, effectively wiping it out of the record.

**HEATTER, Gabriel**—A native of New York City, born 17 September 1890, Gabriel Heatter began his media career in print journalism and graduated to radio in the 1930s. He earned a special note of thanks from J. EDGAR HOOVER in December 1942, for an unsolicited on-air declaration that the FBI director was doing "a marvelous job" and that America owed Hoover "a debt that could not be repaid." Somehow forgotten over the next decade, Heatter was called to Hoover's attention once more by CLYDE TOLSON, in a 1953 memo urging that Heatter "be kept in mind as a special friend who can be helpful." Hoover replied:

"Yes. I am at a loss as to how we have overlooked him all this time." Thereafter, Heatter was graced with inside "highlights" of various FBI cases, once informing a field agent that he "wanted to be sure that the Director knows that he stands ready to do anything for the FBI at any time." The memo informed Hoover that Heatter had "emphasized *anything*." Such media contacts were instrumental in maintaining Hoover's public image throughout the 48 years of his reign as director.

**HECHT, Ben** — The son of Russian Jewish immigrants, born in New York City, Ben Hecht was the author of 35 books and 70 screenplays, perhaps best known for his script *The Front Page*. FBI agents opened a file on Hecht in 1941, after an unnamed INFORMANT reported that Hecht was "either a Communist or a fellow traveler." Four years later, G-men reviewed his screenplay *Notorious*, complaining that an FBI agent portrayed by Cary Grant drank excessively and fell in love with a woman (Ingrid Bergman) assigned to penetrate a Nazi cell in Brazil. (In fact, Grant's character was simply "a cop," and the film included no reference to the FBI.) By 1947, when Hecht became an outspoken champion of Israel, FBI memos labeled him a "dissident." One news clipping included in his file was headlined "U.S. Jews repudiate Hecht," allegedly for his "endorsement" of Irgun "terrorists" led by Menachem Begin. Hecht approached the Bureau twice in 1953, with complaints of threatening phone calls, but G-men referred him to New York police, with the advice that his dilemma involved "no violation of federal law." J. EDGAR HOOVER apparently lost interest in Hecht at that point, and his 24-page file was closed eight years before Hecht's death, in 1961.

**HELD, Richard G.** — Agent Richard G. Held was stationed in Alabama during May 1961, when members of the KU KLUX KLAN collaborated with racist police to attack CIVIL RIGHTS workers involved in integrated "FREEDOM RIDES." Held's personal role in those events is unknown today, but FBI documents released under the FREEDOM OF INFORMATION act confirm that Bureau agents kept Klan-affiliated policemen informed of the demonstrators' itinerary, thus facilitating attacks on their buses at Anniston, Birmingham and Montgomery. G-men observed and filmed the attacks but did not intervene, even when JUSTICE DEPARTMENT advisor JOHN SEIGENTHALER was beaten unconscious by Klansmen.

Held became agent-in-charge of the Minneapolis field office in October 1962. Eight years later, he replaced MARLIN JOHNSON as agent-in-charge of the Chicago field office, in the midst of a cover-up surrounding FBI involvement in the death of FRED HAMPTON, local leader of the BLACK PANTHER PARTY. When Hampton's mother sued Chicago police for killing her son while he slept, Held was called as a witness to explain the Bureau's role in that December 1969 event. Held testified that all relevant FBI documents had been surrendered to the court, whereupon Mrs. Hampton's attorneys produced several memos obtained from other sources, which the Bureau had not released. The threat of perjury charges prompted Held to "reconsider" his position, afterward producing a cache of 100,000 pages previously concealed by his agents. FBI HEADQUARTERS instituted no disciplinary ac-

tion for Held's false testimony under oath, and he remained in command of the Chicago office for six more years.

Much of that time saw him active outside Illinois, after Director CLARENCE KELLEY sent Held to supervise Bureau campaigns against the AMERICAN INDIAN MOVEMENT (AIM) at South Dakota's PINE RIDGE RESERVATION. Held was present as an "observer-consultant" during the 1973 WOUNDED KNEE SIEGE, where he increased FBI support for vigilante GUARDIANS OF THE OGLALA NATION (GOON) squads accused of harassing, assaulting and murdering AIM supporters. On 24 April 1974, after another violent incident on the Pine Ridge Reservation, Held submitted a paper titled "The Use of Special Agents of the FBI in a Paramilitary Law Enforcement Operation in the Indian Country." Held's report lamented that G-men assigned to Pine Ridge had been ordered "to aim to wound rather than kill," further complaining that members of the U.S. MARSHALS SERVICE and other agencies present did not "submit to FBI authority." In future confrontations, Held declared, "the FBI will insist on taking charge from the outset and will not countenance any interference on an operational basis with respect to our actions."

Fourteen months after submitting that paper, Held was back at Pine Ridge (with son RICHARD WALLACE HELD), commanding the investigation of a shootout that left two G-men dead. At the time, Bureau documents identified Held as both the agent-in-charge of Chicago and chief of the Bureau's Internal Security Section, responsible for ongoing "counterintelligence" campaigns in the mold of Director J. EDGAR HOOVER'S illegal COINTELPRO operations. Investigation of the Pine Ridge killings, designated the RESMURS case in Bureau jargon, ultimately led to acquittal of two defendants on a self-defense plea, while AIM activist LEONARD PELTIER was confined to prison for life. Agent Held left Pine Ridge on 16 October 1975, but Bureau documents prove that he was still involved in the case a year later. In June 1976 he penned another position paper, this one titled "Predication of Investigation of Members and Supporters of AIM," which read in part—

> The government's right to continue full investigation of AIM and certain affiliated organizations may create relevant danger to a few citizen's [*sic*] privacy and free expression, but this danger must be weighed against society's right to protect itself against current domestic threats.

A few weeks later, with Held's role in the Hampton whitewash under state and federal investigation, Director Kelley promoted Held to the post of associate director, in effect making him the second most powerful FBI official. Held continued his involvement in the RESMURS case from that position and escaped punishment when his Chicago agents were censured by the 7th Circuit Court of Appeals for obstructing the judicial process and other misconduct in the Hampton case.

**HELD, Richard Wallace** — The son of FBI Associate Director RICHARD G. HELD, Richard W. Held followed in his father's footsteps as a leader of the Bureau's illegal COINTELPRO operations under Director J. EDGAR HOOVER and pursued a similar course of action for 20 years beyond Hoover's death, long after the FBI reportedly abandoned such tactics.

Held's first known involvement in illicit harassment campaigns occurred in the late 1960s, when he served as chief COINTELPRO agent for the Los Angeles field office. There, Held's primary target was the BLACK PANTHER PARTY, "neutralized" by such tactics as the 1972 FRAME-UP of party member ELMER PRATT for a murder he did not commit. (Pratt spent most of 27 years in prison on that charge. During a 1985 habeas corpus hearing, Held repeatedly testified that he "could not recall" various FBI documents related to the case, including some he personally dictated.) Another victim of the L.A. Bureau in that era was actress JEAN SEBERG, hounded to suicide by FBI harassment over her alleged love affair with a Black Panther. In a similar vein, Held launched a similar plot to cause actress Jane Fonda "embarrassment and detract from her status with the general public" by leaking derogatory information to Hollywood gossip columnists.

It was a short drive from Los Angeles to San Diego, where Agent Held was reportedly instrumental in helping local G-men establish the SECRET ARMY ORGANIZATION, a far-right TERRORIST group responsible for several bombings and the attempted murder of a liberal college professor. During the trial of three SAO members for those crimes, testimony from an FBI INFORMANT in the ranks revealed that the Bureau had supplied nearly all of the hit squad's money, firearms and explosives, hiding a rifle used in the murder attempt from local police.

Between 1973 and 1976, Held was active (with his father) against members of the AMERICAN INDIAN MOVEMENT (AIM) at South Dakota's PINE RIDGE RESERVATION. In that campaign, FBI agents and collaborating vigilantes from the GUARDIANS OF THE OGLALA NATION (GOON) killed several AIM members. (GOON members accused of 300 assaults and 64 homicides on federal land were never prosecuted, since the FBI claimed "insufficient manpower" to investigate the charges.) Two FBI agents were also killed at Pine Ridge, in June 1975; AIM activist LEONARD PELTIER was convicted of their murders under circumstances strongly reminiscent of the Pratt case, in Los Angeles.

In 1978, Held was transferred to Puerto Rico as special agent in charge of the San Juan field office. His arrival in San Juan corresponded with an escalation of COINTELPRO-style attacks on various PUERTO RICAN NATIONALIST groups and individuals, including widespread illegal WIRETAPPING later admitted by agents under oath. The home of independence spokesman Juan Mari-Bras was firebombed in 1978; six years later, a former secretary for the San Juan field office testified under oath that FBI agents were responsible for the crime. Held's Puerto Rican tenure climaxed on 30 August 1985, with sweeping raids conducted by some 300 G-men, invading homes, seizing personal property and jailing scores of activists on "John Doe" warrants allegedly related to a 1983 robbery in Connecticut. When Governor Rafael Hernández objected to the paramilitary action, Held's office dismissed the complaint as "lamentable."

From San Juan, Held was next transferred to San Francisco, again serving as special agent in charge. More controversy ensued in 1988, when Held ordered agents to stop using Dr. James Cullen for their yearly physical examinations. Cullen had been diagnosed HIV-positive and subsequently died of AIDS-related illness. His estate filed suit against the Bureau, charging dis-

crimination, and the U.S. Court of Appeals agreed in July 1995, ruling that Held's office had wrongfully terminated dealings with Dr. Cullen "solely because of his handicap." The panel further held that "If the FBI had been legitimately concerned about the risk of transmission, it would have inquired as to the character and effectiveness of the infection-control procedures [at Cullen's office], as it was required to do by the Rehabilitation Act. It made no attempt to do so."

An even more troubling case involved the May 1990 car BOMBING that nearly killed JUDI BARI and Daryl Cherney, activists of the EARTH FIRST! environmentalist organization. Held's G-men and Oakland police charged Bari and Cherney with building the bomb themselves, branding them both "members of a violent TERRORIST group involved in the manufacture and placing of explosive devices." That FRAME-UP attempt was dismantled in court, Bari and Cherney surviving both their wounds and wrongful prosecution to sue the FBI and Oakland Police Department. Held, named as a defendant, retired from the Bureau on 1 August 1993. In a performance strongly reminiscent of the Pratt case, Held "testified throughout his deposition that he did not remember the details of Plaintiffs' case, and that he did not keep abreast of all of the cases in the San Francisco office." Furthermore, Held maintained under oath that he "did not recall any specific conversations" with his various agents concerning the high-profile case. A federal judge released Held from the lawsuit in October 1997, curiously ruling that despite his appointment as special agent *in charge*, "there is no evidence that … Held had any duty to supervise the daytoday [*sic*] activities in any given investigations." Four lesser agents ultimately lost the lawsuit, ordered with their codefendants from Oakland P.D. to pay Bari and Cherney $4.4 million in damages.

**HELLMAN, Lillian** —A New Orleans native, born in 1905 and recognized in life as one of America's premier playwrights, Lillian Hellman also drew fire for her outspoken advocacy of leftist causes. From support for Spanish Loyalists in that nations civil war to criticism of America's military action in Vietnam 30 years later, Hellman endured a half-century of investigation and harassment by the FBI for her political beliefs.

The pursuit began in 1933, when G-men noted Hellman's membership in a New York chapter of the JOHN REED Club. Four years later, she was named with ERNEST HEMINGWAY and others as a leader of the American Committee to Aid Spanish Democracy. In 1938 Hellman spoke at a rally honoring veterans of the ABRAHAM LINCOLN BRIGADE, and she also signed a petition asking President FRANKLIN ROOSEVELT to ban import of goods from Nazi Germany. Hellman admittedly joined the COMMUNIST PARTY in 1938, resigning two years later, around the same time a nameless "reliable source" told G-men that the party had assigned Hellman the task of "smearing the FBI in connection with her work on the newspaper *PM*." A 1941 FBI memo continues that theme, branding her "an outright Communist." (The Bureau also noted her membership in the "subversive" League of Women Shoppers.) Another 1941 memo archly observed that Hellman's play *Watch on the Rhine* seemed to have "great social significance" and had received an "extremely favorable" review in the *Daily Worker*.

In 1942, still maintaining her interest in the Spanish Loyalist cause, Hellman endorsed the Joint Anti-Fascist Refugee Committee to help exiled veterans. A snide FBI memo from the period notes her involvement in the "furious fight against the 'fascists' (meaning anyone who objected to Communist domination)." (In fact, the regime of Gen. Francisco Franco *was* openly fascistic, publicly supported by ADOLF HITLER'S Nazi Germany and Benito Mussolini's Italian fascists.) Another telling observation from the war years noted Hellman's correspondence and visits with longtime paramour DASHIELL HAMMETT. In 1944 J. EDGAR HOOVER ordered the New York field office to photograph Hellman and "if possible to do so in a discreet manner, attempt to obtain a handwriting sample from subject."

Hoover demanded a new report on Hellman in 1949, in light of "the tense international situation," and surveillance was mounted on her New York home. A 1950 memo noted Hellman's membership in the AUTHORS LEAGUE OF AMERICA and her spirited defense of blacklisted writers. Another black mark was added to her record in 1952, when she refused to name "fellow communists" for the HOUSE COMMITTEE ON UN-AMERICAN ACTIVITIES. Some lessening of Hellman's "danger" was apparently perceived in 1955, when the New York field office requested her removal from the top-secret SECURITY INDEX. Still, State Department spies kept Hoover informed of Hellman's movements when she went abroad in 1963 and 1966, while Postmaster Walter Stone helped G-men monitor her mail on Martha's Vineyard.

As late as 1970, an FBI report prepared "in response to Director's request" detailed Hellman's "support of New Left and antiwar groups," and Hoover thanked WILLIAM F. BUCKLEY the following year, for a newspaper column praising the FBI and attacking Hellman's Committee for Public Justice as "a Communist-front organization." At her death in June 1984, Hellman's FBI file included 603 pages, half of them heavily censored prior to release under the FREEDOM OF INFORMATION ACT, with 37 pages withheld altogether.

**HEMINGWAY, Ernest Miller** — Born at Oak Park, Illinois on 21 July 1899, Ernest Hemingway is frequently described as America's foremost novelist of the twentieth century. A combat veteran of WORLD WAR I who spent the early 1920s in Paris, he was called to the FBI's attention in 1935 by an unnamed INFORMANT who inaccurately branded Hemingway "a specialty writer" for the *Daily Worker* and *New Masses*. In fact, Hemingway never joined the COMMUNIST PARTY, but such fine distinctions were lost on J. EDGAR HOOVER when Hemingway served as a correspondent in the Spanish Civil War and returned a bitter enemy of fascism. In 1937, Hemingway joined LILLIAN HELLMAN and other celebrity authors in the North American Committee to Aid Spanish Democracy, and Hoover was further distressed by a 1938 memo advising that Hemingway was "turning away from individualism."

America's entry into WORLD WAR II galvanized Hemingway, then a resident of Cuba. A 1942 report in Hemingway's FBI file identifies him as a spy for the U.S. embassy in Cuba, but Hemingway took the game further that October, when he organized a private spy network which he dubbed "The Crook Factory," field-

ding 26 full- or part-time agents from his home. Hemingway's targets were Nazi agents in Cuba, and he also used his yacht *Pilar* on occasion to hunt for German submarines. At one point, Hemingway rejected a $150,000 Hollywood offer because he considered his amateur spy work to be "of the greatest importance." A U.S. attaché warned Hoover that Hemingway's activities would be "very embarrassing unless something is done to put a stop to them," and Hoover aide Edward Tamm recommended "exposing Hemingway for the phoney [*sic*] that he is," but Hoover demurred, noting that "Hemingway's organization was disbanded and its work terminated as of April 1, 1943."

On balance, Hoover's evident dislike for Hemingway apparently had less to do with politics than with Hemingway's outspoken criticism of the FBI. On various occasions, Hemingway "severely criticized the Bureau," dubbing it "the Gestapo," referring to its activities as "dangerous" and "anti-liberal." Reports on Hemingway's political allegiance are confused and contradictory: memos from 1941 proclaim that Hemingway was "on the outs with the Communists" and had "broken all ties" with the party, while other memos found him in league with "outright communist" Lillian Hellman. In 1959, reports declared that Hemingway had "kissed the Cuban flag" and "announced his support for Fidel Castro."

Hemingway spent his last years convinced (and rightly so) that he was under FBI surveillance, and while close friends regarded such claims as evidence of Hemingway "losing touch with reality," biographer Jeffrey Meyers cited Hemingway's FBI heavily-censored FBI file as proof "that even paranoids have enemies." In 1961 Hemingway entered the Mayo Clinic for a series of electro-shock treatments to cure his suicidal depression, but the treatments may have made his condition worse. Soon after returning to his rural home in Idaho, Hemingway committed suicide on 2 July 1961. Author Dan Simmons, in his novel *The Crook Factory* (1999), suggests that relentless FBI surveillance contributed to Hemingway's death. J. Edgar Hoover, for his part, provided an almost poignant obituary: "Knowing Hemingway as I did, I doubt he had any Communist leanings. He was a rough, tough guy and always for the underdog." Less kind was the final entry in Hemingway's file, a column by WESTBROOK PEGLER that branded Hemingway "one of the worst writers in the English language during his time."

**HERBST, Josephine** — A native of Sioux City, Iowa, born in 1897, novelist Josephine Herbst was initially indexed by the FBI in 1924, with the observation that she had written an article for H.L. MENCKEN'S *American Mercury*. Six years later, Bureau watchdogs reported that Herbst had signed a "Red Scare Protest" and "sent large brown envelopes to the *New Masses* and *Daily Worker* Communistic papers." Furthermore, G-men reported, she "belongs to the Leftist American writing set who resided in France in the 1920s" and "later married John Herrmann, reported a Communist in 1926." Sparing no details, the report observed that Herbst "had an unhappy married life" with Herrmann, who "left her at a time when her writing efforts were not going well with the public." Successive FBI reports brand her a "Communist sympathizer," note that in 1937 she "spent three weeks behind the lines in Spain," and record a nameless INFORMANT's impression of Herbst as "a great follower of Stalin." Mention of her name in ELIZABETH DILLING'S book *The Red Network* was also deemed significant.

In 1941 Herbst went to work on the German desk of the Office of the Coordinator of Information (OCI), later renamed the OFFICE OF STRATEGIC SERVICES. She was dismissed on 21 May 1942, one day after director WILLIAM DONOVAN informed J. EDGAR HOOVER that Herbst had been "giving us concern for sometime." The prime source of "concern" was apparently an FBI interview with novelist KATHERINE PORTER—"Applicant's friend" in Bureau parlance—who denounced Herbst as COMMUNIST PARTY member who sent secret messages to Moscow on behalf of her Red masters. Furthermore, Porter noted, Herbst "has a violent temper, a revolutionist attitude, and has caused trouble whenever the opportunity presented itself," while displaying "the utmost contempt for the American form of government." ELEANOR ROOSEVELT personally questioned Herbst's dismissal, but the First Lady was seemingly satisfied by a letter from Hoover containing "the real facts of the case."

Six years after her dismissal from the OCI, Herbst was named in congressional testimony as an acquaintance of alleged spy ALGER HISS. G-men interviewed Herbst in February 1949 and recorded her denial of knowing Hiss or being present on any occasion when ex-Red Whittaker Chambers photographed classified documents. Interviewed again in November 1949, Herbst reportedly "admitted that between 1932 and 1934 she had been extremely close to the Communist movement," regarding it as a "fashionable thing" to do. G-men added Herbst to their Communist Index in 1951 and considered deporting her two years later, after professional witness ELIZABETH BENTLEY named Herbst as a Soviet spy, but no such option was available for native-born Americans and Herbst was never charged with any crime. She died in 1969.

**HERRICK, Robert**—Born in 1868, novelist and teacher Robert Herrick was praised by critic Alfred Kazin as "one of the most distinguished moral intelligences in the early history of twentieth-century realism." That endorsement would not spare him from FBI scrutiny, however, when G-men noted his membership in the "subversive" AUTHORS LEAGUE OF AMERICA. Herrick's file is brief, a mere 11 pages, but researcher Natalie Robins discovered in 1991—a full 53 years after Herrick's death—seven of those pages were still deemed too "sensitive" for release under the FREEDOM OF INFORMATION ACT. The mystery remains unsolved.

**HERSEY, John Richard**—The son of U.S. missionaries to China, born at Tientsin in 1914, Hersey distinguished himself as both a journalist and novelist. His novel *A Bell for Adano* won the Pulitzer Prize in 1945, and *Hiroshima* (1946) is considered a classic of wartime reportage. Hersey apparently came to the FBI's attention in 1949, when Whittaker Chambers, "a self-confessed former Soviet espionage agent and former senior editor of *Time* magazine, advised ... that John Hersey was chief of the Moscow Bureau of *Time* magazine in the early 1940s and that the information he supplied to *Time* was obviously and quite openly quite favorable to the Union of Soviet Socialist Republics." From there, G-men noted Hersey's membership in (and one-time presidency of) the AUTHORS LEAGUE OF AMERICA. In 1965, when agents infiltrated a University of Michigan conference on the VIETNAM WAR, they found Hersey among the attendees. Three years later, his report on Detroit police murders of innocent blacks in *The Algiers Motel Incident* confirmed J. EDGAR HOOVER'S opinion of Hersey's "subversive" tendencies. Hersey died on 24 March 1993, still ranked among America's most respected authors.

**HICKS, Granville**—A native of Exeter, New Hampshire, born in 1901, novelist and critic Granville Hicks was first indexed by the Bureau in 1926, soon after his graduation from Harvard. G-men noted his speech on war profiteering before a group of Youth for Training in Peace Leadership, deemed by the watchers "a mixture of COMMUNIST PARTY members and intellectual sympathizers." Agents ignored Hicks for the next eight years, until Dilling named him as a party member in *The Red Network*. In 1935, Bureau watchers monitored his speech on Marxism to the Congress of American Revolutionary Writers, and their suspicions were confirmed a year later, when Hicks published a book on JOHN REED. In 1937 agents clipped an article from *Science and Society* that identified Hicks as a "Communist author."

The change for Hicks began in 1939, when Bureau notes identified him as "a self-admitted former [party] member." Collaborating with the FBI thereafter, Hicks lamented that "the Communism to which I was devoted was not the same as the Communism I now hate." In 1953 he told the HOUSE COMMITTEE ON UN-AMERICAN ACTIVITIES that "the Communist Party in the United States was wholly under the domination of the Soviet Union" and that "every member ... is an actual or potential agent of the Soviet Union." J. EDGAR HOOVER appreciated those remarks so much that in October 1954 he consulted Hicks for advice on a pending Bureau efforts to infiltrate the Communist Party. A summary of that interview notes that "In general, Hicks felt that the biggest problem the Agent would have with the Party member would be to convince the Communist that the Agent is not the 'Fascist' Agent that the Party had led the individual to believe. The Agent should attempt to impress on the Communist a feeling of friendliness and sympathy." Hicks died in 1982, his Red days long forgotten and his collaboration with the Bureau yet to be revealed under the FREEDOM OF INFORMATION ACT.

**HILL, James**—A former security analyst for the Bureau's Las Vegas, Nevada field office, James Hill settled in New York following retirement and became a private investigator. On 14 June 2002 he was arrested for involvement in a scheme to sell secret FBI information to members of ORGANIZED CRIME. Hill, age 51, was taken into custody at Oyster Bay, New York after agents caught him faxing information to MICHAEL LEVIN, a G-man in Las Vegas. As charged in their indictments, Hill had provided Levin with hundreds of documents since November 1999, which Levin then sold to mobsters and other subjects of ongoing FBI investigations. Hill pled guilty to conspiracy, obstruction of justice and other charges on 3 September 2002. He faced a maximum of seven years in prison as a result of the plea bargain.

**"HIRED Guns"**—When Congress authorized FBI agents to carry firearms in spring of 1934, J. EDGAR HOOVER found himself confronted with a problem. Many G-men had been illegally armed for decades, and one clumsy agent was responsible for most of the fatalities in the 1933 KANSAS CITY MASSACRE, but pursuit of various "public enemies" under new statutes making BANK ROBBERY and KIDNAPPING federal offenses left no time for training to achieve proficiency with weapons. Accordingly, Hoover recruited a small group of veteran lawmen, known more for their marksmanship than any formal education. Few of those he picked had ever been to college, and none met Hoover's alleged "mandatory" standard of degrees in accounting or law. Assigned to special "flying squads" that operated from FBI headquarters in Washington, these agents soon became known in the Bureau as Hoover's "hired guns."

Drawn chiefly from the Texas and Oklahoma, where lawmen shot first and asked questions later, the members of Hoover's elite team stood out in their Stetsons, cowboy boots and diamond pinky rings, packing personal weapons of choice in defiance of FBI standards. One of the crew, Charles Batsell Winstead, had joined the Bureau in 1926, after a brief stint in business school and service as a deputy sheriff around Sherman, Texas; he was assigned to the Oklahoma City field office when Hoover called him back to Washington. Sharpshooter John Keith had also joined the Bureau in the 1920s, but he never lost his fondness for a matched pair of Colt .45 revolvers. Former Texas Rangers Gus ("Buster") Jones and James ("Doc") White (deaf in one ear from a Texas gambler's ambush) joined the new special unit, as did one-time Dallas chief of detectives Bob Jones and William L. Buchanan, formerly a captain of detectives with the Waco police department. Oklahoma City contributed Chief of Detectives Clarence Hurt, with officers C.G. ("Jerry") Campbell and D.A. ("Jelly") Bryce (slayer of three gunmen in 1927, his first year on the force). Prior to joining the Bureau, Hurt and Bryce participated in the December 1933 shootout that killed "Tri-State Terror" Wilbur Underhill (briefly a suspect in the Kansas City massacre).

Once organized, Hoover's "hired guns" had a dramatic impact on the Bureau's Depression-era "crime war." Jones, White and Winstead worked together on the CHARLES URSCHEL kidnapping case, culminating in the arrest of GEORGE ("MACHINE GUN") KELLY. Jones also played a leading role in the Kansas City massacre investigation, involving a 60-year cover-up of embarrassing ballistic evidence and the probable framing of bandit CHARLES ("PRETTY BOY") FLOYD as one of the killers. Charles Winstead pursued Texas outlaw CLYDE BARROW through 1933 and early 1934; in May 1934 he was reassigned to the Chicago field office with Hurt and Campbell, to track JOHN DILLINGER. Some accounts credit Winstead with personally killing Dillinger on 22 July 1934, while other reports attribute the fatal shot to Agent SAMUEL COWLEY or Detective MARTIN ZARKOVICH. "Doc" White shot and killed bank robber Russell Gibson, a member of the BARKER-KARPIS GANG, IN January 1935. One week later, G-men Winstead and Hurt were present at the Florida shootout that claimed "Ma" Barker and son Fred. (Again, Winstead claimed to have killed "Ma" himself, though many reports call her death

from a single close-range gunshot a suicide.) On 1 May 1936, Winstead and Hurt were again on the scene in New Orleans, facilitating Hoover's "personal" arrest of fugitive Alvin Karpis.

There was little call for quick-trigger FBI "flying squads" after 1936, and Hoover's "hired guns" were thereafter dispersed. John Keith was the first to go, after brief reassignment to the FBI ACADEMY as a firearms instructor, where he was known as much for heavy drinking as for marksmanship. Resigning in 1936 to become a security consultant at Philco, Keith was diagnosed with terminal cancer two years later and shot himself with a souvenir pistol presented to him on retirement from the FBI.

Charles Winstead, notoriously insubordinate, was subjected to rapid-fire transfers, serving short terms in the Birmingham, Dallas, El Paso, Jacksonville, Miami and Orlando field offices. He was exiled to Albuquerque by 1942, the only agent in New Mexico, when he offended a female reporter by remarking that her opinions on Russia were "not worth doodleyshit." Hoover demanded an apology, but Winstead's response—"Go to hell!"—was accompanied by a resignation, instead. Joining the U.S. Army as a captain in Military Intelligence, Winstead directed security for the Manhattan Project at Los Alamos, New Mexico. His request for reinstatement with the Bureau after WORLD WAR II was denied, and Winstead remained in New Mexico, working as a liquor inspector, horse rancher and part-time sheriff's deputy. Winstead died of cancer at the Albuquerque Veteran's Hospital, in August 1973.

Clarence Hurt retired from the FBI in 1955 and became a rancher in his native Oklahoma. He served four years as Pittsburg County's sheriff (1959-62), and served as a consultant on the movie *Dillinger* in 1973. He died of cancer in McAlester, Oklahoma, on 5 November 1975. During Hurt's funeral service, burglars ransacked his home, prompting newspapers to remark that the underworld had finally gotten its revenge.

D.A. Bryce stayed longest with the Bureau, promoted in 1941 to serve as special agent in charge of the San Antonio field office. He later held the same post in Albuquerque and Oklahoma City, while earning a national reputation as a fast-draw artist. FBI publicists downplayed his killing of at least a dozen outlaws, while taking full advantage of "Jelly's" prowess on the target range. *Life* magazine featured a special time-lapse photo spread of Bryce's fast draw in November 1945, noting that he could drop a silver dollar from shoulder height, then draw his pistol and drill the coin with a bullet before it reached waist level. Bryce died at home of a heart attack in May 1974, two days after attending a reunion of retired FBI agents.

**HISPANIC Agents**—The racism of FBI Director J. EDGAR HOOVER was not confined to African Americans. He once advised a congressional committee that Mexicans made unlikely presidential assassins because "they can't shoot straight, but watch out if they come at you with a knife." We can only speculate on the effect such prejudice had on employment of Hispanic FBI agents during Hoover's 48 years as director, but contradictory reports suggest that Hoover's death in May 1972 the Bureau had either 62 or 69 G-men "with Spanish surnames" out of 8,631 (or 8,659)—less than one percent of the total agent force.

MANUEL SOROLA was the first Hispanic G-man, hired as a "special employee" in 1916 and promoted to full agent status six years later. He worked primarily in the Southwest and was placed on "limited duty" status in Los Angeles 11 years before his 1949 retirement. The only known Hispanic to advance beyond mere agent status under Hoover was Julius Lopez, appointed special agent in charge of the Memphis field office in October 1941, later acting special agent in charge at Indianapolis (April 1942) and special agent in charge at San Juan, Puerto Rico (from April 1943 until his retirement in 1960).

Hoover's death cleared the way for more equitable hiring and promotion of Hispanic personnel, as with other ethnic minorities. In February 1992 the FBI claimed 605 Hispanic agents out of 10,422 (5.8 percent), increasing by 1997 to 746 out of 10,816 (6.9 percent). Agent EDMUNDO MIRELES won the Bureau's first Medal of Valor in 1986, following a deadly Miami shootout with bandits WILLIAM MATIX and Michael Platt that left two G-men dead and five others wounded (including Mireles). In March 1988 Julian De La Rosa was promoted to serve as special agent in charge of the St. Louis field office, the first Hispanic to hold that rank in 28 years. James Perez was appointed to run the Bureau's Equal Employment Opportunity office in March 1989, cutting the average response time on personnel complaints from 800 days to 150 days.

Occasional advancement of Hispanic agents through the ranks did not signal widespread contentment, however. In 1987 a group of 311 Hispanic G-men led by BERNARDO PEREZ (no relation to James) filed a class action suit against the FBI, claiming discrimination in promotion and assignments. The plaintiffs declared that too many Hispanic agents were assigned (like Manuel Sorola before them) to field offices located on the Southwestern "Taco Circuit," where they were effectively denied access to advancement in various programs, confronted by superiors who dismissed Hispanic agents as "lazy spics, dirty Mexicans, and wetbacks." (One supervisor mentioned in the lawsuit had criticized an Hispanic WOMAN AGENT for being "too ethnic.") Judge Lucius Bunton ruled for the plaintiffs on 26 September 1988, finding the FBI guilty of "systematic discrimination" against its Hispanic employees. While refusing to award back pay for those denied promotions, Judge Bunton issued an order on 9 May 1989 requiring the Bureau to change its promotion procedures. Director WILLIAM SESSIONS finally accepted the court's ruling in September 1990, a move that led some Anglo G-men to dub him "Con-Sessions." (A curious footnote to the lawsuit was the case of Miami G-man FERNANDO MATA, one of the agents who joined Perez in suing his superiors. Mata was suspended in March 1990, accused of leaking classified FBI material to Cuban intelligence agents. Mata called the suspension illegal retaliation for his courtroom testimony, but he failed to polygraph tests and was ultimately fired. He lost his appeal of that case in 1996.)

The FBI's website offers no ethnic breakdown of the current staff, but it pledges commitment to equal employment opportunities for all Americans, regardless of race. It remains to be seen whether public pledges and real-world behavior have anything in common.

**HISS, Alger** —A Baltimore native, born 11 November 1904, Alger Hiss attended Johns Hopkins University and Harvard Law School, where he became a protégé of future U.S. SUPREME COURT Justice Felix Frankfurter. He graduated from law school in 1929 and served for a year as private secretary to Justice Oliver Wendell Holmes, then entered private practice. In 1933 Hiss joined President FRANKLIN ROOSEVELT's New Deal as an attorney for the Agricultural Adjustment Administration, and two years later he shifted to the STATE DEPARTMENT's Trade Agreements division. By 1944 Hiss was promoted to serve as deputy director of the State Department's Office of Special Political Affairs, in charge of establishing the postwar United Nations. A year later he served as secretary general of the San Francisco conference that established the UN.

His rise to State Department stardom had not gone unnoticed at FBI HEADQUARTERS. A former COMMUNIST PARTY (CP) member, Whittaker Chambers, told State Department officials in September 1939 that Hiss and other New Dealers were members of a secret CP cell in Washington, D.C. G-men obtained the report but delayed their first interview with Chambers until May 1942, when he reported leaving the CP in "early 1937." At his next FBI interview, in March 1945, Chambers promoted Hiss to rank among "the top three leaders of the underground" in Washington, but he still specifically denied that any of those he denounced had been involved in ESPIONAGE of any kind. An eight-hour FBI interview followed on 10 May 1945, producing a 22-page report in which Chambers now claimed to have left the CP at "the end of 1937." Again, as in all previous statements, he denied any knowledge of spying.

On the strength of Chambers's statements, FBI agents tapped the telephones of Alger Hiss and wife Priscilla, placing both under round-the-clock surveillance. The WIRETAPS remained in place from December 1945 through September 1947, but G-men later admitted that "no espionage activities by Hiss were developed from this source." Devoid of solid evidence, the Bureau leaked Hiss's name to Rev. John Cronin, who in turn reported to the Catholic Church hierarchy that Hiss was "an underground member of the Communist Party." In early 1946, at Hoover's suggestion, State Department officials leaked the same stories to various right-wing congressmen, producing untraceable rumors on the Washington cocktail-party circuit. Hiss met with his superiors on 21 March 1946 and denied any affiliation or sympathy with the Communist Party.

Still frustrated, Hoover turned next to the HOUSE COMMITTEE ON UN-AMERICAN ACTIVITIES (HUAC). Chambers was called as a HUAC witness in August 1948, with committee member RICHARD NIXON coordinating the performance through Rev. Cronin and the FBI. (Cronin later served as Nixon's chief speechwriter from 1948 to 1960.) Hiss denied knowing Chambers, so HUAC brought them together on 17 August 1948. Confronted with his accuser, Hiss admitted knowing Chambers as "George Crossley," a freeloader who rented an apartment from Hiss in the mid-1930s and skipped without paying his bills. Hiss denied any communist ties under oath and challenged Chambers to repeat his charges outside the shelter of Congress. This Chambers did ten days later, on television's *Meet the Press*, and Hiss responded with a slander suit for $50,000.

Chambers had thus far continued to deny any knowledge of espionage, including new denials in a deposition by Hiss's attorneys on 4 November 1948. He changed his story two weeks later, though, producing a sheaf of 69 documents allegedly passed to him by Hiss for later delivery to a Soviet agent. (Chambers failed in the latter part of his mission, allegedly hiding the documents for a decade at the home of a relative in Baltimore.) The stash included 69 typed digests of various State Department reports and four short notes in what appeared to be Hiss's handwriting. Since all the documents were dated between 1 January and 1 April 1938, Chambers was forced to change his testimony once again, now claiming that he left the CP on 14 April 1938. FBI headquarters helped the effort by suppressing reports of his earlier contradictory statements.

On 1 December 1948 Richard Nixon telephoned FBI Assistant Director LOUIS NICHOLS to report that Chambers "did not tell the FBI everything he knew" in previous debriefings. There were more documents, Nixon reported, that would "substantiate and vindicate his position which have up to this time not become publicly known." That night, Chambers led HUAC staffers to a rural property where they extracted five rolls of microfilm from a hollow pumpkin. Two of the rolls had already been developed, revealing various State Department cables and documents, some of them in code. On 15 December 1948 a New York grand jury indicted Hiss on two counts of perjury (the three-year statute of limitations on espionage having expired). Specifically, he was charged with lying under oath when he denied passing documents to Chambers and when he denied knowing Chambers after 1 January 1937.

The prosecution hit a snag in January 1949, when Chambers told G-men that he would not testify that Hiss belonged to the Red cell in Washington, since "he was not sure Alger Hiss was in the group." Worse yet, a memo to Hoover (dated 2 February 1949) reported: "It is not clear at this time if Chambers can testify that he received these particular 69 documents from Hiss, but upon establishing the facts of this situation, decision can therefore be reached as to who is in the position to introduce these documents." On 15 February 1949 Chambers handed the Bureau a new confession, this time admitting that he was not only an ex-Red but also an ex-HOMOSEXUAL, who had "conquered" his "affliction" around the same time he left the CP. He denied having sex with any party members, and Hoover hid the embarrassing report from defense attorneys.

While Chambers waffled on his testimony, FBI agents scoured the countryside for Hiss's old typewriter, a Woodstock bearing the serial number 230099. It was finally located in Washington, and members of the Hiss defense team were stunned when a report from the FBI's LABORATORY DIVISION matched the machine to 68 of the documents furnished by Chambers in November 1948. One report had been typed on a Royal machine, the discrepancy never explained since Chambers insisted all 69 had been typed at home by Priscilla Hiss. (Another FBI lab report, exonerating Priscilla as the typist, was illegally withheld from Hiss defense attorneys.) Two decades later, reminiscing in the Oval Office, President Nixon would confide to aides, "The typewriter was always the key. We built one in the Hiss case."

Government handling of the documentary evidence at trial was curious, to say the least. Little mention was made of the Woodstock typewriter, though it sat on an exhibits table in full view of jurors. FBI documents "expert" Ramos Freehan named Priscilla Hiss as the typist of all 69 State Department summaries, thus contradicting the suppressed laboratory analysis. Of the notorious "pumpkin papers," only two film rolls—those already developed—were introduced by the state. The three undeveloped rolls remained mysterious, their contents suppressed on grounds that revelation "would be injurious to the national security." (When finally released in 1975, under the FREEDOM OF INFORMATION ACT, one "sensitive" roll proved to be blank; the other two contained a series of Navy reports on the proper use of fire extinguishers, life rafts and parachutes.)

Hiss's first perjury trial ended with a hung jury in June 1949. He was convicted at a second trial, on 20 January 1950, and received concurrent five-year prison terms on each perjury count. Hiss served 44 months and was released in November 1954. By that time, building on his reputation as "the man who got Alger Hiss," Richard Nixon had advanced to the U.S. Senate and from there to the vice presidency under President DWIGHT EISENHOWER. While remaining philosophical—he told reporters that "three years in jail is a good corrective for three years at Harvard"—Hiss fought tirelessly for vindication throughout the rest of his life. He was disbarred and divorced, but ultimately won reinstatement to the Massachusetts bar in 1975. Hiss died on 15 November 1996, with heated debate still continuing about the details of his case.

**HITLER, Adolf**—Although the FBI was never meant to exercise jurisdiction outside the United States, its authority expanded on the eve of U.S. entry into WORLD WAR II, with creation of the SPECIAL INTELLIGENCE SERVICE. Even then, G-men abroad were theoretically restricted to Latin America by order of President FRANKLIN ROOSEVELT, but one of Director J. EDGAR HOOVER'S wilder schemes, revealed only 40 years after the fact, involved penetration of Adolf Hitler's "Fortress Europe" to kill Der Führer himself.

The plot was described to Hoover biographer Anthony Summers by J. Edgar Nichols, son of long-time Hoover aide LOUIS NICHOLS. As Hoover's namesake explained the event, "Mr. Hoover, my father and a third man whose name I don't know developed a plan to go behind German lines and assassinate Hitler. They actually presented this plan to the White House, and it got bucked to the STATE DEPARTMENT, and they got taken to task by Secretary of State [Cordell] Hull. What they had in mind was a three-man assassination team, and my father talked as though he and Mr. Hoover somehow hoped to take part themselves. My understanding is that this was no joke—they really did hope something would come of it."

The image of Hoover creeping past Nazi guards to kill Hitler invites ridicule, but his evident willingness to participate in what the CENTRAL INTELLIGENCE AGENCY later termed "executive action" fuels concern over the Bureau's role in later political slayings, including the JFK and RFK ASSASSINATIONS, the murders of MARTIN LUTHER KING, JR., and MALCOLM X, and operations of the FBI-funded SECRET ARMY ORGANIZATION.

**HOGAN'S Alley** — A mock town located at the FBI ACADEMY in Quantico, Virginia, "Hogan's Alley" is utilized for training agents in simulated street situations. Its facilities include a simulated bank, pharmacy, pool hall, movie theater, post office, restaurant and bar, pawn shop (with concealed gambling casino), and warehouse, plus residential structures including a motel, trailer park, rooming house and apartments. Some of the buildings are real, containing offices and classrooms, while others are simply false fronts in the nature of a Hollywood movie set. Agents use the facility to practice arrest and pursuit techniques, with other G-men or professional actors cast in the roles of criminals, victims and innocent bystanders. Most of the furnishings in Hogan's Alley are acquired from property seizures conducted by the FBI or the DRUG ENFORCEMENT ADMINISTRATION.

**HOLDEN, Thomas James** — It was fitting that Thomas Holden placed first on the FBI's "TEN MOST WANTED" LIST when that roster was created in 1950, since he symbolized the kind of outlaws who had made crime-busting G-men famous in the Great Depression. Holden launched his career in BANK ROBBERY with partner Francis Keating, in the 1920s, proving that Leavenworth prison could not hold them when they escaped together in 1931, after serving three years of a 25-year sentence for train robbery. Recruited by the violent BARKER-KARPIS GANG, Holden and Keating resumed their felonious ways until they were captured by Bureau agents on 8 July 1932, while playing golf in Kansas City.

Paroled in 1947, Holden returned to his native Chicago and apparently kept his nose clean for the next two years. On 5 June 1949 a drunken family gathering led to angry words between Holden and his wife. Enraged, he drew a gun and killed her with a single shot, then fatally wounded two of her brothers. Fleeing a triple murder charge, Holden was still at large in March 1950, when the Bureau created its "Top Ten" program, branding him "a menace to every man, woman, and child in America." The menace, meanwhile, had gone to ground in Beaverton, Oregon, living quietly as "John McCullough." A local resident recognized Holden's mug shot in the newspaper on 23 June 1951, and agents were sent to arrest him at work. Convicted of murder in Chicago, Holden died in prison two years later.

**HOMOSEXUALITY** — Investigation of private conduct, including sexual behavior, was the very thing feared by congressmen who opposed creation of the FBI in 1908. At the time, they were assured that Bureau scrutiny would be confined to violators of specific federal laws, but that has never been the case in fact. Homosexuals were subject to investigation on two primary grounds, one official and the other unstated. First, it was long assumed that gays in public life were easy marks for blackmail by foreign agents, criminals and such (although no record of any such case in American history). More pertinently, Bureau leaders soon learned that *they* could blackmail gays with threats of exposure, thereby controlling their actions or turning them into INFORMANTS. As one former aide to Director J. EDGAR HOOVER told author Curt Gentry, "If we found out that so-and-so was [gay], and most of them were quite covert about their activities, that person would be 'doubled' and become a listening post for the FBI."

It is unclear exactly when the Bureau began its pursuit of gays. Historian Athan Theoharis reports that G-men collected such information "as early as 1937," but we know today that Hoover opened a special OBSCENE File 12 years earlier, on 24 March 1925. In any case, Theoharis maintains, the Bureau "had not used this information systematically" until the 1940s. The FBI's first gay victim may have been SUMNER WELLES, forced to resign from the STATE DEPARTMENT in 1943 after exposure of a 1940 incident involving black railway porters. Recent evidence suggests that Hoover's men orchestrated the incident specifically to drive Welles from office.

On 20 June 1951 Hoover launched a new Sex Deviates program with the express intent of driving gays from public office in America. All G-men were ordered to collect "allegations concerning present and past" government employees, whereupon the assembled rumors, hints and innuendoes would be sent to designated officials for further action. During the same period, in the presidential campaigns of 1952 and 1956, Hoover was the primary source of "queer" rumors surrounding Democratic candidate ADLAI STEVENSON. Ironically, Hoover was simultaneously working in concert with Red-hunting Senator JOSEPH McCARTHY, whose aides (including chief counsel ROY COHN) were notorious homosexuals. Persistent rumors of gay predilections surrounded McCarthy himself, including reports that his late-life marriage and adoption of a child were merely "covers" for his secret after-hours pursuit of young men.

Hoover's pursuit of gays was tireless. In May 1969 he warned President RICHARD NIXON that "a ring of homosexualists" was active within the White House itself. Based on unfounded reports from a freelance journalist, Hoover named Nixon aides H.R. HALDEMAN and JOHN EHRLICHMAN as primary suspects, but investigation failed to bear out the charges. A year later, in November 1970, Haldeman turned the tables by ordering Hoover to identify gays in the Washington press corps, hoping that embarrassed reporters could be blackmailed into muting their criticism of the Nixon administration. (Hoover enthusiastically agreed to "get right on it.")

The crowning irony of Hoover's lifelong obsession lies in the fact that *he* may have been gay. Throughout his 48 years as FBI director, Hoover was dogged by rumors that he and constant companion CLYDE TOLSON were lovers. One-time fashion model Luisa Steward — pictured in a famous photo of Hoover and Tolson, taken at New York's Stork Club on New Year's Eve 1936 — told author Anthony Summers that Hoover and Tolson held hands in their limousine after the party, en route to another gala event at the Cotton Club. Agent M. WESLEY SWEARINGEN, passing through the FBI ACADEMY in 1951, recalled "jokes in training school about Hoover and Tolson being homosexual." Swearingen also reports that such rumors "continued to permeate the field offices for years, but no agent seemed to have any personal knowledge of an affair." Summers reports that Agent GUY HOTTEL was recruited by Hoover on one occasion in the 1930s, to break off Tolson's budding romance with an unnamed woman; he further claims that field agents routinely derided the Bureau's top men as "J. Edna" and "Mother Tolson."

Stories of Hoover's covert sex life were not restricted to FBI ranks. Indicted pornographer WILLIAM BYARS, JR., and some of his associates allegedly saw Hoover with young male companions on various occasions in the 1950s and 1960s, when he vacationed in California at CLINT MURCHISON's Del Charro Hotel. Author TRUMAN CAPOTE, himself a homosexual and a target of FBI surveillance, told a magazine reporter in the 1960s that Hoover and Tolson were gay. Susan ROSENSTIEL, married to one of Hoover's closest friends, reported meeting Hoover twice at sex parties in 1957-58. She claims Hoover was dressed as a woman on both occasions and that he was introduced to her as "Mary." (Clyde Tolson, Mrs. Rosenstiel maintained, was absent from both parties.)

Rumors persist to this day that Hoover himself was blackmailed by members of ORGANIZED CRIME who possessed photographs of the director in drag. Their price for silence: Hoover's bizarre 40-year insistence that no national crime syndicate existed in the U.S. Anthony Summers floats the theory in his biography of Hoover, *Official and Confidential* (1994), but his "evidence" of a blackmail plot comes down to anonymous hearsay from two "successful professionals in their fields" who allegedly saw compromising photos of Hoover in 1948, at a party in Washington, D.C. The snapshots allegedly showed Hoover in a dress and wearing a blonde wig, but depicted no sexual activity. No further proof of blackmail is offered, but a 1963 WIRETAP recording did catch Philadelphia mobster Angelo Bruno telling a colleague that Attorney General ROBERT KENNEDY "wants Edgar Hoover out of the FBI because he is a fairy. I heard this before."

Former Assistant Director CARTHA DELOACH, still loyal to Hoover in the 1990s, reproached Summers in his own memoirs for presenting a compilation of rumors and lies against Hoover and Tolson. DeLoach notes that Susan Rosenstiel was once cited for perjury in an unrelated matter, and may thus be unreliable in her descriptions of Hoover. Tolson was not gay, DeLoach insists, but merely "sort of an alter ego" who "let Hoover take all the bows, all the credit" for Tolson's achievements. As for Summers's claim that 1930s correspondence between Hoover and Chicago G-man MELVIN PURVIS represents "a homosexual courtship," DeLoach cites the same letters as "the bantering between two bachelors interested in women."

Regardless of his true sexuality, Hoover reacted with towering rage against those who suggested he might be gay. The first known instance involved journalist RAY TUCKER, who wrote in *Collier's* magazine (19 August 1933) that Hoover "walks with mincing steps." FBI HEADQUARTERS launched an immediate counterattack in the press to quell any gay rumors. On 28 August a *Washington Herald* gossip columnist noted that "the Hoover stride has grown noticeably longer and more vigorous" since Tucker's article was published. A short time later, *Liberty* magazine described Hoover as "170 pounds of live, virile masculinity." Assistant Director LOUIS NICHOLS claimed in 1936 that Hoover's "personal capture" of fugitive ALVIN KARPIS "pretty much ended the 'queer' talk," but nothing could be further from the truth.

By 1940 Hoover had ordered a thorough investigation of each new gay rumor, chastising field agents "very forcefully" if they failed to trace and punish those responsible for each "lie." On one occasion, a female FBI clerk in Washington overheard the proprietor of a beauty salon remark that Hoover was "queer." The employee told headquarters, and two G-men were dispatched "to take this scandal monger & liar on." The terrified woman vowed never to "be guilty of such statements again," and the clerk received a commendation for informing on her erstwhile friend.

There were other such incidents during WORLD WAR II. In June 1943 Cleveland's agent-in-charge learned that a woman had told her bridge partners "the Director was a homosexual and kept a large group of boys around him." Summoned to the Cleveland field office for a grilling, the woman was told by the agent-in-charge that "he personally resented such a malicious and unfounded statement." She immediately promised to tell her friends that her comment "was not founded on fact and that she was deeply sorry that she had made it and it should not have been made at all." Furthermore, she swore to inform the Bureau "when this had been done." In January 1944 a Detroit G-man confronted yet another gossiper, warning his subject that if any further tales of Hoover's sexuality were spread, the agent "might take care of him on the spot." Detroit's agent-in-charge assured Hoover that the frightened man "will not repeat such a statement in the future." Later that same year, agents reported that similar stories told by "a prominent New Yorker" were "obviously baseless." Hoover raged in a memo, "I never heard of this obvious degenerate. Only one with a depraved mind could have such thoughts."

Still the rumors persisted. In 1968, under fire from baseless Bureau leaks alleging Mafia connections, New Jersey congressman CORNELIUS GALLAGHER threatened to retaliate with a speech in Congress revealing that Hoover and Tolson "have been living as man and wife for some 28 years at the public's expense." In response, G-men grudgingly admitted that their leaks to *Life* magazine had been false, but the campaign of innuendo persisted until Gallagher was driven from office. As Athan Theoharis observed, Hoover's responses to gay rumors "were invariably vindictive — and all the more so when the suspected offenders were homosexual themselves."

Unfortunately, the FBI's homophobia did not die with Hoover in May 1972. A decade later, under Director WILLIAM WEBSTER, G-men monitored demonstrations by ACT-UP, a gay activist group whose members were charged with no federal crimes. Agent Frank Buttino ran afoul of the Bureau in 1988, when he answered an ad in a gay magazine. Although his letter made no mention of the FBI, someone sent copies to the Bureau and to Buttino's parents. Investigators from the OFFICE OF PROFESSIONAL RESPONSIBILITY subjected Buttino to a polygraph test, which he later described to author Robert Kessler: "They wanted the names of other homosexuals in the FBI, homosexuals I had had sex with outside the Bureau. What kind of sex had I had, details going back to day one." After 20 years of service, Buttino was stripped of his top-secret security clearance in February 1990, then fired four months later (on grounds that all agents must hold top-secret clearance). He filed a lawsuit and the FBI settled out of court in December 1993, paying Buttino $100,000 in legal fees and a pension to age 62. At the same time, Attorney General JANET RENO announced that the JUSTICE DEPARTMENT would no longer discriminate against gays.

**HONORS Intern Program**—Designed to motivate college students toward careers in law enforcement, the Honors Intern Program was inaugurated by Director WILLIAM WEBSTER. In addition to specific (unpaid) work assignments, interns also visit different field offices and the FBI ACADEMY in Quantico, Virginia. No statistics are available on how effective the program has been in producing new recruits for the Bureau or other law enforcement agencies.

**HOOVER, Herbert Clark**—A native of West Branch, Iowa, born 10 August 1874, Herbert Hoover served as U.S. food commissioner during WORLD WAR I, then as Secretary of Commerce under Presidents WARREN HARDING and CALVIN COOLIDGE (1921-28). He became president in his own right on 4 March 1929 and America was stricken by the Wall Street crash seven months later, inaugurating the Great Depression. Fairly or otherwise, Hoover found himself condemned in public for the nation's economic woes, a circumstance which prompted him—with chief aide Lawrence Richey—to retaliate whenever possible against perceived political enemies.

The tool of those reprisals, more often than not, was the FBI. Director J. EDGAR HOOVER accommodated Richey's requests for WIRETAPPING and other forms of surveillance on various adversaries, though Richey sometimes bypassed the Bureau for tasks such as a 1930 BREAK-IN at Democratic Party headquarters. In 1932 G-men were assigned to investigate the "Bonus Army" march on Washington, striving in vain to prove that the demonstrating military veterans were Communists. Hoover lost his re-election bid to FRANKLIN ROOSEVELT in November 1932 and was subsequently targeted for FBI investigation himself in July 1940, after Roosevelt heard rumors that ex-President Hoover and Richey were seeking evidence of illegal U.S. military aid to France. (The probe failed to substantiate those rumors.) Hoover died in New York City on 20 October 1964.

**HOOVER, John Edgar**—The FBI's most famous and longest-serving director was born in Washington, D.C. on 1 January 1895. The nation's capital was then primarily a southern city with typical southern attitudes on race and politics, which young J. Edgar Hoover rapidly absorbed in segregated schools and carried with him for the remainder of his life. In 1913—the year he led a drill team in President WOODROW WILSON'S inauguration parade—Hoover's high school yearbook described him as a "gentleman of dauntless courage and stainless honor."

In October 1913 Hoover found work at the Library of Congress, four blocks from his home, while taking night classes at George Washington University. He graduated with a law degree and passed the bar exam in Washington but never practiced. Two months after the U.S. entered WORLD WAR I, on 26 July 1917, Hoover left his library job for a draft-exempt position as a clerk with the JUSTICE DEPARTMENT, assigned to the ALIEN ENEMY BUREAU. He was promoted to "attorney" at Justice on 18 June 1918 (still trying no cases), and again on 1 July 1919 to serve as special assistant to Attorney General A. MITCHELL PALMER. That move placed Hoover in charge of the Red-hunting GENERAL INTELLIGENCE DIVISION, where he organized and supervised the PALMER RAIDS of 1919-20.

On 22 August 1921 Hoover was promoted again, this time to serve as the Bureau of Investigation's first assistant director under WILLIAM BURNS. Questions about his evasion of military service were resolved in 1922, when Hoover was commissioned as a reserve officer in the Army's Military Intelligence Division. (By the time he "retired" in 1942, without ever serving a day in uniform, Hoover held the rank of lieutenant colonel.) Scandals surrounding the administration of President WARREN HARDING ultimately doomed Burns, but Hoover emerged unscathed from the wreckage at Justice (despite his zealous participation in various illegal activities) and he was appointed acting director of the Bureau on 10 May 1924. He became full-time director on 10 December 1924 and held that position until his death on 2 May 1972, almost 48 years later.

For good or ill, Hoover recreated the FBI in his image, exercising authority over his subordinates which few other Washington bureaucrats enjoyed. At Hoover's insistence, in the name of "national security," Bureau employees were exempt from Civil Service guidelines and thus virtually without recourse in the face of his autocratic, frequently capricious discipline. Under seven presidents and 16 attorneys general, Hoover exercised near-dictatorial power, using "friendly" media sources to make his name a household word in the U.S. For nearly half a century he was literally untouchable, relying on the Bureau's FILES to influence, amuse or blackmail his superiors and guarantee that he remained in office. He briefly cherished higher ambitions, pursuing a failed campaign to become a U.S. SUPREME COURT justice in 1948 and launching an abortive presidential bid in 1956, but Hoover's command of the FBI gave him more covert authority than most public officials in America.

While admirers hailed that fact and looked to Hoover as the savior of conservative America, his flaws were both profound and numerous. One obvious weakness was the director's strident racism, a product of his upbringing thinly veiled in public and blatantly expressed to close acquaintances. Hoover viewed all racial minorities with suspicion and spent the last decade of his career working to "prevent the rise of a 'messiah'" in the black community. He once complained that Supreme Court rulings on the CIVIL RIGHTS of criminal suspects had "gone into the field where police officers must address them in courteous language, particularly in the case of Negroes, and instead of saying, 'Boy, come here,' they want to be addressed as 'Mr.'" On another occasion, the near-pathological nature of his bigotry was revealed when Attorney General TOM CLARK asked Hoover to investigate the attempted murder of (white) labor leader Victor Reuther in 1949. The strange answer came back: "Edgar says no. He says he's not going to get involved every time some nigger woman gets raped."

In addition to his racist-reactionary attitudes, Hoover was also corrupt, a fact effectively hidden from the public until three years after his death. During his tenure as FBI director he used Bureau agents to remodel and maintain his home, while ghost writers in the CRIME RECORDS DIVISION prepared various books and magazine articles for publication over Hoover's by-line. Income from book and film royalties alone exceeded $200,000, "donated" to the FBI RECREATIONAL ASSOCIATION and other funds which Hoover and his top aides used as private slush funds. With constant companion CLYDE TOLSON, he accepted free vacations and gambling junkets each year (officially described as "inspection tours"), with millionaire cronies CLINT MURCHISON, WILLIAM BYARS, SR. and others picking up the tab. Those same friends also guaranteed no-loss investments for Hoover in oil and natural gas corporations, while members of ORGANIZED CRIME funneled cash into the "nonprofit" J. EDGAR HOOVER FOUNDATION. The *Los Angeles Times* described Hoover's legacy in an editorial dated 13 January 1978:

> It was, as corruption goes, pretty piddling stuff, almost embarrassingly so. But that's not the point. The point is that the most powerful law-enforcement official in the world, who would severely discipline or fire underlings for the least infraction of the FBI's rigid rules of personal conduct, could not himself resist the temptation to embezzle from the public purse with routine and unblushing regularity. And because Hoover was corrupt, some of those around him in the upper echelons of the Bureau felt that they too had the right to be corrupt.

Hoover's mental fitness for duty was another question entirely. A hypochondriac who secretly consulted "dozens" of physicians in Washington and New York City for imaginary ailments, Hoover nurtured an obsessive fear of disease, outfitting his home and office with special "bug lights" designed to "electrocute" germs, and he displayed an "almost demented" reaction to flies in his office. Assistant Director WILLIAM SULLIVAN was assigned to scour the media for articles on treatments alleged to prolong human life, "no matter how farfetched the claim," while Hoover displayed peculiar fear of letting anyone step on his shadow. By the mid-1960s a private nurse was employed to give Hoover daily "massive injections of some substance to keep him going." As described by biographer Curt Gentry, Hoover received his shots at 9:00 a.m. each day, thereafter displaying "almost maniacal energy, until he crashed after lunch, often napping until it was time to go home." In 1970, *Time* magazine reporter Dean Fischer found that Hoover was mentally confused, noting that he "had difficulty in responding to a question … without losing himself in a forest of recollections" from the 1930s.

Hoover's death on 2 May 1972 was officially blamed on "hypertensive cardiovascular disease," but rumors persist to this day that he may have been murdered. Be that as it may, his corpse was protected in death by a massive lead-lined coffin guaranteed to frustrate vandals and the ravages of nature. Two of the young servicemen who carried Hoover's casket into the Capitol rotunda, where he lay in state, suffered hernias on the short journey, while a third collapsed unconscious on the steps outside.

Hoover's estate was "conservatively" estimated at $560,000, but a tabulation presented by Curt Gentry — likewise deemed conservative — totaled $732,000. It included a $160,000 house; $70,000 in jewelry and household effects; $160,000 in stocks and bonds; $125,000 in oil, mineral and natural gas leases; and $217,000 in cash. Hoover's legacy suffered from exposure of corruption and illegal activities in the years after his death, with the result that Congress considered a bill to remove his name from the FBI's new headquarters in 1980. That move failed, but the initiative was renewed in 2002 by Indiana congressman Dan Bur-

ton. Thus far, no concrete action has been taken to expunge Hoover's brand from the organization he crafted over nearly half a century as a virtual cult of personality.

**HOPKINS, Louise Macy**—Prior to marrying Harry Lloyd Hopkins, intimate advisor to President FRANKLIN ROOSEVELT and one-time Secretary of Commerce (1938-40), Louise Macy served as Paris editor for *Harper's Bazaar* magazine. President Roosevelt found Mrs. Hopkins so charming that he ignored protests from First Lady ELEANOR ROOSEVELT and invited the newlyweds to live in the White House upon their return to Washington. Over time, however, the relationship soured. By 1944, FDR suspected Mrs. Hopkins of repeating presidential conversations to a friend, *Washington Times Herald* reporter Cissy Patterson. Roosevelt ordered FBI surveillance of Mrs. Hopkins to determine whether she was leaking information to the press, but no proof of any indiscretion was uncovered. Roosevelt then ordered Director J. EDGAR HOOVER to destroy the Hopkins surveillance files, but Hoover kept the paperwork secretly intact. Any blackmail potential was lost in 1946, when Harry Hopkins died and his wife retired from public life.

**HOPPER, Heda**—A Hollywood "journalist" who purveyed movie industry gossip in syndicated newspaper columns and on radio, Heda Hopper launched her career in 1938 but came to the FBI's attention in 1946, after she wrote a letter praising J. EDGAR HOOVER for a recent speech. Hoover scrawled "Write letter to Heda Hopper" in the margin of her letter, and so was launched another "friendly" media relationship, progressing to the point that Hopper became (in one observer's words) "an adjunct of the blacklist process." In 1947, writing once again to praise Hoover's ghost-written book *The Story of the FBI*, Hopper told the director, "I loved what you said about the Commies in the motion picture industry. I'd like to run every one of those rats out of the country, starting with CHARLIE CHAPLIN." Hoover thereafter illegally furnished Hopper with gossip on Chaplin and other celebrities gleaned from the FBI's files. Hopper's cozy relationship with the Bureau continued into the 1960s, but she was also the object of FBI scrutiny, her 116-page dossier including a notation that Hopper's name was found on the mailing list of the American Nazi Party.

**HORAN, Sheila**—Once listed among the FBI's highest ranking WOMEN, Sheila Horan was deputy assistant director of the Bureau's National Security Division until 28 January 2002. Horan was fired on that date, after Director ROBERT MUELLER "lost patience" with her handling of a Chinese ESPIONAGE investigation. FBI spokesmen refused to say whether any actual spying occurred or what (if any) national secrets were compromised, but they reported that Horan was fired "for failing, in [Mueller's] view, to conduct a sufficiently aggressive inquiry into the accusations." The report further stated that Mueller was "especially displeased that [Horan] did not provide him sooner with details of the case." Mueller's action, described as "unusually swift," was couched in terms of a transfer that placed Horan in "an administrative support position" with the FBI, but spokesmen acknowledged that "she was expected to leave the Bureau." Pundits speculated that Horan's ouster was occasioned by recent FBI embarrassment in the cases of WEN HO LEE and Agent ROBERT HANSSEN. Horan had no comment for the press, but friends claimed that Mueller "had unfairly blamed her for longstanding problems in the FBI's counterintelligence operations."

**HORIUCHI, Lon** —As a member of the FBI's HOSTAGE RESCUE TEAM, Lon Horiuchi participated in the RANDALL WEAVER siege at Ruby Ridge, Idaho in August 1992. On 22 August, acting under Bureau rules of engagement stating that FBI snipers "could and should" shoot any armed adults seen on the Weaver property, Horiuchi fired two rifle shots at individuals later identified as Weaver and Kevin Harris. Prior to the shots being fired, one or both targets allegedly brandished weapons as if intending to fire on an FBI helicopter circling over Randall Weaver's cabin. Horiuchi wounded both men, but his second shot also pierced the cabin's door and killed Weaver's wife as she stood with a child in her arms. The siege lasted nine more days, with G-men reportedly unaware that Vicki Weaver had been slain.

Horiuchi appeared as a prosecution witness at Weaver's murder trial, in June 1993, and described the shooting in a performance that led Idaho journalist Dean Miller to describe Horiuchi as "a real piece of work," completely lacking in emotion. Under oath, Horiuchi described his reasons for firing on Weaver and Harris, but Judge Edward Lodge apparently disbelieved him, later instructing jurors that there was no reliable evidence of any threat to the FBI helicopter. Weaver was acquitted and the federal government subsequently paid him $3.1 million for the wrongful death of his wife and son (shot by members of the U.S. MARSHAL'S SERVICE in an earlier skirmish).

A DEPARTMENT OF JUSTICE task force investigated the Weaver stand-off in 1994, concluding that the Bureau's shoot-on-sight rules of engagement deviated from standard procedure and that Vicki Weaver's killing was unlawful. The task force's 300-page report also stated that Horiuchi had "confused his targets" on 22 August 1992 and that he never saw either target fire on the FBI helicopter. Furthermore, the investigators found that no surrender call was made after Horiuchi's first shot and that his targets "were never given a chance to drop their arms to show that they did not pose a threat." Those statements prompted yet another review, this one by the FBI's own Civil Rights Division and OFFICE OF PROFESSIONAL RESPONSIBILITY, which found that Vicki Weaver's death was not unlawful and that criminal prosecution of FBI personnel was unwarranted.

An Idaho prosecutor charged Lon Horiuchi with manslaughter in August 1997, but Judge Lodge dismissed the case in May 1998 with a finding that Horiuchi had shot Vicki Weaver while acting in an official capacity for the FBI and thus could not be tried in state court. No federal charges were filed, thereby effectively dismissing the case. Horiuchi's present status with the FBI is unknown.

**HOSTAGE Rescue Team** — Created by Director WILLIAM WEBSTER in January 1983, the FBI's Hostage Rescue Team (HRT) was conceived as the equivalent of various police department Special Weapons and Tactics (SWAT) teams, albeit with a more "politically correct" title. Regional FBI SWAT teams had existed since the 1970s, active at the siege of WOUNDED KNEE and in similar armed confrontations, but the timing of the HRT's creation was significant, authorized by Attorney General WILLIAM FRENCH SMITH in preparation for the 1984 Los Angeles Summer Olympics, a Worlds Fair in New Orleans, the Democratic Party's national convention in San Francisco, and the Republican national convention in Dallas.

The HRT's first leader was Danny Coulson, assistant special agent in charge of the Washington, D.C. field office. The original complement of 42 agents were meant to work part-time with HRT and spend the rest of their time as street agents in Washington, but FBI officials soon recognized that serving the HRT was a full-time job. It's 90-plus agents are now assigned to the FBI ACADEMY as members of the Bureau's CRITICAL INCIDENT RESPONSE GROUP, theoretically prepared to meet any crisis within four hours of the initial request. Given the nature of their work, it comes as no surprise that HRT agents have been involved in some of the modern FBI's most controversial incidents, including the RANDY WEAVER shootout at Ruby Ridge, Idaho in 1992 and the disastrous BRANCH DAVIDIAN siege at Waco, Texas the following year. On a more positive note, HRT commandos also disarmed members of the covenant, sword and arm of the lord in Arkansas, and captured neo-Nazi members of THE ORDER.

**HOSTY, James P., Jr.** —James Hosty was 28 years old when he joined the FBI in 1952. Eleven years later he was assigned to the Dallas field office, recognized as an expert on the local KU KLUX KLAN while keeping track of various other "subversives" in the process. One of those whom he investigated was LEE HARVEY OSWALD, soon to be named by official sources as the lone gunman in the JFK ASSASSINATION.

According to FBI records, Hosty began working the Oswald case on 11 March 1963, when he made his first unsuccessful attempt to interview Oswald's wife Marina in Dallas. The couple had moved with no forwarding address, but Hosty logged a report from their ex-landlady that Oswald drank heavily and beat his wife. Hosty then "closed" the Oswald FILE, but officially reopened it two weeks later for reasons unknown. In May 1963 he made a second attempt to interview Marina, but the Oswalds had moved again, this time to New Orleans. Louisiana G-men confirmed the move in June and notified Hosty on 3 October 1963 that Oswald had left the Crescent City. On 29 October Hosty visited Dallas resident Dorothy Roberts for "what we call a pretext interview," questioning Roberts about her relationship with the Oswalds and their present whereabouts. Three days later he traced Marina Oswald to Irving, Texas and spoke with her there, at the home of Ruth Paine. Hosty learned that Oswald had moved back to Dallas and found work there, leaving Marina in Irving. Leaving his business card, Hosty asked the women to find and report Lee's new address.

In the 1 November interview, Ruth Paine mentioned Oswald's complaint that "the FBI got him fired from every job he ever had." Hosty denied it, then visited Oswald's new place of employment three days later on another "pretext call," allegedly to obtain Oswald's address. Oddly, he returned to Ruth Paine's home the next day, 5 November, allegedly seeking the address he had received one day earlier. Approximately two days later, Oswald visited the Dallas field office and confronted receptionist Nannie Lee Fenner, asking to speak with Hosty. When told that Hosty was out of the office, Oswald handed Fenner a handwritten message and left. As Fenner recalled the note, it complained of Hosty harassing Marina and warned that if the visits did not cease, Oswald would "either blow up the Dallas Police Department or the FBI office." Assistant agent-in-charge Kyle Clark read the note and told Fenner, "Forget it. Give it to Hosty." Hosty himself later called the note "an innocuous type of complaint" and said "it didn't appear to be of any serious import," though he recalled a vague threat to "take action against the FBI."

Hosty later professed to be stunned by Oswald's arrest on 22 November 1963, on accusations of killing a Dallas policeman (later expanded to include President Kennedy's murder). Still, on his way to interrogate Oswald with Dallas police lieutenant Jack Revill Hosty remarked, "We knew that Lee Harvey Oswald was capable of assassinating the president of the United States, but we didn't dream he would do it." Hosty claimed the 22 November interview was his first meeting with Oswald, and that Oswald "reacted angrily" to their introduction, but Ruth Paine told reporters (on 8 December 1963) that Hosty once met Oswald at her home and that they "spoke at length in his car." Oswald's personal notebook also contained Hosty's name, telephone number and the license number of his car (not shown on the business card Hosty left with Ruth Paine on 1 November 1963). Near Hosty's name, Oswald had written "GANDY"—the surname of FBI Director J. EDGAR HOOVER's longtime personal secretary.

Hosty's comment to Lt. Revill and knowledge that the FBI was tracking Oswald at least eight months prior to Kennedy's assassination (without informing the SECRET SERVICE of any potential danger) posed a potential grave embarrassment for the Bureau. Shortly after Oswald's murder on 24 November 1963, Hosty was ordered by Dallas agent-in-charge Gordon Shanklin to destroy Oswald's threatening letter and the memo Hosty wrote to accompany it. Hosty complied, shredding the documents and flushing them down a toilet. Around the same time, receptionist Nannie Fenner was ordered to "forget about the Oswald note." When G-men reported the contents of Oswald's notebook to the Warren Commission (investigating Kennedy's murder), they deleted Hosty's information and the name "Gandy." Ultimately caught in that deception, FBI HEADQUARTERS admitted the deletions on 27 February 1964 and "explained" the action by stating that "the circumstances under which Hosty's name, et cetera, appeared in Oswald's notebook were fully known to the FBI."

Various Bureau employees were censured for their handling of the Oswald case, including Assistant Director WILLIAM SULLIVAN. Agent Hosty took the brunt of it, suffering what author Curt Gentry termed "the Chinese water torture." On 13 December 1963 Hoover placed Hosty on 90 days' probation. On 28 September 1964—"coincidentally" one day after the Warren Commission's report was released—Hosty was transferred to Kansas City. One week later, on 5 October, he was suspended for 30 days without pay and again placed on probation. Hoover denied Hosty's hardship-exemption request on 8 October (Hosty had a wife and seven children, two of them gravely ill). The following day, Associate Director CLYDE TOLSON put a "stop" on Hosty's personnel file, meaning he would not receive another promotion or pay raise while Hoover and Tolson ran the FBI.

Still Hosty endured, remaining with the Bureau and outlasting both Hoover and Tolson. In 1975 he testified before the CHURCH COMMITTEE, investigating FBI irregularities. Hosty expected a call from the HOUSE SELECT COMMITTEE ON ASSASSINATIONS, but that investigation ignored him. He retired from the FBI on 14 January 1979 and published his memoirs, *Assignment Oswald*, in 1996. His final verdict on the case still cast Oswald as the lone assassin, murdered in turn by a grief-stricken JACK RUBY, but Hosty minced no words about his treatment by the FBI: "I had been sold down the river. The expendable field agent. The classic scapegoat for J. Edgar Hoover."

**HOTTEL, Guy**—Despite 20 years of service with the FBI, most of that time spent as special agent in charge of the Washington, D.C. field office, Guy Hottel is largely forgotten today, ignored by most histories of the Bureau to the point that one author describes him as an official "unperson."

A football star at George Washington University, where he shared a dormitory room with future FBI luminary CLYDE TOLSON, Hottel was employed by the Aetna Insurance Company when Tolson became J. EDGAR HOOVER's second-in-command, in 1936. Two years later, facing an unwelcome transfer with Aetna, Hottel joined the Bureau himself and was named SAC of the Washington office after perfunctory training. Hoover served as best man at Hottel's second wedding, and Hottel frequently accompanied Hoover and Tolson on fishing trips and on their periodic "inspection tours" of various field offices. In 1939, when Tolson reportedly fell in love with a woman from New York City, Hottel was dispatched by Hoover with orders for Tolson to "forget it," and Tolson promptly obeyed.

That assignment backfired on Hottel in the early 1940s, as Tolson's resentment and Hottel's increased drinking combined to exclude him from the Hoover-Tolson inner circle. Known as a gambler and brawler, described by one G-men who knew him as "a terrible roustabout," Hottel embarrassed the Bureau on numerous occasions. As former Washington police inspector Joseph Shimon told author Anthony Summers, "When Hottel went on the drunk, he'd go into different bars and start telling stories about the sex parties at Hoover's house, you know, with the boys." Police were inevitably dispatched to retrieve Hottel and drop him at FBI HEADQUARTERS, where he still retained enough of Hoover's favor to escape punishment for his various indiscretions. The secret of survival undoubtedly lay in Hottel's usefulness to Hoover. In 1952, for example, Democratic Party organizers identified Hottel as the G-man most responsible for spreading rumors of HOMOSEXUALITY against presidential candidate ADLAI STEVENSON.

Upon retirement from the Bureau, Hottel settled in Delaware and refused all interview requests until shortly before his death, in 1990. On that occasion he spoke freely concerning his many "inspection tours" with Hoover and Tolson, in fact lavish vacations financed by wealthy patrons including CLINT MURCHISON, executives of the Ford Motor Company, and the Firestone family. According to Anthony Summers, Hottel described Hoover's gambling addiction, his fondness for a certain nude beach near Miami, and the director's jealous rages sparked whenever Tolson paid attention to third parties of either sex.

**HOUSE Committee on Un-American Activities** — The House Committee on Un-American Activities (HUAC) was created in 1938, with Rep. MARTIN DIES as chairman, to investigate subversive activities in the U.S. At the time, fascist groups like the German American Bund and the CHRISTIAN FRONT were a primary concern, but the far-right political leaning of Dies and company insured that most of those investigated over the next 30-odd years would be suspected members or associates of the COMMUNIST PARTY. HUAC's disregard for law and the U.S. Constitution was revealed a month before its first hearings opened, on 6 July 1938, staff member E.K. Gubin told FBI agents that Dies had ordered "certain of the Investigators to confiscate anything that they wanted in any business office to which they may be sent and … not worry particularly about legal procedure." A case in point occurred in May 1940, when HUAC raiders illegally seized two tons of documents from the Communist Party and the International Workers Order in Philadelphia. By the time three leaders of the raid were jailed and the documents returned by order of a federal judge, HUAC staffers had already photocopied the papers for future reference.

Around the same time, Chairman Dies made the critical mistake of criticizing J. EDGAR HOOVER and the FBI, suggesting that G-men were less than efficient in their pursuit of Reds. On 22 November 1940 Attorney General ROBERT JACKSON accused Dies of interfering with the Bureau's work, but the feud continued for another year, until EDWARD TAMM privately confronted Dies with evidence of a recent $2,000 bribe. Henceforth, while Dies continued his verbal assaults on the New Deal, he never again criticized the Bureau. In fact, as described by journalist Curt Gentry, HUAC soon became "almost an adjunct of the FBI," dominated and manipulated by Hoover "for his own purposes."

The pattern emerged most obviously under Chairman J. Parnell Thomas, when the FBI provided HUAC with classified FILES and testimony from INFORMANTS like ELIZABETH BENTLEY who had outlived their covert usefulness or failed to make their charges stick in court. Targets including WILLIAM REMINGTON and HARRY DEXTER WHITE were subjected to public character assassination by HUAC when G-men found no evidence required for criminal charges, and countless lives were ruined in the process. Rep. RICHARD NIXON joined HUAC in 1947 and subsequently made a national reputation with his pursuit of witness ALGER HISS. Chairman Thomas spoke fondly of the HUAC-FBI partnership in July 1948, telling Congress: "The closest relationship exists between this committee and the FBI…. I think there is a very good understanding between us. It is something, however, that we cannot talk too much about." (Nor would it save Thomas in 1949, when he was convicted of padding his payroll and sentenced to three years in prison.)

HUAC continued to serve the FBI under various chairmen through the years. In 1950, prior to publication of a critical FBI history, the committee grilled author MAX LOWENTHAL's publisher in a failed attempt to find Red connections. During 1965-66, deviating from its pattern of investigating only left-wing targets, HUAC subjected the KU KLUX KLAN to similar treatment. In the process, Chairman Edwin Willis (from Louisiana) deplored Klan violence and underestimated membership by 66 percent, simultaneously praising the FBI's anti-Klan work and exonerating "respectable" segregationists from any involvement in TERRORISM.

In 1969 HUAC was officially renamed the House Internal Security Committee, but its performance under Chairman Richard Ichord ran true to form. The committee worked with G-men and Nixon White House aides to investigate "NEW LEFT" targets, but the WATERGATE SCANDAL and subsequent exposures of federal corruption left the HISC bereft of public support. One of its last investigations, into charges of alleged FBI malfeasance, may best be described as a whitewash. The 1974 report ignored any mention of illegal COINTELPRO operations, blamed recent FBI problems on "an inept [Nixon] Administration," and warned of the danger presented by any future "severe restrictions placed upon the FBI." The committee was formally abolished by Congress in January 1975, its files transferred to the National Archives under seal for a minimum of 50 years.

**HOUSE Select Committee on Assassinations** — Public skepticism concerning lone-assassin verdicts in the 1963 JFK ASSASSINATION and the 1968 murder of MARTIN LUTHER KING, JR., was not assuaged by the Warren Commission's report in 1964 (on the death of President JOHN KENNEDY) or by the FBI's MURKIN investigation (of King's assassination). Revelations of criminal activity by G-men and agents of the CENTRAL INTELLIGENCE AGENCY, exposed by the U.S. Senate's CHURCH COMMITTEE in 1975-76, added fuel to various conspiracy theories surrounding the murders. Congress responded to those widespread doubts in September 1976, with passage of House Resolution 1540, authorizing a new investigation of both crimes by a House Select Committee on Assassinations. The committee was specifically created to answer four questions:

1. Who assassinated President Kennedy and Dr. King?
2. Did the assassin or assassins in either case have assistance — was there a conspiracy?
3. Did the responsible federal agencies perform adequately in sharing information prior to each assassination, in protecting President Kennedy and Dr. King, and in conducting their investigations of the assassinations?
4. Was there a need for new legislation or for amending existing legislation with respect to assassinations?

The committee's initial mandate expired on 3 January 1977, but its life was twice extended by additional House resolutions, finally expiring on 3 January 1979. Chaired by Ohio congressman Louis Stokes, the committee questioned 335 witnesses in public or executive sessions, conducting a total of 4,924 interviews. Immunity orders were secured for 165 witnesses, and two — Chicago mobsters Sam Giancana and John Rosselli — were murdered by persons unknown before they could testify. Critics denounced the committee for its supposed extravagance, but in fact the $5.5 million spent during 30 months of inquiry was barely half of the Warren Commission's for a 10-month investigation in 1964 (adjusted for 1977 dollar values).

The committee published its findings in January 1979, and while various questions remained unanswered (including the role of ORGANIZED CRIME in President Kennedy's murder), the report found "a high probability" of multiple gunmen in JFK's slaying. "A likelihood of conspiracy" was also found in Dr. King's death, with two deceased suspects named as possible sponsors of an alleged murder contract, executed by confessed assassin James Earl Ray.

The committee's report exonerated both the FBI and CIA of direct participation in either slaying, but the Bureau did not escape criticism. In respect to President Kennedy, committee members found that the JUSTICE DEPARTMENT "failed to exercise initiative in supervising and directing" the FBI's assassination inquiry. Specifically, while the Bureau's investigation of LEE HARVEY OSWALD prior to November 1963 was "adequate," and its probe of his role in JFK's murder was "thorough and professional," the FBI was ranked "deficient" in sharing its data with other agencies and furthermore "failed to investigate adequately the possibility of a conspiracy to assassinate the President."

Evidence of federal malfeasance was more voluminous in Dr. King's case, where committee members found that the FBI's COINTELPRO campaigns "grossly abused and exceeded its legal authority and failed to consider the possibility that actions threatening bodily harm to Dr. King might be encouraged by the program." The Bureau had performed "a thorough fugitive investigation" in pursuit of James Earl Ray, but once again G-men had "failed to investigate adequately the possibility of a conspiracy in the assassination." Beyond that failure, the FBI had "manifested a lack of concern for constitutional rights in the manner in which it conducted parts of the [King] investigation." Specific "investigative excesses" noted by the committee included illegal interception and photocopying of several letters exchanged between defendant James Earl Ray and his attorneys. G-men also interviewed Ray on at least one occasion without legal counsel or mandatory advice concerning his right to stand silent. The committee presumed those actions were prompted by "pressure from above," in the form of demands from Director J. EDGAR HOOVER.

Ultimately, the House committee's investigation solved nothing. Its 792-page report failed to convince lone-assassin devotees, while its failure to identify living suspects in either assassination its pro-conspiracy verdicts effectively impotent. None of the committee's recommendations for new legislation were ever enacted by Congress. Controversy surrounding both crimes (and the RFK ASSASSINATION, ignored by the committee's inquiry) endures to the present day.

**HOUSTON, Lenore** — While not the Bureau's first WOMAN AGENT, Lenore Houston holds dubious honor as the first and last hired by J. EDGAR HOOVER during his 48 years as director. Re-grettably, her experience left Houston in a mental institution and apparently convinced Hoover that female agents were detrimental to the service.

Born in 1879, Houston was 45 years old when she joined the Bureau of Investigation as a "special employee" on 14 January 1924. Assigned to the Philadelphia field office, she worked on MANN ACT cases and received a salary equivalent to that of rookie agents ($7 per day plus $4 a day when traveling). Pennsylvania congressman George Graham several times petitioned Director WILLIAM BURNS for Houston's promotion to full-fledged agent status, but Burns refused. Hoover succeeded Burns as acting director in May 1924 and surprised all concerned by appointing Houston as a special agent six months later, on 6 November 1924.

We shall probably never know what went wrong during Houston's last four years with the Bureau. She was transferred from Philadelphia to the Washington, D.C. field office on 29 August 1927 and submitted her resignation on 20 October 1928, effective 7 November 1928. In 1930 she was confined to a psychiatric hospital, suffering from hallucinations and threatening to kill Hoover upon her release. No information on the outcome of her treatment is presently available.

**HOWELLS, William Dean** — Renowned novelist, poet and critic William Howells had been dead for 21 years when the FBI opened a file in his name, during 1941. The cause of that belated interest was an INFORMANT's report that a new owner of *The Daily Worker* once "sat at the feet of Boston's great Novelist, William Dean Howells." The same could be said of authors Stephen Crane, Henry James and Mark Twain, but the Bureau was predictably more interested in "radical" connections. G-men noted that in 1909 Howells had been a charter member of the NATIONAL ASSOCIATION FOR THE ADVANCEMENT OF COLORED PEOPLE, but he was safely beyond their reach, immune to harassment and surveillance

**HUGHES, James Langston** — A native of Joplin, Missouri, born 1 February 1902, Langston Hughes tops the list of black American writers in the first half of the twentieth century, though FBI watchdogs preferred to call him a "Negro pornographic poet." G-men made the first entry to his file in 1925, noting his membership in the All America Anti-Imperialist League and kept after Hughes from there, building a 559-page dossier. Five years later, when Hughes became president of the National Negro Congress, agents branded it "an official Communist subsidiary." In 1933, one nameless INFORMANT told the Bureau he had "loaned" Hughes a COMMUNIST PARTY pamphlet titled "An Appeal to the Negro Voter"; another claimed Hughes "admired the Soviet system for its non-race prejudice [sic]." In 1934 agents noted Hughes's membership in the National Committee of the American League Against War and Fascism." By 1937, demoted in Bureau files to the rank to the status of "alleged poet," Hughes was found to be involved with more "Communist fronts."

Scrutiny of Hughes continued into WORLD WAR II. Watchers noted his 1941 appearance on the Writers' War Board advisory council, with other "subversives" including PEARL BUCK and

QUENTIN REYNOLDS. That same year, a Bureau critic opined that "Good-bye Christ," the author's latest poem, "appears to be of a Communistic nature." (Hoover, in a 1947 speech, deemed it "sacrilegious.") By 1943, Hughes had taken his place in the FBI's secret SECURITY INDEX, listed on grounds that he had allegedly "stated he is a believer in the Russian Soviet form of government and thereby admitted being a Communist." In 1948, when Abington Cokesbury Press sought to include Hoover's 1947 speech in a forthcoming anthology, Hughes denied permission for his poem to be printed. Hoover blamed the publisher and ordered his troops to "Make certain we furnish this outfit no more material for publication. They are too squeamish about offending Commies."

Five years later, Hughes told Senator JOSEPH MCCARTHY's Subcommittee on Investigations that he had grown disillusioned with Russia, but the FBI kept after him, forging his signature on letters used in a 1960 Chicago COINTELPRO campaign. Hughes died in New York City on 22 May 1967, but the FBI vilification continued. Hoover could never speak of Hughes without referring to him as "a colored Communist."

**HURST, Fannie**—The daughter of Jewish immigrants from Bavaria, born in Ohio on 18 October 1889, Hurst was a novelist and playwright identified as "subversive" in ELIZABETH DILLING'S book *The Red Network*. Her 84-page FBI file was opened in 1930, when G-men noted her affiliation with four suspect organizations: the National Unemployment League; the Non-Partisan Committee for Heywood Broun in Congress; the "Norman Thomas New York City Election" [sic]; and "the Recommending Book League of America." Four years later, J. EDGAR HOOVER took particular umbrage to Hurst's role as an organizer of EMMA GOLDMAN'S Welcome Home Tour, and her attendance at a banquet honoring the Soviet ambassador. Another strike against Hurst, in Hoover's mind, was the fact of her close friendship with ELEANOR ROOSEVELT. In the early 1950s, Hoover noted Hurst's affiliation with the NBC television network, while acknowledging that she had "indicated her dislike for certain Communist front organizations." The final entry in her file, from 1956, notes that certain undescribed documents had been forwarded from FBI headquarters to the CENTRAL INTELLIGENCE AGENCY. Hurst died in New York City on 23 February 1968.

**HUSTON Plan**—Named for White House aide Tom Charles Huston, the Huston Plan was an attempt by President RICHARD NIXON to coordinate and consolidate DOMESTIC SURVEILLANCE of his perceived political enemies throughout the U.S. and abroad. The move began on 5 June 1970, when Nixon met with the four chiefs of U.S. intelligence: FBI Director J. EDGAR HOOVER; Director Richard Helms of the CENTRAL INTELLIGENCE AGENCY; Vice Admiral Noel Gaylor of the NATIONAL SECURITY AGENCY; and Donald Bennett, director of the Defense Intelligence Agency. Proclaiming that the nation was beset by an "epidemic of unprecedented domestic TERRORISM," Nixon appointed the four chiefs to an ad hoc committee for development of "a plan which will enable us to curtail the illegal activities of those who are determined to destroy our society." Hoover was placed in charge of the committee, with Huston serving as White House liaison.

Huston's relationship with Hoover broke down three days later, when he met with the chiefs and rejected Hoover's bid to prepare "a historical summary of unrest in the country up to the present." Contradicting Hoover before his peers, Huston dismissed any review of "the dead past," instead demanding a list of techniques for use against left-wing radicals in "the living present." While Bennett, Helms and Gaylor cautiously agreed, Hoover balked at revealing the FBI's illicit methods. In a memo to Assistant Director WILLIAM SULLIVAN, dated 6 June 1970, Hoover declared:

> For years and years I have approved opening mail and other similar operations, but no. It is becoming more and more dangerous and we are apt to get caught. I am not opposed to doing this. I am not opposed to continuing the burglaries and the opening of mail and other similar activities, providing someone higher than myself approves of it. ... I no longer want to accept the sole responsibility. [If] the attorney general or some other high ranking person in the White House [approves] then I will carry out their decision. But I am not going to accept the responsibility myself anymore, even though I've done it for many years.

On 23 June 1970 Hoover severed FBI liaison with the CIA, NSA and DIA, as well as the INTERNAL REVENUE SERVICE, the SECRET SERVICE, and all branches of U.S. military intelligence. When the ad hoc committee's report was presented two days later, it included Hoover's observation that "The FBI does not wish to change its present procedure of selective coverage on major internal security threats as it believes this coverage is adequate at this time. The FBI would not oppose other agencies seeking authority of the Attorney General for coverage required by them and therefore instituting such coverage themselves." One by one, Hoover refused to participate in activities which his G-men had pursued for decades, including "surreptitious entry" and "any covert mail opening because it is clearly illegal."

Historian Theodore White later praised Hoover's stand as a lone hero's resistance to Nixon's criminal activities, but in fact it was nothing of the kind. Hoover simply refused to place himself at risk for a corrupt administration that might—as White House aide JOHN EHRLICHMAN later suggested for Acting FBI Director L. PATRICK GRAY—use him as a scapegoat, "twisting slowly, slowly in the wind." Coordination of domestic spying through the White House was thus derailed by Hoover's instinct for self-preservation, while the nation's chief practitioner of such techniques became (however briefly) an icon to selected civil libertarians. It would be the director's last coup, since he had less than two years to live. Tom Huston was replaced in Nixon's favors by John Dean, and the Nixon regime moved on to the fatal morass of the WATERGATE SCANDAL.

**HUXLEY, Aldous Leonard**—The product of an affluent British family, born 26 July 1894, Aldous Huxley began his literary career as a poet and critic, shifting to novels in 1921. His classic work *Brave New World* was published 11 years later, to worldwide critical acclaim. Huxley was one of several British authors who publicly supported the Loyalist side in Spain's civil war, but that "subversive" stance only came to FBI attention in 1938, when Huxley settled in Los Angeles. G-men studied *An Encyclopedia* *of Pacifism*, edited by Huxley in 1937, which was "found to be distributed by the War Resisters League in New York." (In fact, it was published by Harper & Row.) *Brave New World* was belatedly subjected to "cryptographic examination" in 1943, and while no coded messages were found therein, Huxley still rated an "Internal Security — Alien Enemy Control" dossier that same year. Agents of the CENTRAL INTELLIGENCE AGENCY and Army Intelligence later joined in stalking Huxley until his death on 22 November 1963, news of his passing eclipsed by the JFK ASSASSINATION. Of 130 pages in Huxley's FBI dossier, 89 remain classified today, while most of the remaining 111 were heavily censored before their release under the FREEDOM OF INFORMATION ACT.

# I

**IDENTIFICATION DIVISION** —One of the first "reform" efforts undertaken by Director J. EDGAR HOOVER in 1924 was the consolidation of national fingerprint records under FBI control. Prior to 1924 there were two major fingerprint collections in the U.S.: a substantial file maintained in Chicago by the INTERNATIONAL ASSOCIATION OF CHIEFS OF POLICE (the "National Bureau of Identification"), and the U.S. JUSTICE DEPARTMENT'S National Division of Identification and Information, with some 810,000 fingerprint cards housed at Leavenworth federal prison, in Kansas. The two were combined under Hoover, and the FBI's collection grew rapidly thereafter.

In 1929 the Civil Service Commission began fingerprinting all job applicants, and the FBI absorbed that print collection three years later. The same year, 1932, Bureau headquarters began collecting copies of fingerprint records from state and local police agencies. The U.S. Army and Navy delivered their fingerprint files to the FBI in December 1941, after the PEARL HARBOR attack. Hoover, meanwhile, encouraged *all* Americans to send the FBI their fingerprints for possible use in "emergencies." The Bureau filed its 100-millionth fingerprint card in 1946, and the vast collection had grown to 190 million sets of prints (including many duplicates). By any standard, it was the world's largest fingerprint collection.

But was it practical?

Bureau sources note that fingerprint checks on federal job applicants in 1929 revealed 8 percent of those applicants to have criminal records, a statistic slashed to 2 percent a decade later. Likewise, they note, collecting fingerprints from innocent civilians may be useful in the wake of natural disasters (for identifying corpses) or in cases of amnesia. Critics, however, suggest that vast fingerprint collections are unnecessary, historically utilized by the Bureau as a publicity gimmick. Why, for instance, was it necessary to fingerprint Walt Disney or John D. Rockefeller, Jr., in 1936, and then announce their print donations to the world? Twenty years later, why did the FBI maintain fingerprint files on 60,753,062 blameless civilians and only 29,215,596 convicted criminals? Scotland Yard, by contrast, maintained a file of 1.25 million fingerprints in 1963, nearly all convicted felons, and while that archive gained an average 50,000 fingerprint cards per year, it was also relentlessly "weeded" to remove records of deceased individuals. The FBI, meanwhile, seemed intent on collecting multiple copies of fingerprint records on every American and storing them for eternity. In light of subsequent exposés concerning Hoover's illegal SECURITY INDEX and similar mass-arrest schemes, certain members of society may be forgiven for viewing the Bureau's compulsive fingerprint collection process with suspicion.

In 1993 the Identification Division was absorbed by a Criminal Justice Information Services, a new division of that also includes the FBI Disaster Squad and the NATIONAL CRIME INFORMATION CENTER. Complete automation of the Bureau's fingerprint collection, begun in 1973, was finally achieved in 1996, with relocation to a new operations center in Clarksburg, West Virginia. At that time, the FBI had more than 200 million prints on file, representing some 68 million individuals.

**INDUSTRIAL Workers of the World** —America's first significant "radical" LABOR UNION, the IWW was founded in Chicago, in June 1905, by 200 members of 43 groups that opposed the American Federation of Labor's exclusionist policies. Instead of limiting its membership to white "craft" workers, the IWW (or "Wobblies") sought all American workers, regardless of race or gender, for "One Big Union." Early leaders included William ("Big Bill") Haywood, Daniel De Leon and Eugene V. Debs. Other founding members included ANARCHIST Carlo Tresca and William Z. Foster, later an official of the COMMUNIST PARTY. Factional differences split the group in 1908, with Debs leading advocates of political action into the Socialist Party, while Bill Haywood's militants steered the IWW toward pursuit of a nationwide general strike.

That goal was never attained, but the IWW led numerous strikes around the U.S. between 1909 and the outbreak of WORLD WAR I. Despite their reputation in the press, Wobblies did not seek to initiate violence, but they fought back when attacked and in their 1909 strike against an affiliate of U.S. Steel threatened to kill a policeman for each striker slain by state troopers. Looking beyond local action, IWW spokesmen viewed regional strikes as "mere incidents in the class war … necessary to prepare the masses for the final 'catastrophe,' the general strike which will complete the expropriation of the employers."

Such rhetoric, backed by militant action, was anathema to J. EDGAR HOOVER and the agents of his GENERAL INTELLIGENCE DIVISION. Surveillance and disruption of the IWW was a top priority for the early Bureau of Investigation, though local authorities and right-wing vigilantes fought most of the battles prior to 1917. That year saw passage of the wartime ESPIONAGE ACT, which criminalized any "interference" with (and most public criticism of) the U.S. military. Since IWW leaders stridently opposed American participation in the Great War, they were subject to arrest by G-men as subversive enemies of the state. Acting on instructions from President WOODROW WILSON that "the IWWs certainly are worthy of being suppressed," Attorney General THOMAS GREGORY ordered 166 leaders of the union arrested in April 1918, for obstructing the war effort. Bill Haywood escaped to Russia in the confusion, but 101 Wobblies were convicted in June 1918 and sent to Leavenworth federal prison (where they promptly began recruiting more converts to the cause).

There was no federal armistice for Wobblies in the wake of World War I; in fact, repressive measures from the Bureau and local police intensified, fueled by fears of "black subversion" as the IWW increased its efforts to recruit African American workers. Harassment by G-men and New York police drove one black Wobbly, James Jones, to commit suicide in November 1919. Elsewhere, in Washington and Louisiana, members of the AMERICAN LEGION murdered union activists while authorities turned a blind eye. The DEPARTMENT OF JUSTICE increased its anti-Wobbly efforts in 1920, spearheaded from the Bureau's Chicago field office. There, six agents labored in a special "IWW Room," indexing more than 20,000 members of the "unlawful association" for surveillance and harassment. No Wobbly was too insignificant for federal attention, including the "ultra radical negro [sic] Bolsheviki propagandist and IWW" whom agents hounded from his job as a janitor at Chicago's City Hall.

The campaign took its toll, IWW membership dwindling to the point that no further threat was perceived after 1925. The union survives today, its members scattered in far-flung locals, still espousing the socialist creed of their predecessors, but the glory days are lost beyond recall. Virtual destruction of the Wobblies would rank as one of J. Edgar Hoover's proudest achievement prior to his assumption of absolute control at Bureau headquarters.

**INFORMANTS**—In 1969 authors Harry and Bonaro Overstreet published *The FBI in Our Open Society*, one of the last books devoted entirely to unqualified praise for the Bureau and J. EDGAR HOOVER. Devoting a full chapter to the FBI's employment of covert informers, the authors wrote: "Because they must operate in secret, those for whom the law of our land is *the enemy* have no choice but to hate and fear the informant." [Emphasis in the original.] They proceed from that false premise — i.e., that all opponents of DOMESTIC SURVEILLANCE are criminals or "enemies" of society — to define three categories of informants. They include: (1) individuals like Mafia defector Joseph Valachi, who turn on their former comrades out of personal fear; (2) informants like ex-Klansman DELMAR DENNIS, who become disillusioned with criminal activity by groups they joined in good faith; and (3) agents who infiltrate suspect organizations on behalf of law enforcement.

Even a cursory review of Bureau history, however, indicates that several classes of informant were omitted from the published roster. Those selectively omitted by the Overstreets include:

(1) Active criminals using the FBI to dispose of illicit rivals. A case in point is the Capone gang's fabrication of a kidnapping in 1933 to frame bootlegger ROGER TOUHY and send him to prison, with Bureau complicity, for a crime that never occurred.

(2) Felons awaiting trial or sentencing, who barter testimony in return for official favors. The most notorious such case in Bureau history is JOHN DILLINGER'S betrayal by brothel madam Anna Cumpanas, who sought FBI intervention to prevent her own deportation. A half-century later, contract killer SALVATORE GRAVANO escaped punishment for 19 murders by "rolling over" on Mafia boss John Gotti.

(3) Professional informants like LOUIS BUDENZ, HERBERT PHILBRICK and others who profit from the celebrity of their "born-again" virtue, whether they desert religious cults, political extremist groups or criminal syndicates. Regardless of the target, informant longevity requires continuing disclosures and new "revelations."

(4) Disgruntled spouses, neighbors, co-workers and other grudge-bearers who furnish (or fabricate) derogatory information to punish objects of personal spite. Over time, the FBI has collected thousands of statements, frequently anonymous and unverified, that were circulated as "raw data" to journalists and outside investigators, ruining countless lives and careers.

(5) *Agents provocateur*, employed by unscrupulous agencies to boost arrest statistics and/or "neutralize" specific targets by promoting criminal activity with the full knowledge and approval of their police contacts. The FBI has used *agents provocateur* since the days of the PALMER RAIDS (if not before), and no amount of exposure seems to discourage the practice. An incomplete list of informants who either committed crimes themselves or actively encouraged others to do so includes ALFRED BURNETT, WILLIAM LEMMER, HORACE PACKER, CHARLES GRIMM, GARY ROWE, LARRY GRATHWOHL and MELVIN SMITH.

(6) Informants pressured or intimidated into giving testimony, which sometimes proves to be false. Chicago G-man MELVIN PURVIS was notorious for physical abuse of suspects in custody, and "third-degree" methods have been reported from other Bureau field offices, as well. A central event of FBI history, the 1933 KANSAS CITY MASSACRE, owes its famous (and erroneous)

solution chiefly to informant Vivian Mathias, illegally confined by FBI agents without legal counsel and coached through a series of evolving statements to support the official story.

Ironically, one of the cases cited by the Overstreets in 1969 as an exemplary use of informants actually undermines their case. They refer to the September 1967 arrest of seven persons affiliated with the REVOLUTIONARY ACTION MOVEMENT (RAM) on charges of plotting to kill J. Edgar Hoover and President LYNDON JOHNSON. "Both plots," the authors remind us, "were disclosed by informants who were members of RAM." Strangely, they fail to mention that the charges were dismissed as spurious, for lack of evidence.

The Overstreets' sanitized view of FBI informants presupposes that the Bureau strives to destroy subversive organizations, but even that basic assumption is subject to doubt. Investigation of the 1920 Palmer raids prompted a federal judge to note that the FBI, through its informants, "operates some part of the COMMUNIST PARTY in this country," and the picture had not changed by 1961, when ex-Agent JACK LEVINE revealed that fully one-fifth of all registered U.S. communists drew monthly paychecks from the Bureau. The same was true in Dixie, where FBI informants BILL WILKINSON and EDWARD DAWSON led violent factions of the KU KLUX KLAN; and in California, where defectors from the paramilitary MINUTEMEN created a new SECRET ARMY ORGANIZATION, drawing their money, guns and explosives from the Bureau's San Diego field office.

Writing two years before exposure of the Bureau's COINTELPRO crimes, the Overstreets maintained that "[t]here is nothing to suggest that the use of informants leads to the conviction of innocent persons." Today we know better, informed of the FBI's complicity in deliberate FRAME-UPS ranging from the SACCO-VANZETTI case of 1920 to the fraudulent prosecutions of ELMER PRATT, PETER LIMONE and JOSEPH SALVATI. In light of disclosures now spanning the best part of a century, it is both difficult and dangerous to accept the notion that intelligence agencies should be left to regulate and police themselves.

**INFORMATION Resources Division** — This division of the modern FBI began life in 1972 as the Computer Systems Division (CSD), combining functions of the Bureau's automated payroll with those of the NATIONAL CRIME INFORMATION CENTER. Three years later, the CSD was merged with the FBI LABORATORY to create a new Technical Services Division (including the Communications, Engineering and Special Projects Sections). Director CLARENCE KELLEY extracted the FBI Lab from Technical Services prior to his February 1978 resignation, but Technical Services otherwise continued its functions until 1993, when it was merged with the Information Management Division to create the new Information Resources Division (IRD). The division's employees work in the areas of automated data processing, design and install technical support equipment for FBI field offices, maintain telecommunications services, and perform engineering research.

**INFORMATION Technology Centers** — The FBI's first two Information Technology Centers were established in the 1980s, at obsolete field office headquarters in Butte, Montana and Savannah, Georgia. A third center was established at Pocatello, Idaho in 1998, and Director LOUIS FREEH noted the existence of a fourth (location undisclosed) in his congressional budget requests for 1999-2001. The centers are staffed by technical support personnel, primarily computer experts, who process both administrative information and data required for ongoing field investigations.

**INGE, William** — Born in 1913, William Inge was the author of such noteworthy plays as *Bus Stop*; *Picnic*; *Come Back, Little Sheba*; and *The Dark at the Top of the Stairs*. The FBI opened a brief file on Inge in 1957, after he was mentioned in a State Department intelligence report on Czechoslovakia. The report claimed that certain "inroads" had been made toward relaxing Communist control of the Czech government, illustrated by productions of *Bus Stop*, as well as plays by ARTHUR MILLER and LILLIAN HELLMAN. J. EDGAR HOOVER must have viewed that finding with suspicion, since he regarded both Miller and Hellman as communists. Inge was apparently deemed non-subversive, his FBI dossier consisting of a mere four pages.

**INLET Program** — The Bureau's "INLET" program (for *Intelligence Letters*) had its origins on 9 May 1969, when *New York Times* reporter William Beecher broke the story of President RICHARD NIXON'S secret bombing campaign in Cambodia. Secretary of State HENRY KISSINGER made several urgent calls to Director J. EDGAR HOOVER the same day, demanding "a major effort" to identify the source of leaks using "whatever resources" were necessary. Gen. Alexander Haig followed up on 10 May with specific orders from "the highest authority" for WIRETAPS on an aide to the secretary of defense and three staff members of the National Security Council (NSC). Hoover placed Assistant Director WILLIAM SULLIVAN in charge of the mission, with orders to keep detailed records of the White House requests.

No leaks to the press were uncovered, but Nixon and company enjoyed the flow of illicit intelligence so much that Hoover expanded and formalized the INLET program on 26 November 1969, approving collection of intelligence on national security risks and "items with an unusual twist or concerning prominent personalities which may be of special interest to the President or Attorney General." Nixon deleted Kissinger from the list of recipients in May 1970, by which time the wiretaps had proliferated to cover 17 targets, including at least four prominent journalists. On 25 November 1970, White House aide H.R. HALDEMAN asked Hoover for information documenting HOMOSEXUALITY among Washington newsmen and "any other stuff" of a similar nature. A report from Hoover's office was hand-delivered to Haldeman two days later.

The INLET program was terminated on 10 February 1971, after the *Washington Post* ran a two-part series by Ronald Kessler, detailing illegal FBI wiretaps. President Nixon later told assistant John Dean that "[t]he taps never helped us. Just gobs of material, gossip and bullshitting." Kissinger, long since out of the loop, complained to an interviewer that Hoover "invariably listed some official outside the FBI hierarchy as requesting each wiretap, even in cases where I heard Hoover himself specifically recommend them to Nixon." In the absence of further FBI cooperation, Nixon placed his hopes for future surveillance efforts in the HUSTON PLAN.

**INSPECTION Division**—Created by J. EDGAR HOOVER soon after he assumed control of the Bureau in 1924, the Inspection Division was designed (in theory) to promote Hoover's "cleanup" of the scandal-ridden agency. In fact, however, it was often viewed by agents as a tool of Hoover's private malice, with inspectors dispatched from Washington to perform "hatchet jobs" on a particular target, be it an individual agent or an entire field office whose Special Agent in Charge had somehow angered the director. When not investigating specific complaints, members of the Inspection Division enforced a list of arbitrary, sometimes irrational rules, such as the ban on special agents drinking coffee while on duty. (FBI clerks were allowed to drink coffee at their desks, while on-duty agents were barred from drinking coffee either in their offices or elsewhere. The result: countless wasted hours, sneaking off to remote coffee shops.)

One longtime member of the Inspection Division was W. MARK FELT, assigned as an inspector's aide in 1954, rising to command the division eight years later and remaining as chief of the division until 1968. Felt was later elevated to deputy associate director and briefly served as second in command for Acting Director L. PATRICK GRAY. The quality of his performance in rooting out FBI "bad apples" may be judged by the fact that Felt himself was convicted in November 1980 of personally ordering illegal surveillance techniques, including warrantless BREAK-INS and BUGGING against suspected members of the WEATHER UNDERGROUND. (Felt was later pardoned by President RONALD REAGAN.)

In January 1975, Director CLARENCE KELLEY ordered the Inspection Division to investigate "misuse of office by former Director Hoover" and to report any abuses "irrespective of what the consequences may be." The inspectors examined 300 confidential files maintained in Washington by Hoover, CLYDE TOLSON and CARTHA DELOACH, including derogatory material on 17 past or present members of Congress. Contrary to public denials issued by DeLoach, the inspectors determined that information on 11 senators and congressmen had been illegally disseminated outside the Bureau. Despite Kelley's "new broom" approach, the post-Hoover "reforms" accomplished little or nothing. By 1976, surprise field inspections had been eliminated, with advance lists of written questions furnished to special agents in charge of field offices slated for examination, causing many agents to dismiss the process as a sham.

From 1976 to 1997, the Inspection Division included an OFFICE OF PROFESSIONAL RESPONSIBILITY designed to ferret out and punish incidents of AGENT MISCONDUCT. Despite an appearance of strict enforcement, discipline remains erratic, with relatively minor offenses sometimes receiving disproportionate punishment, while investigation of more serious infractions sometimes appears to be sidetracked or whitewashed. Too often, public exposure in the media seems to dictate FBI reactions to misconduct. As author Ronald Kessler observes in *The FBI*

(1993), "What is needed is a balance between the arbitrary and harsh discipline of the Hoover era and the slap on the wrist that is too often meted out today for lying or for abusing the FBI's awesome power." The division's most recent leader, appointed on 14 May 2002, is Acting Assistant Director John P. O'Connor.

**INTERNATIONAL Association of Chiefs of Police (IACP)**—Founded in 1893 as the National Chiefs of Police Union, the IACP was initially created to apprehend fugitives who fled local jurisdictions in the days before such flight was a federal offense. Today the stated mission is "to advance the science and art of police services; to develop and disseminate improved administrative, technical and operational practices and promote their use in police work; to foster police cooperation and the exchange of information and experience among police administrators throughout the world; to bring about recruitment and training in the police profession of qualified persons; and to encourage adherence of all police officers to high professional standards of performance and conduct." In fact, the group operates as a political lobby on issues deemed critical by its leaders (and ostensibly by police officers nationwide).

Some of the FBI's most famous programs trace their roots to the IACP, although that debt is frequently ignored in Bureau histories. The IACP was a pioneer in fingerprint identification and established a National Bureau of Criminal Identification in 1897, 11 years before the FBI was created and 27 years before the IACP's files were absorbed into the Bureau's new IDENTIFICATION DIVISION. In 1922 the IACP established a uniform crime records reporting system, which the FBI took over (again, using IACP archives) in 1930. In 1934 the FBI and IACP jointly created the FBI NATIONAL ACADEMY for advanced training of state and local police. Six years later the IACP established its national headquarters in Washington, D.C.

That move consolidated FBI Director J. EDGAR HOOVER's de facto control over the IACP. Bureau liaison QUINN TAMM later described for author Sanford Ungar how the Bureau exercised that dominance: "We used to control the election of officers. We had a helluva lot of friends around, and we would control the nominating committee." Various Hoover aides have also admitted that the director used secret FILES on various U.S. police officials to manipulate conduct, including their votes at IACP conventions. Those yearly gatherings sometimes featured Hoover as the keynote speaker, and the IACP resolutions committee never failed to issue proclamations praising "the Honorable J. Edgar Hoover" for his defense of America. (The proclamations were written at FBI HEADQUARTERS, by the CRIME RECORDS DIVISION, and approved by Hoover in advance.) The most blatant example of Hoover's control was recorded in 1959, when an FBI whispering campaign defeated WILLIAM PARKER, chief of the Los Angeles Police Department, in his bid to become IACP president.

Still, the IACP was not always a rubber stamp for Hoover's opinions. In 1956 an informal poll of its members persuaded Hoover to abandon an ill-conceived presidential campaign (initiated by Red-hunting Senator JOSEPH MCCARTHY). Five years later, Quinn Tamm resigned from the FBI to become IACP president in a move opposed by Hoover. The FBI's director was enraged when Tamm won the election despite Bureau opposition, all the more so when Tamm announced his plans to make the IACP the dominant "spokesman for law enforcement in this country." To that end, the IACP hired a full-time Washington lobbyist in 1967, to press for new crime-control legislation that favored local police with new weapons, equipment and increased appropriations.

The break with Hoover did not signify a total rift between the FBI and the IACP, however. Ex-agents were still welcome in administrative positions, chief among them Charles Moore, Jr., an FBI publicist who served during the troubled 1960s as the IACP's publicity director. Under Moore (as with his predecessors and successors), the IACP's monthly *Police Chief* espoused political views that were indistinguishable from Hoover's. In April 1965, on the subject of campus unrest in California, Moore wrote: "One of the more alarming aspects of these student demonstrations is the ever-present evidence that the guiding hand of Communists and extreme leftists was involved. According to those experts who are best informed regarding Communist plans for world domination, a basic objective is to capture the minds of students and whenever possible to take over institutions of higher learning." A detailed investigation by California regents found no evidence of any COMMUNIST PARTY involvement in the demonstrations.

**INTERNATIONAL Law Enforcement Academy**—Located in Budapest, Hungary, this FBI educational facility graduated its first class of 33 officers from former Eastern Bloc nations in November 1993. The academy remains active today, processing five yearly classes with approximately 50 students each. The courses, taught in English, are designed primarily for middle-management administrators, including subject matter such as "Human Dignity and the Police." Critics of the FBI detect a certain irony in the curriculum, concerning the Bureau's history of political repression, ranging from the PALMER RAIDS and COINTELPRO harassment campaigns, through rough handling of the AMERICAN INDIAN MOVEMENT and the BRANCH DAVIDIAN sect in Waco, Texas.

**INTERNET Fraud Complaint Center** *see* **Computer Crimes**

**IREY, Elmer Lincoln**—Born in 1888, Elmer Irey joined the INTERNAL REVENUE SERVICE at age 26 and soon found a place in the organizations enforcement division. By 1919 he was in charge of that unit, and in 1937 he became chief coordinator of the Treasury Department, supervising all of that agency's law enforcement efforts (including the SECRET SERVICE). During Irey's tenure the IRS arrested 15,000 tax evaders, including such notorious ORGANIZED CRIME figures as ALPHONSE CAPONE, Irving Wexler (AKA "Waxey Gordon") and Morris Kleinman (the "Al Capone of Cleveland"). Under Irey, the IRS enjoyed a 90-percent conviction rate which was far superior to the FBI's.

Those facts spawned furious jealousy in FBI Director J. EDGAR HOOVER, but his worst grudge against Irey derived from the LINDBERGH KIDNAPPING. It was Irey's idea to pay the ransom in easily traceable gold certificates, which ultimately led to the arrest of suspect Richard Bruno Hauptmann. Charles Lindbergh Sr. later told Irey, "If it had not been for you fellows being in the case, Hauptmann would not now be on trial and your organization deserves full credit for his apprehension." That compliment is dubious, since Hauptmann was apparently the victim of a FRAME-UP, but Hoover learned of it and harbored a lifelong grudge against both men. Irey's name goes unmentioned in FBI accounts of the Lindbergh case, and the snub enraged him. As colleague Malachi Harney told author Ovid Demaris, "Irey was a good Christian who didn't cuss, but the air would turn blue when the subject of the Lindbergh kidnapping case came up."

In pursuit of their feud, Irey used Hoover's own weapons, including leaks to "friendly" journalists, complaints to his superiors and testimony in Congress. Whenever questioned on the Lindbergh case, Irey took pains to set the record straight and cast Hoover in the role of crass glory hog. In 1935 Irey opposed the Bureau's latest name change on grounds that the new label made Hoover's agency sound like the one and only federal investigative unit, rather than one of a dozen or more. Irey lost that battle, along with his effort to bring the FBI under Civil Service on the eve of WORLD WAR II, but he remained a thorn in Hoover's side until his 1941 retirement from the IRS. Irey died in 1948.

**INTERNAL Revenue Service**—Predating the FBI by 46 years, the IRS has its roots in America's Civil War. Federal income tax was levied for the first time in 1862, to cover war expenses, with a Commissioner of Internal Revenue appointed to collect the money. The tax was repealed 10 years later, then revived by Congress in 1894. The U.S. SUPREME COURT ruled it unconstitutional in 1895, but the 16th Amendment to the U.S. Constitution settled that issue forever in 1913. At its worst, during WORLD WAR I, some Americans paid a yearly income tax of 77 percent. Originally called the Bureau of Internal Revenue, the IRS received its present name in the 1950s.

Various IRS commissioners and criminal investigators have long collaborated with the FBI to investigate (or harass) various targets. FBI Director J. EDGAR HOOVER frequently referred "subversive" groups and individuals to the IRS for tax audits, with members of the COMMUNIST PARTY suffering some of the closest scrutiny. IRS audits have also been a favorite weapon of U.S. presidents since FRANKLIN ROOSEVELT against their perceived political enemies. At the same time, the IRS and FBI have frequently existed in an adversarial relationship, particularly during Hoover's tenure at FBI HEADQUARTERS. Hoover was intensely jealous of IRS investigator ELMER IREY, whose efforts resulted in conviction of Chicago bootlegger ALPHONSE CAPONE and other notorious mobsters. Later, that strain was exacerbated by tension between G-men and agents of the BUREAU OF ALCOHOL, TOBACCO AND FIREARMS (initially a part of the IRS). Two years before his death, in June 1970, Hoover severed the FBI's liaison with the IRS in protest against President RICHARD NIXON'S sweeping HUSTON PLAN, an illicit scheme to unite all federal intelligence agencies under immediate White House control.

**INTERPOL**—Formally known as the International Criminal Police Organization, Interpol was created in 1924 with headquarters in Vienna, Austria. Austrian police effectively dominated the early organization and Interpol fell under Nazi control in the 1930s. German general Kurt Daluege was elected vice president of Interpol in 1937 (and subsequently executed for war crimes in 1946). Around the same time, FBI Director J. EDGAR HOOVER sent Assistant Director H. Lane Dressler to an Interpol meeting in London. Dressler recommended that the U.S. join Interpol, and Attorney General HOMER CUMMINGS passed the recommendation to Congress in 1938, two weeks after ADOLF HITLER annexed Austria. Congress authorized payment of the $1,500 yearly dues on 8 June 1938.

FBI participation in Interpol was limited by the approach of WORLD WAR II in Europe. G-men were invited to attend Interpol's 1939 conference in Berlin, under the auspices of SS leader Heinrich Himmler, but the U.S. STATE DEPARTMENT declined the invitation. Reinhard Heydrich, chief of Hitler's Security Police (SD) became Interpol's new president and the group's headquarters moved to the Berlin suburb of Wannsee in December 1941, one day after the PEARL HARBOR ATTACK in Hawaii. There, Interpol shared quarters with the Gestapo and devoted itself primarily to hunting Jews and other refugees from German occupation. Heydrich was assassinated in June 1942, replaced six months later by Ernst Kaltenbrunner. Despite a pledge to "continue the strictly nonpolitical character" of Interpol, Kaltenbrunner followed Heydrich's example and was sentenced to death for war crimes at the Nuremberg trials.

On the eve of the Third Reich's collapse, Interpol officials transferred their files to neutral Switzerland. The organization resurfaced in 1946 with much of its wartime leadership intact, although a new charter barred investigations of a racial, religious or political nature. Delegates from the U.S. JUSTICE DEPARTMENT were invited to the first postwar conference at Brussels, in May 1946, but Attorney General TOM CLARK officially declined. Spokesmen for the State Department accepted, however, and the conference elected J. Edgar Hoover as Interpol's vice president. President Florent Louwage of the Belgian Political Police had worked directly under Kaltenbrunner and led Interpol for the next decade.

FBI membership in the "new" Interpol was terminated in 1950, when Hoover learned that Czech police officials had used the organization to track down political defectors in West Germany. Unable to tolerate Reds as he did "reformed" Nazis, Hoover resigned his vice presidency of Interpol for "special reasons" on 26 November 1950. The U.S. Treasury Department joined Interpol in 1958 (at an inflated yearly rate of $25,000, approved by Congress), but the FBI remained aloof. Echoes of Interpol's Nazi past were heard in 1968, when SS veteran Paul Dickopf became president. By the time he retired four years later, Interpol had a new French headquarters and nearly 2 billion Swiss francs in its bank account, most of it contributed by supporters in Switzerland, Brazil and Venezuela. Dickopf's vice president was Eugene Rossides from the U.S. Treasury Department. Another T-man on Interpol's executive committee was Edward Morgan, driven from office in 1974 for his role in the WATERGATE SCANDAL.

That same year, Director CLARENCE KELLEY sent Associate Director Nicholas Callahan as the first FBI representative to an Interpol conference since 1958. Interpol was reeling from exposure of charter violations in Northern Ireland (where it helped track political terrorists) and in the Bahamas (where it helped politicians deport "undesirable" delegates to a Black Power Conference in 1969). FBI leaders resisted the lure of formal membership until January 1985, when Interpol officially repealed the charter ban on political investigations to permit activity in cases of TERRORISM. Four years later, Interpol was further embarrassed by news that its Mexican representative, Florentino Ventura, belonged to a drug-dealing voodoo cult responsible for 25 gruesome murders around Matamoros. By 1994, when Bureau liaison was handed to the FBI's International Relations, officials estimated that 90 percent of international police inquiries bypassed Interpol entirely. One journalist described Interpol as "far from being the slick and sophisticated organization of popular mythology." Another was more cynical, reporting: "They just haven't been the same since *der Führer* died."

**ITALIAN-American Civil Rights League**—The FBI's erratic response to ORGANIZED CRIME has prompted widespread criticism of the Bureau, sometimes from curious sources. After decades of denying that the Mafia existed in America, Director J. EDGAR HOOVER changed his mind in 1961 and "discovered" the Italian faction of organized crime sometimes dubbed *La Cosa Nostra* ("our thing," in Italian). Unfortunately, the FBI's new emphasis on "LCN" as the dominant faction of organized crime was both inaccurate and insulting to many Italian-Americans, prompting a new wave of complaints.

Ironically, one who took advantage of the public outcry was Joseph Columbo Sr., boss of a prominent New York Mafia "family." In April 1970, following the federal arrest of son Joe, Jr., Columbo organized a picket line outside the FBI's New York City field office, protesters carrying signs that read ITALIANS UNITE, ITALIAN POWER, and THE FBI FRAMES ITALIAN-AMERICANS. Within days, Columbo had organized the Italian-American Civil Rights League, its stated purposes "to fight the gangster stereotype in the media, make Italian-Americans proud of their heritage, fight, on all fronts, the victimization of Italian-Americans, and persuade the media to refrain from using the terms Mafia and Cosa Nostra."

Columbo, as chief spokesman for the organization, suddenly found himself in the spotlight, tapped for press interviews and an appearance on a nationally televised talk show. Other New York mobsters shunned the sudden glare of publicity, but Columbo forged ahead on his own, addressing a crowd of some 40,000 at Columbus Circle on 29 June 1970, dubbed Italian-American Unity Day. Rival mob boss Carlo Gambino reluctantly agreed to shut down New York's waterfront for the day, thereby freeing thousands of workers to attend the rally. Columbo shared the dais with New York's deputy mayor, a former mayor, and two congressmen. The show of strength was impressive enough that producers of *The Godfather* and *The FBI* television series agreed to delete the terms "Mafia" and "Cosa Nostra" from their dramas.

Law enforcement was less smitten by Columbo's display. In July 1970 the Nassau County district attorney indicted Columbo and 23 of his subordinates for gambling and loan-sharking. By year's end, the FBI had arrested 20 percent of Columbo's men, and grand juries had begun investigating the Gambino family as well. Undaunted, Columbo scheduled his second unity rally for 28 June 1971, with singer FRANK SINATRA tapped to entertain a projected crowd of 100,000 persons.

On the appointed day, when Columbo rose to address his audience, a 24-year-old black photographer, Jerome Johnson, slipped through the crowd and fired several shots into Columbo's head and neck. Killed instantly by a second gunman who then escaped in the crowd, Johnson took the secret of the murder contract to his grave, but there was no shortage of suspects. Long-time Columbo rival "Crazy Joe" Gallo, known to have befriended blacks during a recent prison term, was shot and killed at a Manhattan restaurant on 7 April 1972. Carlo Gambino emerged from the bloodshed as chief among New York's Mafia bosses, reigning unopposed until his death in October 1976. Columbo outlived his old rival but never regained consciousness; he died, still comatose, on 22 May 1978. By then, the Italian-American Civil Rights League had long since ceased to exist.

# J

**JACKSON, Robert Houghwout**—A Pennsylvania native, born at Spring Creek on 13 February 1892, Robert Jackson assumed office as President FRANKLIN ROOSEVELT'S third attorney general on 18 January 1940. Three weeks later, FBI agents arrested members of the ABRAHAM LINCOLN BRIGADE, prompting the *Milwaukee Journal* and other newspapers to denounce the Bureau as a "secret police organization of un-American, anti-American complexion." Jackson defended the arrests, despite criticism from Senators GEORGE NORRIS and BURTON WHEELER, a stance that set the tone for Jackson's relationship with FBI Director J. EDGAR HOOVER. (In the midst of the controversy, Hoover volunteered to resign "at once" if Jackson had "any question as to the Director's administration of the Bureau," but the gesture was predictably declined.)

Subservient to Hoover in all things, by June 1940 Jackson had approved the Bureau's illegal CUSTODIAL DETENTION PROGRAM (launched in 1939), and he soon cleared the way for indiscriminate FBI WIRETAPPING, informing Hoover of his wish to "have no detailed record kept concerning the cases in which wiretapping would be utilized." Any records of illegal taps, Jackson decreed, should be kept in Hoover's "immediate office, listing the time, places, and cases in which this procedure is utilized." In fact, without Jackson's knowledge, Hoover had already created a special "Do Not File" designation for sensitive memos, concealing them even from the attorney general himself. In November 1940 Jackson approved a covert FBI alliance with the AMERICAN LEGION, thereby creating a civilian army of INFORMANTS from coast to coast.

Jackson's only significant clash with Hoover came in February 1941, when ELEANOR ROOSEVELT complained of G-men investigating Edith Helm, her social secretary. Jackson responded to the First Lady's complaint by barring FBI agents from any personnel investigations outside the JUSTICE DEPARTMENT; other background checks would henceforth be conducted by the Treasury Department or the Civil Service Commission. The restriction angered Hoover (and was later reversed by Attorney General FRANCIS BIDDLE), but he only had to live with it for five more months. Jackson resigned as attorney general on 10 July 1941 to fill a vacancy on the U.S. SUPREME COURT. He died in office on 9 October 1954.

**JACKSON State College shooting**—The month of May 1970, following disclosure of President RICHARD NIXON'S covert military campaign in Cambodia, witnessed demonstrations on campuses and in cities across the U.S. The official response was unusually harsh, including the shooting of 13 students (with four killed) by National Guardsmen at KENT STATE UNIVERSITY on 4 May, and police shootings of 86 African Americans (six fatally) in Augusta, Georgia on 11 May. Demonstrations at Mississippi's all-black Jackson State College were marked by scattered incidents of rock- and bottle-throwing on 13 May, and tragedy struck on the following day, when a squad of local police and Mississippi Highway Patrol officers opened fire on the campus, killing two persons and wounding 12 more.

Both police departments involved in the shooting had long histories of racist violence toward blacks and friendly collaboration with the KU KLUX KLAN, a mindset emphasized when Highway Patrol Inspector Lloyd ("Goon") Jones radioed a call for ambulances to transport wounded "niggers" from the campus. Officers involved in the shooting immediately collected their empty shell casings and reloaded their weapons to make it appear that no shots had been fired — this, despite the casualties and evidence of 400 bullet holes in the women's dormitory of Alexander Hall, aside from other damage caused by gunfire. When questioned later, each and every officer present initially denied firing his weapon, a circumstance that led the arch-conservative Mississippi-Louisiana Press Association to pass a resolution condemning the official conspiracy of silence.

FBI investigation of the shooting (code-named JACK-TWO) quickly identified pellets of No. 1 buckshot at Alexander Hall and confirmed that only Jackson police officers had been armed with shotguns on 14 May. All officers involved had denied firing their guns or collecting spent shells at the scene, but the threat of grand jury subpoenas prompted certain highway patrolmen to produce a number of shotgun shells fired by city police. (Meanwhile, the state patrolmen had destroyed their own shell casings.) Confronted with irrefutable evidence, several officers finally admitted firing their weapons but claimed they had done so only in response to "sniper fire" from Alexander Hall. FBI Director J. EDGAR HOOVER made a premature announcement on 18 May, reporting that there seemed "to be substantial proof ... that there was sniper fire on the troops [*sic*] from the dormitory before the troops fired." In fact, there was none, as confirmed by Hoover's agents when their investigation was completed.

President Nixon, declaring himself "deeply saddened" by the Kent and Jackson shootings, appointed a President's Commission on Campus Unrest — better known by the name of its chairman, former Pennsylvania governor William Scranton — to investigate the incidents. The Scranton Commission's report on Jackson State, published on 1 October 1970, called the shooting "an unreasonable, unjustified overreaction." It also accused the Mississippi lawmen of lying and concealing or destroying vital evidence. The report concluded "that a significant cause of the deaths and injuries at Jackson State College is the confidence of white officers that if they fire weapons during a black campus disturbance they will face neither stern departmental discipline nor criminal prosecution or convictions."

That expectation was borne out by subsequent events. Although lying to FBI agents is itself a federal offense, punishable by a maximum $10,000 fine and 10 years in prison, G-men deviated from their normal routine of obtaining signed statements in this case, thereby exempting all suspects from prosecution. A federal grand jury was convened in June 1970 under Judge Harold Cox (a racist known for describing Mississippi blacks as "chimpanzees"), but it returned no indictments after Cox advised the panel that student demonstrators "must expect to be injured or killed." A Hinds County grand jury acknowledged that initial statements taken from police were "absolutely false," but decided that any indictment of police for perjury or worse would be "unwarranted, unjustified and political in nature." Instead, the panel chose a black bystander, 21-year-old Ernest Lee Kyles, and indicted him on 14 October 1970 for arson and inciting a riot. (Charges were later dropped for lack of evidence.)

Despite claims of "sadness" evoked by the shootings in May 1970, President Nixon and company resented any efforts to ex-onerate the victims. Vice President SPIRO AGNEW denounced the Scranton Report as "pabulum for the permissivists" and called on J. Edgar Hoover for any derogatory material "that can ameliorate some of the impact." CIVIL RIGHTS activist RALPH ABERNATHY was a particular target of Agnew's wrath, the vice president seeking information to "destroy his credibility." (Hoover agreed with Agnew that Abernathy, successor to Dr. MARTIN LUTHER KING, JR., as chief of the SOUTHERN CHRISTIAN LEADERSHIP CONFERENCE, was "one of the worst.") Overall, as noted by the Southern Regional Council in *The New South*, "People here think that the way the police handled the students at Jackson State is the way Nixon and Agnew want the students treated."

Litigation arising from the Jackson State shootings dragged on for more than a decade. Relatives of slain victims Phillip Gibbs and James Early Green, assisted by an ad hoc Lawyers Committee for Civil Rights Under Law, sued state and local police for $13.8 million in federal court. At trial, two officers admitted lying in their FBI interviews and five G-men testified that there was no evidence of sniper fire aimed at police, but an all-white jury ruled in favor of the defendants on 22 March 1972. The U.S. Court of Appeals in New Orleans ratified that verdict with a convoluted judgment in October 1974: the panel ruled that there *was* a sniper on campus, then deemed that the police reaction "far exceeded the response that was appropriate," finally declaring that "sovereign immunity" exempted Mississippi police from any lawsuits regardless of their behavior. In January 1982 seven justices of the U.S. SUPREME COURT voted against reopening the case.

**JANKLOW, William John** — A South Dakota native, born 13 September 1939, William ("Wild Bill") Janklow was employed as a tribal attorney for the Rosebud Sioux in January 1967, when he was accused of raping his children's 15-year-old babysitter. The alleged victim, a Brulé Lakota girl named Jancita Eagle Deer, reported the incident to Bureau of Indian Affairs police on 14 January 1967, claiming that Janklow had attacked her while driving her home from his house. BIA authorities recommended prosecution, but the FBI intervened to claim jurisdiction. Minneapolis agent-in-charge RICHARD G. HELD, later revealed as a longtime participant in the Bureau's illegal COINTELPRO campaigns, sent an agent to investigate the charges and received a memo on 16 January 1967 that "it is impossible to determine anything." Six weeks later, apparently without any further investigation, Held informed FBI HEADQUARTERS that there was "insufficient evidence, the allegations were unfounded; we are therefore closing our files on the matter." Janklow left Rosebud (where tribal jurisdiction prevailed), and Jancita Eagle Deer subsequently moved to Iowa.

Six years later, while employed as an assistant prosecutor with the state attorney general's office, Janklow had his first courtroom clash with members of the AMERICAN INDIAN MOVEMENT (AIM). Victorious in that trial, Janklow thereafter billed himself as an "Indian fighter" and campaigned in 1974 to become the state's attorney general. The rape allegations resurfaced, pressed by AIM attorneys, although FBI files were sealed and the Bureau "refused to cooperate in any way." Nonetheless, with barely a month remaining until the November election, tribal judge Mario Gonzales charged Janklow with "assault with intent to commit rape, and carnal knowledge with a female under 16." Two witnesses testified that Janklow had "brooded" over the rape and offered money to Jancita Eagle Deer's grandfather following the incident. Janklow denied the charges and refused to appear in tribal court, thereby frustrating prosecution on the charges. He was elected attorney general and proclaimed the following year that "The only way to deal with the Indian problem in South Dakota is to put a gun to AIM leaders' heads and pull the trigger."

Aggressive pursuit of AIM "radicals" was a ticket to political success for Janklow, who was elected to five terms as South Dakota's governor (1979-87, 1995-2003). During his first gubernatorial term, author PETER MATTHIESSEN published his study of the LEONARD PELTIER case, *In the Spirit of Crazy Horse*, which included pointed criticism of Janklow and a review of the Eagle Deer rape. Two months later, on 19 May 1983, Janklow filed a $24 million libel suit against Matthiessen, his publisher and three Dakota bookstores that offered the volume for sale. Judge Gene Kean dismissed the lawsuit on 13 June 1984, but it was reinstated the following year by South Dakota's Supreme Court. On 25 June 1986 Judge Kean dismissed the three booksellers as defendants, but Janklow forged ahead with his suit against Matthiessen and Viking Press. Judge Kean dismissed that suit again in 1988, and this time the state supreme court upheld his ruling. Despite a public vow that he would fight the case "as long as I live," Janklow chose not to file an appeal with the U.S. SUPREME COURT. (FBI Agent DAVID PRICE filed a similar lawsuit against Matthiessen in 1984 and was likewise unsuccessful.)

**JARRELL, Randall**—A renowned American poet, Jarrell was born in Nashville, Tennessee on 6 May 1914. He joined the U.S. Army in 1942 and established his reputation as a poet while still in uniform, with the 1945 publication of his collection *Little Friend, Little Friend*. Jarrell won the Guggenheim Award twice, in 1946 and 1963; he also received a National Book Award in 1960.

The FBI first took note of Jarrell in 1944, when a car registered in his name was spotted during surveillance of suspected COMMUNIST PARTY members. Investigation showed that he was in the army at the time, and the individual who borrowed his car was never identified. Bureau suspicion of his loyalty deepened in 1946, when Jarrell was hired as poetry editor for *The Nation*. Two years later, agents trailed him to the World Congress of Intellectuals, noting his description as an "advance-guard" poet.

The remainder of Jarrell's 322-page FBI file concerns a 1956 background investigation conducted prior to his appointment as Poetry Consultant for the Library of Congress. G-men noted his 1952 divorce and reported that an unnamed female acquaintance of Jarrell's had once attended "a Communist Party" [*sic*], but nothing was uncovered to block his appointment. Nine years later, on 14 October 1965, Jarrell was struck and killed by a car, authorities speculating that his death may have been suicide. In 1967 a California housewife wrote to J. EDGAR HOOVER, complaining that Jarrell's "gobble de gook" had been assigned in her

son's English class. Hoover replied, perhaps with tongue in cheek, that "It is contrary to my long-standing policy to comment upon material which has not been prepared by personnel of this Bureau."

**J. EDGAR Hoover Foundation**—The original J. Edgar Hoover foundation was established in the spring of 1949, with announcement of a nationwide fund-raising drive to purchase a 530-acre farm in Maryland, for conversion to a school for juvenile delinquents. Columnist DREW PEARSON, still in the Bureau's good graces that year, emerged as the project's chief spokesman. One early contributor was Massachusetts millionaire and former bootlegger Joseph Kennedy, father of future president JOHN KENNEDY. Another was imprisoned Ohio mobster Yonnie Licavoli, who sent his wife and mother to Washington, D.C. with $5,000 for Pearson. The donation failed to achieve Licavoli's hoped-for early parole, but other gangsters soon jumped on the bandwagon—so many, in fact, that Hoover was embarrassed and called a halt to the fund-raising. Pearson announced, in his column of 28 May 1949, that Hoover had withdrawn his support from the foundation because "he does not think a memorial should be built to a living man." Twenty years later, after *Life* magazine published a reference to that episode, Deputy Associate Director CARTHA DELOACH wrote a terse letter to the editors, claiming that "The 'J. Edgar Hoover Foundation' to which you refer in your story was a proposal which was initiated ... without Mr. Hoover's knowledge. Mr. Hoover protested this proposal and refused permission for the use of his name."

By the time DeLoach penned those words in 1969, however, Hoover had discarded his objections to living memorials. The new and approved J. Edgar Hoover Foundation was incorporated on 10 June 1965 and received its tax exemption from the INTERNAL REVENUE SERVICE in record time, four months later. According to the foundation's charter, its purpose was—

1. To safeguard the heritage and freedom of the United States of America, to promote good citizenship through an appreciation of its form of government and to perpetuate the ideals and purposes to which the Honorable J. Edgar Hoover has dedicated his life.

2. To combat communism or any other ideology or doctrine which shall be opposed to the principles set forth in The Constitution of the United States or the rule of law.

Former FBI Assistant to the Director LOUIS NICHOLS, employed since 1957 as an executive of Schenley Industries, served as president of the Hoover Foundation; William Simon, former special agent in charge of the Los Angeles field office, served as vice president; while Cartha DeLoach (still in active FBI service) was appointed secretary. Nichols "convinced" Schenley president (and ex-bootlegger) LEWIS ROSENSTIEL to bankroll the foundation with $10,000 in cash, plus gifts of Schenley stock worth $1,513,543 between 1965 and 1968. The American Jewish League Against Communism, led by former Red-hunter (and underworld associate) ROY COHN, chipped in a modest $500. The new foundation's existence was a closely guarded secret until

WALTER WINCHELL broke the news in 1968, assuring his radio audience that "all donors contributed voluntarily" to the cause.

Passing time has not dimmed FBI devotion to the Hoover foundation. Writing to a Masonic Internet website in May 1997, Cartha DeLoach said of Hoover —

> He elicited such loyalty among his friends and colleagues that 25 years after his death in 1972, Hoover's supporters continue to work to preserve his legacy and the ideals and values by which he lived. To that end, the J. Edgar Hoover Foundation was established to carry on his tradition of service to the public good. The group's selected avenue has been education.
>
> In the past three decades, the Foundation has offered hundreds of grants and scholarships to deserving young men and women across the nation. Several academic institutions and organizations, including Notre Dame, the National College of Criminal Defense Lawyers and Public Defenders, and the National College of District Attorneys, also have been awarded financial aid for specialized programs.

Scholarship donations have not been the foundation's only activity, however. The Hoover Foundation's original incorporation papers declare an intention "to act in conjunction with Freedoms Foundation, a not-for-profit corporation organized under the laws of Pennsylvania, so long as said corporation shall be entitled to exemption from Federal Income Tax." Created in 1949 by Union Oil executives Don Belding and Kenneth Wells, Freedoms Foundation has included among its officers far-right televangelist Billy Hargis; ultra-segregationist Tom Brady, an associate justice of Mississppi's Supreme Court; and Dean Clarence Manion, of the John Birch Society. In 1968, when boxer George Foreman waved a U.S. flag on the Olympic gold-medal victory stand, high-ranking FBI officials encouraged the Freedoms Foundation to give Foreman a special award for patriotism (bestowed in February 1969). According to reporter Hank Messick, the Freedoms Foundation also maintained a J. Edgar Hoover Library at its Valley Forge headquarters, stocked with books about the FBI— most of them purchased and donated by Lewis Rosenstiel.

**JEFFERS, John Robinson**— Born to a wealthy Pittsburgh family on 10 January 1887, Jeffers published his first poetry at age 16, before attending medical school and serving as a professor of physiology. The FBI opened a file on Jeffers in 1935, when he contributed work to the *Pacific Weekly*, forerunner of *People's World* (a West Coast newspaper of the COMMUNIST PARTY). In 1936, G-men noted his attendance at the funeral of LINCOLN STEFFENS, dubbed "a well-known member of the Communist party." Before long, any passing contact with Jeffers was ranked as "subversive" behavior. One individual (name deleted) was considered suspect merely because "several books of poems by Jeffers" reposed in his "library of one thousand volumes." Ironically, Jeffers denounced an open letter condemning the HOUSE COMMITTEE ON UN-AMERICAN ACTIVITIES, signed by 125 fellow members of the National Institute of Arts and Letters in February 1948. FBI agents shadowed Jeffers until 1961, the year before he died at Carmel, California.

**JESUS Christ**— As related by author Curt Gentry in his in-comparable biography of J. EDGAR HOOVER, the FBI's investigation of Jesus Christ sprang from a casual conversation between Hoover and President HARRY TRUMAN. Truman, near the end of his final term in office, expressed his disappointment that some of the men he had appointed to federal office later turned against him. Hoover replied that even Jesus Christ had been betrayed by one of his disciples, whereupon the president corrected Hoover's statement. Jesus, Truman reminded the FBI director, had been betrayed by *three* disciples, not one.

Masking his fury at the perceived insult, Hoover— once a prospect for the ministry, before he turned to law— rushed back to FBI HEADQUARTERS and ordered an investigation to learn if Truman's reading of the Bible was correct. Word swiftly spread throughout the building that "The boss wants us to investigate Jesus Christ!" Within hours, G-men reported back that Truman's version was accurate. In addition to Judas Iscariot, Jesus had also been denied by disciples Thomas and Peter (the latter on three occasions). A report was drafted to that effect, but Hoover's aides were afraid to deliver it, finally delegating the task to Deputy Associate Director WILLIAM SULLIVAN. Instead of the expected rage, however, Sullivan reported that Hoover "just looked thoughtful" after reading the report.

**JEWELL, Richard**— Shortly before 1:00 a.m. on 27 July 1996, private security guard Richard Jewell noticed an abandoned backpack tucked beneath a bench in Atlanta's Centennial Olympic Park. Security was tight during the summer Olympic Games, with countless law enforcement officers assigned to prevent acts of TERRORISM. Jewell reported his find to an agent of the BUREAU OF ALCOHOL, TOBACCO AND FIREARMS, then remained nearby as the agent opened the backpack. Inside was a bomb that exploded moments later— but not before Jewell had escorted more than 100 spectators to safety.

Early reports hailed Jewell as a hero, but the FBI took a different view, publicly declaring him "the chief suspect in the BOMBING." Overnight the global news media pounced on Jewell's story, portraying him as a "bizarre character" who had bombed the park in a sick bid for personal glory. Bureau psychologists even have a name for such behavior: the "recognition (hero)" syndrome. G-men placed Jewell under 24-hour surveillance, questioned him at length without advising him of his legal rights, and searched his apartment with television crews standing by to broadcast the event worldwide. (Raiders confiscated Jewell's guns, his mother's Tupperware, and a collection of Walt Disney videotapes.) Only weeks later, in October 1996, did JUSTICE DEPARTMENT spokesmen finally exonerate Jewell as a potential suspect. Instead, they blamed the bombing on ERIC RUDOLPH, charged with murder and other acts of ANTI-ABORTION VIOLENCE in southern states.

FBI Director LOUIS FREEH disciplined two agents for their conduct in the Jewell affair. Agent Don Johnson received a five-day suspension for failure to advise Jewell of his civil rights during interrogation, while Atlanta agent-in-charge David Johnson (no relation) received a letter of censure. Jewell declined to sue the FBI but he did file civil actions against several media organizations, collecting more than $2 million. As for the Bureau, five years after the circus Jewell told reporters, "Nobody's ever called me, written me a letter, sent me an e-mail, [or] called any of my attorneys" to apologize for the false accusations.

**JFK Assassination**— Murdering a U.S. president was not a federal crime on 22 November 1963, when sniper bullets struck down JOHN F. KENNEDY in Dallas, Texas. FBI agents entered the case nonetheless, on orders from President LYNDON JOHNSON, and Director J. EDGAR HOOVER wasted no time in declaring that the crime was a lone gunman's work. At 2:30 a.m. on 23 November Hoover branded suspect LEE HARVEY OSWALD "a Communist"; that afternoon, Hoover sent the results of a "preliminary inquiry" to the White House, declaring that Oswald had acted alone. That public view did not change when Oswald was murdered by mobster JACK RUBY on 24 November. In fact, the very next day Hoover told reporters, "Not one shred of evidence has been developed to link any other person in a conspiracy with Oswald to assassinate President Kennedy." Officially, that view from FBI HEADQUARTERS has not altered one iota in the decades since the crime.

The White House was equally concerned about killing conspiracy rumors. On 24 November, shortly after Oswald's murder in Dallas, Deputy Attorney General NICHOLAS KATZENBACH sent a memo to press secretary Bill Moyers. It read: "The public must be satisfied that Oswald was the assassin; that he did not have confederates who are still at large; and that the evidence was such that he would have been convicted at trial. Speculations about Oswald's motivation ought to be cut off. Two days later Katzenbach told Hoover that the FBI's report on the assassination "should include everything which may raise a question in the mind of the public or press regarding this matter. In other words, the report is to settle the dust, in so far as Oswald and his activities are concerned, both from the standpoint that he is the man who assassinated the president, and relative to Oswald himself and his activities and background."

On 29 November 1963 Hoover received a telephone call from President Johnson. According to his notes on that conversation, "The President said he wanted to get by with my file and my report" on Kennedy's murder, but public opinion demanded a special inquiry. Hoover opposed "a rash of investigations," but LBJ was determined to pacify America. Accordingly, that afternoon Johnson appointed a special seven-man commission to investigate the assassination, chaired by U.S. SUPREME COURT Chief Justice EARL WARREN. Other members included former CENTRAL INTELLIGENCE AGENCY director ALLEN DULLES, former STATE DEPARTMENT official John McCloy, Senators Richard Russell and John Cooper, with Representatives HALE BOGGS and GERALD FORD (serving as Hoover's clandestine INFORMANT). The Warren Commission's final report, published in September 1964, rubber-stamped Hoover's instant conclusion that Oswald was Kennedy's lone assassin. The commission ignored Jack Ruby's lifelong ties to ORGANIZED CRIME and claimed that his public murder of Oswald was motivated by grief over Kennedy's death and sympathy for the president's widow.

G-men had no part in fabrication of the Warren Commission's "magic bullet theory"—wherein one rifle slug entered Kennedy's back and exited through his throat, then changed course in mid-air before striking Texas Governor John Connally, shattered Connally's ribs, left fragments in his wrist and thigh, then surfaced unscarred on an abandoned stretcher at Parkland Hospital—but FBI marksmen quickly collected (and suppressed) evidence proving that Oswald could not have been Kennedy's assassin. Specifically, while testing Oswald's antique bolt-action rifle, agents discovered that its telescopic sight was inoperable. Before they could test-fire the weapon, they had to repair it and install special braces to make the sight function. That done, they *still* could not make the weapon fire fast enough to get off three shots within the time frame required for Kennedy's slaying.

That critical exculpatory evidence was not the only information which Hoover's agents withheld from the Warren Commission. Johnson's "blue-ribbon" panel never learned of multiple death threats against Kennedy and his brother (Attorney General ROBERT KENNEDY), captured on tape by FBI bugs and wiretaps installed in the homes of high-ranking mobsters from Chicago to Miami and New Orleans. The commission never learned that on 23 November, G-man Hosty told a Dallas police lieutenant, "We knew that Lee Harvey Oswald was capable of assassinating the president of the United States, but we didn't dream he would do it." Instead, the commission accepted Hosty's statement under oath that "Prior to the assassination of the president of the United States, I had no information indicating violence on the part of Lee Harvey Oswald. I wish for the record to so read."

Rumors of Oswald's role as a paid FBI informant *did* reach the Warren Commission, but that information was suppressed (and the commission apparently never learned of similar Bureau contacts with Jack Ruby). Gerald Ford opposed criticizing the FBI for its failure to brief SECRET SERVICE agents on Oswald's extremist activities in Dallas, but Earl Warren insisted on including a mild note of censure in the commission's final report. Hoover retaliated by severing his long friendship with Warren and striking Warren's name from the FBI's "Special Correspondent" list.

The Warren Commission's report failed to erase public doubts about Oswald's "lone gunman" status, Ruby's "grief" motive or the bizarre magic-bullet theory. Over the next decade, numerous books and articles were published dissecting the commission's work, highlighting errors and omissions from its report and 26 volumes of supporting testimony. In 1975 the HOUSE SELECT COMMITTEE ON ASSASSINATIONS was created to examine Kennedy's death and the 1968 murder of Dr. MARTIN LUTHER KING, JR. The committee's report, published in 1979, concluded that Kennedy "was probably assassinated as the result of a conspiracy." Oswald remained the prime suspect, with an observation that "individual members" or organized crime "may have been involved."

In regard to FBI handling of the JFK assassination, the committee found that G-men "adequately investigated Lee Harvey Oswald prior to the assassination and properly evaluated ... his potential to endanger the public safety in a national emergency." They also "conducted a thorough and professional investigation" into Oswald's guilt but "failed to investigate adequately the possibility of a conspiracy to assassinate the president." Furthermore, the FBI was deemed "deficient in its sharing of information with other agencies and departments" prior to Kennedy's murder, and it had "failed to cooperate fully with the Warren Commission." Consideration of a possible conspiracy, the House committee found, had been "a blind spot in the FBI's investigation," through no fault of any particular agent or administrator.

**JOHNSON, Arthur John ("Jack")** — A son of former slaves, born at Galveston, Texas on 31 March 1878, Jack Johnson quit school in fifth grade and worked odd jobs until he discovered his talent for boxing. He turned professional in 1897 and soon became the black heavyweight champion. White champion Jim Jeffries refused to face Johnson, but Johnson went on to beat world champion Tommy Burns in Australia, in 1908. The official world championship title eluded Johnson until 1910, when he defeated Jeffries — called out of retirement by fight promoters as America's "great white hope" — in a bout at Las Vegas, Nevada. Johnson's victory sparked race riots by whites in several U.S. cities, and Texas legislators banned films of his matches with white opponents from the Lone Star State, fearing more violence.

The Bureau of Investigation, charged with enforcement of a federal ban on interstate shipment of prizefight films, apparently noticed Johnson during this period. Passage of the MANN ACT in 1910 offered racist prosecutors an opportunity to break Johnson, whose flamboyant lifestyle and penchant for white women proved even more offensive than his persistent victories over white contenders in the ring. In October 1912 Johnson was arrested in Chicago, on charges of abducting 19-year-old Lucile Cameron from Minneapolis. The charge was filed by a relative of Cameron's, denied by the "victim" herself, and federal prosecutors forged ahead with their case even after Johnson married Cameron in January 1913. At trial, the government's replacement "victim" was a prostitute who claimed Johnson had paid her way from Pittsburgh to Chicago for immoral purposes. Johnson admitted helping the woman financially but denied paying her for sex. An all-white jury convicted Johnson in May 1913; a month later, he was sentenced to one year in prison and a $1,000 fine.

While free on bond pending appeal, Johnson fled to Canada and then to Europe, where he remained at large as a fugitive for seven years. Still recognized as the world heavyweight champion, Johnson defended his title three times in Paris before he agreed to meet contender Jess Willard in Havana, Cuba on 5 April 1915. That match lasted 26 rounds before Johnson was felled by a knockout. He returned to the United States on 20 July 1920 and surrendered to U.S. MARSHALS. Confined at Leavenworth federal prison, Johnson continued boxing and was soon appointed athletic director of the prison. Upon his release, Johnson returned to the ring but fought only exhibition bouts between 1928 and his final retirement in 1945. He died in a car crash near Raleigh, North Carolina on 10 June 1946.

**JOHNSON, Lyndon Baines** — Born near Stonewall, Texas on 27 August 1908, Lyndon Johnson had much in common with FBI Director J. EDGAR HOOVER, including friendship with two of Hoover's financial patrons, Texas oilmen WILLIAM BYARS, SR. and CLINT MURCHISON. Both were contributors to Johnson's various political campaigns, beginning with his first election to Congress in 1936. Johnson served six terms in the House before he was elected to the U.S. Senate in 1948 (by which time his talent for enlisting the dead to vote alphabetically had earned him the nickname "Landslide Lyndon"). Soon after his arrival in Washington, Johnson purchased a home across the street from Hoover, making them both friends and neighbors.

Hoover provided his first known service to Johnson in 1956, when G-men suppressed evidence of vote fraud in the Texas primary elections. Six years later, while Johnson served as vice president under President JOHN KENNEDY, Hoover buried an FBI report detailing the Texan's alliance with various "hoodlum interests." Following the November 1963 JFK ASSASSINATION, Hoover joined LBJ in a concerted effort to suppress conspiracy rumors, producing an overnight judgment that suspect LEE HARVEY OSWALD was the president's lone assassin. Hoover biographer Athan Theoharis described the FBI director's relationship with Johnson over the next five years:

> Although Hoover had willingly serviced the partisan and policy interests of every president since HERBERT HOOVER (inclusive), his services to President Johnson were unique in their scope and nature. For one thing, Johnson did not hesitate to turn to Hoover for information about his administration's critics (which information, for ideological as well as strategic reasons, Hoover generously gave); for another, Johnson, like Hoover, harbored an inordinate interest in derogatory personal information — and, like Hoover, insisted that his requests for such information and the FBI's submissions of it be kept strictly confidential. In that sense, the two men were made for each other.

Hoover's political service to Johnson included extensive surveillance on critical journalists, CIVIL RIGHTS leaders, Republican Party leaders and opponents of the VIETNAM WAR. In August 1964 Assistant Director CARTHA DELOACH led a special 30-man FBI team to monitor LBJ's opposition at the Democratic National Convention in Atlantic City, New Jersey. Two months later, White House aide Bill Moyers requested a special Bureau report on Republican presidential candidate Barry Goldwater, which was hand-delivered on 28 October 1964. In terms of prurient interest, Johnson enjoyed Hoover's stories of celebrity sexual escapades. Assistant Director WILLIAM SULLIVAN later reported that the president's "favorite bedtime reading" included transcripts of Bureau tape recordings obtained by illegally BUGGING hotel rooms occupied by Dr. MARTIN LUTHER KING, JR.

In return for such favors, Johnson granted Hoover the ultimate reward: exemption from retirement at age 70, as required by federal law. In May 1964 a rumor spread that Johnson was preparing to replace Hoover as FBI director. *Newsweek* editor Ben Bradlee (a Johnson critic) prepared a special cover story on the momentous event, but he was surprised on 8 May when Johnson announced that Hoover was exempt from compulsory retirement "for an indefinite period of time." Moments before that Rose Garden press conference, Johnson told Bill Moyers, "You can call Ben Bradlee and tell him, 'Fuck you.'"

Mounting protest against the Vietnam war persuaded Johnson not to seek renomination in 1968. Vice President Hubert Humphrey carried the Democratic standard that year and lost the November election to RICHARD NIXON. Stricken with a heart attack on 22 January 1973, Johnson died en route to a San Antonio hospital. He received a posthumous Presidential Medal of Freedom in 1980.

**JOHNSON, Marlin**— Between 1967 and 1970, while serving as special agent in charge of the Chicago field office, Marlin Johnson supervised a series of illegal COINTELPRO operations that cost two lives and threatened countless others with efforts to incite gang wars in the city's ghetto. Targets of FBI harassment included a variety of black activist groups, ranging from the conservative NATIONAL ASSOCIATION FOR THE ADVANCEMENT OF COLORED PEOPLE to the radical BLACK PANTHER PARTY and the separatist NATION OF ISLAM, but Johnson also mounted campaigns against several NEW LEFT organizations at the same time. A memo from Johnson to FBI HEADQUARTERS, dated 22 January 1969, boasted that "considerable thought has been given and action has been taken with Bureau approval" to disrupt the Nation of Islam, and that "[f]actional disputes have been developed—the most notable being MALCOLM X."

Still, for all that "considerable thought and action," Johnson's crowning achievement was the destruction of the Black Panther Party in Chicago. Under FBI guidance, local Panther chief FRED HAMPTON was charged with 25 separate crimes in the space of two years, convicted of a robbery he almost certainly did not commit, and was finally killed in a raid by CHICAGO POLICE, orchestrated by FBI INFORMANT/*provocateur* WILLIAM O'NEAL. Acting under direct orders from J. EDGAR HOOVER to "destroy what [the party] stands for" and to "eradicate its 'serve the people' programs," Agent Johnson himself led a raid against the local Panther office on 4 June 1969, vandalizing the premises during an alleged search for a fugitive. Johnson's agents also mailed a series of anonymous letters to disrupt friendly relations between the Panthers and the STUDENTS FOR A DEMOCRATIC SOCIETY. When Hampton's Panthers sought to politically educate a local street gang, the BLACKSTONE RANGERS, FBI poison-pen artists fired off more hate mail, hoping—in the words of a Johnson memo to Hoover, dated 10 January 1969—that the Rangers might "take retaliatory action which could disrupt the BPP or lead to reprisals against its leadership." (Seven years later, in a 1976 interview, Johnson denied any intent to provoke homicide, claiming he believed a gangland "hit" to be "something nonviolent in nature.")

On 3 December 1969, the day before Fred Hampton's death, Johnson alerted Hoover to a "positive course of action … being effected under the counterintelligence program." Hours later, with Hampton and comrade Mark Clark in the morgue, Johnson sent another "urgent" teletype to report the outcome. On 8 April 1970, a memo prepared on Johnson's order recorded a promise from the JUSTICE DEPARTMENT, made "in strictest confidence," that no policemen would be indicted on CIVIL RIGHTS charges for killing Hampton while he slept. The same memo noted Illinois State's Attorney Edward Hanrahan's agreement to keep silent concerning FBI involvement in the raid. Johnson retired a short time later, replaced as special agent in

charge of Chicago's field office by COINTELPRO veteran RICHARD G. HELD.

**JONES, James**— Born in 1921, James Jones was best known for his novel *From Here to Eternity*, published in 1951 and filmed two years later (winning eight Academy Awards, including Best Picture). The FBI indexed Jones in August 1963, after he joined a civil rights demonstration led by JAMES BALDWIN in Paris. More than 500 American expatriates, 80 of them published authors, joined in picketing the U.S. embassy to protest racial segregation at home. No further entries were made to Jones's file, and the Bureau ignored his death in 1977.

**JONES, James Wormley**— The son of a Virginia lighthouse keeper, born in 1884, James Jones completed his public schooling at Cambridge, Massachusetts and stopped one year short of obtaining a bachelor's degree from all-black Virginia Union University. He joined the Washington, D.C. police department in January 1905, rising through the ranks from patrolman to detective over the next 12 years. In 1917, with America's entry into WORLD WAR I, Jones joined the U.S. Army and was commissioned as a captain, commanding Company F of the 368th Infantry. His unit saw action in France during 1918, and Jones was back on duty with the Washington police before year's end.

Chief A. BRUCE BIELASKI appointed Jones as the Bureau of Investigation's first black agent on 19 November 1919. The postwar Red Scare was already well advanced, moving toward its climax in the PALMER RAIDS, and Bielaski realized that white agents were handicapped in their efforts to monitor black "radical" groups. Assigned to UNDERCOVER OPERATIONS from the start of his Bureau career, Jones infiltrated the AFRICAN BLOOD BROTHERHOOD and MARCUS GARVEY'S Universal Negro Improvement Association (UNIA), signing his reports with the code number "800." As a trusted UNIA "captain," he sometimes addressed gatherings at Liberty Hall, in Harlem, the *Negro World* observing after one speech that "Mr. Jones, who is very light-complexioned, was mistaken by the audience for a white man."

Garvey trusted Jones enough to have him monitor accounts at the UNIA's Harlem restaurant, but Jones was devoted to putting Garvey in prison. He was the first to suggest a MANN ACT prosecution of Garvey for traveling with girlfriend Amy Jacques, but that effort never came to fruition. An old acquaintance recognized Jones in July 1920, pointing him out the staff at UNIA headquarters as "a former detective," and while Jones retreated to Washington for a time, he remained active in the group. Back on the case by August 1921, Jones emerged as full-blown *agent provocateur*, stirring up feuds between the UNIA and the African Blood Brotherhood, encouraging disgruntled ex-employees to sue the group for back wages.

In January 1923, Jones was one of seven UNIA members whose affidavits permitted federal prosecutors to charge Marcus Garvey with mail fraud. Jones filed his last report with the Bureau on 18 February 1923 and resigned two months later, on 14 April, but several accounts describe him "encouraging" prosecution witnesses during Garvey's trial, in May and June 1923. Jones died in Pittsburgh at age 74, in 1958.

**Jones, LeRoi** *see* **Baraka, Amiri**

**JUNG, Christine M.**—A native of Providence, Rhode Island, born Christine Kaporch on 12 November 1947, Jung grew up in Syracuse, New York and earned a bachelor's degree from the University of Miami at Coral Gables, Florida in 1969. Upon graduation she joined the U.S. Marine Corps and attained the rank of captain before she left the service three years later. On 9 April 1973 Jung became the second WOMAN AGENT hired by the FBI since Director J. EDGAR HOOVER'S death. She served in the Newark and Washington, D.C. field offices before her 1978 transfer to the FBI ACADEMY as a firearms instructor. (Jung was the first woman to hold that post and also the first to shoot a perfect score on the FBI firing range.) In January 1981 Jung was appointed supervisor of the Alexandria, Virginia field office's counterterrorism squad. She held that post until June 1986, when she was moved to FBI HEADQUARTERS and the Inspection Division. Jung became assistant agent-in-charge of the New York City field office in 1991. She resigned from the Bureau on 9 December 1995.

**JUSTICE Department**—While Congress authorized appointment of a U.S. Attorney General in 1789, the department he presently leads was not created until 1870, in the midst of the tumultuous Reconstruction era. Even then, federal prosecutions were so rare that the Justice Department required no detective force of its own for another decade. As responsibilities expanded with passage of the Interstate Commerce Act (1887) and the Sherman Anti-Trust Act (1890), various attorneys general used agents of the PINKERTON DETECTIVE AGENCY on a part-time, case-by-case basis. That relationship was severed in 1892, when Pinkerton's brutal strikebreaking activities prompted a congressional ban on temporary hiring of individuals already employed in the private sector. For the next 16 years, Justice borrowed SECRET SERVICE agents from the Treasury Department, until further abuses led Congress to ban that practice in May 1908. Two months later, in defiance of congressional opponents, Attorney General CHARLES BONAPARTE created a detective force that would become the FBI.

Passage of the MANN and DYER ACTS in 1910 and 1919 further broadened the Justice Department's authority, but investigations took an increasingly political (and often personal) turn after the Russian Revolution of 1917. Fear of ANARCHISTS and the COMMUNIST PARTY drove Attorney General THOMAS GREGORY to create an ALIEN ENEMY BUREAU in 1917, closely followed by Attorney General A. MITCHELL PALMER'S Red-hunting GENERAL INTELLIGENCE DIVISION and the sweeping PALMER RAIDS of 1919-20. J. EDGAR HOOVER, employed with the Justice Department since 1917, escaped censure for his role in those activities and was appointed assistant director of the Bureau under Attorney General HARRY DAUGHERTY. Unfortunately, Daugherty and the rest of President WARREN HARDING'S "Ohio Gang" were so corrupt that Justice soon became known as "the Department of Easy Virtue." Exposure of the TEAPOT DOME SCANDAL nearly sent Daugherty to prison, but Hoover concealed his own involvement in those crimes and was appointed director of the Bureau under

Attorney General HARLAN STONE. (That appointment was conditional on Hoover's agreement to cease pursuit of "radicals," a problem he solved by lying to Stone and continuing his Red hunts in secret.)

Over the next 48 years, Hoover's relationship with his nominal superiors at Justice depended chiefly on the latitude which various attorneys general granted to him in pursuit of his personal agendas. Between 1925 and 1960 most of the attorneys general appointed by Presidents CALVIN COOLIDGE, HERBERT HOOVER, FRANKLIN ROOSEVELT, HARRY TRUMAN and DWIGHT EISENHOWER avoided exercising any supervision over Hoover and the FBI; a few, including Attorneys General HOMER CUMMINGS and HERBERT BROWNELL, JR., actively encouraged expanded DOMESTIC SURVEILLANCE in violation of prevailing federal law. Attorneys general who tried to impose some restraint on the Bureau, including ROBERT KENNEDY and RAMSEY CLARK, were opposed and publicly reviled by Hoover at every turn. By the end of Hoover's life, it seemed that history had come full-circle, with Justice mired in another morass of corruption under Attorney General JOHN MITCHELL and President RICHARD NIXON.

In the wake of Hoover's death and the WATERGATE SCANDAL that toppled Nixon's administration, leaders at Justice have vacillated on priorities and the desirability of continuing widespread FBI spying. Attorneys General EDWARD LEVI and GRIFFIN BELL emphasized prosecution of ORGANIZED CRIME leaders and issued guidelines restricting domestic surveillance on political groups, while successors WILLIAM SMITH, EDWIN MEESE III and RICHARD THORNBURGH took the opposite approach, condemning "subversives" and "terrorists" while mobsters and white-collar criminals were largely ignored. Attorney General JANET RENO was accused of political partisanship in protecting President WILLIAM CLINTON from various investigations, but the same must be said for attorneys general serving Presidents RONALD REAGAN and GEOERGE H.W. BUSH.

In November 2001 President GEORGE W. BUSH and Attorney General JOHN ASHCROFT announced a "wartime reorganization" of the Justice Department to treat TERRORISM as a top priority. Ashcroft's "blueprint for change" reassigned 10 percent of the departments headquarters staff to "front line" field offices nationwide, while declaring that nonpolitical cases would take a backseat. "We cannot do everything we once did," Ashcroft told reporters, "because lives now depend on us doing a few things very well." Critics suggested that the shift in priorities was not only a response to the catastrophic SKYJACKINGS of 11 September 2001, but also a means of retreat from cases that held little interest for the Bush White House, including prosecution of corporate crime. One such critic, Iowa Senator CHARLES GRASSLEY, voiced his concern that the Justice shakeup "won't alter the prevailing culture of arrogance at the FBI. Ending that culture will require real, concrete measures of improvement."

**JUVENILE Delinquency**—FBI Director J. EDGAR HOOVER addressed juvenile delinquency for the first time in 1944, when he publicly blamed "the alarming increase in crime among our young people" on urban sprawl, absence of parents called to military service during WORLD WAR II and "the disintegration of the home as a guiding influence." Two years later, as described by author DON WHITEHEAD in *The FBI Story* (1956):

> Hoover considered the problem so pressing that he directed the organization of an FBI Juvenile Delinquency Instructors School in which special agents were assigned to a broad research project, supplemented by lectures from well-known authorities in the field of juvenile delinquency. The agents equipped themselves to lecture to local police groups on the latest developments in handling juveniles, the psychological problems involved in juvenile delinquency, how to organize boys' clubs, what other agencies were doing in this field and related subjects.

Although the G-men selected for Hoover's new program "had already gained practical experience in dealing with young people in boys' clubs, the Boy Scouts and church work," their efforts were unavailing. Ten years later, Hoover ranked "the juvenile jungle" as a national menace second only to COMMUNIST PARTY subversion. In February 1957 Hoover advocated publishing the names of "young thugs" so that righteous communities could give them a taste of their own medicine. They were not "bad children," he insisted, but rather "young criminals." At the same time, he broke with tradition by opposing federal legislation on the problem, professing fears that such laws might spawn "a national police force." Congress responded to the crisis in 1958 with passage of the Switchblade Knife Act, which demonized inanimate objects and accomplished precisely nothing toward suppression of juvenile crime.

# K

**KACZYNSKI, Theodore John**— Between May 1978 and April 1995, a series of 16 BOMBINGS across the U.S. were blamed on a single elusive offender. FBI agents assigned to the case codenamed the investigation "UNABOM," because the first 10 targets involved *u*niversities or *a*irlines. Some of the bombs were sent by mail, while others were deposited in public places. Despite intensive effort and use of PSYCHOLOGICAL PROFILING, the "Unabomber" remained at large for 18 years, killing three victims and wounding 22 others in his one-man reign of terror.

The first explosion occurred at the University of Illinois in Chicago, wounding a security guard on 25 May 1978. A year later, on 9 May 1979, the bomber wounded a graduate student at Northwest University, in Evanston, Illinois. On 15 November 1979 a bomb detonated aboard American Airlines Flight 444 in Chicago, injuring 12 persons. Seven months later, on 10 June 1980, United Airlines president Percy Wood was wounded by a bomb mailed to his office.

The Unabomber abandoned Illinois after 1980. No one was injured in the next bombing, on 8 October 1981, at the University of Utah in Salt Lake City. A blast at Vanderbilt University (in Nashville, Tennessee) wounded one victim on 5 May 1982. Two months later, another innocent victim was injured by a bombing at the University of California in Berkeley. Three years elapsed before the next attack, on a Boeing Aircraft factory in Auburn, Washington (no injuries). One week later the bomber returned to UC Berkeley for a blast that left one person hospitalized. On 15 November 1985 he surfaced in Ann Arbor, wounding two victims with a bombing at the University of Michigan. Industrial targets came under attack on 11 December 1985, and the Unabomber claimed his first fatality with a bombing at Rentech Company, a computer rental store in Sacramento, California. Perhaps intimidated by the thought of murder charges, he waited 14 months before the next blast, wounding one person at CAAM's Incorporated in Salt Lake City. Six years elapsed before a physician-researcher was injured by the next bomb on 22 June 1993, in Tiburon, California. Two days later, a bombing at Connecticut's Yale University injured a bystander. On 9 December 1994 New York advertising executive Thomas Mosser died in the explosion of a mail bomb at his home in North Caldwell, New Jersey. The Unabomber's final attack, on 24 April 1995, killed a timber lobbyist for the California Forestry Association at his Sacramento office.

FBI agents coordinated their nationwide UNABOM investigation with the U.S. Postal Service and the BUREAU OF ALCOHOL, TOBACCO AND FIREARMS. Thousands of interviews proved fruitless, and the creation of a special task force based in San Francisco brought no useful leads. In 1993 the investigators offered a $1 million reward for information leading to the Unabomber's capture, but there were no takers. Profilers at the FBI ACADEMY, led by Agent JOHN DOUGLAS, dissected the unknown bomber but failed to locate him. (Retired profiler ROBERT RESSLER later told this author, in a February 1998 conversation, that the Douglas profile was "all wrong.")

Finally, in 1995, the bomber mailed a letter offering to cease his attacks if the *New York Times* and *Washington Post* would publish his "manifesto" on the ills of modern industrial society. Some G-men opposed the deal, but both papers ran the 35,000-word diatribe in September 1995 (and Agent Douglas later quoted it verbatim in a book about the Unabomber's case). Still, agents were no closer to their man until early 1992, when New York social worker David Kaczynski named his reclusive brother as a suspect. Investigators found Theodore Kaczynski living in a tiny cabin near Lincoln, Montana and placed him under surveillance for several weeks before finally arresting him on 3 April 1996. Inside the cabin they found bombs and bomb components, together with the typewriter that produced the Unabomber's rambling manifesto.

Ted Kaczynski was born in 1942, a child prodigy who finished high school two years ahead of his class and moved on to Harvard University at age 16. He graduated from Harvard in 1962 and earned a Ph.D. in mathematics from the University of Michigan in 1967. That fall he was hired as an assistant professor at UC Berkeley, but Kaczynski fled academia after three semesters to adopt an odd-job hermit's lifestyle. Briefly employed by his brother in 1978, at a foam rubber factory, he was fired for harassing a female coworker who spurned his romantic attentions. Media analyses of the "mad genius" have thus far failed to explain his lethal grudge against universities, airlines, or society at large.

On 18 June 1996 a federal grand jury in Sacramento indicted Kaczynski on two murder counts; a third capital indictment, in Newark, followed on 1 October 1996. Kaczynski pled not guilty on all charges, then changed his mind on 21 January 1998 and bargained with prosecutors for a sentence of life imprisonment without parole. (His subsequent attempts to revoke that agreement have all been rejected by appellate courts.) David Kaczynski received the $1 million reward for delivering his brother to the FBI.

**KANSAS City Massacre**— No event in Bureau history had a more profound impact than the "massacre" at Kansas City's Union Station on 17 June 1933. It propelled Congress to expand Bureau authority and powers, launching the "war on crime" that would make J. EDGAR HOOVER an international celebrity and turn his "G-men" into Hollywood heroes for nearly four decades. Another 30-odd years elapsed before the legend was exposed as fiction.

The story began with fugitive Frank ("Jelly") Nash. Convicted of robbing a U.S. mail train in 1924, he escaped from Leavenworth federal prison on 19 October 1930 and became an occasional member of the BARKER-KARPIS GANG. In June 1933 Bureau agents traced him to the notorious criminal haven of Hot Springs, Arkansas. Because they lacked arrest powers, the G-men recruited an Oklahoma policeman to give their next move a tenuous air of legitimacy. On 16 June 1933 Nash was snatched by the makeshift posse from a pool hall run by Hot Springs crime boss Dick Galatas. Twice, before they reached Fort Smith and caught a train to Kansas City, they were stopped by deputies seeking a "kidnap victim," but each time the agents bluffed their way through the roadblocks. More agents and local police were waiting to meet the party at Kansas City's Union Station, prepared to escort Nash the final 30 miles to Leavenworth along back roads.

The train with Nash and company aboard arrived at 7:00 a.m. on 17 June. The official version of what happened next, embodied in a single paragraph, is found in the 89th and final volume of the Bureau's 20,000-page file on the Kansas City massacre. (It was clearly written long after the fact, since the initials "FBI" had no meaning before 1 July 1935.) It reads:

> Frank Nash was escorted by the Head of the FBI's Kansas City office [Reed Vetterli], together with Special Agent Raymond J. Caffrey, two other representatives of the FBI [Francis Lackey and Frank Smith], and Otto Reed, chief of police of the McAlester, Oklahoma, Police Department. Police Officers W.J. Grooms and Frank Hermanson of the Kansas City, Missouri, Police Department, were also given important posts of assignment for this transfer. Frank Nash, upon being removed from the train, was immediately taken to the waiting automobile of Special Agent Caffrey, where he was placed in the left front seat in order that the officers might occupy the rear seat. At this instant two Special Agents [Smith and Lackey] took positions in the rear seat with Chief of Police Otto Reed. Police Officers Grooms and Hermanson, together with the Head of the FBI's Kansas City Office, were standing on the right side of Agent Caffrey's automobile during the time Special Agent Caffrey was walking around the car preparatory to entering the driver's seat. It was when Agent Caffrey approached the left door of this automobile that three assassins surprised the officers from a point in front of and about fifteen to twenty feet west of the automobile. These men were observed carrying machine guns and other weapons and in approaching the automobile shouted, "Up, up." An instant later the voice of one of the gunmen was heard to say, "Let 'em have it." Immediately a fusillade of gunfire came from the weapons of the attackers. Shots were fired from the front and from all sides of Agent Caffrey's car. Police officers Grooms and Hermanson were instantly killed in the positions where they stood. Chief of Police Otto Reed was also instantly killed. One agent [Lackey] was severely wounded by bullets which entered his back, and he was confined to bed for several months. Special Agent Caffrey was instantly killed by a bullet which passed directly through his head as he stood beside the car. The prisoner, Frank Nash, was also killed by a misdirected gunshot that entered his skull, thereby defeating the very purpose of the conspiracy to gain his freedom. The other Special Agent [Smith] escaped injury, while the Head of the FBI office [Vetterli] received a wound in the arm. Apparently the assassins started at the front right-hand side of the car and at least two of them proceeded around the vehicle, making a complete circle and firing recklessly as they went.

That was and is today the Bureau's story, but it had problems from day one. Patrolman Mike Fanning, assigned to Union Station that morning, had fired at one of the shooters—a "fat man"—and saw him drop to the ground. "I don't know whether I hit him or whether he fell to escape," Fanning later told the press. "In any event he got up, fired another volley into the car, and ran toward a light Oldsmobile car, which roared west toward Broadway. As the car raced out of the parking lot I saw three men in it, but there may have been more." As the Oldsmobile escaped, Fanning said, "A 1933 Chevrolet car with more gunners swooped past the parked car [Agent Caffrey's] and riddled it from the rear. I ran into the street, fired two shots into the back of that car, and rushed to the parked Chevrolet. I still didn't know the men in it were officers."

Thus, if Officer Fanning's report was correct, there were two cars involved in the shooting, and at least six men (three in the Oldsmobile, plus a driver and "more gunners" in the Chevrolet).

The obvious problem for investigators was identifying those responsible and running them to earth.

Eyewitnesses at the scene were hopelessly confused. Surviving agents Smith and Lackey disagreed on the number of gunmen involved in the ambush, but both initially reported that they had no clear view of the shooters' faces. Agent Vetterli, meanwhile, identified one triggerman from mug shots as Robert Brady, an escaped convict from Kansas who was known to operate with fugitive bank robber Harvey Bailey. That statement seemed to mesh with testimony from two civilian witnesses who named Bailey as one of the shooters. One of those witnesses, Samuel Link, also named the gang's wheelman as bandit WILBUR UNDERHILL, but FBI reports described Link as delusional, claiming personal friendships with ex-president THEODORE ROOSEVELT and various crowned heads of Europe. Another shaky witness, Lottie West from the station's Traveler's Aid booth, identified one of the gunmen as bank robber CHARLES ("PRETTY BOY") FLOYD. West told G-men that Floyd had stopped at her booth before the shooting, giving her a clear look at his face, but her claim was contradicted by several other witnesses who named the man she had seen as Harry Blanchard, a Union Station employee.

Ballistics evidence from the shooting was problematic. Souvenir hunters looted the crime scene before police secured it, leaving only a handful of .45-caliber cartridge cases behind, and even those were useless without suspect weapons for comparison. There were *other* shells, though, found inside the FBI vehicle, where Agent Lackey had fired two rounds from a 16-gauge shotgun, its cartridges specially loaded with steel ball bearings in place of the usual buckshot. Lackey's first shot, whether accidentally or by design, had nearly beheaded Frank Nash. Steel pellets from the shotgun also caused the fatal head wounds suffered by Agent Caffrey and Officer Hermanson, but that evidence was swiftly buried by the FBI. Chief Reed, meanwhile, was struck twice in the head: once by a .45-caliber slug, and once by a .38-caliber round. Either wound was potentially fatal, but the order of impact was never determined, and while investigators claimed the ambushers all used .45-caliber weapons, none of the five .38s carried by lawmen that day were ever test-fired for comparison with the bullet extracted from Reed. The others killed or wounded at Union Station (Grooms, Lackey and Vetterli) were all struck by .45-caliber bullets from submachine guns or pistols—but who did the shooting?

The first real lead came from long-distance telephone records, listing several calls made by Frances Nash from Arkansas to various Missouri numbers on 16 June, in the hours following her husband's arrest. One of those numbers belonged to Vernon Miller, a sheriff-turned-outlaw who lived in Kansas City with a girlfriend, Vivian Mathias. Miller had called Frances Nash from a pay phone at Union Station on Saturday morning, shortly before the ambush. He was long gone when G-men got to his home, but fingerprints confirmed his presence in the house. Agents found other prints, too, but reported no match when they checked them against a list of fugitives including Harvey Bailey, Wilbur Underhill, Pretty Boy Floyd and frequent Floyd accomplice Adam Richetti. Then, on 13 February 1934, agents in Kansas

City "found" new fingerprint evidence and shipped it to Washington. A month later, one of the new prints—allegedly found on a bottle in Verne Miller's basement—was matched to Adam Richetti. Assuming that Floyd must be involved with any action of Richetti's, FBI HEADQUARTERS named Miller, Richetti and Floyd as the Union Station killers. The second carload of gunmen was never thereafter discussed.

The fingerprint "breakthrough" came too late to affect the search for Verne Miller, found beaten to death outside Detroit on 29 November 1933. Vivian Mathias was soon arrested by FBI agents and held incommunicado until she delivered a statement naming the massacre gunmen as Miller, Floyd and Richetti. Floyd had been wounded in the left shoulder during the shootout, Mathias declared, thus accounting for some bloody rags found at Miller's home. Floyd and Richetti hid in Buffalo, New York from September 1933 through early October 1934, then surfaced in Ohio. Richetti was captured there on 19 October; Floyd was cornered by G-man MELVIN PURVIS two days later and killed in what one witness later described as a summary execution.

FBI ballistics experts allegedly matched one of Floyd's .45 automatics to a single shell casing found at Union Station, but his autopsy created more problems. Specifically, there was no shoulder wound to support the story told by Vivian Mathias. Agents returned to Mathias for a new statement, and this time she "remembered" that the bloody rags had nothing to do with Floyd, after all. They were, she said, the remnants of some first-aid treatment given to a wounded Barker-Karpis gangster on some other occasion. As for the rest of her original affidavit, Mathias swore that Floyd's shoulder wound "was the only part I wasn't telling the truth about in the first statement."

It was good enough for J. Edgar Hoover but not for federal prosecutors, who refused to file charges on Richetti. Kansas City prosecutor Michael O'Hearn was likewise "inclined to doubt the fact that there is sufficient evidence to convict Richetti," but his superiors felt otherwise and Richetti was indicted on one murder count, for allegedly killing Officer Hermanson.

Richetti's trial, commencing on 13 June 1935, was something less than a textbook example of justice in action. The only "scientific" evidence against him was a single fingerprint, allegedly recovered not from the crime scene, but from Verne Miller's basement. Ballistically, one cartridge was said to place Pretty Boy Floyd at the murder scene, from which prosecutors inferred that Richetti also must have been present. Agent Vetterli, on the day of the shooting, had reported to FBI headquarters that "I am convinced that the man who first opened fire from our right, with a machine gun, is Bob Brady." Now, two years later, he told the court under oath: "I identify the picture of ... Pretty Boy Floyd as the individual I saw." Agent Smith, in June 1933, reported seeing one machine-gunner and stated unequivocally that he "was unable to obtain any kind of description of him and was unable to see anyone else who did the shooting." In June 1935 Smith examined a photo of Verne Miller and told the jury, "That was the man that shot at my head." Agent Lackey—Officer Hermanson's actual killer—reported to his superiors in 1933 that "there were at least four and possibly more men shooting," although he only glimpsed to and was "not sure that he could identify either of these men," seen only in a "hurried glance" and "through a none too clean window." At trial, Lackey not only identified Richetti as one of the shooters, but denied firing any shots himself, in direct contradiction of physical evidence withheld from the jury.

The verdict was a foregone conclusion: Richetti was convicted of murder on 17 June and sentenced to hang. Progress spared him from the noose, but not from execution: on 7 October 1938 he was the first man executed in Missouri's new gas chamber. The truth about his FRAME-UP was revealed by author Robert Unger in 1997, including an FBI agent's admission to federal judge William Becker: "Our agent sitting in the back seat pulled the trigger on Nash, and that started it. The machine gunners didn't shoot first. Our guy panicked."

**KANTOROWICZ, Alfred**— A leftist German author, born 12 August 1899, Kantorowicz joined the German Communist Party in 1931 and fled his homeland for France when the Nazis came to power, two years later. In 1937 Kantorowicz fought for the Loyalist side in the Spanish Civil War. Four years later he fled the Nazis once again, this time from France to the United States. By the time Kantorowicz arrived in New York, Immigration officials were aware of his communist affiliation. He was threatened with deportation in 1942, but support from ERNEST HEMINGWAY and other prominent writers reversed that decision. Kantorowicz remained under FBI surveillance until he left the U.S. for East Germany in November 1946, notations in his file branding Kantorowicz a "highly dangerous trouble maker" and a "top Comintern agent." Bureau spies noted his membership in the East German Communist Party, between 1949 and 1957, thereafter reporting that Kantorowicz had left East Germany and was "now anti-communist in his beliefs and writings." That observation did not help in 1968, when Kantorowicz sought a U.S. visa to research a book on German exiles in America during WORLD WAR II. Prior membership in the Communist Party was cited as the primary reason for denying Kantorowicz admission to the country.

**KATZENBACH, Nicholas**— A Philadelphia native, born 17 January 1922, Nicholas de Belleville Katzenbach was a Rhodes scholar who served in the U.S. Army Air Force during WORLD WAR II. He subsequently joined the JUSTICE DEPARTMENT and served as deputy attorney general under Attorney General ROBERT KENNEDY (1961-64). When Kennedy left Justice to pursue a higher office, Katzenbach was named Acting Attorney General by President LYNDON JOHNSON on 4 September 1964. He was subsequently confirmed as Attorney General on 1 February 1965.

By that time, Katzenbach was well acquainted with the subterfuge sometimes practiced at Justice and at FBI HEADQUARTERS. It was Katzenbach, in fact, who informed White House aide Bill Moyers of plans to suppress conspiracy theories in the JFK ASSASSINATION. On 24 November 1964, within hours of alleged assassin LEE HARVEY OSWALD'S murder, he told Moyers: "The public must be satisfied that Oswald was the assassin; that he did not have confederates who are still at large; and that the evidence was

such that he would have been convicted at trial. Speculations about Oswald's motivation ought to be cut off."

Katzenbach was successful in that effort, assisted by J. EDGAR HOOVER, but his other contacts with the aging FBI director were less harmonious. Specifically, Katzenbach issued an order on 30 March 1964 that restricted Bureau BUGGING to the same guidelines already imposed for WIRETAPPING, requiring advance approval from Justice for each use of electronic surveillance. Katzenbach found Hoover's former blanket authorization, in an ancient memo from Attorney General HERBERT BROWNWELL, JR., "extremely tenuous" and legally invalid. Hoover retaliated by leaking derogatory information on Katzenbach to the press and blaming the attorney general's office for years of illegal DOMESTIC SURVEILLANCE conducted by G-men. As Katzenbach later told the CHURCH COMMITTEE, "In effect, [Hoover] was uniquely successful in having it both ways: he was protected from public criticism by having a theoretical superior who took responsibility for his work, and he was protected from his superior by his public reputation."

Hoover's feud with Katzenbach went further than mere bureaucratic squabbling, though. Katzenbach told Senate investigators that Hoover routinely lied to his superiors in periodic briefings, employing "terms of art, or euphemisms, without informing the Attorney General that they were terms of art." When shown three memos authorizing microphones in hotel rooms occupied by Dr. MARTIN LUTHER KING, JR., all bearing his alleged signature, Katzenbach stopped short of a forgery accusation but claimed under oath that he could not remember signing the orders. (A report from the FBI's LABORATORY DIVISION predictably confirmed that the signatures were authentic.)

Katzenbach's final quarrel with Hoover was sparked by litigation in the FRED BLACK case, when Katzenbach balked at shouldering responsibility for Hoover's illegal surveillance techniques. Convinced that Katzenbach would "do anything at all" to protect Robert Kennedy's reputation, Hoover escalated his public and private attacks. Finally, Katzenbach told the Church Committee, "My correspondence with Mr. Hoover ... unavoidably became a bitter one and it persuaded me that I could no longer effectively serve as Attorney General because of Mr. Hoover's obvious resentment toward me." Katzenbach resigned on 2 October 1966 and was replaced by Deputy Attorney General RAMSEY CLARK.

### KARPIS, Alvin *see* Barker-Karpis Gang

**KEFAUVER, Carey Estes**— Born near Madisonville, Tennessee on 26 July 1903, Estes Kefauver served five terms in the House of Representatives (1939-49) before he was elected to the U.S. Senate in 1948. Two years later he made national headlines as chairman of the Senate Special Committee to Investigate ORGANIZED CRIME in Interstate Commerce. The investigation placed Kefauver at odds with FBI Director J. EDGAR HOOVER, who had spent a quarter-century denying the mob's existence. On the eve of Kefauver's first hearings, Attorney General J. HOWARD MCGRATH took Hoover's side, publicly declaring that no "national crime syndicate" existed in America.

Kefauver would prove both men wrong in the next 12 months, while Hoover sought to obstruct his efforts at every turn. Denied FBI assistance, Kefauver turned to HARRY ANSLINGER and the FEDERAL BUREAU OF NARCOTICS for support, calling more than 800 witnesses in televised hearings from coast to coast. Americans were captivated by their first glimpse of mobsters including Meyer Lansky, Frank Costello, Moe Dalitz and Mickey Cohen, but public testimony also implicated a number of Hoover's close friends and financial benefactors: CLINT MURCHISON, Joseph KENNEDY, WALTER WINCHELL and LEWIS ROSENSTIEL. When two key witnesses were murdered by gangland assassins, Kefauver sought FBI aid once again, but Hoover remained intractable. He replied, "I regret to advise the Federal Bureau of Investigation is not empowered to perform guard duties."

Kefauver resigned his chairmanship of the crime committee in May 1951, and while he offered various explanations for the move, one he failed to mention was the recent arrest of a friend and campaign contributor, Nashville gambling boss Herbert Brody. Hoover's G-men collected rumors of a $5,000 payoff from Brody to Kefauver, along with other skeletons in the senator's closet. (Author Merle Miller, in his biography of LYNDON JOHNSON, called Kefauver "a boozer, a womanizer, and an eager accepter of bribes from any source.") Despite the potential for embarrassment, however, Kefauver still harbored presidential ambitions. He entered the Democratic field in 1952 and 1956, selected in the latter year as running mate for candidate ADLAI STEVENSON. Hoover used the occasion to provide Republican Vice President RICHARD NIXON with the FBI FILE on Kefauver, as he had with rumors of Stevenson's alleged HOMOSEXUALITY. Kefauver never occupied the White House, but he remained in the Senate until his death from an aortic aneurysm on 10 August 1963. When his safe deposit box was subsequently opened, it revealed $300,000 in stock from various drug companies Kefauver was supposed to regulate.

**KELLER, Oscar Edward**— A native of Helenville, Wisconsin, born 30 July 1878, Oscar Keller moved to Minnesota in 1901 and worked as a merchant before entering politics. In St. Paul he served as a city council member (1910-14), city commissioner (1914-19) and commissioner of public utilities (1914-19). On 1 July 1919 Keller was elected to Congress following the death of incumbent Carl Van Dyke. He was three times reelected to the post, remaining in the House of Representatives until March 1927, and served as chairman of the Committee on Railways and Canals. In that capacity he introduced a resolution calling for the impeachment of Attorney General HARRY DAUGHERTY, after Daugherty used a federal injunction to crush a railroad strike. Bureau agents, presumably acting on orders from Daugherty or Director WILLIAM BURNS, burglarized Keller's Washington office in September 1922 but failed to find any incriminating material. Defeated for reelection in 1926, Keller returned to St. Paul and sold real estate until his death, on 21 November 1927.

**KELLEY, Clarence Marion**— A Missouri native, born 24 October 1911, Clarence Kelley attended high school in Kansas City and graduated from the University of Kansas (at Lawrence), in 1936. Four years later he earned an LL.B. degree from the University of Kansas City School of Law. He joined the FBI on 7 October 1940 and served in various field offices before his 1942 transfer to the FBI ACADEMY as a firearms instructor. Kelley left the Bureau to join the U.S. Navy in 1944, but returned in 1946 to an assignment at the Kansas City field office. In 1953 he was promoted to assistant agent-in-charge of the Houston office, followed by subsequent transfers to FBI HEADQUARTERS, Birmingham and Memphis. Kelley resigned from the FBI in 1961 to become chief of the Kansas City Police Department.

Following the death of FBI Director J. EDGAR HOOVER and Acting Director L. PATRICK GRAY'S resignation in disgrace over the WATERGATE SCANDAL, President RICHARD NIXON nominated Kelley as FBI director in June 1973. Kelley was swiftly confirmed and took over the Bureau on 9 July 1973. Assistant Director Oliver Revell later told journalist Robert Kessler that Nixon chose Kelley in the belief he would be "malleable," but Kelley "was entirely different from that. He was very amiable but also very straight. He brought with him the concept of reorganizing the bureau that today is largely responsible for what we are doing and how we are doing it." His innovations included expanding UNDERCOVER OPERATIONS, instituting a standard of "QUALITY OVER QUANTITY" for FBI investigations, and permitting female employees to wear pant suits instead of dresses.

Publicly, Kelley portrayed himself as an agent of change at the Bureau. In May 1976, speaking at Missouri's Westminster College, he acknowledged that many FBI activities from the Hoover years were "clearly wrong and quite indefensible. We most certainly must never allow them to be repeated." Never again, he insisted, should the Bureau occupy a "unique position that permitted improper activity without accountability." Unfortunately, behind the public façade, Kelley continued Hoover's COINTELPRO campaigns against the "NEW LEFT," black militants and PUERTO RICAN NATIONALIST, using all the illegal techniques he deplored in his speeches. Under Kelley, the covert war also extended to the AMERICAN INDIAN MOVEMENT, including abusive actions during the WOUNDED KNEE SIEGE, FBI sponsorship of the vigilante GUARDIANS OF THE OGLALA NATION at South Dakota's PINE RIDGE RESERVATION, and the apparent FRAME-UP or activist LEONARD PELTIER. Kelley's promotion of COINTELPRO agent RICHARD W. HELD belies statements that the director was "unaware" of abuses committed during his tenure.

Kelley also continued Hoover's tradition of using the FBI to maintain his personal residence, albeit on a smaller scale than his predecessor. Technicians from the FBI Exhibits Section remodeled parts of Kelley's Washington apartment, prompting Special Counsel John Dowd to recommend his dismissal in early 1978, but the final JUSTICE DEPARTMENT report on Kelley's indiscretion stopped short of calling him criminally culpable. Indeed, the report claimed Kelley was "initially unaware" of the work done at his home, and while he received "limited" goods and services from the Bureau, he allegedly reimbursed the government. Still, the scandal was too much in the wake of CHURCH COMMITTEE revelations on FBI impropriety, and Kelley resigned in February 1978. He returned to Kansas City and ran a private security firm for several years. Kelley died on 5 August 1997.

**KELLY, George ("Machine Gun")**—A Chicago native, born George F. Barnes, Jr., on 17 July 1900, this future bank robber and kidnapper moved to Memphis with his family in 1902. He enrolled at Mississippi A&M College in 1917, but left after four months to become a taxi driver. Married at Clarksdale, Mississippi in September 1919, Barnes went to work for his father-in-law's contracting firm, but PROHIBITION beckoned him with promises of easy money and adventure. Barnes logged his first bootlegging arrest, sentenced to six months in jail and a $500 fine. By the time of his divorce, in January 1926, Barnes had begun to call himself "George Kelly."

Jailed again for bootlegging in March 1927, this time in New Mexico, Kelly was free in time to face a vagrancy arrest in Tulsa, four months later. On 13 January 1928 he was caught smuggling liquor onto an Indian reservation, convicted the following month and sentenced to three years at Leavenworth. While there, in February 1930, he allegedly assisted the escape of bank robbers THOMAS HOLDEN and Francis Keating, associates of the BARKER-KARPIS GANG. Himself paroled in June 1930, Kelly joined Holden and Keating for a $70,000 Minnesota bank job the following month. The same gang lifted $40,000 from an Iowa bank on 9 September 1930, and Kelly celebrated the windfall two weeks later, with his marriage to Kathryn Thorne, in Minneapolis.

By most accounts, Kathryn changed Kelly's life, coining his flamboyant nickname and promoting him by word of mouth as a first-rate desperado. Four months after the wedding, Kelly teamed with stickup artist Eddie Doll to kidnap Howard Woolverton, a South Bend, Indiana banker's son. They demanded $50,000 ransom, but Woolverton's family could not raise the money and Kelly released him two days later, with nothing to show for his trouble. Teamed with Doll and Albert Bates, Kelly went back to robbing banks, but he was ready for another fling at KIDNAPPING in July 1933. With Bates, he abducted Oklahoma City oilman CHARLES URSCHEL, stashing him at the Texas farm owned by Kathryn's parents. Kelly was successful this time, collecting $200,000 ransom before Urschel was released on 31 July.

While George and Kathryn decamped for a Mexican vacation, FBI agents entered the case under provisions of the new LINDBERGH Law. By 12 August 1933, when the Kelly's returned to Texas, G-men had arrested Bates and most of Kathryn's family. The Kellys flew to Denver, then Des Moines, then bought a car and made their way to Memphis. Authorities traced them there on 26 September and a raiding party was organized, with local detectives outnumbering FBI agents. Bureau mythology describes Kelly's capture in dramatic terms, the kidnapper cowering before FBI guns and coining a new nickname for the feds as he sobbed, "Don't shoot, G-men!" In fact, however, Memphis detective sergeant W.J. Raney made the arrest, creeping into Kelly's bungalow alone at 6:00 a.m. and jamming a sawed-off shotgun into Kelly's stomach as he ordered the fugitive to drop his pistol. Kelly complied, seeming almost relieved as he told Raney, "I've been waiting for you all night." The "G-men" fable was concocted by FBI press agents and survives to the present day, repeated even by critical historians who should know better.

All concerned in the Urschel kidnapping were later convicted and sentenced to long prison terms. Kelly drew a life sentence, confined first at Leavenworth, then transferred to Alcatraz in September 1934. He was returned to Leavenworth in 1951 and died there, of a heart attack, on 18 July 1954.

**KEMPTON, James Murray**—A Baltimore native, born 16 December 1917, Murray Kempton worked as a reporter and columnist for the *New York Post* from 1942 to 1969, later switching to *Newsday*, where he won a Pulitzer Prize in 1985. He also published several books, including *The Briar Patch*, a study of the BLACK PANTHER PARTY'S official persecution in New York that won the National Book Award in 1973. In 1989 Kempton received the George Polk Career Award "for 45 years of newspaper work that represents the highest standards of journalism."

By that time, the FBI had been on Kempton's trail for over half a century. They somehow missed his two-year membership in the COMMUNIST PARTY, beginning in 1936, but targeted Kempton in 1938, for sponsoring a National Youth Anti-War Congress at Johns Hopkins University. G-men also noted his membership in the Young People's Socialist League. In 1949 Kempton's perceived criticism of J. EDGAR HOOVER landed Kempton on the Bureau's dreaded "Do Not Contact" list, but agents broke the rule in 1953, visiting Kempton to question him about two friends who were former members of the Young Communist League. Following that interview, G-men recommended "no further action" against Kempton, rating him "an effective writer who could be influential in a time of national emergency."

FBI agents continued to clip Kempton's newspaper columns, some from his 401-page file bearing marginal notes in Hoover's own hand. In 1958, while Kempton studied in Italy on a Fulbright scholarship, Hoover demanded a list of the committee members who had chosen him, seeking to learn why "a pseudo Communist ... who belittles the Bureau" should be so honored. Eight years later, when Kempton joined the *New Republic*'s staff, Deputy Associate Director CARTHA DELOACH recommended that the FBI "discreetly" brief friendly journalists on Kempton's "background." Hoover's response: "Yes, do so." Later that year, a 16-page FBI summary of Kempton's career closed with a handwritten note from Associate Director CLYDE TOLSON read, "He is a *real* stinker."

In 1968, following a disorderly conduct arrest at the Democratic Convention in Chicago, G-men considered prosecuting Kempton for "violating antiriot laws," but the attorney general refused to proceed with the case. A year later, while Kempton was writing *The Briar Patch*, FBI sources spread false rumors that he had a "fund raising arrangement" with the Black Panther Party (refuted by statements from the Bureau's own spies in the party). G-men also monitored Kempton's participation in a 1969 Vietnam Peace Parade Committee, noting that he "criticized FBI agents' interference" with reporters during the event. A particularly ghoulish note was filed in 1971, after Kempton's son and daughter-in-law were killed in a traffic accident. Hoover saved their obituary, with a note demanding "subversive references only" on the victims.

Throughout his FBI surveillance, Kempton never lost his

sense of humor. In 1991 he told author Natalie Robins, regarding Hoover, "You think of this lunatic sitting there and saying 'off with their heads'—and there's no axe. There's no executioner. I mean, he presses this button and he says destroy this man's career and the career is not destroyed, thank God." In that respect, unlike so many others, Kempton was very fortunate. He died in New York City on 5 May 1997.

**KENNEDY, John Fitzgerald**—The son of bootlegger-diplomat Joseph Kennedy, born at Brookline, Massachusetts on 29 May 1917, John F. Kennedy was groomed for political office following the death of older brother Joseph, Jr., in WORLD WAR II. He first came to the FBI's attention soon after the PEARL HARBOR ATTACK, when Danish national Inga Arvad (a European beauty queen and friend of ADOLF HITLER) was denounced to G-men as a Nazi spy in the U.S. Agents placed Arvad under surveillance and soon collected evidence (including tape recordings) of Kennedy's illicit love affair with the married journalist. The liaison ended when Kennedy, a Navy officer, was transferred to the South Pacific. The Bureau's investigation of Arvad was closed in March 1945, with a notation that "no subversive activities were discovered."

John Kennedy returned a war hero in 1945 and was elected to Congress the following year. He served three terms in the House (1947-53), then was elected to the Senate in 1952. FBI Director J. EDGAR HOOVER remained on friendly terms with Kennedy's father but despised the various sons, as much for their sexual excesses as for their liberal politics. John Kennedy disliked Hoover in turn, striving in vain to retrieve the Arvad tape recording, and Hoover feared that he might be replaced as FBI director if Kennedy ever reached the White House. Recognizing Hoover's potential danger as a political enemy, JFK endeavored to disguise his feelings toward Hoover. A *New York Times* reporter raised the question of Hoover's replacement on 4 August 1960, less than three weeks after Kennedy's presidential nomination, and Kennedy replied that "he would, of course, retain Mr. Hoover and planned no major changes within the agency." Hoover threw his covert support to Republican RICHARD NIXON, but "assisted" the Kennedy campaign by revealing celebrity supporter FRANK SINATRA'S close ties to ORGANIZED CRIME.

Any threat of Hoover's immediate replacement was eliminated on 10 February 1961, when the director furnished Attorney General ROBERT KENNEDY with a summary of FBI FILES on the president's sexual activities, including "affidavits of two mulatto prostitutes in New York." Hoover also kept tabs on JFK's continuing affairs, including liaisons with actress MARILYN MONROE and Judith Campbell, the sometime lover of Chicago mobster SAM GIANCANA. Those efforts to maintain his job only made the Kennedy brothers more intent on dumping Hoover, but they delayed the move pending John's reelection in 1964. Hoover would reach age 70 (making retirement mandatory under federal law) in January 1965, and President Kennedy planned to celebrate his second inauguration by retiring Hoover with "a great deal of honor." Assistant Director WILLIAM SULLIVAN reported that Hoover learned of the plan and "he was very, very unhappy about it."

Hoover got a reprieve on 22 November 1963, when President Kennedy was shot and killed in Dallas, Texas. It may have been coincidence that prime suspect LEE HARVEY OSWALD and Oswald's own killer, mobster JACK RUBY, were later identified as FBI INFORMANTS. In any case, Hoover did not mourn Kennedy's passing and the FBI's slipshod investigation of the JFK ASSASSINATION served primarily to divert public attention from evidence of a possible conspiracy.

**KENNEDY, Robert Francis**—A brother of future president JOHN KENNEDY, born in Boston on 20 November 1925, Robert Kennedy served in the Navy during WORLD WAR II and followed the family tradition of political service. In the late 1950s he was chief counsel for the U.S. Senate's McClellan Committee, investigating criminal infiltration of national LABOR UNIONS. That experience left him with a determination to fight ORGANIZED CRIME and corrupt leaders of the TEAMSTERS' UNION in particular. When John Kennedy was elected president in 1960, he appointed Robert to serve as his attorney general, pursuing the dual objectives of prosecuting mobsters and securing CIVIL RIGHTS for African Americans.

Both goals were ardently opposed by FBI Director J. EDGAR HOOVER. Although a longtime friend of ex-ambassador Joseph Kennedy, Hoover despised the liberal politics and sexual promiscuity of Kennedy's various sons. Hoover's racism placed him in opposition to all civil rights initiatives, and he feared embarrassment if his 40-year denial of organized crime's existence was exposed as a tissue of lies. Worse yet, Hoover feared that the Kennedy brothers planned to replace him with a younger, more liberal director, and to that end he fought to maintain his position by any means available.

Hoover's preferred weapon was blackmail, using derogatory information from FBI FILES. Beginning within days of President Kennedy's inauguration, Hoover treated the new attorney general to a series of confidential reports detailing sexual affairs and other improprieties of the Kennedy clan. As RFK later described the situation, "every month or so [Hoover] would send somebody around to give information on somebody I knew or members of my family or allegations in connection with myself, so that it would be clear—whether it was right or wrong—that he was on top of all these things." Withheld from Kennedy were a more significant group of reports, including death threats against the president and his brother issued by mobsters including Carlos Marcello, Santo Trafficante, Jimmy Hoffa and SAM GIANCANA.

In retrospect, many of Hoover's clashes with Kennedy involved petty subjects, ranging from corridor lights at the JUSTICE DEPARTMENT (G-men warned the early-rising attorney general that "the Director likes to turn them on"); placement of the telephone connecting Hoover to Kennedy's office on the director's desk (instead of secretary HELEN GANDY'S); and Kennedy's use of the FBI gymnasium (guards barred him for a lack of "proper FBI credentials"). Until RFK ordered a change in the script, tour guides at FBI HEADQUARTERS told visitors that Hoover had become director "the year before the Attorney General was born"; new recruits at the FBI ACADEMY learned that Hoover had rejected Kennedy's application because he was "too cocky." Behind that childish sniping, though, lay bitter opposition that would never fade with passing time. Kennedy may have agreed to FBI BUGGING of Dr. MARTIN LUTHER KING'S hotel suites, after Hoover claimed members of King's entourage belonged to the COMMUNIST PARTY, but Kennedy also forced Hoover to hire BLACK AGENTS for the first time since the 1920s and launched the first prosecutions of high-ranking mobsters in FBI history.

That all changed with the JFK ASSASSINATION of 22 November 1963. Within minutes of the president's death, Hoover ordered the Kennedy hotline returned to Helen Gandy's desk, and RFK would soon remark to aides, concerning Hoover's men, "Those people don't work for us any more." In February 1964, Minneapolis agent-in-charge RICHARD G. HELD reported to Hoover an INFORMANT'S claim that members of "the Kennedy crowd" at Justice had "openly discussed how they were doing everything they could to … embarrass the President [LYNDON JOHNSON] in every way possible." Specifically, they "hoped to create a situation whereby the President would be forced to pick the Attorney General, Robert Kennedy, as his running mate in order to assure his re-election." Worse yet, Held told Hoover that the miscreants "openly criticized you and the FBI, and indicated that they would like to break up the excellent relationship that exists between you and President Johnson." Hoover dutifully passed the news on to Johnson, who fired Kennedy on 3 September 1964.

Undaunted, Kennedy launched a campaign for the U.S. Senate in New York and was elected in November 1964. Choosing racial justice and opposition to the VIETNAM WAR as his primary issues, Kennedy set his sights on the White House in 1968. Observers had no doubt that if elected, he would find a new director for the FBI; some also hinted that the driving motive for his presidential race was a desire to punish his brother's assassins. On 5 June 1968, moments after winning the California primary election, Kennedy was shot and fatally wounded in Los Angeles. He died the following day, and Hoover's investigation of the RFK ASSASSINATION was a carbon copy of the FBI's performance five years earlier. Even in death the director could not resist upstaging Kennedy. On 8 June 1968 Hoover interrupted Kennedy's televised funeral ceremony with a press conference announcing the arrest of James Earl Ray, alleged assassin of Dr. MARTIN LUTHER KING, JR.

**KENT State University shootings**— In May 1970 revelation of President RICHARD NIXON'S covert military action in Cambodia sparked demonstrations on college campuses across the U.S. Students at Ohio's Kent State University rioted on the night of 1 May, prompting Governor James Rhodes to impose an 8:00 p.m. curfew. National Guardsmen occupied the campus after demonstrators burned the ROTC building on 2 May, and another demonstration was in progress on 4 May 1970, when troops opened fire with high-powered rifles, killing four students and wounding another nine.

President Nixon described himself as "deeply saddened" by the deaths at Kent State and others in a similar shooting at Mississippi's JACKSON STATE UNIVERSITY. FBI agents were assigned to investigate the Ohio incident (code-named KENFOUR), while Nixon appointed an independent President's Commission on Campus Unrest (better known by the name of its chairman, former Pennsylvania governor William Scranton) to do likewise. G-men eventually submitted some 8,000 pages of testimony to the Scranton Commission, while Director J. EDGAR HOOVER complained to the U.S. Senate Appropriations Committee that the investigation cost $274,100 in overtime. (Staff members at Kent State complained to their representatives in Congress that G-men spent much of that time examining classroom lesson plans and probing the political beliefs of various professors.) Long before that investigation was finished, though, Hoover telephoned White House aide Egil Krogh to report that "the students invited and got what they deserved."

What they got, according to Hoover's own agents, was an undisciplined and indiscriminate burst of gunfire lasting for 11 seconds, including at least 54 (and perhaps 61) shots fired by 29 of the 78 Guardsmen present. None of the four students killed had been demonstrators; they were shot at distances between 85 yards and 130 yards from the Guardsmen, two with their backs turned and one while lying prone on the ground. Of the nine students wounded, only one appeared to be an active demonstrator, shot while making "an obscene gesture" to the Guardsmen from 20 yards away; the rest were shot at distances ranging from 37 yards to 250 yards from the guns. A JUSTICE DEPARTMENT summary or FBI reports likewise disposed of claims that the Guardsmen believed themselves to be under sniper fire.

> At the time of the shootings, the National Guard clearly did not believe that they were being fired upon. No Guardsman claims he fell to the ground or took any other evasive action and all available photographs show the Guard at the critical moments in a standing position and not seeking cover. In addition, no Guardsman claims he fired at a sniper or even that he fired in the direction from which he believed the sniper shot. Finally, there is no evidence of the use of any weapons at any time in the weekend prior to the May 4 confrontation.

If the physical evidence were not enough, six Guardsmen (including a captain and two sergeants) also "stated pointedly that the lives of the members of the Guard were not in danger and that it was not a shooting situation. As for the 11 Guardsmen who later expressed mortal fear, the Scranton Report concluded: "We have some reason to believe that the claim by the National Guard that they thought their lives were endangered by the students was fabricated subsequent to the event." A report in the Akron *Beacon Journal*, published on 24 May 1970, corroborated that claim of conspiracy with a quote from one of the Guardsmen: "The guys have been saying that we got to get together and stick to the same story, that it was our lives or them, a matter of survival. I told them I would tell the truth and couldn't get in trouble that way."

Reactions from Washington were predictably hostile. Vice President SPIRO AGNEW called the Scranton Report "pabulum for the permissivists," while the commander of Ohio's National Guard found the FBI investigation results "just unbelievable." Even J. Edgar Hoover did not seem to trust his own agents in this case, responding to an article in the Akron *Beacon Journal* with a letter that read in part: "I can assure you that any comments you may have seen in the news media to the effect that the FBI drew conclusions indicating guilt on the part of National Guardsmen in the shooting at Kent State University are absolutely and unequivocally false." Despite the FBI's reported conclusions and those of the Scranton Commission, an Ohio grand jury refused to indict any Guardsmen, instead condemning student "agitators" and Kent State professors who encouraged an "overemphasis on dissent." As for the Guardsmen, the panel's report found that they "fired their weapons in the honest and sincere belief ... that they would suffer serious bodily injury had they not done so."

**KERNER Commission**— On 29 July 1967, days after riots claimed 60 lives in Detroit and Newark, President LYNDON JOHNSON issued Executive Order 11365, establishing the National Advisory Commission on Civil Disorders to study and report the causes of racial outbreaks in 128 U.S. cities since January. The commission is more commonly known by the name of its chairman, Illinois Governor Otto Kerner. Johnson's order not only demanded an investigation of what caused ghetto riots, but also sought recommendations in three related areas: "Short term measures to prevent riots, better measures to contain riots once they begin, and long term measures to eliminate riots in the future."

FBI Director J. EDGAR HOOVER sought to convince the Kerner Commission that American ghetto riots spanning the past four years were the result of a pervasive conspiracy between black militants and the COMMUNIST PARTY, acting through a variety of CIVIL RIGHTS groups, teenage gangs, and the U.S. government's own Office of Economic Opportunity (which Hoover described as being heavily infiltrated by black "radicals"). His testimony stressed the "catalytic effect of extremists" and the "vicious rhetoric" of such organizations as the STUDENT NONVIOLENT COORDINATING COMMITTEE and the SOUTHERN CHRISTIAN LEADERSHIP CONFERENCE. In regard to POLICE BRUTALITY, seen as a spark to most of the 1960s outbreaks, Hoover dismissed such claims as fabrications on the part of "vicious, hate-filled ... black extremists" linked to Moscow. In Hoover's view "the communist policy to charge and protest 'police brutality' ... in racial incidents" was simply part of an "immensely successful ... [and] ... continuing smear campaign." In closing, he recommended strict new legislation to punish ethnic agitators. As Hoover explained, "Any law that allowed law enforcement the opportunity to arrest vicious rabble-rousers would be healthy to have on the books."

The commission flatly rejected Hoover's conspiracy thesis. Its final 425-page report, published on 1 March 1968, listed the primary causes of urban rioting as poverty, racial discrimination and police misconduct. No substantial remedies were forthcoming, however, and the assassination of Dr. MARTIN LUTHER KING, JR., in April 1968 produced riots in 125 cities, leaving 46 persons dead, 2,600 injured, and 21,270 arrested. On 10 June 1968 President Johnson created a National Commission on the Causes and Prevention of Violent Crime (better known as the Eisenhower Commission, after chairman Milton Eisenhower) to investigate the latest outbreaks. That commission, in turn, produced another report blaming poverty, unemployment and substandard housing for much of America's violent crime.

Hoover was appalled by the findings of both commissions and ordered secret "counterintelligence action" to discredit their findings. His first move was to seek investigation of various "black agitators" by the HOUSE COMMITTEE ON UN-AMERICAN ACTIVITIES, but Chairman Edwin Willis declined to participate, expressing concern that such hearings would only reap more sympathy and publicity for subpoenaed witnesses. Hoover's special agent in charge of the Houston field office, lamenting that Kerner's report seemed "to absolve the Negro rioters from any large blame," suggested in March 1968 that the FBI's CRIME RECORDS DIVISION should release a public-opinion poll—"either a true poll or a false poll"—indicating that a majority of Americans blamed "the Negro rioters" for urban violence. Hoover refused to approve that DISINFORMATION campaign and focused instead on his illegal COINTELPRO campaigns against various black activists.

**KGB**— For 37 years, the Soviet Union's Committee for State Security was the FBI's chief rival in the field of ESPIONAGE. Created by Nikita Khrushchev in 1954 to replace and consolidate multiple Stalinist security services, the KGB had 420,000 employees at its peak (excluding thousands of paid INFORMANTS worldwide). It combined functions served by the FBI and CENTRAL INTELLIGENCE AGENCY, with different divisions assigned to handle domestic and foreign intelligence. Its power was such that it has been aptly described as "a state within a state." However, while some authors use the familiar initials to cover every act of Soviet spying from 1917 to the collapse of Communism in 1991, the KGB had nothing to do with such famous 1940s cases as the trials of JUDITH COPLON or JULIUS and ETHEL ROSENBERG.

The FBI got off to a rocky start in its covert war with the KGB, thanks primarily to Director J. EDGAR HOOVER'S naïve obsession with the COMMUNIST PARTY. While hundreds of G-men and informants were employed to keep party members under constant surveillance, KGB agents moved freely in America, usually operating from Soviet embassies where they enjoyed diplomatic immunity (and were thus impervious to arrest). As journalist Robert Kessler observed, "While Hoover had been targeting the Communist Party, the success of the KGB at committing espionage came as a total shock."

The Bureau's first great "victory" against the KGB, the June 1957 arrest of Colonel RUDOLF ABEL, was actually a collaborative effort in which G-men played a relatively minor part. Abel was betrayed by a KGB defector in Europe, who gave his name first to the CIA, and he was initially jailed as an illegal alien by agents of the Immigration and Naturalization Service. Still, official FBI accounts of the case make it seem as if Bureau agents—or Hoover himself—tracked Abel with the skill of a modern Sherlock Holmes.

More substantial victories would follow Abel's trial, and the Bureau did its best work against the KGB under Director WILLIAM WEBSTER (1978-87), but embarrassments were unavoidable. Three FBI agents—RICHARD MILLER, EARL PITTS and ROBERT HANSSEN—have been convicted of spying for Russia since 1986, with Hanssen's treasonous activities spanning two decades. KGB defectors and double-agents were the greatest risk to Russian "moles" inside the Bureau, as they were to traitorous CIA agent ALDRICH AMES. G-men generally overlooked the spies in their midst, and in Hanssen's case the Bureau ignored a written report from another agent (Hanssen's brother-in-law) which named the turncoat as a Russian spy.

The KGB was officially dismantled in December 1991, with the collapse of Russian Communism. Its former duties are today fulfilled by several different agencies, including the Foreign Intelligence Service (FIS), the Ministry of Security (MB), the Main Guard Directorate (GUO) and the Committee for Protection of the Russian Border.

**KIDNAPPING**— America's first "official" ransom kidnapping was the Philadelphia abduction of young Charles Brewster Ross in July 1874. Ross was never found, although a burglar in New York made a deathbed confession to the kidnapping five months later. Hundreds of similar cases were reported over the next 57 years, but kidnapping remained a strictly local crime. Federal agents investigated only those cases where victims were kidnapped on government land, as in national parks or on Indian reservations.

Concerted demands for a federal anti-kidnapping statute began in 1931. The prior decade had witnessed 279 reported abductions in 28 states, including five high-profile murders of children and nine successful ransom kidnappings of affluent businessmen. In December 1931 the St. Louis Chamber of Commerce sent a delegation to Washington, D.C., to lobby for new legislation, and the U.S. House Judiciary Committee opened hearings on 26 February 1932. Three days later, reports of the New Jersey LINDBERGH KIDNAPPING rocked the nation, and Congress was spurred to action. On 10 March 1932 the House passed a bill imposing penalties of 10 years' imprisonment and a $5,000 fine for sending extortion threats through the U.S. mail. Charles Lindbergh, Jr., was found dead on 11 May 1932; eight days later, the House passed a kidnapping bill that included capital punishment, but the Senate deleted that provision prior to final passage. President HERBERT HOOVER signed the "Lindbergh Law" on 22 June 1932, granting FBI agents jurisdiction over interstate abductions. A presumption of interstate flight, sans evidence, allowed G-men to any kidnapping case after seven days.

The first defendants convicted under the new law were the February 1933 kidnappers of Denver millionaire Charles Boettcher II, ransomed for $60,000. (One kidnapper received a 32-year sentence, the other 26 years.) In June 1933, members of the BARKER-KARPIS GANG ransomed William Hamm, a Minnesota brewer, for $100,000, but Chicago G-man MELVIN PURVIS tried to frame bootlegger ROGER TOUHY for the crime. A month later, Oklahoma oilman CHARLES URSCHEL was kidnapped and ransomed for $200,000 by GEORGE ("MACHINE GUN") KELLY, the case enshrined in Bureau mythology until it crumbled in the late 1950s. In October 1933, FBI agents were placed in charge of the ongoing Lindbergh investigation, but they had little to do with its final "solution" in 1935.

Sensational cases continued, despite FBI involvement in pursuing ransom kidnappers. The Barker-Karpis gang doubles its money in January 1934, with the $200,000 snatch of Minnesota

banker Edward Bremer. Four months later, the Lindbergh Law was amended to provide for execution of any interstate kidnapper who harmed his victims, with the "harm" left undefined. Seven days after President FRANKLIN ROOSEVELT signed the amendment into law, on 24 May 1935, a team of husband-wife kidnappers grabbed nine-year-old George Weyerhauser in Tacoma, Washington. He was released on 1 June, after payment of a $200,000 ransom, and the suspects were arrested eight days later. Both pled guilty, receiving sentences of 45 and 20 years, respectively.

Pursuit of kidnappers was initially a boon to FBI Director J. EDGAR HOOVER. In February 1936 he told reporters "kidnapping is well in hand in America.... We haven't had a major kidnapping since the Weyerhauser case last spring." Two months later, pleading with the Senate for a larger budget, he had second thoughts, warning that if piles of cash were not forthcoming, "You would have a wave of kidnapping." Hoover got the money, but it failed to hold the wolves at bay. In December 1936, 10-year-old Charles Mattson was snatched from the same Tacoma neighborhood where George Weyerhauser was kidnapped 19 months earlier. Ransom negotiations broke down in the glare of national publicity, and Mattson was found dead on 11 January 1937. The case remains unsolved, despite FBI investigation of a reported 26,000 suspects.

The Mattson case began another rash of ransom abductions, continuing sporadically into the 1960s. Overall, the Lindbergh Law's death penalty provision produced only four executions between 1936 and 1953. That provision was discarded as unconstitutional in 1967, because it failed to define the "harm" required for a death sentence and because it placed unreasonable pressure on defendants to plead guilty. (Execution was automatically waived for defendants who "copped a plea"; only those who exercised their right to trial faced death.) The Bureau's most prominent kidnapping case of the 1970s involved the SYMBIONESE LIBERATION ARMY'S abduction of newspaper heiress Patricia Hearst. Since the mid-1980s, G-men are best known for "PSYCHOLOGICAL PROFILING" of child-snatchers and suspects linked to SERIAL MURDERS, though the FBI itself rarely participates in an arrest.

**KILMER, Joyce**— A native of New Jersey, born at New Brunswick in 1886, Joyce Kilmer graduated from Rutgers College in 1908. He was a sergeant in the U.S. Army when his most famous poem, "Trees," was published in the August 1913 issue of *Poetry* magazine. A year later, still in uniform, he released the collection *Trees and Other Poems*, which remains a best-seller. Kilmer shipped out to France as a member of the American Expeditionary Force in WORLD WAR I, and died in battle before year's end. The FBI curiously opened a file on him 23 years later, after an entry on his wife appeared in the 1941 edition of *Current Biography*. The file was brief and soon forgotten. When asked about Kilmer, years later, a Bureau spokesman replied, "I don't know her."

**KING, Martin Luther, Jr.**— A third-generation minister, born in Atlanta on 15 January 1929, MARTIN LUTHER KING, JR., was a precocious student who graduated from high school at age 15 and earned a B.A. in sociology from Morehouse College in 1948. King earned a Bachelor of Divinity degree from Pennsylvania's Crozer Theological Seminary in 1951 and moved on to doctoral studies at Boston University, where he received a Ph.D. in systematic theology in June 1955.

King's first pastoral assignment took him to Montgomery, Alabama, where a black boycott of segregated city buses began in December 1955. King was elected president of the Montgomery Improvement Association that month, thus becoming the boycott's official spokesman, and the campaign climaxed with a U.S. SUPREME COURT ban on bus segregation in November 1956. That victory, followed by King's organization of the SOUTHERN CHRISTIAN LEADERSHIP CONFERENCE (SCLC) in 1957, marked King as a primary target for BOMBINGS and murder attempts by the KU KLUX KLAN over the next 12 years. In 1959 King visited India to study Mohandas Gandhi's philosophy of nonviolent civil disobedience. Upon his return to the U.S., King resigned his Alabama pastorate in favor of full-time CIVIL RIGHTS work, directing the SCLC from Atlanta. He logged his first arrest in 1960, during an Atlanta sit-in demonstration, and while sentenced to a four-month jail term, King was freed prematurely thanks to intervention by presidential candidate JOHN KENNEDY.

It is unknown precisely when the FBI first noticed Dr. King. Self-described "FBI hit man" MICHAEL MILAN'S memoirs claim the long pursuit began in 1953, while King was leading a bus boycott "in Mobile, Alabama," but that tale is clearly erroneous. It is more likely the surveillance began sometime in 1961, when King—code-named "Zorro" in FBI FILES—was leading a desegregation campaign in Albany, Georgia. SCLC headquarters issued a report on 8 January 1962, complaining that FBI agents in the South habitually consorted and collaborated with racist police. Bureau Director J. EDGAR HOOVER filed his own report with Attorney General ROBERT KENNEDY the same day, claiming that King and his organization were tools of the COMMUNIST PARTY, embodied in the person of adviser STANLEY LEVISON. Assistant Directors CARTHA DELOACH and WILLIAM SULLIVAN telephoned King, hoping to "set him straight," but King ignored their calls. On 15 January 1962 DeLoach wrote a memo branding King "a vicious liar"; Hoover's marginal note read: "I concur." Ten months later, King told reporters, "One of the great problems we face with the FBI in the South is that the agents are white Southerners who have been influenced by the mores of the community." His statement was technically inaccurate—a narrow majority of G-men stationed in Dixie came from the North—but it perfectly described J. Edgar Hoover.

On 22 June 1963, in the midst of his epic campaign to desegregate Birmingham, Alabama, King met with President Kennedy in Washington. Kennedy cited FBI reports while warning King to dismiss Stanley Levison from his entourage and King reluctantly complied. Two months later, on the eve of King's famous March on Washington, William Sullivan angered Hoover by reporting that the Communist Party was "not the instigator" of the impending demonstration and was likewise "unable to direct or control" it. Hoover's fury at that verdict prompted Sullivan to recant six days later, in a memo (dated 28 August) that read:

The director is correct. We were completely wrong.... Personally, I believe in light of King's powerful demagogic speech yesterday he stands head and shoulders over all other Negro leaders put together when it comes to influencing great masses of Negroes. We must mark him now, if we have not done so before, as the most dangerous Negro of the future in this Nation from the standpoint of Communism, the Negro and national security."

Sullivan also recommended "increased coverage" on King and the SCLC, but Attorney General Kennedy delayed his approval for WIRETAPS and BUGGING of King's hotel rooms until 21 October 1963. Based on past performance, it is safe to assume that illegal surveillance of King was already in place, but for the rest of his life Hoover used Kennedy's limited authorization as an excuse for every excess perpetrated against Dr. King. As later revealed, that campaign included character assassination, efforts to disrupt King's marriage and a bizarre attempt to make him commit suicide.

On 29 December 1963, informed that *Time* magazine's next issue would name King "Man of the Year," Hoover penned a memo saying, "They had to dig deep in the garbage to come up with this one." Two weeks later, while reviewing tapes of King's sexual liaisons with various women, the director gloated, "This will destroy the burrhead." It did not, however, even when Hoover mailed one of the tapes to King's wife. The nature of Hoover's obsession is obvious from another notation in King's file, dated 27 January 1964: "King is a 'tom cat' with obsessive degenerate sexual urges."

When not eavesdropping on King, the FBI did everything possible to deprive him of honors. Officials at Marquette University rescinded their offer of an honorary degree in March 1964, after G-men told them "the truth" about Dr. King, but several other universities were pleased to welcome the civil rights leader. In August 1964 Hoover used Cardinal Francis Spellman to sabotage a scheduled meeting between King and Pope Paul the VI, but the Vatican refused to cancel King's visit. Following the October 1964 announcement that King would receive a Nobel Peace Prize, Hoover hatched his most malicious scheme to date. A letter was prepared at FBI HEADQUARTERS, which read in part:

> King, look into your heart. You know you are a complete fraud and a greater liability to all of us Negroes.... You are no clergyman and you know it. I repeat you are a colossal fraud and an evil, vicious one at that.... But you are done. Your "honorary" degrees, your Nobel Prize (what a grim farce) and other awards will not save you, King, I repeat you are done....
>
> King, there is only one thing left for you to do. You know what it is. You have just 34 days in which to do (this exact number has been selected for a specific reason, it has definite practical significance). You are done. There is but one way out for you. You better take it before your filthy, abnormal fraudulent self is bared to the nation.

An FBI agent mailed the letter, along with a composite tape prepared from various hotel recordings, from Tampa to Atlanta in November 1964. Ironically, by the time it reached King's hands, the 34-day deadline was already past. William Sullivan later explained to author Curt Gentry that the letter was mailed "because King had broken his marriage vows."

Around the same time the letter and tape were sent, on 18 November 1964, Hoover told a group of female reporters that Dr. King was "the most notorious liar in the country." Confronted about the remark by Attorney General NICHOLAS KATZENBACH, Hoover admitted, "I never should have done that," but he was far from repentant. The illegal surveillance and harassment continued, even after a personal meeting between King and Hoover on 1 December 1964.

Following the Selma, Alabama voting rights campaign of 1965, King's message shifted from straightforward attacks on racial segregation to broader dissection of America's socioeconomic ills. He addressed the issues of housing, unemployment, and—after April 1967—the VIETNAM WAR. King's call for peace in Asia was so dynamic that President LYNDON JOHNSON told friends, "That goddamned nigger preacher may drive me out of the White House." Hoover, meanwhile, had launched new COINTELPRO campaigns designed to "prevent the rise of a 'messiah'" in the black community, with King as a primary target.

In early 1968, while planning a controversial Poor People's Campaign in Washington, King became involved in a Memphis garbage workers' strike. His first demonstration ended violently on 28 March, thanks to the activities of black *agents provocateur* in the crowd, but King returned to lead another protest march in April. On the evening of 4 April 1968 he was shot and killed by a sniper on the balcony of his hotel. Ex-agent ARTHUR MURTAGH and others recall G-men celebrating the news at the Bureau's Atlanta field office, cheering, "They got Zorro! They finally got the son of a bitch!" The FBI's subsequent "MURKIN" investigation ignored substantial evidence of a conspiracy behind King's death and named a petty criminal with no racist history as the lone assassin.

Even King's death did not end the long feud, as far as J. Edgar Hoover was concerned. He continued surveillance on the SCLC and on King's successor, Rev. RALPH ABERNATHY, in hopes of proving that the group was run by communists. Until his own death four years later, Hoover also fought efforts to name a national holiday in King's honor, leaking FBI files to right-wing congressmen who opposed the effort. Thanks in large part to FBI obstructionism, the King holiday would not be established until November 1986.

**KISCH, Egon Erwin**—A Czech Jew, born in Prague on 29 April 1885, Egon Kisch fled the Nazi occupation of his homeland in 1939, traveling first to Paris and then to New York, where he spent two months before moving on to Mexico City. FBI files on Kisch bore the headings "Custodial Detention," "Mexico Subversive Matters" and "Internal Security—C" (for Communist). While living in Mexico as a "roving reporter," Kisch remained under constant surveillance by G-men and the U.S. embassy, including a longstanding "mail cover" that enabled agents to read his private correspondence. In July 1942, FBI agents stole a letter addressed to Kisch by FRATISEK WEISKOPF in New York, and delivered it to the Office of Censorship. In February 1946, despite FBI suspicions that Kisch had been earmarked for "a high diplomatic post" in Latin America, he returned to Prague with no official status. Kisch died there on 31 March 1948, but G-men continued collecting rumors of his wartime activities as late as 1956.

**KISSINGER, Henry Alfred**—A German native, born Heinz Alfred Kissinger on 27 May 1923, America's future secretary of state emigrated to the U.S. with his family in 1938, to escape ADOLF HITLER'S persecution of Jews. Upon arrival in New York he changed his given name to "Henry" and quickly emerged as an outstanding student in public school. Kissinger earned a Ph.D. in international relations from Harvard University and joined the faculty there in 1958, remaining until he became President RICHARD NIXON'S assistant for national security affairs in 1969.

While privately describing Nixon as a "basket case" and "meatball mind," Kissinger reveled in his new powers and never hesitated to enlist FBI assistance in pursuance of his broadly-defined duties. In May 1969, after newspapers reported Nixon's illegal bombing campaign in Cambodia, Kissinger ordered Director J. EDGAR HOOVER to "make a major effort" to identify the government sources. He singled out four STATE DEPARTMENT officials for illegal WIRETAPPING, subsequently using those taps to spy on Secretary of State William Rogers and Secretary of Defense Melvin Laird. In June 1969, after protests disrupted Nelson Rockefeller's tour of Latin America, Kissinger ordered the Bureau to investigate "whether they were spontaneous and came from within the countries ... or whether there was a pattern of conspiracy initiated from outside of these countries that led to the disturbances." (Hoover, as always, blamed the demonstrations on a global communist plot.)

In September 1970 Hoover warned the White House of a plot by anti-VIETNAM WAR activists DANIEL and PHILIP BERRIGAN to kidnap Kissinger. While Kissinger scoffed at the story and Attorney General JOHN MITCHELL refused to file charges, Hoover went public with the accusations two months later and forced the JUSTICE DEPARTMENT to pursue a costly, ultimately futile trial. More serious, in Kissinger's mind, was media exposure of the PENTAGON PAPERS in October 1971. As later described by White House aide H.R. HALDEMAN, "Henry got Nixon cranked up, then they started cranking each other up until they were both in a frenzy." The ensuing investigation included a series of illegal BREAK-INS that prefigured the administration's WATERGATE SCANDAL.

Kissinger succeeded Rogers as secretary of state on 22 September 1973 and remained to serve under President GERALD FORD after Nixon resigned in disgrace. His "shuttle diplomacy" in Southeast Asia and the Middle East won Kissinger a Nobel Peace Prize, along with such superlative media descriptions as "the 20th century's greatest diplomatic technician" and "the most admired man in America." After Ford's defeat in 1976, Kissinger joined the faculty of Georgetown University and later chaired a committee on Central America for President RONALD REAGAN in 1983 (during the Iran-Contra scandal). In the mid-1980s Kissinger emerged as a "statesman for hire," leading Kissinger Associates with offices in Washington and New York City. Despite "a complete lack of experience in business," he repaid $350,000 in startup loans within two years and earned a handsome profit in the bargain.

Despite the honors heaped upon Kissinger for his diplomatic service, critics have raised serious questions concerning his involvement in the Vietnam War, the CENTRAL INTELLIGENCE AGENCY'S role in toppling the elected government of Chile (1973), and atrocities committed by U.S.-financed forces in East Timor. A book summarizing his alleged "war crimes"—*The Trial of Henry Kissinger*, by Christopher Hitchens—became a surprise best-seller in 2001. A year later, President GEORGE W. BUSH named Kissinger to lead an "independent" probe into the TERRORIST attacks of 11 September 2001, but the plan was derailed by Kissinger's business interests. Kissinger initially promised to "go where the facts lead us," vowing that "We are under no restrictions and we will accept no restrictions," but he quickly changed his mind when ordered to disclose his list of foreign clients (thus avoiding any real or apparent conflicts of interest). Kissinger met with survivors of the "9-11" attacks on 13 December 2002 and agreed to publish his client list, but he changed his mind hours later and resigned from the commission that same afternoon.

**KLEINDIENST, Richard Gordon**—A Winslow, Arizona native, born 5 August 1923, Richard Kleindienst served in the U.S. Army Air Force during WORLD WAR II and returned to pursue Republican Party politics in his home state as a member of the Arizona legislature (1953-54); Arizona state GOP chairman (1956-60, 1962-63); delegate to the Republican National Convention (1964); and unsuccessful candidate for governor (1964). President RICHARD NIXON brought Kleindienst to the JUSTICE DEPARTMENT in 1969, and he was elevated to serve as acting attorney general on 2 March 1972, after Attorney General JOHN MITCHELL resigned in disgrace. FBI Director J. EDGAR HOOVER died two months later, whereupon Kleindienst chose L. PATRICK GRAY as a successor who would be truly subservient to his superiors.

Confirmed as attorney general on 12 June 1972, Kleindienst soon found himself enmeshed in the WATERGATE SCANDAL and was forced to resign (with White House aides JOHN EHRLICHMAN and H.R. HALDEMAN) on 24 May 1973. In 1974 Kleindienst pled guilty to a reduced perjury charge ("failure to testify fully") lodged after he attempted to mislead a Senate investigation into Nixon's corrupt relationship with the ITT Corporation. His jail sentence was suspended, but a second perjury trial followed in 1981. Kleindienst was acquitted in that case, although his attorney's license was suspended for one year. He died of lung cancer at Prescott, Arizona on 3 February 2000.

**KNOPF, Alfred A.**— Born in New York City on 12 September 1892, Alfred Knopf organized his eponymous publishing house in 1915 and soon emerged as one of America's outstanding publishers of the twentieth century. Few readers know that both the FBI and the CENTRAL INTELLIGENCE AGENCY investigated Knopf on accusations of "disloyalty," primarily because of the authors he published. Some of those, who also drew attention from the FBI themselves, included THOMAS MANN, JOHN HERSEY, T.S. ELIOT, H.L. MENCKEN, DASHIELL HAMMETT, GEORGE JEAN NATHAN and others. Hersey regarded Knopf as "the sworn enemy of hogwash, bunk, gas and rubbish, and a scourge of hypocrites and

shoddyites." Mencken dubbed him, more simply, "the perfect publisher," while Julian Boyd, once president of the American Historical Association, opined that Knopf had "done more for the cause of history than any other publisher."

None of that meant anything to J. EDGAR HOOVER or the HOUSE COMMITTEE ON UN-AMERICAN ACTIVITIES, which found Knopf's name on a 1936 letterhead of the Non-Partisan Committee for the Re-Election of Congressman VITO MARCANTONIO. Sixteen years later, that ancient letterhead moved the U.S. Office of Personnel Management to order a "personal and confidential" FBI investigation of Knopf, to determine whether he was fit to continue in a post on the Advisory Board of the National Park Service which he had held since 1949. In the course of that investigation, a G-man visited Knopf's office in Manhattan and reported back to Hoover that "Books written by authors such as H.L. Mencken, George Jean Nathan, Carl Van Vechten, Katherine Mansfield, Thomas Mann, Charles A. Beard, John Hersey, WILLA CATHER and numerous others were prominently displayed on the wall as published by Knopf." The final FBI report observed that "Bureau files further reflect that the Alfred A. Knopf Publishing Company, New York City ... has published numerous books and articles for authors who have been subjects of bureau espionage and security-matter cases."

Hoover upgraded Knopf's file from "Confidential" to "Secret" in 1955, and tagged his case as "Internal Security — R" (for Russia), after learning that Knopf was a member of the American-Russian Institute, "which organization is on the attorney general's list" of alleged subversive organizations. G-men also reported that Knopf and his wife "have been associated with various COMMUNIST PARTY members and have supported various front organizations." Worse yet, "two individuals reliably reported to have been members of the CP" allegedly worked for Knopf in 1941 and 1943, respectively, though agents found "no indication that Knopf was personally acquainted with these individuals or was made cognizant of their CP activities." A memo from Assistant to the Director Alan Belmont may have pegged the problem more precisely, with its notation that "Mr. Knopf is listed in Who's Who in American Jewry." (Typically careless, the same memo credits Knopf with owning *This Week* magazine, in fact published and distributed by the Crowell-Collier publishing firm.) As late as February 1965, a Bureau report noted that Knopf "has published numerous books written by persons concerning whom allegations have been made which were of such a nature as would raise questions as to their loyalty."

At the same time, a July 1952 report lists Knopf as being "friendly to the bureau," and author HOWARD FAST related an anecdote to historian Natalie Robins that may help to explain the seeming contradiction. During the Red-hunting 1950s, when Hoover mounted a personal campaign to block publication of Fast's novel *Spartacus*, Knopf was among the publishers to whom Fast submitted his manuscript. As Fast recalls the incident, Knopf returned the package unopened, with a noted stating that "he wouldn't even *look* at the work of a *traitor*."

Knopf requested a copy of his FBI file in 1975, under the FREEDOM OF INFORMATION ACT, but he received only a few heavily-censored pages prior to his death in October 1984. Author

Herbert Mitgang subsequently obtained 102 pages with much of their content blacked out, while another 51 were withheld entirely, either to protect confidential sources or "in the interest of national defense or foreign policy."

**KOSTERLITZKY, Emilio** — Although described in some accounts as the Bureau's "first Hispanic agent," Emilio Kosterlitzky was born in Moscow to native Russian parents on 16 November 1853. He studied at a military college in St. Petersburg, then emigrated to Mexico, where he enlisted as a private in the Mexican army. Kosterlitzky rose through the ranks to become a brigadier general, but he was demoted to colonel before he retired and made his way to the United States. He joined the Bureau of Investigation as a "special employee" on 26 March 1917, prized for his fluency in Russian, German, French, Polish, Spanish, Chinese, Korean, Japanese and "three Norse languages." Kosterlitzky resigned from the BI on 1 September 1919, then returned to duty on 1 May 1922, serving as a special agent until his final retirement on 4 September 1926, at age 72. He died on 2 March 1928.

**KRUTCH, Joseph Wood** — A native of Knoxville, Tennessee, born in 1893, Krutch was a distinguished biographer, drama critic, magazine columnist and university professor. The FBI opened a file on his involvement with the American Society for Cultural Relations with Russia in 1928, a year before Krutch achieved national acclaim for his book *The Modern Temper*. In 1941, G-men reviewed the 1928 investigation without adding any new material. The remainder of Krutch's 17-page file strangely involves other subjects: an unnamed former student investigated by the FBI in 1945 ("We failed to contact Professor Joseph W. Krutch."); another unnamed subject, relationship to Krutch unstated, whose visa was reviewed by the CENTRAL INTELLIGENCE AGENCY in 1951; and the 1960 investigation of a United Nations employee's loyalty, again with no reference to Krutch. The Bureau failed to note Krutch's receipt of a National Book Award in 1954 (for *The Measure of Man*) or his death of colon cancer, at Tucson, in 1970.

**KU Klux Klan** — The world's oldest still-active TERRORIST organization began as a Tennessee social club for Confederate war veterans in 1866. Founders of the Ku Klux Klan took its name from the Greek word for "circle" (*kuklos*) and added "clan" (spelled with a K for uniformity). Within a year the KKK was reorganized as a guerrilla force opposed to Reconstruction, the Republican Party and CIVIL RIGHTS for African Americans. Active in 12 states — the old Confederacy plus Kentucky — Klansmen murdered hundreds of victims, tortured and assaulted thousands, until they finally "redeemed" the South for one-party "home rule" by white Democrats in the 1870s.

Over the next 40 years, sympathetic historians (including future president WOODROW WILSON) portrayed Klansmen as "saviors" of Dixie, while veterans of the movement graduated to high public office. (Edward White, ex-Klansman from Louisiana, became Chief Justice of the U.S. SUPREME COURT.) The order was revived in 1915 as a patriotic fraternity, promoting "100-percent Americanism." Modern Klansmen added Catholics, Jews, immigrants and LABOR UNIONS to their list of enemies, but the movement languished until 1920, when a new publicity campaign and a congressional investigation of the Klan attracted national attention. President WARREN HARDING reportedly joined the Klan in 1921; other prominent members included the governors of Alabama, Georgia and Indiana, plus various senators, congressmen and state or local officials. By 1924 the KKK was active in 48 states, with membership estimates ranging from 2 million to 5 million dues-paying bigots.

Popular mythology claims that the FBI destroyed the 1920s KKK. Author DON WHITEHEAD implied as much in *The FBI Story* (1956), and the film version of his book (1961) included a scene wherein agents led by actor James Stewart arrest a truckload of Klansmen for vandalizing a newspaper office. In fact, no such incident ever occurred. Despite a September 1922 complaint from Louisiana Governor John Parker that the Klan dominated his state and committed murder with impunity, Assistant Director J. EDGAR HOOVER achieved nothing by sending G-men to the Pelican State. The Bureau's only victory in that arena was the indictment of "King Kleagle" Edward Clarke on MANN ACT charges. (He pled guilty in March 1924 and paid a $5,000 fine.) And while it is fair to say that Clarke's arrest may have contributed to the KKK's ultimate decline, media exposure of widespread violence and corruption had a much greater impact. The national Klan finally dissolved in 1944, threatened with a tax lien from the INTERNAL REVENUE SERVICE.

Despite the parent organization's collapse, local Klan units survived WORLD WAR II and resurfaced with a vengeance in the late 1940s. FBI HEADQUARTERS generally ignored the new outbreaks of terrorism in Alabama, Georgia and Florida, although agents investigated the Klan murder of Florida CIVIL RIGHTS activist HARRY MOORE in December 1951. (No charges were filed in that case, though six Klansmen were arrested for lying to federal grand juries. Their cases were later dismissed.) Around the same time, a rash of Klan floggings terrorized the Carolinas, and while G-men arrested 24 Klansmen on KIDNAPPING charges, critics charged that the Bureau intervened only when the terrorists shifted from black to white victims.

The Supreme Court's school desegregation rulings of 1954-55 provided the faltering Klans with a new lease on life. Increased violence and recruiting drives failed to impress J. Edgar Hoover, however. In March 1956 he told President DWIGHT EISENHOWER that the KKK — with more than 50,000 active members — was "pretty much defunct." Two years later, Hoover barred his agents from cooperating with a new SOUTHERN CONFERENCE ON BOMBING, created to investigate acts of racial terrorism. FBI INFORMANTS in the Klan, including Alabama's GARY ROWE, were active by 1960, but the Bureau made no effort to prosecute offenders. Worse, in cases like the FREEDOM RIDES of 1961, FBI leaders actively collaborated with Klansmen and Klan-allied police to facilitate violent crimes against civil rights workers. Even when local prosecutors were inclined to try Klansmen for murder, as in the Alabama BAPBOM case or the murder of activist Medgar Evers by BYRON DE LA BECKWITH, FBI agents suppressed confessions and thereby delayed prosecution for 30-odd years.

President LYNDON JOHNSON finally forced Hoover to mount an anti-Klan offensive in 1964, following the "MIBURN" case in Mississippi where three victims were assassinated with police complicity. In response to Johnson's order, the Bureau launched a COINTELPRO campaign against various Klans, using the same illegal techniques it had long employed against the COMMUNIST PARTY and other leftist groups. Thereafter, Klansmen were subjected to BUGGING, WIRETAPPING and BREAK-INS; anonymous letters and "SNITCH-JACKETING" sowed dissent within Klans; *agents provocateur* entrapped Klansmen in illegal activities; and FBI informants were instructed to sleep with Klan wives as a means of destroying marriages. The HOUSE COMMITTEE ON UN-AMERICAN ACTIVITIES cooperated with a public investigation of the KKK (1965-66), and several Klan killers were jailed under civil rights statutes dating from the Reconstruction era.

Even as they plotted to disrupt some Klans, however, G-men supported others. Informant EDWARD DAWSON founded the North Carolina Knights of the KKK in 1969; 10 years later he was implicated in the Klan murders of five demonstrators at Greensboro. Another informant, BILL WILKINSON, led the largest and most violent Klan of the early 1980s, until exposure of his double life drove the group into bankruptcy. Other Klans, like the Communist Party of the 1950s, were so thoroughly infiltrated by Bureau informants that critics claimed only the FBI was keeping them alive with taxpayers' money.

Though greatly reduced in membership and influence today, the KKK remains a threat wherever its activities progress from rhetoric to violence. Klansmen joined THE ORDER in a spree of murder and BANK ROBBERY (1983-85), while collaborating with other violent neo-Nazi groups such as the Aryan Nations and the Aryan Republican Army. Oklahoma City bomber TIMOTHY MCVEIGH was a Klansman before drifting into the far-right MILITIA MOVEMENT. Other crimes committed by the modern KKK include the Alabama LYNCHING of Michael Donald (1981), riots in Georgia (1987), arson attacks on black churches (1996-97), and the Texas torture-slaying of James Byrd, Jr. (1998).

# L

**LABOR Department**—Created by President THEODORE ROOSEVELT in 1905 as the Department of Commerce and Labor, the U.S. Labor Department achieved independence in March 1913, when President WOODROW WILSON divided the parent department in half and appointed WILLIAM WILSON as the first Secretary of Labor. Despite his background as a former coal miner, Secretary Wilson opposed such radical LABOR UNIONS as the INDUSTRIAL WORKERS OF THE WORLD and leftist political groups including the COMMUNIST PARTY and the COMMUNIST LABOR PARTY. His opinion on the matter became critical in 1919, when Attorney General A. MITCHELL PALMER planned mass arrests and deportation of "enemy aliens" from the U.S.

Simply stated, Palmer and young J. EDGAR HOOVER, in charge of the JUSTICE DEPARTMENT's Red-hunting GENERAL INTELLIGENCE DIVISION, lacked jurisdiction to carry out the dragnet arrests under federal law, since the Espionage Act of 1917 was enforceable only in wartime. With the end of WORLD WAR I, no vehicle existed for expelling foreign radicals and ANARCHISTS except the Labor Department's Immigration Bureau. Unfortunately for Palmer's grand design, Secretary Wilson and Assistant Secretary LOUIS POST opposed mass arrests, maintaining that each case should be evaluated on an individual basis before any deportation orders were signed. That view was disregarded in the PALMER RAIDS of 1919-20, jailing thousands without valid warrants or criminal charges, but Wilson and Post successfully blocked most of the deportations planned by Palmer and Hoover. Subsequent congressional investigations of the lawless raids drove Palmer from office and forced Hoover to rewrite history, fabricating a version of events in which he "deplored" the raids and played only a marginal, reluctant role in the events.

**LABOR Unions**—Throughout its history the U.S. JUSTICE DEPARTMENT has generally favored management's side during serious labor disputes and has frequently served as a strikebreaking force, while adopting a pose of neutrality and espousing a simple commitment to "law and order." Before the FBI existed, Justice often hired investigators from the PINKERTON DETECTIVE AGENCY to build cases for trial, but that practice was banned by law in 1892, following exposure of Pinkerton's involvement in violent anti-union activities. It was perhaps inevitable that the fledgling Bureau would follow in its predecessor's footsteps.

G-men launched their first investigations of organized labor in 1914, when the INDUSTRIAL WORKERS OF THE WORLD (IWW) and other leftist groups began protesting the outbreak of a "capitalist war" in Europe. Three years later, America's entry into WORLD WAR I produced a rash of federal legislation aimed at silencing dissent, and Bureau agents used their new tools against the IWW. Sweeping raids in September 1917 closed IWW offices from coast to coast, while 166 leaders of the union were indicted on various charges. At trial, in April 1918, 83 of those defendants were convicted and received prison terms ranging from five to twenty years.

The armistice brought no respite from labor unrest; quite the reverse, in fact. Some 3,600 strikes were recorded in 1919, along with a rash of BOMBINGS blamed on ANARCHISTS. Attorney General A. MITCHELL PALMER viewed the outbreaks as symptoms of impending Bolshevik revolution, and he assigned the department's GENERAL INTELLIGENCE DIVISION, led by young J. EDGAR HOOVER, to ferret out radical strikers along with COMMUNIST PARTY members and insubordinate blacks. The first group targeted for mass arrests and deportations in the PALMER RAIDS, during November 1919, would be the Union of Russian Workers.

Palmer's ultimate embarrassment and removal from office did not discourage his successor from hounding organized labor. Attorney General HARRY DAUGHERTY despised strikers, an opinion shared by Bureau chief WILLIAM BURNS (a former private detective in the Pinkerton mode) and J. Edgar Hoover (now assistant director of the Bureau). Samuel Gompers, president of the American Federation of Labor (AFL), charged Daugherty with building a spy network to entrap and discredit labor organizers, thus allowing the Justice Department to seek injunctions against strikers. The tactic paid off in September 1922, when Daugherty obtained a sweeping injunction barring a national railroad strike. More than 1,200 union members were arrested and the strike was broken. When angry members of Congress threatened to impeach Daugherty, Burns and Hoover sent G-men to search their offices for blackmail fodder.

Hoover had risen to command the FBI by the time a rift in the AFL created a new Congress of Industrial Organizations (CIO) in the mid-1930s. The CIO's blue-collar unions were indeed radical by AFL standards, making no effort at first to purge known communists from their ranks. President FRANKLIN ROOSEVELT opened the door to new union-busting crusades in September 1936, when he authorized FBI surveillance of Nazi and Communist agents inside the U.S. Hoover interpreted that order, in a memo to his troops on 5 September, as a mandate to investigate "general activities — Communist and Affiliated Organizations, Fascist, Anti-Fascist movements, and activities in Organized Labor organizations." By 1940 G-men were pursuing major investigations of the CIO and all of its various member unions. Some of the movement's more outspoken leaders were secretly added to the FBI's illegal CUSTODIAL DETENTION INDEX, slated for mass arrest in the event of an unspecified "national emergency." (WORLD WAR II apparently failed to qualify.)

A case that clearly illustrates Hoover's enmity toward labor unions is that of brothers Walter and Victor Reuther, leaders of the United Automobile Workers in Detroit. In 1949, after Victor survived his second near-fatal shooting within 12 months, the U.S. Senate unanimously passed a resolution asking the FBI to investigate the attacks. Attorney General TOM CLARK supported the resolution, but he had no luck obtaining cooperation from his nominal subordinate at FBI HEADQUARTERS. After broaching the subject to Hoover, Clark regretfully told UAW attorney Joseph Rauh, "Edgar says no. He says he's not going to get involved every time some nigger woman gets raped." (A more courageous attorney general might have fired Hoover on the spot, for insubordination and because the weird non sequitur suggested an unbalanced mind.) Unwilling as he was to investigate murder attempts on the Reuther brothers, Hoover nonetheless kept Walter Reuther under near-constant surveillance from the 1930s until his May 1970 death in a suspicious airplane crash.

The Cold War and the Red scare that followed World War II granted the FBI more latitude in DOMESTIC SURVEILLANCE of organized labor. In 1954 the federal Communist Control Act barred the Communist Party or any Red-infiltrated group from petitioning the National Labor Relations Board for union elections or certification. Three years later, hearings before the Senate's McClellan Committee exposed corrupt links between ORGANIZED CRIME and the TEAMSTERS' UNION led by Jimmy Hoffa, while catapulting brothers JOHN and ROBERT KENNEDY to national prominence. Hoover had no qualms about spying on Teamster leaders, but he withheld recordings that included threats to murder the Kennedy brothers, even after the JFK ASSASSINATION of November 1963.

Suppression of radicals was a top priority for Presidents RICHARD NIXON and GERALD FORD. Under the FBI's illicit COINTELPRO program, *agent provocateur* Joe Burton was sent to Tampa, Florida, where he created a fictitious "Red Star Cadre" with FBI backing. Burton's mission, ultimately fruitless, was to "argue from the left" that leaders of such mainstream unions as the United Farm Workers, the United Electrical Workers and the American Federation of State, County and Municipal Employees were "not militant enough" in pressing their demands. For two years (1972-74) Burton sought to entrap Tampa workers in various violent crimes, but his efforts proved to be a waste of time and taxpayers' money.

A more conventional UNDERCOVER OPERATION was revealed in June 1978, when the FBI's "UNIRAC" sting operation (for *uni*on *rac*keteering) resulted in the indictment of 22 Miami-area labor officials and shipping executives on bribery and other charges. The indictments spread to New York City in January 1979, with charges filed against several Mafia members and associates. Ostensibly, FBI investigations of organized labor are now strictly limited to criminal activities while ignoring the political affiliations of union leaders and members.

**LABORATORY Division** — No aspect of the FBI is more famous than its laboratory, globally renowned for solving some of history's most notorious criminal cases. In any given year, the Bureau's Laboratory Division conducts an average of 15,000 forensic examinations, involving 200,000 individual pieces of evidence — blood and semen samples, paint chips and body parts, photographs and documents, guns and bullets, tire tracks and footprints, arson traces and suspected murder weapons of all kinds. Even critics almost invariably list the Bureau's laboratory among the proud achievements of Director J. EDGAR HOOVER, when he started "cleaning up" the FBI in 1924.

In fact, the lab would not debut for another eight years, until 24 November 1932, and its beginnings were hardly auspicious. The original laboratory's equipment was limited to a fluorescent light and a borrowed microscope, housed in the Southern Railway Building that doubled as the Bureau's smoking lounge. The FBI's reference firearms collection was launched in October 1933, with a Photographic Operations Unit added in 1935. One of the lab's first headline cases, that same year, was the LINDBERGH KIDNAPPING (although few now regard that FRAME-UP as a victory for law enforcement). The FBI lab hired its first full-time chemist, William Magee, in 1937 — the same year that FBI HEADQUARTERS began offering free services to state and local law enforcement agencies without their own lab facilities. A polygraph was added in 1938, then discarded by Hoover after a Florida "lie detector" implicated an innocent kidnapping suspect while exonerating the guilty party. The crime lab achieved division status in 1943, under Assistant Director Edmund Coffey.

The Bureau's crime lab has evolved with the times, though not always for the better. President RICHARD NIXON, obsessed with White House news leaks, demanded resumption of polygraph tests in 1971, and a Polygraph Unit was formally established in 1978 (although the tests remain highly controversial and are inadmissible in most U.S. courts). In 1979 a Special Photography Unit began adapting digital images developed by the National Aeronautics and Space Administration for use in criminal cases. Three years later, the FBI's Forensic Science Research and Training Center opened at Quantico, Virginia (then a subdivision of the Scientific Analysis Section). The FBI lab began accepting DNA evidence for analysis on 1 December 1988 (producing the first DNA identification in a U.S. courtroom nine years later). In August 1991 the Laboratory Division created a Computer Analysis and Response Team to support FBI investigations. Eleven months later, a new DRUGFIRE data base was installed to examine ballistics evidence from unsolved shootings (primarily related to the NARCOTICS trade). By the 1990s, the Laboratory Division included five major sections: Investigative Operations (formerly Documents), Special Projects, Latent Fingerprints, Scientific Analysis, and Forensic Science Research and Training.

Despite its reputation, the FBI lab has not been immune to criticism. In 1996 employee FREDERIC WHITEHURST, a chemist in the explosives unit, went public with complaints of non-scientists dictating laboratory policies. He also alleged that evidence was frequently mishandled and occasionally altered for the benefit of prosecutors. While FBI administrators hounded Whitehurst from his job, an 18-month investigation of his charges was initiated by the JUSTICE DEPARTMENT's Office of the Inspector General. The results of that review, published in April 1997, validated most of Whitehurst's claims and proved so damaging to FBI prestige that prosecutors in the case of Oklahoma City bomber TIMOTHY MCVEIGH feared to put Bureau lab technicians on the witness stand. Criticism of the lab soon spread to Congress, showcased in hearings before Senator CHARLES GRASSLEY, where Gerald Lefcourt (president of the National Association of Criminal Defense Lawyers) declared, "We are left to the conclusion that justice could be perverted by [FBI] alignment with the prosecution."

Clearly, matters had degenerated since the days when Hoover required that any state or local police department submitting evidence for evaluation should promise to accept FBI lab results as final, even if they proved a suspect innocent. Now, NACDL spokesmen charged that all but one of the Bureau's DNA blood technicians had failed a 1989 proficiency test (with those results suppressed at headquarters); that one DNA specialist (later fired) had manipulated test results to convict innocent African American defendants; and that DNA samples were routinely mishandled, sometimes deliberately altered to ensure convictions. The Bureau denied all such claims (while refusing to open its files for review), but on 22 October 1997 Director LOUIS FREEH named an outsider, Donald Kerr, Jr., to head the embattled Laboratory Division. At age 58, Kerr was a physicist and engineer who once directed the Los Alamos nuclear testing facility (1979-85), and he became the first non-agent to supervise the Bureau's lab.

As dust from the latest scandal began to settle, in February 1998, the FBI paid Frederic Whitehurst $1.1 million to settle his claim for harassment and retaliation in the wake of his 1996 disclosures. Four lab supervisors facing censure for negligence or worse were allowed to resign without disciplinary action in June, while mild letters of censure were issued to two others. Former lab unit chief ROGER MARTZ was officially chastised for "negligence, inadequate documentation and overstated trial testimony" in the O.J. Simpson murder case; former lab examiner DAVID WILLIAMS was reprimanded for providing "overstated, inaccurate and unsupported expert opinions" in the WORLD TRADE CENTER and Oklahoma City BOMBING cases. Both men appealed their wrist-slap punishments, while Assistant Attorney General Stephen Colgate told reporters, "The fact that the discipline is minimal should not be viewed as an exoneration of the behavior of these individuals." Senator Grassley countered that view with an observation that "FBI management has succeeded in protecting its rogues in the lab scandal."

**LEE, George Washington**— An African American native of Belzoni, Mississippi, born in 1904, Rev. George Lee supplemented his meager clerical income by running a small grocery store and a printing press for the local black community. In 1954 he joined CIVIL RIGHTS activist GUS COURTS in founding a chapter of the NATIONAL ASSOCIATION FOR THE ADVANCEMENT OF COLORED PEOPLE. Lee's primary concern was registration of black voters, a goal he pursued through personal contacts and circulation of leaflets urging blacks to pay the state poll tax and register despite opposition from whites. Spokesmen for the segregationist CITIZENS' COUNCIL offered to let Lee and his wife vote if they would desist from encouraging others, but Lee rejected the corrupt bargain. By early 1955 he and Courts had registered 92 black voters in Humphreys County.

On the night of 7 May 1955 Lee was ambushed by nightriders, while driving home from his church. Shot in the face and mortally wounded, he died in the ambulance before he could reach a nearby hospital. Sheriff Isaac Shelton impounded Lee's car and initially described the shotgun pellets taken from Lee's head as "fillings from his teeth" jarred loose when his car swerved and crashed. Upon being told that dental fillings are not made from lead, Shelton changed his theory to charge that Lee had been killed by "some jealous nigger."

On 22 May the *New York Times* reported that FBI agents had been asked to investigate Belzoni's latest "traffic fatality," under pressure from the NAACP and the AMERICAN CIVIL LIBERTIES UNION. They traced eyewitness Alex Hudson to Illinois, then barred his lawyer from the interview, recording his statement that Lee had been shot by one of two white men in a passing car. A Belzoni coroner's jury blamed Lee's death on a head wound, "the cause of which is not clear." Sheriff Shelton deemed it "one of the most puzzling cases I have ever had." He reported grilling several "suspects," all black, but never questioned any member of Lee's family, despite repeated statements to the press that "If Lee was shot, it was probably by some jealous nigger. He was quite a ladies' man." Gus Courts carried on in Lee's stead, until he was nearly killed in November 1955. Both crimes remain unsolved today.

**LEE, Wen Ho**— A son of Taiwanese farmers, born in 1940, Wen Ho Lee studied mechanical engineering at Cheng Kun University before emigrating to the U.S. in 1964. He earned his Ph.D. at Texas A&M in 1970 and joined the Los Alamos, New Mexico nuclear laboratory staff in 1978. Two years later Lee was transferred to the lab's X Division, which designs nuclear weapons. FBI spokesmen would later claim that he spent most of the next two decades spying for Communist China, but they were finally unable to prove their case.

The first alarm went off concerning Dr. Lee in 1982, when another Taiwanese-American scientist at Los Alamos was under FBI investigation for ESPIONAGE. A federal WIRETAP caught Lee and the suspect discussing the case, allegedly including Lee's offer to find out who had "squealed." When confronted by G-men, Lee initially denied speaking to the suspect colleague, then offered an innocent explanation for the dialogue. Agents did not pursue the matter and no action was taken by Lee's employers at the Energy Department.

Over the next decade, FBI spokesmen say Dr. Lee made "about a dozen" trips to Beijing, where he allegedly met openly with Chinese scientists involved in nuclear weapons research. The Bureau and journalist Robert Kessler, in his book *The Bureau* (2002), imply a link between Lee's travels and China's detonation of an unexpectedly sophisticated warhead in September 1992. That suspicion was buttressed, they say, when Los Alamos welcomed a team of Chinese weapons researchers in February 1994 and a translator overheard one of the visitors thanking Lee for software and calculations that helped China develop its latest bomb. Los Alamos officials alerted the Bureau and a security case was opened on Lee, assigned to an Albuquerque G-man whom Kessler describes as possessing "no counterintelligence experience." A series of tactical blunders ensued, including a five-year debate on the propriety of searching Lee's office computer (despite a signed waiver from Lee permitting such examinations at any time). It was August 1997 before G-men sought permission to tap Lee's phone, and the request was denied by the Justice Department's Office of Intelligence Policy and Review. A year later, in August 1998, agents set up a "false flag" sting operation using a Chinese-American agent to pose as a Red intelligence officer, but Dr. Lee flatly rejected the overture.

Energy officials subjected Lee to a polygraph test on 23 December 1998, when he returned from a trip to Taiwan, and while the operator judged his answers truthful, FBI critics complained that their competitors had "asked the wrong questions." G-men administered their own polygraph exam on 10 February 1999, without Lee's lawyer present, and branded him a liar. Attorney Mark Holscher later described the test as "chilling. Dr. Lee was threatened that he could be executed if he did not confess to being involved in espionage." Agents finally searched Lee's computer in March 1999, reporting that over the past 70 days he had downloaded some 430,000 pages of sensitive material. Fired from Los Alamos the next day, 8 March 1999, Lee spent the next nine months under 24-hour surveillance, while agents conducted 1,000 interviews with friends and coworkers. Still, no evidence of spying was uncovered.

At last, in December 1999, FBI Director LOUIS FREEH authorized Lee's indictment on charges that he had downloaded classified data with intent "to injure the United States or ... to secure an advantage to [a] foreign power." None of the indictment's 59 counts alleged actual delivery of material to foreign agents, and Freeh's aides later told Kessler that the indictment was based on "vague and unsupportable charges." Still, it carried a maximum life sentence and Lee was denied bail after Agent Robert Messemer told the court that Lee had lied about his reasons for borrowing a Los Alamos computer. Messemer claimed under oath that Lee had told a colleague he wanted to download a résumé, when in fact he was stealing classified files.

Lee spent the next nine months in solitary confinement with a light burning in his cell 24 hours a day, compelled to wear shackles during his brief daily exercise periods. At a second bond hearing, on 17 August 2000, Agent Messemer confessed to lying under oath in December 1999. Dr. Lee had made no mention of a "résumé" when borrowing an office computer; in fact, he had told his colleague frankly that he planned to download documents. Judge James Parker, furious at having been "led astray ... by the executive branch of our government," apologized to Dr. Lee and released him without bail. A month later Lee pled guilty on one reduced count of mishandling classified data; he was sentenced to time served and agreed to 60 hours of debriefing under oath. Prosecutor Ronald Woods told reporters, "There is no disguising defeat in this case."

Still, Justice and the FBI were willing to try. Three weeks after Lee's plea bargain, on 27 September 2000, Freeh and Attorney General JANET RENO told their side of the story before the U.S. Senate. Reno told her audience that "Dr. Lee is no hero," but rather "a felon." Freeh testified in a similar vein, declaring, "It is critical to understand that Dr. Lee's conduct was not inadvertent, it was not careless, and it was not innocent." Eleven months elapsed before Senator CHARLES GRASSLEY, investigating FBI malfeasance, received a heavily-censored Justice Department report on Lee's case from May 2000. That report claimed Energy Department staffers had misled the FBI with false reports, which were uncritically accepted. It read: "The message communicated to the FBI was that the FBI need look no farther within DOE for a suspect. Wen Ho Lee was its man. The FBI never should have accepted this message, as is." The report's author, former federal prosecutor Randy Bellows, called Lee's case "a paradigm of how not to manage and work an important counterintelligence case."

**LEGAL Attaché program** — The FBI's Legal Attaché (Legat) program began in 1940, with creation of the SPECIAL INTELLIGENCE SERVICE to carry out political investigations in Latin America. Around the same time Bureau headquarters began cooperating with British and Canadian intelligence agencies to thwart Axis subversion in those areas. Despite a supposed clear-cut division of labor, leaving domestic security investigations to the Bureau and assigning all foreign operations to the CENTRAL INTELLIGENCE AGENCY after 1947, the FBI continued to post agents (dubbed "legats") in various foreign capitals around the world, where they remain in place to the present day. In theory, legats cooperate with foreign police and intelligence agencies to investigate any matter of shared jurisdiction (international crimes or TERRORISM, fugitives at large); in practice, they perform any duties assigned by FBI headquarters, leaving the director and his staff to decide the fine points of legality.

As of July 2002, FBI agents are active in 52 foreign countries, maintaining 47 Legat offices and four Legat "sub offices." Alphabetically, they are found at U.S. embassies or consulates located in —

| | |
|---|---|
| Almaty, Kazakhstan | Madrid, Spain |
| Amman, Jordan | Manila, Philippines |
| Ankara, Turkey | Mexico City, Mexico |
| Athens, Greece | Monterrey, Mexico (sub office) |
| Bangkok, Thailand | Moscow, Russia |
| Beijing, China | Nairobi, Kenya |
| Berlin, Germany | New Delhi, India |
| Bern, Switzerland | Ottawa, Canada |
| Bogotá, Colombia | Panama City, Panama |
| Brasilia, Brazil | Paris, France |
| Bridgetown, Barbados | Prague, Czech Republic |
| Brussels, Belgium | Pretoria, South Africa |
| Bucharest, Romania | Riyadh, Saudi Arabia |
| Buenos Aires, Argentina | Rome, Italy |
| Cairo, Egypt | Santiago, Chile |
| Canberra, Australia | Santo Domingo, Dominican |
| Caracas, Venezuela |    Republic |
| Copenhagen, Denmark | Seoul, South Korea |
| Frankfurt, Germany (sub office) | Singapore, Singapore |
| Guadalajara, Mexico (sub office) | Tallinn, Estonia |
| Hermosillo, Mexico | Tel Aviv, Israel |
| Hong Kong, China | Tijuana, Mexico |
| Islamabad, Pakistan | Tokyo, Japan |
| Kiev, Ukraine | Vancouver, Canada (sub office) |
| Lagos, Nigeria | Vienna, Austria |
| London, England | Warsaw, Poland |

**LEGAL Instruction Unit** — An FBI training unit, originally created within the OFFICE OF THE GENERAL COUNSEL and later independent, the Legal Instruction Unit (LIU) conducts classes in legal procedures for G-men, agents of the DRUG ENFORCEMENT ADMINISTRATION, and any other law enforcement officers who are admitted to the FBI NATIONAL ACADEMY or various in-service training programs. In the late 1990s, the LIU assumed responsibility for publishing the *FBI Law Enforcement Bulletin*, and while that monthly magazine is now produced by the Law Enforcement Communication Unit, LIU staffers still contribute articles on various aspects of criminal and constitutional law.

**LEMMER, William** — A mentally unstable military veteran, William Lemmer was threatened with a psychiatric discharge from the U.S. Army before he left the service of his own accord. The turmoil had only begun, however: Lemmer's estranged wife had him held for a sanity hearing after he wrote her a letter blaming Vietnam Veterans Against the War (VVAW) for the breakup of their marriage, threatening to "get" the group's members silently, in "tennis shoes" and with a "length of piano wire." Police in Gainesville, Florida detained Lemmer after he was found in possession of two loaded guns, and a local doctor recommended psychiatric treatment.

None of that apparently diminished Lemmer's value as a paid INFORMANT of the FBI, assigned to penetrate and disrupt the VVAW. His first action of record occurred on 4 May 1972, when 12 demonstrators from the War Resisters League were jailed for entering Tinker Air Force Base, near Oklahoma City, to read an anti-war statement. Lemmer planned the demonstration but did not participate. At trial, all 12 protesters were convicted of trespass on a military reservation; four female demonstrators received probation, while eight male defendants served an average of four months in federal custody.

Lemmer's greatest coup occurred in July 1972 and targeted his enemies in the VVAW. Based on Lemmer's testimony to G-men and a federal grand jury in Florida, eight VVAW activists (thereafter known as the "Gainesville 8") were indicted for conspiracy to disrupt the 1972 Republican National Convention in Miami. According to the charges filed against them, the defendants planned to attack the convention with a variety of weapons including crossbows, incendiary devices, homemade grenades, automatic weapons and bazookas. At trial in 1973, however, U.S. attorneys produced no weapons other than slingshots offered for sale in any American sporting goods store. Major Adam Klimkowski, chief of the Miami Police Department's Special Investigation Unit further admitted under oath that one of his agents proposed acquisition of machine guns to the defendants, who flatly rejected the offer. Lemmer's exposure as an FBI informant finally doomed the government's case, and jurors deliberated less than four hours before acquitting the defendants on all charges.

**LENNON, John Winston** — A Liverpool native, born 9 October 1940, John Lennon won international fame as lead singer of a rock-and-roll group, the Beatles, in the early 1960s. Between 1964 and 1969 the Beatles sold more records than any other group in history, leading a "British invasion" of rock bands that found new fans and markets in the United States. By the time the group's breakup was announced in April 1970, Lennon was residing in New York with his second wife, artist-musician Yoko Ono.

It is unknown precisely when the FBI first became interested in Lennon, but several Bureau INFORMANTS filed reports on 10 December 1971, after Lennon performed at a Michigan benefit concert for John Sinclair, an imprisoned leader of the "NEW LEFT" White Panther Party in Detroit. FBI HEADQUARTERS opened a formal "national security" investigation of Lennon on 21 January 1972; one day later, Director J. EDGAR HOOVER reported to President RICHARD NIXON and the head of the CENTRAL INTELLIGENCE AGENCY that Lennon was involved in "movement activities" which "will culminate with demonstrations at the Republican National Convention." The FBI's handiwork was also apparent on 4 February 1972, when Senator Strom Thurmond sent a memo to Attorney General JOHN MITCHELL, urging that Lennon be deported. Immigration officials refused to renew Lennon's visa on 6 March, citing a 1968 guilty plea to misdemeanor marijuana possession in London, and a series of deportation hearings ensued. The FBI formally closed its investigation of Lennon on 8 December 1972, three months before a federal judge ordered Lennon to leave the U.S. within 60 days.

That would not be the end of the story, however. Lennon, a multimillionaire, fought deportation in the courts, filing lawsuits for improper conduct against the Immigration Service, Attorney General Mitchell (himself under indictment by that time), and successor RICHARD KLEINDIENST. A federal appellate court overturned Lennon's deportation order on 7 October 1975, and he was granted permanent U.S. residency on 27 July 1976. Deranged star-stalker Mark David Chapman shot and killed Lennon outside the singer's New York apartment on 8 December 1981.

Revelation of the FBI FILES on John Lennon required 16 years of litigation, dragging on from the initial request filed by author Jon Wiener in February 1981, under the FREEDOM OF INFORMATION ACT, until a federal court ordered release of certain heavily-censored documents in September 1997. Even then, some 10,000 pages were kept under wraps, presumably forever, at the request of FBI and CIA leaders who vowed that further revelations might somehow endanger "national security."

**LEVI, Edward Hirsch**— Born in Chicago on 26 June 1911, attorney Edward Levi spent seven years as president of the University of Chicago before he was appointed to serve as attorney general under President JAMES CARTER, on 5 February 1975. Three weeks later he was called to testify before the House Subcommittee on Civil and Constitutional Rights, where he admitted the existence of late FBI Director J. EDGAR HOOVER's Official and Confidential FILES containing derogatory information on presidents, cabinet members, congressmen and other prominent persons. Upon hearing that Levi had those files in his possession, retired Assistant Director WILLIAM SULLIVAN told author David Wise, "He didn't get the gold."

In the fall of 1975, members of the PIKE COMMITTEE informed Levi that the FBI, since 1963, had purchased all its electronic equipment from the U.S. Recording Company at prices inflated from 40 to 70 percent over fair market value. Top FBI officials allegedly had received kickbacks on the sales from USRC president Jack Tait, a "personal friend" of Assistant Director JOHN MOHR. Levi ordered an investigation, but he deemed the FBI's swift response (reporting no impropriety) as "incomplete" and

"less than satisfactory." A second review, lasting 11 months, confirmed the price-fixing and payoffs, while Bureau spokesmen explained their loyalty to Tait on grounds of confidentiality, calling Tait "an excellent friend of the Bureau [who] would go to any lengths to protect our interests."

In March 1976 Levi issued new guidelines for FBI "domestic security" investigations that limited the Bureau's authority to conduct fishing expeditions and monitor personal beliefs. Under the new rules, 90-day "preliminary" investigations were permitted to confirm or refute "allegations or other information that an individual or group may be engaged in activities which involve or will involve the violation of federal law." No subsequent "full" investigation could proceed without "specific and articulable facts giving reason to believe that an individual or group is or may be engaged in activities which involve or will involve the use of force or violence and which involve or will involve the violation of federal law." Even then, the JUSTICE DEPARTMENT was required each year to review the "results of full domestic intelligence investigations … [and] determine in writing whether continued investigation is warranted."

Levi stepped down as attorney general on 20 January 1977, and while successor GRIFFIN BELL continued strict oversight policies, that practice was abandoned under President RONALD REAGAN, elected in 1980 on a promise to "unleash" the FBI. Edward Levi died of Alzheimer's disease on 7 March 2000.

**LEVIN, Michael**— Michael Levin spent eight troubled years with the FBI's Las Vegas, Nevada field office before he resigned in 1997. In 1994 he was suspended for seven days without pay, "based on a finding that he had used his government credit card for personal purposes." Two years later he received a 30-day suspension without pay and was placed on one year's probation after he allowed an undercover phone bill to become so delinquent that it was referred to a collection agency, "thereby compromising the undercover address." An internal FBI investigation also found that Levin "intimidated telephone company employees in an attempt to have them write off these debts." In 1997, Bureau documents reveal, Levin "[o]nce again … used his government credit card for personal purchases and, when questioned about these purchases, gave statements under oath which were not true." Faced with another 30-day unpaid suspension, Levin resigned instead.

Upon leaving the Bureau, Levin remained in Las Vegas as a private detective, but an FBI background check prompted the Nevada Private Investigators License Bureau to deny him a license in 1998. That ruling was later reversed when Levin asked the PILB to reconsider, a move which critics say indicates a process of "rubber-stamping" applicants in Nevada. With or without a license, Levin was headed for trouble. He filed a federal lawsuit in March 2001 that accused the FBI of invading his privacy and publicly disclosing information from his personnel file (during a 1999 criminal case in which he appeared as a witness). JUSTICE DEPARTMENT attorneys moved to dismiss that case in May 2001, their plea strengthened the following month when Levin was arrested on charges of selling FBI documents to clients facing criminal investigation by the Bureau. As detailed by prosecutors, Levin had recruited 51-year-old JAMES HILL, an analyst at the Las Vegas field office, to steal documents which Levin then sold to his various clients, thereby endangering G-men and civilian INFORMANTS. Hill, also arrested in that case, responded to criminal charges by claiming that he was a "fall guy" for Levin. At last report, Levin had allegedly agreed to testify against Hill. The case remains unresolved at press time for this volume.

**LEVINE, Jack**— A New York native and qualified attorney, Jack Levine entered the FBI ACADEMY as a 26-year-old trainee in September 1960. After graduation he was assigned to the Detroit field office, where his experience appeared to be routine until May 1961. On 18 May Levine received a written reprimand for failure to meet the Bureau's daily quota of "voluntary" (unpaid) overtime. Problems snowballed from there, and Levine resigned from the Bureau on 4 August 1961, returning to private law practice in New York.

Following his separation from the FBI, Levine aired criticism of the Bureau, first in private discussions with JUSTICE DEPARTMENT spokesmen under Attorney General ROBERT KENNEDY, then in a 38-page written report to Assistant Attorney General Herbert Miller, Jr. When those overtures proved fruitless, Levine sat for a series of radio interviews, published an article in *The Nation*, and provided author Fred Cook with inside information for his book *The FBI Nobody Knows* (1964). Levine's complaints about FBI operations under Director J. EDGAR HOOVER, supported by retirees and FBI documents later released under the FREEDOM OF INFORMATION ACT, included observations that —

• Trainees at the FBI Academy were "heavily indoctrinated with radical right-wing propaganda" that was "taken ... as the truth or 'inside story' by reason of the fact that instruction is given by FBI officials." The lessons routinely included attacks on "communists at Harvard" and denunciation of Democratic presidential contender ADLAI STEVENSON. When Levine questioned such statements, he was told that "any comments made by a Bureau official in our training class was in accordance with Bureau thinking or policy and that it would be naïve to think otherwise."

• Trainees were "encouraged" to purchase multiple copies of author DON WHITEHEAD'S book *The FBI Story* and Hoover's ghostwritten *Masters of Deceit* as study aids and gifts for relatives.

• Trainees were also strongly urged to send Hoover adulatory letters on his birthday and the May anniversary of his appointment as FBI director.

• Racism was pervasive within the (then all-white) Bureau, with African Americans frequently described as "niggers."

• Hoover's system of "voluntary" overtime, averaging 2 hours and 45 minutes per day for each G-man, damaged Bureau morale while encouraging agents to waste time on trivial matters.

• FBI INFORMANTS constituted at least one-fifth of American COMMUNIST PARTY membership, keeping the moribund party afloat with taxpayers' money while Hoover bemoaned the "Red Menace."

• Illegal BREAK-INS and other criminal activities were "done every day in the Bureau," with full knowledge and approval from FBI leaders.

Such criticism evoked a predictable response from FBI HEADQUARTERS. Bureau spokesmen initially claimed that Levine had been "fired for cause," but exposure of the lie forced a retraction. Next, Associate Director CLYDE TOLSON told reporters that Levine had tried to rejoin the Bureau a month after resigning, but he was rejected "because his former record was substandard." Thereafter, Tolson claimed, Levine had "launched a campaign of vilification against Mr. Hoover and the FBI." Worse yet, Tolson said, "in pursuing his vindictive course he had utterly disregarded the security of the Nation" in some way never explained.

It was perilous even to offer Levine a forum in those days. After Levine participated in a broadcast over radio station WBAI (New York) in 1962, describing Hoover's FBI as "bizarrely cultlike," FBI spokesmen complained to the Federal Communications Commission that communists had infiltrated the Pacifica Radio network (including WBAI). Three Pacifica stations were stripped of their broadcasting licenses as a result of that allegation, the ruling reversed only after a three-year investigation proved the charges unfounded. Bureau-friendly journalists, meanwhile, dismissed Levine's revelations of illegal WIRETAPPING and other criminal activity with vague references to federal "policy barriers"— a rose-tinted view of FBI integrity thoroughly discredited by revelations of the Bureau's illegal COINTELPRO campaigns in March 1971 and disclosures by the CHURCH COMMITTEE in 1975-76. With hindsight, it is readily apparent that Levine understated the extent of FBI abuses.

**LEVISON, Stanley David**— A New York City native, born in May 1912 Stanley Levison was raised on affluent Long Island. He earned a B.A. from Ohio State University and an LL.B. from St. John's University law school (1938) before joining his family in various successful business ventures around New York. In June 1952 FBI INFORMANT Jack Child denounced Levison to the Bureau as "an important secret financial benefactor of the COMMUNIST PARTY" (CP) since 1945-46, alleged to provide some $50,000 yearly from various sources. FBI memos later revealed under the FREEDOM OF INFORMATION ACT disclosed "electronic surveillances on Levison dating back to 1954" and a series of 29 illegal BREAK-INS at his business office between 1954 and 1964.

Despite all that covert attention, the FBI never secured any proof that Levison was actually a CP member. Jack Child reported Levison's break with the party in July 1955, and the Bureau's New York field office deleted him from a list of CP "key figures" in March 1957. A memo dated 27 November 1959 suggested recruiting Levison as an informant, but he rejected the proposal in two separate interviews, in February and March 1960. By that time, Levison had shifted his interest to CIVIL RIGHTS work on behalf of African Americans, first with a New York-based group called In Friendship, and then with Dr. MARTIN LUTHER KING, JR. It was the latter association that revived FBI interest in Levison, after a lapse of nearly two years.

Levison met King in the summer of 1956 and they became instant friends. Over the next two years, Levison helped King write and sell his first book (*Stride Toward Freedom*); he also prepared King's income tax return in 1958. In November 1959, with BAYARD RUSTIN, Levison drafted King's announcement that he was resigning his Alabama pastorate to pursue full-time civil rights work as head of the SOUTHERN CHRISTIAN LEADERSHIP CONFERENCE (SCLC). Thereafter, Levison helped King screen new employees, advised him on tactics, and served as King's primary speechwriter. As FBI HEADQUARTERS grew increasingly concerned about King's influence over American blacks, Levison provided the perfect excuse for a full-scale investigation of the SCLC.

On 8 January 1962 an FBI report warned Attorney General ROBERT KENNEDY of King's reliance on Levison (habitually described in Bureau documents as "a secret member of the Communist Party"). Days later, on Kennedy's order, Justice aide BURKE MARSHALL warned King of the potential for embarrassment if Levison's rumored Red ties were exposed. On 6 March 1962, FBI Director J. EDGAR HOOVER asked Kennedy for authorization to tap Levison's telephones and Kennedy agreed. G-men broke into Levison's office on 15 March to install a microphone, and the WIRETAPS were initiated four days later (though, as Bureau records indicate, they were not the first). The BUGGING and taps proved that Levison was one of King's closest advisors and his occasional ghostwriter, but they still produced no evidence of links to the Communist Party. Despite that paucity of evidence, the FBI opened a COMINFIL (*Com*munist *infil*tration) dossier on the SCLC in October 1962, but Assistant Director WILLIAM SULLIVAN'S memo to the New York City field office revealed the void of information available: "Exactly what is LEVISON's status within the CP?; is he or is he not a member of the Party?; is he subject to Party discipline, or not?; has he actually broken with GUS HALL and other CP leaders?"

Burke Marshall warned King about Levison a second time in January 1963. Six months later, on 22 June, King met with Marshall and Attorney General Kennedy in Washington to discuss the "problem" of Levison's continued involvement with the SCLC. The public connection was severed in mid-July 1963, but King and Levison remained friendly and Levison still offered advice on King's various campaigns, including the planned Poor People's March on Washington, D.C. in 1968. Following King's murder, widow Coretta King continued the association with Levison and later described him as "indispensable" to SCLC operations. Sporadic FBI reports on Levison's activities continued through the early 1970s. He died in 1979.

Thus far, the Bureau has not been forthcoming on the nature and extent of its Levison FILES. The FBI's official website offers 206 pages for public review, describing the surveillance as a "security investigation … from the 1950's through the early 1970's." It seems impossible that two decades of surveillance would produce so little paperwork, and indeed, another Internet source offers CD-ROM archives containing 1,977 pages on Levison, revealing "heightened [FBI] concern when Levison began to advise King on the VIETNAM conflict." The full extent of Bureau surveillance on Levison may never be known, but its impact was felt long after Hoover's death. In October 1983 Senator Jesse Helms quoted FBI files on Levison in a speech opposing establishment of a federal holiday to honor Dr. King.

**LEWIS, Aubrey C.**— In 1962 U.S. Attorney General ROBERT

KENNEDY ordered FBI Director J. EDGAR HOOVER to begin hiring qualified minorities. Hoover responded to that directive with the same kind of snail's-pace token integration that characterized school desegregation in the South. His first two black recruits were Bureau clerk JAMES BARROW and Aubrey Lewis, a graduate of Notre Dame University who had starred on the school's football team before moving on to play professionally for the Chicago Bears. Recruited by an FBI official active in the Notre Dame Alumni Association, Lewis became a special agent on 25 June 1962. With Barrow, he was the first black employee of the Bureau to complete full training at the FBI ACADEMY, and the first to study any subject there on a desegregated basis. Deceived by Hoover's fiction that black agents were stationed "all over the country," *Ebony* magazine touted Lewis as the Bureau's "newest Negro fledgling, one of the most promising men recruited for action."

Aside from service with the Cincinnati and New York City field offices, Lewis qualified as a firearms expert, a defensive tactics instructor, and a "Bureau speaker" (with the latter duties undefined). Author Kenneth O'Reilly, in his book *Racial Matters* (1989), notes that some civil rights leaders and many of Lewis's fellow G-men regarded him as "a token, an honorary Irishman from Notre Dame among Hoover's heavily CATHOLIC agent corps." That attitude may help explain the brevity of Lewis's FBI career. He resigned on 21 October 1967, at age 32, to pursue a career as vice president of the Woolworth Company. In the 1970s Lewis was a commissioner of the New Jersey Sports and Exposition Authority; in the 1990s he served as vice chairman of the New Jersey Highway Authority and as a commissioner of the Port Authority of New York and New Jersey. He died from complications of chronic heart disease on 10 December 2001.

**LEWIS, Fulton, Jr.**— A nationally syndicated newspaper columnist and radio commentator, Lewis labored as a journalist for 15 years before he first made contact with the FBI, writing in 1938 to request information on "a spy case." No details of the incident remain in his file, but Lewis was added to the Bureau's "general mailing list," and he soon worked his way up from there to rate mention in FBI memos among "anti-Communist writers who have proved themselves to us." That meant praising the FBI, and more particularly J. EDGAR HOOVER, while using leaked material to lambaste Bureau enemies. By July 1938, Hoover appeared on Lewis's radio program, declaring that Lewis had "placed patriotic duty above personal gain and recognition" to provide the FBI with "sensational" evidence of an unspecified "espionage plot."

The relationship blossomed from there, to the point that by July 1939 attorneys from the JUSTICE DEPARTMENT complained about Hoover's illegal leaks to Lewis. (No action was taken.) In 1940 Lewis wrote to Hoover that a group of "radical" journalists who were "very active in support of the Spanish Loyalists" had mounted a campaign to "smear" Hoover as a "publicity seeker," but "we have managed to squelch" the campaign. Nine years later, the shoe was on the other foot when Lewis complained to Hoover that a "character assassin" had denounced Lewis in the pages of the *Princeton Public Opinion Quarterly Review*. Hoover was sympathetic, scouring his private files for derogatory information on the author (a Cornell University professor), but nothing could be found.

Lewis created a furor in 1950, with claims that he possessed a document "prepared by the White House" and seized from a Philadelphia office of the COMMUNIST PARTY, asking Soviet leaders to "direct the North Koreans to cease and desist" in their invasion of South Korea. Aides to President HARRY TRUMAN informed Hoover that the memo had been written by a State Department official, whereupon Hoover launched a fruitless investigation of "White House leaks" to the press. Later that year, after MAX LOWENTHAL published a book highly critical of Hoover and the FBI, Lewis attacked the author as a "red-tinted sinister influence behind the scenes" in Washington, driven by "pro-Communist intents." In 1951, Hoover leaked derogatory information to Lewis on surveillance target WILLIAM CARLOS WILLIAMS, prompting a Lewis tirade on Williams's alleged "association with some of the smelly outfits that have been peddling Moscow propaganda in the U.S. for 25 years." Lewis was also close to Red-hunting Senator JOSEPH MCCARTHY and chief aide ROY COHN, an FBI memo from April 1954 stating that "McCarthy and Lewis are 'thicker than thieves' and that Lewis furnishes McCarthy with information from Mr. [Assistant to the Director LOUIS] NICHOLS of the FBI."

Lewis died in 1966, but the Bureau kept his file open for two more years, finally totaling an impressive 1,754 pages. After his passing, Deputy Associate Director CARTHA DELOACH recalled, "I knew him well. Mr. Hoover knew him well. ... I thought he was a little loose sometimes with his facts, but nevertheless, I knew him well, and he was always very favorable [to the FBI]."

**LEWIS, Harry Sinclair**— A native of Sauk Centre, Minnesota, born in 1885, Sinclair Lewis was a distinguished social critic, the author of 22 novels and three acclaimed plays. The FBI first noted his leftist tendencies in 1923, the year after his second novel (*Babbitt*) was published. Lewis won a Nobel Prize for literature in 1930—the first American to be so honored—but G-men and congressional investigators were more interested in his role as "a member and correspondent" of the Federated Press, publisher of the *Labor News*. Agents also noted his membership on the National Council of the American Birth Control League, and they found four of Lewis's novels housed in The Workers Library, advertised as a collection of "literature most essential to the class-conscious, militant worker in his task of awakening, organizing, and leading the masses." Another black mark was added to Lewis's file in 1935, when he published *It Can't Happen Here*, a view of ascendant American fascism. In 1937 he was found to be a member of the North American Committee to Aid Spanish Democracy, rubbing shoulders with "subversives" such as ERNEST HEMINGWAY and LILLIAN HELLMAN.

Notwithstanding those suspect affiliations, Lewis still rated a private tour of FBI headquarters in October 1939, approved by J. EDGAR HOOVER and guided by Assistant to the Director LOUIS NICHOLS. During the tour Lewis remarked to Nichols that he had broken with the Reds and "now he feels badly if they do not

castigate him in the *Daily Worker* at least once a week." (Lewis also observed that "Hoover is a mere infant. His best years are ahead of him.") Following the tour, Nichols assigned an FBI car and driver to take Lewis and his niece on a visit to nearby Mount Vernon.

Hoover was willing to court a Nobel Prize winner in public, but he never trusted Lewis. In 1940, ignoring the author's disclaimers, Hoover filed a report claiming Lewis was "active as an organizer for the COMMUNIST PARTY." A year later, Jacksonville G-men trailed Lewis from his speaking engagement at a local synagogue to a "notorious joint" where he drank heavily and lost $160 to a "flim flam" artist. That March, agents noted his name on the letter head of the Reader's Club, newly formed in New York City, and agents from the Birmingham field office used false names to enroll as subscribers, keeping tabs on the club's offerings. Still on the job 16 months later, while America fought for its life in WORLD WAR II, they grudgingly admitted that "it appeared that 'The Reader's' would be similar to the well-known 'Book of the Month Club.'" In 1944, Lewis was marked down as suspicious for supporting President FRANKLIN ROOSEVELT'S fourth-term candidacy.

Three years later, the FBI's institutional racism was showcased in a flap over Lewis's latest novel, *Kingsblood Royal*. A California reader wrote the Bureau to complain that it was "the most incendiary book" since *Uncle Tom's Cabin*, and G-men concurred, deeming the novel "very inflammatory due to its references to the question of Negro and White relations." More to the point, an unnamed INFORMANT had cautioned that "The book was stated to be propaganda for the white man's acceptance of the negro [*sic*] as a social equal."

In 1949 agents questioned Lewis about reports that he had denounced the U.S. at an international meeting, only to learn that their source was mistaken. He had, in fact, criticized the Soviet Union. By the time Lewis died in January 1951, a victim of advanced alcoholism, his Bureau file was so "voluminous" that much of it was transferred to the Bureau's "Correlation Section." Despite parallel investigations by Army Intelligence, the Air Force Office of Special Investigations and the SENATE INTERNAL SECURITY SUBCOMMITTEE, G-men ultimately logged "no information that Sinclair Lewis has been involved in espionage activities or that any current espionage investigation is warranted." They did, however, note that he was rumored to have used the names "S. Lewis, Sinclaire Lewis and Saint Clair Lewis," presumably in an attempt to mask some nefarious activity.

**LIBRARY Awareness Program**— In 1962 FBI Director J. EDGAR HOOVER launched a campaign ostensibly designed to identify foreign spies operating in New York City. Personnel in 21 scientific and technical libraries were contacted by G-men and asked to report any patrons with "foreign accents" or "funny-sounding names" who perused specific books or journals. Bureau historian Athan Theoharis reports that "many librarians" protested the intrusive Library Awareness Program and that it was never expanded beyond New York City, but the program was apparently still active in April 1988, when it was publicly exposed and Director WILLIAM SESSIONS felt compelled to defend it, telling reporters, "Our efforts to identify and neutralize the threat posed by hostile intelligence services and their agents in the U.S. must be continued as long as a threat to our national security exists."

A new and expanded version of the Library Awareness Program was specifically authorized in 2001, under terms of the "USA PATRIOT ACT." As reported by the *Washington Post* in June 2002, the FBI was "visiting libraries nationwide and checking the reading records of people it suspects of having ties to terrorists or plotting an attack." The effort apparently began in Florida, where participants in the disastrous SKYJACKINGS of 11 September 2001 resided prior to the attacks. FBI spokesmen declined to explain how reviewing the books read by dead men enhanced national security, and librarians contacted by the Bureau were generally tight-lipped about their dealings with G-men. From the minimal information available, it appears that agents have focused nearly all their recent attention on Middle Eastern immigrants, Arab Americans, and other library patrons with "Arab-sounding" names. So far, no terrorists have been arrested on the basis of library surveillance.

**LIDDY, G. Gordon**— Born in 1931, Gordon Liddy earned a law degree from a Jesuit college before joining the FBI in 1957. (His first choice was a military career, but with no wars in progress Liddy selected the Bureau as "an elite corps" with possibilities for action and intrigue.) Liddy was a gung-ho agent, fond of illegal BREAK-INS and other covert operations, whom fellow agents dubbed a "wild man" and "superklutz"; journalist Fred Emery also describes him as "a gun freak before the term existed." Rising swiftly to become a protégé of Assistant Director CARTHA DE-LOACH, Liddy revered the FBI and ran a background check on his fiancée through Bureau FILES before they were married. Once arrested by Kansas City police in the course of a "black bag job," Liddy was released after telephoning Police Chief CLARENCE KELLEY (himself a former G-man and future FBI director).

Liddy resigned from the FBI in 1962 and served briefly as an assistant district attorney in Poughkeepsie, New York. His tenure was controversial, including one case where Liddy fired a (blank) pistol shot in court to make his point with the jury. His service with RICHARD NIXON'S 1968 presidential campaign earned Liddy an appointment to the White House staff, where JOHN ERHLICHMAN and H.R. HALDEMAN made good use of his skills and FBI contacts. In 1971, following publication of the PENTAGON PAPERS, Liddy collaborated with G-men under Assistant Director WILLIAM SULLIVAN to investigate suspected leaker Daniel Ellsberg. A month later, Liddy planned and supervised a burglary at the office of Ellsberg's psychiatrist, Dr. Lewis Fielding. In October 1971, at the request of White House staffer Egil Krogh, Liddy prepared a list of proposed methods for removing FBI Director J. EDGAR HOOVER from office. Hoover learned of Liddy's plan six months before his death and began purging his confidential files in anticipation of forced retirement.

The year 1972 found Liddy assigned as general counsel for the Committee to Re-elect the President (CREEP). In that role, he hatched a plot (code-named "Gemstone") to disrupt the Democratic Party with a series of burglaries and other "dirty tricks." Journalist Mark Frazier reported (and Liddy denied) that two other break-ins were planned to target Hoover's residence and office. One burglary was allegedly designed to retrieve any potential blackmail files on President Nixon, while the other was said to involve spraying deadly insecticide "on Hoover's personal toilet articles." After Hoover's death in May 1972, Liddy warned the White House to seize the director's private files, which he called "a source of enormous power."

Those files remained elusive, but Liddy had other plots in progress, including a burglary at Democratic National Committee headquarters that started the WATERGATE SCANDAL, ultimately forcing President Nixon to resign in disgrace. As the White House cover-up unraveled, Liddy was charged (and later convicted) for his role in the Fielding and Watergate burglaries, with an additional charge for contempt of court. The Fielding break-in earned him a prison sentence of one to three years for conspiracy. In the Watergate case, he received an 80-month minimum term, with a 20-year maximum. Remaining philosophical, Liddy told reporters, "I really can't be too critical of Judge [John] Sirica [who imposed the sentence] because John Sirica and I think alike. He believes the end justifies the means. He puts that into practice. He does what is necessary."

Liddy served 53 months in prison and emerged to become a media celebrity, best-selling author, right-wing radio pundit and occasional dramatic actor. In 1986 a federal court found Liddy liable for $20,499 in back taxes on unreported Watergate slush-fund money. Seven years later, following the tragic BRANCH DAVIDIAN siege in Texas, Liddy condemned modern FBI agents as "jack-booted thugs" and advised potential arrestees on how best to kill G-men who wore body armor during raids. His prescription to fellow gun enthusiasts: "Head shots! Head shots!"

**LIEBLING, Abbott Joseph**— Born on 18 October 1904, journalist A.J. Liebling studied at Dartmouth, Columbia University and the Sorbonne in the 1920s. He worked as a reporter in Rhode Island and in New York City before joining the *New Yorker* as a columnist in 1935. His "Wayward Press" covered all aspects of American life, and while J. EDGAR HOOVER found the liberal *New Yorker* "unreliable," it was a piece of outside work that first brought Liebling to the FBI's attention.

Specifically, he wrote a satire of FBI investigations that ran in the New York *World-Telegram* on 16 January 1937, comparing Bureau techniques to "a Minsky burlesque opening" and dubbing the director "A. Edwin Doover." G-men clipped the article, branding it a "nasty dig at the Director and the Bureau." Weeks later, in advance of publication, agents noted that Liebling had served as research assistant for a *New Yorker* "special feature article" on Hoover, penned by colleague Jack Alexander.

Liebling served the magazine as an overseas correspondent during WORLD WAR II, reporting from England, North Africa and France, but the FBI somehow ignored that six-year odyssey, resuming its coverage of Liebling in 1947. Agents deemed it sinister when *New Yorker* colleague Richard Owen Bowyer gave Liebling a free copy of his new book on the National Maritime Union. (In respect to Boyer, G-men noted that "it is alleged that he writes articles in which he admits that he is a Communist." No such articles were preserved.) Later in 1947, the Bureau noted

Liebling's attendance at a gathering of the Progressive Citizens of America, protesting HOWARD FAST'S contempt prosecution by the HOUSE COMMITTEE ON UN-AMERICAN ACTIVITIES. A 1948 report in Liebling's file declares that Fast is on his way to jail, but fails to mention Liebling. A 1948 article by Hoover friend and future biographer Ralph De Toledano, clipped from *Plain Talk* magazine and added to Liebling's file, brands Liebling "a careless journalist of the *New Yorker* smart set" who displays "compulsive fellow-travelerism." Other *Plain Talk* clippings dubbed Liebling "an unofficial member of the defense in regard to … ALGER HISS," complaining that he "adopts a ridiculing, deriding, laughter-provoking 'poohpoohisms' attack on [ELIZABETH] BENTLEY and Whittaker Chambers and the House Un-American Activities Committee."

Six years later, in March 1954, an FBI memo noted that "an individual named Liebling" on the *New Yorker* staff "wrote an unfavorable article to [*sic*] Senator [Patrick] McCarran" in which the author "infers [*sic*] McCarran is a liability to the Democratic party." Other reports from the same year note that Liebling's book *The Wayward Pressman* was found in a communist bookstore, shelved with works by Howard Fast "and others who have been identified with Communists." Yet another memo finds Liebling responsible "for the pinko infiltration of *The New Yorker*," prompting one to question why the dossier on such a notable subversive totaled only 18 pages at his death, in 1963.

**LIMONE, Peter J.**— A Massachusetts native, born in 1934, Peter Limone was regarded by Boston G-men in the early 1960s as a "Mafia associate," although his only criminal conviction involved a petty gambling charge. It was a far cry from the murder charges that would send him to prison with three other defendants. Limone spent 32 years in custody before a probe of widespread corruption in the FBI's Boston field office proved that he and his three codefendants were victims of a deliberate FRAME-UP.

The case began with FBI recruitment of Boston-area mobsters for its Top Echelon INFORMANT Program, a belated effort to destroy Italian elements of ORGANIZED CRIME after 40 years of denial from FBI HEADQUARTERS that the Mafia even existed. Two of those recruited to inform on their fellow mobsters in Boston were contract killer Joseph ("The Animal") Barboza and VINCENT FLEMMI (known to underworld associates as "Jimmy"). The Bureau was aware of homicides committed by both men. In fact, a 1964 memo from G-man Dennis Condon notes that another informant had said of Flemmi: "Flemmi told him that all he wants to do now is kill people and that it is better than hitting banks. Informant said Flemmi said that he feels he can now be the top hit man in this area and intends to be."

A few months later, on 10 March 1965, Agent H. PAUL RICO filed a report that Flemmi was planning to kill a small-time Boston mobster named Edward Deegan. As detailed in that document, "Informant advised that he had just heard from Jimmy Flemmi, and Flemmi told the informant that Raymond Patriarca has put out the word that Edward 'Teddy' Deegan is to be 'hit,' and that a dry run has already been made and that a close associate of Deegan's has agreed to set him up." Deegan was killed two days later, and Rico received full details of the murder from his informant on 13 March, including information that the Flemmi and Barboza had committed the crime. G-men suppressed that information for over a year, until Barboza surfaced as an informant and accused four other men of Deegan's slaying.

Those arrested and charged on the basis of Barboza's false testimony included Limone, JOSEPH SALVATI, and two reputed Boston mobsters, Louis Greco and Henry Tameleo. Whatever their previous infractions, none of the four were involved in Deegan's murder, and reports to that effect where sent to FBI Director J. EDGAR HOOVER in Washington, D.C. Still, the Bureau suppressed that information and did nothing as the murder trial proceeded in Boston, with Barboza appearing as a key prosecution witness. All four defendants were convicted and sentenced to life imprisonment. Greco and Tameleo died in prison, serving time for a murder they did not commit. Limone and Salvati would doubtless have shared a similar fate, but investigation of corruption in the Boston field office saved them during 2000, when new agent-in-charge BARRY MAWN discovered an FBI list of the actual suspects and delivered it to attorneys for the innocent men. Joe Barboza was long since dead, gunned down by mob assassins in 1976, but Limone and Salvati filed lawsuits against the FBI for their wrongful imprisonment. When echoes of the case reached Congress, President GEORGE W. BUSH used his powers of executive privilege to conceal Bureau files on the frame-up from members of the House Government Reform Committee, thus ensuring that some aspects of the long cover-up may never be revealed.

**LINDBERGH Kidnapping**— Arguably the most famous American of the late 1920s, "Lone Eagle" Charles Lindbergh earned global fame (and fortune) with his solo transatlantic flight in 1927. His son, born 22 June 1930, was inevitably dubbed "the eaglet" and sometimes described as "America's child." The boy's KIDNAPPING and murder at the tender age of 18 months would be described by journalist H.L. MENCKEN as "the biggest story since the resurrection," and FBI Director J. EDGAR HOOVER meant to have his share of the headlines.

The case began at 10:00 p.m. on 1 March 1932, when a nursemaid found Charles, Jr., missing from his second-floor nursery in the Lindbergh home, near Hopewell, New Jersey. A semiliterate ransom note demanded $50,000 for the boy's safe return. Outside, a crude homemade ladder with a broken step suggested the kidnapper's means of access to the house. (It also bore fingerprints, but they were never identified.)

News of the kidnapping provoked a national outcry, with President HERBERT HOOVER vowing to "move Heaven and Earth" in pursuit of the abductors. Washington had no jurisdiction in the case, but Hoover quickly appointed a special "Lindbergh squad" of G-men to offer "unofficial assistance," but their overtures were rejected by Col. H. Norman Schwarzkopf, commanding the New Jersey State Police. Disdainful of the "federal glory hunters," Schwarzkopf proceeded to manage the case, while the Lindberghs were deluged with crank calls and letters, including multiple ransom demands. A stranger to the family, 72-year-old Dr. John F. Condon of the Bronx, volunteered to serve as go-between in contacting the kidnappers, and his bumbling services were accepted by the Lindberghs for reasons that remain incomprehensible today. Using the code name "Jafsie" (for his initials, J.F.C.), Condon placed an ad in the *Bronx Home News* which led to contact with a purported member of the kidnap gang, known only as "John." A late-night cemetery meeting saw the ransom demand increased to $70,000 since Lindbergh had alerted police and the press, but Condon demanded proof that "John" had the child. Three days later, on 15 March, a package arrived at Condon's home, containing a child's sleeping suit that Lindbergh identified as his son's.

The ransom drop was set for 2 April at St. Raymond's Cemetery in the Bronx. Hoover vetoed a plan to stake out the graveyard and catch the kidnapper red-handed. ELMER IREY of the Treasury Department suggested that the ransom be paid in distinctive U.S. gold certificates, with the serial numbers recorded, and his plan was adopted. On the night of 2 April, Charles Lindbergh waited in the car while Dr. Condon entered the graveyard with two bundles of cash, one containing $50,000, the other $20,000. When "John" called out to him from the shadows, Condon handed over the $50,000 but strangely held back the second parcel. In return, he got a note with direction's to the child's alleged whereabouts, aboard a boat off the Massachusetts coast. An exhaustive search proved fruitless, the Lindbergh baby nowhere to be found. Meanwhile, the first ransom bill surfaced at a New York bank on 4 April 1932, with others popping up around the area in months to come.

The search for Lindbergh's son ended on 12 May 1932, when a child's mutilated corpse was discovered in a wooded area four and a half miles from the family estate. Police had searched the forest thoroughly in March, but if one accepts the prosecution's story, they had somehow missed the body. The child's skull was fractured; its left arm was missing, as were the left leg below the knee and most of the internal organs. Decomposition was so far advanced that even the victim's gender could not be determined. Lindbergh and a governess identified the body, but the family's pediatrician refused to do so. If offered $10 million for a positive verdict, the doctor said, "I'd have to refuse the money."

Congress passed the "Lindbergh Law" on 22 June 1932, making interstate kidnapping a federal offense, and while the statute had no bearing on the present case, President FRANKLIN ROOSEVELT granted the FBI "principal jurisdiction" over the investigation on 13 October 1933. The gesture made no difference: despite recovery of 97 ransom bills between January and August 1934, G-men remained clueless in their search for the kidnappers. Finally, on 15 September 1934, a New York gas station attendant identified one of the gold certificates and recorded his customer's license number, thereby leading authorities to the Bronx apartment of 35-year-old Bruno Richard Hauptmann, a carpenter who came to the U.S. from Germany in 1924.

According to author Ronald Kessler (in *The Bureau*, 2002), FBI agents rushed to Hauptmann's flat but found no one home. Without a warrant, they broke in and searched the place, discovering more than $14,000 of the Lindbergh ransom money stashed in Hauptmann's garage. Realizing that the money would be inadmissible at trial, they replaced it and came back later with

New York police, obtaining permission for a search from Hauptmann's wife and thus "discovering" the cash. In custody, Hauptmann explained that a friend, one Isidor Fisch, had left a shoebox in his care when he (Fisch) returned to Germany and subsequently died there. Hauptmann said he had forgotten the box, stored in his closet, until a leak required attention and he found the box wet. Upon finding the cash inside, he took enough to satisfy a debt Fisch owed him, then stored the rest for safekeeping in case Fisch's heirs came looking for it.

Authorities were naturally skeptical of Hauptmann's "Fisch story," and New York detectives beat Hauptmann repeatedly (a fact confirmed by jailhouse doctor Thurston Dexter on 20 September 1934) in a vain effort to make him confess. J. Edgar Hoover suggested that Hauptmann might crack if forced to copy the ransom notes over and over, but local authorities had already pursued that avenue, compelling him to make seven copies (including misspellings) with three different pens, slanting his writing at various angles in an attempt to match the originals.

When Hauptmann's trial opened at Flemington, New Jersey on 2 January 1935, he confronted a staggering array of evidence. Eight handwriting experts swore that he had written the Lindbergh ransom note and other correspondence. A neighbor of the Lindberghs testified that he had seen Hauptmann scouting the estate before the kidnapping. A New York taxi driver, hired to drop a letter at Dr. Condon's house, identified Hauptmann as the man who paid him. Police described finding Condon's address and telephone number, along with the serial numbers of two ransom bills, written inside Hauptmann's closet. A wood expert testified that the ladder used to kidnap Lindbergh's son included a plank from the floor of Hauptmann's attic. Finally, Dr. Condon and Lindbergh himself would swear under oath that Hauptmann was the "cemetery John" who accepted $50,000 in ransom money on 2 April 1932. Hauptmann was duly convicted on 13 April 1935; his various appeals were denied and he was executed on 3 April 1936.

But was he guilty?

A review of the evidence, coupled with FBI documents declassified long after the fact, suggests a blatant FRAME-UP in the Lindbergh case and proves that G-men were cognizant of that fact. Glaring examples of prosecutorial misconduct include:

*Perjured testimony*: Impoverished Lindbergh neighbor Millard Whited twice told police in 1932 that he had seen no strangers in the area before the kidnapping; by 1934, with reward money in hand and promises of more, he changed his story and "positively identified Hauptmann as the man he had seen twice in the vicinity of the Lindbergh estate." Col. Schwarzkopf also lied, stating falsely that Whited had described the lurking man on 2 March 1932. New York cabbie Joseph Perrone, in 1932, told police that he could not recognize the stranger who gave him a note for delivery to Dr. Condon, since "I didn't pay attention to anything." Schwarzkopf branded Perrone "a totally unreliable witness," but New Jersey prosecutors used him at trial to identify Hauptmann as the note-passer. Dr. Condon spent two years denying any glimpse of "cemetery John's" face and refused to identify Hauptmann's voice at their first jailhouse meeting, when an FBI agent described Condon as being "in a sort of daze."

Later, faced with threats of prosecution as an accomplice to murder, Condon reversed himself and made a "positive" ID under oath. Charles Lindbergh heard two words from "John"—"Hey, Doc!"—in April 1932, and that from 80 yards away. He later told a grand jury, "It would be very difficult for me to sit here and say that I could pick a man by that voice," but he did exactly that at trial, identifying Hauptmann as the speaker.

*Handwriting evidence*: FBI expert Charles Appel, Jr., told reporters that the odds against anyone but Hauptmann writing the Lindbergh ransom notes were "one in a hundred million million," but his grandiose exaggeration flew in the face of logic and the available evidence. Another prosecution expert, 70-year-old Albert Osborn, initially told Col. Schwarzkopf that he was "convinced [Hauptmann] did not write the ransom notes"; at trial, however, he joined seven other experts in stating the exact opposite. Another of the prosecution's expert witnesses was Osborn's son, who in 1971 erroneously certified as genuine alleged writings of billionaire Howard Hughes that were forged by celebrity hoaxer Clifford Irving. (Still, 67 years later, FBI historian Ronald Kessler would insist that "nothing undercut the fact that Hauptmann's handwriting matched the ransom note's.")

*The closet writing*: According to coworkers and friends, New York tabloid reporter Tom Cassidy "bragged all over town" that he wrote Dr. Condon's address and phone number, with the serial numbers of two ransom bills, inside Hauptmann's closet, then reported the "discovery" to police for an exclusive front-page story. Prosecutors accepted the fraudulent writing as evidence, while Cassidy and friends considered it a minor indiscretion, in light of Hauptmann's "obvious" guilt.

*The kidnap ladder*: Crudely manufactured with none of a craftsman's skill, the ladder found at Lindbergh's home bore several latent fingerprints, but they did not match Bruno Hauptmann's. Ignoring that discrepancy, the state called Wisconsin "wood expert" Arthur Koehler to prove that Hauptmann built the ladder. Koehler initially reported, based on nail holes in the ladder, that its planks had not been previously used for flooring, but he changed his story when a lone plank was discovered missing from the floor of Hauptmann's attic. (That "discovery" was made by two state troopers on 26 September 1934, a week after three dozen officers searched every inch of the flat and saw no gaps in any of the floors.) Because the attic plank was two inches wider than any other board used to build the ladder, Koehler surmised that Hauptmann had planed it down to fit. Declassified FBI reports bluntly described Koehler's trial exhibits as "fabricated evidence," but the Bureau made no effort to prevent Hauptmann's wrongful conviction.

If there was any doubt of Hauptmann's innocence in Hoover's mind, it should have been resolved by Col. Schwarzkopf's own behavior. On the day before Hauptmann was electrocuted, another Lindbergh ransom bill surfaced in the Bronx. Schwarzkopf contacted Hoover, urgently requesting that if any further ransom bills were found, they should be secretly destroyed. Hoover's response to the suggestion is unknown, but he made no attempt to interfere with Hauptmann's execution.

Long after Bruno Hauptmann's death, as glaring discrepancies in the state's case began to surface, alternative scenarios for the kidnapping emerged. The suicide of a former Lindbergh maid suggested a possible "inside job." Involvement of ORGANIZED CRIME was another possibility, based on offers from imprisoned gangster AL CAPONE and others to retrieve the Lindbergh baby in return for cash or legal favors. Some theorists surmise, based on tenuous identification of the corpse, that Lindbergh's son survived the kidnapping and grew to manhood in another home. The most unsettling scenario to date, proposed by author Noel Behn in 1994, suggests that Lindbergh's jealous sister-in-law murdered the child as an act of revenge against her sibling, for winning the "Lone Eagle's" affection. In Behn's unsubstantiated tale, Charles Lindbergh then devised the kidnap story to avoid scandal and collaborated in the Hauptmann frame-up to spare his family from social ostracism.

Whatever the truth, today irretrievable, we know that Hoover and his agents were aware of major gaps and outright fabrications in the prosecution's case. It suited Hoover to ignore them, since he was engaged in polishing a fabrication of his own: the enduring myth that G-men "solved" the Lindbergh case virtually unaided by state or local authorities. From author DON WHITEHEAD's rendition in *The FBI Story* (1956) to the modern Bureau's website, the Lindbergh case remains a major segment of the FBI legend.

**LIPPMANN, Walter**— The son of second generation Jewish immigrants from Germany, born in New York City on 23 September 1889, Walter graduated from Harvard in 1910. Two years later, when the Bureau of Investigation launched its first investigation of his political beliefs, Lippmann was already recognized as one of America's foremost journalists. G-men preferred to note his membership in the Harvard Socialist Club and his subsequent service as "secretary to the socialist mayor of Schenectady, New York." Their suspicions were confirmed in 1914, when Lippmann signed on as associate editor for the liberal *New Republic* weekly journal, a post he held until 1920 (when he went to work for the New York *World*). In 1916, agents recorded Lippmann's membership in the Civic Club of New York, an organization the Bureau regarded as "dominated by a radical element."

G-men were confounded by Lippmann's activities during WORLD WAR I. One memo notes his service as an assistant to Secretary of War Newton Baker, while another chides him for assisting civil libertarian ROGER BALDWIN in the "anti-draft propaganda" that sent Baldwin to jail in 1918. A more telling commentary on the Bureau's surveillance techniques, however, is seen in the fact that agents completely missed Lippmann's participation in a covert military intelligence unit, meeting regularly at the New York Public Library on Forty-second Street. Perhaps the agents may be forgiven, though, since Lippmann biographer Ronald Steele reports that the project was so clandestine, "even the head librarian was sworn to secrecy." The same cannot be said of Lippmann's work with President WOODROW WILSON, planning details for the future League of Nations, but the Bureau also missed that small detail of Lippmann's career.

In the 1920s and early 1930s, Lippmann drifted further to the political right, criticizing newspaper censorship in the Soviet Union and finding fault with other aspects of communism. Invited to visit FBI headquarters in 1936, he told his tour guide that Director J. EDGAR HOOVER "must be an administrative genius," lavishly praising the FBI as "the greatest organization he had ever visited." A year later, however, those kind words notwithstanding, Bureau critics condemned Lippmann's latest work, *The Great Society*, vaguely observing that "It has been stated that this book attempts to evaluate the conditions of life under a planned economy."

Scrutiny of Lippmann continued into the Red-hunting days after WORLD WAR II. In 1947, the Bureau planted a spy in the room while Lippmann interviewed ALGER HISS. The following year, memos branded former Lippmann secretary Mary Price a Soviet spy who had "ransacked Lippmann's files." Agents noted that her background "was perfect for an undercover agent since she belonged to an old Southern family and Southerners were the last people suspected of being Communists."

A decade after those disclosures, Hoover was still in full cry, lumping "men like Walter Lippmann" with "coyotes of the press" who betrayed their country. A March 1957 memo on "INFILTRATION OF FABIAN SOCIALISTS INTO HIGH POLICY-MAKING AREAS OF THE UNITED STATES GOVERNMENT" included Lippmann's name on a list of 122 journalists who had published "slanted reports favoring communism" and had "minimized the threat of the Soviet union to peace and democracy" while portraying "Chinese communists as being harmless 'agrarian reformers.'" Two years later, a March 1959 FBI report on "MOLDERS OF PUBLIC OPINION IN THE UNITED STATES" included Lippmann in a list of 100 presumably disloyal reporters, noting Hoover's speculation that "subversive factors in the backgrounds" of such writers might explain and unfairly the modern "prevalence of articles ... which are severely and unfairly discrediting our American way of life and praising ... the Soviet system." Strangely, when those memos were later released under the FREEDOM OF INFORMATION ACT, Walter Lippmann's name was the only one on either list that had not been blacked out.

Deputy Assistant to the Director CARTHA DELOACH later made light of those reports, assuring author Natalie Robins that they were prepared "simply for the Director's information as to what caused these people to write that way—you know, what makes Sammy run—that kind of thing." However, the 1959 memo speaks of "immediate research" conducted "in accordance with the Director's concern," and the memos reportedly involved a crash review of some 9,500 FBI sources within a matter of days. Whatever the urgency of the futile pursuit, it died with Hoover in 1972. Lippmann outlived his "genius" adversary by 31 months and died in New York City on 14 December 1974.

**LIUZZO, Viola Gregg**—A Detroit housewife and mother of five, Viola Liuzzo traveled to Alabama on 19 March 1965, to join in a CIVIL RIGHTS march from Selma to Montgomery. Following the demonstration, on 25 March, she used her car to ferry marchers home from the state capital. While driving through Lowndes County with 19-year-old Leroy Moton, around 8:00 p.m., Liuzzo was killed by gunshots from a carload of KU KLUX KLAN members. Unlike similar crimes in the past, the case was quickly broken when one of the Klansmen, GARY ROWE, identified himself as a paid FBI INFORMANT. The other three were Eugene Thomas, William Eaton, and alleged triggerman Collie Wilkins.

President LYNDON JOHNSON, accompanied by Attorney General NICHOLAS KATZENBACH and FBI Director J. EDGAR HOOVER, announced the arrests at a televised press conference where he praised the "honored public servant, Mr. Hoover" for cracking the case. In fact, Hoover already faced criticism for informant Rowe's failure to prevent the killing, and his first instinct was to avoid embarrassment by slandering the victim. In telephone briefings with President Johnson, Hoover reported that Liuzzo "was sitting very, very close to the Negro [Moton] in the car.... It had the appearance of a 'necking party.'" He went on to say that "the woman had indications of needle marks on her arms where she had been taking dope," and that her husband—a Detroit member of the TEAMSTERS' UNION—had "a shady background." When Johnson called back for more details, Hoover repeated, "On the woman's body we found numerous needle marks indicating she had been taking dope, although we can't say definitely because she is dead."

In fact, Hoover was fabricating lies that made a mockery of his reputation as a peerless detective. There were no needle marks on Liuzzo's body—and even if there had been, posthumous tests routinely find traces of drugs in the blood and tissue of deceased subjects. Hoover's malice was compounded at the Birmingham field office, where G-men leaked a memo to local reporters and Klan informants, claiming falsely that Liuzzo "had puncture marks in her arms indicating recent use of a hypodermic needle." Klan spokesmen soon took the hint from their turncoat members on the FBI payroll, informing racist audiences (again, falsely) that Liuzzo had been infected with venereal disease.

State authorities charged Wilkins, Eaton and Thomas with murder, while the defendants signed autographs at Klan rallies and collected donations for a Whiteman's Defense Fund. Collie Wilkins, defended by ex-FBI agent Arthur Hanes Sr., was acquitted at his second trial, on 22 October 1965. The Klan promptly issued bumper stickers reading "OPEN SEASON," but federal prosecutors stepped in to charge the Klansmen with violating Liuzzo's civil rights. All three were convicted of that crime on 3 December 1965, receiving 10-year prison terms. Those convictions notwithstanding, Eugene Thomas was acquitted of murder on 27 September 1966. William Eaton died of a heart attack in March 1966, without facing trial for murder or serving any time in jail.

While the case made its way through the courts, Hoover's FBI seemed more preoccupied with smearing Liuzzo's memory than with convicting her killers. G-men staked out Liuzzo's funeral in Detroit, after Dr. MARTIN LUTHER KING, JR., announced he would attend. When a class of junior high school students wrote letters praising the FBI's work on the case, Hoover told his staff to ignore them "because a reply would only help build up this character"—but he ordered name checks on the children to ferret out any "subversive" connections. Suspicion lingered that Gary Rowe may have been more than a witness to Liuzzo's slaying, and Lowndes County prosecutors charged him with her murder in 1978, but authorities at his new location refused extradition and the charge was dropped.

**LONDON, Jack**— Born on 12 January 1876, novelist Jack London was best known for his tales of adventure, including *White Fang, The Call of the Wild* and *The Sea Wolf*. He was also a long-time member of the Socialist Party, but Bureau agents seemingly overlooked that fact until after London died (or committed suicide) at his California ranch on 22 November 1916.

The rush to investigate London began on 23 August 1917, one month after J. EDGAR HOOVER joined the JUSTICE DEPARTMENT and four months after the U.S. entered WORLD WAR I. At issue was a pamphlet titled "The Good Soldier," purportedly written by London, that was barred from the mails as "anti-draft matter," including such remarks as "No man can fall lower than a soldier — it is a depth beneath which we cannot go." G-men waited another nine months before questioning London's widow, only to be told the pamphlet was a forgery. That denial notwithstanding, agents labeled the late novelist a "world-famous radical" who "fought with his pen."

**LOS ANGELES Police Dept.** *see* **Parker, William**

**LOWELL, Robert**— The son of a prominent Boston family, born 1 March 1917, Robert Lowell won the first of his three Pulitzer Prizes for poetry in 1930. Twelve years later, after the U.S. entered WORLD WAR II, Lowell tried to join both the army and navy, but was twice rejected on grounds of poor eyesight. Ironically, the army then tried to draft him in 1943, but Lowell refused induction, having decided that the war and Allied tactics were no longer just.

Defiance of his draft board brought Lowell to the FBI's attention, with the first entry in his 36-page dossier dated 17 September 1943. He subsequently pled guilty to draft evasion in federal court, receiving a sentence of one year and one day in prison. (He was paroled after serving four months.) The conviction did not bar him from a second Pulitzer in 1947, and the same year saw Lowell appointed as Consultant in Poetry at the Library of Congress. Around the same time, Lowell was a frequent visitor to the YADDO WRITERS COLONY, another target of FBI surveillance.

In the early 1960s Lowell became an outspoken critic of U.S. involvement in the VIETNAM WAR, thus giving G-men more grounds for suspicion. In 1965 he refused an invitation to participate in President LYNDON JOHNSON'S first-and-only White House Festival of the Arts, and he also signed a "Writers and Artists Protest" message against the ongoing war. Two years later, Lowell was among the leaders of a peace march at the Pentagon. Later that year, agents clipped a *New York Times* article reporting that Soviet poet Andrei Voznesensky had dedicated a poem to Lowell.

Lowell won his third and final Pulitzer in 1974, but the FBI was more interested in his foreign travels, keeping track each time he used or renewed his passport. Lowell died in New York City, of a heart attack, on 12 September 1977. Today, more than a quarter-century after his passing, several pages of his Bureau dossier remain classified "in the interest of national defense or foreign policy."

**LOWENSTEIN, Allard Kenneth**— A Newark native, born 16 January 1929, Allard Lowenstein earned a B.A. from the University of North Carolina in 1949 and an LL.B. from Yale in 1954. After serving in the U.S. Army (1954-56), he taught at Stanford University, North Carolina State University and City College of New York. Throughout the 1960s, Lowenstein channeled many of his students into the CIVIL RIGHTS movement and later into VIETNAM WAR PROTESTS. As a leader of the liberal group Americans for Democratic Action, he launched a "Dump [LYNDON] JOHNSON" movement which later evolved into a "Dump [RICHARD] NIXON" campaign during 1969. Those efforts drew attention from the White House and both presidents authorized FBI surveillance of Lowenstein. (Nixon also initiated a punitive tax audit by the INTERNAL REVENUE SERVICE, which revealed no impropriety on Lowenstein's part.)

Aside from teaching and counseling young activists, Lowenstein also cherished political ambitions of his own. He was elected to Congress in 1968, but lost his reelection bid two years later. In 1972 he mounted a Democratic primary campaign against Rep. JOHN ROONEY, chairman of the House Appropriations Committee and a longtime friend of FBI Director J. EDGAR HOOVER. Anxious to support a crucial ally and curry favor with President Nixon at the same, Hoover ordered a "special investigation" of Lowenstein and furnished derogatory information to Rooney, including a report on Lowenstein's covert HOMOSEXUALITY. Rooney won the June primary by 1,000 votes but Lowenstein contested it, citing proof of fraud that included ballots cast for Rooney by dead voters. Ironically, after the courts ordered a new primary vote, Rooney widened his margin of victory to 1,200 votes.

Lowenstein never regained his seat in Congress, losing subsequent election bids in 1974, 1976 and 1978. President JAMES CARTER appointed him to head the U.S. delegation to the United Nations Commission on Human Rights in 1977 and Lowenstein also served as an alternate U.S. representative for "special political affairs" in the U.N. with the rank of ambassador (1977-78). In his free time, Lowenstein pursued evidence of conspiracy in the JFK ASSASSINATION and the slaying of Dr. MARTIN LUTHER KING, JR. On 14 March 1980, at Rockefeller Center in New York, he was shot seven times and fatally wounded by former protégé Dennis Sweeney. In custody, Sweeney claimed the CENTRAL INTELLIGENCE AGENCY controlled his actions by means of a "telemetric brain device" which transmitted orders through his dentures.

**LOWENTHAL, Max**— An attorney, one-time congressional aide and personal advisor to President HARRY TRUMAN, Max Lowenthal began work on a critical history of the FBI sometime in the late 1930s, spending more than a decade to complete the manuscript. Throughout that protracted effort, J. EDGAR HOOVER knew nothing of the project, learning of the book's impending publication in 1950, from an advance notice in *Publisher's Weekly*. Enraged, Hoover sought to block publication of the book by means of intercession from Morris Ernst, a covert FBI ally in the AMERICAN CIVIL LIBERTIES UNION. Ernst, while loyal to Hoover, declined to approach publisher William Sloane on the grounds that

Lowenthal might reap added publicity if Hoover used "his lawyer" to oppose publication.

Hoover's next move was to marshal his allies in Congress and the media, enlisting them to denounce Lowenthal and his work before the book was published. A copy of advance galleys for *The Federal Bureau of Investigation* were stolen by "persons unknown" from a motorcycle messenger, transporting the proofs from the printer to William Sloane's office, and overnight the manuscript's contents were available to right-wing columnists and commentators including FULTON LEWIS, JR., GEORGE SOKOLSKY, REX COLLIER and WALTER WINCHELL. These and others attacked Lowenthal as a tool of Moscow, "refuting" his work point-by-point with material prepared at FBI HEADQUARTERS.

The Congressional assault on Lowenthal was even more frenetic. Iowa Senator Bourke Hickenlooper blasted the manuscript as "an utterly biased piece of propaganda," while Michigan's Homer Ferguson deemed it "evil, a monstrous libel." In the House of Representatives, Michigan's George Dondero declared that "Lowenthal's book is serving the cause of Moscow. Stalin must be well pleased with Lowenthal." The HOUSE COMMITTEE ON UN-AMERICAN ACTIVITIES (HUAC) subpoenaed Lowenthal in September 1950, the grilling described by HUAC historian Walter Goodman as "a frank effort to discredit the book by discrediting its author." Having failed with Lowenthal, the committee also questioned Sloane, reduced to probing the publisher's affiliation with his wife's brother. (Sloane was moved to ask his inquisitors, "Am I my brother-in-law's keeper?")

Two months after those closed hearings, in conjunction with the book's release, HUAC published its transcript of Lowenthal's testimony in a further attempt to besmirch him. Professor Robert Carr, reviewing HUAC's performance on Hoover's behalf, opined: "That the Committee had any legitimate basis for questioning Lowenthal even in executive session is doubtful, in view of the questions put to him; that it had any justification for making public his testimony, beyond a desire to tar him as a person who had been investigated by the Un-American Activities Committee, is in no way apparent."

Back at Bureau headquarters, Hoover blamed his researchers in the CRIME RECORDS DIVISION for failing to sound an alarm on the book before it was finished. Assistant Director WILLIAM SULLIVAN later told Hoover biographer Curt Gentry of a tense meeting in which LOUIS NICHOLS, in charge of Crime Records, was reduced to tears by Hoover's wrath, sobbing, "Mr. Hoover, if I had known this book was going to be published, I'd have thrown my body between the presses and stopped it." As Sullivan told Gentry, "After that, we developed informants in the publishing houses."

Too late to block release of Lowenthal's work, the Bureau launched a nationwide campaign to spoil its sales. G-men called on bookshop proprietors, urging them not to order the book, and one imaginative agent conceived a plan to steal copies from library shelves. That notion was vetoed on grounds that it might encourage purchase of replacement copies, so a new plan was hatched: agents would visit local libraries and *move* the book to some other section, thus frustrating readers who tried to find it by using the normal Dewey decimal system.

In fact, Hoover need hardly have worried, since *The Federal Bureau of Investigation* sold poorly and soon passed out of print. Even so, Hoover's spite was eternal. Lowenthal was placed under continual FBI surveillance, harassed to the point that he never published again. Nineteen years after the fact, Bureau-friendly authors were still attacking Lowenthal in print. Harry and Bonaro Overstreet, in their book *The FBI in Our Open Society* (1969), scatter anti-Lowenthal remarks over a span of some 225 pages, including some curious index references to pages where Lowenthal does not appear. On pages where they *do* discuss Lowenthal's work, the Overstreets deem it "odd," "improbable," and "nonsense" dredged "out of communism's lexicon." Finally, they urge that the entire book should "be stricken from the record."

**LOYALTY Programs**—While purges of alleged "radicals" and "subversives" have occurred throughout U.S. history, concerted efforts to investigate and guarantee the "loyalty" of federal government employees began during President FRANKLIN ROOSEVELT'S second term in office. The Hatch Act of 1939 restricted political activities by federal employees, and the U.S. Civil Service Commission interpreted that law (on 20 June 1940) to require dismissal of any government employee who belonged to communist or fascist organizations. A few weeks later, Congressman MARTIN DIES, chairman of the HOUSE COMMITTEE ON UN-AMERICAN ACTIVITIES, accused Attorney General ROBERT JACKSON of endorsing Red groups. By March 1941 Dies had issued a demand for President Roosevelt to fire any government employee enrolled in an organization "controlled by a foreign power."

Active investigation of government workers evolved over time. President Roosevelt, in August 1940, required investigations "only upon request of the appropriate Department or Agency." A JUSTICE DEPARTMENT appropriations bill passed on 28 June 1941 gave the FBI $100,000 to seek out any federal employees who were "members of subversive organizations." Martin Dies soon delivered a list of 1,241 alleged "subversives" in government, and Attorney General FRANCIS BIDDLE overruled FDR's order of August 1940 on 21 October 1941, when he commanded the Bureau to investigate any "appropriate complaint," regardless of the source. In April 1942 Biddle created an interdepartmental committee to help department heads evaluate FBI reports, with their frequent references to unnamed INFORMANTS. A short time later, the Civil Service Commission broadened its definition of "subversive" employees, mandating dismissal of any employee for whom G-men reported "a reasonable doubt as to his loyalty to the Government of the United States." Agents scrutinized 273,500 workers before the end of WORLD WAR II, but only 1,180 were actually fired.

War's end only increased the fear of enemies at large in the United States. On 25 July 1946 Congress recommended creation of "a complete and unified program" to protect the federal government from "individuals whose primary loyalty is to governments other than our own." Four months later, on 25 November, President HARRY TRUMAN established a Temporary Commission on Employee Loyalty, declaring that "the FBI alone should have the continuing responsibility" for loyalty investigations. Truman's EXECUTIVE ORDER 9835 established the first federal loyalty program on 22 March 1947, supplemented on 8 July 1947 by a Justice Department directive that Bureau employees could be fired without learning the names of the informants who branded them disloyal. The heads of 25 departments and agencies challenged that apparent violation of the U.S. Constitution's Sixth Amendment, but their protests were dismissed in April 1948. Attorney General HOWARD MCGRATH, in February 1949, limited dismissal to employees who were "at present disloyal," but Truman's Executive Order 10241 (28 April 1951) discarded that standard to permit dismissal on mere suspicion of disloyalty.

Regardless of his efforts to appease right-wing inquisitors, President Truman was inevitably branded "soft on communism" by the likes of Senator JOSEPH MCCARTHY. Republican presidential candidate DWIGHT EISENHOWER promised a more "effective" internal security program as part of his 1952 campaign platform, and he followed through on 27 April 1953 with Executive Order 10450, abolishing the hearing and review procedures of Truman's loyalty program. Federal employment, Ike decreed, was a privilege and not a right. Henceforth, any transient suspicion of disloyalty might cost a federal employee his job. Further executive orders, in October 1953 and April 1954, permitted suspension or dismissal of government workers who claimed their Fifth Amendment rights before any congressional panel investigating "alleged disloyalty or other misconduct."

The U.S. SUPREME COURT intervened on 11 June 1956, with its ruling in *Cole v. Young* that Eisenhower had exceeded his authority by mandating summary dismissal of suspect employees holding "nonsensitive" government positions. Three years later, in *Greene v. McElroy*, the court ruled unconstitutional any procedure that denied employees the right to confront their accusers. Devoted as it was to secret witnesses, the Justice Department spent six months coaching Eisenhower on means of subverting the Supreme Court's order. The result, in February 1960, was Executive Order 10865, permitting department heads to conceal an informant's name whenever "disclosure of his identity would be substantially harmful to the national interest."

President JOHN KENNEDY'S primary contribution to the loyalty-screening program was a June 1963 directive that broadened FBI inquiries to include members of "'rightist or extremist' groups operating in the anti-Communist field." Because such groups constituted a major portion of J. Edgar Hoover's civilian constituency, Bureau investigation of the far-right fringe was half-hearted at best, and it died with Kennedy in November 1963. Successor LYNDON JOHNSON ordered a formal review of the government's loyalty programs in February 1965; eight months later the commission recommended changes to "provide greater uniformity, promote more effective and equitable operation of the program and facilitate the reciprocal use of security clearances among agencies." Johnson approved those limited changes on 3 November 1965, but growing conflict over America's involvement in the VIETNAM WAR prompted congressional calls for liberalization of the loyalty review process. In September 1966 the U.S. Senate convened hearings to "protect the constitutional rights of Government employees and prohibit unwarranted in-

vasions of their privacy." The committee's final report, issued on 21 August 1967, furnished ample proof of abuse but produced no substantive changes prior to President RICHARD NIXON'S inauguration in January 1969.

Nixon's administration was in some respects a throwback to the Red-baiting 1950s. FBI investigation of traditional "subversive" groups was expanded to "NEW LEFT" organizations on the flimsy grounds that "leaders" or those who "joined in membership" should be identified for "future reference," in case they someday attained "a sensitive Government position." By April 1970 the Civil Service Commission had a team of employees hired solely to read various "underground" newspapers and list every person mentioned in their pages — thus creating an index of some 1.5 million "subversive" names. Nixon further revived the moribund SUBVERSIVE ACTIVITIES CONTROL BOARD and expanded the definition of "subversion" to include any person who participated in "civil disorders" or obstructed "the recruiting and enlistment service of the United States."

Nixon's subsequent resignation had no impact on the "national security" juggernaut he had placed in motion. Two weeks after he left office in disgrace, on 16 August 1974, FBI HEADQUARTERS ordered all field offices to report:

> Identities of subversive and/or extremist groups or movements (including front groups) with which subject has been identified, period of membership, positions held, and a summary of the type and extent of subversive or extremist activities engaged in by subject (e.g., attendance at meetings or other functions, fund raising or recruiting activities on behalf of the organization, etc.).

On 11 November 1974 an order from the Justice Department instructed G-men to "detect organizations with a potential" for subversive activity, whether or not said groups had crossed the line into specific action. The order explained:

> It is not necessary that a crime occur before the investigation is initiated, but only that a reasonable evaluation of the available information suggests that the activities of the organization may fall within the prescription of the Order.... It is not possible to set definite parameters covering the initiation of investigations of potential organizations falling within the Order but once the investigation reaches a stage that offers a basis for determining that the activities are legal in nature, then the investigation should cease, but if the investigation suggests a determination that the organization is engaged in illegal activities or potentially illegal activities it should continue.

Since "potentially illegal activities" may spring from any human conduct, every organization was potentially "subversive" under the 1974 guidelines. Those vague standards prevailed until September 1976, when the CHURCH COMMITTEE'S exposure of DOMESTIC SURVEILLANCE abuses sparked national outrage. Federal courts in four states subsequently ruled that questions found on the Civil Service Commission's Federal Job Form 171, pertaining to an applicant's membership in various organizations, violated constitutional protections of the First Amendment. The Hatch Act, substantially amended in 1993, still governs political activity by government workers, but "loyalty" per se no longer qualifies as a litmus test for employment.

**LUCAS, William E.** — A Brooklyn native and combat veteran of WORLD WAR I, born in 1890, William Lucas worked as a Harlem journalist before his 1920 recruitment as an INFORMANT for the Bureau of Investigation. Lucas began writing for the *Crusader*, published by Cyril Briggs and the AFRICAN BLOOD BROTHERHOOD, in March 1920, but since his first report to the Bureau was filed a month later, it remains uncertain whether he took the job as a federal spy or was later persuaded to betray his employers. There is no doubt of his allegiance between April and June 1920, however, his service to the Bureau documented in a series of reports that Lucas signed with the code number "P-135."

Without leaving his post at the *Crusader*, Lucas went on to join MARCUS GARVEY'S Universal Negro Improvement Association and to distribute copies of the *Messenger*, published by FBI target A. PHILIP RANDOLPH. Despite recognition by some of his wartime buddies in Garvey's paramilitary African Legion, Lucas was successful enough as a spy that he worried his FBI handlers might think he was aiding the enemy. Time and time again he reassured them, in respect to his work at the *Crusader* and the *Messenger*, "I am really trying to prevent too extensive a circulation altho [*sic*] I have to make some kind of distribution of the copies that are given [me] for circulation." G-men were happiest when sales declined, and by May 1920 Lucas reported that the *Messenger*'s publishers "are curious as to the reasons of my sudden interest in their various publications." Cyril Briggs, meanwhile, was "very careful to leave nothing about the office that would give any information that he would not wish to get out." Still, Briggs invited Lucas to join the African Blood Brotherhood in late May. It is unknown whether Lucas accepted the invitation, but his service with the Bureau was abruptly terminated for reasons unknown, on 14 June 1920.

**LUSTIG, Victor** — A Czech native, born in 1890, Victor Lustig was a confirmed con artist by age 20, pursued by authorities in several European nations over the next decade. That heat drove him to the U.S., where he billed himself as "Count" Lustig and tackled the most dangerous fraud of his career. Approaching mob boss ALPHONSE CAPONE in Chicago, Lustig invited him to invest $50,000 in a new con game, guaranteed to double Capone's money within two months. Capone took a chance, warning Lustig to expect a one-way ride if he lost the money. Lustig put Capone's investment in a local bank for 60 days, skimming the interest for himself, then returned the principal to Capone with apologies for his failure to pull the scheme off. Capone was so impressed with Lustig's "honesty" that he handed the Count a $1,000 reward.

Lustig returned to France in 1925, posing as the "Deputy Director-General of the Ministry of Mail and Telegraphs" for his next scam, wherein he offered the Eiffel Tower for sale to the five leading scrap metal dealers in Paris. The "winner" signed a bogus contract for the 7,000-ton national monument, whereupon Lustig fled to Vienna with his loot. As it happened, the victim was too embarrassed to report the fraud, so Lustig returned and pulled the con a second time, collecting $100,000 from a second gullible scrap dealer. This one reported the loss to police, however, and Lustig returned to the U.S., where he took a fling at passing counterfeit currency.

That caper brought him to the attention of U.S. Treasury agents, who arrested Lustig in August 1935 and lodged him at the FBI's detention facility in New York City. Lustig escaped from the G-men on 1 September 1935 and fled to Pennsylvania, where Treasury agents found him again. They asked for FBI assistance in the capture, but Bureau agents claimed they were "too busy" to help. T-men captured Lustig themselves, on 29 September 1935, only to be intercepted by FBI agents while en route to Pittsburgh. The Bureau had changed its mind and now sought custody of Lustig, but Treasury refused to relinquish the prisoner. Undaunted by the rebuff, J. EDGAR HOOVER called a press conference to announce Lustig's capture, as if the FBI had bagged another fugitive. It remained for Secretary of the Treasury Henry Morgenthau, Jr., no fan of Hoover's grandstanding, to call a second meeting with the press and set the record straight.

"Count" Victor was convicted of counterfeiting in 1935 and sentenced to 20 years in federal prison. He served 12 years at Alcatraz before pneumonia claimed his life in 1947. In his early days on The Rock, it was reported that his old friend Al Capone kept Lustig safe from cellblock predators.

**LYNCHING** — Lynching is broadly defined as the extralegal execution by a mob of persons who are frequently (but not always) accused of some crime. The practice is named for Charles Lynch, a justice of the peace in 18th-century Virginia whose vigilante court meted out rough justice to Tories, horse thieves and other undesirables in the vicinity. While lynching was a staple of the Western frontier, its most infamous application involved the brutal murders of several thousand African Americans (frequently by torture or burning at the stake) since 1865.

Nearly 1,000 blacks were lynched between July 1908, when the FBI was created, and 1950 (the first year in U.S. history with no reported lynchings). At least 165 of those murders occurred after May 1924, when J. EDGAR HOOVER took charge as the Bureau's director. Lynchers were seldom charged and never convicted, despite the fact that they rarely operated in disguise and often posed for snapshots with the mutilated bodies of their victims. Law enforcement officers, particularly in the South, were often implicated in the crimes, either by delivering victims to the lynchers without resistance or by actively joining in the murders.

In no case prior to 1947 is there any record of an FBI lynching investigation. Bureau apologists note (accurately) that U.S. SUPREME COURT rulings from the 19th century had invalidated most criminal provisions of early CIVIL RIGHTS statutes, exempting private parties from federal trial under most circumstances and exonerating even public officials unless their specific intent while committing a murder involved curtailment of the victim's civil rights "under color of law." Furthermore, Hoover's G-men and the JUSTICE DEPARTMENT at large had no taste for pursuing cases where all-white juries were virtually certain to acquit the defendants, regardless of the evidence arrayed against them. That reluctance to court "embarrassment" is echoed in various Hoover memos from the 1960s, dismissing advice from his agents that the Bureau should pursue violent members of the KU KLUX KLAN.

Still, whatever the logic, it is indisputable that Washington had legal jurisdiction over some lynching cases. The LINDBERGH

LAW empowered G-men to investigate any KIDNAPPING where victims were carried across state lines (or where a 24-hour disappearance created the "presumption" of interstate abduction). Any murder committed on federal land was also fair game, along with cases where police officers joined or assisted a lynch mob while acting "under color of law" to violate a victim's rights. Still the Bureau remained inactive, even in cases like that of lynch victim Claude Neal, driven across the Alabama-Florida border by his killers in 1935 after their plans were announced (complete with an invitation to interested spectators) over local radio stations. In the final analysis, it is impossible to doubt that Hoover's personal racism played a role in his decision to avoid lynching cases whenever possible.

After WORLD WAR II, the FBI was sometimes forced to act against its leader's will, but for another 20 years the federal conviction count remained at zero. The Bureau's handful of postwar lynching investigations included:

*July 1946*— Black victims Roger Malcolm, George Dorsey and their wives were executed by a vigilante firing squad in Georgia. President HARRY TRUMAN ordered an FBI probe of the case, but 2,800 interviews failed to identify any suspects.

*August 1946*— Corporal John Jones was tortured to death by a Louisiana mob that included two deputy sheriffs. The Justice Department filed charges in February 1967 but the defendants were acquitted by an all-white jury, after their attorneys accused the Bureau of using "Gestapo tactics" and claimed "this prosecution has been engineered by minority elements in the East."

*February 1947*— Murder suspect Willie Earle was tortured and slain by lynchers in South Carolina. G-men collaborating with local authorities identified 31 members of the mob, 26 of whom confessed to participating in the murder. At trial in May 1947, a judge directed verdicts of acquittal for three defendants, while jurors acquitted the rest three days later.

*April 1959*— Rape suspect Mack Parker was taken from jail and lynched by a Mississippi mob that included a Baptist minister. Governor J.P. Coleman requested FBI assistance and the lynchers were identified in a November 1959 report. Local authorities refused to file charges.

The FBI finally obtained its first (and only) lynching convictions in October 1967, more than three years after a trio of civil rights workers were murdered by Mississippi Klansmen in the "MIBURN" case. Once again, state authorities refused to file charges, but this time federal prosecutors managed to convict seven of the 18 defendants indicted. Two sheriffs were acquitted, but a deputy was among those sentenced to federal prison in the FBI's last acknowledged investigation of a lynching case.

**LYONS, Leonard**— A licensed attorney who shunned the law to find fame as a high-society gossip columnist, Leonard Lyons began writing his column ("The Lyons Den") for the *New York Post* in 1934 and continued until his death in 1976. He had been on the job one year when FBI agents came calling with questions about a column alleging that "revenue agents were exacting graft from night club owners" in Manhattan. Lyons refused to name his sources without their permission (denied), but J. EDGAR HOOVER forgave him and launched a 37-year collaborative friendship. He also compiled a thousand-page dossier on Lyons, including personal correspondence and copies of columns pertaining to the Bureau.

Attorney ROY COHN once called Lyons "an intimate personal friend of Hoover's," while Lyons's widow disagreed, regarding the director as "an acquaintance, not a friend." The relationship, like all of Hoover's media "friendships," was a matter of personal convenience to Hoover. The FBI director issued an "immediate and favorable" endorsement of Lyons's application to become a war correspondent in 1945, and he once reportedly supplied a reference when Lyons sought to rent a new apartment. On the other hand, Hoover declined an invitation to the 1953 Bar Mitzvah of Lyons's son, and in the same year created a "Secret Correlation Summary" of all known references to Lyons or his "aliases"— "Len Lyons," "Lennie Lyons," "Lenny Lyons" or "L. Lyons." Seven years later, when son Jeffrey Lyons joined a class trip to FBI headquarters, G-men made special note of his remark that "You won't have any trouble with me. I know crime doesn't pay, especially where the FBI is concerned."

In 1970, Lyons sent Hoover a copy of a "black hate letter" bearing his forged signature, including references to "power crazy Blacks" and "the new red front—liberals." For reasons still unclear, Hoover forwarded the letter to White House aide JOHN EHRLICHMAN, who wrote a brief note in reply. The seemingly pointless incident prompted author Natalie Robins to speculate that Lyons may have been used in one of the FBI's strange and convoluted COINTELPRO schemes without his knowledge.

# M

**MacDONALD, Dwight**— A native of New York City, born 24 March 1906, Dwight MacDonald was a leftist author and editor whose sharp tongue never failed to rile conservatives. He became the editor of *Fortune* in 1929, the *Partisan Review* (from 1937), and *Politics* (1944-49). His books included *Against the American Grain* and *Memoirs of a Revolutionist.*

G-men first took notice of MacDonald — whom they dubbed "the ruddy journalist"— in 1936, when he registered to vote "under the COMMUNIST PARTY Emblem." His name was also found that year on the letterhead of the League for Southern Labor. By 1937 Bureau reports called him "well-known in Communist circles" and tagged him as a member of the SOCIALIST WORKERS PARTY. When *Politics* premiered in 1944, agents placed MacDonald and his wife under surveillance, including illegal "mail covers." A March 1946 memo calls *Politics* "an intellectual set-up and part of the Communist transmission belt in this country." When *Politics* reporter Clifton Bennett requested an interview with Hoover in April 1947, Hoover refused and ordered second-in-command CLYDE TOLSON to start "a discreet investigation of the outfit."

MacDonald retaliated by publishing Bennett's critical piece on the FBI, reprinted as a 1948 booklet titled *The FBI— Basis of an American Police State. Politics* also took personal shots at Hoover, noting that "he is obsessed with a persecution complex" and reporting that in high school, "although he was the smallest boy in his cadet class, it has been claimed that during drill he displayed the loudest voice." Hoover responded with a memo ordering G-men to "keep an eye on McDonald [*sic*] & his publication," adding MacDonald's name to the illegal SECURITY INDEX in April 1948 as a "Native-born Communist."

Surveillance of MacDonald, and his retaliatory criticism of the FBI, continued through the 1950s and '60s. In 1969, G-men noted ominously that the 55-year-old editor had turned in his obsolete draft card at a Washington rally against the VIETNAM WAR. Another "discreet inquiry" was ordered, continuing beyond Hoover's death and into 1975, when MacDonald requested his FBI file under the FREEDOM OF INFORMATION ACT. Director CLARENCE KELLEY refused to release the dossier, on grounds that MacDonald had not provided a notarized signature. MacDonald died in New York, still waiting for the file, on 19 December 1982.

**MacDONALD, Jeffrey Robert**— Shortly after 3:30 a.m. on 17 February 1970, military police at Fort Bragg, North Carolina were summoned to the on-post residence of a Green Beret captain and licensed physician, Dr. Jeffrey MacDonald. They found the house ransacked, MacDonald bleeding from a stab wound to his chest. The other members of MacDonald's family — 26-year-old wife Colette, 5-year-old Kimberly and 2-year-old Kristen — had been stabbed and beaten to death in their bedrooms. Dr. MacDonald told investigators that he had awakened in the predawn hours to find four strangers in his home. Three men — two white, one black — attacked MacDonald and his family, while a "hippie-type" woman with long blond hair watched from the sidelines, holding a candle and chanting, "Acid is groovy. Kill the pigs."

Despite the recent Charles Manson cult murders in Los Angeles and Dr. MacDonald's extensive work with drug addicts in nearby Fayetteville, Army investigators quickly dismissed his story and focused on MacDonald as a suspect. FBI agents (responsible for any crimes committed by civilians on a military reservation) found themselves excluded from the crime scene, relegated to questioning local drug dealers and users. One who volunteered to "help" with the investigation was part-time police informant Helena Stoeckley, herself an addict with alleged involvement in occult religious practices. (Despite her strong resemblance to the female assailant described by Dr. MacDonald, Stoeckley was never presented to MacDonald as a possible suspect.) The FBI's turf war with military police produced some curious results, but Bureau documents were suppressed until 1990, when they were finally released under the FREEDOM OF INFORMATION ACT.

MacDonald was charged with killing his wife and daughters in July 1970, but a three-month military hearing revealed so many clumsy errors by Army investigators that the charges were dismissed on 27 October. A memo from FBI Director J. EDGAR HOOVER, dated one day later, declared that he would resist any efforts to involve the Bureau in MacDonald's case because "the Army handled the case poorly from its inception."

Dr. MacDonald subsequently left the Army and entered private practice in California. In 1974 the FBI reversed Hoover's decision and agreed to examine evidence from the MacDonald case, although that evidence had previously been examined in various Army laboratories. (The Bureau's LABORATORY DIVISION had a standing rule against accepting previously-tested evidence, because it might be altered or contaminated; the rule was curiously waived in MacDonald's case.) FBI involvement in the case scarcely improved matters, though. In fact, a review of the FBI's records long after the fact revealed at least 53 items of potentially exculpatory evidence that were either misrepresented or concealed from the defense during MacDonald's 1979 murder trial. The items include:

1. Unidentified candle wax on the living room coffee table.
2. Unidentified wax on a washing machine in the kitchen.
3. Bloodstains on both sides of the washing machine.
4. Fingerprints noted on the washing machine but never collected.
5. Unidentified pink wax on the kitchen floor, near the refrigerator.
6. Blood on the refrigerator door.
7. Three bloody gloves in the kitchen.
8. Blonde wig hairs up to 22 inches long, found on a chair beside the kitchen telephone.
9. Unidentified wax and an unidentified human hair, found on a wall in the hallway.
10. A bloody syringe containing unidentified liquid, found in the hall closet.
11. An unidentified hair, covered with a tarlike substance, found in the bathroom sink.
12. Two unmatched blue cotton fibers and a crumpled pink facial tissue in the bathroom sink.
13. An unidentified hair with root intact, under one of Kimberly's fingernails.
14. Unidentified candle wax on Kimberly's bedding.
15. An unidentified hair on Kimberly's bed.
16. An unmatched black thread on Kimberly's bottom sheet, near a bloody wood splinter.
17. Unmatched pink and blue nylon fibers on Kimberly's bottom sheet.
18. Unmatched purple and black nylon fibers on Kimberly's quilt.
19. Unidentified candle wax on the arm of a chair in Kimberly's bedroom.
20. Unidentified red and blue wax on Kimberly's window curtain.
21. An unidentified red wool fiber and a speck of Type O blood on Dr. MacDonald's reading glasses.
22. Human blood of unknown type from the living room floor near Dr. MacDonald's glasses.
23. An unidentified fingerprint on a drinking glass from the living room end table.
24. An unmatched blue acrylic fiber found in the living room, where Dr. MacDonald claimed to have lain unconscious.
25. Two unmatched black wool fibers found on the murder club.
26. Three hairs that allegedly shook loose from the murder club inside an evidence bag. In 1970 the Army called them "human pubic or body hairs"; in 1974 the FBI Laboratory identified them as "animal hairs."
27. An unidentified bloody palm print on the footboard of the master bed.
28. An unmatched pink fiber from the bed's footboard.
29. Two unidentified human hairs from the footboard.
30. Two unidentified hairs from the master bedspread.
31. An unidentified hair found on a fragment of rubber glove, inside a crumpled blue sheet from the master bedroom.
32. A piece of skin tissue from the same sheet, "lost" after it was cataloged, but reportedly before analysis.

33. An unidentified piece of skin found under one of Colette's fingernails and subsequently "lost."
34. An unmatched blue acrylic fiber found in Colette's right hand.
35. An unidentified hair found in Colette's left hand.
36. An unmatched black wool fiber found near Colette's mouth.
37. An unmatched pink fiber from Colette's mouth.
38. An unmatched purple fiber from Colette's mouth.
39. An unmatched black wool fiber found on Colette's right bicep.
40. Two unidentified body hairs found on the bedroom floor near Colette's left arm, with three bloody wooden splinters.
41. An unidentified hair found beneath Colette's body.
42. An unmatched green cotton fiber found under Colette's body.
43. An unmatched gold nylon fiber stained with blood, found under Colette's body.
44. Two pieces of facial tissue found beneath Colette's body.
45. A clump of fibers, all but one unmatched, found stuck to a bloody hair from Colette's scalp.
46. An unmatched clear nylon fiber stuck to a splinter from the murder club, found on the bedroom floor near the crumpled blue sheet.
47. An unidentified hair with root intact, found under one of Kristen's fingernails.
48. Two unidentified hairs found on Kristen's bed, near her body.
49. An unmatched blue nylon fiber found on Kristen's blanket.
50. Several unmatched clear nylon fibers from the same blanket.
51. A clump of unmatched purple nylon fibers on Kristen's bedspread.
52. Unmatched cotton fibers from Kristen's bedspread.
53. An unmatched yellow nylon fiber stained with blood, found on Kristen's bedspread.

In addition to suppressing physical evidence at trial, the FBI also apparently misrepresented statements from critical witnesses during MacDonald's appeals. A forensic pathologist, Dr. Ronald Wright, reported that Colette MacDonald was clubbed by a left-handed assailant standing in front of her, whereas her husband was right-handed. In 1984, FBI Agent James Reed prepared an affidavit falsely stating that Dr. Wright had "retracted" his opinion. Wright contradicted that claim, but MacDonald's attorneys did not learn of the lie under oath until October 1989. G-men also tinkered with the statements of witness Norma Lane, who reported that suspect Greg Mitchell (a left-handed soldier and addict) had confessed to the murders in her presence, in 1982. An FBI affidavit claimed that Lane was uncertain whether Mitchell had referred to events at Fort Bragg or in Vietnam, a falsehood Lane flatly denies.

Greg Mitchell was not the only suspect who confessed to the MacDonald murders. Mitchell's friend and fellow addict, Helena

Stoeckley, offered multiple confessions to military police, the FBI, and retired G-man TED GUNDERSON, both before and after MacDonald's murder trial. She denied involvement on the witness stand, however, and FBI agents buttressed her denial with reports that she "appeared to be under the influence of drugs" when she made an earlier confession (a claim refuted by hospital blood tests performed the same day). Unfortunately for MacDonald's defense, Stoeckley and Mitchell both died from apparent liver disease (in 1981 and 1982, respectively), before their stories could be verified.

Suggestions of official misconduct continue to surface in the MacDonald case. Prosecutor Jim Blackburn, retired to private practice, received a three-year prison term in December 1993, after pleading guilty to various felony counts that included fabricating a lawsuit, forging court documents (including judges' signatures), and embezzling $234,000 from his law firm. In 1997 MacDonald's attorneys discovered that FBI lab technician MICHAEL MALONE, accused of offering false testimony in other cases, had misrepresented fiber evidence in MacDonald's case. (Specifically, Malone testified that the FBI's "standard sources" revealed that saran fibers could not be used in human wigs; in fact, two of the leading source books in the Bureau's lab stated the exact opposite.)

Despite such revelations of suspicious activity on the prosecution's part, all appeals in MacDonald's case have thus far been denied. The effort to secure a new trial for MacDonald continues.

**MacLEISH, Archibald**— A native of Glencoe, Illinois, born in 1892, MacLeish served as an artillery captain in WORLD WAR I and later graduated from Harvard Law School at the top of his class. A distinguished poet who won the Pulitzer Prize three times (1932, 1952 and 1958), he was also a personal friend of President FRANKLIN ROOSEVELT, variously employed as the Librarian of Congress (1939-44), director of the Office of Facts and Figures (1941-42), assistant director of the Office of War Information (1942-43), and assistant secretary of state (1944-45).

Such eminence did not protect MacLeish from FBI scrutiny; quite the reverse, in fact. In 1936 G-men noted the appearance of his poems in *Common Sense* magazine and sponsorship of the anti-fascist American Friends of Spanish Democracy. A year later, they logged his membership in the AMERICAN CIVIL LIBERTIES UNION, his sponsorship of the Friends of the ABRAHAM LINCOLN BRIGADE, and his seat on the board of trustees of the New School for Social Research (seeking jobs in American schools for refugees from Nazism). In 1939 MacLeish raised Bureau eyebrows by sponsoring the International League Defense Milk Fund and Spanish Refugee Relief.

The FBI snooping continued while MacLeish filled his various posts in the Roosevelt administration. Bureau files on the AUTHORS LEAGUE OF AMERICA call him "another long-time fellow traveler of the Communists," while spokesmen for the HOUSE COMMITTEE ON UN-AMERICAN ACTIVITIES found MacLeish a curious Red who "for some reason does not want to become a member of the COMMUNIST PARTY." In 1940 agents deemed MacLeish suspicious for joining the Committee to Defend America by Aiding the Allies, and for serving on the board of the anti-Nazi American Guild for German Cultural Freedom. The same year saw his name listed under "Communist Activities" — and misspelled "Mac Leach"— for joining LILLIAN HELLMAN in support of a film raising money for Spanish Loyalist veterans. In 1941 and '42, MacLeish infuriated J. EDGAR HOOVER by going over the director's head and writing to Attorney General FRANCIS BIDDLE, with complaints of G-men leaking information to right-wing columnist WESTBROOK PEGLER and for generally being "out of touch with intellectual currents" in America. Another black mark was added to his file in 1943, when MacLeish recommended MURIEL RUKEYSER for a post in the Office of War Information.

The FBI's pursuit of MacLeish continued for another 33 years, without result. In 1962, when MacLeish was nominated for a seat on President JOHN KENNEDY'S Advisory Committee on the Arts, Hoover ordered his men to "determine from persons interviewed their opinion concerning appointee's loyalty from his written works." Those interviews produced only glowing recommendations, and Hoover had to be content with the discovery that MacLeish had been fined $10 in 1928 for "illegal fishing on private property" (fine suspended). His appointment became a moot point in 1963, however, when the JFK ASSASSINATION scuttled plans to create the committee. Agents continued watching MacLeish until 1976, when his file was finally closed, six years before his death.

**"MAGIC Lantern"**— Announced to the public on in November 2001, the FBI's "Magic Lantern" software is designed to monitor Internet traffic by recording every keystroke on suspect computers. Unlike previous advances in the field of DOMESTIC SURVEILLANCE, Magic Lantern went public (after a fashion) because collaboration from various telephone companies is required to install the software. Once in place, it would serve as the same kind of "Trojan horse" program frequently used by outlaw hackers and corporate spies to steal secure data in violation of federal law. While the Bureau's older "key logger system" requires physical BREAK-INS and tampering with a suspect's computer, Magic Lantern would involve no personal contact with persons under surveillance.

FBI spokesmen refused to disclose any details of Magic Lantern's operation, but they revealed that its development was part of a broader program dubbed "Cyber Knight," aimed at decrypting Internet transmissions sent by white-collar criminals, terrorists and other villains found in cyberspace. As one agent noted, "encryption can pose potentially insurmountable challenges to law enforcement when used in conjunction with communication or plans for executing serious terrorist and criminal acts." Civil libertarians, however, were not impressed with the Bureau's assertion that its researchers and agents are "always mindful of constitutional privacy and commercial equities." If anything, Bureau history from 1908 to the present day proves the exact opposite.

**MAILER, Norman Kingsley**— Born at Long Branch, New Jersey on 31 January 1923, Norman Mailer graduated from Harvard at age 20 and was drafted into the U.S. Army a year later, serving in the Philippines. That wartime experience inspired his first best-selling novel, *The Naked and the Dead* (1948). The FBI first noticed Mailer a year later, when he was named as a sponsor of the Cultural and Scientific Conference for World Peace at New York City's Waldorf-Astoria hotel. Covert war was declared 11 years later, after Mailer told a Chicago radio audience that "J. EDGAR HOOVER has paralyzed the imagination of this country in a way Joseph Stalin never could." G-men in the Windy City rushed to Hoover's defense, one reporting to Washington that "A number of persons in Chicago have personally commented to me that Mailer made an ass of himself on the program, and all such comments received have been definitely pro bureau and anti Mailer." A Bureau summary of the broadcast falsely claimed that Mailer had advocated abolition of the FBI because it "was too efficient against communism," and some 10 percent of Mailer's 466-page file is limited to discussion of this single incident.

Once joined, the battle was relentless. Agents tapped Mailer's telephone and monitored his visit to England in 1962. A year later, Mailer retaliated by publicly branding Hoover "the worst celebrity in America." By April 1966, G-men had concocted a COINTELPRO operation against Mailer, planning to send him a forged letter from COMMUNIST PARTY chairman Gus Hall, commending Mailer's opposition to the VIETNAM WAR. Agents hoped Mailer might responded by attacking the party, but Hoover vetoed the scheme, citing fears that the "technique might be compromised." Mailer joined a massive anti-war demonstration at the Pentagon in 1967, and his novelization of that event (*Armies of the Night*) won a Pulitzer Prize the following year.

The FBI ignored Mailer's New York mayoral campaign in 1969, but reported to presidential advisor HENRY KISSINGER that Mailer had joined "negro BAYARD RUSTIN" [*sic*] in a group of "Negro-watchers" who had uttered "sickening obscenities." Two years later, when Mailer's book *The Prisoner of Sex* was published by Little, Brown, G-men reported that "it had been selected by the Book Find Club, proving that it, and Little, Brown know how to find incendiary books." By that time, a friend of Mailer's, Diana Trilling, described the author as "absolutely paranoid on the subject of the FBI," and the feeling appeared to be mutual. When Mailer briefly joined the Committee for Action/Research on the Intelligence Community in 1974, agents worried that he might somehow gain access to classified documents. Four years later, when Mailer obtained his file under the FREEDOM OF INFORMATION ACT, he found it heavily censored. At that, he may have been fortunate that the Bureau never charged him with spying for Russia, since in the early 1950s he had briefly occupied the same Brooklyn apartment house as Soviet spy RUDOLF ABEL.

**MALONE, Michael**— Michael Malone spent 20 years as a microscopy analyst with the FBI LABORATORY DIVISION'S Hairs and Fibers Unit before 1994, when he was transferred to a field position by Director LOUIS FREEH. During his tenure with the Bureau lab he testified in hundreds of cases across the U.S., lecturing juries on the fine points of hair and fiber examination. In retrospect, Malone's critics suggest that he carried the instruction too far and claimed results impossible for modern science in its present state.

Official doubts about Malone's performance first surfaced in July 1989, when FBI metallurgist William Tobin was asked to review Malone's testimony in a federal bribery case. Florida judge Alcee Hastings had been accused of soliciting a bribe from mobsters in December 1980, and while a jury acquitted him in February 1983, Hastings remained the subject of a judicial review by his peers. Agent Malone had testified before the 11th Judicial Circuit in October 1985, concerning tests he had allegedly performed on a purse owned by Hastings. After reviewing that sworn testimony, Tobin drafted a six-page memo listing 27 specific complaints against his lab colleague. He accused Malone of offering the court "false statements" and "contrived, fabricated responses." Malone's scientific conclusions, Tobin said, were "not true," but rather "inaccurate and deceptive," "completely fabricated," and "unfounded and not supported by data." Worst of all, according to Tobin, Malone had even lied about performing tests on the purse himself.

Administrators in the Laboratory Division responded to Tobin's complaint as they had to similar charges from employee FREDERIC WHITEHURST: they ignored his charges, "lost" the memo, and later objected to investigation of the charges by the JUSTICE DEPARTMENT'S Inspector General. Still the review proceeded, powered by complaints from Senator CHARLES GRASSLEY that Malone was frequently known to "provide testimony on hair and fiber that no one else would." Malone specialized in "perfect matches" between hairs and fibers that were scientifically insupportable. Prof. James Starrs, an independent expert, said of Malone's work, "You just cannot draw these conclusions from hair and fiber comparisons." Ed Blake, spokesman for Forensic Science Associates, called Malone's sworn testimony in several cases "fraudulent."

A review of Malone's cases bore out those accusations. In May 1991 he testified that he had "microscopically matched" hairs from murder victim Kathy Wilson to samples found in a van owned by suspect William Buckley. On cross-examination, Malone learned that the hairs in question had not come from Buckley's van after all, but rather from a blanket Buckley used while camping in July 1988 (two months after Wilson was murdered). The samples had been mislabeled by police, and in fact no hairs from Buckley's van had ever been sent to the FBI lab. Confronted with his glaring error, Malone still refused to admit a mistake. "I matched hair on the blanket to Kathy Wilson," he insisted. "I don't know how it got there."

Two years after that performance, Malone "positively" matched hairs from another murder victim's pajamas to suspect John William Jackson, but Jackson's conviction was overturned in August 1997, when a Florida appeals court found that the hairs did not "match" after all. (Fingerprints from another suspect at the crime scene also exonerated Jackson.) Cases of that nature cast doubt on Malone's testimony in other trials, including the North Carolina case of JEFFREY MACDONALD, where dozens of suspicious hairs and fibers were suppressed or misrepresented by the prosecution. Authors John Kelly and Phillip Wearne, in their book *Tainting Evidence* (1998), conclude that "lying was certainly part of the job" for Malone throughout his tenure at the FBI laboratory.

**MANN Act**— Most extensions of the FBI's authority since 1908 have come about through exercise of the U.S. Constitution's so-called "interstate commerce clause," whereby Congress is empowered to exert control over activities occurring between two or more states. As interpreted by federal courts, literal "commerce" need not be involved; the mere crossing of state lines is enough in most cases to offer a pretext for federal intervention. After the Mann Act, FBI authority would be likewise extended to interstate auto theft (1919), KIDNAPPING (1932), and flight to avoid prosecution or confinement for purely local offenses.

The early 1900s witnessed a nationwide panic concerning "white slavery" in America, defined as the forcible abduction of females into lives of prostitution from which there was no escape. Racism played a part in the panic, as many such crimes were attributed to Chinese Tong societies and the Sicilian Mafia. On 25 June 1910, Congress passed the White Slave Traffic Act, more commonly known as the Mann Act (after its primary sponsor, Illinois congressman James Mann). The law provides a maximum 10-year prison sentence and/or fines for anyone convicted of transporting females across state lines "for the purpose of prostitution or for any other immoral purpose."

While congressional debate on the Mann Act made clear its design to crush organized prostitution rings, the law's vague language facilitated prosecution of private "immorality" wherever G-men were particularly zealous. Expanded duties required greater manpower, and the Bureau grew rapidly under the Mann Act, from 64 agents and 9 support personnel in 1910 to 265 agents and 305 support personnel by 1917. Its budget also grew accordingly, from $329,984 in 1911 to $617,534 in 1917. As practiced in those early days, Mann Act enforcement saw Bureau agents polling police chiefs and postmasters around the U.S., to learn which towns hosted brothels. Agents then visited individual houses of prostitution, accompanied by local police and attorneys, to survey the occupants for any interstate travelers. In the process, G-men accumulated reams of information on local corruption and the private lives of prominent citizens, including those who frequented a "very large" red-light district in Chicago. Suppression of private "immorality" was encouraged in 1917, when the U.S. SUPREME COURT affirmed (in *Caminetti v. United States*) that non-commercial sex was also subject to Mann Act restrictions. A noteworthy case, with strong racist overtones, involved the prosecution of black boxer JACK JOHNSON in 1913, for crossing state lines with his white fiancée. A more fortunate defendant was the son of a prominent aide to President WOODROW WILSON, spared from prison when Democratic prosecutors managed to sidetrack his case.

Bureau pursuit of sexual miscreants was energetic between 1910 and 1917, when vice prosecutions yielded to enforcement of the espionage act and arrests of draft dodgers. After WORLD WAR I, Mann Act enforcement resumed along prewar lines, Chief WILLIAM BURNS reporting to Congress in 1922 that while organized vice rings had mostly vanished (untrue), his men were still arresting individuals who crossed state lines in search of private pleasure. One such defendant was KU KLUX KLAN leader Edward Clarke, fined $5,000 for a Mann Act violation in March 1924. (Unlike Jack Johnson, Clarke received no jail time.) Attorney

General WILLIAM MITCHELL told Congress, in 1932, "many non-commercial cases of ordinary immorality, belonging in State tribunals, have been drawn into Federal jurisdiction." Five years later, a committee of the U.S. Senate warned that preoccupation with vice, versus crime, might "become a corrupting influence" on federal agents. J. EDGAR HOOVER disagreed, personally leading a series of controversial vice raids around Baltimore and Miami in 1937 and 1940. After the Maryland raids, Hoover vowed to remain "until Baltimore is completely cleaned up," but he soon retreated to Washington, taking with him the transcripts of illegal WIRETAPS on Maryland state legislators. In a 1938 congressional appearance, Hoover confirmed that his agents frequently arrested Mann Act transgressors in cases where "pecuniary gain is not an element."

Enforcement of the Mann Act continues, though its use is today less publicized. Ex-agent WILLIAM TURNER recalls working "an intensified White Slave Act program" around Knoxville, Tennessee in the early 1960s, and celebrity defendants still occasionally landed in the dock. One such was musician Chuck Berry, indicted in December 1959 for inviting a 14-year-old Arizona girl to work at his jazz club in St. Louis. The girl was soon arrested as a prostitute, and Berry's denials of involvement in her trade were unavailing. Initially sentenced to five years in prison and a $5,000 fine, Berry won a new trial on appeal but was convicted again, finally sentenced to three years and a $10,000 fine.

The Mann Act's original target, sexual slavery, remains an urgent problem in America and around the world. Motorcycle gangs like the BANDIDOS are frequent practitioners of coerced prostitution, and a thriving global trade in sex slaves persists. Reports from the STATE DEPARTMENT, published in the early 1990s, suggest that some 2 million women worldwide are forced into prostitution each year, the flesh trade vying with narcotics as a top money-maker for ORGANIZED CRIME. Hearings before the U.S. Senate Foreign Relations Subcommittee on Near Eastern and Southern Asian Affairs identified the primary "feeder" countries for Western brothels as Albania, Mexico, Nicaragua, the Philippines, Thailand and Ukraine. Mann Act prosecutions in the U.S., meanwhile, have largely been restricted to cases where minors are transported across state lines "for prostitution or any sexual purpose for which any person may be charged with a crime."

In the late 1990s allegations surfaced that the FBI itself might be involved in prostitution, using sex as an instrument of ESPIONAGE. Specifically, *Insight* magazine reporter Tim Maier claimed G-men used underage prostitutes of both sexes to obtain intelligence from foreign diplomats attending the December 1993 Asia Pacific Economic Conference in Seattle. In 1998 another journalist, Charles Smith, filed a FREEDOM OF INFORMATION ACT request concerning FBI use of prostitutes at the Seattle conference. FBI HEADQUARTERS acknowledged possession of 250 relevant documents, but only 13 heavily-censored pages were finally released. None revealed any illegal activity by FBI agents or their INFORMANTS.

**MANN, Thomas**— Born at Lübeck, Germany in 1875, Thomas Mann was arguably the greatest German author of the 20th century. He won the Nobel Prize for literature in 1929, and four years later emigrated to Switzerland, after ADOLF HITLER rose to power in Berlin. Mann visited the U.S. twice, in 1934 and 1935, becoming a personal friend of President FRANKLIN ROOSEVELT, before he settled in Los Angeles for good, in 1938.

Unknown to Mann, the FBI had already been tracking him for 11 years by the time he made his move, building up a 207-page dossier with "approximately 800 references." The first report was filed in 1927, "when information was received that he was a member of the American Guild for German Cultural Freedom." G-men labeled that anti-Nazi group "a racket," for reasons unknown, and they were still watching in 1937, when Mann's daughter Erika read a letter from her father to a New York meeting of the American Artists Congress, the event reported in *Deutsches Volks Echo*, a German-language leftist magazine. The Bureau was watching in 1938, when Mann addressed the Save Czechoslovakia Committee with a speech agents deemed "strongly radical and particularly strongly pro-USSR." Worse yet, it was observed that many in the audience wore lapel pins supporting the Friends of the ABRAHAM LINCOLN BRIGADE. Agents also noted Mann's co-sponsorship of the North American Committee to Aid Spanish Democracy, placing him in company with such alleged "subversives" as ERNEST HEMINGWAY and LILLIAN HELLMAN.

The FBI and OFFICE OF STRATEGIC SERVICES (OSS) were unsure what to make of Mann's politics as WORLD WAR II approached. G-men read his mail occasionally and called him "a warm defender of Moscow," while a 1940 INFORMANT'S report states that "Mann was not a Communist or fellow traveler but has permitted himself to be 'used' several times in recent years." Mann became a U.S. citizen in 1944, but his family's postwar European travels were still closely monitored, FBI agents in various U.S. embassies alerted to keep track of Mann and his kin. In 1951, when Mann became a member of the American Academy of Arts and Letters, FBI headquarters received a mass of "new" evidence, described as including "several hundred clippings, letters, speeches, articles, etc." A note revealed that the material "goes back to WORLD WAR I and is rather complex and not easily understood unless one understands the political setup in Europe since prior to World War One." After receiving that windfall, G-men apparently ignored Mann until his death in 1955.

That is not to say that other members of his clan were overlooked, however. Older brother Heinrich Mann entered the U.S. in March 1941 and acquired a 312-page FBI file over the next nine years, under the heading "Internal Security — R" (for "un-American"). Agents dutifully reported his contributions to *Deutsches Volks Echo*, his membership in the Free German Movement, and his affiliation with the Council for a Democratic Germany (described in FBI memos as "nineteen individuals, considerable of whom [sic] are Communists." The files also recorded wife Nelly's two drunk driving arrests in Los Angeles, during 1943. Heinrich planned a return to Germany in 1950 but he never made it, dying of chronic pulmonary fibrosis on 11 March. Forty years later, 71 pages of his dossier were still deemed too "sensitive" for release under the FREEDOM OF INFORMATION ACT. Heinrich's card in the Bureau's illegal SECURITY INDEX was canceled after his death.

Thomas Mann's children held even more interest for the FBI. Son Klaus and daughter Erika were both deemed "very active agents of the Comintern," described as "very active in Berlin before Hitler seized power." Thereafter, Klaus moved to France, where informants called him "an active agent of Stalin in Paris for many years." Preceding his father to America, Klaus edited *Decision*, an English-language magazine described by FBI sources as a "camouflaged Communist propaganda instrument." Klaus's file was labeled "Internal Security — C" (for Communist), but G-men also filed reports on his sex life, informant "T3" claiming that Klaus "unquestionably ... is a sexual pervert" and possibly a carrier of syphilis. FBI agents vied with Immigration officers, Army Intelligence and Navy Intelligence to keep Klaus under scrutiny. He joined the army in January 1943 and ironically joined Army Intelligence nine months later, becoming a U.S. citizen at the same time. His FBI file was closed on 23 September 1943, but Navy Intelligence went on collecting reports on Klaus until 1956, seven years after his death.

Erika Mann, liker her uncle Heinrich, was tagged by G-men as a contributor to *Deutsches Volks Echo*, a circumstance that encouraged her listing as an "enemy alien." Bureau analysts regarded her as dangerous enough to rate multiple listings, including "Internal Security — C," "Security Matter — C," and "Espionage — C." If her own politics were not bad enough, Erika made things worse by marrying FBI target W.H. AUDEN. (Agents called it a "marriage of convenience," misspelling his name as "Audan.") Strangely, in light of those problems, FBI records also reveal that Erika approached the Bureau in 1940, after nearly a decade of hostile surveillance, to volunteer her services as a confidential informant. G-men who interviewed her in June 1940 found Erika "most cooperative," and she provided information to the FBI through the early 1950s, when she finally returned to Europe. Her relationship with the FBI must have soured by then, since Erika listed the reasons for withdrawing her U.S. citizenship application as "ruined career, reduced means of livelihood and considerable embarrassment from investigations into her loyalty." Four decades later, 100 heavily censored pages from her Bureau dossier were released under the Freedom of Information Act. The Immigration and Naturalization Service, meanwhile. released only 30 pages of its file, withholding another 375.

**MARCANTONIO, Vito Anthony**— A native of New York City, born 10 December 1902, Vito Marcantonio served as a U.S. Representative from 1935-37 and again from 1939-51. His clash with the FBI began in 1939, when Marcantonio learned that Director J. EDGAR HOOVER had revived the Bureau's notorious Red-hunting GENERAL INTELLIGENCE DIVISION. Marcantonio rose in the House to compare Hoover's "system of terror by index cards" with the German Gestapo, branding it "a general raid against CIVIL RIGHTS ... very similar to the activities of the PALMER days." Marcantonio also made the fight personal, denouncing Hoover as "the Stork Club detective" after he saw Hoover dining in Manhattan's swanky nightspot with gossip columnist WALTER WINCHELL.

Hoover did not take lightly to such criticism. He ordered an immediate investigation of Marcantonio's politics and personal life, but the congressman's left-wing affiliations were already well known to his constituents and no private "dirt" was revealed. Red-baiting politics led to Marcantonio's defeat in the general election of 1950, one year after his failed campaign to become New York's mayor. Marcantonio died in Manhattan on 9 August 1954.

**MARCHWITZA, Hans**—A German native, born at Ober-Schlesien in 1890, Marchwitza labored as a miner before turning to left-wing journalism and fiction in the 1920s. An outspoken communist, he fought against right-wing forces that overthrew the Weimar Republic in Germany, and later claimed to be a veteran of the Spanish Civil War (though critics labeled him a "morale commissar" for the Loyalist side). In August 1940, after Nazi troops overran France, Marchwitza was one of 20 German exile writers granted asylum in Mexico. From there, in June 1941, he traveled to Ellis Island and sought entry to the U.S.

Immigration officials were reluctant to admit Marchwitza, grilling him on his leftist beliefs, but he was finally granted a visa (and six extensions, through mid-1946). In New York City, Marchwitza continued his writing, one essay contrasting the Statue of Liberty with the "concrete towers" behind it, "each of them a fortress of devil money." FBI agents indexed Marchwitza as a member of the Exiled Writers Committee and listed him as a prospect for CUSTODIAL DETENTION in September 1944, classifying his file as a "Security Matter—C" (for "Communist"). Marchwitza returned to a defeated Germany in 1947, where he reportedly maintained forbidden contacts in the Soviet occupied zone. He died in East Germany, in 1965.

**MARCUSE, Ludwig**—A German essayist, theater critic and university professor, born in 1894, Marcuse fled Germany for France in 1933, then immigrated to Los Angeles in April 1939. His 29-page FBI file notes that Marcuse spoke "little English" and had listed his race as "Hebrew" on entering the U.S. In 1943, IN-FORMANTS named Marcuse as one of several exiled writers who had gathered at the home of BERTOLT BRECHT to sign a "Moscow manifesto issued by the National Committee for Free Germany," but no evidence of involvement with the COMMUNIST PARTY was produced. Marcuse remained in Los Angeles until 1962, then returned to Germany, where he died in 1971.

**MARQUAND, John Phillips**—A native of Wilmington, Delaware, born in 1893, novelist John Marquand won a Pulitzer Prize in 1937, for *The Late George Apley*, and later created the Japanese detective "Mr. Moto" for a series of short stories published in the *Saturday Evening Post*. The FBI opened a file on Marquand in February 1939, after he signed a petition for the lifting of a U.S. embargo against Loyalist Spain. G-men also noted his membership in the AUTHORS LEAGUE OF AMERICA, but otherwise ignored Marquand until October 1943, when Marquand requested a meeting with J. EDGAR HOOVER in his capacity as director of information for the Federal Security Agency's War Research Service. Specifically, Marquand sought FBI help "in suppressing the publication of stories" about germ warfare, which he feared might ignite "public hysteria and speculation." Hoover's

memo on that meeting labels Marquand a "technical advisor to the FBI," once involved with a top-secret germ warfare project, then curiously notes that he "might possibly be inclined toward the Communist viewpoint." The last addition to Marquand's 14-page file, in June 1956, concerned an FBI investigation of his possible "subversive" role as an editorial board member of the Book-of-the-Month Club. Marquand died in 1960 taking the secrets of his wartime service with him to the grave.

**MARSHALL, Burke**—Born in 1922, Yale University law professor Burke Marshall was recruited by Attorney General ROBERT KENNEDY in 1961 to head the JUSTICE DEPARTMENT's Civil Rights Division. That post soon brought him into conflict with FBI Director J. EDGAR HOOVER, who despised Kennedy and regarded the black CIVIL RIGHTS movement as a thinly veiled vehicle of Communist subversion in America. Although he recognized Hoover's racism, Marshall (and Kennedy) still accepted much of Hoover's "evidence" at face value, particularly in regard to alleged Communist associations of Dr. MARTIN LUTHER KING, JR. Between 1961 and 1963, Kennedy sent Marshall to King with repeated warnings about STANLEY LEVISON, a friend of King's whom Hoover described as "a secret member of the COMMUNIST PARTY." Years later, in the wake of the March 1971 burglary of an FBI RES-IDENT AGENCY in MEDIA, PENNSYLVANIA which revealed details of the Bureau's illegal DOMESTIC SURVEILLANCE operations, Marshall joined former Attorney General RAMSEY CLARK to organize a public conference on FBI abuses at Princeton University. Hoover denounced the meeting's list of speakers as "a group of anti-FBI bigots" and recruited friendly columnist Ray McHugh to discredit the gathering. As part of that effort, in a memo to Associate Director CLYDE TOLSON dated 28 April 1971, Hoover ordered a review of derogatory information on Marshall and Clark from FBI FILES. Hoover wanted that material delivered to McHugh, in a covert bid to help him smear the conference organizers "in any way we can."

**MARTORANO, John Vincent**—A notorious member of Boston's Winger Hill gang, led by JAMES ("WHITEY") BULGER, John Martorano was a contract killer who murdered at least 20 victims scattered across the country from New England to Oklahoma and Florida. Federal agents arrested him in 1994, whereupon he agreed to turn INFORMANT for the FBI and thereby avoid the maximum potential punishment for his crimes. In September 1999 the JUSTICE DEPARTMENT announced that Martorano, then 58 years old, had pled guilty to charges of racketeering, extortion, bookmaking and race-fixing, with no murder counts filed against him. In return for testimony against Bulger, Stephen FLEMMI and other mobsters, Martorano was promised a maximum 15-year prison term (with credit for five years already spent in custody). Oklahoma state authorities later indicted him for the murder of Tulsa millionaire Robert Wheeler, slain on Bulger's orders in May 2001. Martorano received another 15-year sentence for that crime. Bulger remains a fugitive at this writing, having fled Boston in 1995 after corrupt FBI agents warned him of impending federal indictments.

**MARTZ, Roger**— Roger Martz graduated from the University of Cincinnati in 1974, with a degree in biology. He soon joined the FBI and spent most of his career in the LABORATORY DIVISION, where he ultimately rose to head the Chemistry/Toxicology Unit (CTU). He testified in many cases across the U.S. during his tenure at the lab, and he is perhaps best known for using mass spectrometry to identify drug residue in human hair (a technique used to convict Mayor Marion Barry of using cocaine in Washington, D.C.). Martz's cases run the gamut of the FBI's most famous investigations in the 1980s and 1990s. Unfortunately, his findings in most of those cases have now been called into serious question.

Martz's main difficulty was an apparent tendency to stray beyond his field of expertise and overstate the certainty of his lab test results. The first to criticize Martz was lab whistle-blower FREDERIC WHITEHURST, assigned to the Materials Analysis Unit, who protested Martz's testimony in explosive cases where he lacked sufficient training (and CTU lacked the required equipment) to produce results Martz described under oath. Martz had endeared himself to future FBI Director LOUIS FREEH in 1991, with his testimony in the "VANPAC" mail-BOMBING trial (where Freeh served as special prosecutor). Five years later, when VANPAC defendant Walter Moody faced a capital murder charge for one of the bombings in Alabama, Martz was already under investigation for offering false evidence in court. Within two months of Moody's February 1997 death sentence, Martz had been transferred out of the lab and faced censure from the JUSTICE DEPARTMENT's Inspector General.

The FBI had been reluctant to discipline Martz, even so. Complaints against Martz were initially buried, and while Whitehurst faced retaliation for his efforts to expose wrongdoing in the Laboratory Division, Martz was promoted in 1995 to serve as acting chief of the Scientific Analysis Section. It proved to be an unwise move, as bad publicity hounded Martz. In Los Angeles, where he appeared as an expert witness in the O.J. Simpson murder case, Martz stunned defense attorneys by claiming he had erased his raw data from various blood tests because "we only have so much computer space." This, despite specific instructions in the Bureau's *Manual of Administrative Operations and Procedures* that:

> An Agent's notes of a precise character, made to record his/her own findings must always be retained. Such notes include but are not limited to accounts, work papers, notes covering such matters as crime scene searches, laboratory examinations, fingerprint examinations. If a doubtful situation arises, resolve the question in favor of keeping notes.

Around the same time, Martz's work on the 1993 WORLD TRADE CENTER BOMBING was called into question. On 13 September 1995 a televised broadcast of *Prime Time Live* named Martz as "one of the FBI agents who pressured Whitehurst to go along with allegedly altered test results" in that case. Whitehurst maintained that Martz had used only one method to analyze bomb residue from the WTC blast, and that his technique had produced false results. When questioned by the Inspector General, Martz falsely claimed that "[n]o protocol in the Chemistry/Toxicology Unit required any examiner to perform a certain type of analysis." In fact, such a document *did* exist, detailing specific tests for explosive residue — but Martz refused to furnish a copy for review.

Similar doubts arose concerning Martz's work on the 1995 Oklahoma City bombing case, and his work had drawn so much criticism by 1996 that prosecutors declined to call him as a witness at the trial of bomber TIMOTHY MCVEIGH. With colleague DAVID WILLIAMS, Martz was officially censured in August 1998 for "negligence, inadequate documentation and overstated trial testimony" in the Simpson case. Martz appealed the minimal disciplinary action.

**MASTERS, Edgar Lee**— A native of Garnett, Kansas, born 23 August 1868, Edgar Masters spent most of his adult life in Chicago, as a practicing attorney. He was best known for his fiction, however, primarily the 1915 *Spoon River Anthology*. Masters was also an outspoken foe of imperialism in any form, a stance that led him to oppose the Spanish-American War of 1898. He was indexed by the FBI 40 years later, for telling the *Daily Worker*, "I am for Republican Spain, of course." The Masters dossier is brief, a mere 11 pages, but five of those are deemed so "sensitive" that their release under the FREEDOM OF INFORMATION ACT is forbidden, more than a half-century after Masters's death in 1950.

**MATA, Fernando E.**— A decorated counterintelligence agent who joined the FBI in 1972, Fernando Mata served 15 years with the Bureau before he joined 299 other HISPANIC AGENTS in a class-action lawsuit alleging racial discrimination in assignments and promotion. He testified against the FBI in court and was frequently quoted in newspaper stories covering the case — a circumstance which Mata claims prompted his Bureau superiors to retaliate against him after the lawsuit was settled in 1989. Specifically, FBI officials in Miami accused Mata of providing Cuban intelligence agents with classified material (including the location of BUGGING devices sent to Cuba by the CENTRAL INTELLIGENCE AGENCY). Mata reportedly failed two FBI polygraph tests, claiming that he had leaked the material in an attempt to recruit Cuban double-agents for the FBI. Mata was suspended from duty in February 1990, stripped of his security clearance, and finally fired in September 1991 (11 months before he could have retired with full benefits as a 20-year G-man). Mata appealed his dismissal to the U.S. SUPREME COURT, which denied his plea for reinstatement on 10 June 1996.

**MATHIS, Sylvia E.**— Information is curiously sparse on the Bureau's first black WOMAN AGENT. A native of Durham, North Carolina, birth date unpublished, Sylvia Mathis reportedly earned a law degree in May 1975 and was admitted to the North Carolina bar two months later. She joined the FBI on 17 February 1976 and received her first assignment to the New York City field office. No further data is presently available on what should have been a proud (albeit belated) appointment for the Bureau.

**MATIX, William and PLATT, Michael**— Two of America's

most violent modern bandits met, ironically, while serving in the U.S. Army as military police officers. William Russell Matix, an Ohio native born in 1951, was stationed at Fort Campbell, Kentucky in 1975, when he befriended 21-year-old Sgt. Michael Lee Platt. They kept in touch after Matix left the service, in August 1976, settling in Columbus, Ohio. Platt remained in uniform until May 1979, then opened a landscaping business in Miami, Florida.

Grim luck befell the two comrades, a few years later. Matix was widowed in December 1983, after his wife and a female coworker were stabbed to death by an unknown assailant, while working at a Columbus hospital. Matix collected $180,000 life insurance and moved to Miami in April 1984. Eight months later, after multiple complaints of death threats from her husband, Regina Platt "committed suicide" with Michael's shotgun. Miami police suspected Platt of murder but they had no evidence to prove it.

Free of marital encumbrances at last, Matix and Platt launched a spree of violent robberies around Miami. Between April 1985 and March 1986 they struck eight times at banks and armored trucks, killing one guard and wounding two others, stealing an estimated $243,807. They also murdered two strangers, found target shooting at a Dade County rock quarry, in order to steal the victims' cars and guns.

Miami G-men were on alert when the bandits showed themselves on 11 April 1986, driving a car stolen from their latest murder victim. A chase ensued, climaxed by the bloodiest shootout in FBI history, after Platt and Matix were cornered on a dead-end street. An FBI report describes the action.

> [Agents Ben] Grogan and [Jerry] Dove, from the area of Vehicle D [on the FBI's battle map] began firing on the subjects. Following a period of intense gunfire, William R. Matix apparently took Grogan and Dove under fire with a shotgun. This was evidenced by a pattern of #6 shot down the driver's side of Vehicle D. While Matix exchanged fire with Grogan and Dove, Michael Lee Platt left cover of his vehicle and proceeded down the side of car D, leaned over the trunk of it, shooting [Agent John] Hanlon, who was down, in the groin area, and shooting and killing Grogan and Dove. During this period of time, [Agent Ron] Risner was firing on Platt.
>
> Immediately after shooting the Agents, Platt and Matix approached the Bureau vehicle marked as car D, apparently to effect their escape. Both of them entered the vehicle. At this point, [Agent ED] MIRELES, who was apparently semiconscious, and was slightly behind the car, opened fire on the subjects in the FBI car, utilizing his Bureau-issued shotgun. Mireles was forced to fire one-handed. He rolled over on his back, put the shotgun between his legs, racked it with his right hand, forced himself up, pointed it over the rear bumper of the car and fired at the subjects. He apparently fired five rounds of 00 buckshot, puncturing the car in the left front fender, driver's window, and through the windshield. Somehow in this round of fire he hit the subject Platt through both feet. Mireles then rose to his feet, drew his service revolver, and advanced on car #6 firing and inflicting fatal wounds on both subjects.

Ten minutes of fierce action left Platt and Matix dead, along with Agents Dove and Grogan. Of six other G-men involved in the shootout, only Ron Risner emerged without injury. Platt sus-

tained 12 gunshot wounds and "multiple superficial abrasions of the face," while Matix was hit six times (including five shots to the face and neck). In the wake of the firefight, FBI spokesmen speculated publicly that Matix and Platt were members of a larger "loosely organized gang of South Dade armed robbers who specialize in armored car holdups." Director WILLIAM WEBSTER further suggested that they might be linked to some unnamed TERRORIST organization. "We don't have enough information to make a definitive statement," Webster told reporters, "but we are looking at this aspect very, very closely." Another G-man told the media that "many factors," ranging from costumes and choice of weapons to "cold and calculated" behavior in the last moments of their lives, suggested ties to some extremist group. Those factors notwithstanding, no other suspects in the case have been identified since April 1986.

**MATTHIESSEN, Francis Otto**— A California native, born at Pasadena in 1902, F.O. Matthiessen graduated from Yale in 1923, studied at Oxford as a Rhodes Scholar in 1925, and received his Ph.D. from Harvard in 1927. Thereafter, he became a professor of literature at Harvard and was nationally known as a literary critic.

The FBI opened a file on Matthiessen in 1935, after he "spoke at Santa Fe, New Mexico on behalf of Communism." His nickname "Matty" was filed by the Bureau as an "alias," while G-men noted: "Subject known as a Liberal and whenever meetings are held at Harvard University in protest of the activities of the President of the United States, the subject is usually chief worker." Matthiessen sometimes gave his shadows the slip, as demonstrated by the notation "He was absent from Harvard University during 1938 and 1939 for what purpose we cannot say." In 1942 he rated a notation for "promoting the sale" of LILLIAN HELLMAN'S *Watch on the Rhine*, and in 1943 for contributing an article to *The Guardian*, a "negro" magazine.

The Red-hunting years after WORLD WAR II put extra pressure on Matthiessen, harassed both for his politics and his HOMOSEXUALITY. His handwriting was submitted to the FBI LABORATORY for analysis in 1947, purpose unknown, and two years later he was called before a committee of the Massachusetts state legislature, investigating communism. Matthiessen admitted membership in 20 Communist-front groups but informed the committee that "he did not consider them Communist." An FBI report that year claimed that Matthiessen had been caught "publicly defending the USSR Communist seizure of power in Czechoslovakia," further observing that he "upholds the viewpoint of the USSR and criticizes that of the USA" at every given opportunity.

The pressure grew too great for Matthiessen in early 1950. On 1 April he jumped to his death from a 12th-story window of the Hotel Manger in Boston, leaving behind a note that read: "How much the state of the world has to do with the state of my mind I cannot know. But as a Christian and a socialist believing in international peace, I find myself terribly oppressed by the present conditions." Four days later, an attorney handling Matthiessen's estate contacted Boston G-men with personal information that Matthiessen may have been a Red. The Bureau answered with a dismissive note, claiming that it "was not interested in Professor Matthiessen's affairs."

**MATTHIESSEN, Peter**— A native of New York City, born on 2 May 1927, Peter Matthiessen began his professional writing career before he graduated from Yale University. He won a National Book Award in 1979, for *The Snow Leopard*, and the *Dictionary of Literary Biography* recognized him as "one of the shamans of literature." Matthiessen's most controversial book to date is *In the Spirit of Crazy Horse* (1983), a damning exposé of the FBI's long war against the AMERICAN INDIAN MOVEMENT and the 1975 shootout that led to a life prison term for AIM activist LEONARD PELTIER.

Soon after *Crazy Horse* was published, on 19 May 1983, Governor WILLIAM JANKLOW filed a $24 million libel suit against Matthiessen, his publisher (Viking Press), and three South Dakota bookstores, alleging that the book falsely branded him a racist drunkard and contained "factual errors too numerous" to list in his lawsuit. Eight months later, a second libel suit — this one for $25 million — was filed against Matthiessen and Viking Press by FBI Agent DAVID PRICE, who claimed that Matthiessen used false statements from "gangsters, hoodlums and liars" (i.e., members of AIM) to portray Price and other G-men as "corrupt and vicious." Matthiessen considered the latter action a *de facto* lawsuit by the FBI itself, since Price had remarked in a 1979 interview that he took no action of any kind without approval from his superiors. ("Everything I do, the Bureau knows it the day I do it.")

The lawsuits were defended separately. South Dakota judge Gene Kean dismissed Janklow's suit on 13 June 1984, but his ruling was reversed in 1985 by the state supreme court. On 25 June 1986, Kean again dismissed the lawsuit against the three booksellers, but Janklow pursued his case against Matthiessen and Viking. Kean dismissed that lawsuit once again in 1988, and this time the state supreme court upheld the dismissal. Despite public statements that he would press the case "as long as I live," Janklow filed no federal appeals.

Agent Price, meanwhile, initially sought to have his case heard before a "friendly jury" in Rapid City, South Dakota, but that move was foiled by Matthiessen's defense. The case wound up before U.S. District Judge Diane Murphy in Minneapolis, where it was dismissed in January 1986. Price carried his fight to the 8th Circuit Court of Appeals, where Murphy's ruling was upheld on 7 August 1989. From there, Price appealed to the U.S. SUPREME COURT, which twice refused to hear his case. Updated and reissued in 1992, *In the Spirit of Crazy Horse* became a national best-seller. Matthiessen and Viking reportedly spent more than $2 million to defeat the litigation filed by Janklow and Price.

**MAULDIN, William H.**— A New Mexico native, born 29 October 1921, Bill Mauldin was one of America's premier political cartoonists. He joined the U.S. Army in 1940 and thereafter became famous for his "Willie and Joe" cartoons, published in *Stars and Stripes*. The cartoons were nationally syndicated after 1944 and won the Pulitzer Prize in 1945, the same year Gen. George Patton lectured Mauldin for his "scurrilous attempts to under-

mine military discipline." Back in civilian life after WORLD WAR II, Mauldin went to work for the St. Louis *Post-Dispatch*, turning his pen against racism, the KU KLUX KLAN and the HOUSE COMMITTEE ON UN-AMERICAN ACTIVITIES. He won a second Pulitzer in 1959 and went to work for the Chicago *Sun-Times* three years later.

Mauldin's FBI file reveals that G-men began to shadow him while he was still in uniform, keeping track of his artwork and public appearances. In 1948 agents were concerned that Mauldin advocated "a United Nations with teeth in it." A year later, the Bureau had him labeled as a "Security Matter — C" (for Communist), asking field offices to "teletype summary any subversive action known to Bureau." An "urgent" memo from J. EDGAR HOOVER himself noted that Mauldin's "services have been sought in various Communist-front organizations," but he was forced to admit that FBI files "contain no information indicating that Mauldin is a member of the COMMUNIST PARTY." Agents discovered that Mauldin was also being watched by agents of the army's Counterintelligence Corps, but when they questioned the reasons for "this surveillance of a civilian," no answer was forthcoming.

At times, perhaps aware of the ongoing surveillance, Mauldin used his cartoons to lampoon Hoover and the Bureau. One cartoon, with the caption "Word Processor," shows an FBI agent standing behind a newspaper columnist, peering over the writer's shoulder with a magnifying glass as he types. Another, from 1946, depicts two commuters reading a newspaper with the headline: "Still No Clues on Lynchers of 4 in Georgia." In the caption, one man tells another, "I see the FBI cleared up another big postage stamp robbery." Ten years later, when Mauldin ran for Congress in New York, an FBI memo noted that "Bufiles reflect Mauldin had numerous contacts shortly after World War II with Communist-front and other type organizations. Cartoon by Mauldin in October 1946 by inference critical of FBI in lynching investigation." Another report, quoting an unnamed "self-admitted former Communist party member," alleged that "Bill Mauldin was installed in a high position [in an AMERICAN LEGION post] with the purpose of assisting in a Communist domination of the post."

FBI agents were still clipping Mauldin's cartoons and adding them to his file when Hoover died in May 1972. Shortly thereafter, Acting Director CLYDE TOLSON complained that "Mauldin has always resorted to muckraking in portraying the FBI." Mauldin died on 22 January 2003.

**MAWN, Barry W.**— A Massachusetts native, born at Woburn in 1945, Barry Mawn earned a Bachelor of Arts degree from Boston College in 1967 and spent the next year teaching public school in Bourne, Massachusetts. He joined the U.S. Army in 1968 and was commissioned as a second lieutenant the following year. Discharged in 1971, Mawn completed post-graduate work at the University of Massachusetts prior to joining the FBI in 1972. He spent a year with the Detroit field office, then was transferred to New York City in 1973, where he subsequently supervised the FBI/NEW YORK POLICE DEPARTMENT Joint Terrorist Task Force (1980-82). Between 1983 and 1986, Mawn served in various posts at FBI HEADQUARTERS, including a one-year administrative assignment with the DRUG ENFORCEMENT ADMINISTRATION. In June 1986 Mawn was appointed special agent in charge (SAC) of the Chicago field office, followed by terms as an inspector at FBI headquarters (1990-92), SAC of the Knoxville field office (1992-94), SAC of the Newark field office (1994-97), and SAC of the Boston field office (1997-2000). In March 2000, Director LOUIS FREEH promoted Mawn to serve as assistant director in charge of the huge New York City field office, supervising 1,100 agents and 900 support personnel.

Despite Mawn's long and distinguished career with the Bureau, author Ronald Kessler notes that Mawn has acquired a jocular reputation among fellow G-men as a "bad-luck" agent in his various assignments since the mid-1990s. It was during Mawn's tenure as SAC in Newark that "Unabomber" THEODORE KACZYNSKI killed public relations executive Thomas Mosser, on 10 December 1994, with a bomb mailed from California. Five years later, on 31 October 1999, Mawn was SAC in Boston when the copilot of EgyptAir Flight 990 deliberately crashed his aircraft into the sea off Nantucket, killing all 217 persons aboard. Before Mawn left that post, he also had to cope with the unfolding scandal of Boston G-men taking bribes from leaders of ORGANIZED CRIME and collaborating in the FRAME-UPS of innocent defendants for gangland murders. ("We're embarrassed," Mawn told the press. "The system obviously broke down, and it's overshadowed a lot of great work done at this office.") Finally, on 11 September 2001, Mawn was nearly killed in the collapse of the World Trade Centers, after TERRORISTS crashed two hijacked airliners into the twin towers. He retired from the Bureau on 1 March 2002.

**McCARRAN Act**— Passed by Congress over President HARRY TRUMAN'S veto on 23 September 1950, the Internal Security Act is more commonly known by the name of its primary sponsor, longtime Nevada Senator Patrick McCarran (1876-1954). A product of the Red scare that followed WORLD WAR II, the McCarran Act authorized deportation of alien radicals; barred COMMUNIST PARTY members from holding passports or working in defense industries; required communist or communist-front groups to register as "foreign agents" with a newly-created SUBVERSIVE ACTIVITIES CONTROL BOARD; required the publications of said groups to be labeled as communist propaganda; and authorized detention of "dangerous radicals" during national emergencies declared by the president. Such legislation provided an illusion of security by focusing national attention on outspoken leftist groups, while ignoring the threat of covert ESPIONAGE agents. Many states passed legislation modeled on the federal statute, while several southern jurisdictions carried the game a step further by banning the NATIONAL ASSOCIATION FOR THE ADVANCEMENT OF COLORED PEOPLE. FBI Director J. EDGAR HOOVER enthusiastically supported Senator McCarran, not only in his Red-hunting pursuits but in his public denials that ORGANIZED CRIME existed in the U.S.

**McCARTHY, Joseph Raymond**— Born at Grand Chute, Wisconsin on 14 November 1908, Joseph McCarthy was admitted to the state bar and entered private legal practice in 1935. Initially a New Deal Democrat, he lost a campaign for the district attorney's office in 1936 but was elected to a circuit judgeship two years later, in a race marked by flagrant slander of his opponent. (McCarthy lied about the incumbent's age, while accusing him of senility and corruption.) While still a judge, he joined the U.S. Marine Corps in August 1942 and shipped out to the Pacific 10 months later. An airman who never saw combat, McCarthy would later bill himself as "Tail-Gunner Joe," while an accidental foot injury (incurred on shipboard, during a drunken party) became a "war wound." Those heroic trappings failed to place McCarthy in the U.S. Senate on his first attempt, in 1944, but he was more successful as a Republican two years later (ironically supported by Wisconsin's COMMUNIST PARTY).

Soon after his arrival in Washington, McCarthy paid a courtesy call on FBI Director J. EDGAR HOOVER, and the men became great friends. Over the next six years, McCarthy frequently dined with Hoover and Associate Director CLYDE TOLSON at various restaurants and accompanied them on their "inspection tours" of sundry race tracks. McCarthy was also a frequent guest at CLINT MURCHISON'S Del Charro Hotel in California, where he was notorious for getting drunk and swimming naked in the public pool. Somehow, despite his innate moralism, Hoover overlooked McCarthy's glaring faults while they socialized—but he also maintained hefty FILES on the senator's unsavory activities. The information cached in those dossiers included proof of McCarthy's heavy drinking and compulsive gambling; his reputation as a judge who sold quickie divorces; his misuse of campaign contributions to speculate in soybean futures; his acceptance of a $20,000 "loan" from a major soft drink company (earning McCarthy the nickname "the Pepsi-Cola Kid"); and persistent rumors that McCarthy and a number of his aides were HOMOSEXUALS.

Despite such foibles, Hoover's friendship for McCarthy seemed genuine. In February 1948 he invited McCarthy to address the FBI NATIONAL ACADEMY'S graduating class, and in April 1949 Hoover appeared on McCarthy's Wisconsin-based radio interview program. In February 1950, after a series of reckless speeches branding the STATE DEPARTMENT as riddled with "Communist Party members and members of a spy ring," McCarthy turned to Hoover for help in supporting his fabricated charges. Assistant Director WILLIAM SULLIVAN cautioned Hoover to ignore McCarthy, but others told the director, "Senator McCarthy can be very useful to us." Hoover agreed, ordering his staff at FBI HEADQUARTERS to "review the files and get anything you can for him."

Unfortunately, McCarthy's penchant for changing the number of "known" State Department communists with each new speech made his charges even more difficult to support. As Sullivan recalled, "We didn't have enough evidence to show there was a single Communist in the State Department, let alone 57 cases"—or 205, as McCarthy claimed in another address. Still, G-men spent endless hours searching for evidence to buttress McCarthy's claims, while Hoover's ghost writers in the CRIME RECORDS DIVISION began drafting speeches for McCarthy and assistant ROY COHN. At one point, so many agents were attached to McCarthy's staff that his Senate office was nicknamed "the little FBI." As Hoover biographer Curt Gentry aptly observes: "'McCarthyism' was, from start to finish, the creation of one man, FBI Director J. Edgar Hoover."

Hoover's clandestine support for McCarthy continued at least through July 1953, as demonstrated by FBI documents later released. Benefits for the Bureau — as in the "war on terrorism" 50 years later — included more money, more agents, and broader authority under new statutes enacted to contain the "Red menace." At last, however, McCarthy's callous disregard for truth and his worsening alcoholism forced Hoover to sever their relationship in early 1954. McCarthy launched his last series of televised hearings in March of that year, with disastrous results for himself. On 2 December 1954 the Senate voted to censure McCarthy for "contemptuous conduct" and abuse of select committee privilege. Though still a senator, he was a broken man thereafter. A half-hearted bid to nominate Hoover for president in 1956 failed to renew his former close ties with the FBI director, and McCarthy's name went unmentioned that year when author DON WHITEHEAD published *The FBI Story*. McCarthy died of an alcohol-related liver ailment on 2 May 1957.

**McCARTHY, Theresa Mary** — A native of Seattle, born in 1912, Mary McCarthy was a renowned author and critic who also served on the editorial staff of the *Partisan Review* from 1937 to 1948. The FBI apparently ignored her completely until 1959, when she met and married James West, an employee of the U.S. Information Agency stationed in Poland. At that time, State Department sources told the Bureau that McCarthy was a self-described Marxist, which she later acknowledged in letters to author Natalie Robins. Both the FBI and the CENTRAL INTELLIGENCE AGENCY monitored her tour of Vietnam in the mid-1960s, but even then McCarthy described the contents of her dossier, released under the FREEDOM OF INFORMATION ACT, as "disappointingly slight." She died in 1989.

**McCULLERS, Lula Carson** — Born Lula Carson Smith in 1917, this native of Columbus, Georgia married Reeves McCullers in 1937 and achieved literary fame under her married name. (The marriage ended in 1940.) Known for her novels of psychological insight, including *The Heart is a Lonely Hunter* and *Reflections in a Golden Eye*, McCullers was examined briefly by the Bureau after the U.S. Information Agency requested a list of her "subversive references only." None were found, and her FBI dossier consists of a single page. McCullers died of a stroke in New York City, on 29 September 1967.

**McGHEE, Millie LePearl** — An African native of Meridian, Mississippi, born 25 November 1947, Millie McGhee was 51 years old when she began work on a history of her family that took a surprising turn by claiming FBI Director J. EDGAR HOOVER as a relative. McGhee insists that her book, published in 2000, "is not an exposé" of Hoover, but the title is calculated to hook the late director's fans and critics alike.

*Secrets Uncovered: J. Edgar Hoover — Passing for White?* might be a more convincing treatise if 80 percent of its 250 pages was not devoted to dream sequences, wherein author McGhee imagines herself viewing her family's history from 1809 to the early 1900s. Much of that fictional story involves white "Master Hoover's" dalliance with McGhee's female ancestors in Mississippi, producing a line of mixed-race children who disperse after the Civil War, some finding their way to Washington, D.C. in time for J. Edgar Hoover's birth. McGhee concludes that Hoover's mother was a Louisiana-born mulatto who first "shows up" in Washington census reports around 1880. This flies in the face of conventional wisdom that Annie Sheitlin Hoover was the child of Swiss immigrants, but McGhee covers all bases by deducing that Hoover's father was a member of her own (McGhee's) family who moved to Washington after the Civil War and built a housing complex on the fringe of the capital's ghetto.

The book's penultimate chapter raises some intriguing questions about the Hoover family's residence in a mostly-black neighborhood and notes some curious discrepancies in young John Edgar's birth records (listed out of order, the only record on its page to name a child with his parents, bearing a notation of "white" penciled in by a different hand), but the photographs depicting Hoover's "Negroid" features and complexion are murky at best. Finally, the best argument in favor of McGhee's thesis is ephemeral: if Hoover were trying to "pass," it might explain his overt prejudice toward blacks, as rumors of his HOMOSEXUALITY resonate in reports of his lifelong hatred for "queers." On balance, we can only say the case remains unproved.

**McGOVERN, George Stanley** — A South Dakota native, born 19 July 1922, George McGovern served in the U.S. Army Air Force during WORLD WAR II and later entered Democratic Party politics, first as a South Dakota congressman (1957-61), then as a U.S. senator (1963-81). FBI Director J. EDGAR HOOVER despised McGovern as a liberal and outspoken opponent of the VIETNAM WAR, but they avoided open conflict until 1 February 1971, when McGovern raised the case of former G-man JACK SHAW in the Senate, describing Shaw's dismissal as "an injustice that cries out for a remedy." Hoover ordered a review of McGovern's FBI FILE and received an 18-page summary of derogatory information, primarily gossip gleaned from McGovern's prior political opponents. Some of that material was leaked to the press from FBI HEADQUARTERS, including a false tale that McGovern had abandoned a pregnant girlfriend in college.

Undaunted by the smear campaign, McGovern continued criticism of the FBI with predictable results. When McGovern quoted a TWA pilot's criticism of FBI performance in a recent SKYJACKING, Hoover tried to ruin the pilot's career by leaking information from his Air Force personnel file. Later, when McGovern received an anonymous letter on Bureau stationery, purportedly written by 10 current agents who requested an investigation of the FBI "cult of personality," Associate Director CLYDE TOLSON ordered the FBI's 20 top administrators to reply with letters of their own. Tolson's own letter branded McGovern an "opportunist" and went on to say: "You are the first person I have encountered during almost 50 years in Washington whose ambition has far exceeded his ability, and I cannot help wondering how many other esteemed career public servants will be maligned or abused before your political balloon runs out of hot air." Assistant Director JOHN MOHR wrote, in a similar vein, "I cannot help recalling the 'old saw' about political ambition bringing out the worst possible traits of character in weak and expedient men." McGovern, already campaigning for the White House, inserted the letters in the *Congressional Record* and called for Hoover's resignation.

Hoover planned a new campaign of leaks after McGovern secured the 1972 Democratic presidential nomination, including a report that called McGovern "a communist and at least pro-communist and one who attempted to 'tear down' the U.S. Government's position in domestic and foreign relations," but Assistant Director D.J. Dalbey counseled moderation. Dalbey told Hoover, "If [McGovern] wants to be president, he'll have to run on something other than a campaign against the Director. There is no act that would get political sympathy for McGovern quicker than the belief of other politicians that the Director had used the power at his disposal against McGovern. There is no gain here to justify the risk." Hoover reportedly took Dalbey's advice (although the "pregnant girlfriend" fable surfaced again in the 1972 campaign), and McGovern was easily defeated by incumbent RICHARD NIXON. Retired from the Senate in 1981, McGovern sought the presidential nomination once again in 1984 but received only four of 3,933 delegate votes cast at the Democratic National Convention.

**McGRANERY, James Patrick**— A Philadelphia native, born 8 July 1895, James McGranery served as a Pennsylvania congressman (1937-43) and as a federal judge for the Eastern District of Pennsylvania (1946-52) before he took office as President HARRY TRUMAN'S third attorney general, on 27 May 1952. McGranery replaced J. HOWARD MCGRATH, fired by Truman during an investigation of political corruption, and entered office as a "lame duck" attorney general, aware of President Truman's decision not to seek reelection in 1952.

McGranery had previously served as an assistant attorney general under THOMAS CLARK, and his supervisory responsibility for the bungled AMERASIA CASE left him with few illusions where the FBI's record of illegal BREAK-INS was concerned. In April 1952 J. EDGAR HOOVER submitted a list of "hypothetical situations," seeking McGranery's judgment on when and where "trespass was involved." Specifically, Hoover complained to his putative boss that the JUSTICE DEPARTMENT'S present stance "regarding the use of microphones without trespass" was "so highly restricted" and "instances in which we could install microphones without trespass are so few that we have been stripped of this medium of gathering intelligence." Pleading concerns of "national security," Hoover claimed the Bureau had "a definite obligation to obtain and furnish such intelligence [obtained through BUGGING] to responsible officials" and that "if we did not do so, we would be derelict in our duties." In Hoover's view, "all possible means, consistent with good judgment" were required to protect America from "subversive elements" and threats of "foreign invasion." He closed by arguing that strict controls on "investigative techniques in the face of such grave responsibilities

could be considered detrimental to the best interests of this nation.... The Bureau as the responsible agency should be permitted to utilize any reasonable means at its disposal as long as such activity is properly supervised."

There would be no such supervision under James McGranery, however. He accepted Hoover's self-serving argument at face value and approved warrantless bugging "in any case where elements were at work against the security of the United States." A self-addressed memo penned by Hoover on 9 June 1952 noted that McGranery "would leave it to my judgment as to the steps to take. I told the Attorney General that this authority would only be used in extreme cases and only in cases involving the internal security of the United States."

Two more decades would pass before Hoover's abuse of that trust was revealed to the nation at large. As for McGranery, he left office with the rest of President Truman's administration, on 20 January 1953, and died at Palm Beach, Florida on 23 December 1962.

**McGRATH, James Howard**— Born at Woonsocket, Rhode Island on 28 November 1903, J. Howard McGrath took naturally to politics and pursued it throughout his adult life as vice-chairman of the Rhode Island Democratic Party (1928-30), Democratic state chairman (1930-34), U.S. district attorney for Rhode Island (1934-40). Governor of Rhode Island (1941-45), and as a U.S. senator (1947-49). He also served as chairman of the Democratic National Committee in 1947-49, and thus played a prominent role in the 1948 election of President HARRY TRUMAN. Truman repaid his political debt by naming McGrath to replace Attorney General TOM CLARK, when Clark was appointed to the U.S. SUPREME COURT. McGrath took office at the JUSTICE DEPARTMENT on 24 August 1949.

Author Robert Donovan, in his history of the Truman years — *Conflict and Crisis* (1977) — notes that McGrath "was lazy, and it was well known in Washington that he drank too much.... McGrath seems not to have been aware of much that was going on around him." In short, he was the perfect attorney general to feign supervision of the FBI while allowing Director J. EDGAR HOOVER to do what he pleased. Hoover was cordial with McGrath and took the unusual step, in October 1951, of seeking departmental guidance on use of BUGGING and WIRETAPPING. His memo to McGrath read, in part:

> As you are aware, this Bureau has also employed the use of microphone installation on a highly restrictive basis, chiefly to obtain intelligence information. The information obtained from microphones ... is not admissible in evidence....
>
> As you know, in a number of instances it has not been possible to install microphones without trespass. In such instances the information received therefrom is of an intelligence nature only. Here again, as in the case of wiretaps, experience has shown us that intelligence information highly pertinent to the defense and welfare of this nation is derived through the use of microphones.

Having thus informed his nominal superior that the FBI was guilty of criminal BREAK-INS to obtain inadmissible evidence, Hoover requested McGrath's "definite opinion" on whether the lawless activity should continue "or whether we should cease the use of microphone surveillance entirely in view of the issues being raised." On 6 February 1952 McGrath replied:

> The use of microphone surveillance which does not involve a trespass would seem to be permissible under the present state of the law.... Such surveillances as involve trespass are in the area of the Fourth Amendment, and evidence so obtained and from the leads so obtained is inadmissible. ... [P]lease be advised that I cannot authorize the installation of a microphone involving a trespass under existing law.

With that verdict in hand, Hoover restricted (but never ceased) illegal break-ins to install bugging devices. On 18 March 1953 he advised all FBI field offices that "if the contemplated installation is of such importance that it is desired despite the fact that one or more of the requirements for legal microphone surveillance cannot be followed," G-men should obtain Hoover's "specific authorization in each and every instance to make such an installation." In short, agents were required to secure Hoover's blessing before they broke the law.

McGrath, meanwhile, made no attempt to interfere with any illegal activity ordered from FBI HEADQUARTERS. He resigned as attorney general on 7 April 1952 and was replaced the following month by JAMES MCGRANERY. McGrath died in Rhode Island on 2 September 1966.

**McKELLAR, Kenneth Douglas**— A veteran U.S. senator from Tennessee, born in 1869 and elected to his first term in 1917, Kenneth McKellar was no friend of FBI Director J. EDGAR HOOVER. In 1933, Hoover refused to appoint several of McKellar's constituents as G-men, whereupon McKellar complained to Attorney General HOMER CUMMINGS. Far from achieving his goal, McKellar was livid when Hoover retaliated by firing three Tennessee natives already employed with the Bureau. Unfortunately for Hoover, McKellar served as chairman for the Senate Subcommittee on Appropriations, and he was ready for battle when Hoover appeared before the committee in early 1936, requesting nearly twice his previously estimated budget for the year.

McKellar launched his attack with stinging criticism of recent "G-men" films produced in Hollywood, which "virtually advertised the Bureau" on theater marquees. Hoover replied that he had objected to such films "in every instance," but grudgingly admitted that his photo appeared on many of the movie posters. (He also failed to mention a recent brainstorm, opposed by his aides, that would have seen the Bureau producing its own action movies and banking the profits.) Hoover also denied the existence of any paid publicity agents "in the Bureau of Investigation," while neglecting to mention those — including HARRY SUYDAM and COURTNEY RYLEY COOPER — who drew salaries from the JUSTICE DEPARTMENT.

Moving on, McKellar criticized Bureau performance in a recent series of high-profile KIDNAPPING cases, which Hoover claimed were solved by his agents. Under pressure, the director acknowledged that several had been cleared by local agencies or with assistance from civilian tipsters. After noting that fugitive ALVIN KARPIS had escaped three FBI traps in recent weeks, while G-men killed eight other bandits and lost four of their own to

enemy fire, McKellar declared, "It seems to me that your Department is just running wild, Mr. Hoover.... I just think that, Mr. Hoover, with all the money in your hands you are just extravagant."

The worst embarrassment, however, came when McKellar forced Hoover to admit that he had never made an arrest in his 19 years with the Justice Department. Instead, Hoover countered, he had "made investigations"— whereupon he named two ANARCHISTS deported by immigration officials during the PALMER RAIDS of 1920. Biographer Ralph de Toledano observes that Hoover left the Senate chamber feeling "that his manhood had been impugned"— which was doubtless McKellar's intention. In short order, Hoover arranged the "personal" arrests of Alvin Karpis and HARRY BRUNETTE, thereby employing the very publicity apparatus whose existence he denied to salvage his battered reputation.

Senator McKellar, meanwhile, recommended a $225,000 cut in Hoover's budget request. FBI supporters raised the specter of a new crime wave if Hoover was denied the cash. The final vote not only approved Hoover's budget request but also raised his salary from $9,000 to $10,000 per year. McKellar, himself the subject of several FBI dossiers, never again opposed Hoover. In 1943 he attended graduation ceremonies at the FBI NATIONAL ACADEMY and praised "this great instrument of law and order that has been built up by the grand man who is your director." McKellar retired from the Senate 10 years later and died at home, in Tennessee, in 1957.

**McREYNOLDS, James Clark**— Born at Elkton, Kentucky on 3 February 1862, James McReynolds was 51 years old when he took office as President WOODROW WILSON'S first attorney general, on 5 March 1913. The Bureau of Investigation withered under McReynolds, losing 213 of its 335 special agents and 10 of its 39 support personnel during his 17 months in office. The new attorney general's inactivity is further indicated by the fact that the FBI's official timeline lists no significant events during his term. McReynolds resigned in August 1914 (replaced by THOMAS GREGORY) and took a seat on the U.S. SUPREME COURT, where he served without particular distinction until 1941. He died in Washington, D.C. on 24 August 1946.

**McVEIGH, Timothy James**— At 9:02 a.m. on 19 April 1995 a truck loaded with 4,800 pounds of homemade explosives detonated outside the Alfred P. Murrah Federal Building in Oklahoma City. It demolished the edifice, killing at least 168 persons (some reports say 169) and injuring 850. After the WORLD TRADE CENTER BOMBING of 1993, public assumptions first blamed Islamic TERRORISTS for the blast. More than 1,000 agents from the FBI and the BUREAU OF ALCOHOL, TOBACCO AND FIREARMS were assigned to investigate the case, including explosive analysts flown into Oklahoma City from the FBI's LABORATORY DIVISION in Washington, D.C.

The crime scene investigation was curious in some respects, later described by some critics as fatally flawed. FBI explosives expert DAVID WILLIAMS reportedly ordered his search team to ignore small pieces of evidence, telling them, "If you can't see it at rake's length, it's not worth picking up." Hours later he called off the search completely, with the announcement: "We've got thousands of pieces, we don't need to pick up any more." FBI Agent Ed Kelso was "shocked" by the order (and later called Williams a "laughingstock" at the Washington lab), but he obeyed the command. Two other colleagues from the FBI Explosives Unit, Jim Lyons and Wallace Higgins, reportedly left the site in disgust over Williams's mishandling of evidence.

While the search was still ongoing, some 90 minutes after the blast, 26-year-old Timothy McVeigh was stopped by an Oklahoma state trooper in Noble County, 60 miles north of Oklahoma City. McVeigh's car had no license plate, and he was arrested when the officer noticed a pistol concealed under his shirt. McVeigh was jailed at Perry, Oklahoma pending criminal charges, but a check on his name through the FBI's national computer system showed no outstanding warrants.

Meanwhile, a serial number found on truck debris in Oklahoma City led G-men to a rental agency in Junction City, Kansas. The truck had been rented to "Robert Kling," whose name proved to be false. Agents obtained descriptions of Kling and a male companion. Scouring local motels, they found that Kling's description matched that of Timothy McVeigh, registered at a local establishment on the night of 14 April. When his name was checked a second time through Washington, the agents learned of his arrest in Noble County. McVeigh's "home address" on the motel registration led agents to a Michigan farm owned by James Nichols, whose brother Terry was a friend of McVeigh's from the Army. (Neither Nichols brother matched the description of "John Doe No. 2," who remains unidentified to this day.)

Timothy McVeigh was a native of Lockport, New York, born 22 April 1968. A combat veteran of the Gulf War, he had displayed racist attitudes in military service and had briefly joined the KU KLUX KLAN. Returning to civilian life, he had drifted into the paranoid world of the far-right MILITIA MOVEMENT, pouring over the fictional *Turner Diaries* (which inspired THE ORDER'S 1980s crime wave and described a truck-bombing of government buildings in Washington). He was obsessed with the government's role in the BRANCH DAVIDIAN siege of 1993, and the Oklahoma City bombing was timed to occur on the second anniversary of that standoff's fiery climax. Terry Nichols shared McVeigh's anti-government feelings. A search of his home revealed explosives, blasting caps, blue plastic barrels similar to those used in building the truck bomb, and a receipt for 2,000 pounds of ammonium nitrate (also used in making the bomb).

On 11 August 1995 a federal grand jury indicted both suspects for conspiracy and the murders of eight federal agents killed in the bombing. Massive publicity prompted Judge Richard Matsch to grant a change of venue in February 1996, moving the trial to Denver, Colorado. Eight months later, Matsch granted a motion that McVeigh and Nichols should be tried separately. Before those trials convened, however, the prosecution had to deal with serious problems at the FBI laboratory, where technician FREDERIC WHITEHURST had gone public with a series of complaints about negligent mishandling of evidence and deliberate skewing of test results to convict accused suspects. The JUSTICE DEPARTMENT'S Inspector General launched a full-scale investigation and corroborated most of Whitehurst's charges, but inspectors had to overcome a pattern of obstruction at the lab. Agent ROGER MARTZ, involved in the explosive analysis despite his lack of training in chemistry, told inspectors who questioned his methods that "[n]o protocol in the Chemistry/Toxicology Unit requires any examiner to perform a certain type of analysis." In fact, there *was* a protocol (withheld from inspectors by Martz) which detailed specific steps for the analysis of explosive residue. In respect to David Williams, the Inspector General found that he "tilted" evidence against defendants and based some findings on speculation rather than scientific analysis. Authors John Kelly and Phillip Wearne were more plainspoken in their book *Tainting Evidence* (1998), reporting that Williams's September 1995 report on the Oklahoma bombing "showed all the hallmarks of his tendency to work backward, draw unscientific conclusions, and overstate results, all in aid of the incrimination of the only suspects."

Opening arguments in McVeigh's trial began two days after his 29th birthday, on 24 April 1997. Prosecutors presented 137 witnesses and reviewed 7,000 pounds of physical evidence over 18 days. FBI lab technicians were excluded from the proceedings, to avoid further embarrassment, but some of the remaining witnesses were even worse. Michael and Lori Fortier, called as key witnesses for the government, were habitual drug users who had lied repeatedly to FBI agents after the bombing. In media interviews, they had denied any knowledge of the blast and proclaimed McVeigh innocent. Their story had only changed after Michael Fortier was charged with transporting stolen weapons and with failure to report the bomb plot in advance. A plea bargain on those counts (and a grant of full immunity for Lori) had turned the Fortiers into cooperative state witnesses. As Michael told his brother, recorded for posterity on an FBI WIRETAP, "I can tell a fable, I can tell stories all day long…. The less I say now, the bigger the price will be later."

McVeigh's battery of 14 court-appointed lawyers presented a more modest case, calling 25 witnesses in four days. Jurors convicted him of all counts on 2 June 1997 and recommended a death sentence on 13 June. Terry Nichols faced trial in Denver on 3 November 1997. Prosecutors were finally unable to place him at the crime scene, prompting a compromise verdict from the jury. Nichols was convicted of conspiracy and eight counts of involuntary manslaughter (reduced from murder), acquitted on charges of destruction by explosives and using a weapon of mass destruction. The jury deadlocked on penalty deliberations, and Judge Matsch settled the matter by imposing a life prison term. Oklahoma authorities announced their intent to try Nichols on capital murder charges, but no further prosecution has yet materialized.

Six days before McVeigh's scheduled execution, on 10 May 2001, FBI HEADQUARTERS announced that certain FILES on his case had been "inadvertently" withheld from defense attorneys. The dribble soon became a flood, with 4,500 documents retrieved from 46 Bureau field offices. Agent Danny Defenbaugh, lead investigator on the case, blamed the problem on "archaic" FBI computers, then admitted knowing of the "misplaced" documents for several months. The announcement was delayed, Defenbaugh said, because he "wanted to ascertain the magnitude of the problem." Attorney General JOHN ASHCROFT granted McVeigh a 30-day stay of execution, but the documents were soon deemed immaterial to his defense and McVeigh was executed by lethal injection on 11 June 2001.

Justice released another report by the Inspector General's office on 19 March 2002, this one concerning mishandling of documents in McVeigh's case. The report recommended disciplinary action against two FBI supervisors and reported the following errors:

• Nine Bureau field offices destroyed documents that should have been delivered to McVeigh's defense team.

• At least two field offices began destroying documents before permission was granted by records archive officials in late 2000.

• The FBI's Oklahoma City BOMBING task force lost various documents and pieces of physical evidence between 1995 and 2000.

• There was "confusion and differing interpretations" within the Bureau concerning which documents should be delivered to defense attorneys.

• FBI supervisors waited five months to alert Justice officials to the problem, then delayed two more days before informing the court and defense attorneys.

**MEANS, Gaston B.** — Little is known about the early life of Gaston Means, but his adult escapades were so notorious that it hardly matters. In 1923 the *New York Sun* summarized his achievements as follows:

> Means has been in the papers for a long time.... He was an agent of Germany (in 1916) paid to embarrass British commerce. In 1917 he was accused of the murder of a rich widow, Mrs. Maude A. King, who was killed by a pistol bullet while in North Carolina with ... Means. He was acquitted of the killing, only to be denounced in another court for filing a forged will which would have put the King estate practically at his disposal. Next we find this fellow an investigator in the Department of Justice....

Even that synopsis failed to cover all of Means's shady achievements. In the early years of WORLD WAR I he had actually been paid by Germany *and* England, each nation employing him to spy on the other. When not immersed in ESPIONAGE, Means liked to boast that he had been tried and acquitted for every crime known to man. He was appointed to the Bureau of Investigation by Director WILLIAM BURNS, a close friend who had used Means as a private detective in the past. Though officially paid only $7 per day, Means compiled a fortune as a G-man, including a lavish home and a chauffeur-driven Cadillac. As historian Francis Russell later described the situation: "At his disposal were badge, telephone, official stationery, an office, and the complete files of the Bureau of Investigation. That was all he needed."

Operating in the shadow of President WARREN HARDING'S corrupt "Ohio Gang," Means fixed federal cases, sold liquor licenses and pardons to PROHIBITION-era racketeers, and pursued various "special assignments of a confidential nature" for the Harding administration. Many of those "special" tasks involved blackmailing political opponents, as Means later explained to congressional investigators.

> There is a servant working in this house. If she is a colored servant, go and get a colored detective woman [to] take her out; have this colored detective to entertain her, find out the exact plan of the house, everything they discuss at the table, the family, write it down, make a report. And any information you find that is — report what you find ... and then if it is damaging, why of course it is used. If it is fine, why you cannot use it. It does no damage.

Means eventually grew too flamboyant for his own good, whereupon Attorney General HARRY DAUGHERTY suspended him from duty on 9 February 1922 "until further notice." Director Burns compensated for the embarrassment by hiring Means back as a Bureau INFORMANT, but that cut both ways. In October 1923 Means appeared as a key witness before a Senate committee investigating the TEAPOT DOME SCANDAL, led by Senators THOMAS WALSH and BURTON WHEELER. He described clandestine Bureau surveillance of the senators themselves, including an attempted FRAME-UP of Wheeler on corruption charges, but Means himself was soon bound for prison, drawing a two-year term for larceny and conspiracy in a jury-tampering case. Incredibly, Director Burns kept him on the payroll as a "temporarily suspended" agent, but J. EDGAR HOOVER corrected that error by firing Means once and for all in May 1924.

Hoover had not heard the last of Means, however. In 1930 the con man published a book, *The Strange Death of President Harding*, which became a surprise best-seller. Two years later he surfaced in the midst of the LINDBERGH KIDNAPPING case, to bilk newspaper heiress Evalyn McLean of a $100,000 "ransom" and $4,000 in "expenses." Informed of the swindle by McLean's attorney, G-men were present and listening when cronies of Means returned to ask McLean for another $35,000. (They also requested a peek at the famous Hope diamond, which McLean habitually carried in her purse.) Means was arrested for embezzlement on 5 May 1932 and was later sentenced to 15 years in prison. He survived six years in confinement, then died in 1938. His last $100,000 score was never recovered.

**MEDIA, Pennsylvania burglary** — On the night of 8 March 1971 a group of unknown burglars entered the FBI's two-man RESIDENT AGENCY in Media, Pennsylvania, on the second floor of the Delaware County Building. For reasons of economy, the office had no security alarms, and its tamper-proof filing cabinets were used to store weapons rather than papers. The prowlers fled with more than 1,000 documents related to the Bureau's work on "national security." Director J. EDGAR HOOVER was furious, initially ordering all 538 of the FBI's resident agencies closed, but Assistant Director JOHN MOHR persuaded him to close only 103 of the local offices, while beefing up security at the rest. Meanwhile, a massive effort was initiated to identify the thieves.

Two weeks later, a group calling itself the Citizens Committee to Investigate the FBI mailed photocopies of selected stolen documents to various legislators, journalists and individuals who had been targeted for FBI surveillance. Some of those who received the papers returned them to the Bureau, but others proved less accommodating. Attorney General JOHN MITCHELL threatened legal action to prevent publication of the documents, but the *Washington Post* and the *New York Times* forged ahead with front-page stories regardless.

More mailings followed at weekly intervals, treating G-men to a kind of Chinese water torture while they scoured the nation in vain for suspects. In each case, the recipients were carefully selected. African American congressman Parren Mitchell received Hoover's order for investigation of all black student unions in the U.S. The president of Swarthmore College learned that several of his trusted staff members were FBI INFORMANTS, while Rep. Henry Reuss discovered that his daughter was under surveillance at Swarthmore, apparently due to her father's "dovish" views on the VIETNAM WAR. Members of the BLACK PANTHER PARTY in Philadelphia received transcripts of an FBI WIRETAP on their telephones. The Boy Scouts of America found that G-men had investigated a scoutmaster who inquired about a possible field trip to Russia. Leaders of NEW LEFT groups were treated to details of the FBI's illegal COINTELPRO operations, designed to "harass, disrupt and neutralize" their organizations. Some of the documents were sinister, while others verged on hilarious—like the memo on hiring of clerks that read: "Please, when interviewing applicants, be alert for long hairs, beards, pear shaped heads, truck drivers, etc. We are not that hard up yet."

Assistant Director W. MARK FELT—himself later convicted of approving illegal BREAK-INS around New York City—described the Media burglary as "a watershed event" which "changed the FBI's image, possibly forever, in the minds of many Americans." It also prompted Hoover to officially cancel all ongoing COINTELPRO operations after 28 April 1971, although identical techniques would remain in use nationwide (and some agents would still use the COINTELPRO name in memos as late as 1973). The dribbling revelations were bad enough for FBI prestige; worse yet was the inability of G-men to apprehend the burglars. The "MEDBURG" case remains unsolved today, the night-prowling thieves still unidentified.

**MEESE, Edwin III**—Born on 2 December 1931, conservative attorney Edwin Meese III served as executive assistant to California governor RONALD REAGAN (1967-75) and later as White House chief of staff when Reagan was elected president in 1980. In that role, Meese recommended the appointment of JACKIE PRESSER—an eighth-grade dropout and Ohio leader of the TEAMSTERS' UNION under federal investigation for corruption—as a "senior economic adviser" to Reagan's transition team. Meese continued his friendly relationship with Presser over the next three years, but it rebounded to his disadvantage in January 1984, when Reagan named Meese as his choice to replace outgoing Attorney General WILLIAM SMITH.

Meese's confirmation was delayed for over a year by investigations of his Teamster connections, charges of political patronage, various interest-free loans and investments in a Nevada slot machine business. Finally confirmed in February 1985, Meese took office as attorney general on 25 March. Barely four months later, the JUSTICE DEPARTMENT abandoned its pending case against Jackie Presser in a move which prompted widespread criticism. Meese appeared on *Good Morning America* to deny any role in that decision and to say, "It's very clear [that] at no time was there any political influence or any undue influence." Others disagreed, and a January 1986 report from the President's Commission on ORGANIZED CRIME criticized the Reagan administration for its close ties to the Teamsters. Meese immediately called another press conference, declaring, "At no time have I, nor to my knowledge any member of the administration, done anything which was designed to assist or aid anyone involved with organized crime. The fact that people did meet with labor leaders was certainly not designed or intended to in any way interfere with the proper investigation of organized crime."

Meese's only contribution to the FBI was his 1987 recommendation of WILLIAM SESSIONS to replace Director WILLIAM WEBSTER. President Reagan accepted that choice and Sessions was confirmed, serving until his 1993 dismissal on charges of abusing his authority for personal gain. Attorney General Meese, meanwhile, resigned on 12 August 1988 and was replaced by RICHARD THORNBURGH.

**MEHEGAN, Albert D.**—A Hoosier native, born 2 May 1886 and raised at Lafayette, Indiana, Albert Mehegan received a bachelor's degree in mechanical engineering from Purdue University in 1909. After graduation he taught high school mathematics, held various positions in the railway industry, and spent WORLD WAR I as a member of the U.S. Shipping Board. Mehegan joined the FBI as a special agent on 20 March 1922 and served for 53 years, longer than any other G-man in the Bureau's history. His career encompassed work in at least seven states, including a role in the pursuit of 1930s "public enemies" JOHN DILLINGER and GEORGE ("BABY FACE") NELSON. He retired on 30 April 1975, after several years in an advisory capacity to younger, less experienced agents. Mehegan died on 31 January 1983, at age 96.

**MENCKEN, Henry Louis**—A Baltimore native, born on 12 September 1880, H.L. Mencken earned renown as an editor, essayist and satirical observer of the American scene. In the course of his career, Mencken was co-founder and co-editor of *Smart Set* magazine, editor-columnist for the Baltimore *Sun*, and founding co-editor of *American Mercury* magazine. He also published several books, including *The American Language*, long recognized as the standard survey of "American" English.

Mencken's German background made him an object of suspicion for some during both world wars, although the Bureau of Investigation managed to ignore him during WORLD WAR I. The first reference in his file is a letter from the U.S. SECRET SERVICE, dated 14 October 1922, referring to Mencken's "alleged interview" with former German Crown Prince Friederich Wilhelm, purportedly containing a suggestion that "Germany is planning still to regain the power she had prior to 1914, with sinister motives regarding America." (In fact, the "alleged interview" had been published four days earlier and was readily available for examination.) Twelve years later, in 1934, J. EDGAR HOOVER was so impressed with Mencken's *Liberty* magazine article on "What to

Do with Criminals" that he placed Mencken on the list of journalists favored with regular FBI press releases.

In 1941, shortly before the U.S. entered WORLD WAR II, an anxious correspondent (name withheld) wrote the White House to complain that Mencken was a "fifth columnist," urging the JUSTICE DEPARTMENT to "do something" about his writing. Hoover's reply, in the form of a letter stamped "Secret," noted that while Mencken "was deemed by some to be a suspicious person [during World War I] and information was received that he was of pro-German sympathies ... there was no indication according to the records of this bureau that Mencken was involved in espionage activities." Be that as it may, when 57 pages of Mencken's file were released under the FREEDOM OF INFORMATION ACT, some 30 years after his death in January 1956, various documents were still withheld in the "interest of national defense or foreign policy."

**"MIBURN"** — In 1964 a coalition of CIVIL RIGHTS groups targeted Mississippi for a "Freedom Summer" project intended to register black voters and thereby overturn the state's longstanding policy of white supremacy. One of the early volunteers was Michael Schwerner, a bearded New York Jew whom members of the Mississippi KU KLUX KLAN nicknamed "Goatee." Operating from a small office in Meridian, Schwerner and his wife enlisted local blacks to register new voters, coaching applicants in preparation for their state-mandated "literacy" tests (which frequently included such bizarre questions as "How many bubbles are there in a bar of soap?"). Klan leader Samuel Bowers hatched a plot to kill Schwerner, enlisting a group of Klansmen that included Neshoba County deputy sheriff Cecil Price.

On 16 June 1964, while Schwerner attended a training seminar in Ohio, Klan members assaulted black parishioners of the Mt. Zion Methodist Church outside Philadelphia, Mississippi and burned the church. Schwerner learned of the attack on his return and visited the site on 21 June, with colleagues Andrew Goodman (from New York) and James Chaney (a Meridian native). Deputy Price arrested the trio on a spurious traffic charge, then released them after nightfall. Moments later, Price stopped their car a second time and delivered the young men to a Klan lynching party. All three were killed and buried on a farm owned by Klansman Olen Burrage.

The crime was unusual only because two of its victims were white. With national attention focused on Mississippi, President LYNDON JOHNSON ordered FBI Director J. EDGAR HOOVER to launch an investigation that was code-named "MIBURN" (for *Mississippi burning*"). That operation, in turn, sparked a nationwide COINTELPRO campaign of FBI harassment against various Klan factions and affiliated organizations such as the American Nazi Party. Intimidation and bribery of Mississippi Klansmen led agents to the victims' corpses on 4 August 1964, but another four months passed before 21 Klansmen were jailed for complicity in the murders. Those arrested included three lawmen (Deputy Price among them) and a Baptist minister. Two of the suspects confessed, naming their accomplices, but U.S. Commissioner Esther Carter nonetheless dismissed all charges on 10 December 1964.

G-men rearrested 16 of the original Klansmen plus a new suspect (another policeman) on 16 January 1965, but federal judge Harold Cox dismissed all felony charges on 25 February, ruling that the defendants could only be charged with a misdemeanor count of conspiracy. New charges were filed by the JUSTICE DEPARTMENT in June 1965, but Judge Cox — who once described black voters as "chimpanzees" — dismissed the case three months later, ironically on ground that the grand jury had excluded minorities. A new grand jury indicted 18 Klansmen on civil rights charges in February 1967, with the new list of defendants including Sam Bowers and yet another sheriff. Six of those charged, including Bowers and Deputy Price, were convicted at trial in October 1967. Their appeal was rejected in July 1969 and the U.S. SUPREME COURT declined to review the case in February 1970, whereupon the convicted defendants finally began serving their prison terms.

**"MILAN, Michael"** — It is always difficult to assess the declarations of an author, writing under a pseudonym, who describes "secret" events without supporting evidence of any kind. Such is the case with "Michael Milan," a self-described Hollywood stunt man, boxer, and fringe associate of ORGANIZED CRIME in New York City, whose 1989 autobiography (*The Squad*) describes the activities of an "FBI execution squad" allegedly active from 1947 to 1971. According to Milan, J. EDGAR HOOVER created the team after deciding "that the courts of the United States did not properly administer justice the way he thought they should." Recruiting a mixed bag of policemen, Mafia hit men and former agents of the OFFICE OF STRATEGIC SERVICES (OSS), Hoover allegedly dispensed summary justice for a quarter-century without being caught in the act.

Nothing in Hoover's history or personality rules out such a notion, but Milan's account contains certain errors, inconsistencies and improbable anecdotes that make his work sound more like lurid fiction than fact. He has trouble remembering his own birth date (it shifts from 1924 to 1925 within 35 pages), but that is the least of Milan's problems. Sent to infiltrate the Georgia KU KLUX KLAN in 1953, he observes that Rev. MARTIN LUTHER KING, JR., "was organizing black congregations in Mobile" — two full years before King became active in *Montgomery*, Alabama — and he then reports a series of "front-page" Klan incidents never reported in the press. Next, Milan has gangster Benny Siegel murdered "a few years" after the Georgia assignment, when he was actually killed in June 1947. Sent to Dallas after the JFK ASSASSINATION, Milan identifies the sniper as a taxi driver, one Gerard Brinkman, and executes him in a junkyard. (Back in Washington, Hoover tells Milan that the mastermind of the assassination was "[LYNDON] JOHNSON. No doubt. We stand away.")

Hoover's behavior strains credibility even further in Milan's account of early 1970s events. After the KENT STATE SHOOTINGS left four college students dead in May 1970, Hoover telephoned the White House to report that "the students invited and got what they deserved." In Milan's version, though, Hoover "hit the ceiling" when he learned of the shootings, convinced that "either the National guard had been infiltrated by fifth columnists who were out to incite students by shooting them down and then giving them weapons to fight back with, or by Nazis who were inciting college students just to create enough chaos to influence elections." Milan allegedly determined that live ammunition was issued to Ohio Guardsmen by an incompetent commander. Hoover refuses to take action, leaving Milan to plot the unsanctioned murder of "General Smith" on his own.

Milan's last case for The Squad allegedly involved Hoover's plot to assassinate antiwar clergymen DANIEL and PHILIP BERRIGAN. Milan trails his targets to a small parish church in Pennsylvania and catches the brothers in rapt conversation, oblivious to the stranger watching them with gun in hand. "I could have killed them right there," Milan writes, but he opts to abort the assignment. "Whatever they were," he concludes, "they certainly were no threat." Later, Milan persuades Hoover to prosecute the Berrigans instead of simply killing them. Their indictment in January 1971 convinced Milan that "the Old Man had listened to me."

Perhaps, but on balance *The Squad* reads more like sensational fiction than fact. Without resolution of its many errors or evidence to support its sensational charges, it must be taken with a hefty grain of salt. Hoover's abuses of power were sufficiently plentiful and egregious that they require no embellishment from the Twilight Zone.

**MILITIA Movement**— Far-right extremists in the U.S. have long been obsessed with military weapons, uniforms, and the trappings of guerrilla warfare. Factions of the KU KLUX KLAN have maintained paramilitary "security" squads for decades, and the MINUTEMEN organization (1959-73) prepared itself to defend America against invasion by Russian, Chinese or United Nations troops. In 1983 a militant neo-Nazi group, THE ORDER, declared war against the "Zionist Occupation Government" in Washington, D.C. Still, such groups were small and widely scattered until the 1990s, when self-styled patriots received a "wake-up call" from the FBI.

Two incidents that sparked the latter-day militia movement were the RANDALL WEAVER siege of August 1992, in Idaho, and the tragic 51-day standoff between G-men and members of the BRANCH DAVIDIAN religious sect at Waco, Texas in 1993. In the wake of those encounters, right-wing groups across the country organized as "militias" with no official standing, stockpiling weapons and training for the day when they would do battle against the menace of a totalitarian "New World Order." At its peak in 1997, the movement included 858 "patriot" groups nationwide, declining to 194 by the end of 2000. A review of criminal activity by militia-type groups or individuals during that period includes:

*4 August 1994*— Two members of the Minnesota Patriots Council were jailed for manufacturing the deadly toxin ricin. In March 1995 four MPC members were convicted of conspiracy to poison law enforcement officers.

*14 November 1994*— After testifying in favor of an environmental ordinance at Everett, Washington, a member of the Audubon Society was threatened with LYNCHING by local militiamen.

*19 April 1995*— A truck bomb demolished the Oklahoma

City federal building, killing 168 persons. Militia associates TIMOTHY MCVEIGH and Terry Nichols were later convicted of the crime.

*25 March 1996*— The MONTANA FREEMEN organization began an 81-day standoff with FBI agents after its leaders were arrested for a multimillion-dollar fraud.

*27 July 1996*— A bomb planted by militia activist ERIC RUDOLPH killed two persons and injured more than 100 others at the Atlanta Olympic Games. (G-men initially blamed an innocent security guard, RICHARD JEWELL, for the crime.)

*29 July 1996*— Eight members of the Washington State Militia were jailed for building illegal bombs. All were convicted on weapons charges but a mistrial was declared on additional conspiracy charges.

*11 October 1996*— Seven members of the Mountaineer Militia were arrested for conspiring to bomb the FBI's national fingerprint records center in West Virginia. Leader Floyd Looker received an 18-year prison term, while three of his disciples were sentenced to shorter periods of confinement. (Looker claimed the FBI center was actually an intelligence center for the "New World Order.")

*26 March 1997*— Militia activist Brendon Blasz was arrested for constructing bombs and plotting to destroy various public buildings in Michigan. He received a three-year sentence after turning state's evidence against accomplices.

*23 April 1997*— Florida police jailed Todd Vanbiber, a member of the League of the Silent Soldier, after he was wounded by a homemade bomb. Vanbiber later received a six-year sentence after colleagues described his role in three politically motivated BANK ROBBERIES.

*29 January 1998*— Eric Rudolph bombed a Birmingham abortion clinic, killing an off-duty policeman and critically wounding a nurse.

*18 March 1998*— Three members of the North American Militia were jailed in Michigan on firearms charges after plotting to kill federal agents and bomb various public buildings around Kalamazoo.

*4 December 1999*— Two militia members were arrested in Sacramento, California for plotting to bomb giant propane tanks and blame the crime on blacks, in an effort to start a "race war." One suspect was also linked to an abortive 1998 jailbreak plot involving the Montana Freemen.

*12 March 2001*— Gerald Payne, mastermind of a militia-influenced swindle called Greater Ministries International, was convicted by a federal court in Florida of operating a pyramid scheme that bilked $448 million from thousands of investors.

**MILLAY, Edna St. Vincent**— Born at Rockland, Maine on 22 February 1892, Edna St. Vincent Millay tapped her creative impulse at an early age, serving as editor of her school's literary magazine (1905-09) and publishing verse poems in similar venues (1906-10) before her first poem saw widespread release in 1912. She released her first collection of poems in 1917, the same year she graduated from Vassar, and won a Pulitzer Prize for her work five years later.

Bureau agents noticed Millay for the first time in 1923, when her name appeared among those entering a "Free Trip to Russia" contest sponsored by the Friends of Soviet Russia. The group sought to raise $40,000 toward purchase of tractors for impoverished Russian farmers, and the link was enough to brand Millay as "Red" in the eyes of most G-men. Curiously, no further reports were filed for a decade, as Bureau spies completely missed Millay's involvement with the defense of condemned radicals NICOLA SACCO and BARTOLOMEO VANZETTI. In the 1930s, agents noted ominously that "Miss Millay used the analogy of the mole boring under the garden" in her exposition of the alien menace. Their suspicion was compounded in 1941, when she joined the War Writers Board, its membership list a veritable *Who's Who* of authors under FBI surveillance. That same year, a friend sent Director J. EDGAR HOOVER a recording of actor Ronald Coleman reading Millay's "Poem and Prayer for an Invading Army." Hoover replied to his friend that "I will count it among my treasures," then sent the record to the FBI LABORATORY for analysis.

Millay suffered a nervous breakdown in 1944 and died on 10 October 1950. Portions of her 94-page dossier were later released to author Natalie Robins under the FREEDOM OF INFORMATION ACT, documenting the Bureau's conviction that she was a leftist "subversive."

**MILLER, Arthur Aster**— Born in New York City on 17 October 1915, Arthur Miller entered the University of Michigan as a journalism major in 1934, but switched to English two years later, after his first play won the Hopwood Award for drama. He graduated in 1938 and continued writing to critical raves, though his first commercially successful play (*All My Sons*) was not produced until 1947. Two years later, Miller won the Pulitzer Prize for his masterpiece, *Death of a Salesman.*

FBI agents began tracking Miller the year he graduated from college, noting his sponsorship of the American Relief Ship for Spain, his membership in the American Youth Congress, and his signature on a telegram sent by the League of American Writers. In 1939 the Bureau filed (and answered) a letter Miller wrote to President FRANKLIN ROOSEVELT, protesting America's failure to aid Loyalist forces in the Spanish Civil War. Exempted from the draft in WORLD WAR II by knee and wrist injuries, Miller remained under FBI scrutiny for his involvement with the American Labor Party, described by one INFORMANT as having "found Communism in the sifting search for a philosophy of life."

When *All My Sons* premiered in 1947, featuring a manufacturer who sells defective engines to the Air Force, G-men denounced the play as "party line propaganda." Two years later, while the FBI could find no "overt Communist propaganda" in *Death of a Salesman*, Bureau critics still condemned the play as "a negative delineation of American life.... [It] strikes a shrewd blow against [American] values." Around the same time, leaders of the Catholic War Veterans reported their collection of "a detailed file" on Miller's subversive activities, including attendance at a Bill of Rights conference where attendees "would bluntly speak up against the police state methods of certain Army and FBI officials." The same year found G-men reporting archly that Miller's new cottage in Connecticut was not merely a summer home, but was "sufficient for all year round living."

In 1950, professional ex-Red LOUIS BUDENZ told the HOUSE COMMITTEE ON UN-AMERICAN ACTIVITIES (HUAC) that Miller was a "concealed Communist." Three years later, when his play *The Crucible* premiered in Brussels and Miller was invited to attend, RUTH SHIPLEY of the State Department's Passport Office reviewed Miller's FBI file and refused to renew his passport, on grounds that his travel abroad was "not in the national interest." By 1954, AMERICAN LEGION spokesmen were pressuring J. EDGAR HOOVER to take action on Miller's "red ties." Hoover continued the surveillance, but decided against questioning Miller directly. The 1955 report on that decision calls Miller "one of America's greatest writers," while alleging that "he was a member of the CP [COMMUNIST PARTY] in 1946 and 1947."

HUAC spokesmen contacted the Bureau in May 1956, stating that "the committee knows [Miller] was a member of the party in 1943 but is unable to find a live witness that can put him in the Party." Asked to produce a "photostat of Miller's Communist Party card," Associate Director CLYDE TOLSON was unable to comply, since no such document existed. Embarrassed, Hoover replied with a letter falsely stating that "due to a new department ruling," the Bureau could not supply the information requested. Miller appeared before HUAC on 14 June 1956 but refused to name others who attended leftist meetings with him in the 1940s. Cited for contempt of Congress a month later, he was convicted in 1957, but a federal appeals court reversed the conviction in 1958.

The year 1956 also witnessed Miller's marriage to actress MARILYN MONROE, herself a subject of FBI scrutiny (though for different reasons) prior to their divorce in 1962. G-men continued stalking Miller after his HUAC conviction was thrown out. In 1960 they reported that Miller and WILLIAM FAULKNER had been "honored by Polish critics, and that a Soviet journal had praised Miller's play *A View from the Bridge*, calling it "one of the greatest anti-American plays ever written in America in recent years." Such overseas reviews, the Bureau felt, placed Miller in "first place" among friends of the USSR. Two years later, agents panned the TV dramatization of Miller's novel *Focus* as "strictly Communist propaganda," striving to "foster race hatred between Jews and Gentiles."

As the 1960s waned, G-men recorded Miller's opposition to the VIETNAM WAR, including attendance at an anti-war rally on the campus of his alma mater, where he shared the dais with author JOHN HERSEY. Two years later, Miller joined NORMAN MAILER, JESSICA MITFORD and other writers in further protest of the ongoing conflict. The last entry in his 654-page dossier concerns an anti-war rally in New York City, where Miller appeared as a featured speaker.

**MILLER, Edward Samuel**—A Pennsylvania native, born near Pittsburgh on 11 November 1923, Edward Miller joined the FBI on 27 November 1950, spending the next 11 years at field offices in Los Angeles and San Francisco. In March 1962 he was transferred to FBI HEADQUARTERS, serving in various divisions until February 1966, when he was named assistant agent-in-charge of the Mobile, Alabama field office. Between December 1966 and November 1969 Miller held the same post in Honolulu and

Chicago, then he returned to headquarters as deputy assistant director of the Inspection Division. From September 1971 to October 1973 he served as assistant director in charge of the Domestic Intelligence division, then he was promoted to deputy associate director, the position he held until retiring in 1974.

It was during his stint with Domestic Intelligence that Miller ordered a series of illegal BREAK-INS to install BUGGING devices in the homes of certain individuals whose friends or relatives were members of the radical WEATHER UNDERGROUND organization. Records of the burglaries and bugging were supposed to be destroyed at six-month intervals, by order of FBI Director J. EDGAR HOOVER, but 25 volumes of documents describing the FBI's crimes were found in a safe at the New York City field office in March 1976. Agent John Kearney was indicted for some of the break-ins on 7 April 1977, but the JUSTICE DEPARTMENT dropped those charges a year later, indicting Miller, former Assistant Director W. MARK FELT and former Acting Director L. PATRICK GRAY on 10 April 1978. Miller and Felt were convicted of CIVIL RIGHTS violations on 6 November 1980, while Gray's case was severed from theirs and subsequently dropped. The court fined Miller and Felt, but they were pardoned by President RONALD REAGAN (himself a former FBI INFORMANT who had promised to "unleash" the Bureau if elected to the White House) on 26 March 1981.

**MILLER, Henry**— A native New Yorker, born on 26 December 1891, Henry Miller titillated and scandalized America with his sexually explicit prose in novels such as *Tropic of Cancer* and *Tropic of Capricorn*. The FBI opened a file on Miller in 1945, after columnist WALTER WINCHELL sent J. EDGAR HOOVER a warning on Miller's alleged "collaboration" with Nazi Germany. The tale came from an unnamed INFORMANT, who allegedly observed Miller at Dartmouth College, remarking to a group of students that "the Nazis were just the same sort of people as the Americans and they were fighting for the same thing." G-men found nothing to support the claim, but they nonetheless dubbed Miller "a phoney [*sic*] writer," noting that he "has a following among pseudointellectuals in this country." No mention is made in his file of the controversy over his "obscene" novels. The worst agents could finally say about Miller was that he "is considered somewhat of a pacifist as is the case with practically all of the true artists." Miller died at his home in Pacific Palisades, California, on 7 June 1980.

**MILLER, Richard W.**— Richard Miller barely made it through training at the FBI ACADEMY in 1964, emerging as a mediocre agent of slovenly habits, seemingly incapable of submitting proper reports on deadline. Still, he lasted 20 years with the Bureau and was assigned to a foreign counterintelligence team at the San Francisco field office in 1984, when he finally distinguished himself as the first G-man ever arrested for ESPIONAGE.

Fellow agents discovered Miller's illicit activity while they were investigating Russian émigrés Nikolai and Svetlana Ogorodnikov, both of whom worked for the KGB. In the course of their surveillance on the couple, G-men discovered that Richard Miller was having an affair with Svetlana, including occasions when she

performed oral sex on him in Miller's car. Recruited as a Russian spy in August 1984, Miller had delivered a classified FBI manual to the Ogorodnikovs, then demanded $15,000 in cash and $50,000 in gold. They refused to meet his price, but by that time it hardly mattered. After failing a polygraph test, Miller admitted his crime. He was fired and then arrested on 3 October 1984, the sequence of events allowing FBI HEADQUARTERS to report that a "former agent" had been jailed for espionage.

On 26 June 1985 the Ogorodnikovs pled guilty on charges of conspiracy to receive stolen FBI documents. Both agreed to testify against Miller, but convicting the traitorous G-man was not a simple task. His first trial ended in a hung jury, in November 1985, after Miller claimed his dealings with Svetlana were part of a clumsy attempt on his part to infiltrate the KGB. He was convicted of espionage and conspiracy in a second trial, on 19 June 1986, and received two concurrent life sentences. An appeals court quashed that verdict on 25 April 1989, finding that the trial judge had erred by admitting evidence of Miller's failed polygraph test. A third jury convicted Miller on six counts of espionage in October 1990 and he received a 20-year sentence. That judgment was affirmed on appeal, in January 1993.

**MINUTEMEN**— A forerunner of the 1990s MILITIA MOVEMENT, the paramilitary Minutemen organization was founded in 1959 by Missouri chemist Robert DePugh. Members stockpiled weapons in preparation for an expected invasion of the U.S. by Russian, Chinese or United Nations military forces. Many who joined the group were also members of the KU KLUX KLAN or other racist groups, promoting agendas that were not restricted to simple anti-communism. (Dennis Mower, second in command of the California Minutemen, was a close friend of KKK "Wizard" Samuel Bowers, arrested by G-men for multiple murder in the 1964 "MIBURN" case.)

Despite the group's extremist philosophy, racist ties and history of collecting illegal weapons, FBI agents were slow to investigate the Minutemen. In fact, as of early 1967 it appeared that FBI HEADQUARTERS knew nothing about the Minutemen beyond what was published in national newspapers. Writing for the *Washington Post* on 18 November 1964, journalist J. Harry Jones reported:

> DePugh shrugs off the responsibility of trying to prove that all he says of the Minutemen, their activities or their size is true.... DePugh has never offered any real evidence that the Minutemen are anything more than essentially a paper organization with just enough followers over the country so that they can occasionally snag a headline somewhere, usually because of their preoccupation with weapons of war.

Six months later, on 19 May 1965, FBI Director J. EDGAR HOOVER told the House Appropriations Committee, "We have long been aware of the Minutemen organization and our investigation is continuing." Unfortunately, his "awareness" was limited to plagiarism of Jones's article from the *Post*. Quoting nearly verbatim, Hoover told Congress:

> DePugh ... avoids the responsibility of trying to prove that all he says of the Minutemen, their activities or their size is true....

There is little real evidence that the Minutemen are [*sic*] anything more than essentially a paper organization with just enough followers over the country so that they can occasionally attract a headline, usually because of their preoccupation with violence, or weapons of war.

Hoover used identical language to describe the Minutemen in another congressional address, on 10 February 1966. By February 1967 he had dropped the "paper organization" phrase, stating that the group had 500 active members. A year later, in February 1968, he reduced that estimate to "less than 50 persons upon whom Minutemen leaders can call for overt action." By that time, DePugh was a fugitive from federal charges in Seattle, where he and other Minutemen had plotted to bomb a police station and rob four banks. Captured in July 1969, DePugh received an 11-year sentence and was paroled in May 1973, declaring that prison had taught him "a little humility." While DePugh was imprisoned, G-men recruited some of his California veterans for an FBI-sponsored TERRORIST group, the SECRET ARMY ORGANIZATION, linked to BOMBINGS and attempted murders around San Diego.

MIRELES, Edmundo, Jr.— A Texas native, Edmundo Mireles joined the FBI in 1979, soon after earning a bachelor's degree in business administration from the University of Maryland. He served first in the Washington, D.C. field office, then was transferred to Miami in 1985. There, on 11 April 1986, he joined other agents in pursuit of fugitives WILLIAM MATIX and MICHAEL PLATT, wanted in connection to a series of murders and violent armed robberies around Miami. The chase turned into a bloody firefight when Matix and Platt were cornered on a dead-end street, their gunfire killing two G-men and wounding five others. Agent Mireles, with one arm disabled by gunshots, still managed to kill both gunmen in a fierce exchange of fire. As a result of his actions, Mireles received the FBI's first Medal of Valor and was named Police Officer of the Year by the INTERNATIONAL ASSOCIATION OF CHIEFS OF POLICE. While recuperating from his wounds, Mireles served as an instructor at the FBI ACADEMY, then briefly returned to Miami before he was transferred to the Omaha field office.

MISKO, Joanne E. Pierce— With SUSAN ROLEY, Joanne Misko was one of the first WOMAN FBI AGENTS appointed following the death of Director J. EDGAR HOOVER. A native of Niagara Falls, New York, Misko earned a bachelor's degree in history from Medaille College (at Buffalo) and a master's in history from St. Bonaventure University (also in New York). She spent 11 years as a Catholic nun in Buffalo, teaching history and economics at various parochial high schools. Misko joined the Bureau as a researcher on 23 March 1970, working at the FBI ACADEMY until she became an agent on 17 July 1972. One of her first assignments involved a posting to the PINE RIDGE INDIAN RESERVATION in South Dakota, scene of the 1975 shootout that sent AMERICAN INDIAN MOVEMENT activist LEONARD PELTIER to prison for the murders of two G-men. Misko later served in the Philadelphia, St. Louis and Washington, D.C. field offices, eventually becoming one of the Bureau's first female supervisors at FBI HEADQUARTERS. Near the end of her career, Misko transferred to the Miami field office with her husband (also an FBI agent). She retired in September 1994 to work as a bank security supervisor in Boca Raton, Florida.

MITCHELL, John Newton— Born 15 September 1913, John Mitchell served in the U.S. Navy during WORLD WAR II, then practiced law in New York. He met RICHARD NIXON there in 1963 and they became partners. When Nixon was elected president in 1968, he chose Mitchell as attorney general (taking office on 21 January 1969). Observers recall Mitchell as Nixon's primary confidant, described in one account as "the uniquely intimate counselor to whom Nixon turned on every subject from minor political matters to Supreme Court appointments."

Mitchell also appeared to enjoy a close relationship with FBI Director J. EDGAR HOOVER. Both men shared Nixon's view of "subversives" and political "enemies," prompting Mitchell to approve many illegal WIRE-TAPS and BREAK-INS directed at a wide range of targets including White House aides, reporters, Democrats, black militants and members of various "NEW LEFT" organizations. Mitchell was fond of mass "conspiracy" indictments as a means of silencing VIETNAM WAR PROTESTS, and he made no effort to restrain Hoover's illegal COINTELPRO campaigns. On one occasion, when a female reporter asked Hoover if he had any plans for retirement, Mitchell warned her, "You're so far off base I'm going to belt you one." When Rep. HALE BOGGS accused Hoover of tapping his phones, Mitchell "categorically" denied that G-men had ever WIRETAPPED members of Congress, "now or in the past," further demanding that Boggs retract his "slanderous falsehoods" and "apologize to a great American." Hoover, for his part, described Mitchell as "a very able man, a very down-to-earth individual."

Mitchell resigned as attorney general on 1 March 1972, replaced by RICHARD KLEINDIENST, to head Nixon's Committee to Re-Elect the President (CREEP). He hired G. GORDON LIDDY to coordinate CREEP's "dirty tricks," including a series of burglaries and other criminal activities that precipitated the WATERGATE SCANDAL. On 10 May 1973 Mitchell and others were indicted by a federal grand jury for conspiracy, obstructing justice and lying under oath in their efforts to conceal Nixon's illegal actions. Mitchell was convicted in 1974, with former White House aides JOHN EHRLICHMAN and H.R. HALDEMAN, all of whom received prison terms of 20 months to five years. Mitchell finally served only 19 months and was acquitted in a second case, on charges of accepting a $250,000 bribe to protect stock swindler Robert Vesco. The publishing house of Simon and Schuster sued Mitchell in 1981, for failure to deliver a contracted Watergate memoir. Mitchell died in New York on 9 November 1988. Ex-president Nixon led the funeral procession for his friend and loyal accomplice.

MITCHELL, William DeWitt— Born on 9 September 1874, William Mitchell was 54 years old when he assumed the attorney general's office on 5 March 1929, under President HERBERT HOOVER. A "dry" Protestant who favored PROHIBITION, Mitchell curiously opposed expansion of federal authority into other areas of law enforcement traditionally left to the states. In 1932, opposing passage of the LINDBERGH Law that made interstate KID-NAPPING a federal offense, Mitchell told Congress, "You are never going to correct the crime situation in this country by having Washington jump in." FBI Director J. EDGAR HOOVER disagreed strenuously, pursuing ever greater jurisdiction (and publicity) for the Bureau. Mitchell left office with the inauguration of President FRANKLIN ROOSEVELT, on 3 March 1933, and left no visible mark on the JUSTICE DEPARTMENT. He died on 24 August 1955.

**MITFORD, Jessica ("Decca")** — An affluent British subject, a daughter of Lord Redesdale born in 1917, Mitford married Esmond Romilly (a nephew of Winston Churchill) in 1937 and left England for Miami, where they briefly ran a restaurant. FBI agents opened a file on Mitford two years later, as a suspected Nazi sympathizer, based on information that her sister Diana had married British fascist leader Oswald Mosley (true), while sister Unity was an "alleged girlfriend of HITLER" (absurdly false). In fact, as agents soon discovered, while Mitford's sisters were indeed pro-Nazi, Jessica herself leaned sharply toward the left. In 1942, after Romilly joined the Royal Canadian Air Force and was lost at sea, Mitford applied for a clerical post with the Office of Emergency Management in Washington. G-men ran a background check, reporting that she not only "talked fluently in favor of Communism," but that it was "rather difficult to become accustomed to her peculiar English mannerisms." On arrival in Washington, they claimed (again, falsely) that "Jessica was engaged as an entertainer."

Mitford moved to San Francisco in 1943, agents trailing along to report her involvement with the United Federal Workers Union and the Joint Anti-Fascist Refugee Committee. A year later, shortly after Mitford became a U.S. citizen, an unnamed INFORMANT reported her enlistment as a member of the COMMUNIST PARTY. New husband Robert Treuhaft was a party member and practicing lawyer, but FBI observers asserted that Mitford "enjoyed membership in the Communist Party because she liked to 'play games,' and that she viewed the party as an 'ornamental façade.'" That judgment notwithstanding, by 1945 Mitford was listed in the Bureau's illegal SECURITY INDEX, perhaps for her involvement with the Civil Rights Congress, contesting rape charges filed against black defendant Willie McGhee in Mississippi. J. EDGAR HOOVER debated the prospect of "canceling" her naturalization in 1948, but settled two years later for a warning that "Decca Treuhaft was one of the group of Communist Party members in Alameda County considered to be most dangerous to the national security of the United States." Agents reported that she had "entered a building where a regional CP meeting was being held" in December 1957, and claimed she was "reportedly disinherited by her father and cut off from his will."

Mitford resigned from the Communist Party in April 1958, but FBI agents remained on her trail, occasionally tapping her telephone in an effort to keep abreast of events. Mitford joined the integrationist FREEDOM RIDES in 1961, and two years later published her best-selling critique of the funeral industry, *The American Way of Death*. G-men lamented that the book "resulted in considerable publicity for her," and California congressman James Utt was even more outraged, calling it "pro-Communist, un-American, and another blow at the Christian religion." It was no surprise to FBI headquarters when Mitford joined in mass protests against the VIETNAM WAR, throughout 1967-69, or that she wrote articles criticizing government harassment of the BLACK PANTHER PARTY. The last entry to her 570-page dossier noted the publication of her latest book, *The Trial of Dr. Spock*. Mitford died in 1996, shortly after recounting her years of harassment to author Natalie Robins. In that interview she remarked, "They — the FBI — live in a dream world, don't they?"

**MITRIONE, Daniel A., Jr.** — Daniel Mitrione Sr. was an FBI NATIONAL ACADEMY graduate who worked for the CENTRAL INTELLIGENCE AGENCY in Uruguay, schooling police and military officers in torture techniques. As a result of that activity, he was kidnapped and executed by leftist Tupamaros guerrillas in August 1970. His son, Daniel, Jr., joined the FBI a few years later and was assigned to the Miami field office. There, in 1985, he became the first G-man convicted and sentenced to prison for trafficking in NARCOTICS.

Mitrione was regarded as a model FBI employee until his arrest, and former colleagues attribute his downfall to the pressures of an UNDERCOVER OPERATION involving cocaine smugglers. As reconstructed from court documents, Mitrione accepted a Rolex watch and other expensive gifts from one of his INFORMANTS, gradually coming to regard the drug smuggler as "the father he barely knew." Over time, Mitrione accepted cash and other rewards to permit distribution of cocaine in Florida, Pennsylvania and other states. When his informant finally suggested that they steal drugs from an incoming shipment and sell it themselves, with Mitrione earning $850,000 for his part in the plot, Mitrione agreed. On 14 March 1985 Mitrione pled guilty to possessing and distributing 92 pounds of cocaine, as well as taking bribes to ignore other shipments. He received a 10-year prison sentence, but obtained leniency by returning nearly $1 million in illegal assets and agreeing to testify against other conspirators in the case. Mitrione ultimately spent three years in a Catholic monastery normally reserved for discipline of wayward priests.

Others indicted in the same cocaine conspiracy included Florida ringleader Hilmer Sandini, Pennsylvania drug kingpin Eugene Gesuale, and several Latin American smugglers. One of the relative small-fry, Vincent Ciraollo of Deerfield Beach, Florida, was accused of trying to murder Sandini with a car bomb. Ciraollo countered with a claim that Agent Mitrione had planted the bomb in Sandini's car, while he (Ciraollo) later glimpsed its dangling wires and disarmed the device. No mention of that "rumor" was permitted at Ciraollo's trial, where he received a six-year sentence on drug charges. Years later, after his release from prison, Ciraollo obtained various FBI documents related to his case under the FREEDOM OF INFORMATION ACT. Included was an "Informative Note" from the Bureau's Criminal Investigative Division, written two days before Ciraollo's indictment, admitting that Mitrione planted the bomb and describing his act as an "attempted homicide." That document was illegally withheld from Ciraollo's defense counsel, JUSTICE DEPARTMENT spokesmen later claiming that Ciraollo's prosecutors never saw it either, since the note was sent directly from the Miami field office to FBI HEADQUARTERS. Whatever the truth of the matter, no charges were filed against Mitrione for the attempted murder.

**MOHR, John Philip**— A New Jersey native, born 28 April 1910 in West New York, John Mohr attended American University and obtained his law degree from Columbus Law School (both in Washington, D.C.) He joined the FBI on 2 October 1939 and enjoyed one of those meteoric careers reserved for aides hand-picked by Director J. EDGAR HOOVER. Mohr spent a mere 16 months at field offices in San Francisco and Los Angeles before he was recalled to FBI HEADQUARTERS in February 1941, to serve as a supervisor in the Administrative Division. In 1947 he was named assistant to Associate Director CLYDE TOLSON and remained in that post until 1 June 1954, when he was placed in charge of the Administrative Division. His last promotion, on 30 December 1959, made Mohr assistant to the director for Administration, granting him effective control over the FBI's budget.

That position gave Mohr a great deal of power (and opportunity for personal profit) within the Bureau. He mimicked Hoover by compiling secret files to protect himself—"a few goodies of my own," as he sometimes told friends — but his main strength came from holding the FBI's purse strings. In that capacity he arranged an exclusive contract with the U.S. Recording Company, run by personal friend Joseph Tait, to make Tait's firm the only authorized source of FBI electronic equipment. Unfortunately for taxpayers, the gear was marked up 40 to 70 percent on each sale, and rumors persist of kickbacks to FBI brass on the sweetheart deal.

In personal terms, Mohr again followed Hoover's corrupt example, using FBI agents and technicians to maintain his family's cars, remodel his home, install and repair electronic appliances, prepare a coat of arms, and indulge a personal craving for walnut furniture, including gun cases and a $2,000 wine rack. With NICHOLAS CALLAHAN, Mohr administered the FBI's various slush funds, including the SPECIAL AGENTS MUTUAL BENEFIT ASSOCIATION (SAMBA) and the FBI RECREATIONAL ASSOCIATION'S notorious "Library Fund." (Soon after Hoover's death in May 1972, Mohr and Callahan dissolved the fund and destroyed its financial records.)

Mohr was on borrowed time after Hoover's demise, but he did not leave the Bureau empty-handed when he retired on 17 July 1972. SAMBA threw him a going-away party and gave Mohr a small fishing boat — along with a new career as paid consultant for retirees. Stories flourished of Mohr helping himself to personal items from Hoover's home, but Mohr admitted taking only "several boxes of spoiled wine." Around the same time, in June 1972, he drafted a new will for Clyde Tolson and named himself executor of Tolson's estate. The will was redrafted two months later, including an executor's fee for Mohr, and various codicils were added over the next three years.

It was finally the Tolson will that exposed Mohr's chicanery. When Tolson died in April 1975, his brother Hillory challenged the will, claiming that "Tolson suffered physical and mental de-

bility" which made him "easy prey for the undue influence and coercion exhibited upon him by [Mohr] and those in concert with [Mohr].... As a result of [Tolson's] weakened condition, physically and mentally, [Mohr] and those in collaboration with him prevented others, including [Hillory Tolson] from seeing [Clyde Tolson], who became a virtual recluse." Depositions in the lawsuit revealed that Tolson's signature had been forged by long-time secretary Dorothy Skillman, acting on orders from Mohr and without consulting Tolson. A hasty conference avoided further litigation when Hillory Tolson was awarded $100,000 and other beneficiaries agreed to donate part of their bequests to charity. Thus, Mohr received $23,244 from Tolson's estate, rather than the original $26,000. Mohr died in Virginia on 25 January 1997.

**MOHR, Reinhold**— Two years after the KENT STATE SHOOTINGS, in April 1972, members of Vietnam Veterans Against the War (VVAW) warned police in Kent, Ohio that "there's a nut running around out there with a bunch of automatic weapons." In fact, a VVAW spokesman told authorities, the "nut" — supposed student radical Reinhold Mohr, had offered various illegal weapons for sale to the VVAW's Kent State chapter as a means of "furthering the armed struggle against imperialism." When police found Mohr, he had a rocket launcher and a submachine gun in his car, both weapons banned by state and federal law. In custody, Mohr identified himself as a covert member of the Kent State University police force, his credentials promptly endorsed by the chief of campus security. A further vote of confidence came from FBI agents, who told Kent police that Mohr had "only followed orders" in peddling illegal weapons to the VVAW. Mohr was thereafter released without charges to pursue his law enforcement career.

**MOLEY, Raymond Charles, Jr.**— An Ohio native, born in 1886, Raymond Moley spent a dozen years as a university professor in his home state and New York before serving as an economic advisor to New York Governor Alfred Smith in 1928. From there, he became a trusted advisor to future president FRANKLIN ROOSEVELT, emerging as a central figure of FDR's "Brain Trust" and winning appointment as assistant secretary of state in 1933. It was the latter post that enabled Moley, a strong admirer of J. EDGAR HOOVER, to save Hoover's job in the early days of the New Deal.

As Moley later recalled in his book *After Seven Years* (1939), there was "tremendous pressure on Roosevelt by various city politicians to replace Hoover with this or that police chief whom they believed would be more amenable to their patronage.... [Presidential advisor] Louis Howe threw his weight behind the demands of the bosses." Also "lurking around" Washington, Moley reported, were various ex-Bureau agents "who were anxious to see Hoover removed and thus open the way for their reinstatement. One of these was brought to me, and he complained about the iron discipline which Hoover maintained over his subordinates. This sort of argument to me was the best commendation Hoover could have had."

In July 1933, Roosevelt asked Moley to review the Bureau's performance to date and evaluate its ability to cope with future challenges. Moley later wrote that "part of what remained in Roosevelt's mind, I knew, was a doubt about the desirability of continuing J. Edgar Hoover in office—a doubt placed there by Louis [Howe].... When the administration had come into office in March, there were many rumors that Hoover was to be ousted from office in favor of a Democratic politician. I had vehemently defended the magnificent work of Hoover to the president.... I like to think that what I did in August 1933 gave me the opportunity to strengthen Hoover still more.... At least I secured a stay of execution, and the decision was passed over to [Attorney General HOMER] CUMMINGS. It was not long before Cummings realized that Hoover was indispensable, and Hoover was retained."

The same could not be said for Moley, though. He soon broke with FDR over the president's liberal New Deal policies and resigned to become a professional critic of the Roosevelt administration, first as editor of *Today* magazine (1933-37) and then as associate editor of *Newsweek*. Hoover appreciated both the defense of his job and Moley's defection from liberalism. Three decades later, when Moley published a glowing history of the AMERICAN LEGION, Hoover contributed a foreword filled with superlatives. Moley died nine years later, in 1975.

**MONROE, Marilyn**—Arguably the most famous movie actress of all time, Marilyn Monroe was a Los Angeles native, born Norma Jeane Mortensen on 1 June 1926. After spending two years in an orphanage (1935-37), she moved through a series of foster homes and married for the first time at age 16. She graced her first national magazine cover in April 1944 and signed a contract with Fox studios four months later, officially adopting her world-renowned screen name at the same time.

Monroe was as famous for the details of her personal life as for any work on stage or screen. Biographer Anthony Summers suggests a love affair with rising political star JOHN F. KENNEDY in the early 1950s, and any such liaison would have drawn attention from the FBI. Ex-agent G. GORDON LIDDY told Summers, years later, that "[t]he stuff on the [Kennedy] brothers and Monroe was very, very closely held" in Director J. EDGAR HOOVER'S personal FILES. Monroe certainly enjoyed a brief affair with Kennedy after the 1960 presidential election, reportedly meeting him more than once at the home of Kennedy brother-in-law Peter Lawford. Hoover, in turn, warned President Kennedy that Lawford's home "had very likely been bugged by the Mafia," but he neglected to mention that G-men were also BUGGING the actor's residence. JFK reportedly saw Monroe for the last time on 19 May 1962, in New York City.

The break-up did not signal an end to Monroe's links with the Kennedy clan, however. She soon proclaimed herself in love with the president's brother, Attorney General ROBERT KENNEDY, once claiming that Robert had promised to leave his wife and marry Monroe. Recounting other conversations with the high and mighty, Monroe told friends that the Kennedys wanted to replace Hoover with a new FBI director, but the move had been postponed until after JFK won reelection in 1964. Monroe's housekeeper afterward claimed that Robert Kennedy visited Monroe's home on 27 June 1962. Six weeks later, on 4 August 1962, the actress was found dead from an apparent prescription drug overdose, variously reported as accidental, suicide, or murder.

Controversy surrounding Monroe's death persists to the present day. Assistant FBI Director CARTHA DELOACH once claimed that a Kennedy telephone number was found at Monroe's bedside, then suppressed to spare the president from scandal. Columnist WALTER WINCHELL, a frequent recipient of classified FBI material, penned an article virtually accusing Robert Kennedy of Monroe's murder, while a half-brother of Chicago mobster SAM GIANCANA claimed that Giancana ordered Monroe's death in a bid to embarrass Robert Kennedy. The young attorney general, once committed to dethroning J. Edgar Hoover, told the press on 7 August 1962, "I hope Hoover will continue to serve the country for many, many years to come." Ten days later, two men flashing FBI badges visited the New York offices of Globe Photos, confiscating Globe's thick file on Monroe "for the presidential library." To date, only 80 heavily censored pages of the Bureau's dossier on Marilyn Monroe have been released under the FREEDOM OF INFORMATION ACT.

**MONSERRATE, Frank and Suzanne**—A husband-wife team of FBI agents assigned to the Miami field office, Frank and Suzanne Monserrate had outstanding service records prior to the night of 3 January 1987. On that date, while leaving the Playhouse, a club in suburban Perrine, they were accosted by habitual felon Chester Williams, who brandished a weapon and demanded cash. Gunfire ensued, leaving Williams dead and Suzanne Monserrate wounded. FBI investigators soon discovered that the Playhouse was a "swingers" club, with facilities including an adult movie theater, an Orgy Room, an Oral Room, and a Mattress Room with wall-to-wall beds.

The Monserrates initially claimed that 3 January marked their first visit to the Playhouse, but under persistent questioning they admitted a two-year membership ostensibly designed to enhance their marriage. The couple first claimed only a voyeuristic interest in the club, then admitted having intercourse in a private cubicle but denied swapping partners with other club members. Finally, as revealed in an FBI memo, Frank Monserrate "disclosed that he and his wife did, in fact, fully participate in sexual activities at [the club], to include swapping spouses." Another statement from Frank, on 18 January, acknowledged spouse-swapping parties at another couple's home. Suzanne, meanwhile, belatedly confessed that she and her husband "engaged in sexual intercourse with other people" at the Playhouse, adding that she "also participated in oral sex and engaged in sexual activity with other females at the club." Acting Director JOHN OTTO fired the couple in July 1987, rejecting their defense that the club's activities were legal and violated no FBI regulations. "It was more than going to a sex club," Otto said. "There was lack of candor. There were a variety of other things that were tied up in that. There was no justification for the whole conduct situation from beginning to end."

The Monserrates appealed their dismissals to the Equal Employment Opportunity Commission, claiming that Suzanne was fired because of her gender, while Frank was dismissed for being Hispanic. FBI HEADQUARTERS was stunned when the EEOC ordered both agents reinstated in 1992. The Monserrates returned to the FBI ACADEMY, pending assignment to a new field office. Disgusted by the ruling, one Bureau administrator told journalist Robert Kessler, "If we can't fire agents for lying as they did, we might as well forget about discipline in the Bureau."

**MONTANA Freemen**—A spin-off from the far-right MILITIA MOVEMENT, this political fringe group was organized in 1994 by aging con man Leroy Schweitzer, with headquarters at Jordan, Montana (population 450). Aside from the paranoia common to militia groups nationwide, the "Freemen" argued that the Preamble to the U.S. Constitution excludes "the colored races and Jews" from full citizenship. The group first made headlines in 1994, when armed members briefly occupied the Garfield County courthouse for a "common law" meeting. Authorities failed to punish that crime, and the group soon expanded its activities to include issuance of arrest and death warrants for various local, state and federal officials. At the same time, Schweitzer ran a prolific mail-order business, charging correspondents $100 each to learn the fine points of patriotic fraud.

In essence, the scam involved creation of fake financial instruments, allegedly supported by "common-law liens" against government officials and property. Schweitzer had pocketed "tuition" from at least 800 gullible disciples by late 1995, when a federal grand jury indicted various Freemen on 51 counts of fraud and threatening public officials. Remembering hard lessons from the RANDAL WEAVER and BRANCH DAVIDIAN sieges, G-men set up a sting operation in lieu of a frontal assault on the Freemen's ranch outside Jordan. Schweitzer and cohort Daniel Peterson were thus arrested on 26 March 1996, but other Freemen barricaded themselves at the ranch and refused to surrender. With 100 FBI agents surrounding the compound at a distance, the standoff lasted for 81 days until the last holdouts surrendered on 13 June 1996.

At trial, Schweitzer's patriots refused to recognize the court's jurisdiction, but it made no difference to the final outcome. In July 1998 Schweitzer, Petersen and a third defendant were convicted of threatening Montana's chief justice; six other Freemen were convicted of defrauding banks and sundry businesses of nearly $2 million. Schweitzer received a 22-year prison term, while the others drew lesser terms. Except among militia groups, the FBI was praised for its restrained handling of the siege.

**MOORE, Harry**—Harry Moore was newly employed as a schoolteacher in Brevard County, Florida, when he founded a chapter of the NATIONAL ASSOCIATION FOR THE ADVANCEMENT OF COLORED PEOPLE (NAACP) in 1934. Threats and violence by the KU KLUX KLAN failed to deter him from pursuing registration of black voters in the county and statewide. In 1945 he organized the Progressive Voters' League to press the campaign despite stiff white resistance. That move cost Moore and his wife their teaching jobs, but still they persevered. Finally, at Christmas 1951, a bomb demolished Moore's home, killing him instantly and mortally wounding his wife.

Florida governor Fuller Warren (a former Klan member) assigned a policeman with Klan ties to head the state's investiga-

tion of the bombing. FBI agents, operating independently, identified several suspects, while reporting that Florida law enforcement was riddled with KKK members. Suspect Joseph Cox, secretary of an Orlando Klan chapter, killed himself in March 1952, shortly after his second FBI interview. Two other suspects died within the next nine months, reportedly of natural causes. The case remains officially unsolved today, despite sporadic reports of "new leads" as late as 1992.

**MOORE, Henry**—The son of a Yorkshire coal miner, born at Castleford on 30 July 1898, Henry Moore was wounded in WORLD WAR I and used his veterans benefits to attend the Leeds School of Art (1919-21) and later the Royal College of Art in London (1921-25). His performance at the latter school was so impressive that he was retained as a teacher there from 1925 through 1932. Primarily a sculptor, whose works became internationally famous, Moore held his first solo exhibition in London, in 1928. Like most British artists, Moore supported the Loyalist side in Spain's civil war, and he also served on the Artists Refugee Committee, helping to resettle refugees from Nazism. Unlike many of his colleagues, though, Moore declined to join the COMMUNIST PARTY, calling membership "an active role which I didn't want to have."

The FBI ignored Moore until October 1944, when a dispatch from the Overseas News Agency (ONA) listed him among the organizers of a new International Arts Guild, created "to strengthen the spiritual and artistic intercourse of artists of all nations." G-men noted that the ONA's news items were "received principally through leftist émigré channels, official and unofficial," a false statement which then allowed the Bureau to brand anyone mentioned in those dispatches as "leftists." Six years later, agents clipped an article from the January 1951 *Daily Worker* that included Moore's name on a list of 16 prominent Londoners who had signed a statement condemning use of the atomic bomb. The article bears a typical Bureau notation: "Clipped at the Seat of Government"—i.e., J. EDGAR HOOVER'S office in Washington, D.C. Henry Moore died at Hertfordshire on 31 August 1986, presumably unaware of the FBI's long-distance interest in his "un-American" politics.

**MOORE, Marianne**—A St. Louis native, born Marianne Craig in 1887, poet and essayist Marianne Moore was denounced to the FBI in 1935, her name appended to a "list of Communist writers" which arrived at Bureau headquarters sans signature, in "a plain envelope." Ever vigilant, G-men investigate the claim and reported that Moore was "a descendant from Revolutionary heroes." That was no great endorsement, from J. EDGAR HOOVER'S viewpoint, and his file on the "Poetess of Brooklyn" remained active for three decades, including such items as her signing of a 1948 letter condemning the HOUSE COMMITTEE ON UN-AMERICAN ACTIVITIES and her protest that same year against the prosecution of Chilean author Pablo Neruda. Agents spent the better part of 1949 scouring Moore's poems, only to report that they "failed to indicate anything on [her] political sympathies." Still the file remained open, until the late 1960s. Moore died in 1972, perhaps unaware of the Bureau's scrutiny.

**MOORE, Sarah Jane**— Born in 1930, five times married and the mother of four children, Sarah Jane Moore has been described in media reports as "the picture of mental instability." She dropped out of nursing school to join the Women's Army Corps, but later became a successful certified public accountant. In 1972 Moore abandoned her career and family to "go underground" as a member of the "NEW LEFT" counterculture—and, unknown to her radical comrades, as a paid INFORMANT for the FBI. As Moore later explained it, "The original reason the FBI recruited me was the search for Patty Hearst and the [SYMBIONESE LIBERATION ARMY], so I stayed very much interested in and active among the angry and dispossessed the theorist[s] only talked about." Over time, she recalled, "The FBI directed me to people and organizations seriously working for radical change whose dreams I found I shared, whose dedication I envied and whose goal [of] socialism seemed not only necessary but possible."

On 22 September 1975, outside San Francisco's St. Francis Hotel, Moore tried to shoot President GERALD FORD with a .38-caliber pistol. A bystander grabbed Moore's arm and deflected the shot, causing her bullet to ricochet and wound a bystander. Investigators found a poem Moore had written the previous day, which read:

> Hold-Hold, still my hand.
> Steady my eye, chill my heart,
> And let my gun sing for the people.
> Scream their anger, cleanse with their hate,
> And kill this monster.

In custody, Moore denied claims that she was insane and told authorities, "The impression is being deliberately fostered that I am a poor demented woman who went off her rocker and in a moment of madness fired a shot at Gerald Ford. The success of the FBI is people like me … for whom the American dream has worked [until] we find out that for a majority of Americans it is not only a myth, but that our very comfort and success is dependent on the oppression and repression, even the blood of others…. Gerald Ford's life is no more valuable than … an American soldier killed in Vietnam…. When any government uses assassination … it must expect that tool to be turned back against it." Moore pled guilty to a charge of attempted presidential assassination and received a life term in federal prison.

**MORRIS, Newbold**—A New York lawyer, former president of New York's city council and a renowned political reformer, Newbold Morris was tapped by President HARRY TRUMAN in January 1952 to spearhead an investigation of alleged malfeasance in the JUSTICE DEPARTMENT. Appointed as a special assistant to Attorney General J. HOWARD MCGRATH, Morris began his task by interviewing various bureau heads. FBI Director J. EDGAR HOOVER initially refused to speak with Morris unless specifically ordered to do so by Truman, but he later granted Morris a "10-minute" audience that turned into a four-hour monologue. "I don't believe I got to open my mouth more than twice," Morris said of that meeting, "and we never got around to the subject I wanted to discuss." Instead, Hoover treated Morris to a rambling lecture

on FBI history and the Bureau's most famous cases. "Let me say," Morris later observed, "that if I had been my 12-year-old son it would have been the most exciting afternoon of my life."

Morris would not be diverted from his course, however. On 10 March 1952 he told the press that his investigation was proceeding, and that he would use no past or present G-men to assist him. Six days later, fueled by leaks from Hoover's office, columnist WALTER WINCHELL alleged that Morris had fallen under the sway of "subversive" FBI critic MAX LOWENTHAL. Various congressmen echoed that charge in the House of Representatives, and while the claim was false, Morris recognized the fact that he was overmatched. On 19 March he issued another press release, declaring that the FBI would be the only agency at Justice exempt from his investigation.

The proffered olive branch was too little and too late. On 3 April 1952 Attorney General McGrath addressed a press conference, with Hoover at his elbow, and announced that he had fired Morris. President Truman retaliated by dismissing McGrath four days later, but Hoover remained untouchable at FBI HEADQUARTERS, and the abortive probe of Justice went no further.

**MUELLER, Robert Swan III**—A native of New York City, born 7 August 1944, Robert Mueller III received a B.S. degree from Princeton University in 1966, then served in the Marine Corps (1967-70) before pursuing further education. He earned an M.A. in international studies from New York University in 1972, and a law degree from the University of Virginia in 1973. Thus prepared, he served as a federal prosecutor in San Francisco (1973-76); a U.S. attorney in Boston (1986-87), assistant attorney general (1990-93); chief of the U.S. attorney's homicide section in Washington, D.C. (1996-98); and as U.S. attorney in San Francisco (1998-2001). In July 2001 he was chosen by President GEORGE W. BUSH to replace LOUIS FREEH as director of the FBI. At his Senate confirmation hearing Mueller declared, "We must tell the truth and let the facts speak for themselves. The truth is what we expect in our investigations of others, and the truth is what we must demand of ourselves when we come under scrutiny."

Officially installed as FBI director on 4 September 2001, Mueller found his campaign to "fix" the scandal-ridden Bureau interrupted one week later by the catastrophic SKYJACKINGS of 11 September. In the wake of those attacks and the announcement of a global "war on TERRORISM," the FBI found itself immersed in new controversy. Media sources found G-men active with security forces in Pakistan, but FBI HEADQUARTERS denied it. Bureau spokesmen debated the possibility of torturing terrorist suspects for information in "emergency" situations—or perhaps having foreign police do it for them. Incessant terror "alerts" and warnings from Mueller and Attorney General JOHN ASHCROFT soon lost their impact when no attacks materialized (and one alert, complete with photos of five alleged terrorists roaming at large in America, was retracted in January 2003 as a "hoax"). Civil libertarians worried that Mueller's FBI, granted sweeping new powers of DOMESTIC SURVEILLANCE by the "USA PATRIOT ACT," might commit abuses surpassing those of late Director J. EDGAR HOOVER. It remains to be seen whether those fears are justified, but the FBI announced reactivation of its LIBRARY AWARENESS PROGRAM in 2001, professing to believe that a review of books and magazines read by Arab Americans or library patrons with "Arab-sounding" names may somehow prevent acts of terrorism.

**MUHAMMAD, Elijah**— A Georgia native and the son of former slaves, born 7 October 1897, Elijah Poole left home at 16 to adopt a nomadic lifestyle. Settled in Detroit by 1923, he joined the NATION OF ISLAM (NOI) and subsequently helped the sect's founder — Wallace Fard, aka Wali Farad — organize a second congregation in Chicago. Fard renamed Poole "Elijah Muhammad," and upon Fard's disappearance in 1934 (still unexplained) Muhammad emerged as leader of the NOI. Officers of the NOI movement, better known as Black Muslims, were already under FBI investigation in 1933 for consorting with known or suspected Japanese agents. G-men arrested Muhammad on 20 September 1942, for counseling draft evasion, and conviction on that charge left him imprisoned until 24 August 1946.

The Bureau apparently kept Muhammad under surveillance for the rest of his life, although the first acknowledged WIRETAPS were not placed on his telephones in Chicago until 1957. Four years later, when Muhammad bought a winter home in Arizona, G-men rushed to install more taps and BUGGING devices. They kept track of his rift with former NOI spokesman MALCOLM X from 1963 until Malcolm was murdered in February 1965, and the interest at FBI HEADQUARTERS only increased thereafter, as ghetto riots and militant demands for "black power" supplanted the nonviolent civil disobedience of Dr. MARTIN LUTHER KING, JR. A memo from Director J. EDGAR HOOVER, dated 25 August 1967, named Muhammad as one of four black leaders targeted for "intensified attention" under a new COINTELPRO harassment campaign against "Black Nationalist — Hate Groups." Six months later, on 4 March 1968, Hoover ranked Muhammad among five top targets when he ordered G-men to "prevent the rise of a 'messiah' who could unify, and electrify, the militant black nationalist movement."

The FBI's interest in Muhammad did not die with Hoover in May 1972. Two and a half years later, on 20 October 1974, agents tried to interview Muhammad on his return from a trip to Mexico, but he was too ill for interrogation. They returned to question him on 12 November 1974, without result. By January 1975, when Muhammad made another trip to Mexico, FBI headquarters had begun to speculate on how long he would live and who would succeed him at the NOI's helm. Muhammad died in Chicago on 25 February 1975. Louis Farrakhan assumed control of the NOI, while Muhammad's son became leader of a new faction, the Muslim American Community.

**MUMFORD, Lewis**— Born at Flushing, Long Island on 19 October 1885, Lewis Mumford enjoyed a varied career as a social critic, author, urban planner and university professor. Best known for his writing and lectures on city life and architecture, he is broadly described in some quarters as an "urban theorist," but Mumford's FBI file describes him as "a writer by occupation," noting darkly that he "has been engaged in that type of work and its associated ramifications since approximately 1923."

That year marked the opening of Mumford's Bureau dossier, occasioned by his role as cofounder of the Regional Planning Association of America. He was also a member (and one-time president) of the American Academy of Arts and Letters, but G-men were more interested in Mumford's reported affiliation with something called "The Advising Council Book of Union," otherwise labeled "the Communist Book of the Month Club" in FBI memos. Agents also noted Mumford's service on a committee established to aid Loyalist forces in Spain, while he was teaching at City College of New York, and an anti-fascist speech he delivered to the Council for Pan American Democracy. It is all the more curious, then, that a March 1941 Bureau critique of Mumford's latest book, *Faith for Living*, reports that "what Mr. Mumford proposes is a brand of medicine that looks, smells and tastes like fascism."

The FBI pursued Mumford for nearly half a century, without finding any evidence of criminal wrongdoing. As late as February 1965, G-men tapped his phone to eavesdrop on a call inviting him to address an April civil rights convention. Mumford declined, citing a pressing book deadline, but agents made a point of noting that he was "very sympathetic" to the cause. Mumford died on 26 January 1990, and his 47-page dossier was later released under the FREEDOM OF INFORMATION ACT.

**MURCHISON, Clint William, Sr.**— A native of Tyler, Texas, born 11 April 1895, Clint Murchison Sr. is hailed in his official biography for a "remarkable talent as a trader with original approaches to financing." The eldest son of a wealthy banking family, Murchison emerged from military service in WORLD WAR I to carve a substantial niche for himself in oil and natural gas exploitation. Over time he held controlling shares of such major petroleum firms as American Liberty Oil Company, Delhi Oil Corporation, Southern Union Gas Corporation, and Trans Canada Pipeline Inc. The oil business produced some strange bedfellows in those days, and by the early 1950s some 20 percent of Murchison's Oil Lease Corporation was owned by New York City's Genovese Mafia family. By the end of that decade, FBI wiretaps had revealed other Murchison ties to ORGANIZED CRIME, including financial involvement with Chicago mobsters, Las Vegas gamblers, and TEAMSTERS UNION president Jimmy Hoffa.

Most of those revelations went no further than FBI HEADQUARTERS, since Murchison was a close and very generous friend of Director J. EDGAR HOOVER. Murchison owned the Del Charro Hotel in La Jolla, California, where Hoover and Associate Director CLYDE TOLSON stayed free of charge, running up huge bills on their periodic southern California gambling junkets — euphemistically described within the Bureau as "inspection tours." Other favored guests at the Del Charro included JOSEPH MC-CARTHY, RICHARD NIXON, and Arizona Senator Barry Goldwater (the only Jew permitted to stay in the hotel). Aside from free room and board, Murchison engineered a series of loss-proof investments for Hoover in oil, railroads, and various insurance companies. Murchison also held a controlling interest in the Henry Holt publishing house, commanding the firm to grant Hoover "an especially favorable contract" for his ghost-written *Masters of Deceit* in 1958.

Murchison and Hoover shared a common interest in right-wing politics and cultivating officials who could safeguard their respective fortunes. Murchison supported LYNDON JOHNSON'S 1948 senate campaign, and Hoover visited Murchison's home in Austin that winter, during an FBI investigation of alleged irregularities in that election. Observers in Texas noted that the FBI probe of Johnson proceeded "with a notable lack of investigative and prosecutorial vigor" and soon "disappeared without a trace." Hoover and Murchison also offered joint support to 1950s Redhunters Richard Nixon and Joseph McCarthy, but some of Murchison's political connections were even more extreme. In the 1960s a leader of the paramilitary MINUTEMEN organization identified Murchison as a major financial supporter of the American Nazi Party.

The Hoover-Murchison collaboration served both men. Hoover repaid Murchison's generosity by tipping Murchison to government investigations in the offing and forewarned him of pending actions by federal regulatory agencies. During WORLD WAR II, after G-man-turned-lobbyist J.G.C. Corcoran publicly accused Hoover of plotting to "set him up" on a false bribery charge, Corcoran died in a plane crash on Spanish Cay, a Caribbean island owned by Murchison. Twenty years later, when former Del Charro Hotel manager Allan Witwer disclosed Hoover's freeloading to *Life* reporter William Lambert, Lambert's editors killed the story. A subsequent report to Attorney General ROBERT KENNEDY was likewise ignored.

Such friendship notwithstanding, Hoover still maintained FILES "loaded with derogatory material" on Murchison, including Murchison's rumored links to the JFK ASSASSINATION. Four days after President Kennedy was killed in Dallas, on 26 November 1963, FBI headquarters received information from Thomas Webb (an ex-agent hired by Murchison at Hoover's request) that Murchison and Hoover crony WILLIAM BYARS, SR. were both personally acquainted with underworld figure JACK RUBY, slayer of alleged assassin LEE HARVEY OSWALD. An associate of Murchison, D.H. Byrd, also owned the Texas Book Depository from which Oswald supposedly fired three shots at Kennedy's motorcade. Those reports were withheld from the Warren Commission, appointed to investigate Kennedy's murder, and Murchison went on to fund Richard Nixon's successful presidential campaign in 1968. He died at Athens, Texas on 19 June 1969.

**"MURKIN"** — On 4 April 1968 Dr. MARTIN LUTHER KING, JR., was killed by a sniper's bullet on the balcony of a motel in Memphis, Tennessee. After years of FBI surveillance and harassment, numerous arrests, multiple BOMBINGS and murder plots by the KU KLUX KLAN, America's foremost CIVIL RIGHTS leader was dead on the eve of a scheduled Poor People's March on Washington, D.C. Ex-agent ARTHUR MURTAGH described a scene of wild celebration when news of King's death reached the Atlanta field office, with agents cheering, "They got Zorro! [King's FBI code name] They finally got the son of a bitch!"

As ghetto rioting erupted nationwide, President LYNDON JOHNSON — who once described King as "that goddamned nigger preacher" — ordered an FBI investigation of the murder. Hoover complied and his agents took charge of various items, including

a rifle, that were found discarded on a Memphis street moments after the shooting. Those articles bore fingerprints, but two weeks passed before FBI HEADQUARTERS identified their owner as James Earl Ray, a 40-year-old habitual criminal who had escaped from Missouri's state prison on 23 April 1967. Since the Bureau had no legal jurisdiction in King's murder, Ray was charged with charged with conspiring to violate King's civil rights. Conspiracy requires two or more participants, but JUSTICE DEPARTMENT spokesmen later dismissed the charge as a simple pretext for sending G-men after Ray. His name was added to the FBI's "TEN MOST WANTED" LIST on 20 April 1968. Seven weeks later, British police captured Ray at London's Heathrow Airport, as he attempted to board a flight for Brussels.

If the conspiracy charge against Ray was mere fiction, there seemed to be ample evidence suggesting multiple participants in King's murder. Eyewitnesses reported a gunman in a vacant lot across the street from King's motel, while Ray allegedly fired from the bathroom window of a nearby rooming house. Tenants of that seedy establishment, meanwhile, described a sniper who bore no resemblance to Ray. Two white Ford Mustangs had been parked outside the rooming house on 4 April, only one of them Ray's, and a hoaxed CB radio report of a car chase had diverted Memphis police from Ray's escape route. When Ray's car was found in Atlanta, its ashtray overflowed with cigarette butts — but Ray did not smoke.

The case became even stranger as G-men traced Ray's movements since April 1967. He had traveled widely in the U.S., Canada and Mexico, spending more than $10,000 overall, but he had no source of income. (Justice spokesmen later claimed Ray "probably" robbed banks to pay his way, but he was never linked to any unsolved holdups.) In Birmingham, the week before King's murder, Ray purchased a .243-caliber rifle, then returned a day later to exchange it for a more powerful .30-06, explaining that "his brother" had told him he bought the wrong gun for "deer hunting." After the murder, while hiding in Canada, Ray had obtained false passports in the names of three living Canadians whom he did not know, but who closely resembled him. Between 25 April and 2 May 1968, Toronto witnesses saw Ray with unidentified male companions on at least four occasions.

Still, despite the mounting evidence, the FBI's "MURKIN" investigation (for *mur*der and *Kin*g) revealed no other suspects. Why not? Agent Murtagh reports, "We conducted a straight criminal investigation. We never even looked for a conspiracy." In fact, he claims, evidence of conspiracy was "washed out consistently and deliberately" by G-men in the Atlanta field office. Ex-agent WILLIAM TURNER found a similar attitude in Los Angeles, where a Bureau supervisor told his men to ignore evidence suggesting a plot. "We've got our man and that's it," the supervisor declared. "The Director didn't exactly light any candles when King was killed."

James Ray seemed to resolve the issue on 10 March 1969, when he pled guilty to King's murder in Memphis and accepted a 99-year prison term. In fact, however, he maintained from the first that he was simply a pawn in the plot to kill King, manipulated by a contact he knew only as "Raoul" — the man who paid his bills and directed his travels, promising safe passage to a country with no U.S. extradition treaty upon completion of what he described as a "gun-running" deal. Ray explained his guilty plea as a product of coercion, forced upon him by Texas attorney Percy Foreman (who also represented JACK RUBY in his trial for the murder of LEE HARVEY OSWALD). Foreman, Ray said, had loaned money to Ray's relatives on the condition of a guilty plea with no "unseemly conduct" in court and had badgered Ray with threats of execution if he refused a plea bargain.

Ray's later appeals were denied and he died in prison on 23 April 1998 (ironically, the 31st anniversary of his Missouri jailbreak), but the case will not rest. In 1975 Congress created a HOUSE SELECT COMMITTEE ON ASSASSINATIONS to review King's murder and the JFK ASSASSINATION. That committee's report, issued in 1979, found "a likelihood of conspiracy in the death of Dr. King." Congressmen named Gerald Ray and JOHN LARRY RAY as probable conspirators with brother James, allegedly plotting King's death in hopes of collecting a rumored $30,000 "bounty" placed on King by two St. Louis businessmen, John Kauffmann and John Sutherland. Both suspects died before the House committee was created, and were thus unable to defend themselves. Still, investigators speculated that Ray's hypothetical "share" of the payoff might explain his spending on the road—assuming he had collected the money from Kauffmann and Sutherland in advance. The House committee found no evidence of FBI complicity in King's murder, but reported that Hoover's G-men "failed to investigate adequately the possibility of conspiracy in the assassination."

The House report solved nothing, and reports of a MURKIN conspiracy continued to proliferate. In 1993 retired Memphis businessman Lloyd Jowers claimed that he had been the middleman in a murder contract on King, sponsored by members of ORGANIZED CRIME (which opposed King's meddling in a Memphis garbage workers strike), the FBI and the CENTRAL INTELLIGENCE AGENCY (opposed to King's protests against the VIETNAM WAR). Jowers named the shooter as Earl J. Clark, a deceased Memphis policeman who won marksmanship awards at the FBI ACADEMY. King's family sued Jowers for a nominal $100, seeking a court's endorsement of the conspiracy tale, and a Memphis jury agreed on 8 December 1999. (As part of that civil case, Ray's original trial judge testified that he did not believe the rifle found in Memphis on 4 April 1968 and later tested by the FBI was actually used to kill King.)

Nor did that verdict exhaust the MURKIN conspiracy theories. In July 2001 a former Missouri deputy sheriff, Jim Green, told reporters that he was part of a "hit team" assigned to kill King for the "Missouri Mafia" based at Caruthersville. Green claimed to have the murder rifle "safely hidden," but it has not been produced thus far. (Testing may be impossible in any case, since the bullet that struck King fragmented on impact.) "I hope to change a lie in history to the truth about that day in Memphis," Green said, adding that King's murder was committed "with the full knowledge of the FBI."

Nine months later, on the 34th anniversary of King's death, G-men in Florida announced that they were chasing yet another lead in the MURKIN case. A local minister, 61-year-old Rev. Ronald Wilson, had called a press conference to name his late fa-ther—Henry Clay Wilson, deceased in 1990—as the triggerman in King's assassination. As explained by Rev. Wilson, "My dad told me James Earl Ray had nothing to do with the shooting other than to buy a rifle for them." Henry Wilson allegedly "believed Dr. King was a communist and was trying to cause an uprising." Agent Ron Grenier, speaking for the Jacksonville field office, told reporters, "We take statements like this seriously." Still, he admitted, the lead was unlikely to prove anything. "The crime was committed a number of years ago. All the parties are now deceased," Grenier said. "It's just not the type of thing you're going to be able to resolve rather quickly."

**MURPHY, Francis William**—A Michigan native, born 13 April 1890, Frank Murphy served as a state judge (1923), mayor of Detroit (1930-33), governor of the Philippines (1933-35) and governor of Michigan (1937-39) before he was appointed to act as President FRANKLIN ROOSEVELT'S third attorney general. His appointment was announced in December 1938, and by the time Murphy took office on 2 January 1939, FBI Director J. EDGAR HOOVER had already compiled a secret dossier of derogatory information on Murphy's political beliefs and private life, keeping the file open and active long after Murphy left the JUSTICE DEPARTMENT for a seat on the U.S. SUPREME COURT.

We can only speculate on the extent to which Hoover's file made Murphy a malleable tool of his FBI subordinate, but Murphy had been in office barely two months when he approved a plan to greatly expand the Bureau's DOMESTIC SURVEILLANCE powers, while cutting the STATE DEPARTMENT out of such cases. On 16 March 1939 Hoover petitioned Murphy to give the FBI total control over investigations "intended to ascertain the identity of persons engaged in ESPIONAGE, counter-espionage, and sabotage of a nature not within the specific provisions of prevailing statutes." Under current policy, Hoover complained, G-men required "specific authorization" from Assistant Secretary of State George Messersmith to pursue such cases. Murphy discussed the matter with President Roosevelt, who in turn issued a directive on 26 June 1939, ending State Department oversight and requiring that "all espionage, counterespionage, and related matters" would henceforth be "controlled and handled" by the FBI or military intelligence units. All other agencies were thereafter ordered to give the FBI "any data, information, or material … bearing directly or indirectly on espionage, counterespionage, or sabotage."

Having won the new authority he coveted, Hoover set out to jealously protect it. On 6 September 1939 he alerted Murphy to the creation of a 50-man "special sabotage squad" within the NEW YORK POLICE DEPARTMENT, expected to gain another 100 officers in the "rather near future." Hoover complained of publicity surrounding the squad, sparking fears that "consequently much information in the hands of private citizens concerning sabotage and saboteurs will be transmitted to the New York City Police Department rather than the FBI." Hoover requested that President Roosevelt issue "a statement or request addressed to all police officials in the United States and instructing them to turn over to the nearest representative of the Federal Bureau of Investigation any information obtained pertaining to espionage, counterespionage, sabotage, subversive activities and neutrality regulations." Murphy complied, and Roosevelt's subsequent order authorized the Bureau to "take charge of investigative work in matters relating to espionage, sabotage, and violations of the neutrality regulations." To guarantee that such work would be handled in a "comprehensive and effective manner on a national basis," Roosevelt further commanded all state and local police "promptly to turn over any information obtained by them relating to espionage, sabotage, subversive activities, and violations of the neutrality laws."

Attorney General Murphy added his own postscript to the president's order, praising the FBI's professionalism and vowing that "if you want this work done in a reasonable and responsible way it must not turn into a witch hunt. We must do not wrong to any man." Hoover ignored that proviso and sent a letter to all U.S. police commanders, reminding them of their duty to "immediately notify ... the nearest representative of the Federal Bureau of Investigation of any information received relating to cases in the above classifications." Frank Murphy, meanwhile, would not remain to witness the sweeping abuses he had helped to institutionalize. He resigned as attorney general on 18 January 1940, to fill a vacancy on the Supreme Court, and held that post until his death on 19 July 1949.

**MURTAGH, Arthur**— A G-man with 25 years of service in the FBI, Arthur Murtagh has become most noted since retirement for the candor of his memories concerning life inside the Bureau. From congressional hearings to media interviews, he was always ready with sound byte that illuminated the darker corners of FBI operations during his tenure. One of the earliest incidents occurred in 1958, when Murtagh wrote a letter to Director J. EDGAR HOOVER, addressing FBI personnel issues. The letter was intercepted by Murtagh's supervisor, who told him, "Art, I can't let you send that letter.... You don't understand Bureau politics.... You must understand that you're working for a crazy maniac and that our duty is to find out what he wants and to create the world that he believes in and to show him that's the way things are."

When it came to FBI recruiting, Murtagh told Senate investigators, Hoover's employment guidelines were often discarded to obtain the right kind of agent, defined as "a good white Anglo-Saxon, preferably an Irishman with conservative views ... another good WASP, and have him apply to the Bureau and see he gets the job — to hell with the qualification."

Assigned to the Atlanta field office in 1968, Murtagh noted that his fellow agents "literally jumped for joy" when Dr. MARTIN LUTHER KING, JR., was murdered. During the subsequent "MURKIN" investigation, he recalled, "I was told we weren't to talk about conspiracy." More to the point, he says, conspiracy leads were "washed out consistently and deliberately" by the Atlanta office.

Agents were more industrious in collecting derogatory material on public figures, however. As Murtagh explained to the Senate in 1978, "It was not uncommon to learn of some politically damaging information about some leading figure in politics as having been developed by the Bureau; and then, always at a time when it would be most damaging to the individual, the information would in some way show up in the *Chicago Tribune* or some other friend of the Bureau."

In 1975, before the PIKE COMMITTEE, Murtagh related a comment made by Assistant Director CARTHA DELOACH to agents in training at the FBI ACADEMY. DeLoach allegedly told the group, "The other night, we picked up a situation where this senator was seen drunk, in a hit-and-run accident, and some good-looking broad was with him. We got the information, reported it in a memorandum, and by noon the next day the senator was aware that we had the information, and we never had trouble with him on appropriations since." (DeLoach's response to Murtagh's claim: "That is absolutely false. No such thing ever happened. I would not have made any statement lecturing to agents like that.")

Murtagh's most often-quoted comment is an observation on Hoover himself, lifted from a 1990 interview in which he said: "I certainly do not want to indicate that Hoover did not have some unusual ability in structuring an organization designed to perpetuate a sort of dictatorial control of both the FBI and, so far as he could manage it, the minds of the American citizens — but so did ADOLF HITLER."

# N

**NARCOTICS**— Throughout his tenure as FBI director, J. EDGAR HOOVER successfully resisted all suggestions that the FBI should pursue narcotics traffickers or otherwise enforce federal anti-drug legislation. His reasons were twofold: first, he believed (correctly, as we know today) that exposure to drug dealers would increase the likelihood of bribery among his G-men; and second, because

Hoover stubbornly denied the existence of anything resembling ORGANIZED CRIME in the U.S. Drug enforcement thus fell to the FEDERAL BUREAU OF NARCOTICS and Hoover's hated rival HARRY ANSLINGER, who denounced the Mafia at every opportunity.

Hoover had been 10 years in his grave when President RONALD REAGAN declared a national "War on Drugs," appointing vice president GEORGE H.W. BUSH to lead the crusade. On 28 January 1982 Attorney General WILLIAM SMITH assigned the FBI and the DRUG ENFORCEMENT ADMINISTRATION (DEA) to joint jurisdiction in federal drug cases. It was a curious effort from the beginning, with Reagan slashing funds for drug enforcement even as he proclaimed the new "war." Despite the president's professed determination to make America drug-free, he cut the FBI's budget by six percent and the DEA's by 12 percent (forcing dismissal of 211 agents and 223 support personnel). Senator Joseph Biden noted the cutbacks, coupled with an astounding 60-percent drop in criminal cases prosecuted by the JUSTICE DEPARTMENT under Reagan, and demanded an investigation by the General Accounting office, but Reagan and Attorney General Smith refused to cooperate by providing the necessary documents. By March 1982 some Coast Guard officers in Florida had branded the new war on drugs "an intellectual fraud."

Still, G-men tried to shoulder their new burden, shifting agents from white-collar crime investigations to the narcotics front. An uneasy alliance with the DEA found FBI agents focused primarily on top-level dealers and cartel bosses, while the DEA pursued smugglers and street-level dealers. By 1986 approximately 10 percent of the FBI's field programs were related to drug enforcement, and that mission ranked among the Bureau's top priorities in 1987. Some of the milestones in the endless campaign include:

*April 1984*— Arrests in the "Pizza Connection" case jailed 18 underworld figures for smuggling heroin into the U.S. and laundering drug money through a chain of pizza parlors. The defendants, including a former leader of the Sicilian Mafia, were convicted in March 1987.

*June 1984*— Collaborating with the DEA, FBI leaders created the DRUG DEMAND REDUCTION PROGRAM to educate young people on the perils of drug abuse. Shuffled from one division to another over the next decade, the program had no demonstrable effect on society's appetite for drugs.

*March 1985*— FBI Agent DANIEL MITRIONE, JR., assigned to the Miami field office, pled guilty to possessing and distributing 92 pounds of cocaine and to accepting $850,000 in cash as his part of the deal. He was sentenced to 10 years in prison.

*November 1986*— A joint FBI/DEA investigation culminated with indictments of nine Medellin drug cartel leaders for smuggling 58 tons of cocaine into the U.S. None of those indicted was in custody, but cartel leader Carlos Lehder Rivas was captured and extradited to the U.S. for trial in February 1987.

*February 1988*— Panamanian dictator Manuel Noriega and 16 associates were indicted for drug smuggling and money laundering. Noriega remained at large and in control of Panama until President George H.W. Bush sent troops to forcibly extract him in December 1989.

*December 1988*— FBI agents cooperating with the DEA,

U.S. Navy, Customs and the Coast Guard launched a nationwide sweep, arresting members of the Medellin cartel in seven cities nationwide, seizing millions of dollars in cash, drugs and personal property. The operation was dubbed CATCOM, for "*catch communications.*"

*February 1989*— G-men and officers of the NEW YORK POLICE DEPARTMENT closed out Operation WHITE MARE by seizing 820 pounds of heroin in Queens, New York. The record seizure cracked a Southeast Asian drug cartel.

*August 1993*— A National Drug Intelligence Center was established at Johnstown, Pennsylvania, administered by the FBI and Justice Department with cooperation from the DEA, Coast Guard and the BUREAU OF ALCOHOL, TOBACCO AND FIREARMS.

On 20 August 2001 Attorney General JOHN ASHCROFT proclaimed success in the long "drug war," noting that 30,000 defendants were charged with federal drug offenses in 1999 (by his Democratic predecessors). That figure more than doubled the arrest total for 1986, and 91 percent of those convicted at trial were charged with trafficking (versus simple possession). Critics responded to Ashcroft's victory proclamation by noting that 10 percent or less of all drug smugglers were apprehended, and the FBI faced a new embarrassment two days after the attorney general's press conference, when Indianapolis G-men arrested 30 Mexican nationals, seizing weapons and a cache of drugs including marijuana, cocaine and methamphetamines. The problem: No one in authority notified Mexican diplomats of the arrests, as required by treaty, thus provoking an international incident with some two dozen Mexican children were left in state care.

Such considerations vanished for the most part, three weeks later, with the disastrous SKYJACKINGS of 11 September 2001. Overnight, TERRORISM became the FBI's professed top priority, while drug enforcement vanished entirely from the Top Ten list of missions posted on the Bureau's website. Director ROBERT MUELLER assured reporters that the FBI would "remain involved" in narcotics enforcement and other traditional cases, but he warned that the bulk of such cases would be left in future to the DEA.

**NASH, Frederic Ogden**— Born at Rye, New York on 19 August 1902, Ogden Nash sold his first poem to the *New Yorker* in 1930 and subsequently published 19 books of humorous verse. The FBI opened a file on Nash in 1941, clipping his entry from *Current Biography*. Another 16 years elapsed before G-men noted a speaking engagement by the "master of bouffe rime, adroit user of Americana as spoken in subway and cocktail conversations," and a final entry was added in 1962, when the sponsors of a National Poetry Festival questioned his suitability to participate. Nash died in Baltimore, presumably oblivious to the FBI's brief examination of his work, on 19 May 1971.

**NATHAN, George Jean**— A native of Fort Wayne, Indiana, born 14 February 1882, Nathan was a longtime partner/collaborator of social critic H.L. MENCKEN. Together, they founded *Smart Set* magazine in 1914 and co-edited it until 1923, when they again teamed to create a new journal, *American Mercury*. Nathan later founded *American Spectator*, serving as its editor from 1932 to 1935. After 1943 he wrote a regular column for the New York *Journal-American*.

The Bureau of Investigation first targeted Nathan (and somehow overlooked Mencken) in September 1922, when their joint "Repetition Generale" column in *Smart Set* lampooned corrupt PROHIBITION agents and satirically suggested that "before many moons have waxed and waned mob justice" might erupt against the officers "universally regarded in America as ... licensed blackmailer[s] and scoundrel[s]." Bureau chief WILLIAM BURNS had no role in Prohibition enforcement, but he opened a file on Nathan anyway, apparently taking the humorous column as a serious threat against government agents in general.

Nathan's file remained inactive until 1937, when G-men noted his membership in Jersey City's Committee on Civil Liberties. The Bureau, in its wisdom, determined that Nathan and other committee members (including REX STOUT and WALTER LIPPMANN) were "hiding behind labor as a screen for their communistic activities." That view of Nathan apparently changed three years later, when a 1940 *Daily Worker* article condemned him as a "phony socialist" and "phony liberal." In 1946, another blast from the *Daily Worker* attacked Nathan for alleged racism against blacks. Nathan died in 1958, still vaguely suspect in J. EDGAR HOOVER'S eyes.

**NATHAN, Harold**— A native of New York City, born in 1880, Harold ("Pop") Nathan entered federal service at age 23, variously working for the Navy and LABOR DEPARTMENTS before he joined the JUSTICE DEPARTMENT'S Immigration Service. He became an FBI agent on 21 March 1917, spending the next four years at field offices in Norfolk, Charleston and Baltimore. In 1921 he was promoted to serve as agent-in-charge of the Baltimore office, then held the same post in Pittsburgh. He was recalled to FBI HEADQUARTERS by Director J. EDGAR HOOVER and named assistant director for Investigations on 1 May 1925, holding that position until 1941.

For many years Nathan was the only Jew to attain significant rank within the FBI, a fact Hoover's aides explained by claiming that "Jews are not attracted to law enforcement." His unique position and flair for storytelling made him a popular speaker before the B'nai B'rith and other Jewish organizations, but Nathan's real value to the Bureau was his ability to dissuade Hoover from pursuing some of his wilder ideas to fruition. As Assistant Director EDWARD TAMM told author Curt Gentry that Nathan was "like the roll fins on a vessel. He kept us from rolling too far from one side to the other. His was always the word of caution: 'Don't go overboard.'" One classic case, in 1936, occurred when Nathan talked Hoover out of a scheme to have the FBI compete with Hollywood by producing its own "G-men" movies for profit.

Although Hoover relied on Nathan for guidance, their relationship was not always a smooth one. In 1935 Hoover ordered Nathan and G-man CHARLES APPEL to write an official history of the FBI. They took the job seriously, interviewing dozens of former agents and reviewing "many, many" documents to prepare the final manuscript. When Hoover read it, though, he found that Nathan and Appel had honestly credited various Bureau employees for achievements Hoover claimed as his own, whereupon he suppressed the document. Two more decades passed before author DON WHITEHEAD passed muster with *The FBI Story* (1956), crediting Hoover with every Bureau victory on record (and some that rightfully belonged to other agencies).

In 1941 Nathan was transferred to San Diego, California as agent-in-charge of that city's field office. He was briefly recalled during WORLD WAR II, to serve as assistant director of the IDENTIFICATION, TRAINING and LABORATORY DIVISIONS, but the atmosphere at headquarters no longer suited him. In 1944 he was sent to Richmond, Virginia as agent-in-charge. Nathan retired to San Francisco the following year, after 42 years of government service, and he died there on 9 July 1963. Assistant Director Alex Rosen replaced Nathan as the Bureau's unofficial Jewish raconteur.

**NATION of Islam**— The Nation of Islam, better known as the Black Muslim sect, was founded in Detroit during 1930, by an itinerant evangelist named Wallace Fard (aka "Wali Farad," "Farrad Mohammed," "F. Mohammed Ali," "Professor Ford," etc.). Starting as a door-to-door raincoat salesman, Fard progressed to Bible studies and then the "true religion" of Africa — in fact, a curious amalgam of traditional Islam and apparent science fiction, wherein "blue-eyed devils" (whites) were "grafted" from "Original Man" (blacks) by a prehistoric mad scientist. Doubts remain as to whether Fard himself was black or white, and one Chicago newspaper report later described him as "a Turkish-born Nazi agent [who] worked for ADOLF HITLER in WORLD WAR II."

Fard vanished mysteriously in June 1934, soon after naming disciple ELIJAH MUHAMMAD as his heir apparent. Operating from a new Chicago headquarters, Muhammad was arrested by FBI agents for sedition in 1942. He had allegedly consorted with Japanese agents, and while the Bureau's Chicago field office admitted "no definitive connection had been found ... between Negro organizations and Japanese activity in this country, Muhammad was "alleged to have taught Negroes that their interests were in a Japanese victory, and that they were racially akin to the Japanese." Muhammad spent four years in federal prison and emerged to a martyr's acclaim from his followers.

FBI surveillance on the Nation of Islam (NOI) apparently continued for the next three decades. A memo from Director J. EDGAR HOOVER to Attorney General HERBERT BROWNELL, dated 31 December 1956, requested authorization for WIRETAPS on "ELIJA MOHAMMED [*sic*], INTERNAL SECURITY-MUSLIM CULT OF ISLAM [*sic*]," and Brownell agreed. G-men later extended their campaign of taps and BUGGING to Muhammad's winter home in Arizona, and they reported to Hoover on the 1963 rift between Muhammad and prominent NOI minister MALCOLM X. In fact, as we shall see below, the Bureau seemed to take credit for that rift, suggesting the possibility that FBI INFORMANTS were actively sowing dissension inside the sect.

If such efforts were not ongoing in the early 1960s, they certainly began in 1967, when a Hoover memo dated 25 August launched a COINTELPRO campaign against "Black Nationalist-Hate Groups." The new effort was meant "to expose, disrupt, misdirect, discredit, or otherwise neutralize" six black organizations, including the NOI. In addition to general disruption, Hoover instructed his agents that "efforts ... to consolidate their forces or to recruit new or youthful adherents must be frustrated."

Another directive from Hoover, dated 4 March 1968, listed the NOI among four "primary targets" of the ongoing campaign. All FBI field offices were reminded of the program's "long-range goals," including:

1. Prevent the coalition of militant black nationalist groups....

2. Prevent the rise of a "messiah" who could unify, and electrify, the militant black nationalist movement....

3. Prevent violence on the part of black nationalist groups....

4. Prevent militant black nationalist groups and leaders from gaining respectability by discrediting them....

5. A final goal should be to prevent the long-range growth of militant black nationalist organizations, especially among youth.

Item number 4 on the list was presumably cosmetic, since G-men did everything within their power to *encourage* violent conflict between militant groups including the BLACK PANTHER PARTY, US and the BLACKSTONE RANGERS. As discussed in a separate entry, FBI collusion has also been suggested in the February 1965 murder of Malcolm X. In regard to the NOI, a memo to Hoover from the Chicago field office (dated 22 January 1969) details FBI progress in its campaign to "disrupt and neutralize":

> Over the years considerable thought has been given, and action taken with Bureau approval, relating to methods through which the NOI could be discredited in the eyes of the general black populace or through which factionalisms among the leadership could be created. Serious consideration has also been given towards developing ways and means of changing NOI philosophy to one whereby the members could be developed into useful citizens and the organization developed into one emphasizing religion—the brotherhood of mankind—and self improvement. Factional disputes have been developed—the most notable being MALCOLM X LITTLE. Prominent black personages have publicly and nationally spoken out against the group—U.S. District Judge JAMES BENTON PARSONS being one example. The media of the press has played down the NOI. This appears to be a most effective tool as individuals such as MUHAMMAD assuredly seek any and all publicity be it good or bad; however, if the press is utilized it should not concentrate on such aspects as the alleged strength of the NOI, immoral activities of the leadership, misuse of funds by these officials, etc. It is the opinion of this office that such exposure is ineffective, possibly creates interest and maybe envy among the lesser educated black man causing them [*sic*] out of curiosity to attend meetings and maybe join, and encourage the opportunist to seek personal gain—physical or monetary—through alignment with the group. At any rate, it is felt such publicity in the case of the NOI is not overly effective.

Agents in Florida apparently disagreed, as an October 1969 memo to Assistant Director WILLIAM SULLIVAN reported that "a television source was helped in the preparation of a program exposing the Nation of Islam." Hoover himself reviewed that memo and penned a marginal note congratulating the G-men on their "excellent" work.

FBI agents questioned Elijah Muhammad for the last time in November 1974, three months before his death. The movement fragmented thereafter, one faction led by Louis Farrakhan, while Muhammad's son controlled a smaller off-shoot of the NOI. In early 1995 G-men accused Qubilah Shabazz, Malcolm X's daughter, of hiring a killer to slay Farrakhan. Media outlets trumpeted allegations that Farrakhan may have plotted Malcolm's death in 1965, but no proof of either conspiracy was forthcoming. Subsequent review of videotapes made by the FBI reveal that Michael Fitzpatrick, Farrakhan's alleged would-be killer, actually proposed the plot to Shabazz, while she resisted the suggestion. In the past, it was disclosed, Fitzpatrick had been jailed on cocaine charges and was once expelled from an ANARCHIST group for carrying weapons to meetings and urging the group to plot BOMBINGS—in short the typical behavior of an FBI *agent provocateur*. Shabazz attorney William Kunstler told the press, "There's a puppeteer pulling the strings and there are lots of puppets out there." Retired FBI Agent Dan Scott, meanwhile, admitted "handling" Fitzpatrick as an informant in the 1970s and called him "a highly credible witness." The preliminary charge against Shabazz was later dropped, thereby renewing charges of an abortive FBI FRAME-UP.

**NATIONAL Association for the Advancement of Colored People**—America's oldest black CIVIL RIGHTS organization was founded on 12 February 1909 by a multiracial group of activists who initially called their group the National Negro Committee. Within a year, the NAACP inaugurated a tradition of providing legal services for impoverished African Americans, particularly those falsely accused of crimes in racist southern courts. A new career of public protest was launched in 1913, when "progressive" President WOODROW WILSON segregated every aspect of the federal government, and continued through 1915 with demonstrations against D.W. Griffith's film *The Birth of a Nation*, which glorified the KU KLUX KLAN. By 1917, NAACP attorneys had won a concession from the U.S. SUPREME COURT (in *Buchanan v. Warley*) that states could not legally force blacks to live in segregated neighborhoods. A year later, under pressure from the NAACP, President Wilson reluctantly condemned LYNCHING.

Such activities smacked of "Bolshevism" to J. EDGAR HOOVER and the agents of his GENERAL INTELLIGENCE DIVISION. Already suspicious of the NAACP's collaboration with attorneys from the NATIONAL CIVIL LIBERTIES BUREAU, convinced that any opponent of white supremacy must be "subversive," Hoover ordered a full investigation of the NAACP in 1919. Walter White, the group's second in command (and later chief, from 1931-55), volunteered information to the Bureau, but Hoover preferred a more critical view. In fact, Hoover began the search for evidence convinced that the NAACP was a "radical" group, its newspaper (the *Crisis*) published solely "to create unrest among the negro [*sic*] element." Bureau INFORMERS like HERBERT BOULIN and ARTHUR CRAIG eavesdropped at meetings, collected issues of the *Crisis*, and shadowed NAACP spokesmen ranging from executive secretary James Johnson's to Dr. W.E.B. DuBois. A G-man in Louisville, Kentucky spoke for Hoover when he opined that "the existence of this organization may be for no good purpose." Another, in Toledo, reported that "Dr. DuBois is in favor of" the INDUSTRIAL WORKERS OF THE WORLD, whereupon Hoover issued an August 1919 order that "all connections financially and otherwise of this Association with the radical element and the IWW should be looked into." Arthur Craig, meanwhile was busy searching the group's Manhattan headquarters for gun parts allegedly stolen from a Connecticut arms factory, but he came away empty-handed.

By 1920, Bureau agents worried over the NAACP's growth, expanded to 100,000 members in 350 chapters nationwide. A Boston G-man reported that Dr. DuBois did "his utmost to incite riots and cause bloodshed," but no evidence was forthcoming. The New York field office found nothing of interest to report on the group after mid-1922, but Hoover ordered the surveillance to resume in September 1923. A year later, continued spying was justified in Bureau memos as part of a campaign to learn "what every radical organization in the country is doing." What Hoover learned over the next 18 years could have been gleaned more easily from newspaper headlines. In 1930, NAACP protests blocked the appointment of outspoken segregationist John Parker to the U.S. SUPREME COURT. Five years later, NAACP attorney Thurgood Marshall forced the University of Maryland to accept its first black student. In 1941 the group threw its weight behind President FRANKLIN ROOSEVELT's order to desegregate federal jobs and war-related industries.

It may have been coincidence that Hoover chose the same year, 1941, to launch an escalated surveillance campaign, spanning the next quarter-century. His goal, ostensibly, was to weed out COMMUNIST PARTY "contamination and manipulation of the NAACP," but the root of his real fear lay closer to home. Hoover had opened discussions with Walter White in August 1946, to "aid us in out relations with the Negro race," but after White pressed Hoover to integrate his agency, Hoover lamented the "blunder made in committing me to this outfit." Thurgood Marshall added insult to injury in January 1947, telling reporters he had "no faith in either Mr. Hoover or his investigators." Small wonder, then, that in a March 1956 address to President DWIGHT EISENHOWER's cabinet, Hoover accused the NAACP of preaching "race hatred." Nine months later, an FBI report to the White House—based on years of illegal BUGGING, WIRETAPPING and reports from 151 anonymous informers—found "communist activity" in NAACP chapters scattered from Florida to Alaska. When pressed for proof, though, Hoover was found wanting. An official FBI census, issued on 27 January 1960, found only 467 past, present or "suspected" communists among 300,000 NAACP members nationwide.

In fact, future executive secretary ROY WILKINS took steps to purge the NAACP of Reds in the early 1950s, telling Walter White, "We do not want a witch hunt, but we do want to clean out our organization." The FBI collaborated in that effort, checking names submitted for review, but no housecleaning could satisfy Hoover, as long as the NAACP campaigned for racial justice. In 1964, Assistant Director CARTHA DELOACH supervised

the bugging of suites occupied by NAACP delegates to the Democratic National Convention, and illegal surveillance continued through 1966 (if not beyond).

In retrospect, the worst part of Hoover's long war against the NAACP may be the FBI's failure to punish TERRORISTS who maimed and murdered southern leaders of the group over a period of 16 years. Activist HARRY MOORE and his wife were killed by Klan bombers in Florida, at Christmas 1951, and while G-men reportedly identified the men responsible, none was ever prosecuted. Four years later, when nightriders shot and killed NAACP spokesman GEORGE LEE in Mississippi, agents refused to examine the evidence. An arrest *was* made in the 1963 assassination of Mississippi field secretary Medgar Evers, but gunman BYRON DE LA BECKWITH escaped punishment with two hung juries, while FBI HEADQUARTERS suppressed evidence of his public confession to the murder. Car bombs crippled Mississippi NAACP leader George Metcalfe in 1965 and killed his successor, Wharlest Jackson, two years later; again, while author DON WHITEHEAD reported that FBI agents identified the bombers, no charges were filed. In light of such apparent negligence, the 1968 federal conviction of one Mississippi Klansman for killing NAACP activist Vernon Dahmer in 1966 seems too little and too late. (Fifteen other defendants were charged in that case: three were acquitted and charges against the other 12 were dismissed.)

**NATIONAL Center for the Analysis of Violent Crime**—Established on 10 July 1984, at the FBI NATIONAL ACADEMY in Quantico, Virginia, the National Center for the Analysis of Violent Crime (NCAVC) is an outgrowth of the Bureau's early Behavioral Science Unit (now Investigative Support Services). The unit employs PSYCHOLOGICAL PROFILING in an effort to pinpoint unidentified offenders and maintains the VIOLENT CRIMINAL APPREHENSION PROGRAM (VICAP) computer network to assist local law enforcement agencies in tracking unsolved "pattern crimes." The center's work has been publicized (and greatly exaggerated) in Hollywood productions ranging from *The Silence of the Lambs* to TV's *Profiler* series. In fact, NCAVC staff members do not pursue suspects and rarely visit a crime scene, working primarily in the Profiling and Behavioral Assessment Unit of the Forensic Science Research and Training Center. Well-known pioneers of the NCAVC include retired agents JOHN DOUGLAS and ROBERT RESSLER.

**NATIONAL Civil Liberties Bureau**—Founded on 1 October 1917 by ROGER BALDWIN and Crystal Eastman, the National Civil Liberties Bureau replaced a faltering parent organization, the American Union Against Militarism. It was created specifically to defend conscientious objectors after Congress authorized military conscription for service in WORLD WAR I. More specifically, NCLB lawyers argued that provisions of the 1917 Espionage Act which criminalized any opposition to the military draft violated the First Amendment's guarantee of free speech. Conservative courts were not impressed by the argument, and neither was the Bureau of Investigation. On 31 August 1919, G-men joined civilian members of the "Propaganda League" to raid the NCLB's New York office, seizing records and arresting Baldwin with several others. (Ironically, as "dollar-a-year" auxiliary agents of the JUSTICE DEPARTMENT, the Propaganda League's militant patriots were automatically exempt from military service.)

The NCLB survived World War I and remained sharply critical of Bureau activities, particularly during the illegal PALMER RAIDS of 1919-20. Attorney Isaac Schorr, representing the NCLB, wired a protest to Attorney General A. MITCHELL PALMER after G-men beat and otherwise abused their prisoners in New York City. Palmer routinely sent the complaint to young J. EDGAR HOOVER, in charge of the raids, and Hoover replied that he was unaware of any violence. That claim spoke ill of his intelligence-gathering skills, since the beating of detainees was already front-page news in New York's major daily papers. No redress for the assaults was forthcoming, but the NCLB persevered and in 1920 evolved into the still-active AMERICAN CIVIL LIBERTIES UNION.

**NATIONAL Computer Crime Squad** *see* **Computer Crimes**

**NATIONAL Crime Information Center**—Arguably the FBI's most valuable service to state and local law enforcement agencies, the National Crime Information Center (NCIC) has been operational since January 1967, providing a nationwide link-up for arrest and identity records. An ever-expanding Computerized Criminal History File went online in November 1972, but NCIC's files are not limited to arrest and conviction records; they also include information on stolen vehicles, firearms, securities, and any other property identified by serial numbers. A Missing Person File was added in October 1975, followed by an Unidentified Person File in June 1983, and the two were cross-referenced in February 1984.

Like most other units of the FBI, has been shuffled from one division to another throughout its history. It began life as part of the Uniform Crime Records Division, then was transferred five years later to the new Computer Systems Division. In 1992 it was shifted again, to the fledgling Criminal Justice Information Services Division, where a new and improved NCIC 2000 was launched in 1999.

At last report, 99 percent of all NCIC information requests were processed for state and local agencies or other federal agencies outside the FBI, but the system still pays dividends for the Bureau. On 23 July 1970, a computer "hit" enabled Michigan authorities to capture Lawrence Plamendon, a fugitive leader of the White Panther Party and the first member of the FBI's "TEN MOST WANTED" LIST arrested thanks to NCIC. A quarter-century later, following the catastrophic Oklahoma City bombing of 19 April 1995, terrorist TIMOTHY MCVEIGH was arrested for driving a car with no license plate and carrying a concealed pistol. A scan of NCIC records revealed no outstanding warrants, but the system helped G-men locate McVeigh two days later, tracing him to the Noble County jail in Oklahoma after independent evidence identified him as a bombing suspect. Without that rapid link-up, McVeigh might have posted bail on the local charges and vanished into the murky MILITIA MOVEMENT he revered, after the fashion of bomber ERIC RUDOLPH.

**NATIONAL Drug Intelligence Center** *see* **Narcotics**

**NATIONAL Lawyers Guild**—Founded in 1937, the National Lawyers Guild (NLG) was America's first racially integrated bar association, organized as an alternative to the American Bar Association (which then excluded black attorneys). It supported President FRANKLIN ROOSEVELT'S New Deal and assisted in creation of several LABOR UNIONS, including the United Auto Workers (UAW) and the Congress of Industrial Organizations (CIO). Several NLG attorneys left their practices to fight with Loyalist forces in the Spanish Civil War, and at home the NLG established a reputation for defending minorities and "radicals" which rivaled that of the AMERICAN CIVIL LIBERTIES UNION. In the wake of WORLD WAR II, with the onset of the MCCARTHY era's Red Scare, NLG leaders refused to demand that their members sign anti-communist "loyalty" oaths.

That all sounded like subversion to FBI Director J. EDGAR HOOVER, and his suspicions were confirmed in June 1949, when NLG president Clifford Durr petitioned President HARRY TRUMAN to initiate a full-scale investigation of the Bureau's illegal DOMESTIC SURVEILLANCE. FBI WIRETAPS revealed that the NLG was preparing a detailed report on illicit Bureau activities, but G-men kept abreast of its progress through a series of BREAK-INS, stealing successive drafts of the report. In response, FBI HEADQUARTERS prepared a 300-page report of its own on the NLG, leaking selected portions of it in advance to the HOUSE COMMITTEE ON UN-AMERICAN ACTIVITIES (HUAC). HUAC, in turn, published a 50-page pamphlet titled "Report on the National Lawyers Guild: Legal Bulwark of the COMMUNIST PARTY." Hoover learned in advance that the NLG planned a press conference to air its findings on 23 January 1950, but he got the jump on his adversaries once again. One day before the conference, Rep. RICHARD NIXON called for a HUAC investigation of the NLG.

In 1951 American Bar Association president Austin Canfield launched his own attack on the NLG, chairing an ABA committee "to study Communist tactics, strategy, and objectives, particularly as they relate to the obstruction of proper court procedure and law enforcement." (More specifically, he was concerned with the NLG's habit of representing indigent defendants and accused Reds.) Hoover authorized Assistant Director LOUIS NICHOLS to furnish Canfield a series of "blind" memos listing alleged subversive activities of the NLG's leaders, but Canfield still had trouble purging various state and local bar associations. In January 1952 he complained to Nichols that "the National Lawyers Guild is whooping it up and they [his committee] have to decide whether to take them on or not." Nichols urged Canfield to persevere, opining that the ABA "would probably have trouble as long as the National Lawyers Guild remained in operation." Hoover also approved further leaks from FBI FILES on the NLG's support for SMITH ACT defendants in California. Nichols reported back that "there will be a special meeting of his Committee in an attempt to move the American Bar Association into action against the National Lawyers Guild," and while the NLG's influence diminished in the 1950s, it would not disappear.

In the 1960s NLG attorneys provided legal support for CIVIL RIGHTS workers in the South, including the families of three activists murdered by KU KLUX KLAN members in the FBI's

"MIBURN" case. Opponents of the VIETNAM WAR sought aid from the NLG through the late 1960s and early 1970s, while foreign offices in Asia represented U.S. soldiers opposed to the ongoing conflict. Other guild lawyers defended members of the BLACK PANTHER PARTY and various "NEW LEFT" groups targeted by the FBI's illegal COINTELPRO campaigns. In 1976, exposure of a Surreptitious Entries file at the FBI's New York field office revealed what NLG leaders had long suspected—that their group had been under continuous Bureau surveillance since the mid-1950s, at least.

**NATIONAL Police Academy** *see* **FBI National Academy**

**NATIONAL Security Agency**—Beginning in WORLD WAR II as the Army Security Agency, this body concerns itself primarily with cryptography—the interception and decoding of intelligence data. In 1948 the ASA began collaborating with the FBI on a project code-named "Venona," which involved eavesdropping on communications between the Soviet Union and its various consulates abroad. That campaign helped identify Russian agent Klaus Fuchs and ultimately led to the trial of alleged nuclear spies JULIUS and ETHEL ROSENBERG. In 1952 the ASA was formally detached from the Army and renamed the National Security Agency, but its function remained the same. FBI Director J. EDGAR HOOVER remained suspicious of the NSA, as with all potential competitors in the U.S. intelligence community. In July 1970, under terms of the HUSTON PLAN, President RICHARD NIXON sought to unify the FBI, NSA, the CENTRAL INTELLIGENCE AGENCY and various military intelligence groups into one unit commanded from the White House, but Hoover balked at surrendering his personal authority and severed liaison with the other agencies en masse. Three years after Hoover's death, the NSA was scrutinized for potential abuses by congressional investigators from the CHURCH and PIKE COMMITTEES.

**NATIONAL Security Division**—The FBI's oldest major division, this unit was known as the Radical Division when future director J. EDGAR HOOVER joined the Bureau in 1917. It was renamed the GENERAL INTELLIGENCE DIVISION in time for the scandalous PALMER RAIDS of 1919-20 and compiled index cards on some 450,000 alleged "subversives" before it was abolished in 1924, by Attorney General HARLAN STONE. Hoover revived the unit as Division Five, under President FRANKLIN ROOSEVELT, thereafter changing its name to the National Defense Division (1941) and the Security Division (1943). "National security" operations multiplied rapidly in the years after WORLD WAR II, with establishment of the Federal Employees Loyalty Program (1947), plus investigations launched by Senator JOSEPH MCCARTHY and the HOUSE COMMITTEE ON UN-AMERICAN ACTIVITIES. In the chaotic 1960s, Hoover renamed the unit yet again, and as the Domestic Intelligence Division it coordinated his various illegal COINTELPRO operations.

After Hoover's death and the exposure of his crimes, Director CLARENCE KELLEY created a new Intelligence Division to handle foreign counterintelligence cases, while domestic security matters were assigned to the General Intelligence Division

(thereby recapturing the initials, and some say preserving the spirit, of Hoover's original Red-hunting squad). Kelley's Intelligence Division was, in turn, renamed the National Security Division (NSD) in October 1993 and retains that name today. It supervised both ESPIONAGE and TERRORISM cases until November 1999, when Director LOUIS FREEH divided those functions and created a Counterterrorism Division to deal with political violence.

A significant portion of the modern NSD's time and energy is devoted to a program dubbed "Awareness of National Security Issues and Response" (ANSIR), formerly known as "Developing Espionage and Counterintelligence Awareness" (DECA). By any name, ANSIR disseminated FBI "awareness" bulletins to governments, corporations, civic organizations and individuals who contact the Bureau with requests for information. The ANSIR Fax program was inaugurated in 1995 for faster communication, supplanted a year later by ANSIR E-mail as technology exceeded Bureau expectations. By 2001, the ANSIR E-mail program had 30,000 regular subscribers on the Internet.

**NATIVE Americans**—Most Americans know of the FBI's dealings with Native Americans only from a chapter in author DON WHITEHEAD'S *The FBI Story* (1956) or from the further-fictionalized portrayal offered in the Hollywood version of that story five years later. The case involved William Hale, "King of the Osage Hills" in Oklahoma, who hired assassins to kill Osage Indians for their oil-rich lands in the 1920s. As described by Whitehead, G-men mounted an UNDERCOVER OPERATION that cracked the case and sent Hale to prison for life in January 1929. (He was released in July 1947.)

Hale's case did not establish FBI jurisdiction over crimes committed on Indian reservations. That move began during WORLD WAR II, when budgetary shortfalls handicapped investigations normally conducted by the Bureau of Indian Affairs (BIA). Initially, G-men were supposed to provide "investigative assistance" for the BIA's police, but they steadily claimed more authority. By 1953, according to the *Arizona Law Review*:

> ...apparently because of FBI leadership, most U.S. Attorneys, and U.S. District Judges, recognized the FBI as having primary investigative jurisdiction for Federal law violations committed in Indian country, notwithstanding the wording of Congressional appropriation acts since FY-1939 and Opinion M.29669 dated August 1, 1938, issued by the Solicitor, U.S. Department of the Interior [assigning primary jurisdiction to BIA Special Officers].

"FBI leadership," of course, meant Director J. EDGAR HOOVER, who coveted authority in every sphere of law enforcement. Five years after his death, a federal report summarized the tense relationship between the FBI and BIA in "Indian Country":

> The BIA has trained criminal investigators on most reservations. These special officers conduct the initial investigation for the majority of serious crimes which occur on Indian reservations. Most U.S. Attorneys however, will not normally accept the findings of a BIA special officer as a basis for making a decision on whether to prosecute. Instead, most U.S. Attorneys require that the FBI

conduct an independent investigation, often duplicative of the BIA investigation, prior to authorizing prosecution.

The worst example of FBI performance on "the rez" is its long pursuit of the AMERICAN INDIAN MOVEMENT (AIM), apparently beginning with infiltration by INFORMANTS and *agents provocateur* in 1972. FBI misconduct during the WOUNDED KNEE SIEGE of 1973 resulted in dismissal of federal charges against AIM's leaders, while Judge Fred Nichol declared from the bench, "It's hard for me to believe that the FBI, which I have revered for many years, has fallen to this low estate." One G-man, unimpressed, was overheard in a local saloon afterward, telling colleagues, "Half the stuff that went on out there isn't even on paper."

That was certainly true at South Dakota's PINE RIDGE RESERVATION, where G-men aided, armed and financed a brutal anti-AIM vigilante movement called GUARDIANS OF THE OGLALA NATION (GOON). Although believed responsible for dozens of murders and numerous other violent crimes, GOON members were rarely investigated by FBI agents who claimed to be "understaffed" on the reservation. Still, there was no shortage of manpower when it came to raiding homes of AIM supporters, destroying their personal property and orchestrating FRAME-UPS of prominent activists. Four AIM members were charged with murder after a pair of FBI agents were killed at Pine Ridge, in June 1975. Two of the defendants admitted firing shots at Agents Jack Coler and Ronald Williams, but jurors acquitted them on grounds of self-defense. Charges against a third defendant were later dropped, and only LEONARD PELTIER was finally convicted of the slayings, under circumstances reminiscent of cases involving documented frame-up victims ELMER PRATT, PETER LIMONE, JOSEPH SALVATI and others.

G-man RICHARD G. HELD, assistant agent-in-charge at Rapid City, South Dakota, appeared to speak for the FBI at large when he described the Bureau as "a colonial police force" and said of Native Americans: "They are a conquered nation, and when you are conquered, the people you are conquered by dictate your future. This is a basic philosophy of mine. If I'm part of a conquered nation, I've got to yield to authority." Held, a veteran COINTELPRO agent echoed those sentiments in April 1975, with his memo to FBI HEADQUARTERS titled "The Use of Special Agents of the FBI in a Paramilitary Operation in the Indian Country." That call for stern action on the reservation closed with an ironic observation:

It should be clearly stated that the FBI does not desire to become involved in any political situations and definitely not participate [*sic*] in any discussion where it is obviously political in nature.

Politics aside, the Bureau has also received poor marks for its investigation of "normal" crimes on Indian land nationwide. A case in point is the rash of apparent SERIAL MURDERS reported from Washington's Yakima reservation since 1987. At least 15 Native American women were reported dead or missing by 1993, but the FBI's Seattle field office deemed it "highly unlikely" that a serial killer was stalking the reservation. Agent William Gore cited "logical suspects" and "significant evidence" in three of the

cases, but no charges have yet been filed. Local police and tenants of the reservation, meanwhile, contrasted the FBI's expenditure of energy on Seattle's "Green River" murders (a strictly local case, involving mostly Caucasian victims) with the Bureau's seeming lack of interest at Yakima.

**NAZI Saboteurs in the U.S.**—The FBI's most famous case from WORLD WAR II involved the capture of eight Nazi saboteurs who landed on Long Island from a German submarine in June 1942. Wartime mythology, bolstered by author DON WHITEHEAD in *The FBI Story* (1956) presented a scenario of tireless sleuths pursuing clues and tracking down the foreign agents in a race against time that rivaled anything in fiction, but the truth was rather different—and was concealed even from the White House.

Around midnight on 13 June 1942, Coast Guardsman John Cullen was patrolling a beach near Amagansett, Long Island, when he saw four men dragging a rubber raft ashore. Confronted, the men first claimed to be shipwrecked fishermen, but one of them spoke German and another quickly offered Cullen a $260 bribe to forget their meeting. After glimpsing weapons and the low outline of a submarine sitting 50 yards offshore, Cullen accepted the money and fled to his duty station, where he reported the incident to a superior.

Prompt action might have ended the threat then and there, since the submarine was stranded on a sand bar and the German agents dawdled at the local railroad station until 6:00 a.m., waiting for a train to New York City. Unfortunately, Cullen's superiors doubted his report and feared embarrassment if they sounded a false alarm. Instead of responding at once, they waited for dawn, by which time the Germans had caught their train to Manhattan and high tide had rescued the U-Boat. Even so, the patrol unearthed several caches of contraband buried near the beach, including German uniforms, cigarettes, brandy, and large quantities of explosives. It was noon before FBI HEADQUARTERS learned of the landing, not from the Coast Guard, but rather from a Long Island police chief. Hoover informed Attorney General FRANCIS BIDDLE that the saboteurs had disappeared.

In fact, they had split into pairs and found rooms in New York, but team leader George Dasch had a change of heart on 14 June, informing partner Ernst Burger that he planned to surrender. (Dasch had spent nearly 20 years in the U.S. before ADOLF HITLER'S rise to power, and his sympathy with Nazism was tenuous, to say the least.) Burger agreed to abandon their plan, but announced his intention to flee with $84,000 in cash provided by the Abwehr (German intelligence). On hearing that, Dasch seized the money and telephoned the FBI's New York field office. He identified himself and briefly told his story, but the agent he was speaking to refused to believe it. "Yesterday Napoleon called," the G-man declared—and he slammed down the phone.

Dasch next decided to visit J. EDGAR HOOVER in person. Bearing the money in a suitcase, he caught a train to Washington and presented himself at the JUSTICE DEPARTMENT. Assistant Director D.M. Ladd, chief of the FBI's Domestic Intelligence Division, listened skeptically to Dasch's story, then began to push him from the office. Finally, in desperation, Dasch "seized the suitcase that had been lying on the floor, tore its snaps, and dumped the contents on the desk. The three feet of polished wood were [*sic*] too narrow to hole the eighty-four thousand dollars in cash. Packets of bills cascaded over the sides to create the illusion of a miniature waterfall."

After confirming that the money was not counterfeit, the FBI began to take Dasch seriously. He told G-men where to find his comrades, and all three were arrested without incident on 20 June 1942. Dasch and Burger also pointed agents to another team of saboteurs who had landed near Jacksonville, Florida, placing a total of eight men in custody by 27 June. On that date, Hoover prepared a memo for President Roosevelt which read:

> On June 20, 1942, Robert Quirin, Heinrich Heinck, and Ernst Peter Burger were apprehended in New York City by Special Agents of the Federal Bureau of Investigation. The leader of the group, George John Dasch, was apprehended by Special Agents of the FBI on June 22, 1942, at New York City.

By thus revising history, placing the "capture" of Dasch four days after his voluntary surrender and confession, Hoover secured the operation's glory for himself. Dasch was in no position to quibble, as the eight defendants faced a military tribunal convened in a classroom at Justice. All eight were swiftly convicted, facing imminent execution. At their sentencing, on 8 August 1942, a good word from Hoover saved INFORMANTS Dasch and Burger. While their six companions were condemned, Dasch received a 30-year prison term and Burger was sentenced to life.

**NELSON, George ("Baby Face")**— A Chicago native, born 6 December 1908, Lester Gillis despised his name and small stature, insisting that friends call him "Big George" Nelson. His volatile (perhaps psychotic) temper was exacerbated by journalists who dubbed him "Baby Face" Nelson instead. In 1934 Nelson killed three G-men and wounded a fourth, making him the bureau's single most dangerous adversary prior to 1982.

A reputed street gang member in his teens, Nelson launched his adult criminal career in early 1930, with a series of Chicago home invasions that netted his gang $80,000 in jewels. BANK ROBBERY proved less profitable, scoring a mere $8,600 for Nelson's team in three heists, during October and November 1930. Arrested for armed robbery on 15 January 1931, Nelson was convicted six months later and received a prison term of one year to life. Another 20 years was added for a second bank robbery conviction, on 15 February 1932, but Nelson escaped two days later, from the train bearing him back to Joliet prison.

Various authors claim Nelson worked as a contract killer over the next 18 months, serving gang leaders in Chicago, San Francisco and Reno, Nevada. Given his temperament, Nelson might have enjoyed such duties, but no source documents the claim or describes any specific murders. On 18 August 1933, with a new gang, Nelson stole $30,000 from a Michigan bank, rebounding on 22 October to loot a Minnesota bank of $32,000. On 4 March 1934 Nelson killed a total stranger in St. Paul, perhaps because the man saw him with notorious fugitive JOHN DILLINGER. Two days later, Nelson teamed with Dillinger and others to lift $49,500 from a bank in Sioux Falls, Iowa. On 13 March they did even better, stealing $52,344 in Mason City, Iowa.

Nelson and his wife were present, with the rest of the Dillinger gang, when MELVIN PURVIS tried to surround them at Little Bohemia Lodge, in Wisconsin, on 22 April 1934. The raid was a fiasco: agents shot three innocent bystanders, while the entire gang escaped, leaving only their women behind. Fleeing on foot to a nearby hamlet, Nelson ambushed three lawmen, killing BI agent W. Carter Baum, wounding Baum's partner and a local constable. Gang members reunited on 30 June 1934, to steal $29,980 from a bank at South Bend, Indiana. A policeman was killed in the holdup, and while some sources accuse Nelson of the murder, others blame Dillinger crony Homer Van Meter.

Nelson allegedly celebrated in October 1934, when the violent deaths of Dillinger and CHARLES ("PRETTY BOY") FLOYD elevated him to "Public Enemy No. 1," but the title came with a heavy price. Spotted by a bureau stakeout team in Illinois, on 27 November 1934, Nelson fled with his wife and accomplice John Paul Chase. Another pair of G-men overtook Nelson near Barrington, then lost him after wrecking their car. Finally, agents SAMUEL COWLEY and Herman Hollis stopped Nelson's car and engaged the bandits in a pitched battle. Both G-men were mortally wounded, as was Nelson, with 17 hits. Helen Gillis stripped her husband's corpse and left it near a local cemetery, then surrendered to agents in Chicago on 29 November. (They concealed the fact and claimed she was "captured.")

Fugitive John Paul Chase was arrested by police at Shasta, California on 27 December 1934. The first defendant tried under new legislation making it a federal crime to kill FBI agents, he was convicted on 18 March 1935 and sentenced to life at Alcatraz. FBI protests delayed his parole until 31 October 1966, when Chase was finally released over the objections of J. EDGAR HOOVER. He died of cancer in California, on 5 October 1973.

**NESS, Eliot**— A Chicago native, born 19 April 1903, Eliot Ness received a bachelor's degree in business administration from the University of Chicago at age 22. In August 1926 he was hired as a trainee with the Treasury Department's Chicago Division, one of 300 agents assigned to the Windy City during PROHIBITION. Ness was promoted to the rank of "special agent" in the Prohibition Bureau during June 1928, nine months before President HERBERT HOOVER launched a campaign to imprison notorious Chicago bootlegger ALPHONSE CAPONE.

Because FBI Director J. EDGAR HOOVER refused to tackle Capone (or even acknowledge the existence of ORGANIZED CRIME in America), the task fell to "T-men" of the Treasury Department. ELMER IREY and the INTERNAL REVENUE SERVICE pursued Capone for income tax evasion, while Ness led a 10-man team against Capone's illegal breweries and distilleries. Dubbed "the Untouchables" for their alleged immunity to bribes, Ness's men ultimately failed in their effort to "dry up" Chicago, and the local mob lived on after Capone's 1932 tax conviction, thriving for decades thereafter. Meanwhile, Prohibition was repealed in December 1933 and Ness sought new employment opportunities in law enforcement.

His attempts to join the FBI were blocked by Hoover, who resented any competition for "gang-busting" headlines. Hoover ordered a secret investigation of Ness, exposed decades later under the FREEDOM OF INFORMATION ACT. The file contains numerous memos from Hoover, commanding his agents to shun any contact with Ness on the dubious grounds that Ness ignored legal procedures during criminal investigations. Ness biographer Paul Heimel holds the opposite view, that Hoover disdained Ness's commitment to "play by the rules," while G-men operated on a theory that "the end justifies the means."

In either case, Ness remained with Treasury's Alcohol Tax Unit (later the BUREAU OF ALCOHOL, TOBACCO AND FIREARMS) until December 1935, when Cleveland mayor Harold Burton hired him as that city's public safety commissioner. Over the next five years Ness compiled an impressive record of achievements, transforming Cleveland into the self-proclaimed "safest city in America" (though once again, organized crime remained largely unscathed by his efforts). In 1940-41 local newspapers began to snipe at Ness for his divorce and remarriage, as well as his frequent absences from Cleveland. A March 1942 auto accident sparked further criticism, with suggestions that Ness had been driving while intoxicated, and he resigned on 30 April 1942.

Ness spent the remainder of WORLD WAR II with the U.S. government's Social Protection Program, fighting venereal disease and prostitution in the neighborhood of military bases, then retired to a desultory career in private enterprise after 1945. He died on 16 May 1957, six months before publication of his memoirs. *The Untouchables* was a surprise best-seller, fictionalized as a two-part television movie in April 1959. A TV series of the same title (1959-63) and two more TV movies transformed Ness into a mythic hero, sending him in pursuit of every major gangster from the 1930s plus a host who never lived outside a scriptwriter's imagination. In Washington, Hoover assigned G-men to watch and summarize each of the program's 118 episodes, fuming with rage when the writers credited Ness with FBI achievements such as capture of the TRI-STATE GANG and the BARKER-KARPIS GANG.

**NEUMANN, Alfred**— A native of Vienna, born in 1910, playwright Alfred Neumann fled his homeland for the U.S. around the time Nazi Germany annexed Austria, in 1938. He settled in Los Angeles, where the FBI collected sketchy biographical details on Neumann without uncovering any derogatory information. An agent from the OFFICE OF STRATEGIC SERVICES (OSS) questioned Neumann in May 1945, seeking "information about the Communist political cells in Hollywood," but Neumann claimed to be "out of touch" with political trends among European exiles. An OSS memo observes: "It is obvious that either Neumann did not want to talk, or was not asked the right questions." Neumann became a naturalized U.S. citizen in December 1947 and soon moved to Denver, where he served as director of the Jewish Family and Children's Service of Colorado from 1948 to 1976. In 1976 he retired to Sun City, Arizona and died there on 3 March 2002.

**"NEW LEFT"**— The "New Left" was a loose coalition of anti-establishment groups active in the 1960s and early 1970s (as opposed to the "old left" of the COMMUNIST PARTY and the SOCIALIST WORKERS PARTY). Although collaborating with various militant minorities including the BLACK PANTHER PARTY and the AMERICAN INDIAN MOVEMENT, New Left groups were predominantly white, campus-based, and devoted much of their energy to VIETNAM WAR PROTESTS. While scores (or hundreds) of New Left groups were eventually organized, the movement's origin is normally dated from the creation of STUDENTS FOR A DEMOCRATIC SOCIETY (SDS) in 1960-61, and its most volatile group was an SDS spin-off, the WEATHER UNDERGROUND.

Encouraged by Presidents LYNDON JOHNSON and RICHARD NIXON, FBI Director J. EDGAR HOOVER responded to the New Left as he had to every dissident and left-of-center movement organized since 1917—with infiltration, surveillance, harassment, entrapment and disruption. Assistant Director WILLIAM SULLIVAN, in his memoirs, described the Bureau's first fumbling investigation of the SDS following student demonstrations at Columbia University.

> I teletyped the New York office and asked them what was behind all this and demanded to know what information they had. That afternoon I received a memorandum from New York that had attacked to it a number of newspaper articles. I teletyped New York again, saying, "I don't want newspaper clippings. I want to know what you have in the FILES about the student uprising at Columbia University." New York got back to me again with the terse response, "We don't have anything."

That response provoked a flurry of activity at FBI HEADQUARTERS. On 9 May 1968 the Bureau launched a new COINTELPRO campaign designed "to neutralize the New Left and the Key Activists" (defined as "those individuals who are the moving forces behind the New Left and on whom we have intensified our investigations." All field offices were ordered to submit proposed "counterintelligence" actions by 1 June 1968, with a reminder that "[t]he purpose of this program is to expose, disrupt and otherwise neutralize the activities of this group and persons connected with it. It is hoped that with this new program their violent and illegal activities may be reduced if not curtailed."

Still, the target(s) remained elusive, as detailed in a memo from Hoover on 27 May 1968:

> It is believed that in attempting to expose, disrupt, and otherwise neutralize the activities of the "new left" by counterintelligence methods, the Bureau is faced with a rather unique task. Because, first, the "new left" is difficult to actually define; and second, of the complete disregard by "new left" members for moral and social laws and social amenities.
>
> It is believed that the nonconformism in dress and speech, neglect of personal cleanliness, use of obscenities (printed and uttered), publicized sexual promiscuity, experimenting with and the use of drugs, filthy clothes, shaggy hair, wearing of sandals, beads, and unusual jewelry tend to negate any attempt to hold these people up to ridicule....
>
> It is believed therefore, that they must be destroyed or neutralized from the inside. Neutralize them in the same manner they are trying to destroy and neutralize the U.S.

To that end, aside from the standard use of hired INFORMANTS and *agents provocateur*, a special squad of G-men was assigned to grow long hair and infiltrate the New Left personally. Dubbed "the BEARDS" by colleagues, they infiltrated campuses and sundry organizations to identify leaders and objectives, but the final result was not anticipated by Hoover. As later described by Agent CRIL PAYNE, the Beards became immersed in a subculture of drugs and sex that would have appalled the FBI's director — and which, for all practical purposes, rendered their testimony worthless in future court proceedings.

One time-honored technique employed by G-men on the New Left beat was "SNITCH-JACKETING," aptly described in Hoover's memo of 27 May 1968:

> Certain key leaders must be chosen to become the object[s] of a counterintelligence plot to identify them as government informants. It appears that this is the only thing that could cause these individuals concern; if some of their leaders turned out to be paid informers. Attacking their morals, disrespect for the law, or patriotic disdain will not impress their followers, as it would normally to other groups, so it must be by attacking them through their own principles and beliefs. Accuse them of selling out to "imperialistic monopoly capitalism."

The first New Left activist proposed for such treatment was Tom Hayden, later indicted as one of the "Chicago 7" conspiracy defendants (and later still a U.S. Senator, married for a time to actress Jane Fonda). Other candidates would soon be recommended, their radical credentials challenged in anonymous letters and phone calls, rumors spread by FBI *provocateurs* in private conversations, and in political cartoons penned by FBI artists.

Such activities were justified by Hoover's (and President Nixon's) claim that New Left groups engaged in systematic TERRORISM. There can be no doubt that many demonstrations planned by New Left activists degenerated into violence, and several groups were linked to BOMBINGS of various targets around the U.S., including military installations, government buildings, police cars, corporate offices and campus facilities linked to the Vietnam war effort. The FBI's official history, presented on its website, describes a veritable revolution in America, reporting that "in 1970 alone, an estimated 3,000 bombings and 50,000 bomb threats occurred in the United States." While some of those acts were committed by far-right groups, including the KU KLUX KLAN and the MINUTEMEN, FBI publicists lay them all at the New Left's doorstep.

But is it true?

Today, after 30 years of revelations from the FBI's own files, we know that a small army of *provocateurs* was employed to arm New Left activists and persuade them to commit violent crimes (which would then produce arrests and convictions). Such entrapment is generally illegal (and always unethical), but it was not the worst of the FBI's transgressions under the long COINTELPRO-NEW LEFT campaign. Bureau informant THOMAS TONGYAI "constantly talked violence, carried a grenade in his car, showed students how to use an M-1 rifle and offered advice on how to carry out bombings." HORACE PACKER, acting under FBI orders, supplied campus radicals with drugs, weapons and materials for making Molotov cocktails. ALFRED BURNETT paid black war veteran Larry Ward to plant a bomb (which Burnett built and provided) in Seattle, leading to Ward's fatal shooting by police. LARRY GRATHWOHL taught bomb-making to SDS members and personally bombed a Cincinnati school in 1969. When the "Cam-

den 28" invaded a New Jersey draft board, informant ROBERT HARDY provided "90 percent" of the burglary tools, plus his "expertise at breaking and entering." These criminals and many others like them operated with full knowledge and approval of their FBI handlers.

Bureau attacks on the New Left were exposed in March 1971, by the MEDIA, PENNSYLVANIA BURGLARY that revealed a sampling of covert memos, and while Hoover officially canceled the COINTELPRO operations a month later, identical tactics were used against anti-war groups until American withdrawal from Vietnam finally robbed the New Left of its raison d'être. Two retired FBI officials, W. MARK FELT and EDWARD MILLER, were convicted in 1980 of authorizing illegal break-ins against New Left groups and sympathizers, but they were later pardoned by President RONALD REAGAN — himself a former FBI informant who battled the same groups as governor of California.

**NEW York City Police Department** — Like the Los Angeles Police Department, New York's "finest" have a history of competition and conflict with the FBI. The NYPD began tapping telephones in 1885, and in 1906 — two years before the Bureau was created — officers inaugurated a special ANARCHIST Squad to harass and arrest "radicals" on any available pretext. The targets in those days included LABOR UNION organizers, plus advocates of women's suffrage and birth control. As anarchists (or government *provocateurs*) grew more violent, NYPD created a Bomb Squad in 1914 — not to defuse explosive charges, but to pin the blasts on leftists. Bomb Squad agents infiltrated the INDUSTRIAL WORKERS OF THE WORLD and other groups. A report published in 1916 revealed that police WIRETAPPING had extended to some 350 local telephones. In 1930 the Bomb Squad was renamed the Radical Bureau, a name it maintained until the 1950s, when it became the Bureau of Special Services (BOSS).

With such a background, NYPD leaders felt that J. EDGAR HOOVER's G-men were mere upstarts in the field of DOMESTIC INTELLIGENCE. Their initial conflict with the FBI, however, emerged from "normal" criminal cases. In 1935, New York police beat federal agents to the punch by arresting Bruno Hauptmann as a suspect in the LINDBERGH KIDNAPPING. A year later, Hoover double-crossed NYPD in the case of bank robber HARRY BRUNETTE, prompting Police Commissioner Lewis Valentine to call Hoover "a hunter of headlines" as well as criminals. The rivalry intensified on 1 September 1939, when ADOLF HITLER invaded Poland and agents of the Bureau's New York field office warned Hoover that NYPD had already created its own 50-man Sabotage Squad. Five days later, Hoover sought and obtained a statement from President FRANKLIN ROOSEVELT "to all police officials in the United States," commanding them to give the FBI "any information obtained pertaining to ESPIONAGE, counterespionage, sabotage and neutrality violations."

Still, NYPD went its own way in fighting "subversion." In June 1940, 28 rookie officers were trained to infiltrate the COMMUNIST PARTY, which maintained its headquarters in New York. One of those spies, Margaret Disco, remained in the party for 15 years and attained high rank while betraying her "comrades" at every turn. Twenty years later, BOSS launched a new Black Target Infiltration Program that anticipated the FBI's own COIN-TELPRO campaign against black militants nationwide. NYPD refused to collaborate in FBI harassment of the BLACK PANTHER PARTY, trusting its own INFORMANTS to do a better job, but conspiracy charges filed against the "Panther 21" in April 1969 failed to produce the sweeping felony convictions expected at police headquarters.

In their daily routine, BOSS agents mimicked FBI techniques. By 1968 they had compiled a master index listing 1,220,000 "subversive" individuals and 125,000 suspect organizations. In April 1969 they infiltrated a VIETNAM WAR PROTEST and committed violent acts to "justify" police beatings of marchers (a tactic held over from 1930, when Commissioner Grover Whalen first used it against the Communist Party). In 1970, after J. Edgar Hoover blocked implementation of the HUSTON PLAN in Washington, White House aide JOHN EHRLICHMAN increasingly used NYPD officers to service his intelligence needs. John Caulfield, a former New York policeman, was hired full-time to handle intelligence matters "too sensitive" for the FBI. In September 1972, four BOSS officers were flown to Langley, Virginia for a special training session with the CENTRAL INTELLIGENCE AGENCY.

BOSS harassment victims filed a class action lawsuit against NYPD in May 1971. NYPD offered a half-hearted settlement in December 1980, but the case dragged on until March 1985, when federal judge Charles Haight prepared guidelines strictly limiting NYPD's political surveillance activities. The department agreed, but soon forgot its binding promise. In 1987 another lawsuit revealed more of the same abuses, targeting minority victims. As in the past, department leaders lied about their criminal activities at first, then recanted in December 1987 and confessed ongoing violations of the 1985 court order. Civil libertarians are understandably skeptical of NYPD's subsequent promises to obey the laws it is pledged enforce.

**NICHOLS, Louis Burrous**—An Illinois native, born 13 January 1906, Louis Nichols was raised in Michigan and graduated from Kalamazoo College before obtaining a law degree from George Washington University in 1934. He joined the FBI on 30 July 1934, serving in the Birmingham field office before he was recalled to FBI HEADQUARTERS in March 1935. Someone in authority had learned that Nichols paid his way through law school by working as a public relations officer for the Young Men's Christian Association, and Director J. EDGAR HOOVER needed a press agent. Nichols was assigned to the CRIME RECORDS DIVISION, and became its chief in November 1935. His subsequent promotions — to inspector (July 1938); assistant to Associate Director CLYDE TOLSON (August 1939); assistant director of the ADMINISTRATIVE DIVISION (May 1941); and assistant to the director (October 1951) — never changed the nature of Nichols's assignment.

Crime Records was the FBI's publicity department, responsible for all contacts with Congress and the news media. Agents in Crime Records also served as ghost writers, preparing books and articles for Hoover, writing speeches for various FBI spokesmen and members of Congress, drafting "blind" press releases for friendly journalists to use without attribution to the Bureau. One of Nichols's early successes, in May 1936, was the myth that Hoover "personally arrested" fugitive ALVIN KARPIS in New Orleans. The incident was staged in response to congressional criticism of Hoover's inexperience with police work, and also to counteract rumors of his HOMOSEXUALITY. Nichols could never silence those rumors, however, and he was clearly overstating the case when he told author Curt Gentry that Karpis's arrest "pretty much ended the 'queer' talk" about Hoover.

Nichols suffered his first major gaffe 13 years later, when President HARRY TRUMAN allegedly debated plans to fire Hoover. Nichols hoped to generate sympathy for Hoover with a "backfire" rumor that Hoover planned to resign. The planted story made headlines in the *New York Times* on 15 June 1949, but the anticipated groundswell of demands for Hoover to remain never materialized. Instead, Hoover was forced to scramble for his job and deny the stories circulated by his own PR department. Columnist DREW PEARSON publicly identified the source of the story as "J. Edgar Hoover's public relations man, Lou Nichols, a smart and likable Greek-American, formerly Nicholopolous, who, in his zeal to protect his boss, sometimes outsmarts himself."

Ghost writing for Hoover was sometimes a lucrative job. Assistant Director WILLIAM SULLIVAN recalled that after Hoover's *Masters of Deceit* was published, Hoover "put many thousands of dollars [from] that book ... into his own pocket, and so did Tolson, and so did Lou Nichols." Other tasks were simply part of the job, including preparation of speeches for Red-hunting Senator JOSEPH MCCARTHY and his chief aide ROY COHN; leaking news to the press of ELEANOR ROOSEVELT'S alleged romantic affairs; coordinating media attacks on critical author MAX LOWENTHAL; or conducting Hoover's correspondence with attorney MORRIS ERNST of the AMERICAN CIVIL LIBERTIES UNION. In December 1950, Nichols even wrote a *Reader's Digest* article for Ernst, entitled "Why I No Longer Fear the FBI."

Profits and promotions aside, Nichols harbored loftier ambitions. On 14 January 1957 Drew Pearson leaked the news that "Lou Nichols has been busy ingratiating himself with key senators, who have the impression he is grooming himself to be Hoover's heir apparent. To this Lou modestly replied: 'My only desire is to serve Mr. Hoover.'" Eight months later, on 5 September 1957, Pearson wrote again: "The FBI's amiable press agent, Lou Nichols, is cozying up to Vice President [RICHARD] NIXON. Lou has his eye on J. Edgar Hoover's job, is keeping close to the powers-that-be." In the wake of each column, Nichols suffered Hoover's silent treatment. When Nichols left the Bureau on 2 November 1957, taking with him a copy of the FBI's Washington contacts, Hoover furiously branded him "a Judas."

The perceived betrayal was compounded when Nichols moved directly from the FBI to a post as executive vice president of Schenley Industries, serving Hoover financial patron LEWIS ROSENSTIEL. In his first year on the job, Nichols lobbied successfully for passage of the Foran Bill, saving Rosenstiel and Schenley at least $40 million in liquor excise taxes. A major part of Nichols's job was defending Rosenstiel before various government investigating committees that probed his 30-year links to

ORGANIZED CRIME. In each case, Nichols declared under oath that Rosenstiel had "never, directly or indirectly, had any dealings or associations with Meyer Lansky, Frank Costello, or any other underworld characters." (In fact, Rosenstiel was friendly with both mobsters, their contact dating from his role as a bootlegger in PROHIBITION.) In 1965 Nichols orchestrated Rosenstiel's $1 million donation to establish the J. EDGAR HOOVER FOUNDATION.

In 1968, while still employed at Schenley, Nichols was tapped to serve as chief of campaign security for presidential candidate Richard Nixon. He recruited former G-men and attorneys nationwide for "Operation Eagle Eye," to guard against a recurrence of the Democratic vote fraud that scuttled Nixon's White House race in 1960. Nichols retired from Schenley in 1969, and columnist JACK ANDERSON reported on 12 April of that year that "Nichols believes he has the inside track with President Nixon, who is expected to keep Hoover on one more year, then retire him at last at the age of 75." Nichols swiftly called Hoover to deny the report, but Hoover refused to speak with him. Instead, on 8 May 1969, Hoover issued a statement that "I may have plans and aspirations for the future. None includes retirement." In his declining years, Nichols maintained homes in Florida and Virginia. He died in Miami, in 1977.

**NIN, Anaïs**— Born at Neuilly, outside Paris, in 1903, Anaïs Nin came to New York with her siblings and divorced mother in 1914. She married in 1923 and returned to France with her husband a year later, living in Paris for the next 15 years while writing novels and diaries. (She also conducted a long-term romantic affair with novelist HENRY MILLER.) Nin returned to New York City in 1939, and the FBI opened a file on her soon thereafter, but no criminal or "subversive" information was ever collected. Nin died in 1977, Associate Director CARTHA DELOACH later suggesting to author Nancy Robins that "sometime or other [Nin] she probably made some reference to the FBI or about Mr. [J. EDGAR] HOOVER, or perhaps she was a member of the [COMMUNIST] PARTY, and the FBI put her up as a possible source of information." If so, no such information remained in Nin's file when it was released under the FREEDOM OF INFORMATION ACT.

**NIXON, Richard Milhous**— Born at Yorba Linda, California on 9 January 1913, Richard Nixon graduated from Whittier College in 1934 and from Duke University Law School in 1937. He applied for a position with the FBI, but he was rejected when investigators learned that he had lied on his application. Specifically, Nixon denied ever being arrested (he was jailed in 1933, for a student prank at Whittier) and claimed that he had been the "manager" of a California gas station whose owner told G-men that Nixon had merely "done odd jobs for him from time to time." Agents in North Carolina also learned that Nixon had burglarized a Dean's office at Duke, seeking an advance copy of forthcoming tests.

That trademark dishonesty followed Nixon into legal practice, when he joined the California firm of Wingert and Bewley in 1946 (following service with the U.S. Navy during WORLD WAR II). His first courtroom appearance, in a probate case, prompted Judge Alfred Paonessa to say, "Mr. Nixon, I have serious doubts whether you have the ethical qualifications to practice law in the state of California. I am seriously thinking of turning this matter over to the Bar Association to have you disbarred." It proved to be a bluff, and Nixon was undaunted. That fall he defeated incumbent Congressman Jerry Voorhis in a campaign marked by false accusations that Voorhis was a communist. Nixon's campaign manager in that race and subsequent contests was Murray Chotiner, an attorney with strong ties to ORGANIZED CRIME.

In Congress, Nixon quickly attached himself to the HOUSE COMMITTEE ON UN-AMERICAN ACTIVITIES and secured his Red-hunting reputation with the perjury conviction of ALGER HISS. In 1950 he won a Senate seat with identical tactics, branding opponent Helen Gahagan Douglas "the Pink Lady." Republican presidential candidate DWIGHT EISENHOWER tapped Nixon as his running mate in 1952, avoiding personal involvement in the campaign's mud-slinging while Nixon and Senator JOSEPH MCCARTHY did the dirty work. Together, they branded Democratic opponent ADLAI STEVENSON a Red, an "egghead" and a closet HOMOSEXUAL— the latter charge drawn from FILES provided by FBI Director J. EDGAR HOOVER. Even then, Nixon's personal corruption nearly cost Eisenhower the election, when his $18,000 covert slush fund was exposed, but Nixon's tearful "Checkers speech" of 23 September 1952 saved the day with a surprise outpouring of public sympathy.

Nixon lost his 1960 presidential bid to opponent JOHN KENNEDY, despite covert support from FBI HEADQUARTERS, and he was defeated again two years later in a California gubernatorial race. That embarrassment prompted him to tell reporters, "You won't have Richard Nixon to kick around any more," but the lure of the campaign trail would finally prove irresistible. Before that happened, though, the FBI's LEGAL ATTACHÉ in Hong Kong reported that Nixon was involved in an extramarital affair with a Bureau INFORMANT, one Marianna Liu. Hoover filed the information, along with Liu's admission that she went on "many dates" with Nixon (although she denied that they ever had sex). Nixon ran for President again in 1968, employing retired FBI Assistant Director LOUIS NICHOLS as chief of campaign security, and this time he emerged victorious in another close contest.

Nixon's tenure in the White House was an era of corruption unrivaled since the administration of President WARREN HARDING, climaxed by the WATERGATE SCANDAL that finally drove Nixon from office in August 1974. Before that, Vice President SPIRO AGNEW and Attorney General JOHN MITCHELL would face criminal charges, along with White House aides JOHN EHRLICHMAN, H.R. HALDEMAN and others. In the early days of the Nixon administration, Hoover did his best to accommodate White House demands for WIRETAPS on reporters and political opponents, but he balked at surrendering authority under the HUSTON PLAN of June 1970. According to insider accounts, Nixon scheduled multiple meetings with Hoover in 1971-72, intending each time to dismiss the FBI director, but Nixon repeatedly lost his nerve. On the last occasion, when retirement was finally mentioned, author Sanford Ungar reports that Hoover "immediately resisted, making threats and veiled references to material about

Nixon in the Director's private files." It was enough to put dismissal plans on hold, until the problem was solved by Hoover's death in May 1972. Thereafter, Nixon chose L. PATRICK GRAY to head the FBI, but scandal snared him as well, and he was replaced by Director CLARENCE KELLEY in 1973.

Threats of impeachment prompted Nixon to resign on 8 August 1974, and President GERALD FORD pardoned Nixon on 18 September 1974 for any and all crimes he may have committed prior to that date. Critics denounced the "corrupt bargain," and New York's Supreme Court disbarred Nixon in July 1976 for obstructing justice during the Watergate scandal, but memories of his corruption soon faded. Over the next two decades, Nixon wrote a series of best-selling books and appeared frequently on national TV programs, where he was consulted in the role of elder statesman. By the time he died, on 22 April 1994, he was effectively "rehabilitated" in the media, curiously eulogized by leaders of both major parties.

**NOISETTE, Samuel**— One of roughly a dozen African Americans employed by Hoover's FBI prior to the advent of Attorney General ROBERT KENNEDY, Samuel Noisette entered service as a messenger on 27 April 1927. After brief service in that capacity, he was transferred to Hoover's office as a clerk. Hoover formally named Noisette an "information receptionist" on 28 March 1954, and promoted him to "special agent" on 30 June 1957. Although Noisette received only three days of training (on firearms) and never left the office to investigate a single case, Hoover frequently cited him as "proof" that the FBI was fully integrated. *Ebony* magazine, in its issue of 29 September 1962, came closer to the truth than its editors realized when it said that Hoover's relationship to Noisette "virtually sets the race relations pattern for the huge agency."

In fact, as Noisette himself made clear, his actual duties consisted of escorting visitors into Hoover's office, helping the director don his coat, and handing towels to Hoover in his private bathroom. Noisette once said that roughly half his FBI career was spent in the latter pursuit, as an aging Hoover became increasingly obsessed with germs, washing his hands compulsively throughout the day. That fear of disease also brought Noisette on the run with a swatter, whenever a fly found its way into Hoover's inner sanctum. Once, as recalled in the memoirs of Assistant Director WILLIAM SULLIVAN, Noisette was called to slay a fly, only to watch it land on Hoover. As Hoover shouted, "Hit him! Hit him!" Noisette sprang forward and struck the insect "a hell of a lot harder than necessary."

Aside from daily visitors, Noisette also escorted new graduates of the FBI ACADEMY to their first audience with the director, sometimes befriending individual agents and advising them of Hoover's idiosyncrasies. Agent NORMAN OLLESTAD recalled Noisette's warning that "the walls of Justice have ears," and that agents were watched in the headquarters men's room due to Hoover's fear of "queers." In his spare time, Noisette was an accomplished artist who held yearly exhibitions of his work. He retired from the FBI on 19 January 1968, but he was not forgotten. When Hoover died in 1972, his will left half of the director's used clothing to Noisette, with the rest bequeathed to servant JAMES CRAWFORD.

**NORRIS, George William**— An Ohio native, born at Sandusky on 11 July 1861, George Norris later settled in Nebraska, where he served as a district judge (1895-1903) and as a congressman (1903-13) before he was elected to the U.S. Senate in 1913. As an independent liberal, he had no patience with government infringement of CIVIL RIGHTS, and he watched the FBI's expansion under President FRANKLIN ROOSEVELT with great concern. When his complaints to Attorney General FRANK MURPHY failed to curb FBI DOMESTIC SURVEILLANCE, Norris carried his battle to the Senate floor in a series of speeches lambasting the Bureau and Director J. EDGAR HOOVER.

Between February and May 1940 Norris publicly accused the FBI of "overstepping and overreaching the legitimate object for which it was created," warning that if its activities continued "there will be a spy behind every stump and a detective in every closet in our land." As for Hoover, Norris branded him "the greatest hound for publicity on the North American continent," reporting that a personal friend — the editor of a Midwestern daily newspaper —"received an average of one letter a week from Mr. Hoover" seeking further public recognition. The FBI, Norris claimed, would rather try its cases in the press than in court. He went on to state that:

> Mr. Hoover has an organization, maintained at public expense, writing speeches for him to make or for anyone else to make who will take the speeches. When he makes a speech a copy is sent to practically every newspaper in the United States.
>
> No organization that I know of meets in Washington without having some person appear before it to tell what a great organization the FBI is. The greatest man of all, who stands at the head of it, never made a mistake, never made a blunder. In his hands lie the future and the perpetuity of our institutions and our Government.

In a subsequent speech, Norris declared:

> Unless we do something to stop this furor of adulation and praise as being omnipotent, we shall have an organization — the organization of the FBI — which, instead of protecting our people from the civil acts of criminals, will itself in the end direct the Government by tyrannical force, as the history of the world shows has always been the case when secret police and secret detectives have been snooping around the homes of honest men.

Anticipating a backlash from Hoover's apologists, Norris told the Senate that he expected various reporters and public figures to accuse him of trying to "smear ... one of the greatest men who ever lived and who now held the future life of our country in the palm of his mighty hand." That prediction was entirely accurate, as Assistant Director LOUIS NICHOLS enlisted WALTER WINCHELL, DREW PEARSON and other friendly columnists to attack Norris in editorials penned by the Bureau's CRIME RECORDS DIVISION. NBC commentator Earl Godwin told his radio audience that "[i]n many cases an attack on Hoover is an attack on the president of the United States and what's more, an attack on the safety of the government." Hoover himself responded to Norris and other critics in more than a dozen speeches, proclaiming, "The Communists hope that with the FBI shackled, they can proceed without interference as they go about their boring, undermining way to overthrow our government."

Undaunted, Norris pursued his campaign with unrelenting vigor. In December 1940 FBI HEADQUARTERS learned that Norris "was engaged in preparing another blast at the Bureau," scouring JUSTICE DEPARTMENT reports from 1911 onward, with "particular interest in documents covering the period from 1918 to 1922." In reference to the lawless PALMER RAIDS of 1919-20, Norris reminded America that the G-men involved were "all, without exception agents under the control and supervision of Mr. Hoover." We can only speculate what role Hoover may have played in the 1942 election campaign, but Norris was defeated for reelection that year and his voice in the Senate was finally silenced. He died in 1944.

# O

**O'BRIAN, John Lord**— A progressive attorney, born at Buffalo, New York on 14 October 1874, John O'Brian served as a member of the New York state assembly (1908-09) and as U.S. attorney for the Western District of New York (1909-14). In 1917 Attorney General THOMAS GREGORY chose him as a special assistant, to head the JUSTICE DEPARTMENT'S War Emergency Division during WORLD WAR I. In that capacity, O'Brian came to know a young attorney named J. EDGAR HOOVER, whom he characterized in 1918 as "a conscientious and honest fellow." So impressed was O'Brian with Hoover's work ethic, in fact, that he promoted Hoover three times "simply as merits," finally placing Hoover in charge of the department's Enemy Alien Registration Section.

O'Brian left Justice at war's end, while Hoover sought a transfer to the Immigration Service. Rejected there, he tried the Bureau of Investigation next, and was rebuffed again, until O'Brian recommended him to Attorney General A. MITCHELL PALMER. O'Brian praised Hoover as a subordinate "willing to carry out orders at any time," but he soon had reason to regret his endorsement, as Hoover helped coordinate the sweeping PALMER RAIDS of 1919-20. O'Brian was among the critics of those lawless roundups, but he either mistook Hoover's role in the raids or else chose to ignore it. In 1924 O'Brian again recommended Hoover, this time in communication with Attorney General HARLAN STONE, as the best man to supplant disgraced Bureau director WILLIAM BURNS.

Though initially grateful, Hoover turned on O'Brian almost at once, when O'Brian made another recommendation to Attorney General Stone, suggesting WILLIAM DONOVAN'S employment as assistant attorney general in 1924. Hoover despised Donovan — described by some gossips as "O'Brian's eyes and ears at Justice" — and his malice spilled over to anyone associated with Donovan's rise. The FBI director's silent feud with O'Brian continued through 1941, when O'Brian once again endorsed Donovan, this time recommending that President FRANKLIN ROOSEVELT pick Donovan to lead the OFFICE OF STRATEGIC SERVICES in WORLD WAR II. O'Brian, meanwhile, had failed in his 1938 bid to represent New York in the U.S. Senate, and he retired to private practice. Shortly before his death in 1974, O'Brian recalled his promotion of Hoover as "something I prefer to whisper in dark corners. It is one of the sins for which I have to atone."

**ODETS, Clifford**— A Philadelphia native, born in 1906, Clifford Odets emerged as one of America's leading dramatists in the Great Depression, known for his socially conscious plays. The FBI opened a dossier on him in 1935, after he penned an article for the *Daily Worker*. Two years later, tagged "the darling of the left" by G-men, Odets was listed as a member of such suspect organizations as the National Writers Union, the New Theatre League, and the Citizens Committee to Aid Striking Seamen. Odets (or "O'Dets," as the Bureau sometimes spelled his name) also joined the AUTHORS LEAGUE OF AMERICA and served on the War Writers Board in WORLD WAR II. A report filed in LILLIAN HELLMAN'S dossier named Odets as one of five authors considered "extremely close to the COMMUNIST PARTY in recent years," and a 1944 memo repeated that claim, listing him with PEARL BUCK and others as an affiliate of unnamed Red organizations. Called to testify before the HOUSE COMMITTEE ON UN-AMERICAN ACTIVITIES (HUAC) eight years later, Odets admitted joining the party in 1934, but dropped out the following year because he found the meetings "silly." ARTHUR MILLER and other acquaintances condemned Odets for "naming names" in his HUAC appearance, but his cooperation failed to pacify the FBI. G-men maintained their file on Odets until 1964, a year after his death.

**OFFICE of Congressional and Public Affairs**—The FBI's Office of Congressional and Public Affairs (OCPA) is a descendant of the old CRIME RECORDS DIVISION, which once "ghosted" books and magazine articles for the personal profit of Director J. EDGAR HOOVER. Today, as its name suggests, the OCPA is responsible for FBI communications with Congress, the media and the public at large. In addition to various press releases and participation in television programs such as *America's Most Wanted* and *Unsolved Mysteries*, the OCPA publishes an internal magazine for FBI employees only (*The Investigator*), conducts public tours of FBI HEADQUARTERS, and administers the Bureau's "TEN MOST WANTED" LIST. Additionally, in November 1996, OCPA was made responsible for handling all information requests filed under the FREEDOM OF INFORMATION ACT. Based on the tenor of recent FBI press releases, it appears that a major job of the OCPA—as of old—involves damage control and deflection of outside criticism.

**OFFICE of Equal Employment Opportunity Affairs**—Initially created as a section within the FBI's ADMINISTRATIVE SERVICES DIVISION, Equal Employment Opportunity (EEO) was elevated to "office" status in March 1989, thus theoretically providing "greater autonomy and access to the FBI director." Based on the subsequent volume of complaints from minority employees, including class-action lawsuits filed against the Bureau by BLACK and HISPANIC AGENTS in the 1990s, it appears that little was accomplished. Author Robert Kessler, in *The FBI* (1993), calls EEO "essentially useless," with investigation of specific complaints dragging on from 150 to 800 days.

The office was apparently abolished sometime after 1993, since it appears nowhere on the modern FBI's website. Instead, a search under "Equal Employment Opportunity" produces this generic statement: "Except where otherwise provided by law, there will be no discrimination because of color, race, religion, national origin, political affiliation, marital status, disability, age, sex, sexual orientation, membership or nonmembership in an employee organization, or on the basis of personal favoritism."

**OFFICE of General Counsel**—Director LOUIS FREEH created the Office of General Counsel (OGC) in October 1993, during a general overhaul at FBI HEADQUARTERS. Former assistant U.S. attorney Howard Shapiro was hired in an effort to provide the Bureau with a top legal officer who had experience in both litigation and investigation. As of 2002, the OGC employed "approximately 60 attorneys," their mission officially described on the FBI's website.

> The Office of the General Counsel (OGC) provides legal advice to the Director and other FBI officials. In addition, OGC personnel research legal questions regarding law enforcement and national security matters and coordinate the defense of civil litigation and administrative claims involving the FBI, its personnel, and its records.

The OGC presently includes four subdivisions. The Litigation Branch defends civil lawsuits filed against the FBI, including actions arising under the FREEDOM OF INFORMATION ACT. The Administrative and Technology Law Branch advises FBI leaders on a variety of matters including, but not limited to "considerations of: constitutional law, agency authority and organization, fiscal law, ethics and standards of conduct, information law, federal personnel law, facilities and property, contracting and procurement, computer intrusion, infrastructure protection, and

communications and technology law." The Legal Advice and Training Branch schools G-men and agents of the DRUG ENFORCEMENT ADMINISTRATION in the legal fine points of their duties. The National Security Law Branch confines itself to matters including "foreign counterintelligence (FCI), international terrorism, and domestic security/terrorism (including weapons of mass destruction, and counter-proliferation)."

**OFFICE of Investigative Agency Policies**—An innovation of Attorney General JANET RENO, created in November 1993, the Office of Investigative Agency Policies (OIAP) was designed to coordinate actions and policies among various investigative branches of the U.S. JUSTICE DEPARTMENT, chaired by the FBI's director. In that capacity, Director LOUIS FREEH announced a five-year summary of the OIAP's activities in 1998, including creation of uniform policies on shooting incidents and use of deadly force, together with coordination of congressional budget requests "to ensure the Department gets the most impact from its resources." No further reference to the OIAP appears in FBI press releases since 1998, suggesting that the office was dissolved.

**OFFICE of Professional Responsibility**—Created by Director CLARENCE KELLEY in October 1976, to investigate allegations of AGENT MISCONDUCT, the Office of Professional Responsibility (OPR) was part of the FBI's INSPECTION DIVISION until March 1997, when Director LOUIS FREEH made it an independent office headed by an assistant director. Under Freeh, the OPR issued sketchy reports on FBI employees disciplined for misconduct in the years 1997-99, but that practice has apparently been discontinued. At last report, in July 2000, the OPR's staff included 28 special agents and 41 support personnel, assigned to conduct "about one-fourth of the investigations of employees for serious misconduct." (Responsibility for the other three-fourths remained officially unassigned.) As of May 2002, Assistant Director Michael DeFeo commanded the OPR.

**OFFICE of Strategic Services**—In July 1941, five months before the PEARL HARBOR ATTACK drew America into WORLD WAR II, President FRANKLIN ROOSEVELT created the office of a Coordinator of Information to collect and analyze strategic data from abroad. He chose WILLIAM DONOVAN to fill the post, despite strenuous protests from FBI Director J. EDGAR HOOVER (who despised Donovan from his earlier days at the JUSTICE DEPARTMENT). Donovan's group did not assume its more familiar name—the Office of Strategic Services (OSS)—until June 1942, when an order from Roosevelt commanded it to "plan and operate such special services as may be directed by the United States Joint Chiefs of Staff."

By that time, Donovan had already fought a series of petty skirmishes with Hoover and FBI HEADQUARTERS. First, Hoover complained about COI/OSS agents operating in the United States, in competition with the FBI. In January 1942 Roosevelt banned Donovan's men from conducting DOMESTIC SURVEILLANCE inside the U.S. and further compelled them to clear all Western Hemisphere operations with the FBI in advance. (G-men from Hoover's own SPECIAL INTELLIGENCE SERVICE were already active in Latin America.) Donovan obeyed the order long enough to realize that Hoover would never cooperate with the OSS in any way, whereupon Donovan resumed his own clandestine activities in the U.S. In April 1942, learning that OSS men planned to burglarize the Spanish embassy in Washington, Hoover dispatched an FBI car to park outside the embassy with siren wailing, thus alerting the guards and forcing Donovan's men to run for their lives. Next morning, when Donovan took his complaint to Roosevelt, he found that Hoover had been there ahead of him. The OSS was ordered to surrender all its U.S. FILES and operations (including INFORMANTS) to the FBI.

There was no limit to Hoover's vindictive pursuit of the OSS. For months, his friends in the STATE DEPARTMENT stamped "OSS" on passports issued to Donovan's agents, thus endangering their lives, until President Roosevelt intervened to stop the harassment. Hoover opened dossiers on Donovan's employees and their relatives, seeking any derogatory information he could find. Whenever he perceived a slip-up by the OSS, Hoover fired off multiple complaints to the White House, State and Justice. (In February 1944, after Donovan negotiated an exchange of anti-Nazi information with the NKVD [Stalinist secret police], Hoover claimed Donovan had unleashed hordes of Russian agents in the U.S. "attempting to obtain highly confidential information concerning War Department secrets.") Even Congress displayed favoritism, approving Hoover's $49 million budget request uncut in 1944 while Donovan's plea for $45 million was cut to $23 million. On balance, Donovan told friends, "The Abwehr (German intelligence) gets better treatment from the FBI than we do."

Still, Donovan persevered. In fall 1944 he proposed to Roosevelt that the OSS should continue operations after World War II. Hoover learned of the plan and coordinated a series of news leaks, producing nationwide headlines on 9 February 1945 that condemned Donovan's blueprint for a "Super Gestapo Organization." Roosevelt, embarrassed, vetoed the plan. One month later, on 11 March 1945, OSS agents broke the AMERASIA CASE in New York, but they followed procedure and handed it off to the FBI on 14 March. Hoover's men established illegal WIRETAPS, staged illegal BREAK-INS, and finally arrested six ESPIONAGE suspects in June 1945, but the case was thrown out in September, once the Bureau's lawless tactics were exposed.

President HARRY TRUMAN dissolved the OSS on 20 September 1945, with EXECUTIVE ORDER 9621, but he lacked the nerve to confront Donovan personally and passed the job off to Budget Director Harold Smith. Smith, in turn, summoned an aide to do the dirty work, telling him, "The president doesn't want to do it and I don't want to do it, but because I can, I'm ordering you to do it." It was Hoover's final triumph over Donovan, but he would soon face even greater competition in the form of Truman's OSS successor, the CENTRAL INTELLIGENCE AGENCY.

**O'HARA, John Henry**—A native of Pottsville, Pennsylvania, born in 1905, John O'Hara began his literary career as a reporter for the Pottsville *Journal*, at age 19, but he was fired the following year "because of habitual tardiness." Better known for fiction, he went on to publish such best-selling novels as *Appointment in*

*Samara* (1934), *Butterfield 8* (1935), and *Pal Joey* (1940). The FBI opened a file on O'Hara in June 1939, noting his membership in the League of American Writers (described as a Communist front by the HOUSE COMMITTEE ON UN-AMERICAN ACTIVITIES). O'Hara left the group after the Soviet Union invaded Finland, and was thereafter generally considered a "loyal American."

In 1942, following rejections by both the army and navy, O'Hara briefly went to work as chief story editor for the motion picture division of the Office of Coordinator of Inter-American Affairs. Tiring of that post, he entered training as an intelligence officer for the OFFICE OF STRATEGIC SERVICES (OSS), but dropped out due to "health reasons." He next came to the FBI's attention in June 1949, after applying for a post with the OSS's successor, the CENTRAL INTELLIGENCE AGENCY (CIA).

CIA recruiters made the standard request for an FBI background check on O'Hara and G-men hastened to comply. They noted O'Hara's membership in the "Communist infiltrated" AUTHORS LEAGUE OF AMERICA, but compensated with reports that he had been "active in trying to throw out the leftist wing of the [Screen] Writers Guild." Unnamed informers deemed O'Hara "free of any leanings toward Communism," but they also judged him "a very heavy drinker," "highly opinionated," "quarrelsome," "hot-tempered and temperamental," and "a little wild." In July 1949 a "mature, experienced and well qualified" agent was assigned to question *New Yorker* editor Harold Ross about O'Hara, but no report of the interview has survived. The references listed on O'Hara's CIA application placed him "in the class with such authors as ERNEST HEMINGWAY and [WILLIAM] FAULKNER"—no great endorsement, from the Bureau's viewpoint—but they also said O'Hara "would not be intrigued by such asinine concepts as Communism."

The CIA rejected O'Hara's application, thus excluding him from the cloak-and-dagger set. He died in 1970, but his dossier remained classified 15 years later, denied to author Herbert Mitgang "in the interest of the national defense or foreign policy." An 18-month appeal under the FREEDOM OF INFORMATION ACT finally saw 91 censored pages released in 1987, while at least seven more pages were withheld entirely.

**O'KEEFFE, Georgia Totto**—Born at Sun Prairie, Wisconsin on 15 November 1887, Georgia O'Keeffe moved to Virginia with her family in 1903 and settled in New York City four years later. She met photographer-critic Alfred Stieglitz there in 1916, and his gallery was the first to exhibit her drawings. They embarked on a scandalous affair in 1918, living together for six years before Stieglitz obtained a divorce from his wife. O'Keeffe married Stieglitz (23 years her senior) in December 1924, but continued to travel widely, spending most of her time in New Mexico from the mid-1920s onward. Stieglitz died in July 1946 and O'Keeffe buried his ashes at her home in Abiquiu, New Mexico, where she lived and painted in solitude.

The FBI took interest in O'Keeffe during the Red scare that followed WORLD WAR II. A 1953 report described O'Keeffe as "the only person in Abiquiu who was pro-[HENRY] WALLACE in the 1948 election," further quoting an unnamed informer who recalled "that the subject had made remarks which were not with his line of thinking and remarks that would not be made by a loyal American." Specifically, the informer had called presidential candidate Wallace "a bolschevick," whereupon O'Keeffe allegedly "replied that she believed in Wallace's theory that we should have closer relations with Russia." With that in mind, and "due to the closeness of Abiquiu to Los Alamos" (where nuclear weapons were built and tested), the FBI opened a "case" on O'Keeffe under the heading "Security Matter — Communist." Aside from the first semiliterate critic, agents quoted another "confidential informant of known reliability" to the effect that O'Keeffe once entertained a guest who "appeared to be either Chinese or Filipino and did not speak any English." G-men studied her mail for a time, but apparently lost interest in 1954, when O'Keeffe made no effort to attack the Los Alamos test site.

The artist's file was reopened in 1981 and inflated to five volumes after a grand-nephew of O'Keeffe's pled guilty to forgery and attempting to sell her paintings as signed lithographs. O'Keeffe died at her home on 6 March 1986, and author Herbert Mitgang later obtained 117 heavily-censored pages of O'Keeffe's "security" file under the FREEDOM OF INFORMATION ACT, but 28 pages remain classified "in the interest of national security."

**OLLESTAD, Norman T.**— California attorney Norman Ollestad spent only one year in the FBI before resigning to practice law, but he caused the Bureau no end of difficulty. The vehicle for that distress was a book, *Inside the FBI*, which Ollestad published in 1967, describing his days at the FBI ACADEMY and afterward, when he was assigned to the Miami field office. One anecdote described the day when Ollestad's supervisor discovered that Ollestad was dating the daughter of underworld financier Meyer Lansky. Ordered to explain himself, Ollestad told his boss that he was cultivating the young lady as a "CI"— confidential informant. The supervisor thereupon hatched a plan for Ollestad to clog Lansky's toilet on his next visit to the family home. An FBI "plumber" responded to the emergency and bugged Lansky's bathroom, producing what Ollestad described as "hours of recording tapes of running water, flushed toilets and an occasional emission of gas."

The Bureau's reaction was immediate and furious. Ollestad was expelled from the SOCIETY OF FORMER SPECIAL AGENTS OF THE FBI for writing a book "detrimental to the good name or best interest of the Society." Social ostracism was not deemed sufficient punishment for Ollestad's sin, however, and G-men also sought to ruin his career. Alan Furth, vice president in charge of the Southern Pacific Railroad's legal department, told ex-agent WILLIAM TURNER that FBI leaders tried to prevent Southern Pacific from hiring Ollestad as an attorney. That harassment prompted a lawsuit, which the Bureau settled out of court in November 1978: Ollestad received $10,000 in legal fees and a promise that his FBI personnel file would be purged of derogatory material. Three months later, on 19 February 1979, Ollestad and flight instructor Bob Arnold were killed when their airplane crashed in the San Gabriel Mountains. A survivor of the crash, 30-year-old Sandra Cressman, died of exposure that night, while Ollestad's 13-year-old son escaped with a broken hand. Internet

conspiracy theorists blame the plane crash on sabotage, but no evidence of tampering has been produced.

**O'NEAL, William**— A black Chicago resident, William O'Neal was arrested twice in early 1968, for auto theft and for impersonating a G-man with homemade FBI credentials. Rather than take his chances with the federal courts, O'Neal agreed to become a paid INFORMANT of the Chicago field office's Racial Matters Squad, taking orders from Agent Roy Mitchell and others. His assignment, as part of the Bureau's ongoing "COINTELPRO" campaign against black militants, was to infiltrate and disrupt the local BLACK PANTHER PARTY.

One of O'Neal's first tasks, in December 1968, was helping the Bureau foil a proposed coalition between FRED HAMPTON'S Panthers and a Chicago street gang, the BLACKSTONE RANGERS. O'Neal attended meetings between Hampton and Blackstone leader Jeff Fort, providing information that enabled the FBI to prepare a series of anonymous letters, threatening "hits" and reprisals between the two groups. While tension dramatically increased, no violence was reported until 2 April 1969, when O'Neal personally provoked the first shooting incident between the two groups.

By that time, Agent Mitchell had reported O'Neal's promotion to "number three man" in the Chicago Panthers, in line for a national party office. O'Neal received a cash "merit bonus" on 11 March 1969, "for quality of services rendered" to the FBI. Those services included further agitation to disrupt relations between the Panthers and radical groups including the Vice Lords, the Mau Maus, and the mostly-white STUDENTS FOR A DEMOCRATIC SOCIETY (accomplished by a series of anti-white cartoons penned by FBI artists and falsely credited to the Panthers). O'Neal also hatched a "security plan" for the Chicago office and built an electric chair "to deal with informers," but Hampton vetoed its use. Hampton also rejected O'Neal's plans to "bomb city hall" with a mortar and to manufacture nerve gas, but a busy speaking schedule often kept Hampton away from the office. In his absence, O'Neal bullwhipped one Panther he accused of being a police informant and taught others the fine points of "fundraising" via armed robbery. A member who took his advice, Robert Bruce, became a fugitive and fled to Canada — where O'Neal delivered guns and explosives to him at FBI expense. By June 1969 O'Neal had collected a small arsenal and demanded that Panther cadres "always go armed" on the streets.

O'Neal's big news for 1969 was the November announcement that Hampton would replace David Hilliard as national chief of staff, if Hilliard was convicted on charges of threatening President RICHARD NIXON. Galvanized by FBI Director J. EDGAR HOOVER'S order to "prevent the rise of a 'messiah'" in the black community, Agent Mitchell laid new plans to "neutralize" Hampton. O'Neal provided a floor plan of Hampton's apartment, which Mitchell passed on to local police with false information that Hampton was stockpiling "illegal weapons." After various delays, raiders struck Hampton's flat in the predawn hours of 4 December 1969, killing him in his bed. An autopsy revealed that Hampton had been drugged before the raid, thereby rendering him helpless to defend himself. Chicago's field office took credit for the raid, while rewriting history in a memo to Hoover, dated 11 December 1969 (emphasis added):

> Information set forth in Chicago letter and letterhead memorandum of 11/21/69, reflects *legally purchased firearms* in the possession Black Panther Party (BPP) were stored at 2337 West Monroe Street, Chicago. A detailed inventory of the weapons and also a detailed floor plan of the apartment were furnished to local authorities. In addition, the identities of BPP members utilizing the apartment at the above address were furnished. *This information was not available from any other source and subsequently proved to be of tremendous value* in that it subsequently saved injury and possible death to police officers participating in a raid at that address on the morning of 12/4/69. *The raid was based on information furnished by informant.* During the resistance [*sic*] by the BPP members at the time of the raid, the Chairman of the Illinois Chapter, BPP, FRED HAMPTON, was killed and a BPP leader from Peoria, Illinois [Mark Clark] was also killed. A quantity of weapons and ammunition were recovered.
>
> It is felt that this information is of considerable value in consideration of a special payment for informant requested in re. Chicago letter.

**O'NEILL, Eugene Gladstone**— The son of a popular touring actor, born in a Broadway hotel room on 16 October 1888, Eugene O'Neill traveled the world as a merchant seaman and plumbed the depths of alcoholism before he turned to writing in 1912, while recovering from tuberculosis. His first play was produced in 1916, and the FBI opened a file on him (habitually misspelling his surname) a year later, when his play *The Long Voyage Home* was staged in Provincetown, Massachusetts. "O'Niel" and a friend were arrested as "espionage suspects" on that occasion, because "some person alleged that he had seen them in the vicinity of the Provincetown lighthouse," but "they were released, there being no foundation for any charge."

Mere innocence never discouraged the Bureau, however, and 1919 found "one E. O'Neil" [*sic*] indexed as an editor of a magazine titled *The Pagan*. Five years later, in April 1924, G-men filed another memo on "Eugene O'Neil" garbled the titles of several plays, while noting that "The central figure of 'The Emperor Jones' is a negro [*sic*], this seeming to be a favorite theme of O'Neil's [*sic*]." Twelve years after that report showcased the Bureau's institutional racism, O'Neill became the first American playwright to win a Nobel Prize (and thus the first Nobel laureate condemned by FBI critics as "subversive." In June 1942, agents dutifully clipped a *Chicago Tribune* article "exposing" O'Neill, PEARL BUCK and 20 other prominent writers from the AUTHORS LEAGUE OF AMERICA for their alleged disloyalty by public references to "winning the war at home." A degenerative brain disease rendered O'Neill incapable of writing after 1944, and he died in 1953, still suspect in the Bureau's eyes.

**O'NEILL, John Patrick**— A native of Atlantic City, born in 1952, John O'Neill was a teenager when he set his sights on an FBI career, enamored with actor EFREM ZIMBALIST, JR.'s performance on the weekly *FBI* television series. He worked as a Bureau fingerprint clerk after graduating from high school, then served as a tour guide at FBI HEADQUARTERS while completing a master's program in forensics at George Washington University.

O'Neill became a full-fledged G-man in 1976, assigned to the Baltimore field office. In early 1991 he was appointed chief of the FBI's government fraud unit in Washington, D.C. That July he was transferred again, this time to Chicago as assistant agent-in-charge. The move ended O'Neill's marriage, but he thrived in Chicago, establishing a Fugitive Task Force and supervising cases related to ORGANIZED CRIME. Clearly pleased with his career thus far, O'Neill was fond of telling friends, "I *am* the FBI."

Soon after moving to Chicago, O'Neill began a long-term romantic affair with fashion sales director Valerie James. Their relationship continued when O'Neill returned to Washington in January 1995, promoted to serve as chief of the FBI's Counterterrorism Section, serving as chief liaison between the Bureau and the CENTRAL INTELLIGENCE AGENCY. Two years later, on 1 January 1997, he was transferred again, this time as assistant agent-in-charge of counterterrorism and national security for the New York City field office, supervising some 350 agents. The stress of his new position began to tell on O'Neill, producing a series of careless incidents that damaged his professional reputation. Once, he left his Palm Pilot at Yankee Stadium, filled with contacts for police agencies around the world; a short time later, O'Neill lost his cell phone in a New York taxi. The crowning incident occurred in summer 1999, when he drove with Valerie James to the Jersey shore and his car broke down. O'Neill exchanged the vehicle for an FBI car. Found out and accused of using a government vehicle for personal reasons, O'Neill was reprimanded and docked 15 days' pay. James later told journalists that the incident preyed on his mind. "The last two years of his life," she said, "he got very paranoid. He was convinced there were people out to get him."

The disciplinary action stalled O'Neill's career. In the next 12 months he applied for promotion three times, and was three times refused. In July 2000, while attending an FBI retirement conference in Orlando, Florida, O'Neill left a briefcase filled with official documents in a room with other G-men while he went to make a phone call. Returning to find the case gone, he alerted police and the bag was recovered with only a pen and a cigarette lighter missing, but the incident produced further criticism of his judgment. A friend of O'Neill's later told TV's *Dateline*, "He felt that some people were going to use it — and they did — as a wedge, as a way of painting him in a bad light."

By early 2001, O'Neill seemed convinced that he had reached a dead-end with the FBI. His frustration was exacerbated by new President GEORGE W. BUSH, who ordered the Bureau to "back off" its investigation of fugitive terrorist USAMA BIN LADEN and his Al-Qaeda organization. In July 2001 O'Neill was offered a post as chief of security for the World Trade Centers in New York City, at a starting salary of $300,000 per year. He left the Bureau to assume his new position on 22 August 2001, but maintained his interest in international TERRORISM. On the night of 10 September 2001 O'Neill told a friend, Jerry Hauer, "We're in for something big. I don't like the way things are lining up in Afghanistan."

The next day, at 8:46 a.m., the first of two airliners SKY-JACKED by Middle Eastern terrorists crashed into the World Trade Centers. A second plane struck while O'Neill was en route to the scene, telephoning his son while in transit to say that "he was on his way out to assess the damage." O'Neill entered the crippled structure moments before the Twin Towers collapsed. His corpse was found by searchers a week later.

**ORANGEBURG Massacre**— In February 1968 black students from South Carolina State University, in Orangeburg, launched a series of protests against a whites-only bowling alley located near campus. The vehicle of protest was a Black Awareness Co-ordinating Committee (BACC), founded by Cleveland Sellers, Jr., a 22-year-old member of the STUDENT NONVIOLENT COOR-DINATING COMMITTEE, though most BACC members were affiliated with the NATIONAL ASSOCIATION FOR THE ADVANCEMENT OF COLORED PEOPLE. On the night of 5 February 1968 students built a bonfire near the bowling alley, which was doused by firefighters after a piece of timber fell and struck Highway Patrolman David Shealy in the face. Five minutes later, officers opened fire on the unarmed protesters, killing three and wounding 27 as they fled.

Official statements claimed that the shooting occurred "only after an extended period of sniper fire from the campus and not until an officer had been felled during his efforts to protect life and property," yet no weapons were found on the campus and the one policeman injured had been hurt by accident. FBI agents joined state police in a search of the scene and found several .22-caliber bullets embedded in the wall of a nearby railroad warehouse, but ballistic tests could not reveal when they were fired. Examination of the scene *did* prove the slugs originated from a point more than 100 feet away from where the demonstrators had been shot.

The conduct of G-men involved in the Orangeburg case was suspect, at best. Agent Nelson Phillips, a Georgia native with 11 years in South Carolina, was unusually close to the officers involved. In fact, he had helped to train them in riot-control techniques and was present at the shooting (though he later falsely denied it to JUSTICE DEPARTMENT attorneys). At least two other agents also witnessed the shooting but claimed they were elsewhere when questioned by investigators from the Civil Rights Division. Those same agents told Col. Frank Thompson, commander of the state highway patrol, that they thought his men had "acted with restraint," while members of the state police announced that G-men would "support the patrol's account of what happened." Relations between the FBI and state police were so cordial, in fact, that the officers would speak with no one else about the case, flatly refusing interviews with Justice Department investigators.

Attorney General RAMSEY CLARK was admittedly "distressed" by the Bureau's obstructionist tactics. "It was a shame," he later said, "that we probably had quite a bit of trouble with a number of FBI agents as to what they said at different times and we had trouble getting all the interviews we wanted. We also had a terribly difficult time finding out where the FBI people were on the night of February 8 — where they were, what they were doing, whether they were eyewitnesses." Governor Robert McNair, meanwhile, emerged from a closed-door meeting with G-men to declare that the FBI's final report would be "very interesting and very surprising" to police critics. State spokesmen hinted at a

black conspiracy and tried to pin it on "outside agitator" Cleveland Sellers (a native of Denmark, South Carolina, 20 miles south of Orangeburg in neighboring Bamberg County). Sellers was charged with "inciting a riot," but the state granted an "indefinite delay" in January 1970 and he never faced trial.

Nine police admitted firing on the demonstrators in their statements to FBI agents. Lt. Jesse Spell — soon promoted to captain — declared, "I ordered my squad to fire their weapons to stop the mob," yet none of the admitted shooters could recall a verbal order and most of their 30 victims were shot in the back, while running away. A federal grand jury indicted the nine officers on 19 December 1968, for violating CIVIL RIGHTS by means of summary punishment inflicted "under color of law." Their trial convened at Florence, in May 1969.

That proceeding was marked by a curious clash between FBI agents, as two testified for the defense and another from the Bureau's LABORATORY DIVISION was called to rebut the statements of his fellow G-men. Agents Nelson Phillips and William Danielson swore they heard "small arms fire" from the crowd of demonstrators before police started shooting. Danielson also reported Cleveland Sellers "walking around" and "talking to groups," though he admitted "I never heard him say one word because there was a lot of noise." Phillips described (but could not produce) "a little vial that you have around the laboratory," which was allegedly thrown at police during the demonstration. He said it had contained an unidentified "yellow substance," which "we sent ... to our lab and the lab report showed it was highly explosive." Agent Robert Zimmers, dispatched from the Washington lab, contradicted Phillips and Danielson on the source of the gunfire while making no reference to any mysterious "explosive." After brief deliberation, jurors acquitted the officers on all counts. For years afterward, the Orangeburg case was cited as proof of Dr. MARTIN LUTHER KING'S contention that G-men often collaborated with southern officers to suppress evidence of POLICE BRUTALITY toward blacks.

**The ORDER**— Spawned by decades of racist, anti-Semitic propaganda from groups on the far-right lunatic fringe, the Order was America's first example of a hard-core neo-Nazi TERRORIST group. Its leaders publicly declared war against "ZOG" — the so-called "Zionist Occupation Government" in Washington, D.C. — and supported themselves by armed robbery, distributing much of their loot to like-minded fanatics around the country.

The Order's founding father, Texas native Robert Jay Mathews, drew his inspiration from *The Turner Diaries* (1978), a racist novel that also prompted TIMOTHY MCVEIGH to carry out the BOMBING of an Oklahoma City federal building in April 1995. A gadfly associate of various hate groups, Mathews recruited his followers from the KU KLUX KLAN, the Aryan Nations, the neo-Nazi National Alliance, and the Arkansas-based covenant, sword and arm of the lord. Organized in October 1983, the group soon robbed a Seattle video shop, then cranked out stacks of counterfeit $50 bills so inferior that member Bruce Pierce was arrested on his first attempt to pass the funny money.

Next, the Order turned to BANK ROBBERY and armored truck holdups, with greater success. Between December 1983 and July

1984, the "Aryan warriors" stole more than $3.9 million, donating much of the loot to the KKK, Aryan Nations, White Aryan Resistance, and various "Christian Identity" sects (a cult that believes Jews are the literal spawn of Satan). Members of the Order also murdered Alan Berg, a Jewish talk-show host in Denver, and killed one of their own as a suspected informer.

FBI agents got their first clue to the Order's existence on 16 July 1984, when Mathews dropped a pistol registered to sidekick Andrew Barnhill at the scene of a California armored truck heist. Another member, Thomas Martinez agreed to betray his comrades in October 1984, thus escaping trial on counterfeiting charges. Martinez arranged a meeting with Mathews for 29 November, in Portland, Oregon, but Mathews shot his way out of the trap and escaped. (Another Order member, Gary Yarbrough, was captured.) Furious at the betrayal, Mathews penned a declaration of war against the U.S. government, signed by nine of his cohorts.

Instead of launching new offensives, though, the "warriors" fled into hiding. Mathews and four others were cornered by G-men at a compound on Whidbey Island, in Puget Sound, on 7 December 1984. His companions surrendered, but Mathews fought to the death, incinerated when flares set fire to his ammunition stockpile. Sweeping arrests netted most of the Order's survivors over the next four months. The most elusive quarry, Richard Scutari, remained at large as a feature of the Bureau's "TEN MOST WANTED" LIST until March 1986. Twenty-eight members of the Order were indicted for various state and federal crimes. Of those, 15 pled guilty; five received suspended sentences, while 10 others faced prison terms ranging from six months to 20 years. Twelve took their chances at trial and all were convicted, their sentences ranging from five years to 250 years in prison. Defendant David Tate, already serving life for the murder of a Missouri policeman, was not tried for crimes committed as a member of the Order.

A copycat group, calling itself the Order II, surfaced in early 1986. Its members were affiliated with the Aryan Nations and their activities — counterfeiting, several bombings and at least one murder — were confined to the vicinity of that group's Idaho headquarters. Five members were indicted on federal racketeering charges in October 1988. All pled guilty and received prison terms ranging from six to 20 years; the sentence of one female member was suspended in favor of five years' probation.

**ORGANIZED Crime**— Organized crime as we know it in the U.S. today began with PROHIBITION (1920-33) and the coalition of various regional bootlegging gangs. A national crime syndicate grew out of organizational meetings held in Cleveland (1928), Atlantic City (1929), Chicago (1932) and New York City (1934)— all apparently conducted without FBI knowledge or scrutiny. For the first 38 years of his tenure as FBI director, J. EDGAR HOOVER publicly denied the existence of a Mafia or other nationwide crime syndicate in the U.S.; he also bitterly opposed investigations of organized crime by Senator ESTES KEFAUVER and HARRY ANSLINGER (director of the FEDERAL BUREAU OF NARCOTICS).

Hoover's seeming inability to see the obvious has been variously explained as a product of blackmail (various sources alleging that top-level mobsters possessed photographs or other evidence of Hoover's HOMOSEXUALITY) or by Hoover's personal relationship with wealthy individuals (CLINT MURCHISON, LEWIS ROSENSTIEL, etc.) who had close ties to the mob. Certainly, Hoover's fondness for gambling, free lodging at mob-owned hotels, and his willing acceptance of underworld donations to the J. EDGAR HOOVER FOUNDATION suggest a symbiotic relationship with organized crime that had little to do with blackmail or coercion. As late as 1960, Hoover lobbied to defeat a resolution from the INTERNATIONAL ASSOCIATION OF CHIEFS OF POLICE, calling for a federal offensive against organized crime nationwide.

Public denials notwithstanding, Hoover clearly possessed *some* knowledge of syndicated crime before he finally acknowledged its existence in the 1960s. In their 1946 "CAPGA" investigation, G-men scrutinized the Chicago mob until they were ordered to stop by Attorney General TOM CLARK. Eleven years later, after numerous Mafia leaders were arrested at a November 1957 meeting in Apalachin, New York, Hoover launched a new "TOP HOODLUM" PROGRAM that required each field office to open FILES on 10 local gangsters (no more, no less). Even then, the Bureau was unprepared for Attorney General ROBERT KENNEDY'S national war on organized crime. (When Kennedy asked Assistant Director John Malone to provide an update on mob activities in New York City, Malone replied, "I'm sorry, but I can't, because we've been having a newspaper strike.")

The testimony of Mafia INFORMANT Joseph Valachi finally forced Hoover to admit the Mafia's existence, but the director found a semantic loophole which allowed him to save face. According to Valachi, members of the New York Mafia referred to the organization as *La Cosa Nostra* ("our thing"), and Hoover seized upon the nickname — shortened to "LCN" in FBI memos — to pretend that he had discovered a new criminal menace. Forewarned that Valachi would testify publicly before the U.S. Senate on 27 September 1963, Hoover published a ghost-written article in *Reader's Digest* 12 days earlier, telling America that "La Cosa Nostra, the secret, murderous underworld combine about which you have been reading in the newspaper, is no secret to the FBI." Soon after, in an editorial for the FBI's *Law Enforcement Bulletin*, Hoover claimed that Valachi's testimony merely "corroborated and embellished the facts developed by the FBI as early as 1961." Unfortunately for the Bureau's reputation, that was still no great achievement, since events related by Valachi dated from the early 1930s.

Once finally launched in pursuit of organized crime, G-men employed the same tactics they had used for decades against political dissidents — namely, illegal BREAK-INS, BUGGING and WIRETAPPING. Physical surveillance was frequently intrusive, prompting Chicago mobster SAM GIANCANA to sue the FBI and win a judgment forcing agents to keep a respectable distance. At the same time, FBI taps and bugs recorded numerous threats against Attorney General Kennedy and his brother in the White House. Neither Kennedy was warned by Hoover of potential danger from the mob, and Hoover buried evidence of a possible gangland conspiracy in the November 1963 JFK ASSASSINATION.

Federal mob prosecutions declined under Presidents LYNDON JOHNSON and RICHARD NIXON, both of whom had noteworthy syndicate connections, but the Bureau was not entirely inactive. In October 1966 FBI HEADQUARTERS inaugurated "Operation Hoodwink," designed to generate violent conflict between the Mafia and the COMMUNIST PARTY in New York City. As in previous illegal COINTELPRO operations, G-men used anonymous letters and bogus leaflets to promote dissension in the garment industry. Hoodwink was still ongoing in 1968, but Arizona G-men DAVID HALE used a more direct method to harass Mafiosi, hiring a pair of thugs to plant 17 bombs on property owned by rival mobsters in Tucson. When that failed to touch off a gang war, Hale suggested that his stooges execute one of their targets with a crossbow. His plot was revealed before murder resulted, and Hale was forced to resign (though never prosecuted for his crimes).

Hoover's death cleared the way for new FBI leadership to experiment with different approaches to cracking organized crime. Director WILLIAM WEBSTER (1978-87) favored use of UNDERCOVER OPERATIONS, with some noteworthy successes. Some of those breakthroughs included:

*1976*— Agent JOSEPH PISTONE infiltrated the Bonanno Mafia family in New York City, remaining under cover for the next six years, then emerging to testify at a series of federal trials during 1982-86.

*April 1981*— Operation BRILAB climaxed with the indictment of New Orleans Mafia boss Carlos Marcello and various associates, including highly-placed Louisiana politicians.

*April 1984*— The "Pizza Connection" case produced federal indictments of 31 persons for heroin trafficking, including a prominent Bonanno family member and a leader of the Sicilian Mafia. While nine fugitives remained at large, 22 defendants faced trial in September 1985. Four soon pled guilty and one was murdered by confederates; the other 17 were convicted in March 1987, after one of the longest trials in Justice Department history.

*February 1985*— Federal prosecutors in New York indicted eight members of the Mafia's national commission, including prominent members of the Bonanno, Colombo, Genovese and Lucchese crime families. All were convicted in November 1986. Seven defendants received 100-year prison terms, while the eighth was sentenced to 40 years.

*January 1987*— Philadelphia crime boss Nicodemo Scarfo and a city councilman were indicted for extortion. Four months later, Scarfo and 11 associates were indicted for the murder of a judge in New Jersey. A third set of indictments, issued in January 1988, charged Scarfo and 16 other mobsters with murder, attempted murder, extortion and other crimes. Convicted on those counts in 1989, Scarfo received a 55-year prison term, while his associates drew sentences ranging from three years to 45 years.

*March 1990*— New England's mob was targeted, with federal indictments of 21 defendants from the Patriarca crime family. Six pled guilty prior to trial and the other 15 were convicted in two separate trials during 1991-92.

*December 1990*— FBI agents arrested New York mobster John Gotti for the 1985 murder of his predecessor, Paul Castellano. Despite acquittals in three previous racketeering trials (1986, 1987 and 1990), the "Teflon Don" ran out of luck at last, thanks to testimony from turncoat associate SALVATORE GRAVANO. Convicted on all counts in April 1992, Gotti was sen-

tenced to life without parole and subsequently died in prison.

*June 1996*— G-men arrested 19 members of the Genovese crime family on charges including murder, extortion, labor racketeering, loan-sharking, gambling, money laundering and tax evasion. Subsequent conviction at trial dismantled the leadership of America's largest surviving Mafia family.

While those victories boosted FBI morale and polished the Bureau's public image, a festering scandal in Massachusetts threatened to undo much of the agency's good work elsewhere. In 1990 it was revealed that Boston G-men had enjoyed a 15-year corrupt relationship with members of JAMES ("WHITEY") BULGER'S deadly Winter Hill gang. While Bulger and various associates were recruited to inform on rivals from the Patriarca mob, they also found agents receptive to bribes and other favors. Before the criminal alliance was exposed, agents helped the gang frame four innocent men on murder charges and send them to prison for over three decades; two defendants died in custody, while victims JOSEPH SALVATI and PETER LIMONE survived to win vindication and sue the FBI. Agent JOHN CONNOLLY was convicted of bribery and received a 10-year prison term, while other G-men escaped punishment under the statute of limitations.

**OSWALD, Lee Harvey**— Lee Harvey Oswald was born in New Orleans on 18 October 1939, two months after the death of his father. He joined the Civil Air Patrol at age 16, in July 1955, and there met instructor David Ferrie (a known associate of ORGANIZED CRIME and a self-proclaimed member of far-right groups including the paramilitary MINUTEMEN). Oswald dropped out of high school twice, in October 1955 and again in September 1956. His first attempt to join the U.S. Marine Corps was rebuffed in October 1955, but the Corps accepted him a year later and he was shipped to Japan as a radar operator in August 1957.

Oswald's tenure in the Marine Corps was a troubled one. In October 1957 he accidentally shot himself in the arm with an unauthorized pistol. He was court-martialed in April 1958 for possession of another illegal weapon, and again two months later for assaulting a superior. That offense cost him two months in the brig, released on 13 August 1958. Transferred to Taiwan a month later, Oswald suffered a nervous breakdown and was returned to Japan. Back in California by November, he was assigned to the El Toro military base. In August 1959 Oswald requested a dependency discharge, due to an injury suffered by his mother, and he was released from service (though still technically a Marine) on 11 September 1959.

Instead of living with his mother, Oswald left the U.S. for the Soviet Union, arriving in Moscow on 16 October 1959. Five days later he attempted suicide and was hospitalized, then renounced his U.S. citizenship on 31 October. Still, the Marine Corps waited another 11 months before issuing Oswald an "undesirable" discharge, on 13 September 1960. Oswald's fascination with Russia apparently soured over the next five months, and he made his first bid for a return to the U.S. in February 1961. On 30 April 1961 he married Marina Prusakova, the niece of a known KGB officer, and their first child was born in February 1962.

The Oswalds left Russia four months later, arriving in Fort

Worth, Texas on 14 June 1962. FBI agents interviewed Oswald for the first time on 26 June and again on 16 August 1962. They were presumably unaware when he purchased a rifle and pistol by mail, receiving both weapons on 25 March 1963. Oswald left Marina and their daughter in Texas when he traveled to New Orleans on 17 April 1963. A month later he established a one-man chapter of the Fair Play for Cuba Committee, a leftist group supporting Fidel Castro's communist government, but the address printed on his fliers was that of an office occupied by former FBI agent GUY BANISTER, known for his anti-Castro activities and ties to far-right groups. Former friend David Ferrie also worked with Banister, and Oswald met him again at Banister's Camp Street office, frequently accompanied by members of the Minutemen and the KU KLUX KLAN. New Orleans G-man John Quigley interviewed Oswald on 10 August 1963, one day after a televised scuffle between Oswald and an anti-Castro Cuban exile. In September 1963 Oswald allegedly visited Mexico City, calling on the Cuban and Russian embassies there, but the man using his name was photographed by agents of the CENTRAL INTELLIGENCE AGENCY — and those photos reveal that he bore no resemblance to Oswald.

October 1963 found Oswald in Dallas, where he found work at the Texas School Book Depository on the 16th. FBI Agent JAMES HOSTY went looking for Oswald but allegedly failed to find him on any of three visits between 29 October and 5 November 1963. (This despite testimony from Oswald's landlady that Oswald and Hosty met and spoke outside her house, in Hosty's car.) On 12 November Oswald delivered a threatening letter to the Dallas field office, but it was later destroyed on orders from agent-in-charge Gordon Shanklin. Rumors persist to this day (denied by the Bureau) that Oswald was a paid FBI INFORMANT or *agent provocateur*, employed to gather information on pro-Castro elements in New Orleans and Texas.

That speculation assumed critical significance on 22 November 1963, when news of the JFK ASSASSINATION rocked America. President JOHN KENNEDY was killed by sniper fire at 12:30 p.m., followed by the fatal shooting of Dallas policeman J.D. Tippit 46 minutes later. Oswald was arrested for the latter crime at 1:50 p.m., in a local theater. He was arraigned for Tippit's murder at 7:10 p.m., then charged with Kennedy's murder at 11:26 p.m. Throughout his marathon interrogation and a meeting with the press on 23 November, Oswald steadfastly denied any part in the crimes and described himself as a "patsy" for the actual killers. Any question of trial was eliminated at 11:21 a.m. on 24 November, when lifelong mobster JACK RUBY shot Oswald in the basement of the Dallas Police Department.

The shooting silenced Oswald, but it only increased proliferation of conspiracy theories in Kennedy's death. FBI Director J. EDGAR HOOVER had already proclaimed the assassination a one-man crime committed by "a Communist," and he never wavered from that verdict, bending or suppressing evidence to persuade a blue-ribbon panel chaired by Chief Justice EARL WARREN that his hasty judgment was correct. Above all else, Hoover labored to suppress speculation that Oswald had been on the FBI's pay-

roll. Long after the fact, in 1979, the HOUSE SELECT COMMITTEE ON ASSASSINATIONS reported "a high probability that two gunmen fired at President John F. Kennedy," but Oswald remained the only identified suspect. The committee ignored reports from the FBI's FIREARMS AND TOOLMARKS UNIT, filed in 1963, which proved that Oswald's mail-order rifle was incapable of hitting any target at substantial range, much less firing three shots in the time allotted for Kennedy's murder.

**OTTO, John**—Born in St. Paul, Minnesota on 18 December 1938, John Otto served two years in the U.S. Marine Corps after high school, then earned a bachelor of science degree from St. Cloud State College in 1960. While pursuing graduate studies in educational administration, he served with the Ramsey County Sheriff's Department and the Arden Hills Police Department (both in Minnesota). Otto joined the Oakland (California) Police Department in 1963 and was recruited by the FBI a year later, confirmed as an agent on 12 October 1964. After service in Texas and New Jersey, Otto was recalled to FBI HEADQUARTERS in March 1971, filling various positions there through December 1974. In January 1975 he was named special agent in charge of the Portland, Oregon field office, later holding the same position in Minneapolis (1977) and Chicago (1978).

Back at headquarters in August 1979, Otto remained there for the rest of his career. He served as acting director between 26 May 1987, when Director WILLIAM WEBSTER stepped down to lead the CENTRAL INTELLIGENCE AGENCY, and 2 November 1987, when WILLIAM SESSIONS assumed control of the Bureau. On 6 April 1990 Sessions gave Otto the FBI's first Medal of Meritorious Achievement for "extraordinary and exceptional meritorious service in a duty of *extreme* challenge and *great* responsibility." [Emphasis in the original.] Otto retired soon after claiming the award, to become a security agent for Delta Airlines.

**OVERMAN Committee**—This subcommittee of the U.S. Senate's Judiciary Committee, known by the name of Chairman Lee Overman, was initially created in 1918 to investigate charges from Alien Property Administrator A. MITCHELL PALMER that one of his political opponents, Pennsylvania Senator Boies Penrose, had accepted political contributions from the brewing industry. Palmer claimed that since many brewers were German immigrants (and thus presumably disloyal to the U.S. during WORLD WAR I), Senator Penrose must be a traitor. The armistice of November 1918 rendered the committee's investigation moot, but Overman was reluctant to disband the panel. In January 1919 he shifted the investigation to bolshevism, on the tenuous grounds that "German socialism ... is the father of the Bolsheviki movement in Russia, and consequently the radical movement which we have in this country today has its origin in Germany." The investigation reiterated conservative beliefs in the evils of radicalism but failed to identify any actual spies or subversives in America. Palmer subsequently became attorney general and collaborated with J. EDGAR HOOVER to lead the PALMER RAIDS of 1919-20.

# P

**PACKER, Horace L.**—A civilian INFORMANT paid by the FBI to infiltrate the STUDENTS FOR A DEMOCRATIC SOCIETY and the WEATHER UNDERGROUND at the University of Washington in Seattle, Horace Packer later admitted under oath that he supplied campus radicals with drugs, weapons and the components for incendiary Molotov cocktails. He also supplied (and his FBI control agents paid for) the paint used by student demonstrators to vandalize Seattle's federal courthouse during demonstrations staged in February 1970. That incident became a key element in the charges of conspiracy to damage U.S. government property, filed against defendants known locally as the "Seattle Eight." At their trial in Tacoma, Packer testified that his FBI handlers told him to "do anything to protect my credibility" as an informant. Pursuant to those orders, Packer "smoked dope all the time" and used other illegal drugs, including "acid, speed, mescaline" and cocaine while active on FBI business. He was arrested several times in campus demonstrations and violated the terms of a suspended sentence he received for his role in a Weatherman attack on campus ROTC headquarters. Packer's credibility collapsed in court after the following exchange with defendant Chip Marshall (serving as his own counsel):

MARSHALL: Did you recruit others into violent acts?
PACKER: The answer would have to be yes.
MARSHALL: While with the FBI, have you ever encouraged anyone to violate a law?
PACKER: Yes.
MARSHALL: You feel very strongly that we are bad people and should be brought to justice?
PACKER: That's one way of putting it.
MARSHALL: So you would go to almost any length of trickery to bring us to justice?
PACKER: Yes, any length.
MARSHALL: Are you willing to lie to get us?
PACKER: Yes.
MARSHALL (turning to the jury): That's what he said.

All charges against the Seattle Eight were eventually dismissed and Packer faded into obscurity. The trial was one in a series of judicial defeats for the FBI and President RICHARD NIXON'S "law and order" administration during the early 1970s.

**PALEY, Grace**—A native of the Bronx, born in 1922, Grace Paley did not turn her hand to poetry and short fiction until the 1950s, thereafter publishing three acclaimed collections between 1959 and 1985. The FBI spotted her much earlier, in a 1941 report describing her as a secretary of New York University's Young Com-

munist League. (Paley insists the G-men were mistaken, and that it was really the Karl Marx Society.) While acknowledging that most members of the group were communists, Paley described herself as "a wide-open member," more specifically a "somewhat combative pacifist and cooperative ANARCHIST."

It was all the same to J. EDGAR HOOVER and his successors, who kept Paley's dossier open for nearly half a century. A 1948 report noted her membership in the New York Emergency Committee on Rent and Housing." Nineteen years later, agents followed her to numerous protests against the VIETNAM WAR. In 1969, her visit to prisoners of war in North Vietnam was monitored. Copies of her file were sent to the CENTRAL INTELLIGENCE AGENCY and the Office of Naval Intelligence in 1971; a year later, her photo was "disseminated to the SECRET SERVICE," with a notation that Paley was "potentially dangerous because of background, emotional instability or activity in groups engaged in activities inimical to the U.S." G-men also placed her name in ADMINISTRATIVE INDEX that year (1972), but it was removed after Hoover's death. Despite a "case closed" notation in Paley's 78-page dossier, she believes that her 1987 invitation to address the writers' festivals in Australia and New Zealand, sponsored by the U.S. Information Agency, was rescinded on political grounds, specifically her activity in the protest movement against nuclear weapons.

**PALMER, Alexander Mitchell**—A Pennsylvania Quaker, born 4 May 1872, A. Mitchell Palmer was an ambitious politician whose sights remained fixed on the White House throughout his career. He served three terms in the House of Representatives (1909-15) and there described himself as a "radical friend" of LABOR UNIONS, but later suppressed half a dozen major strikes as attorney general. A religious pacifist, Palmer rejected President WOODROW WILSON'S urging that he serve as Secretary of War, then proved so belligerent in his role as Alien Property Custodian that acquaintances dubbed him "the fighting Quaker."

Late in Wilson's second term, Palmer was named to serve as attorney general. He took office on 5 March 1919 and the following month received a mail bomb apparently sent by ANARCHISTS. That charge failed to explode, but the bombers tried again on 2 June 1919, detonating a charge that wrecked Palmer's house in Washington and killed two terrorists in the blast. Soon after that incident, Wilson cautioned Palmer in a cabinet meeting, "Palmer, do not let this country see red!" On 1 July 1919 Palmer appointed WILLIAM FLYNN, whom he called the nation's top "radical chaser," to lead the Bureau of Investigation. A month later, on 1 August, he created a new Red-hunting GENERAL INTELLIGENCE DIVISION, led by young J. EDGAR HOOVER. Together, that trio planned a series of mass arrests memorialized as the PALMER RAIDS, which rounded up suspected anarchists and communists in November 1919 and January 1920. A few hundred "enemy aliens" were deported, but most of those seized without warrants or charges were later released, to a fanfare of critical publicity.

The raids doomed any hopes Palmer may have cherished for a presidential nomination in 1920. He spent the rest of his public career defending himself in federal court (April 1920), before the House Rules Committee (June 1920), and finally before the Senate Judiciary Committee (January to March 1921). Still defiant as his star waned, Palmer told the Senate:

> I apologize for nothing the Department of Justice has done in this matter. I glory in it. I point with pride and enthusiasm to the results of that work; and if, as I said before, some of my agents out in the field, or some of the agents of the Department of Labor, were a little rough or unkind, or short or curt, with these alien agitators whom they observed seeking to destroy their homes, their religion and their country, I think it might well be overlooked in the general good to the country which has come from it. That is all I have to say.

Palmer left the Justice Department two days after delivering that speech, on 5 March 1921. He served as a delegate to the Democratic National Convention in 1932, but public office had slipped forever beyond his grasp. He died in Washington on 11 May 1936.

**PALMER Raids**— The federal government was obsessed with rooting out foreign "radicals" in the early decades of the 20th century. In February 1919 Attorney General THOMAS GREGORY announced plans to deport at least 7,000 "alien ANARCHISTS and trouble makers" before year's end. The apparent need for such action was reinforced during April and June 1919 by a series of BOMBINGS and attempted bombings blamed on unknown anarchists. One target of a blast in June, Attorney General A. MITCHELL PALMER, determined to follow through on the plan hatched by his predecessor. To carry out the mass arrests, he enlisted young J. EDGAR HOOVER, then in charge of the JUSTICE DEPARTMENT'S Red-hunting GENERAL INTELLIGENCE DIVISION.

Hoover decided, for the sake of symbolism, to stage the first arrests on 7 November 1919 — the second anniversary of the Russian revolution. The initial targets, chosen as test cases, were members of the Union of Russian Workers. Palmer and Hoover ostensibly suspected them of plotting the spring bombings, but no terrorists were identified and the crimes remained forever unsolved. The LABOR DEPARTMENT, responsible for deportations of "enemy aliens," issued 600 arrest warrants for the November dragnet, but legal niceties were generally ignored as G-men accompanied by local police staged simultaneous raids in 12 cities nationwide. Raiders jailed 650 persons in New York City alone (with 27 warrants issued), and another 150 were swept up in Newark (on 36 arrest warrants). No figures were published for total arrests, but several thousand persons were certainly detained, the vast majority without valid warrants. The *New York Times* reported from Manhattan that "[a] number in the building were badly beaten by the police during the raid, their heads wrapped

in bandages testifying to the rough manner in which they had been handled." Of those arrested, only 249 were finally deported aboard the SS *Buford* (dubbed the "Soviet Ark") on 21 December 1919.

By that time, Palmer and Hoover were already planning the next round of arrests, intended to dwarf the first effort. Their new targets were the COMMUNIST PARTY (CP) and its chief competitor, the COMMUNIST LABOR PARTY. On 14 December 1919 Hoover submitted 3,000 blank arrest warrants to Secretary of Labor WILLIAM WILSON. Despite misgivings, Wilson agreed that membership in communist organizations constituted legal grounds for deporting aliens under the Immigration Act of 1917. Solicitor General John Abercrombie signed the warrants on 16 December, while Hoover laid plans for nationwide raids to occur on 2 January 1920. Hoover drafted a letter which was signed by Frank Burke, assistant director of the Bureau of Investigation on 27 December 1919 and sent to G-men in 33 cities. That letter read:

> If possible you should arrange with your under-cover INFORMANTS to have meetings of the Communist Party and the Communist Labor Party held on the night set. I have been informed by some of the bureau officers that such arrangements will be made. This, of course, would facilitate the making of arrests.
>
> ... I leave entirely to your discretion as to the methods by which you gain access to such places. If, due to the local conditions in your territory, you find that it is absolutely necessary for you to obtain a search warrant for the premises, you should communicate with the local authorities a few hours before the time of the arrests.
>
> ... On the evening of the arrests, this office will be open the entire night, and I desire that you communicate by long distance to Mr. Hoover any matters of vital importance or interest which may arise during the course of the arrests.... I desire that the morning following the arrests you should forward to this office by special delivery, marked for the "Attention of Mr. Hoover," a complete list of the names of the persons arrested, with an indication of residence, or organizations to which they belong, and whether or not they were included in the original list of warrants.... I desire that the morning following the arrests that you communicate in detail by telegram "Attention Mr. Hoover," the results of the arrests made, giving the total number of persons of each organization taken into custody, together with a statement of any interesting evidence secured.

Hoover would later be embarrassed by that letter, when he tried to distance himself from the planning and conduct of the Palmer raids, but his central role was clear. Likewise, another "extremely confidential" message from Burke to all field offices, sent just before midnight on 31 December 1919, reminded G-men that "Arrests should be completed ... by Saturday morning, January 3, 1920, and full reports reported by Special Delivery addressed to Mr. Hoover."

At least 10,000 suspected communists were arrested on the night of 2 January 1920, with some 6,500 released when they proved to be U.S. citizens or were identified as relatives of party members jailed without charges to ensure the raids proceeded in utmost secrecy. Hoover ignored those figures in his first interview with the *New York Times*, boasting that 3,000 out of 3,600 aliens arrested were "perfect" deportation cases, with party cards seized at the time of arrest. In regard to the other 600, "Hoover said it was believed that their membership would be proved by other evidence." (He was wrong again. Of all those arrested in the final Palmer raids, only 556 were ultimately deported.)

Media reactions to the raids were initially gleeful. The *New York Times* editorialized: "If any or some of us ... have ever doubted the alacrity, resolute will, and fruitful intelligence of the Dept. of Justice in hunting down the enemies of the United States, the questioners and doubters now have cause to approve and applaud." A legal journal, the *Bench and Bar*, went even further, declaring that "the need for repression is great, and the time for repression is now." Palmer and Hoover were greeted with applause when they appeared before Congress on 14 January 1920, but federal lawmakers refused Palmer's call for passage of a peacetime sedition act to permit further mass arrests.

By mid-February the façade of confidence began to crumble. A "confidential" memo from Hoover to Frank Burke, dated 21 February 1920, acknowledged that there was "no authority under the law permitting this Dept to take any action in deportation proceedings relative to radical activities." In March, Assistant Secretary of Labor LOUIS POST had canceled hundreds of the December arrest warrants, and by 14 April 1920 he had canceled 1,141 or the department's 1,600 pending deportation orders. At the same time, in Boston, federal judge GEORGE ANDERSON denounced G-men for their performance in the roundups, publicly refusing to "adopt the contention that government spies are more trustworthy or less disposed to make trouble in order to profit therefrom than are spies in the private industry.... The spy system destroys trust and confidence and propagates hate."

Hoover responded to that criticism by ordering an investigation of Judge Anderson's politics and private life. In public, he issued a series of alerts predicting a nationwide communist revolt on 1 May. Troops were called out in various cities on May Day, but when the insurrection failed to materialize on schedule, many newspapers turned from praising Palmer's efforts to denouncing him as a modern Chicken Little. On 5 May 1920 Secretary Wilson canceled the first deportation warrant on a member of the Communist Labor Party, finding that the group's membership oath required no dedication to overthrowing the U.S. government. In short order, the other CLP deportation orders were likewise dismissed, releasing another batch of detainees. The month ended badly for Hoover, with a report from the National Public Government League denouncing Bureau tactics in the raids. (True to form, Hoover ordered a probe of the NPGL and its members, seeking derogatory information.)

Palmer was called before the House Rules Committee on 1 June 1920 to answer "Charges Made Against the Department of Justice by Louis F. Post and Others." Journalist Curt Gentry described the attorney general's performance in his book *J. Edgar Hoover: The Man and the Secrets* (1991):

> He denied that the recording secretary of a CP local in Buffalo, who'd been especially active in recruiting new members, was a "confidential informant," as charged by Post; he was, Palmer said, a "special agent of the Bureau of Investigation." He admitted that arrests had been made without warrants but denied there was anything illegal about this, since police could make warrantless arrests when they observed a crime taking place. He denied that

his agents used force or violence; only radical publications had made this charge, Palmer said, ignoring the articles and photographs which had appeared in the *New York Times* and other non-radical publications. He admitted that counsel had been denied in the early stages of the proceedings, but when lawyers were present the prosecution "got nowhere." He denied that his agents had forged a signature on a confession, but later admitted that his agents had added the signature "for identification purposes only."

January 1921 found Palmer and Hoover before the Senate Judiciary Committee, where Palmer seemed strangely unable to answer many of the questions posed by Senator THOMAS WALSH and other members of the panel. When pressed for details of the raids, he passed the buck with a reminder that "Mr. Hoover was in charge of this matter." Hoover, for his part, drew an embarrassing blank when asked how many arrests warrants were issued prior to the January 1920 raids and on other salient points. It scarcely mattered by that time, since Republican presidential candidate WARREN HARDING had already been elected on a promise to restore "normalcy" in America, and Palmer's tenure as attorney general ended on 5 March 1921, two days after the conclusion of his Senate testimony.

J. Edgar Hoover remained with the Bureau, rising to command it in May 1924, and he was busily rewriting history. In 1940 an aide to Hoover, G-man Alexander Holtzoff, declared that "Mr. J. Edgar Hoover was not in charge of, and had nothing to do with, the manner in which the arrests were made of the so-called radicals under the administration of Attorney General A. Mitchell Palmer." Seven years later, Hoover himself told the *New York Herald Tribune*, "I deplored the manner in which the raids were executed then, and my position has remained unchanged."

## PARKER, Bonnie *see* BARROW, Clyde

**PARKER, Dorothy Rothschild**— Born at West End, New Jersey on 22 August 1893, Dorothy Rothschild joined the staff of *Vogue* magazine in 1916, then left a year later to work as a drama critic for *Vanity Fair*. She also married husband Edwin Parker II in 1917, keeping his name when they divorced in 1928. Dismissed from *Vanity Fair* in 1920, for the relentless acerbity of her reviews, Parker turned freelance thereafter and before the decade's end joined other renowned New York writers to create the "Algonquin Round Table."

It was that group, apparently, that first brought Parker to the Bureau's attention, opening a dossier that would exceed 1,000 pages. In 1927 she was indexed, with JOHN DOS PASSOS and others, "because of a demonstration in which they were involved protesting the execution of SACCO Vanzetti [sic]." Eight years later, she joined the League of Women Shoppers, created "to provide information relative to labor conditions under which goods are manufactured." In 1937, an "anonymous outside source" named Parker as a writer for the *New Masses*, claiming she had "contributed to the Communist movement." Another informer dubbed her "one of the leading characters in the Communist movement in Hollywood in the early thirties." Thereafter, FBI memos referred to Parker variously as the "cream of the crop of

Communists" or the "queen of Communists," noting her "monumental scorn for the FBI."

As WORLD WAR II began, Parker's activities attracted more interest. Agents from the Office of Naval Intelligence shadowed her in 1939, while Army Intelligence listed her as a COMMUNIST PARTY member in 1940. J. EDGAR HOOVER noted her contributions to *PM* that year, dismissing the liberal newspaper as "banal, amateurish and confusing." Hoover's own confusion on the subject of communism was showcased in 1941, when he drew an X beside Parker's name on a list of "fellow travelers" and scrawled a note that "the ones marked X are Communist pure and simple, no matter what their position is on the business and social world of today." By 1942, as chairperson of the Joint Anti-Fascist Refugee Committee, Parker qualified as a target of FBI "technical surveillance."

That scrutiny continued during the postwar Red panic. In 1950, Hoover ordered the New York field office to investigate Parker as "a concealed Communist," and G-men in Philadelphia filed memos under the heading "Security Matter — C" (for Communist). Parker was added to the FBI's Communist Index a year later, though the descriptions of her affiliation remained chaotic, variously dubbing Parker "an open Communist," "an undercover Communist," and "a Communist appeaser." WALTER WINCHELL complained to Hoover in 1951 that "mad fanatic" Parker had led "a Communist group attack on me" (in fact a joint effort with DASHIELL HAMMETT and others to place more liberal commentators on U.S. radio stations). G-men watched Parker's every move, noting her various addresses. One agent, trailing Parker on a vacation in Mexico, described her as "a very able authoress and also a valuable element in the idealistic fight on behalf of communism." Bureau watchdogs counted 33 alleged Communist front groups in Parker's background, including the Hollywood Anti-Nazi League, the Civil Rights Congress and Friends of the ABRAHAM LINCOLN BRIGADE, but New York's special agent in charge still suggested her removal from the illegal SECURITY INDEX in 1955, on grounds that Parker was "not dangerous enough to be listed."

Hoover complied with that request, but the surveillance continued. In 1965, two years before Parker's death, a high school student writing a term paper on her work wrote to FBI headquarters, asking if Parker was a communist. Hoover replied that "FBI files are confidential," but the stack of right-wing literature enclosed with that response left no doubt of his actual feelings. Parker biographer Marion Meade obtained 900 heavily-censored pages from Parker's FBI dossier in 1987, while another 100 pages remained classified "in the interest of national security" and other unspecified documents were "under review."

**PARKER, William Henry**—A South Dakota native, born in 1902, William Parker moved to California and joined the Los Angeles Police Department in 1927. He studied law at night and earned his degree in 1930, thereafter rising swiftly through the graft-ridden department's ranks. Parker joined the army during WORLD WAR II and was wounded in the Normandy invasion, recovering in time to help liberate Paris from Nazi occupation. After V-E Day he helped establish a new police system in Ger-

many, before he was discharged as a captain in 1945. Back in Los Angeles, he found the police department torn by scandal, embarrassed by gangland killings and unsolved crimes like the grisly "Black Dahlia" murder. Elevated to chief in 1950, Parker instituted sweeping changes, including a requirement that all new recruits possess a minimum IQ of 110.

Soon, LAPD began earning kudos for its spit-and-polish professionalism, but there was also a dark side to the force. Parker was an alcoholic racist who encouraged repressive violence against racial minorities and who once described black protesters as "monkeys in a zoo." Likewise, despite persistent claims that "Los Angeles has no ORGANIZED CRIME," mobsters Mickey Cohen and Jack Dragna waged war under Parker's very nose, while earning millions from illicit gambling, prostitution and narcotics.

It was probably Parker's celebrity that marked him as a target of J. EDGAR HOOVER'S enduring hatred, since their political and racial views were virtually identical. Their 16-year feud was legendary among law enforcement officers, marked by Hoover's ban on Los Angeles officers attending the FBI's NATIONAL ACADEMY for advanced training. Year after year, L.A. applicants were told the Academy's classes were "full," while officers from neighboring departments were readily accepted. In 1959, Hoover torpedoed Parker's bid to become vice president of the INTERNATIONAL ASSOCIATION OF CHIEFS OF POLICE, throwing the FBI's decisive weight behind dark horse candidate Philip Purcell of Newton, Massachusetts. Four years later, Parker was outraged when G-men invaded L.A. to arrest the kidnappers of Frank Sinatra, Jr., without involving local police.

For all its heat, the Hoover-Parker feud also provided some comic relief. Attorney General ROBERT KENNEDY, himself a target of Hoover's malice, enjoyed needling his adversary by slipping notes that read "Parker for FBI director" into Hoover's personal suggestion box. Shaken by the 1965 Watts riots and subsequent reports that blamed the violence on POLICE BRUTALITY, Parker began to drink more heavily at home. On 16 July 1966 he collapsed and died, after accepting a plaque at a U.S. Marine Corps testimonial dinner in Los Angeles. When word of his death reached Washington, Hoover immediately lifted the ban on LAPD officers attending the National Academy.

**PARSONS, Louella**—Born Louella Oettinger in 1881, at Freeport, Illinois, America's foremost gossip columnist began her journalistic career as drama editor of the *Dixon* (Illinois) *Morning Star* while she was still in high school. As a Hollywood columnist for the Hearst newspapers, between 1922 and 1965, Parsons was rivaled only by HEDA HOPPER in the realm of salacious celebrity hearsay. J. EDGAR HOOVER favored Parsons with frequent leaks throughout her career, but their evident friendship did not stop the FBI director from collecting a 178-page dossier on Parsons herself. In 1949, Hoover launched an investigation of the movie *Big Country*, based on a comment from Parsons that its plot would "stress feats of the foreign-born." In 1960, a Las Vegas wire tap revealed that Parsons maintained a suite of rooms, free of charge, at the gangster-owned Tropicana hotel and casino, available for use at need by mobsters on the lam. Parsons faded from the public eye after her column was terminated, in 1965, and her death in December 1972 was largely ignored by the media.

**PAYNE, Cril**— A native of Denton, Texas, born 28 May 1943, Cril Payne earned a bachelor's degree in business administration from Texas Technical University in 1965 and a doctor of jurisprudence degree from the University of Texas Law School in August 1968. He joined the FBI two months later and was assigned to the Seattle field office in February 1969. A transfer to Los Angeles followed in November 1969, and Payne was still assigned there in October 1970, when his superiors recruited him for an UNDERCOVER OPERATION against the "NEW LEFT."

As an active member of the Bureau's latest COINTELPRO campaign, Agent Payne became one of the "BEARDS"—a group of long-haired, bearded G-men assigned to infiltrate and disrupt the WEATHER UNDERGROUND and similar radical groups. By Payne's own admission in his published memoirs (*Deep Cover*, 1979), his work for the Bureau included various criminal acts (ingesting LSD and other outlawed drugs) and unethical behavior (sexual acts with female INFORMANTS and surveillance subjects) that would have invalidated any prosecution arising from his wide-ranging investigations. However, since COINTELPRO's goal was the "disruption" and "neutralization" of various targets, rather than traditional prosecution, Payne's lapses made no practical difference.

As it was, Payne suffered incidents of POLICE BRUTALITY (while infiltrating demonstrations at the 1972 Republican National Convention) and wound up posing as a fugitive draft-dodger in Canada. A transfer to the Dallas field office ended his service with the Beards in August 1973, and Payne returned to the FBI ACADEMY six months later, for certification as an instructor in legal matters. Finally disillusioned by the FBI's evasive response to exposure of its COINTELPRO crimes, Payne resigned on 30 July 1976. While preparing his memoirs, he found FBI HEADQUARTERS unwilling to release his own personnel file under the FREEDOM OF INFORMATION ACT.

**PEARL Harbor Attack**— In 1940, wealthy Yugoslav playboy Dusan ("Dusko") Popov was recruited to spy for the Nazi Abwehr intelligence network. He reported the overture to Britain's MI-6 intelligence unit and was encouraged to proceed as a double agent, code-named "Tricycle." In August 1941 the Abwehr sent Popov to the United States, with orders to visit Hawaii "as soon as possible." His mission, described as rating "the highest priority," involved surveillance of the Hawaiian islands for ADOLF HITLER'S Japanese allies. Before departing, Popov was given a detailed questionnaire including demands for specific information about defenses for the U.S. naval base at Pearl Harbor. Believing that Japanese plans for a raid on Pearl Harbor had already "reached an advanced state," MI-6 leaders approved Popov's trip to the U.S., instructing him to share his information with the FBI.

Arriving in New York City on 12 August 1941, Popov revealed his mission and the questionnaire (in plain text and microdot form) to FBI Assistant Director Earl Connelly and PERCY FOXWORTH, special agent in charge of the New York field office.

Foxworth complained to Popov that the information "all looks too precise." Because the Japanese questionnaire "spells out in detail exactly where, when, how and by whom we are to be attacked," Foxworth concluded "it sounds like a trap." Still, a meeting was arranged between Popov and Director J. EDGAR HOOVER at Foxworth's office. Popov later described the meeting as a one-sided tirade, with Hoover "yelping" denunciations of Popov's lifestyle while his face "turned purple." Hoover complained that Popov was "like all double agents. You're begging for information to sell to your German friends so that you can make money and be a playboy." Rejecting Popov's offer of assistance, Hoover replied, "I can catch spies without your or anyone else's help." As Popov left the office, Hoover shouted after him, "Good riddance!"

It was not the end of Hoover's peevish performance. The FBI barred Popov from traveling to Hawaii and insisted that MI-6 withdraw him from the U.S. On 3 September 1941, Hoover sent a report to President FRANKLIN ROOSEVELT, claiming credit for discovery of the Japanese microdot but omitting any reference to Hawaii or Pearl Harbor and the Japanese attack plans.

In fact, Popov's information was not Hoover's first warning of an impending attack on Hawaii. Four months before the explosive scene in Percy Foxworth's office, MI-6 had intercepted a report from an unknown German agent (code-named "Konrad"), including detailed maps and photos of Pearl Harbor's defenses. The Bureau had suppressed that report as well, and the catastrophic bombing raid of 7 December 1941 appeared to take FBI HEADQUARTERS by complete surprise.

Eight separate investigations were made of the Pearl Harbor disaster during WORLD WAR II, but none of the reports mentioned "Konrad's" report or Dusan Popov's revelations with the FBI. Hoover testified in the last of those investigations, in November 1945, and somehow emerged as a hero, while U.S. military leaders took the blame. Speaking to the *New York Times*, California congressman Bertrand Gearhart opined, "If the Army and Navy had been as aware of the situation as Mr. Hoover was, there probably would have been no necessity for this investigation at this time."

Dusan Popov published his memoirs in 1974, prompting a furious reaction from FBI headquarters. Director CLARENCE KELLEY claimed that Bureau files showed Popov "never personally met Mr. Hoover," and that the Bureau "certainly did not receive information which indicated the Japanese would attack Pearl Harbor." Retired officers of MI-6 refute those denials, and the U.S. Navy also harbored doubts. Rear Admiral Edwin Layton, stationed at Honolulu as Fleet Intelligence Officer in 1941, declared that Hoover "dropped the ball completely" in his handling of Popov's report. "His failure," Layton wrote, "represented another American fumble on the road to Pearl Harbor."

**PEARSON, Drew**— A native of Evanston, Illinois, born 13 December 1897, Drew Pearson taught geography before turning to journalism in the early days of the Great Depression. The *Baltimore Sun* initially carried his "Washington Merry-Go-Round" column, prepared with colleague Robert Allen, but they were fired as too controversial in 1932. The column was nationally syndicated thereafter, with Allen remaining on board until 1942, replaced in 1947 by JACK ANDERSON. The FBI opened a file on Pearson in 1934 and shadowed him until 1968, the year before his death. Aside from a general file (3,260 pages), Pearson was one of only four writers included in J. EDGAR HOOVER'S private "Official and Confidential" files. He was also the subject of a secret "June Mail" file, containing information gathered by G-men via illegal wire tapping and BREAK-INS.

Pearson did not start off in Hoover's bad graces. In fact, he was initially charmed by the director and did his part to promote "Hoover's bulldog reputation." By the end of WORLD WAR II, however, Pearson had grown disillusioned with FBI tactics and found himself posted to the Bureau's "Do Not Contact" list. Between 1951 and 1953, when Pearson criticized Red-baiting Senator JOSEPH MCCARTHY, Hoover clipped and filed each column wherein Bureau-friendly columnist WESTBROOK PEGLER "discredited" Pearson. The intensely personal nature of Hoover's malice toward Pearson is showcased in Hoover's memos, branding Pearson an "eel," a "pathological liar," a "psychopathic liar," and a "real stooge for [Soviet Premier Nikita] Khrushchev." Hoover once referred to Pearson's "muckraking yellow dog style of journalism for which he has become notorious," and in 1961 complained that "This whelp still continues his regurgitation."

The roots of Hoover's feud with Pearson apparently date from 1938, when Pearson and Allen wrote that a Guatemalan diplomat had told them that Hoover "uses a distinctive and conspicuous" perfume. Hoover failed in his effort to have the diplomat dismissed, but thereafter waged relentless war against Pearson and his co-authors. Robert Allen, dubbed the "worst of the two" by Hoover, was targeted for an anti-Semitic smear in 1940, after "a reliable source" told Hoover that Allen's "true name" was Ginsberg. Hoover suggested that the information be used in some derogatory fashion, but the outcome of that plot is unknown. Seven years later, the Bureau opened a file on Jack Anderson, and kept him under surveillance for years after Pearson died in 1969.

A curious item, from 30 years earlier, involved the occasion when Pearson printed a rumor of Hoover's impending retirement. Chastised for that error, Pearson apologized and requested a personal tour of FBI headquarters. Hoover penned a note approving the tour, as long as Pearson was denied access to "the cells in the basement." It remains unclear whether Hoover was displaying a rare flash of wit, or if another Bureau secret still waits to be revealed.

**PEEL, Harry L.**— A popular G-man assigned to the Jacksonville, Florida field office, Harry Peel was employed as a polygraph operator in 1983, when he logged his first arrest for soliciting sex from a male undercover police officer. Jacksonville's agent-in-charge reported the incident to Paul Minor, the FBI's senior polygrapher in Washington, with a request that he "keep Harry close to home" and thus avoid further trouble. (Peel's indiscretion had occurred while traveling on FBI business.) Minor in turn reported Peel's arrest to the chief of the Polygraph Unit, recommending that Peel be reassigned to regular investigative duties. "Ultimately," he told journalist Robert Kessler, "it was de-

cided not to do that, not to do anything. I thought it was pretty amazing."

Indeed, FBI HEADQUARTERS has traditionally shown no tolerance for HOMOSEXUALITY, but an exception was made in Peel's case. Two years later he was arrested again, this time at a Florida beach frequented by gays. The second arrest prompted Agent Minor to review Peel's work in recent cases, revealing that "his truthful rate [on polygraph tests] was higher than average." In fact, Minor noted "major anomalies" in Peel's style of questioning subjects and he suspected "a trade-off for sex." Under questioning, Peel "admitted he had falsified the charts," but claimed he did so only with innocent persons. "Once he decided they were telling the truth," Minor said, "he wanted to make sure the charts had no trouble at headquarters when they came through for review."

It was a strange explanation, at best. Minor concluded that Peel's "secret life may have made him feel defensive and inadequate," but none of the subjects he questioned were later proved guilty. It hardly mattered by that time, since the FBI's OFFICE OF PROFESSIONAL RESPONSIBILITY had started a review of Peel's arrests. On 2 May 1986, after returning from a trip to headquarters, Peel shot himself in his car, parked outside a Jacksonville shopping mall. Fellow agents found a suicide note in his office desk.

**PEGLER, James Westbrook**— A self-described "member of the rabble in good standing," Minneapolis native Westbrook Pegler was born in 1894 and launched his career as a columnist for the New York *World-Telegram* in the 1930s. He won a Pulitzer Prize for exposing labor racketeers in 1940, and ten years later lost a $175,000 libel suit spawned by his reckless disregard for fact and common decency. Pegler's relationship with the FBI was equally erratic, his treatment by the Bureau dependent in equal parts on Pegler's handling of the news and on the whims of Director J. EDGAR HOOVER.

The Bureau opened a file on Pegler in 1935, the first time he was added to Hoover's mailing list of "friendly" journalists. Pegler earned that favor with a column that described the JUSTICE DEPARTMENT as "the most fascinating of all the government bureaus to those who like adventure stories and detective comic-strips," but he was crossed off the list a month later, for referring to FBI agents as "trigger men." Back on the list in May 1936, Pegler requested a tour of FBI headquarters, but he was struck from the roll again on 3 June 1936, establishing a pattern that endured for the next three decades.

Pegler was nothing, if not volatile. He despised President FRANKLIN ROOSEVELT and branded pro-FBI columnist WALTER WINCHELL "dangerous." Winchell responded by dubbing his enemy "Peglouse," and Hoover cheerfully sided with Winchell, referring to "Westcrook Pegler" as a "creature" who "suffers from mental halitosis." A 1940 Hoover memo reads: "Be very circumspect in dealing with Pegler. The rat will twist anything around to serve his own purpose." At the same time, Pegler's 810-page dossier contains columns clipped by G-men and forwarded to Hoover, with Hoover's cheers of "Terrific!" penned in the margins, hailing some attack on a mutual enemy like DREW PEARSON.

A 1942 FBI report claimed Pegler was "either in contact with Nazi sources or obtained certain information therefrom"; a year later, the New York field office referred to "documentary proof" that "Pegler is in the pay of the German government," further alleging that "Nazi officials bailed him out" in 1936, when Pegler had some financial problems.

Despite those alleged ties to America's enemies in WORLD WAR II, Pegler still receives occasional off-the-record tips from FBI sources and the HOUSE COMMITTEE ON UN-AMERICAN ACTIVITIES. FBI Assistant Director LOUIS NICHOLS once opined that "the way to handle Pegler is to completely ignore him and ignore the articles," but Nichols himself recommended in 1947 that the FBI "furnish Pegler for use without attribution" certain information about the mob-owned Flamingo Hotel in Las Vegas. The same year, however, witnessed an FBI plan to embarrass Pegler by unearthing details of a New York arrest, but the charges are blacked out in Pegler's file and the plan was never implemented. Six years later, in 1953, millionaire Hoover ally Joseph Kenney was recruited "to set Pegler straight" on criticism of the FBI's performance in CIVIL RIGHTS cases.

Such critiques notwithstanding, Pegler seemed more often a would-be friend of the Bureau. In August 1946 he addressed a personal letter to Hoover, noting that "Apparently the move to get your job and hand it to some Communist that we observed last winter was blocked before it really got under way. I hope it is dead." Four years later, when author MAX LOWENTHAL published his own critical history of the FBI, Pegler's voice was among the loudest in a journalistic chorus questioning Lowenthal's morality and patriotism.

By 1962, when Pegler began writing tracts for the paranoid John Birch Society, Deputy Associate Director CARTHA DELOACH summarized a personal interview by noting that "Pegler as usual was most incoherent in conversation." Two years later, one of the last "limited" press releases Pegler received from the Bureau's CRIME RECORDS DIVISION bore a handwritten note that "over the years our relations with Pegler have become strained." The strain ended with Pegler's death, in 1969.

**PELTIER, Leonard**— On 26 June 1975 a shootout occurred on South Dakota's PINE RIDGE INDIAN RESERVATION, between FBI agents and members of the AMERICAN INDIAN MOVEMENT (AIM). G-men later claimed that they were trying to arrest an unnamed AIM member for assault and theft, resulting from an earlier incident provoked by members of the vigilante GUARDIANS OF THE OGLALA NATION (GOON). Before the battle ended, Agents Jack Coler and Ronald Williams were killed, along with AIM member Joe Stuntz Killsright. Coincidentally or otherwise, on the day after the shootout, members of the U.S. Senate's CHURCH COMMITTEE canceled plans to hear testimony on the FBI's long-running harassment of AIM.

The Coler-Williams slayings sparked a massive manhunt, code-named RESMURS (for "*res*ervations *mur*ders"). On 25 November 1975 a federal grand jury indicted four AIM members for the murders. Defendants DARELLE BUTLER, James Eagle and Robert Robideau were already in custody, while 31-year-old Leonard Peltier remained at large, his name appended to the

FBI's "TEN MOST WANTED" LIST. Canadian police captured Peltier at Hinton, Alberta on 6 February 1976, and he was held pending extradition to the U.S. A Pine Ridge resident, Myrtle Poor Bear, provided G-men with two affidavits (dated 19 and 23 February 1976) which described Peltier as the lone triggerman in the double killing. At the time she signed those statements, Poor Bear had been held *incommunicado* by FBI agents for over a month, and Canadian authorities later acknowledged her statements were probably false, but Peltier was still extradited on 18 December 1976.

By that time, the JUSTICE DEPARTMENT was desperately in need of a conviction. Defendants Butler and Robideau freely admitted to firing on Agents Coler and Williams, but they claimed the G-men had started the shootout and jurors acquitted both men on 16 July 1976, accepting their plea of self-defense. Prosecutors dropped all charges against James Eagle on 8 September 1976, leaving Peltier as the only defendant in the case. At his murder trial, beginning in March 1977, the government claimed Peltier alone had shot both agents, killing them execution-style with rifle bullets fired at point-blank range. The main evidence against him was a .223-caliber shell casing found in the open trunk of Agent Coler's car, allegedly linked to Peltier's rifle. To prove that case, prosecutors illegally suppressed an FBI memo of 2 October 1975, stating that Peltier's weapon "contains a different firing pin than that in [the] rifle used at [the] RESMURS scene." Deprived of that exculpatory evidence, jurors convicted Peltier on 18 April 1977. Six weeks later, on 1 June 1977, Judge Paul Benson sentenced Peltier to two consecutive life terms. (A separate case, for the attempted murder of a Milwaukee policeman, ended with Peltier's acquittal in February 1978).

Once convicted, Peltier's fate rested in the hands of the federal appellate system. The Eighth Circuit Court of Appeals affirmed his conviction on 14 September 1978, and the U.S. SUPREME COURT declined to hear his case on 10 March 1979. Two months later, Peltier had new worries on his mind. Confined at Lompoc, California, Peltier found himself stalked by convicts including a member of the South Dakota GOON squad (imprisoned for killing another AIM member at Pine Ridge in 1976). Convinced that political enemies and prison officials planned to murder him, Peltier escaped from Lompoc with three other inmates on 20 July 1979. Recaptured on 26 July, Peltier faced trial on 14 November 1979 for additional charges of escape, conspiracy to escape, auto theft and armed robbery. He was convicted on 22 January 1980 and received the maximum seven-year sentence. (Fellow escapee Bobby Garcia, sentenced to five years, was murdered in prison on 13 December 1980.)

The long appeals process continued. On 21 March 1982 the Ninth Circuit Court reversed Peltier's escape conviction on grounds that the trial court improperly denied Peltier's right to question state witnesses about personal bias against him. A writ of habeas corpus was filed in federal court on 11 April 1982, citing suppression of exculpatory evidence and use of perjured testimony at Peltier's murder trial, but Judge Benson remained in charge of the case. On 30 December 1982 he refused to recuse himself or to release 6,000 pages of classified FBI documents on Peltier; the next day Benson predictably denied Peltier's motion for a new trial.

The tide appeared to turn in April 1984, with the Eighth Circuit Court ordered Benson to hold an evidentiary hearing based on the 2 October 1975 FBI teletype excluding Peltier's rifle as the Pine Ridge murder weapon. That hearing documented further instances of federal perjury but once again failed to secure a new trial. Oral arguments before the Eighth Circuit began on 15 October 1985, with lead prosecutor Lynn Crooks frankly admitting, "We don't know who killed those agents." Crooks contradicted his courtroom statements from 1977, claiming now that Peltier was merely convicted of "Aiding and abetting whoever did the final shooting. Perhaps aiding and abetting himself. And hopefully the jury would believe that in effect he did it all. But aiding and abetting, nevertheless." Judge Gerald Heaney replied:

> It seems to me that this would have been an entirely different case, both in terms of the manner in which it was presented to the jury and the sentence that the judge imposed, if the only evidence that you have was that Leonard Peltier was participating on the periphery of the fire fight and the agents got killed. Now that would have been an entirely different case. But the evidence here is that the agents were killed at close range and that Peltier was at the vehicles so he could have done the killing and that even though somebody else may have pulled the trigger, he had the AR-15 and was there with those other two men ant that therefore they were directly implicated. Because I doubt that if all he had been was ... shooting from the periphery, I don't think this would have been the same case at all.

On 11 September 1986 the Eighth Circuit panel declared that Crooks's "aiding and abetting" argument had no merit, since Crooks had earlier called Peltier "the principal" in a first-degree murder. The court also dismissed federal claims that only Peltier had carried an AR-15 rifle in the shootout, finding that "several" such weapons were present on 26 June 1975. Having thus demolished the prosecution's case, the judges still refused to overturn Peltier's conviction. Their reasoning: although ballistics evidence suppressed by the government would "possibly" have changed the trial jury's verdict, recent Supreme Court rulings demanded a judgment that the verdict "probably" would have been altered. The panel's motive for that verdict may be found in this paragraph from the court's final judgment:

> There are only two alternatives ... to the government's contention that the .223 casing was ejected into the trunk of Coler's car when the Wichita AR-15 was fired at the agents. One alternative is that the .223 casing was planted in the trunk of Coler's car either before its discovery by the investigating agents or by the agents who reported its discovery. The other alternative is that a non-matching casing was originally found in the trunk and sent to the FBI laboratory, only to be replaced by a matching casing when the importance of a match to the Wichita AR-15 became evident....We recognize that there is evidence in this record of improper conduct on the part of some FBI agents, but we are reluctant to impute even further improprieties to them.

Thus, to preserve the FBI's already tarnished reputation, Peltier's conviction was affirmed. Subsequent appeals, writs of habeas corpus and pleas for executive clemency have uniformly been denied. FBI HEADQUARTERS still resists applications for release of Peltier's FILES to defense attorneys under the FREEDOM OF INFORMATION ACT. By November 2002 federal authorities in both Canada and the U.S. admitted that the affidavits used to secure Peltier's 1976 extradition were fraudulent, but admission of the government's criminal activity has thus far failed to free Peltier. At this writing (in March 2003) he has served 27 years in prison for a crime he almost certainly did not commit.

**"PENTAGON Papers"**—During 1967-68 Secretary of Defense Robert McNamara ordered preparation of a secret report on America's military involvement in Southeast Asia, titled *History of U.S. Decision-Making Process on Viet Nam Policy*. The document, classified top-secret, revealed embarrassing facts about U.S. complicity and duplicity in events leading up to the VIETNAM WAR. It was never intended for public dissemination, but the *New York Times* obtained a copy and serialized it, with the first installment published on 13 June 1971. Revelation of the so-called "Pentagon Papers" infuriated President RICHARD NIXON, prompting him to order a full FBI investigation of the leak on 15 June.

Director J. EDGAR HOOVER had little enthusiasm for the assignment, fearing that it would drag the Bureau deeper into Nixon's web of political corruption. G-men easily identified the leaker as Daniel Ellsberg, a former researcher for the Defense Department and Rand Corporation whose political sentiments on the war had shifted radically in recent years, transforming him from a "hawk" to a "militant dove." Hoover's reservations about the investigation were compounded by the fact that Ellsberg's father-in-law, wealthy toy manufacturer Louis Marx, was a member of Hoover's "Special Correspondents" list who sent the director a shipment of toys each Christmas, for charity and the children of friends. When G-man Charles Brennan (in charge of the Ellsberg case) sought permission to question Marx, Hoover scrawled "NO" on the memo, but Brennan read the message as "OK" and proceeded with the interview. Hoover promptly slapped Brennan with a punitive transfer to Alexandria, Virginia, eliciting a protest from Brennan's superior, Assistant Director WILLIAM SULLIVAN. Hoover rejected Sullivan's appeal, whereupon Sullivan took his complaint to Assistant Attorney General Robert Mardian, in charge of the JUSTICE DEPARTMENT's Internal Security Division. Mardian convinced Attorney General JOHN MITCHELL to order Brennan's reinstatement, claiming that he needed Brennan on the Ellsberg case. Hoover complied—but only after he demoted Brennan to inspector, censured him and placed him on probation.

The furor at FBI HEADQUARTERS disturbed President Nixon no end. He later wrote of the event:

> Even as our concern about Ellsberg and his possible collaborators was growing, we learned that J. Edgar Hoover was dragging his feet and treating the case on merely a medium-priority basis; he has assigned no special task forces and no extra manpower to it. He evidently felt that the media would make Ellsberg look like a martyr, and the FBI like the "heavy," if he pursued the case vigorously....
> I did not care about any reasons or excuses. I wanted someone to light a fire under the FBI in the investigation of Ellsberg, and to keep the departments and agencies active in the pursuit of leakers. If a conspiracy existed, I wanted to know, and I wanted

the full resources of the government brought to bear to find out. If the FBI was not going to pursue the case, then we would have to do it ourselves.

Nixon's solution, on 17 July 1971, was the creation of a special "plumbers" squad to find and fix the ever-multiplying White House leaks. One of those recruited for the team was ex-FBI agent G. GORDON LIDDY. The units work began with a BREAK-IN at the office of Ellsberg's psychiatrist, Dr. Lewis Fielding, and climaxed 11 months later with a burglary that triggered the WATERGATE SCANDAL, thereby dooming Nixon's presidency.

The Justice Department sought to make an example of Ellsberg for future leakers, indicting him and confederate Anthony Russo on charges of ESPIONAGE, conspiracy and theft of government property. At their trial in 1973, it was revealed that G-men had placed WIRETAPS on various reporters while seeking to trace the Pentagon leak, and Judge W. Matt Byrne ordered prosecutors to reveal whether the defendants or their attorneys had been tapped in the process. Retrieval of that information was retarded by FBI security procedures, since logs of the 17 relevant wiretaps had not been filed with other records of national security taps. Instead, they had been hand-delivered to William Sullivan—who in turn gave them to Robert Mardian "for safekeeping" when Hoover forced Sullivan's resignation in October 1971. Mardian, for his part, reported that the logs were passed on to President Nixon. Citing prosecution failure to comply with his discovery order, Judge Byrne dismissed all charges in the Ellsberg-Russo case on 11 May 1973.

**PEONAGE**—While the U.S. fought a bloody four-year civil war to end slavery and enacted a constitutional amendment (the 13th) banning enslavement of human beings in 1865, the practice was not entirely eradicated. In many states of the former Confederacy "Black Codes" were passed in 1866, requiring former slaves to hold steady jobs under terms dictated by whites and mandating terms of forced labor in case of unpaid debts to their employers. The bitter era of Reconstruction that followed included passage of federal laws to ban peonage—the legal term for slavery in societies where it officially does not exist—but southern legislators soon devised the "convict lease system," under which blacks were imprisoned for petty crimes (and often as victims of FRAME-UPS), then "leased" to private contractors who used the prisoners as slave labor on farms, construction projects and the like.

In 1921 G-men George Brown and A.J. Wismer, assigned to the Atlanta field office, were asked by FBI HEADQUARTERS to estimate the extent of peonage in the modern South. Author Gregory Freeman reports that Brown and Wismer "had seen plenty of examples of peonage, either personally, in reports from Washington, or in complaints from Georgia that they never bothered to follow up," and yet:

> ...[T]hey found the task difficult because [peonage] was relegated to distant rural communities and not well documented in any way. They had no doubt, however, that it was practiced extensively. They came across research from 1907 that estimated that a third of all farmers in Georgia, Alabama and Mississippi used

forced labor, and peonage was reported in every county in Alabama between 1903 and 1905. When a South Carolina farmer was acquitted of peonage charges in 1910, a local newspaper stated that the acquittal was "not at all surprising, for while everybody knows that he is guilty, it is equally well known that he is not any more guilty than scores or perhaps hundreds of other men."

In February 1921 Agents Brown and Wisner began to investigate Georgia farmer John Williams on peonage charges. Williams killed at least 11 of his slaves to prevent them from testifying against him in court, and finally a state murder charge sent Williams to prison for life. Peonage cases remained difficult to prosecute in Dixie, as demonstrated by the subsequent acquittal of ex-governor Sidney Catts in Florida.

It should not be supposed that peonage disappeared in the early 20th century. In March 1978 a retired Florida college professor and his wife were jailed for enslaving a 10-year-old African girl, working her 12 to 18 hours a day in their Okeechobee home on a bare subsistence diet of rice and water. Three years later, in Raleigh, North Carolina, migrant labor contractor Dennis Warren and two of his foremen were indicted on federal charges of kidnapping workers and enslaving them at a camp where one victim collapsed and died; the three defendants were convicted at trial in January 1982. Another Florida couple, Kishin Matani and Shashi Gobindram, pled guilty on 4 December 1996 to enslaving a 23-year-old female immigrant from their native India. The defendants admitted torturing their captive for minor infractions with punishments that included burns and near-drowning.

The scourge of slavery continues in the new millennium. On 28 October 2000 President WILLIAM CLINTON signed federal legislation providing a maximum penalty of life imprisonment for peonage. (Ironically, a Clinton appointee from Arkansas was even then awaiting trial on charges that he twice dispatched procurers to China in search of personal sex slaves.) In August 2001 a University of Texas research assistant and his wife, Sardar and Nadira Gasanov, were accused with luring young women to the U.S. from their native Uzbekistan with promises of lucrative modeling jobs, then forcing them to work in strip clubs while the Gasanovs claimed all their earnings. In lieu of peonage, FBI agents charged the couple with conspiracy, money laundering and smuggling aliens for profit. If convicted on all counts, they faced up to 36 years in federal prison.

**PÉREZ, Bernardo Matias**—A California native, born 26 September 1939, Bernardo Pérez joined the FBI as a headquarters messenger in 1960, then became an agent in September 1963, after graduating from Georgetown University with a degree in Spanish literature. Over the next eight years, he was assigned to field offices in Tampa, San Antonio, Miami and Washington, D.C. In January 1971 he was promoted to supervisor in the Intelligence Division at FBI HEADQUARTERS, later transferred to the Inspection and Records Management Divisions. In March 1977 Pérez was assigned as a supervisor in the Los Angeles field office. In 1979 he was moved to San Juan, Puerto Rico, then back to Los Angeles as assistant agent-in-charge.

Pérez viewed his subsequent transfer to El Paso, Texas as a

demotion, although he held the same rank as he had in Los Angeles. Persistent transfers on the so-called "taco circuit" prompted him to file a formal complaint with headquarters in 1987, alleging racial discrimination. Other HISPANIC AGENTS soon joined in the complaint, which became a full-blown class-action lawsuit. On 26 September 1988 federal judge Lucius Buntun found that the Bureau systematically discriminated against Hispanics in promotions and working conditions. On 5 May 1989 Judge Bunton ordered changes in FBI promotion procedures but declined to award the plaintiffs retroactive pay raises. In a move that angered many white G-men, Director WILLIAM SESSIONS accepted the court's ruling without filing an appeal. Pérez was appointed deputy assistant director of the FBI's LABORATORY DIVISION on 22 May 1989, and on 6 March 1991 he became agent-in-charge of the Albuquerque field office. Perez retired from the Bureau in 1994.

**PERRY Franklyn**— Born in 1940, Franklyn Perry was a longtime resident of Las Vegas, Nevada who had difficulty staying out of prison. In 1985 he was convicted of operating an illegal pyramid scheme and defrauding 50 investors of $3.3 million. At the time of his arrest, authorities declared their belief that Perry had "at least $40 million" stashed from various con games and rip-offs, but they never found the money. Convicted of his latest indiscretion, he received a 25-year prison sentence and served 12 years, winning parole in 1989.

The FBI's Las Vegas field office recruited Perry as an INFORMANT upon his release from prison. His specific target was Jerald Burgess, long suspected in the disappearance and presumed murder of six-year-old Cary Sayegh, missing from Las Vegas since 1978. Burgess had been charged with Sayegh's KIDNAPPING, but a jury acquitted him in 1982. Still, G-men thought that with Perry's help they could obtain enough evidence to charge Burgess with the boy's murder. It never happened, but they did charge Burgess with firearms violations and convicted him in August 2001.

By that time, Frank Perry had more problems of his own — enough, in fact, that he was rendered useless to the Bureau and was stricken from the witness list at Burgess's trial. On 18 July 2001, without informing the Bureau, Las Vegas police arrested Perry for his latest fraud, seizing "at least $22 million" in cash from his home and office. The new scam involved soliciting $10,000 minimum contributions from "partners" around the world, who were promised returns of 60 to 100 percent on their investments. Perry claimed the money would be given to "high rollers" in Las Vegas who had exceeded their credit limits at major casinos, but who were expected to win big money. In fact, the gamblers never existed and Perry's was the only jackpot in the game.

In addition to eight counts of fraud, local authorities charged Perry with 48 sex offenses, including seven counts of sexual assault on a minor below age 14; five counts of attempted sexual assault on a minor under 16; six counts of lewdness with a child under 14; 15 counts of unlawfully using a minor to produce pornography; and 15 counts of possessing child pornography. Police claimed that Perry had telephoned underage girls and coached them through a series of sexually explicit acts while their friends snapped photographs. Perry, through his lawyer, claimed he had collected the smut "as part of his work as an informant for the FBI." At a hearing in late July 2001 Perry told the court, "They [G-men] told me I could take it and turn it over to them." Perry's trial was still pending as of March 2003, delayed by various legal maneuvers.

**PERSONNEL Division**—Prior to 1993, all FBI personnel matters were handled by the Administrative Services Division. Since FBI employees are exempt from provisions of the U.S. Civil Service code (a rule imposed by Director J. EDGAR HOOVER to cement one-man rule of the Bureau under his tenure), many complaints of arbitrary and capricious discipline have been logged through the years, from agents and support personnel alike. Director LOUIS FREEH created the separate Personnel Division in October 1993, one month after he assumed command of the FBI. At last report, in April 1998, the division was led by Assistant Director Ruben Garcia, Jr.

**PHILBRICK, Herbert**— In 1940 Boston advertising agent Herbert Philbrick joined a local organization opposed to the spreading war in Europe, but he soon suspected that the group included members of the COMMUNIST PARTY. At first Philbrick planned to resign, but he first reported his suspicion to G-men, who asked him to join the party as an INFORMANT. Over the next nine years Philbrick rose through the party's middle ranks and emerged as one of the JUSTICE DEPARTMENT's key witnesses in 1949, when 11 party leaders were prosecuted for SMITH ACT violations. With his adventure behind him, Philbrick published a best-selling memoir in 1952, *I Led Three Lives*, which later became a popular television drama of the same title (1953-56).

**PIKE Committee**— Established on 19 February 1975, the House Select Intelligence Committee — better known by the name of its chairman, New York congressman Otis Pike — was the House counterpart of the U.S. Senate's CHURCH COMMITTEE. While the Church Committee focused primarily on illegal (and frequently sensational) activities of the FBI and the CENTRAL INTELLIGENCE AGENCY (CIA), the Pike Committee took a more subtle approach by reviewing the "intelligence community's" expenses and effectiveness. That angle of attack prompted immediate hostility from President GERALD FORD, as well as leaders of the FBI and CIA. When the investigation was complete, the same Congress which had authorized the probe voted to suppress its findings. The full report has never been published, but CBS newscaster Daniel Schorr was suspended for leaking portions of it to the *Village Voice*. Mainstream newspapers, including the *New York Times* and the *Washington Post*, refused to publish the extracts in deference to "national security."

**PINE Ridge Indian Reservation**— Located in southwestern South Dakota, spanning Jackson and Shannon Counties, the Pine Ridge Indian Reservation was a site of concerted FBI activity in the 1970s. G-men first made their presence felt in large numbers during the WOUNDED KNEE SIEGE of 1973, marking the onset of a long Bureau campaign to destroy the AMERICAN INDIAN MOVEMENT (AIM). In pursuit of that goal, FBI leaders armed and financed a private vigilante organization — GUARDIANS OF THE OGLALA NATION (GOON) — whose members harassed, assaulted and murdered AIM activists over the next three years. (FBI agents assigned to Pine Ridge claimed inadequate manpower prevented them from solving those crimes.) Bureau attempts to prosecute AIM's leaders after Wounded Knee proved unsuccessful, as illegal FBI activities caused the case to be thrown out of court. In June 1975, following an incident provoked by GOON vigilantes, two G-men were shot and killed on the reservation. Four AIM members were charged with the killings, but two won acquittal at trial with a self-defense plea, and all charges against a third defendant were dropped. AIM activist LEONARD PELTIER was finally convicted and sentenced to life in prison, in a case which many observers regard as a FRAME-UP.

**PINKERTON Detective Agency** — Organized in 1852 by Allan Pinkerton, a Chicago deputy sheriff, the Pinkerton Detective Agency was America's first private investigation agency. In 1861 its agents were hired to protect President Abraham Lincoln, thus anticipating the U.S. SECRET SERVICE (which Pinkerton led during the Civil War). In the later 1860s and 1870s, Pinkerton detectives were best known for pursuing train robbers, including Jesse James and the Younger brothers. At the same time, Pinkerton agents signed on as strikebreakers for various "robber barons" of the 19th century, actively suppressing various LABOR UNIONS across the nation.

Allan Pinkerton died in 1884, leaving the agency to sons Robert and William. Pinkerton detectives were hired by the JUSTICE DEPARTMENT on a case-by-case basis, since Justice had no investigators of its own, but Congress banned that practice by law in 1893, after Pinkerton gunmen fought (and lost) a pitched battle with strikers at Homestead, Pennsylvania, leaving 16 persons dead on 5 July 1892.

**PISCATOR, Erwin Friedrich** — A German native, born at Ulm on 17 December 1893, Piscator was renowned for his stage productions during the pre-Nazi era of the Weimar Republic. He joined the German COMMUNIST PARTY in 1918 or 1922 (reports vary), and resigned from membership in 1923 over personal dissatisfaction with the party's program. Unwelcome in ADOLF HITLER'S Third Reich, Piscator fled to Canada in 1939 and later made his way to New York City, where he founded the Dramatic Workshop in a failed effort to establish himself on Broadway. The FBI came looking for Piscator in October 1943, serving a search warrant on his Manhattan apartment, scanning the contents of his library and noting that the U.S. attorney general's office had granted Piscator permission to own a camera. Despite his resignation from the Communist Party, G-men considered Piscator's link with the anti-Nazi group Free Germany as proof he was a "fellow traveler," his case classified as "Alien Enemy Control — G" (for German).

V-E Day brought Piscator no respite from FBI scrutiny. No longer classified as an enemy alien, he was now ranked as a "Security Matter — C" (for Communist) in Bureau files. Piscator's application for U.S. citizenship had been rejected in 1944, but when J. EDGAR HOOVER urged Immigration officials to deport him three years later, they could find no grounds to do so. Hoover finally got his wish in October 1951, when Piscator left the country to avoid a subpoena from the HOUSE COMMITTEE ON UN-AMERICAN ACTIVITIES. Settled in West Germany, Piscator was denied a reentry permit to visit his wife in New York. The State Department considered granting Piscator a visa in December 1965, "in view of the compassionate and humanitarian aspects of the case," but the petition was rejected. Piscator died at Starnberg on 30 March 1966.

**PISTONE, Joseph D.** — Pennsylvania native Joseph Pistone joined the FBI in July 1969 and spent his first 18 months assigned to the Jacksonville, Florida field office. His legendary undercover work began in 1971, when he was transferred to Alexandria, Virginia, and from there to New York City in 1974. Two years later, posing as jewel thief "Donnie Brasco," Pistone became the first FBI agent in history to penetrate the Mafia. Working his way into the Joseph Bonnano crime family (though never inducted as a "made" member), Pistone remained undercover until January 1981, collecting sufficient evidence for some 200 indictments and more than 100 felony convictions. (He also provided information leading to the subsequent "pizza connection" case.) Pistone received the U.S. Attorney General's Distinguished Service Award in January 1983 and remained with the Bureau for three more years, playing a peripheral role in FBI penetration of the BANDIDOS MOTORCYCLE GANG. Persistent death threats finally moved Pistone to leave the FBI in 1986 and take his family into hiding. Two years later he published an account of his greatest case — *Donnie Brasco: My Undercover Life in the Mafia*. A film was made of the book in 1997, starring Johnny Depp, but Pistone staunchly refutes the scenes that show his character assuming the personality and ethics of a mobster.

**PITTS, Earl Edwin** — Earl Pitts joined the FBI in 1983 and four years later began a career as a double-agent, spying for the Soviet KGB. His betrayal was a deliberate choice, initiated in July 1987 when Pitts wrote a letter to the Soviet Mission to the United Nations, offering his services as a spy. At the time, he was assigned to counterintelligence operations with the New York City field office, later transferred to the Bureau's Legal Counsel Division in Washington, D.C. KGB officers paid Pitts a total of $224,000 for various documents including a list of FBI INFORMANTS who were providing information on the Soviet Union.

Pitts's career in ESPIONAGE stalled in December 1991, when the Soviet Union abandoned communism and subsequently disintegrated. FBI HEADQUARTERS obtained cooperation from Pitts's original Russian contact, and while Pitts was transferred to a post at the FBI ACADEMY where he could do no further damage, a "false flag" sting operation was mounted against him. A former contact, now collaborating with the Bureau, approached Pitts with an offer to resume spying for the new Russian Foreign Intelligence Service (successor to the KGB). Pitts agreed and accepted $15,000 in cash. Surveillance led to his arrest on 18 December 1996, charged with conspiracy to commit espionage, attempted espionage, communication of classified information and conveyance without authority of government property. Pitts pled guilty in February 1997, calling a psychiatrist to testify that anger had pushed him "beyond his limits." Judge T.S. Ellis III dismissed the argument slapped Pitts with a 27-year prison term, three years longer than the prosecution had requested.

**POLICE Brutality**— The FBI is charged with investigating acts of police brutality whenever law enforcement officers willfully deprive any person of his or her constitutional rights while "acting under color of law" (i.e., in an official capacity). Historically, thousands of well-documented violations have occurred throughout the U.S.— many involving racial, religious and political minorities — but the Bureau has been extremely reluctant to intervene in such cases. Under Director J. EDGAR HOOVER (1924-72), the hands-off attitude toward brutal police derived from a combination of Hoover's personal racism, his ultra-conservative political philosophy, and the FBI's reliance on local officers to help compile favorable arrest statistics (thereby impressing congressional appropriation committees).

The first known case of G-men filing charges in a police brutality case occurred in January 1943, when Georgia sheriff Claude Screws and two of his deputies fatally beat a black prisoner named Robert Hall. The three were convicted in federal court and the Circuit Court of Appeals upheld their conviction, but the U.S. SUPREME COURT overturned the verdicts in 1945, ruling that federal law only applied to murderous police if they killed a victim "with the specific intent and purpose of denying their prisoner a Constitutional right." The defendants were acquitted at a second federal trial and state authorities declined to file charges. Sheriff Screws was later elected to the Georgia state legislature.

The Screws case may have frustrated some G-men, but it gave FBI HEADQUARTERS the perfect excuse to do little or nothing in future cases. Throughout the epic CIVIL RIGHTS struggles of the 1950s and 1960s, FBI agents generally remained on the sidelines, taking notes and snapping photographs while demonstrators were beaten, tear-gassed, mauled by police dogs, and sometimes shot. Arrests of brutal officers were rare, convictions even more uncommon. When Dr. MARTIN LUTHER KING, JR., complained that G-men seemed friendly with racist police in the South, Hoover denounced King as "the most notorious liar in the country," yet examples abounded. The most infamous, in 1968, was the ORANGEBURG MASSACRE, in which South Carolina police shot 30 student demonstrators, killing three. At the trial of nine officers indicted on civil rights charges, FBI agents falsely claimed the unarmed victims had directed "small arms fire" and lobbed nonexistent "high explosives" at police before they were shot.

If the FBI has been deficient in policing lawless law enforcement agencies, there is also reason to believe G-men themselves sometimes brutalize their prisoners. Beatings were routine during the PALMER RAIDS of 1919-20, as reported in New York's daily newspapers and admitted before Congress by Director WILLIAM BURNS. In the 1930s, agents from the Chicago field office were notorious for use of "third-degree" tactics that included dangling suspects from the open windows of their 19th-story offices. Kidnapping suspect ROGER TOUHY was subjected to such

treatment on orders from agent-in-charge MELVIN PURVIS, and while he survived to serve time for a KIDNAPPING he did not commit, others were less fortunate. Prisoners ANDREA SALSEDO in New York (1920) and JAMES PROBASCO in Chicago (1934) both plunged to their deaths from FBI windows in what the Bureau described as unpreventable "suicides."

Such tactics, unfortunately, are not confined to the distant past. On 30 September 1965 FBI agents arrested two BANK ROBBERY suspects at a Brooklyn motel owned by Anthony Polisi, a businessman with no criminal record who denied any knowledge of the crime or previous acquaintance with his two paying customers. Four days later, Polisi claims, a quartet of G-men returned and drove him to a secluded site where:

> The agent in the front passenger seat turned and kneeling on the seat grabbed my tie and pulled it tight choking me. He said, "You ——, you'll talk today or you're a dead man." While he was pulling my tie, the agent on my left held my left hand and was pulling my hair. They said, "Give us the information or we'll kill you." They kept asking about guns and where did I have them. Every time I told them I didn't know anything about any guns they put more pressure on my fingers and pulled tighter on my tie. I asked them if they knew what they were doing, that I had a heart condition. The agent in front who was holding my tie said, "Good, we'll give you an attack right now" and started to punch me in the area of my heart.... I told them they had made a mistake and had the wrong man and begged them to stop before they had a corpse on their hands. When I said this he again punched me three or four times in the same spot. The agent on my left punched me in the face with his left.
>
> ...The agent on my left took his gun out and put it to my temple. [He] said, "Tell us where the guns are or you're a dead ——." The agent on my right, still bending my fingers back, said, "If you want to see your grandchildren again you better talk." I told them the only thing I could say was that I was being tortured as much as Jesus Christ. The agent on my left said, "What kind of Catholic are you?" and again punched me in the face.... The driver kept saying to let him do it his way, let me get out and run away so they could shoot me trying to escape.... They said, "Oh you won't get out huh? We'll get you out." The agent on my right opened the door and started to pull me out while the agent on my left pushed. The agent in front was pulling me by my tie towards the door. I tripped over the floor hump and they dragged me out onto the ground, told me to get up and run. They were punching and kicking me while I was lying there. Someone tried to pick me up by my hair while two others took my arms. After standing they were pushing me away from the car, telling me to run. They were pointing their guns at me. By this time I was completely terrorfied [sic] and begged them to leave me.
>
> ...They pushed me back into the car and started back towards the hotel. They told me that if I said anything to anybody about what happened they would put me and my son in jail for life, my grandchildren would have a father and grandfather in prison, and we would never see them or our wives again. They said that they would get us one way or another, even if they had to plant something in the hotel or put a sack of dope in my pocket....They pushed me out of the car and drove away fast.... I had severe pains in my chest and blacked out. The next thing I remember is hearing my son call for an ambulance.

Hospital reports confirm that Polisi showed bruises and other injuries typical of a beating. He reported the assault to the NEW YORK POLICE DEPARTMENT, but a detective assigned to the case later told Polisi's attorney that "the FBI denies any knowledge or implications of any assault on him and that his complaint should be lodged with the FBI."

In October 2001, following the catastrophic SKYJACKINGS of "9-11" and President GEORGE W. BUSH'S declaration of a global "war on TERRORISM," FBI spokesmen made the startling declaration that they were debating use of torture to extract information from terrorist suspects. The *Toronto Star* (11 October 2001) quoted an unnamed senior FBI official as saying, "We're into this thing for 35 days and nobody is talking. Frustration has begun to appear. We are known for humanitarian treatment. So, basically, we are stuck.... Usually, there is some incentive, some angle to play, what you can do for them. But it could get to that spot where we could go to pressure ... where we won't have a choice, and we are probably getting there." According to the *Star*'s anonymous source, strategies under discussion "include using drugs or pressure tactics, like those Israeli interrogators sometimes employ, to extract information." (Israeli "pressure tactics" reportedly include beatings and application of electric shocks to extract confessions.) As an alternative to personally soiling their hands, FBI spokesmen also suggested that terrorist suspects might be delivered to police of other nations "like France or Morocco," where information could be extracted by force and then transmitted to the JUSTICE DEPARTMENT in Washington.

**PORTER, Katherine Anne**— A descendant of pioneer Daniel Boone, born at Indian Creek, Texas in 1890, Porter was an essayist and author of short stories who published her only novel (*The Ship of Fools*) at age 72. Her political life was a study in contradictions, vacillating from the revolutionary left to Nazism, with a 1940s stint as an informer for the FBI.

Porter traveled widely during her career, extolling the virtues of revolutionary Mexico in 1918-21, but G-men first took note of her in 1927, after she signed a telegram dispatched to President CALVIN COOLIDGE by the Citizens National Committee for SACCO and VANZETTI. The late 1920s and early 1930s found Porter in Europe, where she seemingly discarded any leftist sympathies to become a personal friend and confidante of German Nazi leader Hermann Göring. Back in the U.S. before WORLD WAR II erupted, Porter was interviewed by G-men in 1942, denouncing "best friend" JOSEPHINE HERBST as a Depression-era courier for Moscow, possessed of "the utmost contempt for the American form of government," who "has a violent temper, a revolutionist attitude, and has caused trouble whenever the opportunity presented itself."

Notwithstanding that collaboration, the FBI still viewed Porter with suspicion. In 1945, agents noted her membership in the National Council of Soviet American Friendship and the League of American Writers. Three years later, another memo remarked on her signing of a letter condemning the HOUSE COMMITTEE ON UN-AMERICAN ACTIVITIES. One document from her file, exempted from release under the FREEDOM OF INFORMATION ACT, is a February 1951 memo from the CENTRAL INTELLIGENCE AGENCY, classified 50 years after the fact "in the interest of national defense." Porter died in 1980, but the document remains a closely guarded secret.

**POST, Louis Freeland**— A New Jersey native, born 18 November 1849, Louis Post worked as a journalist before he studied law and was admitted to the New York bar in 1870. A year later, he served as aide to the U.S. attorney in Charleston, South Carolina, taking statements from indicted members of the KU KLUX KLAN and preparing transcripts of their trials for acts of TERRORISM. Back in New York after Reconstruction, Post resigned his JUSTICE DEPARTMENT position to escape from corrupt political bosses and became a columnist for *Truth*, a daily paper sympathetic to LABOR UNIONS which successfully campaigned for establishment of a federal Labor Day holiday in September 1882.

It was no accident, then, that President WOODROW WILSON selected Post to serve as assistant secretary of labor under Secretary WILLIAM WILSON (no relation to the president). Post was skeptical when Attorney General A. MITCHELL PALMER and J. EDGAR HOOVER hatched plans for mass deportation of alien "radicals" in November 1919, but Secretary Wilson approved the original PALMER RAIDS in principle and Post (in Wilson's absence, due to illness) signed deportation orders for 246 of those arrested in the first roundup. He clashed with Justice in 1920, however, when Palmer and Hoover arrested another 10,000 persons, most without warrants or any legitimate charges. In April 1920 Post personally canceled 1,141 of 1,600 outstanding deportation orders and thereby earned a permanent place near the top of Hoover's enemy list.

Palmer and Hoover attacked Post on two fronts, publicly and privately. While Palmer urged the House Rules Committee to impeach Post, Hoover worked behind the scenes, pursuing the erroneous idea that he could link Post to America's most radical union, the INDUSTRIAL WORKERS OF THE WORLD. G-men in Chicago were ordered to scour their files on the IWW and report any mention of Post, but none was found. Before Congress, meanwhile, Post defended himself so ably against Palmer's "deportation delirium," reporting that "the Department of Justice has broken all the rules of law in its activities against the Reds and ... these acts were committed with the knowledge and approval of the Attorney General." One of those acts was labeled "the Salsedo homicide" by Post, a pointed reference to the alleged suicide of ANARCHIST suspect ANDREA SALSEDO, held illegally by G-men in New York until he plunged from a 19th-story window in May 1920, two days before Post testified.

The House committee agreed with Post, dismissing impeachment charges and turning its spotlight on Palmer. The attorney general argued that Post nurtured a "habitually tender solicitude for social revolutionaries and perverted sympathy for the criminal anarchists of the country," but that slander would not stick to a man who had signed the deportation orders for anarchists ALEXANDER BERKMAN and EMMA GOLDMAN, among others. Those hearings, and another round before the U.S. Senate in early 1921, doomed Palmer's political hopes, although Hoover clung to his post at Justice and went on to bigger things. Post retired and spent his final years in Washington, where he died in 1928.

**POTTS, Larry A.**— Larry Potts joined the FBI on 6 May 1974, serving initially with the Pittsburgh and Denver field offices. He was later named assistant agent-in-charge of the Boston field office, before returning to FBI HEADQUARTERS as a supervisor in the Criminal Investigative Division. In 1990 he served as field commander for a multi-agency task force investigating the "VAN-PAC" case (prosecuted by future FBI Director LOUIS FREEH). With that case completed, Potts returned to headquarters in 1991 as assistant director of the Criminal Investigative Division.

In that role, Potts was responsible for supervising agents involved in the RANDALL WEAVER siege at Ruby Ridge, Idaho in August 1992. Controversy surrounding that incident, specifically the slaying of Weaver's wife by FBI sniper RON HORIUCHI, prompted Director Freeh to censure Potts for "failure to provide proper oversight," but it was a temporary setback, followed by promotion to deputy director of the FBI on 2 May 1995. That strange reversal brought criticism from the media, and Potts was demoted when Congress launched an investigation of the Weaver incident in 1995. A two-year review by the JUSTICE DEPARTMENT found no grounds for prosecuting Potts, but the department's August 1997 report failed to win his reinstatement as deputy director. Potts retired before year's end to become executive vice president of Investigative Group International.

**POUND, Ezra Weston Loomis**— Born at Hailey, Idaho on 30 October 1885, poet Ezra Pound left the U.S. for London in September 1908, and moved on from there to Italy in July 1911. His massive Bureau dossier was opened that same year, with an erroneous report that "Dr. Ezra Pound … left the United States in February 1911 and proceeded to Rapallo, Italy." His file remained inactive until 1935, when information was received concerning Pound's admiration for fascist dictator Benito Mussolini. A 1941 notation reveals that "Pound is known to have been very pro-Fascist for a number of years, and to have spoken over the Italian radio system against the policies of the United States."

When the U.S. entered WORLD WAR II, Pound made a series of radio broadcasts meant to discourage American soldiers from battling with Mussolini's troops. An FBI memo of 9 May 1942 acknowledged a "need to investigate Pound further," and he was indicted for treason on 26 July 1943. Anti-fascist partisans captured Pound in 1945 and delivered him to U.S. forces. After six months' confinement at a "disciplinary training center" near Pisa, Pound was returned to the United States on 18 November 1945. A court found him mentally unfit for trial in 1946, whereupon he was confined to St. Elizabeth's Hospital in Washington, D.C. (One of his frequent correspondents, Frederick John Kasper, was imprisoned in 1956 for inciting southern race riots on behalf of the CITIZENS' COUNCIL and the KU KLUX KLAN.) Pound remained hospitalized until 1958, and returned to Italy upon his release. He died in Venice on 1 November 1972.

**POWELL, Lewis Franklin, Jr.**— A Suffolk, Virginia native, born 19 November 1907, Lewis Powell, Jr., obtained his B.A. and law degrees from Virginia's Washington and Lee University, then went on to obtain his master's degree from Harvard Law School. He practiced corporate law in Virginia for 34 years (1937-71) and simultaneously served as chairman of Richmond's school board during the period when southern schools were compelled to desegregate by order of the U.S. SUPREME COURT (1952-61). In December 1971 he "reluctantly" accepted President RICHARD NIXON'S nomination to serve on the Supreme Court and was sworn in as an associate justice on 7 January 1972. While Nixon craved a conservative court, Powell adopted a centrist position and frequently cast the critical swing vote of 5-to-4 decisions during his 15 years in Washington. He retired from the court in 1987 and died on 25 August 1998.

Two years after Powell's death, FBI documents were released disclosing that Powell had conducted a long and friendly correspondence with FBI Director J. EDGAR HOOVER, predating the years when Powell served as president of the American Bar Association (1964-65) and continuing through the early 1970s. In one note to Hoover, penned in April 1971, Powell hailed the director as "a great American" and denounced "irresponsible charges" aired in the media "against one who has served his country with such dedication, devotion and distinction as you have over so many years." Hoover responded to the praise by placing Powell on the Bureau's "Special Correspondents" list, and the information flowed both ways, with Powell serving as a full-fledged FBI INFORMANT. A memo from April 1965 confirmed that:

> Mr. Powell has always been most cooperative with the Richmond Office. He is contacted very frequently for information concerning persons under investigation, particularly in connection with Special Inquiry matters, and always furnishes reliable information. On several occasions he has offered the services of the American Bar Association to the FBI, and he has made many speeches throughout the country, as President of the American Bar Association, and has commended the Director and the Bureau, and urged support for the Bureau in its war on crime. It is also known that Mr. Powell has carried on a very favorable and complimentary correspondence with the Director for several years.

Despite his service to the Bureau, Hoover kept Powell under close surveillance, compiling a 1,500-page dossier on his "special correspondent." In 1964 two G-men visited Powell to question him concerning a recent speech in which he allegedly criticized the FBI for being overzealous in pursuit of the COMMUNIST PARTY. Powell explained that his remarks were misinterpreted by the nameless informant who denounced him.

**PRATT, Elmer Gerard**— A Louisiana native, born in 1948, Elmer ("Geronimo") Pratt joined the U.S. Army at age 17 and served two combat tours in Vietnam, honorably discharged in 1968 as a sergeant with multiple decorations for valor. Settling in Los Angeles, he attended college under the G.I. Bill and simultaneously joined the BLACK PANTHER PARTY. That choice brought him to the FBI's attention and his veteran's benefits were canceled in November 1968. Two months later, after L.A. chapter head Alprentice Carter was murdered by members of the FBI-infiltrated US organization, Pratt became the leader of the local Panther unit. Under terms of the Bureau's illegal COINTELPRO efforts to destroy the party, he was immediately marked for "neutralization."

A series of trumped-up arrests quickly followed. On 4 April 1969 Pratt and colleague Roger Lewis were arrested by officers of the Los Angeles Police Department "on a tip" that they were carrying a pipe bomb in their car. Three weeks later, on 23 April, Pratt was arrested with FBI INFORMANT Julius Butler and three other Panthers on charges of KIDNAPPING party member Ollie Taylor. (All were acquitted in April 1971.) On 15 June 1968 Pratt and others were questioned concerning the murder of local party member Frank Diggs, found shot to death on 19 December 1968, but no charges were filed. Los Angeles police raided the Panther office on 8 December 1969, sparking a shootout that left Pratt and 12 others in jail, charged with conspiracy to assault and kill law enforcement officers. All were acquitted of those charges in July 1970, though Pratt and eight fellow Panthers were convicted on a lesser charge of conspiring to possess illegal weapons.

While appealing that conviction, Pratt left California and missed his trial date on the pipe-bomb charge. (Defendant Lewis was convicted and received a three-year sentence.) On 14 September 1970 federal authorities charged Pratt with unlawful flight to avoid prosecution. FBI agents and members of LAPD's Criminal Conspiracy Section (CCS) met in Pratt's absence, discussing ways to take him off the street, and finally decided to convict him of murder in a deliberate FRAME-UP. By the time they selected a suitable case, on 8 December 1970, Pratt was located in Texas. Police informant Louis Tackwood described what happened next in *The Glass House Tapes* (1973):

> ...[W]hen the FBI found out ... where G was hiding, they didn't bust him, they called here [to Los Angeles]. And you know who busted him?... Not the FBI, but the CCS, and in Texas! And brought him back. No extradition whatsoever.... With all those charges, he could have fought extradition for years. They kidnapped him. Arrested down there, and they kidnapped him.... CCS, they're like federally sponsored. Like J. EDGAR HOOVER says, "They're my boys, they're my boys."

Pratt did not learn of his own murder indictment until 16 December 1970, when he was formally arraigned in Los Angeles. The crime dated from 18 December 1968, when Kenneth and Caroline Olsen were robbed by two black men on a Santa Monica tennis court. Mrs. Olsen was fatally shot as the bandits fled, her husband surviving to examine mug shots of potential suspects. Over the next year he "positively" identified one shooter and "tentatively" fingered three others—none of them Elmer Pratt. Kenneth Olsen changed his story only under pressure from Los Angeles police, who described Pratt's role with the Panthers and explained that a car resembling Pratt's had been sighted near the murder scene. The clincher was a statement from Julius Butler that Pratt had confessed to the Olsen murder in jail, while they were confined in the wake of the December 1969 shootout.

Butler was the key prosecution witness at Pratt's murder trial in May 1972. A month earlier, G-men assigned to the L.A. field office's Racial Squad told colleague M. WESLEY SWEARINGEN how they planned to avoid exposure of his Bureau ties in court: "We will close our informant file on Butler during the trial so that Butler can say he is not an FBI informant." So they did, and so Butler testified under oath, falsely informing the court that he had never worked for law enforcement during his tenure with the Panthers. In fact, his Bureau dossier—hidden from defense attorneys and the jury—revealed that Butler was recruited by COINTELPRO agent Richard G. Held in July 1970 and remained in frequent contact with the FBI until April 1972. His file was reopened, indicating further contacts, in the wake of Pratt's trial. (In 1994, serving as the pastor of a black church in Los Angeles, Butler *still* denied ever working for the FBI.)

Supporting Butler's perjury was not the Bureau's only criminal offense in framing Pratt. Agent Swearingen would later write, "My supervisor and several agents on the racial squad knew Pratt was innocent because the FBI had wiretap logs proving that Pratt was in the San Francisco area several hours before the shooting of Caroline Olsen and that he was there the day after the murder." In fact, there were three separate WIRETAPPING records that exonerated Pratt—a daily log of taps on the Los Angeles Panther office between 15 November and 20 December 1968 (destroyed by G-men prior to trial), another tap on the party's San Francisco office, and an illegal tap in Oakland, where Pratt placed several calls on the day after Olsen's murder. Deprived of that evidence, jurors convicted Pratt of murder and he received a life prison term.

In May 1980 FBI Director WILLIAM WEBSTER announced that the Bureau had completed an "exhaustive" review of Pratt's case, albeit without interviewing any of the COINTELPRO agents assigned to destroy the Panther Party in the late 1960s and early 1970s. Ex-agent Swearingen wrote to Webster on 30 May 1980, observing that Webster's "credibility has fallen to new depths even beyond the imagination of Jules Verne." He closed with the telling indictment: "Mr. Webster, you are either a fake or you are being deceived by your associates, if you think there has been an 'exhaustive' internal investigation of the Pratt case. Or could it be that you believe, as some others from squad two believe, that because a man is black he deserves to be in jail?" Webster promptly sent to agents to grill Swearingen in Honolulu, but the interview consisted chiefly of their denials that agents would ever behave as Swearingen described.

After 25 years of battling frustration and legal delays, including five years spent in solitary confinement, Pratt was vindicated when a court ordered his release in June 1997. California prosecutors appealed that decision in February 1998, claiming that evidence of Pratt's guilt was "overwhelming," but a state appeals court affirmed Pratt's exoneration in February 1999. By that time, he had already filed a civil lawsuit against the FBI and City of Los Angeles (on 29 May 1998), seeking unspecified damages for false imprisonment and violation of his CIVIL RIGHTS. The guilty parties settled that action in April 2000, with FBI HEADQUARTERS agreeing to pay $1.75 million, while Los Angeles kicked in another $2.75 million.

**PRESLEY, Elvis Aaron**—A Mississippi native, born 8 January 1935, Elvis Presley was "discovered" after recording two songs as a birthday gift to his mother in 1953. There followed a meteoric rise to stardom that enshrined him as "The King" of rock-and-roll, and in the process he was several times investigated by the FBI. The Elvis dossier was opened at FBI HEADQUARTERS in April 1956, with the first of several letters complaining to Director J. EDGAR HOOVER about Presley's deleterious impact on morals in

America. The author (from Memphis) reminded Hoover that "[m]ost of this entertainment becomes interstate, and hence should become a Federal Government problem," but Hoover replied that the FBI had no authority to ban musical performances.

Beginning in August 1956, the Bureau investigated various death threats sent to Presley through the U.S. mail. The first such message, a handwritten post card reading "If you don't stop this shit we're going to kill you," was postmarked from Niagara Falls, New York and was never traced to its author. A Bureau teletype from Louisville, dated 7 November 1956, warned Hoover that Presley and Bill Haley's Comets were slated for simultaneous concerts on 25 November, a scheduling conflict that had reportedly sparked teenage riots in California, Connecticut, Florida and New Jersey. G-men thereafter collected a series of bizarre letters from Elvis fans and enemies, accompanied by various newspaper clippings (including observations from March 1957 of a "strong press campaign in Mexico City to ban music and propaganda of Elvis Presley in view of [an] alleged statement by him belittling attractiveness of Mexican women."

More serious matters arose in March 1959, when a letter from Canton, Ohio claimed that "a red soldier in East Germany" planned to kill Presley (then serving with the U.S. Army in West Germany. Nine months later, FBI agents in Germany interviewed Presley concerning a blackmail threat he received from a South African dermatologist. The disgruntled physician "threatened to expose Presley by photographs and tape recordings which are alleged to present Presley in compromising situations." (No resolution to the matter is revealed in Presley's file.) Sporadic threats continued for the remainder of Presley's life, including a scrawled letter from Alabama, addressed to "President Elvis Presley," that warned "You will be next on my list." An FBI memo of 30 December 1970 advised Hoover that:

> Bufiles reflect that Presley has been the victim in a number of extortion attempts which have been referred to the Bureau. Our FILES also reflect that he is presently involved in a paternity suit pending in Los Angeles, California, and that during the height of his popularity during the latter part of the 1950s and early 1960s his gyrations while performing were the subject of considerable criticism by the public and comment in the press. The files of the IDENTIFICATION DIVISION fail to reflect any arrest record for Presley.

In December 1970 Presley wrote to President RICHARD NIXON, asking that he be appointed "a Federal Agent At Large" with an eye toward "helping this country out … by doing it my way through my communication with people of all ages." By way of qualifications, Presley told Nixon, "I have done an in depth study of drug abuse and Communist Brainwashing Techniques and I am right in the middle of the whole thing." Presley closed with the post script: "I have a personal gift for you also which I would like to present to you and you can accept it or I will keep it for you until you can take it." A memo to Hoover from one of his aides, dated 30 December 1970, observed:

> Presley's sincerity and good intentions notwithstanding he is certainly not the type of individual whom the Director would wish

to meet. It is noted at the present time he is wearing his hair down to his shoulders and indulges in the wearing of all sorts of exotic dress.

Thus forewarned, Hoover refused to meet with Presley when the singer's entourage toured FBI headquarters, but the director sent his form-letter regrets on 4 January 1971. Nixon, meanwhile, arranged for the Bureau of NARCOTICS and Dangerous Drugs to furnish Presley with an "honorary" badge, which Elvis later flashed in private photos (complete with shoulder holster and pistol). The grim irony of that appointment was driven home on 16 August 1977, when the drug-addicted singer died of an overdose at his palatial home in Memphis.

**PRESSER, Jack**— The son of Cleveland racketeer and TEAMSTERS' UNION official Bill Presser, born out of wedlock on 6 August 1926, Jack Presser struggled for 16 years to reach seventh grade, then dropped out of school the following year. He found corrupt union politics more rewarding, rising rapidly through Teamster ranks with assistance from his father and various leaders of ORGANIZED CRIME. In 1970 he was recruited as an FBI INFORMANT, described over the next 13 years as the Bureau's most valuable underworld spy of all time.

Presser's rise to Teamster vice president, in charge of the lucrative Ohio Conference, placed him in contact with various politicians including President RICHARD NIXON and future president RONALD REAGAN (himself a former FBI informant from the 1940s). Reagan's race for the White House included a private meeting with Presser and Teamster Vice President Roy Williams (twice indicted for embezzlement, later imprisoned in another case) on 27 August 1980. After 45 minutes behind closed doors, Reagan emerged to address Presser's Ohio Teamsters Conference and accept their official endorsement. Three months later, on their first visit to Washington since the November election, President-elect Reagan and running mate GEORGE H.W. BUSH attended another private meeting with Presser, Williams and Teamster president Frank Fitzsimmons. Before year's end, Presser was named as "senior economic adviser" to Reagan's transition team, telling the press that he would henceforth screen appointments for "the LABOR DEPARTMENT, Treasury, and a few other independent agencies." Reagan and Bush apparently saw no conflict in the fact that Presser was then being sued   by the Labor Department for making illegal loans to Mafia bosses and Nevada casinos.

Presser's career as an FBI informant ended on 22 April 1983, one day after he was elected president of the Teamsters Union. FBI Director WILLIAM WEBSTER terminated Presser's services out of concern for his close White House ties and a fear that critics might suspect the Bureau actually ran the Teamsters Union. Still, FBI protection was hardly needed as long as Presser had friends in the White House. Federal prosecutors sought to indict him in May 1984, but their move was blocked by superiors in the JUSTICE DEPARTMENT. On 23 April 1985 Presser pled the Fifth Amendment 15 times, when questioned about his illegal activities before the President's Commission on Organized Crime. If that performance embarrassed the Reagan-Bush White House, no criticism of Presser was forthcoming. New efforts to indict Presser in July 1985 were blocked once again, a circumstance that prompted Attorney General EDWIN MEESE to tell reporters he played no role in the decision "because we wanted to avoid any possibility of anyone claiming that there was any political influence." Presser died from a blood clot in his lung on 9 July 1998.

**PROBASCO, James J.**—James Probasco was a sometime prize fighter, con man and "fence" for thieves in Chicago, operating on the fringes of ORGANIZED CRIME. In 1921 he was arrested for burglary and receiving stolen property, but the charges were dropped. Several years later, he was linked to a successful ring of diamond thieves, rumored to have paid $40,000 in bribes to corrupt officers of the CHICAGO POLICE DEPARTMENT. Probasco was jailed at least once for selling liquor during PROHIBITION, and in 1927 a police search of his home revealed $10,000 in loot stolen from a wealthy Lake Forest family—but again, the charges were dismissed.

Probasco made his last mistake by opening his home to fugitive JOHN DILLINGER in spring 1934. It was in Probasco's house, according to later reports, that Dillinger underwent plastic surgery to alter his features on 28 May 1934, remaining afterward to convalesce for nearly a month.

Dillinger accomplice Homer Van Meter also went under the knife at Probasco's cottage, a week after Dillinger's surgery. Three days after Dillinger's death, on 25 July 1934, G-men led by SAMUEL COWLEY arrested Probasco and took him to their office in Chicago's Bankers Building. The next morning, around 10:00 a.m., Probasco plunged to his death from one of the suite's 19th-story windows.

Agent's claimed Probasco seemed "despondent" during their all-night interrogation and committed suicide by leaping from the window, despite their best efforts to save him. Rumors circulated that the elderly suspect was beaten to the point of death by G-men seeking a confession, then tossed from the window to disguise his injuries; an alternate story depicted agents dangling Probasco from the window to frighten him, losing their grip accidentally. Agent Cowley denied the accusations, seconded by Doris Lockerman, secretary for Agent MELVIN PURVIS. Writing to a Chicago newspaper, Lockerman asked, "Is it likely that the agents, even had they been in the habit of hanging prisoners out the windows, which they were not, would have hung a kicking, yelling, 250 pound man out in broad daylight, in full sight of the office workers across the way?"

In fact, there were no "office workers across the way" in 1934—adjacent structures were not as tall as the Bankers Building—and Probasco weighed barely 125 pounds. Melvin Purvis, absent on the day Probasco died, muddied the waters further by claiming the suspect, caught up in "an emotional crisis," lunged past agents to leap out the window of Purvis's private office. Again, it was untrue: Purvis's windows faced Clark Street, while Probasco's body was found on the opposite side of the building.

Testimony from two other suspects, while naturally open to question, supported the theory that G-men themselves killed Probasco. Arthur O'Leary, questioned about his own involve-

ment with Dillinger, later told crime historian William Helmer that he heard agents discussing Probasco's death. From their conversation, he related, "it sounded like Cowley had been battering the old man around but was dissatisfied with his answers," whereupon he tried to hang Probasco from the window ledge but lost his grip. A year later, hauled in for questioning about his ties to the BARKER-KARPIS GANG, suspect John McLaughlin reported that he, too, was dangled from a 19th-story window by his wrists.

Probasco's death was ruled a suicide.

**PROHIBITION**—The so-called "Noble Experiment" of Prohibition had its roots in America's 19th-century temperance movement, exacerbated by distrust of German immigrants (who dominated the brewer's trade) during WORLD WAR I. The U.S. Constitution's 18th Amendment, ratified in 1919, banned sale, manufacture or transportation of intoxicating beverages (with narrow religious and medical exceptions). Penalties for violation were spelled out in the federal Volstead Act, effective as of 1 January 1920. Enforcement was initially assigned to the Treasury Department's new Prohibition Bureau, but that unit was transferred to the JUSTICE DEPARTMENT in 1930, following multiple corruption scandals and the resignation of six different directors. Democratic presidential candidate FRANKLIN ROOSEVELT campaigned in 1932 on a promise to repeal Prohibition, and Congress passed a 21st Amendment—repealing the 18th—in February 1933. Still, ratification by two-thirds of the U.S. states was required to make the new amendment effective, a process which was not completed until early December 1933.

In the meantime, on 10 June 1933, President Roosevelt signed an executive order merging the Bureau of Investigation and the Prohibition Bureau in a new Divison of Investigation at Justice. Director J. EDGAR HOOVER protested that his 326 G-men would lose their identity among 1,200 Prohibition agents, and that the Prohibition Bureau's endemic corruption would soon infect his own "clean" agency. Attorney General HOMER CUMMINGS accepted Hoover's recommendation that 82 of the Prohibition Bureau's 105 field offices should be closed, with a chief Prohibition agent assigned to administer the unit under Hoover's general supervision. Thus the future FBI remained untainted by contact with free-spending bootleggers, while the lame-duck Prohibition Bureau passed its final months in relative peace and quiet.

Subsequent mythology notwithstanding, the FBI played no role whatsoever in Prohibition enforcement and waged no campaign against organized racketeers in America during the "dry" era. It is true that G-men arrested Chicago mobster ALPHONSE CAPONE in March 1929, for ignoring a federal grand jury's subpoena, but his conviction on that minor charge played no part in Capone's eventual downfall. It was ELMER IREY'S band of agents from the INTERNAL REVENUE SERVICE who finally nabbed Capone for tax evasion and sent him to federal prison.

While Capone distracted most of America with his flamboyant lifestyle and bloody gang wars, other bootleggers around the country were busy laying the foundation for a national crime syndicate. East Coast smugglers were the first to organize, around 1926, in a coalition dubbed the "Big Seven." Before Prohibition ended, those and other racketeers met in a series of gangland conventions at Cleveland (1928), Atlantic City (1929) and Chicago (1932) to hammer out details of their alliance and carve the U.S. into specific "territories" ruled by local gangs. The Atlantic City conference made newspaper headlines, and G-men can hardly have missed it. Still, Hoover would publicly deny the existence of organized crime in America for another 34 years, until mobster Joe Valachi's testimony forced FBI HEADQUARTERS to admit the obvious. Prohibition's legacy — and the result of FBI inaction — was a crime syndicate infesting and corrupting every aspect of American life.

**PSYCHOLOGICAL Profiling**— Psychological "profiling" of unknown subjects at large — UNSUBs, in FBI parlance — is a controversial investigative tool, used for the first time in the 1950s. Profilers are often portrayed in fiction as virtual psychics, picking up "flashes" from a killer's mind with every visit to a crime scene, tracking down their man (or woman) as inexorably as if they could read the subject's name and address in a crystal ball.

Unfortunately, nothing could be further from the truth.

In fact, FBI profilers make no arrests, engage in no shootouts, and rarely leave their offices to visit a crime scene. Instead, they scrutinize evidence submitted by local police departments, seeking clues to a suspect's personality and motive. At best, the results are educated guesswork, drawing on experience from previous cases to refine a portrait of the UNSUB. Some of those character sketches prove eerily accurate; others are worse than useless, leading detectives down false trails while their quarry goes free. Most profiles fall somewhere between the two extremes, providing a general description of the subject without supplying any details needed for his capture.

The first application of psychological profiling, in 1956, was also the only case to date where a profiler has contributed directly to a subject's arrest. Psychiatrist James Brussel prepared an amazingly accurate sketch of New York's "Mad Bomber," including a correct prediction that the subject would be wearing a double-breasted suit (with the jacket buttoned!) on the day of his arrest. More important to the case, an open letter from Dr. Brussel provoked bomber George Metesky to a written response, which in turn led police to his doorstep. No other profiler to date has rivaled Brussel's feat, and even where specific profiles proved accurate in hindsight, apprehension has come through routine police investigation.

A dramatic failure of profiling was witnessed in 1975, when an "expert panel" was assembled in Los Angeles to analyze the elusive "Skid Row Slasher." The psychologists described their man as a "sexually impotent coward, venting his own feelings of worthlessness on hapless drifters and down-and-outers." They tagged the slasher as a friendless loner, probably a homosexual and possibly deformed, "driven by a frenzy to commit these murders as a substitute for normal heterosexual relations." Sketches drawn to fit the profile showed a white male in his late twenties or early thirties, six feet tall, 190 pounds, with shoulder-length stringy blond hair framing an angular face. At his arrest, two days later, the killer proved to be a black man with no apparent deformi-

ties, whose murders sprang from ritual occultism, complete with blood-drinking and sprinkling of salt around the corpses.

Two cases often cited as success stories by retired FBI profilers demonstrate the gap between hype and reality. In Sacramento, California, G-men profiled an UNSUB blamed for six grisly murders during January 1978. At his arrest, defendant Richard Chase was found to match the profile in every respect, but the analysis played no part in his capture. Rather, a former high-school classmate saw Chase wandering the streets in blood-soaked clothes and notified police, who picked him up for questioning and found incriminating items at his home. Six years later, Florida serial killer Robert Long was the subject of another FBI profile, which again proved remarkably accurate once the suspect was in custody. G-men hail their achievement as if they had caught Long themselves, but in fact he sealed his own fate by releasing his penultimate victim alive, whereupon she described Long and his car to local police.

It is worth noting that profilers themselves disagree on the value of their work. Psychologist Russell Boxley, at Boston University, declares: "I think the people who do profiles are bastardizing their discipline with a lot of mumbo-jumbo, without really knowing what they're doing. You know, it's a mystical thing, and people are very impressed. It's also a media thing." Boxley concludes that forensic psychologists tracking an UNSUB "can't do any better than a college student could with the same materials in front of him." Across the continent, one of the Skid Row Slasher panelists, Dr. Norman Barr, was even more critical. He told reporters, "I don't think my statements would make any more sense than those of the average housewife."

In April 1999 a Common Pleas Court judge in Pennsylvania barred former G-man Roy Hazelwood from introducing testimony on psychological profiling at the murder trial of defendant Christopher Distefano. Prosecutors called Hazelwood to testify that Distefano "exhibited the traits of a murderer," but Judge Carlon O'Malley rejected the evidence. O'Malley declared, "This court finds that the Commonwealth has failed ... to establish that profiling testimony has gained general acceptance in the scientific community to form the basis of Mr. Hazelwood's expert testimony. Furthermore, Mr. Hazelwood's report and related testimony evidences little probative value and is extremely prejudicial to the defendant. Such testimony is akin to an expert eyewitness account that the defendant committed the murder. This court will not allow such an account."

**PUERTO Rican nationalists**— The United States seized Puerto Rico from its Spanish masters in 1898, in the same military action that stripped Spain of her colonies in Cuba, Guam and the Philippines. For the next half-century, America ruled the island as a colonial protectorate. Puerto Ricans were granted U.S. citizenship in 1917, but critics said the move was simply a ploy to make them eligible for military conscription in WORLD WAR I. Island residents who called for independence from U.S. rule were ignored or forcibly silenced. An FBI field office in San Juan kept track of "agitators" and "subversives."

The Puerto Rican National Party (NPPR) was organized in 1922. Eight years later, with the economy mired in depression, party leader Pedro Albizu Campos called for "direct action" to break America's hold on the island. G-men teamed with the insular police, led by Col. E.F. Riggs, to ferret out rebels. Riggs declared his force engaged in "war to the death with all Puerto Ricans," prompting a threat from the NPPR that "for every Nationalist killed, a continental American would die." On 24 October 1935, police fired on student demonstrators at the University of Puerto Rico, killing five. Four months later, on 23 February 1946, guerrillas retaliated by executing Col. Riggs. FBI agents raided NPPR headquarters on 3 March 1936, arresting Albizu Campos and most of his aides. All were convicted on vague "conspiracy" charges, receiving 2-to-10-year prison terms. A federal grand jury in San Juan subpoenaed other party leader, jailing them for contempt when they refused to betray their comrades.

The sweeping arrests and convictions only produced more violence. On 31 March 1937 police fired on a peaceable NPPR parade, killing 20 persons and wounding at least 150 others. Observers from the AMERICAN CIVIL LIBERTIES UNION called it "a massacre," but FBI leaders ignored the mayhem until June 1937, when nationalists tried to kill Albizu's trial judge. A month later, gunmen bungled their attempt to slay Governor Blanton Winship, bagging a colonel of the National Guard instead.

Puerto Rico won the right to elect its own governor in 1948, but *independistas* complained that President HARRY TRUMAN'S "Operation Bootstrap" favored U.S. corporations with huge tax breaks, while forcing the sale of native-owned enterprises. Two thousand nationalists staged an uprising against Gov. Luis Muñoz, followed one day later by an attempt to kill President Truman at Blair House, in Washington, D.C. One of the gunmen died in that effort; the other was wounded, captured, and sentenced to life in prison.

Granted an alternative to colonial rule in 1951, Puerto Ricans voted three-to-one to become a U.S. commonwealth. Independence was not on the menu, however, and committed nationalists continued their fight, both at home and on the American mainland. Anglo support for the movement waned after 1 March 1954, when four Puerto Rican gunmen shot up the House of Representatives. All were imprisoned for life, while FBI agents arrested 17 nationalist leaders in Puerto Rico and local police jailed 40 more.

In 1959 the Puerto Rican Civil Rights Commission reported that *independistas* had been under constant government surveillance for 60 years, since 1899, but mere observation did not satisfy FBI Director J. EDGAR HOOVER. A memo from Hoover to the San Juan field office, dated 4 August 1960, announced that the Bureau was "considering the feasibility of instituting a program of disruption to be directed against organizations which seek independence for Puerto Rico through other than lawful, peaceful means." Hoover instructed his agents to "bear in mind that the Bureau desires to disrupt the activities of these organizations and is not interested in mere harassment." As detailed in subsequent memos, the means to that end would include recruitment of spies to "raise controversial issues" at nationalist meetings, false accusations that nationalist leaders were pawns of Fidel Castro, and leaflets printed by the FBI, wherein

one nationalist group appeared to brand others as traitors to the cause. Other forged letters and leaflets sought to alienate Puerto Rican activists from U.S. leftist groups, including the Progressive Labor Party and the SOCIALIST WORKERS PARTY. The campaign was, in short, another of Hoover's unauthorized and illegal COINTELPRO operations.

After four years of nonstop FBI disruption, on 21 April 1964, nationalist leader Juan Mari-Bras suffered a near-fatal heart attack. A memo to Washington from the San Juan field office boasted that a recent flurry of anonymous letters mailed by G-men "certainly did nothing to ease his tensions." Furthermore, the agent in charge advised Hoover, "This particular technique has been outstandingly successful and we shall be on the lookout to further exploit our achievements in this field. The Bureau will be promptly advised of other positive results of this program that may come to our attention." Twelve years later, when Mari-Bras's son, Santiago Mari-Pesquera, was murdered by unknown gunmen in Puerto Rico, another agent-in-charge wrote from San Juan that "It would hardly be idle boasting to say that some of the Bureau's activities have provoked the situation of Mari Bras [*sic*]."

Beginning in 1970, militant nationalist groups including the Independence Revolutionary Armed Comrades (MIRA), the Armed Forces of National Liberation (FALN), and the Puerto Rican People's Army (EPB, aka "*Los Macheteros*") carried their fight to mainland America with a series of BOMBINGS across the U.S. Most of the targets were government or corporate offices, accompanied by demands for Puerto Rican independence and release of the five would-be assassins jailed in 1950 and 1954. Personal injuries were rare in the explosions, but a notable exception was the bombing of New York's popular Fraunces Tavern on 24 January 1975, which killed four persons and wounded 53. The FALN took credit for that blast, calling it retaliation for the recent bombing of a nationalist meeting at Mayaguez, Puerto Rico, where two persons died.

In fact, the Mayaguez bombing was merely the tip of the iceberg. Throughout the 1970s, Puerto Rican nationalists were subjected to relentless right-wing TERRORISM at home. *Claridad*, the official newspaper of the Puerto Rican Socialist Party, was firebombed in 1973; another 170 beatings, shootings and bombings were documented over the next 15 years, not counting mass assaults on nationalists during public assemblies. The still-unsolved murder of Santiago Mari-Pesquera was part of the terror. So was the apparent kidnap-murder of activist Juan Caballero in 1977. FBI agents produced the wrong body in that case, claiming Caballero had been murdered by his nationalist comrades, but the corpse's fingers were "lost" en route to Washington for confirmation of the body's true identity. In July 1978, a government provocateur persuaded two youths, Arnaldo Dario and Carlos Soto, to bomb a Puerto Rican TV tower; arrested on 25 July, the two were shot dead while kneeling with hands cuffed behind their backs. (In February 1987, relatives of the two murdered youths received $1.15 million in compensation from the government.) Some *independistas*, recalling illegal FBI collaboration with vigilante groups including the KU KLUX KLAN, the SECRET ARMY ORGANIZATION and the GUARDIANS OF THE OGLALA NATION, accused G-men of actively supporting the terrorists. Others wondered why the crimes were never solved, when the *victims* were under constant FBI surveillance. (In December 1984, a sworn affidavit from a former secretary at the San Juan field office stated that G-men conspired to firebomb the home of Juan Mari-Bras in 1978.)

The militant bombing campaign in America played out against that backdrop of right-wing terror in Puerto Rico, rarely reported in the U.S. "mainstream" media. A memo to the White House, dated 9 May 1978 and signed "YFC," detailed 15 years of FBI harassment and "disruption" campaigns in Puerto Rico, closing with a rhetorical question for President JAMES CARTER: "Is this self-determination?" The memo may have influenced Carter's decision of 7 September 1979, to finally release four surviving activists imprisoned in the 1950s. A year later, FBI agents arrested eight alleged FALN members, who ranged in age from 19 to 34 years. Tried on a hodge-podge of conspiracy and SEDITION charges, with little or no evidence linking them to specific bombings, the eight were convicted and sentenced to federal prison for terms between 35 and 105 years. Critics noted that the sentences were unusually severe: 87 percent of all federal prisoners sentenced between 1966 and 1985 received prison terms of 20 years or less, while U.S. murderers received an average 22 years and rapists averaged 12 years.

G-men were galvanized again on 12 September 1983, when alleged "*Macheteros*" stole $7.1 million from a Connecticut armored car depot. Three peripheral suspects were quickly arrested and convicted, drawing 35-year-prison terms, but most of the bandits were still at large two years later. (One fugitive, Victor Gerena, set a Bureau record in 2002 for spending for spending 18 years on the "TEN MOST WANTED" LIST.) Their escape provided an excuse for sweeping raids in Puerto Rico, carried out by FBI agents on 30 August 1985. Planned by San Juan agent-in-charge RICHARD WALLACE HELD, a 15-year veteran of illegal COINTELPRO operations, the raids swept up 48 *independistas*, arrested by agents who ransacked their homes and seized most of their personal papers (inexplicably "lost" before a court ordered their return). None of those detained were charged with participation in the robbery. In Washington, Attorney General EDWIN MEESE told reporters, "We're sending a message to terrorists that their bloody acts will not be tolerated." As those cases slowly made their way to court, G-men submitted affidavits confessing the use of such tactics as "SNITCH JACKETING," illegal WIRETAPS, false accusations of *independista* involvement with Cuban arms smugglers, and subornation of perjury from informers who traded testimony for exemption on a wide range of felony charges.

Twelve years after those revelations, Governor Pedro Rosselló announced that Puerto Rican police had compiled dossiers on thousands of law-abiding residents simply because their political views were unorthodox. Rosselló denounced the "corrupt practice" and apologized to its victims on behalf of the Puerto Rican government, but no corresponding apology issued from FBI HEADQUARTERS. Professor Félix Ojeda, an active *independista* at the University of Puerto Rico, used the FREEDOM OF INFORMATION ACT to obtain FBI documents proving that he had been under surveillance since age 17. The CENTRAL INTELLIGENCE AGENCY denied holding any files on Prof. Ojeda, but his FBI dossier contained CIA collected by the Bureau years earlier. (An FBI memo of 23 August 1968 confirmed that the Bureau was sharing its files on various *independistas* with other agencies, including the CIA and the Office of Naval Intelligence.)

In September 1999, President WILLIAM CLINTON offered clemency to 11 Puerto Rican nationalists imprisoned in the 1980s, but freedom came with a price tag attached. Those accepting the deal were required to cut all ties with "known felons" and groups thought to "advocate violence," a restriction that barred the defendants — including several related by blood or marriage — from meeting each other outside prison walls. Other conditions of release included ongoing FBI supervision, with random drug testing. Two of the inmates refused Clinton's offer; one of the nine accepting it was required to serve five more years of his sentence prior to release.

While agitation for full independence continues, Puerto Rican nationalists have found another cause in the U.S. Navy's practice shelling of Vieques, a coastal island. Supported by Governor Sila Calderon, 100,000 Puerto Ricans demonstrated against the continue bombardment from February 2000 through May 2001. In June 2001, President GEORGE W. BUSH agreed to phase out military operations on Vieques over the next two years, but he rescinded that promise after the terrorist attacks of 11 September 2001.

**PURVIS, Melvin Horace, Jr.**— The son of an affluent southern planter, Melvin Purvis, Jr., was born at Timmonsville, South Carolina on 24 October 1903. He graduated from the University of South Carolina with a law degree in 1925 and spent the next two years in private practice, before joining the FBI under curious circumstances. Although two years below the minimum age for prospective G-men set by Director J. EDGAR HOOVER, Purvis was accepted after Hoover received a personal call from South Carolina's senior U.S. Senator and New Deal champion Ed "Cotton" Smith, thus disproving once more (as in the case of THOMAS DODD) Hoover's lifelong claim that the Bureau was immune to political patronage after he took charge in 1924.

Purvis enjoyed rapid advancement through the ranks, ensconced by 1932 as special agent in charge of the Chicago field office. His startling rise, bested only by that of CLYDE TOLSON, owed more to personal friendship with Hoover than any outstanding performance by Purvis, a fact supported by their correspondence between 1927 and 1934. Initially in awe of Hoover, Purvis addressed him with all due respect until Hoover penned an order to "stop using MISTER" in written salutations. Henceforth, Purvis addressed his boss as "Dear Chairman" or "Dear Jayee" (after Hoover's initials). Hoover's jocular letters to Purvis include observations on one U.S. attorney's "mental halitosis" and suggestions that Hoover secretary HELEN GANDY carried a torch for Purvis. If Purvis turned up for 1932's Halloween Ball, Hoover suggested, Ms. Gandy might be persuaded to greet him in a "cellophane gown." Author Anthony Summers deemed the letters evidence of "a HOMOSEXUAL courtship"; Assistant Director CARTHA DELOACH, by contrast finds them "clearly part of the bantering between two bachelors interested in women." In either case, the warm relationship would not endure.

Purvis might have passed his FBI career as an executive nonentity but for a geographic accident. His Chicago assignment placed him at the heart of bandit country in the Great Depression, and Purvis was involved in some of the era's most notorious cases. Unfortunately for the Bureau's reputation and his own, Purvis had a tendency to bungle manhunts or veer to the other extreme and plot FRAME-UPS of innocent defendants.

An early example of Purvis's ineptitude was seen in his search for outlaw Frank Nash, an escapee from Leavenworth prison who had joined the BARKER-KARPIS GANG. Purvis employed an American Indian ex-convict, one War Eagle, as his primary INFORMER on the case, with humiliating results. War Eagle not only fingered the wrong man, but he also loaned Purvis a stolen car for use in the abortive raid. It was small consolation to Purvis when other G-men captured Nash in June 1933, then died in the bloody KANSAS CITY MASSACRE while returning Nash to prison.

Purvis saw a chance to redeem himself that same month, when brewer William Hamm, Jr., was kidnapped from St. Paul, Minnesota and ransomed for $100,000. Hamm's abductors were members of the same Barker-Karpis gang that sheltered Frank Nash, but Purvis fixed his sights on Chicago bootlegger ROGER TOUHY and three associates, arrested with automatic weapons on 19 July 1933, after an auto accident near Elkhorn, Wisconsin. There was no clear reason to suspect the Touhy gang of snatching Hamm, but they were wanted in Chicago for the alleged ransom kidnapping of career criminal Jerome Factor, later proved to be a gangland hoax.

It was enough for Purvis. He pushed for indictments under the new LINDBERGH Law that made interstate kidnapping a federal offense. In the absence of anything resembling evidence, Purvis fell back on a combination of third-degree tactics and perjured testimony to make his case. Touhy later described a series of beatings administered by G-men in jail, and his complaint might be dismissed as grousing from a lifelong felon were it not for Purvis's own description of how the FBI handled its prisoners. "The escaped prisoner was 'invited' to accompany the special agent to the federal building," Purvis gloated, "and sometimes these invitations were engraved on the minds [sic] of the escape[e] in a very definite manner and they were accepted." Nor were innocent witnesses safe from such tactics. In the Hamm case, prospective defense witness Edward Meany was told by agents, "If you go to St. Paul to testify for Touhy you'll be sorry — and maybe you won't come back."

It was all in vain, despite public claims by Purvis that "We have an ironclad case." Touhy and his codefendants were acquitted of Hamm's abduction on 28 November 1933. Instead of being freed, however, they were held for delivery to Chicago authorities, for trial in the fabricated Factor kidnapping. Purvis labored long and hard on the state's behalf in that case, but the first jury failed to reach a verdict. Finally, with a cast of new witnesses (who later recanted their perjured testimony), prosecutors finally convicted Touhy and three codefendants, sending them to prison for 99 years. J. Edgar Hoover cheered the frame-up as "a credit to the entire Bureau," ranking Touhy among the "most vicious and dangerous criminals in the history of American crime."

Another quarter-century would pass before a federal judge exposed the FBI's malfeasance in Touhy's case. Meanwhile, Purvis had found a new "public enemy" to pursue, in the person of fugitive bandit JOHN DILLINGER. Chicago was the center of Dillinger's violent universe, and Purvis recognized the stakes involved in catching him, dead or alive. If there were any doubts, "Jayee" Hoover dispelled them in a letter dated 3 April 1934, advising Purvis: "Well, son, keep a stiff upper lip and get Dillinger for me, and the world is yours."

Purvis had his chance three weeks later, when tips placed Dillinger's gang at the Little Bohemia Lodge, near Rhinelander, Wisconsin. Bypassing local authorities, Purvis led a team of G-men north to raid the lodge on 22 April 1934, but the outcome was a grim fiasco. FBI agents opened the battle by shooting three innocent civilians, killing one of them, while Dillinger and company fled unscathed into the wood. One of the gangsters, GEORGE ("BABY FACE") NELSON, ambushed three officers at a nearby store, killing Bureau agent W. Carter Baum and fleeing in a stolen car. Purvis arrested Nelson's wife and two other "gun molls," charged with harboring federal fugitives, but they received suspended sentences in May 1934. Purvis further compounded his embarrassment on 29 May, with a premature announcement of Dillinger's death.

Hoover's relationship with Purvis changed dramatically in the wake of Little Bohemia. The director's "Dear Mel" letters were supplanted by terse communiqués addressed to "Dear Mr. Purvis," their tone accusatory. On 4 June 1934 Hoover chastised Purvis for failure to implement some unspecified order, noting that "You have absolutely no right to ignore instructions." Twelve days later, when Purvis went golfing and missed a call from Washington, Hoover cabled that "There is no reason why the Agent in Charge should not leave word where he can be reached at any time." Agent SAMUEL COWLEY was dispatched from FBI HEADQUARTERS to supervise the Dillinger manhunt, undermining Chicago's star agent to the point that subordinates soon dubbed him "Nervous Purvis."

Purvis redeemed himself, after a fashion, when Dillinger was cornered and killed in Chicago on 22 July 1934. Hoover had long since forgotten his promise to give Purvis "the world" in exchange for Dillinger's scalp, but he managed a private note to Melvin's father in South Carolina, noting that Purvis "conducted himself with that simple modesty that is so characteristic of his makeup.... He has been one of my closest and dearest friends." Hoover soon regretted that mild praise, however, when Purvis bagged another trophy. This time the quarry was CHARLES ("PRETTY BOY") FLOYD, lately named a prime suspect in the Kansas City massacre of June 1933. Purvis personally led the firing squad that killed Floyd on 22 October 1934, near East Liverpool, Ohio. Four decades passed before a member of the posse, Patrolman Chester Smith, accused Purvis of having Floyd executed by point-blank gunfire while he lay wounded. Long before that revelation, though, Hoover took steps to quell the "lurid" story that Purvis "personally interviewed Floyd" as the bandit lay dying. "As a matter of fact," Hoover assured journalists, "Mr. Purvis never spoke one word to Floyd."

With or without conversation, Floyd's death put Purvis on the media fast track. Eleven weeks later he personally arrested

Arthur ("Dock") Barker in Chicago, thereby finally capturing one of the real Hamm kidnappers. Purvis scored another publicity coup on 1 June 1935, with the Chicago arrest of Barker-Karpis gangster Volney Davis, sought on multiple murder and robbery charges. New indictments were filed — against the right suspects, this time — in the Hamm kidnapping and the January 1934 abduction of banker Edward Bremer. Conviction on Lindbergh charges sent most of the gang up for life.

It was too much for J. Edgar Hoover. Never one to share the limelight gladly, the director sent a "Dear Sir" note to Purvis in March 1935, accusing Purvis of public drunkenness. Purvis denounced the charge as an "unmitigated and unadulterated lie," his protest undercut by newspaper accounts of Purvis brandishing his pistol in a Cincinnati store, botching a phone call to headquarters, then staggering off to his car. Friends and relatives of Purvis believe Hoover planted the story himself, but the damage was done. Hounded by reports of poor performance, Purvis left the FBI in mid-summer. (Contradictory accounts date his resignation from 10 July, 12 July and 5 August 1935.)

Hoover wasted no time in expunging Purvis from the official FBI record. Once named as Dillinger's slayer, Purvis vanished from Bureau accounts of the shooting, variously replaced by Sam Cowley, Agent CHARLES WINSTEAD, or East Chicago detective MARTIN ZARKOVICH. No mention of Purvis appeared in DON WHITEHEAD's book *The FBI Story*, published with Hoover's full cooperation in 1956, or in the movie version released three years later. Officially, at least around FBI headquarters, Purvis had ceased to exist.

In real life he enjoyed somewhat greater success, moving from Chicago to San Francisco, where he returned to legal practice. In 1936 Purvis published his memoirs, *American Agent*, while lending his famous face and name to promotion of various products ranging from cars to razor blades. He introduced a radio series, *Top Secrets of the FBI*, and served as chairman of the Post Toasties "Junior G-Man Club," thousands of American children mailing box tops in return for badges, cap guns, codes and passwords, microscopes and "G-man" baseball mitts. A more ambitious move was directed toward Hollywood, where Purvis sought work as a technical advisor on gangster films, but Hoover blocked that initiative, offering active-duty agents "free of charge" while telling studio heads that he would "look with displeasure, as a personal matter" on anyone who hired Purvis.

In 1938 Purvis returned to his native South Carolina as a full-time lawyer. Three years later, with America's entry into WORLD WAR II, he was called for active duty in the U.S. Army Reserve, working with military intelligence through the North African and Italian campaigns, later briefly assigned to the War Department's War Crimes Office. Discharged in 1946, Purvis returned to legal practice in Florence, South Carolina, dividing his time between courtrooms and operation of local radio and television stations. Purvis was nominated for a federal judgeship in 1952, but negative reports from Hoover scotched the deal.

The Touhy case returned to haunt Purvis in 1954, when a federal judge declared the Factor case a mockery of justice, noting that the FBI had "worked and acted in concert to convict Touhy of something, regardless of his guilt or innocence." Still,

Touhy remained in prison until November 1959, enjoying three weeks of freedom before Chicago mobsters gunned him down on 16 December. Purvis outlived his victim by 75 days, killed by a self-inflicted gunshot wound at home, in Florence, on 29 February 1960. A local coroner described his death as accidental; FBI spokesmen countered with a whispering campaign that it was suicide. In either case, the gun involved was not, as frequently reported, the pistol Purvis carried on the night John Dillinger was killed. Rather, it was a .45-caliber automatic presented to Purvis by Chicago G-men at his retirement in 1935.

**PUTNAM, Mark Steven**— Mark Putnam seemed to be the stereotypical "all-American boy." Born 4 July 1959 in Coventry, Connecticut, he grew up bright, strong and handsome. A B-average student at the University of Tampa, where he majored in criminology, Putnam also led the school's soccer team to an NCAA Division II championship in 1982. Married to the daughter of a wealthy real estate developer, he was delighted by the birth of their first daughter. Finally, in October 1986, Putnam fulfilled a lifelong dream by graduating from the FBI Academy as a special agent.

Rookie G-men are assigned at the bureau's discretion, and Putnam's first posting sent him to the tiny two-man resident agency in Pikeville, Kentucky, some 120 miles southeast of Lexington. His wife, then pregnant with their second child, hated the backwater district on sight and soon began demanding that he seek a transfer, but Putnam threw himself into the job with gusto, mindful of the fact that the surest way to impress his superiors and earn promotion was to compile an impressive arrest record.

He saw his golden opportunity in a series of local bank robberies. The prime suspect was a 32-year-old ex-convict who rented rooms in Pikesville from Ken and Susan Smith, a young divorced couple who still lived together, pursuing a life style steeped in drugs and petty crime. Putnam arranged a meeting with the Smiths to solicit their cooperation in the case and found himself instantly attracted to Susan. The feeling was mutual, and the cocaine-addicted eighth-grade dropout soon confided to her sister that she planned to make Putnam fall in love with her.

First, however, they established a professional relationship of sorts. Susan quickly accepted Putnam's offer of $5,000 for testimony against her boarder, remaining on the FBI payroll even after the defendant was convicted and imprisoned in January 1988. Several more weeks passed before Putnam and Smith began their love affair, but her frequent boasts of the romance were ignored by most who knew her, based on Smith's established reputation for lying. At one point Smith confronted Putnam's wife, but her disclosures failed to wreck the marriage. Finally, reasoning that a child would force Putnam to divorce his wife, Smith stopped using contraceptives in December 1988.

By that time, Putnam had established himself as a rising star within the FBI, solving another bank robbery and closing down a local "chop shop" where stolen cars were stripped or modified for black-market sale. By early 1989 he had planned his next move, phasing out Susan Smith as an informant, reporting alleged bomb threats against himself and his family. Putnam moved his wife and children out of Pikesville "for their safety," convinced that he would soon win appointment to a larger, more prestigious FBI field office. In later March 1989 he informed Smith of his impending transfer to Miami, and she countered with news that she was pregnant. Putnam initially denied the child was his, then vaguely offered to "take care" of Smith. Resettled in Florida, he was bombarded with calls from Smith, threatening to go public with her pregnancy if Putnam ignored his obligations. Putnam promised to discuss the problem with her when he returned to Pikesville in June, for testimony in the chop-shop case.

Susan Smith had been missing for nine days when her sister filed a police report on 16 June 1989, and she was officially listed as missing three days later. Given her background and lifestyle, police were not greatly concerned by her absence from Pikesville, but relatives demanded a full-scale investigation. Ex-husband Ken Smith was quickly cleared by a polygraph test, and Kentucky state police asked Putnam to take a similar test in February 1990. His evasive response aroused suspicion, and Kentucky authorities teamed with FBI agents for a joint investigation beginning on 1 May 1990. Interviewed at length on 16 May, Putnam denied any link to Smith's disappearance, but an 18 May polygraph test suggested he was lying. Putnam confessed to his wife on 22 May, then resigned from the FBI and ordered his lawyer to seek a plea bargain.

Over the next three weeks, a deal was negotiated whereby Putnam agreed to confess Smith's murder and lead detectives to her body, in exchange for a maximum charge of first-degree manslaughter and a guaranteed maximum sentence of sixteen years, to be served in a federal prison. The state's attorney in charge of the case explained his acceptance of the bargain by noting that conviction without a corpse was unlikely. Putnam's affidavit of 4 June 1990 included an admission of strangling Smith, then five months pregnant, when they met on 8 June 1989. According to his story, they were driving around Pikesville in a rented car when he offered to adopt Smith's baby and take the child into his home. Smith then allegedly slapped him, prompting Putnam to choke her in a fit of rage.

On the afternoon of 4 June, Putnam led investigators to an old mining road nine miles from Pikesville, where Smith's skeletal remains were found in a weed-choked ravine. Eight days later, Putnam received his prearranged sentence, thus becoming the only FBI agent to date convicted of criminal homicide.

**PYLE, Ernest Taylor**— A Midwest farmer's son, born near Dana, Indiana on 3 August 1900, Ernie Pyle studied journalism at Indiana University and afterward went to work at the *Washington Daily News*, ultimately rising to the rank of managing editor. J. EDGAR HOOVER noticed Pyle in 1937, after Pyle met Alaska's resident G-man on a boat trip from Seattle to Juneau and published a column about their encounter. Hoover wrote a letter of appreciation to Pyle on 1 July 1937, but a survey of FBI files reveals an ulterior motive. Prior to writing the letter, Hoover had learned from his agent in Alaska that Pyle and "the Scripps-Howard management" felt Hoover "discriminated against their representatives" and favored the rival *Washington Star*. Hoover's memo on the subject dismissed the notion that he "favors any particular representative of the press" as wholly "untrue." (In fact, it was completely accurate.) Pyle earned his greatest fame in WORLD WAR II, as a front-line correspondent with U.S. troops in Europe and the Pacific. He was killed by a Japanese sniper during the battle for Okinawa, on 17 April 1945.

# Q

**"QUALITY over Quantity"**— Compilation of statistics was an FBI obsession under Director J. EDGAR HOOVER (1924-72), superceded in importance only by the punishment of Bureau critics. Indeed, statistics were the very lifeblood of the FBI, since Hoover based the Bureau's reputation and his yearly budgetary requests on ever-increasing numbers of arrests, cases investigated (as opposed to *solved*), hours of "voluntary" overtime worked without pay by his agents, and so forth. If some tabulations— including the yearly number of fugitives captured and stolen cars recovered— involved taking credit for actions performed by local police departments, so be it. Hoover's ego and the FBI's financial needs took precedence over any considerations of honesty or fairness.

Director CLARENCE KELLEY sought to change that image and create a more proactive Bureau in 1975, with his demand for "quality over quantity" in FBI investigations. Abandoning the Hoover system, wherein agents were assigned to case squads (BANK ROBBERY, counterintelligence, etc.) and waited in their offices for complaints to arrive, Kelley ordered his troops to select targets in advance— e.g., a corrupt politician or member of

ORGANIZED CRIME— and actively pursue that subject through undercover work, "sting" operations, and the like. The concept was

formalized in 1977, with specific Bureau goals enumerated in a series of National Priority Programs.

# R

**RABBLE Rouser Index**— The FBI's Rabble Rouser Index was created on 25 August 1967, to collect the names of "individuals who have demonstrated a potential for fomenting racial discord." Guidelines promulgated by J. EDGAR HOOVER defined a "rabble rouser" as any person "who tries to arouse people to violent action by appealing to their emotions, prejudices, et cetera; a demagogue." (Although that definition clearly fit many white southern politicians in the 1960s, none were included on the list.) As administered by Assistant Director WILLIAM SULLIVAN'S Division 5, in charge of illegal COINTELPRO operations, the racial definition was soon expanded to include any form of disorder affecting "national security" as defined by Bureau leaders. Thus, the rabble-rousing categories included "black nationalists, white supremacists, PUERTO RICAN NATIONALISTS, anti-VIETNAM demonstration leaders, and other extremists."

In March 1968 Hoover changed the title of his newest DOMESTIC SURVEILLANCE program, renaming it the Agitator Index. All field offices were ordered to "estimate" the presumed "propensity for violence" among black activist groups, collecting data for "target evaluation" as well as "record purposes." Focus was directed toward "the most violent radical groups and their leaders," although Hoover ordered particular attention to such nonviolent crusaders as Rev. Jesse Jackson, MARTIN LUTHER KING, JR., and his SOUTHERN CHRISTIAN LEADERSHIP COUNCIL, deemed to be as "violent" as more militant groups including the NATION OF ISLAM and the STUDENT NONVIOLENT COORDINATING COMMITTEE. Fred Hampton, leader of the BLACK PANTHER PARTY in Chicago, was listed on 16 November 1969, 15 days before he was killed in his sleep by CHICAGO POLICE, acting in conjunction with an FBI INFORMER. G-men in Newark listed Tom Hayden, a leader of STUDENTS FOR A DEMOCRATIC SOCIETY, on grounds that he "worked with and supported the Negro people in their program." Omaha's field office, by contrast, found no "extremists" active in its territory.

In their pursuit of radicals, Bureau field offices were specifically ordered to submit "visual material relating to violence by black extremists," ideally including "clear, glossy, 8" by 10" photographs." Those photos were added to the bureau's ever-growing BLACK NATIONALIST PHOTO ALBUM for nationwide circulation, to facilitate tracking subjects around the country. The

Agitator Index ultimately included profiles on 1,191 persons. It was abolished in spring 1971, absorbed (with contents of the parallel SECURITY INDEX) by the larger and more detailed ADMINISTRATIVE INDEX.

**RAINBOW Farm**— Operated by founder Grover T. Crosslin at Vandalia, Michigan, the 34-acre Rainbow Farm was openly dedicated to support for "the medical, spiritual and responsible recreational uses of marijuana for a more sane and compassionate America." That stance brought Crosslin into conflict with local, state and federal authorities when he crossed the line between simple advocacy and practice of his beliefs. A two-year investigation of alleged drug use at the campground climaxed in May 2001 with the arrests of Crosslin and five others, shortly before a "Hemp Aid 2001" celebration planned for Memorial Day. Crosslin, age 47, was charged with felony possession of a firearm, growing marijuana and maintaining a drug house. Released on $150,000 bond, he subsequently violated terms of his release by holding a festival on 17-18 August 2001 and failing to appear for a bond hearing on 31 August. Cass County sheriff's deputies visited the Rainbow Farm that afternoon, after neighbors reported that Crosslin and others were burning buildings on the property, but the camp's occupants refused to admit them.

A stand-off ensued, with 50-odd deputies and state troopers surrounding the campground. Shots were fired at a television news helicopter on 31 August and at an unmarked state police plane the following day. No gunman was identified in either case, and neither aircraft suffered any damage, but FBI agents joined the siege on 1 September, since firing at aircraft is a federal offense. John Bell, special agent in charge of the Bureau's Detroit field office, told reporters on 2 September that "It is the goal of all three agencies to resolve this matter peacefully." Those plans went awry on the night of 3 September, when Crosslin reportedly aimed a rifle at FBI agents and was killed where he stood. Police killed a second occupant of the farm, 28-year-old Rolland Rohm, at 6 a.m. on 4 September, when he emerged from one of the farm buildings with a rifle and ignored orders to drop his weapon. A third subject, identified in press reports as Brandon Peoples, suffered "minor injuries" as officers and agents raided the farm in the wake of the second shooting. Rumors of bombs and booby traps planted on the property proved groundless.

**RANDOLPH, Asa Philip**—A Florida native, born at Crescent City on 15 April 1889, A. Philip Randolph moved to New York City in 1911 and soon converted to socialism. In 1917, with colleague Chandler Owen, Randolph founded a black socialist newspaper, *The Messenger* (later *Black Worker*). Their outspoken opposition to white supremacy and WORLD WAR I, coupled with frank Socialist editorials (and brief support for Bolshevism) marked Randolph and Chandler as natural targets for the early Bureau of Investigation, repeatedly accused in federal memos of spreading "race hatred" (defined by J. EDGAR HOOVER and company as any support for desegregation and racial equality).

G-men and federal prosecutors saw their chance to strike in 1918, when Randolph and Chandler embarked on a national speaking tour, sponsored by the Socialist Party. Their remarks included references to "pro–Germanism among Negroes," interpreted under the espionage act of 1917 as criminal "interference with the efficiency of the military forces." Facing 20-year prison terms, Randolph and Owen ironically benefited from the racist paternalism of a white judge who could not believe that a pair of 29-year-old black "boys" had written the "inflammatory" editorials and speeches published under their names. Accordingly, the charges were dismissed and circulation of the *Messenger* increased by 50 percent in the "Red Summer" of 1919.

Smarting from his defeat in court, Hoover sent a memo to assistant Bureau chief Frank Burke on 12 August 1919, naming the *Messenger* as the primary target of Hoover's GENERAL INTELLIGENCE DIVISION. Leaving his sources anonymous, Hoover claimed the newspaper "is stated to be the Russian organ of the Bolsheviki in the United States and to be the headquarters of revolutionary thought." To meet that threat, Hoover ordered his agents to check the citizenship of all *Messenger* staff members, while staying alert to any links to Bolshevik agents or activists from the INDUSTRIAL WORKERS OF THE WORLD. Various black INFORMERS, including ARTHUR CRAIG and WILLIAM LUCAS, infiltrated the *Messenger*'s staff, seeking to prove the JUSTICE DEPARTMENT'S claim that "there can be no excuse for its publication" except to "inflame" blacks and create "an intense hostility toward the forces of law and order."

Hoover's infiltrators searched in vain for evidence of criminal conspiracy, finally reduced to agitating disgruntled ex-employees, urging them to sue Randolph and Owen for back wages. Undeterred by such harassment, Randolph and Owen founded the Friends of Negro Freedom in March 1920, dedicated to pursuing CIVIL RIGHTS by more militant means than those employed by the NATIONAL ASSOCIATION FOR THE ADVANCEMENT OF COLORED PEOPLE. A year later, both were still listed in Bureau files as "well known radical agitators with Bolshevik tendencies." Black G-man JAMES AMOS interviewed Randolph and Chandler in 1922, but found no evidence of criminal activity. Owen renounced socialism in 1923, while Randolph went on to found the Brotherhood of Sleeping Car Porters in August 1925.

Hoover's agents were distracted by other threats in the 1930s, but Randolph captured the Bureau's attention again during WORLD WAR II, with a series of marches on Washington, D.C. during 1941-43, 20 years before the famous demonstration led by MARTIN LUTHER KING, JR. He also lobbied President FRANKLIN ROOSEVELT to ban segregation in federal bureaus and defense industries—a move that threatened Hoover's all-white FBI—and persuaded President HARRY TRUMAN to desegregate the U.S. military in 1948. Elected vice president of the newly combined AFL-CIO in 1955, Randolph joined Dr. King's boycott of segregated buses in Montgomery, Alabama that same year, then rebounded in 1960 by creating the Negro American Labor Council (NALC) to fight discrimination within the AFL-CIO itself.

Randolph's new prominence as one of the nation's "Big Six" civil rights leaders left Hoover in a quandary. On one hand, Randolph publicly denounced the COMMUNIST PARTY'S program for black American's as "specious" and accepted FBI advice for screening officers of the NALC; on the other, he remained a close associate of Stanley Levison, an alleged communist on Dr. King's staff with the SOUTHERN CHRISTIAN LEADERSHIP CONFERENCE. Randolph sometimes provided G-men with information and copies of his personal travel itinerary, but Hoover still regarded him as a subversive influence (though never on a scale with Dr. King). Randolph survived the FBI's director by seven years; he died in New York City on 16 May 1979.

**RANSOM, John Crowe**—A native of Pulaski, Tennessee, born in 1888, conservative poet and literary critic John Crowe Ransom was 74 years old when G-men noticed him for the first time, in 1962. The occasion was Ransom's participation in a National Poetry Festival, infiltrated by the FBI because various attendees were regarded as leftists or "subversives." Ransom fit neither category, but agents discovered that his name had never been indexed before, and they felt obliged to correct that situation. Thus, as described by author Natalie Robins in *Alien Ink* (1992), Ransom's three-page dossier was opened simply "because he didn't have a file." Ransom died in 1974, without evoking any further interest from the FBI.

**RARICK, John Richard**—An Indiana native, born at Waterford on 29 January 1924, John Rarick served with distinction in the U.S. Army during WORLD WAR II, earning several decorations after his escape from a German prison camp. Rarick graduated from Louisiana's Tulane University Law School in 1949 and entered private practice the same year. An outspoken segregationist during the South's CIVIL RIGHTS crisis, he was elected to a district judgeship in June 1961 and served until May 1966, when he resigned to oppose 12-term incumbent James Morrison in the Democratic congressional primary. Morrison accused Rarick of belonging to the KU KLUX KLAN, and Rarick responded with a $500,000 libel suit, rolling on to defeat his opponent before the case was settled out of court. The *New York Times* reported that Morrison's charges had prompted an FBI investigation of Rarick, and a 1973 Bureau report later confirmed that Rarick once served as "Exalted Cyclops" (chapter leader) of a KKK "klavern" in St. Francisville, Louisiana.

Klan affiliations notwithstanding, Rarick served the Bayou State in Congress from 1967 through 1974, when he lost his fourth re-election bid and returned to private legal practice. Despite Rarick's background (or because of it), J. EDGAR HOOVER favored him with leaks from "confidential" Bureau files, used by Rarick to launch a posthumous attack on Dr. MARTIN LUTHER KING, JR., in the House of Representatives, in June 1969. Rarick continued his extremist associations after retiring from Congress. In 1980 he was the far-right American Independent Party's presidential candidate, polling 41,000 votes out of some 87 million ballots cast, and he was listed in 1991 as a member of the neo-Nazi Liberty Lobby's Populist Action Committee.

**RAY, John Larry**— Born in 1931, John Ray followed his brothers into a life of petty crime as a teenager. His first conviction, for burglarizing a gas station in December 1949, earned him a two-to-five-year sentence at Indiana's Pendleton Reformatory. In June 1953 he pled guilty to car theft in Illinois and received a sentence of five to ten years in state prison. Paroled in the early 1960s, he moved to St. Louis and there operated a tavern, described by local police as a "nice, quiet saloon."

Ray's last round of trouble with the law began in June 1968, after his older brother James was arrested for killing America's foremost civil rights leader, Dr. MARTIN LUTHER KING, JR. James Ray pled guilty to that crime under peculiar circumstances, on 10 March 1969, but the case did not end there. According to James Ray's affidavit in a later civil lawsuit —

> ...[O]n or about March 12, 1969 in the prison segregation building Plaintiff was confronted through a ruse by special agent Robert Jensen of the Memphis, Tennessee, Federal Bureau of Investigation office. The thrust of R. Jensen's conversation was seeking cooperation of Plaintiff in furthering the FBI investigation of said [conspiracy] indictment. When Plaintiff refused the cooperation offer Mr. Jensen upon departing said Plaintiff could expect Plaintiff['s] brothers (John and Jerry Ray) to join him in prison or words to that effect.

As allegedly forecast by Agent Jensen, both of Ray's brothers were soon in trouble with the law. Jerry Ray was subsequently charged — and acquitted — in the shooting of a burglar at Savannah, Georgia. It was John Ray, however, who bore the brunt of federal wrath against his famous younger sibling. John's ordeal began in October 1970, when three armed men robbed a bank in St. Peters, Missouri, making off with $53,000. They fled — alone, according to eyewitnesses — in a waiting car. An hour later, Ray was stopped by police on the highway seven miles from St. Peters; he was alone, unarmed, and had no more than $500 cash in his possession. Still, he was promptly charged with bank robbery, FBI agents claiming that he gave the three bandits a ride between the time they abandoned their first car and boarded a second waiting vehicle to complete their getaway.

Indicted for the actual robbery were defendants James Benney, Ronald Goldstein and Jerry Miller. Benney was later shot and killed in Portland, Oregon, with Goldstein arrested as a material witness to his slaying. Miller remained at large when Goldstein was transferred to Missouri for trial with John Ray, before U.S. District Judge WILLIAM WEBSTER. In the course of that trial, Ray proclaimed his innocence and described threats he received from FBI agents in 1968 and 1969. "They threatened me with the penitentiary," Ray said, "and told me not to visit my brother in Tennessee or attend his trial." Jurors disbelieved the claim and convicted both defendants. Curiously, while Goldstein received only thirteen years for armed robbery, Judge Webster sentenced Ray to eighteen years on the lesser charge of aiding Goldstein's escape.

The strange story was only beginning, however. In March 1972, Goldstein won a new trial on appeal, proving that authorities had illegally searched his hotel room in pursuit of evidence; Ray's corresponding appeal was rejected. At his second trial in October 1972, Goldstein was acquitted on all charges. Jurors deliberated for barely an hour, the *St. Louis Post-Dispatch* reporting that "No evidence was presented by the government establishing Goldstein's presence in the bank at the time of the robbery." John Ray, meanwhile, remained in jail, describing himself as "the only prisoner in the federal prison system serving a sentence for picking up a person who was found not guilty of robbing a bank."

FBI agents remedied that deficiency a few weeks later, when they bagged Jerry Miller at his hideout in Fresno, California. Unlike Goldstein, however, Miller was not returned to Missouri for trial; instead, his case was assigned to a federal court in Fresno, more than 2,000 miles from the scene of the crime. (John Ray insisted that the change of venue was designed "to keep it from me and the news media.") In January 1973, Miller pled guilty to bank robbery and received a three-year sentence to a minimum-security prison; two months later, the court reduced his prison term to eighteen months. John Ray received no such favors, but he was quietly paroled in late 1977 — an event he believed was connected to Judge Webster's appointment as FBI director in January 1978.

Although released, John Ray continued to live in the shadow of Dr. King's murder. Called to testify before the HOUSE SELECT COMMITTEE ON ASSASSINATIONS in 1978, he denied any knowledge of the case. The committee's final report failed to name him as a participant in the slaying, but several journalists have hinted strongly at John's peripheral involvement with the crime. Most recently, Gerald Posner's *Killing the Dream*— a book devoted to the lone-assassin theory of King's murder — suggests that John profited from his brother's sale of contraband at Missouri's state prison; that he helped James escape in 1967; that he provided James with the "Eric Galt" alias used when James fled into Canada that year; and that he "may have" tipped James to a Missouri businessman's standing $50,000 "bounty" on Dr. King. Finally, Posner notes darkly that John "had no alibi" for the days immediately following King's murder, suggesting that John may have helped his fugitive brother flee from the United States to England, where he was captured in June 1968. Despite exhaustive searches by the FBI and Congress, no evidence has been revealed supporting any of those speculative theories.

**REAGAN, Ronald Wilson**— Born at Tampico, Illinois on 6 February 1911, Ronald Reagan graduated from Eureka College in 1932 and spent the next five years as a radio sports announcer, before signing a movie contract with Warner Brothers studios in 1937. He spent WORLD WAR II in California, making propaganda films for the U.S. Army, and was discharged as a captain in December 1945. During the 1940s and 1950s Reagan also served as an FBI INFORMANT (code name "T-10"), reporting on alleged COMMUNIST PARTY activities in Hollywood. In 1947, during his first term as president of the Screen Actors Guild, he appeared as a friendly witness before the HOUSE COMMITTEE ON UN-AMERICAN ACTIVITIES. Reagan announced his switch from the Democratic to the Republican Party in 1962, and two years later received national acclaim for a televised speech on behalf of presidential candidate Barry Goldwater. On the strength of that performance and his right-wing political/industrial connections, Reagan was elected twice as governor of California (1967–75).

Reagan's tenure in Sacramento was a preview of his later performance as president. Already linked to various ORGANIZED CRIME figures, he established a pattern of appointing ultra-conservative friends to high office and persecuting political dissenters. Reagan fired instructor ANGELA DAVIS from her college teaching post because she was a communist and proclaimed his willingness to crush campus demonstrations with violence. ("If they want a bloodbath, let it be now.") Thirty years later, declassified FBI documents would reveal Reagan's collaboration with the Bureau and the CENTRAL INTELLIGENCE AGENCY in an illegal campaign of harassment and DOMESTIC SURVEILLANCE at the University of California in Berkeley. The FBI/CIA activities supported by Governor Reagan included harassment of students, faculty and members of the Board of Regents, coupled with a drive to oust UC President Clark Kerr. To that end, false derogatory information was fabricated and leaked to the press, with several reports dispatched to the White House. Assistant Director CARTHA DELOACH admitted that Reagan was "very helpful" to the FBI, but insisted that the Bureau gave Reagan "no special treatment."

The same could not be said of Reagan's years as president. As in California, Reagan campaigned by soliciting aid from various members of organized crime, particularly the corrupt TEAMSTERS UNION. Reagan and running mate GEORGE H.W. BUSH held various closed-door meetings with Teamster officials — most of them under indictment — both before and after the November 1980 election. Teamster vice president, mobster and FBI informant JACKIE PRESSER was named a "senior economic adviser" to Reagan's transition team, despite the fact that he had dropped out of eighth grade and was currently facing litigation by the LABOR DEPARTMENT for corrupt activities. Less than a month after Reagan's first inauguration, in February 1981, *Organized Crime Review* publisher Ryan Emerson declared:

> About six months before the presidential election I received word that certain individuals within the Reagan camp were negotiating with key people in Las Vegas, Nevada, who were involved in the casino industry, the Teamsters Union, and organized crime. The basis for the discussions was the acute desire of the Teamsters Union to obtain relief from the aggressive probes by the United States Department of Justice organized crime strike forces and the Federal Bureau of Investigation. There was also a continuing grave concern about the FBI's productive court-approved wiretaps that had revealed the hidden interest in many Las Vegas hotels and casinos by some of the country's most powerful organized crime figures.

While Reagan announced a "vigorous war" on crime in America and a parallel "war on drugs," his actions belied public statements. Reagan's courtship of the Teamsters continued unabated, while Nevada mob investigations by the FBI and the INTERNAL REVENUE SERVICE were sharply curtailed. Raymond Donovan, a New Jersey contractor with known mob connections who raised $600,000 for Reagan's 1980 campaign, was nominated to serve as Secretary of Labor. (During his protracted confirmation hearings, Attorney General Smith refused to let the U.S. Senate hear tapes of his conversations with gangsters, secured via FBI WIRETAPS.) Reagan took credit for the conviction of 1,100 mobsters indicted under President JAMES CARTER, but he refused to allow any new UNDERCOVER OPERATIONS against organized crime in 1982. The White House also slashed budgets for federal law enforcement across the board, forcing dismissal of 434 employees from the DRUG ENFORCEMENT ADMINISTRATION, and Reagan tried to eliminate the BUREAU OF ALCOHOL, TOBACCO AND FIREARMS completely. Overall, federal investigative agencies lost a total of 19,609 employees in 1981-82, prompting sources as diverse as the Coast Guard and the AMERICAN CIVIL LIBERTIES UNION to dub the White House war on crime and drugs "a fraud."

Only in the field of political repression did Reagan favor aggressive investigations. His administration witnessed escalation of illegal FBI harassment tactics against PUERTO RICAN NATIONALISTS and saw widespread surveillance directed at critics of Reagan's foreign policy in Central America and the Iran-Contra scandal (notably the COMMITTEE IN SUPPORT OF THE PEOPLE OF EL SALVADOR). One of Reagan's first official acts was the granting of pardons to ex-FBI officials EDWARD MILLER and W. MARK FELT, convicted in 1980 of authorizing illegal BREAK-INS against suspected "NEW LEFT" adherents in New York City. Strangely, despite his criminal connections, repressive police tactics and economic policies that left the nation burdened with a crushing deficit, Reagan still ranks among the most popular U.S. presidents in various public opinion polls.

**RECORDS Management Division** — The FBI's Records Management Division (RMD) was created in 1976, from the Records and Communications Division, to handle inquiries filed under the FREEDOM OF INFORMATION ACT (FOIA). The unit was also assigned to prepare yearly Uniform Crime Reports, formerly prepared by the CRIME RECORDS DIVISION. In 1993 the RMD was absorbed by the FBI's Information Management Division. Three years later, in November 1996, responsibility for FOIA requests was transferred to the OFFICE OF PUBLIC AND CONGRESSIONAL AFFAIRS, but Director ROBERT MUELLER "recommissioned" the RMD in March 2002, in an effort to "ensure executive direction and full-time oversight over all records policy and functions, consolidating all records operations to ensure consistency, thoroughness and accountability." The RMD is presently divided into three sections: the Records Maintenance and Disposition Section, the Records Review and Dissemination Section, and the Freedom of Information/Privacy Acts Section. As of July 2002, the division is commanded by Assistant Director William Hooton.

**REED, John Silas**— The son of a wealthy Portland, Oregon family, born in 1887, John Reed graduated from Harvard in 1910 and became managing editor of *The Masses* three years later. That affiliation was enough to open a file on Reed with the Bureau of Investigation, which mistakenly credited him with founding the magazine in 1911. Reed served as an overseas correspondent during WORLD WAR I and became a good friend of Bolshevik leader Vladimir Lenin. Back in New York on 30 May 1917, Reed was spotted by G-men at the First American Conference for Democracy and Terms of Peace, at Madison Square Garden. Three months later, he traveled to Russia and witnessed the revolution against Czar Nicholas II, later described in his best-selling book *Ten Days that Shook the World* (1919).

The feds were waiting when Reed came home in 1918. They seized his notes, grilled him, and filed reports claiming that Reed had been "named as Russian Consul General of the Russian Soviet government." Subsequent memos dubbed him "not only a fanatic Communist but also an eccentric romantic." Be that as it may, G-men were correct in calling Reed "one of the earliest Communist leaders in the United States," since he played a critical role in founding the small Communist Labor Party. (Prior to 1919, no COMMUNIST PARTY existed in the U.S.) Shadowed relentlessly by agents — he was "observed shaving" on 16 May 1919 — Reed was finally indicted for sedition, but he fled the country with a bogus passport and returned to Russia. Reed contracted typhus there and died on 17 October 1920. He was buried just outside the Kremlin wall. Twelve years later, historian Theodore Draper reports, Reed's widow told an "incredible story," claiming that he had never been a communist at all, but rather served his homeland as a U.S. secret agent. No documentation exists to support the story. Long after his death, the FBI used Reed's name to implicate others in presumed acts of "subversion," opening files on anyone foolish enough to join local chapters of the John Reed Club.

**REGIONAL Computer Support Centers** *see* **Computer Crimes**

**REMARQUE, Erich Maria**— A German native, born at Osnabrüumick on 22 June 1898, Remarque was drafted during WORLD WAR I and suffered several wounds in combat, later using his experience to pen the best-selling novel *All Quiet on the Western Front* (1929). Remarque moved to Switzerland in 1932, and the newly ascendant Nazi government of Germany burned his books a year later. In 1939, he entered the U.S. at San Ysidro, California and joined a growing colony of exiled German writers in Los Angeles. Remarque seemed apolitical for the most part, any gossip limited to his affair with movie star Marlene Dietrich, but G-men dutifully filed a letter addressed to J. EDGAR HOOVER on 6 October 1942. Signed "I am just a true American," the semi-literate letter expressed concern to "Dear Edgar" about Remarque and his fellow exiles: "I hope it is not a crime to be suspicious … but … these german men what are they doing here in our country?" For once, the Bureau declined to investigate, and Remarque became a U.S. citizen five years later. He returned to Switzerland in 1949 and died at Locarno on 25 September 1970.

**REMINGTON, William W.**— A native of Ridgewood, New Jersey, born to an affluent family in 1917, William Remington freely admitted that his politics "moved left quite rapidly" during his years at New Hampshire's Dartmouth College. As an economist with the U.S. Department of Commerce, Remington passed an FBI background check and seemed above suspicion until 1948, when professional ex-Communist ELIZABETH BENTLEY named him as a Russian spy before the SENATE INTERNAL SECURITY SUBCOMMITTEE. According to Bentley, she met Remington a dozen times in 1942-43, always alone and in secret, receiving from him certain notes on his work but no classified documents. Remington admitted meeting Bentley once, in early 1948, but denied allegations of ESPIONAGE. He was suspended while a Loyalty Board reviewed his case, reinstated on 10 February 1949 with all charges dismissed, after Bentley twice broke dates to testify before the board. Though suddenly shy of testifying under oath, Bentley repeated her charges on "Meet the Press," prompting Remington to sue her, the NBC television network, and the program's sponsors for $100,000. NBC and General Foods settled the case for $10,000, in a decision that threatened Bentley's credibility and the entire 1940s Red Scare.

Bentley's rehabilitation was essential, not only for the ongoing purge of "subversives" in government, but to permit publication of a newly-finished book that named Remington as a Soviet spy. In April 1950 the HOUSE COMMITTEE ON UN-AMERICAN ACTIVITIES (HUAC) accused Remington of belonging to the COMMUNIST PARTY in 1936-37, while he was employed by the Tennessee Valley Authority. Remington denied it under oath, and HUAC moved to charge him with perjury. Two successive grand juries in Washington refused to indict him on the flimsy evidence available, but a third panel in New York — chaired by John Brunini, a party to Bentley's publishing contract — returned an indictment on 8 June 1950. Prosecutor Thomas Donovan, a former G-man, was assigned to try the case.

At trial, Bentley changed her original story, secure in the knowledge that friendly witnesses were immune from perjury charges. Instead of solitary meetings with Remington, she now recalled that his wife had been present on several occasions. Mrs. Remington, lately divorced from the defendant, was bullied into reporting that her ex-husband had passed on "top secret" government papers — yet another change in Bentley's original version. A third witness, Howard Bridgman, told the court he saw Remington at a Communist meeting in Knoxville, Tennessee, some time in "winter or early spring" of 1937. Defense attorneys proved that the alleged host of the meeting had not lived in Knoxville prior to mid-June 1937, but jurors ignored such details. They convicted Remington of perjury on 7 February 1951, but the conviction was soon overturned on appeal.

Unwilling to gamble on the same evidence a second time, authorities dismissed the original charge against Remington, then indicted him on 25 October 1951 for five counts of perjury in testimony at his recent trial. Remington's second jury acquitted him on three counts, but convicted him on two others: false denial of receiving secret documents from Bentley, and for lying in denials he "had knowledge" of the Young Communist League at Dartmouth. (He was not accused of *joining*, merely knowing it existed.) A federal appeals court upheld Remington's conviction, and the U.S. SUPREME COURT declined to review the case. Remington entered the federal prison at Lewisburg, Pennsylvania on 15 April 1953.

A year later, in his application for parole, Remington tried to placate authorities by admitting that he had furnished unspecified information to "unauthorized persons," one of whom "was a dedicated Communist party member." The confession would not save him, though. On 22 November 1954 Remington was attacked and savagely beaten by three fellow inmates at Lewisburg. He died without regaining consciousness, at age 37. Six weeks later, on 5 January 1955, New Hampshire attorney general Louis Wyman completed an 18-month review of the case and filed a 289-page report with the state legislature. It included testimony from multiple witnesses that Remington had never joined the Communist Party.

**RENN, Ludwig**— "Ludwig Renn" was the pen name of Arnold Friedrich Vieth von Golssenau, a German native born in 1889. A career military officer who saw action in WORLD WAR I, Renn ran afoul of his superiors during the German Revolution of October 1918, when he refused to fire on striking workers. Thereafter known as a political novelist, he fought with Loyalist forces in the Spanish Civil War and toured the U.S. in 1937 to raise money for the Spanish Republican Army. Two years later, he was shadowed by New York G-men when he returned to address a League of American Writers meeting. Briefly interned in France after fascist forces won the Spanish conflict, Renn was released in 1940 and left for Mexico, where he established himself as a leader of *Alemania Libre*— the Free Germany Movement.

The FBI was doubly suspicious of Renn, for his Loyalist sympathies in Spain (deemed "communist" by J. EDGAR HOOVER), and because *Alemania Libre* corresponded freely with Moscow's Free Germany Committee. Renn later denied that the groups were identical, although admitting to "cordial and sympathetic contact" between the two. Agents of the FBI's SPECIAL INTELLIGENCE SERVICE tracked Renn tirelessly, reporting that he "speaks English awkwardly and stutters," debating the prospects for a BREAK-IN at his office, and noting that rumors of his HOMOSEXUALITY were "common talk among the Mexican foreign colony." Renn was placed on the Bureau's "Special Watch" list, but in an era when the FBI dubbed exiled German writers "Communazis," reports on his politics were predictably confused. A June 1942 memo branded him "a Communist suspect in Mexico," but a year later Hoover informed his SIS agents that Renn "is in reality working in behalf of the Nazis." Agents thereafter described him as a "leader of the Seventh Column in Mexico," while the U.S. naval attaché confided to agents that Renn's "espousal of Communism and loyalty thereto may well be a cloak of opportunism."

Whatever Renn believed, the Bureau was determined to disrupt his communication with exiles in the U.S. Renn's mail was intercepted so often that he finally complained to the Office of Censorship, but no answer was forthcoming. An internal memo cautioned that "No reply should be made to the protest, as such an organization is not justified in expecting an explanation of

measures undertaken in time of war by an agency of the United States Government." Renn left Mexico for Europe on 17 February 1947, and later played a public role in East Germany. A month after he left, the Bureau closed its 290-page file on his "Mexico Subversive Activities" and "Security Matter — C" (for Communist). Forty years later, when his dossier was released under the FREEDOM OF INFORMATION ACT, 97 pages remained classified for reasons of "national security."

**RENO, Janet**— A Miami native, born 21 July 1938, Janet Reno graduated from Cornell University in 1960 and received her LL.B. from Harvard Law School three years later. In 1971 she was named staff director of the Judiciary Committee of the Florida House of Representatives. Two years later Reno joined the Dade County State's Attorney's office, but left public service in 1976 to become a partner in a private law firm. In November 1978 she was elected to the first of four terms as state's attorney for Dade County, working to reform the juvenile justice system and establish a Miami Drug Court. President WILLIAM CLINTON selected Reno as the nation's first female attorney general, and she assumed control of the JUSTICE DEPARTMENT on 12 March 1993.

Reno arrived at an inauspicious moment, with FBI Director WILLIAM SESSIONS accused of professional misconduct and the BRANCH DAVIDIAN siege already under way at Waco, Texas. In April 1993 she approved the Bureau's plan to rout the barricaded Davidians with tear gas, an effort which ended tragically with close to 80 persons dead. (In 1996 a House report branded Reno's approval of the FBI attack plan "premature, wrong, and highly irresponsible.") Reno seemed to enjoy a good relationship with new FBI Director LOUIS FREEH until the Bureau and Congress began investigating charges of Clinton financial corruption during the 1994 midterm elections. Thereafter, Reno and Freeh were often at odds, with some of their clashes played out in the media. Reno was widely criticized for protecting her boss in the White House, and while some of those charges are well documented, her defensive behavior never matched the level of obstructionism practiced by attorneys general under Presidents RICHARD NIXON, RONALD REAGAN and GEORGE H.W. BUSH.

Reno left office with the inauguration of President GEORGE W. BUSH and was replaced by Attorney General JOHN ASHCROFT. She lost Florida's Democratic gubernatorial primary election in September 2002. The onset of Parkinson's disease rendered her political future uncertain.

**RESERVE Index**— Throughout his 55-year career with the JUSTICE DEPARTMENT, from his early days with the GENERAL INVESTIGATION DIVISION to the last chaotic years under President RICHARD NIXON, FBI Director J. EDGAR HOOVER was a compulsive collector of enemies' lists. Usually, those lists included persons whom Hoover hoped to someday arrest en masse for confinement to detention centers in the heat of some unspecified "national emergency." Hoover maintained such lists despite a total absence of authority and in defiance of direct orders from his superiors. When Attorney General FRANCIS BIDDLE banned Hoover's illegal CUSTODIAL DETENTION INDEX in 1943, Hoover simply transferred the names to a new SECURITY INDEX and continued as before.

The Reserve Index was an appendix of sorts to that forbidden roster, formerly called the Communist Index but renamed by Hoover on 21 June 1960. It included names of individuals who were not "dangerous" enough to rate inclusion in the main Security Index, but "who, in a time of emergency, are in a position to influence others against the national interest or are likely to furnish material financial aid to subversive elements due to their subversive associations and ideology." While membership in a "revolutionary" or "subversive" group (so judged by Hoover's standards) was sufficient to place a person's name in the Reserve Index, others were also listed where "investigation has failed to substantiate allegations of membership in a revolutionary organization within the past five years, coupled with some evidence or information indicating activity, association, or sympathy for the subversive cause within the same period, and no reliable evidence of defection."

"The subversive cause," in FBI jargon, included any show of liberalism, sympathy for the CIVIL RIGHTS movement or VIETNAM WAR PROTESTS—and any public criticism of the Bureau.

Individuals listed in the Reserve Index included Dr. MARTIN LUTHER KING, JR., novelist NORMAN MAILER, and various "teachers, writers, lawyers, etc." who were "influential in espousing their respective philosophies." In October 1971, with approval from Attorney General JOHN MITCHELL, Hoover merged the illegal Security and Reserve Indexes into a new ADMINISTRATIVE INDEX and continued filing names as before. Assistant Attorney General Robert Mardian ordered the list destroyed on 9 February 1972, but Hoover ignored the command. Acting Director L. PATRICK GRAY found the list intact in September 1972, four months after Hoover's death.

**RESIDENT Agencies**— While major investigations are coordinated from FBI HEADQUARTERS in Washington, D.C., through a network of 56 field offices, agents also toil in a far-flung system of smaller offices known as resident agencies (RAs). Typically a one- or two-agent operation, located in smaller towns and reporting to the nearest FBI field office, each RA pursues local matters as they arise and may be called upon to assist in wider investigations. Historically, and particularly under the regime of Director J. EDGAR HOOVER, remote RAs located in areas known for harsh weather were used to facilitate punitive actions, assignment to such a post being the equivalent of banishment. The FBI's most notorious resident agency was located in MEDIA, PENNSYLVANIA, where burglars from a self-styled Citizens' Commission to Investigate the FBI looted classified files in 1971, thereby exposing Hoover's illegal COINTELPRO harassment campaigns. In the wake of that embarrassment, Hoover closed 103 of the Bureau's 538 resident RAs.

The FBI provides no detailed list of its resident agencies, although a private estimate published in 2000 referred to "approximately 400" RAs scattered throughout the U.S. As of July 2002, the Bureau's official website offers locations for only 103 resident agencies. They include 15 in Texas; 12 in Oklahoma; 9 in Indiana; 8 each in central Florida and northern California; 7 in Minnesota; 6 each in Maryland, New York and Ohio; 5 each in Alabama and Iowa; 4 each in Nebraska, North Dakota and South Dakota; 2 in Hawaii; plus 1 each on the Pacific islands of Guam and Saipan. Others may be located by checking telephone directories for specific regions of the U.S.

**RESPONSIBILITIES Program**—FBI Director J. EDGAR HOOVER initiated his so-called "Responsibilities Program" on 12 February 1951, in the midst of the post-WORLD WAR II Red scare. The program involved a four-year series of clandestine leaks from FBI files, through which derogatory information on alleged "subversives" was supplied to various state governors and other civic leaders — police chiefs, school administrators, Red Cross officials, etc. (For some unknown reason, ex-president HERBERT HOOVER was also included on the list of favored recipients.) Most of the targets were employed in state or local government, utilities, or in the field of education (including teachers at all levels, in both public and private schools).

Hoover named his illegal whispering campaign for the FBI's alleged "responsibility" to root out subversives in every walk of life. In his rationale, because "public utilities, public organizations and semi-public organizations" served "large portions of the public," Hoover and the Bureau had "an obligation for the protection of the facilities when we have information of a subversive nature affecting them." He insisted on utmost secrecy regarding the leaked material, and canceled the program in 1955 after several recipients breached his terms of confidentiality, thereby subjecting the FBI to potential embarrassment.

**RESSLER, Robert K.**— A Chicago native, born in 1937, Robert Ressler joined the FBI in 1970, after serving with the U.S. Army's Criminal Investigative Division (which illegally assigned him to infiltrate the leftist STUDENTS FOR A DEMOCRATIC SOCIETY while he completed his master's degree at the University of Michigan). In his fourth year of service with the Bureau, Ressler was appointed to teach at the FBI NATIONAL ACADEMY, where he soon joined the Behavioral Science Unit assigned to PSYCHOLOGICAL PROFILING of unidentified offenders. In that capacity, and during a lecture tour of England in 1974, Ressler claims to have coined the term "SERIAL MURDER." (In fact, the term was first used eight years earlier, by British author John Brophy, in his book *The Meaning of Murder*.) Between 1979 and 1983, Ressler participated in prison interviews with 36 sexually motivated killers compiling a database later utilized by the FBI's VIOLENT CRIMINAL APPREHENSION PROGRAM.

Retired from the FBI in 1990, Ressler kept up a busy schedule of lectures and writing, police-training seminars, private consulting on criminal cases, and frequent appearances on television talk shows. He has co-authored several books, including *Sexual Homicide* (1988), the FBI's *Crime Classification Manual* (1992), *Whoever Fights Monsters* (1992), and *I Have Lived in the Monster* (1997).

**REVOLUTIONARY Action Movement**— The Revolutionary Action Movement (RAM), led by Maxwell Sanford, was founded in Philadelphia during the winter of 1963. As a militant ghetto organization whose philosophy merged the teachings of MALCOLM X and ROBERT F. WILLIAMS with Marxist revolutionary theory, calling for the overthrow of capitalism as a racist-exploitive system, RAM was a natural target for surveillance and disruption under the FBI's illegal COINTELPRO campaign. G-men followed RAM's tracks to New York City in February 1965, when member Robert Collier was among four persons charged with plotting to bomb the Statue of Liberty, the Washington Monument and the Liberty Bell. (All four were convicted on 14 June 1965.) Two years later, RAM was one of six black organizations slated for "intensified action" in a memo from J. EDGAR HOOVER, directing all FBI field offices to harass and disrupt "Black Nationalist — Hate Groups." A second Hoover memo, dated 4 March 1968, listed RAM as one of the Bureau's four "primary targets"; Max Sanford joined the short list of five black leaders targeted in Hoover's campaign to "prevent the rise of a 'messiah' who could unify, and electrify, the militant black nationalist movement." Hoover's memo boasted that:

> The Revolutionary Action Movement (RAM), a pro-Chinese communist group, was active in Philadelphia, Pa., in the summer of 1967. The Philadelphia Office alerted local police, who then put RAM leaders under close scrutiny. They were arrested on every possible charge until they could no longer make bail. As a result, RAM leaders spent most of the summer in jail and no violence traceable to RAM took place.

Hoover's message failed to note that no "violence traceable to RAM" had ever been recorded in Philadelphia. Indeed, if the group had been involved in criminal activity, local police would hardly have needed an FBI "alert" to RAM's existence. Seven RAM members *were* jailed in Philadelphia on 30 September 1967, after an FBI INFORMANT accused them of plotting to murder Hoover, President LYNDON JOHNSON and various local officials, but the charges were soon dismissed for lack of evidence and the defendants pled guilty to misdemeanor disorderly conduct. Hoover's subsequent congressional testimony, accusing RAM of ubiquitous involvement in 1967's ghetto riots, was unsupported by anything resembling evidence.

False charges aside, the FBI's disruption campaign had the desired effect, when Sanford formally dissolved RAM in 1968 and advised its members to "go underground." Some, like Bobby Seale and Robert Collier, had already shifted their allegiance to the BLACK PANTHER PARTY, though subsequent claims that RAM "founded" the party are clearly overstated. Sanford himself jumped bail on charges filed in New York City and converted to Islam in hiding, changing his name to Muhammad Ahmad before he was recaptured in 1973. Robert Collier, meanwhile, was among 21 New York Panthers arrested in 1969, charged with conspiracy to bomb various public buildings; all were acquitted at trial in 1971.

**REYNOLDS, Quentin James**— A famous American journalist and author, born 11 April 1902, Quentin Reynolds traveled widely in Europe during the Great Depression, reporting on the rise of ADOLF HITLER and other events that would precipitate global conflict. The FBI first indexed Reynolds in 1938, as a supporter of Loyalist Spain, and another memo was filed in 1939, when his name appeared on a letterhead of the American Union for Con-

certed Peace. Best known as a foreign correspondent during WORLD WAR II, he published a series of popular books including *The Battle of Britain*, *The Wounded Don't Cry*, and *The Curtain Rises*.

Reynolds enjoyed curious and contradictory relations with the post-war FBI. G-men classified him as an "Internal Security" threat in 1946, after he praised the Soviet Union at a town hall meeting in Phoenix, but Reynolds and his wife were granted a private tour of Bureau headquarters the same year, their tour guide reporting that "Mr. Reynolds stated that he is probably the only person who calls the Director 'John,' as everybody else either calls him 'Speed' or 'Edgar.'" Despite that suggestion of friendship, Hoover launched a new investigation of Reynolds in 1947, on behalf of the Defense Department. The Bureau's report on that occasion called Reynolds "a confirmed liberal," noting that while he was "closely associated with a number of Communist front organizations," Reynolds "is definitely not a Communist." Two years later, when columnist WESTBROOK PEGLER attacked Reynolds in print, Hoover filed the article and penned "This is terrific!" in the margin. (Reynolds won his libel suit against Pegler and collected $175,000.)

In 1953, when Reynolds signed to write a children's book about the FBI for Random House, publisher Bennet Cerf requested the Bureau's assistance and G-men pitched in to oblige. Reynolds submitted the first draft to Hoover's office in December 1953 and received a long list of suggested revisions, including one observation that "the story depicted in this entire chapter is contrary to Bureau policy." Assistant to the Director LOUIS NICHOLS deemed the original manuscript "impossible," but cheerfully reported that the "second draft was excellent, although chapters three and four ... will have to be rewritten. I think the book will then be in excellent condition and will serve a useful purpose." Hoover agreed and wrote a foreword for the book. He also demanded a discount price for FBI employees and thereafter kept track of sales figures.

By the time *The FBI* was published in 1954, Louis Nichols regarded Reynolds as "an old friend of the Bureau," Hoover still had reservations. In 1963, when the editor of Reynolds's autobiography wrote Hoover for "at least one anecdote" to spice up the book, Hoover not only declined but also opened a file on the editor. Reynolds died on 17 March 1965, but G-men kept his file open for another year. Today, 330 pages of his 580-page dossier remain classified, exempted from release under the FREEDOM OF INFORMATION ACT.

**RFK Assassination**— Following his September 1964 dismissal as Attorney General by President LYNDON JOHNSON, ROBERT KENNEDY won election to the U.S. Senate from New York (also in 1964). Four years later he sought the Democratic Party's presidential nomination on a platform calling for U.S. withdrawal from the VIETNAM WAR. He won the party's crucial California primary on 4 June 1968, thereby obtaining a guaranteed 174 delegate votes for the August convention in Chicago, but Kennedy would not survive to complete the campaign. Gunned down by an assassin on primary night, in the kitchen pantry of the Ambassador Hotel in Los Angeles, Kennedy died at 1:44 p.m. on 6

June 1968. The circumstances of his death remain mysterious, the controversy unresolved despite "exhaustive" investigations by the FBI and the Los Angeles Police Department.

This much is known with certainty: Around midnight on 4 June, Kennedy's entourage (including bodyguard Bill Barry, an ex-FBI agent) left the hotel's Embassy Room and proceeded through the kitchen pantry toward a rear exit. Shots were fired en route, wounding Kennedy and five other persons. A young Palestinian, Sirhan Bishara Sirhan, was disarmed after firing eight rounds from a .22-caliber pistol and held for police. Sirhan was subsequently convicted of Kennedy's murder and sentenced to death; his sentence was commuted to life imprisonment in 1972, when the U.S. SUPREME COURT ruled current capital punishment statutes unconstitutional.

Comparisons to the 1963 JFK ASSASSINATION were inevitable, and so apparently was the official rush to judgment. Within 24 hours of the shooting, while Kennedy still clung to life, Los Angeles police chief Tom Reddin told reporters that based on information "gleaned from dozens of interviews," he was convinced that Sirhan had acted alone in the shooting. FBI Director J. EDGAR HOOVER soon reached an identical conclusion, that verdict seemingly confirmed at Sirhan's murder trial.

But was it true?

Glaring problems with the "lone assassin" verdict were apparent by the time Chief Reddin made his public statement, though most of the troubling facts were initially buried in the rush to convict and execute Sirhan. Ballistics, for example, posed a major hurdle on two fronts, including both the number and direction of the shots fired on 4 June 1968. First, Sirhan's .22-caliber revolver held eight cartridges, and he had no chance to reload before he was tackled and disarmed. If more than eight shots were fired in the Ambassador's pantry, then a second gunman *must* have been involved. Second, if Senator Kennedy's wounds were inflicted from a direction or distance impossible for Sirhan (as observed by those who witnessed the shooting and captured the gunman), then he *cannot* be the killer. Even in the death of Kennedys, the basic laws of physics and mathematics still apply.

In regard to the number of shots fired, we know that three bullets were removed from Kennedy and four more from wounded bystanders; the eighth and final bullet was described in official reports as being "lost in the ceiling interspace." In fact, police later claimed that two shots pierced the pantry's ceiling tiles, one of the bullets ricocheting downward to strike bystander Elizabeth Evans in the head. Despite that official finding, Los Angeles Police Department ballistics expert DeWayne Wolfer later told Deputy Chief Robert Houghton, "It's unbelievable how many holes there are in the kitchen ceiling." Official photographs and affidavits further confuse the issue, including reports and photos of two or three bullet holes in the pantry's door frame *with bullets still visible inside the holes*. Police removed and destroyed the offending door frame and ceiling panel, dismissing the crime scene pictures as photos of "nail holes," but FBI photos released in 1976 under the FREEDOM OF INFORMATION ACT clearly show four marks on the pantry door frame labeled "bullet holes." (As late as 1977, ex-FBI agent William

Bailey confirmed that two holes he saw in the pantry door frame "were definitely not nail holes," and the metal objects imbedded therein "were not nails.") Expert Wolfer's own affidavit, filed in 1971, includes references to bullet holes and bullets which officially did not exist.

> I went to the scene of the crime and I explored the trajectory of all the holes in the wall and the walls of the victims [*sic*].... I was there immediately after the death of the Senator [*sic*]. I retrieved and was in charge of the crime scene and I recovered the bullets that were recovered.

That statement is crucial, since LAPD and the FBI insist to this day that *no* bullets were recovered from the pantry and there were no "holes in the wall." Indeed, Wolfer himself denied the existence of those bullets and holes in other public statements, but his expertise and credibility are highly suspect. In a sworn affidavit of 28 December 1970, Wolfer claimed that all shots fired in the Ambassador Hotel pantry on 4 June 1968 came from a pistol bearing the serial number H-18602. The serial number of Sirhan's pistol was H-53725. By the time his "mistake" was challenged in October 1971, the pistol in question had been destroyed.

As for the gunman's position and distance from his target, all witnesses agree that Sirhan fired from in front of Kennedy, never coming closer than two or three feet from his target. Hotel maitre d' Karl Uecker further testified (and others confirmed) that he grabbed Sirhan's arm after the second shot and forced it upward, toward the ceiling. Strangely, however, Kennedy was struck by three shots, while a fourth passed through his jacket sleeve, and five other persons were wounded (only one of them by an alleged ricochet from the ceiling). Stranger still, postmortem examination revealed that Kennedy was killed by a shot fired into his head *behind* the right ear, from a range of less than two inches.

In 1968 the FBI had no legal jurisdiction in the murder of a presidential candidate, but agents were nonetheless assigned to "assist" the police investigation. Chief prosecutor Lynn Compton would later tell jurors that "The FBI and the Los Angeles Police Department have interviewed literally thousands of people, running out every suggestion, lead or possibility, and they have failed to find any connection between Sirhan and anyone else." In fact, G-men and detectives collected (and then suppressed) testimony from multiple witnesses who stated the exact opposite.

Consider the case of "the woman in the polka-dot dress." Moments after the Kennedy shooting, witness Sandra Serrano saw a woman in a polka-dot dress running from the scene, crying, "We shot him! We shot him!" When asked who was shot, the woman replied, "Senator Kennedy." G-man Richard Barris reported to FBI HEADQUARTERS on 10 June 1968 that Serrano had agreed to a polygraph test. Ten days later, even as the polygraph exam was under way in Los Angeles, J. Edgar Hoover filed the following memo describing his same-day report to Attorney General RAMSEY CLARK:

> I said we were checking various lines as to [James Earl] Ray and Sirhan Sirhan in the Robert F. Kennedy case as to the mysterious woman in the pantry of the Ambassador Hotel and so far they have all fallen through. I said the girl in the Sirhan case has refused to take a lie detector test, but I thought the police were

going to give her one although so far she has refused to take one. The Attorney General asked if this were the woman in the polka-dot dress and I told him it was the one who claimed she saw the woman in the polka-dot dress. The Attorney General said he had read the report on her and got the feeling she was unbalanced. I commented that she was seeking publicity.

It is unclear why Hoover would be "checking" James Earl Ray, the alleged slayer of Dr. MARTIN LUTHER KING, JR., for links to the Kennedy shooting, but his statements regarding Serrano were simply untrue. Transcripts of her Los Angeles polygraph test — which Serrano allegedly failed — show police badgering the witness, telling her to let Kennedy "rest in peace," and warning that persistence in her story would "make an old woman out of you before your time."

Serrano finally recanted under that pressure, but she was not alone in reporting Sirhan's connection to unidentified strangers. In fact, eight other witnesses described the mysterious woman (and her dress) at the Ambassador Hotel, either standing with Sirhan and a second unidentified man or behaving suspiciously on her own. Susan Locke described a woman in a polka-dot dress lurking about the Embassy Room on the night Kennedy was shot, specifically noting that she did not have the required security badge. Jeannette Prudhomme and George Green saw the woman with Sirhan and a second man loitering in the Embassy Room half an hour before the shooting. Green and security guard Jack Merritt later saw the woman and her unidentified male companion flee the hotel pantry, after Kennedy was shot; Merritt told FBI agents that the couple "seemed to be smiling." Photographer Evan Freed saw *two* armed men in the hotel pantry, describing them as "very similar in appearance," and noted that FBI agents "seemed to be avoiding asking me questions about the second gunman." (Viewing his September 1968 statement for the first time in 1992, Freed found that G-men had changed his story, falsely reporting that "Sirhan was the only person Freed saw shooting.")

Hotel waiters Angelo and Vincent DiPierro (father and son) both witnessed the shooting on 4 June 1968; Vincent stood close enough that his face was spattered with Kennedy's blood. He also saw the woman in the polka-dot dress and reported his sighting to a local radio station. A few days after that call, reporter Art Kevin visited the DiPierro's and found them "all shook up" by a visit from the FBI. According to Angelo, the G-men had "explained in great detail" the thoroughness of their investigation and its lone-gunman conclusion. Despite that finding, Angelo DiPierro "hinted [to Kevin] that he had some reason to believe there was some threat to his son's life." Vincent DiPierro later told author Philip Melanson that Los Angeles police had protected him "when his life was in danger" — but from whom, if Sirhan was the lone assassin?

Indeed, the FBI and local police seemed mutually intent on suppressing any hints of a conspiracy from the moment Kennedy was shot. Pantry witness Nina Rhodes told G-men that she heard 12 to 14 shots on the night of 4 June 1968, but her statement on file (shown to Rhodes for the first time in 1992) contained a false statement that she heard "eight distinct shots." Kennedy campaign volunteers Laverne Botting and Ethel Creehan saw a man

resembling Sirhan, accompanied by a woman and a second man, loitering about campaign headquarters on 30 May 1968. Both witnesses believed they could identify Sirhan if they saw him in person, but police refused to stage a lineup. Similarly, witness Albert LeBeau, manager of a restaurant where Kennedy's entourage dined on 20 May 1968, reported Sirhan and an unidentified woman attempting to join the party without the required tickets. LeBeau offered to identify Sirhan in person, but once again the offer was declined.

Reviewing FBI files on the Kennedy assassination was itself a challenge, since the Bureau seemed intent on keeping them secret. Researcher Bernard Fensterwald won release of 3,000 pages in 1975, using the Freedom of Information Act, but another decade passed before authors Philip Melanson and Greg Stone secured an additional 32,000 pages from Bureau headquarters. Even then it was impossible to question G-men who had filed (or falsified) the various reports, since all agents' names were deleted. Melanson and Stone appealed that censorship, but a federal court upheld it on grounds that the agents deserved "freedom from possible harassment."

**RICE, Elmer Leopold**—A native of New York City, born Elmer Reizenstein in 1892, Elmer Rice graduated from New York Law School in 1912 and thereafter practiced law sporadically while pursuing an alternate career in drama. His first play, *On Trial*, was produced in 1914. He won a Pulitzer Prize in 1929, for *Street Scene*, and afterward continued to distinguish himself with plays known for their socio-political content.

The Bureau of Investigation opened Rice's file in 1925, when he was identified as a contributing editor to *New Masses*. Four years later, memos noted his name change and reported that "he has never to that time voted in any election." Sometimes referring to his birth name as an "alias," G-men monitored Rice's support for an injunction barring interference with a veteran's Hunger March on Washington (1932) and his alleged remark at Columbia University that "Russia is the only place where the theater is really important" (1934). By 1936, Rice was the New York regional director of the Federal Theatre Project, but he resigned in protest when the government forbade depiction of Ethiopia's invasion by Italian fascists. Rice was also deemed suspicious for joining such groups as the AMERICAN CIVIL LIBERTIES UNION, Russian War Relief, the National Council on Freedom from Censorship, and the Committee to Defend America by Aiding the Allies. In 1938, an anonymous witness before the HOUSE COMMITTEE ON UN-AMERICAN ACTIVITIES condemned Red influence on the Playwrights' Company and members like Rice, "about whose radicalism there can be little question."

FBI scrutiny of Rice continued during WORLD WAR II, while he served on the War Writers Board and as president of the AUTHORS LEAGUE OF AMERICA. He was specifically condemned in 1942, with other League members, for public references to "winning the war at home." It was enough to rate a listing of "Internal Security — C" (for Communist) on Rice's file and to list him for CUSTODIAL DETENTION. Two years later, a "security-type investigation" by the New York field office judged Rice "A trifle to the left, recently a liberal, never orthodox in his radicalism, inclined more toward those who have renounced the revolutionary attitude in favor of one more moderate to our native tradition, a persistent experimentalist, and revolutionist in things pertaining to the arts and theater. He has stated that he is not a Communist and considers them a pretty futile, feeble people. He is, by his own statement, left wing, not a Communist, but a Socialist since he was eighteen. Rice had been openly critical of the Russian-German nonaggression pact and the Soviet mass executions. He is a strong supporter of all things anti-Fascist." (The same report also noted of Rice: "Wears glasses, Jewish appearing features.")

The post-war Red scare showcased Rice's opposition to censorship. He withdrew a play from television production after learning that the primary sponsor screened writers through the far-right publication *Red Channels*, and in 1951 Rice led a committee of the Authors League that publicized network blacklisting. A year later, the FBI opened its second "security-type investigation" of Rice, noting for the record that he "always wears glasses," adding to his file an anonymous letter that declared the Authors League "Communist infiltrated, but not Communist dominated." Rice survived the Red panic with his career intact and died in 1967. Twenty years later, 46 heavily censored pages of his dossier were released to author Herbert Mitgang under the FREEDOM OF INFORMATION ACT. A 10-page report from the CENTRAL INTELLIGENCE AGENCY was withheld in the interest of "national defense or foreign policy," along with a report from the OFFICE OF STRATEGIC SERVICES curiously dated 17 April 1957 (12 years after the OSS ceased to exist).

**RICHARDSON, Elliot Lee**— A Boston native, born 20 July 1920, served in the Army during WORLD WAR II and practiced law prior to entering government service. Over time he variously served as U.S. district attorney for Massachusetts (1959-61), lieutenant governor (1965-67) and state attorney general (1967-69). Richardson resigned the latter office to join President RICHARD NIXON'S cabinet where he served first as Secretary of Health, Education and Welfare (1970-73), then briefly as Secretary of Defense (1973). On 25 May 1973 he was named attorney general, replacing RICHARD KLEINDIENST after Kleindienst was tainted by the widening WATERGATE SCANDAL.

Richardson's tenure at the JUSTICE DEPARTMENT was brief. On the day of his appointment, he named Archibald Cox as special prosecutor to probe Watergate. That move caused immediate tension between Richardson and the White House, but he tried to proceed despite obstructions from Nixon and White House chief of staff Alexander Haig. Under pressure to fire Cox, Richardson himself resigned on 20 October 1973. His legacy, in terms of the FBI, was a July 1973 EXECUTIVE ORDER authorizing historical researchers to peruse Bureau files more than 15 years old. Richardson later served President GERALD FORD as ambassador to Great Britain (1975-76), secretary of commerce (1976-77) and ambassador at large (1977). His U.S. Senate race in 1984 was unsuccessful, but he received a Presidential Medal of Freedom in 1999. Richardson died of a stroke on 31 December 1999.

**RICHEY, Lawrence**— Described by author DON WHITEHEAD as "a mystical and even sinister figure" with "a special gift for turn-

ing up embarrassing tidbits about political figures," Lawrence Richey began his career with the U.S. SECRET SERVICE at age 14. The circumstances were peculiar — Richey spied a gang of counterfeiters in action while peering through a basement window — but the T-men thought enough of him to use Richey for BREAK-INS and surveillance assignments where adult agents would have been too conspicuous. Added to the payroll full-time at 16, Richey later served as a bodyguard for President THEODORE ROOSEVELT five years later, and he was one of the Treasury agents "loaned" to Roosevelt's JUSTICE DEPARTMENT before Congress banned that practice in 1907.

Upon retirement from the Secret Service, Richey formed his own private detective agency. The date of his first meeting with J. EDGAR HOOVER is uncertain, but we know that Richey belonged to the same Masonic lodge as Hoover, in Washington, D.C.; they were also fellow members of the University Club. During WORLD WAR I Richey met U.S. Food Administrator HERBERT HOOVER and became his secretary, a position Richey maintained while Hoover was secretary of commerce (1921-28) and president of the U.S. (1929-33). In May 1924 Richey recommended J. Edgar Hoover to Attorney General HARLAN STONE, a replacement for disgraced Bureau director WILLIAM BURNS. Stone took Richey's advice, thus prompting author J.R. Nash to call Richey "the most important friend J. Edgar Hoover ever had."

That friendship would not endure, however. Under President Hoover, Richey led a "dirty tricks" department that prefigured later abuses orchestrated by RICHARD NIXON and his White House aides in the WATERGATE SCANDAL. Unlike Nixon and company, however, Richey managed to keep most of his illicit activities secret. (The burglary of Democratic Party headquarters in New York City which Richey ordered in June 1930 was not revealed until 1983.) Richey kept a "black list" of President Hoover's enemies marked for surveillance, and while he apparently borrowed G-men to spy on those targets occasionally, Richey also had friends in the Secret Service and in the murky world of "private eyes."

FRANKLIN ROOSEVELT had occupied the White House by April 1933, when Attorney General HOMER CUMMINGS warned J. Edgar Hoover that Richey was running a spy operation from Washington's Shoreham Hotel, "assembling information that could be used against the private and official lives of public officials connected with the Democratic administration." Hoover promised "an appropriate investigation," but the results are unknown. Seven years later, in July 1940, the STATE DEPARTMENT asked Hoover to determine whether Richey and his ex-president boss had sent "certain cablegrams" to French officials in the wake of France's recent surrender to ADOLF HITLER. G-men examined recent trans-Atlantic cable traffic, but their search "failed to disclose that any such messages were sent." Richey remained active in politics until 1949; he died in 1960, at age 74.

**ROBIDEAU, Robert** *see* **Butler, Darelle**

**ROEMER, William, Jr.**— Born in August 1916, William Roemer, Jr., earned his bachelor's degree from Notre Dame University before joining the U.S. Marine Corps for service in WORLD WAR II.

Back in civilian life, he returned to Notre Dame and completed legal studies there in 1950. He joined the FBI in 1952 and was assigned to the Chicago field office, where he remained until 1978. After 1957 Roemer worked full-time on the Bureau's "TOP HOODLUM" PROGRAM and other details pertaining to ORGANIZED CRIME. Remembered as "one of the first agents to put a WIRETAP in hoodlum headquarters," he also pioneered the lock-step surveillance that prompted Chicago mobster SAM GIANCANA to sue the FBI in federal court. In 1975 Roemer was the primary case agent assigned to investigate the disappearance of former TEAMSTERS UNION president James Hoffa. Three years later he transferred to Tucson, Arizona and remained there after his 1980 retirement.

Upon leaving the FBI, Roemer established a private detective agency in Tucson and testified occasionally on behalf of reporters facing libel suits from organized crime figures. In 1989 Roemer published his first book, titled *Roemer: Man against the Mob*. Other true-crime volumes followed, including *War of the Godfathers* (1990), *The Enforcer* (1994) and *Accardo: The Genuine Godfather* (1995). Curiously, while marketed as a nonfiction account, *War of the Godfathers* included various fictional events, notably the 1986 "murder" of Las Vegas mobster Moe Dalitz (who actually died of natural causes in 1989). Roemer died of lung cancer in August 1996, two days short of his 70th birthday.

**ROETHKE, Theodore**— Born at Saginaw, Michigan on 25 May 1908, Roethke graduated from the University of Michigan in 1929 and went on to win numerous awards for his poetry, including two Guggenheim Fellowships (1945 and 1950), the Eunice Tietjiens Memorial Prize (1951), two Ford Foundation grants (1952 and 1958), a Pulitzer Prize (1954), a Fullbright grant (1955), the Bollingen Prize (1959), two National Book Awards (1959 and 1965), and the Shelley Memorial Award (1962).

The FBI opened its file on Roethke in 1941, with a notation that he suffered from "mental trouble." That observation was apparently born out by another report, in 1949, citing Roethke's numerous phone calls to the Seattle field office, observing that "he fancys [sic] himself as a highly placed espionage agent in close contact with Army and Navy intelligence." G-men described Roethke as "a near genius ... nationally known in educational fields," who strangely imagined "himself working for the Bureau."

Agents thereafter ignored Roethke until 1963, when an FBI employee reading *Harper's Bazaar* in a beauty salon discovered an article wherein Roethke and novelist NORMAN MAILER "expressed disparaging comments" about J. EDGAR HOOVER. Specifically, Roethke dubbed Hoover the "head of our thought police — a martinet, a preposterous figure, but not funny," while Mailer called Hoover "the worst celebrity in America." Hoover ordered his staff to "check the files" on both miscreants, receiving a summary that branded Roethke "an ardent pacifist" and "a mental defective" who "at one time ... was placed in a local sanitarium for the insane." Before Hoover had a chance to use the information, Roethke died at Bainbridge Island, Washington, on 1 August 1963.

**ROGERS, William Pierce**— A native of Norfolk, New York,

born 23 June 1913, William Rogers served in the U.S. Navy during WORLD WAR II and afterward practiced law until he was recruited for the JUSTICE DEPARTMENT by President DWIGHT EISENHOWER. Rogers initially served as a deputy to Attorney General HERBERT BROWNELL, and in that capacity issued an order that curtailed illegal leakage of FBI FILES to the Red-hunting SENATE INTERNAL SECURITY SUBCOMMITTEE (SISS). Rogers required that G-men limit their assistance to "public source" material, but Director J. EDGAR HOOVER was not so easily foiled. Days later, in early 1955, Hoover inaugurated an "informal" liaison with the SISS, whereby trusted aides were privately briefed in defiance of Rogers and without his knowledge.

Rogers replaced Brownell as attorney general on 8 November 1957 and held that post until President JOHN KENNEDY was inaugurated in January 1961. Like Brownell before him, Rogers granted Hoover virtual autonomy to choose his targets and pursue them by any means he deemed fitting. In fairness to Rogers, he apparently knew little or nothing of the FBI's illegal BREAK-INS, BUGGING and WIRETAPPING during his tenure, since Hoover made no effort to seek advance approval for such actions. Instead, Hoover decided on his own that Brownell's May 1954 authorization for wiretaps in cases of national security actually "covered both Security and Criminal matters." With that problem thus resolved, Hoover reported that he enjoyed a "very close" relationship with Rogers, often dining with his nominal superior and joining Rogers for Christmas vacations in Miami Beach. Rogers, for his part, seemed to have no qualms about FBI DOMESTIC SURVEILLANCE. Discussing Hoover's reputation for political blackmail, Rogers told author Ovid Demaris in 1974:

> I think that's an overpublicized concept. I don't know many persons who are fearful about disclosures of their files. You have fear of your FBI file? It never occurred to me. I can't think of anyone in my acquaintanceship who's been worried about his FBI file. Certainly the idea that Congress supported Hoover and the FBI so wholeheartedly was because they feared disclosure of their files is nonsense.

That view seems naïve in retrospect, all the more so after revelation of the fact that Hoover sabotaged Rogers's nomination to the U.S. SUPREME COURT in 1969, persuading President RICHARD NIXON to choose Warren Burger instead. Rogers served Nixon as secretary of state from January 1969 until September 1973, when the heat from the worsening WATERGATE SCANDAL prompted him to resign, taking with him a Presidential Medal of Freedom. Rogers died at Bethesda, Maryland on 2 January 2001.

**ROLEY, Susan Lynn**— A native of Long Beach, California, born 13 May 1947, Susan Roley was one of two women (with JOANNE MISKO) appointed to serve as FBI agents shortly after the death of Director J. EDGAR HOOVER. Prior to joining the Bureau, Roley earned a degree in history from California State College, Fullerton in 1968 and thereafter joined the U.S. Marine Corps. She was discharged as a first lieutenant on 14 July 1972, and Acting Director L. PATRICK GRAY installed her as a special agent three days later, apparently waiving standard instruction at the FBI ACAD-

EMY. Roley remained with the Bureau for seven years, then resigned in 1979 to join a private security firm in Washington, the Defense Investigative Agency.

**ROONEY, John James**— A Brooklyn native, born 29 November 1903, John Rooney was elected to the U.S. House of Representatives in 1944 and served for the next 30 years. He became chairman of the critical House Appropriations Committee, and thus emerged as one of J. Edgar Hoover's most prized congressional allies. Rooney was fond of boasting that he never cut a penny from one of Hoover's budget proposals, and that he sometimes gave the Bureau more money than Hoover requested.

Hoover's annual appearances before Rooney's committee were a veritable love fest. Rooney's praise for Hoover in 1957 provides a typical example.

> We are delighted that you have dealt so successfully with the Communist menace. I do not know what we would have done in this country if it had not been for the FBI. Your foresightedness and efforts certainly reflect upon you and the personnel of your agency who have been persistent in combating those elements that would undermine or threaten our internal security. In the absence of your Bureau, the goal sought by these subversive elements could have well been achieved in this Nation.

Hoover, for his part, used the committee as a forum for promoting the FBI, lambasting his enemies, and floating conspiracy theories (which inevitably dovetailed with the FBI's request for extra cash). In 1964, stung by revelations of Mafia INFORMANT Joe Valachi, Hoover assured Rooney's panel that Valachi's testimony included "very little ... that [we] have not known for years." Four years later, after the KERNER COMMISSION blamed ghetto rioting on racism, Hoover warned the committee against "troublemakers, extremists, and ... subversive groups who attempt to inject themselves into the turmoil once it has started." In 1971, after Hoover branded ex–Attorney General RAMSEY CLARK "a jellyfish," Rooney chimed in to describe Clark's conduct as "a little sickening." (Clark returned the favor, dubbing Rooney "a terrible restraint on a good Department of Justice.") Hoover's last appearance before the committee, two months before his death, featured florid warnings against women's liberation, gay activists, the Black Liberation Army and the WEATHER UNDERGROUND.

Rooney's payoff for supporting Hoover through the years included free access to FBI surveillance tapes (including one alleged to reveal a HOMOSEXUAL relationship between Dr. MARTIN LUTHER KING, JR., and associate RALPH ABERNATHY), and covert support against political opponents. In Rooney's last primary race (1972), Hoover ordered an investigation of opponent Allard Lowenstein's political and personal activities, producing derogatory material that included allegations of closet homosexuality. Rooney won that election, and his eulogy for Hoover in the House cast the late FBI director as a veritable saint. Rooney died in Washington three years later, on 26 October 1975.

**ROOSEVELT, Anna Eleanor**— Born in New York City on 11 October 1884, a niece of future president THEODORE ROOSEVELT,

Eleanor Roosevelt married fourth cousin FRANKLIN ROOSEVELT in 1905 and thus became America's First Lady when her husband was elected president in 1932. Known as a liberal social activist, concerned for the poor and various minorities, Eleanor Roosevelt soon found herself on a collision course with ultra-conservative FBI Director J. EDGAR HOOVER. Ironically, their first clash (and the 20-year Hoover vendetta that followed) was set in motion by President Roosevelt's secret orders authorizing widespread FBI DOMESTIC SURVEILLANCE.

In January 1941 Mrs. Roosevelt learned that G-men had conducted an investigation of her longtime social secretary, Edith Helm. She complained to Hoover and received a note assuring her that if the Bureau had known Helm's identity "the inquiry would not have been initiated." Two days later, Mrs. Roosevelt wrote Hoover again, this time reporting the investigation of another aide, Malvina Thompson. "I cannot help deeply resenting the action in these two cases," she wrote, "and if you have done this type of investigation of other people, I do not wonder that we are beginning to get an extremely jittery population." In fact, she told Hoover in closing, "This type of investigation seems to me to smack too much of the Gestapo methods."

Never one to forget or forgive an insult, Hoover spent the next two decades stalking and maligning Mrs. Roosevelt at every opportunity. Assistant Directors EDWARD TAMM and WILLIAM SULLIVAN later denied that Mrs. Roosevelt was "the subject" of an FBI investigation, claiming instead that information on her private life found its way into FBI FILES serendipitously, through investigation of others. Be that as it may, Hoover amassed fat dossiers on the First Lady and never hesitated to leak derogatory material where it would do the most harm. As late as 1960, in casual conversation with rookie G-man GORDON LIDDY, Hoover launched into a tirade describing Mrs. Roosevelt as the "most dangerous enemy of the Bureau." But for his close friendship with FDR, Hoover declared she "might well have succeeded in interfering with the Bureau's ability to contain the Communist menace in the United States."

In fact, a month after their first clash, Mrs. Roosevelt persuaded Attorney General ROBERT JACKSON to ban FBI investigations of any government employees outside the JUSTICE DEPARTMENT. Hoover suffered the restriction until September 1941, when Jackson was replaced by FRANCIS BIDDLE. Before year's end he had convinced Biddle that the background checks were essential to national security and the process was resumed with approval from President Roosevelt. In January 1942 G-men staged a BREAK-IN at the New York office of the American Youth Congress, snapping photos of Mrs. Roosevelt's correspondence with AYC leaders. The material was rushed to Washington, where Hoover ordered it "carefully reviewed and analyzed." Nine months later, Hoover's racism was aroused by results of an FBI "survey concerning foreign inspired agitation among the Negroes in this country," specifically "concerning the formation of Eleanor or Eleanor Roosevelt Clubs among the Negroes." A memo from Assistant Director D. Milton Ladd warned Hoover:

> Such incidents as Negro maids allegedly demanding their own terms for working and at the same time stating they were mem-

bers of an Eleanor Roosevelt Club are typical of the rumors reported to the Savannah Field Division. No substantiating information, however, has been received concerning these rumors. However, it is stated that complaints are received that the cause of the agitation among the Negroes in this area is largely attributed to the encouragement given Negroes by Mrs. Roosevelt. The Birmingham Field Division has received a report ... that attempts in that area are being made to form Eleanor Clubs by a strange white man and a large Negro organizer traveling in an automobile. The unverified information indicates that only female domestics are desired for membership. The alleged slogan of the club is "A White Woman in the Kitchen by Christmas" inferring [sic] that Negroes work only part of the day. Similar clubs are claimed to be in operation in other cities in Alabama.

Galvanized by the nightmare of black maids seeking more time off, Hoover ordered G-men throughout Dixie to pursue evidence of the "Eleanor Clubs," but late October brought only Ladd's admission that the "inquiries have met with negative results." Two months later, agents burglarized offices of the International Students Service, retrieving information that "Mrs. Roosevelt was always on hand to use her personal influence on those who threatened to oppose openly the Great Power line." Once, she allegedly intervened to prevent a Lithuanian student from denouncing "Russian aggression and atrocities in Lithuania." (Hoover's marginal note read: "This is nauseating.") In early 1943 Mrs. Roosevelt inflamed the director once more, with an accusation that G-men and the HOUSE COMMITTEE ON UN-AMERICAN ACTIVITIES were "hounding" veterans of the ABRAHAM LINCOLN BRIGADE.

Over time, Hoover convinced himself (on the flimsiest of "evidence") that Mrs. Roosevelt was a promiscuous bisexual whose lovers included high-ranking members of the COMMUNIST PARTY. One suspect was Joseph Lash, an officer of the American Student Union who met Mrs. Roosevelt in November 1939. A liberal journalist who once described himself as "practically a [CP] member" in his youth, Lash was drafted by the Army in April 1942 and thus fell under scrutiny by agents of military intelligence. They tracked him to a Chicago hotel in March 1943, where Lash met privately with Mrs. Roosevelt and later entertained a woman named Trude Pratt. Eavesdropping via WIRETAPS and BUGGING devices, the Army spies somehow convinced themselves that the weekend tryst "indicate[d] a gigantic conspiracy participated in not only by Subject and Trude Pratt but also by E.R., [Agriculture Secretary HENRY] WALLACE, [Treasury Secretary Henry] Morgenthau, etc."

When Army spokesmen reported the "conspiracy" to President Roosevelt, he transferred or demoted most of those involved, shipped Lash to the Pacific theater and ordered all files on his wife destroyed. Lash later reported, in *Love Eleanor* (1982), that FDR demanded the "dismemberment of counterintelligence corps, G-2" and decreed that "anyone who knew about this case should be immediately relieved of his duties and sent to the South Pacific for action against the Japs until they were killed." Instead of burning their files, however, Army intelligence agents passed them to Hoover at FBI HEADQUARTERS, where Hoover declared that the Chicago tapes "indicated quite clearly that Mrs. Roosevelt and Lash engaged in sexual intercourse."

Unable to challenge FDR's authority, Hoover stored the material for future use. In early 1953, when President DWIGHT EISENHOWER considered naming Mrs. Roosevelt as a U.S. delegate to the United Nations, Assistant Director LOUIS NICHOLS briefed White House aides on the "Lash affair" and thus scuttled the nomination. A year later, Hoover had Nichols carry the word to Eisenhower himself, on grounds that "Joe Lash is working for the *New York Post* which has been exceedingly critical of the President as well as of us." Around the same time, Hoover obtained from comedian W.C. FIELDS certain obscene drawings of Mrs. Roosevelt which became a prized exhibit for select visitors to Hoover's home. The malicious slurs continued until Mrs. Roosevelt's death, in New York City, on 7 November 1962.

**ROOSEVELT, Franklin Delano**—Born at Hyde Park, New York on 30 January 1882, Franklin Roosevelt was a fourth cousin (once removed) and a nephew by marriage of President THEODORE ROOSEVELT. Drawn irresistibly to politics, he served in the New York state senate (1911-13) and was an unsuccessful Democratic candidate for vice president in 1920. Roosevelt contracted polio in August 1921, and while his legs were paralyzed thereafter, the disability did not keep him from seeking public office. He served as governor of New York (1929-33) and was elected president of the U.S. for the first time in November 1932. Occupying the White House during the Great Depression and most of WORLD WAR II, he rallied the nation like no chief executive before or since and was the country's only four-term president.

Conflicting stories describe a curious relationship between Roosevelt and FBI Director J. EDGAR HOOVER. While Assistant Director EDWARD TAMM described the men as "very, very friendly," Roosevelt's son Elliot later recalled that "Father dealt with the bullet-headed boss at arm's length. He recognized [Hoover's] efficiency ... though he suspected that in many matters Hoover was not a member of the administration team." That was certainly true, since Hoover regarded the New Deal as a step toward Socialism and he personally despised First Lady ELEANOR ROOSEVELT. Still, Hoover was amenable to White House requests for investigation of Roosevelt's political opponents—and occasional allies, as well. Furthermore, Hoover owed the dramatic expansion of FBI DOMESTIC SURVEILLANCE to an order he received from Roosevelt in 1936.

Specifically, Roosevelt met with Hoover at the White House on 24 August 1936 to discuss investigation of America's enemies. Only Hoover's notes on the meeting remain, asserting that Roosevelt sought "a broad picture" of "subversive activities in the United States, particularly Fascism and Communism." Elaborating (and perhaps fabricating), Hoover added that Roosevelt wanted information on any groups that might "affect the economic and political activity of the country as a whole." Hoover demurred, claiming the FBI had no authority for such investigations (though G-men had pursued dissenters virtually from the Bureau's creation in 1908). Rather than disappoint FDR, Hoover noted that current legislation permitted such inquiries if they were requested by the STATE DEPARTMENT. Accordingly, Hoover and Roosevelt met with Secretary of State Cordell Hull on 25 August and explained the problem, whereupon Hull reportedly told Hoover, "Go ahead and investigate the hell out of those cocksuckers."

Once empowered to act (albeit with dubious legal authority), Hoover swiftly expanded the scope of his investigation. On 5 September 1936 he ordered all FBI field offices to seek information "from all possible sources" concerning Reds, Fascists and "representatives or advocates of other organizations or groups advocating the overthrow or replacement of the Government of the United States by illegal methods." Ed Tamm was ordered to list "general classifications" of targets, which clearly broadened the scope of investigation beyond anything Roosevelt or Hull had imagined. Tamm's list included:

> Maritime Industry, Government affairs, steel industry, coal industry, newspaper field, clothing, garment and fur industry, general strike activities, Armed Forces, educational institutions, general activities — Communist and Affiliated Organizations, Fascisti, anti- Fascisti movements, and activities of Organized Labor organizations.

Hoover praised the all-inclusive list as a "good beginning" and set out to investigate America at large, belatedly informing Attorney General HOMER CUMMINGS of his new crusade on 10 September 1936. That memo to Cummings included a lie, claiming that Roosevelt had issued his order on 1 September, rather than 24 August. The attorney general, ever trusting, "verbally directed" Hoover to proceed "in a most discreet and confidential manner." Two years later, on 2 November 1938, Roosevelt granted the FBI $150,000 in discretionary funds to continue its domestic spying (albeit without knowledge that the targets now included Eleanor Roosevelt), and on 29 June 1939 the president gave Hoover sole authority to coordinate domestic intelligence. Their political differences aside, Hoover had much to thank Roosevelt for by the time the president died, from a stroke, on 12 April 1945.

**ROOSEVELT, Theodore**— A New York native, born in 1858, Theodore Roosevelt served as New York City's police commissioner (1895-97), assistant secretary of the navy (1897-98) and governor of New York (1899-1901) before he was elected vice president in 1900. Six months after taking office, on 14 September 1901, he became president in the wake of William McKinley's assassination by the ANARCHIST Leon Czolgosz.

It was during Roosevelt's last year in office, in June 1908, that Attorney General CHARLES BONAPARTE defied Congress to create a detective force within the JUSTICE DEPARTMENT. Roosevelt approved the unit's creation a month later, and STANLEY FINCH was appointed to serve as its first commander. Known simply as the "special agent force" during its first nine months of operation, the future FBI began with 34 agents and no support staff, specifically empowered to investigate crimes committed on U.S. government property and violations of anti-trust laws. The first federal NARCOTICS prohibition act was passed in February 1909, a month before Roosevelt left office, but members of the new detective squad played no role in its enforcement. The "special agents" were also barred (at least on paper) from carrying firearms or making arrests.

**ROSENBERG, Julius and Ethel**— The Cold War's most sensational ESPIONAGE case began in September 1945, when cipher clerk Igor Gouzenko defected from the Soviet embassy in Ottawa, Canada. Gouzenko brought with him a cache of documents and names of numerous Russian agents: 21 were ultimately prosecuted, nine of them convicted; 50 more resigned from various government posts or were transferred to nonsensitive positions. While searching the home of suspect Israel Halperin, officers of the Royal Canadian Mounted Police discovered a notebook containing the name and address of Klaus Fuchs, a German physicist living in Edinburgh, Scotland. Copies of the notebook were dispatched to FBI HEADQUARTERS and British Intelligence, but four years would pass before they recognized Fuchs as a spy.

Author DON WHITEHEAD, in *The FBI Story* (1956) presents a straightforward account of how the case unraveled: G-men followed the spy trail from Fuchs to a Philadelphia chemist, Harry Gold, and on from there to David Greenglass, a 28-year-old soldier assigned to the Los Alamos nuclear test site. Greenglass, in turn, implicated his wife Ruth, along with his sister Ethel and her husband, Julius Rosenberg. Julius, Greenglass insisted, was the head of a vast Russian spy ring inside the U.S.

Whitehead's version of events was not entirely accurate, however. Greenglass was initially suspected of stealing uranium samples — apparently a common pastime for soldiers at Los Alamos — and he confessed that relatively petty crime one day *before* Klaus Fuchs named Harry Gold as his American contact. FBI agents showed Greenglass's photo to Gold by pure chance, mixed with pictures of other Los Alamos servicemen, and they were surprised when Gold picked him out as a spy. Greenglass subsequently fingered Julius Rosenberg as the agent who seduced him into treason, but he staunchly denied Ethel's involvement until 25 February 1951, ten days before commencement of her trial.

G-men, meanwhile, were busy building their case. They arrested Julius Rosenberg on 17 July 1950, and Assistant Director Alan Belmont issued a memo the same afternoon, urging the Bureau to "consider every possible means to bring pressure on Rosenberg to make him talk ... including careful study of Ethel Rosenberg, in order that charges may be placed against her, if possible." Two days later, Director J. EDGAR HOOVER advised Attorney General J. HOWARD MCGRATH that "There is no question that if Julius Rosenberg would furnish the details of his extensive espionage activities it would be possible to proceed against other individuals." Hoover added that "proceeding against his wife might serve as a lever in this matter."

The only stumbling block to that scenario was a total lack of evidence against Ethel Rosenberg. David Greenglass had told G-men that he passed atomic data to Julius on a New York street, and that Ethel had no knowledge of her husband's covert activity. Still, agents arrested her on 11 August 1950 and she was held, like her husband, in lieu of $100,000 bond.

Once committed to the FRAME-UP, authorities spared no energy in concocting their case. Twenty high-ranking officials met to discuss the matter on 8 February 1951, with JUSTICE DEPARTMENT spokesman Myles Lane confessing for the record that his case against Ethel was "not too strong." Still, he declared, it was "very important that she be convicted too and given a stiff sentence." Lane sought out "the strongest judge possible" to hear the case, finally settling on Irving Kaufman, a former U.S. attorney and aide to Attorney General TOM CLARK who reportedly "worshipped J. Edgar Hoover."

David Greenglass made the case for his jailers in late February, when he changed his story to implicate Ethel. Forgetting his original tale of streetcorner meetings with Julius, Greenglass now "remembered" sessions at his sister's apartment, where she watched him pass notes to Julius and afterward "typed them up" in the bedroom. Agents granted Greenglass a private meeting with Harry Gold, to coordinate their statements, and both men promptly turned state's evidence against the Rosenbergs, thereby escaping the electric chair. Ruth Greenglass also joined the prosecution team, contradicting her previous statements to support David's newfound memories.

A sideshow to the main event was acted out by MORRIS ERNST, legal counsel for the AMERICAN CIVIL LIBERTIES UNION (and a covert FBI INFORMANT). A memo to Hoover from Assistant to the Director LOUIS NICHOLS advised that Ernst had volunteered to represent the Rosenbergs "on one ground only, namely, that he could make a contribution" to the prosecution! As explained by Nichols, Ernst thought "this would be a terrific story and probably would be most helpful to the Bureau." As luck would have it, the Rosenberg's declined Ernst's "help"—and fared even worse with another attorney.

The Rosenbergs and codefendant Morton Sobell (a researcher at General Electric Laboratories) faced trial for their lives on 6 March 1951. Defense attorney Emanuel Block refused to cross-examine Harry Gold, then tackled David and Ruth Greenglass without knowledge of their earlier conflicting statements. Julius and Ethel Rosenberg were the only defense witnesses; both denied spying for Russia, then Julius torpedoed their case by pleading the Fifth Amendment (on Block's advice) to questions concerning his alleged Communist ties. The guilty verdicts, delivered on 29 March 1951, were a foregone conclusion.

So far, all had gone as planned from FBI headquarters, but the psychodrama was not finished yet. Hoover addressed another letter to Attorney General McGrath on 2 April 1951, recommending death for Julius Rosenberg and Sobell, with 30 years' imprisonment for Ethel. (Gold and Greenglass had been promised terms of 30 and 15 years, respectively.) In fact, it would appear in retrospect that no one in the Bureau anticipated executions would be carried out. The electric chair was simply one more "lever," intended to squeeze names and secrets out of Julius Rosenberg. As retired Hoover aide Robert Lamphere confessed in June 1978, "We didn't want them to die. We wanted them to talk."

Judge Kaufman had other ideas. On 5 April 1951 he condemned both Rosenbergs and sentenced Sobell to 30 years in prison. All appeals were denied, and the double execution was scheduled for 18 June 1953. Six G-men made the trip to Sing Sing Prison that morning, setting up shop in two cells on death row, still hopeful that Julius might crack. They waited in vain, however, and the executions were carried out on schedule.

**ROSENSTIEL, Lewis Solon**—A self-made millionaire who earned his initial fortune as a PROHIBITION-era bootlegger, Lewis Rosenstiel hatched plans to "go legit" while sale of alcoholic beverages was still illegal. He organized the Schenley Products Company in 1927, purchasing a distillery and 4,000 barrels of outlawed whiskey; over the next three years he bought another 240,000 cases of liquor from various sources. On 14 November 1933, Rosenstiel joined New York mobster John Torrio (mentor of AL CAPONE), to create the Prendergast-Davies corporation. With the advent of Repeal one month later, Rosenstiel and Torrio unleashed a flood of alcohol from coast to coast, and reaped more millions for their effort.

It is unclear precisely when Rosenstiel forged his enduring friendship with J. EDGAR HOOVER, but the FBI director was surely aware of Rosenstiel's political activity by 1948, when Rosenstiel joined FBI media ally GEORGE SOKOLSKY to create the American Jewish League Against Communism. Sokolsky introduced Rosenstiel to "gangbuster" THOMAS DEWEY, a self-described "very good friend" of Rosenstiel who became Schenley's chief counsel after he retired from politics. Rosenstiel was also friendly with G-man turned senator THOMAS DODD, and he funded the campaigns of yet another Hoover ally, Red-hunting Senator JOSEPH MCCARTHY.

Hoover's friendship with Rosenstiel—as with CLINT MURCHISON and other wealthy men—proved beneficial to both parties. In the 1950s, Rosenstiel purchased 25,000 copies of DON WHITEHEAD'S *The FBI Story* and Hoover's ghostwritten *Masters of Deceit*, thereby placing both books on the best-seller list. In 1965 he donated $50,000 to the J. EDGAR HOOVER FOUNDATION; three years later, Rosenstiel gave the foundation $1 million in bonds of the Glen Alden Corporation (successor to Schenley Industries). Rosenstiel also purchased most of the books shelved in the J. Edgar Hoover Library, at Gettysburg's Freedom Foundation Center. Assistant to the Director LOUIS NICHOLS retired to join Rosenstiel's staff in 1957, and Hoover welcomed Rosenstiel to FBI HEADQUARTERS in 1958, while Congress was debating repeal of an "excessive" tax on whiskey.

Lou Nichols, serving Rosenstiel in the same public relations capacity he had performed as chief of the FBI's CRIME RECORDS DIVISION, long (and falsely) denied that Hoover and Rosenstiel knew one another. He also went to bat for Rosenstiel in 1965, ironically calling for a total ban on WIRETAPPING in his testimony before Sen. Edward Long's committee probing invasions of privacy by the FBI and the INTERNAL REVENUE SERVICE. Five years later, Nichols teamed with attorney ROY COHN to defend Rosenstiel's reputation before the New York Joint Legislative Committee on Crime. Under oath, Nichols proclaimed that he had "found no information, much less credible evidence, of Mr. Rosenstiel's alignment with the underworld." In fact, he declared, Rosenstiel had "never, directly or indirectly, had any dealings or associations with Meyer Lansky, Frank Costello, or any other underworld character." Susan Rosenstiel, lately divorced, told a very different story, recalling visits to Cuba where Lansky and other mobsters greeted her husband as a longtime friend, habitually referring to him as "Supreme Commander." Rosenstiel, in turn, had described Lansky and Costello to Susan as "very good friends of his."

Long after Rosenstiel's death, Susan surfaced again with another story, this time telling author Anthony Summers that her husband and Hoover had cavorted together at HOMOSEXUAL orgies, including one soiree in New York where Hoover appeared in "a fluffy black dress," introduced to Susan by Roy Cohn as "Mary." Mrs. Rosenstiel also reported a second sighting of Hoover in drag, "dressed like an old flapper, like you see on tintypes." Retired assistant director CARTHA DELOACH, refuting those stories in his 1995 memoirs, reports that Susan Rosenstiel was briefly jailed for perjury during her bitter divorce, suggesting that "apparently she blamed Hoover for damaging information her husband obtained concerning her activities, which weighed against her in court."

**ROTTON, Alan H.**—Alan Rotton was assigned to the Bureau's Kansas City field office in 1979, when fellow agents discovered his involvement with a confidential INFORMANT who stole shipments of air conditioners, automobile tires and bicycles from railroad boxcars. Surveillance and WIRETAPS revealed that Rotton's partner, G-man Stephen S. Travis, also profited from the hijacking. Following their indictments in October 1979, both agents were fired. Rotton committed suicide two days later. Travis pled guilty to theft charges in January 1980 and received a four-year prison term.

**ROWE, Gary Thomas, Jr.**—A native Savannah, Georgia, born in 1933, Gary Rowe settled in Birmingham as a young man and soon developed a fixation on police work. He loved spending time with policemen, preferably in bars, and in September 1956 he was fined $30 for impersonating an officer. Birmingham FBI agent-in-charge CLARENCE KELLEY took advantage of Rowe's obsession, recruiting him as an INFORMANT on 18 April 1960. Specifically, the Bureau wanted information on the KU KLUX KLAN, which Rowe joined on 23 June 1960. Less than two months later, on 18 August, he was appointed "Nighthawk-in-Chief" for Birmingham's Eastview klavern, one of Alabama's most violent Klan chapters. By November 1960 Rowe's file acknowledged information of "unusual value," including reports on Klan ties to law enforcement and an Alabama congressman.

In April 1961 Rowe graduated to "missionary work," the Klan euphemism for beatings, BOMBINGS and other acts of TERRORISM. Agent-in-charge Thomas Jenkins knew of Rowe's assignment but screened his file to delete any mention of criminal activities. A month later Rowe alerted G-men to a plot hatched by Birmingham police commissioner EUGENE ("BULL") CONNOR, wherein Klansmen would be granted 15 minutes to assault CIVIL RIGHTS workers participating in desegregated "FREEDOM RIDES." FBI HEADQUARTERS withheld that information from Attorney General ROBERT KENNEDY and passed a copy of the Freedom Ride itinerary to a Birmingham detective known for his links to the Klan. Rowe participated in beatings of demonstrators on 14 May 1961, but the action backfired when one of his victims stabbed Rowe in the neck with near-fatal results. That incident too was erased from his record, while Rowe received a $125 bonus from his FBI handlers.

In September 1963 Rowe was a suspect in the bombing of a black church that killed four young girls. G-men assigned to the "BAPBOM" case, fearful that Rowe might be fingered as one of the killers, warned him to stay clear of the crime scene for at least a week. When showing photographs of known Klansmen to neighborhood witnesses, agents omitted all photos of Rowe and his automobile. Their worries may well have been justified, since Rowe failed two polygraph tests on the bombing and told Birmingham detective W.W. Self, "They will never solve the Sixteenth Street church bombing because me and another guy handled it."

In 1964, when the FBI launched its illegal COINTELPRO campaign against various KKK factions, Rowe claims he was ordered to have sex with as many Klan wives as possible, as a means of disrupting the organization and sparking personal quarrels. While boasting of great success on the romantic front, Rowe is best known for his presence in a car with three other Klansmen on the night of 25 March 1965, when civil rights worker VIOLA LIUZZO was shot and killed in Lowndes County. Soon after the shooting, Rowe told Birmingham officers Lavaughn Coleman and Henry Snow that *he* had shot Liuzzo, explaining, "We had to burn a whore." That story soon changed, however, when Rowe emerged as the key prosecution witness against fellow Klansmen Collie Wilkins, William Eaton and Eugene Thomas.

The Liuzzo trials in 1965-66 exposed Rowe as an FBI informant and he vanished into the federal witness protection program. In 1975 he surfaced, masked for anonymity, to testify before the CHURCH COMMITTEE on his dealings with the FBI. An Alabama grand jury indicted Rowe for Liuzzo's murder in September 1978, but he never stood trial since the governor of his new home state refused extradition. By then, Rowe had achieved minor celebrity, accepting a $25,000 advance for his memoirs, *My Undercover Years with the Ku Klux Klan* (1976). The story was later filmed (and greatly fictionalized) as *Undercover with the KKK* (1978), with athlete-actor Don Meredith portraying Gary Rowe.

**ROWLEY, Coleen**—Iowa native Coleen Rowley earned her law degree from the University of Iowa at age 26, in 1980. She then joined the FBI and was initially assigned to ORGANIZED CRIME cases in the New York City field office. By 2001 she was settled in Minneapolis, a mother of four, employed as legal counsel for the Bureau and frequently quoted as a spokesperson for the local field office. Despite that semi-public role, Rowley kept a low profile for the most part—until May 2001, when she penned an explosive 13-page letter to Director ROBERT MUELLER, with copies addressed to members of the Senate Intelligence Community.

In sum, Rowley's letter charged that officials at FBI HEADQUARTERS had erected "roadblocks" to a Minneapolis investigation of TERRORIST suspect Zacarias Moussaoui, subsequently identified as a conspirator in the tragic SKYJACKINGS of 11 September 2001, and thereby allowed the attacks to proceed at a cost of some 3,500 American lives. Moussaoui was arrested by Minneapolis G-men in August 2001, while training at a Minnesota flight school, but headquarters refused to authorize a search warrant for his apartment and he was subsequently released. Frustrated agents who bypassed Washington to seek information on Moussaoui from the CENTRAL INTELLIGENCE AGENCY were reprimanded for their efforts, and Rowley further claimed that Director Mueller had attempted to conceal those facts from Congress and the media. Among her charges, the following stand out:

> It is obvious, from my firsthand knowledge of the events and the detailed documentation that exists, that the agents in Minneapolis who were closest to the action and in the best position to gauge the situation locally, did fully appreciate the terrorist risk/danger posed by Moussaoui and his possible co-conspirators even prior to September 11th. I think it's very hard for the FBI to offer the "20-20 hindsight" justification for its failure to act!
>
> Even after the attacks had begun, the [Washington supervisor] in question was still attempting to block the search of Moussaoui's computer, characterizing the World Trade Center attacks as a mere coincidence with (Minneapolis') prior suspicions about Moussaoui.
>
> The fact is that key FBI [headquarters] personnel whose jobs it was to assist and coordinate with field division agents on terrorism investigations and the obtaining and use of (classified search warrants) continued to almost inexplicably throw up roadblocks and undermine Minneapolis' by-now desperate efforts.
>
> When, in a desperate 11th-hour measure to bypass the FBI [headquarters] roadblock, the Minneapolis division (notified) the CIA's Counter Terrorism Center, FBI (headquarters) personnel actually chastised the Minneapolis agents for making the direct notification without their approval!
>
> Although I agree that it's very doubtful that the full scope of the [11 September] tragedy could have been prevented, it's at least possible we could have gotten lucky and uncovered one or two more of the terrorists in flight training prior to Sept. 11, just as Moussaoui was discovered, after making contact with his flight instructors.
>
> I know I shouldn't be flippant about this, but jokes were actually made that the key FBI personnel had to be spies or moles, like ROBERT HANSSEN, who were actually working for OSAMA BIN LADEN to have so undercut Minneapolis' effort.

Unable to conceal Rowley's complaints, Director Mueller admitted that the FBI would need a "different approach" to fighting terrorism in the future. Senator CHARLES GRASSLEY was more critical, telling reporters, "The FBI for too long has discouraged agents from using anything besides outdated tactics from the era of chasing Bonnie and Clyde."

Rowley repeated her charges in June 2002, before the Senate. "Mistakes are inevitable," she said, "but a distinction can and should be drawn between those mistakes made when trying to do the right thing and those mistakes ... due to selfish motives." While many proclaimed her a hero, there were others who questioned Rowley's loyalty to the FBI. Charles George, president of the SOCIETY OF FORMER SPECIAL AGENTS OF THE FBI, deemed Rowley's public statements "unthinkable" and compared her behavior to that of G-man Robert Hanssen, lately convicted of spying for Russia. The editors of *Time* magazine disagreed, naming Rowley and two corporate whistleblowers as that journal's "Persons of the Year" for 2002.

**ROYER, Jeffrey**—A former G-man who left the FBI in December 2001, 39-year-old Jeffrey Royer (born 26 November 1962) was subsequently indicted for his alleged role in a Wall Street insider trading conspiracy. Federal prosecutors claim that Royer provided confidential Bureau information to Amr Elgindy, described in media reports as a "self-styled Wall Street whistleblower and noted short seller of stocks." Elgindy himself was charged, on 24 May 2002, with being the mastermind of a conspiracy that involved Royer and another FBI agent, Lynn Wingate (placed on administrative leave pending disposition of charges filed against her). The three defendants were charged with conspiracy and obstruction of justice; Elgindy and two other defendants faced additional charges of extortion.

Royer and Wingate were arraigned in Brooklyn's federal court on 28 May 2002. At that hearing, U.S. Attorney Kenneth Breen requested that Royer be held without bond as a flight risk, partly due to information on "another subject matter" found during an FBI search of his home. Breen declined to elaborate publicly, but said the material included confidential data which Royer had no right to possess and that it might lead to "something more serious." Judge Raymond Dearie referred the bond issue to a special court reserved for classified information, and Royer remained at liberty for the moment, compelled to wear an electronic tracking device on his ankle. Elgindy was held without bond, while Agent Wingate was released on $100,000 bail pending trial. In a previous hearing, Breen suggested that Elgindy's efforts to liquidate his children's trust accounts on 10 September 2001 might indicate foreknowledge of TERRORIST attacks carried out the following day, but defense attorney Jeanne Knight dismissed the remark as an attempt to smear Elgindy (a naturalized U.S. citizen born in Egypt) with empty "terrorist innuendos." Despite their courtroom statements, prosecutors emphasize that indictments are merely accusations of criminal behavior and all defendants are presumed innocent until convicted at trial.

**RUBY, Jack**—Chicago native Jacob Rubinstein was born sometime in 1911. Various official records list eight different dates of birth, between 3 March and 23 June of that year, but no precise determination is possible, since Chicago did not require birth records prior to 1915. His parents separated in 1921 and finally divorced in 1937. Jacob apparently quit school at age 16, after completing eighth grade. Between 1937 and 1940 he worked as a LABOR UNION organizer in Chicago, allied with known members of ORGANIZED CRIME. The Army Air Force drafted Rubinstein in May 1943 and he was honorably discharged in February 1946, without seeing any foreign action during WORLD WAR II. Back in Chicago, he resumed his underworld contacts in 1946, then moved to Dallas, Texas the following year (shortly after he was questioned by agents from the FEDERAL BUREAU OF NARCOTICS).

In Dallas, Rubinstein legally changed his name to "Jack Ruby," operating various nightclubs heavily patronized by police officers. Ruby's partner in the Singapore Club was convicted of heroin trafficking in 1947, but investigation of Ruby produced no indictment. Despite his friendship with lawmen, Ruby still logged repeated arrests for disturbing the peace (February 1949), carrying a concealed weapon (July 1953), selling liquor after hours (December 1954), permitting dancing after hours (June 1959 and August 1960), assault (February 1963), and ignoring traffic tickets (March 1963). He was twice placed on six months' probation as a frequent traffic violator (1956 and 1959), and his liquor license was suspended six times between 1949 and 1961 on charges ranging from after-hours service to "moral turpitude." His last and most famous arrest occurred on 24 November 1963, when Ruby crept into the basement of the Dallas police station and murdered LEE HARVEY OSWALD, the alleged triggerman in the JFK ASSASSINATION.

In custody, Ruby declared that he shot Oswald out of sympathy for the widow of President JOHN KENNEDY, to spare her from testifying at Oswald's murder trial. A special investigative commission chaired by Chief Justice EARL WARREN accepted that motive (and ignored Ruby's plea for a hearing in Washington, where he promised to reveal evidence of a conspiracy). One matter that troubled the Warren Commission was a memo from FBI Director J. EDGAR HOOVER, dated 27 February 1964, admitting that FBI agents had contacted Ruby nine times in 1959, quizzing him for "knowledge of the criminal element in Dallas." Hoover asked the commission to keep that information secret, and Warren agreed. The panel's final report included no mention of Ruby's links to organized crime or his role as an FBI INFORMANT. Ruby received a death sentence for Oswald's murder in 1964 and died in prison three years later, apparently of cancer, with his case still on appeal.

## RUCKELSHAUS, William D.

**RUCKELSHAUS, William D.**—An Indiana native, born 24 July 1932, William Ruckelshaus graduated from Princeton University and Harvard Law School. In 1966 he was elected to the Indiana state legislature and became House majority leader, prompting an unsuccessful run for the U.S. Senate in 1968. President RICHARD NIXON named him assistant attorney general in charge of the JUSTICE DEPARTMENT's Civil Division, then tapped Ruckelshaus as the new Environmental Protection Agency's first administrator in December 1970. He held that post until 27 April 1973, when he replaced L. PATRICK GRAY as acting director of the FBI.

Bureau historian Robert Kessler reports that Ruckelshaus "had little interest" in the FBI and permitted Acting Associate Director W. MARK FELT to make most of the administrative decisions until Felt retired on 22 June 1973. Ruckelshaus left the Bureau 17 days later, replaced by Director CLARENCE KELLEY, and moved on to become Nixon's deputy attorney general under ELLIOT RICHARDSON. Pressured by Nixon to fire special WATERGATE prosecutor Archibald Cox, both Ruckelshaus and Richardson resigned their Justice posts in the "Saturday Night Massacre" of 20 October 1973.

Ruckelshaus thereafter retired to private law practice in Washington, D.C., but returned to lead the Environmental Protection Agency once more under President RONALD REAGAN, from May 1983 until January 1985. Since breaking with the Reagan administration, Ruckelshaus has been an associate of Seattle's largest law firm and chief executive officer of the nation's second-largest waste handler, Houston-based Browning-Ferris Industries. He serves on the boards of various other corporations and social-policy think tanks in Washington.

## RUDOLPH, Eric Robert

**RUDOLPH, Eric Robert**—A Florida native, born at Merritt Island on 19 September 1966, Eric Rudolph developed a fixation on the "Christian Identity" cult in his early twenties, absorbing the racist and anti-Semitic doctrines that regard Jews as the literal offspring of Satan and nonwhite "mud people" as the products of demonic race-mixing experiments. Relatives recall that Rudolph enjoyed violent movies but denounced television as "the Electronic Jew," explaining, "You sit your children down in front of it and it fills their heads with crap."

In the mid-1990s Rudolph apparently gravitated toward the MILITIA MOVEMENT, whose leaders shared his paranoid view of history and current events. JUSTICE DEPARTMENT spokesmen blame him (and he has been indicted for) a series of BOMBINGS in southern states, committed between 1996 and 1998. Those crimes include:

*27 July 1996*—A nail-packed bomb exploded in Atlanta's Centennial Olympic Park, killing two persons and wounding more than 100 others. FBI agents initially blamed an innocent security guard, RICHARD JEWELL, for the bombing, but later identified Rudolph as the probable culprit.

*16 January 1997*—Two anti-personnel bombs exploded outside an abortion clinic in the Atlanta suburb of Sandy Springs, injuring seven persons. Letters signed by the "Army of God," a group frequently active in ANTI-ABORTION VIOLENCE, claimed responsibility for the blasts, but FBI agents today blame Rudolph for planting the charges.

*21 February 1997*—An explosion rocked the Otherside Lounge, an Atlanta gay bar, followed by further correspondence from the Army of God on 22 February. Once again, G-men ultimately named Rudolph as the bomber.

*29 January 1998*—A nail bomb exploded at an abortion clinic in Birmingham, Alabama, killing an off-duty policeman and critically wounding a nurse. Witnesses reported a man running from the scene and removing a wig. The license plate of his getaway car identified Rudolph as a suspect and led FBI agents to a wilderness region of North Carolina, where they found the truck abandoned. The FBI believe that he found shelter with anti-government activists in that isolated mountain region.

Rudolph was placed on the MOST WANTED list in 1998, but despite that publicity and a massive manhunt in North Carolina's Nantahala National Forest and the surrounding area, he remained at large for five years.

About 4:00 a.m. on May 31, 2003, a police officer in Murphy, North Carolina, was on a routine patrol when he spotted a man acting suspiciously in a grocery store parking lot. The man fled from the officer and hid behind some milk crates. The officer called him out, and the man came out and was arrested. During the arrest, another officer who had been called for backup recognized the man as Eric Rudolph.

Rudolph was arraigned in Asheville on June 2 and taken to Birmingham, Alabama, to stand trial for the clinic bombing.

## RUDOLPH, Terry

**RUDOLPH, Terry**—With a Ph.D. in analytical chemistry, Terry Rudolph had no difficulty qualifying as an explosives analyst for the Materials Analysis Unit of the FBI's LABORATORY DIVISION in December 1978. One of his first cases was the "UNABOMBER" investigation, which climaxed two decades later with the arrest of suspect THEODORE KACZYNSKI. Rudolph testified in many cases and helped prosecutors secure numerous convictions, despite the fact that FBI HEADQUARTERS had ample cause to doubt his findings and professional qualifications.

FBI whistleblower FREDERICK WHITEHURST was one of the first to complain about Rudolph's laboratory procedures. Assigned to Rudolph for training in June 1986, Whitehurst soon observed glaring irregularities in Rudolph's handling of explosive residue evidence. As summarized by authors John Kelly and Phillip Wearne in *Tainting Evidence* (1998), Rudolph "rarely did confirmatory tests, only occasionally ran standard tests for comparison purposes on the lab machinery, and never seemed to clean his workbench." In short order, "Whitehurst was convinced that Rudolph drew conclusions that were not justified scientifically by the data from his examinations and seemed to relish having a work area that resembled a pigsty." Whitehurst's complaints were nonetheless ignored by his superiors until one of Rudolph's cases came back to haunt the FBI.

BOMBING suspect Steven Psinakis had been convicted in 1982, largely on the basis of Rudolph's scientific testimony, but he was granted an evidentiary hearing on appeal in 1989. Rudolph was called to testify, his description of "time-saving" shortcuts in standard lab procedure so embarrassing that Psinakis was exonerated and Judge Robert Schnacke wryly observed, "Even with the FBI, completion of all necessary processes is an awfully good idea." An April 1997 report on the case from the JUSTICE DEPARTMENT'S Inspector General declared that "Rudolph's approach represents a fundamental misunderstanding of the role of a forensic scientist. At best, Rudolph's explanation for his opinion in *Psinakis* represents incompetence."

In the wake of the Psinakis case, lab supervisor Jerry Butler penned a memo (dated 2 August 1989) that listed insufficient notes, missing charts and weak analytical procedures among the worst of Rudolph's "numerous administrative shortcomings." Technician ROGER MARTZ was picked to review those findings and initially decreed that Rudolph's methods were sufficient to "base an opinion as to the results that were provided." Seven years later, himself under fire for identical negligence, Martz reversed himself, claiming he never considered the "sufficiency of Rudolph's work to support his stated conclusions." On second thought, Martz found that 10 percent of Rudolph's cases had no supporting notes at all, while the remainder displayed "the very minimum work to come to a conclusion."

Jim Corby, chief of the lab's Materials Analysis Unit, pressed for a full-scale review of Rudolph's work in 1993, but administrators stalled authorization for the study until June 1995. Five months later, Corby's report disclosed that 36 percent of Rudolph's cases "did not meet the administrative or technical guidelines at the time the cases were worked." Lab results in a total of 157 cases, he found, "would not be acceptable under close judicial scrutiny, or past or present peer review." One of those was the Kaczynski case, where prosecutors told the press in April 1997, "We concluded that a qualified explosives examiner should review all of Rudolph's work on Unabom before it is used in the case." In fact, lead prosecutor Robert Clear announced, "To the

extent that the government will offer explosives residue evidence in the Kaczynski case, it will be relying upon conclusions of non-FBI experts." Kaczynski spared the FBI further embarrassment by pleading guilty in 1998, by which time Terry Rudolph was no longer employed in the lab.

**RUKEYSER, Muriel**— A native of New York City, born 15 December 1913, future poet and essayist Muriel Rukeyser first drew FBI attention in 1932, as an 18-year-old student, when G-men reported that she "took two courses, one entitled The Revolutionary Spirit in Literature and another entitled The History of International Sociology, at the Rand School of Social Sciences, which has a reputation of being communistically inclined." Four years later, writing for *The Nation* and *New Masses*, Rukeyser reported on Alabama's Scottsboro rape case, then traveled to Spain in time for the outbreak of civil war between loyalist forces and fascist insurgents. At the same time, she was indexed as a member of the JOHN REED Club.

The Bureau seemingly lost track of Rukeyser for a half-dozen years, but she was rediscovered in March 1943, while working for the Office of War Information's Bureau of Publications and Graphics. That spring, the FBI launched "a complete investigation" of Rukeyser and some 1,300 other OWI employees who had somehow been hired despite "Red" taints in their backgrounds. Rukeyser resigned from her post in May 1943, but the Bureau's investigation continued into 1945. One phase, anticipating the later LIBRARY AWARENESS PROGRAM, saw agents enlist a librarian at the University of California in Berkeley to provide a list of books checked out by Rukeyser a year *after* she left the OWI. ("On February 7, 1945," the Internal Security report noted, "she obtained a renewal of her library card.")

The FBI continued its pursuit of Rukeyser into the postwar era, branding her "a well-known poetess who is alleged to have mixed considerable left-wing politics with her iambic pentameters." In 1950, professional ex-communist LOUIS BUDENZ "advised that Rukeyser was one of 400 concealed Communists." Her name was added to the FBI's Communist Index in 1951, then removed four years later without explanation. In 1958, the AMERICAN LEGION sought Rukeyser's dismissal from Sarah Lawrence College on the basis of her "Communist-Front record." G-men opened another investigation of Rukeyser in 1963, but its subject is blacked out on copies released under the FREEDOM OF INFORMATION ACT. Ten years later, she was cited for unspecified involvement with the AMERICAN INDIAN MOVEMENT'S demonstrations at WOUNDED KNEE, South Dakota, yet Rukeyser's file was officially closed before year's end, citing her "lack of extremist activity." She died in New York City on 12 February 1980.

**RUNYON, Alfred Damon**— Born in Manhattan, Kansas on 4 October 1884, Damon Runyon served in the Spanish-American War as a teenager and later moved to New York City, where he established himself as a journalist and author of short fiction, best known for his portrayal of Broadway characters (*Guys and Dolls, Blue Plate Special*, etc.). Runyon died on 10 December 1946, and a nine-page FBI dossier was released to author Natalie

Robins two decades later. Based on the content of that meager file, including references to a cousin of Runyon's accused of subversive activity in 1953, Robins concludes that "it is simply not possible that the nine pages released are all that exist on Runyon." That assertion is presently impossible to verify, but if true, it would indicate willful violations of the FREEDOM OF INFORMATION ACT.

**RUSTIN, Bayard**— A Quaker native of West Chester, Pennsylvania, born in 1912, Bayard Rustin trained for his lifelong career as a social activist with the American Friends Service Committee. In 1937, while enrolled at City College in New York, he joined the Young Communist League as a youth organizer, focusing primarily on anti-war activism and the problem of racial segregation. Rustin quit the League four years later, when the COMMUNIST PARTY devoted itself to support for the Soviet Union in WORLD WAR II, joining instead the CONGRESS OF RACIAL EQUALITY (CORE) and the Fellowship of Reconciliation (FOR). He also worked extensively with A. PHILIP RANDOLPH, then president of the Brotherhood of Sleeping Car Porters. While a participant in Randolph's March on Washington Movement, Rustin also became CORE's first field secretary. A committed pacifist, he refused to register for the draft in World War II and served three years in federal prison (1943-45).

Upon release, Rustin campaigned for the FOR's Free India Committee, promoting India's struggle for independence from Great Britain. A committed disciple of Gandhi's nonviolent civil disobedience, Rustin thereafter logged multiple arrests for protesting Britain's colonial policies in Africa. In 1947 he helped to plan the original FREEDOM RIDES, seeking enforcement of a U.S. SUPREME COURT ruling that banned segregation in interstate transportation. As part of that campaign, Rustin was arrested in North Carolina and served three weeks on a chain gang. In the same period, he was instrumental in securing President HARRY TRUMAN's promise to desegregate the U.S. military. In 1951 Rustin helped organize the Committee to Support South African Resistance, later the American Committee on Africa. Rustin's HOMOSEXUALITY brought dismissal from the FOR in 1953, after his arrest on a "morals charge" in Washington, D.C., but he soon found another vehicle in the form of the War Resisters League.

Such activities marked Rustin as a prime candidate for FBI surveillance prior to the advent of the 1950s CIVIL RIGHTS movement, but he took the harassment in stride. In February 1956 Rustin traveled to Montgomery, Alabama and assisted Dr. MARTIN LUTHER KING, JR., with a boycott of segregated city buses. Prior to Randolph's arrival, King had not embraced the concept of nonviolence, and in fact kept guns at his home, along with armed guards to repulse attacks by the KU KLUX KLAN. Under Randolph's guidance, King matured as a spokesman for civil disobedience and the SOUTHERN CHRISTIAN LEADERSHIP CONFERENCE. Rustin subsequently organized the Prayer Pilgrimage for Freedom (1957) and two National Youth Marches for Integrated Schools (1958-59). In 1963 he served as deputy director and chief organizer for the most famous March on Washington (to promote new civil rights legislation), and in 1964 co-founded the A. Philip Randolph Institute (which he served as president from 1966 through 1979).

FBI memos concede that surveillance of Rustin disclosed no "direct evidence placing him in the Communist party" after 1941, but G-men continued to paint him as a "Red" throughout the 1960s. As New York's special agent in charge wrote to Director J. EDGAR HOOVER on 25 April 1964: "While there may not be any direct evidence that he is a Communist, neither is there any substantiated evidence that he is anticommunist." Hoover requested permission to tap Rustin's telephones, and Attorney General ROBERT KENNEDY agreed. Those taps extended to Rustin's Atlantic City hotel room in August 1964, when he attended the Democratic National Convention as a supporter of the Mississippi Freedom Democratic Party. G-men leaked derogatory information on Rustin to civil rights leaders ROY WILKINS and WHITNEY YOUNG, seeking to promote dissension in the movement, and critical stories on Rustin were planted in various publications ranging from *Time* magazine to the *New York Daily News*. In one of his yearly appearances before the House Appropriations Subcommittee, Hoover also saw fit to mention that Rustin was "convicted for sodomy" in 1953.

The Bureau was ultimately unsuccessful in its efforts to destroy Rustin's reputation. Rustin outlived Hoover by 15 years, continuing his "radical" activities through the 1970s and 1980s at home, as well as in Africa and Southeast Asia. At the time of his death in 1987, Rustin served as co-chairman of the A. Philip Randolph Institute and president of the A. Philip Randolph Educational Fund; he was also chairman of Social Democrats USA and a member of the U.S. Holocaust Memorial Council.

# S

SACCO-VANZETTI Case—America's most controversial holdup-murder of the 20th century occurred in South Braintree, Massachusetts on 15 April 1920. At three o'clock that afternoon, a paymaster and armed guard for the Slater & Morrill shoe factory were shot and killed by two bandits, the gunmen escaping with $15,776.51. The robbers, seen by several witnesses, tossed their loot into a car occupied by several other men and fled the scene. Their vehicle was found abandoned two days later, in some nearby woods.

Police in Bridgewater, 10 miles to the south, were already investigating a similar holdup, committed without loss of life on 24 December 1919. In both cases the thieves were described as probable Italians. Authorities suspected ANARCHIST roommates Mario Boda (or Buda) and Ferrucio Coacci in the Bridgewater case, further noting that Coacci—arrested as an "enemy alien" in the recent PALMER RAIDS—had failed to report for his scheduled deportation on the day of the South Braintree holdup. Boda was questioned by police on 20 April, but they released him in hopes that he would lead authorities to his accomplices. Officers lay in wait at a garage, springing their trap on 5 May, when Boda, Coacci and three other men came to retrieve the car. Boda escaped in the confusion, while police arrested Coacci, Riccardo Orciani, Nicola Sacco and Bartolomeo Vanzetti. Boda was never caught, Coacci was belatedly deported without further charges being filed, and Orciani provided an iron-clad alibi for both holdup dates, leaving Sacco and Vanzetti to face trial alone.

Modern FBI spokesmen insist that the Bureau became involved in the Sacco-Vanzetti case only *after* the defendants were convicted of murder and robbery, fearing that groups sympathetic to the pair "were making plans to take action against U.S. government officials in order to influence state officials to overturn the conviction of Sacco and Vanzetti." Some 2,189 pages of FBI records, released under the FREEDOM OF INFORMATION ACT, appear to document that claim, detailing surveillance of pro-defense groups between 1921 and 1927—but they do not tell the whole story. In fact, Sacco and Vanzetti were objects of Bureau surveillance before their arrest in Massachusetts, and G-men took an active role in sending them to the electric chair.

Sacco and Vanzetti arrived in the U.S. from their native Italy in 1908, when Sacco was 17 years old and Vanzetti was 20. Both were avid readers of the anarchist newspaper *Cronaca Sovversiva*, active by 1916 in support of "radical" labor unions. Vanzetti logged his first arrest that year, for joining a rally in support of striking Minnesota miners. Both fled to Mexico in 1917, thereby avoiding military conscription when the U.S. entered WORLD WAR I. By 1919, they were listed in the Bureau of Investigation's files as "radicals to watch," but there was insufficient evidence to justify their deportation in the Palmer raids. On 25 April 1920, Vanzetti visited New York City, in an effort to see fellow anarchist ANDREA SALSEDO, illegally confined at the Bureau's Manhattan office on suspicion of participation in terrorist BOMBINGS. Salsedo plunged to his death from a 14th-story window on 3 May, in what G-men described as a suicide. Sacco procured passports for his family's return to Italy the day after Salsedo's death, but his arrest on 5 May spoiled their travel plans.

Spokesmen for the Bureau's Boston field office had initially described the South Braintree holdup as a professional job, but they changed their minds overnight when Sacco and Vanzetti were arrested. Instead of searching for hardened criminals, G-men delivered their files on Sacco and Vanzetti to state prosecutors and infiltrated the Sacco-Vanzetti Defense Committee with INFORMANTS who reportedly looted its treasury. Another spy was planted in jail with Sacco and Vanzetti, eavesdropping in vain for admissions of guilt. Vanzetti was indicted for the Bridgewater holdup on 11 June 1920, convicted on 1 July and sentenced on 16 August to a prison term of 12 to 15 years.

The main event began in Dedham, Massachusetts on 21 May 1921, before Judge Webster Thayer, a bitter enemy of radicals who deemed anarchism "cognate with the crime." Prosecutor Frederick Katzmann cast ethics to the wind in his pursuit of a conviction, while defense attorney John Vahey proved so inept that he was later accused of collusion with the state. (Coincidentally, Vahey also became Katzmann's legal partner in 1924.) Judge Thayer, for his part, welcomed prosecution arguments alluding to the defendants' nationality, their religious and political beliefs, overruling the few objections offered by Vahey.

The resultant trial was a travesty. Witnesses who had refused to identify either defendant in 1920 had changed their mind in the meantime, naming both in court as the South Braintree bandits; one who glimpsed the fleeing getaway car for three seconds or less described Sacco in intimate detail, including "a good-sized [left] hand ... that denoted strength." Ballistics experts agreed that five of the seven fatal bullets came from pistols other than those confiscated from Sacco and Vanzetti, but State Police Captain William Proctor found one .32-caliber slug "consistent" with Sacco's gun. A second expert witness for the state, Charles Van Amburgh, agreed with Proctor. Both defendants were convicted of murder on 14 July 1921. Judge Thayer sentenced them to die, afterward crowing to friends, "Did you see what I did to those anarchist bastards?"

Protests against the verdict and sentence were immediate, both in the U.S. and in Europe. While G-men devoted themselves to surveillance of the protesters, the state's case began to unravel. Captain Proctor recanted his ballistics testimony in 1923, blaming the "confusion" on Prosecutor Katzmann. It was all a matter of semantics, Proctor said: "Had I been asked the direct question, whether I had found any affirmative evidence whatever that this so-called mortal bullet had passed through this particular Sacco's pistol, I should have answered then, as I do now without hesitation, in the negative." Judge Thayer declined to reopen the case, and he stood firm again in 1924, when "expert" Charles Van Amburgh was exposed as a perjurer who frequently lied under oath to please prosecutors. Next, in November 1925, career criminal Celestine Madeiros confessed to driving the South Braintree getaway car for Joe Morelli's holdup gang, confirming that "Sacco and Vanzetti was not in said crime." Six months later, on 12 May 1926, the Massachusetts Supreme Court upheld the original verdict and Judge Thayer's sentence.

Disturbed by the ongoing protests, Governor Alvan Fuller appointed a special commission to review the case in June 1927. Despite noting Judge Thayer's "grave breach of official decorum" at trial, the commission found no reason to recommend clemency. On 15 August, JUSTICE DEPARTMENT spokesmen refused to open Bureau files for the Sacco-Vanzetti Defense Committee, insisting that no proof of guilt or innocence was found therein, much less evidence of collusion between federal agents and the prosecution. Sacco and Vanzetti were executed eight days later. Another 45 years would pass before the redacted files were finally opened, in 1974. Three years later, on the fiftieth anniversary of their death, Sacco and Vanzetti were officially exonerated by proclamation of Massachusetts Governor Michael Dukakis.

**SALSEDO, Andrea**—In early 1920 the Bureau of Investigation was desperate to identify the persons responsible for a June 1919 bomb blast at the home of Attorney General A. MITCHELL PALMER. The resultant PALMER RAIDS had jailed thousands of "radical" suspects and resulted in deportation of several hundred "enemy aliens," but the bombers remained at large. The Bureau's only clue was a flier, titled "Plain Words" and printed on pink paper, found at the scene of the BOMBING.

By February 1920, G-men had focused their attention on a Brooklyn print shop known to publish ANARCHIST literature. Employee Robert Elia was arrested on 25 February, co-worker Andrea Salsedo 11 days later, on 7 March. One report says the two men were arrested on deportation warrants; another claims the agents had no warrants (and thus no legal authority for the arrests). In either case, the prisoners were not delivered to immigration authorities, as a deportation warrant would require, but found themselves confined for the next eight weeks to a suite of JUSTICE DEPARTMENT offices on Park Row, in Manhattan.

Agents later claimed their (illegal) search of the print shop had yielded pink paper "similar" to the "Plain Words" flier, but they never produced it. Instead, they went to work on Salsedo with third-degree tactics, working to extract a confession. Elia later signed an affidavit that he heard Salsedo screaming from an interrogation room, afterward appearing with bruises on his face. Salsedo told Elia the agents beat him with a bloody shoe, allegedly found at the Palmer bomb site, while demanding that he name the bombers. Bureau chief WILLIAM FLYNN was reportedly present throughout those proceedings. On 9 March 1920, after consulting attorney Narcisco Donato, Salsedo "confessed" to printing the "Plain Words" flier, but admitted nothing more. The G-men seemed happy. According to Elia, he and Salsedo were "very well treated" thereafter—but they were not released.

Around 25 April 1920, a friend of Elia and Salsedo, Boston fishmonger BARTOLOMEO VANZETTI, came looking for his vanished friends in New York. He traced them to the Justice building but was sent away by agents who informed him the pair had been detained on official business. Vanzetti went home and recruited anarchist colleague NICOLA SACCO to organize a protest rally, scheduled for 9 May 1920. The rally would never take place, because Sacco and Vanzetti—both targets of Bureau surveillance, themselves—were arrested on charges of robbery and murder, stemming from an incident in April.

By that time, Andrea Salsedo was dead.

Federal agents called it suicide, claiming Salsedo leaped from a 14th-story window of the Bureau offices at 4:20 a.m. on 3 May 1920, reason unknown. Elia said only that Salsedo had "a terrible headache" on the night before his death, "groaning and lamenting" at bedtime. Attorney Donato arrived, later that morning, in response to an official promise that the prisoners "would be freed about this time." An agent met him at the door and said, "Well, your client, Salsedo, is free."

Richard Rohman, then a reporter for the socialist *New York Call*, later told author Fred Cook that he entered the Justice offices on the night of 2 May 1920 and heard "subhuman cries from a man in terrible pain." Following the sounds to an inner office, Rohman saw two G-men standing over Salsedo with blackjacks. The agents chased him downstairs, to the street, where Rohman shook them off. Returning to the *Call*'s press room, he wrote a story on what he had seen, but it was never published.

One official who rejected the suicide story was Assistant Secretary of Labor LOUIS POST, a critic of the Palmer raids who had vetoed many deportation orders. Post described the incident as "the Salsedo homicide," and certain members of Congress were equally suspicious. Attorney General Palmer and a young aide, J. EDGAR HOOVER, appeared before the House Rules Committee to defend the Bureau's conduct on 1 June 1920. Contradicted by attorney Donato and by simple logic, they claimed Salsedo had remained in custody for eight weeks "by his own choice" and was "well treated" throughout his stay. Outside the hearing room, Bureau spokesmen also claimed that Salsedo had named the 1919 bombers, but none was ever identified or arrested.

**SALVATI, Joseph**—With co-defendants Louis Greco, PETER LIMONE and Henry Tameleo, Joseph Salvati was the victim of a criminal FRAME-UP in Boston. The four were charged with killing a small-time member of ORGANIZED CRIME, Edward Deegan, in 1965. Boston FBI agents knew of the murder in advance and failed to prevent it; they also knew that the actual team of killers included two Bureau informants, VINCENT FLEMMI and Joseph ("The Animal") Barboza. Still, the Boston field office raised no objection when Salvati and company were indicted for the slaying and later convicted at trial on the basis of perjured testimony from Barboza. Greco and Tameleo died in prison, while Salvati and Limone were exonerated after serving 30-plus years for a crime they did not commit. Lawsuits against the FBI for false imprisonment and other violations of their CIVIL RIGHTS are pending as this volume goes to press.

**SAMPSON, Gary Lee**—A 41-year-old Massachusetts native, ex-convict, alcoholic and drug addict, Gary Sampson was a fugitive from BANK ROBBERY charges in North Carolina when he telephoned the FBI's Boston field office on 23 July 2001 and attempted to surrender. He would later tell authorities that an FBI operator "blew off" his call and hung up the phone. The next day, Sampson launched a week-long murder spree that claimed three lives in Massachusetts and New Hampshire.

Sampson's one-man crime wave began in Weymouth, Massachusetts, where he commandeered 69-year-old Philip McCloskey's car and then slashed McCloskey to death outside Marshfield. Sampson soon abandoned McCloskey's car and resumed hitchhiking. Nineteen-year-old Jonathan Rizzo picked him up in Plymouth on 26 July, whereupon Sampson pulled a knife and directed Rizzo to nearby Abington. There, he tied the youth to a tree, stabbed him repeatedly and slashed his throat. In Rizzo's car, Sampson fled to Meredith, New Hampshire, where he strangled 58-year-old Robert Whitney in a lakefront home. Captured at last, Sampson confessed his crimes in custody and informed court-appointed attorneys of his abortive attempt to surrender.

An investigation by the FBI's OFFICE OF PROFESSIONAL RESPONSIBILITY failed to make headway at first. Agent Gail Marcinkiewicz, speaking for the Boston office on 30 August 2001, denied that any call had been received from Sampson. G-men were "still trying to get phone records" on 8 September, but six days later they acknowledged receipt of a 55-second call from an Abington pay phone on 23 July, as described by Sampson. No recording was made of the call, and media reports noted that "the FBI has refused to say whether any agents have been disciplined" for hanging up on Sampson. The killer, meanwhile, was indicted on state murder charges and on federal charges that imposed a potential death sentence for fatal carjackings.

Finally, on 18 December 2001, U.S. Attorney Michael Sullivan announced that the FBI had traced Sampson's phone call to an unnamed clerk with 17 years of Bureau service, suspended on 13 December for lying about receipt of the call. The clerk was later identified as 44-year-old William H. Anderson, reportedly substituting for another employee who had gone to lunch when Sampson phoned the Boston office. As explained to the media, Anderson accidentally disconnected Sampson while trying to transfer his call to an FBI agent. Fearful of losing his job, Anderson lied about the call in an oral interview and a subsequent written statement, but confessed after failing a polygraph test on 12 December 2001. "You have so many phone calls," he explained, "you don't know how many are legit or not. It's not up to you to determine what calls are legit or not. I said 'hold on' and tried to transfer it to the agent. It would help if phone calls were recorded. The equipment they had was old."

In June 2002 Anderson pled guilty to lying in his sworn statement. Four months later, federal judge Mark Wolf rejected the JUSTICE DEPARTMENT'S description of Anderson's crime as "making a false statement" and ordered sentencing calculations based on the more serious crime of perjury. In January 2003 Judge Wolf rejected Gary Sampson's attempt to exchange a guilty plea for a guaranteed sentence of life imprisonment, commanding Sampson to stand trial and face a potential death sentence.

**SANDBURG, Carl**—A native of Galesburg, Illinois, born 6 January 1878, Carl Sandburg was a literary Renaissance man: poet, journalist, film critic, novelist and presidential biographer, winner of the Pulitzer Prize for both poetry and history. As a young man he campaigned for the Social Democratic Party, but also served in the Spanish-American War. His multi-volume study of Abraham Lincoln remains the most popular presidential biography of the twentieth century.

The Bureau of Investigation noticed Sandburg for the first time in 1918, while he worked as a foreign correspondent for the Newspaper Enterprise Association (NEA). En route to Stockholm, Sandburg stopped in New York City, where G-men noted his friendly visits with radical author JOHN REED. Returning from Sweden on 11 November 1918, seven weeks after the armistice was signed ending WORLD WAR I, Sandburg was stopped by Customs agents who seized his books, notebooks and manuscripts. NEA editor S.T. Hughes complained to Secretary of War Newton Baker that Sandburg had been treated "like a dog or a traitor"; Baker responded that Sandburg's luggage had been filled with "revolutionary literature," much of it in Russian, plus a $10,000 draft payable to *Anteri Nuorteva*, a Finnish revolutionary group in the U.S. The papers were eventually returned, after federal translators satisfied themselves that the haul contained no orders for an insurrection in the States, but Sandburg was forever marked as "disloyal" in the FBI's view.

No derogatory item was too trivial for inclusion in Sandburg's dossier. In 1939 he was listed as a sponsor of the ABRAHAM LINCOLN BRIGADE. Two years later, Chicago G-men reported that "Sandberg" had "manifested an unfriendly attitude" toward the Bureau at a luncheon sponsored by *March of Time* filmmakers. In 1942 Sandburg shared the dais with CHARLES CHAPLIN at a rally to salute "our Russian ally" in WORLD WAR II. Reports from 1942 and 1944 note his affiliation with the Joint Anti-Fascist Refugee Committee. In 1945 Sandburg sponsored the Midwest division of the Independent Citizens Committee of the Arts, Sciences and Professions, cited by the names as a communist front by the HOUSE COMMITTEE ON UN-AMERICAN ACTIVITIES. Two years later, agents filed a clipping from the *Daily Worker*, reporting that a CBS television documentary on Abraham Lincoln had been prepared "with advice from Carl Sandburg." Another 1947 issue of the *Daily Worker* carried Sandburg's warning that America's "hate Russia" campaign posed a threat of catastrophic global war. A 1948 memo from some anonymous INFORMANT claimed Sandburg "was reported to be a well-known Communist in Chicago" and further stated (falsely) that he owned a building used as national headquarters of the Young Workers League of America.

FBI pursuit of Sandburg continued into the Red-hunting 1950s. A 1952 report from J. EDGAR HOOVER'S office to the STATE DEPARTMENT rehashed Sandburg's "subversive" citations, while continual updates added more derogatory mentions from the distant past. In May 1956, G-men clipped and filed a WESTBROOK PEGLER column that described Sandburg, with apparent disapproval, as "a prosperous commercial biographer of Abraham Lincoln." The same year witnessed Sandburg on the presidential campaign trail for good friend ADLAI STEVENSON, opposing incumbent DWIGHT EISENHOWER. In 1958 the FBI upgraded Sandburg's file to the rank of "Internal Security — C" (for Communist), noting that he "will reportedly write the introduction to [deleted] new book." A year later, Hoover tried to block Sandburg's participation in a cultural exchange program with the Soviet Union, on grounds that "activities that occurred after the first World War" made it "extremely undesirable to permit him to go to Russia." As late as June 1964, agents saw fit to file a "confidential" memo listing Sandburg's date and place of birth, but the dossier failed to stop President LYNDON JOHNSON from awarding Sandburg the Medal of Freedom in a special White House ceremony. Sandburg died at his North Carolina home, still under FBI surveillance, on 22 July 1967.

**SARGENT, John Garibaldi** — Born at Ludlow, Vermont on 13 October 1860, John Sargent served as the state's attorney general from 1908 to 1912. A personal friend and frequent card-playing partner of President CALVIN COOLIDGE, Sargent took office as U.S. attorney general on 17 March 1925. Already in poor health, Sargent disliked Washington, D.C. and spent as little time as possible in the nation's capital. As a consequence, he generally left J. EDGAR HOOVER to run the Bureau of Investigation as he pleased, without supervision. (In the words of Hoover biographer Athan Theoharis, Sargent "saw even less evil than [HARLAN] STONE had seen before him.") In matters of protocol, Hoover dealt primarily with WILLIAM DONOVAN, head of the JUSTICE DEPARTMENT'S Antitrust Division, who likewise did little or nothing to curb Bureau abuses. Years later, in a press interview, Hoover listed Sargent as one of his all-time favorite attorneys general. Sargent left office on 5 March 1929 and died 10 years later to the day, in Ludlow, Vermont.

**SAROYAN, William** — Born in Fresno, California on 31 August 1908, novelist and playwright William Saroyan published more than 60 books in his career. He first drew notice from the FBI in 1940, a year after he declined the Pulitzer Prize for his play *The Time of Your Life*. On that occasion, an unnamed INFORMANT told G-men that Saroyan had addressed "a committee of Publishers Pan-American Dinner for Writers in Exile," described as "an extremely left-wing affair" in which "all the speakers were in one way or another known front people for the COMMUNIST PARTY." A year later, Saroyan and others organized the Free Company "to prepare dramatic broadcasts as a counter-attack against foreign propaganda" in America, but the AMERICAN LEGION condemned them for plotting to broadcast "Red plays designed to encourage radicalism in the United States."

Saroyan served with the U.S. military in Europe during WORLD WAR II, but his service and honorable discharge went un-

noticed by the FBI. The next entry in his file dates from 1948, when Saroyan signed an open letter from the National Institute of Arts and Letters denouncing the HOUSE COMMITTEE ON UN-AMERICAN ACTIVITIES. (G-men retaliated by informing a California legislative body that the Institute was a "Communist front.") A decade later, in 1959, agents clipped and filed a GEORGE SOKOLSKY column "exposing" Saroyan's visits to Russia, reporting that Saroyan had "witnessed an utterly brainwashed society." (J. EDGAR HOOVER penned a marginal note that read: "This pretty well pegs Saroyan.") In 1960, while Saroyan again toured Russia, Armenia and India, the FBI reported that tax problems "drove Saroyan out of the United States." Five years later, responding to a "name check" request from LYNDON JOHNSON'S White House, Hoover curiously claimed that the Bureau had never investigated Saroyan. In 1967, a "secret" entry from the latest edition of *Who's Who* was clipped and added to the file, reporting that Saroyan was living in Paris. Sporadic memos were filed for another decade, the last being dated 28 February 1977.

Saroyan returned to the U.S. in time to die of cancer, within a mile of his California birthplace, on 18 May 1981. When author Herbert Mitgang petitioned for release of his file under the FREEDOM OF INFORMATION ACT, 13 heavily-censored pages were released, including an "Internal Security" memo with its whole text blacked out. The 32 pages still classified for reasons of "national security" include an undated report from the CENTRAL INTELLIGENCE AGENCY, subject unknown.

**SAXBE, William Bart** — Born at Mechanicsburg, Ohio on 24 June 1916, William Saxbe served in the U.S. Army during WORLD WAR II and entered politics upon returning to civilian life. Over the next quarter-century he was elected to the Ohio state legislature (1947-54), as state attorney general (1957-59, 1963-69) and to the U.S. Senate (1969-74). Despite his concerns over President RICHARD NIXON'S foreign policy (Saxbe once said Nixon had "left his senses" in regard to the VIETNAM WAR) and the deepening WATERGATE SCANDAL, Saxbe accepted Nixon's offer to become attorney general and he assumed command of the JUSTICE DEPARTMENT on 4 January 1974.

Saxbe was the last of Nixon's four attorneys general and the only one not driven from office by Watergate. After Nixon resigned in August 1974, Saxbe remained in his post under President GERALD FORD until 3 February 1975 (when he was replaced by EDWARD LEVI. Saxbe's only significant action in regard to the FBI was his release, in November 1974, of an abridged Justice Department report on various illegal COINTELPRO activities carried out under late Director J. EDGAR HOOVER. Following his departure from Justice, Saxbe served as the U.S. ambassador to India (1975-76).

**SCHWARTZ, Delmore** — A lifelong resident of New York City, born 18 December 1913, "city poet" Delmore Schwartz represents the rare case of an individual who invited FBI scrutiny in an apparent bout of mental illness. Before his descent into alcoholism and paranoid insanity, Schwartz published his first collection of poems in 1938 and later served as editor of the *Partisan Review* from 1943 to 1955. He was, nonetheless, ignored by G-men until 13 September 1961, when he sent a telegram to Attorney General

ROBERT KENNEDY reading: "I need help badly Please Please help." A pair of agents called on Schwartz in New York the next day, afterward reporting that he had told "a rambling disjointed story of personal problems relating to marital difficulties and inability to obtain work." The agents deemed him "aberrant," as well as "dirty, slovenly and unkept [sic]." In parting, Schwartz told his visitors that he was moving to a hotel in Cambridge, Massachusetts, but when asked how long he planned to stay there, Schwartz replied, "When one starts doing what the FBI says, one hasn't a very clear sense of how long one will stay anywhere."

In fact, no travel orders from the Bureau were forthcoming, as headquarters decided "no further action" was warranted on Schwartz's case. Schwartz biographer James Atlas later described his subject as "obsessed with [President] JOHN F. KENNEDY" and the author of similar odd telegrams to one-time presidential contender ADLAI STEVENSON. Schwartz died in New York City on 12 July 1966.

**SEBERG, Jean**—A native of Marshalltown, Iowa, born on 13 November 1938, Jean Seberg made her first cinematic appearance as Joan of Arc in *Saint Joan* (1957). She completed another 34 films by 1976 and was best known for her starring role in *Paint Your Wagon* (1969) and *Airport* (1970). In April of the latter year, around the same time that Vice President SPIRO AGNEW requested personal access to "especially graphic incidents" from FBI files, the Los Angeles field office alerted FBI HEADQUARTERS to Seberg's alleged support for the militant BLACK PANTHER PARTY. On 27 April Agent RICHARD W. HELD, in charge of COINTELPRO operations for Los Angeles, proposed a campaign to destroy Seberg's career and reputation. He wrote:

> Bureau permission is requested to publicize the pregnancy of JEAN SEBERG, a well-known movie actress, by [deleted] Black Panther Party (BPP) [deleted] by advising Hollywood "Gossip-Columnists" in the Los Angeles area of the situation. It is felt that the possible publication of SEBERG's plight could cause her embarrassment and serve to cheapen her image with the general public.
> It is proposed that the following letter from a fictitious person be sent to local columnists:
> "I was just thinking about you and remembered that I still owe you a favor. So—I was in Paris last week and ran into Jean Seberg, who was heavy with baby. I thought she and [estranged husband] Romaine [Gary] had gotten together again, but she confided the child belonged to [deleted] of the Black Panthers, one [deleted]. The dear girl is getting around!
> "Anyway. I thought you might get a scoop on the others. Be good and I'll see you soon.
> 　　　　　　　　　　　　　　　　　　"Love, Sol"
> Usual precautions would be taken by the Los Angeles Division to preclude identification of the Bureau as the source of the letter if approval is granted.

Director J. EDGAR HOOVER replied to Held on 6 May 1970, approving the smear campaign on grounds that Seberg "has been a financial supporter of the BPP and should be neutralized." A refinement of the scheme was ordered: "To protect the sensitive source of information from possible compromise and to insure the success of your plan, Bureau feels it would be better to wait

approximately two additional months until Seberg's pregnancy would be obvious to everyone."

Bureau spokesmen later claimed the plot against Seberg was canceled prior to execution, but the sequence of events suggests otherwise. On 19 May 1970 gossip columnist Joyce Haber treated readers of the *Los Angeles Times* to the story of "Miss A" and her pregnancy by "a rather prominent Black Panther." Seemingly untroubled by the L.A. field office's failure to follow his orders, Hoover clipped the column and sent a copy to the White House. The *Hollywood Reporter* identified Seberg as "Miss A" on 8 June 1970. Two months later, on 7 August, she attempted suicide with an overdose of sleeping pills. As a result, on 23 August, Seberg delivered a premature infant weighing barely four pounds. One day later, *Newsweek* magazine named the baby's father as "a black activist she met in California," presumably Black Panther Ray ("Masai") Hewitt. (Another Panther candidate named in FBI reports was Allen ["Hakim Jamal"] Donaldson, a cousin of the late MALCOLM X.) Seberg's daughter died on 25 August 1970, whereupon Held reported to Washington the loss suffered by this "alleged promiscuous and sex perverted white actress."

The FBI's vendetta against Seberg included a racist and sexual component. David Richards, author of *Played Out: The Jean Seberg Story* (1981), recalled the comment of one California G-man in regard to Seberg and Ray Hewitt: "I wonder how she'd like to gobble my dick while I shove my .38 up that black bastard's ass?" Unsatisfied with the damage already done, Hoover added Seberg's name to the FBI's SECURITY INDEX on 29 December 1970, thus ranking her among the "dangerous" persons slated for mass arrest in the event of a national emergency.

Blood tests proved that Seberg's child had indeed been fathered by Romain Gary, whereupon both sued *Newsweek* and other publications, collecting minimal damages ($8,333 for Seberg and $2,777 for Gary). Subsequent disclosure of the fact that she had been a COINTELPRO target exacerbated Seberg's paranoia, and she committed suicide in Paris, with an overdose of barbiturates and alcohol, on 8 September 1979. Critics may quarrel with Romain Gary's assessment that Seberg was "destroyed by the FBI," but her treatment by the Bureau clearly exceeded any legitimate activity of an "investigative agency" pledged to pursue only those persons who violate federal criminal statutes.

**SECRET Army Organization**—In February 1970 members of the disintegrating MINUTEMEN organization met in an effort to cut their losses and form a more viable group. The result was a self-styled "Secret Army Organization" (SAO) based in San Diego, California. It took more than a year to map out the group's command structure, but by early 1971 the SAO was publishing how-to manuals on bombs, booby traps and burglary techniques. In short order the right-wing warriors would match their printed words to action.

A particular sore spot with the SAO was San Diego State College, with its small coterie of liberal professors. One in particular, Professor Peter Bohmer, offended SAO sensibilities by joining radical organizations and attending VIETNAM WAR PROTEST rallies on campus. By the fall of 1971, the SAO had launched a reign of terror in San Diego, beginning with a spate of anonymous phone calls and threatening letters. The action quickly escalated, and on 13 November a car was firebombed outside Bohmer's house. Two days after Christmas, the SAO issued a "Special Bulletin" on Bohmer, recounting his antiwar activities, listing his address, telephone and auto license numbers "for any of our readers who may care to look up this Red Scum and say hello." A facetious warning followed: "Now, in case you don't believe in hitting people who wear glasses, I guess we will have to tell you that he wears contact lenses." On 6 January 1972 anonymous callers warned Bohmer's friends to tell him good-bye. Later that night, shots were fired into his home from a passing car, seriously wounding a visitor, Paula Tharp.

The terror continued in San Diego until June 1972, when a bomb wrecked the Guild Theater, a local porno house. After several false starts, police arrested suspect William Yakopec, a former member of the far-right John Birch Society. Continuing investigation unraveled the SAO's curtain of secrecy, revealing that the army's membership included San Diego firemen and police officers, some of them on the FBI payroll as INFORMANTS.

Thus far, there had been no real surprises. Police involvement in right-wing TERRORISM dated from the Know-Nothing movement of the 1840s, and it seemed only natural that the Bureau, having shadowed the Minutemen since 1964, should pursue its descendants as well. Investigators were not prepared, however, for emerging evidence that G-men had guided and controlled the SAO almost from its inception.

When William Yakopec went to trial on BOMBING charges, the defense was stunned to find one of the SAO's top men, Howard Berry Godfrey, listed as a prosecution witness. Godfrey testified that he had been an FBI informant since 1967, drawing a monthly stipend of $250 for services rendered. He was a Minuteman until the San Diego branch dissolved, and he had joined the SAO in November 1971. He further testified that FBI agents knew of and approved all his SAO activities, including the following:

• Godfrey gave explosives to defendant Yakopec with instructions to "save them for after the communist takeover of the country." Some of those explosives prematurely found their way into the Guild Theater, in June 1972.

• On 6 January 1972, Godfrey drove the car from which SAO member George Hoover fired shots into Peter Bohmer's home. After the shooting, Godfrey met with Agent Steve Christiansen, handing over Hoover's gun and jacket. Christiansen destroyed the jacket and hid the weapon for six months before delivering it to local police. (The FBI averted prosecution of Christiansen; he was permitted to resign and move to Utah.)

• The FBI provided Godfrey with $20,000 worth of weapons and explosives for delivery to the SAO.

• Godfrey himself had planned the Guild Theater bombing, for which Yakopec stood accused. The plot was hatched in October 1971, after Godfrey met with Donald Segretti, an aide to President RICHARD NIXON. In the wake of that meeting, Godfrey concocted plans to firebomb cars owned by "leftists," spike the punch at antiwar rallies with LSD or cyanide, and to bomb various targets including homes, businesses, and the office of Vietnam Veterans Against the War.

Godfrey's bizarre testimony led to further revelations about the FBI's private terrorist army. Informant John Rasperry, retired from the San Diego Police Department, told reporter Joe McMahon in 1975 that he had infiltrated the Center for Radical Education, where Peter Bohmer worked part-time. After several failed attempts to entrap Bohmer in criminal activities, Rasperry's FBI contacts ordered him to "eliminate" and "get rid of" Bohmer, whom they deemed a threat to national security. Rasperry was unclear as to the meaning of those orders; he told McMahon that he would gladly have killed Bohmer, if only his instructions had been more specific.

Courtroom revelations about the SAO led Bohmer and Paula Tharp to seek assistance from the AMERICAN CIVIL LIBERTIES UNION in suing the FBI for $10.6 million. The terror campaign had cost Bohmer his job at San Diego State, but still G-men were not satisfied. According to a report filed by the ACLU with the U.S. Senate's CHURCH COMMITTEE,

> On at least three occasions FBI agents and informers have planned and ordered the assassination of Mr. Bohmer, and in one such instance, an attempt was actually made, resulting in a severe bullet wound to Ms. Tharp. Other FBI-directed abuses against [ACLU's] clients have included repeated threats, both telephonic and printed, against their lives, firebombings of cars, burglaries, the opening and reading of mail, attempts to entrap them in criminal conduct, false arrests, infiltration and monitoring of peaceful and entirely lawful political associations, continuous physical surveillance and repeated, unjustified visits to their friends, relatives and places of employment.

The SAO fiasco ultimately had no consequences for the FBI. While Yakopec, George Hoover and a third terrorist went to prison, Howard Godfrey was rewarded for his "service" with a job in the California fire marshal's office. (He was later indicted for planting a bomb on a busy road near his home, phoning a threat to authorities, then volunteering to lead the investigation.) Ex-agent Christiansen, retired in Utah, refused to discuss the case with reporters but told them, "The FBI is taking good care of us."

**SECRET Service**—The U.S. Secret Service was created as a division of the Treasury Department on 5 July 1865, to suppress counterfeit currency. Two years later its mission was broadened to include "detecting persons perpetrating frauds against the government." That assignment included pursuit of bootleggers, smugglers, mail robbers, individuals responsible for land fraud and members of the KU KLUX KLAN. Secret Service agents began informal part-time protection of President Grover Cleveland in 1894, but that service did not become an official full-time job until 1902, after the assassination of President William McKinley. Over time, Secret Service protection was extended to the vice president, other constitutional successors to the presidency, certain foreign diplomats and (after the 1968 RFK ASSASSINATION) major presidential candidates.

The Secret Service also played a role in the formation of the FBI. Initially, the JUSTICE DEPARTMENT borrowed Secret Service agents to investigate federal crimes, but Congress banned that practice on 27 May 1908. The new restriction prompted Attorney General CHARLES BONAPARTE to created his own detective force at Justice (over congressional opposition) and to staff it with a team of former Secret Service men. That common origin would not prevent the agencies from engaging in a sometimes bitter rivalry, particularly during the 48-year tenure of FBI Director J. EDGAR HOOVER. Envious of the close daily contact with presidents — and the potential for spying — enjoyed by Secret Service agents, Hoover made his first bid to absorb the presidential security detail in 1935. Although angrily rebuffed by Treasury Secretary Henry Morgenthau, Hoover pursued his goal for nearly three decades, until the JFK ASSASSINATION of 1963 drove home the potential embarrassment of failure to protect the chief executive.

President Kennedy's murder was a watershed event for both the FBI and Secret Service. The Warren Commission's report criticized FBI HEADQUARTERS for failure to share information on alleged assassin LEE HARVEY OSWALD with the Secret Service, while members of Kennedy's protection detail were found to have been drinking late on the night before his assassination. Sixteen years later, the HOUSE SELECT COMMITTEE ON ASSASSINATIONS found the FBI "deficient in its sharing of information with other agencies" before the murder, while the Secret Service was chastised for inadequate preparation and failure to properly analyze intelligence before the fatal trip to Texas.

Relations between the FBI and Secret Service have apparently improved since Hoover's death in May 1972. Today the agencies share joint responsibility for investigation of various COMPUTER CRIMES, including various forms of fraud and transmission of child pornography. Secret Service agents also participate with G-men, agents of the DRUG ENFORCEMENT ADMINISTRATION and the BUREAU OF ALCOHOL, TOBACCO AND FIREARMS in a combined Child Abduction and Serial Killer Unit designed to track mobile predators at large. Since the catastrophic SKYJACKINGS of 11 September 2001, the Secret Service also plays an enhanced role in the federal government's proclaimed "war on TERRORISM."

**SEGHERS, Anna** — "Anna Seghers" was the pen name of Netty Radvány (née Reiling), a German Jew born at Mainz in 1900. Unlike so many authors investigated by the FBI, Seghers actually was a member of the German COMMUNIST PARTY, recruited in 1928. Her party membership and the content of her novels prompted Germany's new Nazi masters to ban Seghers's work in 1933, and she fled to Austria the following year, making her way to Spain in time for that country's civil war in 1936-37. A resident of France when German troops invaded that nation in 1940, she escaped with her family to Ellis Island the following year, but Seghers was refused entry to the U.S. and afterward settled with other exiled writers in Mexico, during June 1941.

The FBI was well aware of Seghers by that time, although G-men frequently dubbed her "Hungarian," after her husband's nationality. Bureau critics were disturbed when one of her novels, *The Seventh Cross*, reigned as a Book-of-the-Month Club best-seller from 1942 through 1946, and they enlisted New York bankers to keep tabs on her royalty payments. Any and all derogatory information available was collected by FBI field offices in

New York, Boston and Los Angeles; other material was gathered from the U.S. embassy in Mexico, Army and Navy Intelligence, and (after 1947) the CENTRAL INTELLIGENCE AGENCY. The wartime Office of Censorship intercepted Seghers's mail in the U.S. and sent most of it to the FBI laboratory, where letters were "examined for secret ink by means which would not alter their appearance with negative results." G-men also monitored various publications, including those which published Seghers's work and others to which she merely subscribed, including the *Daily Worker*, *New Masses*, and the *New York Times*. One source was INFORMANT Margarita Nelken, herself expelled from the German Communist Party, who "branded Anna Seghers and other prominent 'free' Germans opportunists and weaklings." Another informant visited Seghers in Mexico City, pretending to offer a publishing contract, and then reported back to FBI headquarters on her appearance ("Peculiarities: Extremely nervous and suspicious.") Agents monitored her public speeches, reported on a daughter's illness, and intercepted manuscripts bound for Seghers's publisher. No evidence of criminal activity was found, but J. EDGAR HOOVER noted ominously that Seghers had sent "greetings to Russia" in November 1942, on the "occasion of the twenty-fifth anniversary of the October Revolution."

The FBI continued to monitor Seghers after she left Mexico for Germany, with a stopover in New York City, during January 1947. She assumed a public role in East Germany, serving as president of the national writer's union from 1952 to 1978. Seghers died in East Berlin three years later, on 1 June 1983. More than a decade later, after much delay in Washington, author Alexander Stephan received 730 heavily-censored pages of Seghers's FBI file, released under the FREEDOM OF INFORMATION ACT, but another 103 pages remain classified, allegedly in the interest of "national security or foreign policy."

**SEIGENTHALER, John** — Journalist John Seigenthaler spent 43 years as a member of the Nashville *Tennessean*'s staff, first as an award-winning reporter, later as editor, retiring in 1991 as publisher and chief executive officer. He took a brief leave from newspaper work in the early 1960s to serve as an administrative assistant to Attorney General ROBERT KENNEDY in the JUSTICE DEPARTMENT. Concerned primarily with the struggle for black CIVIL RIGHTS, Seigenthaler later recalled that activists in the South "couldn't get the FBI to answer them," whereupon Kennedy provided telephone numbers for Seigenthaler and assistant BURKE MARSHALL. At the same time, Seigenthaler was aware of FBI efforts to infiltrate civil rights groups with INFORMANTS, and he reported to author Kenneth O'Reilly that the Bureau had excellent sources "within the civil rights movement."

Seigenthaler's most dramatic contribution to the cause of integration came in May 1961, when he was assigned to serve as Kennedy's negotiator with Alabama Governor John Patterson during the controversial "FREEDOM RIDES." Kennedy seemed to think that Seigenthaler's mere presence in Alabama "might prevent violence," but that judgment proved erroneous. Seigenthaler was present in Montgomery on 20 May 1961, when a mob of KU KLUX KLAN members attacked freedom riders at the city bus depot. Beaten unconscious while trying to rescue two white female protesters, Seigenthaler lay unconscious on the pavement for nearly a half-hour, while FBI agents stood by and took notes "for the specific purpose of observing and reporting to the Department of Justice in order that the Department will have the benefit of objective observations." Lester Sullivan, Montgomery's commissioner of public safety, explained the delay in medical treatment by claiming that "every white ambulance in town" had simultaneously broken down.

Seigenthaler survived the assault without permanent injury and later reminisced on his several meetings with FBI Director J. EDGAR HOOVER for Hoover biographer Curt Gentry. As reported by Gentry in *J. Edgar Hoover: The Man and the Secrets* (1991), Kennedy and Seigenthaler made a running joke of Hoover's mood swings and apparent mental lapses, remarking after one diatribe or another that "He's really out of it today."

In September 1982 Seigenthaler became the founding editorial director of *USA Today*, serving in that position for a decade while continuing his service with the *Tennessean*. Retired from both local and national papers in 1991, he founded the First Amendment Center at Vanderbilt University to encourage national debate and dialogue on First Amendment issues. At this writing (in September 2002) he also serves on the 18-member National Commission on Federal Election Reform and is a member of the Constitution Project Initiative on Liberty and Security, created in the wake of TERRORIST attacks on 11 September 2001.

**SENATE Internal Security Subcommittee**—Established in January 1951 as the U.S. Senate's version of the Red-hunting HOUSE COMMITTEE ON UN-AMERICAN ACTIVITIES (HUAC), the Senate Internal Security Subcommittee (SISS) was initially chaired by Nevada Senator Patrick McCarran (author of the MCCARRAN ACT). Upon McCarran's death in September 1954, he was succeeded as chairman by Indiana's William Jenner (1954-59) and Mississippi segregationist James Eastland (1959-73). A prominent member of the committee was former FBI agent THOMAS DODD.

From its creation onward the SISS enjoyed a close working relationship with the FBI's CRIME RECORDS DIVISION, which created a "McCarran special squad" to assist with various investigations. The collaboration was formalized on 15 March 1951, when McCarran met with Attorney General J. HOWARD MC-GRATH and FBI Director J. EDGAR HOOVER. As later explained by Assistant Director LOUIS NICHOLS, "Our cooperation was being solicited to help the committee whittle out the chaff, provide the committee with leads and to prevent the committee from needless effort, as well as to provide the committee those matters which we had already investigate, which would not be necessary for them to cover." Nichols described the FBI-SISS relationship as "very satisfactory," operating "to the mutual benefit of both the [JUSTICE] DEPARTMENT and the Bureau, as well as Congress and the general public."

Those benefits were realized in various ways. The FBI provided monographs and FILES on various "disloyal" groups and persons, including STANLEY LEVISON (an aide to Dr. MARTIN LUTHER KING, JR., in the SOUTHERN CHRISTIAN LEADERSHIP CONFERENCE). In March 1953 Hoover ordered his G-men to prepare

dossiers on "subversive persons" at 56 American universities, afterward furnishing files on 23 Philadelphia teachers to the SISS while others went to HUAC. In May 1958, as part of a new campaign against "Use of Lawyers and Courts to Further Communist Propaganda," the Bureau sent the committee blind memos detailing "pertinent subversive activities" by 70 lawyers who had represented COMMUNIST PARTY members in court or before congressional panels. Senator Eastland returned the favor in 1962, issuing subpoenas for seven officers of the Pacifica Foundation after Pacifica's radio stations carried interviews with FBI agent-turned-critic JACK LEVINE.

Investigation of "un-American activities" fell out of favor in the 1970s, following exposure of lawless DOMESTIC SURVEILLANCE in the WATERGATE SCANDAL and before the CHURCH COMMITTEE. In 1977 the SISS was quietly merged with the Senate Criminal Activities Subcommittee and thereafter ceased to exist.

**SERIAL Murder**—Most homicides are local crimes, investigated and prosecuted by city, county or state authorities. FBI agents have no jurisdiction in murder cases unless (a) the crime occurs on U.S. government property; (b) the victim is a federal employee; or (c) the killing results from a federal offense, such as interstate KIDNAPPING, CIVIL RIGHTS violation, or an act of TERRORISM. Most serial murder cases fall outside those guidelines, and fictional portrayals of FBI agents pursuing homicidal maniacs are simply that: fiction.

Serial murder is defined by the National Institute of Justice as "a series of two or more murders, committed as separate events, usually, but not always, by one offender acting alone." Many such crimes are sexually motivated, but others spring from motives including greed, revenge, racism, and religious or political fanaticism. While such crimes are as old as human history, their numbers have greatly increased since the 1960s, with some 85 percent of all identified serial killers found in the United States.

Members of the FBI's Behavioral Science Unit and the VIOLENT CRIMINAL APPREHENSION PROGRAM have been involved with PSYCHOLOGICAL PROFILING of serial killers since the late 1970s, but their efforts sometimes confuse the issue. Agents JOHN DOUGLAS and ROBERT RESSLER, writing in the Bureau's *Crime Classification Manual* (1992), insist that a genuine serial murder case requires victims killed at "three or more separate locations," but that rule excludes prolific slayers like Jeffrey Dahmer and Donald Harvey, who kill repeatedly at home or in the workplace. (Agent Ressler also claims to have coined the term "serial murder" in 1974, eight years after its first publication by author John Brophy.) Various serial killers have been posted to the Bureau's "TEN MOST WANTED" LIST, from Richard Marquette in 1961 to Rafael Resendez-Ramirez in 1999, but only three of those were captured by FBI agents, the last in 1966.

**SESSIONS, William Steele**—Born at Fort Smith, Arkansas on 27 May 1930, William Sessions was raised in Kansas City and served in the Air Force from 1951 to 1955. He graduated from Baylor Law School (Waco, Texas) in 1958 and spent 11 years in private practice, then joined the JUSTICE DEPARTMENT's Criminal Division as chief of the Government Operations Section in

September 1969. In August 1971 Sessions became U.S. attorney for western Texas. President GERALD FORD nominated him to the federal bench in 1974 and Sessions served with various federal courts throughout Texas until President RONALD REAGAN named him FBI director in July 1987. Sessions was confirmed two months later and took office on 2 November 1987.

Veteran aides recommended that Sessions spend time at FBI HEADQUARTERS learning his job, but the new director preferred traveling — a total of 126 trips with his wife, at Bureau expense, over the next six years. Some of his quirks — like wearing his FBI badge on the lapel of his suit or interrupting Bureau briefings to sing jingles from TV commercials — were curious at best. G-men noted that Sessions "just babbled" when he spoke, stringing non sequiturs together in a form of "gibberish" Bureau insiders soon dubbed "Sessions-speak." Some FBI veterans also thought him weak in dealing with personnel problems; they called him "Con-Sessions" after he settled class-action lawsuits for discrimination filed against the Bureau by BLACK and HISPANIC AGENTS.

Other problems were more serious, beginning with Sessions's appropriation of FBI vehicles and resources for personal use (including work done around Sessions's home, in the tradition of late director J. EDGAR HOOVER). Alice Sessions took advantage of her husband's position, demanding passes for herself to "secure" areas at FBI headquarters, interfering with Bureau security procedures, and so forth. A longtime Sessions aide, Sarah Munford, also basked in the director's reflected power, flashing FBI credentials to beat speeding tickets, violating various state and federal laws with seeming impunity.

Attorney General WILLIAM BARR received two letters complaining of Sessions's abuses in June 1992. One came from Washington journalist Robert Kessler, posing a series of questions about recent incidents; the other, anonymous but purportedly written by an active-duty agent, detailed the director's practice of masking personal travel as "FBI business." Both letters were delivered to the Bureau's OFFICE OF PROFESSIONAL RESPONSIBILITY, precipitating an investigation that made national headlines in October 1992. A month later, seemingly oblivious, Sessions and his wife flew to Atlantic City in the FBI's Sabreliner jet for a ballet performance, with their tickets "comped" by gambling bosses at the Sands Hotel and Casino. President GEORGE H.W. BUSH, though briefed on the problem with a recommendation that he fire Sessions, did nothing. Barr settled for a stinging memo, penned on 15 January 1993: "Given that you are a former U.S. attorney and federal judge, and that you are currently director of the premier federal law enforce agency, I must conclude that there is no excuse for your conduct."

Refusing to step down voluntarily, Sessions blamed aides and subordinates for his own conduct, noting that FBI counsel had "approved" his many trips on the FBI's tab. The OPR published a critical report on Sessions one day before President WILLIAM CLINTON was inaugurated, but even then relief took another six months. Clinton fired Sessions on 19 July 1993 and replaced him with Director LOUIS FREEH.

**SHAFER, Harry and Jill** — A married team of FBI INFORMANTS, Harry E. Shafer III and his wife Jill apparently began their covert careers in 1969, when they infiltrated the STUDENTS FOR A DEMOCRATIC SOCIETY. They subsequently settled in New Orleans and founded a bogus radical group called the Red Star Collective, which served the FBI's interests by gleaning information from "NEW LEFT" activists while diverting their energies into fruitless work on behalf of a government front group. By 1973 the Shafers had attached themselves to the AMERICAN INDIAN MOVEMENT (AIM) and were present at the WOUNDED KNEE SIEGE, afterward volunteering to "help" with AIM's legal work. Although non-Indians, they were accepted as comrades at face value, later boasting that they had managed to "divert" substantial amounts of money donated for AIM's defense in court. (G-men and their civilian collaborators had used the same tactic more than 50 years earlier, in the SACCO-VANZETTI CASE.)

**SHANAHAN, Edwin C.** — A Chicago native, born in 1898, Edwin Shanahan graduated from high school before serving in the U.S. Army during WORLD WAR I. He joined the Bureau of Investigation in February 1920 and spent his entire term of service in the Chicago field office. On 11 October 1925, while trying to arrest car thief Martin James Durkin for DWYER ACT violations, Shanahan was shot in the chest and fatally wounded.

The resulting manhunt was intense, a matter of pride and personal security for every G-man on the job. Director J. EDGAR HOOVER reportedly summoned an aide to his office and ordered, "We've got to get Durkin. If one man from the Bureau is killed, and the killer is permitted to get away, our agents will never be safe. We can't let him get away with it."

True or not, the story accurately captured Hoover's attitude. The manhunt went national after Durkin shot two Chicago policemen (killing one), then fled the Windy City for parts unknown. Bureau agents tracked him to California, where he was linked to a San Diego car theft, then back through Arizona and New Mexico, into Texas. A sheriff stopped Durkin and his female traveling companion in El Paso, driving a stolen Cadillac with a pistol on the front seat, but Durkin claimed to be a California lawman. Released to fetch his mythical credentials from a local hotel, Durkin and his girlfriend fled into the Texas desert. G-men descended on El Paso and soon found Durkin's car abandoned in the wasteland. A farmer admitted giving the couple a ride to Girvin, Texas and recalled their plans to visit nearby Alpine, in hopes of catching a train. An Alpine ticket clerk directed agents to San Antonio, where Durkin had boarded a train for St. Louis on 20 January 1926. Authorities were waiting when the train arrived at 11:00 a.m. that same day, and they collared Durkin before he could offer resistance.

In custody, Durkin admitted killing Agent Shanahan, but it was not a federal crime to murder G-men in the 1920s, so Illinois tried him on state murder charges and handed Durkin a 35-year prison term. A federal court soon added 15 years for driving stolen cars across state lines. Durkin was paroled from the Illinois state prison on 8 August 1945, transferred directly to the federal lockup at Leavenworth, where he remained until 28 July 1954. Edwin Shanahan's son joined the Bureau in August 1948 and served for 28 years, the same length of time his father's killer spent behind bars.

**SHAPIRO, Karl**—A Baltimore native, born 13 November 1913, Karl Shapiro wrote poetry from an early age, privately publishing his first collection of poems in 1935, but he won fame only during WORLD WAR II, while serving as a sergeant in the U.S. Army overseas. (His fiancée submitted the poems for publication without Shapiro's knowledge.) By that time, however, Shapiro had already earned a place in the FBI's "subversive" files. Specifically, a G-man writing to headquarters in 1940 noted that Shapiro had "produced an edition of *The Exiles Anthology*," including a brief three-paragraph introduction that "may be of interest to the Bureau." No specific text was singled out for study, but one obvious contender is the observation that "Since we are not exiles from this planet of disorder, our participation amid its ruins is one of pamphleteering for the valid activities of a demilitarized world." (Ironically, Shapiro later told author Natalie Robins, "I don't remember the book and can't imagine what 'produced' is supposed to mean. He speculated that he may have *edited* the work, but since no copies have apparently survived, the mystery remains.)

FBI agents continued filing reports on Shapiro from 1945 to 1966, including a list of some 25 "subversive" affiliations and the observation of one nameless INFORMANT that Shapiro was "as red and radical as they come." During the same "radical" period, Shapiro served as Consultant in Poetry at the Library of Congress (1946-47), then edited *Poetry* magazine (1950-56) and *Prairie Schooner* (1956-66). In 1965 agents reported that Shapiro had participated in a teach-in protest against the VIETNAM WAR at the University of Nebraska, and that he demonstrated against South African apartheid the following year. He also invited Bureau target ALLEN GINSBURG to speak at the university, but failed to attend the rally himself, since he "couldn't get through the crowds." Some 20 years later, Natalie Robins obtained portions of Shapiro's dossier under the FREEDOM OF INFORMATION ACT, but 43 pages remained classified "in the interest of national security." Shapiro died in New York on 14 May 2000.

**SHAW, Irwin**—A child of Russian-Jewish immigrants, born in the Bronx during 1913, Irwin Gilbert Shamforoff was known to his legions of fans as Irwin Shaw, best-selling novelist, playwright and Hollywood screen writer. His FBI file opened with allegations of "Communist activities" in 1935, the year before his antiwar play *Bury the Dead* premiered in New York. There is no reason to believe that G-men ever viewed the play, but nameless INFORMANTS reported that the script "followed the antiwar COMMUNIST PARTY line of the period 1933-1936." Two years later, agents noted that Shaw's "hopes are completely with the people of Republican Spain" (as opposed to the troops of Nazi Germany and fascist Italy attempting to crush Spain's legitimate government). Shaw's play for 1939, *The Gentle People*, was a parody of fascism, prompting another unnamed informant to report that Shaw had been "unusually active in the affairs of Communist fronts in Los Angeles, California, since 1937." A 1942 FBI report logged Shaw's membership in the American Committee for the Protection of the Foreign Born, ranking him as a "Lieutenant" (with author LILLIAN HELLMAN) in the "furious fight against the 'fascists' (meaning anyone who objected to Communist domina-

tion)." Before year's end, a nameless informant warned G-men that "the motion picture industry is the greatest medium for subversive activity there is. It is in the writers' hands and comes under the guise of a story." Shaw was singled out by name as a Hollywood writer in need of "watching."

By the time J. EDGAR HOOVER received that report, Shaw had joined the U.S. Army, serving as a private in the Mediterranean theater, later in England and France. He wrote military scripts, until Hoover noticed his activity in 1944 and dispatched a message to the War Department—"Confidential, by Special Messenger"—warning that "Colonel" Shaw was a "Communist sympathizer." The alert resulted in Shaw's name being placed on a secret list of "Subversive and Disaffected Military Personnel," vaguely defined as servicemen "who lack affection for or loyalty to the government and Constitution of the United States." The alert scuttled Shaw's assignment to the staff of *Stars and Stripes*, with Hoover's condemnation trailing Shaw for the remainder of his wartime service.

Back in civilian life after WORLD WAR II, Shaw briefly contributed work to *Salute*, a magazine for military veterans which FBI informants dubbed a "shrewdly camouflaged publication" that criticized the military and "follow[ed] the Communist party line to the letter." His first best-selling novel, *The Young Lions*, was published in 1948 (and filmed 10 years later). A series of best-seller followed, including *Rich Man, Poor Man* (1970), which spawned a popular television series. Despite his commercial success—or because of it—Shaw remained a subject of interest to the FBI and the HOUSE COMMITTEE ON UN-AMERICAN ACTIVITIES (HUAC). The U.S. Information Agency twice requested background information on Shaw, in 1956 and again in 1961, the Bureau responding with summaries from its own files and references to HUAC's. The Red hunters apparently were unaware of Shaw's action in the 1960s, denying a Soviet theater company permission to revive *Bury the Dead*, based on Shaw's concern that the play might be used as anti-U.S. propaganda. Shaw died at Davos, Switzerland on 16 May 1984. When author Herbert Mitgang obtained portions of Shaw's FBI dossier a few years later, 27 pages were blacked out by censors "in the interest of national defense or foreign policy."

**SHAW, John ("Jack")**—In 1970, while completing graduate work at New York City's John Jay College of Criminal Justice, veteran FBI agent Jack Shaw took exception to certain critical remarks about the FBI and Director J. EDGAR HOOVER, uttered in class by Professor Abraham Blumberg. In response, Shaw wrote a 15-page letter to Blumberg and unfortunately sent it to the Bureau's typing pool rather than typing it himself. Eight pages of the letter were subsequently discovered in a routine wastebasket inspection and his superiors were alarmed. While most of the letter strongly defended the Bureau, it included admissions that Hoover focused too much attention on "dime-a-dozen" BANK ROBBERIES, and that he sometimes used a "sledgehammer" approach to public relations. Shaw refused orders to provide the full letter (which he never mailed) on demand, and he was thereupon suspended and his weapon and credentials confiscated.

Hoover, enraged by even the mildest criticism, ordered

Shaw's punitive transfer to Butte, Montana — the FBI's "Siberia" — and explained his motive in a private memo.

> Ordinarily I would dismiss him but he is a veteran and you have to go through a long procedure and they have indicated dismissal would not be sustained because he didn't mail the letter. I said I wanted his transfer to Butte because I hope he will resign as I understand he has four children and the working conditions of the Butte office would be difficult for him in his circumstance.

Shaw's "circumstance" included the fact that his wife was dying of cancer. Confronted with the transfer order, he requested a postponement and advised his supervisor that "if he is fired with prejudice, he will have to fight it and, if he is transferred, the condition of his family is such that he will have to resign." Hoover ordered New York's agent-in-charge to "go ahead and suspend him for 30 days and then transfer him and we will be well rid of him." When Shaw kept his promise to resign, Hoover vengefully accepted "with prejudice," thus effectively precluding any future employment for Shaw in government service.

Unsatisfied with Shaw's departure from the Bureau, Hoover also demanded that John Jay College dismiss Dr. Blumberg. When the school refused, Hoover pulled 15 other G-men from their classes at the school, and when a teacher at Washington's American University criticized his action, agents were forced to withdraw from that school as well. Jack Shaw, meanwhile, complained about his treatment to various members of Congress, including Senator GEORGE MCGOVERN, who made the matter public in January 1971. At the same time, with assistance from the AMERICAN CIVIL LIBERTIES UNION, Shaw sued the Bureau for violation of various CIVIL RIGHTS. Shaw's wife died in March 1971 and the FBI settled his case out of court on 16 June 1971 for a lump payment of $13,000. Shortly after Hoover's death, former Assistant Director WILLIAM SULLIVAN hired Shaw as an investigator for the JUSTICE DEPARTMENT's new Office of National NARCOTICS Intelligence.

**SHEEAN, James Vincent** — A renowned foreign correspondent whose early work helped create the genre of book-length journalism, Vincent Sheean was born in 1899 and three decades later joined EDGAR SNOW as one of the few U.S. reporters with profound insight on the tumultuous politics of China. FBI agents opened a file on Sheean in 1927, following some comment (missing from the dossier) that he had made to a U.S. consular official in Berlin. His file then remained inactive until 1937, when he was indexed as a member of multiple "subversive" groups including the ABRAHAM LINCOLN BRIGADE, the American Committee for Yugoslav Relief, and the Committee for a Democratic Far Eastern Policy. Two years later, agents clipped a *Daily Worker* article referring to Sheean's address before the Third American Writers Congress at Carnegie Hall. In the 1940s, G-men added the Council on African Affairs and the India League of America to Sheean's suspect résumé.

In their pursuit of derogatory information, FBI agents questioned INFORMANTS, read Sheean's mail and sifted through his household trash for clues. In 1943 the Bureau noted Sheean's attendance at a birthday party for singer and reputed communist Paul Robeson. Four years later, J. EDGAR HOOVER was pleased to find Sheean's name on "Master Sucker List" published in the New York *World-Telegram*, citing "persons who had been used by the COMMUNIST PARTY." Lacking any evidence that Sheean himself belonged to the party, FBI memos variously branded Sheean "a Communist," "a liberal," and "the most pathetic figure in the whole gang of pink intellectuals." A 1948 report notes Sheean's awareness of the surveillance, noting that he "did not think much of these agents" and believed "their reports meant nothing." Two years later, another memo identified Sheean as belonging to a "clique of friends of the Chinese Communists, which included STATE DEPARTMENT officials as well as well-known journalist and others." Hoover believed that this group held a "monopoly in book reviewing in the China field," and that Sheean personally "was poisoning the wells of information in America about the Communists and about the Chinese Communists in particular." FBI surveillance of Sheean continued until 1973, two years before his death.

**SHERWOOD, Robert Emmet** — Born at New Rochelle, New York in 1896, Robert Sherwood ranks as one of America's most prestigious poets and biographers, a friend to presidents and four-time winner of the Pulitzer Prize (1936, 1938, 1940 and 1948), whose play *The Best Years of Our Lives* won an Academy Award in 1946. Despite such honors and connections, Sherwood was shadowed by the FBI throughout his long career.

G-men opened their file on Sherwood in 1917, the year before he graduated from Harvard, after a "confidential informant" reported Sherwood's enlistment in the Canadian Black Watch Expeditionary Forces, organized to fight in WORLD WAR I. Two years later, a memo named him as the "dramatic editor" of *Vanity Fair*, and agents kept track of his transfer to *Life* magazine, where Sherwood started as an associate editor (1920) and rose to the rank of full editor (1924-28). "Derogatory" reports piled up in the 1930s, including a notation of Sherwood's membership in the AMERICAN CIVIL LIBERTIES UNION, his 1935 foundation of the New Theatre School (branded a "Communist front" and "the mainspring of the Agitprop theater movement" in 1944, by the HOUSE COMMITTEE ON UN-AMERICAN ACTIVITIES), his 1936 service as secretary of the Dramatists Guild, and his signing (with other prominent writers) of a 1938 letter asking President FRANKLIN ROOSEVELT to end America's economic trade with Nazi Germany.

That criticism of U.S. foreign policy did not prevent FDR from drafting Sherwood as his chief speech writer or placing him in positions of trust during WORLD WAR II. From 1940 to 1945, Sherwood served as an aide to both the secretary of war and the secretary of the navy, while simultaneously directing the Overseas Division of the Office of War Information. It is characteristic of the FBI's political myopia that one report from the same period identifies Sherwood simply as "a dramatist who lives in the White House with [Secretary of Commerce] Harry Hopkins." In 1941, G-men interviewed Sherwood after he told Hopkins a journalist friend had reported "a possible line on important Nazi activities in New York," but the investigation went no further. Agents were apparently more interested in noting that the AMER-

ICAN LEGION was "considerably aroused" by Sherwood's radio plays, including *An American Crusader*, starring Orson Welles. No one from the Bureau actually heard the broadcast, but memos based on commentary from unnamed INFORMANTS note that "The play reportedly made it appear that it was almost impossible for a man to publish a thought or theory which was contrary to the thoughts of the majority." By 1942, after "a highly confidential source" identified Sherwood as a COMMUNIST PARTY member, the Bureau tagged his file "Internal Security — C" (for Communist).

FBI pursuit of Sherwood continued into the Red-hunting 1950s. In 1950 he offended federal sensibilities by signing a telegram to the U.S. Supreme Court, seeking reversal of contempt citations filed against the blacklisted "Hollywood Ten." Two years later, a memo noted, "Various sources have stated that Sherwood is a Communist, appears to favor Socialist organizations, etc., and was believed to be a member of the National Council of the Arts, Sciences and Professions." Collection of material stopped only with Sherwood's death, in 1955. Three decades later, when author Herbert Mitgang obtained 80 pages of the Sherwood dossier under the FREEDOM OF INFORMATION ACT, it was heavily censored, with some pages entirely blacked out in the "interest of national security."

**SHIPLEY, Ruth Bielaski** — A sister of one-time Bureau chief A. BRUCE BIELASKI, Ruth Shipley presided for 25 years as director of the STATE DEPARTMENT's Passport Office, employing information from "secret" FBI files to arbitrarily deny passport applications from various alleged "subversives." Two of her more prominent targets were novelist NELSON ALGREN and playwright ARTHUR MILLER. Algren's passport application was rejected in 1952 "because of allegations of COMMUNIST PARTY activity" (never substantiated, the sources undisclosed). A year later, Miller was denied a passport to attend the premiere of his play *The Crucible* in Belgium, because Shipley believed his travel abroad was "not in the national interest." Miller filed a new application in 1956, offering a sworn affidavit that he had never belonged to the Communist Party, but Shipley rebuffed him again.

Ironically, Shipley's devotion to the whims of J. EDGAR HOOVER was so complete that she herself subverted the national interest during World War II, stamping passports issued to the secret agents of Hoover enemy WILLIAM DONOVAN with the letters "OSS" (for OFFICE OF STRATEGIC SERVICES) until an order from the Roosevelt White House stopped her from placing the lives of American spies in danger. (That malicious behavior was particularly strange, in light of the fact that another of Shipley's brothers, Frank Bielaski, was director of investigations for the wartime OSS.) Upon Shipley's retirement, Hoover continued his harassment of various suspects with aid from her successor, Frances Knight.

**SINATRA, Francis Albert Sr.** — A native of Hoboken, New Jersey, Frank Sinatra was probably born on 12 December 1915 (some reports claim 1916 or 1917). In 1938 Bergen County authorities charged him with seduction under a false promise of marriage, but that charge and a count of adultery later filed in the same case

were subsequently dismissed. Sinatra cut his first hit record in May 1940, and the FBI opened a FILE in his name — "for the purpose of filing miscellaneous information" — on 13 August 1943. Six months later G-men launched a "limited inquiry" into rumors that Sinatra paid $40,000 to escape military service in WORLD WAR II, but they found no evidence to support the charge. (In fact, Sinatra had a perforated eardrum; a psychologist had also judged the celebrity crooner "neurotic" — specifically, terrified of crowds!)

In November 1945 FBI HEADQUARTERS became concerned over Sinatra's alleged Communist sympathies. On 1 November, Sinatra addressed a rally sponsored by the Anselm Forum, opposing white efforts to segregate a school in Gary, Indiana. According to an FBI report on that event, "It was said that many of the leaders of the Anselm Forum were CIO leaders and 'so-called liberals.'" A month later, on 12 December 1945, an anonymous INFORMANT told G-men that Sinatra had joined the COMMUNIST PARTY in New York. A memo from Assistant to the Director LOUIS NICHOLS, describing a May 1946 Sinatra concert in Detroit where members of the audience jeered truant officers, bears a terse marginal notation from J. EDGAR HOOVER: "Sinatra is as much to blame as the moronic bobby-soxers." A September 1950 FBI report linked Sinatra to 15 alleged "Communist front organizations," including such hotbeds of subversion as Veterans of the ABRAHAM LINCOLN BRIGADE, the Joint Anti-Fascist Refugee Committee, and the American Crusade to End LYNCHING. Yet strangely, when the U.S. STATE DEPARTMENT requested a background check on Sinatra in December 1954, FBI headquarters reported no Red links "aside from his membership in the Independent Citizens Committee of the Arts, Sciences, and Professions in 1946."

While Sinatra's communist connections proved ephemeral, the same could not be said for his links to ORGANIZED CRIME. A memo dated 7 September 1950 records Sinatra's offer to become an FBI informant, and while the subject matter of his call remains unknown, a follow-up report of 29 September documented Sinatra's ties to nine prominent mobsters, including Charles ("Lucky") Luciano, Mickey Cohen, Willie Moretti and a brother of ALPHONSE CAPONE. Throughout 1960, agents tracked Sinatra's relationship with presidential candidate JOHN F. KENNEDY, including Sinatra's role in arranging liaisons between Kennedy and Judith Campbell, a sometime girlfriend of Chicago mobster SAM GIANCANA. Hoover was pleased to inform Attorney General ROBERT KENNEDY of Sinatra's mob ties in February 1961, prompting estrangement from the Kennedy clan that turned Sinatra overnight from a liberal Democrat to a conservative Republican.

In the meantime, agents kept watch on Sinatra's underworld connections, reporting his "command performance" for Giancana at Chicago's Villa Venice in November 1962. Two months later, G-men questioned Sinatra about a TEAMSTERS UNION loan that bankrolled his purchase of the Cal-Neva Lodge, at Lake Tahoe. Giancana's frequent appearances at the Cal-Neva cost Sinatra his Nevada gaming license in February 1963, but "Old Blue Eyes" clung defiantly to his underworld alliances. An internal FBI memo, dated 17 April 1964, suggested that the Bureau should "explore the possibilities of developing [Sinatra] as an informant," but Assistant Director Alan Belmont vetoed the idea, responding, "I don't think the leopard will change his spots." Seven months later, a report to President LYNDON JOHNSON confirmed that Sinatra was still a "close friend" of Sam Giancana. In May 1967 Sinatra was named national chairman of gangster Joe Columbo's ITALIAN-AMERICAN CIVIL RIGHTS LEAGUE. (A sideshow to the main event was the December 1963 ransom KIDNAPPING of Sinatra's son, Frank Jr. G-men swiftly apprehended the kidnappers, prompting Sinatra to buy them gold watches. The agents repeatedly declined his gifts until Sinatra got the message and sent a more expensive watch to J. Edgar Hoover.)

Sinatra's mob ties may have embarrassed Democrats, but prominent Republicans had no such qualms. California governor RONALD REAGAN welcomed Sinatra's support in 1966 and 1970 (and later, in his successful bid for the White House). President RICHARD NIXON courted Sinatra in 1969, and the crooner socialized frequently with Vice President SPIRO AGNEW — this notwithstanding his subpoenas to testify before state commissions investigating underworld corruption in New Jersey (1969) and Massachusetts (1972), and before a congressional panel probing mob influence in professional sports (1972). Sam Giancana was murdered in June 1975, shortly before he was scheduled to testify before the HOUSE SELECT COMMITTEE ON ASSASSINATIONS, but Sinatra maintained consistency, posing for photos with New York mob boss Carlo Gambino the following year.

Curiously, Sinatra's relationship with the federal government appeared to thaw from that time forward. When his mother died in January 1977, FBI Director CLARENCE KELLEY sent condolences. Sinatra organized President Reagan's inaugural celebration in 1981, and Nevada officials restored his gaming license the same year, thanks to a character reference from the White House. The last entry in Sinatra's FBI file, from March 1985, recorded a death threat from a deranged female fan. Three months later, President Reagan favored Sinatra with the Medal of Freedom. Sinatra died on 14 May 1998, at age 83. In December 1998 the FBI released 1,275 pages of his dossier under the FREEDOM OF INFORMATION ACT.

**SINCLAIR, Upton** — A Baltimore native, born 20 September 1878, Upton Sinclair moved to New York City with his family at age 10. An active Socialist in the early 1900s, Sinclair published his first novel in 1901 and scored his first critical acclaim four years later, with publication of *The Jungle*. That scathing exposé of the meat packing industry prompted passage of the 1906 Pure Food and Drug Act (and prompted President THEODORE ROOSEVELT to denounce the journalistic trend he termed "muckraking"). Sinclair ran for Congress in New Jersey as a Socialist, then quit the party during WORLD WAR I, but returned to the fold in 1926.

The Bureau of Investigation opened its file on Sinclair in 1923, when his name appeared on the advisory committee of the Friends of Soviet Russia. The same year, G-men noted that Sinclair had criticized the AUTHORS LEAGUE OF AMERICA for its failure to endorse the AMERICAN CIVIL LIBERTIES UNION. Sinclair's dossier remained inactive thereafter, until he ran for governor of California in 1934. On 13 September of that year, President FRANKLIN ROOSEVELT telephoned J. EDGAR HOOVER to report that first lady ELEANOR ROOSEVELT had received a letter from Sinclair, complaining of threats against his life and seeking federal protection. At Roosevelt's request, Hoover agreed to "have somebody see him" and discuss the matter, uncovering "alleged threats" against Sinclair by an enemy described as "a former playboy" and "an extremely dissipated youth of many years." Hoover finally declined to offer Sinclair FBI protection, and no attempt was made on the candidate's life. Sinclair lost the gubernatorial race but continued as an active writer, publishing more than 90 books prior to his death in November 1968.

**SKYJACKING** — Widely regarded as a modern crime, committed principally by TERRORISTS, the hijacking of aircraft — dubbed "skyjacking" in the late 1960s — has in fact kept pace with the growth of civilian aviation since the 1930s. And while political activists have dominated the field, skyjackings are committed for a wide variety of reasons including the time-honored standby of simple greed.

The world's first two skyjackings occurred in Peru, during February 1931. The first U.S. incident was recorded on 1 November 1958, when Cuban rebels diverted a Cubana Airlines plane from Miami to Havana. (It crashed in transit, killing 17 of the 20 persons aboard.) The first American aircraft seized by skyjackers — National Airlines Flight 337 — was rerouted to Cuba by Antulio Ramirez Ortiz on 1 May 1961. A federal grand jury indicted Ramirez three months later, and FBI agents found him in Miami 24 years later, on 11 November 1975. G-men caught their first skyjacker in the act on 3 August 1961, after a nine-hour siege at the El Paso, Texas airport.

The dozen years between January 1968 and December 1979 were the "golden age" of skyjacking, with 370 incidents reported worldwide for an average of one seizure every 12 days. The U.S. suffered 144 skyjackings during that era, with 78 planes diverted to Cuba and 66 others held hostage within national borders. A federal statute on aircraft piracy gave the FBI primary jurisdiction in such cases, but the Bureau's performance got mixed reviews. G-men arrested 27 skyjackers during the 12 years in question, while 69 escaped and remain fugitives. (The other 48 either surrendered voluntarily or were arrested by local police.) In cases where agents employed DEADLY FORCE, they left nine persons dead and seven wounded. Those killed included a crewman and three passengers; the injured included two crew members and an FBI agent.

Casualties notwithstanding, FBI HEADQUARTERS tolerated no criticism of its performance in skyjacking cases. During an incident in Denver, on 1 November 1969, Captain Donald Cook barred two G-men from sneaking aboard his plane to attack hijacker Raphael Minichiello (a Marine combat veteran armed with an automatic rifle). Crew members charged that the agents made no effort to speak with Minichiello and that their behavior endangered all aboard the plane. Director J. EDGAR HOOVER responded to Capt. Cook's "outrageous action" by sending furious protests to TWA, the Federal Aviation Administration and the Airline Pilots Association, attempting to have Cook dismissed. More than two years later, Hoover was still pursuing the fruitless vendetta. In a memo dictated on 26 April 1972, six days before his death, Hoover commanded that the FBI must "be aggressively pertinent when we are communicating with that organization [TWA]."

Skyjacking incidents dropped off dramatically in the 1980s, as new security measures made smuggling weapons aboard commercial aircraft more difficult. Still, loopholes in security remained, and one of them — a regulation permitting small knives aboard U.S. flights — backfired catastrophically on 11 September 2001. That morning, 19 Muslim extremists devoted to fugitive terrorist USAMA BIN LADEN boarded four airliners lifting off from East Coast airports for various destinations. Armed only with simple box cutters, the flight-trained terrorists killed or overpowered crew members and seized control of the jets. Two subsequently crashed into New York City's WORLD TRADE CENTER, claiming more than 3,300 lives, while a third plunged into the Pentagon and killed 189 persons. The fourth flight, presumably intended for another Washington target, crashed outside Pittsburgh, Pennsylvania with loss of all 44 persons aboard. In the wake of that tragedy, FBI agent COLEEN ROWLEY disclosed that Minneapolis G-men had arrested a conspirator in the skyjackings one month prior to the attacks, but they were forced to release him when officials at FBI HEADQUARTERS refused to authorize a search of his apartment and computer. Subsequent revelations that some of the terrorists had plotted their crimes and trained at U.S. flight schools since 1998 — some of them under sporadic FBI scrutiny — did nothing to enhance the Bureau's reputation.

**"SLACKER" Raids (1918)** — The Selective Service Act of 1917, passed by Congress on 6 April and enacted the following month, imposed military conscription on American men for the first time since the Civil War. All males between the ages of 21 and 30 were required to register with local draft boards no later than 15 June 1917. Enforcement of the new law fell to Enoch Crowder, judge advocate general of the War Department, with assistance from Attorney General THOMAS GREGORY and Chief A. BRUCE BIELASKI's Bureau of Investigation. In July 1917, convinced that many draft-age men had either failed to register or had deserted soon after induction, Gregory ordered Bielaski to investigate the scope of noncompliance nationwide. Discovery of "slackers" was assisted by the offer of a $50 bounty for each draft-evader reported, and by the efforts of such private vigilante groups as the AMERICAN PROTECTIVE LEAGUE (APL).

In March 1918 Crowder ordered the Bureau to begin arresting draft dodgers. Teamed with "auxiliary" agents from the APL, G-men staged their first dragnet raids in Minneapolis that month, accosting men wherever they were found in public and detaining any who could not produce a draft card or a birth certificate to prove themselves exempt from service. Additional sweeps were conducted that summer in Birmingham, Cleveland, Dayton, Detroit, Philadelphia, St. Louis and San Francisco, with the mixed bag yielding some 20,000 draft dodgers. Crowder and Gregory were sufficiently pleased with that result to order a more ambitious roundup, scheduled to begin on 3 September 1918.

Beginning that morning and continuing through 5 September, a strike force of 35 G-men, 2,000 APL vigilantes, plus several hundred civilian and military police fanned out through the boroughs of New York City, ultimately broadening their search to include Jersey City and Newark, New Jersey. Within three days they arrested 75,000 suspected slackers, confining the prisoners in rough "corrals" without food, water or sanitary facilities. Some would remain caged for 48 hours until they were proved draft-exempt, while others — including a 75-year-old man on crutches — were released more expeditiously. No final statistics for the New York sweep were ever released, but anonymous sources inside the JUSTICE DEPARTMENT told reporters that only one of every 200 persons arrested proved to be a draft dodger.

Where the earlier raids had been widely commended, those in New York and New Jersey were swiftly condemned by the press as examples of lawless excess. Criticism in the U.S. Senate drove President WOODROW WILSON to order a Justice Department investigation. Gregory assigned the task to Assistant Attorney General JOHN LORD O'BRIAN, who completed a hasty inquiry in 48 hours. O'Brian's report blamed APL members and military police for the worst abuses, noting that APL members had no authority to serve as law enforcement officers. That judgment notwithstanding, Bielaski continued to use the APL as backup in subsequent slacker raids, including a three-day sweep through the state of Washington in September 1918. Fourteen months later, the abuses of the draft roundups were repeated and compounded in the PALMER RAIDS of November 1919 and January 1920.

**SMITH Act** — The Alien Registration Act, more commonly known by the name of Virginia congressman Howard Smith (who authored its sedition provisions) was enacted by Congress on 28 June 1940. It provided a maximum five-year prison term (later amended to 20 years) for anyone who "knowingly or willfully advocates, abets, advises or teaches the duty, necessity, desirability or propriety of violently overthrowing" the U.S. government or the government of any particular state. Although regarded by FBI HEADQUARTERS as a tool for jailing communists and other leftist "radicals," the law was initially used against fascist and Nazi sympathizers during WORLD WAR II. The first group of 26 defendants, indicted in July 1942, were acquitted when the JUSTICE DEPARTMENT failed to prove they had plotted revolution. A second batch of 30 defendants were indicted in 1944, but charges were dropped after a chaotic trial that climaxed with the judge's death.

Following the armistice and onset of the Cold War, FBI Director J. EDGAR HOOVER prepared a 1,350-page history of the Communist Party (with 546 "exhibits"), presented to Attorney General TOM CLARK in an effort to spur Smith Act prosecution of party leaders. At the same time, in February 1948, the HOUSE COMMITTEE ON UN-AMERICAN ACTIVITIES contacted Clark, demanding to know why no indictments had yet been filed under the law. A federal grand jury in New York subsequently indicted 12 members of the party's national board on 29 June 1948, but Clark sealed the indictments for a month and announced them on 20 July, after five of the 12 were arrested in New York City. Hoover freely admitted that the arrests were "a political move ... timed to break just before the [HENRY] WALLACE for President convention in Philadelphia," and complained that more Reds had not been indicted.

Prosecution of defendant William Foster was deferred due to poor health, while the other 11 defendants faced trial in New York on 17 January 1949. Key prosecution witnesses were professional ex-communist Louis Bundenz and HERBERT PHILBRICK, an FBI INFORMANT who broke cover at the trial to testify against his former comrades. All defendants were convicted on 14 October 1949, with 10 receiving the maximum sentence from Judge Harold Medina. (The lone exception was a highly decorated war veteran whose medals won him a reduced sentence.) Their convictions (and the Smith Act's dubious constitutionality) were upheld by the U.S. SUPREME COURT in 1951.

That finding on appeal was Hoover's signal to begin a round of "second echelon" roundups and prosecutions against lower-ranking party officers. Over the next three years 126 Communist Party members were indicted for Smith Act violations, with 93 convicted at trial. Hoover's enthusiasm for the round-ups paled in 1954, when he realized that continued exposure of hired informants in court jeopardized "the highly essential intelligence coverage which this Bureau must maintain in the internal security field." Effectively choosing secrecy over prosecution of alleged subversives, Hoover recommended that future prosecutions should be limited to prominent party leaders.

The Supreme Court changed its view on Smith Act prosecutions in October 1955, accepting one of the "second echelon" cases for review on a writ of certiorari. The final decision in 1957, effectively overturning all but the original dozen convictions, held that mere advocacy of revolution without supporting action should not be prosecuted. A Justice Department ruling, dated 15 March 1956, agreed that any future indictments must include "an actual plan for violent revolution" instead of mere theory. No further Smith Act charges were filed, though the law remains in effect and is used by G-men to justify DOMESTIC SURVEILLANCE in some cases. An attempt to prosecute neo-Nazi leaders for sedition, relative to their involvement with THE ORDER, resulted in the April 1988 acquittals of all defendants.

**SMITH, Melvin**—On 8 December 1969, four days after police officers killed FRED HAMPTON and Mark Clark in a raid on the Chicago office of the BLACK PANTHER PARTY, officers of the Los Angeles Police Department staged a similar raid on the Panther office in L.A. Using an armored car, tear gas and dynamite, SWAT team officers stormed the fortified structure at 5:30 a.m. Besieged Panthers fought back for nearly four hours, until television crews arrived to observe their surrender. Six party members were wounded and a total of 13 arrested, including local leader ELMER ("GERONIMO") PRATT and his security chief, Melvin ("Cotton") Smith. As author Jo Durden-Smith explained the clash:

> The pretext of the raid was twofold. The police, first of all, claimed that on November 28, 1969, George Young and Paul Redd had thrown a police sergeant out of Panther headquarters at gunpoint, and that, later in the day, Geronimo Pratt had taken a bead on a passing police car with a machinegun. Arrest warrants for all three were sworn out a week before the raid. Second, the SWAT assault group was armed with a search warrant ... for stolen weapons.... [I]n getting the search warrant, police deliberately misled Municipal Court Judge Antonio Chavez. The reason ... Sergeant Raymond Callahan gave for the prospective search was that he wanted to look for six machineguns and thirty M-14s stolen from Camp Pendleton marine base, as well as the weapons used in what he called "the assault on officers." In an affidavit under oath, Callahan told Judge Chavez that George Young had been at Camp Pendleton when the machineguns and M-14s were stolen and that he later went AWOL. What he didn't tell him was that Young was in the stockade at the time of the theft and [Callahan] knew it. "I didn't think it was important," he later said.

Thirteen of the Panthers arrested in December 1969 faced trial seven months later, on charges of conspiracy to assault and murder policemen and conspiracy to possess illegal weapons (though none were found in the raid). The defendants were surprised by Cotton Smith's appearance as a prosecution witness against them, and while the state claimed Smith had only "rolled over" since his arrest to avoid prison time, another witness — police INFORMANT Louis Tackwood — testified on 22 November 1971 that Smith had been his FBI contact in the Panthers since fall 1969, months before the raid. That revelation was a crucial blow to the prosecution, as jurors acquitted all 13 defendants on the most serious charges, but Pratt and eight others were oddly convicted of conspiring to stockpile weapons police could not find. Melvin Smith vanished into obscurity after the trial, while Pratt was later sentenced to life imprisonment for murder in a case later proved to be a FRAME-UP. Suspicion lingers that Smith may have coordinated the December 1969 raid, as another Panther "security chief"—WILLIAM O'NEAL— did in Chicago the night Fred Hampton was slain.

**SMITH, William French**—A New Hampshire native, born at Wilton on 26 August 1917, William Smith spent most of his adult life as a California attorney specializing in labor matters (on the side of management). His best-known client was RONALD REAGAN, former governor of California (1967-75), and Smith joined Reagan's campaign for the White House in 1980. His chief contribution was introducing Reagan to Raymond Donovan, a New Jersey contractor with ORGANIZED CRIME connections who gave the campaign $200,000 and was subsequently nominated to serve as secretary of labor. Smith, for his part, was named attorney general and assumed control of the JUSTICE DEPARTMENT on 23 January 1981.

Reagan's emotional "law-and-order" campaign had included vows to "unleash" the FBI and permit unfettered DOMESTIC SURVEILLANCE of alleged "subversive" elements in the U.S. To that end, in March 1983, Smith rescinded the guidelines earlier established by Attorney General EDWARD LEVI, requiring that "national security" investigations of groups or individuals should require some evidence of criminal activity and furthermore must be reviewed by the attorney general "at least annually," with a verdict "in writing" as to whether each investigation should continue. Smith scrapped those rules across the board, permitting the Bureau to initiate "domestic security/TERRORISM" probes whenever "facts or circumstances reasonably indicate that two or more persons are engaged in an enterprise [to further] political or social goals wholly or in part through activities that involve force or violence and a violation of the criminal law of the United States." Surveillance was thus extended to those who merely "advocate criminal activity or indicate an apparent intent to engage in crime," while oversight by the attorney general was henceforth purely discretionary.

In practice, the Smith guidelines revived the essence of President RICHARD NIXON'S campaigns against political "enemies," and many of those slated for surveillance were critics of Reagan's illegal activities in Central America (including the Iran-Contra Scandal). Under Smith, groups such as the COMMITTEE IN SOLIDARITY WITH THE PEOPLE OF EL SALVADOR and various PUERTO RICAN NATIONALIST organizations were subject to harassment indistinguishable from the Bureau's COINTELPRO campaigns of 1956-71.

On other fronts, Attorney General Smith moved to eliminate the Ethics in Government Act, the Foreign Corrupt Practices Act and major portions of the FREEDOM OF INFORMATION ACT. He echoed Reagan by proclaiming a "vigorous" war on crime and NARCOTICS, but simultaneously slashed the budgets of various federal investigative agencies while reshuffling FBI priorities to emphasize "violent crime" over organized crime. Critics ranging from the U.S. Coast Guard to the AMERICAN CIVIL LIBERTIES UNION denounced the Reagan-Smith crime war as "fraudulent," noting the president's enduring ties to leaders of the corrupt TEAMSTERS UNION, but Smith was undeterred. In January 1982, ignoring the protests of FBI Director WILLIAM WEBSTER, Smith ordered the Bureau to share jurisdiction in narcotics cases with the DRUG ENFORCEMENT ADMINISTRATION. Later, in June 1984, he inaugurated the DRUG DEMAND REDUCTION PROGRAM in support of First Lady Nancy Reagan's wholly ineffective "Just Say No" anti-drug campaign. (At the same time, White House aides and leaders of the "Contra" terrorist organization were smuggling cocaine into the U.S. and using the proceeds to finance Reagan's illegal proxy war in Nicaragua.) Poor health compelled Smith's resignation on 25 February 1985, whereupon he was replaced by EDWIN MEESE. Smith died on 29 October 1990.

**"SNITCH Jacketing"**—One of many methods utilized by the FBI in its campaigns to disrupt alleged subversive groups is the technique known as "snitch jacketing" (or "bad jacketing"). Snitch jacketing occurs whenever law enforcement officers or their civilian collaborators falsely identify specific individuals as INFORMANTS, thereby attempting to discredit them among their comrades in a particular movement or organization. This technique was especially popular with G-men assigned to the Bureau's illegal COINTELPRO operations and similar campaigns pursued through the years under different names.

Methods for applying a snitch jacket vary from one case to another. Agents sometimes approach their target in public, behaving in a friendly manner for the benefit of bystanders. Likewise, in the case of group arrests, one or two individuals may be released while others remain in jail, making those incarcerated think their friends have "cut a deal" with the authorities. In a variation on that theme, suspects in custody may be allowed to "overhear" staged broadcasts on a police radio, seeming to arrange clandestine meetings between authorities and some trusted member of their organization. Author DON WHITEHEAD described with approval various cases where G-men parked their government cars overnight near the homes of known KU KLUX KLAN members, leading other Klansmen to suspect them as traitors. When agents wish to distance themselves from such tactics, paid informants may circulate false accusations. Anonymous letters and pamphlets have also been used to breed mistrust within various "undesirable" organizations.

While a threat of snitch jacketing may be employed to "turn" an individual, coercing him or her into becoming an informant, once the label is applied, the subject is theoretically "neutralized," shunned by former comrades as a turncoat. The COMMUNIST PARTY was an early target of such methods, as were various CIVIL RIGHTS and "NEW LEFT" groups in later years. In some cases, snitch jacketing efforts may continue even after the target's demise, as witnessed in repeated claims that deceased LSD guru Timothy Leary was an FBI informant throughout the period when he advised America's youth to "tune in, turn on, and drop out." In a similar vein, rumors persist that a 1968 FBI memo (never produced for examination) says that the Bureau hired Jerry Garcia's Grateful Dead rock band "to politicize the counterculture with drugs."

In cases where a particular group or its members are known to be violent, the effects of snitch jacketing may extend beyond mere social ostracism. A member of the Mississippi Klan, suspected of "snitching" on his comrades, was beaten to death by persons unknown near his Meadville home on 16 August 1965. (A sheriff allied with the Klan ruled the death "accidental" and closed the case.) Eleven years later, in February 1976, unknown gunmen killed ANNA MAE AQUASH on South Dakota's PINE RIDGE RESERVATION, where she was known as an active member of the AMERICAN INDIAN MOVEMENT (AIM). FBI memos reveal a campaign to make AIM leaders think Aquash was a Bureau informant, though her killers were probably members of an anti-AIM vigilante group supported by the FBI, the so-called GUARDIANS OF THE OGLALA NATION. In 1992, when eight alleged Minnesota members of the Vice Lords street gang were charged with killing a police informant, testimony demonstrated that victim Ed Harris had himself been a target of snitch jacketing by local police, working in concert with the FBI. Such lethal violence is predictable in many cases, and FBI memos from the COINTELPRO years make it clear that G-men considered the murder of various subjects a "positive result" of their covert campaigns.

**SNOW, Edgar**—Born in Kansas City on 19 July 1905, Edgar Snow began his writing career with a New York advertising agency in 1924, then left the U.S. to wander Asia from 1928 to 1941, reporting on the tides of war and revolution wracking that vast continent. A friend of Mao Zedong and Chou En-lai two decades before they led the successful communist revolution in China, Snow became a target of federal investigation in 1931, when Bureau headquarters received Shanghai police files branding him a "radical journalist" who was "believed to be receiving Communist literature from [COMMUNIST PARTY] agents in Shanghai." Six years later, G-men reviewed Snow's best-selling *Red Star Over China*, concluding that "anyone who would write a book" of that title "would definitely be referring to the Soviet government." In May 1945, after Snow published an article titled "Must China Go Red?" in the *Saturday Evening Post*, J. EDGAR HOOVER branded him "an ingenious fellow-traveler" and asked the STATE DEPARTMENT to cancel Snow's passport.

FBI suspicion of Snow only deepened in 1949, after China "went Red" in reality, and agents sometimes found themselves working at cross-purposes with the State Department, which valued Snow as a priceless resource. U.S. officials picked Snow's brain throughout the 1960s, seeking advice on matters ranging from Mao Zedong's health to his opinions on the JFK ASSASSINATION and the attitude of average Chinese citizens to communist rule. Through it all, the FBI regarded Snow simply as a threat to national security, noting that "although he was not an actual Party member, the Party knew just how to use him." Sporadic surveillance of Snow continued through 1971. He died in Switzerland on 15 February 1972.

**SOCIALIST Workers Party**—Founded in 1938, the Socialist Workers Party (SWP) was under FBI scrutiny by 1940, if not sooner. In addition to its socialist program (despised as "communism" by FBI Director J. EDGAR HOOVER, the SWP also doggedly opposed American involvement in WORLD WAR II. The Bureau's first concerted anti-SWP action occurred on 28 June 1943, when G-men raided the party's Minneapolis headquarters and seized thousands of documents. Twenty-nine officers of the party were subsequently indicted for SMITH ACT violations, with 18 convicted at trial and sentenced to prison. The U.S. SUPREME COURT declined to review their convictions, leaving them incarcerated for the duration of the war.

While surveillance of the SWP was unrelenting, Hoover took the next step on 12 October 1961, with his announcement of an illegal COINTELPRO disruption campaign. His rationale for trying to destroy a legitimate public organization was that the SWP:

> ... has, over the past several years, been openly espousing its line on a local and national basis through the running of candidates for public office and strongly directing and/or supporting such causes as Castro's Cuba and integration problems arising in the South. The SWP has been in frequent contact with international Trotskyite groups stopping short of open and direct contact with these groups.... It is felt that a disruption program along similar lines [to that mounted against the COMMUNIST PARTY in 1956] could be initiated against the SWP on a very selective basis. One of the purposes of this program would be to alert the public to the fact that the SWP is not just another socialist group but follows the revolutionary principles of Marx, Lenin and Engels as interpreted by Leon Trotsky.... It may be desirable to expand the program after its effects have been evaluated.

And expand it they did. In May 1962 G-men sought to drive a wedge between the SWP and the NATIONAL ASSOCIATION FOR THE ADVANCEMENT OF COLORED PEOPLE in support of ROBERT WILLIAMS and other black defendants framed for KIDNAPPING at Monroe, North Carolina. Everywhere they ran for office, SWP candidates across the U.S. were slandered by FBI whispering campaigns and anonymous letters. In 1968, when SWP presidential candidate Fred Halstead announced an impending tour of Vietnam battle fronts, the Bureau's New York City field office recommended planting inflammatory items in U.S. military newspapers, inciting servicemen to physically attack him. Two years later, FBI artists prepared a series of crude sexual cartoons to disrupt alliances between the SWP and various "NEW LEFT" groups involved in VIETNAM WAR PROTESTS. Overall, the FBI would finally admit 46 separate disruption campaigns against the SWP between 1961 and 1971; G-men also staged more than 90 BREAK-INS at SWP offices during the years 1960-66, photographing more than 8,000 documents (including financial records and personal correspondence). Nor did those efforts end with the alleged termination of COINTELPRO in May 1971: a memo dated 20 June 1973 describes items stolen from an SWP office in Denver.

SWP leaders filed a federal lawsuit against the FBI on 18 July 1973. Bureau lawyers stalled the trial until 2 April 1981, and final judgment was not rendered until 25 August 1986. On that date, Judge Thomas Greisa ruled that the SWP's CIVIL RIGHTS had indeed been violated by "the FBI's disruption activities, surreptitious entries and use of INFORMANTS." Greisa awarded the party $246,000 in damages and went even further on 17 August 1987, issuing an unprecedented injunction that barred the FBI from ever using any of the estimated 1 million pages of investigative documents compiled on the SWP since 1940.

**SOCIETY of Former FBI Women** *see* **FBI Alumni Association**

**SOCIETY of Former Special Agents of the FBI**—Created in June 1937 as a social organization for retired G-men, the Society of Former Special Agents committed an immediate faux pas by selecting early Bureau chief A. BRUCE BIELASKI as its first president. Stung by the perceived insult, Director J. EDGAR HOOVER harbored a silent grudge against the society for three decades, refusing to address its annual conventions until 1968, despite yearly invitations to speak.

The society's constitution offered membership to "men of good moral character ... who served with due fidelity their oaths of office and with loyalty to the service and to their fellow agents." Retired WOMEN AGENTS were also (theoretically) eligible to join, but Hoover hired none during his administration of the Bureau (1924-72), and there appears to be no record of a woman joining the society before his death.

The Bielaski indiscretion was not Hoover's only quarrel with the Society of Former Special Agents. He also objected to admission of retired G-men who left the Bureau under a cloud of personal disfavor, but that stumbling block was removed by the creation of a "double blackball" system, wherein candidates for membership were screened both by the current membership and by FBI HEADQUARTERS, to weed out targets of Hoover's malice.

Hoover's final qualm — that ex-agents used their former FBI affiliation to launch lucrative second careers, was never resolved.

Indeed, a major function of the society has always been easing its members into profitable non-retirement. *The Grapevine*, a society newsletter published since April 1938, proudly reported in its issue of 18 July 1969 that society had lately helped 39 members find jobs with an average yearly income of $19,750. Others fared better still, including the seven ex-agents found in Congress during 1970 (with Senator THOMAS DODD the best known). Elsewhere, the FBI was well represented in the security and "labor relations" departments of various banks, heavy industry, casinos, the Mormon church, and on the staff of reclusive billionaire Howard Hughes. President RICHARD NIXON chose two former G-men, Robert Lee and Randolph Thrower, to head the Federal Communications Commission and Internal Revenue Service (investigating and harassing Nixon's many "enemies"). Lloyd Wright, a former agent turned Los Angeles attorney, also counted Nixon among his clients. George Wackenhut spent only three years in the Bureau before resigning to create his own security team, hired by Florida governor Claude Kirk in the 1960s as what some critics called a "private Gestapo." Another security firm led by ex-FBI men, Dale Simpson & Associates of Dallas, served various major oil companies. One of their agents, Vincent Gillen, was caught spying on consumer activist Ralph Nader in 1966.

Despite the long cold-shoulder treatment from FBI headquarters, the Society of Former Special Agents still revered Hoover and all he stood for. Members sold thousands of Hoover's ghost-written books, along with miniature bronze busts of the director. In 1955, a group of ex-agents created the private American Security Council, using "the largest private files on Communism in this country" to screen employees for such mega-clients as Sears Roebuck and General Electric. The society attacked Hoover's critics wherever they appeared, and member NORMAN OLLESTAD was expelled in 1967 for publishing a book that criticized the FBI. As late as October 1992, when the society's headquarters moved from New York City to Quantico, Virginia, spokesmen still objected to media descriptions of the "old" vs. "new" FBI, suggesting that for some loyal veterans at least, the Bureau is incapable of change.

**SOKOLSKY, George**—Arguably J. EDGAR HOOVER'S favorite gossip columnist of the 1940s and '50s, described by Hoover in 1958 as "a member of our FBI team," George Sokolsky was born at Utica, New York on 5 September 1893, raised by his immigrant parents in the Jewish ghettos of Harlem and New York City's East Side. He was expelled from Columbia University in 1917, on charges of "immoral behavior," variously reported as involving left-wing radical activity or indiscretions with a young woman whose parents disapproved of Sokolsky. He immediately left for Russia, writing for the *Russian Daily News*, an English-language newspaper, while revolution raged around him, presumably tempering Sokolsky's youthful attraction to radical causes.

Sokolsky's relationship with the FBI got off to a rocky start in January 1926, when the American consul in Shanghai sent the FBI a copy of Sokolsky's latest article from the *North China Daily News*, suggesting that Sokolsky was "a Bolshevik agent." Four years later, G-men received tips that Sokolsky was "very active in Communist work," busily planning "a propaganda tour of the United States." The story had altered somewhat by 1934, with an unnamed INFORMANT branding Sokolsky a Japanese spy "endeavoring to obtain information about the fleet in New York." A 1942 memo found in the journalist's 906-page FBI dossier notes that "it was common gossip that Sokolsky had been kicked out of China for being on the Japanese payroll."

Communist or Axis spy? By 1944, Sokolsky was writing for the New York *Sun* and receiving letters of praise from Hoover. The price of Bureau endorsement was a series of fawning columns and personal correspondence that praised the FBI and vilified its critics. By the end of WORLD WAR II, Sokolsky had also completed his transformation into a professional Red-baiter who, as described by Victor Navasky in *Naming Names*, "indicted, convicted, pardoned, paroled and granted clemency according to his own rules of evidence. Sokolsky strayed on occasion, as with his 1947 suggestion that Congress should investigate the Bureau "to point out who was responsible for tying the Director's hands," but FBI contacts "straightened out" his thinking, advising Sokolsky that "rooting out communism in the schools, the churches, publications, and thinking … was the real field where writers such as he could lend a great service."

Once corrected, Sokolsky fell to it with a will—and managed to turn a handsome profit in the bargain. A confidante of Red-hunting Senator JOSEPH MCCARTHY, Sokolsky recommended former U.S. attorney ROY COHN as chief investigator for McCarthy's inquisition and afterward served double duty for the crusade, leaking "confidential" FBI documents to McCarthy, then trumpeting McCarthy's use of the material in print. Sokolsky led the Bureau's hue and cry against critical author MAX LOWENTHAL in 1950, and three years later he received the ultimate kudos from Hoover, in the form of a private note declaring that Sokolsky had "done an exceedingly effective job over the years in arousing public interest in the menace of Communism." Furthermore, Hoover gushed, "reading your column each day is a 'must' for me." The same year saw Sokolsky lined up on Hoover's side against rival columnist WESTBROOK PEGLER. After Pegler mildly criticized the FBI's performance in CIVIL RIGHTS cases, Associate Director CLYDE TOLSON informed assistant LOUIS NICHOLS that "George has told me that he is patiently waiting to pay Pegler back in kind." A year later, Sokolsky joined Hoover's guerrilla war against the CENTRAL INTELLIGENCE AGENCY, criticizing the CIA for "closing out" the FBI's "very effective secret intelligence organization" in Latin America.

When not engaged as a Bureau press agent, Sokolsky found time to moonlight as a professional blacklister, screening employees and job applicants for the entertainment industry. Actors and writers deemed "Red" by Sokolsky were fired, but forgiveness was available to some, in return for confessions (and rumored cash payments) that persuaded Sokolsky of their resurrected patriotism. As late as 1961, Sokolsky fired a typist in his office when her friendship with an unnamed "very high government official" was revealed, prompting Hoover to fear exposure of his illegal leaks to Sokolsky. A year later, at Sokolsky's December 1962 funeral, archenemies Roy Cohn and Attorney General ROBERT KENNEDY put aside their feud long enough to serve as pallbearers.

**SOROLA, Manuel**—A Texas native, born near San Antonio on 4 December 1880, Manuel Sorola studied at Alamo Business College before pursuing diverse careers as a bookkeeper, an insurance agent and a private investigator for various railroads throughout the Southwest. He joined the Bureau of Investigation as a "special employee" on 27 April 1916, valued for his fluency in Spanish and knowledge of Mexican politics at a time when guerrilla fighters led by Pancho Villa staged sporadic raids across the U.S. border. Sorola was elevated to full agent's status on 1 July 1922, thereafter serving with field offices in El Paso, Los Angeles, New Orleans, Oklahoma City, Phoenix and San Antonio. He was placed on "limited duty" in 1938, but continued to serve as a Bureau liaison with Los Angeles police until his retirement on 31 January 1949. Sorola died on 29 November 1957, at age 76.

**SOUTHERN Christian Leadership Conference**—Founded by Dr. MARTIN LUTHER KING, JR., and other black CIVIL RIGHTS activists in 1957, the Southern Christian Leadership Conference (SCLC) was devoted to opposing racial segregation via Gandhian principles of nonviolent civil disobedience. FBI Director J. EDGAR HOOVER regarded such efforts as "communist action" and found tenuous support for his prejudice in the person of SCLC adviser STANLEY LEVISON, named in FBI memos as "a secret member of the COMMUNIST PARTY." Dr. King and the SCLC were under FBI surveillance before Attorney General ROBERT KENNEDY authorized WIRETAPS on King's telephones in 1962, and the harassment intensified in 1967, when King added his voice to national VIETNAM WAR PROTESTS. On 25 August 1967 an FBI memo listed the SCLC among six groups marked for "intensified attention" under a new COINTELPRO campaign against "Black Nationalist—Hate Groups."

FBI efforts to disrupt and "neutralize" the SCLC continued beyond Dr. King's assassination in April 1968. A month later, striving to disrupt the SCLC's Poor People's Campaign in Washington, the Bureau's CRIME RECORDS DIVISION planted false stories with "friendly" journalists to create petty dissent between SCLC leaders and Quaker participants in the demonstration. In 1969-70 FBI HEADQUARTERS collaborated with Vice President SPIRO AGNEW in a campaign "to destroy [RALPH] ABERNATHY's credibility, and long after Hoover's death the Bureau opposed efforts to dedicate a federal holiday in Dr. King's name.

**SOUTHERN Conference on Bombing**—The U.S. SUPREME COURT's school desegregation orders of 1954-55 produced a wave of racist TERRORISM in the South unprecedented since the days of Reconstruction following the Civil War. Between January 1957 and May 1958 a series of 46 BOMBINGS struck various southern targets, including schools, synagogues, churches, and homes owned by African Americans. Most such crimes were traceable to factions of the KU KLUX KLAN or other racist groups, but the rare cases of arrest invariably led to acquittals by all-white juries.

The Southern Conference on Bombing (SCB) was founded in response to those crimes, on 3 May 1958. Police officials from 21 southern cities gathered in Jacksonville, Florida, at the invitation of Mayor Haydon Burns, to compile dossiers on likely bombing suspects and offer rewards that finally totaled $55,700 for information leading to arrests. The FBI refused to participate, but a former G-man employed by the Anti-Defamation League of B'nai B'rith, Milton Ellerin, compiled a list of prominent racists deemed likely to plot terrorist bombings. Conference participant EUGENE ("BULL") CONNOR, the Klan-allied public safety commissioner from Birmingham whose police had failed to solve 30-odd bombings since 1949, was embarrassed to find his own name on the list.

Agents of the SCB reportedly infiltrated several racist groups, but no arrests resulted from their efforts. Indeed, while some participants were doubtless sincere in their wish to halt bombing, the inclusion of Klan-friendly members like Connor and Jacksonville's Mayor Burns (who favored Klansmen with parade permits while jailing black demonstrators) prompted suggestions that the SCB may have been created as a publicity measure, rather than a serious attempt to curb racist terrorism.

**SPECIAL Agents Mutual Benefit Association**—A private organization ostensibly created to provide health and life insurance for FBI employees, the Special Agents Mutual Benefit Association (SAMBA) was in fact a slush fund used to purchase football season tickets, provide wedding and anniversary gifts, and to fund Christmas and retirement parties. Assistant Director JOHN MOHR's 1972 going-away party, for example, cost SAMBA $635.21 (including the price of a new fishing boat from Sears & Roebuck). The group's financial irregularities were uncovered during an audit in 1976, by which time the men responsible were either deceased or retired.

**SPECIAL Intelligence Service**—Created in 1940, by order of President FRANKLIN ROOSEVELT, the FBI's Special Intelligence Service (SIS) was assigned to disrupt Axis activity in Latin America. Bureau operations outside the U.S. placed Director J. EDGAR HOOVER in direct (and often hostile) competition with America's other foreign spy network, the OFFICE OF STRATEGIC SERVICES led by WILLIAM DONOVAN. While G-men had no legal jurisdiction outside United States territory, they collaborated with friendly governments south of the border to seek out German spies and propagandists during WORLD WAR II. At its peak of operation, the SIS maintained a staff of some 500 persons, including 360 FBI agents. Matching wits with Nazis in South America, where Argentina's Juan Perón and other dictators admired ADOLF HITLER and sheltered fugitive war criminals, was a potentially hazardous pastime. Still, only four agents lost their lives on SIS duty, all of them in airplane crashes (two in Dutch Guiana, one in Argentina, and one in Colombia). Dissolution of the SIS in 1946 presumably canceled any further FBI actions abroad, but agents remained on duty in various foreign capitals as part of the Bureau's LEGAL ATTACHÉ PROGRAM.

**SPECIAL Investigative Division**—After decades of denial and false starts like the abortive Chicago CAPGA operation, the FBI created its Special Investigative Division (SID) in 1961, to participate in Attorney General ROBERT KENNEDY's campaign against ORGANIZED CRIME. Initially led by Courtney Evans, Director J.

EDGAR HOOVER'S personal liaison to the Kennedy JUSTICE DEPARTMENT, the SID had its own assistant director in charge after 1967, with its duties expanded to include pursuit of federal fugitives (the Fugitive Section) and background investigations on government employees or contractors (the Employees Security and Special Inquiry Section), while mob investigations remained the province of the Criminal Intelligence-Organized Crime Section. In 1977 Director CLARENCE KELLEY abolished the SID, combining its function with those of the former Domestic Intelligence Division and General Investigative Division in a new Criminal Investigative Division.

**SQUAD 47**—Established by the FBI's New York City field office in 1970 and active into 1974, Squad 47 was a special "black bag" unit created for the specific purpose of committing illegal BREAK-INS. Its primary targets were suspected members of the WEATHER UNDERGROUND, some of them fugitives, but friends of the elusive subjects also suffered burglaries in which their homes were searched and their mail was opened. Agent John Kearney commanded the squad's 68 agents and selected their targets. On 7 April 1977, Kearney was indicted for ordering illegal break-ins, mail-openings and WIRETAPS, whereupon his former agents responded with angry letters to Attorney General GRIFFIN BELL and picketed the New York field office. Charges against Kearney were dismissed in April 1978, with new indictments issued against former acting director L. PATRICK GRAY, former acting associate director W. MARK FELT, and former assistant director EDWARD MILLER. Gray petitioned for a separate trial, and the charges were later dismissed. Felt and Miller were convicted in November 1980, then pardoned four months later by new president (and one-time FBI informant) RONALD REAGAN.

**STABILE, Joseph**—Agent Joseph Stabile was assigned to the FBI's New York City field office, where his fluency in the Sicilian language made him a natural choice for Mafia investigations. Assigned to the ORGANIZED CRIME squad, he was used to translate conversations gleaned from WIRETAPS and BUGGING devices all over New York and New England. Soon, Stabile knew which mobsters were under surveillance, what they talked about, and who the Bureau's paid INFORMANTS were. And as he quickly learned, that information could be very valuable to the mob.

In 1970 Agent Tony Villano developed evidence that Stabile had accepted a $10,000 bribe from the New York Mafia. When he confronted Stabile with the accusation, Stabile offered to cut him in on the payoffs. "There's a fortune to be made out there," Stabile explained. "Like a hundred grand in no time at all. It's better than being assigned to Las Vegas." Villano declined the offer and reported Stabile to his superiors, whereupon a team of inspectors were sent from FBI HEADQUARTERS to resolve the problem. Despite their conflicting stories, both Stabile and Villano passed polygraph tests. Director J. EDGAR HOOVER used that inconsistency as an excuse to close the case, thus preserving his fiction that no G-man had ever taken a bribe. Villano resigned in disgust, while Stabile remained with the Bureau.

Director CLARENCE KELLEY reopened the case eight years later and Stabile was finally indicted on 15 September 1978. The charges filed against him included eight counts of perjury, conspiracy and obstructing justice. He thus became the first G-man indicted while on active duty. (Others had been fired or forced to resign before they were charged, allowing the Bureau to claim indictment of a "former agent.") Stabile pled guilty to obstructing justice on 9 November 1978, while the other charges were dropped. On 17 January 1979 he was sentenced to one year and a day in federal prison.

**STARSKY, Morris J.**—Morris Starsky, a professor at Arizona State University in Phoenix, drew FBI attention in 1968 via his membership in the SOCIALIST WORKERS PARTY (SWP), a group marked for harassment and disruption under the Bureau's illegal COINTELPRO program, on personal orders from Director J. EDGAR HOOVER. Unsatisfied with surveillance and "neutralization" of the party at large, G-men sought to earn Hoover's approval by targeting individual SWP members across the country. A memo from the Phoenix field office to FBI HEADQUARTERS, dated 31 May 1968, observed that local COINTELPRO targets were "pretty obvious. It is apparent that NEW LEFT organizations and activities in the Phoenix metropolitan area have received their inspiration and leadership almost exclusively form the members of the faculty in the Department of Philosophy at Arizona State University (ASU), chiefly Assistant Professor MORRIS J. STARSKY." A second communiqué to Hoover, on 1 October 1968, detailed the motives of the FBI's campaign to ruin Starsky's career.

> MORRIS J. STARSKY, by his actions, has continued to spotlight himself as a target for counterintelligence action. He and his wife were both named as presidential electors by and for the Socialist Workers Party when the SWP in August, 1968, gained a place on the ballot in Arizona. In addition they have signed themselves as treasurer and secretary respectively of the Arizona SWP. Professor STARSKY's status at Arizona State University may be affected by the outcome of his pending trial on charges of disturbing the peace. He is alleged to have used violent, abusive and obscene language against the Assistant Managing Director of Gammage Auditorium at ASU during memorial services for MARTIN LUTHER KING [JR.] last April. Trial is now scheduled for 10/8/68 in Justice Court, Tempe, Arizona.

That case failed to result in Starsky's dismissal as Hoover desired, but the FBI was persistent. In 1970 the Phoenix field office proposed (and Hoover approved) mailing anonymous letters to members of the ASU Faculty Committee on Academic Freedom and Tenure, assigned to review Starsky's actions. One such letter read as follows:

> Dear Sir:
>     It seems appropriate that you should be informed of one of the most recent activities of Morris J. Starsky. Starsky learned of a suicide attempt by one of his close campus co-workers, David Murphy. Feeling that Murphy could no longer be trusted as a member of the campus Socialist group, Starsky demanded that Murphy return all literature and other materials belonging to the Socialist group. Murphy refused to give Starsky a quantity of the Socialist literature in his possession until Starsky would pay him a sum slightly in excess of $50 which was owed for telephone calls charged by Starsky to Murphy's telephone. Morris Starsky was in-

dignant at Murphy's independent attitude and at 2:00 A.M. on April 5, 1970 he, accompanied by his wife Pamela and two young male associates, invaded Murphy's apartment and under threat demanded return of the socialist literature. When Murphy refused unless Starsky paid the phone bill, Starsky told him that his two associates would beat him unmercifully. Murphy, convalescing from a recent hospital stay, was under great fear of bodily harm and surrendered the literature.

I find this episode interesting. Where did Starsky learn of the effectiveness of smashing into a person's home at 2:00 A.M.? Also, of utilizing four persons to threaten the health or life of someone? Is this an example of academic socialism? Should the ASU student body enjoy the guidance of such an instructor? It seems to me that this type of activity is something that Himmler or Beria could accept with pride. If Starsky did not enjoy the prestige and sanctuary of his position he would be properly punished for such a totalitarian venture.

/s/ A concerned ASU alumnus

While committee members were not deceived by the FBI's smear campaign, ASU's regents declined to renew Starsky's contract, thereby terminating his employment in June 1970. Some 250 professors and 3,000 ASU students signed a petition calling for Starsky's reinstatement, but red-baiting hysteria carried the day. In Professor Starsky's words, the incident was "sort of like being found innocent and executed anyway." After his dismissal from ASU, Starsky lost two subsequent teaching posts for what he termed "political reasons."

**STATE Department**—One of the original executive departments of the U.S. government, created in 1789, the State Department has at different times maintained both a cooperative and antagonistic relationship with the FBI. In 1936, approval from Secretary of State Cordell Hull was required (and freely given) to implement President FRANKLIN ROOSEVELT'S plans for widespread DOMESTIC SURVEILLANCE on alleged "subversive" groups and individuals. Fourteen years later, it was State's turn to be under scrutiny, as Senator JOSEPH MCCARTHY claimed secret knowledge of 57 (or 205) COMMUNIST PARTY members spying for Russia within the department and "known to the secretary of state." (No such spy ring was ever documented, and McCarthy was censured by the U.S. Senate for his irresponsible behavior in 1954.)

On a practical level, FBI Director J. EDGAR HOOVER maintained a cordial relationship with State Department passport directors RUTH SHIPLEY and Frances Knight, enabling him to harass selected individuals at will by having State suspend, revoke or deny passports on request from FBI HEADQUARTERS. Other suspects were allowed to travel freely, but their names were placed on an FBI "watch list," meaning that their movements abroad were monitored by State Department employees in various U.S. embassies. The era of mutual suspicion returned under President RICHARD NIXON (1969-74), when Hoover's G-men were ordered to place WIRETAPS on various State Department employees, seeking the sources of media leaks. Today, State and the JUSTICE DEPARTMENT presumably cooperate once more to facilitate President GEORGE W. BUSH'S "war on TERRORISM" at home and abroad.

**STEIN, Gertrude**—Born at Allegheny, Pennsylvania on 3 February 1874, avant-garde writer and certified eccentric Gertrude Stein moved to Paris at age 29 and returned to the U.S. only once, briefly, in 1934. She was still of interest to the FBI, rating a dossier dating from 1937. The first report noted that Stein "didn't seem to be pro-any nationality, but she was anti-[FRANKLIN] ROOSEVELT." Still, G-men noted that "her sympathies were not very strongly with America else she would not have stayed abroad so long." Four years later, with Stein still residing in Nazi-occupied Paris, another FBI report noted that "no action is contemplated ... at the present time" against Stein or another unnamed individual, "in the absence of more complete and definite information concerning [their] left-wing activities." Another memo added to Stein's dossier in 1941 refers in passing to artist Helen Rose, whom "Stein considered ... to be the greatest painter since Pisasso [sic]." Despite allegations of leftist activity, a 1945 FBI report (never followed up) reports that Stein was "definitely pro-Nazi." Author MALCOLM COWLEY also described Stein as "a collaborationist," but her dealings with German occupation troops were apparently more a matter of personal convenience than ideological commitment to fascism. Stein died in Paris on 27 July 1946.

**STEINBECK, John**—Born at Salinas, California on 27 February 1902, John Steinbeck published his first novel in 1929. The FBI officially took note of him seven years later, filing reports on his participation in a western writers' conference and his contributions to *Pacific Weekly*, regarded by Bureau headquarters as a "Red" magazine. Colleague HOWARD FAST later informed author Natalie Robins that Steinbeck was a COMMUNIST PARTY member at the time, but "then he sold out" with publication of *The Grapes of Wrath* in 1939. Spokesmen for the AMERICAN LEGION, whose members were frequently hired to terrorize the same California farm workers portrayed in the novel, branded it "Red propaganda," and G-men reported its sale at a Communist Party gathering held in Los Angeles on 1 May 1940.

By that time, Steinbeck had approached the Bureau himself, concerning a series of 1939 extortion letters, but no charges were filed against their author. Three years later, finally aware of ongoing FBI surveillance, Steinbeck wrote to Attorney General FRANCIS BIDDLE, asking him, "Do you suppose you could ask Edgar's boys to stop stepping on my heels? They think I'm an enemy alien. It's getting tiresome." When queried on the matter, J. EDGAR HOOVER lied outright to his nominal superior, reporting that "Steinbeck is not being and has never been investigated by this Bureau."

Surveillance of Steinbeck continued, meanwhile. In 1943, when the novelist applied for a commission with Army Intelligence, Hoover scuttled the bid with a confidential report citing "substantial doubt as to [Steinbeck's] loyalty and discretion." Another 1943 report noted that Steinbeck's novels were "used in discussions of history" at the "official Communist party school" in New York City. A year later, when the HOUSE COMMITTEE ON UN-AMERICAN ACTIVITIES (HUAC) reported that the National Maritime Union "toes the Communist line," G-men pitched in with a report that in many shipboard libraries "*The Grapes of*

*Wrath* is naturally present, as it would be in any Communist's selection."

Steinbeck found no respite from pursuit in the Red-baiting decade after WORLD WAR II. In June 1953 a HUAC witness claimed that Steinbeck "has done more through his novel about the agricultural workers than anyone else for the Communist party." Nine months later, FBI headquarters took time from its Cold War spy hunting to compile a list of "Instances Wherein America's Enemies Have Used or Attempted to Use Steinbeck's Writings and Reputation to Further Their Causes." G-men ignored Steinbeck's receipt of a Nobel Prize for Literature in 1962, but they were standing by the year after, to record his comment that he was "impressed by the changes" in Soviet Russia since the 1940s. (Agents also claimed Steinbeck "had received the sum of $420 as an author's fee from the Soviet publication, Novyi Mir.") In 1964, an FBI memo reported that Steinbeck's works were "translated into foreign languages and distributed by enemies of the United States," but found communists "at odds" with Steinbeck over his adverse portrayals of the party. Ironically, an illegal FBI wiretap on the Chicago chapter of STUDENTS FOR A DEMOCRATIC SOCIETY found those "NEW LEFT" radicals rejecting Steinbeck as an ally because he was "conservative."

FBI surveillance of Steinbeck continued until his death in New York City, on 20 December 1968. Deputy Associate Director CARTHA DELOACH justified the investigation years later, to author Natalie Robins, by claiming (without any proof) that *The Grapes of Wrath* "was used as a code book in some espionage cases." Researcher Herbert Mitgang eventually received 94 pages of Steinbeck's dossier under the FREEDOM OF INFORMATION ACT, while another 23 pages remained classified. The CENTRAL INTELLIGENCE AGENCY also withheld two documents on Steinbeck from release, citing concerns for their impact on "national defense or foreign policy."

**STEVENSON, Adlai Ewing II** — A Los Angeles native, born 5 February 1900, Adlai Stevenson was a prominent liberal member of the Democratic Party from the 1940s until his death in 1965. In early 1946 he attended the first session of the United Nations General Assembly, then meeting in London, with ELEANOR ROOSEVELT and ALGER HISS. Stevenson served as governor of Illinois (1949-53) and as a delegate to Democratic National Conventions in 1948, 1952, 1956 and 1960. He was the party's unsuccessful presidential candidate in 1952 and 1956, running against DWIGHT EISENHOWER.

Stevenson's presidential ambitions exposed him to covert FBI harassment for the first time, though he may have been subject to prior surveillance. In early 1952, when Stevenson emerged as the Democratic favorite, Eisenhower met with Director J. EDGAR HOOVER and Texas financier CLINT MURCHISON to discuss Stevenson's candidacy. Murchison emerged from that meeting concerned that Stevenson might be "used by radicals to destroy America's proud traditions." In July 1952, on the same day Stevenson announced his candidacy, a senior FBI official prepared a 19-page memo accusing Stevenson of HOMOSEXUALITY and communist sympathies. GUY HOTTEL, in charge of the Washington field office, spread the "queer" rumors with help from the

FBI's CRIME RECORDS DIVISION, leaking false reports of Stevenson's alleged arrests for homosexual activity to various local police departments, whence they were soon transmitted to the media. Hoover opened a "Sex Deviate" file on Stevenson in Washington, including baseless rumors that the candidate was known as "Adeline" within the gay community. Eisenhower refrained from participating in the smear campaign, but running mate RICHARD NIXON and Senator JOSEPH MCCARTHY collaborated in the Bureau's fling at character assassination.

On balance, Eisenhower hardly needed the FBI's help, since he won 83 percent of the U.S. electoral vote. Stevenson's margin in 1956 was even smaller, 73 electoral votes to Ike's 457, but Hoover revived the gay smear nonetheless. The second round spelled disaster for one of Hoover's primary media allies. Right-wing commentator WALTER WINCHELL found himself devoid of television sponsors after airing the opinion that "a vote for Adlai Stevenson is a vote for Christine Jorgensen" (a renowned 1950s transsexual).

President JOHN KENNEDY appointed Stevenson as a U.S. representative to the United Nations in 1961, and Stevenson held that post until he died in London, of a heart attack, on 14 July 1965. Ironically, the year before Stevenson's death, Hoover sought to use him as a pawn in yet another FBI smear campaign, providing Stevenson with derogatory material on Dr. MARTIN LUTHER KING, JR., in an effort to make Stevenson shun celebration of King's Nobel Peace Prize. Stevenson, to his credit, ignored the director's overture.

**STEWART, Donald Ogden** — Born at Columbus, Ohio on 30 November 1894, novelist and playwright Donald Stewart moved to Hollywood in 1930 and won an Academy Award for his screenplay of *The Philadelphia Story* 10 years later. In between those two events, he drew attention from the FBI, which marked him as "one of the principal leaders of the Communist element in the motion picture industry." Stewart apparently joined the COMMUNIST PARTY as a "secret member" in 1936, the same year G-men filed the first entry in his Bureau dossier. In 1937 he became president of the League of American Writers, and soon addressed a telegram to J. EDGAR HOOVER, requesting a public statement on anti-Semitism, but the telegram was misfiled in BOOTH TARKINGTON'S FBI file and no record remains of Hoover's reply (if any). Two years later, Stewart married ELLA WINTER, ex-wife of LINCOLN STEFFENS and a subject of long-term FBI surveillance in her own right. Stewart and Winter suspected (rightly) that agents were reading their mail and tapping their phone lines. One letter, intercepted by the Bureau in 1944 discussed creation of "a code which they could use, and which would circumvent censorship in future correspondence."

It was all in vain, as the surveillance continued for decades, sometimes including round-the-clock surveillance on Stewart and his wife. G-men noted the color of Stewart's dog, recorded the times when Winter went shopping, and trailed the couple on outings to the theater, all in vain. J. EDGAR HOOVER'S interest was piqued in 1945, when Winter met ELEANOR ROOSEVELT at a party and addressed the president's wife by her first name. Five years later, the FBI placed Stewart in a "special section" of the illegal

SECURITY INDEX, after Hollywood director Sam Wood "named the subject as a Communist" in testimony before the HOUSE COMMITTEE ON UN-AMERICAN ACTIVITIES. In 1952, when Stewart and Winter moved to London, Hoover's STATE DEPARTMENT ally RUTH SHIPLEY revoked their passports, to frustrate any further travel plans. The passports were renewed in 1957, but Hoover asked the U.S. embassy in London to monitor their travels until he seemingly lost interest and closed Stewart's 915-page dossier in June 1970. Stewart died in London on 2 August 1980.

**STONE, Harlan Fiske** — A Chesterfield, New Hampshire native, born 11 October 1872, Harlan Stone served as dean of Columbia Law School before President CALVIN COOLIDGE tapped him as attorney general to replace HARRY DAUGHERTY on 7 April 1924. Stone would serve less than a year at the JUSTICE DEPARTMENT, but he made a fateful and enduring decision when he chose J. EDGAR HOOVER as acting director of the FBI on 10 May 1924. Various sources have reported (and mythologized) their terse conversation as follows:

STONE: Young man, I want you to be Acting Director of the Bureau of Investigation.
HOOVER: I'll take the job, Mr. Stone, on certain conditions.
STONE: What are they?
HOOVER: The Bureau must be divorced from politics and not be a catch-all for political hacks. Appointments must be based on merit. Second, promotions will be made on proved ability and the Bureau will be responsible only to the Attorney General.
STONE: I wouldn't give it to you under any other conditions. That's all. Good day.

True or false, Stone clearly intended to end the Bureau's long-running investigation of political opinions and its harassment of so-called "radicals." On 13 May 1924 he sent Hoover six-point memo detailing policy changes which he required of the new acting director. Five dealt with personnel matters, but the first was most telling in light of Hoover's Red-hunting background: "The activities of the Bureau are to be limited strictly to investigations of violation of law, under my direction or under the direction of an Assistant Attorney General regularly conducting the work of the Department of Justice."

Hoover pretended to agree, and weeks later he assured Senate investigators that "[i]nstructions have been sent to officers in the field to limit their investigations in the field to violations of the statutes." When the AMERICAN CIVIL LIBERTIES UNION complained to Stone that FBI DOMESTIC SURVEILLANCE of dissidents continued unabated, Hoover called the report "untrue and misleading." A "small portion" of the Bureau's work involved "ultra-radicals," Hoover admitted, but he vowed that inquiries "are made [only] when there is indication of a possible violation of a federal statute."

It was a blatant lie, but Stone trusted his new subordinate beyond reason and his own days at Justice were numbered in any case. Stone confirmed Hoover as full-time FBI director on 10 December 1924, and three months later he was gone, resigning on 2 March 1925 to fill a vacancy on the U.S. SUPREME COURT.

After 16 years as an associate justice, Stone was elevated to Chief Justice in 1941 and held that post until his death on 22 April 1946. Author Curt Gentry notes that Hoover "deified" Stone and kept a portrait of his benefactor in his office at FBI HEADQUARTERS for the remainder of his life.

**STOUT, Rex Todhunter** — Born at Noblesville, Indiana in 1886, Rex Stout was the child of Quaker parents who initially rejected his parents' pacifism to join the U.S. Navy, then left the service in 1908 to become a freelance writer. He published 73 novels in all, and was most famous for the 46 mysteries starring investigator Nero Wolfe. By the time the first episode of that series was published, in 1936, Stout had been under FBI investigation for 16 years.

The Bureau opened its dossier on Stout in 1920, when he joined the fledgling League for Mutual Aid, created (in FBI terms) to provide financial help for "political prisoners and radical agitators and workers temporarily in distress." Six years elapsed before Stout rated his next FBI memo, as an executive board member for *The New Masses*. In fact, Stout had already resigned from the board, protesting its inclusion of several communists, but G-men neglected to mention that fact and the "Red" connection dogged Stout to the end of his days. Further suspicion accrued from his membership in (and occasional leadership of) the AUTHORS LEAGUE OF AMERICA, regarded by the FBI as a thinly veiled communist front. Confusion arose over Stout's politics in 1940, when an unnamed informant told G-men that Stout's short story "Sisters in Trouble," published in *American Magazine*, was "a deliberate attempt to convey a meaning other than the solution of a mystery story.... [N]ote the almost exclusive German cast of characters." Before agents could brand Stout pro-Nazi, however, he confused them with a radio speech urging America to "declare war now" on ADOLF HITLER'S Germany. That outburst landed Stout a ranking as "No. 49" on the FBI's "General Watch List," and scrutiny extended to the Writers War Board in 1941, when Stout emerged as the founding leader. A year later, he was back in the Red column, with memos branding him "a Communist fellow traveler and one of the prize exhibits of the [MARTIN] DIES [HOUSE] COMMITTEE ON UN-AMERICAN ACTIVITIES."

Agents continued their surveillance of Stout after WORLD WAR II, dubbing him a "joiner" who had compiled "approximately" 500 citations for membership in such groups as the Joint Anti-Fascist Refugee Committee, the National Council of Soviet-American Friendship, the Americans for Democratic Action (opposed to Hollywood blacklisting in 1947), Friends of the Spanish Republic, the National Federation for Constitutional Liberties, and the Society for the Prevention of World War III (opposing proliferation of nuclear arms). Still, for all his "Red" connections, Stout's primary sin was public criticism of the FBI, as demonstrated by the Bureau's reaction to publication of *The Doorbell Rang*, in 1965.

The novel's plot finds Nero Wolfe employed to end FBI harassment of a wealthy New York matron, and was thus guaranteed to provoke J. EDGAR HOOVER's wrath. Stout's book had barely arrived on store shelves when Hoover demanded a Bureau review, with predictable results. Agent M.A. Jones served as critic in residence, reporting to Hoover that "this vicious book depicts the FBI in the worst possible light.... The false and distorted picture of the FBI which Stout sets forth is an obvious reflection of his leftist leanings as indicated in our files." The good news, Jones opined, was that "The plot of this book is weak and it will probably have only limited public acceptance despite Stout's use of the FBI in an apparent bid for sensationalism to improve sales." All FBI field offices were immediately warned of the novel's existence "and its placement in the CRIME RECORDS DIVISION."

Stout compounded his sin six months later, with an appearance on *The Today Show*, where he called Hoover a "tinhorn autocrat" who was "on the edge of senility," proceeding from there to denounce the blackmail potential of FBI files maintained "on thousands of individuals." The warning was timely — in fact, overdue — but Hoover noted only the personal jibes. Furious, the 72-year-old director penned a note on his transcript of the program, noting that "Stout has a nerve in referring to me as close to seventy and on the edge of senility. He was born in December 1886." Unfazed by Hoover's rage, Stout told interviewers, "If he wants to get at me for writing this book, I wish he would try. He can't hurt me at all, so to hell with him."

Surveillance of Stout continued until Hoover's death in 1972, and his case remains a sensitive subject at FBI headquarters. Stout died in October 1975, but 118 pages of his 301-page dossier were still classified in 1987, the rest heavily censored before its release to author Herbert Mitgang under the FREEDOM OF INFORMATION ACT. Historian Natalie Robins fared slightly better with her FOIA request, obtaining 183 pages, but comments in her book *Alien Ink* (1992) suggest that she was deceived concerning the full extent of Stout's file.

**STUART, Lyle** — New Yorker Lyle Stuart created his eponymous publishing house in 1956 and found himself subjected to FBI scrutiny five years later, over his public support for the Fair Play for Cuba Committee. Deputy Associate Director CARTHA DE-LOACH described Stuart in one memo as "a New York publisher whose book lists are dominated by earthy novels, sex-technique manuals and pro-Castro books." A subsequent FBI leak to the press, timed to coincide with Stuart's appearance before a Senate subcommittee, featured a "representative" list of titles, including *Diary of a Nymph*, *Transvestism*, and *Pleasure Was My Business*. Stuart was also first to publish *The Anarchist's Cookbook* (1971), presenting drug recipes along with instructions on bomb-making and urban sabotage techniques. After selling off his first company and founding Barricade Books, Stuart faced (and lost) a $3.1 million libel suit filed by Las Vegas casino mogul Steve Wynn, over published statements in the biography *Running Scared*, which purported to link Wynn with ORGANIZED CRIME.

**STUDENT Nonviolent Coordinating Committee** — Prior to 1960, African American campaigns for CIVIL RIGHTS were fought primarily in the courts, by attorneys for such organizations as the NATIONAL ASSOCIATION FOR THE ADVANCEMENT OF COLORED PEOPLE. The movement entered its "direct action" phase on 1 February 1960, when a group of black college students staged the first "sit-in" at a whites-only lunch counter in Greensboro, North Carolina. Two months later, on the weekend of 16-17 April, the Student Nonviolent Coordinating Committee (SNCC, pronounced "Snick") was founded on the campus of Raleigh's Shaw University. SNCC held its first official gathering on 13-14 May 1960, electing Marion Berry (future mayor of Washington, D.C.) as chairman. Over the next five years, SNCC's young activists spearheaded many of the civil rights movement's most dramatic campaigns, including the FREEDOM RIDES (1961); protests against segregation in Albany, Georgia (1962); a perilous effort to register black voters in Mississippi (1963-64); and the Selma, Alabama registration drive (1965).

The FBI's website offers 2,887 pages of edited memos and reports on SNCC, released under the FREEDOM OF INFORMATION ACT, with an explanation that "[a]n investigation was opened in 1964 to establish the extent of communist infiltration in the SNCC." In truth, however, the Bureau began to monitor SNCC meetings in the latter part of 1960, emulating its surveillance of the SOUTHERN CHRISTIAN LEADERSHIP CONFERENCE and other groups devoted to peaceful eradication of Jim Crow laws throughout America. SNCC members in Dixie provided G-men with "a steady flow of information" on their movement, hoping protection against acts of racist TERRORISM, but those hopes were in vain. An incident from Mississippi illustrates the point: after racist gunmen wounded four SNCC workers at Greenwood, on 6 March 1963, a G-man sent to investigate asked the victims, "Are you boys sure you didn't shoot up this car?" As activist Randolph Blackwell recalled, it was "like talking to a member of the KU KLUX KLAN."

In 1965, as SNCC began to shift its focus from the rural South to urban ghettos in the North, Attorney General NICHOLAS KATZENBACH approved J. EDGAR HOOVER'S request for wiretaps on the telephones of all identified SNCC officers. At the same time, Hoover ordered full-scale infiltration and "disruption" of SNCC under the Bureau's illegal COINTELPRO campaign. STOKELY CARMICHAEL'S election as chairman of SNCC in 1966 marked a shift toward more radical rhetoric and action, including declarations that SNCC would henceforth be "an all black project" devoted to "Black Power." By 1967 SNCC was active in VIETNAM WAR PROTESTS, pointedly deleting "Nonviolent" from its title to become the Student National Coordinating Committee. J. Edgar Hoover responded to those moves on 25 August 1967, with a memo demanding "intensified attention" to SNCC and similar "Black Nationalist — Hate Groups." SNCC thereafter rated its own section in the Bureau's RABBLE ROUSER INDEX, while 66 individual members were listed in the larger SECURITY INDEX for potential arrest in the event of a national emergency. Assistant Director WILLIAM SULLIVAN'S Division 5 listed SNCC with the NATION OF ISLAM and the Southern Christian Leadership Conference as ranking among "the most violent and radical groups" in the nation.

FBI pressure increased after 17 February 1968, when Carmichael and SNCC announced a merger with the militant BLACK PANTHER PARTY. Two weeks later, on 4 March 1968, Hoover renewed efforts to crush the organization. Houston G-men promptly burglarized SNCC's local office and photographed "all the SNCC records" for posterity. Agents in South Carolina found only two SNCC members in the state, but one of them, Cleveland Sellers, was named as a ringleader of demonstrations leading to the ORANGEBURG MASSACRE, subsequently sentenced to five years in federal prison for violating the Selective Service Act. Carmichael's successor as chairman, H. RAP BROWN, was subsequently charged with arson and inciting a riot in Maryland.

When prosecution of its leaders failed to destroy SNCC, the Bureau fell back on familiar covert techniques. SNCC's alliance with the Panthers had disintegrated by October 1968, one spokesman for the group remarking that "the difference between a panther and other large cats is that the panther has the smallest head." FBI Associate Director George Moore drafted a memo to William Sullivan, noting that the observation "is biologically true," recommending that the Bureau circulate a series of derisive "Panther Pinhead" cartoons to widen the rift between the two groups and "help neutralize Black Panther recruiting efforts." A SNCC activist working to politicize black youths in St. Louis, Rev. Charles Koen, was "neutralized" by an FBI letter-writing campaign, accusing him of sexual liaisons with female members of a local street gang, the Black Liberators.

Matters went from bad to worse in September 1969, when SNCC spokesmen voiced sympathy for Palestinian activists in the Middle East conflict. The FBI drafted another series of anonymous letters, these accusing SNCC of anti-Semitism, and sent them to the violent Jewish Defense League (JDL) in New York City. Internal memos reveal the Bureau's hope that JDL terrorists would be driven "to act" against SNCC, and two associates of chairman H. Rap Brown were killed by a car bomb four months later, on 10 March 1970, outside Bel Air, Maryland. G-men and local police agreed that the victims were killed while transporting illegal explosives, but in retrospect the case seems nearly identical to the 1990 car-bombing of EARTH FIRST! activists JUDI BARI and Daryl Cherney. (FBI agents tried to frame the victims in that case on bomb-making charges, but their efforts were exposed and cost the plotters $4 million in a civil lawsuit.)

Whoever planted the bomb in Bel Air, charges of anti-Semitism undercut SNCC's financial support, and worse publicity followed when Chairman Brown skipped bail on his riot charges on 4 May 1970, winning a place on the FBI's "TEN MOST WANTED" LIST two days later. He was captured in October 1971, after an apparent holdup in Manhattan, and later sentenced to prison. By early 1972, SNCC had ceased to exist.

**STUDENTS for a Democratic Society** — First and foremost among countless "NEW LEFT" groups of the 1960s, the SDS was founded in 1960 as an educational association intended to advance liberal-left ideology throughout academia and American society at large. The group's 1962 "Port Huron Statement" called for students nationwide to join in a movement for "participatory democracy" — which FBI HEADQUARTERS regarded as a synonym for communism. That belief was reinforced when COMMUNIST PARTY leader Gus Hall described the SDS as a group the party had "going for us," and FBI Director J. EDGAR HOOVER henceforth never mentioned SDS without including Hall's comment as "proof" of a sinister conspiracy.

Hoover's personal distaste notwithstanding, the FBI was slow to begin its investigation of the SDS. The organization grew from 10,000 members in October 1965 to 80,000 in November 1968, but the Bureau's FBI field office was completely unprepared for an outbreak of student demonstrations led by SDS at Columbia University in April 1968. When Assistant Director WILLIAM SULLIVAN asked New York to provide details on the protest, New York's agent-in-charge had nothing on file but press clippings. To counter that alarming situation, a full-scale COINTELPRO operation was launched against the New Left on 9 May 1968, with the SDS and founder Tom Hayden named as key targets of the illegal disruption campaign.

Offensive politics aside, Hoover also despised SDS members for their "beatnik dress," long hair, profanity and use of drugs. The open rejection of conservative morals hampered FBI efforts to embarrass SDS members, since public exposure of drug use or sexual promiscuity carried no stigma amongst New Left organizations. Instead, the Bureau resorted to "SNITCH-JACKETING" (falsely portraying various targets as government INFORMANTS) and made extensive use of hired *agents provocateur* to encourage criminal behavior. Reluctantly, Hoover also approved UNDERCOVER OPERATIONS by a small group of G-men who were dubbed "The BEARDS" after they grew long hair and whiskers to infiltrate the SDS. With agents inside and out working overtime to "neutralize" the SDS, it suffered internal dissension and rifts with various other groups, all encouraged by the FBI. Agents disrupted unity meetings between the SDS and the BLACK PANTHER PARTY, while penning anonymous letters (often signed "SDS member") attacking black student groups as racist. In another case, at Princeton University, the FBI delivered anti-SDS pamphlets to a member of the far-right John Birch Society for distribution on campus via the school's Conservative Club.

It is impossible to say how much credit the FBI deserves for the final SDS break-up in June 1969. More than 2,000 members attended the group's national convention in Chicago that month, engaged in divisive arguments over the role of women and racial minorities in the "worldwide fight against U.S. imperialism." The result was a fatal rift, with militant members seceding to join a new WEATHER UNDERGROUND faction or the Revolutionary Youth Movement, while more "conservative" loyalists gravitated toward the Progressive Labor Party. The SDS clung tenuously to life for a few more months, but it had essentially ceased to exist by the time aides to President RICHARD NIXON named it a priority target of the abortive HUSTON PLAN in June 1970. A year later, the burglary of an FBI RESIDENT AGENCY at MEDIA, PENNSYLVANIA revealed Bureau investigation and harassment of the SDS, along with many other groups and individuals.

**SUBVERSIVE Activities Control Board** — Created by the MCCARRAN ACT in September 1950, the Subversive Activities Control Board (SACB) existed to identify and register the members of "Communist-action, Communist-front or Communist-infiltrated" organizations. To that end the SACB relied primarily on FBI FILES and hearings which featured a variety of Bureau INFORMANTS, professional ex-Communists and hostile witnesses subpoenaed from suspect groups. Although bound in theory by federal rules of evidence, SACB hearings mimicked those of the HOUSE COMMITTEE ON UN-AMERICAN ACTIVITIES (HUAC) and the SENATE INTERNAL SECURITY SUBCOMMITTEE by providing a forum for rumor, innuendo and character assassination.

A series of U.S. SUPREME COURT rulings in 1956-57 curtailed the SACB's perceived campaign of "outlawing the COMMUNIST PARTY without becoming involved in the constitutional complications of actual outlawry," and while its influence faded thereafter, the board persevered in its heavy-handed efforts through the 1960s. On occasion it was able to assist kindred spirits, as in its investigation of the National Committee to Abolish HUAC, but the SACB generally failed to intimidate "NEW LEFT" activists and organizers of VIETNAM WAR PROTESTS. Public discontent with DOMESTIC SURVEILLANCE and the broadening WATERGATE SCANDAL prompted abolition of the SACB in 1973. The Attorney General's list of subversive organizations was abolished the following year.

**SULLIVAN, Jerome**—A G-man with 20 years of service to the Bureau, Jerome Sullivan worked at the New York City field office on cases involving ORGANIZED CRIME. Unfortunately, he was also a compulsive gambler who ran up massive debts to bookies associated with the Lucchese Mafia family—and which he sought to cover by embezzling some $400,000 from the FBI and his criminal INFORMANTS. The sums which Sullivan later admitted to stealing included $196,000 seized during a probe of Colombian NARCOTICS dealers, $100,000 in syndicate money stolen from an FBI safe, another $100,000 taken from an informant in a money-laundering investigation, and $5,200 from the sale of contraband cigarettes by a Lucchese family member. Sullivan was indicted in June 1997 on 10 counts of embezzling government funds, making false statements, deceiving his colleagues and obstructing justice. He pled guilty to all counts on 24 November 1998 and received a five-year term in federal prison, plus an order to reimburse the FBI $191,250.

**SULLIVAN, William Cornelius**—A Bolton, Massachusetts native, born 12 May 1912, William Sullivan earned a B.A. from American University in Washington, then taught school in his hometown before moving on to graduate studies in Boston. He first joined the INTERNAL REVENUE SERVICE, then transferred to the FBI on 4 August 1941, serving at six different field offices over the next three years. In June 1944 Sullivan moved to FBI HEADQUARTERS and supervised FOREIGN OPERATIONS of the SPECIAL INTELLIGENCE SERVICE for the remainder of WORLD WAR II.

Sullivan, nicknamed "Crazy Billy" within the FBI, was assigned to Phoenix in August 1953, then recalled to headquarters 10 months later as an inspector with the Domestic Intelligence Division (where he became assistant director in June 1961). In 1956 he penned the monograph that launched the FBI's first illegal COINTELPRO campaign against the COMMUNIST PARTY. Briefly detailed to the CRIME RECORDS DIVISION in 1962, he was the principal ghost writer for Director J. EDGAR HOOVER's latest book, *A Study of Communism*. In his post at Domestic Intelligence (Division 5) Sullivan ran the intelligence side of the JFK ASSASSINATION case, the 1968 "MURKIN" investigation, and most of the

FBI's COINTELPRO operations against black militants, the "NEW LEFT" and the KU KLUX KLAN. He was a pivotal figure at headquarters, regarded by many observers as Hoover's heir apparent to command of the Bureau.

That vision began to unravel on 12 October 1970, when Sullivan told a gathering of newspaper editors that the Communist Party was "not in any way causing or directing or controlling the unrest we suffer today." Afterward, he claimed that Hoover raged at him in private, "How do you expect me to get my appropriations if you keep downgrading the Party?" Increasingly fed up with FBI politics, Sullivan wrote the first of several "honest memos" to Hoover in June 1971, recommending prompt reduction in the number of LEGAL ATTACHÉS, cutbacks in unproductive investigations, and relegation of foreign work to other agencies. A conference of FBI executives, held on 18 June 1971, warned Hoover that Sullivan seemed "more on the side of the CIA, STATE DEPARTMENT and Military Intelligence Agencies, than the FBI." Two weeks later, Hoover promoted W. MARK FELT over Sullivan, with orders to watch Sullivan "very carefully." When White House operative G. GORDON LIDDY spoke to Sullivan on 2 August 1971 he found the assistant director "very insecure in his position, almost frightened."

On 28 August 1971 Sullivan wrote a letter to Hoover outlining their recent points of disagreement, assuring Hoover "that those of us who disagree with you *are trying to help you and not hurt you*." (Emphasis in the original.) A three-hour meeting on 31 August failed to resolve their argument, and four days later Hoover wrote Sullivan to request his resignation. Sullivan went on leave but declined to resign. When they met again on 30 September, Hoover allegedly called Sullivan "a Judas." Sullivan recalled his own reply: "I'm not a Judas, Mr. Hoover, and you certainly aren't Jesus Christ." Fired on the spot for insubordination, Sullivan spent the next five days typing a long letter to Hoover, including detailed criticism on such points as "Concealment of the Truth," "Senator JOSEPH MCCARTHY and Yourself," "Leaks of Sensitive Material," and "FBI and Politics." Sullivan recommended that Hoover "sit down quietly ... and work out a plan to reform, reorganize and modernize the Bureau." Failing that, he wrote:

> Mr. Hoover, if for reasons of your own you cannot or will not do this may I gently suggest you retire for your good, that of the Bureau, the intelligence community and law enforcement. More than once I told you never to retire; to stay on to the last, that you would live longer being active. It looks now that I may have been wrong. For if you cannot do what is suggested above you really ought to retire and be given recognition due you after such a long and remarkable career in government.

While Hoover fumed over that "betrayal," Sullivan leaked various stories to major newspapers, magazines and television networks, critical of Hoover's tenure at the FBI. He went public for the first time on 10 January 1972, remarking to the *Los Angeles Times* about Hoover's "fossilized" bureaucracy. Shortly after Hoover's death in May 1972, Attorney General RICHARD KLEINDIENST named Sullivan to lead a new Office of National NARCOTICS Intelligence, a post he held until June 1973. Retired to a

New Hampshire farm, Sullivan revisited Washington to testify before the CHURCH and PIKE COMMITTEES in 1975-76. Any possibility of Sullivan testifying before the HOUSE SELECT COMMITTEE ON ASSASSINATIONS was canceled on 9 November 1977, when he was shot and killed in New Hampshire. Authorities named the shooter as a policeman's son and called Sullivan's death a hunting accident.

**SUYDAM, Henry**—U.S. Attorney General HOMER CUMMINGS was disturbed by media reactions to the death of bandit JOHN DILLINGER in July 1934. Some editorials romanticized Dillinger's violent life, while others criticized the FBI's careless use of DEADLY FORCE, resulting in the death or injury of several unarmed suspects and innocent bystanders during the Dillinger manhunt. Anxious to remedy that situation, Cummings met with several prominent newsmen, including columnist DREW PEARSON, to find a solution. As Pearson recalled that meeting 34 years later, in an article for *True* magazine, "[H]e believed the best cure ... was to build up the FBI, not only in actual strength but in the strength of public opinion behind it.... He asked our opinion about the appointment of a top-notch public relations man and those of us present, including Cummings, all agreed on Henry Suydam."

A respected war correspondent and Washington reporter for the *Brooklyn Eagle*, later chief of *Life* magazine's Washington bureau, Suydam was also a personal friend of President FRANKLIN ROOSEVELT. In April 1934 he had interviewed J. EDGAR HOOVER and produced a laudatory profile of the FBI, prompting Hoover to command that Suydam's name be placed "on the list of persons to receive various releases and documents issued" by FBI HEADQUARTERS. That memo was the first documentation of Hoover's file on "friendly" journalists, and the director raised no objection to Suydam's employment as official FBI press agent.

For the record, Suydam was appointed on 29 August 1934 to serve as a "special assistant to the attorney general," drawing his salary from the JUSTICE DEPARTMENT. That subterfuge would permit Hoover to tell the U.S. Senate under oath, in April 1936, that no publicists were employed "in the Bureau of Investigation." Meanwhile, as Drew Pearson recalled in 1968, Suydam "did a terrific job. He really went to town with Hollywood, the radio industry and everyone else to make the FBI invincible." In fact, Pearson observed, Suydam "performed so spectacularly that within a year he had transformed Hoover, previously a barely known bureaucrat, into an omnipotent crime-buster whose name was familiar to every American."

Suydam's campaign was so successful, in fact, that Hoover soon began to emulate his efforts, working closely with novelist COURTNEY RYLEY COOPER and various right-wing journalists to create his own publicity network. By early 1937, Hoover regarded Suydam as superfluous; biographer Curt Gentry suggests that Hoover also resented Suydam's occasional mention of Attorney General Cummings as the real leader of America's "war on crime." In 1937 a last-minute rider attached to the Justice Department's annual appropriation from Congress provided that no salary should be paid to any "special assistant to the Attorney General who is not a qualified attorney." Henry Suydam was the only department employee affected by the new rule, and he was forced to resign. As Drew Pearson later observed, "No one had any doubt regarding the original author [of the amendment]. J. Edgar Hoover had learned how to get the publicity and did not need help any more."

**SWEARINGEN, M. Wesley**—A Steubenville, Ohio native, born 20 May 1927, Wesley Swearingen served in the U.S. Navy during 1945-46 and emerged from that experience "bubbling over with patriotism." His parents recommended an FBI career, and Swearingen entered the FBI ACADEMY in May 1951. He spent his first year as a G-man with the Memphis field office, then transferred to Chicago in July 1952. There, under the leadership of agent-in-charge GUY BANISTER, Swearingen joined a special squad created to perform illegal BREAK-INS as part of the FBI's campaign against the COMMUNIST PARTY. Over the next 11 years he was immersed in various aspects of the Bureau's illicit COINTELPRO campaigns and witnessed first-hand the corruption of various high-ranking Bureau officials.

It was finally love, rather than law-breaking, which drove Swearingen from the Chicago field office. Late in 1962, despite warnings from Bureau officials, he married a divorcée whose first husband had supported presidential candidate HENRY WALLACE in 1948. Swearingen's defiance and marriage to an alleged "subversive" prompted a punitive transfer to Kentucky in January 1963 (the FBI's motive was confirmed in 1979, by documents released under the FREEDOM OF INFORMATION ACT). Swearingen spent five years in exile, twice passed over for promotion, before he was forgiven and transferred to New York City in 1968. There, he resumed his career as a burglar with a badge, this time focused primarily on targets of the "NEW LEFT." A move to Los Angeles in May 1970 placed Agent Swearingen in the midst of covert operations against the BLACK PANTHER PARTY, the WEATHERMAN UNDERGROUND, actress JEAN SEBERG, and others.

Finally disillusioned, Swearingen left the Bureau on his 50th birthday—20 May 1977—and prepared a 212-page summary of his career entitled *FBI Chicanery*, which he shared with various investigators, journalists and attorneys, beginning in 1978. December of that year brought a warning from friends that Swearingen was under active FBI investigation. A team of 16 G-men raided his home and safe-deposit box on 14 December 1978, seizing his typewriter, various papers, and other personal effects, but no charges were ever filed against him.

Harassment and surveillance only made Swearingen more vocal in his criticism of the FBI's illegal activities. The publishing house of William Morrow purchased Swearingen's memoirs in 1980, then declined to publish the book "for business reasons," but Swearingen would not be silenced. His assistance proved critical for various groups and individuals suing the FBI over its COINTELPRO crimes, including members of the SOCIALIST WORKERS PARTY and relatives of murdered Black Panther FRED HAMPTON. Thus far, all Bureau efforts to discredit Swearingen have failed, and his testimony has forced FBI leaders to admit illegally withholding evidence from federal courts and congressional investigators. His memoir, *FBI Secrets: An Agent's Exposé*, was finally published in 1995.

**SYMBIONESE Liberation Army** — America's most notorious radical clique of the 1970s sprang from a failed social experiment at California's Vacaville State Prison. The Black Cultural Association was initially created to provide education and prerelease counseling for inmates nearing parole, but white radicals William Wolfe and Russell Little seized control of the program in 1972, collaborating with 30-year-old convict Donald DeFreeze to teach their students Maoist politics. DeFreeze was later transferred to Folsom prison and escaped from that facility's minimum security wing on 5 March 1973. Joining Wolfe and Little in Oakland, the fugitive dubbed himself "Cinque" (after the leader of a 19th-century slave revolt) and proclaimed himself "field marshal" of the Symbionese Liberation Army (SLA). The name apparently derived from a novel by Sam Greenlee, *The Spook Who Sat by the Door* (1959), which portrays an armed insurrection in Chicago's ghetto and uses the term *symbiology* in passing to describe collaboration among disparate organisms.

Cinque's battle plan for the SLA involved himself giving orders to a handful of naïve white radicals. Despite its origins and professed dedication to oppressed minorities, the SLA apparently had no black members other than DeFreeze. His disciples were unanimously white and thoroughly ashamed of it, to the extent that they shunned their given "slave names" and adopted more exotic monikers. (Wolfe, for instance, called himself "Cujo," a word of unknown derivation that supposedly meant "unconquerable.") Female recruits — a majority of the SLA's tiny membership — went even further in rejecting their ethnicity, affecting dark makeup and Afro wigs to make themselves "look black."

By autumn 1973 DeFreeze had recruited 11 would-be warriors for his "army," seven of them women. Aside from charter members Wolfe and Little there was disaffected VIETNAM WAR veteran Joseph Remiro; James Kilgore; Nancy Ling Perry; Patricia Soltysik; Camilla Hall; Wendy Yoshimura; Angela Atwood; Kathleen Soliah; and a married couple, William and Emily Harris. The SLA made its first move on 9 November 1973, when Little and Remiro ambushed Oakland's black school superintendent, Marcus Foster, and killed him in a fusillade of cyanide-tipped bullets. Foster's "crime," according to DeFreeze, was sponsorship of a program to photograph each member of Oakland's mostly-black student body. DeFreeze regarded the plan as an attempt to isolate and persecute black militants, thus prompting the elimination of a "people's enemy." (Little and Remiro were captured in Concord, California on 10 January 1974, later convicted of murder and sentenced to life imprisonment.)

So far, the FBI had nothing to do with the SLA, but that changed on 5 February 1974, when four masked members kidnapped 19-year-old Patricia Hearst (granddaughter of late newspaper magnate William Randolph Hearst) from her Berkeley apartment. Two days later, a local radio station received one of Hearst's credit cards and a letter from the SLA, decorated with a seven-headed cobra, explaining that Hearst was being held in "protective custody." On 12 February a second letter demanded that Hearst's family distribute $70 million worth of groceries to "all people [in California] with welfare cards, food stamp cards, disabled veteran cards, medical cards, parole or probation papers, and jail or bail release slips." Randolph Hearst agreed on 13

February to "set up some kind of food distribution system," but warned that he could not meet the estimated $400 million cost of implementing the SLA's plan. A tape recording of Patricia's voice was received three days later, telling her father, "It was never intended that you feed the whole state. Whatever you come up with is okay."

Authorities and members of the Hearst family were stunned on 15 April 1974, when SLA members robbed a San Francisco bank of $10,960. Security cameras captured the event — and revealed one of the bandits to be Patricia Hearst, armed with a .30-caliber carbine. Controversy erupted over the videotape, relatives noting that two other robbers appeared to keep their weapons trained on Hearst throughout the holdup, while U.S. Attorney General WILLIAM SAXBE declared, "The entire group we're talking about is common criminals…. And Miss Hearst is part of it." Randolph Hearst called Saxbe's comment irresponsible, but eyewitness Edward Shea disagreed. Hearst was "absolutely a participant," Shea told reporters. She wasn't scared, I'll tell you that…. She had a gun and looked ready to use it. She had plenty of command in her voice. She was full of curse words. She let it be known that she meant business."

Federal arrest warrants issued on 17 April 1974 named Hearst as a material witness to the BANK ROBBERY; those named as active participants included DeFreeze, Nancy Perry, Patricia Soltysik and Camilla Hall. On the same day, state authorities indicted SLA members William Wolfe, Angela Atwood, William Harris and Emily Harris for giving false information on their California driver's license applications.

While family members insisted that Patty Hearst had been brainwashed by her captors, another audio tape was received on 24 April. In that recording, Hearts identified herself as "Tania," called her father a "pig," and denounced the brainwashing claims as "ridiculous." Randolph Hearst dismissed the tape as a product of coercion, but a federal grand jury disagreed, indicting Patricia for bank robbery on 6 June 1974.

By that time, half of the SLA's soldiers were already dead. Authorities traced DeFreeze and company to Los Angeles on 17 May 1974, surrounding the gang's rented hideout. A pitched battle erupted and the house caught fire, allegedly from tear gas canisters (although a reporter for *The Nation* described FBI agents lobbing military hand grenades into the house). Hours later, police and firefighters removed the charred remains of DeFreeze, Wolfe, Perry, Hall and Soltysik from the smoldering rubble. On 7 June 1974, yet another tape recording was received from "Tania" Hearst, this one proclaiming her passionate love for William Wolfe, whom she called "the most beautiful man I've ever known." Once again she denied allegations of SLA brainwashing and pledged her devotion to the revolutionary cause.

Hearst remained at large for another 15 months, during which the SLA robbed another bank at Concord, California, stealing $15,000 and killing customer Myra Opsahl on 21 April 1975. Five months later, on 18 September, G-men captured William and Emily Harris in San Francisco's Mission District. Moments later, agents raided a nearby apartment, where they found Patty Hearst and 32-year-old Wendy Yoshimura (wanted for conspiracy to bomb a Naval ROTC center in 1972). Bail was denied, while defense attorneys tried in vain to have Hearst transferred from jail to a psychiatric hospital. Judge Oliver Carter deemed Hearst competent for trial, and the proceedings convened on 4 February 1976. Convicted of bank robbery and sentenced to seven years' imprisonment, Hearst was paroled after serving 28 months.

SLA survivors William and Emily Harris, meanwhile, faced trial on multiple kidnapping charges. On 9 August 1976 they were convicted of snatching two hostages during the April 1974 robbery of a Los Angeles sporting goods store. Indicted for Hearst's abduction on 29 September 1976, they delayed trial until August 1978, then pled guilty to a reduced charge of "simple kidnapping," rather than "kidnapping for ransom and with great bodily harm." With credit for time served before trial, William Harris was paroled on 26 April 1983; his wife was released one month later, on 27 May.

SLA fugitive Kathleen Soliah defied the odds, remaining at large for a quarter-century and building a respectable life for herself in St. Paul, Minnesota as suburban housewife Sarah Jane Olson. Finally arrested in June 1999, she was returned to California for trial on charges of conspiracy to bomb Los Angeles police cars in 1974. A guilty plea on charges of attempted murder earned Soliah/Olson a sentence of 20 years to life, imposed on 18 January 2002. The sole remaining SLA fugitive, James William Kilgore, eluded capture until 8 November 2002, when he was arrested in Cape Town, South Africa. Since fleeing the U.S., Kilgore had established himself as university lecturer "Charles William Pape" and raised a family in Cape Town. News of Kilgore's capture was "coincidentally" announced by G-men one day after four of his SLA comrades — Sarah Olson, Michael Bortin, William Harris and his ex-wife Emily Montague — pled guilty to the Opsahl murder in Sacramento. Those defendants received prison terms ranging from six to eight years.

# T

**TAFT, William Howard** — The Bureau of Investigation gained its name (from Attorney General GEORGE WICKERSHAM) and enjoyed its first growth spurt under President William Howard Taft. The original force of 34 agents was increased to 64 in 1909, to 81 in 1911, and to 158 in 1912, with a budget of $354,596 during Taft's last year in office. The primary impetus for that growth was passage of the MANN ACT to suppress "white slavery" in 1910. A. BRUCE BIELASKI replaced STANLEY FINCH as head of the Bureau in April 1912. Taft was defeated by WOODROW WILSON in his 1912 campaign for reelection. He was appointed to the U.S. SUPREME COURT in June 1921 and resigned in February 1930, a month before his death.

**TAMM, Edward A.** — A native of St. Paul, Minnesota, born 4 April 1906, Edward Tamm earned a degree in accounting from the University of Montana before attending Georgetown University Law School in Washington, D.C. He joined the FBI in 1930 and was soon promoted to serve as special agent in charge of the Pittsburgh field office. In 1934 Tamm replaced SAMUEL COWLEY as chief aide to Assistant Director of Investigations HAROLD NATHAN. While occupying that post, in 1936, he coordinated Director J. EDGAR HOOVER'S "personal arrest" of bandit ALVIN KARPIS, and was then assigned to outline the Bureau's new program of DOMESTIC SURVEILLANCE. His list of targets, accepted by Hoover as a "good beginning" for future expansion, read as follows:

Maritime Industry, Government affairs, steel steel industry, coal industry, newspaper field, clothing, garment and fur industry, general strike activities, Armed Forces, educational institutions, general activities — Communist and Affiliated Organizations, Fascisti, Anti-Fascisti movements, and activities in Organized Labor organizations.

In 1940 Tamm was promoted to serve as assistant to the director, a post that soon found him defending FBI arrests of the ABRAHAM LINCOLN BRIGADE against harsh criticism from Senator GEORGE NORRIS. In January 1941 Hoover assigned Tamm to investigate Undersecretary of State SUMNER WELLES; that December, he confronted Rep. MARTIN DIES with evidence of a recent $2,000 bribe, thereby securing eternal loyalty from the chairman of the HOUSE COMMITTEE ON UN-AMERICAN ACTIVITIES (HUAC). Before his 1948 retirement to become a federal district judge in Washington, Tamm was also credited with coining the FBI's motto: "Fidelity, Bravery, Integrity."

Such achievements notwithstanding, Hoover regarded Tamm as a traitor for leaving the Bureau, and he spread a rumor that Tamm had received his judicial appointment in exchange for whitewashing President HARRY TRUMAN'S well-known links to Missouri's Pendergast political machine. Hoover's anger cooled over time, partly assuaged in 1965 when Tamm alerted Hoover to a Congressional resolution calling for HUAC's abolition. Tamm was called to lecture on occasion at the FBI ACADEMY, and the CRIME RECORDS DIVISION finally acknowledged him as a "distinguished FBI alumnus," but Hoover's pardon was transitory, colored by anger at yet another "defector," Tamm's younger brother, QUINN TAMM. Edward saw Hoover for the last time on 26 April 1972, a mere six days before the director's death. He found Hoover "just as sharp as ever, and just as cold and anti."

**TAMM, Quinn** — A Seattle native, born in 1910, Quinn Tamm was the younger brother of FBI Assistant to the Director ED-WARD TAMM. He joined the Bureau in 1934, after graduating from the University of Virginia, and four years later became the youngest agent thus far appointed to the rank of inspector by J. EDGAR HOOVER. After 17 years in command of the IDENTIFICA-TION DIVISION, Tamm was again promoted to serve as assistant director of the combined Training and Inspection Division. In that post, and later as chief of the LABORATORY DIVISION, Tamm also served as Hoover's liaison to the INTERNATIONAL ASSOCIA-TION OF CHIEFS OF POLICE, rigging elections so that only officers approved by FBI HEADQUARTERS were chosen to lead the IACP. It was Tamm, in 1959, who engineered the defeat of WILLIAM PARKER, chief of the Los Angeles Police Department, and selected in his place as IACP president a virtual unknown.

Quinn Tamm remained in Hoover's good graces after brother Edward left the Bureau to become a federal judge, but that ended in 1961, when he resigned to become executive director of the IACP. Hoover tried to block Tamm from filling the post, but this time his efforts failed. Under Tamm, the IACP assumed certain law enforcement training functions and challenged FBI headquarters as the primary representative of American police officers. The gauntlet was thrown down in 1962, at the association's annual convention in St. Louis, when Tamm declared that the IACP had once been — and should be again — "the dominant voice in law enforcement. This, I fear, has not been true." He did not mention Hoover's name, but left no doubt of his intentions when he declared that the IACP "must be the spokesman for law enforcement in this country." Seven years later, in Honolulu, Tamm challenged Hoover more directly, warning that a recent plan to "centralize police training in the hands of the director of the FBI could become the first step toward a national police." The feud continued until Hoover's death in May 1972.

**TARKINGTON, Newton Booth** — An Indianapolis native, born in 1896, Booth Tarkington is best remembered for his lighthearted novels of Midwestern life, beginning with *The Gentleman from Indiana* (1899). He collected two Pulitzer Prizes, for *The Magnificent Ambersons* (1918) and *Alice Adams* (1921), long before the FBI took an interest in him and his work.

The Bureau opened its Tarkington file in December 1936, noting his membership in the Authors Guild (a division of the AUTHORS LEAGUE OF AMERICA), and two years later G-men recorded his affiliation with the League of American Writers. In 1940, agents recorded Tarkington's involvement with the American Defenders of Freedom and the North American Spanish Aid Committee. In 1941, his interest in the Negro Cultural Committee raised federal eyebrows, and 1943 found Tarkington cited again (with ALBERT EINSTEIN and others) for sending a telegram

to President FRANKLIN ROOSEVELT, urging the White House to quash ongoing race riots in Detroit. Tarkington died in 1946, but not before his name was dragged into the backwash of the LIND-BERGH KIDNAPPING case. Specifically, Charles Lindbergh sent the FBI two letters from an unidentified correspondent, suggesting that Tarkington had handled the 1932 ransom money and insisting "it is high time to dig into Booth Tarkington's past." FBI headquarters dismissed the letters' author as deranged, but filed the correspondence in Tarkington's dossier for posterity, just in case.

**TATE, John Orley Allen** — Born at Winchester, Kentucky in 1899, poet Allen Tate illustrates the manner in which FBI domestic intelligence gathering has often failed, despite the best efforts of agents and clerks to collect as much data as possible on anyone of note (and many who were not) in the United States. Tate was appointed in 1943 to serve as Consultant in Poetry at the Library of Congress, a position which then required an FBI background check for "suitability" and "loyalty," but no trace of the mandatory investigation could be found 13 years later, when the U.S. Information Agency sought a report on his possible subversive connections in August 1956. Tate's one-page dossier, opened that month, contains only a report that no citations could be found in Bureau files. Tate died in 1979, without accumulating any further paperwork.

**TATUM, Roosevelt** — Between 1947 and 1963 racial BOMBINGS by the KU KLUX KLAN were so common in Birmingham, Alabama that black residents nicknamed the city "Bombingham." Police led by Commissioner EUGENE ("BULL") CONNOR were widely suspected of involvement in the TERRORISM and none of the crimes were solved. FBI agents rarely investigated and made no arrests, although the CIVIL RIGHTS Act of 1960 gave them primary responsibility for such crimes.

On the night of 11 May 1963, following a large Klan rally in Birmingham, another blast rocked the city's black neighborhood known as "Dynamite Hill." Residents flocked around a smoking crater outside the home of Rev. A.D. King, the brother of civil rights activist MARTIN LUTHER KING, JR. Moments after the first explosion, a second bomb detonated on King's porch, demolishing part of his home. A witness to the bombing, black laborer Roosevelt Tatum, told King that he had seen a Birmingham police car stop in front of King's house, its uniformed driver crossing the lawn to place a package on King's porch. Seconds later, driving away, the officer had tossed another parcel from his window, resulting in the evening's first explosion. King listened to the story, then reported Tatum's statement to the FBI.

It should have been easy to trace the suspect officer's movements on 11 May, since Tatum had identified the vehicle as Car 22. G-men questioned Tatum, but the inquiry apparently went no further, despite police lieutenant Maurice House's conviction that members of his own force were "deeply involved" in Birmingham's long reign of terror. On 20 August 1963 another bombing struck the home of black attorney Arthur Shores and neighbors reacted with outrage, stoning police cars sent to the scene.

Birmingham's white newspapers blamed Roosevelt Tatum's "false charges" for the violent reaction, ignoring the 16 years of Klan mayhem that proceeded it.

The FBI, likewise, displayed no interest in solving the crimes. Six days after the Shores bombing, a federal grand jury indicted Tatum for lying to FBI agents. Three months later, on 18 November, Tatum pled guilty before Judge Clarence Allgood and received a one-year prison term. By that time, G-men were busy suppressing evidence in the "BAPBOM" case — yet another bombing, this one fatal to four young girls in a Sunday school class. A quarter-century would pass before state officials obtained their first conviction in that case, and no federal charges have ever been filed in a Birmingham bombing, aside from the apparent FRAME-UP of witness Roosevelt Tatum.

**TEAMSTERS Union** — Arguably the most notorious LABOR UNION in U.S. history, the International Brotherhood of Teamsters was organized in August 1903, in a convention held at Niagara Falls, New York. Cornelius Shea was elected general president, holding that office until 1907, when he was unseated by Boston organizer Daniel Tobin. Tobin, in turn, ran the union and nurtured strong ties with ORGANIZED CRIME until 1952, when he retired and was succeeded by Dave Beck. (The union honored Tobin by creating a new position, "president emeritus," which paid the same $50,000 yearly salary received by active-duty general presidents.)

Nationwide links between the Teamsters Union and various mobsters were already well known to law enforcement (albeit ignored at FBI HEADQUARTERS, where Director J. EDGAR HOOVER denied the existence of organized crime in America), but those corrupt ties became public knowledge under Dave Beck's regime. Senate investigations of the union propelled brothers JOHN and ROBERT KENNEDY to national prominence in 1957, while sending Beck to federal prison for five years. Beck's replacement, James Hoffa, was questioned in the same public hearings and nurtured a hatred of the Kennedys that may have led directly to the JFK ASSASSINATION of November 1963. Hoffa was sentenced to an eight-year prison term for jury tampering in 1964, remaining at large for three years until his appeals were exhausted with a rebuff from the U.S. SUPREME COURT.

Despite incessant publicity surrounding the union's mob ties, multimillion-dollar "loans" to Las Vegas casinos and felony convictions of numerous Teamster officials, national politicians still courted the IBT's money and 1.4 million voting members. President RICHARD NIXON was elected with Teamster support and rewarded Hoffa successor Frank Fitzsimmons with a private sweetheart contract: to keep Teamster votes and guarantee Fitzsimmons control of the union, Nixon granted clemency to Hoffa in 1972 but barred him from holding any union office for the next 10 years. Hoffa was fighting that restriction when he disappeared in 1975, a presumed gangland murder victim.

Fitzsimmons ruled the Teamsters for another decade, long enough to see another presidential hopeful, RONALD REAGAN, pledge his support to the union in exchange for cash and votes. Reagan named IBT Vice President JACKIE PRESSER (an eighth-grade dropout, racketeer and FBI INFORMANT) as a "senior eco-

nomic adviser" to his White House transition team, while lavishing praise on the union at large. (Reagan told one IBT gathering, "I want to be in team with the Teamsters.") Fitzsimmons died of cancer in May 1981, replaced as general president by Reagan ally Roy Williams. Less than two weeks after his election, Williams was indicted for conspiracy to bribe Nevada Senator Howard Cannon. Convicted of attempted bribery in 1982, he remained free on appeal after resigning his union presidency. (In 1985, still seeking leniency, Williams turned informer and provided details on the IBT's long symbiotic relationship with organized crime.)

Jackie Presser replaced Williams as Teamster president in April 1983, continuing the union's support for President Reagan and successor GEORGE H.W. BUSH. Presser's links to the Bureau finally could not prevent his May 1986 indictment for racketeering and embezzling $700,000 through a "ghost" employee scam. Six months later, four Mafia leaders were indicted for rigging Presser's IBT election and controlling his decisions in office. Mounting legal bills and failing health at last persuaded Presser to step down as president, two months before his death in July 1988. William McCarthy replaced him as president, while FBI memos continued to describe the union as "substantially controlled" by leaders of organized crime.

In 1988 the JUSTICE DEPARTMENT filed a civil racketeering lawsuit against the Teamsters Union, code-named "Liberatus" after the FBI investigation that collected information on mob infiltration of the IBT. Union leaders and Justice officials reached a settlement on 13 March 1989, agreeing that the union's next general president would be chosen in 1991 by popular vote of convention delegates (as opposed to rigged election by the union's national committee, composed of or influenced by racketeers). The Bureau's website hails "Liberatus" as a major victory, claiming it "has been largely successful at removing extensive [underworld] influence" from the IBT, but the 1991 election of president Ronald Carey was overturned six years later and Carey was barred from seeking reelection in November 1997, on grounds of corrupt campaign funding. Carey was later indicted on seven counts of perjury concerning that campaign, charges alleging that he lied to a federal grand jury and to various other bodies established to end mob control of the union. Though acquitted at trial in October 2002, Carey was barred from IBT office while James Hoffa, Jr., assumed control of the union once led by his father from prison.

**TEAPOT Dome Scandal** — In 1920 Congress passed the Oil Land Leasing Act, permitting private companies to lease oil-drilling rights on reserves owned by the U.S. Navy. The following year, on 31 May 1921, President WARREN HARDING issued an EXECUTIVE ORDER transferring control of those reserves from the Navy to the Interior Department controlled by Secretary Albert Fall, a member of Harding's corrupt "Ohio Gang." Two months later, without competitive bidding (and in return for a $100,000 bribe), Fall granted drilling rights on the 40,000-acre Elk Hills, California reserve to an old friend, Edward Doheny of Pan American Petroleum. In April 1922 another of Fall's cronies, Mammoth Oil boss Harry Sinclair, obtained exclusive drilling rights to the

9,481-acre oil reserve at Teapot Dome, Montana. Fall's payoff in that case included $70,000 in cash and $233,000 in Liberty bonds.

Rumors of Fall's corruption soon reached the ears of Montana senators THOMAS WALSH and BURTON WHEELER, but Attorney General HARRY DAUGHERTY sidetracked requests for a JUSTICE DEPARTMENT investigation. There matters rested until 2 August 1923, when President Harding died unexpectedly in San Francisco. Senator Wheeler opened a formal investigation of the suspect oil leases in October 1923, while Walsh launched a Senate probe of the Justice Department three months later. Daugherty and FBI Director WILLIAM BURNS did their best to obstruct the investigation, with help from Assistant Director J. EDGAR HOOVER. As described by Senator Thomas Heflin:

> These detectives went through the office of the Senator from Arkansas [Thaddeus Caraway] and they read his correspondence; they went through the office of the Senator from Wisconsin [Robert La Follette]; and God only knows how many other offices they went through. That was a "general fishing expedition"; it was fishing at night, when Senators were at home asleep; but the Department of Justice was awake, and its smooth and alert detectives were quietly going through the offices of United States Senators.

Walsh and Wheeler were primary targets, for their leadership role in the Teapot Dome investigation. G-men orchestrated a FRAME-UP of Wheeler on false corruption charges, but he was acquitted and pressed on with the inquiry, scoring a major coup against Daugherty and Burns with the testimony of ex-Agent GASTON MEANS. President CALVIN COOLIDGE fired Daugherty on 28 March 1924, while Harry Sinclair was fined $1,000 and sentenced to three months in jail for contempt of Congress. Still, another three years elapsed before the U.S. SUPREME COURT annulled Sinclair's and Doheny's oil leases in 1927.

By then, Hoover had replaced Burns at FBI HEADQUARTERS and had launched his famous "clean-up" of the Bureau. Doheny and Fall faced trial for conspiracy on 28 November 1926, but both were acquitted. Fall and Sinclair went to court on identical charges, on 17 October 1927, with agents from the Burns Detective Agency shadowing jurors. Their intrusive surveillance produced a mistrial, and Fall was deemed too sick to appear in court when Sinclair was tried again, in April 1928. Again the verdict was acquittal, though Sinclair still had to serve his trifling time for contempt. Albert Fall was finally convicted of bribery on 25 October 1929, four days before the Wall Street crash and onset of the Great Depression. He was fined $100,000 and sentenced to a year in prison, though appeals delayed his incarceration until July 1931.

**"TEN Most Wanted" List** — Late in 1949 a feature writer for the International News Service (predecessor of United Press International) asked the FBI to name the "toughest guys" whom G-men were pursuing at the moment. The resultant story proved so popular and generated so much positive publicity that Director J. EDGAR HOOVER inaugurated the Bureau's "Ten Most Wanted" program a few weeks later, on 14 March 1950. Since then (as of 1 August 2002), 475 fugitives have graced the roster,

all but 30 of them located by a collaborative effort of watchful citizens and various law enforcement agencies.

Criteria for the selection of a "Top Ten" fugitive is specialized, befitting designation as among the worst of several hundred thousand criminals at large on any given day. First, the individual must either have a lengthy history of conflict with the law or else be counted as a special danger to society because of pending charges. Sheer ferocity is not enough, however. It must also be determined that publicity afforded by the program will be useful in apprehending a subject. Thus, the SYMBIONESE LIBERATION ARMY abductors of heiress Patty Hearst were not listed in 1974, since they generated ample publicity on their own. Terrorist kingpin Usama bin Laden, by contrast, was listed two years *before* the disastrous attacks of 11 September 2001 and remains on the list today. Since many of those listed are fugitives from local charges (murder, rape, etc.), a federal count of unlawful flight to avoid prosecution (or confinement, in the case of escaped convicts) is often added to legitimize FBI pursuit.

As noted earlier, not every Top Ten fugitive is apprehended. Fourteen have been found dead, their names removed from the list once identification of their remains was confirmed. Fifteen others have been dropped after federal charges were dismissed, either because the fugitive is presumed dead or his capture is deemed so unlikely that space must be cleared for another candidate. Fugitive cop killer Donald Eugene Webb holds the record for evading manhunters to date, listed in May 1981 and still on the roster today. Billy Bryant, by contrast, was captured two hours after his "Most Wanted" listing was announced in 1969. Seven fugitives to date have been arrested prior to the public announcement of their Top Ten listing, but they are still considered official members of the FBI's dishonor roll.

Its title notwithstanding, the Ten Most Wanted list has been expanded several times to include more than 10 fugitives. Of 13 such "special additions," seven were NEW LEFT radicals listed in September and October 1970, nearly doubling the "Top Ten" list to include 16 fugitives. That inflation said more about Hoover's obsession with the "Red menace" than any real danger to society at large, and "special" eleventh fugitives have been added only twice since Hoover's death (serial killer Alton Coleman in 1984, and World Trade Center bomber Ramzi Yousef in 1993). Six other fugitives have been listed twice in different years, for separate offenses.

Top Ten fugitives have been captured in 47 states and some two dozen foreign countries. At last count, 120 captures were linked directly to publicity from the Ten Most Wanted program, including 23 fugitives jailed after their stories were broadcast on television and one from the Internet. The Bureau offers a minimum $50,000 reward for information leading to the arrest of any Top Ten fugitive. (See the appendix for a complete list of Most Wanted fugitives.)

**TERRORISM** — The FBI's response to terrorism — generally defined as any use of threats or violence to achieve social or political objectives — has varied since the term entered common usage in the 1960s. Throughout that decade and the next, Bureau spokesmen commonly branded as "terrorists" any group or individual targeted for DOMESTIC SURVEILLANCE or "neutralization" under various illegal COINTELPRO programs. Frequently, FBI charges of violent behavior were either spurious (as when leveled at the SOUTHERN CHRISTIAN LEADERSHIP CONFERENCE in 1967-68) or else the fraudulent product of criminal acts by paid INFORMANTS and *agents provocateur*. At the same time, FBI HEADQUARTERS actively sponsored certain right-wing terrorist groups, including the SECRET ARMY ORGANIZATION and factions of the KU KLUX KLAN. That picture changed in the 1980s and 1990s, as G-men were confronted by real threats from abroad (as in the WORLD TRADE CENTER BOMBING) and from domestic groups including THE ORDER and the far-right MILITIA MOVEMENT.

Following the catastrophic SKYJACKINGS of 11 September 2001, the FBI shuffled its declared priorities to make the foremost goal protection of America from future terrorist attacks. Attorney General JOHN ASHCROFT instantly called for new authority to pursue suspected terrorists, embodied in terms of the "USA PATRIOT ACT." FBI Director ROBERT MUELLER likewise declared the Bureau in need of more money, equipment and agents to cope with the threat, while President GEORGE W. BUSH created an Office of Homeland Security led by former Pennsylvania governor Tom Ridge, coordinating the activities of several dozen federal agencies.

The FBI was not included in that shakeup, but its post-"9/11" activities still gave some cause for alarm. Within two weeks of the September attacks, Muslims and Arab-Americans across the U.S. complained of harassment by federal agents, including arrests and detentions without warrants, coercive interviews, and surveillance that verged on outright intimidation. The offices of Muslim charities were raided in a search for evidence of links to USAMA BIN LADEN or other terrorist leaders, and Ashcroft (echoing the words of A. MITCHELL PALMER in 1919-20) urged his men to be "relentless" in their pursuit of "enemy aliens." At the same time, state and local authorities throughout the U.S. complained that the Bureau refused to share information on its continuing terrorist manhunt, thereby preventing any meaningful cooperation toward the common goal of national security. By 30 December 2001 FBI spokesmen described "more than 150 U.S. terror investigations" in progress — none of them finally resulting in arrests or convictions. In late November 2002 G-men blamed shoddy Immigration records for their failure to locate 4,334 of 5,046 illegal aliens from Middle Eastern countries, known to be residing in the United States.

Despite the flurry of post-9/11 activity, it is clear that leaders of the FBI and CENTRAL INTELLIGENCE AGENCY fumbled their anti-terrorist duties before the attacks. A 450-page report, issued by the Senate Intelligence Committee in December 2002, revealed that a year before 9/11 FBI agents intercepted telephone calls from one of the skyjackers (then living in San Diego, California) to a terrorist facility in the Middle East. No action was taken in that case, and FBI headquarters likewise ignored warnings from an Arizona G-man that suspected terrorists were training at U.S. flight schools. A CIA-FBI rivalry dating from the days of FBI Director J. EDGAR HOOVER reared its head again in early 2000, when CIA agents learned that two Al-Qaeda terrorists had entered the country — and then withheld that information from the Bureau. FBI whistle-blower COLEEN ROWLEY also revealed that agents in Minneapolis arrested one of the 9/11 plotters months in advance of the raids, but were forced to release him when headquarters refused to authorize a search of his home and computer.

As if to compensate for those failures, the FBI followed 9/11 with an endless series of media "terrorist warnings," none of which proved to be valid. Among those were the following:

*October 2001*— Director Mueller warned U.S. authorities and civilians to "be on the highest alert" for possible attacks over the next week, based on undisclosed information that was "deemed credible" but which was "not specific as to intended targets or as to intended methods."

*November 2001*— After a warning that terrorists "might attack West Coast bridges," Bureau spokesmen belatedly acknowledged that the "raw intelligence" behind the alert "was not credible."

*December 2001*— Mueller issued another "general alert" for terrorist attacks. When none occurred, local officials across the U.S. denounced the continuing alarms as "needless provocations of public anxiety" which "contained so little information or specific guidance for how people should act that they are useless at best, disruptive at worst." One day after those complaints were aired (on 11 December 2001), FBI headquarters reported another vague threat suggesting two people "may retaliate against a Texas school for the U.S. bombing in Afghanistan."

*May 2002*— FBI headquarters warned of "a possible terrorist threat to the Orlando, Florida water supply." Local authorities told reporters on 21 May that the threat "was so vague that officials did not know what contaminants to check for." In fact, none were found.

*July 2002*— Admitting that their lead was "very vague," FBI spokesmen issued a national warning that "people with ties to terrorist groups are downloading images of U.S. stadiums from the Internet." The alleged terrorists engaged in that legal activity remain unidentified today.

*October 2002*— Vague as ever, FBI headquarters issued a nationwide alert about "a possible attack soon against transportation systems, particularly railroads." No such attacks occurred.

*November 2002*— "Despite a lack of specific credible evidence," the Bureau warned Americans that unnamed members of Usama Bin Laden's Al-Qaeda group were "likely to attempt a 'spectacular' attack intended to inflict large-scale casualties and damage the U.S. economy." Days later, the FBI reported "unconfirmed information from intelligence sources overseas that hospitals in four U.S. cities could be the targets of a terrorist threat." No cities were named, and no attacks occurred.

*December 2002*— The Bureau broadcast photos of four alleged Muslim terrorists said to be at large in the U.S. and seeking targets. On 2 January 2003 a Pakistani jeweler in Lahore, one Mohammed Asghar, identified himself as the man depicted in one photo. By 7 January G-men had called off their search for the "terrorists," ruefully confessing that the latest alarm was a hoax "fabricated by an informant."

*February 2003*— Unfazed by the January fiasco, FBI headquarters issued its first-ever "National Threat Assessment" to Congress, listing various terrorist groups worldwide and describing "the chemical and biological agents that U.S. officials believe are the most likely to be used in a terrorist attack."

The result of so much attention to terrorism was dramatic. Between 11 September and 30 November 2001, the number of criminal cases recommended for prosecution by FBI agents dropped 76 percent across the U.S. According to JUSTICE DEPARTMENT records, only 263 "ordinary" cases (including NARCOTICS, BANK ROBBERY, ORGANIZED CRIME and white-collar crime) were referred for prosecution in the last half of September 2001, versus more than 1,400 cases for the same two-week period in 1999 and 2000. That boon for criminals was balanced, Director Mueller claimed in December 2002, by the fact that "nearly 100 terrorist attacks, some intended to take place on U.S. soil, have been thwarted" since 9/11. None of those cases was further described, and some inkling of the FBI's methods is provided by James Moore, a retired agent for the BUREAU OF ALCOHOL, TOBACCO AND FIREARMS:

> FBI "achievements" in the field of terrorism generally fall into two categories: cases they "adopt" without disclosing that the most critical aspects of the case were actually accomplished by other agencies; and instances where the "accomplishment" is described as "preventing a terrorist act." The latter, translated into what the FBI actually *did*, consists of having a tip and interviewing the alleged would-be terrorists—informing them that "we know what you're planning" and warning of the consequences, should they choose to carry out the reported plot. Receiving tips is no accomplishment—considering the $3.5 million the FBI paid to informers in 1975 and their mandate, which makes it every police agency's duty to report such rumors to the FBI. "Resolving" the situation through aggressive questioning and dire warning is something any officer could do. Result: No one knows whether there was really a plot, so no one goes to jail.

Even so, a federal commission chaired by former Virginia governor James Gilmore voiced concerns in December 2002 that the FBI might become "a kind of secret police" if its agents continued long-term pursuit of terrorists while also maintaining their normal law enforcement duties. The panel recommended creation of a new National Counter Terrorism Center to "separate the intelligence collection function from the law enforcement function to avoid the impression that the U.S. is establishing a kind of 'secret police.'" Attorney General Ashcroft and Director Mueller predictably opposed any surrender of their new powers granted under the USA Patriot Act. Recent failures and cutbacks notwithstanding, Ashcroft voiced his belief "that the FBI is well suited to serve as the domestic intelligence and terrorism-prevention agency in the United States," while Mueller deemed the Bureau "uniquely positioned" to perform all jobs at once. It remains to be seen if their faith is well-founded.

**THOMPSON, Linda C.**—A 39-year-old agent assigned to the Bureau's Miami field office, Linda Thompson joined in an UNDERCOVER OPERATION during 1991. The target was Michael Guibilo, a violent felon then confined at the South Dade Metropolitan Correctional Center. Thompson was ordered to pose as a paralegal and as Guibilo's "girlfriend" in an effort to obtain information on his criminal activities and associates. Specifically, the FBI wanted Guibilo to tape conversations with another inmate who was plotting to murder a federal prosecutor.

Trouble began for Thompson when guards complained that she and Guibilo were "kissing passionately" during jailhouse visits. Miami's agent-in-charge removed Thompson from the case and ordered her to sever her relationship with Guibilo, but Guibilo subsequently telephoned her several times, with one call lasting for 38 minutes. The Bureau's OFFICE OF PROFESSIONAL RESPONSIBILITY investigated Thompson and she passed a polygraph test, explaining that she maintained contact with Guibilo out of fear that his criminal cohorts might harm her if she broke off the relationship. Thompson was eventually vindicated, after filing a complaint of sexual discrimination under Equal Employment Opportunity statutes. Meanwhile, Guibilo's cooperation produced a 50-year sentence for James Monaco, convicted of drug conspiracy and plotting to murder Assistant U.S. Attorney Barbara Petras.

**THORNBURGH, Richard Lewis**—Born 16 July 1932, Richard Thornburgh served as U.S. attorney for the western district of Pennsylvania in 1969-75 and later as governor of Pennsylvania (1979-87). He was sworn in as President RONALD REAGAN'S third attorney general on 12 August 1988, replacing EDWIN MEESE. He remained to serve under President GEORGE H.W. BUSH. Thornburgh assisted both presidents in seeking to derail prosecution of conspirators in the Iran-Contra scandal, including a failed effort to dismiss charges filed against defendant Oliver North. Thornburgh treated FBI Director WILLIAM SESSIONS with complete disdain, frequently refusing to accept his telephone calls, but he was willing to expand the Bureau's FOREIGN OPERATIONS in defiance of international law. On 12 June 1989 Thornburgh authorized G-men to arrest suspected TERRORISTS, drug traffickers and other fugitives abroad without consulting police in the nations where they reside—an order having no legal effect outside the U.S., which might indeed be treated as an act of war by various hostile regimes. Thornburgh resigned as attorney general on 15 August 1991 and was replaced by WILLIAM BARR.

**THURBER, James Grover**—Born in Columbus, Ohio on 8 December 1894, James Thurber found his true vocation after serving with the U.S. Army in WORLD WAR I, returning to civilian life as a journalist, playwright, cartoonist and short story writer. He joined the *New Yorker*'s staff in 1927, but it took the FBI 11 years to notice him, opening Thurber's dossier in 1938, after he attended the Third American Writers Congress. Self-appointed infiltrator Leland Stowe, himself the author of three books, sent J. EDGAR HOOVER a list of conference attendees with a note reading: "Dear Edgar, Here's a pretty good dictionary of Communists." In 1939, G-men noted Thurber's name among 400 signatures on a letter seeking closer U.S. cooperation with the Soviet Union against fascism, and Hoover noted Thurber's contribution of several cartoons to an auction held for the benefit of Spanish refugees. A year later, Thurber was listed among 125 signatories of a letter to the White House, condemning FBI persecution of the ABRAHAM LINCOLN BRIGADE.

Such "radical" activities on Thurber's part continued after WORLD WAR II. In 1946 he joined THOMAS MANN and others calling for "a clearcut break" with fascist Spain. Leland Stowe returned that same year, providing derogatory information on Thurber to the HOUSE COMMITTEE ON UN-AMERICAN ACTIVITIES (HUAC), and G-men reported that Thurber had helped to raise money for the blacklisted "Hollywood Ten," facing contempt charges for their refusal to collaborate with HUAC inquisitors. Agents also clipped a *Daily Worker* gossip column in 1947, alleging that Thurber was "disgusted" with the anti-communist activities of former coauthor Elliott Nugent. Three years later, agents worried over reports that a Thurber short story, "The Catbird Seat," would be filmed with suspected "fellow traveler" José Ferrer in a starring role. Thurber's dossier contained 105 pages of gossip and innuendo at the time of his death, in 1961.

**THURMAN, James ("Tom")**—A former U.S. Army officer and commander of an ammunition company in South Korea, James Thurman joined the FBI in 1977 and was assigned to the LABORATORY DIVISION as an explosives analyst in 1981. That assignment was problematic, since coworker FREDERICK WHITEHURST later recalled (and informed his superiors) that as of 1989 "Thurman had no idea what an explosive material was composed of or how the different components functioned in the chemical reaction of an explosion." That deficiency did not prevent him from testifying as a key government witness in the "VANPAC" case, prosecuted by U.S. Attorney LOUIS FREEH, and the subsequent conviction of defendant Walter Moody firmly established Thurman in the JUSTICE DEPARTMENT circle known as "Friends of Louie."

In 1992 Whitehurst complained to his superiors that Thurman had systematically altered his (Whitehurst's) lab reports over the past five years, "apparently to slant the conclusions and opinions in favor of guilt," while agent ROGER MARTZ pressured Whitehurst to accept the changes. Supervisor James Corby found that Whitehurst had in fact altered text in 31 of Whitehurst's 52 explosives reports since 1988; in 13 of those cases, the findings were "materially altered" to the point that Corby felt Whitehurst's conclusions had been compromised. Corby's boss, James Kearney, agreed that Thurman had "significantly altered Whitehurst's dictation" in 12 reports, and in one had "reported technical results without supporting laboratory analysis." Corby recommended formal censure, but Kearney refused, concluding that Thurman's revisions were not made to "bias the reports in favor of the prosecution" but rather to "clarify the reports by integrating the findings … into the full context of the report." Later, Kearney told authors John Kelly and Phillip Wearne, "No doubt about it, Tom Thurman shouldn't have been doing what he was doing, but the changes did not really change the consistency of the reports, so I thought they were making a big deal over nothing."

Corby disagreed, calling Thurman's changes "clearly intentional" and stating that Thurman "does not understand the scientific issues involved with the interpretation and significance of explosives and explosive residue composition. He therefore should realize this deficiency and differentiate between his personal opinions and scientific fact." Any question of censure was settled with Louis Freeh became director of the FBI in September 1993. Ten months later, deficiencies notwithstanding, Thurman was promoted to acting chief of the FBI lab's Explosives Unit, directing the work of Fred Whitehurst and others.

A second trial in the VANPAC case brought Thurman back to the spotlight in 1995. He initially testified that all the various mail bombs allegedly built by defendant Moody were "identical," then confessed numerous differences on cross-examination, while insisting that a common "signature" linked all the devices. Moody was convicted again, in a verdict that prompted Whitehurst to make his complaints public. During a subsequent investigation by the FBI's Inspector General (IG), Thurman took offense to various questions and walked out of the interview. The IG's final report found a persistent pattern in Thurman's reports, overstating evidence in a fashion favorable to the prosecution, yet strangely concluded that Thurman merely "erred" repeatedly, but had not "intended to write reports with a prosecutorial bias." Still, the mild rebuke was enough to remove Thurman from the Laboratory Division in January 1997. At last report he was still employed as an FBI agent.

**TICKEL, H. Edward, Jr.**—The son of a retired G-man, Edward Tickel, Jr., earned his bachelor's degree from Henderson State University (in Arkansas) and then obtained a master's in forensic sciences from George Washington University. He joined the FBI in 1969 and was assigned to the TECHNICAL SERVICES DIVISION, soon recognized by his peers as "the FBI's top BREAK-IN artist." A master with locks of all kinds, Tickel bugged Soviet embassies and carried out other sensitive assignments, including a change of locks at the home of WILLIAM WEBSTER following Webster's 1978 appointment as FBI director.

At 5:30 a.m. on 16 April 1980, janitor Earl Thornton unlocked the FBI Credit Union, on the eighth floor of FBI HEADQUARTERS, and prepared to vacuum the floor. He saw Tickel crouched before an open safe with $260,000 inside, but before he could speak Tickel leaped to his feet and arrested Thornton for attempted burglary. The clumsy cover fell apart when Tickel failed a polygraph test, and following investigation by the OFFICE OF PROFESSIONAL RESPONSIBILITY (OPR) his case was referred to the JUSTICE DEPARTMENT for further study. U.S. Attorney John Hume soon discovered that Tickel had been investigated by the OPR in a previous case, for using his authority to help a friend suspected of stealing jewelry worth $200,000 in North Carolina. Hume procured Tickel's credit card letters and found Tickel had lied when he denied being present in North Carolina at the time of the theft. Soon, Hume learned that Tickel was involved in selling the stolen jewelry, as well as fencing stolen cars and stealing FBI two-way radios for various friends.

Tickel was acquitted of breaking into the FBI Credit Union but he pled guilty in Washington to theft of the radios. At a second trial in Alexandria, Virginia, Tickel was convicted and sentenced to eight years in prison for tax evasion, making false statements, obstructing justice and transporting stolen property (the Carolina jewels) across state lines. That conviction earned him an eight-year prison sentence. A third jury in Loudon County, Virginia subsequently convicted Tickel of receiving $120,000 in stolen cars and other contraband.

**TITUS, Earl E.** —Born in 1867, Earl Titus graduated from high school and spent five years as a patrolman with the Indianapolis Police Department, before retiring from law enforcement to work as a barber in the early 1900s. He was 55 years old when he joined the Bureau of Investigation in 1922, assigned to work "black radical" cases from the New York City field office under supervision from Agent JAMES AMOS. Titus focused primarily on MARCUS GARVEY'S Universal Negro Improvement Association and the AFRICAN BLOOD BROTHERHOOD, enjoying his greatest success with the latter. Titus befriended leader Cyril Briggs in August 1923 and soon rose into the Brotherhood's leadership circle, assisting in distribution of the group's publications. Titus was summoned to a meeting with Bureau Director WILLIAM BURNS in New York, on 20 November 1923, and he was packed off to Washington two days later. Transferred to the Chicago field office before year's end, Titus resumed his work with the Brotherhood, but its local chapter had shriveled to 13 members by January 1924 and dissolved entirely two months later. Titus left the Bureau soon thereafter, with no records surviving to indicate if he resigned voluntarily or was dismissed as unneeded. J. EDGAR HOOVER'S rise to control of the Bureau in May 1924 marked the beginning of a 38-year lapse before the FBI hired its next African American agent.

**TOLSON, Clyde Anderson** —A Missouri native, born near Laredo on 22 May 1900, Clyde Tolson moved to Cedar Rapids, Iowa as a youth and spent a year (1917) at Cedar Rapids Business College. Somehow avoiding the draft in WORLD WAR I, he moved to Washington, D.C. in 1918 and enrolled in night classes at George Washington University, while working days at the War Department. In 1920 Tolson was appointed confidential secretary to Newton Baker, the secretary of war. Tolson finally earned his law degree in October 1927 and joined the FBI six months later, on 2 April 1928. On his application, Tolson warned that he was only passing through the Bureau, planning to quit as soon as he had enough money to start a law practice in Cedar Rapids. Director J. EDGAR HOOVER was reportedly amused, telling an aide, "Hire him, if he measures up after the examination and investigation. He will make us a good man."

In fact, he did much more. Within the last six months of 1928 Tolson was stationed in Washington, D.C., then transferred to Boston, and finally recalled to FBI HEADQUARTERS as chief clerk. On 31 July 1929 Hoover placed him in charge of the Buffalo, New York field office, then recalled him to Washington one week later with a promotion to inspector. On 16 August 1930 Tolson was named assistant director for Personnel and Administration. Less than a year later, Hoover created the new post of assistant to the director (later associate director) for Tolson, thus making him the FBI's number-two man within two short years of joining the Bureau.

Tolson's meteoric rise, coupled with his lifelong bachelorhood and inseparability from Hoover, nurtured rumors that the two men were HOMOSEXUAL lovers. While never definitely proven, the stories were common currency among G-men nationwide and were also widely taken as "common knowledge" among outsiders ranging from gossip columnists to members of ORGANIZED CRIME. Whatever the true nature of their personal relationship, from 1928 onward the two men followed a lock-step course through life, even vacationing together on "inspection tours" of race tracks and lavish hotels (all "comped" by wealthy benefactors, many with underworld connections).

Tolson's power grew with that of Hoover and the FBI. In 1936, after Senate critics challenged Hoover's prowess as a lawman, the director staged "personal arrests" of federal fugitives for himself and Tolson: Hoover "captured" ALVIN KARPIS, while Tolson followed a small army of G-men to clap handcuffs on HARRY BRUNETTE. In 1939 Tolson followed Hoover's example by accepting a commission as a lieutenant commander in the Naval Reserve (though he had no duties and never spent a day on active duty during WORLD WAR II). Tolson's health began to fail in the 1960s, with strokes in 1966-67 leaving him partially disabled. Although he survived and remained on the job, his mental acuity was reduced to the point that he no longer caught all of Hoover's mistakes and he could not restrain his old friend's erratic fits of rage. Following Hoover's death on 2 May 1972, Tolson spent one day as acting FBI director, then ceded his post to L. PATRICK GRAY. Tolson retired from the Bureau on 16 May 1972 and lived in Hoover's former home (which he inherited) until his death on 14 April 1975.

**TONGYAI, Thomas** —Nicknamed "Tommy the Traveler" after his penchant for rambling around New York state, Thomas Tongyai posed as a "NEW LEFT" radical when he visited various college campuses in the late 1960s. Financed simultaneously by the FBI and local police departments, Tongyai furnished leftist student groups with radical speakers and literature, urging each audience in turn to kill police, build bombs and demolish selected targets. At one point, Tongyai tried without success to organize a Rochester chapter of STUDENTS FOR A DEMOCRATIC SOCIETY, and he encouraged New York students to visit Chicago in October 1969, for the WEATHERMAN UNDERGROUND'S riotous "Days of Rage." An obsessive proponent of illegal violence, Tongyai habitually traveled with firearms and hand grenades, instructing campus dissidents in marksmanship and counseling them on construction of bombs. Students at Hobart College apparently took his advice and bombed the campus ROTC office, whereupon Tongyai's activity as an *agent provocateur* was revealed. Even so, he escaped indictment by the grand jury that charged nine of his followers, and Tongyai retired from UNDERCOVER OPERATIONS to become a policeman in Pennsylvania.

**TOP Hoodlum Program** —On 14 November 1957 police officers surprised 63 Italian-American gangsters who had gathered for a "convention" of sorts at the Apalachin, New York estate of Joseph Barbara Sr. Media reports of that event embarrassed FBI Director J. EDGAR HOOVER, who had denied since 1924 that the Mafia or anything resembling ORGANIZED CRIME existed in the U.S. Confronted with proof of his error, Hoover responded days later by inaugurating the FBI's "Top Hoodlum Program."

As dictated from FBI HEADQUARTERS, each Bureau field office was required to prepare a list of 10 "top hoodlums"—no more, no less—from each respective region of the country. The fallacy of that order was readily apparent, since major urban areas teemed with hundreds of mobsters, while other areas — e.g. Butte, Montana—might have none at all. Still, each office without exception was commanded to prepare a list of ten felons marked for intensive surveillance, including the same BREAK-INS, BUGGING and WIRETAPPING that characterized FBI investigation of groups like the COMMUNIST PARTY. Few prosecutions resulted, since illegal evidence was inadmissible in court, but the Bureau soon amassed intelligence that would prove useful when Attorney General ROBERT KENNEDY (1961–64) forced Hoover to pursue the mob in earnest.

**TOUHY, Roger**—Illinois bootlegger Roger ("The Terrible") Touhy holds the dubious distinction of being the only man framed by FBI agents for two separate crimes. When they failed to convict him in the first case, G-men collaborated with members of ORGANIZED CRIME to imprison Touhy and three others for a second crime, which never occurred.

Touhy's legal problems stemmed from his illegal competition with mobster ALPHONSE CAPONE in Chicago's beer wars. Unable to kill Touhy off as he had so many other rivals, Capone hatched a plot with corrupt Chicago police to frame Touhy for the staged kidnapping of British con artist John Factor. Factor proved agreeable, since the diversion postponed his extradition to England for trial on fraud charges. Allegedly kidnapped on 30 June 1933, Factor surfaced 12 days later, telling police that Touhy's gang had snatched him for $70,000 ransom. Touhy and three associates—Eddie McFadden, Gus Schaefer and Willie Sharkey—were arrested on 19 July, but Factor failed to identify them, claiming he was blindfolded throughout his captivity.

G-man MELVIN PURVIS, meanwhile, had somehow convinced himself that Touhy and company were responsible for the June 1933 kidnapping of Minnesota brewer William Hamm. That crime was actually committed by the BARKER-KARPIS GANG, but Purvis did not know that gang existed, despite its long history of violent BANK ROBBERIES. Instead, he told reporters that the Bureau had "an ironclad case" against the Touhy gang for Hamm's abduction. Touhy described the FBI's investigative technique years later, in an autobiography aptly titled *The Stolen Years*.

> I went into jail in excellent physical shape. When I came out I was twenty-five pounds lighter, three vertebrae in my upper spine were fractured, and seven of my teeth had been knocked out. Part of the FBI's rehabilitation of prisoners, I supposed....
>
> They questioned me day and night, abused me, beat me up, and demanded that I confess the Hamm kidnapping. Never was I allowed to rest for more than half an hour. If I was asleep when a team of interrogators arrived at my cell, they would slug me around and bang me against the wall....

On 12 August 1933 a federal grand jury in St. Paul indicted Touhy and his three associates for the Hamm kidnapping. At trial, prosecutor Joseph Keenan called witnesses who swore they had seen Touhy's gang loitering outside Hamm's brewery, and later in a field where Hamm was released after payment of $100,000 ransom. John Factor was brought in "to aid the government" with a series of press conferences, wherein he claimed Touhy had kidnapped and tortured him. Despite such antics, jurors acquitted all four defendants of Hamm's kidnapping on 28 November 1933. Purvis, undaunted, announced that the four would be held for trial in Chicago, for kidnapping Factor. It was too much for Willie Sharkey, and he hanged himself in jail two days later.

The lineup of defendants was revised for Factor's case. Eddie McFadden was released, while another gang member, August Lamarr, was charged with kidnapping Factor. Two suspects still at large, Basil Banghart and Charles Connors, were accused of demanding $50,000 for Factor's release in August 1933, a month *after* he returned safely home. A strike force of 300 cops and G-men had tried to capture Banghart and Connors at the "ransom" drop, on 12 August 1933, but the two gunmen shot their way clear and were still at large in January 1934, when Touhy's second trial began.

At those proceedings, prosecutor Tom Courtney called half a dozen witnesses to finger Touhy, Schaefer and Lamarr as Factor's kidnappers. Factor changed his original story, claiming now that his blindfold was removed long enough for him to glimpse Touhy's face. The defendants countered with alibi witnesses and a reporter who noted that Factor seemed curiously well-groomed for a kidnap victim, on the day of his "release." Hopelessly confused, jurors deadlocked and a mistrial was declared on 2 February 1934.

Prior to the start of Touhy's third trial, Basil Banghart was arrested with cohort Ike Costner, for robbing a mail truck in North Carolina. Forgetting Charles Connors (found murdered in Chicago on 14 March 1934), Touhy's prosecutors drafted Costner as a witness to the Factor kidnapping, while Banghart took his place at the defendant's table. Coached by the prosecution (and promised immunity for the mail holdup), Costner identified Touhy as the mastermind of Factor's abduction. This time, all four defendants were convicted and sentenced to 99-year prison terms. Touhy and Banghart escaped from prison in October 1942, but G-men led by J. EDGAR HOOVER recaptured them two months later and 199 years was added to Touhy's sentence for the breakout.

In 1954 Ike Costner recanted his story and signed an affidavit confessing to perjury at Touhy's second Chicago trial. Federal judge John Barnes reviewed the case, declaring that Chicago police had suppressed "important evidence," while prosecutors engaged in "numerous stratagems and artifices ... consistent only with a design to bring about the conviction of Touhy at any cost." The bottom line, according to Judge Barnes: "John Factor was not kidnapped for ransom or otherwise.... Roger Touhy did not participate in the alleged kidnapping of John Factor.... Perjured testimony was knowingly used by the prosecution to bring about Touhy's conviction—this being the case, his conviction cannot stand, regardless of the motive."

Touhy was freed, then returned to prison when the state appealed Judge Barnes's ruling on grounds that Touhy had not exhausted his legal remedies in state court before proceeding to the federal level. An appellate court found the argument persuasive, and Touhy remained in custody until his eventual parole on 16 December 1959. He was free just 16 days when gunmen shot him down outside his sister's home in Chicago. As he lay dying, Touhy said, "I've been expecting it. The bastards never forget."

**TRAINING Division**—Fans and critics alike generally agree that J. EDGAR HOOVER'S greatest contribution to law enforcement was the establishment of training facilities to create a standard of professional behavior, not only within the FBI but among thousands of U.S. and foreign police officers trained at FBI facilities since 1935. The fact that Hoover frequently ignored the law himself and commanded his agents to engage in criminal behavior, or that foreign trainees returned home to serve brutal despots, takes nothing away from the sterling instruction provided by the FBI's Training Division.

Formal training for G-men was a haphazard affair prior to 1935, when Hoover established the internationally famous FBI ACADEMY at Quantico, Virginia. Even then, advances notwithstanding, the temptation to inflate Bureau achievements proved irresistible. It was never true, as frequently suggested in FBI press releases from the Hoover era, that "all"—or even "most"—G-men were distinguished by their college degrees in law or accounting. Such applicants may be "preferred," as DON WHITEHEAD claimed in *The FBI Story* (1956), but they are by no means the norm. As late as 1993, author Robert Kessler found that "close to 15 percent" of FBI applicants held legal degrees, and a similar percentage were accountants—less than one-third of all applicants combined.

Aside from training FBI agents, Hoover also opened the FBI Police Training School (also at Quantico) in 1935, renamed the FBI National Police Academy a year later and known simply as the FBI NATIONAL ACADEMY since 1945. (Admission to the National Academy was sometimes offered as a reward for outstanding officers, or withheld from whole police departments out of spite, as during Hoover's long feud with Los Angeles police chief WILLIAM PARKER.) Training of the Bureau's first Special Weapons and Tactics (SWAT) teams began at Quantico in July 1973, renamed the HOSTAGE RESCUE TEAM in January 1983. Facilities and programs housed at the FBI's Quantico complex include:

*Executive Training Program*—Created in 1976 for high-ranking administrators of America's large police departments. A parallel course for leaders of mid-sized agencies, the *Law Enforcement Executive Seminar*, was launched in 1981.

*National Center for the Analysis of Violent Crime*—Incorporating the Behavioral Science Unit (now Investigative Support Services) and the Bureau's VIOLENT CRIMINAL APPREHENSION PROGRAM (VICAP), this unit seeks to assist in capture of unidentified felons by means of PSYCHOLOGICAL PROFILING. Its methods remain controversial and do not involve active pursuit of fugitives by FBI agents.

*CRITICAL INCIDENT RESPONSE GROUP*—Created in April 1994 to facilitate a rapid FBI response in emergency situations throughout the nation.

*Child Abduction and Serial Killers Unit*—Placing FBI agents on a collaborative team with agents from the BUREAU OF ALCO-HOL, TOBACCO AND FIREARMS; the DRUG ENFORCEMENT ADMINISTRATION; the U.S. MARSHALS SERVICE; the U.S. SECRET SERVICE; the U.S. Postal Service; and the U.S. Customs Service. Although serial murder and most child abductions lie outside federal jurisdiction (except where state lines are crossed by the offenders or their crimes occur on government property), public hysteria surrounding such incidents was sufficient to produce congressional action in 1994, creating this team whose "primary objective is the safe return of the victim."

*Justice Training Center*—Opened in 2000, specifically for the training of Drug Enforcement Administration agents, the new facility was envisioned as a cost-cutting measure and a step to "strengthen the bond between the FBI and the DEA."

**TRAVIS, Stephen** *see* **ROTTON, Alan**

**TRILLING, Lionel**—A native of New York City, born in 1905, essayist Lionel Trilling graduated from Columbia University in 1925, went on to earn his Master's there a year later, and joined the staff while completing his Ph.D. (1938), remaining as a professor at the university until his death in 1975. With wife Diana Rubin Trilling, he was a key figure in "the New York intellectual" circle, prominent from the 1930s through the 1950s. The FBI opened a file on Trilling in 1937, widow Diana later expressing amazement that agents had somehow overlooked her husband's period of "most ardent commitment" to leftist causes in 1932-33.

Tardy they may have been, but once G-men focused on Trilling there was no letting go. In 1949 they noted his collaboration, with other Columbia professors, in providing legal aid to student ALLEN GINSBERG, orchestrating a psychiatric defense that spared Ginsberg from indictment and trial for a suspected Long Island burglary. Around the same time, Bureau headquarters pored over Trilling's novel *The Middle of the Journey*, worried that its portrayal of certain individuals within the American COMMUNIST PARTY "could possibly be of use to [ALGER] HISS and his attorneys" in a forthcoming perjury trial. Agents also clipped a *Daily Worker* review of the novel, which ironically branded it "a cold calculated slander of the Communist party."

Several documents filed in Trilling's dossier oddly make no mention of his name, including a 1950 memo on the AUTHORS LEAGUE OF AMERICA (of which he was a member) and a 1952 "Internal Security" report that seems to have no bearing whatever on Trilling. Three years later, agents noted that Trilling had signed a letter to President DWIGHT EISENHOWER, protesting the expulsion of an Indonesian diplomat. In 1958 the Bureau used an open letter to the *New York Times*, signed by Trilling and others in protest of treatment afforded to Soviet Jews, in a COINTELPRO operation aimed at stirring up dissension between Reds and intellectual "fellow travelers." Two documents filed in 1959 remain classified today for reasons of "national security," including a memo from the CENTRAL INTELLIGENCE AGENCY and an "Internal Security" report on Russia and Poland. (Trilling would visit Poland three years later, but had not been there previously.)

The tumultuous 1960s saw more documents added to

Trilling's dossier. A report filed in 1960 warned that Trilling "is a potential participant in an exchange between Columbia and Moscow University," though in fact he never went to Russia. A 1961 report on the Fair Play for Cuba Committee was blacked out prior to release under the FREEDOM OF INFORMATION ACT, but Diana Trilling reports that her husband had no sympathy for the Castro regime in Havana. Another document from 1961, headed "Communist Security Matter and Fraud Against the Government," notes that the Bureau sent a Trilling book review to agents of Naval Intelligence. In 1964, around the time the Trillings went to Oxford, a name check was ordered by officers of the U.S. Information Agency, with the routine repeated (adding a fingerprint check) in 1965, at the request of White House aides. Overall, 28 years of FBI investigation failed to disclose any criminal or "subversive" activity on Trilling's part.

**TRI-STATE Gang** — The Tri-State Gang was a band of Depression-era desperadoes active primarily on the Eastern Seaboard, where they committed armed robberies, murders, and at least one ransom KIDNAPPING. Gunmen Walter Howard Mais and Walter Legurenza shared leadership of the gang, which included 15 other bandits at its peak.

The gang's first recorded crime was a mail robbery at Union Station in Washington, D.C., committed on 5 December 1933. Three months later the outlaws stole $60,000 and killed one employee during a Richmond, Virginia BANK ROBBERY. On 4 April 1934, the crew hijacked a truckload of cigarettes valued at $17,000 in North Carolina, abducting the drivers and leaving them handcuffed to trees at Bowling Green, Virginia.

That violation of the LINDBERGH Law gave G-men a reason to track the gang. One member, William Phillips, was killed by Bureau agents and police in Washington, on 12 April 1934. Three weeks later, a federal grand jury in North Carolina indicted Legurenza, John Kendrick and Morris Kauffman for theft of a shipment in interstate commerce. Kauffman was found dead in Philadelphia on 23 May, the victim of a gangland execution. Ten days later, the gang raided a National Guard armory at Hyattsville, Maryland, to replenish its stockpile of weapons, but the guns did no good on 4 June 1934, when Mais, Legurenza and girlfriend Marie McKeever were captured at Baltimore's fairgrounds.

The gang appeared to be on its last legs. Mais and Legurenza were convicted of murder in Virginia and sentenced to die. Gang member Salvatore Serpa, sought by police for a triple murder in Chicago, was killed by rival Windy City gangsters on 25 July 1934. Then, just as authorities prepared to brand the gang defunct, Mais and Legurenza shot their way out of Richmond's jail on 29 September 1934, killing a policeman in the process.

A month later, on 26 October, the gang kidnapped Philadelphia racketeer William Weiss, demanding $100,000 for his safe return. Bargained down to $12,000, the kidnappers went to pick up their ransom on 5 November, but the money was wrapped in two packets and they overlooked the smaller one, containing $4,000. Seething at the "betrayal," they executed Weiss and dumped his body near Doylestown, Pennsylvania on 6 November 1934. Bureau agents were tipped off to the kidnap-murder on

19 November, but they still had no leads to the gang's whereabouts.

The Tri-State Gang robbed another National Guard armory on 11 December 1934, this one at Morristown, Pennsylvania. Two days later, Philadelphia police raided a mob hideout, capturing five gang members, but Mais and Legurenza escaped in the confusion, Legurenza fracturing both feet in a leap from an elevated train platform. Marie McKeever drove the fugitives to New York City, while federal prosecutors in Baltimore charged the fugitive trio with theft of government property.

The end came swiftly, in January 1935. G-men traced Legurenza to New York's Presbyterian Hospital on the 17th and arrested him there, seizing two more gang members the same afternoon. A flying squad of agents and police trapped Mais and McKeever in their New York apartment on 18 January, arresting both without resistance. Mais and Legurenza were returned to Richmond, where they kept their date with the electric chair on 2 February 1935.

**TRUDEAU, Pierre** — In January 2001, pursuant to requests filed by Canadian journalists under the FREEDOM OF INFORMATION ACT, FBI HEADQUARTERS released documents demonstrating that G-men had spied on Pierre Trudeau, Canada's one-time prime minister, for at least two decades. The full parameters of that surveillance are difficult to judge, since 161 heavily-edited pages were declassified but media reports claim "numerous pages were withheld in their entirety." The file as viewed reveals no justification or legal jurisdiction for such a FOREIGN OPERATION by the FBI.

Bureau investigation of Trudeau apparently began in January 1952 with a query from Director J. EDGAR HOOVER to agents in Ottawa and Paris. (The entire text of the letter is blacked out.) Subsequent documents chart Trudeau's political career and private life (including the loss of his first wife's purse on a U.S. visit), collected under the dubious heading of "Domestic Security." Surveillance was especially tight after Trudeau's election to serve as prime minister, during the tenure of President RICHARD NIXON. G-men kept Nixon informed of Trudeau's dealings with China, including a visit to Beijing in 1973, and clipped articles from far-right journals branding Trudeau "the Canadian Castro." Later, in the 1980s, agents investigated threats against Trudeau from individuals in California, Colorado, Georgia and Michigan. Trudeau died of prostate cancer in September 2000.

**TRUMAN, Harry S** — A Missouri native, born at Lamar on 8 May 1884 and raised in Independence, Harry Truman served as an Army major in WORLD WAR I. Back in civilian life, he ran a haberdashery before aligning himself with the corrupt machine of boss Tom Pendergast to launch a new career in politics. Truman served first as a Jackson County judge (1922-24, 1926-24), and was then elected to the U.S. Senate (1935-45). He applied for membership in the KU KLUX KLAN around 1923 but reportedly changed his mind before going through with the initiation. President FRANKLIN ROOSEVELT chose Truman as his third vice president in 1944, and Truman thus became president when Roosevelt died on 12 April 1945.

Roosevelt's death surprised FBI Director J. EDGAR HOOVER.

He scoured the Bureau for an agent with some connection to Truman, finally locating G-man Morton Chiles, Jr. (the son of a lifelong Truman friend from Independence). Chiles was dispatched to the White House, bearing Hoover's standard offer of assistance, whereupon Truman sent back a terse message: "Anytime I need the services of the FBI, I will ask for it through my attorney general." Hoover followed up with a personal visit on 23 April, to brief Truman on the FBI's current cases, but Truman passed him off to an aide, Brigadier General Harry Vaughn, with orders to communicate through Vaughn in the future. As later recounted by Assistant Director WILLIAM SULLIVAN, "From that time on Hoover's hatred of Truman knew no bounds."

The Hoover-Truman feud escalated in September 1945, when Truman sought to limit FBI FOREIGN OPERATIONS (a plan evaded by Hoover via his network of LEGAL ATTACHÉS abroad) and in 1946, when Truman slashed $6 million from the FBI's budget. Truman further enraged Hoover by refusing to fire various federal employees (notably HARRY DEXTER WHITE) whom Hoover regarded as sympathetic to the COMMUNIST PARTY. Truman drove another wedge between the White House and FBI HEADQUARTERS in 1947, when he created the CENTRAL INTELLIGENCE AGENCY over Hoover's objections. Hoover threw his weight behind Republican candidate THOMAS DEWEY in the 1948 presidential election, and was so enraged by Dewey's loss that he feigned a bout of pneumonia to avoid Truman's inauguration ceremony.

Truman declined to seek reelection in 1952, but his departure from the White House did not reduce Hoover's spite. Unable to resist a parting slur, Hoover joined Attorney General HERBERT BROWNELL before the SENATE INTERNAL SECURITY SUBCOMMITTEE on 17 November 1953, quoting from FBI FILES in an effort to prove that Truman's administration was riddled with traitors. Truman finally outlasted his old enemy, dying in Kansas City on 26 December 1972.

**TUCKER, Ray**—The Washington, D.C. bureau chief for *Collier's* magazine, Ray Tucker ran afoul of the FBI on 19 August 1933, when he published an article challenging the recent spate of pro-Bureau publicity. After noting how easily subjects were able to dodge federal "tails," Tucker continued: "Despite all this burlesque and bombast, there is a serious and sinister side to this secret federal police system. It had always been up to its neck in personal intrigue and partisan politics." Under J. EDGAR HOOVER, Tucker wrote, the Bureau was run in a Prussian manner as the director's "personal and political machine. More inaccessible than presidents, he kept his agents in fear and awe by firing and shifting them at whim; no other government agency had such a turnover of personnel." Furthermore, Tucker wrote, "The director's appetite for publicity is the talk of the Capital, although admittedly a peculiar enterprise for a bureau which, by the nature of its work, is supposed to operate in secrecy. Although Mr. Hoover issued strict orders against publicity on the part of his agents, he was never bound by them."

Tucker was also the first reporter to raise the subject, albeit indirectly, of Hoover's rumored HOMOSEXUALITY. The article noted in passing that "In appearance Mr. Hoover is utterly unlike the story-book sleuth.... He dresses fastidiously, with Eleanor

blue as the favored color for the matched shades of tie, handkerchief and socks.... He is short, fat, businesslike, and walks with a mincing step." Tucker closed by observing that "President [FRANKLIN] ROOSEVELT ... may reorganize this miniature American Cheka, and Mr. Hoover may have been replaced by the time this article is published."

It was too much for Hoover to bear, and he struck back with the aid of friendly journalists. While G-men launched an investigation of Tucker, leaking derogatory material on his private life to adversaries in the press, *Liberty* magazine challenged Tucker's description of Hoover, reporting that his "compact body, with the shoulders of a light heavyweight boxer, carries no ounce of extra weight—just 170 pounds of live, virile masculinity." As for his walk, a gossip columnist for the *Washington Herald* noted on 28 August 1933 that "the Hoover stride has grown noticeably longer and more vigorous" since Tucker's piece was published.

Hoover never forgave an insult, and he had another chance to punish Tucker in 1940, when President Roosevelt reported rumors that U.S. Postmaster General JAMES FARLEY was providing material for Tucker's attacks on the New Deal. Aides recall that Hoover declined a request to tap Farley's telephones, but he readily volunteered to tap Tucker's. No incriminating conversations were recorded, but we may assume that surveillance of Tucker continued until Hoover finally tired of nursing the grudge.

**TURNER, Jane**—A veteran agent with 24 years of service to the Bureau, Jane Turner was assigned to the Minneapolis field office in 2002, when she noticed a peculiar object on the desk of one FBI secretary. Looking closer, she recognized a damaged Tiffany paperweight apparently taken from the rubble of New York's World Trade Center following the catastrophic TERRORIST attacks of 11 September 2001. The paperweight normally sold for $115, but its link to a historic disaster bumped the value to $5,000 or more. Turner promptly informed her superiors, who took no action. She subsequently wrote a letter to the Senate Judiciary Committee, in September 2002, which created a substantial furor. In addition to more unwelcome publicity, closely following the complaints of Bureau whistle-blower COLEEN ROWLEY, Turner's revelation spotlighted a conflict of interest that removed Minneapolis agents from their ongoing investigation of a Minnesota firm allegedly involved in thefts of World Trade Center rubble from a dump on Staten Island.

Turner, as it happened, had endured a troubled career with the FBI even before her revelations in Minneapolis. In August 2001 she filed a sex-discrimination lawsuit, still pending at press time, alleging unfair treatment both in Minneapolis and at her former post in Minot, North Dakota. Turner claims that when she was transferred from Minot to Minneapolis, her supervisors isolated her and warned other agents to avoid contact with her whenever possible. In the wake of her latest complaints, on 22 October 2002, Turner's Minneapolis supervisor informed her that her job performance "does not meet expectations" on some "critical element"—typically the first step toward dismissal with prejudice. Attorney Stephen Kohn, representing Turner, told reporters his client had been singled out for persecution as a whistle-blower. "It is ethically repugnant," Kohn said, "for them to expect Jane to ignore the theft of the globe while holding civilians under investigation to a different standard." Ignoring recent history, including the cases of Rowley and FREDERICK WHITEHURST, Bureau spokesman Paul McCabe assured the media that "the FBI does not retaliate against its employees."

**TURNER, William W.**—A Buffalo, New York native, born in 1927, William Turner joined the U.S. Navy at age 17 and served in the Pacific theater during WORLD WAR II. He earned a bachelor's degree in chemistry, in 1949, and entered the FBI ACADEMY on 5 February 1951. Initially assigned to the St. Louis field office, Turner was next transferred to San Francisco, where he soon became disillusioned with FBI practices that included imposition of mandatory (unpaid) overtime on all agents and manipulation of auto theft statistics to inflate recoveries and convictions under the DWYER ACT. A quarrel with his supervisor brought Turner a disciplinary transfer to Seattle, where his fortunes seemed to improve. In 1959 he received three commendations within as many months, including praise for solving a BANK ROBBERY and for successful completion of a difficult WIRETAPPING assignment. Turner was scheduled for a meritorious pay increase, but he lost it when a visiting inspector found "nonofficial property"—a vacation travel brochure—in Turner's desk drawer.

Matters went from bad to worse in October 1960, with Turner's transfer to Oklahoma City under agent-in-charge WESLEY GRAPP. Unhappy with the post, Turner requested assignment to Los Angeles, despite warnings from colleagues that "Grapp will take it personally." That proved to be the case, as Grapp denied the transfer and hounded Turner with "unsatisfactory" performance ratings. A memo from Grapp to FBI HEADQUARTERS, dated 16 December 1960, read:

> It appears that SA [Special Agent] Turner is a spoiled, self-centered individual who is trying to pick his assignments in this division, as well as what division he will work in. In my opinion he needs a good "jolt" to enable him to place himself in the proper perspective with the Bureau's needs. My recommendations for administrative action are as follows: 1. SA TURNER be placed on probation. 2. He remain assigned to this division for the present and if he ever be transferred from this division that he be assigned to another rural area, possibly including Alaska. To do otherwise would be rewarding him for his poor attitude.

Director J. EDGAR HOOVER accepted Grapp's recommendation, sending Turner a letter on 27 December 1960 that read in part: "You apparently place your personal preferences and conveniences above the welfare and needs of the FBI and your conduct in this matter is definitely not in keeping with the standards expected of Special Agents of this Bureau." A confidential footnote on Grapp's copy of the letter read: "For *your* information, on SA Turner's anniversary 2/5, no Ten Year Key or letter from the Director will be sent in view of his unsatisfactory attitude. For *your* information only."

Rather than apologize to Grapp and Hoover for requesting a transfer, Turner teamed with Agent NELSON GIBBONS (also enduring harassment at the Oklahoma City field office) to file a complaint against Grapp. Hoover retaliated by suspending both

agents for 30 days without pay; Turner was transferred to Knoxville, Tennessee, while Gibbons drew a punitive transfer to Butte, Montana. Turner's new supervisor was ordered not to let him leave the Knoxville area for any reason, including vacations. When Turner complained to Attorney General ROBERT KENNEDY and Tennessee's elected representatives about his "house arrest," the Bureau mobilized its friends in Congress to neutralize his efforts. Headquarters filed six charges against Turner in June 1961, seeking his dismissal, and the Civil Service Commission upheld two of the counts in October 1961. Specifically, Turner was found guilty of making "untrue or unverified statements" in his complaints to Congress, and of showing "a poor attitude toward the Federal Bureau of Investigation and its Director." A federal court in Washington upheld his dismissal, and the U.S. SUPREME COURT declined to review the case.

Following expulsion from the FBI, Turner became a journalist specializing in exposés of the FBI and illegal government activities. FBI agents and their media allies tracked his progress, furnishing derogatory information to reviewers and the hosts of various radio or television programs that scheduled Turner as a guest. Failing to silence Turner by intimidation, Bureau leaders plotted to incarcerate him on a trumped-up charge. In 1970, while Turner was researching an article on the FBI's 1933 FRAMEUP of Kathryn Kelly in the CHARLES URSCHEL kidnapping case, G-men tried to charge Turner with impersonating an FBI agent. When that effort failed, Hoover scrawled an angry memo: "It is a shame we can't nail this jackal." In fact, they never could. Turner went on to publish numerous articles and several books, including *Hoover's FBI: The Men and the Myth* (1970).

**TWA Flight 800**—On the evening of 16 July 1996, TWA Flight 800, en route from New York to Paris, crashed in the sea off Long Island with loss of all 230 persons aboard. Eyewitness reports of a midair explosion and a "streak of light" pursuing the plane from ground level raised the possibility of TERRORISM, whereupon an FBI investigation was initiated in conjunction with the standard crash review conducted by the National Travel Safety Board (NTSB). Nearly a decade after the event, despite agreement by both agencies that the crash was accidental and involved no hostile action, many facts about the case remain obscure, contributing to charges of an official cover-up.

One sticking point with critics of the FBI verdict is the acknowledged presence of a "mystery boat" in the vicinity where Flight 800 crashed. According to radar plots contained in the NTSB's Airplane Performance Study, the closest vessel to Flight 800 on 16 July—only 2.9 nautical miles from the jet when it lost electrical power—was an unknown craft traveling south-southeast at 30 knots, tracked for 16 minutes while speeding out to sea. Despite 16 months of investigation, including some 7,000 interviews, FBI HEADQUARTERS reported that the Bureau "has been unable to identify this vessel."

Crash investigators found chemical traces of explosives on various fragments of Flight 800, but FBI officials attributed those findings to a canine bomb detection exercise allegedly conducted on the aircraft in St. Louis five weeks before the crash. According to G-men, particles of the explosives PETN and RDX were "inadvertently deposited" on the jet during that exercise and they remained in significant quantities despite continual exposure to the elements.

In addition to the explosive traces, at least 89 of the 230 crash victims were found to have foreign objects resembling shrapnel embedded in their corpses. FBI agents seized all such fragments and reportedly submitted them for laboratory analysis, but the various objects *and* the resultant reports have mysteriously disappeared. In October 2000 an FBI affidavit filed with a federal court in Springfield, Massachusetts declared that the evidence and lab reports could not be found despite a "thorough search."

The NTSB held a week-long public hearing on the crash in Baltimore, starting on 8 December 1997, with various eyewitness accounts of the disaster scheduled for review. However, five days prior to the hearing's commencement, FBI Assistant Director James Kallstrom wrote to the NTSB, declaring: "The FBI objects to requests to disclose or include in the public docket ... the results of any interviews or reinterviews of the 244 eyewitnesses whose reports were examined by the CIA in connection with its analysis and to calling any eyewitnesses to testify at the public hearing." Without objection, NTSB Chairman Jim Hall agreed to the Bureau's demand for secrecy and excluded all eyewitness testimony from the hearing.

The Bureau's suppression of eyewitness testimony was not limited to public hearings. For 13 months after the event, FBI leaders withheld statements made by 278 witnesses from the NTSB itself. Included in that mass of suppressed evidence were *all* statements from witnesses who claimed they saw a "streak" shoot upward from the ground or sea toward Flight 800 on the night it fell. Likewise, a letter from FBI Assistant Director Lewis Shiliro to the NTSB, dated 25 August 1998, declared that G-men were "unable to locate" results of their study to determine the origin of an alleged surface-launched object seen by witnesses before the crash.

In November 1996, even as Assistant Director Kallstrom declared the theory of a mid-air BOMBING "unproven," ABC News reporter Pierre Salinger advanced the theory that a U.S. Navy missile was responsible for the disaster in a reckless case of "friendly fire." Salinger cited radar images and documented naval maneuvers in the area on 16 July 1996, but the FBI and NTSB jointly dismissed his concerns. A report from the BUREAU OF ALCOHOL, TOBACCO AND FIREARMS (dated 20 January 1997) concluded that Flight 800 crashed after a mechanical flaw caused its central fuel tank to explode. Andrew Vita, BATF's assistant director of field operations, told the U.S. Senate in May 1999 that he "met resistance" from the FBI when he tried to submit that report in March 1997, but FBI spokesmen later endorsed the findings. Senator CHARLES GRASSLEY termed the crash investigation "a model of failure, not success"; he further dubbed the FBI's performance "a disaster" and charged that the Bureau "risked public safety" by manipulating crash site evidence.

# U

**UHSE, Budo**—A German national, born in 1904, author Budo Uhse joined the COMMUNIST PARTY at some point prior to his enlistment as a Loyalist soldier in the Spanish Civil War. Unwelcome at home under ADOLF HITLER'S Nazi regime, Uhse made his way to the U.S. and settled briefly in California where the FBI took immediate notice of his politics and activities. Most of his 521-page dossier remains classified today, but the snippets finally released—including descriptions of Uhse as "unattractive, sly, shifty-eyed"—are sufficient to convey the Bureau's personal malice.

Uhse left the U.S. for Mexico on 26 May 1940, whereupon J. EDGAR HOOVER informed President FRANKLIN ROOSEVELT that an agent would be sent to keep an eye on the alleged "organizer of Stalin immigration into Mexico." A year later, Uhse met and married Alma Agee, ex-wife of novelist James Agee and herself an object of FBI investigation. Mere contact with Uhse was

enough to open Bureau files on new subjects, as witnessed by the case of exile ERNST BLOCH in New York, targeted after government censors intercepted a telegram sent to Bloch by Uhse in February 1942. Bloch never saw the telegram, but he became a suspect nonetheless.

After WORLD WAR II, Uhse returned to East Germany and assumed a public role that seemed to confirm Hoover's darkest suspicions. The FBI and STATE DEPARTMENT delayed Alma Uhse's passport as long as possible, but she joined him in 1947. They separated in May 1963, and G-men dutifully noted her return to the U.S. By that time, Uhse was tagged in Bureau files as both a "German communist writer" and "currently a communist official," but his time was running out. He died before year's end, yet federal interest in him lingers, 40 years after his death. When author Alexander Stephan sought release of Uhse's file under the FREEDOM OF INFORMATION ACT, FBI clerks delivered 167 pages "almost completely blacked out" and withheld another 354 entirely. The U.S. Army also retained 57 documents, classified in the "interest of national security."

**ULTIMA Spa**—The Ultima Spa, a Lodi, New Jersey massage parlor that offered illicit sexual services to its patrons, was opened by FBI INFORMANT Luke Hoffman in the mid-1990s. Targets for the ongoing sting operation included local policemen who frequented the brothel. In February 1998 Hoffman accused Lodi police lieutenant Vincent Caruso of assaulting him and threatening his life after Caruso learned of his role as a federal informant. Caruso denied the assault, while admitting that he had "acquaintances" in ORGANIZED CRIME, the charge was subsequently dismissed.

Meanwhile, 24-year-old Millie Nevin applied for a job at the Ultima Spa in 2000, afterward complaining to Lodi police that Hoffman told her she would only be hired if she agreed to service patrons as a prostitute. Officers charged Nevin with making a false report, but Bergen County prosecutor William Schmidt dismissed the charge as false, claiming Lodi police were coerced into the FRAME-UP by FBI agents and an assistant U.S. attorney from Newark. "I feel there was a terrible abuse of power," Schmidt told reporters.

Authorities raided the Ultima Spa and arrested 137 persons, including Hoffman, on 29 March 2001. Patrons found inside the brothel included 21 off-duty policemen, but none were charged since they were not engaged in sex acts when the raiders arrived. Lodi's mayor, Gary Paparozzi, declared that the brothel had been left untouched for years by local officers because Hoffman was known as an FBI informant. Bureau spokesperson Sandra Carroll declined to comment on Hoffman's status, but she promised that all charges of unethical behavior would be fully investigated by the FBI's OFFICE OF PROFESSIONAL RESPONSIBILITY. No results of that study have yet been announced, but on 2 August 2002 a Bergen County municipal judge reinstated charges of aggravated assault, terroristic threats and witness tampering against Acting Police Chief Vincent Caruso. No disposition of that case was available at press time.

**UNDERCOVER Operations**—Undercover operations are distinguished from the use of civilian INFORMANTS by involving sworn law enforcement agents who adopt false identities ("covers") to penetrate suspected criminal organizations and gather evidence from the inside. Such operations in the FBI's early history (1917-24) were generally limited to a handful of black agents who infiltrated groups including the AFRICAN BLOOD BROTHERHOOD and MARCUS GARVEY's United Negro Improvement Association. Director J. EDGAR HOOVER discontinued the practice during his tenure (1924-72), eschewing any plan that violated the strait-laced FBI dress code or placed G-men at risk of potential corruption. (The lone exception was a small team dubbed "THE BEARDS," who were assigned to infiltrated "NEW LEFT" organizations near the end of Hoover's life.)

FBI policy changed dramatically following Hoover's death, as subsequent directors relied heavily on undercover operations for "stings" involving ORGANIZED CRIME, political corruption,

NARCOTICS and white-collar crime. A sampling of those cases includes the following operations:

"*ABSCAM*"—Initiated as a sting of criminal "fences" in New York and New Jersey, the Abscam operation soon expanded to Washington, D.C. and implicated various members of Congress on bribery charges. Twenty-seven officials were indicted when the campaign went public in February 1980.

"*BRILAB*"—An investigation of bribery in LABOR UNIONS, centered on New Orleans, which resulted in the April 1981 convictions of Mafia boss Carlos Marcello and a former aide to Louisiana's governor.

"*Bullpen*"—In a sequel to Operation Foul Ball (below), the Bureau's San Diego field office pursued vendors of fraudulent sports memorabilia across the U.S. Multiple defendants were indicted in April 2000.

"*Candyman*"—An international sting targeting pedophiles and Internet purveyors of child pornography, by March 2002 this operation had indicted 86 defendants including clergymen, law enforcement officers, a school bus driver and a teacher's aide. Of those charged, 27 admitted molesting children in previous cases.

"*Catcom*"—In collaboration with the DRUG ENFORCEMENT ADMINISTRATION and other agencies, G-men used a Miami electronics firm to supply Colombian drug dealers with communications gear, thus intercepting their secret messages and seizing millions of dollars in cash and contraband in December 1988.

"*Cyber Loss*"—A major COMPUTER CRIMES investigation spanning the U.S. climaxed in May 2001 with indictments of 90 individuals and companies on charges that included wire fraud, mail fraud, bank fraud, money laundering and copyright violations.

"*Disconnect*"—Revealed in March 1993, this operation identified 123 companies and 584 individuals involved in shady telemarketing practices across the U.S.

"*Dragon Chase*"—Penetration of a major Asian narcotics syndicate and its allies in New York, resulting in a January 1991 heroin seizure and indictments of 10 defendants, including several in Thailand.

"*Equine*"—A combined effort of the FBI, DEA and Royal Canadian Mounted Police, resulting in the August 1992 arrests of 40 persons charged with using or distributing black-market steroids.

"*Foul Ball*"—A nationwide fraud investigation targeting purveyors of sports memorabilia bearing forged autographs. Seven vendors were indicted in July 1996, all later convicted at trial.

"*Gambat*"—A follow-up to Operation Greylord (below), revealing more corruption in Chicago courts and political circles. Five defendants were indicted in October 1990, including a judge, a state senator and a city alderman. Four were later convicted, while the fifth died prior to trial.

"*Gold Pill*"—Launched in 1990, the two-year probe of corrupt physicians and other health providers led to seizure of assets in more than 50 U.S. cities.

"*Greylord*"—An investigation of bribery in the Chicago courts, producing indictments of 88 judges, lawyers, clerks and police officers in 1984. Two of those charged committed suicide; all but four of the remaining defendants were convicted at trial.

"*Illwind*"—A probe of procurement corruption in the U.S. Department of Defense ended in September 1986 with the indictment of 54 government employees and civilian defense contractors on charges of bribery and fraud. All were convicted in 1989, with two corporations (Unisys and United Technologies) fined for illegal activities.

"*Incubator*"—One more in a series of FBI stings targeting corrupt Chicago politicians, this one resulting in the November 1986 indictments of 14 public officials. Those charged with bribery included a deputy water commissioner, Cook County's clerk, four aldermen and a former mayoral aide.

"*Lost Trust*"—A probe of legislative vote-selling in South Carolina, exposed in August 1990 with indictments of five state legislators. Five more were later indicted, with all 10 forced to resign their positions.

"*Mayban*"—A three-year investigation of bank fraud in Knoxville, Tennessee during the 1980s, climaxed in January 1983 with of six defendants on various counts in relation to the failure of a 26-bank conglomerate.

"*Pretense*"—A sting operation targeting corrupt Mississippi officials in the 1980s, this operation indicted supervisors from 57 of the state's 82 counties for embezzling funds by means of kickbacks and false purchase orders.

"*Recoup*"—A sting operated under the DYER ACT, targeting interstate vendors of stolen cars, by October 1982 this campaign had seized vehicles from more than 250 buyers who purchased them in good faith.

"*Silver Shovel*"—Yet another investigation of civic corruption in Chicago, this one producing indictments of six aldermen and 12 other local officials in December 1995. All were subsequently convicted.

"*UNIRAC*"—Initiated in Miami as a probe of corrupt labor unions, Unirac climaxed with indictment of 22 union officials and shipping executives in June 1978. It later expanded to New York and resulted in conviction of top-level organized crime figures.

"*White Mare*"—Collaborating with the NEW YORK POLICE DEPARTMENT, FBI agents infiltrated a narcotics syndicate, climaxing in February 1989 with the largest heroin seizure in U.S. history.

"*White Spider*"—A probe of organized prostitution, conducted by the Knoxville field office, which indicted 21 persons on racketeering charges in July 2002. Those charged operated Korean massage parlors, modeling studios and "health studios" in Tennessee and five other states.

Undercover operations frequently smack of entrapment, and lawsuits have resulted from several campaigns (such as Operation Recoup, where more than 250 good-faith purchasers bought stolen cars). By 31 December 1981 FBI sting operations had already resulted in 29 lawsuits against the JUSTICE DEPARTMENT, with damage claims logged at $424.3 million. To remedy that situation, in January 1981 Attorney General BENJAMIN CIVILETTI divided undercover operations into two broad categories labeled Group I (including "sensitive" cases requiring supervision by the FBI's Undercover Operations Review Committee) and Group II (wherein authority for launching sting operations was granted to the agents-in-charge of various field offices). Group I operations included any investigation of a foreign government, any public official, the news media or any political-religious organizations; any "domestic security" investigation; any case where agents might break the law (excluding sale or purchase of stolen property or concealing his/her identity); any case requiring an agent to pose as a lawyer, doctor, journalist or clergyman; any investigation requiring agents to attend meetings between suspects and their lawyers; and any operation with a risk of significant financial loss to any person. Civiletti also established three general guidelines for undercover activity:

1. Operations are permissible whenever reasonable suspicion of criminal activity exists.

2. Targeted individuals must clearly understand the illegal nature of the operation.

3. Undercover operations must be "modeled on the real world," rather than fabricating some improbable scenario unlikely to occur without impetus from the Bureau.

Those guidelines failed to satisfy the Oregon Supreme Court, which in August 2000 issued a judgment requiring all law enforcement agents to obey a list of ethical rules established by Oregon statute—including a ban on "dishonesty, fraud, deceit or misrepresentation." Henceforth, agents in Oregon were barred from adopting "covers" to purchase drugs or otherwise trap their targets in criminal activity. Interim U.S. Attorney Mike Mosman called that verdict "a terrible problem" for G-men, terming it "the single greatest challenge" of his career. Defense attorney John Hingson III, of Oregon City, was more philosophical. "They went rumbling for a fight," he told reporters in July 2001, "and they got kicked."

**UNDERHILL, Wilbur**—A native of Joplin, Missouri, born in 1901, Wilbur Underhill was the youngest of four criminal brothers. His mother blamed a childhood accident in Wilbur's case, complaining that "I don't think it left him quite right." Convicted of burglary at age 17, by 1923 he was notorious (albeit anonymously) as Joplin's "Lover's Lane Bandit." A short time later, Underhill's explosive temper got him expelled from Oklahoma's Kimes-Terrill bank-robbing gang. Teamed with sidekick Ike Atkins, Underhill shot a bystander during a holdup at Picher, Oklahoma on 12 December 1926. Two weeks later, he killed a teenage boy during another robbery, at Okmulgee. Arrested in Tulsa on 7 January 1927, Underhill and Atkins escaped three weeks later. Atkins was killed by police on 12 February and Underhill was recaptured on 20 March, convicted of murder and sentenced to life imprisonment in June 1927.

Wilbur served four years of that term before escaping from Oklahoma's state prison, on 14 July 1931. He fled to Kansas and killed a Wichita policeman on 13 August, but was wounded and captured by other officers the same day. That murder earned Wilbur his second life sentence, this one in Kansas. On 30 May 1933, he joined bank robbers Harvey Bailey, Bob Brady and nine other convicts in a mass escape from the state pen at Lansing, armed with pistols smuggled in by federal fugitive Frank ("Jelly") Nash.

The escapees were short on cash and itching for action. They robbed a bank at Black Rock, Arkansas on 16 June 1933 and were named as suspects in the following day's KANSAS CITY MASSACRE, which claimed the lives of Frank Nash and four lawmen. On 3 July the gang stole $11,000 from a bank in Clinton, Oklahoma. Underhill was alone when he robbed a Canton, Kansas bank two days later, but he rejoined the gang for a holdup at Kingfisher, Oklahoma on 3 August 1933. Over the next two months, the raiders looted banks at Stuttgart, Arkansas (22 September); at Baxter Springs, Kansas (9 October); and at Okmulgee, Oklahoma (2 November).

On 18 November 1933, Underhill purchased a marriage license at Coalgate, Oklahoma, brazenly using his real name and that of his intended bride, Hazel Hudson. More bank holdups followed, to finance their honeymoon, at Frankfort, Kentucky (23 November); at Harrah, Oklahoma (11 December, foiled by bank guards); and at Coalgate, Oklahoma (13 December).

The day after Christmas 1933, Underhill and his bride rented a house in Shawnee, Oklahoma, sharing quarters with outlaw Ralph Roe and his girlfriend, Eva Nichols. Four days later, a strike force of 24 G-men and local police surrounded the house, touching off a pitched battle. Eva Nichols was killed and Ralph Roe wounded before Underhill fled barefoot, clad only in his underwear. Hit five times before he cleared the yard, Wilbur ran 16 blocks and broke into a furniture store, where pursuers found him sprawled on one of the beds. Underhill survived for six days, shackled to a bed in the state prison infirmary. His last words to the jailers at his bedside: "Tell the boys I'm coming home."

**UNIDENTIFIED Flying Objects**—Millions of persons who know nothing else about the FBI believe today that its files contain vast stores of classified information on unidentified flying objects (UFOs) and visitors from outer space. They draw this impression from a popular television program, *The X-Files* (1993-2002), which portrays the efforts of two stalwart agents to breach an intergalactic conspiracy of silence. Long before that drama premiered, in July 1966, a writer for another television program asked FBI HEADQUARTERS for help in tracing a source of UFO information. Director J. EDGAR HOOVER replied, for the record, that "the investigation of unidentified flying objects is not, and never has been, a matter within the investigative jurisdiction of the FBI."

Today it is no great surprise to learn that Hoover lied.

While UFO reports date back to Biblical times, the first modern report—which also coined the term "flying saucers"— was logged by pilot Kenneth Arnold, over Washington state, on 24 June 1947. Two weeks later, on 9 July, Brigadier General George Schulgen of the Army Air Corps asked the FBI to investigate recent UFO reports, specifically to determine if they were part of a plot by communists or Red sympathizers "to cause hysteria and fear of a secret Russian weapon." Assistant Director CLYDE TOLSON opined, "I think we should do this." Hoover agreed with a proviso, writing: "I would do it, but first we must have access to all disks recovered. For example, in the La. case the Army grabbed it and would not let us have it for cursory ex-amination." (The case referred to was a UFO hoax at Shreveport, on 7 July 1947.)

By the time of Gen. Schulgen's request for help, Hoover had already learned of the now-famous incident at Roswell, New Mexico on 8 July 1947. Initially reported as the "capture" of an alien craft, the story was revised a day later to describe the crash-landing of a weather balloon. An "urgent" FBI memo from Texas, however, contradicted the official Air Force version of events. That message noted that the Roswell craft allegedly "resembles a high altitude balloon with a radar reflector," but "telephonic communication … [with] Wright [F]ield has not borne out this belief." Rather, the field agent reported, unidentified material was "being transported to Wright Field by special plane for ex-amination."

On 30 July 1947, a message from headquarters ordered all Bureau field offices to "investigate each instance which is brought to your attention of a sighting of a flying disc in order to ascertain whether or not it is a bona fide sighting, an imaginary one, or a prank…. The bureau should be notified immediately by teletype of all reported sightings, and the results of your inquiries." Over the next two months, field agents filed some two dozen reports of UFO sightings around the U.S., including two reports from Portland, Oregon, made by a navy pilot and the chief of police. Many of the memos bear the heading "Security Matter — X."

The FBI's investigation of UFOs hit a snag on 3 September 1947, when an Air Force lieutenant colonel gave the San Francisco field office a copy of a letter signed by the assistant chief of staff for intelligence, a Lt. Gen. Stratemeyer, explaining to various Air Force commanders that "whereas the Air Defense Command Air Forces would interview responsible observers," the FBI "would investigate incidents of discs being found by civilians on the ground." Thus, Stratemeyer hoped "to relieve the numbered Air Forces of the task of tracking down all the many instances which turned out to be ash can covers, toilet seats and whatnot." Predictably furious, Hoover cut a new order on 1 October 1947, decreeing that "All future reports connected with flying discs should be referred to the Air Force, and no investigative action should be taken by Bureau agents."

That resolve on Hoover's part held fast until 20 February 1948, when a letter from headquarters to the San Francisco field office instructed agents to collect any UFO reports volunteered by witnesses and furnish them to the Air Force, in addition to which the FBI would "receive any information which the Air Forces volunteer." A few reports were exchanged between April and July 1948, but the Bureau's UFO probe remained largely dormant until 10 January 1949, with the receipt of an "Internal Security — X" alert from the Knoxville field office, reporting that saucers had been sighted over the nuclear research facility at Oak Ridge, Tennessee. Three weeks later, San Antonio's agent in charge filed a report on "Protection of Vital Installations," after "balls of fire" were sighted near Kirtland Air Force Base and the Los Alamos nuclear test site.

On 25 March 1949, FBI headquarters issued a letter to all field offices, reading in part: "For your confidential information, a reliable and confidential source has advised the Bureau that flying discs are believed to be man-made missiles rather than natural phenomenon. It has also been determined that for approximately the past four years the USSR has been engaged in experimentation on an unknown type of flying disk." That "confidential" letter somehow found its way to FBI-friendly journalist WALTER WINCHELL, who announced on 3 April that UFOs were "definitely" Russian aircraft. Air Force spokesmen requested an FBI investigation to identify Winchell's source, but Hoover refused on 26 April 1949, perhaps afraid that he would be revealed as the leak.

That near-miss discouraged further UFO investigations until March 1950, when Washington agent-in-charge GUY HOTTEL reported that "an investigator for the Air Force" had admitted recovery of three crashed saucers in New Mexico, containing nine corpses of three-foot-tall alien beings. Hot on the heels of that shocker, the *New York Times* of 4 April reported that UFOs were actually experimental U.S. warplanes.

Hoover remained aloof from that debate and ignored the matter until October 1950, when he ordered the Los Angeles field office to "discreetly determine from appropriate sources" whether Frank Scully, author of *Behind the Flying Saucers*, had been "actively engaged in Communist activities since the late nineteen thirties." Despite three urgent messages from Hoover, FBI files released under the FREEDOM OF INFORMATION ACT contain no answer to that query.

Two months later, on 8 December 1950, an "urgent" message from the Richmond field office advised Hoover that agents of Army Intelligence "have been put on immediate high alert for any data whatsoever concerning flying saucers." The FBI provided no assistance in that quest, and only one UFO report was logged at headquarters over the next nine months, concerning a September 1951 sighting by pilots and radar operators at Fort Monmouth, New Jersey. Reports of UFO activity trickled in from various field offices over the next 16 years, including a North Carolina sighting logged by a Bureau employee on 9 April 1956, but the last known FBI report on UFOs dates from 18 January 1967, when a resident of Chesapeake, Virginia reported being "taken into [a] craft which he recalls as being made of a glass-like substance and being transparent." The see-through UFO was "manned by several individuals who appeared to be undersized creatures similar to members of the human race, probably not more than 4 feet tall." G-men ran a check on the witness, but reported that "Bureau indices did not disclose any information which could be identified with Mr. [name deleted]."

**UNIFORM Crime Reports** — On 11 June 1930 Congress authorized the Bureau of Investigation to collect and publish crime statistics voluntarily supplied by local law enforcement agencies throughout the U.S. By 1940, 4,164 city and county agencies were involved in reporting, with the results published quarterly. In 1957, 6,808 agencies reported crime statistics to the FBI, their combined jurisdiction covering 97 percent of the U.S. population. Today, some 16,000 law enforcement agencies report to FBI HEADQUARTERS with statistics on murder, forcible rape, robbery, aggravated assault, burglary, larceny-theft, motor vehicle theft and arson. In 1992, Congress further ordered the Bureau to begin collecting data on HATE CRIMES, but local reporting remains voluntary and private watchdog groups have noted extreme reticence by some local agencies to report on this category of offenses.

While the FBI's Uniform Crime Reports were intended to provide a reliable portrait of criminal trends in America, critics — including some within the Bureau — suggest that crime statistics are manipulated either to enhance the FBI's reputation (by presenting unrealistic declines in specific crime categories) or to increase the Bureau's annual appropriations (by suggesting some new crime wave in progress). The late J. EDGAR HOOVER was particularly prone to playing numbers games in his yearly visits to Congress, claiming extravagant conviction rates (seldom less than 96 percent) and a yearly "profit" of nearly $1.50 from fines and recovery of stolen goods for every dollar spent on the FBI.

Those figures were grossly misleading, as noted by ex-agent WILLIAM TURNER in his book *Hoover's FBI* (1970). A case in point was the year 1968, during which the FBI investigated 483,000 criminal cases and secured 13,000 convictions (2.7 percent). Nonetheless, by counting only "persons brought to trial" — as opposed to those who plead guilty or whose charges are dismissed — Hoover claimed a 1968 "conviction rate" of 96.5 percent. The FBI's record for CIVIL RIGHTS cases was even worse, 14 convictions out of 11,328 cases handled between 1960 and 1964 (barely one-tenth of one percent).

Hoover's statistics on "fines, savings and recoveries" were likewise inflated by means of creative accounting. Each year, under the DYER ACT (forbidding interstate transportation of stolen automobiles), Hoover claimed credit for "recovering" thousands of hot cars retrieved by local police. Huge savings were also reported under the federal Tort Claims Act, involving civil lawsuits filed against the U.S. government. When FBI agents investigated such cases, frequently involving accidents with government vehicles, Hoover claimed a "savings" even when the plaintiffs were awarded money by the court. Thus, if a lawsuit for $100,000 was settled for $75,000, Hoover told Congress that his agents had "saved" the government $25,000.

**UNIRAC** — The Bureau's UNIRAC operation (named for labor *uni*on *rac*keteering) began in 1975, after Joe Teitelbaum, owner of a Miami stevedoring company, complained of shakedowns by members of the International Longshoremen's Association (ILA). Various state and federal investigators had documented ILA links to ORGANIZED CRIME since the 1930s, but UNIRAC would be the first concerted move against the corrupt union. Teitelbaum agreed to record his future conversations with ILA extortionists and to place UNDERCOVER FBI agents in his business as observers.

Evidence gathered in Miami led agents farther afield, securing warrants for WIRETAPS and BUGGING of various syndicate targets ranging from Boston to Texas. Controlled by the Gambino crime family of New York, ILA strong-arm artists forced dockworkers to kick back a portion of their daily income, orchestrated bogus claims for workmen's compensation, rigged bids on ship repairs, charged ship owners as much as $35,000 per day to unload their cargoes, and fingered some of that same merchandise for hijackers. On 7 June 1978 a federal grand jury in Miami indicted 22 ILA officials and shipping executives for bribery, embezzlement, kickbacks and other felonious activities. It was only the first round of UNIRAC charges, culminating in 110 convictions around the U.S. by 1981.

The biggest fish caught in the UNIRAC net was Anthony Scotto, a member of the Gambino family and boss of Brooklyn ILA Local 1814, identified as the number three man in the union. Linked to criminal activities ranging from New York to Norfolk, Virginia, Scotto was convicted in a $250,000 payoff scheme and sentenced to prison in 1979. New York Governor Hugh Carey tried to intercede on Scotto's behalf, as did former New York City mayors John Lindsey and Robert Wagner, but all in vain. Scotto served three years of a five-year sentence and was treated to a welcome-home banquet by his political friends on release from custody. Little changed with the ILA, meanwhile; a later FBI bug was eavesdropping when mobster Paul Castellano declared, "It's our International."

**UNITED Negro Improvement Association** *see* **GARVEY, Marcus**

**UNRUH, Fritz von**—The son of a Prussian general, born at Koblenz on 10 May 1885, Fritz von Unruh served as a German officer in WORLD WAR I but emerged from the experience a dedicated pacifist. Acclaimed thereafter for his antiwar plays and poetry, Unruh opposed the militarism of ADOLF HITLER and thus was forced to flee his homeland, passing through France and Portugal before reaching the U.S. in August 1940. Passports for Unruh and his wife were provided by French defense minister Edouard Daladier, with assistance from U.S. Secretary of State Cordell Hull, but no high-flown connections would spare the new arrival from FBI scrutiny.

Ironically, considering his flight from Nazi Germany, Unruh was denounced to the FBI in early 1942, by an unnamed "generally reliable and highly confidential source" as being somehow "connected to the Gestapo." Thereafter, much of Unruh's 102-page Bureau dossier consisted of press clippings, including an article clipped from the liberal *New Republic*, complete with J. EDGAR HOOVER'S marginal note that "this publication has been unable to make a harmonious adjustment in capitalistic America." Finally deciding that Unruh's political allegiance lay somewhere on the left, rather than the Nazi right, G-men clipped a New York *Herald Tribune* story recounting an invitation from the mayor of Frankfort for Unruh to settle there in January 1947. In fact, Unruh drifted back and forth between the U.S. and Europe until 1962, when he finally settled abroad. The Bureau closed his file in March 1959, "in view of subject's advanced age and inactivity," though Unruh in fact survived for nearly 12 more years, dying at Diez, Germany on 28 November 1970.

**UNTERMEYER, Louis**—A native New Yorker, born 1 October 1885, Louis Untermeyer dropped out of high school to work in his father's jewelry shop, but later emerged as a left-wing poet and anthologist. He helped produce *The Masses* prior to WORLD WAR I, but FBI agents somehow overlooked him until 1921, when they noted his name on the masthead of a successor publication, *The Liberator*. Intense surveillance followed, reports that Unter-

meyer "has been of great help to the [COMMUNIST] PARTY in raising finances mixed with observations of his "small pot belly." G-men were still on the case 30 years later, despite Untermeyer's public statements that he was "unequivocally opposed to communism." J. EDGAR HOOVER thought otherwise, based on information from an unnamed "highly confidential source," adding Untermeyer's name to the Bureau's illegal SECURITY INDEX.

That listing and the collateral FBI whispering campaign cost Untermeyer his job as a weekly panelist on the television program *What's My Line?* According to ARTHUR MILLER, in *TimeBends*, producers of the show told Untermeyer, "The problem is that we know you've never had any left connections, so you have nothing to confess to, but they're not going to believe that. It's going to seem that you're refusing to be a good American." Thereafter, Miller writes, Untermeyer "didn't leave his apartment for almost a year and a half," kept housebound by "an overwhelming and paralyzing fear."

Hoover removed Untermeyer's name from the Security Index in 1955, warning agents not to contact Untermeyer directly "in view of his age, his prominence in the literary field, and the fact that although he is retired, he continues to write and occasionally goes on a lecture tour." Four years later, Hoover briefly placed Untermeyer in the FBI's Communist Index, removing his name before year's end, but FBI machinations were insufficient to prevent Untermeyer's 1961 appointment as Consultant in Poetry at the Library of Congress, where he remained until 1963. Untermeyer died in New York on 18 December 1977.

**URSCHEL, Charles F.**—Oklahoma City resident Charles Urschel was a prime target for ransom kidnappers during the Great Depression, the trustee of a $32 million oil estate, his wife the widow of another oilman and a millionaire in her own right. On 22 July 1933 Urschel was snatched from his home by two gunmen who later demanded $200,000 ransom. The money was delivered in Kansas City, on 30 July, and Urschel was released at Norman, Oklahoma the following day.

FBI publicists later described Urschel as a veritable Sherlock Holmes, listening for sounds that betrayed his location, timing the daily passage of airplanes overhead, recalling rainstorms and the mineral taste of water served at the hideout where he was held captive. Clever G-men took those clues and worked a feat of virtual magic, examining roads and bridges, comparing daily weather reports with airline flight plans, until they zeroed in on a ramshackle farm outside Paradise, Texas. That farm, as luck would have it, belonged to the parents of Kathryn Kelly, wife of fugitive bank robber GEORGE ("MACHINE GUN") KELLY. Urschel, armed with a shotgun, joined the raiding party on 12 August 1933, when agents arrested farmer R.G. Shannon, his wife Ora, and son Armon. Also captured was bank robber Harvey Bailey, hiding out with the Shannons between holdups, charged with kidnapping when G-men found some of the Urschel ransom loot in his pocket. (In fact, Bailey got the money from George Kelly, in payment of a debt, but he would still face life in prison for a crime he did not commit.) Kidnap accomplice Albert Bates was captured in Denver on 12 August, but the Kellys remained at large until 26 September 1933, when they were arrested in Memphis.

All directly involved in the crime (plus Bailey) were later convicted under the new LINDBERGH Law and sentenced to life imprisonment. Several lesser accomplices received shorter terms for helping pass the ransom money.

Subsequent revelations suggest that solution of the Urschel kidnapping had less to do with brilliant deductions than with a tip from Texas police. Prior to the crime, the Kellys had cultivated a pair of Fort Worth detectives, Ed Weatherford and J.W. Swinney, buying them drinks and discussing their criminal plans with the officers. Weatherford and Swinney warned one intended kidnap victim, Texas millionaire Guy Waggoner, before the Kellys could grab him, and they met with Kathryn after the Urschel snatch, afterward relaying their suspicions to the FBI, directing G-men and local officers to the Shannon ranch outside Paradise.

Worse problems arise with the FBI's claim that Kathryn Kelly wrote the Urschel ransom letters, which she staunchly denied. At trial in 1933, amateur handwriting "expert" D.C. Patterson identified Kathryn Kelly as the author of two ransom notes, and the judge refused to permit examination of the letters by independent experts, telling the defense, "I am not going to continue this case all fall." In 1958 Kathryn found a lawyer willing to reopen the case, with an appeal that she had been denied due process. The appeal was granted in June 1959, Kathryn and her mother released on bond pending a new trial, while the court demanded access to FBI files on the case. Bureau leaders refused to comply with the order, and the charges were finally dismissed, leaving the two women at liberty.

Years later, ex-agent WILLIAM TURNER explained the Bureau's strange reluctance to re-try Kathryn Kelly. According to Turner, a search of FBI files in Oklahoma City revealed a September 1933 report from handwriting analyst Charles Appel that read: "The handwriting on the [ransom] letters … is not identical with that of Mrs. Kelly. There are a great many similarities which on casual examination would lead one to think that these handwritings are the same. However, detailed analysis indicated that Mrs. Kelly did not write the letters." Appel further determined that George Kelly "may have written these letters," but the evidence was inconclusive. In October 1959, agent WESLEY GRAPP, in charge of the Oklahoma City field office, reported to FBI HEADQUARTERS that Bureau files "do not indicate that the [U.S. attorney's] office was ever made aware of the fact that the two letters … had been submitted to the FBI Laboratory in 1933 for handwriting examination or that the FBI Laboratory conclusion was contrary to that of Patterson." Furthermore, Grapp warned, "Should action be taken at this time to acquaint the U.S. Attorney with these circumstances, it is not improbable he might take the position that he was obligated to acknowledge to the Court and the defendants at this time that the testimony of the Government witness on this particular point of evidence was possibly based on an erroneous conclusion." The truth was therefore suppressed, out of fear that it might cause "some embarrassment to the Bureau."

**US ("United Slaves")**—Founded in 1965 by Los Angeles resident Maulana Ron Karenga (née Ron Everett), US was described by its spokesmen as a black "cultural nationalist" organization, thus setting itself apart from groups espousing political nationalism or traditional Marxism. US members affected African dress, studied the Kiswahili language, and otherwise forged visible links to their African heritage. On 26 December 1966 Karenga inaugurated the quasi-religious festival of Kwanzaa, a seven-day feast celebrating the principles of unity, self-determination, collective responsibility, cooperative economics, purpose, creativity, and faith.

Karenga and US might have followed a quiet path, but for the emergence in 1967 of the militant BLACK PANTHER PARTY. Panther spokesmen espoused Maoist revolutionary principles and ridiculed US members for their costumes and "African" mannerisms. Agents with the FBI's Los Angeles field office monitored the feud, seeking opportunities to make matters worse as part of their ongoing COINTELPRO campaign against "Black Nationalist—Hate Groups." In April 1968, after Karenga met with Governor RONALD REAGAN and leaders of the Los Angeles Police Department, seeking to reduce ghetto tension after the murder of Dr. MARTIN LUTHER KING, JR., G-men saw their opportunity to strike. First, they spread rumors that Karenga was a police INFORMANT—a technique commonly known as "SNITCH JACKETING"—and then escalated hostile interviews with known Black Panthers "in the hope that a sate of distruct [sic] would remain among the members and add to the turmoil presently going on within the BPP." On 25 November 1968 Hoover issued an order to all field offices that read:

> For the information of recipient offices a serious struggle is taking place between the Black Panther Party (BPP) and the US organization. The struggle has reached such proportions that it is taking on the aura of gang warfare with attendant threats of murder and reprisals.
>
> In order to fully capitalize upon BPP and US differences as well as to exploit all avenues of creating further dissension in the ranks of the BPP, recipient offices are instructed to submit imaginative and hard-hitting counterintelligence measures aimed at crippling the BPP.
>
> Commencing December 2, 1968, and every two-week period thereafter, each office is instructed to submit a letter under this caption containing counterintelligence measures aimed against the BPP. The bi-weekly letter should also contain accomplishments obtained during the previous two-week period under the captioned program.
>
> All counterintelligence actions must be approved at the Bureau prior to taking steps to implement them.

Four days later, another memo from FBI HEADQUARTERS offered an example of "imaginative and hard-hitting" police work.

> The Los Angeles Office is currently preparing an anonymous letter for Bureau approval which will be sent to the Los Angeles Black Panther Party (BPP) supposedly from a member of the "US" organization in which it will be stated that the youth group of the "US" organization is aware of the BPP "contract" to kill RON KARENGA, leader of "US," and they, "US" members, in retaliation, have made plans to ambush leaders of the BPP in Los Angeles.

It is hoped this counterintelligence measure will result in an "US" and BPP vendetta.

G-men got their wish in early 1969. The key dispute between US and the Panthers in Los Angeles was a competition for leadership of the new Afro-American Studies Department at UCLA, with each group backing a different candidate. An estimated 150 students gathered to discuss the matter on 17 January 1969, at a meeting where Panthers Alprentice Carter and John Huggins rose to denounce Karenga. Gunfire erupted, killing Carter and Huggins. Three US members were later convicted and imprisoned for the murders.

Two months after the shootings, agents of the San Diego field office prepared two cartoons, which they mailed to local Panthers and the offices of two "underground" newspapers. One of the crude sketches showed US members gloating over the corpses of Carter and Huggins; the other depicted Panthers referring to US as a group of "pork chop niggers." At the same time, G-men made a series of anonymous calls to San Diego Panther headquarters, denouncing various loyal party members as police informants. On 16 March in San Diego, Panthers shot up the home of a US member, followed shortly by reprisals that left one Panther wounded. When leaders of the two groups scheduled a meeting "to talk out their differences," San Diego agents sought and received permission to mail more scurrilous cartoons. As a result, in May 1969, Panther John Savage was fatally shot by US gunmen. When members of US began drilling with weapons in June, G-men mailed a series of inflammatory letters to keep the pot boiling. In August, Panthers bombed the San Diego office of their rivals and US retaliated by shooting three Panthers, killing victim Sylvester Bell. In the midst of that violence, on 20 August 1969, Hoover received a memo from his San Diego office listing "Tangible Results" of the latest COIN-TELPRO campaign.

> Shootings, beatings, and a high degree of unrest continues to prevail in the ghetto area of southeast San Diego. Although no specific counterintelligence action can be credited with contributing to this over-all situation, it is felt that a substantial amount of the unrest is directly attributable to this program.
>
> In view of the recent killing of BPP member SYLVESTER BELL, a new cartoon is being considered in the hopes that it will assist in the continuance of the rift between BPP and US. This cartoon, or series of cartoons, will be similar in nature to those formerly approved by the Bureau and will be forwarded to the Bureau for evaluation and approval immediately upon their completion.

G-men also orchestrated a series of police raids in San Diego, including one staged in response to false reports of "sex orgies" at Black Panther headquarters. In the wake of that raid, agents were pleased to note that "the brothers" beat a woman who opened the door for police. By March 1970 the San Diego Panther office had dissolved, while agents in Los Angeles still sought means to promote "internecine struggle" between US and the Panthers, bringing the hostile groups together and giving "nature the opportunity to take her course." (San Diego's COIN-TELPRO agents, meanwhile, received monetary "merit incentives" for their role in promoting murder on the streets.)

Decades after the fact, it remains unclear whether Ron Karenga was, in fact, a government informant. Louis Tackwood, a longtime *agent provocateur* for the Los Angeles Police Department, wrote in 1973 that he "contacted Ron Karenga and gave him orders to the effect that was given to me, that he was to curtail the Panther party's growth no matter what it cost." Be that as it may, the US-Panther conflict clearly drove Karenga to the brink of paranoia. On 9 May 1970, he and two other US members allegedly tortured two women, Deborah Jones and Gail Davis, whom Karenga suspected of placing suspicious "crystals" in his food and water. Convicted of felonious assault and false imprisonment in September 1971, Karenga received a sentence of one to 10 years in prison.

Paroled in a more moderate state of mind, leading a revamped Organization Us, Karenga was hired in 1978 by California State University at Long Beach. Armed with two doctorates (in political science and social ethic), he was soon promoted to chair both the university's Black Studies Department and the President's Task Force on Multicultural Education and Campus Diversity. The holiday he created in 1966, meanwhile, is now globally honored. The U.S. Postal Service has released a Kwanzaa stamp, and Hallmark offers special Kwanzaa greeting cards. Only surviving veterans of the Panther Party still recall the bad old days and sound a sour note against Kwanzaa. As ex-Panther James Coleman observes, "By only stressing the unity of black people, Kwanzaa separates black people from the rest of Americans. Americans must unify on whatever principles ensure we live in a safe, prosperous, God-loving country, with the race and ethnicity of any American seeking to abide by those principles being of no consequence."

**"USA PATRIOT Act"**—The U.S. has a long tradition of passing federal legislation in response to crises, including from the MANN ACT of 1910 (attacking "white slavery"), the LINDBERGH Law of 1932 (aimed at KIDNAPPING), the National Firearms Act of 1934 (intended to disarm gangsters), the SMITH ACT of 1940 (targeting the COMMUNIST PARTY), the McCARRAN ACT of 1950 (punishing "subversives"), and the Gun Control Act of 1968 (spawned by the JFK ASSASSINATION, the "MURKIN" case and the RFK ASSASSINATION). It was probably inevitable, then, that the catastrophic SKYJACKINGS of 11 September 2001 would produce new legislation seeking to prevent future acts of TERRORISM. Critics, however, charge that the law enacted by Congress and signed by President GEORGE W. BUSH on 26 October 2001 is a step — or a leap — toward erosion of basic American CIVIL RIGHTS.

Possessed of a flair for melodrama, the law's authors titled it the *Uniting and Strengthening America by Providing Appropriate Tools Required to Intercept and Obstruct Terrorism* (USA PATRIOT) Act. Its major provisions include:

• *Expansion of WIRETAPS and warrants.* Requirements for secret warrants under the Foreign Intelligence Surveillance Act of 1978 are broadened and loosely redefined.

• *Expansion of government authority to search computers.* Requirements for showing "probable cause" of a criminal act are eliminated. Henceforth, agents need only claim that information is "relevant" to an ongoing criminal investigation.

• *Exposing confidential records.* The FBI is granted broad new powers to review medical, mental health, financial and educational records without court orders or producing any evidence of criminal activity.

• *Reviving CIA DOMESTIC SURVEILLANCE.* The CENTRAL INTELLIGENCE AGENCY is empowered to designate priority targets for surveillance within the U.S., thus violating the agency's original charter restrictions to foreign intelligence collection.

• *Detention of foreign suspects.* The U.S. attorney general is empowered to arrest and detain suspected foreign terrorists for seven days without filing criminal or immigration charges. (President Bush and Attorney General JOHN ASHCROFT initially sought power to detain foreign suspects indefinitely.)

• *Designation of terrorist groups.* The attorney general and secretary of state are empowered in their sole discretion to identify "terrorist" organizations and to bar any non-citizen member of those groups from entering the country. Resident aliens holding membership in designated groups may be deported.

• *Secret searches.* Federal agents may obtain warrants and search private property without informing the owner(s).

• *Biological agents and toxins.* Civilian possession is restricted to quantities "justified by a peaceful purpose" (such as medical research). Any possession by non-resident aliens from "countries that support terrorism" is banned.

• *Removing legal barriers between foreign intelligence gathering and domestic criminal investigations.* Henceforth, at their sole discretion, domestic law enforcement agencies are free to share any information gathered during routine criminal investigations (including unverified testimony offered before grand juries) to agencies engaged in foreign intelligence work.

• *Banking provisions.* Banking secrecy regulations are revised to prevent foreign account holders from concealing their identity. Depositors in foreign "shell" banks (existing only on paper) are barred from opening parallel deposits in U.S. banks. American banks are required to monitor transfers from foreign accounts and are penalized for dealing with foreign banks alleged to have "terrorist" ties (as defined by the attorney general or the secretary of state).

• *Border surveillance.* The number of border-watching agents from the Customs Service, Border Patrol and the Immigration and Naturalization Service will be tripled.

• *Defining "domestic terrorism."* Domestic terrorism is defined as including any effort "to intimidate or coerce a civilian population" or "to influence the policy of a government by intimidation or coercion." Critics note that the broad definition could be applied any socio-political demonstration, since no specific acts of criminal violence are required.

As administered by Attorney General Ashcroft, the USA PATRIOT Act has already sparked a series of lawsuits. Mass detention of Muslim immigrants who registered with Immigration authorities as required by post-"9/11" regulations have prompted class-action litigation by the AMERICAN CIVIL LIBERTIES UNION and other groups (still unresolved at this writing in March 2003). It seems certain that various provisions of the law will face challenges in court for years to come.

**U.S. Marshals Service**—President George Washington appointed the first U.S. Marshal and deputy marshals in 1789, under terms of the federal Judiciary Act. Members of the service were initially assigned to support federal courts and to enforce any lawful order of a federal judge—i.e., serving writs, subpoenas and warrants; making arrests and handling prisoners; renting courtrooms and jail space; hiring bailiffs, criers and janitors. Before creation of the FBI in 1908 the Marshals Service was the primary agency responsible for tracking federal fugitives, registering enemy aliens, and (prior to 1860) capturing runaway slaves. In modern times, the Marshals Service has been charged with exchanging captured spies and overseeing the Federal Witness Protection Program.

Over time, the FBI and the Marshals Service have been both allies and competitors. Both agencies were present at the WOUNDED KNEE SIEGE in 1973, where members of the Marshals Service displayed superior restraint and were several times chastised by G-men for trying to disarm vigilante GUARDIANS OF THE OGLALA NATION. A year later, marshals joined the FBI; the DRUG ENFORCEMENT ADMINISTRATION; the BUREAU OF ALCOHOL, TOBACCO AND FIREARMS (BATF); and other agencies to create the EL PASO INTELLIGENCE CENTER. The deadly RANDALL WEAVER siege of 1992 began after BATF agents passed Weaver's case to the Marshals Service, declaring him a "dangerous fugitive"; later, after Weaver's son and Marshal William Deegan were killed in a shootout on 21 August 1992, FBI agents were summoned to make the final arrests. In 1994 the Marshals Service collaborated once again with the Bureau, the DEA, BATF and the SECRET SERVICE to organize the Child Abduction and Serial Killer Unit in Washington, D.C.

**U.S.S. *Iowa* explosion**—Launched in August 1942, the battleship *Iowa* saw action in three wars before it was mothballed as obsolete in April 1958. President RONALD REAGAN'S campaign pledge to strengthen the U.S. military saw the *Iowa* recommissioned in April 1984. Five years later, while performing a routine gunnery exercise in the Caribbean on 19 April 1989, the ship was rocked by an explosion from one of its 16-inch gun turrets, claiming 47 lives.

Naval investigators treated the blast as a tragic accident until 8 May 1989, when they received a letter from relatives of 24-year-old Clayton Michael Hartwig, gun captain of the demolished turret and a victim of the deadly explosion. Hartwig's family wrote to ask if they could share the $100,000 payoff from a life insurance policy Hartwig had recently purchased, naming shipmate Kendall Truitt as his sole beneficiary. The Navy had no jurisdiction over life insurance, but the question sparked suspicion that the *Iowa*'s tragedy might be something more than a random accident.

The ensuing naval inquiry portrayed Clayton Hartwig as a "religious kid" and a quiet loner, whose only true friend aboard ship had been Truitt. They were so close, in fact, that rumors of HOMOSEXUALITY circulated aboard the *Iowa*, but both denied the allegations and neither was charged under the Navy's strict rules banning gays. Soon after Hartwig purchased the $50,000 life insurance policy, with a double-indemnity clause for accidental death, he had quarreled with Truitt over Truitt's marriage plans and their friendship had suffered. Truitt survived the *Iowa* explosion on 19 April 1989, only to face an inquisition concerning his relationship with Hartwig.

Navy brass never determined the cause of the *Iowa* explosion, but prevailing suspicion centered around some murky murder-suicide scenario with Hartwig cast as the villain. On 23 May 1989 naval investigators turned to the FBI's Behavioral Science Unit, requesting limited assistance. Spokesmen for FBI HEADQUARTERS later told Congress that Navy technicians "had ruled out the possibility of an accidental explosion" and ranked Hartwig's death as "equivocal." G-men would not review the Navy's investigation in detail; rather, they were asked to prepare a PSYCHOLOGICAL PROFILE of Hartwig, presuming his guilt in the blast and determining motive.

Agents Richard Ault and Roy Hazelwood discovered that Hartwig kept a scrapbook of maritime disasters and owned a book on Japanese *kamikaze* attacks during WORLD WAR II. Acquaintances spoke of his lifelong interest in explosives and his alleged desire to die on duty, thus earning a grave plot at Arlington National Cemetery. By early June the agents had profiled Hartwig as "a very troubled young man who had low self-esteem and coveted power and authority he felt he could not possess. The real and perceived rejections of significant others emotionally devastated him. This, combined with the inability to verbally express anger and faced [*sic*] with a multitude of stressors had he returned from the cruise, virtually ensured some type of reaction. In this case, in our opinion, it was a suicide. He did so in a place and manner designed to give him the recognition and respect that he felt was denied him."

Navy commanders accepted that judgment and issued their final verdict to the media on 7 September 1989. Rear Admiral Richard Milligan told the press conference: "The explosion in center gun, Turret 2, U.S.S. *Iowa*, on 19 April 1989 resulted from a wrongful intentional act. Based on this investigative report and after full review of all Naval Investigative Service's reports to date, the wrongful intentional act that caused this incident was most probably committed by CMG2 Clayton M. Hartwig, USN."

The outcry was immediate. Hartwig's family called him an innocent scapegoat, suggesting that Navy investigators sought to whitewash the dangers of obsolete equipment aboard other battleships still afloat. Television's *60 Minutes* "magazine" showcased the claim, and a committee was appointed in the House of Representatives to review the *Iowa* disaster. That inquiry began with selection of 14 notable psychologists from the American Psychological Association, enlisted to critique the FBI's profile of Hartwig. Even before the experts went to work, committee chairman Nicholas Mavroules predicted that the House investigation would reveal "a very different picture of Hartwig" than that presented by G-men Ault and Hazelwood.

In fact, the psychological review gave mixed results. Of 14 analysts consulted, three pronounced Hartwig innocent, five were skeptical of suicide or found insufficient evidence to support a conclusion, and six deemed the FBI's verdict "plausible" or "reasonable." Technicians had found "no trace elements" of an explosive device in Hartwig's gun turret, but Navy spokesmen remained "sure that foreign material was in that propellant charge." The final House report, titled *U.S.S.* Iowa *Tragedy: An Investigative Failure*, avoided any final verdict on the source of the explosion, while blasting Quantico's "mindhunters." It read, in part:

> The FBI psychological analysis procedures are of doubtful professionalism. The false air of certainty generated by the FBI analysis was probably the single major factor inducing the Navy to single out Clayton Hartwig as the likely guilty party. The FBI should consider revamping its entire equivocal death analysis system.

Senator William Cohen (R-Maine) offered his own terse verdict from the sidelines: "The Navy came to the FBI with a preordained conclusion, and the FBI comes back with the *Good Housekeeping* Seal of Approval."

In the wake of those congressional rebukes, Navy investigators performed a new series of tests on artillery powder bags, concluding that the explosion may have been accidental, after all. Naval spokesmen apologized to the Hartwig family on 16 October 1991, but the reversal failed to salve hurt feelings. Hartwig's survivors filed a $12 million lawsuit against the Navy, claiming emotional distress from the original description of Hartwig as a suicidal homosexual, but a federal court dismissed the case in November 1999. Retired G-men Ault and Hazelwood stand by their original posthumous judgment of Hartwig.

**U.S. Supreme Court** —America's first and foremost federal court bears the ultimate responsibility for interpreting U.S. statutes and determining their constitutionality. In that respect, its decisions frequently affect law enforcement techniques of arrest, search and seizure, and various forms of intelligence gathering. Techniques used by the FBI and JUSTICE DEPARTMENT have been expanded or curtailed by many of the high court's rulings. The most noteworthy include:

• *Nardone v. U.S.* (1939)— Interpreted the 1934 Federal Communication Act's ban on WIRETAPPING to prohibit both divulgence of "the exact words heard through forbidden interception" and any "derivative use" of evidence which the court deemed "fruit of the poisonous tree."

• *Dennis v. U.S.* (1949)— Upheld the SMITH ACT convictions of 12 COMMUNIST PARTY leaders and thus endorsed the law itself as constitutional, encouraging further prosecutions over the next five years.

• *Irvine v. California* (1954)— Sharply criticized local police for BUGGING the home of a suspected gambler, thus prompting Director J. EDGAR HOOVER to seek authorization for FBI BREAK-INS from Attorney General HERBERT BROWNELL.

• *Communist Party v. SUBVERSIVE ACTIVITIES CONTROL BOARD* (1956)— Ruled that party members could not legally be forced to register with the SACB. That protection was extended to "Communist front" groups and members in 1965, with *Albertson v. Subversive Activities Control Board*.

• *Yates v. U.S.* (1957)— Effectively reversed the court's ruling in *Dennis v. U.S.* and overturned the majority of Smith Act convictions obtained on basis of advocacy alone, with no evidence of actual intent to overthrow the U.S. government.

• *Jencks v. U.S.* (1957) — Reversed the conviction of a LABOR UNION organizer jailed for perjury after signing a non-Communist affidavit. The court held that defendants are entitled to see the statements of accusing witnesses, even if those witnesses are confidential government INFORMANTS.

• *U.S. v. U.S. District Court* (1972) — Ruled that the U.S. president has no authority to order warrantless wiretaps in "domestic security" cases. Failure to address the parallel matter of foreign intelligence created a great deal of ongoing controversy.

J. Edgar Hoover expended a great deal of energy contesting or evading Supreme Court rulings which he viewed as detrimental to the FBI and "proper" law enforcement. His greatest single victory in that regard was a counterattack on the 1957 *Jencks* decision, wherein Hoover lobbied successfully for passage of a law designed to protect FBI FILES from "fishing expeditions" by defense attorneys. The bill was duly passed by Congress and signed by President DWIGHT EISENHOWER. The Supreme Court upheld it in July 1959, thus effectively negating *Jencks* and demonstrating Hoover's covert power in Washington.

In 1948 Hoover threw his considerable weight behind Republican presidential candidate THOMAS DEWEY, in return for Dewey's promise that Hoover would be named attorney general in 1949 and subsequently guaranteed a place on the Supreme Court. Those dreams were dashed in November, with incumbent HARRY TRUMAN'S surprise victory, and Hoover henceforth limited his judicial aspirations to selecting or removing justices from the Supreme Court. The full scope of Hoover's influence can only be surmised, but his role has been amply documented in respect to the following justices:

• *EARL WARREN* — A friend of Hoover's from the early 1930s, Warren was selected by President Eisenhower (with Hoover's hearty endorsement) to fill the vacancy left by Justice Harold Vinson's death in 1953. Regarded as politically conservative, Warren did a sharp turnabout once installed on the court and as chief justice later produced a series of liberal rulings that mortified Hoover.

• *Potter Stewart* — When Justice Harold Burton announced his impending retirement in May 1958, Hoover ordered his staff to prepare a short list of suitable replacements. Heading the list was Potter Stewart, praised at FBI HEADQUARTERS for his "clear appreciation of the problems of law enforcement" and fact that he "has not rendered any opinions which can be construed as anti-law enforcement or anti-Bureau." Hoover recommended Stewart to President Eisenhower on the day of Burton's retirement (6 October 1958), and Ike announced Stewart's appointment the following day.

• *Abe Fortas* — Despised by Hoover as a liberal, Justice Abe Fortas resigned under fire in May 1969, after media sources broke the story of his financial ties to Lewis Wolfson, a millionaire industrialist convicted of violating federal securities statutes. The news leaks were coordinated by Hoover and Attorney General JOHN MITCHELL, as part of a plan to purge liberals from the court and let President RICHARD NIXON appoint more conservative judges.

• *WILLIAM O. DOUGLAS* — Another liberal marked for removal by Hoover, Mitchell and Nixon, Douglas was attacked for his financial dealings and the fact that he had published an article in a journal Hoover deemed "pornographic." In June 1970 Congressman (and FBI informant) GERALD FORD mounted a fruitless effort to impeach Douglas in the House of Representatives, citing derogatory information gleaned from FBI files. Douglas believed (correctly, as we know today) that G-men had tapped various telephones at the Supreme Court for years before the abortive impeachment campaign.

• *Lewis Powell* — Appointed to the court by President Nixon in 1971, Powell corresponded frequently with Hoover from the early 1960s onward and had been an FBI informant for at least five years preceding his appointment to the court. The secret relationship, with its apparent conflict of interest, was revealed after Powell's death, through documents obtained under the FREEDOM OF INFORMATION ACT.

# V

**VAN DOREN, Carl Clinton** — A native of Vermillion County, Illinois, born in 1885, Carl Van Doren obtained his Ph.D. from Columbia University in 1911 and remained on campus as an associate in English until 1930. He also served as literary editor for *The Nation* from 1919 to 1922, and at *Century Magazine* from 1922 through 1925. Despite his membership in the American Society for Cultural Relations with Russia, FBI agents overlooked him until 1929, two years after they opened a dossier on his brother MARK VAN DOREN.

Once focused, though, G-men applied their usual intensity to tracking Van Doren's movements. In 1937 they noted his attendance at a banquet held to raise money for "the defense of the

Spanish government." A year later, the FBI ignored Van Doren's Pulitzer Prize for biography of Benjamin Franklin, citing him instead for sponsoring the American Committee for the Protection of the Foreign Born. In 1939 agents recorded his participation in the Third National Congress of the League of American Writers, claiming that "at least fourteen" of the 72 attendees were COMMUNIST PARTY members, while the rest were "fixtures on Stalinist manifestos and whitewash documents." Agents were concerned in 1940, when a copy of Van Doren's stock lecture on Franklin was sold at an auction to benefit exiled writers, and again in 1940, when he joined SINCLAIR LEWIS and others to review famous books for the Readers Club, offering classic novels to the public for one dollar each. Agents joined the club under false names and reported on its activities through 1942.

Following Pearl Harbor, Van Doren and other members of the AUTHORS LEAGUE OF AMERICA organized the Writers War Board, thereby causing still more worry at FBI headquarters. As late as 1944, agents compiled lists of board members with alleged communist affiliations, listing Van Doren with the likes of PEARL BUCK and CLIFFORD ODETS. At war's end, in 1945, both Van Doren brothers were cited for joining HOWARD FAST on a committee which "urged that the U.S. accept the Bretton-Woods [sic] Economic Plan for recovery of Europe." (FBI observers somehow failed to realize that Bretton Woods is a town in New Hampshire, where Allied leaders met in July 1944 to plan creation of the World Bank and other postwar economic strategies. By promoting it, the Van Dorens and Fast were in fact supporting U.S. foreign policy, but the Bureau's garbled understanding apparently derived from a column in the *Daily Worker*, devoid of any background research.) Agents continued shadowing Van Doren, branding him a "dupe" of the Reds, until 1948. He died in 1954.

**VAN DOREN, Mark**—An Illinois native, born in 1894, Carl Van Doren received his Ph.D. from Columbia University in 1920 and remained as a long-term professor, highly regarded by colleagues and students. He also served as literary editor of *The Nation* from 1924 to 1928, and again from 1935 through 1938. The FBI opened a file on Van Doren in 1927, based on his membership in the American Society for Cultural Relations with Russia, and thereafter dubbed him "a Red-ucator at Columbia University."

Reports found in Van Doren's file are similar to those logged on his older brother, CARL VAN DOREN. In 1932 he was cited for supporting the National Student League, and two years later for joining the National Committee for the Defense of Political Prisoners. In 1936 G-men called Van Doren a "writer" for the Book Find Club and noted that "he made statements approving the employment of Communists as teachers." The year 1938 found Van Doren "in agreement with the Communist viewpoint in the Spanish situation"—i.e., opposed to a fascist overthrow of the elected government, supported by Nazi German troops—but agents overlooked his 1939 Pulitzer Prize for *Collected Poems*.

Van Doren reached out to the FBI in 1942, with a letter suggesting investigation of some person whose name was blacked out prior to later release of the file, but his warning was routinely passed on the Postmaster General. Agents were back on track in

1945, recording the word of an "anonymous source" that Van Doren "was one of the nice cozy Reds that are around most all intellectual outfits." They also reviewed an "undated typewritten report received from an unidentified source," blithely accepting its claim that Van Doren belonged to some nameless "High Toned Red Group." Black marks were also added to the files of both Van Doren brothers in 1945, after they publicly supported President HARRY TRUMAN's plan for economic recovery in postwar Europe.

The Red-hunting 1950s rejuvenated FBI pursuit of Van Doren. A "new main file" was opened in his name during 1951, as part of a "security-type investigation." That file listed 15 variations of his name as aliases, author Natalie Robins later discovering that separate files existed for at least nine of the variant names (including "M. Doren" and "One Van Doren"). By 1953, Van Doren was listed in the Bureau's illegal SECURITY INDEX, remaining on file there until 1955, when agents belatedly admitted he had never been an "actual member of the COMMUNIST PARTY." Still, his file(s) remained active for another decade, with reports periodically added through 1965. Van Doren died in 1972.

**"VANPAC"**—On 16 December 1989 a pipe bomb, sent through the mail, exploded at the Mountain Brook, Alabama home of Robert Vance, a judge with the 11th Circuit Court of Appeals. Vance was killed instantly, his wife badly wounded by shrapnel and roofing nails packed with the bomb. Two days later, a similar bomb was intercepted and deactivated at 11th Circuit Court headquarters in Atlanta, Georgia. Later that afternoon, 18 December, a third bomb killed attorney Robert Robertson at his office in Savannah. Next morning, the fourth and last bomb was found and defused at the Jacksonville, Florida office of the NATIONAL ASSOCIATION FOR THE ADVANCEMENT OF COLORED PEOPLE (NAACP).

The murder of a federal judge and use of the U.S. mail to deliver explosives made the "VANPAC" case (for "*Vance package*") a priority for FBI HEADQUARTERS and the Treasury Department's BUREAU OF ALCOHOL, TOBACCO AND FIREARMS (BATF). The two agencies shared responsibility for such crimes under the Federal BOMBING Statute, but in this case they followed very different paths. G-men focused on an Alabama racist, one William O'Ferrell, who had once shared lodgings with relatives of a KU KLUX KLAN member convicted of murder in Birmingham's infamous "BAPBOMB" case. O'Ferrell had also written several letters using the same typewriter which produced notes mailed with the December 1989 bombs. G-men led by Agent JAMES THURMAN from the Bureau's LABORATORY DIVISION raided O'Ferrell's home in January 1990 and found no evidence linking him to the case. O'Ferrell also passed two polygraph tests, explaining that he had sold his typewriter months earlier, to an unidentified patron at his Alabama junk shop.

BATF agents, meanwhile, recalled a 1972 bombing similar to the recent crimes. The defendant in that case was Walter Leroy Moody, Jr., of Rex, Georgia. Furious with an Atlanta car dealer who had repossessed his vehicle, Moody built a pipe bomb which he meant to send through the mail, but it exploded prematurely and injured his wife. Convicted of possessing a pipe bomb,

Moody was sentenced to five years in prison, paroled after three. His marathon appeal of that conviction was rejected by the 11th Circuit Court of Appeals in 1988, thus providing a motive for two of the recent bombings. While investigating Moody, the BATF uncovered evidence that he coached and bribed witnesses during his 1988 appeal, thereby leaving himself vulnerable to another federal charge.

Back at the FBI lab, the VANPAC case was being handled in a curious manner. A desire for quick results prompted Agent Thurman, in charge of the case, to reject an offer of help from FREDERICK WHITEHURST, a member of the Materials Analysis Unit described as the Bureau's "only qualified explosives residue examiner at the present time." Instead of Whitehurst, Thurman assigned the case to ROGER MARTZ, an agent in the Chemistry and Toxicology Unit who had no experience with explosives. Both Thurman and Martz would later be accused of tailoring their testimony to favor prosecutors — a charge that resulted in both men being removed from the FBI lab.

BATF agents briefed the FBI on their suspicions concerning Moody and electronic surveillance was authorized on 1 April 1990. WIRETAPS proved fruitless, but a BUGGING device in Moody's home caught the suspect talking to himself, muttering, "Now you've killed two. Now you can't pull another bombing." A subsequent search of the house revealed nails, pipes and other components resembling those used in the recent blasts. Moody was indicted for the bombings on 7 November 1990; he and his wife were also charged with obstructing justice in the 1988 appellate case. Facing trial on that charge in July 1990, Susan Moody pled guilty and cooperated with her husband's prosecutors. Walter Moody was convicted on 13 counts in December 1990 and received a 15-year prison term.

Publicity surrounding the bombings won Moody a change of venue for his next trial, beginning on 4 June 1991 in St. Paul, Minnesota. Future FBI Director LOUIS FREEH served as lead prosecutor on the case. Moody testified in his own behalf, blaming the KKK for his alleged crimes and claiming that he was visiting Florida when the bombs were mailed in Georgia. Still, his penchant for talking to himself betrayed him, as a court-authorized bug in his cell recorded Moody saying, "Kill those damn judges … I shouldn't have done it. Idiot!" That bitter commentary might have sealed his fate, but G-men pulled out all the stops in their effort to convict Moody on scientific evidence. Agents Thurman and Martz were among the key witnesses, but a review of their testimony discloses crucial discrepancies.

The FBI had long claimed that "Moody's [bomb] design is unique," but in fact it was not. His 1972 effort was a four-rod aluminum pipe bomb; three of those mailed in 1989 were made from single-rod steel pipes, while the Vance bomb featured steel pipe with cast-iron caps. Unlike the 1989 bombs, Moody's 1972 construction had no detonator, using instead a flashlight bulb to ignite the charge. The 1972 bomb used a single D-cell battery, while those mailed in 1989 each used two C-cell batteries. Agent Thurman told the St. Paul jury there were "lots of similarities," but he glossed over a greater number of discrepancies. As authors John Kelly and Phillip Wearne note in their book *Tainting Evidence* (1998):

Thurman testified that the bombs that killed Judge Vance and Robinson were "essentially identical." Then he said that all four 1989 devices were identical. "The conclusion I reached is that these devices were … made by one individual, working off the same plans, using essentially the same type of materials," he pronounced to the court. Yet … one of the bombs sported such an obvious difference that a child could have remarked on it. The Birmingham bomb that killed Judge Vance had no welded end plates but cast iron caps on the end of the steel tube. It was cut from a different piece of tube, being 1½ inches in diameter, not 2 inches, and was shorter than the other tube, 5½ inches rather than 7 inches.

Agent Martz admitted under oath that he was unable to "successfully compare" residue from the four 1989 bombs, but he hedged his testimony in terms that made jurors believe he had linked the four devices to Moody. A 1997 report from the FBI's Inspector General declared that "Martz was ambiguous.… [H]e should have stated more directly that he found differences and similarities." It hardly mattered by then however, since Moody was convicted on 71 counts in June 1991, receiving seven life terms plus 400 years without parole. In October 1996, the same evidence was used to convict him of murder in Alabama, whereupon he received a death sentence. The Inspector General's report was filed less than three months after that second conviction, prompting FBI leaders to remove Martz and Thurman from their laboratory assignments.

**VIDAL, Gore Eugene Luthar** — Born at West Point military academy in 1925, the son of an instructor there, Gore Vidal published his first novel, *Williwaw*, at age 21, while serving in the U.S. Army. His second book, *The Pillar and the City*, was widely condemned by conservative critics for its frank portrayal of HOMOSEXUALITY, but FBI agents were more concerned with the novel's review in the *Daily Worker*. That clipping opened Vidal's 38-page dossier, and the Bureau kept him under sporadic surveillance thereafter. In 1960, G-men judged him "on the pink side" and noted that his play *A Best Man* included an "unnecessary jibe" at J. EDGAR HOOVER. Vidal compounded that sin in 1961, by condemning the HOUSE COMMITTEE ON UN-AMERICAN ACTIVITIES, and again three years later, when he criticized the FBI during a television interview. (Headquarters encouraged agents to swamp the network with letters demanding that the program, *Hot Line*, be canceled.)

In 1970, agents tuned in to *The David Frost Show*, where they caught Vidal making "unnecessary remarks" about Vice President SPIRO AGNEW. Later that year, an unnamed correspondent warned agents that Vidal had urged critics of the RICHARD NIXON administration to "blow up the Capitol," but no charges were filed (unlike the case of a BLACK PANTHER PARTY spokesman who allegedly threatened Nixon's life). One of the last reports in Vidal's dossier summarized his public altercation with right-wing columnist WILLIAM BUCKLEY, JR. Buckley sued Vidal for libel, seeking $500,000 in damages, after Vidal called him a "crypto-Nazi" in a televised debate. Vidal counter sued, but his case was summarily dismissed. Director Hoover died four months before Buckley withdrew his lawsuit, in September 1972, and the Bureau thereafter lost interest in watching Vidal.

**VIERTEL, Berthold** —A native of Vienna, born in 1885, Berthold Viertel made his first visit to Hollywood in 1928, a decade before ADOLF HITLER annexed Austria for the Third Reich. By 1932, Viertel and his wife (actress/writer Salomea "Salka" Viertel) were settled full-time in Los Angeles, though Berthold traveled frequently abroad on film-related business. Salka Viertel was naturalized as a U.S. citizen in 1939, but Berthold's application was delayed by FBI investigation into his alleged "communist" activities.

The Viertel file was opened in 1942, with a report that actress Greta Garbo (another target of FBI surveillance) "received a great deal of mail" at Viertel's home address. A "30 day mail cover" on Viertel was extended through 1946, G-men intercepting letters from various exiled writers including ANNA SEGHERS, BERTOLT BRECHT, and members of the Joint Anti-Fascist Refugee Committee. Viertel's telephones were also tapped in California, and again when he moved to New York. J. EDGAR HOOVER explained the surveillance by claiming Viertel was "a known contact of agents of the Soviet Secret Intelligence (NKVD)." Of particular concern was a meeting of a "Russian-German Committee" held at Viertel's home in August 1943, with THOMAS MANN and others in attendance, to prepare a telegram endorsing the National Committee for a Free Germany's "Moscow manifesto."

Ironically, Viertel served the U.S. government during WORLD WAR II through the Office of the Coordinator of Information, and his citizenship application was finally cleared in March 1944, after prominent sponsors interceded with Attorney General FRANCIS BIDDLE. It was a small victory, and ultimately wasted. Viertel returned to Austria in 1949, and while Hoover failed in his effort to revoke Viertel's U.S. citizenship that year, Viertel died in Vienna four years later, on 24 September 1953.

**VIETNAM War Protests** —While U.S. diplomats and military personnel were involved in various aspects of the Vietnam War virtually from the closing days of WORLD WAR II, a serious military commitment did not begin until Congress passed the Gulf of Tonkin Resolution in August 1964, followed by President LYNDON JOHNSON's bombing of North Vietnam in February 1965 and deployment of U.S. Marines two months later. Protests on the home front were immediate, and the FBI's annual report to Attorney General NICHOLAS KATZENBACH in 1964 noted the COMMUNIST PARTY's "intensive campaign for the withdrawal of American forces from South Vietnam." Within days of the first Marines arriving in Vietnam, on 17 April 1965, members of the STUDENTS FOR A DEMOCRATIC SOCIETY (SDS) led the nation's protest demonstration, with 25,000 anti-war marchers. Ten days later, presidential adviser McGeorge Bundy asked FBI Director J. EDGAR HOOVER for any available data on Communist involvement in protests against the war. Hoover met with Johnson on 28 April and later reported:

> that he was quite concerned over the anti-Vietnam situation that has developed in this country and he appreciated particularly the material that we sent him yesterday containing clippings from various columnists in the country who had attributed the agitation in this country to the communists as there was no doubt in his mind but that they were behind the disturbances that have al-

ready occurred. [The CIA had] stated that their intelligence showed that the Chinese and North Vietnamese believe that by intensifying the agitation in this country, particularly on the college campus levels, it would so confuse and divide the Americans that our troops in South Vietnam would have to be withdrawn in order to preserve order here and it would enable North Vietnam to move in at once.

No evidence of any such global conspiracy existed, but Hoover believed in it all the same, and current events exacerbated his worries. Four hundred campus demonstrations were recorded in the 1966-67 school year, escalating to 3,400 in 1967-68. In April 1967, spurred by remarks from Dr. MARTIN LUTHER KING, JR., some 200,000 anti-war protesters marched in New York City, while another 65,000 paraded in San Francisco. In October 1967 the National Mobilization to End the War in Vietnam rallied 200,000 protesters at the Pentagon, including author NORMAN MAILER (whose subsequent account of the event won a Pulitzer Prize). That year, in his annual appearance before the House Appropriations Committee, Hoover declared:

> I do not believe that everybody who is opposed to the foreign policy in Vietnam is necessarily a Communist. That, of course, would be ridiculous as a charge, but there are many gullible people who are against the policy in Vietnam as a result of the propaganda put out by some college professors who are naïve and some students lacking in maturity and objectivity who are constantly agitating and carrying on demonstrations in some of our largest universities.

Chief among those enemies on Hoover's list were leaders of the SDS, which Hoover regarded as a tool of the Communist Party (based on one tenuous remark from CP leader Gus Hall). To counter that "menace," Hoover launched the last of his illegal COINTELPRO disruption campaigns against the SDS and other "NEW LEFT" organizations. He regarded the threat as so critical, in fact, that the Bureau's "TEN MOST WANTED" LIST was expanded to accommodate 16 fugitive radicals, while a special team of G-men (dubbed "THE BEARDS") were granted permission to grow long hair and penetrate the SDS in Hoover's first-and-only UNDERCOVER OPERATION.

The FBI's war against anti-war activists escalated under President RICHARD NIXON, with the KENT STATE SHOOTINGS in Ohio and a mad scramble to identify those responsible for leaking the "PENTAGON PAPERS" to reporters from the *New York Times*. G-men hired *agents provocateur* like JOE BURTON to provoke violent acts by normally peaceable groups including Vietnam Veterans Against the War, in hope of producing arrests, and Hoover was finally reduced to fabricating bizarre conspiracy charges against protest leaders DANIEL and PHILIP BERRIGAN, claiming they had schemed with "radical nuns" to kidnap presidential aide HENRY KISSINGER. Hoover died before Nixon declared "peace with honor" in Vietnam and withdrew American troops in 1972, thus eliminating any need for further protests.

**VIOLENT Criminal Apprehension Program (VICAP)** — VICAP was the brainchild of retired Los Angeles homicide detective Pierce Brooks, a veteran of SERIAL MURDER investigations who recognized the glaring lack of any information network geared to track nomadic killers on the move. Computers offered the obvious solution, and Brooks told anyone who would listen of his plans for a nationwide network designed to collect and compare details of unsolved crimes, thus charting patterns that might otherwise be missed. Retained by the FBI in 1981, Brooks and former Seattle detective Robert Keppel hammered out the VICAP framework, drafting an investigative questionnaire for local officers, but they still had far to go in terms of winning support from the federal bureaucracy. Funding was approved by the U.S. Senate in 1983, but another year passed before President RONALD REAGAN announced creation of a new NATIONAL CENTER FOR THE ANALYSIS OF VIOLENT CRIME, including the VICAP computer system.

Unlike fictional G-men, the VICAP team is paid to analyze crimes from a distance, rather than conducting active field investigations. With fewer than a dozen full-time agents, the program is not equipped for staging manhunts, raiding suspect hideouts, or gunning down desperate killers. (Besides which, the vast majority of serial murders are state offenses, involving no federal violations.) On the rare occasions when VICAP agents do visit a crime scene, their function is purely advisory, reviewing local task force operations and suggesting more efficient means of handling information. The national program's success or failure ultimately hinges on cooperation from local agencies, where jealousy, resentment, or simple fatigue sometimes conspire to frustrate VICAP.

Six months of operation was enough to highlight VICAP's problems in the field. Overworked police considered the 44-page questionnaire too cumbersome and time consuming. If a killer claimed 10 or 15 victims and the FBI required a separate questionnaire for each, some locals chose to ignore the federal team and spare themselves a case of writer's cramp. The current VICAP forms [see the Appendix] are two-thirds shorter than their predecessors, but reduced paperwork has not solved all the Bureau's problems in coordinating manhunts. Many local officers still regard the FBI as a headline-grabbing agency more interested in claiming credit for a high-profile case than helping out the average working cop. Federal bungling of cases like the notorious YOSEMITE MURDERS and failures of PSYCHOLOGICAL PROFILING prompt many homicide investigators to regard VICAP's aid as a mixed blessing.

# W

**WALKER, John Anthony, Jr.**—A mercenary spy whose sole motive was profit, John Walker, Jr., began feeding classified U.S. Navy documents to the Soviet KGB in 1967, continuing until his retirement in 1976, then recruiting other spies within the service who included his son, his brother, and a close friend of the family. Upon retirement from the navy, Walker remained in the Norfolk, Virginia region where he had last been stationed (as a naval intelligence officer) and opened a private detective agency. In his spare time, Walker also joined a faction of the KU KLUX KLAN led by "Imperial Wizard" BILL WILKINSON, who was employed throughout his KKK career as a secret FBI INFORMANT.

Wilkinson played no role in Walker's eventual exposure and arrest, however. That honor belonged to Walker's ex-wife, who approached FBI agents in 1985, with tales of watching her husband exchange stolen classified papers for cash. G-men placed him under surveillance, trailing Walker through a series of suspicious meetings and deliveries before they finally arrested him for ESPIONAGE on 20 May 1985. Walker was indicted on 28 October 1985 and soon struck a bargain with federal prosecutors, trading a full confession for leniency in the case of his son, Michael. As a result of that confession, Walker and his brother (Arthur Walker) received life prison terms. Son Michael was sentenced to 25 years, while Walker's friend and fellow spy Jerry Whitworth received a 365-year sentence. FBI agents were not alone in overlooking Walker's 18-year career as a Soviet spy. His navy personnel records reveal that Walker was cleared by multiple security checks while still on active duty, between 1967 and 1976.

**WALLACE, Henry Agard**—A native of Adair County, Iowa, born 7 October 1888, Henry Wallace was a prominent member of President FRANKLIN ROOSEVELT's "New Deal" administration. He served variously as Secretary of Agriculture (1933-40) and as Roosevelt's third-term vice president (1941-45), then briefly as Secretary of Commerce under President HARRY TRUMAN (1945-46). In 1948 he challenged Truman for the White House, as the candidate of the Progressive Party.

FBI Director J. EDGAR HOOVER apparently despised Wallace

from the early 1930s onward, though the reason for his animosity remains unclear. In 1940, after choosing Wallace as his running mate, Roosevelt asked Hoover to recover certain "embarrassing" personal letters Wallace had written to Nicholas Roerich — a "psychic medium" — and others, discussing his interest in the occult. G-men performed the chore, but Hoover had the letters copied for his FILES before delivering the originals to the White House. The habit of reading Wallace's mail proved impossible to break; agents continued to open and photograph his private correspondence after he became vice president in 1941, also tapping his telephones and those of his aides. Wallace lived under constant FBI surveillance, at home and abroad. When he addressed a LABOR UNION rally in Los Angeles, G-men informed FBI HEADQUARTERS that "many well known Communists were in the audience." In 1943, while Wallace toured South America, Hoover alerted Attorney General FRANCIS BIDDLE to "information from a confidential source which indicates the possibility that Vice President Wallace is being unknowingly influenced by Bolivian Communists."

President Roosevelt took such warnings with a grain of salt, but his successor viewed the charges more seriously. On 29 May 1946, Hoover warned President Truman that the FBI had uncovered "an enormous Soviet ESPIONAGE ring in Washington," with Wallace numbered among 13 alleged spies. Four months later, on 28 September, Averell Harriman replaced Wallace as Secretary of Commerce. In 1948 Hoover maintained consistency by furnishing Truman with derogatory material on Wallace and the Progressive Party. Among those items were Wallace's stolen correspondence with medium Nicholas Roerich, leaked to columnist WESTBROOK PEGLER as a means of humiliating Wallace. On election day, Wallace trailed the field of four major candidates, running behind Truman, Republican contender THOMAS DEWEY, and Dixiecrat candidate Strom Thurmond.

Wallace's defeat and subsequent retirement from politics failed to placate Hoover. Indeed, the mere mention of Wallace's name was enough to spark the director's rage. Agent M. WESLEY SWEARINGEN received a punitive transfer from the Chicago to Kentucky in 1963, after he spurned Bureau advice and married a divorcée whose first husband had campaigned for Wallace 15 years earlier. Henry Wallace, perhaps unaware of Hoover's enduring hatred, died at Danbury, Connecticut on 18 November 1965.

**WALSH, Thomas James** — A Wisconsin native, born 12 June 1859, Thomas Walsh was elected to the House of Representatives from Montana in 1906, and then to the U.S. Senate in 1913. He was a vocal critic of the PALMER RAIDS in 1920, condemning the JUSTICE DEPARTMENT and the Bureau of Investigation for the "indignities and outrages" suffered by thousands of persons wrongfully arrested in those dragnets. In 1923, with fellow Montana senator BURTON WHEELER, Walsh spearheaded an investigation of the TEAPOT DOME SCANDAL, and thus ran afoul of the Bureau once more. G-men ransacked Walsh's office, tapped his telephone and read his mail in a fruitless effort to discredit him; they also accosted his daughter on the street, while she pushed her baby in a pram, and warned her that the Teapot Dome investigation should be terminated. Agent Blair Coan sought dirt on Walsh in Montana but found nothing; when Senator Wheeler was framed on corruption charges, Walsh successfully defended him in court. Three years later, armed with inside information from ex-agent Franklin Dodge, Walsh publicly denounced the Bureau's illegal domestic surveillance, exposed leakage of classified material to right-wing journalists, and condemned Director J. EDGAR HOOVER'S frequent "junketing around the country."

Hoover's hatred of Walsh turned to fear on 28 February 1933, when president-elect FRANKLIN ROOSEVELT announced his plan to name Walsh as the next attorney general. Walsh, for his part, told the *New York Times* that "he would reorganize the Department of Justice when he assumed office, probably with an almost completely new personnel." No one doubted that Hoover would be among the first to go when Walsh began cleaning house. It appeared that only a miracle could save Hoover's job — and he got one on 2 March 1933.

Widowed in 1917, a bachelor for 15 years since his wife's death, 73-year-old Thomas Walsh had recently married the daughter of a prominent Cuban family. The couple was returning from a visit to Havana when Roosevelt announced Walsh's nomination for attorney general, and they boarded a train from Daytona Beach to Washington the next day, en route to Roosevelt's inauguration ceremony. In the predawn hours of 2 March, as the train passed through Wilson County, North Carolina, Mrs. Walsh woke to find her husband sprawled unconscious on the floor of their compartment. A doctor was summoned, but Sen. Walsh was dead before help arrived. Conspiracy theories flourished when Walsh's death certificate listed "Cause unknown, possibly coronary thrombosis." Critics of the finding noted that a recent Florida checkup had revealed no heart trouble, and the *New York Times* pronounced Walsh in "vigorous health." Whatever the cause, his passing saved Hoover from a near-miss with dismissal, even as he planned new ways to make his name a household word throughout America.

**WARREN Commission** *see* **JFK Assassination**

**WARREN, Earl** — A Los Angeles native, born 19 March 1891, Earl Warren emerged from military service during WORLD WAR I to pursue a career in Republican politics. He met FBI Director J. EDGAR HOOVER in 1932, while serving as district attorney of northern California's Alameda County. Four years later, Hoover watched approvingly as Warren engineered the FRAME-UP of three "radical" LABOR UNION leaders for the murder of a ship's engineer. (When the three were paroled in 1941, Warren charged that Communists had secured their release from prison.) Hoover added Warren to his "special correspondents" list, closely following Warren's subsequent career as state attorney general (1939-43), California governor (1943-53), and unsuccessful candidate for vice president of the U.S. (1948).

Hoover's relationship with Warren was not strictly passive. In 1948 Hoover decreed that FBI HEADQUARTERS should furnish any information requested by Warren "in strictest confidence," with a proviso that "none of the information can be attributed to the FBI." Three years later, Hoover penned an order reading:

"Whatever the Governor requests I want prompt attention accorded to it." That attention included FBI cars and drivers, furnished free of charge on Warren's visits to New York and Washington, and Bureau background checks on young men dating Warren's daughters during 1954 and 1955.

By that time, Warren had already taken his place as chief justice of the U.S. SUPREME COURT, but his unexpected liberal stance on CIVIL RIGHTS and police handling of criminal suspects quickly soured Hoover's admiration for the one-time anti-Red crusader. FBI records reveal that G-men WIRETAPPED Warren's telephones at least seven times while he was active on the court (1953-69), and congressman GERALD FORD reported directly to Hoover on Warren's conduct as chairman of the Warren Commission, appointed to investigate the JFK ASSASSINATION in 1963-64. While Warren and his fellow panelists accepted Hoover's revisionist history in that case, he remained at odds with other FBI practices. In December 1966, while considering an appeal by convicted TEAMSTERS UNION president James Hoffa, Warren called the FBI's use of INFORMANTS "an affront to the quality and fairness of Federal law enforcement." Warren resigned from the Supreme Court in 1969 and died five years later, on 9 July 1974. He was awarded a posthumous Presidential Medal of Freedom in 1981.

**WASKY, Ted**—Identified in press releases as the assistant special agent in charge of the FBI's Indianapolis field office, Ted Wasky embarrassed himself and the Bureau on 17 July 2001, when an unknown thief stole his car keys from an unlocked locker at a local gym, then removed Wasky's FBI identification and his .40-caliber service pistol from a car parked outside. An anonymous telephone tip led G-men to the missing gun on 18 July, but Special Agent in Charge Robert Reilley told reporters that Wasky might still face disciplinary action. The gun was stolen from beneath the driver's seat of Wasky's car, whereas FBI regulations mandate that weapons left in vehicles must be secured in a locked gun rack, in a metal container with a case-hardened lock, or with a case-hardened chain inside an alarmed car trunk. The theft proved even more embarrassing than usual, as it came on the same day when JUSTICE DEPARTMENT spokesmen announced that 449 other weapons (pistols and machine guns) were missing from FBI arsenals, along with 180 stolen computers. The action finally taken against Agent Wasky (if any) remains unknown at press time for this volume, but a media report of 4 September 2002 revealed that he was still assistant special agent in charge of Indianapolis.

**WATERGATE Scandal**—The morass of scandal and corruption surrounding President RICHARD NIXON takes its popular name from events transpiring on 17 June 1972 at the Watergate office complex in Washington, D.C. In the predawn hours of that fateful day, five men with ties to the CENTRAL INTELLIGENCE AGENCY were captured during a BREAK-IN and attempted BUGGING at the office of the Democratic National Committee. Thus began the investigation that journalist Ronald Kessler describes as "the FBI's biggest case since the assassination of John F. Kennedy."

All five Watergate burglars were soon identified as employees of CREEP — the Committee to Re-Elect the President — and rumors swiftly circulated that their actions had been dictated by higher-ups in the Republican Party. Serial numbers on money they carried were traced to party contributors via a Mexican money laundry. The five were indicted for conspiracy on 15 September; charged in the same indictment were two accomplices, White House consultant E. Howard Hunt and CREEP employee (and former FBI agent) G. GORDON LIDDY. At trial in January 1973, five of the seven pled guilty and their codefendants were convicted. They were sentenced on 23 March, with Liddy receiving the longest jail term (six years). At the sentencing, Judge John Sirica revealed a letter from defendant James McCord (CREEP's chief security officer) alleging that other persons were involved in the conspiracy and that the seven had been pressured to plead guilty.

Thus began the broader investigation into Nixon crimes and scandals collectively dubbed "Watergate." An early casualty was Acting FBI Director L. PATRICK GRAY, who withdrew his nomination of 27 April 1973 after admitting he destroyed documents related to the Watergate investigation. Three days later, Nixon accepted the resignations of Attorney General RICHARD KLEINDIENST and three top White House aides: H.R. HALDEMAN, JOHN EHRLICHMAN, and former attorney general JOHN MITCHELL. On 10 May 1973 a federal grand jury indicted Mitchell and former Commerce Secretary Maurice Stans for obstructing justice in the Watergate case. Two weeks later, on 23 May, Attorney General ELLIOT RICHARDSON appointed Archibald Cox to serve as special prosecutor in charge of the widening investigation. A parallel (and televised) review of the facts was initiated by a Senate Select Committee on Presidential Campaign Activities.

Curiously, it was later disclosed that much of the Watergate scandal sprang from late FBI Director J. EDGAR HOOVER's 1970 rejection of the White House HUSTON PLAN (consolidating illegal DOMESTIC SURVEILLANCE in a single agency) and his failure to pursue the "PENTAGON PAPERS" case with enough zeal to satisfy Nixon. That reticence, which ironically led some historians to name Hoover a champion of civil liberties, prompted Nixon's aides to organize a special security team (dubbed "plumbers") and to pursue a regimen of "dirty tricks" (i.e., crimes) throughout the 1972 presidential campaign. Ongoing revelations and White House pressure to conceal the truth drove Attorney General Richardson and Acting FBI Director WILLIAM RUCKELSHAUS from office in 1973, while sending Nixon staffers Mitchell, Haldeman and Ehrlichman to prison (with others). Vice President SPIRO AGNEW resigned in disgrace on 10 October 1973 and later pled guilty to charges of corruption. The House Judiciary Committee recommended three articles of impeachment against Nixon on 30 July 1974, and Nixon resigned 10 days later. President GERALD FORD granted Nixon a blanket pardon for all crimes on 8 September 1974.

**WEATHER Underground Organization**—The Weather Underground Organization (WUO)—more commonly known as the "Weathermen"—emerged from a factional rift in the STUDENTS FOR A DEMOCRATIC SOCIETY on 20 June 1969. It was one of four factions surviving the SDS split, and the only one to have a significant impact on U.S. politics thereafter. The group took its name from the lyrics of a popular Bob Dylan song, *Subterranean Homesick Blues*: "You don't need a weatherman to know which way the wind blows."

Having pledged themselves to revolution, members of the WUO wasted no time putting their program in action. Weatherman exploits are frequently exaggerated, but the group's semi-official history (published in 1997) claims credit for the following actions:

*7 October 1969*—BOMBING of Chicago's Haymarket statue, honoring 19th-century policemen allegedly killed by ANARCHISTS.

*8-12 October 1969*—Window-smashing "Days of Rage" riots in Chicago.

*December 1969*—Firebombing of Chicago police cars in retaliation for the 8 December slayings of BLACK PANTHER PARTY members FRED HAMPTON and Mark Clark.

*January 1970*—Attempted bombing of a Reserve Officers Training Corps office at the University of Washington, landing two WUO members in jail.

*6 March 1970*—Accidental detonation of a WUO "bomb factory" in a Greenwich Village (New York) townhouse. Three members were killed, while two others escaped and became fugitives.

*May 1970*—Bombing of the National Guard's headquarters in Washington, in response to the KENT STATE SHOOTINGS.

*June 1970*—Bomb detonation at headquarters of the NEW YORK POLICE DEPARTMENT.

*26 July 1970*—Bombing at the U.S. Army's Presidio base in San Francisco.

*13 September 1970*—Prison break extricating LSD guru Timothy Leary from custody.

*August 1971*—Bombing of prison offices in San Francisco, following the 21 August death of Black Panther spokesman George Jackson in a riot at nearby San Quentin prison.

*September 1971*—Bomb explosion at the office of New York's Commissioner of Corrections in Albany.

*October 1971*—Bombing of VIETNAM WAR planner McGeorge Bundy's office at the Massachusetts Institute of Technology.

*28 September 1973*—Bombing of ITT's Latin American section in New York City, responding to the company's role in the recent overthrow and murder of Chilean President Salvador Allende.

*23 January 1975*—Bombings of U.S. government offices in Washington, D.C. and Oakland, California.

*16 June 1975*—Explosion at the New York City office of Banco de Ponce, targeted for its "superexploitation" of labor in Puerto Rico.

*10 October 1975*—Bombing of Kennecott Corporation's headquarters in Salt Lake City.

*3 February 1977*—Bombing of the Immigration and Naturalization Service's office in San Francisco.

*7 November 1983*—Bombing of the U.S. Capitol building by a WUO offshoot, the Armed Resistance Unit, to protest America's military invasion of Grenada.

Despite those claims of violent action, questions remain concerning the WUO's responsibility for various crimes. Subsequent trials and release of documents under the FREEDOM OF INFORMATION ACT demonstrate that the group's more outrageous crimes were often planned and carried out by FBI or police *agents provocateur*. One such, FBI hireling HORACE PACKER, provided Seattle Weathermen with drugs, weapons and the ingredients for Molotov cocktails; he also furnished the paint used to deface a federal courthouse in February 1970—a key element in later indictments for conspiracy to damage government property. At trial, Packer testified under oath that G-men knew of his crimes and told him to "do anything to protect my credibility."

Another FBI *provocateur*, LARRY GRATHWOHL, was ranked among the WUO's "most militant members" in Detroit, where he gave bomb-making lessons to fellow radicals. Grathwohl was among the Weathermen indicted by a federal grand jury in March 1970, on charges of conspiring to bomb police and military installations. His charges were later dropped, while the other defendants escaped and became WEATHERFUGS (FBI jargon for "Weatherman fugitives"). In a subsequent press interview, Grathwohl admitted personally bombing an Ohio school in 1969.

Yet another Bureau agitator, THOMAS TONGYAI, was nicknamed "Tommy the Traveler" for his incessant roaming across country, seeking out WUO members with pleas for violent action. He recruited young rioters for the Chicago "Days of Rage," provided other radicals with weapons, and volunteered to plant various bombs. At the same time, *provocateurs* employed by the CHIGACO POLICE DEPARTMENT did their part to entrap Weathermen. One was expelled from Northwestern University after assaulting the school's president; another admitted supplying explosives to the WUO; a third admitted assaulting a uniformed policemen in the Days of Rage demonstrations; and a fourth tried unsuccessfully to form a WUO sniper team, with the purpose of killing police.

Thus infiltrated and bedeviled by police and the FBI's illegal COINTELPRO operators, it is no surprise that the WUO suffered a fatal rift in the summer of 1976. Gender, race and organizational issues prompted a split in the ranks, producing the rival Central Committee and Revolutionary Committee. At year's end, the Revolutionary Committee expelled its more "conservative" critics, and three months later created a Prairie Fire Organizing Committee to speak for the WUO "above ground." Few were listening by then, although the FBI kept hunting WEATHERFUGS without success. Five members surrendered in New York, in November 1977, and others slowly surfaced over the next two decades, with the last arrest reported in 1996.

FBI pursuit of the WUO was relentless, if rarely successful. Director J. EDGAR HOOVER feared the Weathermen so much that he relaxed the Bureau's dress code for the first time in his left and let a group of G-men (dubbed "THE BEARDS") grow shaggy hair to infiltrate the group. In New York City, FBI SQUAD 47 burglarized the homes of individuals related to known WEATHERFUGS, but the campaign backfired in 1978, when FBI officials EDWARD MILLER and W. MARK FELT were indicted for authorizing illegal BREAK-INS. Both were convicted in 1980, then pardoned months later by President RONALD REAGAN. The crowning embarrassment came when two WUO veterans, Dana Biberman and Judy Clark, sued the Bureau from prison for alleged CIVIL RIGHTS violations. Although the defendants were serving life terms for robbery and murder, FBI HEADQUARTERS still lost its case and was forced to pay an undisclosed "monetary settlement favorable to the plaintiffs."

**WEAVER, Randall Claude**—A native of Villisca, Iowa, born 3 January 1948, Randall Weaver graduated from high school at Jefferson, Iowa in 1966 and enrolled at Iowa Central Community College. There he met his future wife, Vicki Jordison, in 1967. A year later Weaver quit school and joined the U.S. Army, with the announced goal of fighting in the VIETNAM WAR, but even after qualifying for the Special Forces he received a stateside posting and was discharged in October 1971 without seeing action. Weaver wanted to join the FBI, but with a wife and children on the way he could not afford to finish college. By the late 1970s, the Weavers had drifted into "Christian Identity," a racist, anti-Semitic sect much favored by neo-Nazis and members of the KU KLUX KLAN. In 1983 they moved to Ruby Ridge, Idaho, near Aryan Nations headquarters.

The Weavers' politics became increasingly extreme over the next decade. In February 1985 they filed an affidavit with the Boundary County court, claiming to be victims of a smear campaign initiated by the FBI, the SECRET SERVICE and the county sheriff. Specifically, Weaver claimed:

> My accusers set me up as a criminal member of the Aryan Nations. They accused me of having illegal weapons. They accused me of saying I was going to assassinate the president of the United States and the Pope. Very possibly a threatening letter was sent to the president with my name or initials forged. My accusers hoped that the FBI would "rush" my home with armed agents hoping I would feel the need to defend myself and thus be killed or arrested for "assault on a federal official." Fortunately bad weather (the first part of Feb. 1985), witnesses to this plot, and our God, the Lord Jesus Messiah, King of Israel, prevented a disaster.

In 1988 Weaver ran for sheriff and lost. A year later, while attending the Aryan World Congress, he met an undercover agent from the BUREAU OF ALCOHOL, TOBACCO AND FIREARMS (BATF) who persuaded Weaver to sell him two illegal sawed-off shotguns. In June 1990, according to Weaver, BATF agents threatened to prosecute him unless he served as an INFORMANT within the Aryan Nations. Weaver refused and was subsequently arrested on 17 January 1991. His court date was set for 20 February, but the notice sent to Weaver's home mistakenly listed the date as 30 *March* 1991. He failed to appear for trial on 20 February, and a federal grand jury convened on 14 March—still six days before the trial date printed on his formal notice—to indict Weaver as a fugitive. Although informed of the clerical error by a deputy sheriff, Judge Harold Ryan signed the arrest warrant.

Regarding the "mistake" as further proof of a conspiracy against him, Weaver holed up at his isolated cabin. Agents from the U.S. MARSHALS SERVICE invaded his property on 21 August 1992 and a chaotic shootout erupted, killing Marshal William Degan, Weaver's 14-year-old son, and the family dog. A day later, 50 members of the FBI's HOSTAGE RESCUE TEAM surrounded Weaver's cabin, including 11 snipers acting under orders that any armed adult seen on the property "could and should be the subject of DEADLY FORCE." It was, in effect, a "shoot on sight" order that clearly violated standard FBI procedure in such cases.

The source of that order remains unclear today, but its tragic result is well known. On the afternoon of 22 August, Randall Weaver and a friend, Kevin Harris, emerged from the cabin with rifles. FBI agents later testified (some say falsely) that Weaver and Harris aimed their weapons at a Bureau helicopter passing overhead. FBI sniper LON HORIUCHI fired on both men as they ran back toward the cabin, wounding Harris and killing Vicki Weaver as she stood inside the cabin, holding her 10-month-old daughter. A nine-day siege ensued, with Harris evacuated on 30 August, while Weaver and his three surviving children surrendered peacefully the following day.

Weaver and Harris were charged with killing Marshal Degan; Weaver also faced additional charges of assaulting federal officers, possessing illegal weapons, and failure to appear on the original firearms charge, while Harris was charged with "harboring" a federal fugitive. On 8 July 1993 jurors acquitted both defendants of murder; Harris was acquitted of harboring Weaver; and Weaver was acquitted on all remaining counts except the minor charges of failure to appear in court and committing a crime while on release. He received am 18-month prison sentence (less 14 months served prior to trial), with a $10,000 fine and three years' probation upon release.

The case, however, was far from resolved. Conservative outrage over the FBI's conduct helped spawn the far-right MILITIA MOVEMENT in 1994, while criticism of Bureau tactics echoed in the press and in Congress. Director LOUIS FREEH announced in January 1995 that while no criminal violations had been found, 12 G-men would be disciplined for "inadequate performance, improper judgment, neglect of duty, and failure to exert proper managerial oversight." One of those censured, siege commander Eugene Glenn, complained to the JUSTICE DEPARTMENT that field agents had been singled out as scapegoats, while higher-ups at FBI HEADQUARTERS (including Larry Potts, promoted by Freeh while still under investigation) were whitewashed. In August 1995 the Bureau's OFFICE OF PROFESSIONAL RESPONSIBILITY (OPR) announced an investigation of suspected criminal misconduct by six FBI administrators (including Potts), who were accused of destroying various documents relevant to the case. Freeh suspended the six pending resolution of the matter, while the government paid Weaver $3.1 million for the wrongful deaths of his wife and son.

Congress launched its own parallel investigation of the siege and produced a sharply critical report, but the FBI's internal probe was more methodical. A full two years elapsed before the OPR issued its final report in August 1997, exonerating five of the six official suspects. Only Michael Kahoe faced criminal charges, for destroying a critical "after action" report prepared in November 1992. Kahoe pled guilty to the charge in October 1997; he received an 18-month prison sentence, with a $4,000 fine and two years' probation on release from custody. Idaho prosecutors, meanwhile, indicted sniper Lon Horiuchi for manslaughter in Vicki Weaver's death, but federal judge Edward Lodge ruled in May 1998 that any charges against Horiuchi should be filed and tried by the federal government.

And still the case would not die. In August 2001 the *Washington Post* reported that Justice officials had launched yet another review of the Ruby Ridge standoff, this time investigating charges that FBI leaders illegally retaliated against three agents who reported official misconduct in the case. G-men Frank Perry, John Roberts and John Werner, assigned to review the Hostage Rescue Team's performance in 1992, claimed that their findings of malfeasance were ignored and that they were threatened or passed over for promotion as a result of their findings. Thus far (as of March 2003), no results of that inquiry have been published.

**WEBSTER, William H.**—A native of St. Louis, born 26 March 1924, William Webster served with the U.S. Navy in WORLD WAR II, then received his B.A. degree from Amherst College (Massachusetts) in 1947 and earned his J.D. degree from Washington University Law School two years later. He thereafter practiced law in St. Louis from 1949 to 1969, with an interval of naval duty during the Korean War and brief service as a federal prosecutor in Missouri (1960-61). President RICHARD NIXON appointed Webster a federal judge in 1970, his cases including the peculiar BANK ROBBERY prosecution of defendant JOHN LARRY RAY. In 1973 Nixon elevated Webster to the 8th Circuit Court of Appeals, where he remained until President RONALD REAGAN chose him to serve as FBI director. Webster officially replaced Director CLARENCE KELLEY on 23 February 1978.

Webster's tenure as director was marked by some dramatic changes in FBI procedures. He emphasized diversity in hiring, greatly increasing the number of BLACK, HISPANIC and WOMAN AGENTS employed by the Bureau. Webster also expanded the FBI's range of UNDERCOVER OPERATIONS, emphasizing pursuit of white-collar crimes and ORGANIZED CRIME until President Reagan sharply curtailed those activities. Under Webster, use of court-ordered WIRETAPS more than tripled, rising from 326 (in 1977-80) to 733 (in 1983-84). He once boasted to journalist Ronald Kessler that since J. EDGAR HOOVER's death in 1972 there had not been "a single proven case of a violation of constitutional rights" by FBI agents, but Webster and Kessler — who called the director "a legend" — both ignored the Bureau's persecution of PUERTO RICAN NATIONALISTS and the AMERICAN INDIAN MOVEMENT (the latter instance resulting in outspoken condemnation of a federal judge for illegal tactics employed in the WOUNDED KNEE SIEGE of 1973). Likewise, at the time Webster spoke to Kessler, his G-men were pursuing an identical campaign against the COMMITTEE IN SOLIDARITY WITH THE PEOPLE OF EL SALVADOR and harassing other critics of Ronald Reagan's foreign policy in Central America.

Reagan, for his part, admired Webster enough to name him director of the CENTRAL INTELLIGENCE AGENCY in 1987. Webster left the FBI on 26 May and spent four years in his new post, retiring in May 1991. A decade later, on 29 August 2001, Attorney General JOHN ASHCROFT named Webster chairman of a commission to study security policies for sensitive and classified information at the FBI. The commission was scheduled to complete its review by 31 March 2002, but its work was interrupted two weeks later, by the catastrophic TERRORIST attacks of 11 September 2001. The Webster Commission's final report offered various prescriptions for improvement in FBI performance and closed with the following observations:

> Our report is critical of the FBI and with justification. However, we recognize that the Bureau has taken many steps, in light of ROBERT HANSSEN'S treason, to improve security. Furthermore, in consistently finding the Bureau's security policy and practice deficient when compared with security at other entities within the Intelligence Community, we do not mean to single out the FBI for criticism. The security programs in most agencies to which we turned to develop a best-practices model have resulted from radical restructuring made necessary as one after another agency discovered that its core had been penetrated by disloyal employees working for foreign interests. Had the FBI learned from the disasters these agencies experienced, perhaps Hanssen would have been caught sooner or would have been deterred from violating his oath to the Bureau and his country. But it is equally true that, had those agencies learned from disturbing patterns of espionage across the Intelligence Community, other treacherous moles might have been caught or deterred. Consequently, in addition to the particular recommendations about Bureau policies we make in our Report, we also make a more global recommendation: a system should be established whereby security lapses in particular entities lead to improved security measures throughout the entire Intelligence Community.
>
> In sum, we do not mean to gainsay the steps the Bureau has taken since Hanssen's arrest to safeguard national security information. Many of those steps have been significant, as has the Bureau's cooperation as we conducted our review. However, before the Bureau can remedy deficiencies in particular security programs, it must recognize structural deficiencies in the way it approaches security and institutional or cultural biases that make it difficult for the FBI to accept security as a core function.

**WEISKOPF, Frantisek Carl**—Born at Prague (then a part of Bohemia) in 1900, F.C. Weiskopf joined the Czech COMMUNIST PARTY in 1920 and rose to a post on its central committee, while emerging as a prominent journalist, later penning several novels. Marked for extermination by ADOLF HITLER'S Nazi regime, Weiskopf fled to France in 1938, and from there to the United States. He arrived in New York on 1 June 1939, as a guest of the League of American Writers, planning a "short stay" that lasted for nearly a decade.

Despite their reputation for sniffing out "Reds," FBI agents had no inkling of Weiskopf's political connections until July 1942, when they intercepted a letter from surveillance target EGON KISCH. By 1943, Weiskopf had earned a place on both the Bureau's "key list" and in the illegal SECURITY INDEX, various hyperbolic memos describing him as a "comintern dictator" and a "commissar in the 'League of American Writers'," accusing Weiskopf (with no supporting evidence) of working for Hitler's Gestapo between 1939 and 1941. G-men collected samples of his handwriting and speculated on Weiskopf's undocumented links to an anti-Nazi resistance group called *Rote Kapelle* ("Red Chapel"), described in FBI documents as a "Western European Soviet-espionage network."

Weiskopf became a Czech diplomat in 1947, protected by his status from arrest, if not continuing surveillance. STATE DEPARTMENT agents followed his career abroad, including his 1949 appointment as the Czech ambassador to Mao Zedong's China. Weiskopf died in Berlin in 1955. His FBI dossier included more than 1,000 pages at his death, fully 800 of them withheld four decades later, "in the interest of national security or foreign policy."

**WELLES, Benjamin Sumner**—A New York City native, born 14 October 1892, Sumner Welles was a longtime friend of FRANKLIN ROOSEVELT, serving as a member of the future president's wedding party in March 1905. Roosevelt appointed Welles ambassador to Cuba in 1933, and later Undersecretary of State, sometimes preferring his advice to that of Secretary Cordell Hull. Welles supported FDR's unprecedented third-term bid in July 1940, as a Maryland delegate to the Democratic National Convention. Two months later, he became embroiled in a scandal that prematurely ended his career.

The incident occurred in September 1940, as Welles was returning to Washington by train, from the Alabama funeral of House Speaker William Bankhead. Official reports, long suppressed, claim that Welles invited several black Pullman porters to his sleeping compartment and offered them money for sex. A whispering campaign ensued, and presidential aide Harry Hopkins ordered an FBI investigation in January 1941. Director J. EDGAR HOOVER assigned EDWARD TAMM to handle the inquiry, allegedly confirming the allegations and revealing prior incidents of HOMOSEXUAL activity between Welles and various black men in Washington, D.C. Hoover briefed Roosevelt on 29 January 1941, but the president remained skeptical.

What happened next remains a matter of ongoing controversy. Welles maintained his STATE DEPARTMENT post for two more years, but rumors of his sexual behavior circulated freely in Washington and beyond. Hoover denied any part in spreading those rumors, but Harold Ickes (Secretary of the Interior, 1933-46) has said that Hoover approached him with claims of "absolute proof that Welles is a homosexual ... and he did not ask that I hold this information in confidence.... To my surprise, I found that Hoover was very talkative." There is also reason to believe that Hoover may have engineered the 1940 incident himself, to remove the liberal Welles from office. A retired FBI agent told author Charles Higham that G-men paid the Pullman porters to entrap Welles, and Assistant Secretary of State Adolf Berle confirmed that the September incident was "a put-up job." Years later, Berle's widow told author Anthony Summers that President Roosevelt was enraged by the FRAME-UP. "After it was all over," she claimed, "Roosevelt told Hoover to get out, and he never received him again."

Be that as it may, there was no saving Welles from the Washington rumor mill. He resigned from the State Department in August 1943, citing an illness in the family, but government insiders knew the truth. Welles later served as a member of the Council on Foreign Relations. He died on 24 September 1961.

**WERFEL, Franz**—A Jewish native of Prague, born in 1890, Franz Werfel is best known for his plays and novels celebrating heroism, human brotherhood, and religious faith. The carnage of WORLD WAR I converted him to pacifism. Residing in Germany when ADOLF HITLER'S Nazis rose to power in 1933, Werfel fled first to Austria, then Paris (1938), and finally to the United States (1940), where he settled in southern California. He published his most famous novel, *The Song of Bernadette*, a year later, around the same time that an unnamed "reliable source" informed FBI agents (falsely) that Werfel had been "a leader of the COMMUNIST PARTY in Germany, involved "for many years ... with radical activities" in Berlin and Vienna. A second INFORMANT, hopelessly confused, claimed Werfel as involved with a Mexican group of "Fifth Columnists ... closely connected with either Nazism, Fascism or Communism." G-men were suspicious of Werfel's involvement with the Joint Anti-Fascist Refugee Committee, and noted ominously that his wife, although a Roman Catholic, "had twice married Jews." The Bureau apparently lost interest in Werfel following his death in California, on 26 August 1945.

**WHARTON, Edith**—Born Edith Jones on 24 January 1862, novelist Edith Wharton spent most of her life in France and died there in 1937. Another eight years passed before the FBI saw fit to open a file in her name, after her 1921 Pulitzer Prize-winning novel *The Age of Innocence* appeared on a list of books owned by an unnamed target of a Bureau "loyalty" investigation in Kansas City. Agents noted that the list also included novels by presumed "subversives" JOHN STEINBECK, JOHN HERSEY, ERNEST HEMINGWAY, SINCLAIR LEWIS, THOMAS WOLFE and RICHARD WRIGHT.

**WHEELER, Burton Kendall**—Born at Hudson, Massachusetts on 27 February 1882, Burton Wheeler later settled in Montana and entered politics there, serving in the state legislature (1911-13) and as a federal prosecutor (1913-18) before he was elected to the U.S. Senate in 1922. His arrival in Washington, D.C. coincided with exposure of the TEAPOT DOME SCANDAL and investigations launched by Montana Senator THOMAS WALSH. Wheeler soon led his own investigation of the JUSTICE DEPARTMENT and Attorney General HARRY DAUGHERTY, recalled long after the fact in his memoirs.

> When I first came to Washington and began the investigation of the Department of Justice, Mr. [J. EDGAR] HOOVER was present at the investigation and hearings, and sat through them during the time the charges against Mr. Daugherty were being heard. Agents of the Department raided my offices; they broke into my offices ... they stationed men at my house, surrounded my house, and shadowed my wife.... During all that time there were in the Department of Justice ... [Director WILLIAM] BURNS and Mr. Hoover.

When surveillance and intimidation failed to halt Wheeler's investigation of Justice, G-men arranged to catch him in a hotel room with a woman other than his wife, but friends warned Wheeler of the trap and he avoided it. Next, four weeks into the hearings, a federal grand jury in Great Falls, Montana indicted Wheeler for bribery, but he was cleared of those charges with Senator Walsh serving as his defense counsel. During the trial, 30 FBI agents circulated through Great Falls, reporting nightly to Hoover in Washington, while a turncoat at Justice delivered the phone logs to Wheeler.

In March 1924 Wheeler asked Attorney General Daugherty for his files on the Teapot Dome investigation. Daugherty refused to permit a "fishing expedition," but his defiance backfired, prompting his dismissal by President CALVIN COOLIDGE. New Attorney General HARLAN STONE delivered the files in April, but Wheeler found that "they appeared to have already been emasculated." Publicity from the Senate hearings won Wheeler a place as the Progressive Party's vice presidential candidate in 1924, and while the ticket collected nearly 5 million votes, that was still below one-third of Coolidge's winning majority.

In March 1933, soon after Senator Walsh died en route to accept appointment as President FRANKLIN ROOSEVELT'S attorney general, friends in the Democratic Party told Wheeler that Roosevelt had agreed to dismiss Hoover from the FBI at Wheeler's request. Three decades later, Wheeler wrote, "Hoover got wind of this talk and came to see me. He insisted he played no part in the reprisals against me. I had no desire to ask for Hoover's head on a platter—and I'm glad I didn't." Still, they would never be friends, and Assistant FBI Director WILLIAM SULLIVAN recalled that Wheeler "started off distrusting Hoover and he ended up distrusting him."

That mistrust was showcased in March 1940, when Wheeler chaired a committee investigating U.S. police misconduct since the outbreak of WORLD WAR II in Europe. While the FBI was never specifically named, Wheeler made clear in private that Hoover and the Bureau were his primary targets. The committee's final report condemned the "resurgence of a spy system" targeting persons for their political belief and catalogued various abuses including illegal searches, "third-degree" interrogations and detentions without legal counsel. Two months later, Wheeler's name headed the list of 131 administration critics slated for renewed investigation by the FBI.

Defeated in his 1946 reelection bid, Wheeler left the Senate in January 1947 and returned to private legal practice. He outlived J. Edgar Hoover by nearly three years, and died in Washington on 6 January 1975.

**WHITE, Harry Dexter**—A Boston native, born in 1892, Harry White served as a first lieutenant during WORLD WAR I and later taught economics for six years at Harvard University, while working toward his Ph.D. (awarded in 1930). Appointed as an aide to Secretary of the Treasury Henry Morgenthau in 1934, White was later promoted as Assistant Secretary of the Treasury. President HARRY TRUMAN subsequently nominated White to serve as executive director of the International Monetary Fund, in January, but a heart attack forced his retirement from government service in 1947. Another full year passed before White, then retired, was publicly accused of spying for the Soviet Union.

The accusation came from ELIZABETH BENTLEY, a former COMMUNIST PARTY member turned professional INFORMANT. Bentley raised White's name before the HOUSE COMMITTEE ON UN-AMERICAN ACTIVITIES (HUAC) on 30 July 1948, asserting that while she could not verify his party membership, White had several times furnished her with government documents via Red go-between Nathan Silvermaster. Four days later, ex-Communist Whittaker Chambers (later a key witness in the ALGER HISS case) told HUAC that White was "a fellow traveler so far within the fold that his not being a Communist would be a mistake on both sides." White addressed the committee on 13 August 1948, denying under oath that he ever met Bentley or Chambers, refuting all charges of ESPIONAGE and subversive activity. Three days later, another heart attack claimed his life at home, in Fitzwilliam, New Hampshire.

White's death opened the floodgates of a posthumous smear campaign spanning the next eight years. Whittaker Chambers, having initially denied any personal involvement in espionage, produced in November 1948 four pages of handwritten notes allegedly furnished by White years earlier, but the documents contained no classified information and were riddled with suspicious erasures, apparently made by Chambers himself. Indeed, the timing of the Bentley-Chambers accusations was apparently no accident: authors Curt Gentry and Anthony Summers suggest that FBI Director J. EDGAR HOOVER coordinated the HUAC revelations in a failed bid to ensure President Truman's November defeat by Republican contender THOMAS DEWEY.

Truman declined to seek reelection in 1952, leaving ADLAI STEVENSON to face war-hero opponent DWIGHT EISENHOWER, but Hoover was unwilling to let the president retire without a parting salvo of charges that Truman had been "soft on Communists" in federal service. On 6 November 1953, armed with information from FBI FILES, Attorney General HERBERT BROWNELL, JR., told assembled businessmen from the Executive Club of Chicago:

> Harry Dexter White was a Russian spy. He smuggled secret documents to Russian agents for transmission to Moscow. Harry Dexter White was known to be a Communist spy by the very people who appointed him to the most sensitive and important position he ever held in Government service.
>
> The FBI became aware of White's espionage activities at an early point in his Government career and from the beginning made reports on these activities to the appropriate officials in authority. But these reports did not impede White's advancement in the Administration....
>
> I can now announce officially, for the first time in public, that the records of my department show that White's spying activities for the Soviet Government were reported in detail by the FBI to the White House ... in December 1945.

Eleven days later, on 17 November 1953, Brownell and Hoover appeared together before the SENATE INTERNAL SECURITY SUBCOMMITTEE, expanding their previous charges. Hoover now claimed that he filed a total of seven reports on White's treasonous activities with the Truman White House, between November 1945 and July 1946. When hard proof was requested, though, Brownell drew the line, declaring, "We will never impair the most important work of the FBI by making public FBI reports." Unsubstantiated charges remained the order of the day in 1956, when author DON WHITEHEAD repeated Hoover's accusations against White in *The FBI Story*. To this day, no proof of White's employment as a spy for Russia (or for any other foreign power) has been revealed.

**WHITEHEAD, Don** — A coal miner's son, born at Inman, Virginia in 1908, Don Whitehead nurtured a lifelong interest in newspaper work, logging his first journalistic experience in high school. He left college in 1928 to work as a reporter, and so distinguished himself as a combat correspondent in WORLD WAR II that he was nicknamed "Beachhead Don," for his frequent presence at Allied amphibious landings. Whitehead won two Pulitzer Prizes for his coverage of the Korean war, in 1951 and 1952, before assuming Stateside roles as a feature writer for the Associated Press and Washington bureau chief of the New York *Herald Tribune*.

Whitehead's association with the FBI began in April 1954, when he interviewed J. EDGAR HOOVER in honor of Hoover's impending thirtieth anniversary as director. Their three-hour meeting spawned a series of laudatory articles that endeared Whitehead to Hoover, and someone raised the notion of an "authorized" Bureau history, considered at FBI headquarters since MAX LOWENTHAL published his critical treatment in 1950. Memories differ on whether Whitehead or someone else conceived the original project — Assistant to the Director LOUIS NICHOLS later claimed the idea was his; Whitehead disagreed — but the end result was guaranteed to win Hoover's unstinting approval. Nichols himself admittedly "reviewed the … manuscript, as it went along," and while he claimed the final result was "100 percent Whitehead," it might have been written by Hoover himself. Published by Random House in 1956, *The FBI Story* regurgitated every myth concocted by Bureau press agents over the past four decades, while slighting Hoover's enemies at every opportunity. (MELVIN PURVIS disappeared completely, and is nowhere mentioned in the text.) Hoover, in a brief foreword, pronounced himself "deeply grateful" for Whitehead's efforts to counteract "a campaign of falsehood and vilification … directed against the FBI by some ignorant and some subversive elements."

As a boost to sales, Hoover's ghost writers in the CRIME RECORDS DIVISION took over advance publicity for *The FBI Story*, recruiting WALTER WINCHELL and other media allies to book a guaranteed best-seller. Millionaire ex-bootlegger and Hoover crony LEWIS ROSENSTIEL shelled out $100,000 for 25,000 copies (and an equal number of Hoover's *Masters of Deceit*), for distribution to educational institutions. Whitehead's first-run printing of 50,000 copies sold out a week before the book's official publication date, with orders averaging 3,000 per day. *The FBI Story* stood on various best-seller lists for 38 weeks and was serialized in 170 newspapers. At the FBI ACADEMY, a captive audience of new trainees in every class was "encouraged" to purchase multiple copies as gifts for friends and relatives.

Hoover and Whitehead scored a second triumph in 1959, with a cinematic version of *The FBI Story*. Slipping even further into fiction, the film cast James Stewart as a heroic G-man assigned to every major Bureau case from the 1920s through WORLD WAR II. FBI headquarters hand-picked director Mervyn LeRoy for the film, and he in turn recalled that "Everybody on that picture, from the carpenters and electricians right to the top, everybody, had to be okayed by the FBI." The premiere reportedly left Hoover in tears.

Don Whitehead earned enough from book and movie sales to retire from newspaper work and finish his days as a full-time freelance author. Encouraged by his success with *The FBI Story*, he pursued other official histories, including a 1964 treatment of the U.S. Customs Service (*Border Guard*) and a puff piece on the Dow Chemical Corporation (*The Dow Story*, 1968) written at the height of protests against Dow's manufacture of napalm for use in the VIETNAM WAR. Whitehead revisited the Bureau's files in 1970, to whitewash Hoover's handling of CIVIL RIGHTS cases in *Attack on Terror: The FBI Against the Ku Klux Klan in Mississippi*. Whitehead tried to follow up with a biography of Hoover, after the director's death in 1972, but Acting Director CLYDE TOLSON vetoed the project. Whitehead died in 1981.

**WHITEHURST, Frederic** — Born in 1948, Fred Whitehurst earned four Bronze Stars for bravery in the VIETNAM WAR and displayed special valor on the night he stopped four fellow U.S. soldiers from torturing and raping a female villager. Back in civilian life, he earned a Ph.D. in chemistry and joined the FBI in 1982. Four years later he was assigned to the Bureau's LABORATOY DIVISION and spent most of the next decade as an explosives residue analyst with the Materials Analysis Unit.

Whitehurst encountered problems at the lab almost from the moment he was assigned to supervisor TERRY RUDOLPH for training. It soon became apparent that Rudolph and others cut corners in their work, skipping various tests required or "suggested" by FBI lab protocols, and that they often phrased reports in terms favoring the prosecution. Whitehurst was pressured to do likewise and complained repeatedly, without result. Finally, at the 1989 federal trial of defendant Steve Psinakis (accused of shipping explosives to the Philippines in an effort to topple U.S.-supported dictator Ferdinand Marcos), Whitehurst aired his concerns to the defense. Psinakis's attorney first suspected Whitehurst was "some kind of weirdo," but he soon embraced the G-man as an expert witness. Psinakis was acquitted, whereupon his prosecutors complained to the JUSTICE DEPARTMENT, expressing "serious questions" about "the FBI laboratory's procedures."

Still, slipshod work continued at the lab despite that episode and Whitehurst's ongoing complaints. In February 1993 he met twice with FBI Director WILLIAM SESSIONS, who promised a full investigation by the Bureau's OFFICE OF PROFESSIONAL RESPONSIBILITY (OPR). When nothing came of that, Whitehurst contacted the National Whistleblower Center (NWC) in Washington, sitting for interviews with the group's attorneys in October and December 1993. NWC lawyer Stephen Kohn wrote to FBI HEADQUARTERS in February 1994, demanding a full investigation of Whitehurst's charges, and Whitehurst personally took his complaints to the OPR around the same time. Attorneys from the OFFICE OF GENERAL COUNSEL interviewed Whitehurst in May 1994, reporting back to Justice that all of Whitehurst's complaints had been fully investigated and resolved except for charges he leveled against Terry Rudolph.

The falsity of that claim was revealed in 1995, when Whitehurst was subpoenaed as a defense witness in the second trial of defendants charged in the 1993 WORLD TRADE CENTER BOMBING. Judge Lance Ito refused to permit a similar appearance at the O.J.

Simpson murder trial, but Whitehurst's allegations went public in September 1995, with his appearance on ABC-TV's *Prime Time Live*. That broadcast named lab supervisor ROGER MARTZ as "one of the FBI agents who pressured Whitehurst to go along with allegedly altered test results." Lab spokesmen refused to be interviewed on camera, but they faxed ABC a statement claiming that the Bureau had thoroughly investigated Whitehurst's "concerns about forensic protocols and procedures" and "reviewed more than 250 cases involving work previously done by the Laboratory." The end result of that supposed investigation: "To date, the FBI has found no evidence of tampering, evidence fabrication or failure to report exculpatory evidence."

In fact, ABC's broadcast triggered the first real investigation so far, conducted over the next 18 months by the Inspector General's office. A 517-page draft report was submitted to Justice in January 1997, but its contents were withheld in a seeming effort to avoid further problems with the upcoming trial of Oklahoma City bomber TIMOTHY MCVEIGH. Whitehurst filed suit to compel publication in March 1997, supported by the NWC and the National Association of Defense Lawyers. Only then was a publication date fixed for 15 April 1997, with the McVeigh trial already in progress.

As a result of the Inspector General's findings, Roger Martz and DAVID WILLIAMS were removed from their posts at the lab; two other agents criticized in the report, JAMES THURMAN and MICHAEL MALONE, had already retired. Whitehurst was penalized at the same time, suspended and placed on administrative leave in a move that violated terms of the 1989 Whistleblower Protection Act. He sued the FBI again and won his case on 26 February 1998, when the Bureau agreed to pay him $1,166,000 for unlawful retaliation. Two weeks later, the Bureau settled a second lawsuit filed by Whitehurst under the Privacy Act. While most such claims are settled for $5,000 or less, the FBI agreed to pay Whitehurst $300,000 ($258,580 in legal fees plus the equivalent of salary and pension benefits he would have earned if still employed by the Bureau to retirement age). As part of the March settlement, FBI officials also promised to release 180,000 pages of lab reports prepared by analysts whom Whitehurst had publicly criticized.

**WICKERSHAM, George Woodward** —A Pittsburgh native, born 19 September 1858, George Wickersham assumed office as U.S. Attorney General on 5 March 1909, under President WILLIAM TAFT. Eleven days later, Wickersham formally named his department's small detective force the Bureau of Investigation, the name it would carry until June 1930. Under Wickersham the Bureau grew rapidly, its agent force more than doubling in size from 64 to 158. Most of that expansion was occasioned by passage of the MANN ACT in 1910, making G-men responsible for investigation of interstate car thefts. Wickersham left office on 5 March 1913 and returned to the private practice of law in New York. In 1929 President HERBERT HOOVER appointed him to chair the National Commission on Law Observance and Law Enforcement (better known as the Wickersham Commission). As the first federal assessment of nationwide law enforcement, the Wickersham Commission examined problems ranging from PROHIBITION vi-olations to POLICE BRUTALITY. Its final report was issued in 1931. Wickersham died in New York City on 26 January 1936.

**WILDER, Thornton** —A native of Madison, Wisconsin, born 17 April 1897, Thornton Wilder served as an army corporal in WORLD WAR I and as a lieutenant colonel with air corps intelligence in WORLD WAR II. He also won the Pulitzer Prize three times, for his novel *The Bridge at San Luis Rey* (1928) and for two plays: *Our Town* (1938) and *The Skin of Our Teeth* (1943). Wilder's case also illustrates the character of FBI duplicity under J. EDGAR HOOVER, 21 years of surveillance neatly summarized in a 1954 report that opens with a lie, proclaiming that "No investigation has been conducted by the bureau of Thornton Wilder."

In fact, as Wilder's dossier makes clear, G-men began to shadow him in 1933, when they identified him as a member of the National Committee of the American Committee for Struggle Against War, labeled a Soviet front by the HOUSE COMMITTEE ON UN-AMERICAN ACTIVITIES (HUAC). Two years later, Wilder earned another Bureau citation by joining the American League Against War and Fascism. In 1937 agents noted his participation in the Second National Congress of the League of American Writers. The following year, G-men ignored his second Pulitzer award but preserved Wilder's "subversive" comment that "I am unreservedly for the legal government and Loyalist party in Spain" (then under assault by ADOLF HITLER and Benito Mussolini). The year 1938 also witnessed Wilder's signing, with 38 other noted writers, of a letter asking President FRANKLIN ROOSEVELT to end U.S. trade with Nazi Germany. FBI agents pointedly observed that while Wilder's name was found "on the Republican voting list," he had "boosted for President Roosevelt" in the 1936 campaign. In 1939, Wilder earned another black mark by signing a letter from the League of American Writers, supporting a new Federal Arts project.

The Bureau's non-investigation of Wilder took a bizarre turn in 1940, when agents mistook him for "the mysterious Captain" said to command a German spy brigade operating from an Austrian refugee camp at Keene, New Hampshire. They also suspected Wilder of "dominating" an unnamed "elderly lady whose home was originally in Cambridge, Mass." The year-long search for evidence went nowhere, probably because the Bureau's lead INFORMANT was "the girl at the Eskimo stand on the road leading up to the camp." The most incriminating information uncovered in 1940-41 was Wilder's membership in the American Committee for the Protection of the Foreign Born, the National Committee for People's Rights (condemned by HUAC), and the National Council of American-Soviet Friendship. Even so, agents concluded that Wilder was "good mainly for signatures to open letters ... but 'not much action.'"

That view seems to have changed with the onset of WORLD WAR II, when Wilder joined the War Writers Board, then enlisted with the army air corps. In June 1942, a *Chicago Tribune* editorial included Wilder's name on a list of prominent authors, suspected of treason because they had publicly spoken of "winning the war at home." Throughout Wilder's service in uniform, he was subject to a special "FBI Watch" that included interception of his mail, branded as a "Suspect" with no offense specified.

The non-investigation continued through the postwar Red scare, with a notation of Wilder's signature on a 1948 letter denouncing HUAC and three FBI "name checks" in the 1950s, one each for the Air Force, the STATE DEPARTMENT, and the CENTRAL INTELLIGENCE AGENCY. Three more name checks, complete with fingerprint reviews, were ordered by the White House in the 1960s. Hoover was still circulating documents from Wilder's file to other agencies as late as 1970, five years before the writer's death. A decade later, when author Herbert Mitgang sought release of Wilder's dossier under the FREEDOM OF INFORMATION ACT, 90 pages were delivered, all heavily censored, while eight more were withheld "in the interest of national security."

**WILKINS, Roy Ottoway**—A St. Louis native, Roy Wilkins was born in St. Louis on 30 August 1901. (His father missed the event, having fled town a short time earlier to avoid LYNCHING, after he ignored demands to step aside and yield the public sidewalk to a white man.) Raised in St. Paul, Minnesota, Wilkins attended integrated schools and earned a bachelor's degree in sociology from the University of Minnesota in 1923. He worked as a journalist for black newspapers over the next eight years, before joining the NATIONAL ASSOCIATION FOR THE ADVANCEMENT OF COLORED PEOPLE (NAACP) as assistant executive secretary in 1931. In 1955, as the U.S. CIVIL RIGHTS movement entered its most active phase, Wilkins succeeded Walter White as national leader of the NAACP.

Despite his ranking as one of America's "Big Six" civil rights leaders in the 1950s and 1960s, Wilkins was naturally conservative, unable to discard the term "Negro" in favor of "black" as his colleagues became increasingly militant. FBI agents had monitored the NAACP almost from its beginnings in 1909, treating it as a "radical" organization, but Bureau leaders acknowledged that Wilkins "has been strongly anti-communist, and has done everything possible to keep the NAACP clear of communist infiltration." Those efforts included cooperation with the FBI in purging alleged COMMUNIST PARTY members during the early 1950s, when J. EDGAR HOOVER ordered Assistant to the Director LOUIS NICHOLS to furnish Wilkins classified material "regarding Communist activities directed at the NAACP."

At the same time, Hoover increased surveillance on the NAACP and circulated derogatory information on Wilkins to the U.S. Civil Rights Commission, striving to undercut his standing with the federal government. Smear campaigns notwithstanding, Hoover also sought to manipulate Wilkins, using him in an effort to disrupt the broader civil rights movement. Prior to the 1963 March on Washington, G-men leaked adverse material on colleague BAYARD RUSTIN to Wilkins, prompting Wilkins to complain of Ruskin's role in the march and links to "subversive elements in the larger society." Hoover also capitalized on Wilkins's well-known dislike for Dr. MARTIN LUTHER KING, JR., treating him to sex tapes recorded via illegal BUGGING of King's hotel rooms.

In January 1964, as part of the Bureau's ongoing COINTELPRO campaigns, Assistant Director WILLIAM SULLIVAN recommended Dr. King's replacement with the "right kind" of African American, nominating Wilkins as "a man of character" who fit the bill. Assistant Director CARTHA DELOACH met Wilkins that summer, afterward reporting to FBI HEADQUARTERS that Wilkins was willing to help remove King "from the national picture." DeLoach claimed that Wilkins had promised to tell King "he can't win a battle with the FBI" and that "the best thing for him to do is to retire from public life." Hoover passed that word to President LYNDON JOHNSON on 30 November 1964, while Wilkins later denied it, calling DeLoach's account "self-serving and filled with inaccuracies." Whatever the truth of that encounter, FBI memos from March 1965 describe Wilkins as an FBI "source," laying plans for a meeting of "reputable Negroes" that would preach "the facts" of Bureau civil rights achievements while promoting "the stature of Roy Wilkins." (The meeting never occurred.)

Throughout the latter 1960s, FBI spokesmen hailed Wilkins as a "restraining influence" on ghetto rioters, and President Johnson regarded him as one of the civil rights movement's "real leaders" (in contrast to Dr. King and other "loudmouths" who had lately joined in VIETNAM WAR PROTESTS). King's 1968 assassination and the rapid shift of secondary spokesmen from nonviolence to "Black Power" scuttled any further plans for elevating Wilkins to command of the movement. President RICHARD NIXON requested a Bureau "name check" on Wilkins in 1970, presumably for inclusion on one of the various White House "enemies" lists. Wilkins retired from leadership of the NAACP in 1977 and died in New York City on 8 September 1981.

**WILKINSON, Elbert Claude ("Bill")**—A native of Galvez, Louisiana, Bill Wilkinson graduated from high school at age 16 and immediately joined the navy, serving as a cryptographer aboard the nuclear submarine *USS Simon Bolivar*. He retired from the service after eight years and settled in Denham Springs, Louisiana, where he soon joined David Duke's Knights of the KU KLUX KLAN. Wilkinson rapidly won promotion to serve as the state's "grand dragon," doubling as editor of Duke's *Crusader* newsletter. In August 1975 Wilkinson quarreled with Duke over money and defected to lead his own Invisible Empire Knights of the KKK.

By 1979 Wilkinson's faction ranked as the largest Klan in the U.S., its membership including one-fifth to one-third of all active Klan members. It was also the most violent, known for public displays of firearms and Wilkinson's statements that "These guns ain't for rabbit hunting; they're to waste people." Wilkinson proved adept at capitalizing on black CIVIL RIGHTS demonstrations, using a method his rivals called "ambulance chasing." His Klansmen clashed violently with protesters in Oklona and Tupelo, Mississippi, and in Decatur, Alabama. In autumn 1980 Wilkinson announced that his Klan was expanding beyond Dixie, with recruiting drives in Pennsylvania and Connecticut.

The end came for Wilkinson in early 1983, when articles in the Nashville *Tennesseean* named him as a longtime FBI INFORMANT. Wilkinson acknowledged reporting to the Bureau since 1974, but claimed he had given G-men no information they could not have gleaned from the mainstream media. Hundreds of Klansmen resigned in the wake of that exposé, and Wilkinson declared his Klan bankrupt on 27 January 1983. Observers familiar with the FBI's COINTELPRO campaigns professed to see the Bureau's hand at work in Wilkinson's downfall.

**WILLIAMS, David**—Although his major field of college study was zoology,, David Williams spent his first five years with the FBI (1977-82) in the Explosives Unit of the LABORATORY DIVISION. He was then transferred to a field office for five years, but returned to the crime lab in 1987. Six years later, Williams was assigned as the agent in charge of analyzing evidence from the WORLD TRADE CENTER BOMBING. In that capacity, he clashed with explosive residue analyst FREDERICK WHITEHURST, editing Whitehurst's lab reports to eliminate any qualifying remarks on the possible sources of chemicals found at the blast site. As Williams later explained his actions to investigators from the Inspector General's office, "I felt that was fluff, that wasn't necessary.... And the fact that he's putting in any possibility of where this material could have come from was bullshit. If he was going to go into where these chemicals could have originated from, why didn't he make an opinion that this World Trade Center could have been damaged by an act of God or lightning?" Williams was a key witness at both Trade Center bombing trials, and the *New York Times* had this to say about his testimony in 1995:

> The purpose of a criminal trial is of course to determine guilt. The issue of guilt is the ultimate question to which all others are directed. In contrast Williams began with a presumption of guilt as a foundation on which to build inferences.... The agent simply assumed that the perpetrators produced a 1,200 pound bomb at the Trade Center using the urea and nitric acid missing from the defendants' facility and that the yield (the amount used at the bombing divided by the amount missing) informed his testimony about "non-laboratory yield."

Williams delivered a similar performance in the Oklahoma City bombing case that saw defendant TIMOTHY MCVEIGH executed for mass murder. While supervising a search of the crime scene, Williams amazed other experts by declaring, "If you can't see it at rake's length, it's not worth picking up. We've got thousands of pieces. We don't need to pick up any more." Ed Kelso, an Explosives Unit colleague, dubbed Williams "a laughingstock" for those pronouncements, but his errors did not end with the search. At trial it was revealed that Williams had essentially destroyed the crucial chain of custody by instructing subordinates to scratch his initials on virtually every piece of evidence collected, whether he personally saw it or not.

After numerous complaints from Fred Whitehurst, the Inspector General's office finally launched an investigation of FBI lab procedures in 1995. When the IG's final report was submitted in January 1997, Williams and two other analysts (ROGER MARTZ and JAMES THURMAN) were removed from their lab assignments. Even then, another 16 months elapsed before Williams received a written censure for providing "overstated, inaccurate and unsupported expert opinions in the World Trade Center and Oklahoma City" cases. Senator CHARLES GRASSLEY, an outspoken critic of Bureau malfeasance, complained that "The FBI has succeeded in protecting its rogues in the lab scandal." Williams,

meanwhile, found the wrist-slap punishment too harsh and announced his intent to appeal in August 1998.

**WILLIAMS, Robert Franklin**—A grandson of former slaves, born at Monroe, North Carolina in 1925, Robert F. Williams led his first political action (a machinist's strike) at age 16. Two years later, he was working at a Detroit auto plant when white mobs and police attacked the city's black community, leaving 34 persons dead and 700 injured in the wake of a two-day riot. Discharged from the U.S. Marine Corps in 1955, Williams returned to Monroe and was chosen to lead the local chapter of the NATIONAL ASSOCIATION FOR THE ADVANCEMENT OF COLORED PEOPLE. Violent opposition from the KU KLUX KLAN soon escalated to the point where Williams felt obliged to purchase rifles (with donations from the NATION OF ISLAM) and mount guards to repel nocturnal invasions of the black community. Reports of the local resistance movement were broadcast nationwide after Williams and company traded shots with Klan terrorists on the night of 5 October 1957.

Racial violence in Monroe peaked during 1961, when Williams led a campaign to desegregate the town's public swimming pool. Participants in the integrated "FREEDOM RIDES" came to join the protests on 25 August 1961 and new rioting followed, with more Klan raids on the black Newton district. On the night of 27 August a white couple unwittingly drove into the combat zone and found themselves caught in the cross-fire. Williams escorted them to his home and sheltered them for several hours, until it was safe for them to leave. Local authorities seized the opportunity to file KIDNAPPING charges against Williams and four other defendants.

Williams and his wife promptly fled Monroe, beginning a 12-year exile that included residence in Cuba, China, North Vietnam and Tanzania. FBI agents scoured the U.S. for Williams, and after failing in that pursuit they launched a COINTELPRO disruption campaign against the multi-racial Committee to Aid the Monroe Defendants, organized by members of the NAACP and the SOCIALIST WORKERS PARTY (SWP). In May 1962 the Bureau's New York City field office suggested (and J. EDGAR HOOVER approved) a series of anonymous telephone calls to create friction between the SWP and the NAACP. Williams, meanwhile, broadcast "Radio Free Dixie" bulletins from Cuba and persuaded Chinese leader Mao Zedong to make public statements supporting the black liberation struggle in America. At home, various groups including the Deacons for Defense and the BLACK PANTHER PARTY followed Williams's example by adopting postures of armed self-defense in the latter 1960s.

Williams and his wife returned to the U.S. in 1969, settling in Baldwin, Michigan. He successfully fought extradition to North Carolina, and all charges against him were finally dropped in January 1976. Williams died at Grand Rapids, Michigan on 15 October 1996.

**WILLIAMS, Tennessee**—A native of Columbus, Mississippi, born Thomas Lanier Williams on 26 March 1911, Tennessee Williams began writing at age sixteen and saw his first play produced in Memphis, during 1937. The FBI noticed him for the first time a decade later, after the *Daily Worker* praised his Pulitzer Prize-winning play *A Streetcar Named Desire*. (Agents mistook the play for a novel in their early memos.) In 1948, Williams earned another citation for sending personal greetings to the Moscow Art Theatre, at a time when the U.S. government was considering a cultural exchange program with Russia. (The troupe finally reached America in 1965.) Another *Daily Worker* clipping was filed in 1950, this one listing Williams among several "top show business cultural names" who opposed blacklisting of writers in Hollywood. A year later, agents found it noteworthy that his name appeared on the board of trustees for the Dramatic Workshop and Technical Institute.

In the 1960s, FBI agents abandoned their interest in Williams's politics and focused instead on his alleged HOMOSEXUALITY. A 1964 report, prepared at the STATE DEPARTMENT'S behest, declares that "the bureau ascertained that Thomas Lanier Williams has the reputation of being a homosexual." The same document also notes that "the Office of Naval Intelligence, in a separate inquiry, secured statements from individuals who admitted participating in homosexual acts with Williams." The motive for FBI investigation of a civilian playwright's sex life is anyone's guess. It remains unexplained in the seven-page dossier, stamped "Security Information — Confidential," that was released to author Herbert Mitgang under the FREEDOM OF INFORMATION ACT, several years after Williams's death in February 1983. Mitgang's requests for further information from the DEPARTMENT OF JUSTICE were uniformly rejected, allegedly to protect "confidential informants."

**WILLIAMS, Wayne Bertram** *see* ATKID

**WILLIAMS, William Carlos** — A native of Rutherford, New Jersey, born 17 September 1883, Williams studied medicine at Princeton and entered practice as a country doctor while completing his first book of poetry, published in 1909. Bureau agents first took note of Williams in 1930, when *New Masses* published a letter he sent to the magazine, reading in part:

> I like the JOHN REED number. Here's money. Send me more. The only thing is, what the hell? I feel in a false position. How can I be a Communist, being what I am. Poetry is the thing which has the hardest hold on me in my daily experiences. But I cannot, without an impossible wrench of my understanding, turn it into a force directed toward one end, Vote the Communist Ticket, or work for the world revolution.

G-men ignored the poet's protestation, noting that he wrote for *Partisan Review* "during the period of its domination by the COMMUNIST PARTY." In 1937 they reported that Williams had signed the Golden Book of American Friendship with the Soviet Union, and a year later he endorsed a statement calling for greater U.S. cooperation with Russia. Williams appended his signature to a similar letter in 1939 and earned another black mark by supporting the U.S. government's own Federal Arts Project (coincidentally endorsed by the *Daily Worker*). Surveillance was tightened in September 1942, after an unnamed source gave the Bureau "seventeen sheets bearing typewriting of a suspicious na-

ture." One FBI critic suspected Williams's poems might contain subversive coded messages, remarking that "they appear to have been written by a person who is very queer or possibly a mental case." Another five months of investigation was required to brand Williams "a sort of absent minded professor type but certainly 100% American," the confusion arising from his use of "an 'expressionistic' style which might be interpreted as being 'code.'"

The "100% American" endorsement was fleeting, at best. By 1943 Williams was under renewed investigation, this time for his college friendship with expatriate poet EZRA POUND. Suspicion of disloyalty lingered into 1951, when Williams was nominated to serve as Consultant in Poetry at the Library of Congress. J. EDGAR HOOVER scuttled that offer with a derogatory report, ironically handing the job to another target of Bureau surveillance, RANDALL JARRELL. A short time later, FBI sources leaked information to "friendly" journalist Fulton Lewis, Jr., who devoted a column to Williams's alleged "association with some of the smelly outfits that have been peddling Moscow propaganda in the U.S. for 25 years." Williams died on 4 March 1963, prior to receiving a Pulitzer Prize for literature in the same year.

**WILSON, Edmund** — Born at Red Bank, New Jersey on 8 May 1895, Edmund Wilson graduated from Princeton University in 1916 and served as a U.S. Army intelligence officer in WORLD WAR I. That experience may have contributed to a leftward political drift in the postwar years, including an outspoken devotion to socialism that spanned the next three decades. Regarded by many as the preeminent critic and literary historian of his day, Wilson served variously as the managing editor of *Vanity Fair*, as associate editor of the *New Republic*, and as a book critic/essayist for the *New Yorker*. He also published several books, some of which — like 1940's *To the Finland Station* — reveal a Marxist influence.

The FBI's investigation of Wilson remains shrouded in deliberate confusion. Author Natalie Robins reports, in *Alien Ink* (1992), that Wilson's "fourteen page file" was started in 1946 and that "certain documents" were still classified in 1987, 15 years after Wilson's death. Herbert Mitgang, meanwhile, writes in *Dangerous Dossiers* (1988) that 15 heavily-censored pages were released to him under the FREEDOM OF INFORMATION ACT, the earliest dating from 1951, and that "a second, smaller file on Wilson" was withheld entirely "in the interest of the national defense or foreign policy." Which version, if either, is correct? Given the FBI's propensity for evasion, no definitive answer is possible.

Whatever the truth, it is remarkable that G-men overlooked Wilson during the 1930s, when he was most active in left-wing causes. In 1932, Wilson visited striking coal miners in Harlan County, Kentucky, joined by WALDO FRANK and others whose presence was recorded by the FBI. Three years later, Wilson visited Soviet Russia, but the Bureau missed that trip as well. A pair of agents finally interviewed Wilson in 1951, feigning interest in a third party, recording Wilson's admission that he "tried to give Stalin the benefit of the doubt" in 1935, but later "realized that the Soviet Union under Stalin could never improve the plight of the masses and that the Russian Revolution had failed." J. EDGAR HOOVER passed that information along to the STATE DEPARTMENT in 1953, responding to a "name check" request on Wilson. Four years later, answering a similar request from the CENTRAL INTELLIGENCE AGENCY, Hoover reported that "Wilson was a Trotskyite during earlier years but is now actively anti-Communist."

The director had cause to regret that judgment in May 1961, when Wilson joined others in signing an open letter to the *New York Times*, asking President JOHN KENNEDY to withdraw U.S. support from trigger-happy gangs of Cuban exiles seeking to depose Fidel Castro. Four years later, Wilson was among the signers of a "Writers and Artists Protest" against the escalating VIETNAM WAR. The last known entry in his dossier dates from 1966, yet another name (and fingerprint) check requested by White House aides to President LYNDON JOHNSON, presumably related to Wilson's anti-war statements. Wilson died in New York City on 13 June 1972.

**WILSON, William Bauchop**—A native Scotsman, born at Blantyre on 2 April 1862, William Wilson immigrated to the U.S. with his family as a child and subsequently entered Democratic politics, serving three terms as a Pennsylvania congressman (1907-13). In March 1913 President WOODROW WILSON (no relation) tapped him as the first Secretary of Labor, a post he retained (albeit with some difficulty) until March 1921.

It was Wilson's misfortune to head the new LABOR DEPARTMENT (formerly Commerce and Labor, divided by President Wilson) during an era of unprecedented upheaval. Conservative businessmen and politicians lived in dread of an imminent revolution by ANARCHISTS or "Bolsheviks" (after 1917), and events seemed to bear out their worst fears. Radical LABOR UNIONS such as the INDUSTRIAL WORKERS OF THE WORLD (IWW) staged 3,600 strikes across the U.S. in 1919 alone, and the same year was marked by a series of still-unsolved bombings attributed to anarchist conspirators. To his credit, Secretary Wilson opposed most federal moves against the IWW, but autumn 1919 found him in a weakened state, stricken with illness, his wife and mother dying. Frequently absent from Washington, he met with Attorney General A. MITCHELL PALMER and J. EDGAR HOOVER long enough to agree that membership in the COMMUNIST PARTY should be a deportable offense under the Immigration Act of 1918, but he still did not foresee the massive dragnets planned by the JUSTICE DEPARTMENT. Examining the first 3,000 arrest warrants submitted by Hoover, Wilson dismissed many of the supporting affidavits as "flimsy," but he finally agreed to support Justice on the condition that Acting Secretary of Labor John Abercrombie review each case individually prior to deportation.

The resultant PALMER RAIDS of December 1919 were a chaotic nightmare. Wilson returned to find that Abercrombie had ignored his orders and sanctioned mass arrests, many conducted without proper warrants. Wilson protested to Palmer in vain, but further illness prevented him from blocking a new round of dragnet sweeps in January 1920. Labor's collaboration with Justice was undercut by Acting Secretary LOUIS POST, who reviewed and dismissed a majority of the deportation cases in Wilson's absence. Subsequent congressional hearings on the raids doomed Palmer's presidential hopes, while Hoover revised history to claim that he opposed and "deplored" the raids. William Wilson

mounted an unsuccessful U.S. Senate race in 1926, and he died eight years later, while traveling through Georgia by train on 25 May 1934.

**WILSON, Thomas Woodrow**—An Ohio native, born in 1822, Woodrow Wilson spent 14 years as a college professor (1888-1902) and served two years as governor of New Jersey before his presidential election in 1912. (J. EDGAR HOOVER led his high school drill team in Wilson's inaugural parade.) Remembered as "progressive," Wilson was nonetheless an outspoken racist who admired the KU KLUX KLAN (revived in 1915), segregated all aspects of the federal government, and used the U.S. military extensively to enforce his will throughout Latin America and the Caribbean.

Under Wilson, the Bureau of Investigation grew from 335 agents and 27 support personnel (1913) to 579 agents and 548 support personnel (1920). Its yearly budget increased from $415,452 to $2,457,104 in the same period. A. BRUCE BIELASKI continued as chief until February 1919, succeeded in turn by Acting Chief WILLIAM ALLEN and Chief WILLIAM BURNS (in July 1919). America's entry into WORLD WAR I greatly accelerated Bureau activity, first with passage of the Selective Service Act (prompting the "SLACKER" RAIDS of 1918), then the Espionage and Sedition Acts of 1917-18. J. Edgar Hoover joined the JUSTICE DEPARTMENT in 1917 and would soon find himself in the thick of the action against spies and "subversives."

President Wilson was particularly frightened of "enemy aliens," once declaring that they had "poured the poison of disloyalty into the very arteries of our national life. America has never witnessed anything like this before.... Such creatures of passion, disloyalty and anarchy must be crushed out!" The Russian Revolution of 1917 only increased his paranoia. At a cabinet meeting in the fall of 1918, Wilson ordered Attorney General A. MITCHELL PALMER, "Do not let this country see red!" A spate of radical BOMBINGS in spring 1919 seemed to be the signal for a Bolshevik uprising, but a series of strokes disabled Wilson before the PALMER RAIDS and subsequent deportations. National PROHIBITION took effect in the last year of Wilson's administration, marked by unbridled lawlessness before regional bootlegging gangs merged to create the embryonic form of modern ORGANIZED CRIME.

**WINCHELL, Walter**—A native New Yorker, born 7 April 1897, Walter Winchell entered Vaudeville at age 13 and later supplied items to the *Vaudeville News*, a pastime that led him to a new career as full-time celebrity gossip columnist for the *New York Daily Mirror*. Winchell's newspaper column was nationally syndicated until 1963, and he also had a weekly radio program from 1932 through the early 1950s. Winchell met FBI Director J. EDGAR HOOVER in 1934 and they became close friends by 1938, with Winchell addressing many "Dear John" letters to FBI HEADQUARTERS. Winchell often dined with Hoover and top aide CLYDE TOLSON at New York's Stork Club, and they sometimes vacationed together in Florida. Hoover favored Winchell with countless "leaks" of classified information, but when confronted on the subject he denied it, once telling the *New York Times*, "The truth is that Winchell gets no tips from me of a confidential nature. I cannot afford to play favorites."

In return for Hoover's covert generosity, Winchell performed as an unofficial FBI press agent, praising the Bureau and its director at every opportunity, attacking on cue such FBI targets as ALGER HISS, HARRY DEXTER WHITE, MAX LOWENTHAL and Democratic presidential contender ADLAI STEVENSON. The latter effort doomed Winchell's foray into television, when sponsors rebelled at his 1956 comment that "a vote for Adlai Stevenson is a vote for Christine Jorgensen" (a prominent 1950s transsexual). It was Winchell who arranged for Hoover to "capture" fugitive mobster LOUIS BUCHALTER in 1939, but his underworld connections later proved embarrassing. In 1950, hearings chaired by Senator ESTES KEFAUVER revealed that Winchell was on a first-name basis with New York gangsters Meyer Lansky and Frank Costello (whom Winchell habitually addressed as "Francisco").

Winchell biographer Lately Thomas notes that near the end of his career, Winchell "sounded more strident. His prejudices overshadowed everything. He seemed less like the breathless reporter of old and more like a garrulous, opinionated eccentric." His last media job, in those days, involved voice-over narration of *The Untouchables*, a television series that infuriated Hoover by crediting Treasury agent ELIOT NESS with some of the FBI's most sensational captures. Winchell was diagnosed with prostate cancer in October 1971 and died four months later. The FBI subsequently released 3,900 pages of his dossier under the FREEDOM OF INFORMATION ACT, including many of Winchell's letters to Hoover.

**WINGATE, Lynn** *see* **ROYER, Jeffrey**

**WINSTEAD, Charles** *see* **"Hired Guns"**

**WINTER, Ella**—A lifelong radical socialist, born in Melbourne, Australia, to German-Jewish immigrants in 1898, Ella Winter moved to London with her family in 1910. Winter married FBI surveillance subject LINCOLN STEFFENS in 1924 and returned with him to the U.S., but G-men ignored her for another three years, finally deciding that Winter deserved her own dossier in 1927. She divorced Steffens two years later, but continued sporadic correspondence while agents intercepted and copied the letters. (Several make it clear that Winter suspected her mail was under surveillance.) In 1930, Winter visited Russia and returned to write a book—*Red Virtue*—that confirmed the Bureau's opinion of her "disloyalty" to America. Nine years later, Winter married another subject of FBI scrutiny, DONALD OGDEN STUART, and the mail thefts resumed, one purloined letter from 1944 discussing the creation of a private code to frustrate snoopers.

That same year, after visiting Russia a second time for the *New York Post*, Winter received another letter—this one in Russian, including a "German game of Guess the Numbers"—that sent G-men into a panic. Suspecting treason, the Bureau opened a "highly confidential Comintern case" on Winter and Stewart, including 24-hour surveillance and interrogation of acquaintances. Friends of Winter were quizzed concerning her political views and her involvement with the YADDO WRITERS COLONY,

while agents logged the couple's shopping trips, visits to the theater, even the appearance of "a delivery boy from the University Cleaners." Stewart and Winter moved to England in 1952, agents of the STATE DEPARTMENT confiscating their passports to limit further travels. The passports were restored in 1957, over objections from J. EDGAR HOOVER, followed by an FBI request for the U.S. embassy in London to track any movements by Stewart and Winter. Winter survived the FBI director by eight years, and died in 1980.

**WIRETAPPING**—Wiretapping — the interception of messages transmitted by wire — has been used by police and criminals alike virtually from the day of the telegraph's invention in 1837. The first telephones, in 1876, were also easy prey for eavesdroppers and have remained so to the present but for "scrambling" devices used to frustrate interception. G-men were no strangers to wiretapping in the Bureau's first quarter-century, their targets including suspected criminals, ANARCHISTS and radicals, along with such critics of government corruption as Senators THOMAS WALSH and BURTON WHEELER.

Congress made its first effort to regulate wiretapping on 20 June 1934, with passage of the Communications Act. Section 605 banned "interception and divulgence" of any communication "transmitted by wire," but since it failed to specifically mention federal agents, FBI Director J. EDGAR HOOVER felt free to continue tapping phones in defiance of the statute. The U.S. SUPREME COURT closed that loophole on 20 December 1937, with its ruling in *Nardone v. U.S.* that G-men were included in the statutory ban. Another door was slammed shut two years later, in a second *Nardone* ruling on 11 December 1939, when the court banned use at trial of evidence derived in any way from illegal taps (dubbed "fruit of the poisonous tree"). In response to the *Nardone* rulings, Attorney General ROBERT JACKSON publicly declared, "Wire tapping, entrapment, or the use of any other improper, illegal, or unethical tactics will not be tolerated by the Bureau." Hoover, meanwhile, continued to do as he pleased, albeit with a bit more caution.

As WORLD WAR II raged in Europe and fascist groups paraded across the U.S., President FRANKLIN ROOSEVELT sought means of suppressing enemies at home. On 21 May 1940 he issued a secret directive to Hoover, declaring that he was "convinced that the Supreme Court never intended any dictum ... to apply to grave matters involving the defense of the nation." Acting without legal authority, Roosevelt approved FBI use of "listening devices" to intercept "conversation or other communications of persons suspected of subversive activities against the Government of the United States, including suspected spies." Each wiretap required direct approval from the attorney general "after investigation of the need in each case," and Roosevelt added: "You are requested furthermore to limit these investigations so conducted to a minimum and to limit them insofar as possible to aliens."

Attorney General Jackson, less concerned with oversight than with deniability, met privately with Hoover to discuss the matter on 28 May 1940. Hoover's memo of that meeting reports that Jackson said "he would have no detailed record kept concerning the cases in which wiretapping would be utilized. It was agreeable to him that I would maintain a memorandum book in my immediate office, listing the time, places, and cases in which this procedure is to be utilized." Hoover's "memorandum book" quickly became a massive file of index cards. When finally revealed, after his death, it would include the names of 13,500 persons and organizations wiretapped between 1941 and 1971.

For all his posturing, President Roosevelt in fact had no more scruples about illegal wiretapping than did Hoover himself. In August 1945, Naval aide James Vardaman complained to the FBI of ongoing media leaks and ordered G-men to "secure all information possible on White House employees." Specifically, he "requested that the FBI investigate suspected White House aides, wiretap Treasury Department aide Edward Pritchard, and study the operation of the White House with the objective of offering recommendations to improve its efficiency." Mindful of the risks, Vardaman warned that while "intercepts of the phone conversations of those employees would be of extreme value … if it became known that we were investigating these people, it would be incumbent upon both the President and [Vardaman] to deny that any such investigation had been ordered."

Roosevelt's order approving "national security" wiretaps carried no legal weight with the courts, and evidence thus obtained was still inadmissible. Hoover tried to disguise the source, describing wiretaps as "confidential sources" in various FBI reports, but disclosure of the Bureau's illegal techniques still jeopardized cases at trial. The *AMERASIA* CASE was thrown out of court in 1945, with probable Axis agents released, when illegal FBI wiretaps were exposed. In July 1946 President HARRY TRUMAN approved expanded use of taps to root out "subversive activities," but federal judges still insisted on observance of the law, dismissing ESPIONAGE charges filed against JUDITH COPLON in 1949 when more illegal wiretaps were revealed.

Hoover's dogged persistence in wiretapping despite those judicial rebukes suggests that he was more interested in gathering "intelligence" than prosecuting spies or criminals. Increasingly, as shown in memoranda and private conversations, his mind turned toward individual blackmail or "disruption" and "neutralization" of targeted organizations, eschewing due process in favor of covert guerrilla warfare. Hoover paid lip service to the law and Constitution while holding himself and the Bureau above their restrictions on criminal conduct.

In that respect, despite their personal distaste for one another, Hoover found a kindred spirit in Attorney General ROBERT KENNEDY (1961-64). Dedicated to full-throttle pursuit of ORGANIZED CRIME, Kennedy lobbied Congress to legalize wiretaps, while illicitly authorizing FBI taps on targets including "TOP HOODLUMS," Dr. MARTIN LUTHER KING, JR., and various reporters who disclosed or criticized U.S. foreign policy in the Caribbean. Ironically, Kennedy was freshly dead — the victim of an assassin's bullet — when Congress granted his wish in June 1968, with passage of the Omnibus Crime Control and Safe Streets Act. The statute authorized court-ordered wiretapping and BUGGING in criminal cases, while stipulating that the warrant requirement was not intended to "limit the constitutional powers of the President" in regard to national security.

President RICHARD NIXON stretched those ill-defined powers to the breaking point and beyond during his scandal-ridden regime, climaxed by the WATERGATE SCANDAL that finally drove him from office in disgrace. At Daniel Ellsberg's trial for leaking the "PENTAGON PAPERS" in 1973, FBI documents revealed that G-men had tapped phones belonging to 17 persons on White House orders, between May 1969 and February 1971. The targets included reporters and White House staff members, placed under surveillance (as in Roosevelt's day) to determine the source of persistent media leaks. Further revelations by the CHURCH COMMITTEE (1975-76) hinted at the scope of illegal wiretapping under the FBI's COINTELPRO campaigns. Bureau spokesmen admitted tapping the telephones of 2,305 "subversives" between 1960 and 1974, but claimed statistics for 1956-59 were "not available."

The Foreign Intelligence Surveillance Act of 1978 created a special secret court to review and authorize requests for wiretaps and bugs in cases allegedly dealing with espionage or foreign TERRORISM. The 11-judge panel examines requests for electronic surveillance and (theoretically) grants warrants on the merits of each case. Because the standards of evidence required for eavesdropping are much lower in most intelligence investigations than in criminal cases, Congress banned divulgence of intelligence information to criminal investigators or prosecutors, but that limitation was removed in 2001 with passage of the sweeping "USA PATRIOT ACT." Even before the change, however, there was evidence of G-men playing fast and loose with the rules of the game. In August 2001— three weeks before the tragic "9/11" terrorist attacks and three months before passage of the Patriot Act — the secret court announced that FBI spokesmen had misrepresented facts while seeking warrants in 75 different cases. The lies included "erroneous statements" about "the separation of the overlapping intelligence and criminal investigators and the unauthorized sharing of FISA information with FBI criminal investigators and assistant U.S. attorneys." The report concluded with a notation that "How these misrepresentations occurred remains unexplained to the court."

Law enforcement constantly struggles to keep pace with criminals in the field of new technology. On 7 October 1994 Congress passed the Digital Telephony Act, responding to the shift from analog to digital communications systems by requiring all providers to honor court-ordered wiretaps in criminal investigations. FBI pursuit of COMPUTER CRIMES raised new privacy concerns at the turn of the millennium. The Bureau's "CARNIVORE" and "Magic Lantern" software programs have extended wiretapping into the nebulous realm of cyberspace. Alleged Mafia figure Nicodemo Scarfo, Jr., challenged FBI surveillance in August 2001, after a computer "key logger" system was used to indict him on bookmaking charges. Ironically, the same month witnessed accusations that G-men had subpoenaed telephone records of John Solomon, an Associated Press reporter who published a story on the 1996 federal wiretapping of a U.S. senator. Sandra Rowe, former president of the American Society of Newspaper Editors called Attorney General JOHN ASHCROFT'S conduct in the case "reprehensible," while current ASNE president Tim McGuire declared: "The case makes me wonder if seizing phone records has become a first resort rather than last resort. It appears to me that the JUSTICE DEPARTMENT has seriously overreacted in search of a leak."

**WOLFE, Thomas Clayton** — Born at Asheville, North Carolina in 1900, Thomas Wolfe was a precocious child who entered the University of North Carolina at age 15. He published the first of four autobiographical novels (*Look Homeward, Angel*) in 1929. After visiting Germany in the mid-1930s, Wolfe seemed briefly enamored of ADOLF HITLER'S regime, but he later spoke out forcefully against Nazi brutality. Wolfe died on 15 September 1938, three days after undergoing surgery for suspected tuberculosis of the brain at Johns Hopkins Hospital, in Baltimore.

Extensive censorship and alleged concerns for "national security" make it impossible to know when the FBI opened its file on Wolfe, but memos were still being added as late as 1957, nearly two decades after his death. Author Biographer David Donald received the FBI's assurance in 1985 that no file existed on Wolfe, but he was deceived. Two years later, author Herbert Mitgang obtained 42 heavily-censored pages, released under the FREEDOM OF INFORMATION ACT, but another 81 acknowledged pages were withheld entirely. Wolfe's name appeared in blacked-out "Espionage" reports dating from 1947, 1949 and 1957, leaving Mitgang to suggest that Wolfe's novels had appeared in the classrooms of suspected "communist" schools.

That speculation is supported by three FBI reports that survive from the Red-baiting 1940s, more or less intact. The first, filed in 1944, suggests that a copy of Wolfe's novel *The Web and the Rock*, found "with no visible markings or writing," was "possibly a code book." (Nothing left in the report suggests who owned the book, or why G-men suspected it.) A year later, the Kansas City field office reported that Wolfe's *You Can't Go Home Again* was found on a list of novels "assigned by [name deleted]" to unknown readers. Finally, a 1947 "Security Matter" filed by the Boston field office noted that Wolfe's *Of Time and the River* was advertised for sale at a local COMMUNIST PARTY bookshop, along with novels by Mark Twain, HOWARD FAST and JACK LONDON. Ironically, the "godless" Red proprietors sought to lure customers with an ad urging them to "Give Books for Christmas."

**WOMEN Agents** — J. EDGAR HOOVER regarded law enforcement as man's work (and work best performed by white men, at that). During his 48 years as FBI director, Hoover appointed only one female agent, and that experiment failed so dramatically that he never hired another.

The Bureau's first two G-women were ALASKA DAVIDSON (hired in 1922, confined to investigation of MANN ACT cases) and Jessie Duckstein (promoted to agent status in November 1923, after two years as a typist for Bureau Chief WILLIAM BURNS). Neither lasted long after Hoover became acting director in May 1924: he demanded Duckstein's resignation on 26 May, followed by Davidson's on 10 June. Although details are scarce, it seems likely that one or the other was the anonymous female employee described by Hoover biographer Athan Theoharis in *The Boss* (1988), dismissed for breaking silence on illegal investigative techniques, when called to testify before a U.S. Senate committee.

The only woman ever appointed to serve as an FBI agent by Hoover, LENORE HOUSTON, entered the Bureau as a "special employee" in January 1924 and was promoted to full agent status that

November. Houston served with the Philadelphia field office until August 1927, when she was transferred to Washington, D.C. Things went badly for Houston at the "seat of government," though details remain elusive. She resigned in October 1928, effective the following month, and by 1930 Houston was confined to a mental institution, reportedly delusional and threatening to shoot Hoover if she was ever released.

No other women agents would be hired until July 1972, when JOANNE MISKO and SUSAN ROLEY were appointed by Acting Director L. PATRICK GRAY. (The longest-serving Bureau employee, though not an agent, was Mildred Parsons, secretary to the assistant special agent in charge of the Washington, D.C. field office; she served more than 57 years, beginning in September 1939, and never took a single sick day in that time.) SYLVIA MATHIS was the first black woman agent, hired in February 1976. Two years later, Christine Jung became the Bureau's first female firearms instructor. Carolyn Morris, an African American, became the FBI's first woman deputy assistant director in November 1984. Eleven months later, ROBIN AHRENS was the first G-woman killed on duty (shot by fellow agents while attempting to capture a fugitive). Burdena Paseneli was promoted from assistant special agent in charge of the Houston field office to serve as the Bureau's first female special agent in charge (at Anchorage, Alaska) in February 1992. In July 1995, Julianne Slifco was posted to Vienna, Austria as the FBI's first woman LEGAL ATTACHÉ.

Overall, employment of female agents has shown steady improvement since the long drought of the Hoover years, though it required a complaint from agent Christine Hansen, in 1981, to produce an order from the Equal Employment Opportunity Commission, requiring the FBI ACADEMY to recruit women more aggressively and modify their physical training requirements. A survey in February 1992 found 1,177 G-women among 10,422 agents nationwide (11.3 percent). Numbers declined the following year, with only 10,273 agents on staff, but 1,167 women remained in that total (for 11.4 percent). By 1997, the 1,617 female agents employed represented 15 percent of the total — still not a tremendous showing in a country where women make up 52 percent of the population. The FBI's website offers no breakdown of agents by gender today, but it includes a promise of equal-opportunity hiring without regard to sex or race.

Female agents pose some special problems for the FBI, as for other law enforcement agencies and military units where they are employed. An internal survey conducted in 1988 revealed that 13 percent of all female FBI employees (including support personnel) had suffered incidents of sexual harassment on the job; 40 percent of the 196 responding employees were special agents, but only 10 percent had filed official complaints with the Bureau. A San Antonio G-man was quietly fired in 1992, for raping a new female agent the previous year; his dismissal followed two previous complaints of sexual harassment and assault in 1990, one of which was ignored, while the other resulted in some unspecified (and clearly ineffective) disciplinary action.

Male agents, for their part, frequently complain that their female counterparts have it "too easy" in respect to Bureau discipline. (Two percent of male Bureau employees also reported incidents of sexual harassment in the 1988 survey, without providing sufficient details for analysis.) One case often cited is that of a female agent suspended for 30 days in 1988, after she was caught bringing marijuana and drug paraphernalia into the U.S. after a vacation abroad. Male agents, the complainants note, are routinely fired for drug offenses. G-women respond with complaints of their own, including discriminatory treatment during UNDERCOVER OPERATIONS. Miami agent LINDA THOMPSON, assigned to infiltrate a criminal gang by posing as the leader's girlfriend, was disciplined on charges of having sex with her target (though Thompson insists their romantic liaison never progressed beyond kissing).

It may well be unreasonable to expect the FBI to set a shining example where gender issues are concerned in American society, but there is likewise no doubt that Hoover's longstanding prejudice against female agents outlasted his tenure at FBI HEADQUARTERS, surviving into the 21st century. The Bureau passed a double milestone on 5 February 2002, when Director ROBERT MUELLER appointed 17-year FBI veteran Cassandra Chandler to serve as assitant director in charge of the TRAINING DIVISION, the first black female agent to achieve that exalted rank.

**WOODRIFFE, Edwin R.**—A Brooklyn native, born 22 January 1941, Edwin Woodriffe, Jr., earned a bachelor of science degree from New York's Fordham University and worked as a criminal investigator for the U.S. Treasure Department before he joined the FBI in May 1967. He worked briefly in Cleveland before he was transferred to the Washington, D.C. field office in February 1968. On 8 January 1969, Woodriffe and partner Anthony Palmisano were fatally wounded while trying to capture Billy Austin Bryant, an escaped convict sought for multiple counts of BANK ROBBERY. Bryant was immediately placed on the Bureau's "TEN MOST WANTED" LIST, captured later the same evening. Convicted of double murder on 27 October 1969, Bryant received two consecutive life sentences.

**WOOLLCOTT, Alexander**—Born at Phalanx, New Jersey in 1887, Alexander Woollcott served as a medical orderly in WORLD WAR I, then tried his hand at journalism and became America's highest-paid drama critic by age 35. His reviews, combining praise and scorn in a style that led JAMES THURBER to dub Woollcott "Old Vitriol and Violets," appeared variously in the *New York Times*, the *New York World*, and the *New Yorker*. He was also a founding member of New York's Algonquin Round Table and aired his reviews on radio from 1929 until his death, from a stroke at the close of a broadcast, on 23 January 1943.

Confusion surrounds the FBI's interest in Woollcott. Author Natalie Robins reports that his "two-page file" was started after Woollcott's death, and that it contains only two newspaper clippings. One reports that Woollcott edited an anthology of stories written by such Bureau targets as ERNEST HEMINGWAY, BOOTH TARKINGTON and DOROTHY PARKER. The other notes his death, with a marginal handwritten note that Woollcott was "previously removed from the [FBI] mailing list" for unstated reasons. While empty files prove nothing, Woollcott may have been ostracized by the Bureau in March 1941, when G-men found him listed with surveillance subjects SINCLAIR LEWIS and CARL VAN DOREN, reviewing books for The Reader's Club, which offered classic novels to subscribers for one dollar each. Since J. EDGAR HOOVER viewed the club with suspicion and assigned agents to join under false names, he can hardly have missed Woollcott's participation, even though no mention of it lingers in the critic's dossier.

**WOOTEN, Terry L.**—A protégé of South Carolina senator Strom Thurmond, federal magistrate Terry Wooten was nominated for lifetime appointment as a U.S. district judge by President GEORGE W. BUSH in 2001. Controversy surrounding his nomination erupted on 24 August, when one-time conservative journalist David Brock told the Senate Judiciary Committee that Wooten had furnished him with classified FBI documents in 1991, for Brock's book on the nomination hearings for U.S. SUPREME COURT justice Clarence Thomas. Specifically, Brock charged that Wooten—then Republican chief counsel for the Judiciary Committee—had illegally leaked documents intended to discredit witness Angela Wright. Wright, in conjunction with Anita Hill, accused Thomas of sexual harassment in September 1991, while confirmation of his Supreme Court appointment was pending. Brock was hired by Republican activists a month later, to write a book "exposing" both women as liars, and he now maintains that aides to President GEORGE H.W. BUSH sent him to Wooten for FBI documents containing derogatory material on Wright. As Brock described their meeting, "Mr. Wooten handed me copies of several pages of Ms. Wright's raw FBI FILES. This material included FBI interviews with Ms. Wright's former employers and former co-workers. With Mr. Wooten's agreement, I removed the FBI material from his office."

Brock used the classified material to write an article that appeared in the March 1992 issue of *American Spectator*, an ultraconservative magazine. His subsequent book on the Thomas hearings (*The Real Anita Hill*, 1993) also quoted from "an FBI file" that described Wright as "vengeful, angry and immature." As Brock told the Senate panel in August 2001, "There's no way I could have gotten this if Wooten hadn't given me the files."

Mindy Tucker, speaking for the JUSTICE DEPARTMENT, refuted Brock's allegations, telling reporters, "Based on all of our information and investigation, there is absolutely no basis for any allegation that Judge Wooten provided Brock with FBI materials related to Ms. Wright. I think it would be unfortunate if the desire for book sales promulgated a charge involving a man's integrity, such as this might." In fact, Wooten had nothing to fear. He denied any impropriety at his senate confirmation hearing and he was duly confirmed, presently serving on the federal bench in Florence, South Carolina. Critics maintain that his appointment was a reward from President Bush, for services rendered to his father and the Republican Party during the Thomas confirmation hearings.

**WORLD Trade Center bombing (1993)**—At 12:18 p.m. on 26 February 1993, a massive explosion rocked the basement garage of the World Trade Center in Lower Manhattan. The blast killed six persons, injured more than 1,000 and trapped thousands more in the Twin Tower office complex while emergency workers swarmed over the scene. Initial speculation centered on a transformer explosion, but technician DAVID WILLIAMS from the FBI's LABORATORY DIVISION read the scene differently. "I knew we had a bomb the moment I walked in," he later said. Before performing a single scientific test, he continued, "I knew within two hours of entering the World Trade Center what type of bomb we had and how big it was." Williams seized control of the crime scene by shouting, "I'm in charge here!" and subsequently led FBI explosives residue analysts Steven Burmeister and FREDERIC WHITEHURST on a tour of the crime scene. Before day's end, 300 G-men would be teamed with detectives from the NEW YORK POLICE DEPARTMENT and agents from the BUREAU OF ALCOHOL, TOBACCO AND FIREARMS to investigate the crime code-named "TRADEBOM."

Investigators found the shattered wreckage of a van in the garage which seemed to be the focal point of the explosion. A partial vehicle identification number led G-men to a Ryder Truck Rental office in Jersey City, where the 1990 Ford Econoline van had been rented on 23 February to Mohammed Salameh, a 25-year-old Palestinian from Jordan. Soon after the bombing, Salameh had returned to the rental office, reporting the van stolen and demanding a refund of his $400 fee. Ryder employees told him a police report was needed to document the theft, and Salameh had left in a huff. A background check on Salameh identified him as a participant in demonstrations on behalf of El-Sayid Nosair, a Muslim acquitted in 1991 on charges of murdering militant rabbi Meier Kahane. Salameh and Nosair both attended the Jersey City mosque of Sheik Omar Abdel Rahman, a cleric expelled from Egypt in 1981 for advocating overthrow of the Egyptian government. Many of Rahman's disciples had been under FBI surveillance since Kahane's murder in November 1990.

Without a clue to Salameh's whereabouts, G-men staked out the Ryder office in hopes he might return. While they waited, the *New York Times* received a letter claiming credit for the BOMBING for the "Liberation Army Fifth Battalion." It read: "This action was done in response for the American political, economical and military support to Israel, the state of terrorism, and to the rest of the dictator countries of the region." Two days later, on 4 March 1993, Salameh returned to the Ryder office and was arrested by an agent posing as an employee. A search of Salameh's apartment and a self-serve storage unit yielded chemicals which David Williams and his lab team suspected were used in the Trade Center bombing. Agents also found a business card from Nidal Ayyad, a 25-year-old chemical engineer linked to Sheik Rahman's mosque. At his arrest, G-men found a letter "similar" to the *New York Times* note of 2 March on Ayyad's home computer.

The FBI lab, meanwhile, had run into problems with the analysis of evidence from the crime scene. Agent ROGER MARTZ, with the Chemistry and Toxicology Unit (CTU) identified urea nitrate in the blast debris, but experts Whitehurst and Burmeister disagreed. When David Williams overruled them, Whitehurst and Burmeister wrote to lab chief John Hicks, complaining that:

In the rush to find the perpetrators of the crime a number of novel methods of investigation and crime scene handling were conducted and mistakes made. One of those mistakes was the identification by this laboratory by mass spectrometry alone of urea nitrate in explosives residue.

When Hicks ignored the memo, Whitehurst and Burmeister mounted a sting operation against CTU, dehydrating some of Whitehurst's own urine and submitting it as evidence. When CTU identified it as explosives residue, the analysts reported that failure to Al Robillard, chief of the Scientific Analysis Section. Whitehurst later described Robillard's reaction in court:

Mr. Robillard became extremely loud and extremely angry at Mr. Burmeister. He advised us that he would now have to embarrass his Chemistry and Toxicology Unit chief [Martz] and that we were never, ever again to do something like that to him.

Whitehurst further claimed that he was pressured to revise his findings to conform with CTU's report and that his report was changed by others at the lab when he refused. That experience prompted his first contact with the National Whistleblowers Center in November 1993, leading to worldwide publicity on the FBI lab's many failings two years later.

While the technicians fought amongst themselves, two more Trade Center suspects were identified. One, 27-year-old Ahmed Mohammed Ajaj, had been incarcerated since his arrest with bomb-making manuals at JFK Airport, on 1 September 1992, but G-men still named him as part of the plot. The fourth defendant, Mahmud Abouhalima, was captured by police in Cairo and returned to the U.S. for trial. The four were charged collectively with conspiracy, explosive destruction of property and interstate transportation of explosives. Their trial began in September 1993 and lasted five months, including testimony from 207 witnesses.

Some of those called by the prosecution were suspect, at best. One witness, Peter Wolpert, was the president of a Jersey City chemical company who claimed suspect Ramzi Ahmed Yousef (still at large in 1993) had paid $4,000 for three large orders of chemicals, including urea and nitric acid. On cross-examination, however, it was revealed that Wolpert's company was itself under investigation for violating New Jersey fire and environmental laws, prompting Wolpert to testify under a grant of government immunity. Another witness, Willie Moosh, was a former gas station attendant from Jersey City. He claimed to have gassed up a Lincoln Town Car occupied by suspects Yousef, Salameh and Abouhalima around 4:00 a.m. on 26 February 1993, thus placing them together near the scene of the explosion. Unfortunately for his credibility, Moosh fingered a trial juror as the Lincoln's driver in court (correcting himself a day later), and admitted taking $40,500 from the FBI to "stay available" as a witness. Prosecutors revealed defendant Salameh's fingerprint on a parking stub from the Trade Center garage, but a closer look found it was dated 10 full days before the bombing. Agent Williams spoke for the FBI lab, and while his testimony sounded professional, he was later removed from his post and censured (in 1997) for offering "overstated, inaccurate and unsupported expert opinions" in the Trade Center case.

Such problems notwithstanding, jurors were overwhelmed by the sheer mass of testimony and physical evidence. They convicted all four defendants on 4 March 1994; two months later, Judge Kevin Duffy sentenced the quartet to matching prison terms of 240 years without parole.

That victory behind them, with two alleged Trade Center plotters (Yousef and Eyad Ismoil Najim) hiding abroad, FBI HEADQUARTERS still believed there were more conspirators dwelling in New Jersey. That sense derived primarily from 43-year-old Emad Salem, a former Egyptian Army officer and confidant of Sheik Rahman who was also an INFORMANT for the FBI and the New York police. Salem had supplied his handlers with information on the mosque's militant congregation for nearly two years, and he now reported a series of terror attacks in the planning stage, with targets including the United Nations building, the FBI's New York field office, the George Washington Bridge, plus the Holland and Lincoln Tunnels. He arranged for his comrades to rent a "safe house" bugged by G-men, where their every word was captured on tape. Raiders arrested five of the would-be terrorists on 24 June 1994, allegedly while building more bombs. Sheik Rahman and seven others were picked up later, all 14 charged with conspiracy to bomb New York landmarks and to murder various prominent persons in the U.S. and Egypt. None were charged with participation in the Trade Center bombing, though its shadow overlay the whole proceeding and complicity was widely assumed. Defense attorneys countered with a charge that Rahman and his followers had been indicted to repair the FBI's tarnished reputation.

If that were true, the eight-month conspiracy trial, begun on 30 January 1995, did nothing of the sort. Fred Whitehurst, still an active-duty G-man and explosives analyst, testified as a witness for the defense, doing his best to counteract lab reports he denounced as deliberately inaccurate. Worse yet, when Emad Salem took the witness stand, it was revealed that he had secretly recorded many conversations with his FBI and NYPD handlers. Among the startling revelations on those tapes were a New York policeman's suggestion that Salem should demand a $1.5 million informant's fee from the FBI and "settle" for $1 million, followed by curious suggestions that some of the money Salem received was raised by unnamed private parties. Most shocking, however, was the dialogue indicating that FBI agents knew of the Trade Center bombing in advance and did nothing to stop it.

On one undated tape, Agent John Anticev was heard instructing Salem to learn where the defendants stored their explosives, telling Salem, "We'll just know where stuff exists and where it is, and then we'll make our move. There's no danger, you know. We can be sneaky and take our time." After the Trade Center blast, on 1 April 1993, Salem seemed to rebuke Anticev for failing to prevent the bombing. "They told me that 'we want to set this,'" he declared. "'What's the right place to put this?' You were informed. Everything is ready. The day and the time. Boom. Lock them up and that's that. That's why I feel so bad." Salem challenged Anticev on tape, "Do you deny your supervisor is the main reason of bombing the World Trade Center? We was handling the case perfectly well until the supervisor came and messed it up, upside down."

According to Salem, the unnamed supervisor had proposed a plan to arrest the bombers without damage to the World Trade Center. "He requested to meet me in the hotel," Salem reminded Agent Anticev on tape. "He requested to make me to testify and if he didn't push for that, we'll be going building the bomb with a phony powder and grabbing the people who was involved in it. But since you, we didn't do that." Later, speaking to Agent Nancy Floyd about Anticev, Salem told her, "He [Anticev] said, 'I don't think that the New York [FBI] people would like the things out of the New York office to go to Washington, D.C.'" Agent Floyd replied, "Well, of course not, because they don't want to get their butts chewed." Salem told Floyd, "Since the bomb went off I feel terrible. I feel bad. I feel here is people who don't listen." Her response: "Hey, I mean it wasn't like you didn't try and I didn't try. You can't force people to do the right thing."

FBI spokesmen acknowledged using Salem as an informant, but claimed they dispensed with his services prior to the Trade Center bombing (ironically, because he refused to wear a microphone.) Tapes notwithstanding, they insisted that he "never provided detailed information of the attack in advance." For reasons best known to the Bureau, Salem was rehired in time to help the Bureau arrest Sheik Rahman and his followers. Four of those defendants pled guilty at trial, one turning state's evidence against his comrades, and the other 10 were convicted on 1 October 1995. Three months later, Rahman and defendant El-Sayid Nosair received life sentences with no parole; the rest drew prison terms ranging from 25 to 57 years.

While the New York conspiracy trial was in progress, on 7 February 1995, Trade Center fugitive Ramzi Yousef was captured in Pakistan and returned to the U.S. for trial. The last alleged plotter, Eyad Najim, was subsequently caught in Jordan and delivered to U.S. authorities on 2 August 1995. The pair faced trial together in August 1997, and both were convicted on 12 November 1997. Najim and Yousef received 240-year prison terms; they were also slapped with uncollectable $250,000 fines and ordered to pay $10 million in restitution to their victims.

In a turn of grim irony, New York's Twin Towers were destroyed in another terrorist attack, with massive loss of life, on 11 September 2001. As in the first Trade Center bombing, evidence would later surface (from FBI Agent COLEEN ROWLEY and others) that G-men knew some of the terrorists in advance but failed to apprehend them, either through negligence or "miscommunication."

**WORLD War I**—Intelligence agencies typically profit from national emergencies, and the FBI is no exception. At the time World War I began in Europe, in August 1914, the Bureau had 122 agents and 39 support personnel operating on a budget of $455,698. Three years later, when America was drawn into the conflict, the agency boasted 265 agents and 305 support staff, with a budget of $617,534. By the time the armistice was signed in 1919, there were 301 G-men and 329 support staffers, working with a $2,272,658 budget allotment.

The wartime Bureau gained more than staff and money, however; it also gained power by leaps and bounds. The Selective Service Act of 1917, imposing the first U.S. military conscription since 1865, placed G-men in charge of tracking draft evaders and deserters. That mandate led directly to the chaotic "SLACKER RAIDS" of 1918, wherein reckless tactics were exacerbated by collaboration with the vigilante AMERICAN PROTECTIVE LEAGUE. Attorney General THOMAS GREGORY approved that unwise alliance, and Bureau Chief A. BRUCE BIELASKI was pleased to make use of the APL in any way possible.

Aside from hunting "slackers," the Bureau was also assigned to enforce the Espionage Act of 1917 and the Sedition Act of 1918. The Espionage Act proscribed theft of government secrets with intent of aiding the enemy, required fingerprinting of resident aliens from enemy nations, and further banned any oral or written statements designed to "interfere with the operation or success of the military of naval forces of the United States or to promote the success of its enemies … cause insubordination, disloyalty, mutiny, or refusal to duty" or to "willfully obstruct" military recruiting. The Sedition Act went even further, banning "any disloyal, profane, scurrilous, or abusive language" concerning the government, Constitution or U.S. military, "or any language intended to … encourage resistance to the United States, or promote the cause of its enemies." Together, those statutes effective canceled the First Amendment guarantees of free speech and a free press, permitting imprisonment of nearly anyone who criticized the war effort. Socialist presidential candidate Eugene Deb was the most prominent of those convicted and jailed for denouncing the war, but he was not alone. Other targets included the INDUSTRIAL WORKERS OF THE WORLD and various African American organizations marked by the JUSTICE DEPARTMENT as "radical."

The Russian Revolution of 1917 stunned America and the world at large, tipping the balance of power in war-torn Europe. Following the armistice, it also sparked an hysterical Red Scare in the U.S., fueled by Attorney General A. MITCHELL PALMER, Bureau Director WILLIAM FLYNN and "patriotic" groups such as the AMERICAN LEGION. While the NATIONAL CIVIL LIBERTIES BUREAU tried to restrain government excess in the Red-hunting post-war era, it made little headway and could not prevent the sweeping PALMER RAIDS of 1919-20, meant to crush "subversive" groups including the COMMUNIST PARTY and the COMMUNIST LABOR PARTY. The illegal and abusive tactics used in those raids created a backlash that finally swept Palmer and Flynn from office, installing President WARREN HARDING in the White House with a promise to restore "normalcy" in the U.S.

**WORLD War II** — As with WORLD WAR I, America was not immediately drawn into the global conflict that began with ADOLF HITLER'S invasion of Poland on 1 September 1939, but the FBI was an early beneficiary of "war fever." President FRANKLIN ROOSEVELT had already approved new campaigns of DOMESTIC SURVEILLANCE in 1936 (illegally expanded even further by FBI Director J. EDGAR HOOVER on his own authority), and the new assignment had produced steady growth. The Bureau grew from 609 agents and 971 support personnel (with a budget of $5 million) in 1936 to a force of 713 agents and 1,199 support staff (operating with a budget of $6,578,076) in 1939. By the time America entered the war in December 1941, Hoover had 1,596 G-men and 2,677 support personnel, working on a budget of $14,743,300. At war's end, the Bureau boasted 4,370 agents, 7,422 additional staff, and a $44,197,146 budget.

Despite its dramatic growth, the FBI's wartime performance left much to be desired. Hoover was warned in August 1941 of the impending PEARL HARBOR ATTACK but rejected the information in a fit of petty malice toward the messenger and failed to alert the White House. His foreign branch, the SPECIAL INTELLIGENCE SERVICE, collected information on Axis spies in Latin America but spent much of its time feuding with agents from the OFFICE OF STRATEGIC SERVICES (again, because of Hoover's personal hatred for OSS commander WILLIAM DONOVAN). That sibling rivalry hampered America's wartime intelligence efforts and allowed a group of apparent Axis spies to escape prosecution in the *AMERASIA* CASE.

Hoover's agents won kudos for their capture of eight NAZI SABOTEURS on U.S. soil in 1942, but the case was chiefly a media event. Far from running the enemy agents to earth, G-men merely accepted a turncoat's surrender and followed his lead to seven accomplices — and even that slim victory was nearly bungled, when FBI officials twice rejected the penitent German's confession, dismissing him as a crank. FBI HEADQUARTERS subsequently altered dates and falsified reports to make it seem as if the eight arrests had sprung from great detective work. On balance, though, Hoover's agents showed more interest in harassing the COMMUNIST PARTY (then allied with the U.S. war effort), prosecuting veterans of the ABRAHAM LINCOLN BRIGADE (who fought against Hitler in the Spanish Civil War), and spying on First Lady ELEANOR ROOSEVELT than in tracking Axis spies.

**WOUK, Herman** — Born in New York City during 1915, a child of Russian Jewish immigrants, Herman Wouk grew into a best-selling novelist whose works often explore American dilemmas and the experience of Jews in the U.S. He won a Pulitzer Prize for *The Caine Mutiny* (1941), and FBI agents opened a dossier on Wouk the same year, when he applied for a job with the government's Office of Production Management. G-men found him "arrogant and cocky for a young man," noting that his "only hobby is reading classical works," but they forgave him that weakness and finally deemed Wouk "thoroughly American."

That verdict was borne out in his wartime service with the U.S. Navy, and in Wouk's celebration of the military through such novels as *The Winds of War* and *War and Remembrance*. FBI agents noted with pleasure that in 1949, the *Daily Worker* deemed his play *The Traitor* "quite unacceptable," condemning its "description of U.S. Communists as atom spies." Still, Wouk was not perfect in the Bureau's eyes. A memo from May 1962 noted that his novel *Youngblood Hawke* "is reportedly critical of the FBI," and agents confirmed it by reading a copy. One fictional G-man was described as "an ex-football player gone to fat," while another was simply "a small man." Outraged, Bureau leaders decided to "take action," described in a surviving memo: "Since we knew Jerry O'Leary at the 'Star' was reviewing Wouk's book, efforts were tactfully made through him to counteract the critical part of the book. This undoubtedly resulted in the comment by O'Leary, in his review of the book several days ago, (5/20) that the attack against the FBI was unwarranted."

**WOUNDED Knee Siege (1973)**—Wounded Knee, South Dakota was the site of the last official "battle" in America's long-running Indian wars. There, on 29 December 1890, U.S. troops killed at least 150 Sioux (some accounts say 300 or more), while losing 25 of their own (mostly killed by inept "friendly fire"). Eighty years later, Wounded Knee was a small village on the PINE RIDGE INDIAN RESERVATION, and it still was not at peace. Problems included extensive strip mining of reservation land by companies licensed from Washington and a virtual civil war between traditional and "progressive" Indians. The latter sought stronger ties to the federal government and tried to enforce their will by means of an armed vigilante force, the GUARDIANS OF THE OGLALA NATION (GOON) that was supported by the FBI and the Bureau of Indian Affairs (BIA). GOON violence was opposed by members of the newly-formed AMERICAN INDIAN MOVEMENT (AIM).

On 27 February 1973 an armed group of 200 AIM members and supporters occupied Wounded Knee, announcing reclamation of the village in the name of the Lakota people. They soon found themselves surrounded by a much larger force of G-men, BIA police, deputies from the U.S. MARSHALS SERVICE, National Guardsmen and GOONs packing military weapons supplied by the FBI. Blockades were erected by both sides, with the standoff enduring for 71 days. The siege featured near-daily gunfire that killed two AIM members (Frank Clearwater and Buddy Lamont) and left several others wounded. One federal marshal was also wounded, apparently by GOONs. (When other marshals tried to disarm the vigilantes, G-men countermanded the order.) Rumors persist that 12 other AIM supporters were captured by GOONs while smuggling food into Wounded Knee "and were never heard from again," but a cursory FBI search for "mass graves" revealed no evidence to support the charges.

The siege ended on 6 May 1973. Rapid City's G-men compiled, though persistently unable to solve crimes committed on the Pine Ridge Reservation, and spent the past 71 days compiling more than 316,000 investigative FILE classifications on known AIM members. A total of 1,162 persons were finally arrested, including 562 siege participants and 600 others detained across the country for supporting AIM. Of the 1,162 initially jailed, only 185 were finally indicted, some of them on multiple felony charges. Trials spanned the next two years, but the most important (from the government's perspective) was the trial of AIM leaders Dennis Banks and Russell Means in 1974. Each defendant was charged with 13 counts, including arson, burglary, criminal conspiracy, theft, interfering with federal officers, and possession of illegal weapons. If convicted on all counts, each faced a potential prison term exceeding 150 years.

The JUSTICE DEPARTMENT'S key witness at trial was Louis Moves Camp, a former AIM member expelled by Banks and Means after he was accused of rape in South Dakota. At the time he agreed to testify for the government, Moves Camp also faced felony charges carrying a 20-year maximum sentence, which were waived in return for his cooperation. G-men refused to permit a polygraph test on Moves Camp before he appeared as an "eyewitness" to events in South Dakota that apparently occurred while he was 1,300 miles away, in California. Prosecutor R.D. Hurd misrepresented Moves Camp's rape charge to the court,

describing it as "only a minor matter" similar to "public intoxication," and the government illegally suppressed at least 131 pieces of exculpatory evidence. At the same time, FBI INFORMANT Douglass Durham (serving as AIM's national security director) leaked information from the defense team to his Bureau paymasters. It was all in vain, however, as Judge Fred Nichol discovered the Bureau's illegal tactics and dismissed all charges, lamenting from the bench that "the FBI I have revered so long, has stooped so low." Nichol added:

> Although it hurts me deeply, I am forced to the conclusion that the prosecution in the trial had something other than attaining justice foremost in its mind.... The fact that the incidents of misconduct formed a pattern throughout the course of the trial leads me to the belief that this case was not prosecuted in good faith or in the spirit of justice. The waters of justice have been polluted, and dismissal, I believe, is the appropriate cure for the pollution in this case.

Overall, 185 indictments and two years of trials produced only 15 convictions on minor charges, but the exercise was not a total loss for the FBI. As described by authors Bruce Johansen and Robert Maestas in their book *Wasi'chu: The Continuing Indian Wars* (1979):

> [B]efore Wounded Knee the full-time staff of the Rapid City [FBI] office had been three agents; after Wounded Knee eleven were assigned there. On the reservation, agents conspicuously walked the streets of Pine Ridge Village, looking appropriately colonial with their short haircuts and shiny black, round-toed shoes. Paramilitary gear, such as tanks and armored personnel carriers, reminders of Wounded Knee, sometimes stood on street corners.

The GOON campaign of TERRORISM continued at Pine Ridge, and climaxed with the shooting deaths of two FBI agents in June 1975 and the eventual imprisonment of AIM activist LEONARD PELTIER in an apparent FRAME-UP for that crime.

**WRIGHT, Richard Nathaniel**—Mississippi native Richard Wright was born on a plantation 20 miles from Natchez, on 4 September 1908. He later settled in Chicago, working part-time for the U.S. Postal Service in the early 1930s, while he joined the JOHN REED Club and the COMMUNIST PARTY, earning a reputation for his revolutionary verse. FBI agents noticed Wright in 1935, while he was working for the Federal Writers Project in Chicago, and their suspicions were confirmed two years later, when he moved to New York City as editor of the *Daily Worker*. Reunited with the Federal Writers Project in New York, Wright remained under surveillance by Bureau INFORMANTS while he published the novels *Uncle Tom's Children* (1938) and *Native Son* (1940). In 1941, Wright's name appeared on an FBI list of persons deemed "extremely close to the Communist party in recent years"; others listed included DASHIELL HAMMETT, LILLIAN HELLMAN and CLIFFORD ODETS. Later that year, when Wright received a prize for *Native Son* at the Fourth Writers Conference in New York, G-men called it "definitely a Communist gathering."

Wright left the Communist Party in 1942, but his public break came two years later, with denunciation of the Reds as "narrow-minded, bigoted, intolerant and frightened by new ideas which don't fit into their own." Encouraged, J. EDGAR HOOVER ordered a "discreet" interview with Wright, and word came back from New York that "his interest in the problem of the Negro has become almost an obsession." The following year, Hoover penned a memo citing Wright's "militant attitude toward the Negro problem" and placed his name in the Bureau's illegal SECURITY INDEX. Later in 1945, the Kansas City field office noted the presence of *Uncle Tom's Children* on a list of books "assigned by [name deleted]" to some unknown reader. Other writers on the list included Bureau targets HOWARD FAST, JOHN STEINBECK, ERNEST HEMINGWAY and JOHN HERSEY.

Wright moved to Paris in 1947, but the FBI continued its surveillance, joined by agents of the CENTRAL INTELLIGENCE AGENCY. G-men were alarmed by Wright's contributions to left-wing French journals, reporting that "wittingly or not he has been serving Communist Party ends." A report from 1951 listed Wright's affiliation with "Communist fronts" overseas, and he was interviewed repeatedly, throughout the decade, by the U.S. consul in Paris. In 1956, KAY BOYLE warned Wright of a rumor that he was "working for the STATE DEPARTMENT or the FBI as an informer," to retain his passport. The rumor may represent an example of malicious FBI "SNITCH-JACKETING," but a 1956 State Department memo, released 30 years later, confirms that Wright approached the embassy "to express certain concern over the leftist tendencies" of the First Congress of the Présence Africaine (a group of black scholars in Paris). Wright allegedly asked the embassy to help him promote U.S. delegates to the Congress, as a moderating influence, but his nomination of FBI target LANGSTON HUGHES reveals no great drift to the right.

Interviewed a last time by embassy officials in 1958, Wright acknowledged belonging to the Communist Party from 1932 to 1942. He died in Paris two years later, on 28 November 1960, still listed in FBI files as a "possible subversive among U.S. personnel in France." Kay Boyle reported new rumors — this time that Wright was "put out of the way by the government" — but biographer Addison Gayle found no evidence of assassination. All things considered, Wright's Bureau dossier was relatively modest, described by author Natalie Robins as containing a mere 181 pages.

# X

**X, Malcolm** — An Omaha, Nebraska native, born 19 May 1925, Malcolm Little was the son of an outspoken black separatist. His father was active in MARCUS GARVEY's Universal Negro Improvement Association and later led the UNIA's East Chicago, Indiana chapter. The family settled in East Lansing, Michigan in January 1928, where they endured successive tragedies: their house burned on 7 November 1929, and Malcolm's father was killed by a streetcar on 28 September 1931. (Malcolm heard rumors that the "accident" was really murder, planned by the Black Legion, an offshoot of the KU KLUX KLAN.)

Discouraged in school and consigned to a juvenile home in August 1939, Malcolm drifted through odd jobs and a life of petty crime. The Army spurned him in October 1943 with the notation "psychopathic personality inadequate, sexual perversion, psychiatric rejection." Convicted of larceny and other charges in January 1946, he converted to the teachings of ELIJAH MUHAMMAD while serving time in a New York prison. Upon his release in August 1952, Malcolm traveled to Chicago and joined the NATION OF ISLAM (NOI), adopting the name "Malcolm X." Three weeks after his recruitment, on 23 September 1952, an INFORMANT gave the FBI three letters written by Malcolm at various times. In one of them, penned from prison in June 1950, he declared, "I have always been a Communist."

The FBI kept Malcolm under surveillance from that day forward, charting his rise to assistant minister in Detroit and "first minister" in Boston (1953), then Philadelphia and New York (1954). G-men followed him to temples throughout the U.S. and eavesdropped on his conversations with illegal WIRE-TAPS. On 8 June 1964, FBI HEADQUARTERS added his name to the Bureau's "COMSAB" (*Com*munist *Sab*otage) and "DETCOM" (*Det*ention of *Com*munists) lists, slating him for potential arrest under terms of the MCCARRAN ACT. Seven months later, on 10 January 1955, two agents approached Malcolm at home, requesting a list of all NOI temples, officers and members. Malcolm told them to "go back to Hell"; the memo of that interview describes him as "uncooperative."

As Malcolm X became more prominent, he kept FBI agents busy. On 28 January 1961 he met with Georgia Klan leaders, seeking aid in the purchase of land for an all-black community. He also subscribed to a newsletter published by the Fair Play for Cuba Committee (later made famous by LEE HARVEY OSWALD). G-men, reading Malcolm's mail, mistook the newsletter's subscription renewal date for a "membership number" and reported him to Washington as a dues-paying member of the FPCC. Elijah Muhammad suspended Malcolm in December 1963, after Malcolm publicly described the JFK ASSASSINATION as a case of "chickens coming home to roost." A month later, on 6 January 1964, Malcolm was formally "isolated" from the sect, with an order from Muhammad that barred any NOI members from contact with Malcolm. The rift became irreparable in February 1964, when a former aide in New York warned Malcolm of an NOI plot to bomb his car.

On 9 March 1964 Malcolm announced the foundation of a new religious order, the Muslim Mosque, Incorporated. The next day, he told *Ebony* magazine that Muhammad's Black Muslims have "got to kill me. They can't afford to let me live.... I know where the bodies are buried, and if they press me, I'll exhume some." Three weeks later, on 31 March, FBI Director J. EDGAR HOOVER asked Assistant Director WILLIAM SULLIVAN for recommendations in the "high-priority" case of Malcolm X. Sullivan responded with a suggestion that Attorney General ROBERT KENNEDY be asked to authorize wiretaps on Malcolm (already maintained illegally for the past decade). Hoover sent the request to Kennedy on 1 April, claiming that he sought "information concerning the contacts and activity of Little, and activity and growth of the Muslim Mosque, Incorporated." Kennedy approved the tap request after reading Hoover's report that Malcolm encouraged "the possession of firearms by members of his new organization for their self-protection." On the same day, Justice aide BURKE MARSHALL asked the CENTRAL INTELLIGENCE AGENCY for a report on Malcolm. CIA headquarters replied that it "had nothing which would shed light on Subject's recent breakaway from the Black Muslims nor anything reflecting on where he might be getting financial support."

Shadowed by the FBI and CIA, Malcolm traveled widely through Africa and the Middle East in April and May 1964. Back in New York, on 28 June 1964 he announced the creation of the Organization of Afro-American Unity. Death threats were by now routine, but they struck close to home when Malcolm's home was firebombed at 2:46 a.m. on 14 February 1965. One week later, on 21 February, Malcolm was shot and killed while addressing a crowd at New York's Audubon Ballroom. Two gunmen linked to the Nation of Islam were arrested at the scene, and a third was jailed two days later. On the night of Malcolm's death, an FBI informant gave G-men one of the pistols used in his murder.

The judicial resolution of Malcolm's slaying solved nothing. Suspects Talmadge Hayer, Norman 3X Butler and Thomas 15X Johnson were indicted for murder on 10 March 1965. At trial in March 1966, Hayer testified that he and three others were hired to kill Malcolm, while insisting that Butler and Johnson were innocent. Johnson's wife also swore he was not present at the shooting, but jurors convicted all three defendants on 11 March 1966. A month later, on 14 April, all three were sentenced to life imprisonment. Conspiracy theories later surfaced, suggesting that Malcolm was slain by some combination of the FBI, CIA and/or New York mobsters who resented his June 1964 call for "an all-out war against ORGANIZED CRIME" in black communities. On 29 May 1980 New Jersey congressman William Hughes asked FBI Director WILLIAM WEBSTER to review Malcolm's assassination, but the plea was ignored.

# Y

**YADDO Writers Colony**—A classic retreat for authors and others of artistic leanings, the Yaddo colony was founded in 1900 by financier Spencer Trask and his wife Katrina, herself an accomplished poet. The childless couple bequeathed their mansion and 400-acre estate at Saratoga Springs, New York as a perpetual sanctuary "to nurture the creative process by providing an opportunity for artists to work without interruption in a supportive environment." In the century since its creation, Yaddo authors have won 56 Pulitzer Prizes, 55 National Book Awards, one Nobel Prize, and countless other literary honors. Noteworthy guests at Yaddo have included JAMES BALDWIN, TRUMAN CAPOTE, MALCOLM COWLEY, LANGSTON HUGHES, ROBERT LOWELL, KATHERINE ANNE PORTER and ELLA WINTER.

A retreat like Yaddo naturally proved irresistible to J. EDGAR

HOOVER in the Red-hunting 1940s and '50s. Yaddo board members claimed that G-men had begun investigating the colony in 1942, and Yaddo director Elizabeth Ames's secretary was recruited as an FBI informer two years later. She reported that a friend of Ames and frequent guest at Yaddo, journalist Agnes Smedley, hosted a reception for COMMUNIST PARTY officials at Yaddo in February 1948. Ten months later, columnist DREW PEARSON accused Smedley of being a Soviet spy, and poet Robert Lowell demanded that Ames resign as director of Yaddo for consorting with alleged traitors. By 14 February agents were on the scene at Yaddo, telling board members that they hoped "to find people off guard and make discoveries." Malcolm Cowley reported that the G-men seemed most interested in interviewing anti-communist guests at the colony, who "leaped to the conclusion that

Yaddo had been the scene of a Stalinist plot." Director Ames refused to step down, and the board declined to remove her. Board member Acosta Nichols, writing to Cowley, reported that the accusations "can now be discounted in view of Lowell's condition. His insanity is indeed a sad matter."

Yaddo survived the inquisition, outliving both Lowell and J. Edgar Hoover. The colony's latest award-winning author, poet Carl Dennis, won a Pulitzer Prize in 2002 for his collection *Practical Gods*.

**YOSEMITE murders** —On 12 February 1999, 42-year-old Carole Sund left Eureka, California with her 15-year-old daughter Julie and a friend of the family, 16-year-old Silvina Pelosso, en route to Yosemite National Park for a brief vacation. They drove a rented car and were supposed to meet Sund's husband in San Francisco four days later. The women registered at the Cedar Lodge in El Portal, near Yosemite, on 12 February but missed their rendezvous with Jens Sund on the 16th. They were still missing on 19 February, when the credit card insert from Carole's wallet was found on a street in Modesto, 86 miles northeast of Yosemite. None of the cards were missing, and the last charge had been made at Cedar Lodge on 14 February.

FBI agents entered the case eight days later, with 50 G-men assigned to the search, but some critics later claimed that the Bureau's efforts did more harm than good. Task force headquarters was established at a Modesto motel, state and federal officers fielding more than 2,000 tips in pursuit of the three missing women. On 26 February, Agent James Maddock told reporters "there's a likelihood they're dead," but he was still no closer to the victims or their theoretical killers. PSYCHOLOGICAL PROFILING was attempted, by two agents summoned from the FBI ACADEMY, producing a suggestion that two or more young white males were involved in the KIDNAPPING. Meanwhile, 110 full-time searchers found nothing as they scoured Yosemite and environs.

Bureau agents arrested their first suspect, 39-year-old ex-convict Billy Joe Strange, on 5 March 1999. A janitor at Cedar Lodge, Strange had served prison time for assault and domestic violence. Nine days later, G-men jailed Strange's roommate, paroled rapist Darrell Stephens, and held him in lieu of $125,000 bond for failure to register as a convicted sex offender. Despite press leaks suggesting that a search of the Strange-Stephens residence had produced vital evidence, nothing was found to implicate either man in the case.

On 18 March 1999, Carole Sund's burned-out rental car was found at Sonora Pass, 90 miles north of El Portal. Inside the trunk were two charred bodies, identified from dental records as Carole Sund and Silvina Pelosso. Both had been strangled, their vehicle apparently set afire twice, several days apart, by a killer striving to incinerate the corpses. Julie Sund was still missing on 24 March, when agents in Modesto received an anonymous letter, postmarked nine days earlier but delayed in transit by the postal service. The letter included a gloating confession to Julie's murder — "We had our way with her"— and a hand-drawn map led searchers to nearby Don Pedro Reservoir, where Sund's body was found on 25 March. She was nude, ankles bound with duct tape, her throat slashed so deeply that she was nearly decapitated.

Arrests of various suspects continued into early June 1999, and while some were later convicted of unrelated crimes, none were linked to the triple murder at Yosemite. On 21 July, around 5:00 p.m., 26-year-old teacher and naturalist Joie Armstrong left her job at the Yosemite Institute. She missed an appointment with her boss's wife 90 minutes later, and friends who checked her house the next morning found the front door open, a stereo playing inside, with no trace of Armstrong. Searchers found her headless body, the severed skull missing, in a drainage ditch several hundred yards from her cabin. Witnesses recalled a blue-and-white sport utility vehicle parked near the cabin on the night of 21 July.

Local police arrested a suspect, 22-year-old Cary Anthony Stayner, at 4:30 p.m. on 22 July, after they found his blue-and-white SUV on a mountain road near Yosemite. Stayner was nude at the time, and smoking marijuana. Tire tracks, fingerprints and a fresh cut on his hand linked him to the Anderson murder. Still, Agent Maddock told reporters there was "absolutely no reason to believe there is a connection" between the Anderson beheading and the Sund-Pelosso murders. Stayner embarrassed his captors a few hours later, announcing himself as the lone perpetrator of all four homicides.

A federal grand jury indicted Stayner for Anderson's murder (committed on U.S. government property) on 5 August 1999. Seven weeks later, on 16 September, the same grand jury added charges of KIDNAPPING and sexual assault. On 20 October 1999, the district attorney of Mariposa County filed state charges of multiple murder, burglary, robbery, forcible oral copulation and attempted rape in the Sund-Pelosso case. Investigation of Stayner's background suggested possible involvement in other California murders, dating from the early 1980s, but no further charges were filed. Stayner pled guilty to Anderson's murder on 20 November 2000 and received a life sentence in federal prison. In state court, Stayner was convicted of triple murder and one count of kidnapping on 26 August 2002. The jury sentenced him to death on 9 October 2002.

**YOUNG, Whitney Moore, Jr.**—A Kentucky native, born in 1921, Whitney Young, Jr., earned his bachelor's degree from Kentucky State College, followed by a master's from the University of Minnesota in 1947. He joined the staff of the National Urban League's St. Paul chapter that same year, and was elected to lead the Omaha chapter in 1950. In 1961 Young was chosen as the group's national leader, a post he held until his untimely death in 1971.

Leadership of the Urban League ranked Young as one of America's "Big Six" CIVIL RIGHTS leaders in the 1960s, but his political stance was more conservative than that of Dr. MARTIN LUTHER KING, JR., thereby gaining Young a degree of conditional sympathy from FBI Director J. EDGAR HOOVER. Bureau documents from that era describe Young as "a very expedient person" and "a restraining influence" on blacks during the ghetto riots of 1965-67. President LYNDON JOHNSON regarded Young and NAACP leader ROY WILKINS as the "real leaders" of the civil rights movement, while despising the "opportunistic loudmouths using [King] as their front man" in protests against the VIETNAM WAR. Hoover, for his part, would only describe Young as "one stripe above" Dr. King.

Still, it was something. Young praised FBI agents for their arrest of KU KLUX KLAN members in the "MIBURN" case, and he accepted information from the Bureau on alleged efforts by the COMMUNIST PARTY to infiltrate the Urban League. In 1963, seeking to disrupt the historic March on Washington in its planning stages, G-men leaked derogatory information on colleague BAYARD RUSTIN to Young and Roy Wilkins; they also treated Young to a series of sex tapes recorded via illegal BUGGING of Dr. King's hotel rooms. Two years later, Young was approached by Jay Kennedy, a minor functionary of King's SOUTHERN CHRISTIAN LEADERSHIP CONFERENCE who also had ties to the CENTRAL INTELLIGENCE AGENCY. Kennedy suggested that Young should urge King to surrender his position as nominal head of the civil rights movement, but Young declined to participate in the coup. FBI memos from the same period suggest that Hoover hoped to replace King with a more "reliable" spokesman, though he favored Roy Wilkins over Young.

Young survived the Bureau's machinations and surveillance, emerging from the turbulent 1960s with his reputation intact. His work took him to Africa in 1971, but he would not return. While swimming with friends at Lagos, Nigeria, Young drowned on 11 March 1971. He was succeeded at Urban League headquarters by activist Vernon Jordan.

# Z

## ZARCOVICH, Martin

A sergeant with the East Chicago (Indiana) Police Department, born in 1896, Martin Zarcovich managed to keep his badge despite a 1930 conviction for smuggling liquor during PROHIBITION. He was notorious for his corrupt association with various underworld figures, including brothel madam Anna Sage (née Cumpanas), who operated in East Chicago from 1919 to 1927. Her financial and romantic dealings with Zarcovich led the sergeant to divorce court, and Zarcovich continued their illicit liaison after Sage moved her operation across the state line to Chicago. It was there, in early 1934, that Sage recognized one of her regular patrons as fugitive bandit JOHN DILLINGER, lately ranked as America's "Public Enemy No. 1."

Sage, a Romanian native, faced deportation in 1934 as an undesirable alien. Scheming with Zarcovich she devised a plan to betray Dillinger (aka "Jimmy Lawrence") to the FBI in return for cash rewards and Bureau intercession with U.S. Immigration officials. Agent MELVIN PURVIS, anxious to redeem himself after a bungled effort to capture the Dillinger gang left one of his G-men and an innocent bystander dead in April 1934, welcomed the offer from Sage and Zarkovich to put his quarry "on the spot." Some published sources claim that Purvis agreed to kill Dillinger on sight, at Zarcovich's urging, and while nothing in the G-man's style or record rules out such a bargain, no transcript of their meeting exists to prove the assertion.

By the time he met Purvis, Zarcovich was already responsible for one lethal shootout involving Dillinger. According to crime historian William Helmer, East Chicago officers Lloyd Mulvihill and Martin O'Brien threatened to expose "Zark's" illegal activities in May 1934, whereupon he arranged for them to roust a couple of "suspicious characters" on the night of 24 May. Confronted by Dillinger and sidekick Homer Van Meter, Mulvihill and O'Brien went down in a blaze of machine-gun fire, while Zarcovich's secrets were preserved. Now, two months later, Zarcovich engineered Dillinger's death to keep the outlaw from telling tales of police corruption to the FBI.

Zarcovich and East Chicago police captain Tim O'Neil were present when G-men laid their trap for Dillinger outside Chicago's Biograph Theater on 22 July 1934. Their presence takes on special significance when we remember that members of the CHICAGO POLICE DEPARTMENT were excluded from participation in the stakeout. Dillinger was killed when he emerged from the theater with Anna Sage and prostitute Polly Hamilton, but the fatal shot was never traced to a specific weapon. Several authors have suggested that Zarcovich delivered a point-blank *coup de grâce* as Dillinger lay wounded on the pavement, afterward rifling his pockets and stealing several thousand dollars. (One author, Jay Robert Nash, goes further yet, claiming that "Jimmy Lawrence" was a substitute for Dillinger, silenced by Zarcovich as part of a corrupt bargain that let Dillinger escape.) FBI Director J. EDGAR HOOVER allegedly blamed Zarcovich for killing Dillinger, criticizing Purvis in an interview with newsman Russell Girardin for letting Zarcovich and O'Neil join the ambush party, but in public Hoover blessed the East Chicago officers with his "highest esteem and best regards" for their assistance.

Zarcovich and O'Neil split a $5,000 reward for their role in the Dillinger set-up, and while both testified on behalf of

Anna Sage at her deportation hearing, it did no good. Sage was deported to Romania on 29 April 1936. Zarcovich was subsequently demoted for refusing to discuss the Dillinger case with Indiana's governor, but it was a minor setback. He was later promoted to chief of detectives and served as East Chicago's police chief from 1947 to 1952. Upon retirement Zarcovich became a probation officer, never straying far from East Chicago. He died there, at age 73, on 30 October 1969.

**Z-COVERAGE** — Initiated by J. EDGAR HOOVER in 1940, the "Z-Coverage" program involved FBI interception and reading of all mail addressed to the German, Italian and Japanese embassies in Washington, D.C. Later, following the PEARL HARBOR attack and America's entry into WORLD WAR II, scrutiny was extended to mail received by the embassies of Axis-friendly nations Spain, Portugal and Vichy France, plus the Soviet Union (by then a U.S. ally). In a parallel operation, Hoover also arranged for various international telegraph companies to delay transmission of all messages sent from the U.S. to those seven nations by 24 hours, until they could be copied and examined by G-men and agents of U.S. Army Intelligence.

**ZEISS, George** — George Zeiss joined the FBI in 1942 and joined the teaching staff at the FBI ACADEMY the same year, remaining at Quantico, Virginia until his retirement in 1977. He was best known in the Bureau (and outside it) as an internationally famous trick-shot marksman. His stunts included firing a pistol at the thin edge of a playing card and cutting it in half with one bullet; using the reflection in a diamond ring to aim at targets behind him; and firing at the sharp edge of an axe, splitting the bullet to strike a pair of targets.

In addition to marksmanship, Zeiss also instructed FBI recruits in other forms of self-defense, but he was not strictly limited to the academy. In 1959 he served as a technical advisor and bit player in the film version of DON WHITEHEAD'S Bureau history, *The FBI Story*. Nine years later, Zeiss was sent to retrieve fugitive James Earl Ray (the alleged killer of Dr. MARTIN LUTHER KING, JR.) from British custody in London. Upon retirement, Zeiss joined the staff of Wackenhut Corporation, a private security firm founded by former G-men whose clients included reclusive billionaire Howard Hughes.

**ZIGROSSI, Norman** — A protégé of COINTELPRO Agent RICHARD G. HELD at the Bureau's Chicago field office, Norman Zigrossi accompanied Held to South Dakota's PINE RIDGE INDIAN RESERVATION in June 1975, as part of the team assigned to investigate the deaths of two agents in a shootout with presumed members of the AMERICAN INDIAN MOVEMENT (AIM). Zigrossi replaced George O'Clock as assistant special agent in charge of the Rapid City office, while Held operated behind the scenes as coordinator of the FBI's ongoing anti-AIM campaign. During July and August 1975 Zigrossi, Held and the U.S. Attorney used federal grand jury subpoenas and contempt citations to imprison various AIM supporters and members of the WOUNDED KNEE Legal Defense/Offense Committee (WKLDOC), which Zigrossi publicly described as a "revolutionary organization." On 4 Oc-

tober 1975 Zigrossi led a raid on WKLDOC headquarters, ostensibly seeking a federal fugitive, and used the pretense to confiscate various records and legal documents, while leaving the office in a shambles.

While in command of the Rapid City office, Zigrossi vowed that any local G-man who abused his authority would be relieved of duty immediately. That promise notwithstanding, dozens of complaints against Agent DAVID PRICE were met with Zigrossi's assurance that Price was "a model agent." Zigrossi revealed his true attitude toward the South Dakota assignment in a comment to *Rolling Stone* magazine, published on 7 April 1977. In that interview he declared, "They [Indians] are a conquered nation, and when you are conquered, the people you are conquered by dictate your future. This is a basic philosophy of mine. If I'm part of a conquered nation, I've got to yield to authority.... [The FBI] must function as a colonial police force."

Despite Zigrossi's best efforts, however, AIM defendants DARRELLE BUTLER and Robert Robideau were acquitted of murder in the Pine Ridge shootings on a plea of self-defense, after convincing jurors that their lives were endangered by illegal FBI actions. In the wake of that verdict, Zigrossi complained that "the system beat us," but he was not defeated. Ten days later, he drafted a teletype to Director CLARENCE KELLEY, seeking to explain the jury's unexpected verdict. His review of the trial included complaints that "over strong objections by government, the defense was allowed freedom of questioning of witnesses"; that "the court allowed testimony concerning past activities of the FBI relating to the cointel pro [*sic*] and subsequently allowed the CHURCH [COMMITTEE] report into evidence"; and that "the court continually overruled government objections and allowed irrelevant evidence: for example, introduction of seven Bureau documents ... which were disseminated at headquarters level to other law enforcement agencies. As a result, the defense inferred [*sic*] the FBI created a climate of fear on the reservation which precipitated the murders." Zigrossi also found it suspect that "the defense utilized ... the services of nine attorneys, many of which were vastly experienced in criminal defense." (Defendant LEONARD PELTIER was later convicted of the Pine Ridge murders, under circumstances many critics describe as a FRAME-UP.)

Following his COINTELPRO activities in Chicago and South Dakota, Zigrossi was promoted to serve as special agent in charge of the Washington, D.C. field office. Upon retirement from the Bureau he was hired as chief administrative officer for the Tennessee Valley Authority, at a yearly salary of $118,000. His retirement from that position in November 2000, at age 64, sparked controversy when the Nashville *Tennessean* reported that Zigrossi would receive $1.08 million in deferred compensation and other benefits, plus yearly pension payments of $136,000 for life, upon leaving his post in December 2000. Tennessee congressmen Zach Wamp and John Duncan, Jr., long critical of the benefits received by other TVA managers, promptly renewed their call for increased public disclosure and congressional oversight of the TVA. "Ninety-nine percent plus of TVA employees never get anything even remotely close to what Mr. Zigrossi has gotten," Duncan told reporters. "They can get top-notch, high-quality people to do those jobs without paying ridiculously excessive compensation."

**ZIMBALIST, Efrem, Jr.**—Born in New York City on 30 November 1918, Efrem Zimbalist, Jr., was the son of a world-renowned violinist and an opera singer. Educated at expensive New England preparatory schools, he briefly enrolled at Yale University, then left to study acting at New York's Neighborhood Playhouse. After combat service (and a Purple Heart) in WORLD WAR II, Zimbalist performed on Broadway and made the first of many film appearances in *House of Strangers* (1949). Television beckoned in the late 1950s, and Zimbalist enjoyed a six-season run on the weekly series *77 Sunset Strip* (1958-64). In 1965 he was tapped to play Inspector Lewis Erskine on a new weekly drama, *The FBI.*

Director J. EDGAR HOOVER dominated the ABC television series from its inception, permitting use of the FBI name and official seal only after ABC paid $75,000 for screen rights to Hoover's ghost-written *Masters of Deceit* (never filmed) and agreed to pay the director $500 per episode. With 191 episodes aired before Hoover's death in May 1972, that meant another $95,500 for the director—$170,500 in all. (Payments were made to the FBI RECREATIONAL ASSOCIATION, which operated as Hoover's private slush fund.) Hoover also screened the cast and crew for potential "subversives," including a two-hour interview with Zimbalist at FBI HEADQUARTERS. Zimbalist recalled that Hoover "had this marvelous old colored man [SAMUEL NOISETTE] who takes you in." As for the director himself, Zimbalist found Hoover "very sweet" and "a breath of fresh air." In fact, he opined, Hoover was "the ideal, he was a benevolent ruler."

Despite the hand-picked cast and crew, Hoover and Associate Director CLYDE TOLSON were still shocked by *The FBI*'s premiere episode, which featured a killer driven to violence by a fetish for women's hair. Tolson recommended cancellation of the series, and Hoover scrawled a marginal note on the memo: "I concur." Assistant Director CARTHA DELOACH, having signed a five-year contract with the program's sponsor (Ford-Mercury, which also supplied all cars used on the show), calmed Hoover and ran interference with various media critics who had panned the initial episode. The series ultimately outlived Hoover, running until April 1974 and portraying an all-white band of G-men who never once investigated (or even mentioned the existence of) ORGANIZED CRIME.

Zimbalist attended Hoover's funeral on 4 May 1972, and the demise of *The FBI* two years later did not harm his career. Roles followed in numerous films and television series, climaxing with a stint of voice-over work for various animated features and programs since 1997. Zimbalist's on-camera appearances have recently been limited to armchair Bible readings on the Christian fundamentalist Trinity Broadcasting Network.

**ZUCKMAYER, Carl**—Born at Nackenheim, Germany on 27 December 1896, Carl Zuckmayer served as an army lieutenant in WORLD WAR I, but made his reputation as a dramatist in postwar civilian life. He left Germany for Austria when ADOLF HITLER came to power, and later fled to the United States. Bureau spokesmen assured author Alexander Stephan, in November 1994, that Zuckmayer "was not the subject of an FBI investigation," but 76 pages including references to his name were still found in various files. Stephan received 66 of those documents, under the FREEDOM OF INFORMATION ACT, but 10 others remain classified today, suggesting that the Bureau's disavowal may have been untrue.

Zuckmayer and his wife resided both in Hollywood and New York City (where informants described him living "like a prince" at the home of an American sponsor), before retreating to a farm at Barnard, Vermont. Their mail was subject to occasional interception and scrutiny during WORLD WAR II, but it remains unclear which agency initiated the snooping. The FBI memos contain no subversive allegations, but many of Zuckmayer's friends were exiled writers subject to constant FBI surveillance. Zuckmayer became a U.S. citizen in December 1945, while living in Vermont, but traveled frequently to Europe in the 1950s. He returned to Austria in 1957 and his U.S. citizenship was revoked five years later. A frequent outspoken critic of the Cold War, Zuckmayer died at Visp, in Switzerland, on 18 January 1977.

**ZUKOFSKY, Louis**—Born in New York City on 23 January 1904, poet Louis Zukofsky received his master's degree from Columbia University at age 20. FBI agents initially overlooked his articles in *The New Masses* and his membership in the League of American Writers, but they opened a file on Zukofsky in 1935, when an anonymous letter "described him as a Communist writer." Six years later, Zukofsky's application to work as an FBI translator was rejected. Another decade passed before Whittaker Chambers, a professional ex-communist and lead prosecution witness in the ALGER HISS case claimed, in 1951, that he had personally recruited Zukofsky into the COMMUNIST PARTY at age 21. G-men found no corroboration for that claim, and Chambers later modified his statement to say that Zukofsky "only stayed in the Party one month." Zukofsky and his wife were "guarded in their answers" when agents came calling at their home, and the poet's file was closed in 1953, devoid of any solid evidence. Zukofsky died at Port Jefferson, New York on 12 May 1978.

# Appendix A: Abbreviations and Acronyms

ALF — anonymous letter file
ASAC — assistant special agent in charge (of an FBI field office)
ASD — Administrative Services Division
BNDD — Bureau of Narcotics and Dangerous Drugs
CALEA — Communications Assistance for Law Enforcement Agencies
CASKU — Child Abduction and Serial Killers Unit
CCH — Computerized Criminal Histories
CCIPS — Computer Crime and Intellectual Property Section
CID — Criminal Investigative Division
CJIS — Criminal Justice Information Services
CIRG — Critical Incident Response Group
COINTELPRO — counterintelligence programs
CRS — Community Relations Service
DEA — Drug Enforcement Administration
DOJ — Department of Justice
FBIHQ — FBI headquarters (Washington, D.C.)
FBIRA — FBI Recreation Association
FBN — Federal Bureau of Narcotics
GID — General Intelligence Division
HRT — Hostage Rescue Team
IDIU — Interdivisional Information Unit
IEC — Intelligence Evaluation Committee
IFCC — Internet Fraud Complaint Center
IRD — Information Resources Division
ITOM — interstate transportation of obscene material
ITSMV — interstate transportation of stolen motor vehicles
ITSP — interstate transportation of stolen property
LCD — Legal Counsel Division
LCN — La Cosa Nostra (the Mafia)
LEAA — Law Enforcement Assistance Administration
Legats — Legal attachés (FBI foreign liaison offices)
LHM — letterhead memorandum (circulated outside FBI)
LIU — Legal Instruction Unit
NA — FBI National Academy
NCAVC — National Center for Analysis of Violent Crime

NCIC — National Crime Information Center
NDIS — National DNA Index System
NDPO — National Domestic Preparedness Office
NIBRS — National Incident-Based Reporting System
NIPC — National Infrastructure Protection Center
NLETS — National Law Enforcement Telecommunications System
NSD — National Security Division
NW3C — National White Collar Crime Center
OEEOA — Office of Equal Employment Opportunity Affairs
OGC — Office of the General Counsel
OLIA — Office of Liaison and International Affairs
OO — office of origin (primary case investigators)
OP — office of preference (on requests for transfer)
OPCA — Office of Public and Congressional Affairs
OPE — Office of Planning and Evaluation
OPR — Office of Professional Responsibility
RA — resident agency (or resident agent)
SA — special agent
SAC — special agent in charge (of an FBI field office)
SEARCH — System for Electronic Analysis and Retrieval of Criminal Histories
SID — Special Investigative Division
SIS — Special Intelligence Service
SOG — "seat of government" (FBI headquarters)
SRA — senior resident agent
TFIS — theft from an interstate shipment
TIO — time in office (vs. field investigations)
UFAC — unlawful flight to avoid confinement
UFAP — unlawful flight to avoid prosecution
unsub — unknown subject (unidentified offender)
VCMOP — Violent Crimes and Major Offenders Program
VICAP — Violent Criminal Apprehension Program
VOT — "voluntary" overtime (required of all agents under J. Edgar Hoover)

# Appendix B: Chronology

**24 September 1789**— Office of the Attorney General created by Congress. Edmund Randolph appointed to fill the post.

**22 June 1870**— Department of Justice created to enforce federal laws.

**3 March 1871**— Congress grants the Justice Department $50,000 for "detection and prosecution" of federal crimes. Attorney General George Williams appoints the department's first investigator.

**1 January 1895**— J. Edgar Hoover born in Washington, D.C.

**27 May 1908**— Congress bars Secret Service agents from assisting the Dept. of Justice.

**29 June 1908**— Attorney General Charles Bonaparte creates a Special Agent Force within the Justice Department.

**26 July 1908**— Stanley Finch appointed chief of the Special Agent Force.

**16 March 1909**— Attorney General George Wickersham renames the Special Agent Force the Bureau of Investigation (BI).

**25 June 1910**— BI jurisdiction expands with passage of the White Slave Traffic Act (Mann Act) by Congress.

**30 April 1912**— A. Bruce Bielaski appointed as BI chief.

**20 March 1917**— Chief Bielaski approves cooperation with the privately organized American Protective League.

**6 April 1917**— America enters World War I; President Woodrow Wilson authorizes arrest and detention of "enemy aliens."

**15 June 1917**— Espionage Act passed by Congress, expanding BI jurisdiction to investigate "sedition" and opposition to the war.

**26 July 1917**— J. Edgar Hoover joins the Justice Department as a filing clerk.

**5 September 1917**— BI agents arrest leaders of the Industrial Workers of the World for violating the Espionage Act.

**3 September 1918**— BI agents and APL vigilantes conduct nationwide dragnet arrests of "slackers" caught without draft cards in their possession. Abuses produce widespread criticism.

**10 February 1919**— William Allen replaces Bielaski as acting chief of the BI.

**28 April 1919**— Mail bombs are sent by persons unknown to 29 prominent Americans, all but one defused before exploding.

**2 June 1919**— Bomb explodes at the Washington home of Attorney General A. Mitchell Palmer. Several other bombs are found and defused.

**30 June 1919**— Attorney General Palmer appoints William Flynn chief of the BI.

**1 August 1919**— Palmer creates a new Radical Division (later renamed the General Intelligence Division) within the BI, placing J. Edgar Hoover in charge.

**28 October 1919**— BI jurisdiction expands with passage of the Motor Vehicle Theft (Dyer) Act by Congress, banning transportation of stolen cars across state lines.

**7 November 1918**— BI agents and others raid meetings of the Union of Russian Workers, detaining them for deportation under the 1918 Immigration Act.

**1 December 1919**— First *Bureau Bulletin* issued to BI field offices, detailing official procedures.

**21 December 1919**— 249 "Bolsheviks" arrested in the November dragnets are deported to Russia aboard the SS *Buford*.

**2 January 1920**— "Palmer Raids" resume with mass arrests of suspected Communist Party and Communist Labor Party members in 33 cities. Of thousands detained, fewer than 600 are deported over the next 18 months.

**27 April 1920**— The House Rules Committee begins impeachment hearings on Assistant Labor Secretary Louis Post, for his role in the Palmer raids and deportations. Testimony highlights BI conduct and abuses in the raids.

**25 May 1920**— Reports issued by the Interchurch World Movement and the National Popular Government League criticize abuses by the BI and Immigration Bureau in the Palmer raids.

**21 August 1920**— The Chicago field office opens, commanded by SAC James Rooney.

**16 September 1920**— A massive bomb explodes on Wall Street, New York City. J. Edgar Hoover takes personal charge of the case, which remains unsolved.

**28 September 1920**— Chief Flynn issues the first *SAC Letter*, updating BI special agents in charge on new policies.

**19 January 1921**— A U.S. Senate committee launches hearings on the planning and conduct of the Palmer raids.

**22 August 1921**— William Burns replaces Flynn as BI director; J. Edgar Hoover promoted to assistant director. BI agents raid a Communist Party meeting in Bridgman, Michigan, delivering confiscated literature to state authorities.

**9 November 1921**— The Milwaukee field office opens, with SAC Henry Stroud commanding four agents and one support employee.

**1 September 1922**— Attorney General Harry Daugherty obtains an injunction against striking railroad workers and orders BI agents to collect evidence for prosecution, resulting in arrest of 1,200 strikers.

**September 1922**— BI agents raid the offices of Congressman Oscar Keller, an outspoken critic of Attorney General Daugherty's attack on striking railroad workers.

**10 March 1924**— Edward Y. Clarke, "Imperial Kleagle" of the Ku Klux Klan, pleads guilty to Mann Act charges.

**7 April 1924**— Harlan Fiske Stone replaces Daugherty as Attorney General.

**May 1924**— A special U.S. Senate committee begins investigation of former Attorney General Daugherty for abuse of power, including use of the BI to investigate critics of the Harding administration.

**9 May 1924**— Attorney General Stone demands resignation of William Burns as BI director.

**10 May 1924**— J. Edgar Hoover appointed acting director.

**1 July 1924**— Hoover creates the BI Identification Division, charged with creating a national fingerprint registry.

**July 1924**— F.H. Hessler is appointed as the first special agent in charge of the new Detroit field office.

**10 December 1924**— Hoover confirmed as full-time BI director.

**20 February 1925**— Hoover reorganizes the BI with six headquarters divisions governing administrative and investigative affairs nationwide.

**24 March 1925**— Hoover creates an OBSCENE file for collection of alleged "obscene and improper" materials.

**11 October 1925**— Edwin Shanahan becomes the first BI agent killed on duty, shot by car thief Martin Durkin in Chicago.

**15 August 1926**— BI agents join Border Patrol officers and California police to disrupt an illegal invasion of Mexico, arresting Major General Enrique Estrada and his staff.

**15 September 1927**— The BI's first *Manual of Investigation* is issued, detailing approved procedures.

**1 January 1928**— A two-month training course for new BI agents is inaugurated at the Washington, D.C., field office.

**1 April 1928**— Bureau agents receive their first Manual of Rules and Regulations.

**2 April 1928**— Clyde Tolson becomes a BI agent.

**12 January 1929**— The Minneapolis field office is established with Werner Hanni as special agent in charge.

**13–15 May 1929**— Leaders of various Midwestern and East Coast bootleg gangs meet in Atlantic City, N.J., in the first of several conferences designed to organize a national crime syndicate. FBI spokesmen will deny the existence of any such group until 1961.

**11 June 1930**— Congress authorizes collection and publication of national crime statistics by the BI's Division of Identification and Information.

**5 December 1931**— BI agents organize the Recreation Association (later FBI Recreation Association) to promote social activities within the bureau.

**1 March 1932**— International exchange of fingerprint data with friendly foreign governments is initiated.

**22 June 1932**— Congress passes the "Lindbergh Law," making interstate kidnapping a federal crime under BI jurisdiction.

**1 July 1932**— The BI is renamed the United States Bureau of Investigation.

**1 September 1932**— First issue of the BI's periodical, *Fugitives Wanted by Police*, published.

**25 October 1932**— "The Lucky Strike Hour" premieres as the first national radio program based on BI cases.

**24 November 1932**— BI crime laboratory established in Washington, D.C.

**10 June 1933**— President Franklin Roosevelt announces merger of the BI, Prohibition Bureau and the Bureau of Identification into a new Justice Department Division of Investigation (DI).

**17 June 1933**— Four lawmen are killed in Kansas City, Mo., while escorting prisoner Frank Nash to Leavenworth prison; Nash also dies in the shooting. DI agent Raymond Caffrey is among those slain. Bureau leaders suppress evidence that several of the dead were accidentally shot by a surviving federal agent.

**10 August 1933**— Over objections from J. Edgar Hoover, the scandal-ridden Prohibition Bureau is transferred from the Treasury Department to Justice.

**26 September 1933**— George "Machine Gun" Kelly arrested for kidnapping in Memphis. Publicists fabricate Kelly's introduction of the "G-man" nickname for federal agents.

**1 October 1933**— The DI establishes a reference collection of firearms confiscated from arrested suspects.

**10 November 1933**— Civil File of fingerprints from nonarrested persons established by the DI in Washington.

**5 December 1933**— Prohibition is repealed by the 21st Amendment to the U.S. Constitution.

**20 March 1934**— Attorney General Homer Cummings appeals to Congress for passage of new federal laws against bank robbery and extortion, with expanded jurisdiction in kidnapping cases.

**22 April 1934**— Melvin Purvis leads DI agents to arrest the Dillinger gang at a lodge near Rhineland, Wisconsin. Agents shoot three innocent men, killing one, while the bandits escape. Gang member "Baby Face" Nelson kills one DI agent and wounds two other lawmen.

**3 May 1934**— DI agents notify Scotland Yard that Dillinger may be aboard the SS *Duchess of York*, sailing for Glasgow. The tip is a hoax, but police arrest another passenger, fugitive Trebilsch Lincoln, sought for fomenting rebellion in India.

**8 May 1934**— President Roosevelt orders Hoover to begin surveillance of suspected Nazi groups and sympathizers in America.

**19 May 1934**— Congress enacts six of the statutes promoted by Attorney General Cummings.

**18 June 1934**— Congress officially empowers DI agents to make arrests and carry firearms (with special authorization from headquarters).

**20 June 1934**— The federal Communications Act bans wiretapping. Subsequent Supreme Court decisions specifically apply the ban to federal agents.

**22 July 1934**— John Dillinger is killed by DI agents outside a Chicago theater.

**11 October 1934**— The FBI belatedly names "Pretty Boy" Floyd as the ringleader of the Kansas City massacre, citing previously undisclosed ballistics evidence. Floyd is killed by DI agents in Ohio, on 22 October.

**27 November 1934**— Baby Face Nelson dies in a shootout with DI agents near Barrington, Ill.; two agents are also killed.

**16 January 1935**— "Ma" Barker and son Fred are killed by DI agents near Oklawaha, Florida.

**1 July 1935**— The Division of Investigation is officially renamed the Federal Bureau of Investigation.

**10 July 1935**— Melvin Purvis resigns from the FBI.

**29 July 1935**— The FBI National Police Academy is established in Washington, D.C.

**October 1935**—*Fugitives Wanted by Police* becomes the *FBI Law Enforcement Bulletin*.

**30 April 1936**— FBI agents arrest fugitive Alvin Karpis in New Orleans, crediting Hoover with a "personal" capture.

**24 May 1936**— President Roosevelt orders FBI investigation of fascists, communists and other "subversives" in the U.S.

**24 August 1936**— President Roosevelt cites legislation from World War I to authorize sweeping FBI investigation of communist and fascist sympathizers in America.

**5 September 1936**— Hoover directs FBI field offices to collect and report information on "subversive activities" across the nation, "regardless of the source from which this information is received."

**1 May 1937**— The Knoxville, Tennessee field office opens.

**May 1937**— The Bureau's Juneau, Alaska field office opens. It closes in April 1938, due to lack of funding.

**26 June 1939**— A secret directive from FDR assigns responsibility for "espionage, counterespionage, and sabotage matters" to the FBI, the War Department's Military Intelligence Division, and the Navy Department's Office of Naval Intelligence.

**July 1939**— The Juneau, Alaska field office reopens, primarily due to an increase in espionage investigations.

**2 September 1939**— Hoover authorizes creation of a Custodial Detention list, including names of aliens and U.S. citizens deemed "dangerous" in the event of war or national emergency.

**6 September 1939**— FDR publicly orders the FBI to take charge of espionage and sabotage investigations, along with violations of neutrality statutes.

**21 May 1940**— A secret directive from FDR authorizes FBI wiretaps in the course of "national defense" investigations, requiring prior approval from the attorney general.

**5 June 1940**— The FBI assumes responsibility for "internal security" investigations, relegating Military Intelligence and Naval Intelligence to cases involving military personnel and bases.

**15 June 1940**— Hoover seeks permission from Attorney General Robert Jackson for a new list of individuals marked for preventive detention in wartime.

**24 June 1940**— FDR secretly expands FBI jurisdiction to include intelligence and counterintelligence matters throughout the western hemisphere. Hoover creates the Special Intelligence Service to handle cases in Latin America.

**27 June 1940**— National emergency declared.

**28 June 1940**— Passage of the Alien Registration (Smith) Act by Congress forbids any group or individual from advocating violent overthrow of the U.S. government.

**17 October 1940**— Passage of the Foreign Agent Registration (Voorhis) Act requires all foreign-controlled groups advocating overthrow of the U.S. government to register with the attorney general's office.

**1 January 1941**— The FBI Disaster Squad is created to assist civilian authorities in identifying victims of a Virginia airplane crash (including FBI personnel).

**28 June 1941**— Congress appropriates $100,000 for FBI investigation of federal employees linked to "subversive" organizations. FBI agents arrest 33 persons on charges of spying for Nazi Germany.

**8 September 1941**— The Minneapolis field office closes. A new St. Paul field office begins operation with 16 special agents and 880 pending investigations.

**1 October 1941**— Hoover establishes a "Confidential File" system in his office, supervised by Assistant Director Louis Nichols.

**7 December 1941**— Japanese attack on Pearl Harbor; U.S. declares war on the Axis powers. Attorney General Francis Biddle authorizes FBI detention of "enemy aliens."

**22 June 1942**— Hoover orders the nationwide investigation of "agitation among Negroes" by Axis agents and/or members of the Communist Party.

**9 October 1942**— FBI agents in Clinton, Maryland, establish the first of several international radio monitoring stations. The operation is transformed into a "domestic emergency network" after 1947, when the CIA assumes responsibility for foreign intelligence gathering.

**14 January 1943**— The Justice Department authorizes to run background checks on suspect individuals for the American Red Cross. The liaison system soon expands to include collaboration with various other organizations across the country.

**13 July 1943**— Attorney General Biddle orders termination of the FBI's Custodial Detention list.

**14 August 1943**— Hoover technically complies with Biddle's order, but maintains the banned list by renaming it the Security Index.

**20 February 1944**— The Juneau field office transfers to Anchorage, Alaska.

**16 April 1945**— A weekly radio program, "This is Your FBI," begins under close supervision of bureau leaders.

**31 July 1945**— President Harry Truman requests an FBI investigation of White House employees to determine the source of media leaks. Wiretaps are employed to identify the culprits.

**5 September 1945**— FBI investigation of disloyal federal employees intensifies after Soviet embassy clerk Igor Gouzenko defects to Canadian authorities, detailing wartime espionage across North America.

**27 February 1946**— Hoover authorizes a covert "education program" designed to promote "informed public opinion about the seriousness of the Communist threat and their support among liberal elements."

**8 March 1946**— Hoover recommends establishment of a secret Security Index, marking "dangerous" individuals for internment in the event of another war or threat of invasion. Action is deferred on his request, but the FBI begins collecting names.

**17 July 1946**— President Truman authorizes FBI wiretaps during investigation of "subversive activities," later explaining that he meant the rule to apply only in cases "where human life is in jeopardy."

**1 August 1946**— President Truman signs the Atomic Energy Act, mandating FBI investigation of persons having access to restricted nuclear data and those suspected of criminal violations under the law.

**21 March 1947**— Executive Order 9835 establishes the Federal Employee Loyalty System, authorizing FBI investigation of incumbent government employees and new applicants for any taint of "subversive" activity or beliefs.

**13 May 1947**— Hoover secretly approves dissemination of confidential FBI files to the House Committee on Un-American Activities (HUAC) for scheduled hearings on "disloyalty" in Hollywood.

**30 July 1947**— Hoover orders all FBI field offices to investigate UFO sightings nationwide and determine if each is "a bona fide sighting, an imaginary one, or a prank." Agents interview more than a dozen UFO witnesses over the next month.

**3 August 1948**— Attorney General Tom Clark approves FBI plans for the Security Index requested by Hoover in March 1946.

**29 June 1949**— Hoover launches the "JUNE Mail" project, mandating concealment of files obtained by illegal methods in a Special File Room at FBI headquarters. The program remains in effect until November 1978

**8 July 1949**—Hoover inaugurates use of special, disposable "administrative pages" in FBI field reports for recording "facts and information which are considered of a nature not expedient to disseminate, or which could cause embarrassment to the Bureau, if distributed."

**24 September 1949**—The St. Paul field office closes, its operations transferred back to Minneapolis.

**March 1950**—Hoover orders collaboration with Senator Joseph McCarthy's investigations of alleged subversion in the federal government, continuing with strategic advice and delivery of classified files through July 1953.

**14 March 1950**—FBI headquarters launches the "Ten Most Wanted Fugitives" program.

**23 September 1950**—Congress overrides President Truman's veto to pass the Internal Security (McCarran) Act, requiring all communist organizations to register with a new Subversive Activities Control Board. Preventive detention is also approved, the later provision repealed in September 1971.

**12 February 1951**—Hoover establishes the "Responsibilities Program," wherein state governors are furnished derogatory information concerning alleged communists.

**6 March 1951**—The espionage trial of Julius and Ethel Rosenberg, David Greenglass and Morton Sobell begins in New York City. All are convicted on 5 April 1951.

**15 March 1951**—Hoover approves a liaison operation wherein the FBI exchanges information with the U.S. Senate Internal Security Subcommittee (SISS).

**20 June 1951**—Hoover institutes a "Sex Deviates" program to drive identified homosexuals from all branches of federal employment. Later, the program expands to include American universities and state or local police departments.

**26 February 1952**—Attorney General J. Howard McGrath supports use of FBI wiretaps, requiring only that the Justice Department be informed of their use in cases considered for prosecution.

**19 March 1953**—Hoover orders senior FBI officials to destroy the contents of their "office" files at regular intervals.

**26 April 1953**—Executive Order 10450 inaugurates a new test for federal employees, denying jobs to any who cannot prove "unswerving loyalty" to the United States.

**17 November 1953**—Hoover and Attorney General Herbert Brownell testify before the SISS, accusing ex-President Truman of negligence in handling national security matters.

**20 May 1954**—Attorney General Brownell authorizes FBI break-ins and bugging during "national security" investigations. Hoover interprets the ruling to include standard criminal cases.

**28 August 1956**—Hoover launches the first Counterintelligence Program—COINTELPRO—specifically designed to "harass, disrupt, and discredit" the U.S. Communist Party.

**3 June 1957**—The U.S. Supreme Court, in *Jencks v. U.S.*, rules that defense attorneys may examine FBI confidential pretrial reports whenever informers are called to testify at trial. Congress later intervenes on the FBI's behalf, restricting access to "signed" statements relevant to trial testimony.

**14 November 1957**—State police arrest dozens of gangsters during a Mafia conference at Apalachin, New York. The exposure of a national crime syndicate prompts Hoover to create the FBI's "Top Hoodlum" program.

**January 1958**—FBI leaders seek Post Office approval for a "mail cover" program to identify Americans corresponding with persons in the Soviet Union. Post Office officials reveal that the CIA has

maintained such an operation since 1953. From February 1958 onward, the FBI receives copies of mail opened and photocopied by the CIA.

**16 February 1961**—Attorney General Robert Kennedy approves FBI wiretaps on employees of the Agriculture Department and a lobbyist for the Dominican Republic, in respect to proposed amendments to sugar quota legislation.

**27 June 1961**—Attorney General Kennedy requests investigation of leaks to *Newsweek* magazine. FBI agents tap the phone of reporter Lloyd Norman.

**11 October 1961**—Hoover authorizes a second COINTELPRO operation, to "harass, disrupt and discredit" the Socialist Workers Party.

**April-June 1962**—FBI agents plant more wiretaps in Washington, D.C., as part of their investigation into pending legislation on sugar quotas for the Dominican Republic.

**June 1962**—FBI agents tap the phone of *New York Times* reporter Hanson Baldwin, after Attorney General Kennedy orders investigation of news leaks.

**9 June 1962**—President John Kennedy grants supervisory control of all "internal security" matters to his brother, Attorney General Robert Kennedy. FBI autonomy is thus theoretically restricted.

**7 August 1962**—President Kennedy signs National Security Action Memorandum 177, enhancing the U.S. government's foreign police-training program. Hoover agrees to accept up to 20 foreign officers in each session of the FBI National Academy.

**13 February 1963**—Propelled by White House demands that leaders of organized crime be prosecuted, Hoover orders intensified mob investigations nationwide. The Mafia is dubbed "La Cosa Nostra" and proclaimed a new discovery.

**18 October 1963**—Attorney General Kennedy approves 30-day wiretaps on Dr. Martin Luther King Jr. and the Southern Christian Leadership Conference. Hoover maintains the taps until 1965.

**22 November 1963**—President Kennedy is assassinated in Dallas. President Lyndon Johnson orders an FBI investigation, though the Bureau has no jurisdiction over presidential assassinations.

**8 May 1964**—President Johnson exempts Hoover from mandatory retirement at age 70.

**14 May 1964**—Hoover testifies before the Warren Commission, stating that the FBI has found no "scintilla of evidence" suggesting a conspiracy in the death of President Kennedy.

**10 July 1964**—Hoover visits Jackson, Mississippi for the opening of a new FBI field office, in response to acts of terrorism by the Ku Klux Klan.

**23-24 August 1964**—Acting on orders from President Johnson, 30 FBI agents monitor the Democratic National Convention in Atlantic City, New Jersey.

**2 September 1964**—Hoover authorizes a COINTELPRO operation to "expose, disrupt, and otherwise neutralize" the KKK and other white supremacist groups.

**26 October 1964**—Aides to President Johnson request FBI reports on U.S. Senate staff members of GOP presidential candidate Barry Goldwater. The report is delivered on October 28.

**3 February 1965**—The FBI formally agrees to provide Secret Service agents with information necessary to protect the president.

**March 1965**—Attorney General Nicholas Katzenbach issues new guidelines on FBI bugging and wiretaps. Written authorization from the attorney general is now required for each bug or tap, with duration limited to six months.

**10 June 1965**—Millionaire whiskey distiller Lewis Rosenstiel creates the J. Edgar Hoover Foundation at Valley Forge, Pennsylvania, to "perpetuate the ideas and purpose" of the FBI's director.

**August 1965**— Congress enacts legislation making it a federal crime to assault, kidnap or kill the U.S. president, vice president, and other specified government officials.

**19 September 1965**— *The FBI*, first national television series on the bureau, premieres on the American Broadcasting Company network. The show airs through 1974.

**19 February 1966**— President Johnson orders FBI investigation of upcoming Senate Foreign Relations Committee hearings on the administration's Vietnam war strategy "with a view toward determining whether [Chairman William] Fulbright and the other Senators were receiving information from Communists."

**14 March 1966**— President Johnson orders FBI reports on any contact between members of Congress and Eastern bloc embassies. Hoover supplies weekly reports to the White House from 13 May 1966 through 20 January 1969.

**13 June 1966**— The U.S. Supreme Court demands justification of FBI bugging in the case of defendant Fred Black, appealing a conviction for income tax evasion.

**4 July 1966**— President Johnson signs the Freedom of Information Act, providing limited access to files of certain federal agencies. Amendments to the act are passed in November 1974 and October 1986.

**19 July 1966**— Hoover bans future break-ins during FBI investigations.

**September 1966**— The Justice Department orders creation of an "ELSUR Index" to include the names of all subjects whose conversations have been recorded during FBI electronic surveillance.

**December 1966**— Supplied with information by Hoover, Republican congressmen publicly accuse Robert Kennedy of authorizing FBI bugs and wiretaps while he was attorney general.

**1 January 1967**— The FBI's National Crime Information Center (NCIC) becomes operational in Washington, D.C.

**25 August 1967**— Hoover launches a COINTEPLRO operation to "expose, disrupt, misdirect, discredit, or otherwise neutralize" selected "black nationalist hate groups."

**4 April 1968**— Dr. Martin Luther King Jr. is assassinated in Memphis, Tennessee.

**1 June 1968**— Congress enacts Public Law 90351, providing for presidential appointment of the FBI director for a 10-year maximum term. The law has no effect on Hoover's tenure as director.

**4 June 1968**— Senator Robert Kennedy is shot in Los Angeles. He dies from his wounds two days later.

**June 1968**— Congress passes the Omnibus Crime Control and Safe Streets Act, authorizing warranted bugs and wiretaps during criminal investigations, leaving the door open to presidential orders for electronic surveillance in "national security" cases.

**28 October 1968**— Hoover inaugurates a COINTELPRO operation to "harass, discredit, and disrupt" student organizations of the so-called New Left.

**30 October 1968**— The National Security Council requests FBI surveillance of prominent Republican Anna Chennault and the South Vietnamese embassy in Washington, to determine if GOP strategists are obstructing peace talks in Vietnam

**13 November 1968**— President Johnson orders an FBI check of telephone records to learn if GOP vice presidential candidate Spiro Agnew has spoken to Anna Chennault or the South Vietnamese embassy.

**9 May 1969**— President Richard Nixon and Henry Kissinger order FBI wiretaps on four Washington journalists and 13 federal officials,

seeking sources of news leaks to the *New York Times*. The taps continue through February 1971 without identifying the leakers.

**5 November 1969**— The White House orders FBI investigation of syndicated columnist Joseph Kraft, seeking sources of his information on the Paris peace talks.

**26 November 1969**— Hoover creates the INLET program, furnishing President Nixon and his staff with information from FBI files.

**31 March 1970**— Hoover's intermittent feud with the CIA resumes with termination of liaison between the two agencies and a cutback in FBI surveillance instituted at the CIA's request.

**5 June 1970**— President Nixon orders Hoover to assist House minority leader Gerald Ford in his efforts to impeach U.S. Supreme Court Justice William Douglas.

**27 July 1970**— Hoover resumes his weekly reports to the White House, detailing congressional contacts with communist embassies in Washington, D.C.

**15 October 1970**— Congress passes the Organized Crime Control Act, expanding FBI authority to pursue racketeers.

**25 November 1970**— White House aide H.R. Haldeman orders the FBI to provide a list of Washington journalists who are gay or "any other stuff." The list is delivered on 27 November.

**8 March 1971**— Thousands of FBI COINTEPLRO documents are stolen from the resident agency in Media, Pennsylvania, later published by the War Resisters League and the Citizens' Committee to Investigate the FBI. Hoover closes 103 of the FBI's 538 resident agencies, but investigation fails to identify the burglars.

**28 April 1971**— Hoover terminates all COINTEPLRO operations, lately exposed by the Media burglary.

**30 September 1971**— Hoover fires Assistant to the Director William Sullivan and locks him out of his office. Sullivan delivers wiretap transcripts and other sensitive records to the Justice Department.

**22–23 October 1971**— White House aides urge President Nixon to demand Hoover's resignation. Nixon declines.

**29–30 October 1971**— The American Civil Liberties Union and Princeton University's Woodrow Wilson School of Politics and International Affairs host a conference evaluating modern FBI practices.

**2 May 1972**— J. Edgar Hoover is found dead at his home in Washington, D.C.

**3 May 1972**— President Nixon appoints L. Patrick Gray as acting FBI director. Nominated as full-time director in February 1973, Gray later admits destroying records in the Watergate scandal and withdraws his nomination on 23 April 1973.

**4 May 1972**— Longtime Hoover secretary Helen Gandy begins shredding the late director's "Personal and Confidential" files.

**8 May 1972**— The new FBI Academy opens at the U.S. Marine Corps base in Quantico, Virginia. Its first class convenes on June 26.

**June 19, 1972**— The U.S. Supreme Court, in *U.S. v. U.S. District Court*, rules that the president has no authority to order warrantless wiretaps in "domestic security" cases. The question of "foreign intelligence" cases remains unresolved.

**24 October 1972**— Congress passes Public Law 92–539, authorizing FBI investigation of any kidnapping involving foreign officials or official guests on U.S. soil.

**27 February 1973**— 200 supporters of the American Indian Movement seize a strategic hamlet at Wounded Knee, South Dakota. The siege continues until 9 May, with casualties inflicted on both sides during several shootouts between AIM members and FBI agents.

**23 April 1973** — L. Patrick Gray resigns as acting FBI director. President Nixon appoints William Ruckelshaus to replace Gray on 27 April.

**6 June 1973** — President Nixon nominates Clarence Kelley as FBI director. Kelley is confirmed by the U.S. Senate on 27 June and sworn in on 9 July.

**11 July 1973** — Attorney General Elliott Richardson authorizes release of closed FBI records more than 15 years old to historical researchers.

**February 1974** — FBI leaders inaugurate the PRISACT program, to coordinate action with local police in surveillance of militant extremists imprisoned throughout the U.S. Black nationalists are the primary targets.

**17 May 1974** — Six members of the Symbionese Liberation Army die in a shootout with FBI agents and Los Angeles police.

**21 November 1974** — Congress overrides President Gerald Ford's veto of amendments to the Freedom of Information Act, broadening access to FBI records.

**27 January 1975** — The Senate Select Committee on Intelligence Activities is established to investigate operations of the FBI and CIA. Committee hearings reveal numerous instances of abuse by both agencies.

**19 February 1975** — Following the Senate's lead, the House of Representatives creates a committee to investigate U.S. intelligence activities. On 29 January 1976 the House votes to suppress the committee's final report, but a copy is obtained and published by the *Village Voice*.

**21 February 1975** — Congressional testimony by Attorney General Edward Levi reveals that J. Edgar Hoover maintained derogatory dossiers on prominent Americans, including presidents and members of Congress.

**May 1975** — FBI leaders recommend destruction of all closed FBI files in the National Archives. The plan is approved on 26 March 1976, but various civic groups file lawsuits to block the purge of records. In January 1980, a federal court enjoins the FBI and National Archives from destroying the records, mandating development of a plan to preserve any records of "historical value."

**26 June 1975** — FBI agents Jack Coler and Ronald Williams die in a shootout with Indian activists on the Pine Ridge, South Dakota, reservation.

**22 September 1975** — FBI informer Sarah Jane Moore fires a pistol at President Ford in San Francisco.

**30 September 1975** — The J. Edgar Hoover FBI Building is dedicated in Washington, D.C.

**1 October 1975** — The FBI activates its Missing Person File in Washington.

**18 February 1976** — Executive Order 11905 broadly outlines the responsibilities and authority of federal intelligence agencies, including the FBI and CIA.

**10 March 1976** — Attorney General Levy issues guidelines for FBI counterintelligence and domestic security investigations. Counterintelligence guidelines remain secret; domestic security guidelines permit 90-day "preliminary" investigations, while "full" investigations require annual written approval from Justice.

**17 March 1976** — Agents in New York find 25 volumes of documents in the office safe of SAC John Malone, describing illegal FBI break-ins committed between 1954 and 1973. Investigators later report that no such documents exist in any other field office.

**July 1976** — Preliminary hearings on a lawsuit filed against the FBI by leaders of the Socialist Workers Party reveal that FBI agents repeatedly burglarized SWP offices during the 1960s and 1970s.

**4 October 1976** — The FBI establishes an Office of Professional Responsibility to investigate alleged criminal or ethical infractions by FBI agents.

**1 January 1978** — Federal legislation passed in 1976 imposed a mandatory retirement age of 55 on all FBI personnel.

**19 January 1978** — President Jimmy Carter nominates William Webster as FBI director. Webster is confirmed by the Senate on 9 February and sworn in on 23 February.

**24 January 1978** — Executive Order 12036 tightens restrictions on foreign intelligence and counterintelligence activities.

**3 April 1978** — The FBI Laboratory pioneers use of laser technology to detect fingerprints on criminal case evidence.

**28 May 1978** — The elusive "Unabomber" detonates his first explosive device at the University of Illinois in Chicago. G-men pursue the unknown subject for 18 years, until a relative betrays him in April 1996.

**7 June 1978** — The FBI's UNIRAC investigation climaxes with indictment of 22 labor union officials and shipping executives in Miami. More than 110 convictions are finally recorded in the long-running probe of kickbacks, embezzlement and related crimes.

**25 October 1978** — President Carter signs the Foreign Intelligence Surveillance Act, thereby creating a special court to secretly review and approve government requests for bugs and wiretaps.

**18 December 1978** — A computerized Intelligence Information System goes online at FBI headquarters in Washington.

**21 April 1980** — A computerized Organized Crime Information System goes online in the FBI's Detroit field office.

**3 October 1980** — FBI inauguration of a computerized fingerprint search and identification program reduces average processing time from two weeks to 24 hours.

**5 January 1981** — Attorney General Benjamin Civiletti establishes new guidelines for FBI investigation concerning bribery of public officials.

**16 June 1981** — The FBI's Forensic Science Research and Training Center is dedicated at Quantico, Virginia.

**4 December 1981** — Executive Order 12333 outlines new rules for FBI conduct during efforts to "collect foreign intelligence or to support foreign intelligence collection requirements" inside the U.S.

**28 January 1982** — Attorney General William Smith gives the FBI and Drug Enforcement Administration concurrent jurisdiction in federal narcotics cases, ordering the DEA's chief to report to the FBI director.

**January 1983** — The Knoxville field office launches Operation MAYBAN, a three-year investigation of white-collar crime in the banking industry. Six defendants are ultimately charged with conspiracy, bankruptcy fraud and other felonies related to the failure of a 26-bank conglomerate with assets exceeding $3 billion.

**7 March 1983** — Attorney General Smith issues new guidelines for FBI "domestic security/terrorism" investigations. Covert operations to "anticipate or prevent" crime are authorized, while existing requirements for Justice Department review and authorization are rescinded.

**30 June 1983** — The FBI activates its Unidentified Person File, to collate reports of corpses found across the U.S.

**August 1983** — The FBI Hostage Rescue Team is established, in the mold of urban police SWAT teams.

**10 July 1984** — The National Center for Analysis of Violent Crime is established at the FBI Academy, employing psychological profiling to assist local police in unsolved cases.

**3 October 1984** — FBI agent Richard Miller becomes the first G-man arrested for espionage. His Russian accomplices plead guilty and cooperate with the prosecution. Miller is convicted on 19 June 1986.

**12 October 1984**— President Reagan signs the Omnibus Crime Control Act, expanding federal jurisdiction to computer crimes and counterfeit consumer goods, while strengthening federal authority to seize assets of drug dealers.

**11 April 1986**— Seven FBI agents are shot in Miami, two fatally, in a battle with fugitive bank robbers.

**17 October 1986**— The Freedom of Information Act is amended, exempting certain law enforcement investigative information from public scrutiny.

**26 May 1987**— Director Webster resigns to accept appointment as director of the CIA. John Otto becomes acting director.

**24 July 1987**— President Reagan nominates William Sessions as FBI director. Sessions is confirmed by the U.S. Senate on 25 September and sworn in on 2 November.

**26 September 1988**— A federal court finds that the FBI has systematically discriminated against Hispanic agents in promotions and working conditions. On 5 May 1989, Judge Lucius Bunton orders changes in FBI promotion procedures but refuses to award the plaintiffs back pay.

**1 December 1988**— The FBI Laboratory begins accepting DNA samples for analysis from state and local police departments. DNA testing in rape and murder cases soon becomes routine.

**21 June 1989**— Attorney General Richard Thornburgh authorizes FBI agents to arrest suspected terrorists, drug smugglers and other fugitives outside with U.S., without prior consent of the nations where they are found.

**18 January 1990**— FBI agents and local police arrest Mayor Marion Berry for cocaine possession in Washington, D.C. Though charged with 14 counts of possession and perjury, Berry is convicted only on one misdemeanor charge and later wins reelection to office.

**12 June 1990**— FBI agent Mark Putnam pleads guilty to manslaughter in the slaying of his pregnant girlfriend at Pikeville, Kentucky. He receives a 16-year prison term.

**August 1990**— Director Sessions settles a lawsuit filed by Agent Donald Rochon against the FBI, claiming racial harassment suffered at field offices in Chicago, Omaha and Philadelphia. The settlement includes monetary damages and administrative punishment of 11 agents who either harassed Rochon or ignored his complaints.

**August 1991**— The FBI creates a new Computer Analysis and Response Team to assist in various investigations.

**21 December 1991**— The Soviet Union dissolves, officially ending the Cold War. On 9 January 1992, Director Sessions transfers 300 FBI agents from foreign counterintelligence duties to violent crime investigations, under the bureau's Safe Streets program.

**11 March 1992**— An FBI Criminal Justice Information Services Division is established at Clarksburg, Virginia, combining the National Crime Information Center, the Automated Fingerprint Identification System, and the Uniform Crime Reports Program.

**July 1992**— The FBI Laboratory installs a new computerized ballistics database, code-named DRUGFIRE.

**26 February 1993**— A car bomb explodes in the underground garage of New York's World Trade Center, killing six persons and injuring more than 1,000. FBI investigation identifies six Middle Eastern terrorists involved in the bombing.

**19 July 1993**— President Bill Clinton fires FBI Director Sessions, charged with unethical use of his office for personal gain. Deputy director Floyd Clarke is named acting director.

**9 August 1993**— The National Drug Intelligence Center is dedicated at Johnstown, Pennsylvania, consolidating elements of the FBI, DEA, ATF and Coast Guard to apprehend drug traffickers.

**September 1, 1993**— Louis Freeh is confirmed and sworn in as FBI director.

**December 1993**— The FBI makes its first use of the Internet, requesting information on the UNABOM investigation.

**27 January 1994**— Director Freeh transfers 600 supervisory and administrative agents to work on criminal and national security cases.

**7 March 1994**— Director Freeh requires polygraph tests for all FBI job applicants, imposes harsher penalties for agent misconduct, and forbids bias based on sexual orientation.

**April 18, 1994**— Freeh enlarges the Hostage Rescue Team from 52 to 77 agents, appointing a new SAC for Critical Incident Response to oversee emergencies.

**May 1994**— Congress passes the Freedom of Access to Clinic Enterprises Act, making violent interference with abortion clinics a federal crime under FBI jurisdiction.

**28 June 1994**— A delegation of FBI officials meet with senior officers from 11 Eastern European nations to coordinate criminal investigations.

**7 October 1994**— Congress passes the Digital Telephony Act, in response to new technology, requiring the telecommunications industry to cooperate with court-ordered wiretaps in federal investigations.

**18 December 1996**— FBI supervisor Earl Pitts is arrested for selling classified documents to Russian intelligence agents over an eight-year period.

**27 January 1997**— Scandals surrounding the FBI Laboratory, including official reports of negligence and mishandled evidence, prompts the transfer of four senior staff members to posts outside the lab. A new lab director is appointed on 22 October 1997. The National Association of Criminal Defense Lawyers calls for a congressional investigation of the lab's practices on 25 November 1997. On 11 March 1998 the FBI settles a Privacy Act lawsuit filed by the original whistle-blower, with a payment of $300,000. On 8 August 1998, two lab employees receive "minimal" disciplinary censures for mishandling evidence.

**8 December 1997**— The FBI announces its new National DNA Index System (NDIS). On the same day, the FBI Laboratory declares its success in extracting DNA profiles from mitochondrial DNA, thus permitting analysis of minute samples (including strands of human hair).

**26 February 1998**— FBI leaders settle a lawsuit filed by crime lab whistle-blower Frederic Whitehurst, alleging that bureau officials punished him illegally for revealing malfeasance in the FBI Laboratory. Whitehurst receives $1.1 million in damages.

**May 1998**— Director Freeh makes a five-day tour of South America, conferring with authorities in Argentina, Brazil, Chile, Colombia and Venezuela.

**7 August 1998**— Terrorist bombings of U.S. embassies in Nairobi and Dar es Salaam kill hundreds of American, Kenyan and Tanzanian citizens. A Joint Terrorist Task Force, including FBI agents and members of various other agencies, conducts the global investigation. As a result, terrorist leader Usama Bin Laden is added to the Bureau's "Ten Most Wanted" List on 7 June 1999.

**13 October 1998**— The FBI introduces its National DNA Index System.

**30 November 1998**— The FBI's National Instant Check System is inaugurated to screen potential firearms purchasers for criminal records. By 14 December the system has examined 372,565 would-be buyers. That number increases to 1,030,606 by 11 January 1999, with 11,584 sales to ex-convicts prevented.

**1 April 1999**—Investigation by the Cleveland field office results in Four Pillars Enterprises, a Taiwanese company, becoming the first foreign firm convicted under the Economic Espionage Act of 1996.

**27 April 1999**—Operation "Sudden Stop," targeting organized car thieves across the country, results in more than 200 arrests in 22 cities. Federal indictments are filed against 125 suspects in October 1999, with 93 more indicted in February 2000.

**12 June 1999**—Teams of FBI agents and forensic scientists are dispatched to examine mass graves around Kosovo, assisting in prosecution of suspected war criminals. Their investigation is completed on 30 June after examination of nine burial sites.

**23 July 1999**—Public tours of FBI headquarters are suspended indefinitely, pending installation of new security devices.

**10 August 1999**—The FBI inaugurates its Integrated Automated Fingerprint Identification System.

**15 August 2000**—Director Freeh revises the FBI disciplinary system to create a single standard for all Bureau employees, including those in the Senior Executive Service.

**22 September 1999**—FBI agents tell a Senate committee that leaders of the Justice Department blocked investigation of Democratic Party fundraising irregularities in 1997.

**11 November 1999**—A major restructuring of FBI headquarters is announced, including creation of two new divisions—Counterterrorism and Investigative Services.

**8 May 2000**—The Justice Department establishes its Internet Fraud Complaint Center.

**14 November 2000**—The FBI's Regional Computer Forensics Laboratory opens in San Diego.

**5 January 2001**—The FBI and spokesmen for the Justice Department's Infrastructure Protection Center introduce the National InfraGuard Program.

**18 February 2001**—FBI agent Robert Hanssen is arrested and charged with spying for Russia.

**1 May 2001**—Director Freeh announces his retirement, effective on 2 June 2001.

**6 July 2001**—President George W. Bush appoints Robert Mueller as director of the FBI.

**11 September 2001**—Middle Eastern terrorists trained at American flight schools hijack four commercial airliners and use them as weapons in a series of coordinated attacks. Two planes crash into New York's World Trade Center, collapsing both towers and claiming 3,380 lives. A third plane crashes into the Pentagon, in Washington, D.C., killing 189 persons. The fourth plane crashes in rural Pennsylvania, killing all 44 aboard, after passengers and crew try to overpower the hijackers. FBI agents launch the largest criminal investigation in U.S. history, quickly blaming "Top Ten" fugitive Usama Bin Laden for masterminding the attacks.

**18 October 2001**—The FBI and U.S. Postal Service offer a joint $1,000,000 reward for information leading to the arrest of persons responsible for mailing anthrax-contaminated letters to media organizations and congressional offices. The case remains unsolved.

**26 October 2001**—President Bush signs the "USA Patriot" Act into law, granting broad new search and surveillance powers to American police and intelligence agencies.

**19 November 2001**—The FBI and U.S. Army announce construction of a new Hazardous Devices School at Huntsville, Alabama, created to certify bomb technicians for anti-terrorist work.

**3 December 2001**—A reorganization of FBI Headquarters is announced, including appointment of four new executive assistant directors to supervise criminal and anti-terrorist investigations in the wake of the 11 September attacks.

**February 2002**—More than 1,300 FBI personnel collaborate with other federal, state and local law enforcement agencies to provide security at the 2002 Winter Olympic Games in Salt Lake City.

**1 October 2002**—FBI headquarters announces the rehiring of 60 retired agents as "special consultants" to "plug holes" in the Bureau's Counterintelligence and Counterterrorism units, while new agents are hired and trained.

**26 November 2002**—President Bush signs legislation merging 22 federal agencies into a new Department of Homeland Security. The FBI is not affected.

# Appendix C: Agents Killed in the Line of Duty

| Name | Date | Name | Date |
|---|---|---|---|
| Edwin C. Shanahan | 11 October 1925 | Ronald A. Williams | 26 June 1975 |
| Paul E. Reynolds | 9 August 1929 | Trenwith S. Basford | 25 August 1977 |
| Albert J. Ingle | 24 November 1931 | Mark A. Kirkland | 25 August 1977 |
| Raymond J. Caffrey | 17 June 1933 | Johnnie L. Oliver | 9 August 1979 |
| W. Carter Baum | 22 April 1934 | Charles W. Elmore | 9 August 1979 |
| Herman E. Hollis | 27 November 1934 | Jared Robert Porter | 9 August 1979 |
| Samuel P. Cowley | 28 November 1934 | Terry Burnett Hereford | 16 December 1982 |
| Nelson B. Klein | 16 August 1935 | Robert W. Conners | 16 December 1982 |
| Wimberly W. Baker | 17 April 1937 | Charles L. Ellington | 16 December 1982 |
| Truett E. Rowe | 1 June 1937 | Michael James Lynch | 16 December 1982 |
| William R. Ramsey | 3 May 1938 | Robin L. Ahrens | 5 October 1985 |
| Hubert J. Treacy, Jr. | 13 March 1942 | Jerry L. Dove | 11 April 1986 |
| Percy E. Foxworth | 15 January 1943 | Benjamin P. Grogan | 11 April 1986 |
| Harold Dennis Haberfeld | 15 January 1943 | James K. McCallister | 18 April 1986 |
| Richard Blackstone Brown | 14 July 1943 | Scott K. Carey | 10 May 1988 |
| Joseph J. Brock | 26 July 1952 | L. Douglas Abram | 19 January 1990 |
| John Brady Murphy | 26 September 1953 | John L. Bailey | 25 June 1990 |
| Richard Purcell Horan | 18 April 1957 | Stanley Ronquest, Jr. | 11 March 1992 |
| Terry R. Anderson | 17 May 1966 | Martha Dixon Martinez | 22 November 1994 |
| Douglas M. Price | 25 April 1968 | Michael John Miller | 22 November 1994 |
| Anthony Palmisano | 8 January 1969 | William Christian, Jr. | 29 May 1995 |
| Edwin R. Woodriffe | 8 January 1969 | Charles Leo Reed | 22 March 1996 |
| Gregory W. Spinelli | 15 March 1973 | Paul A. Leveille | 1 September 1999 |
| Jack R. Coler | 26 June 1975 | Leonard Hatton | 11 September 2001 |

# Appendix D: Field Offices

## ALABAMA

Birmingham Field Office
2121 8th Avenue N., Room 1400
Birmingham, AL 35203–2396
(205) 326–6166

Mobile Field Office
One St. Louis Centre
1 St. Louis Street, 3rd Floor
Mobile, AL 36602–3930
(334) 438–3674

## ALASKA

Anchorage Field Office
101 East Sixth Avenue
Anchorage, AK 99501–2524
(907) 258–5322

## ARIZONA

Phoenix Field Office
201 East Indianapolis Avenue, Suite
400
Phoenix, AZ 85012–2080
(602) 279–5511

## ARKANSAS

Little Rock Field Office
Two Financial Centre, Suite 200
10825 Financial Centre Parkway
Little Rock, AR 72211–3552
(501) 221–9100

## CALIFORNIA

Los Angeles Field Office
Federal Office Building, Suite 1700
11000 Wilshire Boulevard
Los Angeles, CA 90024–3672
(310) 477–6565

Sacramento Field Office
4500 Orange Grove Avenue
Sacramento, CA 95841–4205
(916) 481–9110

San Diego Field Office
Federal Office Building
9797 Aero Drive
San Diego, CA 92123–1800
(858) 565–1255

San Francisco Field Office
450 Golden Gate Avenue, 13th Floor
San Francisco, CA 94102–9523
(415) 553–7400

## COLORADO

Denver Field Office
Federal Office Building, Suite 1823
1961 Stout Street, 18th Floor
Denver, CO 80294–1823
(303) 629–7171

## CONNECTICUT

New Haven Field Office
Federal Office Building, Room 535
150 Court Street
New Haven CT 06510–2020
(203) 777–6311

## DISTRICT OF COLUMBIA

Washington Metropolitan Field Office
601 4th Street, NW
Washington, DC 20535–0002
(202) 278–2000

## FLORIDA

Jacksonville Field Office
7820 Arlington Expressway, Suite 200

Jacksonville, FL 32211–7499
(904) 721–1211

Miami Field Office
16320 Northwest Second Avenue
North Miami Beach, FL 33169–6508
(305) 944–9101

Tampa Field Office
Federal Office Building, Room 610
500 Zack Street
Tampa, FL 33602–3917
(813) 273–4566

## GEORGIA

Atlanta Field Office
2635 Century Parkway, NE, Suite 400
Atlanta, GA 30345–3112
(404) 679–9000

## HAWAII

Honolulu Field Office
Kalanianaole Federal Office Building,
   Room 4–230
300 Ala Moana Boulevard
Honolulu, HI 96850–0053
(808) 566–4300

## ILLINOIS

Chicago Field Office
E.M. Dirksen Federal Office Building,
   Room 905
219 South Dearborn Street
Chicago, IL 60604–1702
(312) 431–1333

Springfield Field Office
400 West Monroe Street, Suite 400
Springfield, IL 62704–1800
(217) 522–9675

## INDIANA

Indianapolis Field Office
Federal Office Building, Room 679
575 North Pennsylvania Street
Indianapolis, IN 46204–1585
(317) 639–3301

## KENTUCKY

Louisville Field Office
600 Martin Luther King Jr. Place, Room 500
Louisville, KY 40202–2231
(502) 583–3941

## LOUISIANA

New Orleans Field Office
2901 Leon C. Simon Drive
New Orleans, LA 70126
(504) 816–3000

## MARYLAND

Baltimore Field Office
7142 Ambassador Road
Baltimore, MD 21244–2754
(410) 265–8080

## MASSACHUSETTS

Boston Field Office
One Center Plaza, Suite 600
Boston, MA 02108
(617) 742–5533

## MICHIGAN

Detroit Field Office
P.V. McNamara Federal Office Building,
26th Floor
477 Michigan Avenue
Detroit, MI 48226
(313) 965–2323

## MINNESOTA

Minneapolis Field Office
111 Washington Avenue, South, Suite 1100
Minneapolis, MN 55401–2176
(612) 376–3200

## MISSISSIPPI

Jackson Field Office
Federal Office Building, Room 1553
100 West Capitol Street
Jackson, MS 39269–1601
(601) 948–5000

## MISSOURI

Kansas City Field Office

1300 Summit
Kansas City, MO 64105–1362
(816) 512–8200

St. Louis Field Office
2222 Market Street
St. Louis, MO 63103–2516
(314) 231–4324

## NEBRASKA

Omaha Field Office
10755 Burt Street
Omaha, NE 68114–2000
(402) 493–8688

## NEVADA

Las Vegas Field Office
700 East Charleston Boulevard
Las Vegas, NV 89104–1545
(702) 385–1281

## NEW JERSEY

Newark Field Office
1 Gateway Center, 22nd Floor
Newark, NJ 07102–9889
(973) 792–3000

## NEW MEXICO

Albuquerque Field Office
415 Silver Avenue, Southwest, Suite 300
Albuquerque, NM 87102
(505) 224–2000

## NEW YORK

Albany Field Office
200 McCarty Avenue
Albany, NY 12209
(518) 465–7551

Buffalo Field Office
One FBI Plaza
Buffalo, NY 14202–2698
(716) 856–7800

New York Field Office
26 Federal Plaza, 23rd Floor
New York, NY 10278
(212) 384–1000

## NORTH CAROLINA

Charlotte Field Office
400 South Tryon Street, Suite 900
Charlotte, NC 28285–0001
(704) 377–9200

## OHIO

Cincinnati Field Office

550 Main Street, Room 9000
Cincinnati, OH 45202–8501
(513) 421–4310

Cleveland Field Office
Federal Office Building, Room 3005
Cleveland, OH 44199–9912
(216) 522–1400

## OKLAHOMA

Oklahoma City Field Office
3301 West Memorial Drive
Oklahoma City, OK 73134
(405) 290–7770

## OREGON

Portland Field Office
Crown Plaza Building, Suite 400
1500 Southwest 1st Avenue
Portland, OR 97201–5828
(503) 224–4181

## PENNSYLVANIA

Philadelphia Field Office
William Green Jr. Federal Office Building,
8th Floor
600 Arch Street
Philadelphia, PA 19106
(215) 418–4000

Pittsburgh Field Office
U.S. Post Office Building, Suite 300
700 Grant Street
Pittsburgh, PA 15219–1906
(412) 471–2000

## PUERTO RICO

San Juan Field Office
U.S. Federal Building, Room 206
150 Carlos Chardon Avenue
Hato Rey
San Juan, Puerto Rico 00918–1716
(787) 754–6000

## SOUTH CAROLINA

Columbia Field Office
151 Westpark Boulevard
Columbia, SC 29210–3857
(803) 551–4200

## TENNESSEE

Knoxville Field Office
John J. Duncan Federal Office Building,
Suite 600
710 Locust Street
Knoxville, TN 37902–3672
(865) 544–0751

Memphis Field Office
Eagle Crest Building, Suite 3000
225 North Humphreys Boulevard
Memphis, TN 38120–2107
(901) 747–4300

## TEXAS

Dallas Field Office
1801 North Lamar, Suite 300
Dallas, TX 75202–1795
(214) 720–2200

El Paso Field Office
660 South Mesa Hills Drive
El Paso, TX 79912–5533
(915) 832–5000

Houston Field Office
2500 East TC Jester
Houston, TX 77008–1300
(713) 693–5000

San Antonio Field Office
U.S. Post Office Courthouse Building,
Suite 200
615 East Houston Street
San Antonio, TX 78205–9998
(210) 225–6741

## UTAH

Salt Lake City Field Office
257 Towers Building, Suite 1200
257 East, 200 South
Salt Lake City, UT 84111–2048
(801) 579–1400

## VIRGINIA

Norfolk Field Office
150 Corporate Boulevard
Norfolk, VA 23502–4999
(757) 455–0100

Richmond Field Office
1970 East Parham Road
Richmond, VA 23228
(804) 261–1044

## WASHINGTON

Seattle Field Office
1110 Third Avenue
Seattle, WA 98101–2904
(206) 622–0460

## WISCONSIN

Milwaukee Field Office
330 East Kilbourn Avenue, Suite 300
Milwaukee, WI 53202–6627
(414) 276–4684

# Appendix E: Most Wanted Fugitives, 1950–2003

Four hundred seventy-six fugitives have been posted to the FBI's "Ten Most Wanted" list since its creation in March 1950. They are listed below in order of their appearance on the list, with basic information including name, federal charge(s) filed, date of listing, and date of capture (if apprehended). Because selection takes time, some Top Ten fugitives were captured before their listing was publicly announced. FBI abbreviations denote the following crimes:

CRV = conditional release violation
EFP = escaped federal prisoner
FFA = Federal Firearms Act violations
ITOM = interstate transportation of obscene materials
ITSMV = interstate transportation of stolen motor vehicles
ITSP = interstate transportation of stolen property
NFA = National Firearms Act
PV = parole violation
RICO = racketeering influence in corrupt organizations
UFAC = unlawful flight to avoid confinement (with state charge)
UFAP = unlawful flight to avoid prosecution (with state charge)

1. Thomas James Holden: UFAP — murder. Listed: 14 March 1950; Apprehended: 23 June 1951
2. Morley Vernon King: UFAP — murder. Listed: 15 March 1950; Apprehended: 31 October 1951
3. William Raymond Nesbit: UFAC — murder. Listed: 16 March 1950; Apprehended: 18 March 1950
4. Henry Randolph Mitchell: Bank robbery. Listed: 17 March 1950; Dropped from list 18 July 1958
5. Omar August Pinson: UFAC — murder. Listed: 18 March 1950; Apprehended: 18 August 1950
6. Lee Emory Downs: UFAP — burglary. Listed: 20 March 1950; Apprehended: 7 April 1950
7. Orba Elmer Jackson: EFP. Listed: 21 March 1950; Apprehended: 22 March 1950
8. Glen Roy Wright: UFAP — robbery. Listed: 22 March 1950; Apprehended: 13 December 1950
9. Henry Harland Shelton: Kidnapping; ITSMV. Listed: 23 March 1950; Apprehended: 23 June 1950
10. Morris Guralnick: UFAP — assault. Listed: 24 March 1950; Apprehended: 15 December 1950
11. William Francis Sutton: UFAC — armed robbery. Listed: 20 March 1950; Apprehended: 18 February 1952
12. Stephen William Davenport: EFP; ITSMV. Listed: 4 April 1950; Apprehended: 5 May 1950
13. Henry Clay Tollett: EFP. Listed: 11 April 1950; Apprehended: 3 June 1951
14. Frederick J. Tenuto: UFAC — murder. Listed: 24 May 1950; Dropped from list: 9 March 1964
15. Thomas Kling: UFAP — attempted armed robbery. Listed: 17 July 1950; Apprehended: 20 February 1952
16. Meyer Dembin: Bank robbery; ITSMV. Listed: 5 September 1950; Apprehended: 26 November 1951
17. Courtney Townsend Taylor: CRV; ITSP. Listed: 8 January 1951; Apprehended: 16 February 1951
18. Joseph Franklin Brent Jr.: UFAP — robbery. Listed: 9 January 1951; Apprehended: 29 August 1952
19. Harry H. Burton: UFAP — murder. Listed: 9 March 1951; Apprehended: 7 February 1952
20. Joseph Paul Cato: UFAP — murder. Listed: 27 June 1951; Surrendered: 21 June 1951
21. Anthony Brancato: UFAP — robbery. Listed: 27 June 1951; Apprehended: 29 June 1951
22. Frederick Emerson Peters: ITSP; PV. Listed: 2 July 1951; Apprehended: 15 January 1952
23. Ernest Tait: UFAP — burglary. Listed: 11 July 1951; Apprehended: 12 July 1951
24. Ollie Gene Embry: Bank robbery; ITSMV; ITSP. Listed: 25 July 1951; Apprehended: 5 August 1951
25. Fiachino A. Baccolia: Obstructing justice. Listed: 20 August 1951; Apprehended: 10 December 1951
26. Raymond Edward Young: UFAP — burglary. Listed: 12 November 1951; Apprehended: 16 November 1951
27. John Thomas Hill: UFAP — murder. Listed: 10 December 1951; Apprehended: 16 August 1952
28. George Arthur Heroux: Bank robbery. Listed: 19 December 1951; Apprehended: 25 July 1952

29. Sydney Gordon Martin: UFAP — murder. Listed: 7 January 1952; Apprehended: 27 November 1953

30. Gerhard Arthur Puff: Bank robbery. Listed: 28 January 1952; Apprehended: 26 July 1952

31. Thomas Edward Young: Bank robbery. Listed: 21 February 1952; Apprehended: 23 September 1952

32. Kenneth Lee Maurer: UFAP — murder. Listed: 27 February 1952; Apprehended: 8 January 1953

33. Isaie Aldy Beausoleil: UFAP — murder. Listed: 3 March 1952; Apprehended: 25 June 1953

34. Leonard Joseph Zalutsky: UFAC — murder. Listed: 5 August 1952; Apprehended: 8 September 1952

35. William Merle Martin: ITSMV. Listed: 11 August 1952; Apprehended: 30 August 1952

36. James Eddie Diggs: UFAP — murder. Listed: 27 August 1952; Dropped from list 14 December 1961

37. Nick George Montos: UFAP — armed robbery. Listed: 8 September 1952; Apprehended: 23 August 1954

38. Theodore Robert Byrd Jr.: ITSP. Listed: 10 September 1952; Apprehended: 21 August 1954

39. Harden Collins Kemper: ITSMV. Listed: 17 September 1952; Apprehended: 1 January 1953

40. John Joseph Brennan: Bank robbery. Listed: 6 October 1952; 23 January 1953

41. Charles Patrick Shue: Bank robbery. Listed: 15 January 1953; Apprehended: 13 February 1953

42. Lawson David Shirt Butler: UFAC — armed robbery. Listed: 22 January 1953; Apprehended: 21 April 1953

43. Joseph James Brletic: UFAP — robbery. Listed: 9 February 1953; Apprehended: 10 February 1953

44. David Dallas Taylor: UFAC — murder. Listed: 3 March 1953; Apprehended: 26 May 1953

45. Perlie Miller: UFAC — armed robbery. Listed: 4 March 1953; Apprehended: 5 March 1953

46. Fred William Bowerman: Bank robbery. Listed: 5 March 1953; Killed by police: 24 April 1953

47. Robert Benton Mathus: UFAP — armed robbery. Listed: 16 March 1953; Apprehended: 19 March 1953

48. Floyd Allen Hill: UFAP — robbery. Listed: 30 March 1953; Apprehended: 18 April 1953

49. Joseph Levy: PV; CRV; ITSP. Listed: 1 May 1953; Apprehended: 30 April 1953

50. Arnold Hinson: UFAP — murder. Listed: 4 May 1953; Apprehended: 7 November 1953

51. Gordon Lee Cooper: UFAP — armed robbery. Listed: 11 May 1953; Apprehended: 11 June 1953

52. Fleet Robert Current: UFAP — robbery. Listed: 8 June 1953; Apprehended: 12 July 1953

53. Donald Charles Fitterer: UFAP — murder. Listed: 8 June 1953; Apprehended: 21 June 1953

54. John Raleigh Cooke: Kidnapping. Listed: 22 June 1953; Apprehended: 20 October 1953

55. Jack Gordon White: UFAP — armed robbery. Listed: 6 July 1953; Apprehended: 27 August 1953

56. Alex Richard Bryant: ITSMV. Listed: 17 July 1953; Apprehended: 26 January 1954

57. George William Krendich: UFAP — murder. Listed: 27 July 1953; Found dead: 11 October 1953

58. Lloyd Reed Russell: UFAC — murder. Listed: 8 September 1953; Killed: 3 August 1954

59. Edwin Sanford Garrison: UFAC — burglary. Listed: 26 October 1953; Apprehended: 3 November 1953

60. Franklin James Wilson: UFAP — armed robbery. Listed: 2 November 1953; Apprehended: 18 January 1954

61. Charles E. Johnson: Bank robbery. Listed: 12 November 1953; Apprehended: 28 December 1953

62. Thomas Jackson Massingale: UFAP — kidnapping. Listed: 10 November 1953; Apprehended: 26 November 1953

63. Peter Edward Kenzik: UFAP — murder. Listed: 7 December 1953; Apprehended: 26 January 1955

64. Thomas Everett Dickerson: UFAP — robbery. Listed: 10 December 1953; Apprehended: 21 December 1953

65. Chester Lee Davenport: UFAC — robbery. Listed: 6 January 1954; Apprehended: 7 January 1954

66. Alex Whitmore: UFAP — robbery. Listed: 11 January 1954; Apprehended: 10 May 1954

67. Everett Lowell Krueger: ITSMV. Listed: 25 January 1954; Apprehended: 15 February 1954

68. Apee Hamp Chapman: UFAP — murder. Listed: 3 February 1954; Apprehended: 10 February 1954

69. Nelson Robert Duncan: ITSMV; FFA. Listed: 8 February 1954; Apprehended: 21 February 1954

70. Charles Falzone: UFAP — robbery. Listed: 24 February 1954; Apprehended: 17 August 1955

71. Basin Kingsley Beck: UFAP — burglary. Listed: 1 March 1954; Apprehended: 3 March 1954

72. James William Lofton: UFAC — armed robbery. Listed: 16 March 1954; Apprehended: 17 March 1954

73. Clarence Dye: UFAP — armed robbery. Listed: 8 March 1954; Apprehended: 3 August 1955

74. Sterling Groom: UFAP — murder. Listed: 2 April 1954; Apprehended: 21 April 1954

75. Raymond Louis Owen Menard: UFAP — burglary. Listed: 3 May 1954; Apprehended: 5 May 1954

76. John Alfred Hopkins: UFAP — murder. Listed: 18 May 1954; Apprehended: 7 June 1954

77. Otto Austin Loel: UFAP — murder. Listed: 21 May 1954; Apprehended: 17 January 1955

78. David Daniel Keegan: ITSP. Listed: 21 June 1954; Dropped from list: 13 December 1963

79. Walter James Wilkinson: UFAP — kidnapping. Listed: 17 August 1954; Apprehended: 12 January 1955

80. John Harry Allen: UFAP — robbery. Listed: 7 September 1954; Apprehended: 21 December 1954

81. George Lester Bellew: ITSP. Listed: 4 January 1955; Apprehended: 24 January 1955

82. Kenneth Darrell Carpenter: Bank robbery. Listed: 31 January 1955; Apprehended: 4 February 1955

83. Flenoy Payne: UFAP — murder. Listed: 2 February 1955; Apprehended: 11 March 1958

84. Palmer Julius Morset: UFAP — robbery. Listed: 7 February 1955; Apprehended: 2 March 1956

85. Patrick Eugene McDermott: UFAC — murder. Listed: 9 February 1955; Apprehended: 19 July 1955

86. Garland William Daniels: EFP; ITSP. Listed: 18 February 1955; Apprehended: 29 March 1955

87. Daniel William O'Connor: ITSMV. Listed: 11 April 1955; Apprehended: 26 December 1955

88. Jack Harvey Raymond: ITSP. Listed: 8 August 1955; Apprehended: 14 October 1955

89. Daniel Abram Everhart: UFAP — robbery. Listed: 17 August 1955; Apprehended: 9 October 1955

90. Charles Edward Ranels: Bank robbery. Listed: 2 September 1955; Apprehended: 16 December 1956

91. Thurman Arthur Green: ITSMV. Listed: 24 October 1955; Apprehended: 16 February 1956

92. John Allen Kendrick: UFAP — assault. Listed: 2 November 1955; Apprehended: 5 December 1955

93. Joseph James Bagnola: UFAP — murder. Listed: 19 December 1955; Apprehended: 30 December 1955

94. Nick George Montos: EFP. Listed: 2 March 1956; Apprehended: 28 March 1956

95. James Ignatius Faherty: UFAP — armed robbery. Listed: 19 March 1956; Apprehended: 16 May 1956

96. Thomas Francis Richardson: UFAP — armed robbery. Listed: 12 April 1956; Apprehended: 16 May 1956

97. Eugene Francis Newman: UFAP — robbery. Listed: 28 May 1956; Dropped from list: 11 June 1965

98. Carmine Di Biase: UFAP — murder. Listed: 28 May 1956; Apprehended: 28 August 1958

99. Ben Golden McCollum: UFAC — murder. Listed: 4 January 1957; Apprehended: 7 March 1958

100. Alfred James White: UFAP — assault. Listed: 14 January 1957; Apprehended: 24 January 1957

101. Robert L. Green: UFAP — burglary. Listed: 11 February 1957; Apprehended: 13 February 1957

102. George Edward Cole: UFAP — murder. Listed: 25 February 1957; Apprehended: 6 July 1959

103. Eugene Russell McCracken: UFAC — murder. Listed: 26 March 1958; Apprehended: 27 March 1958

104. Frank Aubrey Leftwich: UFAC — armed assault . Listed: 4 April 1958; Apprehended: 18 April 1958

105. Quay Cleon Kilburn: CRV. Listed: 16 April 1958; Apprehended: 2 June 1958

106. Dominick Sciallo: UFAP — murder. Listed: 9 May 1958; Apprehended: 27 July 1959

107. Angelo Pero: UFAP — murder. Listed: 16 June 1958; Warrant dismissed: 2 December 1960

108. Frederick Grant Dunn: UFAP — burglary. Listed: 29 July 1958; Found dead: 7 September 1959

109. Frank Lawrence Sprenz: UFAP — robbery. Listed: 10 September 1958; Apprehended: 15 April 1959

110. David Lynn Thurston: UFAC — robbery. Listed: 8 January 1959; Apprehended: 6 February 1959

111. John Thomas Freeman: ITSMV. Listed: 17 February 1959; Apprehended: 18 February 1959

112. Edward Sanford Garrison: UFAC — robbery. Listed: 4 March 1959; Apprehended: 9 September 1960

113. Emmett Bernard Kervan: Bank robbery. Listed: 29 March 1959; Apprehended: 13 May 1959

114. Richard Allen Hunt: ITSMV. Listed: 27 May 1959; Apprehended: 2 June 1959

115. Walter Bernard O'Donnell: UFAP — robbery. Listed: 17 June 1959; Apprehended: 19 June 1959

116. Billy Owens Williams: UFAP — kidnapping. Listed: 10 July, 1959; Apprehended: 4 March 1960

117. James Francis Jenkins: Bank robbery. Listed: 21 July 1959; Apprehended: 12 August 1959

118. Harry Raymond Pope: UFAP — burglary. Listed: 26 August 1959; Apprehended: 2 September 1959

119. James Francis Duffy: UFAP — armed robbery. Listed: 11 August 1959; Apprehended: 25 August 1959

120. Robert Garfield Brown Jr.: ITSP. Listed: 9 September 1959; Apprehended: 11 January 1960

121. Frederick Anthony Seno: UFAP — armed robbery. Listed: 24 September 1959; Apprehended: 24 September 1959

122. Smith Gerald Hudson: UFAC — murder. Listed: 7 October 1959; Apprehended: 31 July 1960

123. Joseph Lloyd Thomas: Bank robbery. Listed: 21 October 1959; Apprehended: 10 December 1959

124. Kenneth Ray Lawson: UFAC — armed robbery. Listed: 4 January 1960; Apprehended: 20 March 1960

125. Ted Jacob Rinehart: UFAC — armed robbery. Listed: 25 January 1960; Apprehended: 6 March 1960

126. Charles Clyatt Rogers: UFAC — murder. Listed: 18 March 1960; Apprehended: 11 May 1960

127. Joseph Corbett Jr.: UFAP — murder. Listed: 30 March 1960; Apprehended: 29 October 1960

128. William Mason: UFAP — murder. Listed: 6 April 1960; Apprehended: 27 April 1960

129. Edward Reiley: Bank robbery. Listed: 10 May 1960; Apprehended: 24 May 1960

130. Harold Eugene Fields: UFAC — burglary. Listed: 25 May 1960; Apprehended: 5 September 1960

131. Richard Peter Wagner: EFP. Listed: 23 June 1960; Apprehended: 25 June 1960

132. James John Warjac: UFAC — burglary. Listed: 19 July 1960; Apprehended: 22 July 1960

133. Ernest Tait: UFAP — burglary. Listed: 16 August 1960; Apprehended: 10 September 1960

134. Clarence Leon Raby: UFAP — murder. Listed: 19 August 1960; Apprehended: 28 August 1960

135. Nathaniel Beans: UFAP — murder. Listed: 12 September 1960; Apprehended: 30 September 1960

136. Stanley William Fitzgerald: UFAP — murder. Listed: 20 September 1960; Apprehended: 22 September 1960

137. Donald Leroy Payne: UFAP — rape. Listed: 6 October 1960; Dropped from list: 26 November 1965

138. Charles Francis Higgins: UFAC — robbery. Listed: 10 October 1960; Apprehended: 17 October 1960

139. Robert William Schultz Jr.: EFP. Listed: 12 October 1960; Apprehended: 4 November 1960

140. Merle Lyle Gall: UFAP — burglary. Listed: 17 October 1960; Apprehended: 18 January 1961

141. James George Economou: UFAC — robbery. Listed: 31 October 1960; Apprehended: 22 March 1961

142. Ray Delano Tate: Bank robbery. Listed: 18 November 1960; Apprehended: 25 November 1960

143. John B. Everhart: UFAC — murder. Listed: 22 November 1960; Apprehended: 6 November 1963

144. Herbert Hoover Huffman: UFAP — murder. Listed: 19 December 1960; Apprehended: 29 December 1960

145. Kenneth Eugene Cindle: UFAP — armed robbery. Listed: 23 December 1960; Apprehended: 1 April 1961

146. Thomas Viola: UFAC — murder. Listed: 17 January 1961; Apprehended: 27 March 1961

147. William Chester Cole: UFAP — armed robbery. Listed: 2 February 1961; Apprehended: 6 February 1961

148. Willie Hughes: UFAP — murder. Listed: 15 March 1961; Apprehended: 8 August 1961

149. William Terry Nichols: UFAC — robbery. Listed: 6 April 1961; Apprehended: 30 April 1962

150. George Martin Bradley Jr.: Bank robbery. Listed: 10 April 1961; Apprehended: 1 May 1961

151. Philip Alfred Lanormandin: UFAP — armed assault. Listed: 17 April 1961; Apprehended: 17 April 1961

152. Kenneth Holleck Sharp: UFAP — murder. Listed: 1 May 1961; Apprehended: 3 July 1961

153. Vincent Anthony Fede: UFAP — kidnapping. Listed: 22 May 1961; Apprehended: 28 October 1961

154. Richard Laurence Marquette: UFAP — murder. Listed: 29 June 1961; Apprehended: 30 June 1961

155. Robert William Schuette: UFAC — robbery. Listed: 19 July 1961; Apprehended: 2 August 1961

156. Chester Anderson McGonigal: UFAP — attempted murder. Listed: 14 August 1961; Apprehended: 17 August 1961

157. Hugh Bion Morse: UFAP — attempted murder. Listed: 29 August 1961; Apprehended: 13 October 1961

158. John Gibson Dillon: UFAP — narcotics. Listed: 1 September 1961; Apprehended: 2 March 1964

159. John Robert Sawyer: Bank robbery. Listed: 30 October 1961; Apprehended: 3 November 1961

160. Edward Wayne Edwards: Bank robbery. Listed: 10 November 1961; Apprehended: 20 January 1962

161. Franklin Eugene Alltop: UFAP — armed robbery. Listed: 22 November 1961; Apprehended: 2 February 1962

162. Francis Laverne Brannan: UFAP — murder. Listed: 27 December 1961; Apprehended: 17 January 1962

163. Delbert Henry Linaweaver: UFAC — burglary. Listed: 30 January 1962; Apprehended: 5 February 1962

164. Watson Young Jr.: UFAP — murder. Listed: 5 February 1962; Apprehended: 12 February 1962

165. Lyndal Ray Smith: UFAC — robbery. Listed: 14 February 1962; Apprehended: 22 March 1962

166. Harry Robert Grove: UFAC — robbery. Listed: 19 February 1962; Apprehended: 26 January 1963

167. Bobby Randell Wilcoxson: Bank robbery. Listed: 23 February 1962; Apprehended: 10 November 1962

168. Albert Frederick Nussbaum: Bank robbery. Listed: 2 April 1962; Apprehended: 4 November 1962

169. Thomas Welton Holland: UFAC — robbery. Listed: 11 May 1962; Apprehended: 2 June 1962

170. Edward Howard Maps: UFAP — murder. Listed: 15 June 1962; Dropped from list: 1 December 1962

171. David Stanley Jacubanis: Bank robbery. Listed: 21 November 1962; Apprehended: 29 November 1962

172. John Kinchloe DeJarnette: UFAP — Drug fraud. Listed: 30 November 1962; Apprehended: 3 December 1962

173. Michael Joseph O'Connor: UFAP — murder. Listed: 13 December 1962; Apprehended: 28 December 1962

174. John Lee Taylor: UFAP — robbery. Listed: 14 December 1962; Apprehended: 20 December 1962

175. Harold Thomas O'Brien: UFAP — murder. Listed: 4 January 1963; Dropped from list 14 January 1965

176. Jerry Clarence Rush: Bank robbery. Listed: 14 January 1963; Apprehended: 25 March 1963

177. Marshall Frank Chrisman: Bank robbery. Listed: 7 February 1963; Apprehended: 21 May 1963

178. Howard Jay Barnard: UFAP — robbery. Listed: 12 April 1963; Apprehended: 6 April 1964

179. Leroy Ambrosia Frazier: EFP. Listed: 4 June 1963; Apprehended: 12 September 1963

180. Carl Close: Bank robbery. Listed: 25 September 1963; Apprehended: 26 September 1963

181. Thomas Asbury Haddar: UFAP — murder. Listed: 9 October 1963; Apprehended: 13 January 1964

182. Alfred Oponowicz: Bank robbery. Listed: 27 November 1963; Apprehended: 23 December 1964

183. Arthur William Couts: UFAP — robbery. Listed: 27 December 1962; Apprehended: 30 January 1964

184. Jesse James Gilbert: Bank robbery. Listed: 27 January 1964; Apprehended: 26 February 1964

185. Sammie Earl Ammons: UFAP — forgery. Listed: 10 February 1964; Apprehended: 15 May 1964

186. Frank B. Dumont: UFAP — assault. Listed: 10 March 1964; Apprehended: 27 April 1964

187. William Beverly Hughes: UFAC — armed robbery. Listed: 18 March 1964; Apprehended: 11 April 1964

188. Quay Cleon Kilburn: UFAC — robbery. Listed: 23 March 1964; Apprehended: 25 June 1964

189. Joseph Francis Bryan Jr.: Kidnapping. Listed: 14 April 1964; Apprehended: 28 April 1964

190. John Robert Bailey: UFAC — robbery. Listed: 22 April 1964; Apprehended: 4 May 1964

191. George Zavada: Bank robbery. Listed: 6 May 1964; Apprehended: 12 June 1964

192. George Patrick McLaughlin: UFAP — murder. Listed: 8 May 1964; Apprehended: 24 February 1965

193. Chester Collins: UFAP — assault. Listed: 14 May 1964; Dropped from list: 30 March 1967

194. Edward Newton Nivens: UFAP — robbery. Listed: 28 May 1964; Apprehended: 2 June 1964

195. Lewis Frederick Vasselli: UFAP — narcotics. Listed: 15 June 1964; Apprehended: 1 September 1964

196. Thomas Edward Galloway: UFAP — murder. Listed: 24 June 1964; Apprehended: 17 July 1964

197. Alson Thomas Wahrlich: Kidnapping. Listed: 9 July 1964; Apprehended: 28 October 1967

198. Kenneth Malcolm Christiansen: UFAC — robbery. Listed: 27 July 1964; Apprehended: 8 September 1964

199. William Hutton Cable: UFAC — bank robbery. Listed: 11 September 1964; Apprehended: 1 March 1965

200. Lloyd Donald Greeson Jr.: UFAP — murder. Listed: 18 September 1964; Apprehended: 23 September 1964

201. Raymond Lawrence Wyngaard: UFAP — armed robbery. Listed: 5 October 1964; Apprehended: 28 November 1964

202. Norman Belyea Gorham: Bank robbery. Listed: 10 December 1964; Apprehended: 27 May 1965

203. John William Clouser: ITSMV. Listed: 7 January 1965; Dropped from list: 1 August 1972

204. William Lee Parman: UFAP — murder. Listed: 15 January 1965; Apprehended 31 January 1965

205. Gene Thomas Webb: UFAP — attempted murder. Listed: 11 February 1965; Apprehended: 12 February 1965

206. Samuel Jefferson Veney: UFAP — murder. Listed: 25 February 1965; Apprehended: 11 March 1965

207. Earl Veney: UFAP — murder. Listed: 5 March 1965; Apprehended: 11 March 1965

208. Donald Stewart Heien: UFAC — murder. Listed: 11 March 1965; Apprehended: 3 February 1966

209. Arthur Pierce Jr.: UFAP — murder. Listed: 24 March 1965; Apprehended: 25 March 1965

210. Donald Dean Rainey: Bank robbery. Listed: 26 March 1965; Apprehended: 22 June 1965

211. Leslie Douglas Ashley: UFAC — murder. Listed: 6 April 1965; Apprehended: 23 April 1965

212. Charles Bryan Harris: UFAP — murder. Listed: 6 May 1965; Apprehended: 17 June 1965
213. William Albert Autur Tahl: UFAP — murder. Listed: 10 June 1965; Apprehended: 5 November 1965
214. Duane Earl Pope: Bank robbery & murder. Listed: 11 June 1965; Apprehended: 11 June 1965
215. Allen Wade Haugsted: UFAP — murder. Listed: 24 June 1965; Apprehended: 13 December 1965
216. Theodore Matthew Brechtel: EFP. Listed: 30 June 1965; Apprehended: 16 August 1965
217. Robert Allen Woodford: UFAC — robbery. Listed: 2 July 1965; Apprehended: 5 August 1965
218. Warren Cleveland Osborne: UFAP — murder. Listed: 12 August 1965; Apprehended: 9 September 1965
219. Holice Paul Black: UFAP — armed robbery. Listed: 25 August 1965; Apprehended: 15 December 1965
220. Edward Owen Watkins: Bank robbery. Listed: 21 September 1965; Apprehended: 2 December 1965
221. Joel Singer: UFAP — robbery. Listed: 19 November 1965; Apprehended: 1 December 1965
222. James Edward Kennedy: Bank robbery. Listed: 8 December 1965; Apprehended: 23 December 1965
223. Lawrence John Higgins: Bank robbery. Listed: 14 December 1965; Apprehended: 3 January 1966
224. Hoyt Bud Cobb: UFAP — murder. Listed: 6 January 1966; Apprehended: 6 June 1966
225. James Robert Bishop: UFAP — armed robbery. Listed: 10 January 1966; Apprehended: 21 January 1966
226. Robert Van Lewing: Bank robbery. Listed: 12 January 1966; Apprehended: 6 February 1967
227. Earl Ellery Wright: Bank robbery. Listed: 14 January 1966; Apprehended: 20 June 1966
228. Jessie James Roberts Jr.: Bank robbery. Listed: 3 February 1966; Apprehended: 8 February 1966
229. Charles Lorin Gove: UFAC — armed robbery; Bank robbery. Listed: 16 February 1966; Apprehended: 16 February 1966
230. Ralph Dwayne Owen: UFAC — armed robbery. Listed: 16 February 1966; Apprehended: 11 March 1966
231. Jimmy Lewis Parker: UFAC — murder. Listed: 25 February 1966; Apprehended: 4 March 1966
232. Jack Daniel Sayadoff: Kidnapping; ITSMV. Listed: 17 March 1966; Apprehended: 24 March 1966
233. Robert Clayton Buick: Bank robbery. Listed: 24 March 1966; Apprehended: 29 March 1966
234. James Vernon Taylor: UFAP — murder. Listed: 4 April 1966; Apprehended: 4 April 1966
235. Lynwood Irwin Meares: UFAC — larceny. Listed: 11 April 1966; Apprehended: 2 May 1967
236. James Robert Ringrose: Interstate check fraud. Listed: 15 April 1966; Apprehended: 29 March 1967
237. Walter Leonard Lesczynski: UFAP — robbery. Listed: 16 June 1966; Apprehended: 29 March 1967
238. Donald Rogers Smelley: UFAP — armed robbery. Listed: 20 June 1966; Apprehended: 7 November 1966
239. George Ben Edmondson: UFAC — armed robbery. Listed: 21 September 1966; Apprehended: 28 June 1967
240. Everett Leroy Biggs: UFAP — armed robbery. Listed: 21 September 1966; Apprehended: 1 December 1966
241. Gene Robert Jennings: UFAC — armed robbery. Listed: 15 December 1966; Apprehended: 14 February 1967
242. Clarence Wilbert McFarland: Bank robbery. Listed: 22 December 1966; Apprehended: 4 April 1967
243. Monroe Hickson: UFAC — murder. Listed: 17 February 1967; Apprehended: 30 January 1968
244. Clyde Edward Laws: Kidnapping. Listed: 28 February 1967; Apprehended: 18 May 1967
245. Charles Edward Ervin: UFAC — armed robbery. Listed: 13 April 1967; Apprehended: 25 July 1967
246. Gordon Dale Ervin: UFAC — armed robbery. Listed: 13 April 1967; Apprehended: 7 June 1969
247. Thomas Franklin Dorman: Kidnapping. Listed: 20 April 1967; Apprehended: 20 May 1967
248. Jerry Lynn Young: Bank robbery. Listed: 12 May 1967; Apprehended: 15 June 1967
249. Joseph Leroy Newman: EFP; ITSMV. Listed: 2 June 1967; Apprehended: 29 June 1967
250. Carmen Raymond Gagliardi: UFAP — murder. Listed: 9 June 1967; Apprehended: 23 December 1967
251. Donald Richard Bussmeyer: Bank robbery. Listed: 28 June 1967; Apprehended: 24 August 1967
252. Florencio Lopez Mationg: UFAP — murder. Listed: 1 July 1967; Apprehended: 16 July 1967
253. Victor Gerald Bono: UFAP — murder. Listed: 1 July 1967; Apprehended:16 July 1967
254. Alfred Johnson Cooper Jr.: UFAP — robbery. Listed: 27 July 1967; Apprehended: 8 September 1967
255. John D. Slaton: UFAP — assault. Listed: 2 August 1967; Apprehended: 1 December 1967
256. Jerry Ray James: UFAP — armed robbery. Listed: 16 August 1967; Apprehended: 24 January 1968
257. Richard Paul Anderson: UFAP — murder. Listed: 7 September 1967; Apprehended: 19 January 1968
258. Henry Theodore Young: UFAC — armed robbery. Listed: 21 September 1967; Apprehended: 9 January 1968
259. Donald Eugene Sparks: UFAP — armed robbery. Listed: 13 November 1967; Apprehended: 24 January 1968
260. Zelma Lavone King: UFAP — murder. Listed: 14 December 1967; Apprehended: 30 January 1968
261. Jerry Reece Peacock: UFAC — robbery. Listed: 14 December 1967; Apprehended: 5 March 1968
262. Ronald Eugene Storck: UFAP — murder. Listed: 19 January 1968; Apprehended: 29 February 1968
263. Robert Leon McCain: Bank robbery. Listed: 31 January 1968; Apprehended: 23 February 1968
264. William Garrin Allen II: UFAP — murder. Listed: 9 February 1968; Apprehended: 23 March 1968
265. Charles Lee Herron: UFAP — murder. Listed: 9 February 1968; Apprehended: 18 June 1986
266. Leonard Daniel Spears: UFAP — murder. Listed: 13 February 1968; 2 March 1968
267. William Howard Bornman: UFAP — armed robbery. Listed: 13 February 1968; Apprehended: 13 February 1968
268. John Conway Patterson: UFAP — murder. Listed: 26 February 1968; Apprehended: 17 March 1968
269. Troy Denver Martin: Kidnapping. Listed: 8 March 1968; Apprehended: 19 March 1968
270. George Benjamin Williams: Bank robbery. Listed: 18 March 1968; Found dead: 19 June 1968
271. Michael John Sanders: UFAP — armed robbery. Listed: 21 March 1968; Apprehended: 8 April 1968
272. Howard Callens Johnson: UFAP — murder. Listed: 21 March 1968; Apprehended: 24 April 1968

273. George Edward Wells: UFAP—murder. Listed: 28 March 1968; Apprehended: 27 May 1969

274. David Evans: Bank robbery. Listed: 3 April 1968; Apprehended: 26 April 1968

275. Franklin Allen Paris: UFAP—burglary. Listed: 9 April 1968; Apprehended: 21 May 1968

276. David Stuart Neff: Bank robbery. Listed: 18 April 1968; Apprehended: 25 April 1968

277. James Earl Ray: Civil rights conspiracy. Listed: 20 April 1968; Apprehended: 8 June 1968

278. John Wesley Shannon Jr.: Bank robbery. Listed: 7 May 1968; Apprehended: 5 June 1968

279. Taylor Morris Teaford: UFAP—murder. Listed: 10 May 1968; Dropped from list: 24 May 1972

280. Phillip Morris Jones: Bank robbery. Listed: 5 June 1968; Apprehended: 26 June 1968

281. Johnny Ray Smith: ITSMV. Listed: 20 June 1968; Apprehended: 24 June 1968

282. Byron James Rice: UFAP—murder. Listed: 5 July 1968; Apprehended: 2 October 1972

283. Robert Leroy Lindblad: UFAP—murder. Listed: 11 July 1968; Apprehended: 7 October 1968

284. James Joseph Scully: Bank robbery. Listed: 15 July 1968; Apprehended: 23 July 1968

285. Billy Ray White: UFAP—murder. Listed: 13 August 1968; Apprehended: 17 August 1968

286. Frederick Rudolph Yokom: UFAP—armed robbery. Listed: 29 August 1968; Apprehended: 6 September 1968

287. Harold James Evans: UFAC—armed robbery. Listed: 19 September 1968; Apprehended: 2 January 1969

288. Robert Lee Carr: UFAP—burglary. Listed: 18 October 1968; Apprehended: 4 November 1968

289. Levi Washington: Bank robbery. Listed: 15 November 1968; Apprehended: 9 December 1968

290. Richard Lee Tingler Jr.: UFAP—murder. Listed: 20 December 1968; Apprehended: 19 May 1969

291. George Michael Gentile: Racketeering & extortion. Listed: 18 June 1968; Apprehended: 17 December 1968

292. Gary Steven Krist: Kidnapping. Listed: 20 December 1968; Apprehended: 22 December 1968

293. Ruth Eisemann-Schier: Kidnapping. Listed: 28 December 1968; Apprehended: 5 March 1969

294. Baltazar Garcia Estolas: UFAP—murder. Listed: 3 January 1969; Apprehended: 3 September 1969

295. Billy Austin Bryant: UFAC—robbery; bank robbery. Listed: 8 January 1969; Apprehended: 8 January 1969

296. Billy Len Schales: UFAP—murder. Listed: 27 January 1969; Apprehended: 30 January 1969

297. Thomas James Lucas: Bank robbery. Listed: 13 February 1969; Apprehended: 26 February 1969

298. Warren David Reddock: UFAP—murder. Listed: 11 March 1969; Apprehended: 14 April 1971

299. George Edward Blue: Bank robbery. Listed: 20 March 1969; Apprehended: 28 March 1969

300. Cameron David Bishop: Sabotage. Listed: 15 April 1969; Apprehended: 12 March 1975

301. Marie Dean Arrington: UFAP—murder. Listed: 29 May 1969; Apprehended: 22 December 1971

302. Benjamin Hoskins Paddock: EFP. Listed: 10 June 1969; Dropped from list: 5 May 1977

303. Francis Leroy Hohimer: UFAP—burglary. Listed: 20 June 1969; Apprehended: 20 December 1969

304. Joseph Lloyd Thomas: Bank robbery. Listed: 12 September 1969; Apprehended: 8 March 1970

305. James John Byrnes: Kidnapping. Listed: 6 January 1970; Apprehended: 17 April 1970

306. Edmund James Devlin: Bank robbery. Listed: 20 March 1970; Apprehended: 15 August 1970

307. Lawrence Robert Plamondon: Destroying govt. property. Listed: 5 May 1970; Apprehended: 23 July 1970

308. Hubert Geroid Brown: UFAP—arson. Listed: 6 May 1970; Apprehended: 16 October 1971

309. Angela Yvonne Davis: UFAP—murder. Listed: 18 August 1970; Apprehended: 13 October 1970

310. Dwight Alan Armstrong: Destroying government property. Listed: 4 September 1970; Dropped from list: 7 April 1976

311. Karleton Lewis Armstrong: Destroying govt. property. Listed: 4 September 1970; Apprehended: 16 February 1972

312. David Sylvan Fine: Destroying government property. Listed: 4 September 1970; Apprehended 8 January 1976

313. Leo Frederick Burt: Destroying government property. Listed: 4 September 1970; Dropped from list: 7 April 1976

314. Bernadine Rae Dohrn: UFAP—conspiracy. Listed: 14 October 1970; Dropped: 7 December 1973

315. Katherine Ann Power: Bank robbery & murder. Listed: 17 October 1970; Dropped: 15 August 1985

316. Susan Edith Saxe: Bank robbery & murder. Listed: 17 October 1970; Apprehended: 27 March 1975

317. Mace Brown: UFAP—murder. Listed: 20 October 1972; Killed by police: 18 April 1973

318. Herman Bell: UFAP—murder. Listed: 9 May 1973; Apprehended: 2 September 1973

319. Twyman Ford Myers: UFAP—murder. Listed: 28 September 1973; Apprehended: 14 November 1973

320. Ronald Harvey: UFAP—murder. Listed: 7 December 1973; Apprehended: 27 March 1974

321. Samuel Richard Christian: UFAP—murder. Listed: 7 December 1973; Apprehended: 11 December 1973

322. Rudolph Alonza Turner: UFAP—murder. Listed: 10 January 1974; Apprehended: 1 October 1974

323. Larry Gene Cole: Kidnapping. Listed: 2 April 1974; Apprehended: 3 April 1974

324. James Ellsworth Jones: UFAP—armed robbery. Listed: 16 April 1974; Apprehended: 15 June 1974

325. Lendell Hunter: UFAC—rape. Listed: 27 June 1974; Apprehended: 31 July 1974

326. John Edward Copeland Jr.: UFAC—rape. Listed: 15 August 1974; Apprehended: 23 July 1975

327. Melvin Dale Walker: EFP. Listed: 16 October 1974; Apprehended: 9 November 1974

328. Thomas Otis Knight: UFAP—murder & kidnapping. Listed: 12 December 1974; Apprehended: 31 December 1974

329. Billy Dean Anderson: UFAP—attempted murder. Listed: 21 January 1975; Killed by FBI: 7 July 1979

330. Robert Gerald Davis: UFAP—murder. Listed: 4 April 1975; Apprehended: 5 August 1977

331. Richard Dean Holtan: Bank robbery & murder. Listed: 18 April 1975; Apprehended: 12 July 1975

332. Richard Bernard Lindhorst Jr.: Bank robbery. Listed: 4 August 1975; Apprehended: 7 August 1975

333. William Lewis Herron Jr.: UFAP—murder. Listed: 15 August 1975; Apprehended: 30 October 1975

334. James Winston Smallwood: EFP. Listed: 29 August 1975; Apprehended: 5 December 1975

335. Leonard Peltier: UFAP — murder. Listed: 22 December 1975; Apprehended: 6 February 1976

336. Patrick James Huston: Bank robbery. Listed: 3 March 1976; Apprehended: 7 December 1977

337. Thomas Edward Bethea: Kidnapping. Listed: 5 March 1976; Apprehended: 5 May 1976

338. Anthony Michael Juliano: Bank robbery. Listed: 15 March 1976; Apprehended: 22 March 1976

339. Joseph Maurice McDonald: ITSP. Listed: 1 April 1976; Apprehended: 15 September 1982

340. James Ray Renton: PV; UFAP — murder. Listed: 7 April 1976; Apprehended: 9 May 19777

341. Nathaniel Doyle Jr.: UFAC — bank robbery. Listed: 29 April 1976; Killed by police: 15 July 1976

342. Morris Lynn Johnson: EFP. Listed: 25 May 1976; Apprehended: 26 June 1976

343. Richard Joseph Picariello: Terrorist bombings. Listed: 29 July 1976; Apprehended: 21 October 1976

344. Edward Patrick Gullion Jr.: Terrorist bombings. Listed: 13 August 1976; Apprehended: 22 October 1976

345. Gerhardt Julius Schwartz: Bank robbery. Listed: 18 November 1976; Apprehended 22 November 1976

346. Francis John Martin: UFAC — kidnapping & rape. Listed: 17 December 1976; Apprehended: 17 February 1977

347. Benjamin George Pavan: UFAP — armed robbery. Listed: 12 January 1977; Apprehended: 17 February 1977

348. Larry Gene Campbell: UFAP — murder. Listed: 18 March 1977; Apprehended: 6 September 1977

349. Roy Ellsworth Smith: UFAP — murder. Listed: 18 March 1977; Apprehended: 2 June 1977

350. Raymond Luc Levasseur: Bank robbery. Listed: 5 May 1977; Apprehended: 4 November 1984

351. James Earl Ray: UFAC — murder. Listed: 10 June 1977; Apprehended: 13 June 1977

352. Willie Foster Sellers: UFAC — bank robbery. Listed: 14 June 1977; Apprehended: 20 June 1979

353. Larry Smith: UFAP — murder. Listed: 15 July 1977; Apprehended: 20 August 1977

354. Ralph Robert Cozzolino: UFAP — murder. Listed: 19 October 1977; Apprehended: 6 January 1978

355. Millard Oscar Hubbard: Bank robbery. Listed: 19 October 1977; Apprehended: 21 October 1977

356. Carlos Alberto Torres: NFA; UFAP — terrorist bombings. Listed: 19 October 1977; Apprehended: 4 April 1980

357. Enrique Estrada: UFAP — robbery. Listed: 5 December 1977; Apprehended: 8 December 1977

358. William David Smith: UFAP — murder. Listed: 10 February 1978; Apprehended: 27 October 1978

359. Gary Ronald Warden: UFAP — armed robbery. Listed: 10 February 1978; Apprehended: 12 May 1978

360. Theodore Robert Bundy: UFAP — murder. Listed: 10 February 1978; Apprehended: 15 February 1978

361. Andrew Evan Gipson: UFAC — bank robbery & murder. Listed: 27 March 1978; Apprehended: 24 May 1978

362. Anthony Dominic Liberatore: UFAP — murder. Listed: 26 May 1978; Apprehended: 1 April 1979

363. Michael George Thevis: ITOM; UFAP — conspiracy. Listed: 10 July 1978; Apprehended: 9 November 1978

364. Charles Everett Hughes: UFAP — murder. Listed: 19 November 1978; Apprehended: 29 April 1981

365. Ronald Lee Lyons: Air piracy & kidnapping. Listed: 17 December 1978; Apprehended: 10 September 1979

366. Leo Joseph Koury: RICO. Listed: 20 April 1979; Apprehended: 16 June 1991

367. John William Sherman: EFP. Listed: 3 August 1979; Apprehended: 17 December 1981

368. Melvin Bay Guyon: Kidnapping. Listed: 9 August 1979; Apprehended: 16 August 1979

369. George Alvin Bruton: UFAP — burglary. Listed: 28 September 1979; Apprehended: 14 December 1979

370. Earl Edwin Austin: Bank robbery. Listed: 12 October 1979; Apprehended: 1 March 1980

371. Vincent James Russo: UFAP — robbery. Listed: 24 December 1979; Apprehended: 4 January 1981

372. Albert Lopez Victory: UFAC — murder. Listed: 14 March 1980; Apprehended: 24 February 1981

373. Ronald Turney Williams: UFAC — murder. Listed: 16 April 1980; Apprehended: 8 June 1981

374. Daniel Jay Barney: UFAP — sexual assault. Listed: 10 March 1981; Committed suicide: 19 April 1981

375. Donald Eugene Webb: UFAP — murder. Listed: 4 May 1981; Still at large

376. Gilbert James Everett: Bank robbery. Listed: 13 May 1981; Apprehended: 12 August 1985

377. Leslie Edward Nichols: UFAP — murder. Listed: 2 July 1981; Apprehended: 17 December 1981

378. Thomas William Manning: Bank robbery. Listed: 29 January 1982; Apprehended: 8 July 1982

379. David Fountain Kimberly Jr.: Bank robbery. Listed: 29 January 1982; Apprehended: 8 July 1982

380. Mutulu Shakur: UFAP — murder. Listed: 23 July 1982; Apprehended: 11 February 1986

381. Charles Edward Watson: Kidnapping. Listed: 22 October 1982; Apprehended: 25 October 1983

382. Laney Gibson Jr.: UFAP — murder. Listed: 16 November 1983; Apprehended: 18 December 1983

383. George Clarence Bridgette: UFAP — murder. Listed: 13 January 1984; Apprehended: 30 January 1984

384. Samuel Marks Humphrey: Bank robbery. Listed: 29 February 1984; Apprehended: 22 March 1984

385. Christopher Bernard Wilder: Kidnapping; UFAP — murder. Listed: 5 April 1984; Committed suicide: 13 August 1984

386. Victor Manuel Gerena: Bank robbery; ITSP. Listed: 14 May 1984; Still at large

387. Wai-Chiu Ng: UFAP — murder. Listed: 15 June 1984; Apprehended: 24 October 1984

388. Alton Coleman: Kidnapping; UFAP — murder. Listed: 11 July 1984; Apprehended: 20 July 1984

389. Cleveland McKinley Davis: UFAP — murder. Listed: 24 October 1984; Apprehended: 25 January 1984

390. Carmine John Persico Jr.: RICO. Listed: 31 January 1985; Apprehended: 15 February 1985

391. Lohman Ray Mays Jr.: UFAC — murder; bank robbery. Listed: 15 February 1985; Apprehended: 23 September 1985

392. Charles Earl Hammond: UFAP — murder. Listed: 14 March 1985; Apprehended: 4 August 1986

393. Michael Frederic Allen Hammond: UFAP — murder. Listed: 14 March 1985; Apprehended: 4 August 1986

394. Robert Henry Nicolaus: UFAP — murder. Listed: 28 June 1985; Apprehended: 20 July 1985

395. David Jay Sterling: UFAC — rape. Listed: 30 September 1985; Apprehended: 13 February 1986

396. Richard Joseph Scutari: UFAP — armed robbery. Listed: 30 September 1985; Apprehended: 19 March 1986

397. Joseph William Dougherty: Bank robbery. Listed: 6 November 1985; Apprehended: 19 December 1986

398. Brian Patrick Malverty: UFAP — murder. Listed: 28 March 1986; Apprehended: 7 April 1986

399. Billy Ray Waldon: UFAP — murder. Listed: 16 May 1986; Apprehended: 16 June 1986

400. Claude Lafayette Dallas Jr.: UFAC — manslaughter. Listed: 16 May 1986; Apprehended: 8 March 1987

401. Donald Keith Williams: Bank robbery. Listed: 18 July 1986; Apprehended: 20 August 1986

402. Terry Lee Connor: Bank robbery. Listed: 8 August 1986; Apprehended: 9 December 1986

403. Fillmore Raymond Cross Jr.: UFAP — extortion & assault. Listed: 8 August 1986; Apprehended: 23 December, 1986

404. James Wesley Dyess: UFAP — murder. Listed: 29 September 1986; Apprehended: 16 May 1988

405. Danny Michael Weeks: UFAC — kidnapping. Listed: 29 September 1986; Apprehended: 20 March 1988

406. Michael Wayne Jackson: UFAP — murder. Listed: 1 October 1986; Committed suicide: 2 October 1986

407. Thomas George Harrelson: Bank robbery. Listed: 28 November 1986; Apprehended: 9 February 1987

408. Robert Alan Litchfield: EFP. Listed: 20 January 1987; Apprehended: 20 May 1987

409. David James Roberts: UFAC — murder. Listed: 27 April 1987; Apprehended: 11 February 1988

410. Ronald Glyn Triplett: UFAC — armed robbery. Listed: 27 April 1987; Apprehended: 16 May 1987

411. Claude Daniel Marks: Conspiracy — multiple charges. Listed: 22 May 1987; Surrendered: 6 December 1994

412. Donna Jean Wilmott: Conspiracy — multiple charges. Listed: 22 May 1987; Surrendered: 6 December 1994

413. Darren Dee O'Neal: UFAP — murder. Listed: 25 June 1987; Apprehended: 3 February 1988

414. Louis Ray Beam: Sedition. Listed: 14 July 1987; Apprehended: 6 November 1987

415. Ted Jeffrey Otsuki: UFAP — murder. Listed: 22 January 1987; Apprehended: 10 October 1988

416. Pedro Luis Estrada: UFAP — murder. Listed: 15 April 1988; Apprehended: 1 October 1989

417. John Edward Stevens: Bank robbery. Listed: 29 May 1988; Apprehended: 20 November 1988

418. Jack Darrell Farmer: RICO. Listed: 29 May 1988; Apprehended: 1 June 1988

419. Robert Lee Jones: UFAP — child molestation. Listed: 29 May 1988: Apprehended: 4 March 1989

420. Terry Lee Johnson: UFAC — murder. Listed: 12 June 1988; Apprehended: 17 August 1988

421. Stanley Faison: UFAP — murder. Listed: 27 November 1988; Apprehended: 24 December 1988

422. Steven Ray Stout: UFAP — murder. Listed: 27 November 1988; Apprehended: 6 December 1988

423. Armando Garcia: UFAP — murder & drug trafficking. Listed: 8 January 1989; Apprehended: 18 January 1994

424. Melvin Edward Mays: Terrorist conspiracy. Listed: 7 February 1989; Apprehended: 9 March 1995

425. Bobby G. Dennie: UFAP — murder, theft, rape, robbery. Listed: 24 February 1989; Apprehended: 28 October 1989

426. Constabile Farace: UFAP — manslaughter. Listed: 17 March 1989; Murdered: 17 November 1989

427. Arthur Lee Washington Jr.: UFAP — attempted murder. Listed: 18 October 1989; Dropped: 27 December 2000

428. Lee Nell Carter: UFAP — Murder, attempted murder. Listed: 19 November 1989; Apprehended: 20 November 1989

429. Wardell David Ford: UFAP — armed robbery & murder. Listed: 20 December 1989; Apprehended: 17 September 1990

430. Leslie Ibsen Rogge: EFP; bank robbery. Listed: 24 January 1990; Surrendered: 19 May 1996

431. Kenneth Robert Stanton: UFAP — child molestation. Listed: 24 October 1990; Apprehended: 31 October 1990

432. Patrick Michael Mitchell: Bank robbery. Listed: 23 November 1990; Apprehended: 22 February 1994

433. Jon Preston Settle: UFAP — murder. Listed: 9 August 1991; Apprehended: 6 August 1991

434. Robert Michael Allen: UFAP — murder. Listed: 13 September 1991; Found dead: 23 December 1992

435. Mir Aimal Kansi: UFAP — murder. Listed: 9 February 1993; Apprehended: 17 June 1997

436. Ramzi Ahmed Yousef: UFAP — murder. Listed: 21 April 1993; Apprehended: 7 February 1995

437. Joseph Martin Luther Gardner: UFAP — murder. Listed: 25 May 1994; Apprehended: 19 October 1994

438. Gary Ray Bowles: UFAP — murder. Listed: 19 November 1994; Apprehended: 22 November 1994

439. Gerald Keith Watkins: UFAP — homicide. Listed: 4 March 1995; Apprehended: 5 May 1995

440. Juan Garcia-Abrego: Drug trafficking. Listed: 9 March 1995; Apprehended: 15 January 1996

441. Abdel Bassett Ali Al-Megrahi: Terrorist conspiracy. Listed: 23 March 1995; Apprehended: 5 April 1999

442. Lamen Khalifa Fhimah: Terrorist conspiracy. Listed: 23 March 1995; Apprehended: 5 April 1999

443. O'Neil Vassell: UFAP — murder. Listed: 17 July 1995; Apprehended: 16 October 1996

444. Rickey Allen Bright: UFAP — kidnapping & rape. Listed: 15 December 1995; Apprehended: 7 January 1996

445. Agustin Vasquez-Mendoza: UFAP — murder. Listed: 3 August 1996; Apprehended: 9 July 2000

446. Thang Thanh Nguyen: UFAP — murder. Listed: 3 August 1996; Apprehended: 6 January 1998

447. Glen Stewart Godwin: UFAC — drug trafficking. Listed: 7 December 1996; Still at large

448. David Alex Alvarez: UFAP — murder. Listed: 14 December 1996; Apprehended: 20 May 1997

449. Andrew Phillip Cunanan: UFAP — murder. Listed: 12 June 1997; Committed suicide: 23 July 1997

450. Paul Ragusa: Bank robbery & racketeering. Listed: 6 September 1997; Surrendered: 30 January 1998

451. Ramon Eduardo Arellano-Felix: Drug conspiracy. Listed: 24 September 1997; Killed: 10 February 2002

452. Tony Ray Amati: UFAP — murder. Listed: 21 February 1998; Apprehended: 27 February 1998

453. Harry Joseph Bowman: RICO. Listed: 14 March 1998; Apprehended: 7 June 1999

454. Eric Robert Rudolph: UFAP — murder. Listed: 5 May 1998; Apprehended: 31 May 2003

455. James Charles Kopp: UFAP — murder. Listed: 7 June 1999; Apprehended: 29 March 2001

456. Usama Bin Laden: UFAP — murder. Listed: 7 June 1999; Still at large

457. Rafael Resendez-Ramirez: UFAP — murder. Listed: 21 June 1999; Apprehended: 13 July 1999

458. James J. Bulger: RICO & extortion. Listed: 19 August 1999; Still at large

459. Jesse James Caston: UFAP — murder & attempted murder. Listed: 19 August 2000; Apprehended: 20 December 2000

460. Eric Franklin Rosser: Child pornography. Listed: 27 December 2000; Apprehended: 21 August 2001

461. Aurlieas Dame McClarty: Bank robbery & UFAP — murder. Listed: 24 February 2001; Apprehended: February 14, 2001

462. Hopeton Eric Brown: Drug conspiracy; murder. Listed: 17 March 2001; Still at large

463. Maghfoor Mansoor: UFAP — sexual assault; kidnapping.. Listed: 23 May 2001; Apprehended: 11 May 2001

464. Francis William Murphy: UFAC — parole violation. Listed: 6 June 2001; Apprehended: 20 May 2001

465. Dwight Bowen: UFAP — Murder. Listed: 30 August 2001; Apprehended: 22 August 2001

466. Nikolay Soltys: UFAP — murder. Listed: August 23, 2001; Apprehended: August 30, 2001

467. Clayton Lee Waagner: EFP; bank robbery. Listed: September 21, 2001; Apprehended: 5 December 2001

468. Felix Summers: UFAP — homicide & aggravated assault. Listed: October 30, 2001; Apprehended: 13 December 2001

469. Christian Michael Longo: UFAP — murder. Listed: 11 January 2002; Apprehended: 13 January 2002

470. Michael Scott Bliss: UFAP — child molestation. Listed: 31 January 2002; Apprehended: 24 April 2002

471. James Spencer Springette: conspiracy to import cocaine. Listed: 25 April 2002; Apprehended: 7 November 2002

472. Ruben Hernandez Martinez: UFAP — rape & burglary. Listed: 1 May 2002; Apprehended: 2 May 2002

473. Unavailable; apprehended before formal listing.

474. Richard Steve Goldberg: UFAP — child pornography. Listed: 14 June 2002; still at large

475. Robert William Fisher: UFAP — murder and arson. Listed: 29 June 2002; still at large

476. Michael Alfonso: UFAP — murder. Listed: 23 January 2003; still at large

# Appendix F: Films Depicting the FBI

## 1935

*G-Men*—A young FBI agent (James Cagney) seeks revenge after mobsters kill his partner in the FBI's big-screen premiere. Cast: Ann Dvorak, Margaret Lindsay, Robert Armstrong.

*Let 'Em Have It*—Underworld doctors are the targets in this plodding treatment, pursued by a dead-pan FBI agent (Richard Arlen). Cast: Virginia Bruce, Alice Brade, Bruce Cabot.

*Mary Burns, Fugitive*—Hollywood G-men pursue a gun moll forced into a life of crime despite her good intentions. Cast: Sylvia Sidney, Melvyn Douglas, Pert Kelton, Alan Baxter, Wallace Ford, Brian Donlevy, Kernan Cripps, Ivan Miller, Charles Wilson.

*Public Hero Number One*—A stalwart G-man (Chester Morris) goes undercover to trap a criminal loosely based on John Dillinger. Cast: Lionel Barrymore, Jean Arthur, Joseph Calleia.

*Show Them No Mercy*—FBI agents track a gang of sadistic kidnappers in this story inspired by a real-life ransom abduction from 1931. Cast: Cesar Romero, Rochelle Hudson, Bruce Cabot, Edward Brophy, Edward Norris, Warren Hymer.

*Whipsaw*—An FBI agent operating undercover (Spencer Tracy) falls in love with a gangster's gun moll. Cast: Myrna Loy, Harvey Stephens, William Harrigan, Clay Clement.

## 1936

*Public Enemy's Wife*—FBI agents pursue gangsters in another violent tale, paradoxically climaxes when one of the G-men (Pat O'Brien) marries his adversary's ex-wife. Cast: Margaret Lindsay, Robert Armstrong, Cesar Romero.

*Special Investigator*—An underworld lawyer goes straight—and the action goes west—after his G-man brother is murdered by mobsters. Cast: Richard Dix, Margaret Callahan.

## 1938

*Smashing the Rackets*—FBI agents tackle organized crime twenty years before their real-life counterparts catch up, in a drama loosely based on the career of New York state prosecutor Thomas Dewey. Cast: Chester Morris, Frances Mercer, Bruce Cabot, Rita Johnson.

## 1939

*Confessions of a Nazi Spy*—Hitler's blitzkrieg prompts a shift in story lines, as an FBI agent (Edward G. Robinson) pursues Axis saboteurs in America. Cast: George Sanders, Francis Lederer, Paul Lukas, James Stephenson, Sig Rumann.

*Missing Evidence*—Another movie G-man (Robert Preston) falls in love with the enemy, this time a seductive female counterfeiter. FBI incursion on Secret Service jurisdiction remains unexplained. Cast: Irene Hervey, Inez Courtney.

*Persons in Hiding*—Bank robbers Clyde Barrow and Bonnie Parker get their first screen treatment in this film loosely based on J. Edgar Hoover's ghost-written account of 1930s fugitives. Cast: J. Carroll Naish, Patricia Morison, Lynne Overman, William Henry, Helen Twelvetrees, William Frawley.

## 1940

*Queen of the Mob*—Another lift from Hoover's ghost-written *Persons in Hiding*, this one fictionalizing the outlaw career of "Ma" Barker. Cast: Ralph Bellamy, Blanche Yurka, Jack Carson, Richard Denning.

## 1942

*Joe Smith, American*—A munitions worker is kidnapped by Nazi agents but preserves the secrets of his trade, leading FBI agents to arrest his captors. Cast: Robert Young, Marsha Hunt, Harvey Stephens, Darryl Hickman.

## 1943

*They Came to Blow Up America*—A German-American FBI agent (George Sanders) infiltrates a ring of Nazi saboteurs in this fictionalized account of the bureau's war work. Cast: Ward Bond, Anna Sten.

## 1944

*Roger Touhy, Gangster*— A decade after G-men framed him for a nonexistent kidnapping, Touhy allegedly collaborated (from prison) with Twentieth Century Fox to produce this treatment of his case. Cast: Preston Foster, Victor McLaglen, Lois Andrews, Anthony Quinn, Kent Taylor, Harry Morgan, Kent Richmond, Trudy Marshall.

## 1945

*Allotment Wives*— An FBI agent (Paul Kelly) exposes a swindler's scheme to cheat U.S. servicemen out of their paychecks. Cast: Otto Kruger, Kay Francis.

*Dillinger*— Myth triumphs over fact in this send-up of "Public Enemy Number One's" violent career. Cast: Edmund Lowe, Lawrence Tierney, Anne Jeffreys, Elisha Cook Jr., Eduard Ciannelli.

*The House on 92nd Street*— J. Edgar Hoover introduces this Oscar-winning docudrama of the FBI's campaign against Nazi spies in World War II. Cast: William Eythe, Lloyd Nolan, Signe Hasso, Leo G. Carroll, Gene Lockhart.

## 1947

*Ride the Pink Horse*— An FBI agent (Art Smith) intervenes when one crook plots to blackmail another. Cast: Robert Montgomery, Fred Clark, Wanda Hendrix, Thomas Gomes, Rita Conde, Andrea King, Grandon Rhodes.

## 1948

*Street with No Name*— Richard Widmark steals the show with his portrayal of a demented killer, when an FBI agent (Mark Stevens) goes undercover to infiltrate a crime syndicate. Cast: Lloyd Nolan, Ed Begley, Barbara Lawrence, Donald Buka.

*Walk a Crooked Mile*— G-men collaborate with Scotland Yard to crack a ring of post-war nuclear spies. Cast: Louis Hayward, Dennis O'Keefe, Onslow Stevens, Raymond Burr, Louise Allbritton.

## 1949

*Federal Agents vs. Underworld, Inc.*— Title notwithstanding, FBI agents continue to avoid the Mafia in this tale of thieves pursuing ancient artifacts. Cast: Kirk Alyn, Carol Foreman, Rosemary La Planche.

## 1950

*Mister 880*— Comedy supercedes drama—and the Secret Service is ignored again—as an FBI agent (Burt Lancaster) pursues a wily counterfeiter. Cast: Dorothy McGuire, Edmund Gwenn, Monor Watson, Millard Mitchell.

*Southside 1–1000*— FBI agents make their third cinematic foray against counterfeiters, still without so much as a nod to the U.S. Secret Service. Cast: Don Defore, George Tobia, Andrea King, Barry Kelley.

## 1951

*FBI Girl*— A clerk in the bureau's Identification Division (Audrey Totter) saves the day when a gangster tries to remove his fingerprints from FBI files. Cast: Cesar Romero, George Brent, Tom Drake, Raymond Burr.

*Government Agents vs. the Phantom Legion*— G-men pursue uranium thieves in this 12-part serial. Cast: Walter Reed, Dick Curtis, Mary Ellen Kay.

*I Was a Communist for the FBI*— The Cold War kicks in with this fact-based account of an FBI informer (Frank Lovejoy) inside the U.S. Communist Party. Cast: Philip Carey, Dorothy Hart, James Millican.

## 1952

*Walk East on Beacon*— Produced with FBI collaboration, this treatment of the Klaus Fuchs spy case is based on a ghost-written *Reader's Digest* article by J. Edgar Hoover. Cast: George Murphy, Finlay Currie, George Hill, Virginia Gilmore.

## 1953

*Pickup on South Street*— G-men enlist a small-time pickpocket to help them smash a Russian spy ring. Cast: Richard Widmark, Thelma Ritter, Richard Kiley, Jean Peters.

## 1954

*The Atomic Kid*— Child star Mickey Rooney is pursued by foreign spies and FBI agents after he miraculously survives a nuclear explosion. Cast: Robert Strauss, Whit Bissell, Hal March.

*Down These Dark Streets*— An FBI agent (Broderick Crawford) pursues cases left unsolved after his partner's murder. Cast: Ruth Roman, Kenneth Tobey, Martha Hyer, Marisa Pavan.

*Them!*— An FBI agent (James Arness) dons military fatigues to battle giant ants in a tale of nuclear testing run amok. Cast: James Whitmore, Edmund Gwynn, Joan Weldon.

## 1955

*A Bullet for Joey*— G-men face a double dose of drama as a gangster stalks a nuclear scientist. Cast: Edward G. Robinson, George Raft, Audrey Totter.

## 1957

*Baby Face Nelson*— Mickey Rooney plays the title role opposite Leo Gordon's Dillinger, in this fictionalized treatment of 1930s bank robbers. Cast: Carolyn Jones, Cedric Hardwicke.

## 1958

*Machine Gun Kelly*— Another Depression-era desperado gets the Hollywood treatment and comes to the predictable bad end, after pursuing mythical adventures. Cast: Charles Bronson, Susan Cabot, Morey Amsterdam, Barbara Morris, Wally Campo, Jack Lambert, Connie Gilchrist, Frank DeKova.

## 1959

*The FBI Story*— Don Whitehead's FBI-approved best-seller receives further fictional embellishment, spanning bureau history from the 1920s to World War II. James Stewart narrates and stars as Agent Chip Hardesty. Cast: Vera Miles, Murray Hamilton, Nick Adams, Diane Jergens.

*Jet over the Atlantic*— An FBI agent (Guy Madison) escorts a fugitive on his way back from Europe for trial. Cast: George Raft, Virginia Mayo, Llona Massey.

## 1960

*Ma Barker's Killer Brood*— Lurid melodrama rides roughshod over fact in a stock treatment of Depression-era bank robbers. Cast: Lurene Tuttle, Tris Coffin, Nelson Leigh, Paul Dubrov, Myrna Dell.

*Pretty Boy Floyd*— History is among the first casualties in this Hollywood portrayal of another 1930s desperado. Cast: John Ericson, Barry Newman, Joan Harvey.

## 1965

*That Darn Cat*— Walt Disney propels the titular feline into an FBI spy case, playing the story for laughs. Cast: Hayley Mills, Dean Jones, Roddy McDowell, Dorothy Provine, William Demarest, Elsa Lanchester.

*Young Dillinger*— Dillinger teams briefly with Pretty Boy Floyd and Baby Face Nelson in this low-budget melodrama, while G-men (Reed Hadley, Robert Osterloh) pursue them. Cast: Nick Adams, Robert Conrad, John Ashley, Mary Ann Mobley, Victor Buono.

## 1966

*FBI 99*— A routine made-for-television feature, wherein G-men pursue wily crooks. Cast: Marten Lamont, Helen Talbot, George Lewis, Wally Wales, Lorna Gray.

## 1967

*Cosa Nostra, Arch Enemy of the FBI*— Regular characters from the bureau-approved television series *The FBI* confront the Mafia (whose existence J. Edgar Hoover denied for nearly four decades) in this made-for-TV feature. Cast: Efrem Zimbalist Jr., Philip Abbott, Robert Duvall, Celeste Holm, Walter Pidgeon, Telly Savalas, Susan Strasberg.

*The President's Analyst*— A psychiatrist privy to White House secrets is hunted by G-men, CIA agents, and hit men from the telephone company. Cast: James Coburn, Godfrey Cambridge, Severn Darden.

## 1970

*Bloody Mama*— Incest triggers "Ma" Barker's 1930s crime wave in this low-budget treatment from B-movie king Roger Corman. Cast: Shelley Winters, Don Stroud, Robert DeNiro, Pat Hingle, Bruce Dern.

*A Bullet for Pretty Boy*— Bank robber Pretty Boy Floyd returns for another slug-fest, portrayed sympathetically by rock idol Fabian Forte. Cast: Jocelyn Lane, Astrid Warner.

## 1971

*Clay Pigeon*— FBI agents entrap innocent civilians as part of their ploy to convict a drug dealer. Cast: Lane Slate, Tom Stern, Telly Savalas, Burgess Meredith, Robert Vaughn.

## 1973

*Dillinger*— The gang's all here for an action-packed reunion of *Wild Bunch* co-stars Warren Oates (as Dillinger) and Ben Johnson (as G-man Melvin Purvis). Fact takes a backseat to fireworks in the most violent portrayal of Dillinger's legend to date. Cast: Richard Dreyfuss, Harry Dean Stanton, Geoffrey Lewis, Steve Kanaly, Michelle Phillips, Cloris Leachman.

## 1974

*The FBI Story: The FBI versus Alvin Karpis, Public Enemy Number One*— Not to be confused with the 1959 original, this made-for-TV melodrama follows J. Edgar Hoover (Harris Yulin) in pursuit of a 1930s outlaw. Cast: Robert Foxworth, Kay Lenz, Gary Lockwood, Cris Robinson, Anne Francis, Gerald McRaney, Eileen Heckart, Whit Bissell, James B. Sikking.

*Melvin Purvis, G-Man*— Fresh from his portrayal of J. Edgar Hoover, Harris Yulin returns as outlaw Machine Gun Kelly, pursued through mythical adventures by FBI agent Melvin Purvis (Dale Robertson). Cast: Matt Clark, Margaret Blye.

*The Story of Pretty Boy Floyd*— Floyd is exonerated of the Kansas City massacre and Melvin Purvis (Geoffrey Binney) takes a backseat in this sympathetic made-for-television biopic (which also curiously makes a point of getting Floyd's first name wrong). Cast: Martin Sheen, Kim Darby, Michael Parks, Steven Keats, Bill Vint, Rod McCrary.

## 1975

*Attack on Terror: The FBI versus the Ku Klux Klan*— Peter Strauss plays a remarkably lean J. Edgar Hoover in this made-for-television account of the bureau's campaign against Mississippi Klansmen in the 1960s. Cast: Rip Torn, Dabney Coleman, Ned Beatty, John Beck, Billy Green Bush, Andrew Duggan, Ed Flanders, L.Q. Jones, George Grizzard.

*Dog Day Afternoon*— Cold-blooded G-men undermine police negotiations and force a lethal confrontation in this story of a bank heist gone sour. Cast: Al Pacino, John Cazale, Charles Durning, James Broderick, Chris Sarandon.

*Kansas City Massacre*— Dale Robertson reprises his cigar-smoking portrayal of Melvin Purvis in a made-for-television feature that teams Pretty Boy Floyd with John Dillinger and the Barker-Karpis gang. Cast: Bo Hopkins, Mills Watson, Matt Clark, Scott Brady, John Karlen, Robert Walden, Elliott Street, Harris Yulin, William Jordan, Morgan Paull.

## 1977

*The Private Files of J. Edgar Hoover*— Flashbacks illustrate this offbeat portrayal of the aging FBI director (Broderick Crawford), complete with implications of a rumored homosexual relationship with sidekick Clyde Tolson (Dan Dailey). Cast: Rip Torn, Jose Ferrer.

## 1979

*Love and Bullets*— G-men and mobsters alike stalk Charles Bronson through this predictable melodrama filmed on location in Switzerland. Cast: Rod Steiger, Jill Ireland.

*The Lady in Red*— A new take on the Dillinger legend, viewed through the eyes of girlfriend Polly Hamilton — who was *not* the historical "Lady in Red." Also released as *Guns, Sins, and Bathtub Gin.* Cast: Pamela Sue Martin, Louise Fletcher, Robert Conrad, Robert Hogan, Glenn Withrow, Laurie Heineman, Christopher Lloyd, Dick Miller.

*The Ordeal of Patty Hearst*— An FBI agent (Dennis Weaver) pursues the Symbionese Liberation Army and its famous captive-turned-radical in a made-for-television feature. Cast: Lisa Eilbacher, David Haskill, Felton Perry, Tisa Farrow, Anne De Salvo, Karen Landry, Brendan Burns.

## 1980

*Follow That Car*— Children help the bureau crack a case in this improbable feature pitched to the youth market. Cast: Dirk Benedict, Tanya Tucker, Terri Nunn.

## 1981

*No Place to Hide*— FBI agents try to protect a woman stalked by a homicidal maniac. Cast: Mariette Hartley, Keir Dullea, Kathleen Beller.

## 1982

*I Was a Zombie for the FBI*— Science fiction and the supernatural collide when two criminal brothers discover an alien plot to conquer earth and the FBI improbably recruits them to investigate. Cast: Larry Raspberry, James Raspberry, John Gillick, David Hyde, James Ostrander.

*They Call Me Bruce*— A Chinese chef obsessed with Bruce Lee movies finds himself pursued by FBI agents after he is recruited to smuggle narcotics. Cast: Johnny Yune, Ralph Mauro, Margaux Hemingway, Pam Huntington.

## 1983

*Strange Invaders*— Appeals to the skeptical FBI prove fruitless as a tabloid reporter and her boyfriend battle invaders from outer space. Cast: Nancy Allen, Paul LeMat, Diana Scarwid, Louise Fletcher, Michael Lerner, Wallace Shawn, Fiona Lewis, Kenneth Toby, June Lockhart.

## 1984

*Best Defense*— FBI agents and Soviet spies are equally inept in their pursuit of a mysterious super-weapon. Cast: Dudley Moore, Eddie Murphy, George Dzundsa, Kate Capshaw.

## 1985

*Falcon and the Snowman*— Two adventure-loving friends run afoul of the FBI after selling military secrets to the Soviet Union. Cast: Timothy Hutton, Sean Penn.

*To Live and Die in L.A.*— The Secret Service gets short shrift again, as corrupt FBI agents pursue a counterfeiter, committing robberies in the process. Cast: William Peterson, Willem Defoe, John Pankow, John Turturro.

## 1986

*Black Moon Rising*— FBI agents hire a thief to steal blueprints for a revolutionary new car, then give chase when he absconds with the plans. Cast: Tommy Lee Jones, Robert Vaughn, Linda Hamilton, Richard Jaeckel.

*Black Widow*— An FBI statistician (Debra Winger) disobeys orders to pursue a female serial killer. Cast: Theresa Russell, Sami Frey, Dennis Hopper, Nicol Williamson, Terry O'Quinn.

*The Deadly Business*— A mobster with a conscience turns FBI informer upon learning that his boss is dumping toxic waste. Cast: Alan Arkin, Armand Assante, Michael Learned.

*F/X*— G-men hire a Hollywood special effects wizard to stage a mobster's death, then seek to insure his silence by killing him. Cast: Bryan Brown, Cliff DeYoung, Diane Venora, Mason Adams.

*Manhunter*— A retired FBI profiler (William Peterson) pursues a vicious serial killer in the first film treatment of Thomas Harris's best-selling novel *Red Dragon*. Cast: Brian Cox, Tom Noonan, Dennis Farina, Stephen Lang, Joan Allen, Kim Greist.

*Raw Deal*— An ex-FBI agent (Arnold Schwarzenegger) earns his way back onto the bureau payroll by infiltrating the Chicago mob and wiping out most of its members. Cast: Robert Davi, Kathryn Harold, Sam Wanamaker, Paul Shenar, Ed Lauter, Darren McGavin.

*Under Siege*— A fictional FBI director (Peter Strauss) declares war on domestic terrorism in this made-for-television drama. Cast: Mason Adams, Lew Ayres, Hal Holbrook, George Grizzard, E.G. Marshall, Fritz Weaver, David Opatoshu, Paul Winfield, Frederick Coffin.

## 1987

*The Hidden*— An alien doubling as an FBI agent (Kyle MacLachlen) tracks an intergalactic killer who can possess human corpses. Cast: Michael Nouri, Claudia Christian, Ed O'Ross.

*Hoover vs. the Kennedys: The Second Civil War*— John and Robert Kennedy clash with J. Edgar Hoover (Jack Warden) in a made-for-television docudrama of the turbulent 1960s. Cast: Robert Pine, Nicholas Campbell, Richard Anderson, Barry Morse, Brioni Farrell.

*The House on Carroll Street*— An FBI agent (Jeff Daniels) becomes romantically involved with an informant while tracking fugitive Nazis in the 1950s. Cast: Kelly McGillis, Mandy Patinkin, Jessica Tandy.

*The Wild Pair*— Rule books go out the window as an FBI agent (Beau Bridges) pursues white-supremacist drug dealers. Cast: Bubba Smith, Lloyd Bridges, Raymond St. Jacques, Gary Lockwood, Danny De La Paz, Ellen Greer, Lela Rachon.

*Wisdom*— Emilio Estevez directs and stars in this sympathetic treatment of a modern-day Bonnie and Clyde pursued by heartless G-men. Cast: Demi Moore, Tom Skerritt, Veronica Cartwright.

## 1988

*Betrayed*— A female FBI agent (Debra Winger) falls in love with a neo-Nazi killer while investigating a group resembling The Order. Cast: Tom Berenger, John Heard, Betsy Blair, John Mahoney, Ted Levine.

*Die Hard*— Trigger-happy G-men (Robert Davi, Grand L. Bush) jeopardize innocent lives and lose their own during a terrorist stand-off in Los Angeles. Cast: Bruce Willis, Alan Rickman, Bonnie Bedelia, James Shigeta.

*Favorite Son*— An FBI agent (Robert Loggia) is enmeshed in political intrigue while investigating the attempted murder of a vice presidential candidate in this made-for-television drama (also broadcast as *Target: Favorite Son*). Cast: Harry Hamlin, Jason Alexander, James Whitmore, Randi Brooks, Linda Kozlowski, Ronnie Cox.

*Feds*— Female recruits confront sexism and play it for laughs as they progress through the FBI Academy. Cast: Rebecca De Mornay, Mary Gross, Fred Thompson, Ken Marshall, Larry Cedar.

*J. Edgar Hoover*— The director (Treat Williams) looks better than ever in this loose adaptation of late assistant director William Sullivan's tell-all exposé.

*Little Nikita*— An FBI agent (Sidney Poitier) must tell an orphan that his late parents were Soviet agents. Cast: River Phoenix, Caroline Kava.

*Married to the Mob*— Yet another G-man (Matthew Modine) falls in love with his prime suspect while investigating a Mafioso's murder. Cast: Michelle Pfeiffer, Dean Stockwell, Mercedes Ruehl, Alec Baldwin, Joan Cusack.

*Midnight Run*— FBI agents and mobsters alike pursue a bounty-hunter and his bail-jumping prisoner on their cross-country trip to Los Angeles. Cast: Robert DeNiro, Charles Grodin, John Ashton, Yaphet Kotto, Dennis Farina.

*Mississippi Burning*— Mismatched FBI agents (Gene Hackman, Willem Dafoe) team up to investigate the Ku Klux Klan in this fictionalized portrayal of infamous 1960s civil rights murders. Cast: Brad Dourif, Frances McDormand, Gailard Sartin.

*Patty Hearst*— The fugitive heiress gets sympathetic treatment in this film adaptation of Hearst's autobiography, *Every Secret Thing.* Also released simply as *Patty.* Cast: Natasha Richardson, Ving Rhames, William Forsythe, Olivia Barash, Dana Delaney, Jodi Long, Peter Kowanko.

*Running on Empty*— Over-the-hill leftist radicals from the 1960s try to avoid capture by persistent FBI manhunters. Cast: Christine Lahti, Judd Hirsch, River Phoenix, Martha Plimpton.

*Shoot to Kill*— Sidney Poitier returns as an FBI agent pursuing a homicidal kidnapper into the wilderness, with help from an irascible hunting guide. Cast: Tom Berenger, Kirstie Alley, Clancy Brown.

## 1989

*Dead-Bang*— A Los Angeles detective pursues neo-Nazis reminiscent of The Order, obstructed by strait-laced FBI agents who worship procedural guidelines and cringe in the face of profanity. Cast: Don Johnson, William Forsythe, Penelope Ann Miller.

*Johnnie Mae Gibson*— Lynn Whitfield portrays the FBI's first black female agent in this made-for-television drama. Cast: Howard Rollins Jr., Marta DuBois, Richard Lawson.

*The Mighty Quinn*— Years of indoctrination as an FBI agent handicap a retired G-man (Denzel Washington) when he goes to work as a Caribbean police chief. Cast: Robert Townsend, James Fox.

## 1990

*The Arrival*— An FBI agent (John Saxon) battles extraterrestrials who possess humans. Cast: Joseph Culp.

*At Gunpoint*— FBI profilers track a serial murderer. Cast: Frank Kanig, Tain Bodkin, Scott Claflin.

*Flashback*— A gung-ho FBI agent (Keifer Sutherland) undergoes a change of personality while transporting a 1960s radical to trial. Cast: Dennis Hopper, Carol Kane, Paul Dooley.

*I Come in Peace*— An unimaginative FBI agent (Brian Benben) teams with a rogue Houston vice cop to investigate serial murders committed by an alien from outer space. Cast: Dolph Lundgren, Betsey Brantley, Matthias Hues.

*Mr. Hoover and I*— A self-indulgent exercise by militant leftist director Emile de Antonio, interspersing documentary footage with angry reflections on his own FBI file (procured under the Freedom of Information Act) and speculation on J. Edgar Hoover's presumed homosexuality.

*Murder in Mississippi*— History gets better-than-average treatment in the second made-for-television portrayal of 1960s civil rights murders and the FBI's response. Cast: Tom Hulce, Blair Underwood, Jennifer Grey, CCH Pounder, Josh Charles.

*My Blue Heaven*— An introverted G-man (Rick Moranis) learns new social skills from a mobster in the federal witness protection program. Cast: Steve Martin, Joan Cusack, Carol Kane, William Hickey, Bill Irwin, Melanie Mayron.

*A Show of Force*— A journalist exposes murders committed by the FBI in a bid to influence Puerto Rican elections. Cast: Amy Irving, Andy Garcia, Robert Duvall, Lou Diamond Phillips.

## 1991

*The Dark Wind*— Corrupt FBI agents obstruct a Navajo detective's investigation of narcotics trafficking on Southwestern Indian reservations. Cast: Lou Diamond Phillips, Gary Farmer, Fred Ward, Guy Boyd.

*Homicide*— A Jewish police detective rediscovers his heritage while investigating a hate crime left unsolved by inept FBI agents. Cast: Joe Mantegna, W.H. Macy, Natalija Nogulich.

*JFK*— A courageous district attorney investigates conspiracy theories in the murder of President John Kennedy, exposing retired G-man Guy Bannister (Ed Asner) as one of many plotters. Cast: Kevin Costner, Sissy Spacek, Tommy Lee Jones, Kevin Bacon, Laurie Metcalfe, Joe Pesci, Donald Sutherland, John Candy, Jack Lemmon, Gary Oldman, Walter Matthau.

*Point Break*— Unconventional FBI agents (Gary Busey, Keanu Reeves) pursue a gang of bank-robbing surfers in Los Angeles. Cast: Patrick Swayze, Lori Petty, James LeGros, John Philbin, Bojesse Christopher.

*The Rain Killer*— G-men track a serial killer who prowls only during inclement weather. Cast: Ray Sharkey, David Beecroft, Tania Coleridge, Michael Chiklis, Woody Brown.

*The Silence of the Lambs*— Five Oscars were awarded to this story of an FBI recruit (Jody Foster) seeking help from an incarcerated serial killer to capture another still at large. The film also reportedly produced a rash of applications to the FBI Academy. Cast: Anthony Hopkins, Scott Glenn, Ted Levine, Anthony Heald, Brook Smith, Diane Baker.

*Steele's Law*— Hampered by a shortage of black agents, the FBI recruits a Chicago policeman to infiltrate a criminal gang in Texas. Cast: Fred Williamson, Bo Svenson, Phyllis Cicero.

*Stone Cold*— The FBI recruits a suspended police officer to infiltrate a motorcycle gang and disrupt its plans for political assassination. Cast: Brian Bosworth, Lance Henriksen, William Forsythe, Arabella Holzbog.

*The 10 Million Dollar Getaway*— FBI investigation of the 1978 Lufthansa robbery at New York's JFK Airport is dramatized in this made-for-television movie. Cast: John Mahoney, Terrence Mann, Joseph Carberry, Karen Young, Tony Lo Bianco.

## 1992

*Deadly Rivals*— An FBI agent (Andrew Stevens) contends with smugglers and corporate spies. Cast: Joseph Bologna, Richard Roundtree, Cela Wise, Margaux Hemingway.

*Folks!*— A stock trader's life is turned upside-down by an FBI investigation. Cast: Tom Selleck, Don Ameche, Christine Ebersole, Anne Jackson.

*Honor and Glory*— A female FBI agent (Cynthia Rothrock) displays her martial arts prowess while battling nuclear hijackers. Cast: Donna Jason, Gerald Klein, Chuck Jeffreys.

*In the Line of Duty: The FBI Murders*— FBI agents in Miami pursue a pair of violent bank robbers, climaxed with the bureau's worst-ever shootout in this made-for-television treatment of real-life events from 1986. Cast: Ronnie Cox, Michael Gross, David Soul, Doug Sheehan.

*Incident at Oglala*— Robert Redford narrates this documentary, suggesting that federal prisoner Leonard Peltier was framed for the 1975 murders of two FBI agents on the Pine Ridge, South Dakota, Indian reservation.

*Jennifer 8*— While tracking an elusive serial killer, a Los Angeles detective runs afoul of FBI agents who suspect he is the murderer. Cast: Andy Garcia, Lance Henriksen, Kathy Baker, Kevin Conway, John Malkovich, Graham Beckel.

*Lady Dragon*— Cynthia Rothrock returns as a high-kicking FBI agent, tracking the criminals who killed her husband on their wedding day. Cast: Richard Norton, Robert Ginty.

*Live Wire*— An FBI demolitions expert (Pierce Brosnan) must protect his wife's lover, a corrupt U.S. senator, from a terrorist assassin. Cast: Ron Silver, Ben Cross, Lisa Eilbacher, Brent Jennings, Al Waxman, Tony Plana, Michael St. Gerard, Philip Baker Hall.

*Malcolm X*— Director Spike Lee suggests that FBI eavesdroppers had foreknowledge of Malcolm's impending assassination but failed to warn the target. Cast: Denzel Washington, Angela Bassett, Al Freeman Jr., Spike Lee, Albert Hall, Delroy Lindo, Theresa Randle, Debby Mazar, Kate Vernon.

*Rapid Fire*— FBI agents place a murder witness at risk by compelling him to testify against underworld killers, then predictably fail to protect him. Cast: Brandon Lee, Powers Boothe, Nick Mancuso, Raymond Barry.

*Ruby*— A poor man's *JFK* links Dallas mobster Jack Ruby to the FBI and Mafia before his murder of Lee Harvey Oswald in November 1963. Cast: Danny Aiello, Sherilyn Fenn, Joe Cortese, Arliss Howard, Marc Lawrence.

*Teamster Boss: The Jackie Presser Story*— Based on James Neff's *Mobbed Up*, this made-for-television movie follows the parallel careers of Cleveland's Jackie Presser (Brian Dennehy) as a union leader, FBI informer and active member of organized crime. Cast: Jeff Daniels, Eli Wallach, Maria Conchita Alonso, Robert Prosky, Tony Lo Bianco.

*Three Ninjas*— The children of a Chinese-American FBI agent are abducted by an arms smuggler their father is investigating. Cast: Michael Treanor, Max Elliott Slade, Chad Power, Rand Kingsley.

*Thunderheart*— A fictional treatment of real-life events on the Pine Ridge Indian reservation finds a mixed-race FBI agent (Val Kilmer) torn between duty to the bureau and his Sioux heritage. Cast: Sam Shepard, Fred Ward.

*Twin Peaks: Fire Walk with Me*— Director David Lynch adds an incomprehensible postscript to his already-cancelled "Twin Peaks" television series, posing more questions than he answers for the surreal saga of an FBI agent (Kyle MacLachlen) pursuing a small-town serial killer. Cast: Lara Flynn Boyle, Michael Ontkean, Piper Laurie, Sherilyn Fenn, Joan Chen.

*White Sands*— A New Mexico sheriff finds himself unwittingly at odds with an FBI investigation in progress. Cast: Willem Dafoe, Samuel L. Jackson, Mary Elizabeth Mastrantonio, Mickey Rourke, M. Emmet Walsh.

## 1993

*The Firm*— The newest member of an underworld law firm is harassed by an FBI agent (Ed Harris) determined to recruit him as a government witness. Cast: Tom Cruise, Hal Holbrook, Jeanne Tripplehorn, Holly Hunter, Wilford Brimley, David Strathairn, Gary Busey.

*Golden Gate*— Guilt-stricken after his investigation of an alleged communist drives the subject to suicide, FBI agent Matt Dillon bows to cinematic convention by falling in love with the dead man's daughter. Cast: Joan Chen, Bruce Kirby, Tzi Ma.

*Hitwoman: The Double Edge*— Soap opera veteran Susan Lucci plays dual roles as an FBI agent and the contract killer she pursues. Cast: Robert Urich, Michael Woods.

*In the Line of Duty: Ambush at Waco*— Director Dick Lowry strives for balance in this made-for-television docudrama of the 1993 Branch Davidian siege. Cast: Tim Daly, William O'Leary, Dan Luria.

*No Escape, No Return*— G-men and undercover police collaborate to snare a major narcotics trafficker. Cast: Maxwell Caulfield, Dustin Nguyen, Denise Loveday.

*The Outfit*— Hollywood departs from reality as a rogue G-man (Lance Henriksen) caught up in the bootleg wars of 1920s New York. Cast: Billy Drago, Martin Kove.

*Slaughter of the Innocents*— Eerie effects go to waste in this impossible story, as an FBI profiler (Scott Glenn) is consistently outsmarted by his 12-year-old son in pursuit of a serial killer. Cast: Jesse Cameron-Glickenhaus, Darlanne Fluegel, Sheila Tousey, Zitto Kazann.

*Undercover Blues*— A husband-wife team of FBI agents (Dennis Quaid, Kathleen Turner) encounter arms smugglers while vacationing with their infant child in New Orleans. Cast: Tom Arnold, Park Overall.

## 1994

*The Client*— Federal prosecutors send G-men in pursuit of a child who witnessed a gangland murder. Cast: Tommy Lee Jones, Susan Sarandon, Mary Louise Parker, Anthony LaPaglia.

*Holy Matrimony*— FBI pursuit drives a female bank robber to seek refuge in a Hutterite religious community, pledged in marriage to a boy half her age. Cast: Patricia Arquette, Joseph Gordon-Levitt, Armin Mueller-Stahl, John Schuck, Tate Donovan, Lois Smith.

*Shattered Image*— G-men pursue the kidnappers of a modeling agency's proprietor. Cast: Jack Scalia, Bo Derek, Dorian Harewood, John Savage, Ramon Franco, Carol Lawrence, Michael Harris.

*Zero Tolerance*— An FBI agent (Robert Patrick) turns vigilante to execute the leaders of a drug cartel that killed his parents. Cast: Titus Welliver, Mick Fleetwood, Kirsten Meadows, Miles O'-Keefe.

## 1995

*Baby Face Nelson*— C. Thomas Howell turns in a campy performance as the 1930s bank robber driven by ego to his own destruction. Cast: Lisa Zane, F. Murray Abraham, Martin Kove.

*Captain Nuke and the Bomber Boys*— Children recover a lost nuclear device and the FBI mistakes them for members of a terrorist cell. Cast: Joe Montegna, Joanna Pacula, Martin Sheen, Joe Piscopo, Rod Steiger, Ryan Thomas Johnson.

*Dillinger and Capone*— After faking his own death, John Dillinger is called from retirement to pull a bank job for Chicago's mob boss (in fact, already imprisoned when Dillinger was shot). Cast: Martin Sheen, F. Murray Abraham, Don Stroud, Sasha Jenson.

*From the Journals of Jean Seberg*— Mary Beth Hurt plays the title role (and remains the only credited cast member) in this *JFK*-style docudrama, pursuing the theory that FBI harassment drove the actress to commit suicide.

*Nixon*—Director Oliver Stone pursues his conspiratorial vision of American history with this docudrama, wherein J. Edgar Hoover (Bob Hoskins) conspires with the Mafia to blackmail and manipulate President Richard Nixon. Cast: Anthony Hopkins, Joan Allen, Paul Sorvino.

*Panther*—J. Edgar Hoover (Richard Dysart) conspires with the Mafia to promote ghetto drug sales in this provocative docudrama charting the rise and fall of the Black Panther Party. Cast: Courtney Vance, Marcus Chong, Anthony Griffith, Wesley Jonathan.

*Two If by Sea*—G-men and mobsters race to overtake a pair of thieves and recover their stolen loot. Cast: Sandra Bullock, Dennis Leary, Yaphet Kotto.

# 1996

*Chain Reaction*—G-men pursue the inventor of a miracle fuel after he is framed for murder. Cast: Keanu Reeves. Morgan Freeman, Rachel Weisz, Fred Ward, Kevin Dunn.

*Children of Fury*—FBI agents lay siege to a compound occupied by religious fanatics in a drama with strong overtones of the Waco confrontation. Cast: Dennis Franz, Ed Begley Jr., Tess Harper, Paul Le Mat, Kyle Secor.

*Ghosts of Mississippi*—A one-time FBI informant in the KKK (Jim Harley) provides information crucial to the belated prosecution of Klan assassin in this fact-based treatment of the Medgar Evers murder case. Cast: Alec Baldwin, James Woods, Whoopi Goldberg, Craig T. Nelson, William H. Macy, Susanna Thompson, Virginia Madsen.

*Hollow Point*—A female FBI agent (Tia Carrere) teams with a DEA agent and a contract killer to wipe out a criminal syndicate. Cast: Thomas Ian Griffith, Donald Sutherland, John Lithgow.

*Mask of Death*—Plastic surgery enables an FBI agent (Lorenzo Lamas) to pursue a killer more effectively. Cast: Conrad Cunn, Rae Dawn Chong, Billy Dee Williams.

*Maximum Risk*—G-men complicate a vengeful brother's search for the Russian mobsters who murdered his twin. Cast: Jean Claude Van Damme, Natasha Henstridge, Zach Grenier, Jena-Hugues Anglade, Paul Ben-Victor.

*Mulholland Falls*—A squad of vigilante Los Angeles policemen tangle with FBI agents and the U.S. Army while investigating a mysterious homicide. Cast: Nick Nolte, Chazz Palminteri, Michael Madsen, Melanie Griffith, Chris Penn, Jennifer Connelly, John Malkovich.

*Public Enemies*—FBI "gunfighter" Melvin Purvis (Dan Cortese) pursues the Barker-Karpis gang to a bloody showdown. Cast: Theresa Russell, Eric Roberts, Alyssa Milano, Gavin Harrison, Joseph Lindsay.

*The Rock*—An inexperienced FBI agent (Nicolas Cage) teams with an ex-convict to foil a terrorist takeover of Alcatraz island. Cast: Sean Connery, Ed Harris, David Morse, William Forsythe, John Spencer.

*Serial Killer*—An FBI profiler (Kim Delaney) is hounded by a murderer she once sent to prison. Cast: Gary Hudson, Tobin Bell, Pam Grier.

# 1997

*Donnie Brasco*—Based on G-man Joe Pistone's memoir of six years undercover in a New York Mafia family, this thoughtful docudrama examines the moral ambiguity of sting operations. Cast: Johnny Depp, Al Pacino, Michael Madsen, James Russo, Bruno Kirby, Anne Heche.

*Double Tap*—An FBI agent (Heather Locklear) falls in love with hit man (Stephen Rea). Cast: Peter Greene, Mykelti Williamson.

*Face/Off*—The leader of an FBI anti-terrorist squad (John Travolta) surgically switches faces with his prime target to infiltrate the gang and prevent a catastrophic bombing. Cast: Nicolas Cage, Joan Allen, Gina Gershon, Allesandro Nivola.

*In the Line of Duty: Blaze of Glory*—FBI agents pursue a husband-wife team of bank robbers in this fact-based feature made for television. Cast: Bruce Campbell, Lori Loughlin, Brad Whitford, Tom LaSalle.

*The Jackal*—An FBI agent (Sidney Poitier) collaborates with Russian authorities and an imprisoned Irish terrorist to avert a high-level political assassination. Cast: Bruce Willis, Richard Gere, Diane Venora, Mathilda May.

*Murder in My Mind*—A rookie G-woman (Nicolette Sheridan) pursues a serial killer by having cells from a victim implanted in her brain, thus enabling her to see the killer.

*Switchback*—An FBI agent (Dennis Quaid) abandons procedure to find the serial killer who has kidnapped his son. Cast: Danny Glover, Jared Leto, R. Lee Ermey, Ted Levine.

# 1998

*Mercury Rising*—Improbable tale of an outcast FBI agent (Bruce Willis) defending an autistic child against government assassins, after the boy accidentally cracks a top-secret code. Cast: Alec Baldwin, Miko Hughes, Chi McBride, Kim Dickens, Bodhi Elfman.

*Renegade Force*—The commander of an FBI Hostage Rescue Team (Michael Rooker) is pitted against a deadly squad of vigilante policemen. Cast: Robert Patrick, Diane DiLascio, Louis Mandylor, James Kisicki, Darnell Suttles.

*The Siege*—FBI agents (Denzel Washington, Tony Shalhoub) race the clock to capture Arab terrorists in New York, obstructed by CIA machinations and an over-zealous army commander. Cast: Bruce Willis, Annette Bening, Sami Bouajila.

*The X Files: Fight the Future*—Said future includes alien colonization of earth and proliferation of a deadly virus from outer space, as FBI agents Fox Mulder (David Duchovny) and Dana Scully (Gillian Anderson) carry their fight against intergalactic conspirators from television to the big screen. Cast: William B. Davis, Mitch Pileggi, John Neville, Martin Landau, Terry O'Quinn, Blythe Danner.

# 1999

*Arlington Road*—The husband of a murdered FBI agent (Laura Poe) suspects his new neighbors are fugitive terrorists responsible for a series of deadly bombings. Cast: Jeff Bridges, Tim Robbins, Joan Cusack, Robert Gossett.

*Brotherhood of Murder*—Fact-based, made-for-cable TV depiction of The Order, as viewed by FBI informant Thomas Martinez (William Baldwin). Cast: Peter Gallagher, Kelly Lynch.

*Crazy in Alabama*—FBI agents pursue a homicidal racist sheriff in the 1960s, as a subplot to the comic story of a fugitive housewife who murders her abusive husband. Cast: Melanie Griffith, David Morse, Meat Loaf.

*Judgment Day*—An FBI agent (Suzy Amis) teams with a convicted killer to rescue a kidnapped scientist from a religious doomsday cult. Cast: Ice-T, Mario Van Peebles.

*Red Team—* An FBI agent (Patrick Muldoon) tracks a killer whose victims are themselves suspected serial murderers. Cast: Cathy Moriarty, Tim Thomerson, Fred Ward, C. Thomas Howell, David Brown.

## 2000

*A Better Way to Die—* An ex-cop is targeted by mobsters and a vengeful FBI agent. Cast: Joe Pantoliano, Andre Braugher.

*Big Momma's House—* Ethnic humor ensues when an FBI agent (Martin Lawrence) goes undercover to capture bank robbers. Cast: Nia Long, Paul Giamatti, Jascha Washington, Anthony Anderson, Carl Wright.

*Miss Congeniality—* A female FBI agent (Sandra Bullock) chafes at her undercover assignment as a beauty pageant contestant. Cast: Michael Caine, William Shatner, Benjamin Bratt, Candace Bergen.

*Natural Selection—* An eccentric FBI agent (David Carradine) tracks a serial killer to a small Texas town. Cast: Michael Bowen, Joe Unger, Bob Balaban, Darren Burrows, Missy Atwood, Heather Kafka.

*Nostradamus—* An clairvoyant FBI agent (Joely Fisher) helps local detectives solve the murder of a victim who is burned beyond recognition, uncovering an ancient cult in the process. Cast: Rob Estes, Fintan McKeown, David Millbern.

*Our Lips Are Sealed—* Twin sisters enter the FBI witness protection program and flee to Australia after testifying against a mobster. Cast: Ashley Olsen, Mary-Kate Olsen, Jim Meskimen, Robert Miano, Willie Garson.

*Run for the Money—* An FBI agent (Val Kilmer) blackmails thieves into looting a riverboat casino. Cast: Christian Slater, Darryl Hannah.

*The Silencer—* An FBI agent (Brennan Elliott) fakes his own death to infiltrate a terrorist cell. Cast: Michael Dudikoff, Terence Kelly, Peter LaCroix, Gabrielle Miller.

*The Whole Nine Yards—* FBI agents take advantage of a henpecked dentist to obtain evidence against his next-door neighbor, a notorious underworld hit man. Cast: Matthew Perry, Bruce Willis, Natasha Henstridge, Rosanna Arquette, Michael Clarke Duncan.

## 2001

*Corky Romano—* Slapstick comedy ensues after the FBI recruits a Mafioso's bumbling son to infiltrate and disrupt his father's crime family. Cast: Chris Kattan, Peter Falk, Fred Ward, Jennifer Gimenez, Craig Richards, Vincent Pastore.

*Full Disclosure—* A journalist finds himself trapped between Middle Eastern terrorists and FBI agents while investigating a local murder. Cast: Fred Ward, Virginia Madsen.

*Hannibal—* An FBI agent (Julianne Moore) tracks an escaped serial killer in this sequel to *The Silence of the Lambs.* Cast: Anthony Hopkins, Gary Oldman, Ray Liotta, Frankie Faison, Francesco Neri.

*Hearts in Atlantis—* FBI agents pursue a clairvoyant seer, hoping to monopolize his talents in this film version of the Stephen King best-seller. Cast: Anthony Hopkins, Hope Davis, David Morse, Anton Yelchin, Steve Little.

## 2002

*Jackie Chan Presents: Metal Mayhem—* An FBI agent (Paul Rudd) tries to recover a military robot stolen from American scientists in Hong Kong.

*Red Dragon—* An FBI profiler (Edward Norton) comes out of retirement to track a serial killer with help from imprisoned maniac Hannibal Lecter. Cast: Anthony Hopkins, Ralph Fiennes.

# Appendix G: Radio and Television Series

## Radio

*The FBI in Peace and War* (1944) — This radio series based on author Frederick Collins's 1943 book of the same title was sold to CBS without J. Edgar Hoover's permission, thereby infuriating the director who sought to control every aspect of publicity concerning the bureau. So angry was Hoover, in fact — despite having cooperated on production of the book — that he persuaded Congress to pass legislation banning unauthorized use of the FBI name.

*This Is Your FBI* (1945) — Hoover's answer to the Collins radio series, this bureau-controlled offering premiered with ABC on April 6, 1945 and ran until 1953, spoon-feeding listeners an uncritical view of the bureau's sterling achievements.

*FBI, This Week* (1999– ) — The bureau controls every aspect of this weekly program broadcast over more than 3,200 ABC Radio Network affiliated stations. Moderator Neal Schiff interviews FBI spokesmen on general topics ("Hate Crimes," "Cyberspace Crime") and specific cases ("Largest Cash Robbery in History," "Broker Bilked Out of $60,000").

## Television

*I Led Three Lives* (1953–56) — FBI informer Herbert Philbrick (Richard Carlson) is elevated to the status of a bureau "counterspy" in this series dramatizing his nine years in the U.S. Communist Party. Scripts were reviewed and approved by the FBI to insure "accuracy" and "patriotic" content. Regular cast: Virginia Steffen, Joe Zaremba, Ed Hinton, Patricia Morrow.

*The FBI* (1965–74) — The bureau dominated every aspect of this "official" production, from script approval to screening of cast members, thus insuring that the FBI was always shown in a flattering light. Regular cast: Efrem Zimbalist Jr., Philip Abbot, Lex Barker, Stephen Brooks, Lynn Loring.

*Today's FBI* (1981) — This unsuccessful effort to depict a "new," multicultural FBI without addressing any of the scandals or abuses recently exposed in Congress was canceled after one season of poor ratings. Regular cast: Mike Connors, Harold Sylvester, Joseph Cali, Carol Potter, Richard Hill.

*Unsub* (1989) — A mid-season replacement series on CBS, this drama followed the cases of an FBI profiling unit in pursuit of various serial killers. At least one episode was loosely based on a real-life investigation. More realistic than later programs featuring profilers, this series still included one member whose powers of "empathy" verged on psychic mind-reading. Cast: David Soul, M. Emmett Walsh, Kent McCord, Richard Kind, Jennifer Hetrick, Andrea Mann.

*Mancuso, FBI* (1989–90) — Robert Loggia reprises his role as an irascible G-man first seen in the television miniseries *Favorite Son*. Regular cast: Lindsay Frost, Frederic Lehne, Randi Brooks.

*Twin Peaks* (1989–91) — This surrealistic series tracks the efforts of an FBI agent (Kyle MacLachlan) to solve serial murders in a rural town where every resident is either suspect or apparently insane. David Duchovny (see *The X Files* below) appears briefly as a cross-dressing G-man. Regular cast: Lara Flynn Boyle, Michael Ontkean, Piper Laurie, Joan Chen, Sherilyn Fenn, Russ Tamblyn.

*FBI: The Untold Stories* (1991–93) — Despite the title, there are few surprises in this syndicated series hosted and narrated by Pernell Roberts. The FBI collaborated in production (and apparently controlled content) of half-hour episodes dramatizing well-known cases drawn from recent bureau files. Interviews with real-life agents enhance authenticity, while any criticism of the FBI is carefully avoided.

*The X Files* (1993–2001) — Definitely *not* on the bureau's approved list (though it has reportedly increased applications to the FBI Academy), this popular series follows an FBI odd couple (David Duchovny, Gillian Anderson) in pursuit of UFOs, sinister mutants and other weird phenomenon around the world. Along the way, they are obstructed, harassed and endangered by conspirators whose number includes some of their own superiors at bureau headquarters. Regular cast: Mitch Pileggi, William B. Davis, Robert Patrick.

*Millennium* (1996–99) — A retired FBI profiler (Lance Henriksen) is unable to escape the clutches of a parallel organization, the Millennium Group, which stalks serial killers in an effort to head off mass violence in the year 2000. Regular cast: Megan Gallagher, Brittany Tiplady, Terry O'Quinn.

*C-16: FBI* (1997–98)—Agents of the FBI's Los Angeles field office pursue danger and intrigue in this short-lived action series. Regular cast: Eric Roberts, D.B. Sweeney, Christine Tucci, Angie Harmon.

*Profiler* (1996–2000)—A female profiler with the FBI's "Violent Crimes Task Force" (Ally Walker) is both hunter and prey in this series, pursuing serial offenders while a homicidal psychopath follows her every move. After disposing of her enemy, Walker leaves the team and is replaced by Jamie Luner in the final season. Regular cast: Robert Davi, Julian McMahon, Roma Maffia, George Fraley, Dennis Christopher, Traci Lords.

*FBI Files* (1998–2002)—The Discovery Channel presents this straightforward documentary series "revealing the bureau's forensic techniques and investigative grit." Each episode recounts a recent case.

*Cover Me: Based on the True Life of an FBI Family* (2000)—The title insures that this short-lived action series contains more fiction than fact in its portrayal of an undercover FBI agent (Peter Dobson) and the members of his family who are drawn into perilous investigations. Regular cast: Melora Hardin, Cameron Richardson, Antoinette Picatto, Michael Angarano.

*Sue Thomas: F.B.Eye* (2002– )—The PAX network offers family-oriented drama in this fact-based series following the exploits of a deaf G-woman (Deanne Bray) assigned to read lips with the FBI's "elite surveillance unit." Cast: Yannick Bisson, Rick Peters, Mark Gomes, Tara Samuel, Ted Atherton.

*HRT* (200?)—This action series based on the exploits of an FBI Hostage Rescue Team was still "in production" at press time, with no word available on when (or if) it will actually air. Cast: Alejandro Abellan, Michael Rooker, Lillo Brancato, Kimberly Hawthorne.

# Bibliography

"Agents cleared in false 9–11 confession." Associated Press (26 November 2002).

Alexander, Shana. *The Pizza Connection*. New York: Weidenfeld and Nicholson, 1988.

Altimari, Dave, and Jack Dolan. "FBI searches home in anthrax case." *Hartford Courant* (26 June 2002).

American Civil Liberties Union. *Not Moderate, Not Compassionate, Not Conservative*. Washington, D.C.: ACLU. 2001.

"The American OGPU." *New Republic* 102 (March 11, 1940): 330–332.

Anderson, Curt. "FBI: Al-Qaida may try major attack." Associated Press (16 November 2002).

_____. "FBI director: 100 terror attacks stopped." Associated Press (14 December 2002).

Anderson, Terry. *The Movement and the Sixties: Protest in America from Greensboro to Wounded Knee*. New York: Oxford University Press, 1995.

Anson, Robert. *They've Killed the President*. New York: Bantam, 1975.

"Anthrax profile." Associated Press (9 November 2001).

"Ashcroft defends anti-terror campaign." Associated Press (30 November 2001).

"Ashcroft enthusiastic about new powers." Associated Press (26 October 2001).

"Ashcroft: Laws limit wiretaps." *USA Today* (18 September 2001).

"Ashcroft: Religious groups could be monitored." Associated Press (2 December 2001).

Auerbach, Ann. *Ransom: The Untold Story of International Kidnapping*. New York: Henry Holt, 1998.

Ayer, Frederick. *Yankee G-Man*. Chicago: Regnery, 1957.

Bailes, James. *J. Edgar Hoover Speaks*. Washington, D.C.: Capitol Hill Press, 1970.

Bainerman, Joel. *The Crimes of a President: New Revelations on Conspiracy & Cover-Up in the Bush and Reagan Administrations*. New York: S.P.I. Books, 1992.

Baird-Windle, Patricia, and Eleanor Bader. *Targets of Hatred: Anti-Abortion Terrorism*. New York: St. Martin's Press, 2001.

Banda, Solomon. "FBI failed to give McVeigh documents." Associated Press (11 May 2001).

Barron, John. *Breaking the Ring*. Boston: Houghton Mifflin, 1987.

Bartley, Robert. "FBI reform: Connect anthrax dots. The 'lone wolf' theory is evidence of the Bureau's ineptitude." *Wall Street Journal* (3 June 2002).

Bayles, Fred. "Informants put FBI, its practices on trial." *USA Today* (7 January 1998).

Behn, Noel. *Lindbergh: The Crime*. New York: Atlantic Monthly Press, 1994.

Belknap, Michael. *Cold War Political Justice: The Smith Act, the Communist Party, and American Civil Liberties*. Westport, Conn.: Greenwood, 1977.

_____. *Federal Law and Southern Order: Racial Violence and Constitutional Conflict in the Post-Brown South*. Athens, Ga.: University of Georgia Press, 1987.

_____. "The mechanics of repression: J. Edgar Hoover, the Bureau of Investigation and the radicals, 1917–1925." *Crime and Social Justice* 7 (Spring/Summer 1977): 49–58.

_____. "The Supreme Court goes to war: The meaning and implication of the Nazi saboteur case." *Military Law Review* 89 (1980): 59–95.

Bendavid, Naftali. "Reno says credibility hurt by FBI admission." *Chicago Tribune* (27 August 1999).

Bennett, Sara. "New info disclosed on surveillance of lesbians and gays." *Quash* (August/September 1982).

"Bennett given reduced sentence in Cornwell case." Associated Press (16 May 1996).

Benson, Robert, and Michael Warner, eds. *VENONA: Soviet Espionage and the American Response, 1939–1957*. Washington, D.C.: National Security Agency and Central Intelligence Agency, 1996.

Berman, Jerry. "FBI spies on Central American protesters." *Civil Liberties* 363 (Winter 1988): 1, 3.

Berman, Jerry, and Morton Halperin, eds. *The Abuses of the Intelligence Agencies*. Washington, D.C.: Center for National Security Studies, 1975.

Bernikow, Louis. *Abel*. New York: Trident, 1970.

Bernstein, Barton. "The Oppenheimer conspiracy." *Our Right to Know* (Fall/Winter 1984–85): 9–13.

_____. "The road to Watergate and beyond: The growth and abuse of executive authority since 1940." *Law and Contemporary Problems* 40 (Spring 1976): 58–86.

Bernstein, Dan. "Specialist who led probe charged in bombing case." *Sacramento Bee* (16 November 1989).

Bhatt, Sanjay. "FBI to use 60 agents to start questioning 800 tabloid workers." *Palm Beach Post* (13 October 2001).

Bird, Kai, and Max Holland. "The tapping of 'Tommy the Cork.'" *Nation* 242 (February 8, 1986): 129.

Bisson, Terry. *On a Move: The Story of Mumia Abu-Jamal*. London: Litmus Books, 2000.

Blackhurst, Chris. "Anthrax attacks now being linked to US right-wing cranks." *The Independent* (21 October 2001).

419

Blackstock, Nelson. *COINTELPRO: The FBI's Secret War on Political Freedom*. New York: Vintage, 1975.

Blecker, R.I. "Beyond 1984: Undercover in America—Serpico to Abscam." *New York Law School Law Review* 28 (1984): 83–1024.

Blum, Howard. *Gangland: The Secret Wars of the FBI's Gambino Squad*. New York: Simon & Schuster, 1992.

Blum, Richard, ed. *Surveillance and Espionage in a Free Society*. New York: Praeger, 1973.

Blum, William. *Killing Hope: U.S. Military and CIA Interventions Since World War II*. Monroe, Maine: Common Courage Press, 1995.

Blumenthal, Ralph. *Last Days of the Sicilians: At War with the Mafia*. New York: Times Books, 1988.

Blumenthal, Ralph. "Tapes depict proposal to thwart bomb used in Trade Center blast." *New York Times* (28 October 1993).

_____. "Tapes in bombing plot show informer and FBI at odds." *New York Times* (27 October 1993).

Blumenthal, Sid, and Harvey Yazijian. *Government by Gunplay: Assassination Conspiracy Theories from Dallas to Today*. New York: Signet, 1976.

Bock, Alan. *Ambush at Ruby Ridge: How Government Agents Set Randy Weaver Up and Took His Family Down*. Irvine, Calif.: Dickens Press, 1995.

"Bombing suspect said confessed." Associated Press (17 June 1999).

"Bombs, bullets, bodies: The decade in review." *Intelligence Report* no. 97 (Winter 2000): 9–29.

Brady, Erik. "Justice Department poised to blunt Title IX." *USA Today* (28 May 2002).

Branch, Taylor. *Parting the Waters: America in the King Years, 1954–1963*. New York: Simon & Schuster, 1988.

_____. *Pillar of Fire: America in the King Years, 1963–1965*. New York: Simon & Schuster, 1998.

Bratzel, John. "Pearl Harbor, microdots, and J. Edgar Hoover." *American Historical Review* 87 (December 1982): 1342–47.

Bratzel, John, and Leslie Rout. *The Shadow War: German Espionage and U.S. Counterespionage in Latin America during World War II*. Frederick, Md.: University Publications of America, 1989.

Breitman, George, et al. *The Assassination of Malcolm X*. New York: Pathfinder Press, 1976.

Breuer, William. *Hitler's Undercover War: The Nazi Espionage Invasion of the U.S.A.* New York: St. Martin's Press, 1989.

_____. *J. Edgar Hoover and His G-men*. New York: Praeger, 1995.

Bridis, Ted. "Changes in FBI organization expected." Associated Press (28 May 2002).

Broad, William. "Experts see FBI Missteps hampering anthrax inquiry." *New York Times* (10 November 2001).

Brock, David. "Today's FBI: Rating the remake of the G-Men." *Insight* (February 16, 1987): 8–16.

Bronskill, Jim. "FBI spied on Trudeau for 30 years." *Ottawa Citizen* (20 January 2001).

Brown, Charles. "FBI, feds declare war on computer crimes." *Seattle Times* (4 July 1999).

Brune, Tom. "FBI faults archaic computers for slip-up." *Newsday* (12 May 2001).

Bugliosi, Vincent. "None dare call it treason." *Nation* (5 February 2001).

Buitrago, Ann. *Report on CISPES Files Maintained by FBI Headquarters and Released under the Freedom of Information Act*. New York: FOIA, Inc., 1988.

Burnham, David. *Above the Law: Secret Deals, Political Fixes and Other Misadventures of the U.S. Department of Justice*. New York: Scribner, 1996.

_____. *The Rise of the Computer State*. New York: Random House, 1983.

"Bush aides consider domestic spy agency." Reuters (16 November 2002).

Butterfield, Fox. "FBI agent linked to mob is guilty of corruption." *New York Times* (30 May 2002).

Cagin, Seth, and Philip Dray. *We Are Not Afraid: The Mississippi Murder of Goodman, Schwerner and Chaney*. New York: Macmillan, 1988.

Cain, Brad. "Ashcroft to pursue suicide doctors." Associated Press (7 November 2001).

Candeloro, Dominic. "Louis F. Post and the Red Scare of 1920." *Prologue* 11 (Spring 1979): 40–55.

Carson, Clayborne. *Malcolm X: The FBI File*. New York: Carroll & Graf, 1991.

Cary, Lorin. "The Bureau of Investigation and Radicalism in Toledo, Ohio: 1918–1920." *Labor History* 21, no. 3 (1980): 430–440.

Caute, David. *The Great Fear: The Anti-Communist Purge Under Truman and Eisenhower*. New York: Simon and Schuster, 1978.

Chanen, David, and Randy Furst. "Whistleblower Rowley may be hero, but some question her loyalty to FBI." *Minneapolis Star Tribune* (4 August 2002).

Chanen, David, and Jon Trevlin. "Tell-it-like-it-was letter doesn't surprise those who know Rowley." *Minneapolis Star Tribune* (25 May 2002).

Charles, Deborah. "FBI gains new anti-terrorist powers." Reuters (31 May 2002).

Charns, Alexander. *Cloak and Gavel: FBI Wiretaps, Bugs, Informers, and the Supreme Court*. Urbana, Ill.: University of Illinois Press, 1992.

_____. "Cloak and gavel: The secret history of the FBI and the Supreme Court." *Trial Briefs* 21, no. 2 (1989): 46–49.

_____. "Gavelgate." *Southern Exposure* 18 (Fall 1990): 8–11.

Chase, Harold. *Security and Liberty: The Problem of Native Communists*. Garden City, N.Y.: Doubleday, 1955.

Churchill, Ward, and Jim Vander Wall. *Agents of Oppression: The FBI's Secret War against the Black Panther Party and the American Indian Movement*. Boston: South End Press, 1988.

_____ and _____. *The COINTELPRO Papers: Documents from the FBI's Secret War against Dissent in the United States*. Boston: South End Press, 1990.

Clancy, Paul. "The Bureau and the Bureaus, Part I." *Quill* 64 (February 1976): 12–18.

Clayton, Merle. *The Union Station Massacre: The Shootout That Started the FBI's War on Crime*. Indianapolis: Bobbs-Merrill, 1975.

"Clinton passes on vote of confidence to FBI director." Associated Press (17 December 1997).

Coates, James. *Armed and Dangerous: The Rise of the Survivalist Right*. New York: Hill & Wang, 1987.

Cohen, Stanley. *A. Mitchell Palmer: Politician*. New York: Columbia University Press, 1963.

Cohen, William. "Riots, Racism, and Hysteria." *Massachusetts Review* 13 (1972): 373–400.

Conconi, Charles, and Tony House. *The Washington Sting*. New York: Coward, McCann, and Geoghegan, 1979.

Cook, Fred. *The FBI Nobody Knows*. New York: Macmillan, 1964.

_____. *The Nightmare Decade: The Life and Times of Joe McCarthy*. New York: Random House, 1971.

_____. *The Unfinished Story of Alger Hiss*. New York: William Morrow, 1958.

Cooper, Courtney Ryley. "Camps of Crime." *American Magazine* 129 (February 1940): 14–15, 130–32.

_____. *Designs in Scarlet*. Boston: Little, Brown, 1939.

_____. *Ten Thousand Public Enemies*. Boston: Little, Brown, 1935.

Corson, William. *Armies of Ignorance: The Rise of the American Intelligence Empire*. New York: Dial Press, 1977.

Cotter, Richard. "Notes toward a definition of national security." *Washington Monthly* 7 (December 1975): 4–16.

Coulson, Danny, and Elaine Shannon. *No Heroes: Inside the FBI's Secret Counter-Terror Force*. New York: Pocket Books, 1999.

Cox, Donald. *Mafia Wipeout: How the Feds Put Away an Entire Mafia Family*. New York: Shapolsky Publishers, 1989.

Crewdson, John. "Seeing red: an FBI 'Commie hunter' rebels at illegal tactics." *Chicago Tribune Magazine* (March 2, 1986).

Criley, Richard. *The FBI vs. the First Amendment.* Los Angeles: First Amendment Foundation, 1990.

Cromie, Robert, and Joseph Pinkston. *Dillinger: A Short and Violent Life.* New York: McGraw-Hill, 1962.

Croog, Charles. "FBI political surveillance and the isolationist-interventionist debate, 1939–1941." *The Historian* 54 (Spring 1992): 441–58.

"Curtains for semi-nude justice statue." BBC News (29 January 2002).

Davis, Ann. "Under a cloud." *Wall Street Journal* (24 November 2002).

Davis, James. *Spying on America: The FBI's Domestic Counterintelligence Program.* New York: Praeger, 1992.

DeLoach, Cartha. *Hoover's FBI: The Inside Story by Hoover's Trusted Lieutenant.* Washington, D.C.: Regnery, 1995.

DeLong, Candice, and Elisa Petrini. *Special Agent: My Life on the Front Lines as a Woman in the FBI.* New York: Hyperion, 2001.

Demaris, Ovid, ed. *The Director: An Oral Biography of J. Edgar Hoover.* New York: Harper's, 1975.

DeStefano, Anthony. "Feds: Ex-agent had key data." *Newsday* (29 May 2002).

DeToledano, Ralph. *J. Edgar Hoover: The Man in His Time.* New Rochelle, N.Y.: Arlington House, 1973.

Dettlinger, Chet, and Jeff Prugh. *The List.* Atlanta: Philmay, 1983.

Diamond, Sigmund. *Compromised Campus: The Collaboration of the University and the Intelligence Community.* New York: Oxford University Press, 1992.

_____. "The FBI in the yard: Hoover goes to Harvard." *Nation* 253 (October 24, 1981): 393, 405–11.

_____. "God and the FBI at Yale." *Nation* 230 (April 12, 1980): 422–28.

_____. "Kissinger and the FBI." *Nation* 229 (November 10, 1979): 449–66.

Dion, Susan. "The FBI surveillance of the Women's International League for Peace and Freedom." *Journal for Peace and Justice Studies* 3, no. 1 (1991): 1–21.

_____. "Pacifism treated as subversion: the FBI and the War Resisters League." *Peace and Change* 9, no. 1 (1983): 43–59.

Donn, Jeff. "FBI was making deals with the mob." Associated Press (28 July 2002).

Donner, Frank. *The Age of Surveillance.* New York: Knopf, 1980.

_____. "Electronic surveillance the national security game." *Civil Liberties Review* 2 (Summer 1975): 21–23.

_____. "Hoover's legacy: a nationwide system of political surveillance based on the spurious authority of a press release." *Nation* 218 (1 June 1974): 678–99.

_____. "How J. Edgar Hoover created his intelligence powers." *Civil Liberties Review* 3 (February/March 1977): 34–51.

_____. "Intelligence on the attack: the terrorist as scapegoat." *Nation* 226 (20 May 1978): 590–4.

_____. "The new FBI guidelines: rounding up the usual suspects." *Nation* 235 (August 7–14, 1982): 97, 110–16.

_____. *Protectors of Privilege: Red Squads and Police Repression in Urban America.* Berkeley: University of California Press, 1990.

Dorsen, Robert, and Stephen Gillers, eds. *None of Your Business: Government Secrecy in America.* New York: Penguin, 1975.

Douglas, John, and Mark Olshaker. *Journey into Darkness.* New York: Pocket Books, 1997.

_____. *Mind Hunter.* New York: Scribner, 1995.

Duffy, Brian, and Steven Emerson. *The Fall of Pan Am 103: Inside the Lockerbie Investigation.* New York: G.P. Putnam's, 1990.

Dunaway, David. "Songs of subversion: how the FBI destroyed the Weavers." *Village Voice* (January 21, 1980): 39–40, 42.

Earley, Pete. *Family of Spies: Inside the John Walker Spy Ring.* New York: Bantam, 1988.

"Earth First! and the FBI: What the verdict means." *Institute for Public Accuracy* (12 June 2002).

"Earth First! exposes FBI conspiracy." *Slingshot* (Spring 1997).

Eggen, Dan. "Ashcroft aggressively pursues death penalty." *Washington Post* (1 July 2002).

_____. "Blunders detailed in FBI Lee probe." *Washington Post* (27 August 2001).

_____. "Kissinger to withhold client list." *Washington Post* (13 December 2002).

_____. "Senators question agent's bad review." *Washington Post* (23 October 2002).

Elliff, John. "Aspects of civil rights enforcement: the Justice Department and the FBI, 1939–1964." *Perspectives in American History* 5 (1971): 605–73.

_____. "The Attorney General's Guidelines for FBI Investigations." *Cornell Law Review* 69 (April 1984): 785–815.

_____. *The Reform of FBI Intelligence Operations.* Princeton, N.J.: Princeton University Press, 1979.

_____. *The United States Department of Justice and Individual Rights.* New York: Garland Publishing, 1987.

Emerson, Thomas, and David Helfeld. "Loyalty among Government Employees." *Yale Law Journal* 58 (December 1948): 1–143.

English, Raymond. "A counterintelligence and counterterrorism case: CISPES and the FBI." *Harvard Journal of Law and Public Policy* 12 (Spring 1989): 483–94.

Espo, David. "Rowley criticizes FBI bureaucracy." Associated Press (6 June 2002).

Evanzz, Karl. *The Judas Factor: The Plot to Kill Malcolm X.* New York: Thunder's Mouth Press, 1992.

_____. *The Messenger: The Rise and Fall of Elijah Muhammad.* New York: Pantheon Books, 1999.

Farrington, Brendan. "FBI faces renewed police complaints." Associated Press (17 November 2001).

Fass, Paula. *Kidnapped: Child Abduction in America.* Cambridge, Mass.: Harvard University Press, 1997.

"FBI agent arrested on child porn charges." Associated Press (18 October 2001).

"FBI agent knew about documents for months." Associated Press (18 May 2001).

"FBI agent pleads guilty in $400,000 embezzlement case." *Chicago Tribune* (29 January 1998).

"FBI agent's gun stolen, thief sought." Associated Press (19 July 2001).

"FBI agents say superiors hurt fund-raising probe." *USA Today* (23 September 1999).

"FBI alert for five men reportedly based on hoax." Reuters (7 January 2003).

"FBI: Anthrax mailer probably a man with a grudge." Associated Press (9 November 2001).

"FBI as Big Brother." *Christian Century* 100 (April 20, 1983): 361.

"FBI calls off search for illegal immigrants." Associated Press (8 January 2002).

"FBI circulates researcher's photo in anthrax probe." *USA Today* (14 August 2002).

"FBI finds more Oklahoma City bombing records." *USA Today* (15 May 2001).

"FBI finds site where letters were mailed." Associated Press (20 October 2001).

"FBI: Hospitals possible terror targets." *USA Today* (13 November 2002).

"FBI in anthrax probe goes back to scientist's home." Reuters (1 August 2002).

"FBI indicted in Earth First! bomb trial." *Socialist Action* (April 2002).

"FBI investigates similarities in anthrax cases." Associated Press (17 October 2001).

"FBI investigation criticized." Associated Press (28 July 1999).

"FBI, Justice Department bungled case against scientist." Associated Press (6 August 1999).

"FBI: Major reform needed." *Milwaukee Journal Sentinel* (28 May 2002).

"FBI pays $300,000 in privacy lawsuit." Associated Press (12 March 1998).

"FBI probed for treatment of Ruby Ridge critics." Reuters (9 August 2001).

"FBI raids home of ELF spokesmen." Associated Press (6 April 2001).

"FBI reports 19 firings for misconduct." Associated Press (10 December 1998).

"FBI said to target lawmakers in 9/11 leak probe." Reuters (24 August 2002).

"FBI seeking help in anthrax probe." Associated Press (8 November 2001).

"FBI sharpshooter won't be prosecuted." *USA Today* (15 June 2001).

"FBI specialists baffled by bomb." Associated Press (26 April 2001).

"FBI steps up probe of anthrax cases." Associated Press (8 October 2001).

"FBI suspends agent in spy case." *San Diego Union* (5 March 1990).

"FBI talks about anthrax probe woes." Associated Press (10 November 2001).

"FBI: 'Very vague' intelligence bulletin warns of possible threats." Associated Press (3 July 2002).

"FBI warns of possible threat to gas pipelines." Associated Press (27 November 2001).

"FBI wants to beef up Canadian presence." Canadian Press (18 November 2001).

"FBI withheld key evidence in bombing trial." Associated Press (4 May 2001).

"Feds announce anthrax hoax indictment." Associated Press (17 October 2001).

Felt, W. Mark. *The FBI Pyramid from the Inside*. New York: G.P. Putnam's, 1979.

Fenwick, Ben. "The road to Oklahoma City." *Playboy* 44, no. 6 (June 1997): 70–72, 158–160.

Fields, Gary. "FBI lab gets new director, criticism." *USA Today* (22 October 1997).

_____. "Freeh: No plan to step down." *USA Today* (17 December 1997).

_____. "Reno says she is 'great admirer' of Freeh." *USA Today* (5 December 1997).

Fineman, Howard, and Michael Isikoff. "Right from the start." *Newsweek* (22 January 2001): 21–27.

Finucane, Martin. "Man goes free after 32 years in prison." *Indianapolis Star* (6 January 2001).

"Fired FBI agent loses his appeal." Associated Press (14 June 1996).

Fisher, David. *Hard Evidence: How Detectives Inside the FBI's Sci-Crime Lab Have Helped Solve America's Toughest Cases*. New York: Simon & Schuster, 1995.

Fisher, Jim. *The Lindbergh Case*. New Brunswick, N.J.: Rutgers University Press, 1987.

Fleeman, Michael. "Anthrax charges dropped; material was a vaccine." *Louisville Courier-Journal* (24 February 1998).

Flynn, Devin, and Gary Gerhardt. *The Silent Brotherhood*. New York: Free Press, 1989.

Foerstel, Herbert. *Surveillance in the Stacks: The FBI's Library Awareness Program*. Westport, Conn.: Greenwood Press, 1991.

Ford, Corey. *Donovan of OSS*. Boston: Little, Brown, 1970.

"Former FBI agent in Boston sentenced to 10 years for tipping off his top mob informants." Associated Press (16 September 2002).

"Former mob turncoat 'Sammy the Bull' Gravano sentenced to 19 years for drug crimes." Associated Press (30 October 2002).

"Former stripper says Hanssen gave her almost $80,000 in gifts." Associated Press (19 May 2001).

Fournier, Ron. "Kissinger quits as chairman of 9/11 panel." Associated Press (13 December 2002).

Frank, Thomas. "Effort to reform FBI builds momentum." *Newsday* (30 December 2002).

Frasier, David. *Suicide in the Entertainment Industry*. Jefferson, N.C.: McFarland, 2002.

"Freeh wrapping up tenure as director of FBI." *USA Today* (19 June 2001).

Freeman, Gregory. *Lay This Body Down: The 1921 Murder of Eleven Plantation Slaves*. Chicago: Chicago Review Press, 1999.

Friedman, Robert. "FBI: manipulating the media." *Rights* 23 (May/June 1977): 13–14.

"From push to shove." *Intelligence Report* no. 107 (Fall 2002): 20–29.

Garrow, David. *The FBI and Martin Luther King, Jr.: From Memphis to "Solo."* New York: Norton, 1989.

Gearan, Anne. "Feds sued by civil rights groups." Associated Press (5 December 2001).

Gehrke, Robert. "Report: Energy Dept. misled FBI on Lee." Associated Press (14 August 2001).

Gelbspan, Ross. *Break-ins, Death Threats and the FBI*. Boston: South End Press, 1991.

Gentry, Curt. *J. Edgar Hoover: The Man and the Secrets*. New York: Norton, 1991.

Gibbs, Nancy, and Michael Duffy. "The fight for Justice." *Time* (22 January 2001): 20–28.

Gibson, Dick. "The Making of the Hoover myth: a critical analysis of FBI public relations." *Public Relations Quarterly* 33 (Winter 1988): 7.

Giglio, James. *H.M. Daugherty and the Politics of Expediency*. Kent, Ohio: Kent State University Press, 1978.

Gillers, Stephen, and Pat Watters, eds. *Investigating the FBI*. Garden City, N.Y.: Doubleday, 1973.

Gilmore, Christopher. *Hoover vs. Kennedy: The Second Civil War*. New York: St. Martin's Press, 197.

Gleick, Elizabeth. "Agent of change: Suzanne Doucette broke the code of silence at the FBI and is suing over sexual harassment." *People Weekly* 40 (November 1, 1993): 101.

Glick, Brian. *War at Home: Covert Action against U.S. Activities and What We Can Do about Them*. Boston: South End Press, 1988.

Goddard, Donald. *The Insider: The FBI's Undercover "Wise Guy" Goes Public*. New York: Pocket Books, 1992.

Godson, Roy, ed. *Intelligence Requirements for the 1980s: Domestic Intelligence*. Lexington, Mass.: D.C. Heath, 1986.

Goldberg, Carey. "Philip Berrigan: From prison, old militant struggles on." *New York Times* (29 November 1997).

Goldstein, Robert. *Political Repression in Modern America*. Cambridge, Mass.: Schencken, 1978.

Goldwasser, Katherine. "After Abscam: an examination of congressional proposals to limit targeting discretion in federal undercover investigations." *Emory Law Journal* (Winter 1987): 75–77.

Gordon, Gregory. "Judge halts destruction of FBI's investigative dossiers." *New Jersey Law Journal* 105 (February 7, 1980): 9.

Graham, Patrick. "Mob turncoat charged in Phoenix drug ring." Associated Press (25 February 2000).

Green, Ben. *Before His Time: The Untold Story of Harry T. Moore, America's First Civil Rights Martyr*. New York: Free Press, 1999.

Greenberg, Martin, and Mark Sabljak. *Most Wanted: A History of the FBI's Most Wanted List*. New York: Bonanza Books, 1990.

Greene, Robert. *The Sting Man: Inside Abscam*. New York: Dutton, 1981.

Grezlak, Hank. "'Profiling' testimony inadmissible in murder trial." *Pennsylvania Law Weekly* (12 April 1999).

Grimaldi, James. "2 FBI whistle-blowers allege lax security, possible espionage." *Washington Post* (19 June 2002).

Grunwald, Michael. "FBI hurt Flight 800 probe inquiry, critics say." *Washington Post* (27 November 1998).

Gullo, Karen. "Ashcroft grilled on anti-terror plans." Associated Press (7 December 2001).

_____. "Ashcroft issues new terror warning." Associated Press (30 October 2001).

_____. "Ashcroft pledges to use new powers." Associated Press (26 October 2001).

_____. "FBI: Bridges threat not credible." Associated Press (6 November 2001).

_____. "FBI issues new terrorism warning; no specific target or method." Associated Press (29 October 2001).

_____. "FBI's director to leave post, cut term short." Associated Press (2 May 2001).

_____. "GAO: FBI doesn't always share info." Associated Press (16 August 2001).

_____. "Justice Department probes FBI." Associated Press (13 August 2001).

_____. "U.S. announces terror tips program." Associated Press (30 November 2001).

Hall, Angus. *The Crime Busters: The FBI, Scotland Yard, Interpol: The Story of Criminal Investigation*. New York: Verdict Press, 1976.

Halperin, Morton, et al. *The Lawless State: The Crimes of the U.S. Intelligence Agencies*. New York: Penguin, 1976.

Hamm, Mark. *Apocalypse in Oklahoma: Waco and Ruby Ridge Revenged*. Boston: Northeastern University Press, 1997.

Hampson, Rick. "Mueller: New spy agency would be 'step backward.'" *USA Today* (22 December 2002).

Handley, Christine. "2nd-guessing of FBI probe begins in Yosemite killings." Associated Press (28 July 1999).

"Hanssen indicted on capital espionage charges." Associated Press (17 May 2001).

"Hanssen sentenced to life without parole." *Washington Post* (10 May 2002).

Hardy, Dan. "FBI raids homes in Chester in probe." *Philadelphia Inquirer* (14 November 2001).

Harris, Richard. *Freedom Spent*. Boston: Little, Brown, 1976.

Heimel, Pail. *Eliot Ness: The Real Story* 2nd edition. Nashville, Tenn.: Cumberland House, 2000.

Heslam, Jessica. "Former FBI clerk admits he lied about killer's call." Associated Press (21 June 2002).

Higham, Charles. *Trading with the Enemy: The Nazi-American Money Plot, 1933–1949*. New York: Barnes & Noble, 1983.

Hill, Robert. *The FBI's RACON: Racial Conditions in the United States during World War II*. Boston: Northeastern University Press, 1995.

_____. "The Foremost Radical among His Race: Marcus Garvey and the Black Scare, 1918–1921." *Prologue* 16 (Winter 1984): 216–22.

"Hit man pleads guilty to murder." Associated Press (4 May 2001).

Holland, Jesse. "FBI chief says more agents needed." Associated Press (6 June 2002).

_____. "Mueller promises to improve FBI." Associated Press (31 July 2001).

Hoover, J. Edgar. "Crime Trap." *American Magazine* 116 ( November 1933): 64–66, 94–98.

_____. *Masters of Deceit: The Story of Communism in America and How to Fight It*. New York: Holt, 1958.

_____. *Persons in Hiding*. Boston: Little, Brown, 1938.

Hopper, D. Ian. "Memo: FBI destroyed evidence in Bin Laden case after glitch with e-mail surveillance system." *Boston Globe* (28 May 2002).

Horne, Terry. "Diplomatic goof snares FBI drug raid." *Indianapolis Star* (1 September 2001).

Hosty, James, with Thomas Hosty. *Assignment: Oswald*. New York: Arcade Publishing, 1996.

"House panel apologizes to FBI informant wrongly jailed." Associated Press (4 May 2001).

Howe, Russell. *Sleeping with the FBI: Sex, Booze, Russians and the Saga of an American Counterspy Who Couldn't*. New York: National Books, 1993.

Howlett, Debbie, and Toni Locy. "Mayor criticizes FBI handling of anthrax scare." *USA Today* (15 November 2001).

Hurt, Henry. *Shadrin, The Spy Who Never Came Back*. New York: Reader's Digest Press, 1981.

Huston, Luther. *The Department of Justice*. New York: Frederick A. Praeger, 1967.

Hyde, H. Montgomery. *Room 3603: The Story of the British Intelligence Center in New York during World War II*. New York: Ballantine, 1977.

"Indiana colleges turned over information on foreign students." Associated Press (18 October 2001).

"Informer arrested on drug charges." *USA Today* (25 February 2000).

Irons, Peter. "'Fighting Fair': Zechariah Chafee, Jr., the Department of Justice, and the 'Trial at the Harvard Club.'" *Harvard Law Review* 94 (April 1981): 1205–36.

Jackman, Tom. "Handling of anthrax inquiry questioned." *Washington Post* (25 August 2002).

Jaquith, Cindy, and Diane Wang. *FBI vs. Women*. New York: Pathfinder Press, 1977.

Jeffers, H. Paul. *Who Killed Precious? How FBI Special Agents Combine Psychology and High Technology to Identify Violent Criminals*. New York: Pharos Books, 1991.

Jeffreys, Diarmuid. *The Bureau: Inside the Modern FBI*. Boston: Houghton Mifflin, 1995.

Jerome, Fred. *The Einstein File: J. Edgar Hoover's Secret War Against the World's Most Famous Scientist*. New York: St. Martin's Press, 2002.

Johnson, Kevin. "Alleged spy good at covering tracks." *USA Today* (21 February 2001).

_____. "Ashcroft broadens FBI's license to spy." *USA Today* (30 May 2002).

_____. "Ashcroft defends anti-terror tactics." *USA Today* (1 October 2002).

_____. "Bureau suffers another black eye." *USA Today* (14 May 2001).

_____. "FBI agents to undergo more polygraphs." *USA Today* (2 March 2001).

_____. "FBI policing itself more under Freeh." *USA Today* (23 August 2000).

_____. "FBI taps retired agents for 9/11 investigation." *USA Today* (2 October 2002).

_____. "FBI turns to locals to track bombing suspect." *USA Today* (31 May 2000).

_____. "Federal judge backs Oregon suicide law." *USA Today* (18 April 2002).

_____. "Freeh, other FBI leaders to take polygraph tests." *USA Today* (6 April 2001).

_____. "Hanssen helps FBI tighten loopholes in security." *USA Today* (2 April 2002).

_____. "Justice: Papers have no bearing on guilt." *USA Today* (23 May 2001).

_____. "Justice seeks to question 5,000 witnesses." *USA Today* (14 November 2001).

_____. "Lee spent 9 months in solitary confinement." *USA Today* (15 September 2000).

_____. "Letter shifts heat to FBI." *USA Today* (28 May 2002).

_____. "Shoddy records slow 9/11 inquiry." *USA Today* (22 November 2002).

Johnson, Kevin, and Toni Locy. "Apologetic judge frees scientist." *USA Today* (14 September 2000).

_____. "FBI moves counterterrorism to the top of its list." *USA Today* (29 May 2002).

_____. "FBI, Justice cooperation worries some agents." *USA Today* (23 December 2002).

_____. "More facts surface in spy case." *USA Today* (23 February 2001).

Johnson, Kevin, and Richard Willing. "FBI veteran allegedly worked for Russians." *USA Today* (21 February 2001).

Johnston, David. "Anthrax hits Capitol Hill—bin Laden suspected." *New York Times* (16 October 2001).

_____. "FBI director removes official over her handling of spy inquiry." *New York Times* (30 January 2002).

_____. "Fuming FBI expects Reno to end query into president." *New York Times* (24 November 1997).

_____. "Justice Dept. reopens campaign plot case." *New York Times* (11 December 1997).

_____. "Scientist fired after warning on U.S. funds." *New York Times* (6 September 2002).

Jones, Charles, ed. *The Black Panther Party Reconsidered*. Baltimore: Black Classic Press, 1998.

Jones, Stephen, and Peter Israel. *Others Unknown: The Oklahoma City Bombing Case and Conspiracy*. New York: Public Affairs, 1998.

Jonnes, Jill. *Hep-Cats, Narcs, and Pipe Dreams?: A History of America's Romance with Illegal Drugs*. Baltimore: Johns Hopkins University Press, 1996.

"Justice Department backs away from DNA testing program." *Los Angeles Times* (27 December 2001).

"Justice Department reorganized." *Los Angeles Times* (9 November 2001).

Kasindorf, Martin. "Test results weaken anthrax case." *USA Today* (23 February 1998).

Keller, William. *The Liberals and J. Edgar Hoover*. Princeton, N.J.: Princeton University Press, 1989.

Kelley, Matt. "Robert Mueller takes control of FBI." Associated Press (4 September 2001).

Kelly, John, and Phillip Wearne. *Tainting Evidence: Inside the Scandals at the FBI Crime Lab*. New York: Free Press, 1998.

Kennedy, Ludovic. *The Airman and the Carpenter: The Lindbergh Kidnapping and the Framing of Richard Hauptmann*. New York: Viking, 1985.

Kenworthy, Tom. "Struggling to create a homeland defense." *USA Today* (10 October 2001).

Kerby, Phil. *With Honor and Purpose*. New York: St. Martin's Press, 1998.

Kessler, Robert. *The Bureau: The Secret History of the FBI*. New York: St. Martin's Press, 2002.

_____. *The FBI: Inside the World's Most Powerful Law Enforcement Agency*. New York: Pocket Books, 1993.

_____. *Inside the CIA*. New York: Pocket Books, 1992.

_____. *Spy vs. Spy: Stalking Soviet Spies in America*. New York: Scribner's, 1988.

Kesten, Lou. "Justice Dept. rejected Freeh censure." Associated Press (5 August 2001).

Kiel, R. Andrew. *J. Edgar Hoover: The Father of the Cold War*. Lanham, MD: University Press of America, 2000.

King, Colbert. "Sneaking and peeking—then and now." *Washington Post* (8 June 2002).

Kiraly, Andrew. "Who's investigating the investigators?" *Las Vegas Mercury* (21 March 2002).

Klaber, William, and Philip Melanson. *Shadow Play: The Untold Story of the Robert F. Kennedy Assassination*. New York: St. Martin's Press, 1997.

Kimball, Penn. "The History of *The Nation* According to the FBI." *Nation* 242 (March 22, 1986): 399–426.

Knoll, Erwin. "Filed but Not Forgotten." *Progressive* 50 (October 1986): 24–25.

Kornbluh, Peter, and Malcolm Byrne, eds. *The Iran-Contra Scandal: The Declassified History*. New York: New Press, 1993.

Kornweibel, Theodore Jr. *"Seeing Red": Federal Campaigns Against Black Militancy, 1919–1925*. Bloomington: Indiana University Press, 1998.

Krikorian, Greg. "FBI making increasing use of deportation." *Los Angeles Times* (3 November 2002).

Kuntz, Tom, and Phil Kuntz, eds. *The Sinatra Files: The Secret FBI Dossier*. New York: Three Rivers Press, 2000.

Lamphere, Robert, and Tom Shachtman. *The FBI-KGB War: A Special Agent's Story*. New York: Random House, 1986.

Lane, Mark. *Rush to Judgment*. New York: Holt, Rinehart and Winston, 1966.

Langum, David. *Crossing over the Line: Legislating Morality and the Mann Act*. Chicago: University of Chicago Press, 1994.

Lardner, George Jr. "Censure of FBI's Freeh rejected." *Washington Post* (5 August 2001).

Lasalandra, Michael. "FBI probes two anthrax cases tied to Fla. building." *Boston Herald* (9 October 2001).

Lasky, Victor. *It Didn't Start with Watergate*. New York: Dial Press, 1977.

Lavoie, Denise. "Flemmit to be sentenced in racketeering case." Associated Press (21 August 2001).

_____. "Jury deliberates FBI-mob case." Associated Press (24 May 2002).

Lawrence, J.M. "Attorney 'confident' records show accused killer's call to FBI." Associated Press (11 September 2001).

_____. "Devilish deal: Probers unveil memo showing FBI protected killer." Associated Press (12 May 2002).

_____. "FBI aided killer: Hub agents helped mob hit man escape death row." Associated Press (29 August 2001).

_____. "FBI clerk faces prison for lying about Sampson call." Associated Press (7 January 2003).

_____. "Statute of limitations may keep agents out of jail." Associated Press (22 August 2001).

_____. "U.S. attorney praises FBI's Sampson probe." Associated Press (18 December 2001).

Leinwand, Donna, and Deborah Sharp. "After 37 years, 2 more arrests." *USA Today* (18 May 2000).

_____. "Bombing is a wound that has never closed." *USA Today* (18 May 2000).

Lemos, Robert. "FBI Agent: I am Big Brother." ZDNet News (6 April 2000).

Lichtblau, Eric. "Pressure on FBI builds as agents urged to adapt." *Las Vegas Sun* (2 December 2002).

Lockwood, Brocton, and Harlan Mendenhall. *Operation Greylord: Brocton Lockwood's Story*. Carbondale, Ill.: Southern Illinois University Press, 1989.

Locy, Toni. "Attorney protests anthrax case leaks." *USA Today* (15 August 2002).

_____. "Broader domestic spying allowed." *USA Today* (18 November 2002).

_____. "Justice launches a counterattack: 'Lee is no hero.'" *USA Today* (27 September 2000).

_____. "Proof of 'person of interest' sought; Ashcroft asked to define term in anthrax probe." *USA Today* (20 September 2002).

_____. "Witnesses: Blame 'the club' for FBI debacles." *USA Today* (20 July 2001).

Locy, Toni, and Kevin Johnson. "FBI: Al-Qaeda seeks to top Sept. 11." *USA Today* (4 February 2003).

Locy, Toni, and Patrick O'Driscoll. "McVeigh lawyers: FBI guilty of fraud." *USA Today* (1 June 2001).

Louderback, Lew. *The Bad Ones: Gangsters of the '30s and Their Molls*. New York: Fawcett, 1968.

Loven, Jennifer. "Bush names Kissinger to lead 9/11 probe." Associated Press (27 November 2002).

Lowenthal, Max. *The Federal Bureau of Investigation*. New York: Sloane, 1950.

Lukas, J. Anthony. *Nightmare: The Underside of the Nixon Years*. New York: Viking, 1976.

Lysing, Henry. *Men against Crime*. New York: David Kemp, 1938.

Maas, Peter. *Underboss: Sammy the Bull Gravano's Story of Life in the Mafia*. New York: HarperCollins, 1997.

_____. *The Valachi Papers*. New York: G.P. Putnam's, 1968.

Mabin, Connie. "FBI: Vague threat on Texas schools." Associated Press (12 December 2001).

Maccabee, Bruce. *UFO-FBI Connection: The Secret History of the Government's Cover-up*. St. Paul, Minn.: Llewellyn Publications, 2000.

MacDonnell, Francis. *Insidious Foes: The Axis Fifth Column and the American Home Front*. New York: Oxford University Press, 1995.

MacKenzie, Angus. "Sabotaging the Dissident Press." *Columbia Journalism Review* (March-April 1981): 57–63.

Mahoney, Edmund. "Rogue agent on the stand for U.S.: *Hartford Courant* (11 May 2002).

Maldonado, Patricia. "Agent sentenced after admitting embezzlement." Associated Press (24 November 1998).

Marrs, Jim. *Crossfire: The Plot That Killed Kennedy*. New York: Carroll & Graf, 1989.

Marx, Gary. "Some Reflections on Undercover: Recent Developments and Enduring Issues." *Crime, Law and Social Change* 18 (September 1992): 193–217.

_____. *Undercover: Police Surveillance in America*. Berkeley: University of California Press, 1988.

Matthiessen, Peter. *In The Spirit of Crazy Horse: The Story of Leonard Peltier and the FBI's War on the American Indiana Movement*. New York: Penguin, 1992.

May, Gary. *Un-American Activities: The Trials of William Remington*. New York: Oxford University Press, 1994.

Macy, Robert. "2 accused of holding anthrax as weapon." Associated Press (20 February 1998).

McCall, William. "Oregon backed on assisted suicide." Associated Press (21 November 2001).

McClam, Erin. "*Time* names whistleblowers persons of year." Associated Press (22 December 2002).

McCormick, Charles. *Seeing Reds: Federal Surveillance of Radicals in the Pittsburgh Mill District, 1917–1921*. Pittsburgh: University of Pittsburgh Press, 1997.

McGee, Jim. "The rise of the FBI." *Washington Post Magazine* (July 20, 1997): 11–15, 25–28.

McGhee, Millie. *Secrets Uncovered: J. Edgar Hoover—Passing for White?* Rancho Cucamonga, Calif.: Allen-Morris, 2000.

McKnight, Gerald. *The Last Crusade: Martin Luther King, Jr., the FBI, and the Poor People's Campaign*. Boulder, Colo.: Westview, 1998.

McWhorter, Diane. *Carry Me Home: Birmingham, Alabama—The Climactic Battle of the Civil Rights Revolution*. New York: Simon & Schuster, 2001.

Meager, Sylvia. *Accessories After the Fact: The Warren Commission, the Authorities, and the Report*. New York: Bobbs-Merrill, 1967.

Melanson, Philip. *The Robert F. Kennedy Assassination: New Revelations on the Conspiracy and Cover-Up*. New York: S.P.I. Books, 1994.

Mendelsohn, Jack. *The Martyrs: Sixteen Who Gave Their Lives for Racial Justice*. New York: Harper & Row, 1966.

Messerschmidt, Jim. *The Trial of Leonard Peltier*. Boston: South End Press, 1983.

Messick, Hank. *John Edgar Hoover*. New York: David McKay, 1972.

Michel, Lou, and Dan Herbeck. *American Terrorist: Timothy McVeigh & the Oklahoma City Bombing*. New York: Regan Books, 2001.

Mikkelson, Randall. "Bush creates high office of homeland security." Reuters (21 September 2001).

Miller, Greg. "More 9/11 clues were overlooked." *Los Angeles Times* (12 December 2002).

Miller, John. *Crisis in Freedom: The Alien and Sedition Acts*. Boston: Atlantic-Little, Brown, 1951.

Miller, Mark, and Daniel Klaidman. "The hunt for the anthrax killer." *Newsweek* (12 August 2002).

Miller, Nathan. *Stealing from America: A History of Corruption from Jamestown to Reagan*. New York: Paragon House, 1992.

Mitgang, Herbert. "Annals of government: policing America's writers." *New Yorker* 63 (October 5, 1987): 47–90.

_____. *Dangerous Dossiers: Exposing the Secret War against America's Greatest Authors*. New York: Donald Fine, 1988.

Mittelstadt, Michelle. "Reno seeks 'perfect person' to investigate siege at Waco." Associated Press (4 September 1999).

"Mob hit man reaches plea, may be free in eight years." Associated Press (10 September 1999).

Moldea, Dan. *Dark Victory: Ronald Reagan, MCA, and the Mob*. New York: Viking, 1986.

_____. *The Hoffa Wars: Rebels, Politicians and the Mob*. New York: Paddington Press, 1978.

Morgan, Richard. *Domestic Surveillance: Monitoring Dissent in America*.

Morrow, Robert. *The Senator Must Die*. Santa Monica, Calif.: Roundtable Publishing, 1988.

Murphy, Shelley. "Connolly still faces battle in pending civil suits." *Boston Globe* (30 May 2002).

_____. "FBI head testifies to taking bribes." *Boston Globe* (10 May 2002).

_____. "US judge asks for Connolly leniency." *Boston Globe* (2 August 2002).

Murray, Robert. *Red Scare: A Study in National Hysteria, 1919–1920*. Minneapolis: University of Minnesota Press, 1955.

Mustain, Gene, and Jerry Capeci. *Murder Machine: A True Story of Madness and the Mafia*. New York: Onyx, 1993.

Navasky, Victor. *Kennedy Justice*. New York: Atheneum, 1971.

_____. "The FBI's wildest dream." *Nation* 226 (17 June 1978): 716–18.

Neff, James. *Mobbed Up: Jackie Presser's High-Wire Life in the Teamsters, the Mafia and the FBI*. New York: Atlantic Monthly Press, 1989.

Neier, Aryeh. "Adhering to principle: lessons from the 1950s." *Civil Liberties Review* 4 (November-December 1977): 26–32.

Nelson, Jack. *Terror in the Night: The Klan's Campaign Against the Jews*. New York: Simon & Schuster, 1992.

Nelson, Jack, and Jack Bass. *The Orangeburg Massacre*. New York: World Publishing Co., 1970.

Nelson, Jack, and Ronald Ostrow. *The FBI and the Berrigans: The Making of a Conspiracy*. New York: Coward, McCann and Geoghegan, 1972.

Neville, Lewis. "We didn't start the fire." *Fortean Times* 133 (April 2000): 34–38.

Newton, Christopher. "Anthrax clues sought at apartment." Associated Press (1 August 2002).

_____. "FBI begins visiting libraries." *Washington Post* (24 June 2002).

_____. "FBI investigates anthrax researchers." Associated Press (28 June 2002).

Newton, Michael. *Bitter Grain: The Story of the Black Panther Party*. Los Angeles: Holloway House, 1980.

_____. *A Case of Conspiracy: James Earl Ray and the Assassination of Martin Luther King, Jr.* Los Angeles: Holloway House, 1980.

_____. *The Encyclopedia of Kidnappings*. New York: Facts on File, 2002.

_____. *The Encyclopedia of Robberies, Heists and Capers*. New York: Facts on File, 2002.

_____. *The Encyclopedia of Serial Killers*. New York: Facts on File, 2000.

_____. *The FBI Plot*. Los Angeles: Holloway House, 1981.

_____. *The Invisible Empire: The Ku Klux Klan in Florida*. Gainesville, Fla.: University Press of Florida, 2001.

_____. *Still At Large: A Casebook of 20th Century Serial Killers Who Eluded Justice*. Port Townsend, Wash.: Loompanics Unlimited, 1998.

Newton, Michael, and Judy Ann Newton. *The FBI Most Wanted*. New York: Garland, 1988.

_____. *The Ku Klux Klan: An Encyclopedia.* New York: 1991.

_____. *Racial and Religious Violence in America: A Chronology.* New York: Garland, 1991.

Noble, Chris. "Former FBI agent on trial for helping Boston mobsters." Reuters (6 May 2002).

North, Mark. *Act of Treason: The Role of J. Edgar Hoover in the Assassination of President Kennedy.* New York: Carroll & Graf, 1991.

Novak, Robert. "A campaign to blame FBI's Freeh." *Indianapolis Star* (8 September 1999).

_____. "FBI chief being pressed on specifics." *Indianapolis Star* (9 January 1998).

Nowell, Paul. "FBI isn't ruling anything out after bomb blast at N.C. clinic." Associated Press (15 March 1999).

Nunnelley, William. *Bull Connor.* Tuscaloosa: University of Alabama Press, 1991.

O'Brien, Joseph, and Andris Kurins. *Boss of Bosses: The Fall of the Godfather: The FBI and Paul Castellano.* New York: Simon & Schuster, 1991.

O'Connell, Peter. "Man faces sex, fraud charges. *Las Vegas Review-Journal* (28 July 2001).

Oliver, Ryan. "Millions in cash seized in LV arrest." *Las Vegas Review-Journal* (19 July 2001).

_____. "Seized cash estimated at $21.5 million." *Las Vegas Review-Journal* (20 July 2001).

Ollestad, Norman. *Inside the FBI.* New York: Stuart, 1967.

"Oregon arguments delay Ashcroft order." Associated Press (21 November 2001).

O'Reilly, Kenneth. "The FBI — HUAC's Big Brother." *Nation* 230 (January 19, 1980): 42–45.

_____. "The FBI and the politics of riots, 1964–1968." *Journal of American History* 75 (June 1988): 91–114.

_____. "Herbert Hoover and the FBI." *Annals of Iowa* 47 (Summer 1983): 46–63.

_____. *Hoover and the Un-Americans: The FBI, HUAC, and the Red Menace.* Philadelphia: Temple University Press, 1983.

_____. "A New Deal for the FBI: the Roosevelt administration, crime control, and national security." *Journal of American History* 69 (December 1982): 638–58.

_____. "*Racial Matters*": The FBI's Secret File on Black America, 1960–1972. New York: Free Press, 1989.

Overbye, Dennis. "New details emerge from the Einstein files." *New York Times* (7 May 2002).

Overstreet, Harry, and Bonaro Overstreet. *The FBI in Our Open Society.* New York: Norton, 1969.

Pace, David. "Feds preoccupied with terrorism." Associated Press (1 December 2001).

"Pakistani police arrest 3 suspected al-Qaeda operatives." *USA Today* (9 January 2003).

Parker, Laura. "Bioweapons expert defends himself." *USA Today* (12 August 2002).

_____. "Rudolph manhunt only finding a skeptical town." *USA Today* (16 December 1998).

Payne, Cril. *Deep Cover: An FBI Agent Infiltrates the Radical Underground.* New York: Newsweek Books, 1979.

Pearson, Hugh. *The Shadow of the Panther: Huey Newton and the Price of Black Power in America.* Reading, Mass.: Addison-Wesley, 1994.

Pepper, William. *Orders to Kill: The Truth Behind the Murder of Martin Luther King, Jr.* New York: Warner Books, 1995.

Phillips, Charles, and Alan Axelrod. *Cops, Crooks, and Criminologists: An International Biographical Dictionary of Law Enforcement.* New York: Checkmark Books, 2000.

Pileggi, Nicholas. *Wise Guy: Life in a Mafia Family.* New York: Simon & Schuster, 1985.

Pincus, Walter. "Why FBI debates use of torture." *Toronto Star* (22 October 2001).

Pistone, Joseph. *Donnie Brasco: My Undercover Life in the Mafia.* New York: American Library, 1987.

Pizzo, Stephen; Mary Fricker; and Paul Muolo. *Inside Job: The Looting of America's Savings and Loans.* New York: HarperCollins, 1991.

Pogrebin, L.C. "Have you ever supported equal pay, child care, or women's groups? The FBI was watching you." *Ms.* 5 (June 1977): 37–44; 5 (October 1977): 7–8, 37–44.

Potter, Claire. *War on Crime: Bandits, G-Men, and the Politics of Mass Culture.* New Brunswick, N.J.: Rutgers University Press, 1998.

Pound, Edward. "Suspect hacked into FBI system." *USA Today* (22 February 2001).

Pound, Edward, and Kevin Johnson. "Hanssen had no role in Hunt for Ames, officials say." *USA Today* (27 February 2001).

Poveda, Tony. "The effect of scandal on organizational deviance: the case of the FBI." *Justice Quarterly* 2 (June 1985): 237–58.

_____. "The FBI and domestic intelligence: technocratic or public relations triumph." *Crime and Delinquency* 28 (April 1982): 194–210.

_____. *Lawlessness and Reform: The FBI in Transition.* Pacific Grove, Calif.: Brooks/Cole Publishing, 1990.

Powers, Richard. "The G-man and the attorney general: Hollywood's role in Hoover's rise to power." *Southwest Review* 62 (Autumn 1977): 329–47.

_____. *G-Men: Hoover's FBI I American Popular Culture.* Carbondale, Ill.: Southern Illinois University Press, 1983.

_____. "J. Edgar Hoover and the detective hero." *Journal of Popular Culture* 9 (Fall 1977): 257–58.

_____. *Secrecy and Power: The Life of J. Edgar Hoover.* New York: Free Press, 1987.

Pratt, William. "Farmers, Communists, and the FBI in the upper Midwest." *Agricultural History* 63 (Summer 1989): 61–80.

Preston, William. *Aliens and Dissenters: Federal Suppression of Radicals, 1903–1933.* Cambridge, Mass.: Harvard University Press, 1963.

"Prosecutors drop charges in tree-spiking case." Associated Press (13 September 2001).

"Prosecutors file murder charges against Bulger, Flemmi." Associated Press (14 March 2001).

Puit, Glenn. "$18 million returned to investors." *Las Vegas Review-Journal* (28 December 2002).

_____. "Perry indicted on dozens of sex charges." *Las Vegas Review-Journal* (9 August 2001).

_____. "Victims dial in to police about pyramid caper." *Las Vegas Review-Journal* (21 July 2002).

Purvis, Melvin. *American Agent.* Garden City, N.Y.: Doubleday, 1936.

Pyle, Christopher. "A bill to bug aliens." *Nation* 222 (29 May 1976): 645–48.

_____. "Domestic spying catches no one." *Los Angeles Times* (9 June 2002).

Quimby, Myron. *The Devil's Emissaries.* New York: Modern Literary Editions, 1969.

Rabosh, Ronald, and Joyce Milton. *The Rosenberg File: A Search for Truth.* New York: Holet, Rinehart and Winston, 1983.

Ranalli, Ralph. "FBI knew wrong man was convicted of murder." Associated Press (22 December 2000).

_____. "FBI reportedly hid key evidence." *Boston Globe* (21 December 2000).

_____. *Deadly Alliance: The FBI's Secret Partnership with the Mob.* New York: HarperTorch, 2001.

Rashbaum, William. "FBI analyst is charged with theft of documents." Reuters (21 June 2001).

Ratner, Michael, and Michael Smith, eds. *Che Guevara and the FBI: The U.S. Political Police Dossier on the Latin American Revolutionary.* Melbourne: Ocean Press, 1997.

Rauh, Joseph. "Nonconfrontation in security cases: the Greene decision." *Virginia Law Review* 45 (1959): 1175–90.

Reaves, Lynne. "Greylord's uneasy fallout." *ABA Journal* (March 1984): 35–47.

Reeves, Jay. "Design of church bomb a mystery." Associated Press (26 April 2001).

_____. "Ex-Klansman convicted." Associated Press (2 May 2001).

_____. "FBI agent was catalyst in church-bombing case." Associated Press (19 May 2000).

Reid, Robert. "FBI takes place in hunt for terrorists." Associated Press (1 November 2002).

Ressler, Robert, and Tom Schachtman. *I Have Lived in the Monster.* New York: St. Martin's Press, 1997.

_____. *Whoever Fights Monsters.* New York: St. Martin's Press, 1994.

Revell, Oliver, and Dwight Williams. *A G-Man's Journal.* New York: Pocket Books, 1998.

Richman, Josh. "Bombshell verdict: Earth First! activists win $4.4 million from police, FBI." *Oakland Tribune* (12 June 2002).

_____. "Earth First! win in court spurs other activists." *Oakland Tribune* (16 June 2002).

_____. "FBI and police appeal $4.4 million Earth First! verdict." *Oakland Tribune* (8 September 2002).

_____. "Judge offers way out of new Earth First! trial." *Oakland Tribune* (29 June 2002).

_____. "Loose ends need to be tied up in Earth First! case." *Oakland Tribune* (20 June 2002).

Riebling, Mark. *Wedge: The Secret War between the FBI and the CIA.* New York: Knopf, 1994.

Risen, James. "FBI agent says superior altered report, foiling inquiry." Associated Press (25 May 2002).

Ritter, John. "Ashcroft's crackdown outrages many in Ore." *USA Today* (13 November 2001).

_____. "FBI: Yosemite suspect confesses." *USA Today* (27 July 1999).

Robins, Natalie. *Alien Ink: The FBI's War on Freedom of Expression.* New York: Morrow, 1992.

_____. "Spying in the stacks: the FBI's invasion of libraries." *Nation* 246 (April 9, 1988): 481, 498–502.

Roemer, William. *Roemer: Man against the Mob.* New York: Donald Fine, 1989.

Rosenberg, John. "The FBI sheds its files: catch in the Information Act." *Nation* 226 (4 February 1976): 108–111.

_____. "Follow-up: the FBI field files." *Nation* 228 (March 3, 1979): 231–32.

Rosenfeld, Seth. "Secret FBI files reveal covert activities at UC." *San Francisco Chronicle* (9 June 2002).

Rosswurm, Steven, and Tony Gilpin. "The FBI and the farm equipment workers: FBI surveillance records as a source for CIO union history." *Labor History* 27 (Fall 1986): 485–505.

Rowe, Gary. *My Undercover Years with the Ku Klux Klan.* New York: Bantam, 1976.

Rubin, Mitchell. "FBI and dissidents: a First Amendment analysis of Attorney General Smith's 1983 guidelines on domestic security investigations." *Arizona Law Review* 27 (1988).

Sack, Kevin. "Two charged in fatal bombing of Birmingham church in 1963." *New York Times* 18 May 2000).

Safire, William. "A Justice Dept. half slave, half Freeh." *New York Times* (5 December 1997).

_____. "The clash between FBI and Reno." *New York Times* (19 July 1999).

Salant, Jonathan. "FBI criticized for way it disciplines employees." Associated Press (16 November 2002).

_____. "Panel warns FBI could turn into 'secret police.'" Associated Press (17 December 2002).

_____. "Senate seeks Ashcroft 'explanation.'" Associated Press (25 November 2001).

Sanders, James. *The Downing of TWA Flight 800.* New York: Zebra Books, 1997.

Savage, David. "Anita Hill writer says judge leaked FBI files." *Los Angeles Times* (25 August 2001).

Savino, Lenny. "FBI polygraph failure rate 'low.'" *Las Vegas Review-Journal* (29 July 2001).

Scaduto, Anthony. *Scapegoat: The Lonesome Death of Bruno Richard Hauptmann.* New York: Putnam, 1976.

Schardt, Arlie. "FBI conference: a crack in the Hoover fortress." *Nation* 213 (November 22, 1971): 526–30.

Scheim, David. *Contract on America: The Mafia Murder of President John F. Kennedy.* New York: Shapolsky Publishers, 1988.

Schlesinger, Arthur. *Robert Kennedy and His Times.* Boston: Houghton Mifflin, 1978.

Schmidt, Susan, and Dale Russakoff. "FBI agents focus on N.J. mail route." *Washington Post* (19 October 2001).

Schmidt, Susan, and Joby Warrick. "FBI investigates possible financial motive in anthrax attacks." *Washington Post* (21 December 2001).

Schneir, Walter, and Miriam Schneir. *Invitation to an Inquest.* Garden City, N.Y.: Doubleday, 1965.

Schott, Joseph. *No Left Turns: The FBI in Peace and War.* New York: Praeger, 1975.

Schwartz, Richard. "What the files tell: the FBI and Dr. Einstein." *Nation* 236 (September 3–10, 1983): 168–72.

"The secret files of J. Edgar Hoover." *U.S. News and World Report* 95 (December 19, 1983): 45–50.

Sentner, David. *How the FBI Gets Its Man.* New York: Avon, 1965.

Shapiro, Ira. "Civil liberties and national security: the outlook in Congress." *Intellect* 105 (February 1977): 230–33.

Shapiro, Walter. "FBI, Enron memo writers probably felt similar push." *USA Today* (29 May 2002).

Shattuck, John. "You can't depend on it: the Carter administration and civil liberties." *Civil Liberties Review* 4 (January/February 1978): 10–27.

Shahzad, Asif. "Pakistani says he's in FBI wanted photo." Associated Press (2 January 2003).

Shennon, Philip. "Secret court says FBI aides misled judges in 75 cases." *New York Times* (23 August 2001).

Sheridan, Walter. *The Fall and Rise of Jimmy Hoffa.* New York: Saturday Review Press, 1972.

Sifakis, Carl. *Encyclopedia of Assassinations.* New York: Facts on File, 1991.

_____. *The Mafia Encyclopedia* 2nd edition. New York: Checkmark Books, 1999.

Silvergate, Henry. "Courts let FBI run amok." *National Law Journal* (21 May 2001).

Simon, David, and Stanley Swart. "The Justice Department focuses on white collar crime: promises and pitfalls." *Crime and Delinquency* 30 (1984): 107–20.

Simon, Stephanie. "State, local officials say FBI conceals intelligence." *Los Angeles Times* (25 November 2001).

Singular, Stephen. *Talked to Death: The Murder of Alan Berg and the Rise of the Neo-Nazis.* New York: Beech Tree, 1987.

Slevin, Peter. "Ashcroft blocks FBI access to gun records." *Washington Post* (7 December 2001).

Smith, Brent. *Terrorism in America: Pipe Bombs and Pipe Dreams.* Albany, N.Y.: State University of New York Press, 1994.

Smith, Carlton. *Murder at Yosemite.* New York: St. Martin's Press, 1999.

Smith, James. *Freedom's Fetters: The Alien and Sedition Laws and the American Civil Liberties Union.* Ithaca, N.Y.: Cornell University Press, 1956.

Smith, John. *Alger Hiss: The True Story.* New York: Holt, Rinehart and Winston, 1976.

Smith, John L. "Tales attributed to con man as tall as a $22 million pyramid." *Las Vegas Review-Journal* (2 August 2001).

Sniffen, Michael. "FBI director, Reno defend new lab chief." Associated Press (22 October 1997).

Snow, Robert. *The Militia Threat: Terrorists Among Us.* New York: Plenum Trade, 1999.

Sobieraj, Sandra. "Bush hopes new director can fix FBI." Associated Press (6 July 2001).

_____. "McVeigh execution delayed." Associated Press (12 May 2001).

Sokoloff, Brian. "FBI's dragnet frightens Muslims." Associated Press (26 September 2001).

Solomon, John. "Justice: Panel can't see documents." Associated Press (30 August 2002).

_____. "Review details human errors in belated discovery of McVeigh documents." Associated Press (19 March 2002).

Solomon, John, and Larry Margasak. "FBI agent alleges Moussaoui roadblocks." Associated Press (24 May 2002).

Stalcup, Mark. "Environmental activists protest local FBI." *Bloomington Independent* (1 June 2000).

Stanton, Mary. *From Selma to Sorrow: The Life and Death of Viola Liuzzo.* Athens, Ga.: University of Georgia Press, 1998.

Steele, Roland. "Franklin D. Roosevelt and his Foreign Policy Critics." *Political Science Quarterly* 94 (Spring 1979): 15–32.

Stein, Judith. *The World of Marcus Garvey: Race and Class in Modern Society.* Baton Rouge: Louisiana State University Press, 1986.

Steinwall, Susan. "Appraisal and the FBI Files Case: For Whom Do Archivists Retain Records?" *American Archivist* 49 (Winter 1986): 52–63.

Stephan, Alexander. *"Communazis": FBI Surveillance of German Emigré Writers.* New Haven, Conn.: Yale University Press, 2000.

Stevenson, William. *A Man Called Intrepid: The Secret War.* New York: Harcourt, Brace, Jovanovich, 1976.

Stolberg, Gay, and David Johnston. "Senators told of lack of answers in FBI inquiry on bioterrorism." *New York Times* (7 November 2001).

Stone, I.F. *The Killings at Kent State: How Murder Went Unpunished.* New York: Vintage Books, 1970.

Stowe, David. "The Politics of Café Society." *Journal of American History* 84, no. 4 (March 1998): 1384–1406.

"Study: FBI fails to monitor agents' finances." Associated Press (5 April 2002).

Sullivan, William. *The Bureau: My Thirty Years in Hoover's FBI.* New York: Norton, 1979.

Summers, Anthony. *Official and Confidential: The Secret Life of J. Edgar Hoover.* New York: G.P. Putnam's, 1993.

Swaby, Bethany. "Week of Resistance winds up with protests, march. *Herald-Times* (6 April 2001).

Swearingen, M. Wesley. *FBI Secrets: An Agent's Exposé.* Boston: South End Press, 1995.

"Terror alerts criticized, defended." *Newsday* (11 December 2001).

"The FBI's shocking failure." *Washington Times* (9 April 2002).

Theoharis, Athan. "Bell limits FBI prosecutions." *Nation* 225 (10 September 1977): 198–99.

_____. "Bureaucrats above the law: double-entry intelligence files." *Nation* 225 (22 October 1977): 393–97.

_____. "Classification restrictions and the public's right to know: a new look at the Alger Hiss case." *Intellect* 104 (September/October 1975): 86–89.

_____. "Dissent and the State: unleashing the FBI, 1917–1985." *History Teacher* 24 (November 1990): 41–52.

_____. "The FBI and the American Legion contact program, 1940–1966." *Political Science Quarterly* 100 (Summer 1985): 271–86.

_____. "FBI surveillance: past and present." *Cornell Law Journal* 69 (April 1984).

_____. "The FBI's stretching of presidential directives, 1936–1953." *Political Science Quarterly* 91 (Winter 1976–1977): 649–72.

_____. "The FBI's war on gays." *Rights* 37 (April-June 1991): 13–15.

_____. "FBI wiretapping: a case study of bureaucratic autonomy." *Political Science Quarterly* 107 (Spring 1992): 101–22.

_____. "The FDR file: J. Edgar Hoover, Eleanor — and Herbert, too?" *Nation* 234 (February 20, 1982): 200–201.

_____. "How the FBI gaybaited Stevenson." *Nation* 250 (May 7, 1990): 617, 635–36.

_____. "Illegal surveillance: will Congress stop the snooping?" *Nation* 218 (2 February 1974): 138–42.

_____. *J. Edgar Hoover, Sex, and Crime: An Historical Antidote.* Chicago: Ivan Dee, 1955.

_____. "Misleading the presidents: thirty years of wiretapping." *Nation* 212 (14 June 1971): 244–50.

_____. "The presidency and the Federal Bureau of Investigation: the conflict of intelligence and legality." *Criminal Justice History* no. 2 (1981): 131–60.

_____. "Second-term surveillance: the Froehlke affair." *Nation* 215 (18 December 1972): 623–26.

_____. *Seeds of Repression: Harry S. Truman and the Origins of McCarthyism.* Chicago: Quadrangle, 1970.

_____. *Spying on Americans: Political Surveillance from Hoover to the Huston Plan.* Philadelphia: Temple University Press, 1978.

_____. "The Truman administration and the decline of civil liberties: the FBI's success in securing authorization for a preventive detention program." *Journal of American History* 64 (March 1978): 1010–30.

Theoharis, Athan, ed. *Beyond the Hiss Case: The FBI, Congress, and the Cold War.* Philadelphia: Temple University Press, 1982.

Theoharis, Athan, and John Cox. *The Boss: J. Edgar Hoover and the Great American Inquisition.* Philadelphia: Temple University Press, 1988.

Theoharis, Athan, and Elizabeth Meyer. "The 'national security' justification for electronic eavesdropping: an elusive exception." *Wayne Law Review* 14 (Summer 1968): 749–71.

Thevenot, Carri. "Ex-FBI employee had stormy career." *Las Vegas Review-Journal* (21 June 2001).

_____. "Perry details Burgess encounter." *Las Vegas Review-Journal* (12 August 2001).

Thomason, Dan. "The FBI myth is corroded." *Cincinnati Post* (12 April 2002).

Thompson, Don. "Terror threat renews rights debate." Associated Press (29 November 2001).

Toland, John. *The Dillinger Days.* New York: Random House, 1963.

Tonkovich, Emil. "The use of Title III electronic surveillance to investigate organized crime's hidden interests in gambling casinos." *Rutgers Law Journal* 16 (Spring-Summer 1985): 811–29.

Tully, Andrew. *The FBI's Most Famous Cases.* New York: Morrow, 1965.

Turner, William. *Hoover's FBI: The Men and the Myth.* Los Angeles: Sherbourne Press, 1970.

_____. *Power on the Right.* Berkeley: Ramparts Press, 1969.

Turner, William, and Jonn Christian. *The Assassination of Robert F. Kennedy: A Searching Look at the Conspiracy and Cover-Up, 1968–78.* New York: Random House, 1979.

"2 FBI crime lab workers get minimal discipline." *Chicago Tribune* (8 August 1998).

Ungar, Sanford. *FBI.* Boston: Little, Brown, 1976. Vasquez, Daniel. "FBI's methods questioned in Yosemite slayings case." *San Jose Mercury News* (1 March 2002).

Vicini, James. "Ashcroft recuses himself from Enron case." Reuters (10 January 2002).

_____. "Fired researcher in anthrax probe wants apology." Reuters (6 September 2002).

_____. "Report criticizes FBI security in Hanssen spy case." Reuters (4 April 2002).

_____. "U.S. unveils fingerprint plan, angers Arab groups." Reuters (5 June 2002).

Villano, Anthony. *Brick Agent: Inside the Mafia for the FBI.* New York: Quadrangle, 1977.

Vitello, Michael. "The ethics of Brilab." *Howard Law Journal* 27 (Summer 1984): 902–27.

Volkman, Ernest. *Gangbusters: The Destruction of America's Last Mafia Dynasty*. Boston: Faber and Faber, 1998.

Waller, George. *The Story of the Lindbergh Case*. New York: Dial Press, 1961.

Walsh, Edward. "FBI probe of TWA crash criticized." *Washington Post* (11 May 1999).

Washburn, Patrick. "J. Edgar Hoover and the black press in World War II." *Journalism History* 13 (Spring 1986): 26–33.

_____. *A Question of Sedition: The Federal Government's Investigation of the Black Press During World War II*. New York: Oxford University Press, 1986.

"Washington Gestapo." *Nation* 157 (17 and 24 July 1943): 64–66, 92–95.

Washington, Wayne. "Anthrax probe raises doubts on FBI." *Boston Globe* (23 September 2002).

Watson, Paul, and Josh Meyer. "Pakistanis see FBI in shadows." *Los Angeles Times* (25 August 2002).

Watson, Traci. "FBI baffled by anthrax letters' link to town." *USA Today* (23 October 2001).

Wedge, Dave. "FBI defends Sampson handling." *Boston Herald* (9 September 2001).

Wedge, Dave, and Jonathan Wells. "Sampson's alleged FBI call crucial to his fate." *Boston Herald* (31 August 2001).

Weinstein, Allen. *Perjury: The Hiss-Chambers Case*. New York: Knopf, 1978.

Weisberg, Harold. *Frame-Up*. New York: Outerbridge & Dienstfrey. 1969.

Welch, Neil. *Inside Hoover's FBI: The Top Field Chief Reports*. Garden City, N.Y.: Doubleday, 1984.

Wells, Jonathan. "Indictments put abrupt end to FBI's story on informants." *Boston Herald* (29 September 2000).

Wells, Jonathan, and Dave Wedge. "Source: FBI eyes agent in probe of Sampson phone call." *Boston Herald* (30 August 2001).

Weiss, Mike. "Judge rules fingerprints can be used in courts after all." *San Francisco Chronicle* (14 March 2002).

Whitehead, Don. *Attack on Terror: The FBI against the Ku Klux Klan in Mississippi*. New York: Funk and Wagnalls, 1970.

_____. *The FBI Story: A Report to the People*. New York: Random House, 1956.

Wicksham, DeWayne. "Hoover role in bombing case deserves our condemnation." *USA Today* (8 May 2001).

Williams, Daniel. *Executing Justice: An Inside Account of the Case of Mumia Abu-Jamal*. New York: St. Martin's Press, 2001.

Williams, David. "The Bureau of Investigation and its critics, 1919–1921: the origins of federal political surveillance." *Journal of American History* 68 (December 1981): 560–79.

_____. "They never stopped watching us: FBI political surveillance, 1924–1936." *UCLA Historical Journal* no. 2 (1981): 5–28.

Willing, Richard. "Charge: Hanssen foiled '89 spy pursuit." *USA Today* (26 February 2001).

_____. "Director's legacy shows in changes to FBI's mission." *USA Today* (2 May 2001).

_____. "FBI's DNA lab accused of bias, incompetence." *USA Today* (26 November 1997).

_____. "Good idea to be on Hoover's good side." *USA Today* (1 May 2000).

_____. "Justice had ties to FBI; Powell an informant." *USA Today* (1 May 2000).

_____, "Poll: 4 in 10 say FBI held back evidence." *USA Today* (23 May 2001).

_____. "Program for DNA testing of inmates is scrapped." *USA Today* (25 December 2001).

_____. "Psychiatrist says 'demons' pushed ex-FBI agent into spying." *USA Today* (19 June 2001).

_____. "Waco tape brings no letup in furor." *USA Today* (3 September 1999).

Willing, Richard, and Kevin Johnson. "McVeigh might ask for delay." *USA Today* (11 May 2001).

Willing, Richard, and Traci Watson. "FBI portrays Hanssen's double life." *USA Today* (21 February 2001).

Wilson, James. "The changing FBI: the road to ABSCAM." *Public Interest* 59 (Spring 1980): 3–14.

Wise, David. *The American Police State: The Government against the People*. New York: Random House, 1976.

_____. *The Spy Who Got Away: The Inside Story of Edward Lee Howard*. New York: Random House, 1988.

Woodward, Calvin. "Anthrax probe frustrates lawmakers." Associated Press (23 June 2002).

Wright, Lawrence. "The counter-terrorist." *New Yorker* (14 January 2002).

Yardley, Jim. "Critic is described as scrupulous and determined." Associated Press (25 May 2002).

Yost, Pete. "Administration seeks new authority." Associated Press (17 September 2001).

_____. "Justice's record taking questions." Associated Press (29 August 2001).

_____. "FBI scientist explains anthrax delay." Associated Press (23 November 2001).

Zamora, Jim. "After 11 years, jury vindicates Earth First pair." *San Francisco Chronicle* (12 June 2002).

# Index

*Numbers in **boldface** indicate a primary entry.*